ABRIDGMENT

OF THE

DEBATES OF CONGRESS,

FROM 1789 TO 1856.

FROM GALES AND SEATON'S ANNALS OF CONGRESS; FROM THEIR REGISTER OF DEBATES; AND FROM THE OFFICIAL REPORTED DEBATES, BY JOHN C. RIVES.

BY

THE AUTHOR OF THE THIRTY YEARS' VIEW.

VOL. XVI

NEW YORK:

D. APPLETON & COMPANY, 443 & 445 BROADWAY.

1863.

TWENTY-NINTH CONGRESS.—SECOND SESSION.

PROCEEDINGS AND DEBATES

IN THE

SENATE AND HOUSE OF REPRESENTATIVES.

IN SENATE.

MONDAY, December 7, 1846.

In conformity with the constitution, the Second Session of the Twenty-ninth Congress commenced this day.

The Senate was called to order at twelve o'clock, by its presiding officer, the Vice President of the United States.

JOSEPH CILLEY, from New Hampshire, took his seat, and forty-three Senators answered to their names.

Resolutions.

On motion of Mr. BREESE, it was

Resolved, That a committee be appointed, jointly with such committee as may be appointed by the House of Representatives, to wait on the Pressident of the United States, and inform him that quorums of the two Houses have assembled, and that Congress are ready to receive any communication he may be pleased to make.

The VICE PRESIDENT appointed Messrs. BREESE, CRITTENDEN, and FAIRFIELD, a committee on the part of the Senate in accordance with the foregoing resolution.

On motion of Mr. CAMERON, it was

Resolved, That each Senator be supplied, during the present session, with newspapers as heretofore, not exceeding the cost of three daily papers.

Messages from the House.

A message was received from the House of Representatives by its Clerk, BENJAMIN B. FRENCH, Esq., informing the Senate that the House of Representatives had assembled, and was ready to proceed to business.

Also, a message informing the Senate that the House of Representatives had passed a resolution that a committee be appointed, on the part of the House, to join such committee as might be appointed on the part of the Senate, to wait upon the President of the United States, and inform him that a quorum of the two Houses was assembled, and that Congress was now ready to receive any communication he might be pleased to make, and that Mr. HOPKINS and Mr. WINTHROP were appointed said committee on the part of the House.

Report of Committee

Mr. BREESE, on behalf of the committee on the part of the Senate, appointed to wait upon the President of the United States, reported that the committee had performed the duty assigned to them, and that the President had stated in reply that he would send a communication to both Houses of Congress on to-morrow at twelve o'clock.

On motion, the Senate adjourned.

HOUSE OF REPRESENTATIVES.

MONDAY, December 7.

At twelve o'clock the Hon. JOHN W. DAVIS, of Indiana, Speaker of the House of Representatives, took the chair, and called the House to order.

The roll of the members was called over by B. B. FRENCH, Esq., Clerk of the House, when 186 members answered to their names.

A message was received from the Senate by the hands of A. DICKINS, Esq., Secretary, informing the House that a quorum of the Senate had assembled, and that that body was ready to proceed to business.

Mr. PAYNE, of Alabama, announced that his colleague, Mr. JAMES L. COTTRELL, elected to fill the vacancy occasioned by the resignation of WILLIAM L. YANCEY, and FRANKLIN W. BOWDEN, to fill the vacancy occasioned by the death of FELIX G. MCCONNELL, were present.

Mr. JULIUS ROCKWELL, of Massachusetts, announced that his colleague, Mr. ARTEMAS HALE, elected to represent the 9th district of that State, was present.

Mr. CULVER, of New York, announced that his colleague, Mr. THOMAS P. RIPLEY, elected to fill the vacancy occasioned by the death of RICHARD P. HERRICK, was present.

Mr PHELPS, of Missouri, announced that his colleague, Mr. WILLIAM McDANIEL, elected to fill the vacancy occasioned by the resignation of Mr. STERLING PRICE, was present.

These several members elect were respectively qualified, and took their seats.

Letter from the Secretary of the Treasury, Robert J. Walker, Esq.: Estimate of appropriations required for the fiscal year ending June 30th, 1848.

TREASURY DEPARTMENT, *November* 19, 1846.

SIR: Agreeably to the joint resolution of Congress of the 7th January, 1846, I have the honor to transmit, for the information of the House of Representatives, printed estimates of the appropriations proposed to be made for the fiscal year ending the 30th June, 1848, amounting to $41,-717,355 48, viz:

Civil list, Foreign intercourse, and miscellaneous,	$4,477,813 49
Army proper,	6,046,598 25
Volunteers,	17,932,331 00
Fortifications, ordnance, &c.,	1,720,571 00
Indian department,	1,231,614 00
Pensions,	1,303,700 00
Naval Establishment,	9,004,727 74

To the estimates are added statements showing—

I. The appropriations for the service of the fiscal year ending the 30th June, 1848, made by former acts of Congress, of a permanent character, amounting to		3,340,144 72
Viz:		
Civil list, foreign intercourse, and miscellaneous,	$1,046,800 00	
Arming and equipping militia,	200,000 00	
Civilization of Indians,	10,000 00	
Pensions,	675,00 00	
Interest, &c., public debt,	1,408,344 72	
II. The existing appropriations which will be required to be expended in the fiscal year ending 30th June, 1848, amounting to		724,284 31
Consisting of the following items, viz:		
Civil list, foreign intercourse, and miscellaneous,	$519,786 31	
Army proper,	50,000 00	
Harbors and rivers,	24,209 00	
Pensions,	124,990 00	
Indian department,	5,299 00	
		$45,781,784 51

III. There is also added to the estimates a statement of the several appropriations which will probably be carried to the surplus fund, amounting to $721,609 31.

Accompanying the estimates are sundry statements furnished by the Treasury and War Departments, containing the references to the acts of Congress, &c., on which the estimates for the service of those departments are founded.

I am, very respectfully, your obedient servant,

R. J. WALKER,
Secretary of the Treasury.

Hon. JOHN W. DAVIS,
Speaker of the House of Representatives.

The letter was laid upon the table.

IN SENATE.

TUESDAY, December 8.

The following Senators appeared in their seats to-day:

From Connecticut—Hon. JOHN M. NILES.
" New Jersey—Hon. W. L. DAYTON.
" Mississippi—Hon. J. W. CHALMERS.

President's Message.

The Journal having been read—

The following Message from the President of the United States was received by the hands of J. KNOX WALKER, Esq., his Private Secretary:

Fellow-Citizens of the Senate and of the House of Representatives:

In resuming your labors in the service of the people, it is a subject of congratulation that there has been no period in our past history, when all the elements of national prosperity have been so fully developed. Since your last session no afflicting dispensation has visited our country; general good health has prevailed; abundance has crowned the toil of the husbandman; and labor in all its branches is receiving an ample reward, while education, science, and the arts, are rapidly enlarging the means of social happiness. The progress of our country in her career of greatness, not only in the vast extension of our territorial limits and the rapid increase of our population, but in resources and wealth, and in the happy condition of our people, is without example in the history of nations.

As the wisdom, strength, and beneficence of our free institutions are unfolded, every day adds fresh motives to contentment, and fresh incentives to patriotism.

Our devout and sincere acknowledgments are due to the gracious Giver of all good, for the numberless blessings which our beloved country enjoys.

It is a source of high satisfaction to know that the relations of the United States with all other nations, with a single exception, are of the most amicable character. Sincerely attached to the policy of peace, early adopted and steadily pursued by this Government, I have anxiously desired to cultivate and cherish friendship and commerce with every foreign power. The spirit and habits of the American people are favorable to the maintenance of such international harmony. In adhering to this wise policy, a preliminary and paramount duty obviously consists in the protection of our national interests from encroachment or sacrifice, and our national honor from reproach. These must be maintained at any hazard. They admit of no compromise or neglect, and must be scrupulously and constantly guarded. In their vigilant vindication, collision and conflict with foreign powers may sometimes become unavoidable. Such has been our scrupulous adherence to the dictates of justice, in all our foreign intercourse, that, though steadily and rapidly advancing in prosperity and power, we have given no just cause of complaint to any nation, and have enjoyed the blessings of peace for more than thirty years. From a policy so sacred to humanity, and so salutary in its effects upon our political system, we should never be induced voluntarily to depart

The existing war with Mexico was neither desired nor provoked by the United States. On the contrary, all honorable means were resorted to to avert it. After years of endurance of aggravated and unredressed wrongs on our part, Mexico, in violation of solemn treaty stipulations, and of every principle of justice recognized by civilized nations, commenced hostilities; and thus, by her own act, forced the war upon us. Long before the advance of our army to the left bank of the Rio Grande, we had ample cause of war against Mexico; and had the United States resorted to this extremity, we might have appealed to the whole civilized world for the justice of our cause.

I deem it to be my duty to present to you, on the present occasion, a condensed review of the injuries we had sustained, of the causes which led to the war, and of its progress since its commencement. This is rendered the more necessary because of the misapprehensions which have, to some extent, prevailed as to its origin and true character. The war has been represented as unjust and unnecessary, and as one of aggression on our part upon a weak and injured enemy. Such erroneous views, though entertained by but few, have been widely and extensively circulated, not only at home, but have been spread throughout Mexico and the whole world. A more effectual means could not have been devised to encourage the enemy and protract the war than to advocate and adhere to their cause, and thus give them "aid and comfort."

It is a source of national pride and exultation, that the great body of our people have thrown no such obstacles in the way of the Government in prosecuting the war successfully, but have shown themselves to be eminently patriotic, and ready to vindicate their country's honor and interest at any sacrifice. The alacrity and promptness with which our volunteer forces rushed to the field on their country's call, prove not only their patriotism, but their deep conviction that our cause is just.

The wrongs which we have suffered from Mexico almost ever since she became an independent power, and the patient endurance with which we have borne them, are without a parallel in the history of modern civilized nations. There is reason to believe that if these wrongs had been resented and resisted in the first instance, the present war might have been avoided. One outrage, however, permitted to pass with impunity, almost necessarily encouraged the perpetration of another, until at last Mexico seemed to attribute to weakness and indecision on our part a forbearance which was the offspring of magnanimity, and of a sincere desire to preserve friendly relations with a sister republic.

Scarcely had Mexico achieved her independence, which the United States were the first among the nations to acknowledge, when she commenced the system of insult and spoliation, which she has ever since pursued. Our citizens engaged in lawful commerce, were imprisoned, their vessels seized, and our flag insulted in her ports. If money was wanted, the lawless seizure and confiscation of our merchant vessels and their cargoes was a ready resource; and if, to accomplish their purposes, it became necessary to imprison the owners, captains, and crews, it was done. Rulers superseded rulers in Mexico in rapid succession, but still there was no change in this system of depredation. The Government of the United States made repeated reclamations on behalf of its citizens, but these were answered by the perpetration of new outrages. Promises of redress made by Mexico in the most solemn forms, were postponed or evaded. The files and records of the Department of State contain conclusive proofs of numerous lawless acts perpetrated upon the property and persons of our citizens by Mexico, and of wanton insults to our national flag. The interposition of our Government to obtain redress was again and again invoked, under circumstances which no nation ought to disregard.

It was hoped that these outrages would cease, and that Mexico would be restrained by the laws which regulate the conduct of civilized nations in their intercourse with each other, after the treaty of amity, commerce, and navigation, of the 5th of April, 1831, was concluded between the two republics; but this hope soon proved to be vain. The course of seizure and confiscation of the property of our citizens, the violation of their persons, and the insults to our flag, pursued by Mexico previous to that time, were scarcely suspended for even a brief period, although the treaty so clearly defines the rights and duties of the respective parties, that it is impossible to misunderstand or mistake them. In less than seven years after the conclusion of that treaty, our grievances had become so intolerable, that in the opinion of President Jackson, they should no longer be endured. In his message to Congress in February, 1837, he presented them to the consideration of that body, and declared that "the length of time since some of the injuries have been committed, the repeated and unavailing applications for redress, the wanton character of some of the outrages upon the property and persons of our citizens, upon the officers and flag of the United States, independent of recent insults to this Government and people by the late extraordinary Mexican Minister, would justify in the eyes of all nations immediate war." In a spirit of kindness and forbearance, however, he recommended reprisals as a milder mode of redress. He declared that war should not be used as a remedy "by just and generous nations, confiding in their strength, for injuries committed, if it can be honorably avoided," and added, "it has occurred to me that, considering the present embarrassed condition of that country, we should act with both wisdom and moderation, by giving to Mexico one more opportunity to atone for the past, before we take redress into our own hands. To avoid all misconception on the part of Mexico, as well as to protect our own national character from reproach, this opportunity should be given with the avowed design and full preparation to take immediate satisfaction, if it should not be obtained on a repetition of the demand for it. To this end I recommend that an act be passed authorizing reprisals, and the use of the naval force of the United States, by the Executive, against Mexico, to enforce them in the event of a refusal by the Mexican Government to come to an amicable adjustment of the matters in controversy between us, upon another demand thereof, made from on board one of our vessels of war on the coast of Mexico."

Committees of both Houses of Congress, to which this message of the President was referred, fully sustained his views of the character of the wrongs which we had suffered from Mexico, and recommended that another demand for redress should be made before authorizing war or reprisals. The Committee on Foreign Relations of the Senate, in their report, say: "After such a demand, should prompt justice be refused by the Mexican Government, we may appeal to all nations not only for the equity and moderation with which we shall have acted towards a sister republic, but for the necessity which will then compel us to seek redress for our wrongs, either by actual war or by reprisals. The subject will then be presented before Congress, at the commencement of the next session, in a clear and distinct form; and the committee cannot doubt but that such measures will be immediately adopted as may be necessary to vindicate the honor of the country, and insure ample reparation to our injured citizens."

The Committee on Foreign Affairs of the House of Representatives made a similar recommendation. In their report, they say that they "fully concur with the President that ample cause exists for taking redress into our own hands, and believe that we should be justified in the opinion of other nations for taking such a step. But they are willing to try the experiment of another demand, made in the most solemn form, upon the justice of the Mexican Government, before any further proceedings are adopted."

No difference of opinion upon the subject is believed to have existed in Congress at that time; the executive and legislative departments concurred; and yet such has been our forbearance and desire to preserve peace with Mexico, that the wrongs of which we then complained, and which gave rise to these solemn proceedings, not only remain unredressed to this day, but additional causes of complaint, of an aggravated character, have ever since been accumulating.

Shortly after these proceedings, a special messenger was despatched to Mexico, to make a final demand for redress; and on the twentieth July, 1837, the demand was made. The reply of the Mexican Government bears date on the twenty-ninth of the same month, and contains assurances of the "anxious wish" of the Mexican Government "not to delay the moment of that final and equitable adjustment which is to terminate the existing difficulties between the two Governments;" that "nothing should be left undone which may contribute to the most speedy and equitable determination of the subjects which have so seriously engaged the attention of the American Government;" that the "Mexican Government would adopt, as the only guides for its conduct, the plainest principles of public right, the sacred obligations imposed by international law, and the religious faith of treaties;" and that "whatever reason and justice may dictate respecting each case will be done." The assurance was further given, that the decision of the Mexican Government upon each cause of complaint, for which redress had been demanded, should be communicated to the Government of the United States by the Mexican Minister of Washington.

These solemn assurances, in answer to our demand for redress, were disregarded. By making them, however, Mexico obtained further delay. President Van Buren, in his annual message to Congress of the fifth of December, 1837, states, that "although the larger number" of our demands for redress, and "many of them aggravated cases of personal wrongs, have been now for years before the Mexican Government, and some of the causes of national complaint, and those of the most offensive character, admitted of immediate, simple, and satisfactory replies, it is only within a few days past that any specific communication in answer to our last demand, made five months ago, has been received from the Mexican Minister;" and that "for not one of our public complaints has satisfaction been given or offered; that but one of the cases of personal wrong has been favorably considered, and that but four cases of both descriptions, out of all those formally presented, and earnestly pressed, have as yet been decided upon by the Mexican Government." President Van Buren, believing that it would be vain to make any further attempt to obtain redress by the ordinary means within the power of the Executive, communicated this opinion to Congress, in the message referred to, in which he said: "On a careful and deliberate examination of the contents, [of the correspondence with the Mexican Government,] and considering the spirit manifested by the Mexican Government, it has become my painful duty to return the subject as it now stands to Congress, to whom it belongs, to decide upon the time, the mode, and the measure of redress." Had the United States at that time adopted compulsory measures, and taken redress into their own hands, all our difficulties with Mexico would probably have been long since adjusted, and the existing war have been averted. Magnanimity and moderation on our part only had the effect to complicate these difficulties, and render an amicable settlement of them the more embarrassing. That such measures of redress, under similar provocations, committed by any of the powerful nations of Europe, would have been promptly resorted to by the United States, cannot be doubted. The national honor, and the preservation of the national character throughout the world, as well as our own self-respect and the protection due to our own citizens, would have rendered such a resort indispensable. The history of no civilized nation in modern times has presented within so brief a period so many wanton attacks upon the honor of its flag, and upon the property and persons of its citizens, as had at that time been borne by the United States from the Mexican authorities and people. But Mexico was a sister republic, on the North American continent, occupying a territory contiguous to our own, and was in a feeble and distracted condition, and these considerations, it is presumed, induced Congress to forbear still longer.

Instead of taking redress into our own hands, a new negotiation was entered upon, with fair promises on the part of Mexico, but with the real purpose, as the event has proved, of indefinitely postponing the reparation which we demanded, and which was so justly due. This negotiation, after more than a year's delay, resulted in the convention of the eleventh of April, 1839, "for the adjustment of claims of citizens of the United States of America upon the Government of the Mexican republic." The joint board of commissioners created by this convention to examine and decide upon these claims, was not organized until the month of August, 1840, and under the terms of the convention they were to terminate their duties within eighteen months from that time. Four of the eighteen months were consumed in preliminary discussions on frivolous and dilatory points raised by the Mexican commissioners; and it was not until the month of December, 1840, that they commenced the examination of the claims of our citizens upon Mexico. Fourteen months only remained to examine and decide upon these numerous and complicated cases. In the month of February, 1842, the term of the commission expired, leaving many claims undisposed of for want of time. The claims which were allowed by the board, and by the umpire authorized by the convention to decide in case of disagreement between the Mexican and American commissioners, amounted to two million twenty-six thousand one hundred and thirty-nine dollars and sixty-eight cents. There were pending before the umpire when the commission expired, additional claims, which had been examined and awarded by the American commissioners, and had not been allowed by the Mexican commissioners, amounting to nine hundred and twenty-eight thousand six hundred and twenty-seven dollars and eighty-eight cents, upon which he did not decide, alleging that his authority had ceased with the termination of the joint commission. Besides these claims, there were others of American citizens amounting to three million three hundred and thirty-six thousand eight hundred and thirty-seven dollars and five cents, which had been submitted to the board, and upon which they had not time to decide before their final adjournment.

The sum of two million twenty-six thousand one hundred and thirty-nine dollars and sixty-eight cents, which had been awarded to the claimants, was a liquidated and ascertained debt due by Mexico, about which there could be no dispute, and which she was bound to pay according to the terms of the convention. Soon after the final awards for this amount had been made, the Mexican Government asked for a postponement of the time of making payment, alleging that it would be inconvenient to make the payment at the time stipulated. In the spirit of forbearing kindness towards a sister republic, which Mexico has so long abused, the United States promptly complied with her request. A second convention was accordingly concluded between the two Governments on the thirtieth of January, 1843, which upon its face declares that, "this new arrangement is entered into for the accommodation of Mexico." By the terms of this convention, all the interest due on the awards which had been made in favor of the claimants under the convention of the eleventh of April, 1839, was to be paid to them on the thirtieth of April, 1843, and "the principal of the said awards, and the interest accruing thereon," was stipulated to "be paid in five years, in equal instalments every three months." Notwithstanding this new convention was entered into at the request of Mexico, and for the purpose of relieving her from embarrassment, the claimants have only received the interest due on the thirtieth of April, 1843, and three of the twenty instalments. Although the payment of the sum thus liquidated, and confessedly due by Mexico to our citizens as indemnity for acknowledged acts of outrage and wrong, was secured by treaty, the obligations of which are ever held sacred by all just nations, yet Mexico has violated this solemn engagement by failing and refusing to make the payment. The two instalments due in April and July, 1844, under the peculiar circumstances connected with them, have been assumed by the United States and discharged to the claimants, but they are still due by Mexico. But this is not all of which we have just cause of complaint. To provide a remedy for the claimants whose cases were not decided by the joint commission under the convention of April the eleventh, 1839, it was expressly stipulated by the sixth article of the convention of the thirtieth of January, 1843, that "a new convention shall be entered into for the settlement of all claims of the Government and citizens of the United States against the republic of Mexico which were not finally decided by the late commission, which met in the city of Washington, and of all claims of the Government and citizens of Mexico against the United States."

In conformity with this stipulation, a third convention was concluded and signed at the city of Mexico on the twentieth of November, 1843, by the plenipotentiaries of the two Governments, by which provision was made for ascertaining and paying these claims. In January, 1844, this convention was ratified by the Senate of the United States, with two amendments, which were manifestly reasonable in their character. Upon a reference of the amendments proposed to the Government of Mexico, the same evasions, difficulties, and delays were interposed which have so long marked the policy of that Government towards the United States. It has not even yet decided whether it would or would not accede to them, although the subject has been repeatedly pressed upon its consideration.

Mexico has thus violated a second time the faith of treaties, by failing or refusing to carry into effect the sixth article of the convention of January, 1843.

Such is the history of the wrongs which we have suffered and patiently endured from Mexico through a long series of years. So far from affording reasonable satisfaction for the injuries and insults we have borne, a great aggravation of them consists in the fact, that while the United States, anxious to preserve a good understanding with Mexico, have been constantly, but vainly, employed in seeking redress for past wrongs, new outrages were constantly occurring, which have continued to increase our causes of complaint, and to swell the amount of our demands. While the citizens of the United States were conducting a lawful commerce with Mexico under the guarantee of a treaty of "amity, commerce, and navigation," many of them have suffered all the injuries which would have resulted from open war. This treaty, instead of affording protection to our citizens, has been the means of inviting them into the ports of Mexico, that they might be, as they have been in numerous instances, plundered of their property, and deprived of their personal liberty if they dared insist on their rights. Had the unlawful seizures of American property, and the violation of the personal liberty of our citizens, to say nothing of the insults to our flag which have occurred in the ports of Mexico, taken place on the high seas, they would themselves long since have constituted a state of actual war between the two countries. In so long suffering Mexico to violate her most solemn treaty obligations, plunder our citizens of their property, and imprison their persons without affording them any redress, we have failed to perform one of the first and highest duties which every Government owes to its citizens; and the consequence has been, that many of them have been reduced from a state of affluence to bankruptcy. The proud name of American citizen, which ought to protect all who bear it from insult and injury throughout the world, has afforded no such protection to our citizens in Mexico. We had ample cause of war against Mexico long before the breaking out of hostilities. But even then we forbore to take redress into our own hands, until Mexico herself became the aggressor, by invading our soil in hostile array, and shedding the blood of our citizens.

Such are the grave causes of complaint on the part of the United States against Mexico—causes which existed long before the annexation of Texas to the American Union; and yet, animated by the love of peace, and a magnanimous moderation, we did not adopt those measures of redress which, under such circumstances, are the justified resort of injured nations.

The annexation of Texas to the United States constituted no just cause of offence to Mexico. The pretext that it did so, is wholly inconsistent, and irreconcilable with well-authenticated facts connected with the revolution by which Texas became independent of Mexico. That this may be the more manifest, it may be proper to advert to the causes and to the history of the principal events of that revolution.

Texas constituted a portion of the ancient province of Louisiana, ceded to the United States by France in the year 1803. In the year 1819, the United States, by the Florida treaty, ceded to Spain all that part of Louisiana within the present limits of Texas; and Mexico, by the revolution which separated her from Spain, and rendered her an independent nation, succeeded to the rights of the mother country over this territory. In the year 1824, Mexico established a federal constitution, under which the Mexican republic was composed of a number of sovereign States, confederated together in a federal Union similar to our own. Each of these States had its own Executive, Legislature, and Judiciary; and, for all except federal purposes, was as independent of the General Government, and that of the other States, as is Pennsylvania or Virginia under our constitution. Texas and Coahuila united, and formed one of these Mexican States. The State constitution which they adopted, and which was approved by the Mexican confederacy, asserted that they were "free and independent of the other Mexican United States, and of every other power and dominion whatsoever;" and proclaimed the great principle of human liberty, that "the sovereignty of the State resides originally and essentially in the general mass of the individuals who compose it." To the government under this constitution, as well as to that under the federal constitution, the people of Texas owed allegiance.

Emigrants from foreign countries, including the United States, were invited by the colonization laws of the State and of the federal Government to settle in Texas. Advantageous terms were offered to induce them to leave their own country and become Mexican citizens. This invitation was accepted by many of our citizens, in the full faith that in their new home they would be governed by laws enacted by representatives elected by themselves, and that their lives, liberty, and property, would be protected by constitutional guarantees similar to those which existed in the republic they had left. Under a Government thus organized they continued until the year 1835, when a military revolution broke out in the city of Mexico, which entirely subverted the Federal and State constitutions, and placed a military dictator at the head of the Government.

By a sweeping decree of a Congress subservient to the will of the dictator, the several State constitutions were abolished, and the States themselves converted into mere departments of the central Government. The people of Texas were unwilling to submit to this usurpation. Resistance to such tyranny became a high duty. Texas was fully absolved from all allegiance to the central Government of Mexico from the moment that Government had abolished her State constitution, and in its place substituted an arbitrary and despotic central Government.

Such were the principal causes of the Texan revolution. The people of Texas at once determined upon resistance, and flew to arms. In the midst of these important and exciting events, however, they did not omit to place their liberties upon a secure and permanent foundation. They elected members to a convention, who, in the month of March 1836, issued a formal declaration that their "political connection with the Mexican nation has forever ended, and that the people of Texas do now constitute a FREE, SOVEREIGN, and INDEPENDENT REPUBLIC, and are fully invested with all the rights and attributes which properly belong to independent nations." They also adopted for their government a liberal republican constitution. About the same time, Santa Anna, then the dictator of Mexico, invaded Texas with a numerous army, for the purpose of subduing her people, and enforcing obedience to his arbitrary and despotic government. On the twenty-first of April, 1836, he was met by the Texan citizen soldiers, and on that day was achieved by them the memorable victory of San Jacinto, by which they conquered their independence. Considering the numbers engaged on the respective sides, history does not record a more brilliant achievement. Santa Anna himself was among the captives.

In the month of May, 1836, Santa Anna acknowledged, by a treaty with the Texan authorities, in the most solemn form, "the full, entire, and perfect independence of the republic of Texas." It is true, he was then a prisoner of war, but it is equally true that he had failed to reconquer Texas, and had met with signal defeat; that his authority had not been revoked, and that by virtue of this treaty he obtained his personal release. By it hostilities were suspended, and the army which had invaded Texas under his command returned, in pursuance of this arrangement, unmolested, to Mexico.

From the day that the battle of San Jacinto was fought, until the present hour, Mexico has never possessed the power to reconquer Texas. In the language of the Secretary of State of the United States, in a despatch to our Minister in Mexico, under date of the eighth of July, 1842, "Mexico may have chosen to consider, and may still choose to consider Texas as having been at all times since 1835, and as still continuing, a rebellious province; but the world has been obliged to take a very different view of the matter. From the time of the battle of San Jacinto, in April, 1836, to the present moment, Texas has exhibited the same external signs of national independence as Mexico herself, and with quite as much stability of Government. Practically free and independent, acknowledged as a political sovereignty by the principal powers of the world, no hostile foot finding rest within her territory for six or seven years, and Mexico herself refraining for all that period from any further attempt to re-establish her own authority over that territory, it cannot but be surprising to find Mr. de Bocanegra [the Secretary of Foreign Affairs of Mexico] complaining that for that whole period citizens of the United States, or its Government, have been favoring the rebels of Texas, and supplying them with vessels, ammunition, and money, as if the war for the reduction of the province of Texas had been constantly prosecuted by Mexico, and her success prevented by these influences from abroad." In the same despatch, the Secretary of State affirms, that "since 1837, the United States have regarded Texas as an independent sovereignty, as much as Mexico; and that trade and commerce with citizens of a Government at war with Mexico cannot, on that account, be regarded as an intercourse by which assistance and succor are given to Mexican rebels. The whole current of Mr. de Bocanegra's remarks runs in the same direction, as if the independence of Texas had not been acknowledged. It has been acknowledged—it was acknowledged in 1837, against the remonstrance and protest of Mexico; and most of the acts of any importance, of which Mr. de Bocanegra complains, flow necessarily from that recognition. He speaks of Texas as still being 'an integral part of the territory of the Mexican Republic;' but he cannot but understand that the United States do not so regard it. The real complaint of Mexico, therefore, is, in substance, neither more nor less than a complaint against the recognition of Texan independence. It may be thought rather late to repeat that complaint, and not quite just to confine it to the United States, to the exemption of England, France, and Belgium, unless the United States, having been the first to acknowledge the independence of Mexico herself, are to be blamed for setting an example for the recognition of that of Texas." And he added, that "the constitution, public treaties, and the laws, obliged the President to regard Texas as an independent State, and its territory as no part of the territory of Mexico." Texas had been an independent State, with an organized Government, defying the power of Mexico to overthrow or reconquer her, for more than ten years before Mexico commenced the present war against the United States. Texas had given such evidence to the world of her ability to maintain her separate existence as an independent nation, that she had been formally recognized as such, not only by the United States, but by several of the principal powers of Europe. These powers had entered into treaties of amity, commerce, and navigation with her. They had received and accredited her ministers, and other diplomatic agents at their respective courts; and they had commissioned ministers and diplomatic agents on their part to the Government of Texas. If Mexico, notwithstanding all this, and her utter inability to subdue or reconquer Texas, still stubbornly refused to recognize her as an independent nation, she was none the less so on that account. Mexico herself had been recognized as an independent nation by the United States, and by other powers, many years before Spain, of which, before her revolution, she had been a colony, would agree to recognize her as such; and yet Mexico was at that time, in the estimation of the civilized world, and in fact, none the less an independent power because Spain still claimed her as a colony. If Spain had continued until the present period to assert that Mexico was one of her colonies, in rebellion against her, this would not have made her so, or changed the fact of her independent existence. Texas, at the period of her annexation to the United States, bore the same relation to Mexico that Mexico had borne to Spain for many years before Spain acknowledged her independence, with this important difference—that, before the annexation of Texas to the United States was consummated, Mexico herself, by a formal act of her Government, had acknowledged the independence of Texas as a nation. It is true, that in the act of recognition she prescribed a condition, which she had no power or authority to impose, that Texas should not annex herself to any other power; but this could not detract in any degree from the recognition which Mexico then made of her actual independence. Upon this plain statement of facts, it is absurd for Mexico to allege, as a pretext for commencing hostilities against the United States, that Texas is still a part of her territory.

But there are those who, conceding all this to be true, assume the ground that the true western boundary of Texas is the Nueces, instead of the Rio Grande; and that, therefore, in marching our army to the east bank of the latter river, we passed the Texan line, and invaded the territory of Mexico. A simple statement of facts, known to exist, will conclusively refute such an assumption. Texas, as ceded to the United States by France in 1803, has been always claimed as extending west to the Rio Grande, or Rio Bravo. This fact is established by the authority of our most eminent statesmen at a period when the question was as well, if not better understood, than it is at present. During Mr. Jefferson's administration, Messrs. Monroe and Pinckney, who had been sent on a special mission to Madrid, charged, among other things, with the adjustment of boundary between the two countries, in a note addressed to the Spanish Minister of Foreign Affairs, under date of the twenty-eighth of January, 1805, assert that the boundaries of Louisiana, as ceded to the United States by France, "are the river Perdido on the east, and the river Bravo on the west;" and they add, that "the facts and principles which justify this conclusion are so satisfactory to our Government, as to convince it that the United States have not a better right to the island of New Orleans, under the cession referred to, than they have to the whole district of territory which is above described."

Down to the conclusion of the Florida treaty, in February, 1819, by which this territory was ceded to Spain, the United States asserted and maintained their territorial rights to this extent. In the month of June, 1818, during Mr. Monroe's administration, information having been received that a number of foreign adventurers had landed at Galveston, with the avowed purpose of forming a settlement in that vicinity, a special messenger was despatched by the Government of the United States, with instructions from the Secretary of State, to warn them to desist, should they be found there, "or any other place north of the Rio Bravo, and within the territory claimed by the United States." He was instructed, should they be found in the country north of that river, to make known to them "the surprise with which the President has seen possession thus taken, without authority from the United States, of a place within their territorial limits, and upon which no lawful settlement can be made without their sanction." He was instructed to call upon them to "avow under what national authority they profess to act," and to give them due warning "that the place is within the United States, who will suffer no permanent settlement to be made there, under any authority other than their own." As late as the eighth of July, 1842, the Secretary of State of the United States, in a note addressed to our Minister in Mexico, maintains that, by the Florida treaty of 1819, the territory as far west as the Rio Grande was confirmed to Spain. In that note he states that, "by the treaty of the twenty-second of February, 1819, between the United States and Spain, the Sabine was adopted as the line of boundary between the two powers. Up to that period, no considerable colonization had been effected in Texas; but the territory between the Sabine and the Rio Grande being confirmed to Spain by the treaty, applications were made to that power for grants of land, and such grants, or permissions of settlement, were in fact made by the Spanish authorities in favor of citizens of the United States proposing to emigrate to Texas in numerous families, before the declaration of independence by Mexico."

The Texas which was ceded to Spain by the Florida treaty of 1819 embraced all the country now claimed by the State of Texas between the Nueces and the Rio Grande. The republic of Texas always claimed this river as her western boundary, and in her treaty made with Santa Anna, in May, 1836, he recognized it as such. By the constitution, which Texas adopted in March, 1836, senatorial and representative districts were organized extending west of the Nueces. The Congress of Texas, on the nineteenth of December, 1836, passed "an act to define the boundaries of the republic of Texas," in which they declared the Rio Grande from its mouth to its source to be their boundary, and by the said act they extended their "civil and political jurisdiction" over the country up to that boundary. During a period of more than nine years, which intervened between the adoption of her constitution and her annexation as one of the States of our Union, Texas asserted and exercised many acts of sovereignty and jurisdiction over the territory and inhabitants west of the Nueces. She organized and defined the limits of counties extending to the Rio Grande. She established courts of justice, and extended her judicial system over the territory. She established a custom-house, and collected duties, and also post-offices and post roads in it. She established a land office, and issued numerous grants for land, within its limits. A Senator and a Representative residing in it were elected to the Congress of the republic, and served as such before the act of annexation took place. In both the Congress and Convention of Texas, which gave their assent to the terms of annexation to the United States, proposed by our Congress, were representatives residing west of the Nueces, who took part in the act of annexation itself. This was the Texas which, by the act of our Congress of the twenty-ninth of December, 1845, was admitted as one of the States of our Union. That the Congress of the United States understood the State of Texas which they admitted into the Union to extend beyond the Nueces is apparent from the fact, that on the thirty-first of December, 1845, only two days after the act of admission, they passed a law "to establish a collection district in the State of Texas," by which they created a port of delivery at Corpus Christi, situated west of the Nueces, and being the same point at which the Texas custom-house, under the laws of that republic, had been located, and directed that a surveyor to collect the revenue should be appointed for that port by the President, by and with the advice and consent of the Senate. A surveyor was accordingly nominated, and confirmed by the Senate, and has been ever since in the performance of his duties. All these acts of the republic of Texas, and of our Congress, preceded the orders for the advance of our army to the east bank of the Rio Grande. Subsequently, Congress passed an act "establishing certain post routes," extending west of the Nueces. The country west of that river now constitutes a part of one of the congressional districts of Texas, and is represented in the House of Representatives. The Senators from that State were chosen by a Legislature in which the country west of that river was represented. In view of all these facts, it is difficult to conceive upon what ground it can be maintained that, in occupying the country west of the Nueces with our army, with a view solely to its security and defence, we invaded the territory of Mexico. But it would have been still more difficult to justify the Executive, whose duty it is to see that the laws be faithfully executed, if in the face of all these proceedings, both of the Congress of Texas and of the United States, he had assumed the responsibility of yielding up the territory west of the Nueces to Mexico, or of refusing to protect and defend this territory and its inhabitants, including Corpus Christi, as well as the remainder of Texas, against the threatened Mexican invasion.

But Mexico herself has never placed the war which she has waged upon the ground that our army occupied the intermediate territory between the Nueces and the Rio Grande. Her refuted pretension that Texas was not in fact an independent State, but a rebellious province, was obstinately persevered in; and her avowed purpose in commencing a war with the United States was to reconquer Texas, and to restore Mexican authority over the whole territory—not to the Nueces only, but to the Sabine. In view of the proclaimed menaces of Mexico to this effect, I deemed it my duty, as a measure of precaution and defence, to order our army to occupy a position on our frontier as a military post, from which our troops could best resist and repel any attempted invasion which Mexico might make.

Our army had occupied a position at Corpus Christi west of the Nueces, as early as August

1845, without complaint from any quarter. Had the Nueces been regarded as the true western boundary of Texas, that boundary had been passed by our army many months before it advanced to the eastern bank of the Rio Grande. In my annual message of December last I informed Congress that, upon the invitation of both the Congress and Convention of Texas, I had deemed it proper to order a strong squadron to the coasts of Mexico, and to concentrate an efficient military force on the western frontier of Texas, to protect and defend the inhabitants against the menaced invasion of Mexico. In that message I informed Congress that the moment the terms of annexation offered by the United States were accepted by Texas, the latter became so far a part of our own country as to make it our duty to afford such protection and defence; and that for that purpose our squadron had been ordered to the Gulf, and our army to "take a position between the Nueces and the Del Norte," or Rio Grande, and "to repel any invasion of the Texan territory which might be attempted by the Mexican forces."

It was deemed proper to issue this order, because, soon after the President of Texas, in April, 1845, had issued his proclamation convening the Congress of that republic, for the purpose of submitting to that body the terms of annexation proposed by the United States, the Government of Mexico made serious threats of invading the Texan territory.

These threats became more imposing as it became more apparent, in the progress of the question, that the people of Texas would decide in favor of accepting the terms of annexation; and, finally, they had assumed such a formidable character, as induced both the Congress and Convention of Texas to request that a military force should be sent by the United States, into her territory for the purpose of protecting and defending her against the threatened invasion. It would have been a violation of good faith towards the people of Texas to have refused to afford the aid which they desired against a threatened invasion, to which they had been exposed by their free determination to annex themselves to our Union, in compliance with the overtures made to them by the joint resolution of our Congress.

Accordingly, a portion of the army was ordered to advance into Texas. Corpus Christi was the position selected by General Taylor. He encamped at that place in August, 1845, and the army remained in that position until the eleventh of March, 1846, when it moved westward, and on the twenty-eighth of that month reached the east bank of the Rio Grande opposite to Matamoras. This movement was made in pursuance of orders from the War Department, issued on the thirteenth of January, 1846. Before these orders were issued, the despatch of our Minister in Mexico, transmitting the decision of the Council of Government of Mexico, advising that he should not be received, and also the despatch of our consul residing in the city of Mexico—the former bearing date on the seventeenth, and the latter on the eighteenth of December, 1845, copies of both of which accompanied my message to Congress of the eleventh of May last—were received at the Department of State. These communications rendered it highly probable, if not absolutely certain, that our Minister would not be received by the Government of General Herrera. It was also well known that but little hope could be entertained of a different result from General Paredes, in case the revolutionary movement which he was prosecuting should prove successful, as was highly probable. The partisans of Paredes, as our Minister, in the despatch referred to, states, breathed the fiercest hostility against the United States, denounced the proposed negotiation as treason, and openly called upon the troops and the people to put down the Government of Herrera by force. The reconquest of Texas, and war with the United States, were openly threatened. These were the circumstances existing, when it was deemed proper to order the army under the command of General Taylor to advance to the western frontier of Texas, and occupy a position on or near the Rio Grande.

The apprehensions of a contemplated Mexican invasion have been since fully justified by the event. The determination of Mexico to rush into hostilities with the United States was afterwards manifested from the whole tenor of the note of the Mexican Minister of Foreign Affairs to our Minister, bearing date on the twelfth of March, 1846. Paredes had then revolutionized the Government, and his Minister, after referring to the resolution for the annexation of Texas, which had been adopted by our Congress in March, 1845, proceeds to declare that "a fact such as this, or, to speak with greater exactness, so notable an act of usurpation, created an imperious necessity that Mexico, for her own honor, should repel it with proper firmness and dignity. The supreme Government had beforehand declared that it would look upon such an act as a *casus belli;* and, as a consequence of this declaration, negotiation was, by its very nature, at an end, and war was the only recourse of the Mexican Government."

It appears, also, that on the fourth of April following, General Paredes, through his Minister of War, issued orders to the Mexican general in command on the Texan frontier to "attack" our army "by every means which war permits." To this General Paredes had been pledged to the army and people of Mexico during the military revolution which had brought him into power. On the eighteenth of April, 1846, General Paredes addressed a letter to the commander on that frontier, in which he stated to him, "at the present date I suppose you at the head of that valiant army, either fighting already, or preparing for the operations of a campaign;" and "supposing you already on the theatre of operations, and with all the forces assembled, it is indispensable that hostilities be commenced, yourself taking the initiative against the enemy."

The movement of our army to the Rio Grande was made by the commanding general under positive orders to abstain from all aggressive acts towards Mexico, or Mexican citizens, and to regard the relations between the two countries as peaceful, unless Mexico should declare war, or commit acts of hostility indicative of a state of war; and these orders he faithfully executed. Whilst occupying his position on the east bank of the Rio Grande, within the limits of Texas, then recently admitted as one of the States of our Union, the commanding general of the Mexican forces, who, in pursuance of the orders of his Government, had collected a large army on the opposite shore of the Rio Grande, crossed the river, invaded our territory, and commenced hostilities by attacking our forces.

Thus, after all the injuries which we had received and borne from Mexico, and after she had insultingly rejected a Minister sent to her on a mission of peace, and whom she had solemnly agreed to receive, she consummated her long course of outrage against our country by commencing an offensive war and shedding the blood of our citizens on our own soil.

The United States never attempted to acquire Texas by conquest. On the contrary, at an early period after the people of Texas had achieved their independence, they sought to be annexed to the United States. At a general election in September, 1836, they decided with great unanimity in favor of "annexation;" and in November following, the Congress of the republic authorized the appointment of a Minister to bear their request to this Government. This Government, however, having remained neutral between Texas and Mexico during the war between them, and considering it due to the honor of our country, and our fair fame among the nations of the earth, that we should not at this early period consent to annexation, nor until it should be manifest to the whole world that the reconquest of Texas by Mexico was impossible, refused to accede to the overtures made by Texas. On the twelfth of April, 1844, and after more than seven years had elapsed since Texas had established her independence, a treaty was concluded for the annexation of that republic to the United States, which was rejected by the Senate. Finally, on the first of March, 1845, Congress passed a joint resolution for annexing her to the United States, upon certain preliminary conditions to which her assent was required. The solemnities which characterized the deliberations and conduct of the Government and people of Texas, on the deeply interesting questions presented by these resolutions, are known to the world. The Congress, the Executive, and the people of Texas, in a convention elected for that purpose, accepted with great unanimity the proposed terms of annexation; and thus consummated on her part the great act of restoring to our federal Union a vast territory which had been ceded to Spain by the Florida treaty more than a quarter of a century before.

After the joint resolution for the annexation of Texas to the United States had been passed by our Congress, the Mexican Minister at Washington addressed a note to the Secretary of State, bearing date on the sixth of March, 1845, protesting against it as "an act of aggression, the most unjust which can be found recorded in the annals of modern history, namely: that of despoiling a friendly nation, like Mexico, of a considerable portion of her territory," and protesting against the resolution of annexation, as being an act "whereby the province of Texas, an integral portion of the Mexican territory, is agreed and admitted into the American Union:" and he announced that, as a consequence, his mission to the United States had terminated, and demanded his passports, which were granted. It was upon the absurd pretext made by Mexico, (herself indebted for her independence to a successful revolution,) that the republic of Texas still continued to be, notwithstanding all that had passed, a province of Mexico, that this step was taken by the Mexican Minister.

Every honorable effort has been used by me to avoid the war which followed, but all have proved vain. All our attempts to preserve peace have been met by insult and resistance on the part of Mexico. My efforts to this end commenced in the note of the Secretary of State of the tenth of March, 1845, in answer to that of the Mexican Minister. Whilst declining to reopen a discussion which had already been exhausted, and proving again what was known to the whole world, that Texas had long since achieved her independence, the Secretary of State expressed the regret of this Government that Mexico should have taken offence at the resolution of annexation passed by Congress, and gave assurance that our "most strenuous efforts shall be devoted to the amicable adjustment of every cause of complaint between the two Governments, and to the cultivation of the kindest and most friendly relations between the sister republics."

That I have acted in the spirit of this assurance will appear from the events which have since occurred. Notwithstanding Mexico had abruptly terminated all diplomatic intercourse with the United States, and ought therefore to have been the first to ask for its resumption, yet, waving all ceremony, I embraced the earliest favorable opportunity "to ascertain from the Mexican Government whether they would receive an envoy from the United States intrusted with full power to adjust all the questions in dispute between the two Governments." In September, 1845, I believed the propitious moment for such an overture had arrived. Texas, by the enthusiastic and almost unanimous will of her people, had pronounced in favor of annexation. Mexico herself had agreed to acknowledge the independence of Texas, subject to a condition, it is true, which she had no right to impose and no power to enforce. The last lingering hope of Mexico, if she still could have retained any, that Texas would again become one of her provinces, must have been abandoned.

The consul of the United States at the city of Mexico was, therefore, instructed by the Secretary of State on the fifteenth of September, 1845, to make the inquiry of the Mexican Government. The inquiry was made, and on the fifteenth of October, 1845, the Minister of Foreign Affairs of the Mexican Government, in a note addressed to our consul, gave a favorable response, requesting, at the same time, that our naval force might be withdrawn from Vera Cruz while negotiations should be pending. Upon the receipt of this note, our naval force was promptly withdrawn from Vera Cruz. A Minister was immediately appointed, and departed to Mexico. Every thing bore a promising aspect for a speedy and peaceable adjustment of all our difficulties. At the date of my annual message to Congress, in December last, no doubt was entertained but that he would be received by the Mexican Government, and the hope was cherished that all cause of misunderstanding between the two countries would be speedily removed. In the confident hope that such would be the result of his mission, I informed Congress that I forbore at that time to "recommend such ulterior measures of redress for the wrongs and injuries we had so long borne, as it would have been proper to make had no such negotiation been instituted." To my surprise and regret, the Mexican Government, though solemnly pledged to do so upon the arrival of our Minister in Mexico, refused to receive and accredit him. When he reached Vera Cruz, on the thirtieth of November,

1845, he found that the aspect of affairs had undergone an unhappy change. The Government of General Herrera, who was at that time President of the republic, was tottering to its fall. General Paredes (a military leader) had manifested his determination to overthrow the Government of Herrera by a military revolution; and one of the principal means which he employed to effect his purpose, and render the Government of Herrera odious to the army and people of Mexico, was by loudly condemning its determination to receive a minister of peace from the United States, alleging that it was the intention of Herrera, by a treaty with the United States, to dismember the territory of Mexico, by ceding away the department of Texas. The Government of Herrera is believed to have been well disposed to a pacific adjustment of existing difficulties; but, probably alarmed for its own security, and in order to ward off the danger of the revolution led by Paredes, violated its solemn agreement, and refused to receive or accredit our Minister; and this, although informed that he had been invested with full power to adjust all questions of dispute between the two Governments. Among the frivolous pretexts for this refusal, the principal one was, that our Minister had not gone upon a special mission, confined to the question of Texas alone, leaving all the outrages upon our flag and our citizens unredressed. The Mexican Government well knew that both our national honor and the protection due to our citizens imperatively required that the two questions of boundary and indemnity should be treated of together, as naturally and inseparably blended, and they ought to have seen that this course was best calculated to enable the United States to extend to them the most liberal justice. On the thirtieth of December, 1845, General Herrera resigned the Presidency, and yielded up the Government to General Paredes without a struggle. Thus a revolution was accomplished solely by the army commanded by Paredes, and the supreme power in Mexico passed into the hands of a military usurper, who was known to be bitterly hostile to the United States.

Although the prospect of a pacific adjustment with the new Government was unpromising, from the known hostility of its head to the United States, yet, determined that nothing should be left undone on our part to restore friendly relations between the two countries, our Minister was instructed to present his credentials to the new Government, and ask to be accredited by it in a diplomatic character in which he had been commissioned. These instructions he executed by his note of the first of March, 1846, addressed to the Mexican Minister of Foreign Affairs, but his request was insultingly refused by that Minister in his answer of the twelfth of the same month. No alternative remained for our Minister but to demand his passports, and return to the United States.

Thus was the extraordinary spectacle presented to the civilized world, of a Government, in violation of its own express agreement, having twice rejected a minister of peace, invested with full powers to adjust all the existing differences between the two countries in a manner just and honorable to both. I am not aware that modern history presents a parallel case, in which, in time of peace, one nation has refused even to hear propositions from another for terminating existing difficulties between them. Scarcely a hope of adjusting our difficulties, even at a remote day, or of preserving peace with Mexico, could be cherished while Paredes remained at the head of the Government. He had acquired the supreme power by a military revolution, and upon the most solemn pledges to wage war against the United States, and to reconquer Texas, which he claimed as a revolted province of Mexico. He had denounced as guilty of treason all those Mexicans who considered Texas as no longer constituting a part of the territory of Mexico, and who were friendly to the cause of peace. The duration of the war which he waged against the United States was indefinite, because the end which he proposed, of the reconquest of Texas, was hopeless. Besides, there was good reason to believe, from all his conduct, that it was his intention to convert the republic of Mexico into a monarchy, and to call a foreign European prince to the throne. Preparatory to this end, he had, during his short rule, destroyed the liberty of the press, tolerating that portion of it only which openly advocated the establishment of a monarchy. The better to secure the success of his ultimate designs, he had, by an arbitrary decree, convoked a Congress—not to be elected by the free voice of the people, but to be chosen in a manner to make them subservient to his will, and to give him absolute control over their deliberations.

Under all these circumstances, it was believed that any revolution in Mexico, founded upon opposition to the ambitious projects of Paredes, would tend to promote the cause of peace, as well as prevent any attempted European interference in the affairs of the North American continent—both objects of deep interest to the United States. Any such foreign interference, if attempted, must have been resisted by the United States. My views upon that subject were fully communicated to Congress in my last annual Message. In any event, it was certain that no change whatever in the Government of Mexico, which would deprive Paredes of power, could be for the worse, so far as the United States were concerned, while it was highly probable that any change must be for the better. This was the state of affairs existing when Congress, on the thirteenth of May last, recognized the existence of the war which had been commenced by the Government of Paredes, and it became an object of much importance, with a view to a speedy settlement of our difficulties, and the restoration of an honorable peace, that Paredes should not retain power in Mexico.

Before that time there were symptoms of a revolution in Mexico, favored, as it was understood to be, by the more liberal party, and especially by those who were opposed to foreign interference and to the monarchical form of government. Santa Anna was then in exile in Havana, having been expelled from power and banished from his country by a revolution which occurred in December, 1844; but it was known that he had still a considerable party in his favor in Mexico. It was also equally well known that no vigilance which could be exerted by our squadron would, in all probability, have prevented him from effecting a landing somewhere on the extensive gulf coast of Mexico, if he desired to return to his country. He had openly professed an entire change of policy; had expressed his regret that he had subverted the federal constitution of 1824, and avowed that he was now in favor of its restoration. He had publicly declared his hostility, in the strongest terms, to the establishment of a monarchy, and to European interference in the affairs of his country.

Information to this effect had been received, from sources believed to be reliable, at the date of the recognition of the existence of the war by Congress, and was afterwards fully confirmed by the receipt of the despatch of our consul in the city of Mexico, with the accompanying documents, which are herewith transmitted. Besides, it was reasonable to suppose that he must see the ruinous consequences to Mexico of a war with the United States, and that it would be his interest to favor peace.

It was under these circumstances and upon these considerations that it was deemed expedient not to obstruct his return to Mexico, should he attempt to do so. Our object was the restoration of peace; and with that view, no reason was perceived why we should take part with Paredes, and aid him, by means of our blockade, in preventing the return of his rival to Mexico. On the contrary, it was believed that the intestine divisions which ordinary sagacity could not but anticipate as the fruit of Santa Anna's return to Mexico, and his contest with Parades, might strongly tend to produce a disposition with both parties to restore and preserve peace with the United States. Paredes was a soldier by profession, and a monarchist in principle. He had but recently before been successful in a military revolution, by which he had obtained power. He was the sworn enemy of the United States, with which he had involved his country in the existing war. Santa Anna had been expelled from power by the army, was known to be in open hostility to Paredes, and publicly pledged against foreign intervention and the restoration of monarchy in Mexico. In view of these facts and circumstances it was, that, when orders were issued to the commander of our naval forces in the Gulf, on the thirteenth day of May last, the day on which the existence of the war was recognized by Congress, to place the coasts of Mexico under blockade, he was directed not to obstruct the passage of Santa Anna to Mexico, should he attempt to return.

A revolution took place in Mexico in the early part of August following, by which the power of Paredes was overthrown, and he has since been banished from the country, and is now in exile. Shortly afterwards Santa Anna returned. It remains to be seen whether his return may not yet prove to be favorable to a pacific adjustment of the existing difficulties, it being manifestly his interest not to persevere in the prosecution of a war commenced by Paredes, to accomplish a purpose so absurd as the reconquest of Texas to the Sabine. Had Paredes remained in power, it is morally certain that any pacific adjustment would have been hopeless.

Upon the commencement of hostilities by Mexico against the United States, the indignant spirit of the nation was at once aroused. Congress promptly responded to the expectations of the country, and, by the act of the thirteenth of May last, recognized the fact that war existed, by the act of Mexico, between the United States and that republic, and granted the means necessary for its vigorous prosecution. Being involved in a war thus commenced by Mexico, and for the justice of which on our part we may confidently appeal to the whole world, I resolved to prosecute it with the utmost vigor. Accordingly, the ports of Mexico on the Gulf and on the Pacific have been placed under blockade, and her territory invaded at several important points. The reports from the Departments of War and the Navy will inform you more in detail of the measures adopted in the emergency in which our country was placed, and of the gratifying results which have been accomplished.

The various columns of the army have performed their duty under great disadvantages, with the most distinguished skill and courage. The victories of Palo Alto and Resaca de la Palma, and of Monterey, won against greatly superior numbers, and against most decided advantages in other respects on the part of the enemy, were brilliant in their execution, and entitle our brave officers and soldiers to the grateful thanks of their country. The nation deplores the loss of the brave officers and men who have gallantly fallen while vindicating and defending their country's rights and honor.

It is a subject of pride and satisfaction that our volunteer citizen soldiers, who so promptly responded to their country's call, with an experience of the discipline of a camp of only a few weeks, have borne their part in the hard-fought battle of Monterey with a constancy and courage equal to that of veteran troops, and worthy of the highest admiration. The privations of long marches through the enemy's country, and through a wilderness, have been borne without a murmur. By rapid movements the province of New Mexico, with Santa Fé, its capital, has been captured without bloodshed. The navy has co-operated with the army, and rendered important services: if not so brilliant, it is because the enemy had no force to meet them on their own element, and because of the defences which nature has interposed in the difficulties of the navigation on the Mexican coast. Our squadron in the Pacific, with the co-operation of a gallant officer of the army, and a small force hastily collected in that distant country, have acquired bloodless possession of the Californias, and the American flag has been raised at every important point in that province.

I congratulate you on the success which has thus attended our military and naval operations. In less than seven months after Mexico commenced hostilities, at a time selected by herself, we have taken possession of many of her principal ports, driven back and pursued her invading army, and acquired military possession of the Mexican provinces of New Mexico, New Leon, Coahuila, Tamaulipas, and the Californias, a territory larger in extent than that embraced in the original thirteen States of the Union, inhabited by a considerable population, and much of it more than a thousand miles from the points at which we had to collect our forces and commence our movements. By the blockade, the import and export trade of the enemy has been cut off. Well may the American people be proud of the energy and gallantry of our regular and volunteer officers and soldiers. The events of these few months afford a gratifying proof that our country can, under any emergency, confidently rely for the maintenance of her honor, and the defence of her rights, on an effective force, ready at all times voluntarily to relinquish the comforts of home for the perils and privations of the camp. And though such a force may be for the time expensive, it is in the end economical, as the ability to command it removes the necessity of employing a large standing army in time of peace, and proves that our people love their institutions, and are ever ready to defend and protect them.

Whilst the war was in a course of vigorous and successful prosecution, being still anxious to arrest its evils, and considering that, after the brilliant victories of our arms on the eighth and ninth of May last, the national honor could not be compromitted by it, another overture was made to Mexico, by my direction, on the twenty-seventh of July last, to terminate hostilities by a peace just and honorable to both countries. On the thirty-first of August following, the Mexican Government declined to accept this friendly overture, but referred it to the decision of a Mexican Congress, to be assembled in the early part of the present month. I communicate to you, herewith, a copy of the letter of the Secretary of State proposing to reopen negotiations, of the answer of the Mexican Government, and the reply thereto of the Secretary of State.

The war will continue to be prosecuted with vigor, as the best means of securing peace. It is hoped that the decision of the Mexican Congress, to which our last overture has been referred, may result in a speedy and honorable peace. With our experience, however, of the unreasonable course of the Mexican authorities, it is the part of wisdom not to relax in the energy of our military operations until the result is made known. In this view, it is deemed important to hold military possession of all the provinces which have been taken, until a definitive treaty of peace shall have been concluded and ratified by the two countries.

The war has not been waged with a view to conquest; but having been commenced by Mexico, it has been carried into the enemy's country, and will be vigorously prosecuted there, with a view to obtain an honorable peace, and thereby secure ample indemnity for the expenses of the war, as well as to our much-injured citizens, who hold large pecuniary demands against Mexico.

By the laws of nations, a conquered territory is subject to be governed by the conqueror during his military possession, and until there is either a treaty of peace, or he shall voluntarily withdraw from it. The old civil government being necessarily superseded, it is the right and duty of the conqueror to secure his conquest, and to provide for the maintenance of civil order and the rights of the inhabitants. This right has been exercised, and this duty performed, by our military and naval commanders, by the establishment of temporary governments in some of the conquered provinces in Mexico, assimilating them, as far as practicable, to the free institutions of our own country. In the provinces of New Mexico, and of the Californias, little, if any, further resistance is apprehended from the inhabitants to the temporary governments which have thus, from the necessity of the case, and according to the laws of war, been established. It may be proper to provide for the security of these important conquests by making an adequate appropriation for the purpose of erecting fortifications and defraying the expenses necessarily incident to the maintenance of our possession and authority over them.

Near the close of your last session, for reasons communicated to Congress, I deemed it important, as a measure for securing a speedy peace with Mexico, that a sum of money should be appropriated, and placed in the power of the Executive, similar to that which had been made upon two former occasions, during the administration of President Jefferson.

On the twenty-sixth of February, 1803, an appropriation of two millions of dollars was made, and placed at the disposal of the President. Its object is well known. It was at that time in contemplation to acquire Louisiana from France, and it was intended to be applied as a part of the consideration which might be paid for that territory. On the thirteenth of February, 1806, the same sum was in like manner appropriated, with a view to the purchase of the Floridas from Spain. These appropriations were made to facilitate negotiations, and as a means to enable the President to accomplish the important objects in view. Though it did not become necessary for the President to use these appropriations, yet a state of things might have arisen in which it would have been highly important for him to do so, and the wisdom of making them cannot be doubted. It is believed that the measure recommended at your last session met with the approbation of decided majorities in both Houses of Congress. Indeed, in different forms, a bill making an appropriation of two millions of dollars passed each House, and it is much to be regretted that it did not become a law. The reasons which induced me to recommend the measure at that time still exist; and I again submit the subject for your consideration, and suggest the importance of early action upon it. Should the appropriation be made and be not needed, it will remain in the treasury: should it be deemed proper to apply it, in whole or in part, it will be accounted for as other public expenditures.

Immediately after Congress had recognized the existence of the war with Mexico, my attention was directed to the danger that privateers might be fitted out in the ports of Cuba and Porto Rico, to prey upon the commerce of the United States; and I invited the special attention of the Spanish Government to the fourteenth article of our treaty with that power, of the twentieth of October, 1795, under which the citizens and subjects of either nation who shall take commissions or letters of marque to act as privateers against the other "shall be punished as pirates."

It affords me pleasure to inform you that I have received assurances from the Spanish Government that this article of the treaty shall be faithfully observed on its part. Orders for this purpose were immediately transmitted from that Government to the authorities of Cuba and Porto Rico to exert their utmost vigilance in preventing any attempts to fit out privateers in those islands against the United States. From the good faith of Spain, I am fully satisfied that this treaty will be executed in its spirit as well as its letter; whilst the United States will, on their part, faithfully perform all the obligations which it imposes on them.

Information has been recently received at the Department of State that the Mexican Government has sent to Havana blank commissions to privateers, and blank certificates of naturalization, signed by General Salas, the present head of the Mexican Government. There is also reason to apprehend that similar documents have been transmitted to other parts of the world. Copies of these papers, in translation, are herewith transmitted.

As the preliminaries required by the practice of civilized nations for commissioning privateers and regulating their conduct appear not to have been observed, and as these commissions are in blank, to be filled up with the names of citizens and subjects of all nations who may be willing to purchase them, the whole proceeding can only be construed as an invitation to all the freebooters upon earth, who are willing to pay for the privilege, to cruise against American commerce. It will be for our courts of justice to decide whether, under such circumstances, these Mexican letters of marque and reprisal shall protect those who accept them, and commit robberies upon the high seas under their authority, from the pains and penalties of piracy.

If the certificates of naturalization thus granted be intended by Mexico to shield Spanish subjects from the guilt and punishment of pirates, under our treaty with Spain, they will certainly prove unavailing. Such a subterfuge would be but a weak device to defeat the provisions of a solemn treaty.

I recommend that Congress should immediately provide by law for the trial and punishment as pirates of Spanish subjects who, escaping the vigilance of their Government, shall be found guilty of privateering against the United States. I do not apprehend serious danger from these privateers. Our navy will be constantly on the alert to protect our commerce. Besides, in case prizes should be made of American vessels, the utmost vigilance will be exerted by our blockading squadron to prevent the captors from taking them into Mexican ports, and it is not apprehended that any nation will violate its neutrality by suffering such prizes to be condemned and sold within its jurisdiction.

I recommend that Congress should immediately provide by law for granting letters of marque and reprisal against vessels under the Mexican flag. It is true that there are but few, if any, commercial vessels of Mexico upon the high seas; and it is, therefore, not probable that many American privateers would be fitted out, in case a law should pass authorizing this mode of warfare. It is, notwithstanding, certain that such privateers may render good service to the commercial interests of the country by recapturing our merchant ships, should any be taken by armed vessels under the Mexican flag, as well as by capturing these vessels themselves. Every means within our power should be rendered available for the protection of our commerce.

The annual report of the Secretary of the Treasury will exhibit a detailed statement of the condition of the finances. The imports for the fiscal year ending on the 30th of June last were of the value of one hundred and twenty-one million six hundred and ninety-one thousand seven hundred and ninety-seven dollars; of which the amount exported was eleven million three hundred and forty-six thousand six hundred and twenty-three dollars, leaving the amount retained in the country for domestic consumption one hundred and ten million three hundred and forty-five thousand one hundred and seventy-four dollars. The value of the exports for the same period was one hundred and thirteen million four hundred and eighty-eight thousand five hundred and sixteen dollars; of which one hundred and two million one hundred and forty-one thousand eight hundred and ninety-three dollars consisted of domestic productions, and eleven million three hundred and forty-six thousand six hundred and twenty-three dollars of foreign articles.

The receipts into the treasury for the same year were twenty-nine million four hundred and ninety-nine thousand two hundred and forty-seven dollars and six cents; of which there was derived from customs twenty-six million seven hundred and twelve thousand six hundred and sixty-seven dollars and eighty-seven cents; from sales of public lands two million six hundred and ninety-five thousand four hundred and fifty-two dollars and forty-eight cents; and from incidental and miscellaneous sources ninety-two thousand one hundred and twenty-six dollars and seventy-one cents. The expenditures for the same period were twenty-eight million thirty-one thousand one hundred and fourteen dollars and twenty cents, and the balance in the treasury on the first day of July last was nine million one hundred and twenty-six thousand four hundred and thirty-nine dollars and eight cents.

The amount of the public debt, including treasury notes, on the first of the present month, was twenty-four million two hundred and fifty-six thousand four hundred and ninety-four dollars and sixty cents; of which the sum of seventeen million seven hundred and eighty-eight thousand seven hundred and ninety-nine dollars and sixty-two cents was outstanding on the 4th of March, 1845, leaving the amount incurred since that time six million four hundred and sixty-seven thousand six hundred and ninety-four dollars and ninety-eight cents.

In order to prosecute the war with Mexico with vigor and energy, as the best means of bringing it to a speedy and honorable termination, a further loan will be necessary to meet the expenditures for the present and the next fiscal years. If the war should be continued until the 30th of June, 1848—being the end of the next fiscal year—it is estimated that an additional loan of twenty-three millions of dollars will be required. This estimate is made upon the assumption that it will be necessary to retain constantly in the treasury four millions of dollars, to guard against contingencies. If such surplus were not required to be retained, then a loan of nineteen millions of dollars would be sufficient. If, however, Congress should at the present session, impose a revenue duty on the principal articles now embraced in the free list, it is estimated that an additional annual revenue of about two millions and a half, amounting, it is estimated, on the 30th of June, 1848, to four millions of dollars, would be derived from that source; and the loan required would be reduced by that amount. It is estimated, also, that should Congress graduate and reduce the price of such of the public lands as have been long in the market, the additional revenue derived from that source would be annually, for several years to come, between half a million and a million of dollars; and the loan required may be reduced by that amount also. Should these measures be adopted, the loan required would not probably exceed eighteen or nineteen millions of dollars—leaving in the treasury a constant surplus of four millions of dollars. The loan proposed, it is estimated, will be sufficient to cover the necessary expenditures, both for the war and for all other purposes, up to the 30th of June, 1848; and an amount of this loan, not exceeding one-half, may be required during the present fiscal year, and the greater part of the remainder during the first half of the fiscal year succeeding.

In order that timely notice may be given, and proper measures taken to effect the loan, or such portion of it as may be required, it is important that the authority of Congress to make it be given at an early period of your present session. It is suggested that the loan should be contracted for a period of twenty years, with authority to purchase the stock and pay it off, at an earlier period, at its market value, out of any surplus which may at any time be in the treasury applicable to that purpose. After the establishment of peace with Mexico, it is supposed that a considerable surplus will exist, and that the debt may be extinguished in a much shorter period than that for which it may be contracted. The period of twenty years, as that for which the proposed loan may be contracted, in preference to a shorter period, is suggested, because all experience, both at home and abroad, has shown that loans are effected upon much better terms upon long time, than when they are re-imbursable at short dates.

Necessary as this measure is, to sustain the honor and the interests of the country, engaged in a foreign war, it is not doubted but that Congress will promptly authorize it.

The balance in the treasury on the 1st of July last exceeded nine millions of dollars, notwithstanding considerable expenditures had been made for the war during the months of May and June preceding. But for the war, the whole public debt could and would have been extinguished within a short period: and it was a part of my settled policy to do so, and thus relieve the people from its burden, and place the Government in a position which would enable it to reduce the public expenditures to that economical standard which is most consistent with the general welfare, and the pure and wholesome progress of our institutions.

Among our just causes of complaint against Mexico, arising out of her refusal to treat for peace, as well before as since the war so unjustly commenced on her part, are the extraordinary expenditures in which we have been involved. Justice to our own people will make it proper that Mexico should be held responsible for these expenditures.

Economy in the public expenditures is at all times a high duty which all public functionaries of the Government owe to the people. This duty becomes the more imperative in a period of war, when large and extraordinary expenditures become unavoidable. During the existence of the war with Mexico all our resources should be husbanded, and no appropriations made except such as are absolutely necessary for its vigorous prosecution and the due administration of the Government. Objects of appropriation which in peace may be deemed useful or proper, but which are not indispensable for the public service, may, when the country is engaged in a foreign war, be well postponed to a future period. By the observance of this policy at your present session, large amounts may be saved to the treasury, and be applied to objects of pressing and urgent necessity, and thus the creation of a corresponding amount of public debt may be avoided.

It is not meant to recommend that the ordinary and necessary appropriations for the support of Government should be withheld, but it is well known that at every session of Congress appropriations are proposed for numerous objects which may or may not be made, without materially affecting the public interests; and these it is recommended should not be granted.

The act passed at your last session "reducing the duties on imports" not having gone into operation until the first of the present month, there has not been time for its practical effect upon the revenue, and the business of the country, to be developed. It is not doubted, however, that the just policy which it adopts will add largely to our foreign trade, and promote the general prosperity. Although it cannot be certainly foreseen what amount of revenue it will yield, it is estimated that it will exceed that produced by the act of 1842, which it superseded. The leading principles established by it are, to levy the taxes with a view to raise revenue, and to impose them upon the articles imported according to their actual value.

The act of 1842, by the excessive rates of duty which it imposed on many articles, either totally excluded them from importation, or greatly reduced the amount imported, and thus diminished instead of producing revenue. By it the taxes were imposed not for the legitimate purpose of raising revenue, but to afford advantages to favored classes, at the expense of a large majority of their fellow-citizens. Those employed in agriculture, mechanical pursuits, commerce, and navigation, were compelled to contribute from their substance to swell the profits and overgrown wealth of the comparatively few who had invested their capital in manufactures. The taxes were not levied in proportion to the value of the articles upon which they were imposed; but, widely departing from this just rule, the lighter taxes were, in many cases, levied upon articles of luxury and high price, and the heavier taxes on those of necessity and low price, consumed by the great mass of the people. It was a system the inevitable effect of which was to relieve favored classes and the wealthy few from contributing their just proportion for the support of Government, and to lay the burden on the labor of the many engaged in other pursuits than manufactures.

A system so unequal and unjust has been superseded by the existing law, which imposes duties not for the benefit or injury of classes or pursuits, but distributes, and, as far as practicable, equalizes the public burdens among all classes and occupations. The favored classes, who, under the unequal and unjust system which has been repealed, have heretofore realized large profits, and many of them amassed large fortunes, at the expense of the many who have been made tributary to them, will have no reason to complain if they shall be required to bear their just proportion of the taxes necessary for the support of Government. So far from it, it will be perceived, by an examination of the existing law, that discriminations in the rates of duty imposed within the revenue principle, have been retained in their favor. The incidental aid against foreign competition which they still enjoy gives them an advantage which no other pursuits possess; but of this none others will complain, because the duties levied are necessary for revenue. These revenue duties, including freights and charges, which the importer must pay before he can come in competition with the home manufacturer in our markets, amount, on nearly all our leading branches of manufacture, to more than one-third of the value of the imported article, and in some cases to almost one-half its value. With such advantages, it is not doubted that our domestic manufacturers will continue to prosper, realizing in well-conducted establishments even greater profits than can be derived from any other regular business. Indeed, so far from requiring the protection of even incidental revenue duties, our manufacturers in several leading branches are extending their business, giving evidence of great ingenuity and skill, and of their ability to compete, with increased prospect of success, for the open market of the world. Domestic manufactures, to the value of several millions of dollars, which cannot find a market at home, are annually exported to foreign countries. With such rates of duty as those established by the existing law, the system will probably be permanent; and capitalists, who have made, or shall hereafter make, their investments in manufactures, will know upon what to rely. The country will be satisfied with these rates, because the advantages which the manufacturers still enjoy result necessarily from the collection of revenue for the support of Government. High protective duties, from their unjust operation upon the masses of the people, cannot fail to give rise to extensive dissatisfaction and complaint, and to constant efforts to change or repeal them, rendering all investments in manufactures uncertain and precarious. Lower and more permanent rates of duty, at the same time that they will yield to the manufacturer fair and remunerating profits, will secure him against the danger of frequent changes in the system, which cannot fail ruinously to affect his interests.

Simultaneously with the relaxation of the restrictive policy by the United States, Great Britain, from whose example we derived the system, has relaxed hers. She has modified her corn laws, and reduced many other duties to moderate revenue rates. After ages of experience, the statesmen of that country have been constrained by a stern necessity, and by a public opinion having its deep foundation in the suffering and wants of impoverished millions, to abandon a system the effect of which was to build up immense fortunes in the hands of the few, and to reduce the laboring millions to pauperism and misery. Nearly in the same ratio that labor was depressed, capital was increased and concentrated by the British protective policy.

The evils of the system in Great Britain were at length rendered intolerable, and it has been abandoned, but not without a severe struggle on the part of the protected and favored classes to retain the unjust advantage which they have so long enjoyed. It was to be expected that a similar struggle would be made by the same classes in the United States, whenever an attempt was made to modify or abolish the same unjust system here. The protective policy had been in operation in the United States for a much shorter period, and its pernicious effects were not, therefore, so clearly perceived and felt. Enough, however, was known of these effects to induce its repeal.

It would be strange if, in the face of the example of Great Britain, our principal foreign customer, and of the evils of a system rendered manifest in that country by long and painful experience, and in the face of the immense advantages which, under a more liberal commercial policy, we are already deriving, and must continue to derive, by supplying her starving population with food, the United States should restore a policy which she has been compelled to abandon, and thus diminish her ability to purchase from us the food and other articles which she so much needs, and we so much desire to sell. By the simultaneous abandonment of the protective policy by Great Britain and the United States, new and important markets have already been opened for our agricultural and other products; commerce and navigation have received a new impulse; labor and trade have been released from the artificial trammels which have so long fettered them; and to a great extent reciprocity, in the exchange of commodities, has been introduced at the same time by both countries, and greatly for the benefit of both. Great Britain has been forced, by the pressure of circumstances at home, to abandon a policy which has been upheld for ages, and to open her markets for our immense surplus of breadstuffs; and it is confidently believed that other powers of Europe will ultimately see the wisdom, if they be not compelled by the pauperism and sufferings of their crowded population, to pursue a similar policy.

Our farmers are more deeply interested in maintaining the just and liberal policy of the existing law than any other class of our citizens. They constitute a large majority of our population; and it is well known that when they prosper, all other pursuits prosper also. They have heretofore not only received none of the bounties or favors of Government, but, by the unequal operations of the protective policy, have been made, by the burdens of taxation which it imposed, to contribute to the bounties which have enriched others.

When a foreign as well as a home market is opened to them, they must receive, as they are now receiving, increased prices for their products. They will find a readier sale, and at better prices, for their wheat, flour, rice, Indian corn, beef, pork, lard, butter, cheese, and other articles, which they produce. The home market alone is inadequate to enable them to dispose of the immense surplus of food and other articles which they are capable of producing, even at the most reduced prices, for the manifest reason that they cannot be consumed in the country. The United States can, from their immense surplus, supply not only the home demand, but the deficiencies of food required by the whole world.

That the reduced production of some of the chief articles of food in Great Britain, and other parts of Europe, may have contributed to increase the demand for our breadstuffs and provisions, is not doubted; but that the great and efficient cause of this increased demand, and of increased prices, consists in the removal of artificial restrictions heretofore imposed, is deemed to be equally certain. That our exports of food, already increased and increasing beyond former example, under the more liberal policy which has been adopted, will be still vastly enlarged, unless they be checked or prevented by a restoration of the protective policy, cannot be doubted. That our commercial and navigating interests will be enlarged in a corresponding ratio with the increase of our trade is equally certain; while our manufacturing interests will still be the favored interests of the country, and receive the incidental protection afforded them by revenue duties; and more than this they cannot justly demand.

In my annual message of December last, a tariff of revenue duties based upon the principles of the existing law was recommended, and I have seen no reason to change the opinion then expressed. In view of the probable beneficial effects of that law, I recommend that the policy established by it be maintained. It has but just commenced to operate; and to abandon or modify it without giving it a fair trial, would be inexpedient and unwise. Should defects in any of its details be ascertained, by actual experience, to exist, these may be hereafter corrected; but until such defects shall become manifest, the act should be fairly tested.

It is submitted for your consideration whether it may not be proper, as a war measure, to impose revenue duties on some of the articles now embraced in the free list. Should it be deemed proper to impose such duties, with a view to raise revenue to meet the expenses of the war with Mexico, or to avoid to that extent the creation of a public debt, they may be repealed when the emergency which gave rise to them shall cease to exist, and constitute no part of the permanent policy of the country.

The act of the sixth of August last, "to provide for the better organization of the treasury, and for the collection, safekeeping, transfer, and disbursement of the public revenue," has been carried into execution as rapidly as the delay necessarily arising out of the appointment of new officers, taking and approving their bonds, and preparing and securing proper places for the safekeeping of the public money, would permit. It is not proposed to depart in any respect from the principles or policy on which this great measure is founded. There are, however, defects in the details of the measure, developed by its practical operation, which are fully set forth in the report of the Secretary of the Treasury, to which the attention of Congress is invited; these defects would impair to some extent the successful operation of the law at all times, but are especially embarrassing when the country is engaged in a war, when the expenditures are greatly increased, when loans are to be effected, and the disbursements are to be made at points many hundred miles distant, in some cases, from any depository, and a large portion of them in a foreign country. The modifications suggested in the report of the Secretary of the Treasury are recommended to your favorable consideration.

In connection with this subject I invite your attention to the importance of establishing a branch of the mint of the United States at New York. Two-thirds of the revenue derived from customs being collected at that point, the demand for specie to pay the duties will be large; and a branch mint where foreign coin and bullion could be immediately converted into American coin, would greatly facilitate the transaction of the public business, enlarge the circulation of gold and silver, and be, at the same time, a safe depository of the public money.

The importance of graduating and reducing the price of such of the public lands as have been long offered in the market at the minimum rate authorized by existing laws and remain unsold, induces me again to recommend the subject to your favorable consideration. Many millions of acres of these lands have been offered in the market for more than thirty years, and larger quantities for more than ten or twenty years; and being of an inferior quality, they must remain unsalable for an indefinite period, unless the price at which they may be purchased shall be reduced. To place a price upon them above their real value is not only to prevent their sale, and thereby deprive the treasury of any income from that source, but it is unjust to the States in which they lie, because it retards their growth and increase of population, and because they have no power to levy a tax upon them as upon other lands within their limits, held by other proprietors than the United States, for the support of their local governments.

The beneficial effects of the graduation principle have been realized by some of the States owning the lands within their limits, in which it has been adopted. They have been demonstrated also by the United States acting as the trustee of the Chickasaw tribe of Indians in the sale of their lands lying within the States of Mississippi and Alabama. The Chickasaw lands, which would not command in the market the minimum price established by the laws of the United States for the sale of their lands, were, in pursuance of the treaty of 1834 with that tribe, subsequently offered for sale at graduated and reduced rates for limited periods. The result was that large quantities of these lands were purchased, which would otherwise have remained unsold. The lands were disposed of at their real value, and many persons of limited means were enabled to purchase small tracts, upon which they have settled with their families. That similar results would be produced by the adoption of the graduation policy by the United States, in all the States in which they are the owners of large bodies of lands which have been long in the market, cannot be doubted. It cannot be a sound policy to withhold large quantities of the public lands from the use and occupation of our citizens, by fixing upon them prices which experience has shown they will not command. On the contrary, it is a wise policy to afford facilities to our citizens to become the owners, at low and moderate rates, of freeholds of their own, instead of being the tenants and dependants of others. If it be apprehended that these lands, if reduced in price, would be secured in large quantities by speculators or capitalists, the sales may be restricted, in limited quantities, to actual settlers, or persons purchasing for purposes of cultivation.

In my last annual message I submitted for the consideration of Congress the present system of managing the mineral lands of the United States, and recommended that they should be brought into market and sold, upon such terms and under such restrictions as Congress might prescribe. By the act of the eleventh of July last, "the reserved lead mines and contiguous lands in the States of Illinois and Arkansas and Territories of Wisconsin and Iowa," were authorized to be sold. The act is confined, in its operation, to "lead mines and contiguous lands."

A large portion of the public lands containing copper and other ores is represented to be very valuable, and I recommend that provision be made authorizing the sale of these lands, upon such terms and conditions as their supposed value may, in the judgment of Congress, be deemed advisable, having due regard to the interests of such of our citizens as may be located upon them.

It will be important, during your present session, to establish a territorial government and to extend the jurisdiction and laws of the United States over the Territory of Oregon. Our laws regulating trade and intercourse with the Indian tribes east of the Rocky Mountains, should be extended to the Pacific Ocean; and for the purpose of executing them, and preserving friendly relations with the Indian tribes within our limits, an additional number of Indian agencies will be required, and should be authorized by law. The establishment of custom-houses, and of post-offices and post roads, and provisions for the transportation of the mail on such routes as the public convenience will suggest, require legislative authority. It will be proper, also, to establish a surveyor general's office in that territory, and to make the necessary provision for surveying the public lands, and bringing them into market. As our citizens who now reside in that distant region have been subjected to many hardships, privations, and sacrifices in their emigration, and by their improvements have enhanced the value of the public lands in the neighborhood of their settlements, it is recommended that liberal grants be made to them of such portions of these lands as they may occupy, and that similar grants or rights of pre-emption be made to all who may emigrate thither within a limited period, to be prescribed by law.

The report of the Secretary of War contains detailed information relative to the several branches of the public service connected with that department. The operations of the army have been of a satisfactory and highly gratifying character.

I recommend to your early and favorable consideration the measures proposed by the Secretary of War for speedily filling up the rank and file of the regular army, for its greater efficiency in the field, and for raising an additional force to serve during the war with Mexico.

Embarrassment is likely to arise for want of legal provision authorizing compensation to be made to the agents employed in the several States and Territories to pay the revolutionary and other pensioners the amounts allowed them by law. Your attention is invited to the recommendations of the Secretary of War on this subject. These agents incur heavy responsibilities and perform important duties, and no reason exists why they should not be placed on the same footing, as to compensation, with other disbursing officers.

Our relations with the various Indian tribes continue to be of a pacific character. The unhappy dissensions which have existed among the Cherokees for many years past have been healed. Since my last annual message important treaties have been negotiated with some of the tribes, by which the Indian title to large tracts of valuable land within the limits of the States and Territories has been extinguished, and arrangements made for removing them to the country west of the Mississippi. Between three and four thousand, of different tribes, have been removed to the country provided for them by treaty stipulations, and arrangements have been made for others to follow.

In our intercourse with the several tribes particular attention has been given to the important subject of education. The number of schools established among them has been increased, and additional means provided, not only for teaching them the rudiments of education, but of instructing them in agriculture and the mechanic arts.

I refer you to the report of the Secretary of the Navy for a satisfactory view of the operations of the department under his charge during the past year. It is gratifying to perceive, that while the war with Mexico has rendered it necessary to employ an unusual number of our armed vessels on her coasts, the protection due to our commerce in other quarters of the world has not proved insufficient. No means will be spared to give efficiency to the naval service in the prosecution of the war; and I am happy to know that the officers and men anxiously desire to devote themselves to the service of their country in any enterprise, however difficult of execution.

I recommend to your favorable consideration the proposition to add to each of our foreign squadrons an efficient sea steamer, and, as especially demanding attention, the establishment at Pensacola of the necessary means of repairing and refitting the vessels of the navy employed in the Gulf of Mexico.

There are other suggestions in the report which deserve, and, I doubt not, will receive, your consideration.

The progress and condition of the mail service for the past year are fully presented in the report of the Postmaster General. The revenue for the year ending on the thirtieth of June last amounted to three million four hundred and eighty-seven thousand one hundred and ninety-nine dollars, which is eight hundred and two thousand six hundred and forty-two dollars and forty-five cents less than that of the preceding year. The payments for that department during the same time amounted to four million eighty-four thousand two hundred and ninety-seven dollars and twenty-two cents. Of this sum five hundred and ninety-seven thousand and ninety-seven dollars and eighty cents have been drawn from the treasury. The disbursements for the year were two hundred and thirty-six thousand four hundred and thirty-four dollars and seventy-seven cents less than those of the preceding year. While the disbursements have been thus diminished, the mail facilities have been enlarged by new mail routes of five thousand seven hundred and thirty-nine miles; an increase of transportation of one million seven hundred and sixty-four thousand one hundred and forty-five miles, and the establishment of four hundred and eighteen new post-offices. Contractors, postmasters, and others, engaged in this branch of the service, have performed their duty with energy and faithfulness deserving commendation. For many interesting details connected with the operations of this establishment, you are referred to the report of the Postmaster General; and his suggestions for improving its revenues are recommended to your favorable consideration. I repeat the opinion expressed in my last annual Message, that the business of this department should be so regulated, that the revenues derived from it should be made to equal the expenditures; and it is believed that this may be done by proper modifications of the present laws, as suggested in the report of the Postmaster General, without changing the present rates of postage.

With full reliance upon the wisdom and patriotism of your deliberations, it will be my duty, as it will be my anxious desire, to co-operate with you in every constitutional effort to promote the welfare and maintain the honor of our common country.

JAMES K. POLK.

WASHINGTON, *December* 8, 1846.

The reading of the Message occupied upwards of two hours.

On motion of Mr. SPEIGHT, it was

Resolved, That 3,500 copies of the Message, and 1,500 copies of the Message and documents, in addition to the usual number, be printed for the use of the Senate.

WEDNESDAY, December 9.

The Journal of yesterday was read and approved.

Report of Secretary of Treasury.

The VICE PRESIDENT laid before the Senate the annual report of the Secretary of the Treasury on the state of the finances.

Mr. SPEIGHT remarked that the report was probably a lengthened one, and its reading would occupy a large portion of time. Unless, therefore, any Senator desired it should be read, he would move to dispense with the reading.

No Senator desiring the report to be read, the motion was agreed to.

Printing of the Report.

On motion of Mr. SPEIGHT, it was

Ordered, That the report be printed; and that five thousand copies in addition to the usual number be printed for the use of the Senate.

HOUSE OF REPRESENTATIVES.

WEDNESDAY, December 9.

The Journal of yesterday was read and approved.

The following members, in addition to those who were present on the first day of the session, have since appeared in their seats: Mr. SYKES, of New Jersey; Mr. LEAKE and Mr. MCDOWELL, of Virginia; Mr. LIGON, of Maryland; Mr. BELL, of Kentucky; Mr. DELANO, of Ohio; Mr. EWING, of Pennsylvania; Mr. DOBBIN, of North Carolina; and Mr. HOUSTON, of Alabama.

THURSDAY, December 10.

The Journal of yesterday was read and approved.

Messrs. JAMES THOMPSON, of Pennsylvania, TOWNS, of Georgia, and DARGAN, of Alabama, appeared, and took their seats.

Constitution of Iowa.

Mr. DODGE appealed to Mr. BRODHEAD to allow him to present the constitution of the State of Iowa, and have it referred; and Mr. BRODHEAD having yielded the floor—

Mr. DODGE presented the constitution and form of State government adopted by a convention of delegates assembled in Iowa City, on the 18th day of May, A. D. 1846, in pursuance of the provisions of the act of the Territorial Assembly, approved January 17, 1846.

Mr. D. read from the law the following section:

"SEC. 8. That said constitution and form of State government shall, if ratified at the election specified in the 5th section of this act, be presented to the Congress of the United States at the next ensuing session thereof, for admittance into the Union upon an equal footing with the original States, and with such other provisions and conditions as may be provided for by the convention framing said constitution and form of State government, *but shall not be presented for admittance until the same shall be accepted and ratified by the qualified electors of this Territory.*"

Mr. D. said, accompanying the constitution now presented, would be found a letter from the Secretary of the Territory, transmitting a copy of the proclamation of the Governor, declaring the adoption of the constitution by a majority of the qualified electors at the time and in the manner prescribed in the law calling the convention.

Mr. D. said that the vote on the constitution was had on the first Monday in August, the third day of the month, and that Congress had adjourned on the tenth of August. It was therefore impossible to know the result of the vote upon the question of the adoption or rejection of the constitution during the last session; indeed, it was not certainly known in the Territory until some time in September. The 6th section of the 13th article of the constitution provides that "the first general election under this constitution shall be held at such time as the Governor of the Territory, by proclamation, may appoint, *within three months* after its adoption, for the election of a Governor, two members of Congress," &c. Under this provision of the constitution the Territorial Governor issued his proclamation for an election, which took place on the 26th of October last. One of the members elected to this House was in the city, and ready to take his seat as soon as an act or joint resolution could be passed admitting the State.

Mr. D. had seized the earliest moment afforded him, after the appointment of the committees, to present the constitution of his State, and the evidence of its ratification by the people. At the last session an act was passed prescribing the constitution of the State of Iowa, &c. The constitution and the act of Congress referred to were in perfect harmony—the boundaries in each being the same.

Mr. D. said he would call the attention of the Committee on Territories, to whom he should move to refer the subject, to the necessity of speedy action on their part, so that the complete admission of Iowa might be consummated at the earliest day practicable.

The constitution was then referred to the Committee on Territories.

IN SENATE.

WEDNESDAY, December 16.

Return of Santa Anna to Mexico.

Mr. BARROW submitted the following resolution for consideration:

Resolved, That the President of the United States be requested to inform the Senate, if any officer or agent was sent by him or by his direction to Havana, to advise, procure, or in any manner promote the return of Santa Anna to Mexico; and if so, who was the officer or agent, what were his instructions, and when was he sent on such a mission; also that he inform the Senate by what means, and through what channel, Santa Anna was informed that an order was issued to the commander of our naval forces in the Gulf directing said commander not to obstruct his (Santa Anna's return to Mexico; and also that he transmit to the Senate copies of any correspondence in possession of the Government relative to the terms or conditions on which Santa Anna was permitted to pass through our blockading squadron, or in any manner relating to the subject of Santa Anna's return to Mexico.

HOUSE OF REPRESENTATIVES.

Monday, December 21.

Admission of Iowa into the Union.

The pending question was on the engrossment of the bill.

Mr. Douglas, from the Committee on Territories, explained its provisions.

The first section merely declared that the State, having complied with the conditions required by a law of Congress passed last session for her admission, was admitted into the Union.

The second section re-enacted the same provisions which had been contained in the bill passed last year, which was supplemental to a former law.

The people of the State having refused to accept the boundaries prescribed in the law of last session, it was deemed to follow that the law admitting the State with those boundaries of course fell with them; and it became necessary that the enactments should be revived and applied to the State as bounded in the present bill.

Mr. Sims, of South Carolina, observed that before the bill should be ordered to its third reading, he wished to call the attention of the Delegate from Iowa to a clause contained in the tenth article of the State constitution, set forth in the bill, taken in connection with one of the sections of the law of 1841. According to the present bill, the donation from the United States of five hundred thousand acres of public land to each new State to be admitted into the Union should, when received, be applied to purposes of education; but, by the law of 1841, it was required that these lands should be applied to purposes of internal improvement.

Mr. S. thought it proper to bring before Congress and before the Delegate from Iowa this discrepancy, with a view to obviate doubt or difficulty hereafter from the idea that it had escaped notice. Mr. S. approved of the alteration, and had no doubt it would be the duty of the land officers to govern themselves by the provision of the present law as modifying that of the law of 1841. The discrepancy was manifest, and it should not exist without the knowledge and notice of the House, so that if the new application of the land fund was to be made, it should be done with the knowledge and approbation of Congress.

Mr. Dodge said it was very true that the constitution approved by the people of Iowa did make that application of the proceeds of the public lands received from the United States which had been stated by the gentleman from South Carolina; but—

Mr. Sims here said, before the gentleman proceeded, he wished it distinctly to be understood by that gentleman, by the House, and the country, that he was in favor of the admission of Iowa with her constitution thus modified. He approved of the change entirely; he had referred to it not by way of objection to her reception, but merely because he thought it due to all parties that the fact should be known and understood.

Mr. Dodge proceeded to say that the people of Iowa, in accepting the constitution in its present form, considered the five hundred thousand acres of land received from the General Government as a paternal gift which they had a right to apply in any manner they might deem most conducive to their own good. They supposed that the trust had been applied to a proper and praiseworthy object, and that this House would concur in that opinion. They regarded it as the gift of a parent to the child, and that the recipient might lawfully apply it to any proper purpose. He trusted that no difficulty would grow out of the fact which had been brought to the notice of the House.

Mr. Douglas stated that all that had been done under the first law had been rendered null and of no effect by the people's refusal of their first constitution. The boundaries were then altered by a second law; these the people had agreed to; and, under this last law they came, presented their constitution, and asked to be admitted into the Union. This was the first time they had asked it; and, if admitted, they would be admitted by the present law. And this brought him to notice the objection of the gentleman from South Carolina.

Mr. Sims said he again protested against its being understood that he was opposed to the bill. He had raised no objection to it: he should, on the contrary, vote for the admission of the State under the constitution as it stood: all he desired was, that the true state of the fact should be clearly understood.

Mr. Douglas, resuming, said the gentleman seemed to have got hold of the old constitution of 1845. It was possible the same article might be in the present constitution, but if it was he was not aware of it: if it was wrong, he was willing it should be altered As to the second section of the bill, it was necessary, in order to establish Federal courts within the new

State. The provision of the former law to that effect having become inoperative, the same had been inserted in the present bill.

Mr. DODGE said it was only necessary to state what had been the understanding of the people of Iowa in this matter. They supposed that when the former constitution was rejected, the act proposing the rejected boundaries fell of course, for it was on condition of their acceptance, and this they refused. A second convention, therefore, was held in January, 1846, under the law passed in 1845. The eighth section of that law showed the necessity of a new act. By the former act the proclamation of the President of the United States was required: in this act no such requirement was contained.

Mr. SIMS entirely concurred with the gentleman from Ohio (Mr. THURMAN) as to the effect of all trusts imposed upon States, but he wholly dissented from the inference that it was therefore indifferent whether they were expressed in the State constitution or not. This amounted to saying that Congress never would trust a State, because no State was trustworthy. On the contrary, he thought States eminently worthy of trust, because whatever their legal inefficacy, they created a moral obligation which he hoped no State would disregard.

Mr. THURMAN disclaimed having meant to insinuate any thing to the contrary. He admitted trusts created a moral obligation on a State; but it was moral only, and never could be enforced. And he meant to say that he would not limit the State constitution without sufficient reason.

Mr. SIMS repeated his willingness to admit the State and his hope that the bill would pass.

Mr. THOMPSON, of Pennsylvania, asked the yeas and nays; but the House refused to order them. And thereupon the bill was read a third time and passed.

IN SENATE.

MONDAY, December 28.

The Writings of Alexander Hamilton.

The bill for the relief of Elizabeth Hamilton, widow of Alexander Hamilton, was taken up for consideration.

Mr. BREESE called for the reading.

The Secretary read it accordingly. It enacts,

"That the Treasurer of the United States be, and be is hereby, directed to pay to Elizabeth Hamilton, widow of Alexander Hamilton, out of any moneys in the treasury not otherwise appropriated, the sum of twenty thousand dollars, whenever the said Elizabeth Hamilton shall deliver to the librarian of Congress one thousand copies of each of the five volumes which she proposes to publish of the writings of General Hamilton, and shall also deliver to said librarian the entire manuscripts, to be deposited and remain forever among the archives of the Government: *Provided, always*, That such volumes shall be octavo, and substantially bound in leather, and not less than five hundred pages each, and shall be compiled by some suitable person, at the expense of Mrs. Hamilton, and to be by her selected and chosen, with the approval of the Committee on the Library; and that such five volumes shall embrace substantially all the writings of General Hamilton which are of a public and important character."

The question being on ordering the bill to be engrossed for a third reading—

Mr. CHALMERS suggested that the bill should be passed over informally, the chairman of the Committee on the Library, (Mr. PEARCE,) who reported the bill, not being in his seat.

Mr. TURNEY called for the yeas and nays on the engrossment.

Mr. CHALMERS again rose and said he had desired, as the Senator from Maryland who reported this bill was not in his seat this morning, that the bill might be passed over informally. If too late, however, for a postponement, or the Senate was unwilling to postpone, he desired to make a few remarks in explanation. At the last session, this subject was fully examined by the committee which reported this bill, and it passed the Senate by a large majority. The works which were proposed to be published were furnished to the committee at that time for examination, and he became satisfied of their very great importance in regard to the subject of which they treat. They relate to all the important transactions during the revolutionary war, and to many subjects and occurrences subsequent to that war, when General Hamilton was Secretary of the Treasury. He could conceive of no papers more valuable or more desirable to preserve with the archives of the country than those which were offered to them by Mrs. Hamilton. The cost of these papers was not more than they were really worth; and he thought it would be becoming in, nay, that it was the duty of this Government, to obtain possession of these documents, over and above any disposition they might feel to render to the widow of so distinguished a man so small a service. He should feel that the Senate, in rejecting this bill, was not only doing an injustice to the widow of Alexander Hamilton, but was not fulfilling its duty to the Government. He hoped the bill would pass, as at the last session, by a large majority.

Mr. SEMPLE had voted for this bill at the last session, and should do so again; still, he would not object to the postponement of this bill to next week, if desired by Senators, until the Senator from Maryland should return to his seat. He believed these books would be valuable to the country, and therefore he hoped the bill would pass.

The question was then taken on ordering the bill to be engrossed for a third reading, and it was decided in the affirmative, as follows:

YEAS.—Messrs. Archer, Atchinson, Badger, Bagby, Chalmers, John M. Clayton, Thomas Clayton, Corwin, Crittenden, Davis, Evans, Greene, Huntington, Jarnagin, Johnson of Louisiana, Mangum, Morehead, Phelps, Semple, Sevier, Simmons, Speight, Sturgeon, Upham, Woodbridge, and Yulee—26.

NAYS.—Messrs. Allen, Ashley, Atherton, Breese, Bright, Butler, Calhoun, Dix, Fairfield, Niles, Turney, and Westcott—12.

On motion of Mr. SPEIGHT, the bill was read a third time, and, by unanimous consent, was passed.

On motion of Mr. CHALMERS, the title of the bill was changed to "A bill to purchase the Papers of the late Alexander Hamilton."

HOUSE OF REPRESENTATIVES.

MONDAY, December 28.

The Journal of Thursday was read and approved.

Mr. ROBERT TOOMBS, of Georgia, appeared and took his seat.

IN SENATE.

WEDNESDAY, December 30.

Death of Senator Barrow.

On motion of Mr. HUNTINGTON, the reading of the Journal was dispensed with; when—

Mr. JOHNSON, of Louisiana, rose and addressed the Senate as follows:

Mr. President: Louisiana has to mourn the loss of another of her distinguished sons! It is with unfeigned sorrow I announce to the Senate the death of my late friend and colleague, the Hon. ALEXANDER BARROW, who died at Baltimore yesterday morning at five o'clock, after a short and violent attack of illness, which would not yield to the best medical skill. All the relief that medical science and skill could accomplish was applied in vain. He left this city on the 24th instant, on a short visit to Baltimore, apparently in perfect health, and I only heard of his illness the day before his death. Indeed, so sudden and unexpected was the shock produced by the annunciation of the sad event yesterday, that I cannot yet hardly realize the fact, and do not feel sufficiently composed to do justice to the memory of the deceased in the few remarks I propose to make. The deep anxiety felt here not only by the members of both Houses of Congress, but by all classes of the community, when his dangerous situation became known through the telegraph, is now dispelled by the melancholy gloom spread over the whole city. It is, indeed, but too true that ALEXANDER BARROW, the pure patriot and enlightened statesman, is no more.

Three years have not passed away since Mr. BARROW announced in appropriate and eloquent terms the death of his late distinguished colleague; and since then it has devolved on me to present the ordinary resolutions as a mark of respect to the memory of two of my colleagues of the other House of Congress, and a similar resolution will now be offered on this melancholy occasion. In less than three years, two Senators and two Representatives in Congress from the same State have been gathered to their fathers. The death of my late colleague was the most unexpected; for he was not only in the vigor of life, but he possessed a strong constitution.

The ways of Providence are indeed inscrutable. It may with truth be said, that "whilst in life we are in death."

Of Mr. BARROW's early history I know but little. He was a native of Tennessee, and was, I am told, about forty-five years of age. His family and connections are of the highest respectability, and have been long distinguished for their talents and patriotism. After having completed his education, Mr. BARROW studied law, and was admitted to the bar in Tennessee; immediately after which, I believe, he removed to Louisiana, where he pursued his profession for some time with success; and, had he remained at the bar, would have attained the highest distinction. Being independent in his circumstances, and fond of agricultural pursuits, after a few years' practice, he retired from the bar, and became a successful planter, and has since devoted his attention mainly to the cultivation of the earth.

Mr. BARROW served, however, repeatedly in the Legislature of Louisiana with reputation, and was regarded as a distinguished member; and he received from the people of the State many other proofs of their highest respect and confidence. His election to the Senate of the United States, under circumstances the most flattering, is the best evidence of the high estimation in which he was held by the people of his adopted State, by whom his character and services will ever be held in grateful remembrance. The news of his death will produce throughout the State, as it has produced here, the deepest emotions of sorrow.

Mr. BARROW was distinguished for his bland and courteous manners, for his frank and manly deportment, and for his many generous and noble traits of character. No man, in fact, had more sincere and devoted friends whilst living, and no one has died more lamented. He performed his duties here with zeal and ability, and, at the same time, in the most frank and conciliatory spirit; and I am sure that it is no exaggeration to say, that in his intercourse with his brother Senators, his deportment on all occasions was such as to command the respect and confidence of every member of this body. He has now closed his earthly career, but he has gone, I hope, to a better and happier world.

Although he expired far from his home, and from the cherished partner of his bosom, it must be a source of some consolation to her, and to her orphan children, to learn that he was surrounded at that awful moment by devoted friends, from whom he received every attention which friendship could bestow, and that he died as he had lived, without fear and without reproach, relying upon the mercy of his Redeemer. And what shall be said of their bereavement? There is a silence which is more expressive than language. We forbear, in humble submission to the will of Heaven—in grateful recollection, that "He who strikes has power to heal."

The character of the deceased was indeed, sir, of the highest order As a Senator, a citizen, and a gentleman—indeed, in all the relations of public and private life—he was esteemed and beloved. As a patriot, a firm and uncompromising friend of his country and of her constitution, he had no superior. Brave, ardent, and chivalrous in his temperament, and devoted to the principles of civil and religious liberty, had he lived in the days of the early struggles for English freedom, he would have bled by the side of Hampden in the field, or died with Sidney on the scaffold. Yet, sir—

"His life was gentle,
And the elements so mixed in him,
That Nature might stand up,
And say to all the world, 'THIS WAS A MAN.'"

Mr. Benton said: In rising, Mr. President, to second the motion for paying to the memory of our deceased brother Senator the last honors of this body, I feel myself to be obeying the impulses of an hereditary friendship, as well as conforming to the practice of the Senate. Forty years ago, when coming to the bar at Nashville, it was my good fortune to enjoy the friendship of the father of the deceased, then an inhabitant of Nashville, and one of its most respected citizens. The deceased was then too young to be noted amongst the rest of the family. The pursuits of life soon carried us far apart, and long after, and for the first time to know each other, we met on this floor. We met not as strangers, but as friends—friends of early and hereditary recollections; and all our intercourse since—every incident and every word of our lives, public and private—has gone to strengthen and confirm the feelings under which we met, and to perpetuate with the son the friendship which had existed with the father. Up to the last moments of his presence in this chamber—up to the last moment that I saw him—our meetings and partings were the cordial greetings of hereditary friendship; and now, not only as one of the elder Senators, but as the early and family friend of the deceased, I come forward to second the motion for the honors to his memory.

The Senator from Louisiana (Mr. Johnson) has performed the office of duty and of friendship to his deceased friend and colleague. Justly, truly, and feelingly has he performed it. With deep and heartfelt emotion he has portrayed the virtues, and sketched the qualities, which constituted the manly and lofty character of Alexander Barrow. He has given us a picture as faithful as it is honorable, and it does not become me to dilate upon what he has so well presented; but, in contemplating the rich and full portrait of the high qualities of the head and heart which he has presented, suffer me to look for an instant to the source, the fountain, from which flowed the full stream of generous and noble actions which distinguished the entire life of our deceased brother Senator. I speak of the heart—the noble heart—of Alexander Barrow. Honor, courage, patriotism, friendship, generosity—fidelity to his friend and his country—the social affections—devotion to the wife of his bosom, and the children of their love: all—all, were there! and never, not once, did any cold, or selfish, or timid calculation come from his manly head to check or balk the noble impulses of his generous heart. A quick, clear, and strong judgment found nothing to restrain in these impulses; and in all the wide circle of his public and private relations—in all the words and acts of his life—it was the heart that moved first; and always so true to honor that judgment had nothing to do but to approve the impulsion. From that fountain flowed the stream of the actions of his life; and now what we all deplore—what so many will join in deploring—is, that such a fountain, so unexpectedly, in the full tide of its flow, should have been so suddenly dried up. He was one of the younger members of this body, and in all the hope and vigor of meridian manhood. Time was ripening and maturing his faculties. He seemed to have a right to look forward to many years of usefulness to his country and to his family. With qualities evidently fitted for the *field* as well as for the Senate, a brilliant future was before him, ready, as I know he was, to serve his country in any way that honor and duty should require.

Mr. Breese next arose, and spoke as follows:

Mr. President: It is not in my power to add any thing to the eulogies already so eloquently pronounced by the more particular friends of the deceased, in the beautiful language of sincerity and truth. Be it my humble purpose to fling but one flower upon his grave—to add but one slight tribute, among more valued offerings, to his acknowledged worth; a tribute, sir, although slight, perhaps not altogether valueless, coming as it does from a political opponent as ardent and as decided in the support of his principles as he whom we all mourn was known to be in the cause he espoused. It was not my fortune, Mr. President, to know intimately the deceased until after the close of the last long and laborious session of Congress. We met in our journey to our distant homes, at the Falls of Niagara, and proceeded thence through our vast ocean lakes quite to Illinois—he pursuing his way by the rivers to his, and I overland my route to my home. In this intercourse, so cordial and friendly as it was, there were daily developed the most amiable points of his character, winning my regard, and advancing us speedily from mere acquaintances to intimate friends. This I know, sir, from the mutual regrets expressed in parting, and from the warm and cordial welcome on our meeting here at the commencement of this session—he then, in all the pride of his manhood, gazing with joyous and contented eyes upon the beautiful world before him, and which the apparent heathfulness and vigor of his frame gave him promise he should long enjoy. But, Mr. President, what a change a few days have made!

> "All, all, that promise fair
> Has sought the grave, to sleep forever there."

Ardently and sincerely devoted as he was to his party and its principles, it was his good fortune, Mr. President, I take it upon myself to say, to enjoy in the highest degree the unbounded respect of his opponents, and of all his associates here; no matter how amiable, sincere, or kind they may be, he alone, perhaps, of all of them, could say, "I have no personal enemy." Nor could he have; for a kinder or a manlier heart never beat within a human bosom. But now he is no more! Though but in his meridian, life's evening shadows have fallen, and the portals of the tomb will soon close upon him forever! Gone from among us and forever, and from all he loved, is that manly form we delighted to look upon; quenched is the fire and spirit of that eye that so often beamed in kindness; pulseless is now that heart whose every throb was in unison with friendship, fidelity, and with all the generous and captivating qualities that adorn man's best nature. Faults he had—let the grave hide them. The memory of his many virtues will be preserved, if not in brass or marble, upon a more valued and more durable material—the hearts of his friends and his countrymen. I join, Mr. President, with melancholy satisfaction in assent to such resolutions as may be offered, appropriate to the occasion.

Mr. Hannegan remarked: I also desire, with a mournful heart, to add my feeble but sincere testimony to the exalted worth, and noble and manly and generous spirit which in life adorned, and now, as he lies cold and shrouded, sanctify the memory of Alexander Barrow. Come when it may in our midst, Mr. President, death never fails to make its impress upon those who survey its work. There are none so careless, none so indifferent, as to defy its impressions, when even a casual acquaintance falls. But the feeling of awe and of gloom which pervades this chamber to-day is far beyond the usual and ordinary feeling. One of us—one who has long occupied a high place here, in his country's highest place, has been suddenly, and almost without warning, stricken down. But a day or two since—to me it seems but an hour—and he was here, beloved and respected by all; in all the pride of intellect, and in all the royalty of the most vigorous and athletic manhood. Where, sir, shall we look to find a more manly, commanding, and symmetrical form? Where shall we seek a nobler and a more majestic front? Where are we to seek and where to find a loftier nature, a soul more elevated, or a heart more kind, more generous, and more gentle? I know not one—not one.

Heaven had blessed him with that high nature which knows no disguise, and scorns all unmanly concealment. He knew no art; dissimulation, with its fell train of poisons, had no home in his bosom. In all his bearings here, from the hour in which my eyes first rested upon him, I have known nothing of him but what became, proudly became an American Senator. Brave, generous, manly, and highly gifted, he discharged his duties here as a proud representative of a proud people. And how beautifully, how happily were all the elements of our nature commingled in him! He had "a heart formed for pity, and a hand open as day to melting charity." That heart—that heart is cold, and that hand is still, and Barrow—Barrow, the name so often uttered in this chamber, and never but in tones of kindness—Barrow, with his elastic step, with his joyous look, his noble presence, and his winning virtues—Barrow sits with us here no more; yon vacant chair tells the stern reality—Barrow will be with us no more. Strange and mysterious Providence! The most robust of all our number—he who but a week since stood here fit model for an ancient hero or a demigod—he is the first to be gathered to dust, and that, too, before his noon of life was reached, and long, long before the harvest to our eyes seemed ready for the reaper.

It was my happy fortune to contract an acquaintance with him shortly after I entered the Senate, which gradually ripened into a most intimate friendship. I knew him well—I knew him well—I loved him dearly; and, Mr. President, I will say that in private, as in his public life, I found him ever distinguished by the same lofty characteristics, the same scrupulous regard for honor and propriety, the same rare endowment of remarkable common sense, the same sound discriminating judgment, and a perception unusually, singularly clear, quick, and correct. The delight of the social circle, Alexander Barrow was master of all the social virtues. He won all hearts that approached him as with a spell. The last time that I saw him, Mr. President, he came to visit me in my sick room. It was but a few days since, not ten; we were alone for some time; the conversation turned upon home—upon our own homes—and we spoke of distant and dearly beloved friends; and, sir, I shall never forget how his eye lighted up as he talked of his approaching retirement from public life, and dwelt upon his future career of tranquil happiness, when, engaged only in domestic pursuits, he should be surrounded daily and hourly by those endearments which he fondly—but alas! how vainly—fancied were reserved for him through many, many long years at home. He dwelt upon his home, and those who were there—of her, its light, its joy—his wife. He spoke, as

I have often heard him speak of her before, in those tender and respectful terms which tell that the love of the heart borders on idolatry.

> "But alas! nor wife nor children more shall behold,
> Nor friends, nor sacred home."

I have come here to-day, Mr. President, all unfit for the duty, feeble and out of health, to bear a passing, slight, slight tribute to friendship—to give a slight expression of my feelings on this mournful occasion. I come, prompted by those feelings of attachment and respect which I cherished for our deceased friend in life, and by that melancholy regard with which I shall continue to hold him in memory through life. I could not forbear—I could not do less. I will add the expression of the single hope that she to whom I have alluded—the partner of his bosom—when the lapse of time shall have relieved her overcharged heart of its heavy burden—that she may find a mournful consolation in turning back to the proceedings which marked his last hours; and after those hours were gone, the sombre scenes which filled up his little abiding time above the ground. I trust, sir, that when time, and years, and above all, the soothing voice of religion, shall have abated the mighty burden of her grief, and she shall have become calm in her woe, she will find a relief, a sad relief, in the thought, that though it was denied her hand to smooth his dying pillow, to bathe his fevered brow, and to catch from his pallid lips the last fond sigh, yet kind and devoted friends, his best-loved associates and comrades in this chamber, were there to watch, not with her love—ah, no! that could not be—but with the love and sorrow of brothers to watch over the closing scene, and minister to his departing struggles. And I trust, also, that she may find something to break her grief in the thought that at his obsequies strangers of whom she never heard, were eager to pay just tribute to his exalted worth, and embalm with heartfelt homage the memory of her husband

Mr. Crittenden then arose, much affected, and said: I desire, Mr. President, however needless it may be after what has been said, to offer my tribute in a few words. Mr. C. then paused, and, after an evident struggle with his feelings, he could only say, "I beg pardon, Mr. President," and sat down.

Mr. Mangum thereupon rose and moved the following:

Resolved, unanimously, That a committee be appointed by the Vice President to take order for superintending the funeral of the Hon. Alexander Barrow, which will take place to-morrow at the hour of twelve M., and that the Senate will attend the same.

Resolved, unanimously, That the members of the Senate, from a sincere desire of showing every mark of respect due to the memory of the Hon. Alexander Barrow, deceased, late a member thereof, will go into mourning for him one month, by the usual mode of wearing crape on the left arm.

Resolved, unanimously, That, as an additional mark of respect for the memory of the Hon. Alexander Barrow, the Senate do now adjourn.

Ordered, That the Secretary communicate these proceedings to the House of Representatives.

The Senate then adjourned.

HOUSE OF REPRESENTATIVES.

Wednesday, December 30.

Death of Hon. Alexander Barrow.

A message having been received from the Senate announcing the death of the Hon. Alexander Barrow, Senator from the State of Louisiana—

Mr. Morse, of Louisiana, rose and addressed the House as follows:

Mr. Speaker: The melancholy communication which has just been read, and a request from my colleagues in this House, has devolved upon me the painful duty of arresting the ordinary business of your body for the purpose of announcing the solemn intelligence that Alexander Barrow, late one of the Senators from the State of Louisiana, is now no more.

Within the past year Death has reaped a golden harvest, and numbers among his victims some of the brightest ornaments of our Commonwealth

To many of these it has been permitted to give the latest pulsation of their hearts and the last life-drop of their blood in defence of their country—to realize the noblest sentiment that can animate the human heart, "How sweet it is to die for our country." But that death is still more noble when heralded by the shouts of victory, so dearly purchased by their own valor.

Among the many noble sons whose untimely death our common mother now deplores, none, not one, combined in a more enviable form those rare qualities of head and heart which made men love them, than did my departed friend.

A native of the State of Tennessee, born within a few miles of the city of Nashville, the first elements of that chivalric character, that noble bearing, that manly form of vigorous constitution, were in part received from early education and discipline at the Military Academy at West Point.

He pursued his legal studies in Tennessee, and there laid the foundation of a thorough acquaintance with English jurisprudence. He removed soon after to the State of Louisiana, and made himself well acquainted with the principles of the civil law, in which he promised to become one of the most distinguished jurisconsults, had not the partiality of his friends and his own inclinations marked out for him another career.

His fine talents, generous impulses, and integrity of character, soon won for him the esteem and admiration of an enlightened constituency, who selected him as their representative in the Legislature of his adopted State and continued their confidence in him by re-electing him as often as was agreeable to his wishes.

The occasional development of talents which, on ordinary subjects, he seemed unwilling or averse to exhibit, the suavity of his manners in his intercourse with his brother members, and the confidence in the purity of his motives, served still more to increase the admiration of his friends, and extorted homage from his opponents.

In 1840, then not forty years of age, he was elected to a full term in the Senate of the United States, which elevated position he filled in a manner highly honorable to himself and eminently useful to his country.

There was a blunt honesty of purpose and a frank boldness in his manner which, though it might sometimes offend, always commended itself to our respect from the consciousness of its integrity.

He was taken suddenly ill on Friday evening, while on a visit to Baltimore. His disease resisted all the skill and attention which the solicitude of his friends had summoned from Baltimore and Philadelphia, and on Tuesday morning about five o'clock, in the full possession of all his faculties, with a perfect consciousness of his approaching end, with a firmness which marked his whole life, surrounded by numerous friends from both Houses of Congress, perished all but the immortal spirit of ALEXANDER BARROW.

Although his disease was so violent in its course that many of his friends scarcely knew of his illness until after its fatal termination, I had the melancholy satisfaction of being with him a few hours before he died. His last moments were occupied with the tenderest and heart-rending allusions to his wife, children, and country.

When these melancholy tidings shall reach his now happy home, who can penetrate, in imagination, that veil of woe that must enshroud his wife and only daughter, but will offer up to the Disposer of all things one prayer that he will "temper the wind to the shorn lamb."

Two sons, the younger of whom was with him, and the other a student of Harvard College, with his wife and daughter in Louisiana, constitute all his immediate family. A recommendation to his friends to watch over their education, and be as a father to them, one bitter pang that he could not for the last time press her to his bosom who had been to him the most devoted wife, were the last of earthly matters that occupied his thoughts. May his children be only worthy of their sire! His friends ask no more.

When I pressed his cold hand for the last time, he returned that grasp with a strength which even disease seemed scarcely to have weakened, and, in a voice of more than usual firmness, said, "I shall never see Louisiana more." No, brave spirit, you will not again revisit the scenes of so many bright and happy years, but your numerous friends need not the presence of that manly form, nor the marble, nor the canvas, to recall the many kind and delightful associations that will forever be entwined with the name of ALEXANDER BARROW.

Was this dispensation of Providence visited upon us to remind us how frail the tenure of our lives is, the death of our friend forms an impressive lesson.

Among the youngest members of the Senate, blessed with competence, extensive and influential family connections, health, and a constitution not impaired or even approached by disease, there was no member of either House who had a more reasonable expectation in looking forward to a long and brilliant career; and, when the summons shall come to all of us, may the consciousness of a well-spent life enable us to meet it like a "Preux Chevalier, sans peur et sans reproche."

The death of ALEXANDER BARROW is the fourth that has occurred, within the brief space of four years, in the small delegation from Louisiana; and true it is "death loves a shining mark." PORTER, BOSSIER, DAWSON, BARROW! What four names living can outweigh yours dead? The earth that holds you dead, bears not alive four nobler spirits; and, while the mighty Mississippi rolls her tribute to the sea, your memories will live in the hearts of your countrymen.

In conclusion, I move you the adoption of the following resolutions:

Resolved, That this House has heard with deep sensibility the announcement of the death of the Hon. ALEXANDER BARROW, a Senator in Congress from the State of Louisiana.

Resolved, That as a testimony of respect for the memory of the deceased, the members and officers of this House will wear the usual badge of mourning for thirty days.

Resolved, That the proceedings of this House, in relation to the death of the Honorable ALEXANDER BARROW, be communicated to the family of the deceased by the Clerk.

Resolved, That this House will attend the funeral of the deceased in a body; and, as a further mark of respect for his memory, that it do now adjourn.

And the House accordingly adjourned.

IN SENATE.

MONDAY, January 11.

Increase of Army—Lieutenant-General.

BENJAMIN B. FRENCH, Esq., Clerk of the House of Representatives, delivered to the Senate the bill to authorize the raising of additional regiments for a limited period, and for other purposes; and it was read twice by its title, and referred to the Committee on Military Affairs.

Mr. DIX, from the Committee on Military Affairs, reported two bills, as follows:

A bill to provide for an additional military force, and for other purposes; and

A bill to appoint a lieutenant-general to command the military forces of the United States during the war with Mexico.

He moved that these bills be printed, and made the order of the day for to-morrow.

The Secretary read the bills a first time.

The PRESIDENT then stated the question to be on making these bills the special order for to-morrow.

Several Senators: Oh, no, it is too soon.

Mr. DIX urged the necessity of prompt action upon these bills, and reminded Senators that more than one-third of the session was gone already.

Mr. REVERDY JOHNSON suggested to the Senator from New York the propriety of fixing Thursday, instead of Tuesday.

Mr. DIX reiterated, that it was very desirable the bills should be taken up and acted upon immediately; he had therefore named to-morrow as the earliest possible day; and would still prefer that day, unless it was the desire of the Senate to name another.

Mr. SEVIER inquired if the bill reported was like the bill which had just been received from the House of Representatives.

Mr. DIX replied, that there were some differences. He had, however, not carefully examined the bill from the House of Representatives; but he believed their substantial provisions were the same.

Mr. H. JOHNSON suggested Thursday instead of Tuesday, for the reason that the bill would not be printed by to-morrow morning. If it was to be taken up it was desirable that the Senate should know exactly what its provisions were; but he saw not how this could be accomplished by to-morrow. Besides, it could make but little difference whether Tuesday or Thursday were named, as he presumed it would be voted upon during the week in any case.

Mr. HUNTINGTON said, it was important, doubtless, that there should be speedy action on these bills, as the Senator from New York had remarked; but it was unusual to name the day immediately succeeding that on which the bills were reported. By Thursday the Committee on Military Affairs will have had before them the House bill on the same subject, and will have considered its provisions.

Mr. DIX supposed the committee would be ready to report on that bill by Wednesday.

Several Senators: Well, say Wednesday, then.

Mr. DIX. Wednesday has been named, and I accept this suggestion.

The PRESIDENT rose to put the question on making the bills the special order for Wednesday; when

Mr. MANGUM interposed, and said they had not been read a second time, and no disposition could be made of them until they had been read.

The PRESIDENT assented, and added, The bills will now be read a second time, unless objected to

Mr. MANGUM. I object.

After a short pause, Mr. M. withdrew his objection, and the bills were read a second time.

The question then recurred on making the bills the special order for Wednesday.

Mr. BADGER inquired if the Senator from New York intended to make them both the order of the day for Wednesday.

Mr. DIX replied in the affirmative.

Mr. BADGER suggested the propriety of separating them. He saw no reason why they should go together.

Mr. SEVIER briefly explained the features of the bill which had recently come from the House, and remarked that he supposed on that every Senator would be prepared to vote at any time. He hoped, therefore, the Senator from New York would adhere to his original motion, and make them the special orders for to-morrow.

Several Senators: "Oh! no, no, no."

Mr. SEVIER. Well, Wednesday, then.

The PRESIDENT again rose to put the question on the motion to make the bills the special order.

Mr. MANGUM called for the question to put first on the longest day.

The PRESIDENT accordingly put the question on fixing Thursday as the day, and it was agreed to—31 in the affirmative, and 17 in the negative.

So the bills were made the special order for Thursday.

HOUSE OF REPRESENTATIVES.

MONDAY, January 11.

Oregon Territorial Government—Anti-Slavery Ordinance of 1787 extended to the Territory.

The SPEAKER announced the business in order to be the bill to establish the Territorial Government of Oregon, which had been made the special order for this day.

After some conversation on a point of order between Mr. JACOB THOMPSON and the SPEAKER,

The House, on motion of Mr. DOUGLAS, resolved itself into Committee of the Whole on the state of the Union, Mr. HOPKINS, of Virginia, in the chair, and proceeded to the consideration of the bill to establish the Territorial Government of Oregon.

The bill, having been read through, was taken up by sections.

Mr. JAMES THOMPSON said: Mr. Chairman, I rise to make an inquiry of the honorable gentlemen who reported this bill. It will be recollected that at the last session of this Congress, I had the honor to offer to the bill for the organization of the Territory of Oregon an amendment to provide against the introduction of slavery into said Territory. I desire to know what provision this bill contains on that subject: whether it contains the amendment then offered? If not, I desire to renew the amendment.

Mr. Douglas replied by reading the twelfth section of the bill, which extends the provisions of the ordinance of 1787 to the Oregon Territory, and said he presumed the gentleman would find slavery expressly prohibited by that ordinance.

Mr. Thompson said he knew this to be so. If that ordinance was, as he had no doubt it was, in force at this time, he would reflect on the subject until the section came before the committee.

Mr. Douglas, in reply, read the following portion of the twelfth section of the bill, which, he thought, would fully satisfy the gentleman's inquiry, viz:

"Sec. 12. *And be it further enacted,* That the inhabitants of said Territory shall be entitled to enjoy all and singular the rights, privileges, and advantages granted and secured to the people of the territory of the United States north-west of the Ohio river, by the articles of compact contained in the ordinance for the government of said Territory, on the thirteenth day of July, seventeen hundred and eighty-seven; and shall be subject to all the conditions, and restrictions, and prohibitions in said articles of compact imposed upon the people of said Territory."

The second and third sections were passed over without amendment.

The fifth section was then read, as follows:

"Sec. 5. *And be it further enacted,* That every free white male inhabitant above the age of twenty-one years, who shall have been a resident of said Territory at the time of the passage of this act, shall be entitled to vote at the first election, and shall be eligible to any office within the said Territory; but the qualifications of voters and of holding office, at all subsequent elections, shall be such as shall be prescribed by the Legislative Assembly: *Provided,* That the right of suffrage and of holding office shall be exercised only by citizens of the United States, and those who shall have declared, on oath, their intention to become such, and shall have taken an oath to support the Constitution of the United States and the provisions of this act."

Mr. W. W. Campbell moved to amend it, by adding, between the words "the age of twenty-one years" and the words "who shall have been," &c., the words "who is a citizen of the United States."

Mr. C. observed, that as the bill stood at present, every free white male inhabiting the Territory, whether Jew or Gentile, Englishman or American, had the right of suffrage, and this provision would remain in force so long as Oregon should remain under a territorial form of government. However proper it might be that States should enjoy the right of determining on the qualifications of its own voters, he held that, when Congress was legislating for a Territory of its own, it should take care that the right of suffrage should be exercised in a manner conformable to the principles of the constitution. Should the bill remain in its present shape, what would there be to prevent the President of the Hudson Bay Company himself, or any member of that company, from becoming a member of the Legislature of Oregon? We had long been struggling to rescue this Territory from under British dominion; surely we ought not now to adopt a course which might practically throw it back under that dominion in a different form. Were gentlemen prepared to allow to any and every member of the Hudson Bay Company on the north side of the Columbia River the right of suffrage in choosing the Legislature of an American Territory? Were they willing to see aliens of this description taking their seats in such a Legislature, to make laws to bind American citizens? He hoped not; and he should therefore move to amend the bill, so as to require both those voting and those voted for to be American citizens. The bill, to be sure, required that voters should have taken an oath of allegiance to the United States; but this they were all bound to observe whether they took an oath or not. They were also to have made previous oath of naturalization; but this oath did not, in the mean time, release them from allegiance to a foreign Government, and there would be nothing to prevent a British alien from walking in and taking his seat in this American Territorial Legislature. He hoped, now we had at length got peaceable possession of Oregon, that we should do what we could to Americanize it.

Mr. Douglas, in reply, stated that this part of the bill was only in conformity to the known state of the population in that country at this time. It was known to gentlemen that these people had met and formed a sort of temporary constitution for themselves; and, under that constitution, some of the persons now exercising authority there by the choice of the people, were not legally American citizens, but were, in all cases, persons friendly to the American Government, and desirous of the extension of our laws over them. The reason why, though entertaining these feelings, they had, nevertheless, not actually become American citizens, was, that they never had had an opportunity, there being in the Territory no courts of record, or other legal authority, before whom the necessary oaths could be taken.

Mr. Levin was understood to inquire whether these oaths could not have been taken before any magistrate?

Mr. Douglas replied that the bill provided for the establishment of courts of justice and the appointment of judges and justices of the peace, and it allowed that all who had taken the oath of allegiance, and made oath to the purpose of becoming naturalized, might vote for members of the Legislature. So that, even at the first election, they could not vote without this qualification. Nor did it follow that even then they could vote permanently, unless the Legislature so provided. And if the people knew a man to be an alien, and did not wish him to serve, they would make such a provision. He thought that a man who had been an inhabitant of the Territory from the very beginning, and who had always been friendly to our cause, if he was willing to take the oaths prescribed in the bill, ought in fairness to be allowed to have a vote. He hoped the amendment moved by the gentleman from New York would not prevail.

Mr. FICKLIN suggested that the oaths taken should be in conformity with the law of the United States now in force, or to be in force. on the subject of naturalization.

Mr. DOUGLAS said he had no objection to adopt that as a modification of the bill.

Mr. VINTON expressed his concurrence in the views advanced by the gentleman from New York (Mr. CAMPBELL) as to the propriety of requiring that all voters should be citizens of the United States; but was wholly opposed to surrendering to the Territorial Legislature the right of prescribing, permanently, the qualifications of voters. It was allowing a Legislature, that was a mere agent of Congress, virtually to repeal the organic law, or constitution, prescribed by Congress for the Territory.

The question on agreeing to this amendment was taken by tellers, who reported, for the amendment 65, against it 55.

So the amendment was agreed to.

Mr. VINTON moved further to amend the fifth section, by striking out the words "the first election," and inserting in lieu thereof the words "all elections."

Mr. V. also moved to amend the fifth section, by striking out the words "but the qualifications of voters and of holding office, at all subsequent elections, shall be such as shall be prescribed by the Legislative Assembly."

Mr. V. contended that the House should prescribe to this Territory a provision in regard to qualifications of electors which should be its organic law, to be changed by Congress only. The officers to be chosen were paid out of the treasury of the United States, which was an additional reason why Congress only should make the permanent provision.

Tellers were demanded, and being ordered, the result was as follows: 65 in the affirmative, and 55 in the negative.

So the amendment was adopted.

Mr. VINTON moved that the section be further amended, by striking out the words "the first election," and insert the words "all elections." Also, by striking out the words "but the qualification of voters and of holding office at all subsequent elections shall be such as shall be prescribed by the Legislative Assembly."

Mr. MCCLERNAND said he had not expected to have been drawn into the debate by venturing the suggestion he had to his friend from Ohio, (Mr. THURMAN,) for whose opinions he had a high respect. He would say, however, that the views which had been presented by his friend, in answer to the suggestion he (Mr. McC.) had made, had failed to change his opinion upon the constitutional question involved.

After a few remarks by Messrs. THURMAN, CARROLL, BOWLIN, and VINTON,

Mr. ROOT obtained the floor, and on his motion the committee rose and reported.

IN SENATE.

TUESDAY, January 12.

Death of Judge Pennybacker.

Mr. ARCHER then rose and addressed the Senate as follows:

Only a few days, Mr. President, have passed over us, since we witnessed the spectacle of this Chamber clothed with the deepest expression of mourning for the loss of one of our most honored and beloved associates. It was no ordinary enhancement, Mr. President, of that afflicting bereavement that the subject of it was in the prime and vigor of manhood, blessed ordinarily with the highest condition of health, and giving the promise of the maturest and the fullest career of usefulness, and happiness, and honor. Sir, it was my desire on that occasion to have mingled a feeble expression of my regret with the honored lament which burst out from every corner of this Chamber. The subject of this bereavement was reckoned in the number of the very dearest of my friends. I felt myself, however, Mr. President, unequal to the discharge of that office, from the overflowing fulness of my feelings. I felt, sir, that I could not trust myself to attempt to commit to words the emotions which were laboring for utterance in my bosom. Sir, a correspondent occasion has now occurred, from which it is not my option to exempt myself, from the peculiar relation in which I stood to the deceased. Sir, it is not my good fortune—I am not able to say that it is the loss of a particular friend that I have to present to the Senate. My acquaintance was too short to authorize me to claim that distinction, though I might have hoped that a fuller acquaintance would have authorized me to do so. The subject of the bereavement to which I now call your attention, stood to me in the relation of a most esteemed colleague. On this morning, sir, at about four o'clock, the Hon. ISAAC S. PENNYBACKER departed this life—the victim of a relentless disease, which resisted all the ministrations of medical skill, and all the efforts of solicitous affection. Yes, sir, like the lamented BARROW, Mr. PENNYBACKER, too, was in the number of the very youngest of the members of this body, and promised, by the vigor of his general health and constitution, as Mr. BARROW did, a very long protraction of a useful and honorable life. It was in harvest, having just reached the point of maturity, that the sickle has been put which has gathered it to the garner of the grave. Inscrutable dispensation of an overruling and all-wise Providence! Another, sir, in exactly the same circumstances—another associate of our body has been stricken down by the insatiable spoiler, and gathered to his receptacle of trophies—the grave. Sir, it was not my fortune to be personally acquainted with Mr. Pennybacker till he met me on this floor as my colleague; but I learn from others that he was born in the most beautiful region of this widely-extended Union—the mountain valley of Virginia. Sir, the population of that valley, like that, I believe, of all mountain regions in this country, was marked by primitive simplicity and industrial habits, and he seemed to have imbibed from the contact all that purity of character, and those habits of industry, which are the appropriate characteristics of such regions. My honored colleague was no more than forty-one years of age. His merit cannot be better estimated by other evidences than by the fact that he had been a Representative of the State of Virginia upon the floor of the House of Representatives—had filled the office of Federal district judge of his State, and at this early period of life, was elevated to the second highest distinction known under this Government—a seat on the floor of the Senate of the United States. He came, sir, to my acquaintance, heralded by the reputation of the highest probity—the soundest understanding, improved by habits of labor—the kindest affections, expanding themselves in a large domestic and social sphere—manners so felicitously bland and courteous as to prepare the way for that esteem which his character was calculated to impress. Sir, I believe I may appeal to every member who with me has known him upon this floor—he entirely fulfilled the promise of this heraldry in the intercourse which I had with him. I do not affect, Mr. President, to offer consolation to his bereaved and afflicted family, who are here affording the best of all solace—that of solicitous and affectionate attention in his last moments. I refer them, sir, for consolation to that High Power which we read sometimes chasteneth, because He loveth, and who has promised unfailing comfort to those who, with reverence say: "Thy will be done, and not mine." Sir, to that power and to that source of consolation, with all reverence on my part, I refer their distresses. I now move the ordinary resolutions, which will be read by the Clerk, for the adoption of the Senate.

The resolutions were read accordingly, and are as follows:

Resolved, unanimously, That a committee be appointed by the President of the Senate *pro tempore,* to take order for superintending the funeral of the Hon. Isaac S. Pennybacker, which will take place to-morrow, at twelve o'clock M., and that the Senate will attend the same.

Resolved, unanimously, That the members of the Senate, from a sincere desire of showing every mark of respect due to the memory of the Hon. Isaac S. Pennybacker, deceased, late a member thereof, will go into mourning for him one month, by the usual mode of wearing crape on the left arm.

Resolved, unanimously, That as an additional mark of respect for the memory of the Hon. Isaac S. Pennybacker, the Senate do now adjourn.

The committee of arrangements consists of Mr. Sevier, Mr. Mangum, Mr. Breese, Mr. Crittenden, Mr. Benton, and Mr. Webster.

The Senate then adjourned.

HOUSE OF REPRESENTATIVES.

Tuesday, January 12.

Death of Judge Pennybacker.

The Senate notified the House of Representatives by their Secretary of the death of the Hon. Isaac S. Pennybacker, late a Senator in Congress from the State of Virginia.

Whereupon Mr. James McDowell, of Virginia, rose and addressed the House as follows:

I rise, Mr. Speaker, to perform, for an honored and valued colleague, lately representing our native and common State in the other branch of this national assembly, the same sad and melancholy office which he himself performed in his place less than a year ago for my own kinsman and immediate predecessor, here. I rise to say—what I know will be felt with sensibility by those who hear me, and what will send a pang to the hearts of thousands who do not—that Isaac S. Pennybacker, one of the Senators from Virginia, is no more! Whatever, under the guidings of Providence, or in the fulfilled and cheering promise of his outset, he might have become in the lofty career which the confidence of his country had assigned him, that career is now over; his expectations and his efforts in it are now ended, and the silence and seal of death are forever upon him.

He was seized and snatched away from his labors almost before he had begun them, but not before the modest and ingenuous qualities of his nature had been seen, or before he had shown himself, in all the safest, soundest, and purest virtues of a public man, to be worthy of all acceptation. He was comparatively young—less than forty-two years of age—so that he came to the eminent station which he filled precisely at that period of life when the body and mind, in their complex action upon one another, co-operate the best, and when man is most capable of building up the richest monuments of usefulness and fame for his country, and himself. He was born in Shenandoah county, Virginia—was educated to the profession of law, which he entered upon in early manhood, and practised with a high and progressive reputation until he was called upon to represent his native district in Congress, from whence, at the end of his first representative term, he was transferred, by appointment of the President and Senate, to the district court of Western Virginia, and was thence again transferred, but a year ago, by the Legislature of that venerable Commonwealth, to the responsible and final post, from all the honors, and counsels, and toils, of which he has now been removed by that mysterious and Gracious Power which governs us all, to another, and I would reverently hope, to a better world.

He was always a student—an ardent and devoted student. The study of his profession especially, as I learn from his more intimate friends, was both his habit and his enjoyment; and hence it was that he became not only eminently qualified by his learning and his love of investigation for judicial labors, but that the whole texture of his mind became gradually and essentially judicial also. He thought with care, with system, with clearness, with rectitude, and he thought to results. A sound lawyer, a wise judge, a trusted statesman—he was more than all these; he was a sound, irreproachable, trustworthy, and honest man; never—and I speak it with emphatic utterance—never bringing upon any human face, by any act of his, either the blush of shame or the stain of a tear. Wherever his avocations or his duties called him, it was the cheering lot of this excellent man to be always surrounded by friends—friends who respected and who loved him. And, having thus lived a life of probity and of peace upon earth, he has gone, in the meridian of his day, to the tomb, without a solitary reproach to follow, or a solitary enemy to forgive him.

Like his late and lamented colleague from Louisiana, (Mr. BARROW,) he was stricken down in all the pride of his physical power, and in the full maturity of his brightest manhood; like him he was crushed by an unexpected and a startling blow, and sharing side by side with one another, as they did, the hopes of their country and the joys of freshest life, how sad, how strange, how admonitory, is it to us all to see them parted by death for a season, and then grouped and gathered again as companions for the grave! Unlike that Senator, however, my honored colleague breathed his last in the bosom of his family, and had his forlorn and solitary pathway to another world soothed by the presence and comforted by the aid of all who were dearest to him in this. Here it is, in the breaking up of that tender and holy bond which brings wife and children to the pillow of the dying husband and father that we find a bitterness in death to which the rupture of all other relations is as nothing. But it is not for us to look upon this private scene; it is not for us to go into the sanctuary of this sorrow, nor listen to that cry of anguish and brokenness of heart which is there. As frail and dying and Christian men, however, we cannot think upon such distress without sympathy and awe, nor without an involuntary appeal to him who is the Father and Saviour of us all, that he would spread the shelter of his wing for the poor sufferers who are weeping and bleeding under the stroke of his power

To us who are here, this lesson after lesson on our own mortality is too solemn and too sacred to be lost. If we are provident and wise, as we know that we are immortal, let us take these lessons as so many providences, mercifully and seasonably sent for our good; and, flushed as we now are with all the energies and hopes of life, be it our part to seek for and to seize upon that hope, blessed above every other—that hope "which travels through nor quits us when we die;" which unites the last throb of expiring nature with the first one of never-ending joy.

> "To man in this, his trial state,
> The privilege is given,
> When tossed by waves of human fate,
> To anchor fast on Heaven."

With these remarks, Mr. Speaker, I move the resolutions which will be offered by one of my colleagues.

Resolved, That this House has heard with deep sensibility the announcement of the death of the Hon. ISAAC S. PENNYBACKER, a Senator in Congress from the State of Virginia.

Resolved, That as a testimony of respect for the memory of the deceased, the members and officers of this House will wear the usual badge of mourning for thirty days.

Resolved, That the proceedings of this House in relation to the death of the Hon. ISAAC S. PENNYBACKER, be communicated to the family of the deceased by the Clerk.

Resolved, That this House will attend the funeral of the deceased in a body; and, as a further mark of respect for his memory, that it do now adjourn.

The resolutions were adopted, and the House accordingly adjourned

---

IN SENATE.

THURSDAY, January 14.

Lieutenant-General.

Mr. DIX moved that the Senate proceed to the consideration of the bill to appoint a lieutenant-general to command the military forces of the United States during the war.

The motion was agreed to, and the bill was taken up accordingly, as in Committee of the Whole.

Mr. DIX rose and said:

Mr. PRESIDENT: The bill under consideration was introduced in accordance with the recommendation contained in the President's special Message of the 4th instant. The reasons for asking the appointment of a general to command all our military forces in Mexico were briefly explained in that Message. Having introduced the bill as a member of the Committee on Military Affairs, I deem it due to the Senate and to the subject to state the considerations by which I have been governed in giving the measure my support.

Our military operations in Mexico have heretofore been carried on in detached commands, on very extended lines, and in the execution of enterprises not only totally distinct from each other, but at geographical distances so remote as to preclude any thing like direct combination between the forces respectively employed in them. These enterprises have all been successful. Santa Fé and Chihuahua have been overrun and occupied by the military forces under General Kearny; the Californias by Colonel Fremont and our naval forces in the Pacific; New Leon and part of Tamaulipas by General Taylor; and Durango by General Wool and General Worth. The whole of northern and central Mexico, as far south as the mouth of the Rio Grande and the twenty-sixth parallel of latitude, is virtually in our possession. The Mexican authority may by this occupation be considered extinct in this extensive district, constituting, if we include Sonora and Sinoloa on the eastern shore of the Gulf of California, from which I believe the Mexican forces are withdrawn, about two-thirds of the entire territory of the Mexican republic, and about one-tenth of its population. The land forces, by which these acquisitions have been made, are rapidly concentrating upon the southern line of the subjugated territory. Their operations are to be, in some degree, combined, instead of being carried on in separate divisions. General officers, who have heretofore operated independently, are to come together and to act with each other in the accomplishment of common objects. At least four of these generals have the same rank, that of major-general, the highest rank in the service; and precedence among them in their respective arms is, therefore, to be determined by date of commission. In subordinate commands this mode of settling questions of precedence is inevitable, and ordinarily leads to little practical inconvenience. But to permit the right to the chief command over such numerous forces as are now to be combined, and in such extensive operations as are to be carried on, to be determined by mere priority of commission, and not by superiority of grade, is, to say the least, exceedingly undesirable not only in deference to military principles, but because this very circumstance has often proved unfriendly to united and zealous action, and sometimes has led to the frustration of plans of campaigns, and even to defeat, when success would have been certain with proper co-operation on the part of the commander and his subordinates. I might appeal, for the truth of this remark, to our own military history, as well as to that of other countries. I believe I may say, it is a well-settled opinion in respect to military command, and especially in extensive operations, that the chief commander should, if possible, be superior in grade to the other general officers serving under him. The considerations, by which the correctness of this principle is supported, are perfectly compatible with the highest patriotism and honor in the persons holding subordinate commands. It is strictly a question of military organization. We may concede to all the purest devotion and disinterestedness; and yet in the organization of military bodies and in the preparation of plans of campaign, we should be wanting in ordinary prudence if we were not guided by those general principles, which are calculated to render our arrangements proof, as far as human arrangements can be, against all hazard of failure in their execution. If there is a particular form of organization better suited than any other to give efficiency to the movements of military forces, it is the part of wisdom to adopt it; nor should we be content with a less efficient form, even though we have the fullest confidence in the patriotism and zeal of those who are to have part in the contemplated enterprises. Sir, I have entire faith in the devotedness and gallantry of the officers of our army, and of the volunteers; and no one shall surpass me here in attributing to them the praise, and awarding to them the justice to which they are entitled. I consider the proposed measure entirely consistent with the interests of both arms of the service, which are deeply concerned, though not so deeply as the interests of the country, in giving to the military body, of which they are a part, the most judicious and efficient organization.

Looking to the numerical forces to be moved in combination, they will far exceed any number ever commanded in this country—and I believe I may say in any other, except from accident or some temporary necessity—by a major-general, the highest grade in our service. The proper command of an officer of that rank is a division. A major-general and a general of division are convertible terms. A division consists of two brigades; a brigade consists of two regiments in the regular service and three in the volunteers. The command of a major-general, therefore, is from four to six thousand men. The force to be employed in Mexico, if our operations are to be carried on with proper vigor, should not fall short of twenty-five or thirty thousand fighting men in the field. It now exceeds twenty thousand. It is sufficient for four full divisions. To permit it to be commanded by a major-general, having no precedence over his associates except by the date of his commission, is as inconsistent with military principles as it would be to organize a regiment with three or four majors, and without a colonel; or, in other words, without a head. It is far too large a force to be commanded either by a major-general or a general having no higher rank than others serving under him. Such an arrangement is totally inconsistent with military principles and usages, looking to organization in its narrowest sense. When Napoleon was in command of the army of Italy, after his first successes, the Executive Directory determined to associate with him General Kellerman, one of the best commanders of that day. Napoleon remonstrated against it in a letter written in his usual terse and vigorous style; and he concluded by saying, that one bad general was better than two good ones.

Sir, there is great force and truth in the proposition. He intended to intimate that every military body should have a distinct head; and certainly the observation is eminently applicable to cases in which the numerical forces are greatly disproportioned to the rank of the officer commanding them. For these reasons, if there were no others, I should be in favor of the President's recommendation to appoint an officer of higher rank to command our armies in Mexico.

Thus far I have spoken of the proposed measure as connected with sound principles of military organization and command. I desire now to present some considerations of a different nature. Our military commanders in Mexico are operating in an enemy's country of vast extent. They are overrunning provinces, reducing cities and towns, and providing for the security of the subjugated territories under the rules of international law, and according to the usages of civilized States. These are high prerogatives, the incidents of war, having their authority in conventional rule beyond the civil constitution and municipal laws of our own country. It is very desirable that the depositary of these high and extraordinary powers should not only carry with him the requisite military talents, but that he should also possess the experience and the civil qualifications indispensable to enable him to meet his responsibilities intelligently and discreetly. Not only his own Government, but all civilized nations have an interest in the maintenance of rules designed to mitigate the asperities of warfare by applying to the conduct of war the principles of humanity and justice. Errors in the application of these rules may involve his own Government in embarrassment and reproach. These considerations, I am aware, apply rather to the qualifications of the man than to the rank he may happen to hold. I advert to them only for the purpose of indicating the importance of the position occupied by the commander of our armies in Mexico, and the propriety of extending to the President the broadest field for selection.

In the Message of the President, it is recommended that authority be given to appoint a commanding general for our military forces in Mexico, without specifying any rank. The committee, in reporting the bill, proposed to confer on him the rank of lieutenant-general—the grade in other services next above that of major-general, which is the highest in ours. The grade was created in 1798, during our dissensions with the French republic, by an act authorizing the President to raise a provisional army. The office was conferred, by the unanimous vote of the Senate, on General Washington, and was accepted by him, but with the express stipulation, that he should not be called into service until the exigency for which the office was created—an invasion of the United States by France—should actually occur. He did not believe it would occur; he was not deceived in this belief; and he never entered on the discharge of his duties, excepting so far as to give advice with regard to the organization of the army. About a year after this grade was created, and a few months before he died, another act was passed authorizing the appointment of a commander of the army, with the title of "general of the armies of the United States," and thereupon abolishing the office of lieutenant-general. I have not been able to find that the appointment was ever made, and by a return from the War Department in 1800, General Washington was reported as lieutenant-general *dead*. According to the analogies of other services, the rank of general is higher than that of lieutenant-general. I have not thought it material to inquire into the object of the second act; but it may have been designed to confer on him a rank as nearly approaching that which he bore in the revolutionary war (that of general and commander-in-chief) as was consistent with the Constitution of the United States, which declares the President to be commander-in-chief of the armies of the United States.

In other services, the rank of lieutenant-general is, I believe, a part, and an essential part, of the military organization. In France it was formerly conferred on the chiefs of provinces and the individuals holding it were invested with civil as well as military functions. In modern times, I believe, it has become purely a military title, and it confers a rank intermediate between that of major-general which is below, and general, which is above it. As the grade next to that of major-general it seems the proper title, if a higher grade is to be created. On the other hand, though the office of commander of the military forces in Mexico will be purely military, nevertheless, in providing for exigencies which may arise in the occupation of an enemy's territory—and, let me add, with as little disturbance as possible to the local authorities and the ordinary administration of justice—his station becomes one of the highest delicacy and importance. If a new grade is to be created, I repeat, the title of lieutenant-general will be admitted to be proper in a strictly military sense, and it is descriptive of the relation in which the commander of the armies in Mexico will stand to the President as commander-in-chief of the armies of the United States under the constitution. He cannot be in Mexico in person, and he must, therefore, command there by his lieutenant or deputy, by whatever name the latter may be called.

The proposed creation of a new grade in the army, higher than any now known to the service, does not contemplate the creation or delegation of any new authority to the officer who may be appointed to it. He will possess no other powers excepting those now possessed by our military commanders. The act creating the office limits its duration to the war with

Mexico. It is proposed to be created for the extraordinary emergency in which the country is placed, and will cease with it.

I desire it to be distinctly understood that the measure is proposed with a view to the vigorous prosecution of the war, and in this view only I support it. If we were to have a war of posts, or a long and moderate war, the office would be unnecessary, and I should not give it my support. On this point I desire to say a few words more. I concur fully in the sentiments expressed by the Senator from Kentucky (Mr. CRITTENDEN) at a late session of the Senate, with regard to a vigorous prosecution of the war. I see no alternative but to advance with a competent force, and compel Mexico to make peace. Least of all would I approve the policy which has been referred to on this floor, of maintaining our present line of possession, and waiting for peace to come to us. I see in such a policy no beneficial results. On the contrary, I see in it nothing but evil and mischief. I believe it would be a line of war, assassination, and rapine, which neither party would have the ability to put down. It is only a restoration of peace, resting upon the solemn sanctions of a treaty, that can engage either party to treat the perpetrators of outrage with the severity necessary to suppress it. Draw a line across the Mexican territory, and place your soldiery here to guard it, and you will be exposed to the danger, so well described by the Senator from Kentucky, of having your own divided forces attacked by the combined forces of the enemy at any point which he may elect. Besides, sir, take such a line, and let our present hostile relations to Mexico continue, and you give to individual acts of depredation, in some degree, the sanction of law. You convert a war of communities into a war of individuals, without responsibility and without restraint, while the hostile feeling between the two countries will constantly grow more embittered by the repetition of acts of violence. Peace alone, uniting the sovereign power of both countries in the maintenance of order, can terminate a state of things disastrous to both, and at war with all the interests of humanity.

I have but one word more to say in support of the bill. The President has asked the appointment of a commander of the armies in Mexico, with an increased rank. He believes it to be essential to the proper organization and movement of the army. He believes the success of our military operations may depend upon it. Sir, when the public honor and reputation are at stake, I am willing to extend to the Executive, on whom rests the whole responsibility of bringing the war to an honorable termination, any reasonable aid he requires. If we deny him the means he asks, and there shall be any failure in the enterprises set on foot, the responsibility will rest, not on him, but on us. While I am never in favor of enlarging unduly the sphere of executive patronage or power, I am in favor of extending to the President, within the sphere of his existing powers, the fullest command of means. It is a necessary incident to the conduct of war to invest him, in this respect, with a large discretion. Be it for good or for evil, we must give him our confidence. It is always possible an Executive may not respond to it as we think he ought. But it is quite clear that he cannot without it hope for a successful execution of his plans. With these impressions, I shall vote for the men and means, which may be asked to carry on the war with vigor. I shall vote for such an organization of the army as is deemed necessary to give it the greatest efficiency, so long as I see no salutary principle violated. The honorable Senator from Kentucky (Mr. CRITTENDEN) expressed the same determination in respect to men and means at a late meeting of the Senate. Sir, no one appreciates the patriotism of that honorable Senator better than myself; and I sincerely wish the confidence in the Executive, which this determination implies, could consistently with his views of duty, be carried a little farther—that while giving to the Executive all the men and money asked for, he could also vote for such an organization of the army as is deemed necessary to a vigorous prosecution of the war; for means and men avail little without the energy—moral and physical—of an efficient organization. For myself, I perceive nothing objectionable in the measure proposed. On the contrary, I can readily conceive it to be essential to the successful prosecution of our military operations in Mexico. I believe it to be necessary to a proper organization of the army; and I sustain it with cheerfulness, as a measure which is deemed necessary by the Administration to sustain the honor of the country and to insure the success of its arms.

Mr. BADGER said he had the honor of serving on the Military Committee; and when this bill was under consideration in that committee, in the absence of the chairman, (Mr. BENTON,) its members found themselves equally divided. He and the Senator from Kentucky (Mr. CRITTENDEN) were opposed to the plan of creating the office of lieutenant-general; while the other two members of the committee (Messrs. DIX and HOUSTON) were in favor of it. His friend from Kentucky and himself, however, felt bound in courtesy to permit the bill to be reported, as the two gentlemen who were in favor of it undoubtedly represented a majority of the committee, and the majority on this floor; still he felt bound to state his reasons for opposing it. He wished, in his own behalf, (and perhaps he might say on behalf of the honorable Senator from Kentucky,) to state to the Senate briefly, but yet somewhat more in detail than the short summary given by his honorable friend, the reasons which induced him and his colleague (Mr. CRITTENDEN) in committee, and which would induce him now, and he supposed he might say still influenced his colleague, to refuse, from considerations of public duty, to yield their assent to the establishment of the office which the President asked. It was, however, now past three o'clock, the usual hour of adjournment; he would therefore, with the approbation of the Senate, ask for an opportunity to assign his reasons to-morrow; and he now moved that the Senate do adjourn.

The motion was agreed to.

The Senate adjourned accordingly.

MONDAY, January 25.

Lieutenant-General—Vindication of the President.

Mr. BENTON asked the indulgence of the Senate to make an exposition of the circumstances under which the President had proposed the appointment of a lieutenant-general to command the army in Mexico, and with which appointment his name had become connected. It had been intimated, he said, on the floor of the Senate—hypothetically, to be sure, but not the less intelligibly and forcibly on that account—that there might be an ulterior and covert design in the proposition: nothing less than a design on the part of the President to appoint his successor. The Senator from North Carolina, (Mr. BADGER,) in his speech on the lieutenant-general bill, had indulged in that hypothesis; and as no supposition could be more unfounded, or more injurious to the President or to the public service, or could descend from a higher source and as he (Mr. BENTON) happened to be in possession of all the facts necessary to the vindication of the President, he desired to make an exposition which would show the supposition to be unfounded, and would save the President's character and the public service from the injury they would suffer if the intimation was allowed to go out uncontradicted from the floor of the Senate. He asked leave; for, as the bill for the lieutenant-general was laid upon the table, and as he would not have it taken up, (and would not speak to it if it was,) and as he did not choose to commit the irregularity of hanging a speech on some irrelevant bill, he must throw himself upon the indulgence of the Senate for leave to make the exposition of facts which the case required, and which the intimations of the Senator from North Carolina had rendered necessary.

Leave was given, and Mr. BENTON proceeded—

I feel myself called upon by the remarks of the Senator from North Carolina (Mr. BADGER) to vindicate the President from the unconstitutional and dangerous design which the hypothetical observations of that Senator would attribute to him; and shall do so in the simplest form of narrative, repeating to the Senate all that has taken place between the President and myself in relation to this appointment, and thereby enabling the Senate and the people to judge of the justice of the accusation.

It was at the beginning of the month of September last, and in the moment that I was about setting out to the West, that the President sent for me, and informed me that he had done so for the purpose of offering me a high appointment. He named it. It was the mission to France, then becoming vacant by the return of the gentleman (Mr. King, of Alabama) so long an ornament to this Chamber. I declined the appointment, and for reasons which had induced me to decline high appointments from Presidents Jackson and Van Buren. Mr. Polk was kind enough to ask me to take time to consider; but I answered him that there was no need for time; that the answer would still be the same, after any length of consideration; and so, with thanks for the honor he had done me, the appointment to the French mission was definitively declined. This was the beginning of September last; so that, at that time, it is certain that the President could have had no such design as has been attributed to him by the Senator from North Carolina—no design to make me his successor, by virtue of military feats to be performed on the lowlands or the table land of the republic of Mexico. On the contrary, a fertile imagination—such as the Senator from North Carolina so happily possesses—might have seen, or thought it saw, in this proposed amendment, a sort of political deportation—something like an exiling and burying in a foreign Court—for a purpose the very reverse of what the Senator from North Carolina has supposed. I say an inventive imagination might have seen, or thought it saw, all this. Possessing no such imagination, I saw no such thing. And taking the offer in the sense in which it was made, as eminently honorable in itself and a signal evidence of the President's confidence in me, and goodwill for me, I made him my thanks for it privately, as I now do publicly; and the affair was dropped. This, I repeat, was at the beginning of September last—only three months before the meeting of Congress; so that, at that time, it is quite clear the President had no such momentous and fearful design as the Senator from North Carolina has attributed to him. Up to that time—up to the first day of September, in the year 1846—the republic was safe.

Immediately after refusing the mission to France I went off to the West, was gone until the month of November, and had no communication of any kind, direct or indirect, nor upon any subject whatever, during my absence, with President Polk. This makes all safe again for two months more. I returned to this city in November, where my family was, and where Congress was soon to meet. The day after my arrival I called upon the President; and here we approach the dangerous ground! For, in that first interview, he actually asked me my opinion about the future mode of conducting the Mexican war. For reasons not proper now to be stated, but of the validity of which the country will some day have an opportunity of judging, the President saw fit to ask me my opinion upon the future mode of conducting the war. This request did not strike me as being any thing strange or unreasonable—either unbecoming in him to make, or for me to comply with. In my Senatorial capacity I was his constitutional adviser on many great questions, those of peace and war inclusive. In my political capacity, I was the supporter of his administration, and ready to give him my opinion on any subject. As chairman of the Senate's Committee on Military Affairs, and accustomed, in that character, to communicate on military subjects with all Administrations for about a quarter of a century last past, I saw nothing in the nature of the request he had made to implicate either of us. He asked me for my opinion as to the future mode of conducting the war. I gave it to him, first in speech, face to face, and afterwards in writing. And here it is! [holding up a roll of paper,] for I chose to retain the original for myself, while sending a copy to him. Here it is! and at the proper time the public shall see it, but not now; for I do not belong to the school that makes publication of plans of campaign—even dead plans—in time of war.

The President approved the plan: and it so happened that the nature of the plan required a head to the army—one head to the whole body—to unite and combine the whole into one harmonious and consistent movement. It so happened, also, that enough was known of the ideas of the two highest in rank of the officers of the army to know that their plans were different; and it is a maxim of fundamental observance in war, that no general is to be required to execute a plan which he disapproves. A new commander became indispensable; and as any new major-general would be subordinate to all now in commission, the solution of the difficulty lay in the creation of a new rank, superior to that of major-general, and inferior to the constitutional commander-in-chief. The creation of the rank of lieutenant-general, as had been done in the year 1798, at the time of the expected war with France, was the solution of the difficulty. This rank appeared to be the natural and regular derivation from the President's own political and military character, and the proper connecting-link between him and the army. As President, he was both the civil head of the Government and the military head of the army. He was commander-in-chief of the army and navy, and of the militia or volunteers when in service. They were all then in service, and in a foreign country. He could not go to Mexico to command in person: paramount duties required him to remain here. He could not send orders from the closet in this city. That was a folly of which there had been no example since the time that the Prince Eugene (of Savoy) was accustomed to return unopened, at the end of the campaigns, all the orders which the Aulic Council was in the habit of sending to him from Vienna.

The President was bound to command: he could not go to Mexico to command in person; and he could not command from Washington. The solution of the difficulty, which reconciled all contradictions, and permitted the exercise of all duties, civil and military, was the appointment of a military deputy—a legatus—a locum tenens—a lieutenant to take the place of the constitutional commander-in-chief in the field; to give orders in his name, and to take the responsibility of plans and movements, while the generals, at the heads of divisions or columns, would only have the responsibility of execution. This, for reasons too well known to require rehearsal in this chamber, it was thought would be entirely ageeable to the generals of highest rank in our army in Mexico; it would secure their rear at home, and leave them free to contend with the enemy in front. It was not intended to diminish the fighting vocation of the two generals, but to reconcile and accomplish two desirable objects, namely, the execution of the President's plans, and the release of the major-generals from responsibility for plans and movements. This was the view of the *office* of lieutenant-general: as to the proposed *officer*, there was no breach of military rule, law, etiquette, or propriety, in the proposed appointment. The office was original, and belonged to no person. The President had a right to nominate, and the Senate to confirm, whom they pleased. Personally, I would take no concern in it. I only asked the President to make known the name intended for the place to the members of Congress, that all objections to the *officer*, as well as to the *office*, should be open to full inquiry. I forbade my friends to say a word on my account. I would not say a word for myself. I would not even obviate a prominent objection by reminding any one that, in 1812, I was the military superior of every general now in the service, and had a right to have commanded the whole of them if we had chanced to serve together. I was then colonel in the service of the United States, commissioned by President Madison, under a law of Congress, and led a regiment of my own raising from Tennessee to the lower Mississippi, under General Jackson, to meet the British then expected at New Orleans, but who did not come till 1814. I was then of a rank, and in a position to have commanded, if we had met, every general now in service. Even in the regular army, in 1813, I was lieutenant-colonel, while most of the present generals were company officers, and only one of them of the rank of colonel. Yet I scorned to mention these things, even to bosom friends, while the measure was depending, and only do it now for the purpose of rescuing the President from the supposed breach of military decorum which the appoinment of a citizen from civil life (myself being that citizen) to the command of the army would imply in the opinion of the Senator from North Carolina. Sir, if the appointment of a citizen from civil life to the command of the army, would be an insult to it, that army is now already grievously insulted; for the present President is from civil life, and is now the constitutional commander-in-chief of the army, with rather more power than a lieutenant-general would have, and rather less experience in military affairs than the proposed one possesses.

Finally, and to conclude the vindication of the President in this particular, I can say that Mr. Polk is not the first President who proposed to give me the command of the army against Mexico—that General Jackson himself proposed it in 1836, when our affairs with that country looked warlike; and that then, as now, I agreed to take it.

And here, Mr. President, having fulfilled my task of vindicating the Chief Magistrate of the Union from the design, hypothetically imputed to him, of wishing to appoint his successor, in my person, and by means of this lieutenant-generalship, I might close my remarks; but as my name has been coupled with this business, and as I have remained silent, and even left my seat while the measure was depending, I must now take leave, with the kind indulgence of the Senate, to proceed a step further, and to say a word on my own account; and to show that *service*, and not *rank*, was my inducement to agree to the offer of the President; and that there might have been cases in which I would not have accepted the office of lieutenant-general, even if it had been created. I have already said that I will not now show what my own plan was; but I can say of it that it was a plan which looked to a *result*, and promised an *issue*, and that briefly; and that I would have had nothing to do with any plan of any other kind —nothing to do with any plan that contemplated a long and moderate war, or a war of masterly inactivity, or of retreat upon the Rio Grande, or of defending a line; or of attack upon the idle and solitary castle of San Juan of Ulua—especially at the commencement of the season for the black vomit. In no one of these cases would I have been lieutenant-general, or captain-general, or major-general, or colonel-general, or any other sort of a general that ever was heard of. I know very well that the President had no idea of any one of these most amiable plans; but there is a way to give him an idea of them, and even to force them upon him; and that would be, by the simple process of denying him the means of doing any thing else.

I shall not state my plan; but I will say of it, that, besides intending a *result*, it proposed to carry on the war, while there was war, according to the usage of all nations in the case of invasive war—the invaders to be paid and subsisted by the invaded. Contributions regularly levied—duties regularly collected—would accomplish these objects, and leave the United States free, or nearly free, from the expenses of the war.

I can say, further, that my plan was not limited to a mere military view of the subject; that it comprehended a union of policy and of arms—the olive-branch to go with the sword, ministers to treat, as well as an army to fight. A diplomatic mission, nationally constituted both in a geographical and in a political sense, was to attend the head-quarters; and, while the ministers stood ready to negotiate at every step, the army was to make an organization and an attitude to give emphasis to negotiation. And this combination of arms and of policy was not mere guess work, the idle conception of fancy; but the result of a knowledge of the state of parties in Mexico—a peace party, for honorable peace; a war party, for endless war —as was so luminously shown by the Senator from New York (Mr. DIX) a few days ago. My plan was adapted to both of these parties—honorable peace for the one; the sword for the other. The military part of the plan has fallen to the ground: the diplomatic part falls with it: and now it devolves upon those who have frustrated the plan of the President to present him a better.

I counted much on the efficacy of the diplomatic part of this plan; for great errors prevail in Mexico with regard to our designs and feelings towards that country, and which nothing but an authentic mission can remove. The war party is incessant in its calumnies against us, artfully contrived to operate on every class of the people, and to render peace impossible. It has a falsehood for every class. To the religious orders the war is represented as a war of religion—the Protestant against the Catholic —and a war of sacrilege—the spoliation of the churches. To the Crecle Spaniards and the Indians of mixed blood they present it as a war of races—the Anglo-Saxon against the Spanish-American—and the subjugation of the latter intended. To the unmixed Indian race, (nearly the one-half of the whole population, and the sole resource of the army for its rank and file,) it is presented as a war of extinction, or of slavery—their race to be extirpated, like so many tribes in our North America; or to be carried into slavery to work the fields of their masters, like the slaves brought from Africa. And, to all, it is presented as a war of ambition and of conquest, in which there is no peace for Mexico but in the degradation of her citizens and the loss of her independence. A mission, such as I proposed, would authentically contradict all these calumnies, and show the deceived people of Mexico that just and honorable peace is all that we want; and that, far from wishing her degradation, both policy and interest unite in making us wish to see her prosperous, happy, and independent. She is a republic—our neighbor—who did us the honor to copy our form of government, and had a great commerce with us. The injuries of which we complain were the work of a few, while the great majority of the people, who have done us no harm, are willing to do us justice; and every republican in Mexico reciprocates the wish for that close connection, political and commercial, between the two republics, which is necessary to their own prosperity, to the stability of the republican system in all the Spainish American States, and to the complete independence of the New World from the Old.

I counted much on the efficacy of the diplomatic part of the plan, and not less on the military part, if the other failed. Of this I can say nothing but that it was not framed in total ignorance of Mexican character, Mexican country, and Mexican resources. Forty years ago I studied Humboldt, and did not overlook his chapter on the military defences of the country, and especially his imposing development of the great elements of defence with which nature had endowed her; the dangers of the coast when the north wind was blowing, which blows from the autumnal to the vernal equinox—the black vomit when it was not—and the deep defiles of volcanic mountains. The plan may have been bad; but it was not conceived without some knowledge of the subject; and it promised a result—peace to the country, if it succeeded; and to the soldier that died, a death worthy of the soldier—the battle-storm his embrace, the field of honor his bed, the lofty summits of the Cordilleras his monument and his grave!

Tuesday, February 2.

*Three Million Loan.**

Mr. Sevier moved that the Senate proceed to the consideration of the special order, being the bill making appropriations to bring the existing war with Mexico to a speedy and honorable conclusion.

The motion having been agreed to, the bill was taken up for consideration as in Committee of the Whole. After having been read a second time, as follows:

"*Be it enacted, &c.*, That a sum of money, not exceeding three millions of dollars, be, and the same is hereby, appropriated, for the purpose of defraying any extraordinary expenses which may be incurred in order to bring the existing war with Mexico to a speedy and honorable conclusion, to be paid out of any money in the treasury not otherwise appropriated, and to be applied under the direction of the President of the United States, who shall cause an account of the expenditure thereof to be laid before Congress as soon as may be"—

Mr. Sevier remarked, that this bill had been introduced upon the recommendation of the President of the United States, and that the Committee on Foreign Relations, by whom it was reported, in preparing the bill, had resolved to follow the form in which other enactments of a similar character had been framed. One of those enactments to which he referred was passed in the year 1803, at the time of the acquisition of Louisiana, during the Administration of Mr. Jefferson; and another in 1806, when it was proposed to purchase Florida. A similar bill had also passed the Senate at the last session of Congress, the proposition having been first considered with closed doors, and afterwards reported in open session. The design of the committee was to follow those precedents, excluding all extraneous matter, and incorporating nothing that was calculated to excite sectional or party feeling, or to occasion debate. It was the opinion of the committee, and in this opinion he concurred, that all such matter would be ill-timed, and that its introduction could lead to no good result; and he intended, if it were moved from any quarter, to put any thing of that sort into the bill, to oppose it. In looking over the proceedings of the last session, he found that the Committee on Foreign Relations had reported two resolutions on the subject, the first of which declared that the course indicated by the President in his Message received the approbation of the Senate, and was in the following language:

"1. *Resolved*, That the Senate entertain a strong desire that the existing war with Mexico should be terminated by a treaty of peace, just and honorable to both nations; and that the President be advised to adopt all proper measures for the attainment of that object."

This resolution was discussed for several days, and was at length voted on, and was sanctioned by every Senator, on both sides of the Senate, with the exception of two, the Senator from Texas, (Mr. Rusk,) and the Senator from Missouri, (Mr. Atchison.) The second resolution was as follows:

"2. *Resolved further*, That the Senate deem it

---

* This bill was no part of the ordinary support of the war by providing for the army and navy. It was a special appropriation for a special purpose, as its terms imply, and as was made known by the President in a confidential message. It looked to the acquisition of territory, and to the payment of money in advance of the ratification of the treaty of purchase. Santa Anna had returned, and expected this money, and was ready to treat on the assurance of receiving it. The clause in the bill by which the President was to cause an account of the expenditure, made under his direction, to be laid before Congress as soon as may be, sufficiently indicate it to be of the nature of secret service money. This being the character of the appropriation, and evidently intended for territorial acquisition, it became the main topic of the debate of the session—embracing the origin, the conduct, and the objects of the war, and giving a full view both of the opposition and of the administration side of that question. It was to this bill that Mr. Wilmot proposed his *proviso* against the introduction of slavery in the territory which should be acquired, which created so much excitement for some time, and was finally rejected on showing that slavery was then extinct in the territory expected to be acquired.

advisable that Congress should appropriate a sum of money to enable the President to conclude a treaty of peace, limits, and boundaries, with the republic of Mexico, and to be used by him in the event that such treaty should call for the expenditure of the money so appropriated, or any part thereof."

This was agreed to, and the Committee on Foreign Relations were instructed to report to the Senate, in open session, a bill to that effect. Various propositions to amend the bill were made, and the discussion upon it consumed two days. The bill was ultimately passed by a vote of 33 to 19. This proposition having been thus discussed and deliberately voted on, he would consider it a waste of time to go at any length in the matter now, and in regard to the form of the measure. The same course had been adopted in 1803, in the acquisition of Louisiana; in 1806, in the acquisition of Florida; and, lastly, in that body at its last session, in 1846. Unless gentlemen had changed their opinions since that time, there could be no great variety of opinion in any part of this chamber. The object of this bill, as appears upon its face, was to make peace with Mexico; and, in urging its passage, he should abstain from the expression of any opinions regarding the origin of the Mexican war; for his object was to excite no party feelings upon any side on a question of this sort. He had his own opinion on the subject, but he should not introduce it into a discussion. He took it for granted they were all in favor of peace, if it could be obtained upon proper terms; and it was proper that he should say, that he did not see how peace could be brought about, unless one or other of the belligerent parties made an advance towards obtaining it. It was true, we had already made an advance towards that object, by sending a Minister to treat with the Government of Mexico, and had kept our army out of the country which was claimed by us for a considerable time before the commencement of this war, for the express purpose of securing peace, by showing a forbearance and a disposition to avoid a hostile collision.

In making peace, of course the United States would expect to receive indemnity, to some extent at least, for the expenses of the war, and they would expect also the payment of the claims held by our citizens against the republic of Mexico, and this indemnity was expected in the shape of territory. He was not authorized to state precisely what territory this Government would require, but he supposed that no Senator would think that they ought to get less than New Mexico and Upper California. He did not suppose that a treaty of peace with less than this would ever pass that body. However, they would be better prepared when a treaty was proposed to determine as to the quantity.

Having stated then, in as few words as practicable, the object of the bill and its form, the next question that arose was, Whether it was likely that they could effect their purpose upon these terms? In regard to that he would say, that, in coming to the conclusion they had, the committee were governed, to a great extent, by the recommendation of the President; and he, after examining that correspondence, had come to the conclusion that peace could be made upon those terms with Mexico. He believed that Mexico, a large part of it, at all events a large majority of the people, would be glad to make peace on these terms.

Mr. MANGUM said there was no purpose of delay, of any unreasonable delay, on his part; but this was a very important question. They had been engaged during the last few weeks on very important measures, which had occupied their attention exclusively; and not knowing that this bill would be precipitated upon them, they were not prepared satisfactorily to determine those important questions which it involved. He hoped the question would not be pressed. If it were necessary they could go into special session.

Mr. SEVIER said if it was to be debated, that it might share the fate it did last year, he was not willing to have it passed over; but he should not object to reasonable debate. He was not willing, though, to have it spoken to death. They had the appropriation bills yet behind, but he was willing to yield a day or two.

Mr. MANGUM said the object of the President now seemed to be pretty clearly intimated to be the purchase of California and New Mexico. If this were so, he would only say, for one, that, under this aspect, it presented a vastly momentous question. He was unwilling to see Mexico dismembered. He was unwilling to acquire, at the edge of the sword, or the point of the bayonet, a single square inch of territory, though he was disposed to acquire, if practicable, those water facilities which would be of immense advantage to this country. But as to a forcible spoliation of the territory of California, or any other, at the edge of the sword, it was distasteful to him. He was altogether averse to it. The change of phase which this matter had assumed rendered it incomparably of more importance than the proposition of last year; and he was indisposed, therefore, to give a vote which might foreclose him hereafter (the views of the Administration not having been clearly indicated until to-day) from taking such a course as his more mature judgment might dictate.

Mr. SEVIER moved to postpone the further consideration of the subject until to-morrow. He then briefly explained some matters in relation to this subject, from the history of the last session of Congress.

Mr. CALHOUN said Thursday was but day after to-morrow. By the postponement to that day they should gain time, as it would give Senators the opportunity for reflection; and they knew that debates which came on after due reflection were generally the most concise.

He hoped that during every session of Congress every one would have the opportunity at some period of the session to express his views on the general questions before the country. So far as he had observed, the gentlemen on the other side of the chamber had shown no disposition to prolong the debate unnecessarily. He thought there had been rather more consumption of time on his own side. He thought the request now made a reasonable one. Senators desired to be heard without intending to consume time unnecessarily, and what even time a reasonable discussion might take no one could tell. But surely three, four, five, or even six days, could not be considered unreasonable on a great question like this. He should vote for the postponement.

So the bill was postponed.

Mr. BERRIEN then gave notice of his intention to offer an amendment, which was read as follows, and ordered to be printed:

"*Provided, always*, And it is hereby declared to be the true intent and meaning of Congress in making this appropriation, that the war with Mexico ought not to be prosecuted by this Government with any view to the dismemberment of that republic, or to the acquisition by conquest of any portion of her territory; that this Government ever desires to maintain and preserve peaceful and friendly relations with all nations, and particularly with the neighboring republic of Mexico, will always be ready to enter into negotiations, with a view to terminate the present unhappy conflict on terms which shall secure the just rights and preserve inviolate the national honor of the United States and of Mexico; that it is especially desirable, in order to maintain and preserve those amicable relations which ought always to exist between neighboring republics, that the boundary of the State of Texas should be definitively settled, and that provision be made by the republic of Mexico for the prompt and equitable settlement of the just claims of our citizens on that republic."

FRIDAY, February 5.

Three Million Bill.

Mr. SEVIER moved to proceed to the consideration of the special order, being the bill making further appropriation to bring the war with Mexico to a speedy and honorable conclusion; which motion having been agreed to—

Mr. BERRIEN said: I now turn to the consideration of this bill. Sir, the bill which is before you proposes an appropriation of $3,000,000, or rather not exceeding $3,000,000, for the purpose of defraying any extraordinary expenses which may be incurred in bringing the existing war with Mexico to a speedy and honorable conclusion. Now, sir, with a view of bringing this war to a speedy and honorable conclusion, we have already authorized the President of the United States to raise an army of upwards of seventy thousand men; and, in addition to the ordinary revenue of the Government, we have placed at his disposal twenty-eight millions of money; and now it is asked that we shall make an appropriation of three millions of dollars for the purpose specified in this bill, to be applied under the sole discretion and control of the President; and we are asked, with an apparent confidence that the request will be complied with, to let this bill pass without debate or discussion, reserving for some other occasion the examination of those interesting questions which present themselves to the mind of every Senator at the moment when this proposition is made. For myself, I certainly cannot consent; the feelings, the wishes, the just expectations of the American people, combine to forbid it. They desire to know—they have a right to know, as far as we are informed—what is their condition in relation to this foreign power with which we are at war. They have a right to know, as far as we have the means of informing them, what expectation they may entertain of a termination of the conflict in which they have been so unexpectedly involved. Sir, in May last, without any premonition, without any expectation on the part of the American people of such a result, you were suddenly roused by the intelligence that hostilities had commenced between the American and the Mexican armies. These hostilities had been brought about by military movements made in consequence of orders emanating from the commander-in-chief of the American army. In the first moment of excitement, produced by the intelligence that hostilities had been commenced, Congress recognized the existence of the war, and made provision for its vigorous prosecution. Every demand that was made by the President, with a solitary exception, has been acquiesced in. He has been furnished with the means which he has deemed necessary for the prosecution of this war, and our gallant army has nobly sustained the honor of the American name. Wherever our standard has been unfurled—wherever the stars and the stripes which emblazon it have been given to the breeze—the honor of the American name has been vindicated. That army is now in the heart of Mexico; it has, in the phraseology of the day, covered itself with glory as with a mantle. If the military fame of our army were a thing of which we were not before certain, they have won it for themselves. They have triumphed over superior numbers, and Mexico stands now beaten, stricken down by an army inferior in numbers, rebuked in the heart of her own territory. If it be this glory of which we are in search, we have won it. We are inthe heart of Mexico with forces which she shuns to meet.

But what have we done? How, by the advance of the army, have we advanced the interests of the country? How have we advanced that honor of the possession of which we were not certain, but for which the war was entered upon? Who, that witnesses the actual posture of our affairs, is able to tell how much nearer we are to the termination of this war than when we entered it? Sir, I believe that this war may be terminated. I believe that it may be terminated by a course consistent with the honor of the American nation. I believe that it may be terminated by a course which shall not only consist with our interests, but which shall place us in that elevated position which, as the first free nation of the world, we ought to occupy in the eyes of the civilized world. I have asked how much honor shall we have attained at the termination of this war by all the victories we have won? Who does not know that the effect of our military operations has been to unite and to animate a distracted people; and that at this moment a determination for resistance on the part of Mexico is more fixed, more resolute, than at any former moment? On what was that determination founded? Whence did it originate? It was, in his opinion, the determination of despair. It was the result of that desperation to which the Mexican Government were reduced by their belief of the exorbitance of our demands. He would take from them this motive to resist; he would take it from them, not by a renewal of overtures of peace which they had disregarded, but he would take it from them by a declaration of the opinion and feelings of the American Congress as to the purpose for which this war was prosecuted, and as to the terms upon which it might be terminated. It was with a view to this object that he had suggested to the Senate the amendment of which he gave notice the other day.

The question on his motion might be stated now, or at the close of his remarks, which he proposed to submit, at the pleasure of the Chair. He would await its direction, either to pause or to proceed.

Mr. Cass said, if this was the proper moment, he would inform the honorable Senator from Georgia that he had an amendment to submit.

Mr. Berrien remarked, that the Senator could have it read and printed.

The Presiding Officer inquired if the Senator from Georgia desired to have the amendment read.

Mr. Berrien. Certainly.

The Secretary then read the amendment of Mr. Cass, as follows:

Strike out all after the word "provided," and insert: "And it is hereby declared to be the true intent and meaning of Congress, in making this appropriation, that, as by the act of the republic of Mexico, a state of war exists between that Government and the United States, agreeably to the declaration made by this Congress on the 13th day of May last, therefore the interest and honor of this country require that the said war be vigorously prosecuted to a successful issue, and that a reasonable indemnity should be obtained from Mexico for the wrongs she has committed towards the Government of the United States.

"And it is further declared, that the nature and extent of such indemnity are proper subjects, in the first instance, for executive consideration, when negotiations for peace may be opened between this country and Mexico, subject to the action of the Senate on the question of ratification."

Mr. Bagby hoped both amendments would be read, that the Senate might have them before it.

The Secretary read Mr. Berrien's amendment, as follows:

"*Provided, always*, And it is hereby declared to be the true intent and meaning of Congress in making this appropriation, that the war with Mexico ought not to be prosecuted by this Government with any view to the dismemberment of that republic, or to the acquisition by conquest of any portion of her territory; that this Government ever desires to maintain and preserve peaceful and friendly relations with all nations, and particularly with the neighboring republic of Mexico, will always be ready to enter into negotiations, with a view to terminate the present unhappy conflict on terms which shall secure the just rights and preserve inviolate the national honor of the United States and of Mexico; that it is especially desirable, in order to maintain and preserve those amicable relations which ought always to exist between neighboring republics, that the boundary of the State of Texas should be definitively settled, and that provision be made by the republic of Mexico for the prompt and equitable settlement of the just claims of our citizens on that republic."

Mr. Berrien said he wished to ask if the amendment of the Senator from Michigan was offered as a substitute.

Mr. Cass said he should offer it as a substitute at the proper time.

Mr. Berrien continued. The amendment which he had proposed and the substitute which the Senator from Michigan had notified them he should offer, opened the whole question. He desired to say at the outset, in order to avoid any misapprehension, that he was prepared to sustain the Government in the vigorous prosecution of this war, by voting all needful supplies of men and money to bring it to a successful result. In order to avoid any misapprehension of the remarks he was about to submit to the Senate to-day, and the course he designed to pursue, he was ready to sustain the Executive department in a vigorous prosecution of this war, by voting all needful supplies of men and money—all such supplies as were necessary to bring it to a successful result, if Mexico, madly regardless of her own interests and the interests of humanity, should refuse to terminate this controversy upon terms which may consist with her honor and the honor of the United States. This principle had regulated his personal conduct from the commencement of this war. He had voted all the supplies which had been required by the President of the United States, which had received the sanction of their committees, with the single exception of the act of 13th May, 1846, upon which he did not vote. And he did not vote for that bill because it required him to affirm what he did not believe to be true. But it proposed to provide for reinforcing and strengthening our army, then on the confines of Mexico, and apparently in danger from what seemed to be an overwhelming superiority of numbers. He did not, indeed, share the apprehensions felt for the fate of that army, for he had an abiding confidence in the skill and gallantry of its leaders, the bravery and discipline of our soldiers, and the patriotism of both. He cherished, moreover, a grateful recollection of the story of San Jacinto, and he had formed his own estimate of the Mexican army under the guidance of its most distinguished chieftain.

But it was proposed to strengthen and reinforce that army, and to deliver it from the unequal conflict to which it might be subjected; and though that relief might not reach the army before its fate should be decided—so far as a single battle might decide it—he was willing to vote to strengthen and reinforce it at the earliest moment, had that proviso not been connected with the bill.

He entertained then as he entertained now, the belief, the conviction, that we had been unnecessarily involved in this war with Mexico. He believed it had been brought about by military movements on our part, and that it had been forced upon the Mexican Government. He was convinced that the military order which was given by our military commander-in-chief, anterior to the march of our army from Corpus Christi to the Rio Grande, was the real source and practical origin of this war. Though he had since seen it stated in official documents, that it grew out of the indignities inflicted by Mexico upon our citizens, and her determination to invade with a view to regain dominion over Texas, he would call the attention of the Senate to the fact, that as early as the preceding month of June—the 15th day of June, 1845—by an order emanating from the War Department, addressed to General Taylor, and marked "confidential," but which was subsequently communicated to the Senate, it was distinctly announced that he was ordered to take up his line of march from his encampment, with the view of protecting Texas, not then one of the States of this Union; it was then distinctly announced to him that his ultimate destination was the Rio Grande or its vicinity. And yet they were told that the order of January, 1846, was issued under the pressure of indignities offered by Mexico, in her refusal to receive our Minister, and in her menaces of hostilities. He would take from these allegations the foundation on which they rest. He would refer to an order which emanated from the War Department on the 9th of June, 1845, and reiterated, with a single modification, in July. By this he would show that this army was not merely designed for the protection of Texas, which would have been secured by the possession of Corpus Christi, but it was announced that its destination was the Rio Grande, which Mexico claimed to be beyond her boundary. In the order issued in July, 1845, this order was so far modified as this: the preceding order of June had announced that the ultimate destination of the army was the Rio Grande without qualification; in the order which followed, the commander of the American army was told that Mexico had certain posts east of the Rio Grande which she had occupied, and that in the advance of our army to the Rio Grande, which was its ultimate destination, these forces of the enemy were not to be interrupted. Now it seemed to him, with these documents before them, that the war in which we are now involved, is therefore a war resulting from the order which was given by the President of the United States to advance the American army to the Rio Grande from Corpus Christi, in pursuance of the destination which had been confidentially announced to the commander of the American army as early as the preceding June; that the advance of the army to the Rio Grande, the erection of a fort pointing her cannon upon the town of Matamoras, was an indication of hostile intent—no, not of hostility of intent, but an act of hostility, which was the real origin and the commencement of this war. He would put the question to every American Senator—he would put the question to the American people, whether they would not have considered such a movement on the part of Mexico, or any other nation on earth, as an act of hostility to us. If Great Britain, during the existence of the north-eastern boundary question, had advanced her military forces to the disputed territory, and erected forts and planted cannon there, and pointed them on the contiguous villages, should we have waited for her to apply the match to those cannon before we should have considered that Great Britain had committed against us an act of war? And if that would have been the universal feeling of the American people, shall we deny to Mexico, because she is our enemy, a participation in the common feelings of our nature?

This was the view he had entertained of the origin of the war. But it exists. It has been recognized by Congress. They had bound themselves by pledges given by the act of the 13th of May, 1846, vigorously to prosecute it to a successful result. He was willing to participate in the common lot; and so far as depended on him, to perform that portion of the duty which might devolve on him in the redemption of that pledge. He was willing, therefore, he repeated, to vote the men and money which might be necessary for the prosecution of this war, or the termination of it by negotiation in an honorable peace, by such means as Senators might devise.

Mr. SEVIER. I hope the Senator, when he comments on my speech, will read the words

I used as reported in the papers. I said this money was wanted for the purpose of making peace: not as secret-service money, as the Senator throughout his remarks seemed to suppose, but as money for which a return was to be made by the President publicly, openly, before the world. I said I conceived that the honor and the interest of the country required on the part of Mexico two things: indemnity in part for the expenses of the war, in the first place, and in the next, the payment of the claims of our citizens; and to effect this object, that a cession of a part of her territory would be necessary, for it was not to be supposed that she had got the money to pay us with; and I said that I supposed no Senator would be willing to take less for this purpose than New Mexico and Upper California. These were my remarks, in substance, and I hope the Senator will take them as I made them.

Mr. BERRIEN said it seemed to him, without entering into any discussion upon this point—for he was always ready to receive from the honorable Senator his own view of what he said—that, if he had been under a misapprehension, there was some cause for such misapprehension. But to proceed: This was a new principle in the diplomacy of this country, to negotiate with a foreign power, giving to her in advance a certain sum of money to be applied to her exigencies, and to pay her army and other expenses, for the purpose of disposing her to make peace; for the purpose of payments to her army. There, he apprehended, was the real key to this operation. The President of the United States probably felt—the Senator from Arkansas felt probably, what they all felt, that any act of the Mexican rulers, not sustained by the army, would be inevitably unreliable; and it was therefore to propitiate the army in favor of any negotiation into which they might enter, that this money was to be applied. He did not know whether it could properly be called secret-service money; he did not know that it could be properly said to be money given to the Mexican rulers to dispose them to make peace; but this he did know, that the history of this country, so far as he was acquainted, afforded no instance whatever of any case in which money had been appropriated by this Government for such a purpose. In their negotiations with Indian tribes, certainly, they sometimes provided for their sustenance, and, indulging the ancient habits of that people, they sometimes made presents to their chiefs. But he did not know that they had transferred, or were about to transfer, in their dealings with foreign countries, the observances which had been followed in relation to the Indian tribes. Were they disposed to deal with Mexico as with the savage tribes? Were they disposed, in looking to the necessitous condition of Mexico, considering her Government unstable, and insufficient to preserve the stipulations of any treaty, were they disposed to conciliate opposing parties by the payment of money? He apprehended not. He apprehended that the operations of the distinguished chief who was now at the head of the Mexican army might possibly be influenced in a different direction from what was contemplated by this enactment. It might be, if they were permitted to rely, as they were to a certain extent, upon the communications which had been made to the President—it might be that Santa Anna was really disposed to peace; it might be the understanding that the unstable condition of their country rendered it necessary that the army should be propitiated, in order to give permanency to any treaty; it might be that Santa Anna found it necessary to be possessed of a certain fund to enable him to conciliate the army. If this were so, why, then, they had the key to the inactivity of that military chieftain who was now at the head of the Mexican forces—forces vastly superior in numbers to any which we had the power to bring against them. This might be the key to the means by which he has been so mysteriously enabled to pass our blockade. He understood it now to be conceded that the money to be appropriated was to be given to the Mexicans for the purpose of being applied by them to the payment of their army and other expenses, and he presumed that, when the money was paid to the Mexicans, we should at least have lost the security which possession gave us until the conditions for which this money was appropriated were fulfilled.

He desired to remove any impressions which he feared might have resulted from the remarks of the honorable chairman of the Committee on Foreign Relations at the opening of this discussion, that Senators were committed by the vote they had given upon this subject as submitted to them by the President in his Message of the 4th August, 1846. The Senator had, however, corrected a misapprehension under which he was then laboring, that the almost unanimous vote of the Senate was given on the resolution which he had first stated. He feared it was not distinctly understood by the Senator what was the real action of the Senate on that subject.

The President, by his Message, required two millions of dollars, in order to put it in his power to advance a portion of the consideration in money for the cession of any territory which might be made. The President said:

"Under these circumstances, and considering the exhausted and distracted condition of the Mexican republic, it might become necessary, in order to restore peace, that I should have it in my power to advance a portion of the consideration money for any cession of territory which may be made. The Mexican Government might not be willing to wait for the payment of the whole until the treaty could be ratified by the Senate, and an appropriation to carry it into effect be made by Congress; and the necessity for such a delay might defeat the object altogether. I would therefore suggest, whether it would not be wise for Congress to appropriate a sum such as they might consider adequate for this purpose, to be paid, if necessary, immediately upon the ratification of the treaty by Mexico. This disbursement would of course be accounted for at the treasury, not as secret-service money, but like other expenditures."

Now, on this Message of the President, the Committee on Foreign Relations made the following report to the Senate:

"*Resolved*, That the course adopted and proposed by the President, as indicated in his message of the 4th instant, for the speedy termination of the war with Mexico, receives the approbation of the Senate.

"*Resolved*, That in the opinion of the Senate, it is expedient to place two millions of dollars at the disposal of the President, to be used at his discretion in the event of a treaty of peace with Mexico, satisfactorily adjusting the boundaries of the two countries; and that the Committee on Foreign Relations be instructed to report to the Senate, in open session, a bill for that purpose, in conformity to the provision of similar acts passed in 1803 and 1806."

These resolutions were so little acceptable to the Senate, that the then chairman of the Committee on Foreign Relations modified the second resolution in this way:

"*Resolved*, That in the opinion of the Senate, it is expedient to place a sum of money at the disposal of the President, to be used at his discretion in the event of a treaty of peace with Mexico, satisfactorily adjusting the boundaries of the two countries."

"In the event of a treaty of peace with Mexico," and not preliminary to it.

Upon this, on the motion of another Senator, it was proposed to amend by striking out all after the word "Resolved," and inserting as follows:

"That the Senate heartily unite with the President in his expressed desire for a speedy and honorable peace with Mexico, but, as at present informed, they have no further advice to give in the premises."

Still these resolutions were unacceptable to the Senate, and they were recommitted, and the next report was in these words:

"1st. *Resolved*, That the Senate entertain a strong desire that the existing war with Mexico should be terminated by a treaty of peace, just and honorable to both nations, and that the President be advised to adopt all proper measures for the attainment of that object."

Here was a resolution on which he presumed the Senate was unanimous. The second resolution was in these words:

"2d. *Resolved further*, That the Senate deem it advisable that Congress should appropriate a sum of money to enable the President to conclude a treaty of peace, limits, and boundaries, with the republic of Mexico, and to be used by him in the event that such treaty should call for the expenditure of the money so appropriated, or any part thereof."

Now, the vote of the Senate—not that to which the Senator from Arkansas referred—but the vote of thirty to eighteen, was the vote on the second resolution, in which, by that majority, the Senate directed that a sum of money should be placed at the disposal of the President to conclude a treaty of peace, limits, and boundaries, with the republic of Mexico—not to be used by him for the purpose of concluding that treaty, but to be used by him if such treaty should call for the expenditure of the money so appropriated, or any part thereof.

He had referred to these proceedings of the last session for the purpose of showing that no Senator was committed by those proceedings to vote for the bill now under consideraion.

The Senate then adjourned.

SATURDAY, February 6.

Three Million Bill.

On motion of Mr. SEVIER, the special order was taken up, and the Senate resumed the consideration, as in Committee of the Whole, of the bill making further appropriation to bring the existing war with Mexico to a speedy and honorable conclusion.

The question being upon the following amendment submitted by the Senator from Michigan (Mr. CASS) to the amendment of the Senator from Georgia, (Mr. BERRIEN,) and intended as a substitute therefor:

Strike out all after the word "provided," and insert: "And it is hereby declared to be the true intent and meaning of Congress, in making this appropriation, that, as by the act of the republic of Mexico, a state of war exists between that Government and the United States, agreeably to the declaration made by this Congress, on the 13th day of May last, therefore the interest and honor of this country require that the said war be vigorously prosecuted to a successful issue, and that a reasonable indemnity should be obtained from Mexico for the wrongs she has committed towards the Government and the citizens of the United States.

"And it is further declared that the nature and extent of such indemnity are proper subjects, in the first instance, for executive consideration, when negotiations for peace may be opened between this country and Mexico, subject to the action of the Senate on the question of ratification."

Mr. REVERDY JOHNSON then rose, and addressed the Senate to the following effect:

Mr. President: The question pending before the Senate is on the amendment proposed by the Senator from Michigan as a substitute for the amendment offered by the Senator from Georgia to the bill as reported from the Committee on Foreign Relations. The single question, therefore, and properly the only one before the Senate, is as to the propriety of this amendment. But in what I am about to say, it being, perhaps, the only occasion which I may have to trouble the Senate on this subject,

I propose to myself a wider latitude, and to extend my remarks to other matters, as growing out of this proposition. And I will venture to hope for the indulgence of the Senate for what I may thus feel myself called on to say, because I find myself somewhat unexpectedly thrown into the discussion of this bill. Nothing, certainly, was further from my purpose, in this stage of the debate, when the Senator from Georgia concluded his admirable speech yesterday. In my simplicity, I took it for granted that the amendment submitted by the Senator from Michigan would not be suffered by him to go to a vote, without his saying a single word in its support. It is on its face an important proposition; but it is not on its face an amendment obviously connected with this bill. It has been started on the Senate without previous notice, suddenly, and apparently without even consultation with the Senator's own political friends. It embraces, Mr. President, a high and momentous principle of public policy, a principle not only of vital importance in the present condition of the country, but of vital importance in any similar situation in which the country may hereafter be placed. In this situation, seeing the vote about to be taken, even before time was allowed for the presenting of the amendment, I inquired of my friend from Michigan if it was not his purpose to make a statement of the ground on which he had submitted the proposition. I was answered, as I distinctly heard the honorable Senator, that it was not. I could not have been more surprised if our friend Santa Anna had proved true to the promise, either given or implied, under which he was permitted to pass through our blockading squadron to enter Mexico, and to head the troops now marshalled in battle-array against us. I pondered for a moment, and then came to the conclusion that a night's reflection would be sufficient to satisfy the Senator from Michigan that it was no less due to the country, than to his own reputation, that a proposition of such a character should be defended by all the arguments which his ability could present. Under this impression I moved the adjournment. But I have taken nothing by my motion. The honorable Senator is as still as the grave. Why is this? Has the proposition been offered without due reflection? If so, it should be withdrawn. Has it been carefully considered? Does it meet with the concurrence of the Senator's political friends? Does it express the sentiments of the President of the United States? If so, it is due to all that it should be defended with all that ability which the distinguished Senator from Michigan possesses. On this side the chamber, we think we have a right respectfully to ask the aid of lights which we ourselves are not able to furnish. Let the effulgent intellect of the Senator from Michigan shine upon this proposition, that the darkness of our minds may be illuminated, and that we may be enabled to see it in its intrinsic excellence. I do not yet despair that this will be done, although the prospect is exceedingly discouraging. We yet have strong reason for hope. The American people have a right to expect it; the well-earned reputation of the honorable Senator, at home and abroad, invokes it; public feeling will not, should not, be satisfied without it. His high character, his long experience, his mature judgment, his nice sense of honor, public and private, cannot fail to make the world solicitous to learn the grounds on which he places his amendment. And I trust, although a night's reflection has not been able to bring my friend from Michigan on the floor today, that we shall find him in his proper place there on Monday next.

What is the proposition? In order to understand it, it is necessary to see what the bill is which it is proposed thus to amend. During the last session of Congress, the President of the United States, first in secret and then in open session, asked for an appropriation for the purpose of negotiating a peace with Mexico. A bill was accordingly passed by the House, appropriating two millions, but was defeated in the Senate by the termination of the session pending its discussion. In his annual Message at the commencement of this session, he reiterates the request. The chairman of the Committee on Foreign Relations has reported a bill from that committee, appropriating not two, but a sum not exceeding *three* millions, for the purpose of enabling the President to bring the war with Mexico to a speedy and honorable termination: and he has accompanied this with a speech, to which, by and by, I shall pay my respects. What is this bill? [Mr. J. here read the bill.]

To this bill the Senator from Georgia (Mr. Berrien) proposes to append a proviso concerning which it is not my purpose, in this connection, to say any thing. Then comes the amendment, by way of substitute to that amendment, of the Senator from Michigan, (Mr. Cass,) in which he assumes to give the grounds on which this appropriation is to be made. As one of the reasons, reference is made to the causes which have produced the war. Another consists in a statement of the terms on which the war is to be brought to a conclusion, as regards the matter of the indemnity which the United States demand, and without which, I presume, the war is to be interminable. And the third is, that, in order to begin to conclude this war, the President must first act.

In relation to the first of these grounds, I will ask my friend from Michigan to state, at his own good pleasure hereafter, why he deemed it necessary, in a bill appropriating three millions to terminate a war in which we are engaged, to go into any reference to the cause and character of the war? Has he any misgivings in his own breast? Is he apprehensive that his own opinion on the subject will not coincide with the opinions of the people of the

United Sates, and that the world at large has come to a different conclusion as to the character of the contest?

Mr. J. went on to remark on the language of the preamble to the law of May 13, 1846, in which it was declared that the war was brought on by the unauthorized act of Mexico, a proposition to which many Senators objected, but which they were induced to sanction by the spirit of patriotism which prompted them to vindicate the honor of the United States, and to preserve her arms from tarnish. He was not one of those who differed from the President and his friends as to the fact stated in the preamble. He had then given his reasons, and it was not now necessary to reiterate them. A proposition was made at that time to strike out the preamble, but it was voted down, and this he thought ought to have satisfied the Senator from Michigan. But it did not. So far from being satisfactory, on every occasion since, when it could be done, whenever opportunity offered, the same idea has been reasserted, although not with equal success. Even on the resolution of thanks to the commanding general and his gallant army, but a day or two since, this declaration was introduced. The Senator from Michigan had voted to retain it in the resolution, but the effort had failed. And now he insists on retaining the same proposition and incorporating it in this bill. Once again the declaration is to be revived, to which a great portion of the Senate has refused to agree, to drive (although he acquitted the Senator from Michigan of any such purpose) the Senate to sanction by their vote the proposition that the war is a just and necessary war on our part, brought on us by the act of Mexico. He (Mr. J.) could readily understand why such a principle should be adopted in any bill which was germain to the matter; but he could see no propriety in its incorporation in a bill, the sole purpose of which was stated to be the obtaining of a speedy and honorable peace. It was entirely inconsistent with the character and object of that bill. It had nothing to do with the measure with which it was now attempted to be incorporated. The country, however, had before it the language of the preamble of the act of 13th May, and would exercise a correct and independent opinion regarding it.

[Here Mr. J. read the preamble.]

It would be seen that this preamble declares the war to be just on our part, brought about solely by the act of Mexico. The amendment now offered contained a peculiar declaration. Congress, on the 13th May, declared that the war was brought on us by the act of Mexico. We now are called on, in a bill to terminate the war speedily and honorably, to insert a declaration that the interests and honor of the country require that it shall be vigorously prosecuted. It was not necessary to call up the dead to tell us that. A nation involved in war is placed in a position in which it is compelled, without going out of its way to do it, to use every effort to bring it to an honorable termination. But that was not the object of the amendment. It was regarded as necessary to a just and honorable termination of the war, that full indemnity should be obtained from Mexico for the expenditures of the Government, and all the wrongs which had been inflicted on American citizens. What was the indemnity which was looked for? What is the character of the indemnity which is desired? He would quote the language of the President of the United States, in order that the Senate might be reminded of his views on the subject.

[Here Mr. J. read an extract from the President's Message.]

Now, (said Mr. J.,) I am sure my friend from Michigan is not prepared to say that the President claims any thing unreasonable in this part of his Message. If the Senator intends it to be understood that the war is not to be brought to a termination until Mexico shall have given indemnity for all our expenses during its progress, and for all claims due to our citizens, how is this to be obtained? Is it by purchasing a speedy peace, or by a vigorous prosecution of the war? Why, this bill is not reported for the purpose of vigorously prosecuting the war. Whenever that has been submitted to us as the object to be accomplished, on this side of the chamber as well as on the other, no Senator has evinced the slightest disposition to refuse all which has been demanded by the President to bring the war to a termination by this mode. All the appropriations of money which he has demanded have been unhesitatingly granted: even against the sense of some of his own friends, all the troops he has asked for, and precisely of the description he has required, have been given him. And there is an entire disposition to go yet further. And whenever the President shall think more aid necessary, he will find as many advocates on this side the chamber, as he has a right to look for among his own political friends.

What, then, is the character of this bill? Does it look to a termination of the war by a vigorous prosecution of it? No. It rather shows the white feather, to use a common phrase. It fears—and it is clearly founded on that apprehension—that no such peace can be obtained from a vigorous prosecution of the war. The evident object of the bill is not to fight, but to buy a peace.

The Senator from Arkansas goes on to say, that the intelligence possessed by the President gave them reason to believe that peace could be obtained. Unfortunately, the Senate did not enjoy the benefit of that intelligence. The language of the Senator from Arkansas was:

"The intelligence possessed by the President gave them reason to believe, that by a certain advance in money, to be made to them in their exhausted and impoverished condition, to pay off their army and other expenses, they would be willing and able to make peace, and cede, for the objects specified, that portion of the country he had named.

Now, he (Mr. J.) could not for his life see what benefit this was to be to us. But before he proceeded, he would go a little further back. The President of the United States, in his annual Message, in which he is justifying the permission which he authorized to be given to Santa Anna to return to Mexico, told us, among other things, that the day war was declared—the 13th of May, 1846—that very day, he gave the order, or caused the order to be given, that Santa Anna might be permitted to return to Mexico. Now, this was an extraordinary circumstance. The 13th day of May was the very day on which Congress passed the act recognizing the war with Mexico, and on that day the President gave permission to Santa Anna to return. I will read what he says on this subject. It succeeds what I will read hereafter:

"In view of these facts and circumstances it was, that, when orders were issued to the commander of our naval forces in the Gulf, on the 13th day of May last, the day on which the existence of the war had been recognized by Congress, to place the coasts of Mexico under blockade, he was directed not to obstruct the passage of Santa Anna to Mexico, should he attempt to return."

Now what were the circumstances under which the order was given, and what were the reasons which resulted from those circumstances? He tells us in the preceding part of the same Message:

"Our object was the restoration of peace; and with that view, no reason was perceived why we should take part with Paredes, and aid him, by means of our blockade, in preventing the return of his rival to Mexico. On the contrary, it was believed that the intestine divisions which ordinary sagacity could not but anticipate as the fruit of Santa Anna's return to Mexico, and his contest with Paredes, might strongly tend to produce a disposition with both parties to restore and preserve peace with the United States."

The "intestine divisions" in which he might involve Mexico! This was the avowal of the President of the United States, of his reasons for such an extraordinary circumstance. The "intestine divisions" which Santa Anna's return to Mexico was expected to occasion, was to bring peace to the United States! He expected to obtain an "honorable and successful termination of the war" by sending into the country of our adversary a man to produce "intestine divisions!" It was not to be accomplished by our arms and our valor, but by supposing the return of one whose tyranny had compelled the people to drive him into exile, in the hope that his return would be attended with "intestine divisions" and with a revolution, involving the country in a civil war, and creating by a civil war still greater embarrassments than resulted from the contest with us, and thus to induce them to enter into a peace, which, if united, he feared we might not be able to conquer!

Well, he goes there. He goes attended by a troop of officers. He passes our blockade by order of the President of the United States. And the moment he gets there he is found giving "aid and comfort to the enemy;" and he is enabled to do this by this act of our President. The country rises to receive him. All the resources of the nation are put at his command. The dying hopes of the people are revived through the instrumentality of the President of the United States, and Santa Anna now stands their leader, their chosen leader—he who is the most successful and approved soldier that Mexico ever had. He is invested with the command of from forty to fifty thousand well-chosen and well-drilled troops; he has the command of the country, and his will, by the physical power which he is able to wield, must be the will of the nation. Now, what effect must this have on the nation? It must draw closer their union, revive their expiring hopes, reanimate their courage, and create the determination to die in the last ditch in defence of their soil. Of this, no Senator could doubt who had heard, on another occasion, intelligence from journals published in that country, read to this body by the Senator from New York, (Mr. Dix.) And while Santa Anna has been returned to Mexico by the act of our President, we are not able to meet him. In May last fifty thousand men were placed at the command of the President—all he asked; but he called out but a trifling quota. And what was the War Secretary doing? Why, as late as November last, he writes that no more troops will be wanted; but in five days after, ten regiments are called into the field, and soon after this Congress comes together, ten more regiments are asked for. How soon either of these ten regiments can be mustered into the service it will be impossible to say. It will take time. But what was now proposed to be done?

One thing could not avoid suggesting itself to the Senate, and that was the inquiry, how it had happened that in the months of May, June, July, and August last, when Santa Anna had the orders, which had doubtless been communicated to him, that he might return, he never started to go to Mexico until the President here asked them in secret session, and afterwards in public, to give him two millions of dollars for this purpose? The Senator from Arkansas, who is supposed necessarily to consult the President, now asks for three millions of dollars. How was this? Had Santa Anna raised his demands? When the Senator from Arkansas closes this debate, as he supposed that Senator would, he hoped he would inform the Senate why it was that two millions were asked for in August and three millions now? Was this additional sum to be considered as part of the expenses of the war? How, then, were we to be paid for paying the Mexican army? In Mexican territory? Were these three millions to be considered as part of the expenses of the war?

We present the extraordinary spectacle of being willing to have an army of our own in the field, and an army of the Mexican Republic, and of being willing, out of the treasury of the United States, to pay the expenses of both, provided Santa Anna will think proper to cede to the United States at least New Mexico and Upper California. And if he does not do it in a short time, as the Senator intimates, we shall require a great deal more of Mexican territory, if not the whole. Now this appeared to him to be a most extraordinary position. We are to make peace with Mexico, which, by the very confession of the Senator's speech, is broken down by contending factions, and from day to day is afraid of its tyrants, amongst whom she numbered this very Santa Anna that our President returns to them—they are afraid of, they look with dread upon the army, which had been the great cause of the oppressions of these down-trodden and impoverished people—but we are to make peace with them by pouring gifts into the hands of that very army and that very leader, and then transfer them, in spite of themselves, from the institutions in which they have been bred, from the associations in which they have been brought up, and which they value, into our institutions—into one of the portions of the United States—to be subject to our laws. Now there is something wrong in this. The principle is wrong. He was satisfied that the Senator from Arkansas and those who thought with him did so on high and lofty principle; but standing there as an American Senator, he felt called upon to say that a war of dismemberment was revolting to his moral sense of propriety, honor, and justice.

[Mr. Johnson concluded with a vivid representation of the danger to the Union from the slavery agitation arising out of this acquisition of territory, and could see but one way to avoid that danger, and that was by keeping it out in not making the acquisition.]

There was but one way to obviate it, and that way was open to us; it was a way which had hitherto made us a happy, powerful, and united people. It was by keeping the question out: and, in his judgment, it could be done consistently with the national honor. What were one hundred or two hundred millions of dollars expense in which this war may involve us? No man can feel the pressure of it for a moment. No man would know of its existence, unless he were told of the fact. And what was additional territory wanted for? Have we not enough not only for the men of the present day, but for hundreds and hundreds and hundreds of millions, that may come into existence hereafter? Have we not degrees of latitude enough to furnish us with every thing to supply man's wants and minister to his comforts? The progress of the United States thus far has announced that we have. No people that ever breathed in past time or the present, can compare in the prosperity which we have enjoyed and the glory we have acquired by and for the United States with its present territory. The war will have been forgotten except for the splendor of its achievements—and they will tell the world through all time what is the extent and ability of American valor—they will tell to all times that whenever and however assailed, American courage and American skill, under the guidance of American freedom, are equal to any emergency. But great as our prosperity is, and great as is the glory we have heretofore had, they will be still greater if we are but true to ourselves. Who, looking through the vista of time—no matter how fruitful his imagination—no matter how sanguine his temperament—can tell of the power and glory of those that will succeed us if this Union lasts? The South is in no danger from whatever they might term the honest prejudices of the North, or the political fanaticism of the political demagogues of the North, if there be such, who may seek to avail themselves of such fanaticism, if the South was true to itself, and stood together as one man to the territory we now hold, covered as it was with the ægis of protection which the constitution affords. They dare not pass a State line, or the constitution will speak in a voice of authority. Once assail us, and the laws will vindicate our rights. But when a new element is brought into existence—when new States are to be brought in, consisting of a territory equal, as the President says, to the original thirteen States of this Union, by conquest, then an alarming element is created, which is calculated to frighten the most sanguine. In the name of Heaven why was it that they were willing to brave so much danger for such an acquisition? And an acquisition obtained by such means! Were they not satisfied with the Constitution of the United States? Have we not territory enough to answer all the reasonable wants of human society? Has not the constitution given to all the blessings which man can derive from such an instrumentality? It was reared for immortality, if any work of man can aspire to such an existence, but it might perish in an hour by forgetfulness, corruption, or negligence.

What, then, is to be done? He asked Southern men and Northern men, if the question should be forced upon them, what was to be done? The North is firm as the soil upon which her freemen tread: the South is imbued with indomitable courage, and feels impressed with the conviction that their rights are invaded. What, then, is to be the result? One of two things: civil war with all its inconceivable evils, or the disruption of this Union. The cement which keeps us all together, in a Union which dispenses to all every thing that any contrivance of human society can dispense, is to be dissolved; and this glorious and mighty republic, now the pride and admiration of the world, will be broken into withered and scattered fragments; and all by suicidal hands. And all, I again repeat, for what? Because Mexico is unable to pay except by a cession of territory which we will force from her at the point of the bayonet, or failing in that, will buy a peace.

Mr. CASS remarked that he did not rise to make *that* speech—the speech the honorable Senator from Maryland had so much pressed him to make. His honorable friend had paid him a good many compliments; some of them were righthanded, but some of them, Mr. C. feared, were rather lefthanded. Were it not for the confidence he had in the good faith and judgment of the honorable Senator, his modesty would have suggested there was some little humor in what had been said with such outward gravity. However, he was bound to believe he deserved it all. Mr. C. said the honorable Senator had adjured him with unusual solemnity to make a speech—to explain the amendment he had offered—adjured him by the highest moral and political considerations —by his duty to himself, to the Senate, to the country, to the world, and to posterity. He could hardly escape from such invocations. Still he would not make a speech, at any rate at that moment. His resolution appeared to him so plain as to need no explanation. He who runs may read it. Its bearing lay upon the very surface, and could only be misunderstood by talking it into a state of mystery. Mr. C. said he could not flatter himself that the world knew or cared much about him—an ignorance in which posterity would equally partake. Whether he spoke or not, was a matter of the smallest possible consequence to any body but to him. But (he said) he rose for a more serious object, and that was to put himself and his amendment right in the opinion of the Senator from Maryland. That honorable Senator had wholly misunderstood him. He seemed to suppose the amendment was designed to entrap some Senator who might be desirous of voting for the appropriation, but who could not vote for the declaration that Mexico commenced the war. No such unworthy purpose gave birth to his proposition. So far from it, he himself should vote against it on the final question, should it supersede the amendment of the Senator from Georgia. Mr. C. said he desired the naked appropriation, without any restriction as to its application, and he did not design to encumber it with any thing which would impede its passage. He was anxious for a cession of land, and he believed if the matter were left to the President, that a cession would be obtained satisfactory to the American people. In introducing his proposition, he was merely desirous to express his views on the subject as contradistinguished from those of the Senator from Georgia. If a rider must be attached to the appropriation, he desired his own; but he desired still more that nothing of the kind should take place, believing it was wholly unnecessary, and might put to hazard the appropriation itself.

Mr. MOREHEAD rose to address the Senate, but as the hour was late, he gave way for a motion to go into executive session.

MONDAY, February 8.

Three Million Loan.

The Senate proceeded to the consideration of the special order, being the bill making further appropriation to bring the war with Mexico to a speedy and honorable conclusion; the question pending being the amendment of Mr. CASS, to substitute for the amendment of Mr. BERRIEN, the following:

"And it is hereby declared to be the true intent and meaning of Congress, in making this appropriation, that as, by the act of the republic of Mexico, a state of war exists between that Government and the United States, agreeably to the declaration made by act of Congress on the 13th of May last, therefore the interest and honor of this country require that the said war should be vigorously prosecuted to a successful issue; and that a reasonable indemnity should be obtained from Mexico for the wrongs she has committed towards the Government and citizens of the United States.

"And it is further declared that the nature and extent of such indemnities are proper subjects in the first instance for Executive consideration, when negotiations for peace may be opened between this country and Mexico, subject to the action of the Senate on the question of ratification."

Mr. MOREHEAD said the bill proposed to appropriate the sum of three millions, to be applied, under the direction of the President of the United States, to defray such extraordinary expenditures as might be necessary to bring the war to a speedy and honorable conclusion. What these extraordinary expenditures were, the bill did not state, and no information on this point had been given by the chairman of the Committee on Foreign Relations, or by any of the friends of the Administration. Of one thing we must be assured, that this appropriation was beyond all the sums ordinarily necessary for the prosecution of a war, and that it was to be expended for the purpose of bringing the war to a conclusion. Among the various modes by which the war might be terminated, might be named its vigorous and successful prosecution, by the combined efforts of our army and navy, by blockading ports, capturing the enemy's vessels, subduing towns, taking possession of provinces, and overrunning territories. But all these objects might be accomplished by the application of the ordinary expenditures. There might be extraordinary events, growing out of the victories and triumphs of our army; there might be some enterprises in keeping with the former glory of our navy; but these might be met by the ordinary appropriations. Another mode of terminating the war might be by means of negotiation. To effect this, the President might ask for the appointment of a commission, to which he (Mr. M.) did not doubt that the Senate would hasten to give its approbation, for the purpose of opening a negotiation. But the expenses of such a commission would be provided for by the ordinary course of appropriation. There might, however, be other objects than those he had enumerated, other means to be employed, other influences to be brought into action, to be applied without reference to the legislative authority, but exclusively by the President. The bill says, that this sum of three millions shall be expended under the direction of the President. According to the language of the bill, he is to be governed, in its expenditure, only by his personal will and uncontrolled pleasure. It is to be expended, therefore, in some mode of which the people can have no knowledge, and in which the legislative branch can exercise no advisory power. The bill confers on the President an unprecedented and enormous power; a measure not only unexampled in our history, but in opposition to the spirit of our institutions.

We are engaged in a war with a powerless enemy; an enemy so weak and powerless, that, at the commencement of the conflict, it was deemed only necessary to send the few troops we had into the field to insure a compliance with our demands; and now we are called on to sanction an extraordinary expenditure of three millions to bring the war to a close. The contest is not to be terminated by the prowess of our arms, but by the application of money; and the bill proposes to grant this money to the President, to be expended at the will of the President, and without any other restriction than a provision that he shall account for it hereafter. If, after getting us into a war with that weak and powerless foe, we are willing to place these three millions in the hands of the President, how much more would be required of us if we were engaged in a war with either of the most powerful nations in the world—France or Great Britain, or both of them? Would fifty—would a hundred millions be sufficient in such a case? If it would, it would furnish no justification of the appropriation we are at this time required to make, when we have a President without any military talents or skill—he said this without intending any disrespect—without those qualities which would be a security for its wise application. The occasion, the juncture, the position in which we stand, all admonish us of the dangerous tendency of such a course. Here, if we pass this bill, will be a precedent, which will be entitled hereafter to consideration and discussion, which may be wielded to pernicious influences, which, in our Government of checks and balances, cannot be too vigilantly guarded against.

This war with Mexico was about to subject the Constitution of the United States to a still severer trial than those it had heretofore experienced. They were now occupying a new attitude in view of their constitutional powers, and in view also of the course which expediency required. Hitherto the wars in which they had been engaged were wars for human liberty, or in defence of violated rights. Now there was pending a war of conquest. What were the obligations resting upon the Government of the United States in view of such a state of things? Should they, in imitation of the Governments of Europe, prosecute a war for conquest to the dismemberment of a neighboring nation? Did the genius of our constitution permit the adoption of such a course? He thought that the great American doctrine was a doctrine peculiarly applicable to the support and protection of our domestic institutions, totally distinct from any purpose of acquiring foreign territory by conquest. But now it seemed, in view of the attitude in which we were placed, in a war which had been brought on, as they were told by their friends on the other side, by Mexico, and merely recognized by us, that a war of this character was to be prosecuted with vigor and energy, for the purpose of acquiring territory, and of setting up our own civil institutions within the territory thus acquired; thus extending, as it was said, the limits of freedom by the prosecution of this war of conquest. Without inquiring into the fact, whether the war was commenced by Mexico or not, it would have been but the exercise of a proper discretion on the part of the President if he had hesitated before removing the army from Corpus Christi. It would have been a fair subject of inquiry (it seemed to him) on the part of the President, how far it would be expedient and proper to direct such a movement; how far it would be construed into an act of hostility towards the republic of Mexico? He differed with the President as to the propriety even of this incipient movement But, not to detain the Senate with any protracted argument upon this point, he would proceed to the next important act of the President in relation to this war, in permitting Santa Anna to re-enter Mexico; and he would venture to assert that there was no event in the history of the prosecution of war anywhere, so novel and unprecedented as this. The President attempted, in his Message at the opening of this session, to give them his views at large upon this subject, and to assign the reasons which had actuated him in permitting Santa Anna to pass the blockading squadron. These reasons were before them; and, in view of the subsequent events which had happened, and in view of the elevated position which Santa Anna now occupied, of the dangerous nature of that position in relation to the army of the United States, and of the opportunity which he possessed to injure us, he would leave it to the people of the United States to judge in what manner the trust confided to the President had been fulfilled.

There were other great interests involved: interests to which allusion had been made by the Senator from Georgia and the Senator from Maryland; interests growing out of these acquisitions of territory by the dismemberment of Mexico. Besides the principle that was at stake, besides the incompatibility of doctrines of this kind with the interests of the Government of the United States, there were yet unknown and unseen evils that would result from such a policy, which it became their duty to avoid as far as practicable. Let us not push the territorial limits of this Government to such an extent as to bring upon us a collision of interests and feelings which will shake the very foundations of the Government. What sort of policy is it that will lead us into the pursuit of territorial acquisition at the expense of our own domestic peace and concord? What sort of policy is that which will lead us on step by step in the pursuit of conquest, while at home there is such formidable opposition to a policy of this sort as to endanger the very institutions of the Government? Whatever may be the views of the Executive or of American statesmen in regard to this policy, it seems to me to be a subject which requires the utmost deliberation.

It would, he thought, be a poor return for the achievement of a legislative victory on the part of his friends on the other side of the chamber—it would be a poor consolation to the people of this country, after having carried our arms to the Pacific, if the acquisition of territory, which would be the result of that proceeding, should have the effect of creating internal discord, and destroying the institutions of this country. There was a question involved in this consideration which overshadowed them like a cloud. The great question of slavery, as the conscript fathers of the Republic well knew when the Government was first established, would become the more dangerous the more it was agitated.

Why, then, should they pursue a policy that would lead to such agitation? What was the state of things now, as exhibited in the popular branch of the legislature? Was it not plainly to be perceived that there was a majority there that could carry measures which it would be the interest of this country to reject? Should they not, while they had it in their power, avoid a policy which would occasion the agitation of this question? He thought they should announce such a determination at once, from both sides of this chamber, so that the public mind might be set at rest. But, announce to the people of this country that you are about to add one-third of the territory of Mexico to your already extended limits, and one-tenth of her population, and put to them the question as to their approval of your policy, and it will be met by a response which will be felt from one end of this extended continent to the other—a response, the tones of which will be calculated to shake the foundations on which our institutions rest. Sir, are we prepared to encounter hazards like these?

The question of which I am speaking now, and which I almost dread to discuss, agitated the councils of our fathers; and there is, resulting from the policy pursued by them, an example which seems to me worthy of praise—an example of compromise and conciliation, avoiding extremes on either side. I call, therefore, upon our friends on the other side so to leave this question as to promote the sound policy of the Government; as to heal up the wounds which dissension has already made; to quiet the apprehensions of the public mind, and to follow the example of the illustrious fathers of the republic, in announcing that the object of this Administration is not to add territory to the Union by dismembering another nation; that it is not their object to pursue a policy that will shake the public sentiment of this country to a dangerous extent. They owe it to themselves and to the country to place the policy of the present Government upon this ground. Sir, it appears to me that it is the interest of this Executive to quiet the feeling that now exists in this country upon this subject, instead of asking money for the purpose of acquiring territory, which will excite and exasperate that feeling. As you have announced to the country that the war was not commenced for conquest, you should also announce that it is not to end by conquest. Have we not land enough to satisfy any American citizen? Or is there such a pressing necessity to have more, that we will endanger all that is dear to us in the pursuit of this policy?

Sir, there is another branch of this subject to which I will briefly advert. Suppose the President should purchase Upper California and New Mexico; suppose he applies the money to be given to him by this bill in such a way as to secure to us those territories, and presents to the Senate a treaty with the republic of Mexico to that effect; do gentlemen suppose that it is a matter of certainty that the Senate will accede to it? Where, then, is the propriety of urging a measure that can end in no good? Is there any certainty, I ask, that a treaty negotiated upon this basis can ever receive the sanction of the Senate? In view of the great divisions which distract this country, a majority of two-thirds on a question like this is very difficult to be obtained. Suppose, then, a treaty negotiated on this basis should be presented to the Senate and rejected: what, then, is the attitude which you will occupy before this nation and the world? You will indicate to Europe, that while the President has announced that the war at its beginning was not for conquest, you announce that both the beginning and the close of the war has been exclusively for conquest. There is the positive fact presented to the view of the world. There is the result. Negotiation concluded, and a treaty presented to the Senate and rejected, and what will you have gained? Increased divisions, excitement, and disorder throughout the land; dangerous agitation, every thing, sir, which the mind can conceive or the eye look upon, threatening the disturbance of the peace and quiet of the people of this country.

Again: suppose you make a treaty upon this basis, and it is confirmed by the Senate: what do you gain? You have additional territory; what do you propose to do with it? I suppose there is not a citizen of this country who, if the question were put to him, would not say that you have territory enough already. But you acquire additional territory. What else do you acquire? You will have acquired a large number of the population of Mexico, an ignorant, a fanatic, a disorderly people—a population having none of the elements of character in common with the people of this country—a population sprung from a different origin, having none of the blood of the Anglo-Saxons running in their veins—a people differing from you in origin, in character, in feelings, and in principles—having nothing in common with you. What are you to do with them? Are you to govern them as you do your slaves in those States which now tolerate the institution of slavery? Are you to treat them as serfs belonging to the land which you acquire, as attached to the soil? Or will you put them on a level with the people of this country? Will you give them the privileges which your people enjoy, and enable them to regulate and control the destinies of the Government? Will you elevate them to the character of citizens of the United States, though it is now universally believed that the people of Mexico are entirely destitute of the capacity of self-government? Sir, if they are to constitute a portion of your population—if they are to become free citizens side by side with us—it may be that, in displaying those elements of character which render them now the most unstable, unsettled, inefficient population on the face of the globe, you may have the same difficulty in governing them that the authorities in Mexico have. I will acknowledge the energy and power of this Government, but at the same time remember their remoteness from the centre of action; remember the responsibility that you would incur, owing to their distance from the seat of power. You may pass your laws, but you may not be able to control the people and to enforce their obedience.

Sir, in every aspect in which I can view this subject, it does seem to me that it becomes us to pause before adopting a policy like this. Let the President, in his confidential relations with the two Houses, ask us, if he chooses, to receive a Message from him disclosing his policy; let him put this grant of three millions upon a known and recognized basis; let the country be satisfied that the appropriation is intended to accomplish a great national object that will meet their approval; and my word for it, he will not find a dissenting voice. There is no party in this country willing to throw obstructions in the way of beneficial measures—measures for the advancement of the interests and the glory of this country. I know how apt we are to look upon the Representatives in these halls as opposed to each other upon all questions submitted to them, because they represent different portions of the country, and, to some extent, different interests; but, upon a question like this, it will be found that they represent but one people, having a common object to promote the good of the whole nation.

Mr. CALHOUN moved that the subject be informally passed over.

HOUSE OF REPRENTATIVES.

MONDAY, February 8.

Three Million Loan Bill—Wilmot Proviso.

The House resolved itself into Committee of the Whole on the state of the Union, (Mr. NORRIS in the chair,) and took up for consideration the bill appropriating three millions of dollars to bring the war with Mexico to a speedy and honorable termination.

The bill having been read—

Mr. C. J. INGERSOLL, chairman of the Committee on Foreign Affairs, went into a speech at large in explanation and support of the bill, in which he stated, in substance, that the money was wanted to buy New Mexico and California. He then went into some remarks on the proviso which he understood his colleague (Mr. WILMOT) was going to offer to the bill, which he strenuously opposed.

Mr. WILMOT then obtained the floor, and offered as an amendment, a proviso restricting the addition to the United States of any slave territory; and then yielded the floor to

Mr. BOYD, who moved that the committee rise to receive in the House the report of the Committee of Conference on the army bill.

The committee thereupon rose and reported progress.

The House, on motion of Mr. BRODHEAD, returned into Committee of the Whole, (Mr. NORRIS again in the chair,) and resumed the consideration of the three million bill with Mr. WILMOT's proviso; and the question being on the adoption of the proviso—

Mr. WILMOT having the floor, refused to surrender it, and addressed the committee substantially as follows:

I suppose, Mr. Chairman, it will be proper for me to notify the committee that I intend to move to amend the bill by the additional section which has been read, without now designating any particular part of the bill in which I intend it should come. And my anxiety in this matter is not to deprive the gentleman from Virginia, (Mr. DROMGOOLE,) or anybody else of the opportunity to move any amendment to the bill they may wish, but I am embarrassed by these rules of the House, (with which I am little acquainted,) and my object is, the opportunity to be heard upon this question fairly, and not to be deprived, by any parliamentary restrictions, of the opportunity of vindicating this amendment, and vindicating the position which I occupy before the House and the country.

Sir, it will be recollected by all present, that at the last session of this Congress, an amendment was moved to a bill of a similar character by me, in the form of a proviso, by which slavery should be forever excluded from any territory that might be subsequently acquired by the United States from the republic of Mexico.

Sir, permit me to say, that upon that occasion that proviso was sustained by a very decided majority of this House. Nay, sir, more; it was sustained, if I mistake not, by a majority of the republican party on this floor. And I am prepared to show, I think, that the entire South were then willing to acquiesce in what appeared to be, and, so far as the action of this House is concerned, in what was the legislation, will, and declaration of this Union on the subject. It passed in this House. Sir, there were no threats of disunion sounded in our ears. It passed here, and it went to the Senate, and it was the judgment of the public, and of many men well informed, that had it not been defeated there for the want of time, it would have passed that body and become the established law of the land.

Sir, the friends of this Administration, of whom I am one, did not then charge upon me, did not throw the whole burden upon me, nor upon those who acted with me, of having, by the introduction and support of that proviso at an untimely period of the question, defeated a measure especially necessary for the establishment of peace between this country and Mexico. The "Union," sir, the whole Democratic press in the land, charged this upon the unparliamentary conduct of a Senator from Massachusetts. He was charged with having defeated this great measure, by the Administration press, and the "Organ" of the Administration; showing that the Administration and the President were entirely willing to accept of this appropriation under the restrictions imposed by the proviso which I offered.

Yes! no anathemas were fulminated against me then. I was not then denounced as an abolitionist by the correspondents of the "Union," as I have been since, and from which charge I intend to vindicate myself. And I say to its respectable editor, for whom I have high respect and regard, that I am no more an abolitionist than he is a Hartford-Convention Federalist; and of that, no man who knows his history or his character will charge him. I am as far from the one as he is from the other.

I assert, then, that the South was prepared to acquiesce in this restriction.

Mr. Sims, of South Carolina (Mr. W. yielding) said he recollected, when the question was under discussion here, near the close of the last session, that he had made remarks sustaining the propriety of the two-million appropriation; but in the course of these remarks, he deprecated, as untimely and mischievous, the proposition which was likely to come from the gentleman from Pennsylvania; and the entire South, so far as he recollected, (he knew that he did, at least,) when the proviso was voted upon, voted against it; and he voted against his declared sentiments in reference to the appropriation; so unwilling was he to give any countenance to such a proviso.

Mr. Wilmot (resuming.) I was aware that the proviso met with no favor from the South. I did not mean to declare that it did; and if the gentleman so understood me, he misunderstood me. I did not mean to say that the South was favorable in any way to the proviso which I offered. They resisted it, manfully, boldly resisted it. But, sir, it *was passed.* And there was then no cry that the Union was to be severed in consequence. No, sir. But I fear that the hesitation and the warning of Northern men on this question has induced the South to assume a bolder attitude. Why, sir, in God's name, should the Union be dissolved for this? What do we ask in this matter? We ask but sheer justice and right. It was a question of compromise. I would go as far as any man in this House for compromise. Were it a question of concession and compromise, I might perhaps say to the North, Concede again, as you have done before; yield all; bow to the South, as you have done on all previous occasions—yield this also. But it is a question of naked and abstract right; and, in the eloquent language of my colleague from the Erie district, (Mr. Thompson,) sooner shall they draw this right shoulder from its socket, than I will yield one jot or tittle of the ground on which I stand.

What, then, do we ask? Sir, we ask the neutrality of this Government on this question of slavery. I have stood up at home, and fought single-handed—no, I was not single-handed, because my party was with me—but I have stood at home, and fought, time and again, against the Abolitionists of the North. I have denounced them publicly, upon all occasions, when it was proper to do so. I have met them in their own meetings, and assailed them. And, sir, the efforts that may be made, here or elsewhere, to give an abolition complexion to this movement, cannot, so far as my district and my people are concerned, have the least effect. And efforts made to give me the character of an abolitionist, will fall harmless when they reach my constituency. They know me upon this question distinctly. I stand by every compromise of the constitution. I adhere to its letter and its spirit. And I would never invade one single right of the South. So far from it am I, that I stand ready, at all times and upon all occasions, as do nearly the entire North, to sustain the institutions of the South as they exist, with our money and with our blood, when that day comes, as many—many Southern men—fear it may come. When that day comes, sir, the North stands with them. We go for every compromise of the constitution.

But, sir, this is another question—entirely another question. We ask that this Government preserve the integrity of free territory against the aggressions of slavery—against its wrongful usurpations. Sir, I was in favor of the annexation of Texas. I supported it with the whole influence which I possessed, and I was willing to take Texas in as she was. I sought not to change the character of her institutions. Texas was a slave country; and although it was held out to us, in the celebrated letter of Mr. Walker, that two slave and two free States might be made out of it, yet the whole of Texas was given up to slavery, every inch. For although the Missouri compromise line was mentioned in the resolutions of annexation, yet no State can be admitted without the consent of the original State of Texas ; and she, by her refusal to allow any free State to be formed out of her limits, may keep that whole country for slavery. We voted for the annexation of Texas. The Democracy of the North was for it, to a man. We are for it now—firmly for it. Sir, we are fighting this war for Texas, and for the South. I affirm it; here is a matter well known to the Union. We are fighting this war cheerfully, not reluctantly; cheerfully fighting this war for Texas; and as we seek not to change the character of her institutions, slavery was recognized there, and established by law. Now, sir, we are told that California is ours; and so it is. I intend to refer more particularly to this subject before I conclude. But, we are told, California is ours. And all we ask in the North is, that the character of its territory be preserved. It is free; and it is part of the established law of nations, and all public law, that when it shall come into this Union, all laws there existing, not inconsistent with its new allegiance, will remain in force. This fundamental law, which prohibits slavery in California, will be in force; this fundamental law, which prohibits slavery in New Mexico, will be in force. Shall the South invade it? Shall the South make this Government an instrument for the violation of its neutrality, and for the establishment of slavery in these territories, in defiance of law? That is the question. There is no question of abolition here, sir. It is a question whether the South shall be permitted, by aggression, by invasion of right, by subduing free territory and planting slavery upon it, to wrest this territory to the accomplishment of its own sectional purposes and schemes? That is the question. And shall we of the North submit to it? Must we yield this? It is not, sir, in the spirit of the compact; it is not, sir, in the constitution.

IN SENATE.

TUESDAY, February 9.

Three Million Loan.

The Senate proceeded to the consideration of the special order, being the bill making a special appropriation to bring the war with Mexico to a speedy and honorable conclusion —the question pending being the amendment of Mr. CASS.

Mr. CALHOUN rose and addressed the Senate. Never (said he) since I have been upon the stage of action, has this country been placed in a more critical situation than at present. We are not only in the midst of a war, a very difficult and very expensive war, but we are involved in a domestic question of the most irritating and dangerous character. They both claim our serious and deliberate consideration, and I do trust, that before this session closes, late as it is, they will both receive a full discussion. It is due to our constituents that the actual state of things in reference to both should be fully understood. For the present, I purpose to consider the question which is more immediately pending: How shall this war be best conducted in order to bring it most advantageously to a successful termination? or, to express it a little more fully, How shall it be conducted to enable us most advantageously to effect all the objects for which the war was made? for it is only by effecting these objects, that the war can properly be said to be successful.

There are two ways (continued Mr. C.) in which this war may be conducted. The one is, to push on offensive operations until Mexico is compelled to yield to our terms; the other is, to take a defensive position, and to maintain and secure the possession of the country which is already in our military occupation; and the question which I propose now to consider is, which of these two ought to be selected? This is, Mr. President, a great question; in my opinion it is next in importance only to the war itself. I have given it my most deliberate consideration, and the result to which I have come is, that we ought to choose the defensive position, and I shall now proceed to state the reasons on which that conclusion is founded. I believe that such a course is the best calculated to bring this war to a successful termination, or, to express it more fully and more explicitly, (for I wish to be fully comprehended upon this important question,) to bring it to a certain successful termination, and that with the least sacrifice of men and money, and with the least hazard of disasters or sacrifices, or loss of reputation or standing to this country.

If he rightly understood the objects for which this war was declared, he felt a deep conviction, that by assuming this defensive attitude all those objects might be obtained; if he rightly understood, he repeated, for, strange as it might seem, the objects for which the war was commenced were left, even at this late day, to inference. He had examined the Message of the President to Congress, containing his recommendations that Congress should make war—the Messages rather, and the acts of this body arising out of them—for the purpose of discovering the objects for which the war should be undertaken. The result of that examination was, that the objects for which the war was made were threefold: first, to repel invasion; next, to establish the Rio del Norte as the western boundary of Texas; and, thirdly, to obtain payment of the indemnities due to our citizens for claims which they held against Mexico. The two first appeared to him to be the primary objects of the war, and the last only accessory. The President, in his Message, did not recommend Congress to declare war. No; he assumed that the war already existed, and called upon Congress to recognize its existence. The President assumed it to exist, because the country had been invaded, and blood had been spilt on American soil. This assumption he predicated on the ground that the Rio del Norte was the western boundary of Texas; and he alleged that the Mexicans had crossed that boundary—had come to the American side—which he affirmed was an invasion; and the war having been thus entered upon, he recommended likewise that it should be prosecuted in reference to the claims of our citizens. The act of Congress declaring that war had been made by the republic of Mexico recognized the Rio del Norte to be the western boundary of Texas, and affirmed that the crossing of that river by the Mexicans constituted an act of invasion. Hence, both the executive and the legislative branches of this Government were committed to the fact that the Rio del Norte was the western boundary of Texas, and that the crossing it was an invasion on the part of the Mexicans. These were clearly primary objects. But in recommending the war, the President recommended that it be prosecuted for the objects which he had already mentioned, among which was that of indemnity to our citizens, an object which, though not a sufficient cause of war in itself, yet, being involved in war, it appeared to him might properly be made one of the causes for which the war should be prosecuted, that all causes of difference might be settled. These were the three objects of the war.

But (continued Mr. C.) the President now further recommends that the war be prosecuted in order to obtain indemnity for the expenses of the war itself. That can, however, in no sense be considered as one of the primary objects of the war, though it may be said to be a legitimate policy; for it can never be supposed that a country would enter upon a war for the mere purpose of being indemnified for the cost of that war. I hold, then, Mr. President—such being the objects of the war—that all those objects for which it was declared can be accomplished by taking a defensive position. Two of them have been already thoroughly effected. The invasion has been repelled by two brilliant victories; the Rio del Norte is held from its source to its mouth as the American boundary; a single Mexican soldier does not remain within our territory; and such has been the success of our arms, that we have not only acquired enough territory from them, but vastly more than enough to indemnify us for the expenses of the war, if it should be the judgment of this body that it would be a sound, wise, or just policy on our part to seek such indemnity. Here, then, we have the question presented, shall we hold to the line we now occupy, and which we cover by our military forces, comprehending two-thirds of the whole of Mexico, embracing the valley of the Rio del Norte on both sides, as far upward as the Siérra Madre, and down to the extremities of Upper California and New Mexico—shall we hold all this, or shall we select some other position better calculated for the object we have in view? Sir, I am not at all prepared to discuss this point. I have not the requisite information, and, if I had, it would not be necessary, with the object I have in view. What I propose to discuss, in the absence of such information, is, what considerations ought to govern us if this point were determined—if it were determined that a defensive line is the course of policy to be pursued; and this again must be deduced from the objects contemplated by the war.

He would now proceed to state what, in his opinion, those considerations were; the first of which necessarily must be to effect the objects they had in view in declaring the war, viz., to repel invasion, to acquire the territory as far east as the Del Norte, to establish that as our boundary, and to compel the payment of the indemnities due to our citizens. And, as far as these considerations were concerned, they ought not to go an inch beyond them; they ought to avoid the appearance even of taking possession of any portion of the country in the way of conquest. But what was to be demanded by these considerations might be enlarged by others, which he would now proceed to state. And, first, as to forming our boundary: he considered that it should be done in such a manner as would involve the smallest possible sacrifice of men and of money; and that it should possess all the natural advantages that such a boundary ought to possess, in order that supplies of men and provisions could readily be drawn from the adjacent country. The next consideration, in his opinion, which ought to govern them in selecting the line was: it ought to be convenient, to possess all natural advantages, to be tenable at the least expense, and to allow supplies to be introduced with the greatest facility, and such as it would be desirable for us to possess, if, upon the ultimate adjustment of our differences with Mexico, it should become the common boundary between the two countries. And he would go further: he would say that it should be such a line as would not deprive Mexico in the smallest possible degree of her resources and her strength; for, while we consulted our own interests in establishing a defensive line, we should not overlook what was due to Mexico. He held that we ought to be just and liberal towards Mexico, not only because she was our neighbor; not only because she was a sister republic; not only because she was emulous now, and ever had been emulous, of imitating our example in the establishment of free institutions; not only because she was, next to ourselves, the greatest power upon this continent, amidst all the powers which had grown up from Spanish or other European origin; though these were high considerations, which every American ought to feel, and which every generous and sympathetic heart would feel, yet there were others, which referred more immediately to ourselves. Mexico was one of the greatest problems among nations; and, in his opinion, the true policy of this country was, not to repress her power, but, on the contrary, to render her strong, and capable of sustaining all those relations which might exist between her and other nations. He held that there was a mysterious connection between the fate of this country and that of Mexico, and that her independence and respectability, and capability of maintaining all those relations, were almost as essential to us as they were to Mexico. He held that Mexico was to us forbidden fruit; and that, if we should consume that fruit, it would be almost tantamount to the political death of our own institutions.

The next consideration was, that the line should be so set that, if it should be finally established as the boundary between this country and Mexico, it would lead to a permanent peace, and that it should lead to as speedy a peace as possible; and for this purpose it should be eminently pacific.

Now (continued Mr. C.) the question is, What would be such a line as would fulfil all these requisitions? And here, again, I am not fully prepared to pronounce an opinion; for it requires a more accurate acquaintance with the country and more accurate military knowledge than I possess to determine this question. But, while I do not feel myself prepared with the necessary information to enable me to pronounce upon this with accuracy, I am prepared to suggest a line which embraces most of those considerations as nearly, perhaps, as could be desired; and, if I understand the wishes of the Executive, as interpreted to us by the chairman of the Committee on Foreign Relations, it is such a line as the Executive itself considers a proper one. The line which I would suggest is one beginning at the mouth of the Rio del Norte and extending up to the pass of the Del Norte, a southern boundary of New Mexico, and thence due west to the Gulf of California. Such a line will strike the Gulf nearly at its head. Now, I propose to examine this line in reference to the considerations which I have already laid down as being those which ought to govern us in determining upon a line of defence.

[Here Mr. Calhoun examined this proposed defensive line under all the aspects he suggested, and argued that, under every aspect it was preferable to occupy such a line to engaging in a march upon the city of Mexico—that it would be cheapest in money, cheapest in lives, most certain of bringing the Mexicans to terms—and, skirting our settlements nearly all the way, would be easily maintained and defended. He then displayed a view of the expenses and difficulties of a march upon the city of Mexico, and the uncertainty of its success if accomplished.]

Now, (continued Mr. C.,) under this aspect of the question, I put it home to the Senate, is it worth while to pursue a war of this description, an offensive war, even if you were assured that you could reach the city of Mexico during this campaign and dictate such a treaty? Sir, what is to be the strength of the army which you propose to raise in order to accomplish this purpose? And what is the amount of money which will be required to carry on your military operations with that army? You propose to raise upwards of seventy thousand men, and to expend thirty-five or forty millions of dollars. Nay, we will suppose that you have an effective war establishment in the field of but fifty thousand troops. Now, what will be the end of the campaign? Suppose, by a concurrence of favorable circumstances, you have effected the whole that you contemplated by the employment of this force and the expenditure of this money, what then is the state of the case? Why, you will have sacrificed in the first place thirty millions of dollars to get to the city of Mexico to dictate this peace; and what the sacrifice of life will be, may be judged by looking at the past. One-third must be put down as certain to perish, not by the sword, but by disease; fifteen thousand lives, then, must be sacrificed. And I now put this question: Is it worth while that these sacrifices should be made in order to get that which is within your reach without any sacrifice at all? Sir, I put a higher question, thirty millions of dollars to be expended in pushing your war, which must result in obtaining for us no more than we have already? Is there any man here who would give for California fifteen millions of money? Yet we propose to prosecute a war at an expense of thirty millions, which is to produce this result. Sir, I am but touching the shell of this matter as yet. Is there any certainty that you will reach the city of Mexico, or if you reach it, is there any certainty that you can dictate a peace there, even if in possession of the city? These are considerations which command our attention. They are considerations of the utmost magnitude. But there are others which are not to be overlooked. An offensive war looks ultimately to subduing the country against which it is waged; and taking this to be the object of it, we have scarcely commenced an offensive war. It is true we have acquired two-thirds of the Mexican territory by this war, in that part of Mexico that is adjacent to us; and let it be remembered further, that this acquisition gives us a larger extent of country than the whole valley of the Mississippi, and in this immense space we have not more than five or six hundred thousand inhabitants.

Now we have overrun this adjacent country to this vast extent, and with this thin population, hardly a man of whom had joined the forces of the enemy: and what has been the result of thus getting possession? Have we conciliated the Mexicans who occupy that vast country? Not at all. They are more hostile to us than they were at first, and more ready to take advantage of any opportunity to do us injury. Can we hold these possessions, then, without a large force? Not at all. It must require several thousands of our best troops. What, then, have we accomplished? We have hardly approached the confines of populated Mexico; we have but entered her ulterior provinces. Mexico proper consists of that remarkable high land, of which the city may be said to occupy the centre; a vast region extending down to the Pacific, and to the southern side of the Gulf of California, containing seven millions of population—a population ten times as numerous as that of the country which we have captured. Here is the seat of her wealth and of her power; of her strength in defence in resistance to our arms. What description of country is it? It is mountainous as any region in the world. It may well be compared with Mount Atlas in Africa, and with the Caucasus in Europe. These mountains are interspersed with enormous defiles, rendering the approach of an army a work of the utmost difficulty. This is the character of the country we are about to conquer. How are we to overcome these difficulties? The plan is first, as I understand it, to take Vera Cruz. Now, what is the description of country in that region? The country about Vera Cruz, like the province of Yucatan, is a hot and sickly region, the home of the yellow fever for eight months in the year, and, during the months that it is exempt from this scourge, it is subject to the most violent storms, which endanger navigation, and make it difficult for ships to land. April is a very sickly month; March not so sickly. We are now near the middle of February. We may have force enough to take Vera Cruz; but I appeal to Senators on all sides, shall we have force enough to march to the city of Mexico? Sir, I will not say that we have not, but I will say this, there is no certainty that we have. It is altogether a contingency. We may not be able to reach the city of Mexico before the sickly season commences, and, if we do not, all is lost for this campaign. Mexico will be encouraged, and we discouraged, before we can remedy the disastrous effects of this result of our ineffectual attempt to reach the city.

But suppose we do reach the city of Mexico, can we dictate a peace? Whom have we to deal with? A people—a race above all others renowned in history for obstinate resistance when assailed—a people who held out, when their independence was refused to be recognized, for twenty years. These are the people we have to deal with; and is there any certainty that we can bring them to consent to propositions for peace, provided we get there? Well, if there is no certainty, but, on the contrary, there is every probability that another campaign will be inevitable, (and it must be so if either of these contingencies happen,) we must then have a second campaign.

But there was a still deeper, a still more terrific difficulty to be met—a difficulty more vital than those to which he had alluded—a difficulty arising out of a division of sentiment which went to the very foundation of our Government. How should these lands be acquired, if any were acquired? To whose benefit should they enure? Should they enure to the exclusive benefit of one portion of the Union? We were told, and he was feafrul that appearances too well justified the assertion, that all parties in the non-slaveholding portion of the Union insisted that they should have the exclusive control of this acquired territory—that such provision should be made as should exclude those who were interested in the institutions of the South from a participation in the advantages to be derived from the application of these institutions to the territory thus acquired.

Sir, (said Mr. C.,) if the non-slaveholding States, having no other interests in the question except their aversion to slavery—if they can come to this conclusion with no interest in the matter but this, I turn and ask gentlemen, what must be the feeling of the population of the slaveholding States, who are to be deprived of their constitutional rights, and despoiled of the property belonging to them—assailed in the most vulnerable point, for to them this question was a question of safety, of self-preservation, and not a mere question of policy; and thus to be despoiled by those who were not concerned? If there were sternness and determination on one side, they might be assured there would be on the other. If he might judge from what he had heard, from the appearances proceeding from the non-slaveholding States—and he had no reason to doubt it, they being the first to cry out for a vigorous prosecution of the war—could they suppose that less feeling would be exhibited on the part of those who were to be entirely excluded from their rights, and while this radical difference existed between them?

Mr. CASS then rose, and, after complimenting the Senator from South Carolina on the ability and eloquence of his argument, said he desired to make some reply; but as the day was far advanced, and he desired some time for reflection, he hoped the bill would be postponed.

The further consideration of the bill was then informally postponed until to-morrow.

WEDNESDAY, February 10.

Three Million Bill

The Senate proceeded to the consideration of the special order, being the bill making a special appropriation of three millions to bring the war with Mexico to a speedy and honorable conclusion.

The question pending being on the substitute moved by Mr. CASS, as an amendment to the amendment of Mr. BERRIEN.

Mr. CASS said: In the remarks I propose to submit, Mr. President, I shall invert the natural order of arrangement. I intend to present my views of the causes and course of the war thus far, and also the reasons, which will induce me to vote for the appropriation of three millions of dollars. To which I shall add my views of the best mode of proceeding in the prosecution of the war. I shall begin, however, with the two latter subjects.

I do not rise, sir, with the emotions so visibly felt and so eloquently described by the distinguished Senator from South Carolina. I do not consider this country, or its institutions, in the slightest danger. Never was it more free, powerful, or prosperous, than at the present moment, when untimely warnings come to assail us. The public sentinel may sleep upon his watchtower. In the distant horizon, not a cloud as big as the prophet's hand, is to be seen, which is to overspread the heavens, and to burst in thunder and in tempest upon us. We are, indeed, engaged in a foreign war, which demands the solicitude of every good citizen. But the scene of its operations is two thousand miles distant; and, come the worst that may, we can at any time withdraw into our own country. Disgraceful, indeed, would be such a movement; but it would be still better than the evils predicted, and according to the nature of the apprehensions expressed, it would terminate the danger.

Mr. President, it gives me great pain to hear any allusions to the dissolution of this Confederacy; and of all the places in this republic, this high place is the last in which they should be expressed. The constitution is in no danger. It has survived many a shock, and it will survive many more. There are those now in the Senate—and I am among them—who were born before it came into being.

We have grown with our growth and have strengthened with our strength, till the approach of physical infirmities, the kindly warnings of nature, bid us prepare for another and an untried world. And the constitution, too, has grown with its growth and strengthened with its strength, till from three millions it governs twenty millions of people, and has made them the happiest community upon the face of the globe. But it is yet fresh in its strength. No infirmity has come to tell us that its dissolution is near. It is no longer an experiment, but experience; no longer a promise, but performance. It has fulfilled all, and more than all, its most sanguine advocates dared predict. It is at this moment stronger in the affections of the American people, than at any other period of its existence. Like the cliff of eternal granite, which overlooks the ocean, and drives back the ceaseless waves that assail its base, so will this constitution resist the assaults that may be made upon it, come how or when or whence they may. In the providence of God, no such lot as ours was ever conferred upon a people. What we have been and are, the past and the present have told, and are telling us. What we are to be, the future will tell to those who are to come after us, to their joy or sorrow, as we cherish or reject the blessings we enjoy. If we are not struck with judicial blindness, as were God's chosen people of old, and punished for national offences by national punishments, we shall cling to this constitution, as the mariner clings to the last plank, when night and the tempest close around him; and we shall cling to it the stronger, as the danger is greater.

Mr. President, I shall not touch any of the topics before us, as a sectional man. I view them, and shall present them, as an American citizen, looking to the honor and interests of his country, and of his whole country. In these great questions of national bearing, I acknowledge no geographical claims. What is best for the United States is best for me; and in that spirit alone shall I pursue the discussion.

A strong desire pervades this country, that a region, extending west of our present possessions to the Pacific Ocean, should be acquired and become part of our Confederacy. The attempt to purchase it was made during the administration of General Jackson, and the hope of succeeding has never since been wholly abandoned. I will not detain the Senate by spreading out the reasons which render such a measure desirable. It would give to us a large territory, a great deal of it calculated for American settlement and cultivation, and it would connect us with the great western ocean, giving us a front along its shores in connection with Oregon of, perhaps, thirteen or fourteen degrees of latitude. It would give us also the magnificent Bay of St. Francisco, one of the noblest anchorages in the world, capable of holding all the navies of the earth; and from its commanding position, controlling, in some measure, the trade of the northern Pacific. But, sir, besides these advantages, commercial and geographical, there are important political considerations, which point to extension as one of the great measures of safety for our institutions.

In Europe, one of the social evils is concentration. Men are brought too much and kept too much in contact. There is not room for expansion. Minds of the highest order are pressed down by adverse circumstances, without the power of free exertion. There is no starting-point for them. Hence the struggles, that are ever going on, in our crowded communities. And hence the *emeutes,* which disturb and alarm the Governments of the Old World, and which must one day or other shake them to their centre. Questions of existence are involved in them, as well as questions of freedom. I trust we are far removed from all this; but to remove us further yet, we want almost unlimited power of expansion. That is our safety-valve. The mightiest intellects which when compressed in thronged cities, and hopeless of their future, are ready to break the barriers around them the moment they enter the new world of the West, feel their freedom, and turn their energies to contend with the works of creation; converting the woods and the forests into towns, and villages, and cultivated fields, and extending the dominion of civilization and improvement over the domain of nature. This process has been going on since the first settlement of our country; and while it continues, whatever other evils betide us, we shall be free from the evils of a dense population, with scanty means of subsistence, and with no hope of advancement.

We are at war with Mexico, brought on by her injustice. Before peace is established, we have a right to require a reasonable indemnity, either pecuniary or territorial, or both, for the injuries we have sustained. Such a compensation is just in itself, and in strict accordance with the usages of nations. One memorable proof of this has passed in our own times. When the allies entered Paris, after the overthrow of Napoleon, they compelled the French Government to pay them an indemnity of 1,500,000,000 francs, equal to $300,000,000. In the condition of Mexico, there is no disposition in this country to ask of her an unreasonable sacrifice. On the contrary, the wish is everywhere prevalent, and I am sure the Government participates in it, that we should demand less than we are entitled to. No one proposes a rigid standard, by which the indemnity shall be measured. But there are certain territorial acquisitions, which are important to us, and whose cession cannot injure Mexico, as she never can hold them permanently. We are willing, after settling the indemnity satisfactorily, to pay for the excess in money. The Senator from South Carolina has stated the proposition very distinctly, "any excess on our part we are willing to meet, as we ought, by the necessary payment to Mexico."

Information received by the President, during the last session of Congress, induced him to believe, that if an appropriation for this purpose were made, the difficulties between the two countries might soon be terminated by an amicable arrangement. A proposition for that purpose was submitted to us in secret session, debated and approved by this Senate. It was then introduced into the Legislature with open doors, passed the House of Representatives, and came to us. Here it was discussed until the stroke of the clock, when the hand on the dial-plate, pointed to 12, struck its funeral knell. In his Message at the commencement of this Congress, the President renewed his suggestion, and the whole matter is now before us. Such is its history.

It is now objected to, as an immoral proposition, a kind of bribery, either of the Government of Mexico, or of its Commanding General; and the honorable Senator from Maryland, who is not now in his seat, said emphatically and solemnly, "that this project of terminating the war by dismembering a sister republic, is so revolting to my moral sense of propriety, honor, and justice, that I should see my arms palsied by my side, rather than agree to it." The "dismemberment" of which the honorable member speaks is previously defined by himself. That is the term he gives the acquisition, but I call it purchase. He says the money will go to Santa Anna and pay the army, which will thus be secured, and the poor "down-trodden" people be transferred to this country "in spite of themselves," in consequence of this "pouring of gifts into the hands of their tyrants."

Now, sir, there is no such proposition, as I understand it, nor any thing like it. The object of the President has been distinctly stated by himself. It is to have the money ready, and if a satisfactory treaty is signed and ratified, then to make a payment into the treasury of Mexico, which will be disposed of by the Government of that country, agreeably to its own laws. The propositions, both at the last session of Congress and at this, were identical. The difference in the phraseology of the appropriation has been satisfactorily explained by the chairman of the Committee on Foreign Relations, and seems to me of very little consequence. Be that as it may, it is not a subject which can produce of itself any practical difficulty. For if there is any member of the Senate, who is willing to vote for the appropriation in the form in which it was presented last year, and is unwilling to vote for it in this, the Committee on Foreign Relations will cheerfully assent to the substitution of the latter for the former. "The principle is wrong," says the honorable Senator from Maryland. But, in my view, the principle of this appropriation, and of the other appropriation, is precisely the same.

And yet, the honorable Senator from Maryland voted for the former, while he reprobates the present, and a number of Senators on the other side of the chamber voted the last session in the same manner. If the proposition was bribery or unprincipled then, it seems to me it must be so now. Expediency may change with time, but right and wrong undergo no change.

As to the idea that such an arrangement is something like bribery, it seems to me it will not bear the slightest investigation. A strange kind of bribery this! The appropriation called for was preceded by a Message from the President to the Senate in secret session. It was then received in both Houses, and the doors thrown open. It was discussed fully, not to say warmly, and was finally lost by the lapse of time. In secret session thirty-three Senators voted for it. It again takes a prominent place in the President's Message at the commencement of the present session of Congress. It has been before us between two and three months, and has been borne upon the wings of the wind to the remotest portions of our country. It entered Mexico long ago, and has been proclaimed upon every house-top in town and country. It is known to every citizen of that republic, who knows any thing of political affairs, whether the blood in his veins is Castilian, or Moorish, or Aztec. It has passed to Europe, and received the condemnations of many of its journals. Had it been approved there, I should doubt its policy or its justice. And for aught I know, it is travelling along the canals of the Celestial Empire. I repeat, a strange kind of bribery this! That is an offence which does its work in secret. This is a proposition made by one nation to another, in the face of the world. It is not to enable Mexico to carry on the war, as an honorable Senator seems to suppose, for it is not to be paid till the war is over.

Mr. MOREHEAD inquired if the honorable Senator considered the present proposition as confining the President, in the disbursement of the money, to the purposes to be specified in the treaty, as the resolution of the last session did?

Mr. CASS said that his understanding of the proposition was, that the money was not to be paid, until a treaty was agreed upon. The payment was not to precede the treaty, but to follow it.

Mr. WEBSTER, (rising.) Will the honorable Senator allow me—

Mr. CASS. I will hear you with pleasure, but I cannot answer any more questions. I have said that no money is to be paid until a treaty is ratified.

Mr. WEBSTER. I was merely going to remark, that this is the very turning point.

Mr. CASS. I will sit down and hear the honorable Senator, but he must not ask me any questions. If he does, I shall not answer them, till I have concluded my remarks.

Mr. WEBSTER resumed his seat.

Mr. C. continued:

The whole proposition results from the peculiar condition of Mexico. Her Government is ephemeral. Its members are born in the morning and die in the evening. Administrations succeed one another like the scenes of a theatre, rather than the events of life, and still less of events in the life of a nation. The rulers do not dare to do justice in such a case as this. It might cost them their places, to which they hold on as tenaciously as though their tenure were a secure one. There is a strong excitement in that country against us. Nothing shows this more distinctly, than the scene which lately passed there, when their President swore that the nation would never yield one inch of its territory, nor make peace with the invader, till his foot was off the soil. A dangerous resolution to be thus publicly proclaimed, and one more easily proclaimed than kept. The sublime and the ridiculous may so easily touch, that nations should be chary of such exhibitions which may belong to the domain of the one or of the other, as subsequent circumstances stamp their character. Whatever judgment, however, history may pronounce upon this ceremony in Mexico, it is significant enough of the disposition of the people towards us. Hence the difficulty of the Government is increased, and hence the necessity of their strengthening themselves. Their revenues are drying up. They are always in debt in all their departments, civil and military. By a prompt payment into their treasury upon a ratification of a treaty, the Government will be enabled to satisfy the most pressing demands, and thus to do an act of justice at home which will counteract any ill effects of an act of justice abroad. And this is the very point of the whole matter. We may thus tempt them to do right, while so many other strong circumstances tempt them to do wrong. As to the application of this money, after it reaches the treasury of Mexico, it is no question of ours, any more than was the application of the consideration money paid to France and Spain for the purchase of Louisiana and of Florida. We cannot follow it, and it must take its fate with the other resources of the country. It has one advantage, however, and that is its publicity. If the silver or gold were carried by wagons to the palace of the Government, the transaction could have no more publicity than it has now. And this throws upon the authorities a much graver responsibility, than do the ordinary payments, and one less likely to be abused. If all this is bribery, I am fully prepared to take my share in the guilt of it. If it is bribery, let the honest Governments of Europe make the most of it.

As to the comparison, instituted by the honorable Senator from Maryland, between this act and an attempt of the Mexican Government to bribe General Taylor, it certainly gives me very little trouble. We have nothing to do with Santa Anna, as the General of an army. We deal with the Government of Mexico. The very authority that makes the treaty is the authority to which the payment is to be made. If General Taylor were the American Government, and had power to cede away a portion of the American territory, the analogy would then exist in fact, as it now exists but in fancy. And this obvious consideration answers all the objections presented by the Senator, when he expresses such an apprehension, that the money would slip from our fingers, before we secured a consideration. Not a dollar is to be paid, till the treaty is ratified, and the country thus made ours.

Passing now, sir, from the consideration of this subject to the course before us, I would observe, that there are but three plans of operation by which we can escape from the difficulties of our position.

The first, is an abandonment of the war, and an inglorious return to our own country.

The second, is the establishment of a line over such a portion of the enemy's territory as we think proper, and holding the country on this side of it without any further military operations.

The third, is a vigorous prosecution of the war, agreeably to the public expectation, and the experience of the world.

As to the first, sir, I do not place it in the category of things possible, but only in the category of things proposed, and I cast it from me with contempt.

The second, sir, is a very different proposition; supported by high names, civil and military, and was yesterday presented to us, with great power of argument and beauty of illustration, by the distinguished Senator from South Carolina. I shall state as succinctly as I can, the reasons which induce me to consider this as an inexpedient, not to say an impossible, proposition.

A plan of operations, seeking to hold a portion of a country, properly guarded by fortresses, and furnished with the necessary lines of communication, and seeking to do this, without publicly announcing the nature of the plan, and the determination to adhere to it, is one thing. An attempt to occupy another portion of country, open, unfortified, with no natural boundaries, and penetrable in all directions, and publicly proclaiming this system as an invariable one, not to be departed from, is another, and quite a different thing. From the Gulf of Mexico, following the boundaries of the provinces now in our possession, to the Pacific Ocean, is but little short of two thousand miles. Far the greater portion of it is open, and much of it unoccupied. Instead of any lines of communication, natural or artificial, where it must necessarily be crossed, it may be crossed anywhere. It is a mere paper line—a descriptive one. For hundreds of miles on each side of a great part of the line, the country is the same; roamed over rather than possessed by nomadic tribes, and affording subsistence and shelter to the beasts of the earth. If you assume such a boundary, you necessarily place yourself upon the defensive. You must establish troops along it, and these must be scattered, occupying different positions. Your enemy thus acts in masses, while you act in detachments. If he attack you, and succeed, you are destroyed. If he attack you, and is discomfited, he falls back behind his impenetrable barrier. A snake, clutched by an eagle, is one of the emblems of the armorial bearings of Mexico. If this plan of fighting to an air line is adopted, the proud bird will soon be powerless, and the reptile will coil itself up to strike at its leisure and its pleasure. In such a state of offensive-defensive warfare, the enemy chooses his time, when you least expect him, or are least able to resist him. He gains your rear, and cuts off your convoys and supplies, and thus reduces you to weakness and distress. Or he strikes you in a period of sickness, in a climate to which you are unaccustomed, and whose alternations do not affect him. You cannot pursue him into his country, for the moment you do that, you confess the folly of your plan, and abandon it forever. If you cross your boundary, you must cross it to hold on, and then you have a new boundary, or in other words, a system of unlimited operations. If you do not cross to hold on, what will you do? Your very object in crossing is to chastise the enemy; and you must pursue him to his fortresses and capture them, if he has any; or you must fight him in the open field and disperse him. I repeat, if you do not do this, you may as well stop at your boundary; look civilly at the retiring enemy, take off your hats, and say: Good-bye gentlemen; we will wait till you come back again. The riches of Crœsus would melt away before such a system of fighting-no-fighting. The laurels of Napoleon would wither and die. No exchequer could bear the expense. No public sentiment the dishonor. There is but one such campaign, sir, recorded in all history, ancient or modern, sacred or profane, true or fabulous, and that is the campaign of Sisyphus. It was an eternal one. Sanction the plan proposed, and yours will be eternal too. This stone will never be rolled to the top of the mountain. It would be a never-ending, ever-renewing war. The distinguished Senator from South Carolina thinks, that four regiments and three fortresses along this line, and one regiment and a few small vessels for California, "would be ample for its defence." The line, as described by himself, is this: "Beginning at the mouth of the Rio del Norte, and continuing up the Paso del Norte, or southern boundary of New Mexico, which nearly coincide, and then due west to the Gulf of California, striking it, according to the maps before us, nearly at its head."

Here, sir, is a line across the continent from the Gulf of Mexico to the Gulf of California; and this line is to be so protected by five regiments, three fortresses, and a few small vessels, as to be impervious to the rancheros and other light troops of Mexico—the best and most indefatigable horsemen, perhaps, in the world. I have enumerated, in these means of defence, a few small vessels, because they form part of the *projet* of the honorable Senator. How they are to be employed in defending any part of the line, as I do not understand, I will not attempt to explain. If the soldiers were stationed equidistant upon this boundary, they would probably be a mile apart. It seems to me, sir—and I say it with all respect—that we might as well attempt to blockade the coast of Europe by stationing a ship in the middle of the Atlantic. As to the Rio Grande, it is no defensive line at all. Rivers, when best guarded, are found to afford very insufficient protection. But in the great country south and west of us, yet in a state of nature, or slowly emerging from it, streams are entitled to very little consideration in defensive operations. Who is there, that has passed his life in the West, and has not crossed them a hundred times by swimming, in canoes, upon logs, upon rafts, and upon horses? Is it to be supposed, that an active Mexican, accustomed to the woods from his infancy, would hesitate to dash into a stream, and cross it, almost as readily as if it were unbroken ground?

But long defensive lines, even when skilfully constructed and carefully guarded, are but feeble *barriers* against courage and enterprise. How long did the Roman wall keep the North Britons out of England? How long did the Grecian wall of the Lower Empire keep the Turks out of Constantinople, and the horse-tails of their Pashas from the cathedral of Saint Sophia? And the Chinese wall—an immense labor of man—that, too, opened to the Tartars, and enabled the chief of roving bands to ascend the oldest throne in the world. The best wall a country can have is the breasts of its citizens, free, prosperous, and united.

But, sir, there is another consideration, not to be overlooked. How could you keep your own citizens on this side of your imaginary line? The honorable Senator tells us, their spirit of adventure can hardly be restrained in time of peace, and that there is always danger they will push into the Mexican provinces. But in time of war—even of a new kind of war like this—they would feel that the enemy's country was open to them, and their incursions would keep up a continued state of hostilities.

Some of the remarks of the honorable Senator I regretted to hear: those which cast doubts upon the power of this country to prosecute this war to an honorable conclusion—such a conclusion, indeed, as alone will be satisfactory to the American people. I am not going, Mr. President, to subject these views to any severity of investigation. I should do it with reluctance in any case, and I could not do it in this. My unfeigned respect for the distinguished Senator would prohibit it. While I claim for myself and yield to others the most unlimited range of discussion; and while I do not call in question the truth of the sentiment, uttered during the last war, that a public man has a right to speak to his country, though he may be overheard by the enemy, still there are discretionary limits, which it seems to me it were better not to pass. Every word that is spoken here, is heard upon the plateau of Mexico. Legislative discussions, with open doors, are, in this age of progress, discussions before the world. As we watch the indications of public opinion in Mexico, and seek them in the journals of the day, the same universal messengers carry back to that country all we are saying, and doing, and proposing. Far be it from me to question the conduct, or the motives of any honorable Senator. I believe that every member of this body is actuated by as pure intentions as I am myself. But I suggest, is it prudent to say here, that it is uncertain whether we shall be able to reach the city of Mexico during this campaign, and that if we do not, she will be encouraged, and we discouraged; she fortified, and we irresolute? Is it prudent to say, that there are doubts, whether we can raise the means for another, more costly, and at a greater distance? To say that the spirit of volunteering is gone? To say, that for a third campaign, there will be no longer resources in treasury notes? Exhausted, perhaps more than exhausted, by this single campaign? To ask, if we can borrow? If we can lay taxes? What taxes, &c.? To ask, if we can collect them in certain States, that are embarrassed; and to answer, No! To inquire, if there will be sufficient unanimity and zeal in the prosecution of the war, to warrant the belief, that Congress would grant the necessary supplies?

These are irksome inquiries to me, Mr. President, and I shall not pursue them. If all this is so, we are already unfaithful to the trust transmitted to us, purchased by the exertion and blood of our fathers, and left as a precious legacy for those who are to come after us. The lofty position of the distinguished Senator from South Carolina, his reputation—a European one, in fact—his great services, and his pure character, give extraordinary weight to all the sentiments he utters; and the deeper, therefore, is my regret. If these apprehensions are well founded, there is another point of application for the epigrammatic remark of a French statesman, speaking of us in the earlier periods of our history, who said, "*If such is the youth* of that *republic*, what *will be its old age?*"—Sir, it will have no old age.

The eyes of Europe are upon us. Nothing worse can happen to us than to stop ingloriously. That is our last resource. We have, then, but to prosecute this war, as other wars are prosecuted by other nations. We have but to discard dangerous experiments, and to hold on to the experience of the world. We must breast ourselves to the shock. We must continue our occupation of Mexico, and push the invasion still farther. We must do as other people have done—we must attack and disperse her armies, take possession of her towns, and capture her fortresses. There seems to be some analogy between the cities of Paris and Mexico. Both are the native seats of revolutions. Both exert a preponderating influence over their respective countries. I have no right to give an authoritative opinion, respecting the expediency of a demonstration upon the capital. Still, I do not hesitate to say, that I think it would be a wise and probably decisive measure. It would disperse the Government, and weaken, if not break, its hold upon public opinion. It would divert the revenues from them to us. And, in addition to this resource, I agree fully with the honorable Senator from Missouri in opinion, that we should call contributions to our aid, in defraying our military expenses. It is a legitimate means of support for hostile armies. It belongs to the present age, and not exclusively to the past. During all the wars in Europe in our time, almost the first thing the commander of a foreign army does, on entering an enemy's town, is to convene the magistrates, and make requisitions upon them for bread, meat, wine, forage, and such other supplies as are wanted. And this, too, under threat of military execution. And the process has been found effectual, and the practice universal.

But it is said, Mr. President, that the Mexicans will fight till the last extremity. It may be so. There are many desperate deeds recorded in history, and obstinacy is a prominent trait in the Spanish character, and belongs to all the affiliated people of that stock. But men do not fight for the mere purpose of being killed. We do not enter Mexico to conquer her—*only to conquer a peace.* We do not assail her independence. We do not seek her permanent subjugation. We only ask her to do us justice. It seems to me, then, that this is not one of those cases, sometimes prominent in the history of nations, where the public energy is aroused to a fit of desperation, and by which means victories are achieved against all previous calculations. Without government, without trade, without resources, sowing, but not to reap, or reaping but not to enjoy, and with all the evils of hostile occupation, I cannot but think, that the Mexican people may be conquered—to justice.

SATURDAY, February 13.

Further War Measures.

The Presiding Officer laid before the Senate the following Message from the President of the United States:

To the Senate and House of Representatives of the United States.

Congress, by the act of the 13th of May last, declared, that "by the act of the republic of Mexico, a state of war exists between that Government and the United States;" and "for the purpose of enabling the Government of the United States to prosecute said war to a speedy and successful termination," authority was vested in the President to employ the "naval and military forces of the United States."

It has been my unalterable purpose, since the commencement of hostilities by Mexico, and the declaration of the existence of war by Congress, to prosecute the war in which the country was unavoidably involved with the utmost energy, with a view to its "speedy and successful termination" by an honorable peace.

Accordingly, all the operations of our naval and military forces have been directed with this view. While the sword has been held in one hand, and our military movements pressed forward into the enemy's country, and its coasts invested by our navy, the tender of an honorable peace has been constantly presented to Mexico in the other.

Hitherto, the overtures of peace which have been made by this Government have not been accepted by Mexico. With a view to avoid a protracted war, which hesitancy and delay on our part would be so well calculated to produce, I informed you, in my annual message of the 8th December last, that the war would "continue to be prosecuted with vigor, as the best means of securing peace," and recommended to your early and favorable consideration the measures proposed by the Secretary of War, in his report accompanying that message.

In my message of the 4th January last, these and other measures, deemed to be essential to the "speedy and successful termination" of the war, and the attainment of a just and honorable peace, were recommended to your early and favorable consideration.

The worst state of things which could exist in a war with such a power as Mexico, would be a course of indecision and inactivity on our part. Being charged by the constitution and the laws with the conduct of the war, I have availed myself of all the means at my command to prosecute it with energy and vigor.

The act "to raise for a limited time an additional military force, and for other purposes," and which authorizes the raising of ten additional regiments to the regular army, to serve during the war, and to be disbanded at its termination, which was presented to me on the 11th instant, and approved on that day, will constitute an important part of our military force. These regiments will be raised and moved to the seat of war with the least practicable delay.

It will be perceived that this act makes no provision for the organization into brigades and divisions of the increased force which it authorizes, nor for the appointment of general officers to command it. It will be proper that authority be given by law to make such organization, and to appoint, by and with the advice and consent of the Senate, such number of major-generals and brigadier-generals as the efficiency of the service may demand. The number of officers of these grades now in service are not more than are required for their respective commands; but further legislative action during your present session will, in my judgment, be required, and to which it is my duty respectfully to invite your attention.

Should the war, contrary to my earnest desire, be protracted to the close of the term of service of the volunteers now in Mexico, who engaged for twelve months, an additional volunteer force will probably become necessary to supply their place. Many of the volunteers now serving in Mexico, it is not doubted, would cheerfully engage, at the conclusion of their present term, to serve during the war. They would constitute a more efficient force than could be speedily obtained by accepting the services of any new corps who might offer their services. They would have the advantage of the experience and discipline of a year's service, and will have become accustomed to the climate, and be in less danger than new levies of suffering from the diseases of the country. I recommend, therefore, that authority be given to accept the services of such of the volunteers now in Mexico as the state of the public service may require, and who may, at the termination of their present term, voluntarily engage to serve during the war with Mexico, and that provision be made for commissioning the officers. Should this measure receive the favorable consideration of Congress, it is recommended that a bounty be granted to them upon their voluntarily extending their term of service. This would not only be due to these gallant men, but it would be economy to the Government; because, if discharged at the end of the twelve months, the Government would be bound to incur a heavy expense in bringing them back to their homes, and in sending to the seat of war new corps of fresh troops to supply their place.

By the act of the thirteenth of May last, the President was authorized to accept the services of volunteers, "in companies, battalions, squadrons, and regiments," but no provision was made for filling up vacancies which might occur by death, or discharges from the service, on account of sickness or other casualties. In consequence of this omission, many of the corps now in service have been much reduced in numbers. Nor was any provision made for filling vacancies of regimental or company officers who might die or resign. Information has been received at the War Department of the resignation of more than one hundred of these officers. They were appointed by the State authorities, and no information has been received, except in a few instances, that their places have been filled; and the efficiency of the service has been impaired from this cause. To remedy these defects, I recommend that authority be given to accept the services of individual volunteers, to fill up the places of such as may die, or become unfit for the service and be discharged; and that provision be also made for filling the places of regimental and company officers who may die or resign. By such provisions, the volunteer corps may be constantly kept full, or may approximate the maximum number authorized and called into service in the first instance.

While it is deemed to be our true policy to prosecute the war in the manner indicated, and thus make the enemy feel its pressure and its evils, I shall be at all times ready, with the authority conferred on me by the constitution, and with all the means which may be placed at my command by Congress, to conclude a just and honorable peace.

Of equal importance with an energetic and vigorous prosecution of the war are the means required to defray its expenses, and to uphold and maintain the public credit.

In my annual Message of the 8th December last, I submitted for the consideration of Congress the propriety of imposing as a war measure, revenue duties on some of the articles now embraced in the free list. The principal articles now exempt from duty, from which any considerable revenue could be derived, are tea and coffee. A moderate revenue duty on these articles, it is estimated, would produce annually an amount exceeding two and a half millions of dollars. Though in a period of peace, when ample means could be derived from duties on other articles for the support of the Government, it may have been deemed proper not to resort to a duty on these articles; yet, when the country is engaged in a foreign war, and all our resources are demanded to meet the unavoidable increased expenditure in maintaining our armies in the field, no sound reason is perceived why we should not avail ourselves of the revenues which may be derived from this source. The objections which have heretofore existed to the imposition of these duties were applicable to a state of peace, when they were not needed. We are now, however, engaged in a foreign war. We need money to prosecute it, and to maintain the public honor and credit. It cannot be doubted that the patriotic people of the United States would cheerfully, and without complaint, submit to the payment of this additional duty, or any other that may be necessary to maintain the honor of the country, provide for the unavoidable expenses of the Government, and to uphold the public credit. It is recommended that any duties which may be imposed on these articles be limited in their duration to the period of the war.

An additional annual revenue, is is estimated, of between half a million and a million of dollars, would be derived from the graduation and reduction of the price of such of the public lands as have been long offered in the market at the minimum price established by the existing laws, and have remained unsold. And, in addition to other reasons commending the measure to favorable consideration, it is recommended as a financial measure. The duty suggested on tea and coffee, and the graduation and reduction of the price of the public lands, would secure an additional annual revenue to the treasury of not less than three millions of dollars, and would thereby prevent the necessity of incurring a public debt annually to that amount, the interest on which must be paid semi-annually, and ultimately the debt itself, by a tax on the people.

It is a sound policy, and one which has long been approved by the Government and people of the United States, never to resort to loans unless in cases of great public emergency, and then only for the smallest amount which the public necessities will permit.

The increased revenues which the measures now recommended would produce would, moreover, enable the Government to negotiate a loan, for any additional sum which may be found to be needed, with more facility, and at cheaper rates than can be done without them.

Under the injunction of the constitution which makes it my duty "from time to time to give to Congress information of the state of the Union, and to recommend to their consideration such measures" as shall be judged "necessary and expedient," I respectfully and earnestly invite the action of Congress on the measures herein presented for their consideration. The public good, as well as a sense of my responsibility to our common constituents, in my judgment, imperiously demand that I should present them for your enlightened consideration, and invoke favorable action upon them before the close of your present session.

JAMES K. POLK.

WASHINGTON, *February* 13, 1847.

On motion, the Message was referred to the Committee on Military Affairs.

The Senate then adjourned.

HOUSE OF REPRESENTATIVES.

SATURDAY, February 13.

Three Million Loan Bill.

Mr. SEABORN JONES was entitled to the floor, and addressed the committee during the hour. Premising that he did not intend to occupy much of the time of the House with remarks upon the bill immediately under consideration, he (Mr. J.) passed on to a review of the causes which had involved us in the war with Mexico. Whether just or unjust, whether brought on by the Executive of the United States or by Mexico, war *existed;* money was requisite to procure an honorable peace, or to carry on the war, as the case might be; and he did not doubt that a large majority of the House would readily appropriate all the means that were required.

Mr. J. then entered upon a reply to the argument of Mr. STEPHENS, in relation to the causes of the war, which he attributed entirely to the stubborn folly of Mexico herself. He (Mr. J.) was not for a "masterly inactivity," but for a vigorous prosecution of the war, and for cutting off the resources of Mexico, until she came and asked for peace; and then he was for granting peace on liberal terms.

He opposed urgently the adoption of the Wilmot proviso; and in this connection, went into an examination of the Scripture argument on the subject of slavery.

Mr. W. HUNT then obtained the floor, and addressed the committee mainly in opposition to the acquisition, on grounds of public policy, of any further territory.

[Whilst Mr. H. was speaking,

Mr. JOHN QUINCY ADAMS, for the first time since his attack of paralysis, entered the Hall. The committee rose in a body to receive him. Mr. HUNT suspended his remarks; and

Mr. ANDREW JOHNSON then rose, and said: In compliance with the understanding with which I selected a seat at the commencement of the present session, I now tender to the venerable member from Massachusetts the seat which I then selected for him, and will furthermore congratulate him on being spared to return to this House.

Mr. ADAMS responded. It is with much pleasure that I again return to your midst. Had I a more powerful voice, I might respond to the congratulations of my friends and the members of this House for the honor which has been done me. But enfeebled as I am by disease, I beg that you will excuse me.]

Mr. W. HUNT then resumed the floor, and entered into a discussion of the general question of the war, showing that the longer it continued the greater would be the amount of indemnity required from Mexico—thus increasing the difficulties of final adjustment.

[In the course of the day a Message in writing was received from the President of the United States. See Senate proceedings for this Message.]

The Message having been read, some conversation followed; when

Mr. C. J. INGERSOLL offered the following resolution; which was adopted:

Resolved, That so much of the President's Message, this day presented to the House of Representatives, as relates to an increase of military officers, be referred to the Committee on Military Affairs; so much as relates to additional impost, to the Committee of Ways and Means; and so much as relates to the war with Mexico, to the Committee on Foreign Affairs, with instructions to report thereon promptly.

Mr. HUDSON took the floor, and resumed the debate. He discussed the war and connected topics, maintaining that the war was brought upon us by the act of the President in ordering the advance of our army to the Rio Grande—into a territory without our jurisdiction—where Texas had never extended her authority, and had no claim, except a mere paper claim and declaration that it was hers.

A word or two of conversation took place on this point between Mr. HUDSON and Mr. PILLSBURY—Mr. P. controverting the position of Mr. HUDSON, and declaring that Texas had a permanent force which had ranged within that territory for years over the inhabited part of that frontier, and which, with other acts of jurisdiction, constitute the basis of a sound claim on the part of Texas to the Rio Grande.

Mr. HUDSON (resuming) admitted that Texas had settlements in the valley of the Nueces, but never upon the Rio Grande.

He referred to the comparison which gentlemen had attempted to institute between this war and that of 1812—instituted, he said, because this war could not be justified upon its own merits, and maintained that, instead of resembling, this war was the very reverse of the war of 1812; the war of 1812 being just—this, unjust; that being defensive—this, aggressive; that, commenced and prosecuted to extend the freedom of the seas—this, to extend slavery on shore.

He defended the right of Congress to withhold supplies to an unjust war. To deny it was to assert that we were already under a military despotism, and not a free people. The power of the people, through their representatives, to withhold supplies, was their peculiar prerogative under our Government, and was a doctrine "formidable to tyrants only."

He reviewed the course of the Administration in its different stages, and their admissions, to show that this was a war of conquest; and alluded to the various, almost insurmountable, difficulties which stood in the way of our success.

He considered it, then, his duty to withhold supplies of men and money for more extended movements; but would pay our forces already in service. His policy would be to withdraw our army to our own territory; and this not with reference to Mexico, but with reference to ourselves, to self-respect, to truth, and justice; and then proclaim to Mexico and the world that we want none of her territory; that we want nothing but a just and honorable peace, with such indemnity as she may owe our citizens. This proposition would bring Mexico to terms, and secure peace in a very short period. Mr. H. having concluded,

Mr. JENKINS rose and said:

Mr. CHAIRMAN: The remarks which I propose to make at this time will mainly be devoted to the support of the amendment offered by the honorable gentleman from Pennsylvania. Notwithstanding the exciting nature of the subject, I am happy to notice that it has been treated, both by the North and the South, generally, with the cool deliberation suited to its importance. It has been suggested upon this floor, that the support of this proviso is an act hostile to the Administration, and tends to embarrass the Government in the prosecution of the war. For the purpose of showing that this opinion is founded in misapprehension, it is proper to take into consideration the legislation upon the subject of the war.

On the thirteenth day of May last, Congress passed an act recognizing the existence of war with the republic of Mexico. By the same statute, the army and navy were placed in the hands of the President, and the Government authorized to increase the amount of seven millions then in the treasury by the loan of ten millions of dollars, and to raise fifty thousand volunteers, for a vigorous prosecution of the war. Upon the passage of this act one hundred and seventy-four members of this House voted in the affirmative, and fourteen only voted in the negative—making a majority in favor of the measure larger than can be found upon so important a subject from the days of Jefferson to the present time. The confidence of Congress in the Government was further evinced during last session, by the most liberal appropriation bills for the maintenance of our army and navy.

Congress has manifested a similar spirit at the present session. The bill under consideration was made a special order for the first day of March instant. But in order to hasten the passage of some important appropriation bills, the bill in question was postponed to the eighth instant. Aware of the large amount of men and money necessary for a vigorous prosecution of the contest, we have at this session authorized a further loan of twenty-eight millions of dollars, and the raising of ten regiments for the increase of the regular army. Appropriation bills suited to the gigantic undertaking of the Government, have been passed with unexpected unanimity; and every war measure recommended by Government of any considerable importance, has already passed this House. On the part of the Government, the war has been prosecuted with commendable vigor and brilliant success. A large amount of territory, equal to one-third of the whole Mexican republic, is now under our control. It rests with the Executive to direct the further operations. Men and means have been provided by a patriotic country, and a soldiery not less patriotic have given in the past, a pledge of future bravery and renown.

The essential war measures having been provided for, the President has thought proper to invite our attention to the subject of peace. Upon his recommendation, the Committee on Foreign Relations have introduced the bill in question, which provides that "the sum of three millions of dollars be hereby appropriated, out of any money in the Treasury not otherwise appropriated, to enable the President to conclude a treaty of peace with the republic of Mexico; to be used by him in the event that said treaty, when duly ratified by Mexico, shall call for the expenditure of the same, or any part thereof."

This bill is not a war but a peace measure. The money cannot be drawn from the treasury until the republic of Mexico has agreed on terms for adjusting her difficuties with this country. How soon that event will occur is a question of great doubt. Present appearances are not propitious of early negotiation. But it may be wanted at some time; and, before voting for the bill, I shall not fail to inquire, to what specific purpose is this three millions of money to be devoted? When it is remembered that our Government has announced its determination to require of Mexico the payment of the immense amount due our citizens for spoliations long since committed, and an adequate indemnity for the expenses of the war, as conditions of peace; when we consider that Mexico is unable to raise money for that purpose, and that the surrender to us of a portion of her territory is the only way in which she can make the required recompense—we shall not be at a loss to know why our forces have taken possession of that portion of Mexico, which, from its contiguity to our own dominion and its commercial and agricultural advantages invites the hardy industry and resistless enterprise of our people. Our laws are already administered there; the press is scattering intelligence in our own language there; and an army has been sent to California, with express orders to be disbanded west of the Rocky Mountains. When that army shall return they will bring the country with them.

Upon the return of peace and the acquisition of a part of the Mexican territory, it may well be expected that expediency as well as justice will suggest the propriety of paying to the Mexican Government this three millions as a balance due Mexico, over and above her indebtedness to us, for the territory we shall acquire. This is the purpose for which the three millions is wanted. When we consider how much more than she can pay Mexico owes already, it woud be idle to ask, for what other purpose can the three millions be required?

When we are thus taking measures for a permanent acquisition of territory, ordinary prudence forces upon us the inquiry, To what purpose shall this territory be devoted? Shall it be hallowed by free and cheerful toil, or must it be condemned to yield a stinted supply to the reluctant labor of the slave? The proviso under consideration is intended to perform the office of reserving this territory to the enjoyment of free labor. Some effort has been made to brand this movement with hard names, and to impress upon it the odium of Abolitionism. But the day has gone by when men can be driven from the performance of their duty by such expedients. This is no Abolition project. The proviso does not interfere with slavery in the States where it now exists. With that subject we have nothing to do. We take this up as a great national question—a question untrammelled by any vested right—one which addresses itself to us not as mere philanthropists or partisans, but as legislators.

But, Mr. Chairman, I have another case of the highest authority—an authority which honorable gentlemen who take the other side of this question by no means should question. It will be remembered that a few days since, when the bill to organize the Territory of Oregon was in progress through this House, the honorable gentleman from South Carolina (Mr. BURT) proposed an amendment to that bill, fixing the line for slave territory at thirty-six degrees and thirty minutes of north latitude. The honorable mover of that amendment, with those who deny the power generally, voted in favor of that amendment; thus explicitly admitting, by their most solemn acts, the power of Congress to control this question. Acts are better evidence of the real opinions of men than declarations. Thus, upon authority of the highest character, judicial and legislative, am I borne out in the conclusion, that the constitution has vested in Congress the power to prohibit the introduction of slavery in territory thus acquired.

Mr. STEWART opposed the grant of three millions of dollars proposed by the bill under consideration, as intended to ratify any treaty the President of the United States might think proper to make for the acquisition of territory. It was the ratification of a treaty beforehand, and if passed in its present form, would preclude both Houses from objecting to ratify and carry out any treaty whatever which the President might be disposed to make.

He denounced the war as a Presidential war, and a war of conquest, and would vote for the "Wilmot proviso" as the most effectual means, if carried, of bringing it to a speedy termination. The object of the Administration was to acquire new territory to make it slave territory, and if this prohibition of slavery were imposed by Congress, their warlike spirit would quickly subside. Still he had voted supplies because the President, by plunging us into war and our army into danger, had left him no choice. He had done it for the protection of our army.

He commented upon the fatuity and madness of the Administration in involving us in war for the sake of acquiring territory with which we could do nothing when got, and which would but prove an apple of discord, and was fraught with danger to the existence of the Union itself.

Mr. BROCKENBROUGH said, upon the subject of the "Wilmot proviso," unlike many gentlemen from the South, he had no fears for the institution of slavery, or for the dissolution of the Union; not from any wilful blindness, but because, after calm reflection, it appeared to him that whenever the governments of this country, either State or Federal, had undertaken to legislate in advance of public opinion, and prescribe rules for public opinion, their enactments were but a dead letter on the statute book. Any legislation at this time, declaring that lands which may hereafter be acquired by the United States shall be occupied by one portion of the country to the exclusion of the other, would be perfectly futile and ineffectual. From the beginning of the Government down to the present day, the North and the South had been advancing with giant and equal stride towards the West, and no arbitrary line could restrain the advances of the institutions of either. The Missouri compromise line had only been acquiesced in by the South because north of that line slavery could not go, from the nature of the case, so as to be for the interest of the people.

But granting that the principles of the amendment could be enforced, (in case it were adopted,) Mr. B. presented a picture of the blighting influences it would entail upon the South, resulting finally in the extermination of the entire white race in that section; a consequence disastrous in the extreme to the North and of all sections of our country.

On the other hand, if this institution were allowed to take its natural course, and to spread southward and westward, by diffusion it would lose its strength, and in the course of a century, he prophesied, its very existence itself. It was already beginning to ebb in the southern States, and white labor and industry were coming in to take the place of those of the slave.

Advancing to the subject of the war, and premising that it was a just war upon our part, a redress of aggressions and wrongs, Mr. B. did not understand that our Government was, nor would he have it to be, a new-modelled, Quaker sort of a Government, which, with hands bound, was to submit to all public injuries and insults, either because it was too good to present them, or because the Government making them was too poor to make reparation; but he said, if that party had waste lands, (as it made no other indemnity,) he did not see why those waste lands should not be appropriated by us. It might be called dismemberment, robbery, &c.; but nine-tenths of the nations of the present day had no better title to their own territory than that of conquest. Mexico should be made to pay our just demands; and if she had no money, it was no crime to take her land for indemnity to our citizens and to the Government for the expenses of the war she has brought upon us. He did not pretend to designate what portion of her territory; but his objections to taking a particular line, and defending and holding it, were very much removed by the argument of a distinguished Senator from his own section of the country a few days since.

Mr. McCLELLAND signified his intention to vote for the Wilmot proviso, in accordance with what he believed to be the wishes of his constituents; and briefly mentioned the points which he should make in its support, upon constitutional grounds, as well as those of expediency.

Mr. GIDDINGS said he would present a synopsis of what he would have said were there a more general attendance of the committee. He said he desired to call the attention of the country to the fact that the time had arrived when the great question of freedom and slavery was to be passed upon by this body. From that issue no member could escape; each must show whether he be on the side of oppression or freedom.

There is now (said he) no longer doubt as to the objects and ulterior designs of this war. They are now understood through the country. That object (he said) is the acquisition of further slave territory; it is carrying out the policy of the annexation of Texas. He had regarded that measure at the time as fatal to the continuance of the Union. He stated that the policy of territorial aggrandizement, if continued, must end in the overthrow of our Government and separation of the States. He did not regret that an issue so distinct was presented. He was himself prepared to meet it. He rejoiced to see northern men of both parties uniting upon this important question. "No more slave territory" has become the watchword among the free States. They will adhere to that doctrine. They will never permit Texas to extend beyond its actual limits.

He desired particularly to call the attention of the country to the proposition just made by an eminent statesman in the other end of the Capitol. That plan was to take possession of territory large enough to form twelve such States as that of Ohio. He proposes to hold this immense territory under military occupation. That will ensure an emigration into it of slaveholders with their slaves, which will render it *slave* territory. If we should not then obtain it from Mexico, it will be prepared for revolt, after the example of Texas. If we should obtain any portion of the territory it will then be called slave territory; and we shall be told that we must not interrupt the relation of master and slave, and therefore it must remain slave territory. He wished to warn the people of the free States against this insidious proposition. He insisted that not another inch of slave territory should be acquired. The boundaries of Texas must never extend beyond the Nueces; nor must there ever be another slave State admitted to the Union.

He repelled the idea that had been thrown out that the Whig party were in favor of prosecuting the war. He said he represented the strongest Whig district in the Union, and that they had authorized no man to pledge them to the support of the war.

Mr. SEAMAN obtained the floor, and said that some of the measures of this Congress were as extraordinary as important. The acquisition of territory by annexation and compromise—a change in our system of keeping and disbursing the public moneys, and the revenue laws—a war of conquest, and a national debt, are among its prominent features. These he should speak of freely and honestly.

He voted for the two million bill at the last session, with the Wilmot proviso, and should vote for it now. He was willing to go with him that would go farthest in placing at the disposal of the President the means to secure a peace with Mexico. He did not believe the bill would accomplish such a wished-for result; but the Wilmot proviso would lead him to give his vote for the bill, much as he disliked it. He opposed the admission of Texas into the Union on the ground that it extended the institution of slavery. He was opposed to any further extension of it, and thought it ought to be confined within its present limits. He was opposed to the war. It was wrong in principle, and unjust in its inception. It was waged for conquest and to extend slavery. The President provoked it. He was in favor of withdrawing our troops from Mexico to the Rio Grande, or even across the disputed boundary if it would stop the war, and lead to an adjustment of the difficulties between the two Governments. He considered the sub-treasury an unfortunate and an unwise measure. It was condemned by all intelligent merchants as a measure of mischief, and ought to be repealed. The specie clause could not be carried out.

Mr. HARPER then obtained the floor. He briefly gave notice of points which he should discuss more fully in his written speech. In it, he should endeavor to show that this was a presidential war; a war of aggression: that it was caused by the movement, by the order of the President, of our troops to the Rio Grande, into a territory which was not ours, over which, notwithstanding what had been said by the gentleman from Texas, (Mr. PILLSBURY,) Texas had never exercised jurisdiction: that it was not a war for the redress of grievances; but that the failure of Mexico to make payment of indemnities to our citizens, was made the pretext for commencing the war, for the object of a permanent acquisition of territory: that the conduct of this war reflected no honor upon the Administration; but that it was a war upon our brave generals, who had shed lustre upon the arms of our country. He declared himself in favor of the Wilmot proviso: it was not a question with the North; they were decided that no more territory should be acquired, to be made slave territory. He maintained that the whole object of the war was the acquisition of foreign territory, that the South, in all time to come, might have the control of the Government, as had been stated in the public papers there. The orders to the American army and navy, to invade and conquer a portion of Mexican territory, and establish political and civil power therein; the troops sent by Colonel Stevenson to California, with their families, implements of agriculture, &c., were evidences of the fact.

An additional motive was, to gain or secure political power, regardless of the interests to the country. This is clear, from the course pursued by the Administration and its friends in and out of this House, in regard to the conduct of General Taylor in the war.

This bill (he said) was nothing more or less than one to give the President three millions of dollars as secret-service money, to be used, if the President so please, to fulfil any arrangement he may have made with Santa Anna, when he permitted him to return to Mexico, and assume the command of the Mexican army: that this was giving aid and comfort to the enemy far beyond any thing in the whole Whig party to afford: that this money may, and probably will, be used to bribe and corrupt the authorities of Mexico, both civil and military, to procure a *quasi* peace: that this was in direct conflict with the purposes of the party in power made heretofore, which were, to "conquer a peace;" and not only so, but to revel "in the halls of the Montezumas:" that he would not have any agency in furnishing funds for a purpose so profligate and disgraceful. He said we had now a country unoccupied, of an extent sufficient to make several new States: that he was opposed to the purchase of the territory sought by the President, that is, New Mexico and Upper California—an extent of country greater than the original thirteen States of the Union: that the introduction of this territory into the Union would agitate the question of slavery, which, ultimately, and at no very remote period, in his opinion, would shake this Union from its centre to its circumference, and terminate in the subversion of the liberties of the people, and the destruction of the union of the States.

Mr. THOMASSON opposed the three million bill, either with or without the Wilmot proviso, and gave his reasons why he voted for it last year. He then digressed into some discussion of political topics in general.

Mr. PENDLETON then obtained the floor, and moved that the committee rise.

The question was put, and no quorum voted.

The committee rose, and the Chairman reported that fact to the House.

Mr. PENDLETON moved that the House adjourn.

The question was decided by yeas and nays as follows—yeas 13, nays 40.

The House having refused to adjourn—

Mr. DROMGOOLE moved a call of the House.

The question was put, and decided in the affirmative.

The SPEAKER accordingly ordered the Clerk to call the roll.

When the call had progressed a few minutes—

Mr. STROHM moved that the further proceedings of the call be dispensed with.

The question was put and negatived.

The roll being called through, it appeared that fifty-eight members had answered to their names.

The absentees were then called, when it appeared that five other members were present—making sixty-three in all.

The doors of the Hall were now closed, and the list of absentees were then again called for excuses; and Messrs. ABBOTT, JOHN Q. ADAMS, BELL, CULVER, DOBBIN, LEWIS, MCKAY, PETTIT, STARKWEATHER, and YOUNG, were severally excused.

During the call of the absentees several motions to suspend the call and to adjourn were made and rejected.

When the absentees were called through, the following order was adopted:

Ordered, That special messengers, to be appointed for that purpose, be sent for the absent members, and that they be taken into custody and brought to the House.

Mr. FARAN moved to suspend the call, and stated that, as a member of the Committee on Accounts, he had been called on to pass upon accounts of the Sergeant-at-Arms for arresting members during the process of calls of the House. It frequently happened, that during the calls of the House the Sergeant-at-Arms arrested members and had them in attendance at the door of the Hall when the call was suspended, which always released members from custody without the payment of the fine, and the House was then called upon to pay it.

Mr. F.'s motion was then put and agreed to, and the call was suspended.

Mr. GEORGE W. JONES moved that the House adjourn. Rejected.

Mr. COBB moved that the House again resolve itself into Committee of the Whole. Rejected.

Mr. COBB then moved that the House adjourn.

The question was decided in the negative—yeas 22, nays 36.

Mr. SAWYER inquired of the Chair if it was in order for him to make a speech on the Wilmot proviso?

The CHAIR decided that no speech on any subject would be in order at this time, (no quorum.)

Mr. SAWYER said that he did not think that any gentleman would object to his making a speech, as it would be a rich one.

Another motion to adjourn was then made, and, having been decided in the affirmative,

The House, at a very late hour, adjourned.

IN SENATE.

MONDAY, February 15.

The Mexican War—Mr. Webster's Resolutions.

Mr. WEBSTER rose and said that he proposed to lay upon the table two resolutions respecting the Mexican war. It was not his purpose to interfere, by any proposition of his own, with the bill now before the Senate, commonly called the three million bill, either by way of amendment to that bill or otherwise; but he wished, at the proper time, to have an opportunity of addressing the Senate in regard to the existing war, and to say something in favor of the two resolutions he now presented to the Senate. He would therefore offer the resolutions, and ask that they may be laid on the table, until he should call them up. He asked that the resolutions should be read. They were accordingly read by the Secretary as follows:

Resolved, That the war now existing with Mexico ought not to be prosecuted for the acquisition of territory to form new States to be added to the Union.

Resolved, That it ought to be signified to the Government of Mexico, that the Government of the United States does not desire to dismember the Republic of Mexico, and is ready to treat with the Government of that Republic for peace, for a liberal adjustment of boundaries, and for just indemnities due by either Government to the citizens of the other.

Mr. SEVIER expressed the hope that the honorable Senator would call up his resolutions for consideration within the present week.

Mr. WEBSTER. Certainly.

The resolutions were ordered to be printed.

Washington Monument.

On motion of Mr. MILLER, the previous orders were postponed, and the joint resolution for the selection of a suitable site for the erection of a monument to the memory of General George Washington, was taken up—ayes 19, noes 14.

The joint resolution was then considered as in Committee of the Whole.

Mr. MILLER expressed a hope that the joint resolution might be acted on promptly, as the managers wished to lay the corner stone on the 22d instant.

Mr. CALHOUN submitted to the Senator from New Jersey that it would be regarded as discourteous to the Senator from Missouri, who was not in his seat, to urge the passage of this joint resolution in his absence. That Senator, it would be recollected, had opposed this measure at the last session, and expressed his intention to produce some new facts when it should be again brought forward. As an act of courtesy to the Senator from Missouri, therefore, he moved to lay the joint resolution on the table for the present.

The motion was agreed to—ayes 17, noes 16.

War Steamers.

On motion of Mr. FAIRFIELD, the Senate proceeded to the consideration of the bill to build and equip four additional steamers for the use of the navy of the United States.

Mr. DAYTON requested some information as to the cost of these vessels, and by whom they had been asked for.

Mr. FAIRFIELD said the bill contained but a single provision, and required no elaborate explanation. It rested on the recommendation of the President in his annual Message, and on that of the Secretary of the Navy. Mr. F. here read extracts from the public documents. He had also received a letter from the Secretary of the Navy, and another from the Chief of the Bureau of Construction, Commodore Warrington; and on the authority of these recommendations, he had been instructed by the Committee on Naval Affairs to report the bill. The necessity of at least one vessel of this description, to be attached to each of our squadrons, must be obvious to every one. Their utility as a means of communication between different ports, for towing vessels in a calm, or when vessels were exposed to a lee shore, or for the transmission of information, was perfectly apparent. The war in which we were now engaged offered another reason. It was true, they might not be ready for service during the war, the termination of which was doubtful; but as a part of our peace establishment, such vessels were necessary. Whether they were to be built for propellers, or not, the bill did not say; it was a subject which the committee did not feel themselves competent to decide. Experiments were going on, the result of which would determine the character of these vessels. Considering the disposition always manifested to put our naval establishment on a proper footing, and the late period of the session, he hoped the bill would pass without delay.

Mr. DAVIS wished to know the expense of the vessels.

Mr. FAIRFIELD. The estimate was $500,000 each.

Mr. HUNTINGTON. Any time suggested when they will be finished?

Mr. FAIRFIELD. None. The materials are not yet determined on.

Mr. DAVIS. What amount does the bill appropriate?

Mr. FAIRFIELD. One million.

Mr. DAVIS said he had always felt inclined to vote for strengthening our navy. Even if we were in profound peace, and the state of our finances permitted, he would be in favor of these steamers, looking at the extent of our commerce, which finds its way over the whole face of the earth, entering into the markets of all the nations of the world. The use of steam, either for offensive operations or defensive purposes, was important. It had drawn the attention of all commercial nations, and most of the governments of Europe had availed themselves of it. We ought to keep pace with the times, to increase our steam navy, and take every means to obtain greater practical skill in the construction and armament of such vessels. All these considerations would justify this increase even in a state of profound peace. But in the last European journals he saw a new motive for this measure. He believed we had now no squadron, not a single ship in the Mediterranean; and the foreign papers announce that in London there was now an office opened for the sale of letters of marque. The names of three of these vessels were given. They were equipped there for the purpose of cruising against the commerce of the United States. If there was any valuable service in which steamers could be employed, it would be against such vessels striving to assail our commerce on the great highway of nations. They ought now to be ready.

He would not, at this time, go more largely into this subject. But he hoped the bill would be favorably considered, without reference to the war. The state of our finances, it was true, admonished us to be economical, and an appropriation of two millions was a large appropriation. But if they who had the responsibility said they wanted them, he was prepared to accede to their wishes.

Mr. NILES said his friend from Maine had acted very properly in bringing this bill before the Senate. But he (Mr. N.) did not understand this increase to be recommended for the purpose of carrying on war. These vessels were advocated on the ground of their convenience. Were we in a different state of things as to finances, and if the other expenses consequent on the war would admit, he might be disposed to favor this bill. But he was inclined to believe that the best way, unless these vessels were essentially necessary for the war, or for a time of peace, would be to adopt the course commenced last session, and encourage the increase of private steamers. In point of economy this was preferable, as they might be employed at half the expense of construction. There was now a steamer, the Washington, nearly ready, which would be, without question, the best steamship afloat. She had cost $300,000, little more than half which we are asked for, and better than any we have. These vessels would be efficient when needed for service. The Governments of Great Britain and France had adopted this principle, and would not have continued it, had it not been found advantageous. Their example was worthy our imitation. This bill, too, would involve an appropriation of two millions, in the midst of a war, and while we were drawing largely on our treasury. They were not assumed to be necessary for the war, and therefore we should pause before we authorize such a large outlay. The President had, in his Message, recommended that no appropriations should be made, but such as were absolutely necessary, and this was a proposition to enlarge our navy for a time of peace. We had gone on, ever since the commencement of the session, making large appropriations, amounting already to many millions, and we were now required to swell the list further. We were going on, he would not say recklessly, but improvidently, in appropriating thus largely while we had a war on hand, and a force of forty thousand men in the field. Every way we were met by expenses. Appropriations were made almost without limit. And what single thing had been done to sustain the country under these heavy expenditures? None in the world. Only a single proposition had been submitted, and that included not more than half the amount appropriated by this bill. It would be acting unwisely to authorize further expenses unless they are necessary for the war.

Mr. CALHOUN expressed his entire concurrence with these views. It was a great point to restrict our appropriations, and to incur no expenditure which could be avoided. If war was to go on, he knew not how we should get through. Yet from the appropriations, day after day, it might be supposed that our treasury was overflowing. He would postpone this appropriation until after the war. He was opposed to it at this time.

Mr. FAIRFIELD briefly replied, reiterating his former arguments.

The bill was then read a third time, and passed

TUESDAY, February 16.

Three Million Bill.

On motion of Mr. SEVIER, the Senate proceeded to the consideration of the special order, being the bill making an appropriation of three millions of dollars for the purpose of bringing the existing war with Mexico to a conclusion; with the amendments proposed by the Senator from Georgia and the Senator from Michigan.

Mr. BADGER said that the bill now under consideration proposed to make an appropriation for which, as he did not feel himself prepared to vote, he thought it was proper that he should assign to the Senate the reasons which would govern him in the course which he felt compelled to take upon the subject now before them; and as it seemed to be the generally prevailing practice for Senators in the debate upon this bill to give, as far as they deemed proper, an expression of their views in relation to the whole subject of the war, he would follow the example which had thus been set him, and, according to the phrase once fashionable but now somewhat fallen into disuse, define his position, in which he not only differed from those gentlemen who occupied the other side of the chamber, but in some respects from those upon his own side. There was, however, another subject which it seemed to him demanded a preliminary examination. He was fully aware of the responsibility which any member of that body assumed, who undertook at the present day either to vote or to speak against such measures as were pressed upon the consideration of Congress by the Executive Department of this Government; and he thought it would not be a waste of the time of the Senate to draw their attention to what had forced itself upon his mind, as being a systematic effort on the part of the Executive Government of the country to control the freedom of discussion and freedom of action in the Halls of Congress; freedom of discussion and freedom of action in the Legislatures of the several States of this Union; and still further to reach forward a proposal for arresting all freedom of speech, all discussion among the people of this country upon subjects relating to this war. He proposed to produce for the consideration of the Senate some evidence that, whether he was right or not in the conclusion to which he had come on this subject, it was, at all events, a conclusion founded upon strong probable evidence, and that it presented such an aspect of our affairs as should arrest the attention of the American people, and cause them to institute a strict and earnest inquiry, whether, while the forms of their Government continued to be the same as were handed down by our ancestors, there was not imminent danger that the spirit of those institutions should be entirely transmuted, and that we were no longer to stand before the civilized world as a people really and truly free, possessing here, and possessing everywhere, the right of speech, the right of discussion, the right of consideration in regard to the conduct of our rulers. He had said that the conviction had been forced upon his mind. It had been forced upon it, for it was such a conviction as no American would desire to have, because it presented one branch of that Government which claimed his warmest affections, in an attitude hostile to the best interests of the country, in a position of aggression upon the other departments of the Government, and in a position manifesting a desire to take from the people themselves the first fundamental, indubitable right which belonged to them, as the legitimate sovereigns of this country—the consideration of, and free expression of opinion in relation to the measures of those who, by their selection, had been appointed to conduct the affairs of the Government.

He had said that it appeared to him that this action, on the part of the Executive, was first directed towards the control of freedom of discussion and freedom of action in the halls of Congress. Was any proof necessary upon this subject? It appeared to him that the proof was evident to every Senator. Was there a measure introduced here—was there a discussion that took place here, or that took place in the other branch of Congress, upon a measure recommended to the two branches of Congress, or to either of them, on the part of the Executive of this country—that it was not at once made the subject, through the instrumentality of the Executive press of this city, not of inquiry, not of argument, not of discussion, but of instant and summary condemnation towards those who withheld from them their support? Had they not, during the whole of this session, observed that if, under the operation of the peculiar rules which existed in the other branch of the Legislature of this country, every measure that was desired by the Executive passed that body almost without discussion and without consideration, it was immediately held up as an example which we were told it would be wise for us to follow? It was not long ago that they were told that if a day or two days were spent in the discussion of any measure, however important it might be, it was instantly to be reported to the people of this country that Congress were not engaged in the discharge of their proper duties; were not engaged in the duties they owed to the people who sent them here; that they were not engaged, as they ought to be, in passing without debate, a measure proposed to them on the part of the Executive. Not a day—he thought he might say not a day—certainly very few days had passed during this session of Congress, in which one or both branches of the supreme Legislature of the United States had not been exposed to remarks and observations which, to say the least of them, were not very becoming to the source whence they proceeded, and were manifestly calculated (and he presumed therefore clearly designed) to produce upon this body, and upon the other House of Congress, a ready, prompt, unreasoning submission to every demand that was made upon them by the President.

Mr. B., after disposing of these preliminary matters, entered upon the subject of the existing war, and proceeded to demonstrate that the war was commenced by the Executive of the United States. He referred to the Message of the President, wherein was a recital of the act of May 13, 1846, in which it was declared that this war had been brought upon us by Mexico, and proceeded to observe, that notwithstanding this positive declaration, the President himself seemed not very clear on the subject, or else apprehended that those whom he was addressing were not altogether convinced that the proposition as declared was correct. If he had had no misgivings upon the subject, what would have been his course? Why, he would have stated distinctly, and in direct terms, once for all, that Mexico had made war upon us; but it was a remarkable fact, and one which struck him forcibly upon the reading of the Message, that there was scarcely a single portion of that Message in which the President alluded to the war, without adding that the war was commenced by Mexico. He did not mean to impute to the President that he meant to assert that which he believed to be false; but what he meant to say was, that if he were really and fully satisfied of the truth of the proposition, there was no necessity for so frequent a repetition of it. Such repetition could only spring, he thought, either from a desire to strengthen one's own convictions, or to remove the incredulity of others. Again: If the President were satisfied of the fact, to what purpose tended his long recital of the grievances and wrongs which Mexico had inflicted upon us? What had they to do with the subject? If Mexico commenced the war, on our part it could only be defensive, and any recitals of reasons which should induce us to go to war were altogether superfluous.

The present Executive would continue to be the head of the Government but for a short term, and beyond that he would have no more connection with the Government than any other citizen. When he did an act, therefore, by which the country was involved in war, by that act he involved others in a war of which he did not himself share any portion of the responsibility. It was the war of the nation. It was a war in which the people of the country were directly interested; and it was a war, therefore, on which we were not at liberty to turn our backs, and say, You have got us into a war, get out of it as you can. What was Congress to do when the gallant Taylor with his army was placed in a position of peril? What were we to do? Leave our gallant troops in a hostile country to be overpowered, cut in pieces, annihilated, by way of punishing the President of the United States for having brought them into such straits? We have been obliged to recognize the existence of the war, not because we did not understand the wrong which had been committed upon us by the exercise of usurped power on the part of the President, but we felt the wrong the deeper because, in consequence of its commission, we were placed in a position in which duty to our country obliged us to support the war.

But he had voted these supplies for the war. Why? Not because he thought the war was necessary; he thought it was unnecessary. Not because it was commenced by Mexico; he believed it was commenced by the President of the United States. But he had voted the supplies because the interests of his country were at stake in the actual condition of things; because the remedy of withholding the supplies, that *ultima ratio* which was never to be applied until all others failed in controlling the too great extension of executive power, might produce mischievous consequences; and therefore, with great respect to the Senator from Ohio, he must be permitted to say, that when the Senator thanked God he had not voted any supplies for this war, he had better reconsider the source of his thanks, and have voted the supplies which the necessities of the case required, for the benefit of the country, and for the preservation of our gallant little army in the perilous position in which they were placed, and who were entirely guiltless in the matter, and have united with us in a solemn declaration of the purposes for which the supplies were granted, and for the purposes for which we would not support the war.

It would then be time enough to consider, if the President should be so unwise as not to submit to the wishes of Congress. If he should go on upon his own authority in controlling the war in such manner as he pleased; if he did this, he for one, would be found side by side with the Senator from Ohio. Not because he would do it willingly. God knows he would do it very unwillingly; but, from the necessity of the case, he would unite with the Senator from Ohio in refusing the supplies; and he would put it to the country, and to the civilized world, to decide whether the disastrous consequences which must follow from such an unsupported war, ought not to be attributed to the obstinate and arbitrary conduct of the Executive, and not to any factious spirit on the part of Congress. These were his general views in regard to the character of the war. These were the reasons upon which he had supported the war; these were the reasons on which he would continue to vote the necessary supplies for carrying on the war, until that state of things arrived to which he had adverted, when it would be seen whether the President would obstinately persist in prosecuting the war, from mistaken views of benefit to the country, or from views of personal ambition; and then he should stand ready to record his vote against surrendering the authority of the representatives of the people of the United States to direct the purposes and objects of a war sanctioned by them in the exercise of a power which the people of the United States had confided to us, and not to the President.

Mr. B. next adverted to the change which had come over this war in the course of the year which had elapsed since its commencement. It was now plainly and clearly a war of conquest, although the President in his Message informed them that the war was not commenced for the purpose of conquest; that it was not intended to be a war of conquest. He did not intend to impeach the sincerity of the President in making this declaration, but according to every notion which he had on the subject, it was clearly and unquestionably a war of conquest. What did the President say? He told them that he was going to prosecute the war until he had obtained an ample indemnity, not only for the claims of our citizens against Mexico for spoliations, but also for the expenses of the war. Now, in what attitude did this present itself? He supposed it would not be considered extravagant to assume that the expenses of the war up to this time would amount to fifty millions; and if the war were continued for another year, they would amount to one hundred millions. But suppose fifty millions to be the amount for which we were to be indemnified. Mexico had a few years ago shown herself either unable or unwilling to pay a very few millions of dollars by way of indemnity to our citizens. There was every reason to believe that she resorted to forced loans and contributions for the purpose of paying them, without succeeding in discharging the amount. How, then, was it to be expected that she could pay fifty millions of dollars for the expenses of this war? But the President was going to say to Mexico, You must either pay me the money or deliver a part of your territory; I must have satisfaction in money or in land. Was it not evident, then, that the plan of the Administration, that the end and object of the war, was conquest? He had shown, he thought conclusively, that the war had been commenced by the President, and afterwards sanctioned by Congress. Here, then, was a war, commenced by us, in which we have expended fifty millions of dollars; and we say to Mexico, We will now settle this dispute, if you will pay us in land for the expenses we have incurred in prosecuting a war which we have ourselves commenced.

Mr. B., in the course of his remarks, quoted from a Message of Mr. Jefferson, in 1805, to show how he understood the power to declare war to be in the Congress alone. Territory which we had acquired, and which was in our possession, was threatened with invasion; but Mr. Jefferson submitted the matter to Congress.

Mr. CHALMERS moved an adjournment; but gave way to—

Mr. PEARCE, who said that he rose only for the purpose of strengthening a point made by the Senator from North Carolina, (Mr. BADGER,) which had been controverted by the Senator from Arkansas, (Mr. SEVIER.) The Senator from North Carolina had assumed, that if the United States had a clear and indisputable title to a territory which was in the actual occupancy and possession of a *foreign* power, the taking military possession of such territory by the United States would be an act of war. In the case supposed, it would be a rightful act of war, but being such, the authority first must be referred to the legislative and war-making power; that is to say, to Congress; and he quoted, in support of this position, the Message of Mr. Jefferson, in December, 1805, in relation to the posts and territory held by Spain within the limits of Louisiana, in which Jefferson said that Congress alone being constitutionally invested with the power of changing our condition from peace to war, he thought it his duty to await their authority for using force in any degree which could be avoided. The Senator from Arkansas here interrupted the Senator from North Carolina, and denying this proposition, undertook to oppose the authority of Mr. Madison to that of Mr. Jefferson. He referred to the course of Mr. Madison in relation to the occupation of what were then called, and still are frequently, the Florida parishes of Louisiana. I sent for the authority which I am about to submit to the Senate, but did not receive it till the Senator had passed to another point in his argument; and I did not think it proper then to interrupt him. Sir, the Senator from Arkansas is mistaken; Mr. Madison held no doctrine at variance with that of Mr. Jefferson. He did not assume that the Executive, of his sole authority, could take military possession of territory, even rightfully belonging to the United States, if in the actual occupancy of a foreign power. He, equally with Mr. Jefferson, recognized the constitutional power of Congress, and invoked their authority before taking possession of that part of Louisiana of which Spain then held the occupancy. It is true that the Spanish authorities at Baton Rouge were dispossessed by a body of armed indivduals, in the summer of 1810, who declared their independence, and established a government of their own; and that Mr. Madison, by his proclamation of October 16, 1810, took possession of this country in the name of the United States. But this proclamation recited that the territory in question "had always been claimed as being within the territory of Louisiana;" "that a crisis had at length arrived subversive of the order of things under the Spanish authority;" and "that, under the peculiar and imperative circumstances, forbearance on the part of the United States to occupy the territory in question, and thereby guard against the confusions and contingencies which threaten it, might be construed into a *dereliction* of their title," &c.; and "finally, that the acts of Congress, though contemplating a present possession by a foreign authority, have contemplated also an eventual possession of the said territory, and are accordingly so framed as in that to extend their operation to the same."

Now, sir, this instance does not amount to a contradiction of Mr. Jefferson's authority, and the position of the Senator from North Carolina, for the Spanish authority was at an end in this territory; it could not be said to be in the occupancy of a foreign power. And Mr. Madison so well knew this distinction, that General Claiborne was especially instructed not to take possession of any post in which the Spaniards had a garrison; accordingly no attempt was made to take possession of Mobile, or any part of the territory around it. Mr. Madison's proclamation was communicated to

Congress in December, 1810; and on the 15th of January, 1811, a secret resolution, not made public till years afterwards, was passed by Congress and approved by the President, the preamble of which referred to the peculiar situation of Spain and her American provinces, and the body of which declared that a due regard to the safety of the United States compelled them "to provide, under certain contingencies, for the temporary occupation of the said territory," &c.

In January, 1813, the President sent to Congress a confidential communication, which led to the passage of the secret act of February 12, 1813, which authorized the President "to occupy and hold all that tract of country called West Florida, which lies west of the river Perdido, not now in the possession of the United States;" and it also authorized the President to employ the military and naval force of the United States in maintaining the authority of the United States in such territory. Under the sanction of this act, the President sent orders to General Wilkinson, who drove the Spaniards out of Fort Charlotte, established a fortification at Mobile Point, and occupied the country west of the Perdido in the name of the United States.

Mr. SEVIER then briefly noticed some historical circumstances in connection with the act of General Thomas, which had been referred to by Mr. PEARCE, to show that Congress had afterwards sanctioned and approved his conduct, by making him a donation of sections of land.

While he was up, he would take occasion to say, that the removal of our army from Corpus Christi to the Rio Grande was known to Congress; for the Secretary of War had given all necessary information on that subject in his report which accompanied the President's annual Message; and gentlemen could have read the documents with but little attention, who complained that no notification had been given of that movement. It was made known to Congress sufficiently early for steps to have been taken to prevent it, if prevention were deemed necessary.

Mr. CHALMERS then obtained the floor, as was afterwards understood for Mr. COLQUITT, who was absent, and the Senate went into Executive session. After a short time spent therein,

The Senate adjourned.

WEDNESDAY, February 17.

Three Million Bill.

The Senate proceeded to the consideration of the special order, being the bill making an appropriation of three millions of dollars for the purpose of bringing the existing war with Mexico to a conclusion, with the amendments proposed by the Senator from Georgia and the Senator from Michigan.

Mr. COLQUITT, of Georgia, then rose and addressed the Senate as follows:

I will now make some remarks upon the war itself, the fruitful theme for abuse of the Administration. It has been said, and has been reiterated again and again, that the President made this war. The question is, how did he make it? How do you establish the charge? It should be remembered, that if this charge fails—if the proof does not establish it, our Whig friends will have no excuse for their course upon the subject of the war, and must expect the stern rebuke of an insulted and indignant people. How did the President make this war? It is positively certain that he sought very earnestly to make a treaty with Mexico! After the Mexican Minister had left the country, breathing hostility against the United States; after our Minister had been dismissed from his official station by the authorities of Mexico, the President still sought negotiation. This did not exhibit any anxiety for war with that republic. After the threatening tone and attitude of Mexico made it necessary for our vessels of war to hang upon her coast, and be ready for the exigency that was threatened, they were withdrawn by the suggestion of Mexico, that their contiguity was a barrier to any overtures of peace. This, surely, indicated no hostile wish on the part of the President to have a war with Mexico. If he sought only a pretext for hostility, he had enough to justify him in the eyes of the civilized world. He still sued for peace, and by means which would have been humiliating, if we had been in contest with a mightier power; he flattered himself that success would attend the effort. According to agreement, he sent a Minister, with full powers to make a permanent treaty. This certainly bears no mark of a desire upon the part of the President to rush into a war. Herrera, the then President of Mexico, soon heard the murmurings of discontent, and saw the undoubted signs of a revolution, in consequence of his consent to make a treaty of boundary. He endeavored to prolong the existence of his rickety Government, by refusing our Minister, and excusing himself for the refusal by denying the agreement. He agreed to receive a commissioner only, and not a Minister, he said. I do not propose to examine this quibble, although politicians here agreed with Mexico and blamed the President. The revolution in Mexico was not consummated because Herrera agreed to receive a Minister; but because he was friendly to a treaty of boundary. If the quibble to which he resorted had been the cause of complaint, the resolution would have been arrested when he rejected our Minister. Having shown a disposition to treat upon the subject of boundary, the army would not trust him in power. They placed at the head of the Government the master-spirit of the revolution, Paredes, who put the army in motion by his hostility to the United States, and his opposition to any treaty with us upon the subject of boundary. I suppose that the most bitter enemy of the President will not deny but he did all that could be done to make a treaty of peace. He failed. All this I am told is true; but that the war was made by the President, by ordering the army from Corpus Christi to the Rio Grande! If he had suffered the army to remain at Corpus Christi, say they, we should have had no war. This is a supposition, unsupported by a solitary fact; it is a mere conjecture, contradicted by every act and every declaration upon the part of Mexico. Why do you say that we should have had no war, if the army had remained at Corpus Christi? Your only reply must be, that such is your opinion—you think so! You may have high character for wisdom and sagacity, but I prefer to have some data upon which I may examine the correctness of that opinion. That such is your opinion, and so you think, that may be answer sufficient for yourself; but I very much doubt whether your naked assertion, unsupported by a single well-founded reason, and contradicted by repeated acts and declarations upon the part of Mexico, will be considered conclusive by the thinking public. At any rate, I must be excused for my incredulity and unbelief. When the resolutions favorable to the admission of Texas into the Union passed the Congress of the United States, the Mexican Minister demanded his passports, and declared that act a cause of war. During the campaign of 1844, almost every Whig press and Whig orator in the Union opposed the annexation of Texas, assigning, as a prominent reason, the injustice of the act, and that it necessarily involved us in a war with Mexico. I stop but a moment to inquire of gentlemen upon the other side of the chamber how they hope to reconcile the people of this country to their own glaring inconsistency? They made an issue before the people in the Presidential canvass, and received the support of no small number of voters, by proclaiming the act of annexation as a just and certain cause of war. You now throw yourselves before the same people, and tell them, Oh, no; that was no cause of war. Annexation did not produce it; but the war has been made by the President! Will not the people ask an explanation of this inconsistency? Will you not have to acknowledge that your predictions were insincere in 1844, or that your declarations now are unfounded? This clamor about a war with Mexico, and the injustice of annexing Texas to the Union, did not cease with the election. I will call your attention to an extract or two from the New York Tribune, which will more definitely exhibit the position of the Whig party, even after the election of President.

[The honorable gentleman here read several extracts from the New York "Tribune," containing denunciations of the Democratic party on account of annexation.]

With such declarations as these, made prior to the election of President from one end of the Union to the other, how can you now change your position, and charge the war upon the President, because he ordered the army to the Rio Grande? But, sir, not only did the Mexican Minister return home, our Minister there dismissed, and a revolution favorable to Paredes, all showing that Mexico intended war, but I desire to submit two or three circulars, which issued from the War Department in Mexico, that there may be no mistake, no doubt about how and by whom the war was commenced.

[Here the honorable Senator submitted the well-known official declaration of the Mexican Government, denouncing annexation as an act of war, and directing the generals in command of the army to collect troops.]

Here is the declaration of war! Here are the circulars calling for soldiers to prosecute the war! This was all done some twelve months before our army left Corpus Christi. Will gentlemen still insist that the removal of the army was the cause of the war? In obedience to these orders from the Department of War in Mexico, troops were collected, and an invading army, with orders to retake Texas, of which she insisted she had been perfidiously despoiled. This army had its headquarters at Matamoras, waiting more troops and additional preparation. Thus, with war declared, an army collected, all chance for negotiation closed, we are still gravely assured that nothing but the removal of the army caused the war! I am willing that this assertion—no matter by whom made, wholly unsupported by facts, and contradicted by so many circumstances—shall go before the world for what it is worth.

Again: it is urged that the President ought not to have ordered the army on disputed ground. The President might have been very delicately situated, in deciding what was disputed ground. The Mexicans claimed all Texas; and by her the whole ground was disputed, until our army crossed the Sabine. I suppose gentlemen do not mean to insist that it was the duty of the President to abandon Texas, in order to place the army on undisputed territory. At what point do you say the ground was undisputed? Congress has fixed no boundary. The best informed statesmen here may complain, but they cannot define what they themselves call undisputed ground. How was the President to ascertain this boundary? Texas claimed to the Rio Grande. She had never claimed any other boundary. No other was established by either Mexico or Texas. No other boundary was known to the United States or to the world. What was the President to do? By his official oath, he was bound to protect Texas. He had no power to define limits, unless Mexico had entered into treaty, which she refused. I leave this question for those wise statesmen to solve, who could not be satisfied with any act which the President could do. If the ground between the Nueces and the Rio Grande is what gentlemen call disputed ground, and if that were truly the case, I would say that, after every effort to settle the dispute, and every overture of peace had been rejected by Mexico, it was the duty of the President to take possession of the disputed ground; and if it had to be settled by war, let that be the place of settlement.

Much has been said as to the manner in which the war has been conducted, and what should be the course of future operations. The complaints made against the President I could take up, and I think, successfully defend. He has from the first shown great anxiety to prosecute with vigor the war. I doubt not that he has used all the means placed at his disposal as judiciously as the time and circumstances would permit. Many of us are wiser after the happening of events than before they transpired, and not a few delight in showing our wisdom by criticizing actions after their performance, which we could not very well have directed before. It is, however, soothing to our vanity to wind up our criticisms by insisting that it was all plain to our sagacious intellects before. The army has not advanced so rapidly as the President had wished, and a controversy has sprung up as to who is to blame. I think if the American people were polled, and they would all answer truly, that four-fifths of them would say that they believed there would have been no more fighting after the battles of the 8th and 9th of May. Taking into calculation the impoverished and distracted condition of Mexico, the supposition was reasonable. General Taylor thought so, or he would not have complained at the number of soldiers sent to his assistance. The army moved slowly, and I doubt not that the commander confidently expected propositions for peace. He did not desire to shed any more blood than was absolutely necessary to secure an honorable peace. This same expectation prevailed when the army was marched to Monterey. No battle was expected; and the best excuse offered for the capitulation was the belief that even then the Governments might be making terms of peace.

I am in favor of adopting the most effectual course for obtaining peace, and securing the rights of the country. The plan suggested by the Senator from South Carolina (Mr. CALHOUN) it seems to me is the most certain and practicable; and I shall not repeat it. His arguments are strong, if not conclusive. We prosecute the war to procure a peace. It seems to me that a common interest will unite the people of Mexico, as your army advances. If you pause on some safe and convenient line, her dissensions will be more likely to operate in favor of a treaty, than continual invasion. If no treaty shall be made for five years, the additional expense over the ordinary expenses of the Government would not exceed five millions annually in maintaining a sufficient force to maintain our position. At the end of that time there would not be a Mexican on this side the designated line, but such as preferred to be a citizen of our Government. Within the country there would be, by that time, citizens enough to protect themselves without an army. I have full confidence that we can, with our arms, pass through every part of Mexico; but I doubt whether the country would be subdued, and a permanent peace secured. Whatever course may be supposed most efficient, that course will have my hearty co-operation. I shall vote for the bill placing the three millions of dollars at the disposal of the President. If he can use it for the benefit of the country, very well; if not, it will not be lost to the treasury. I regret the amendment proposed by my colleague, and shall vote against it. It appears to me to be nothing but a little display of party tactics, which will defeat the end it is proposed to serve. We are in a war; and can any one point out the propriety of informing Mexico and the world, that when the war is ended we intend to surrender all the advantages which have resulted from the conflict? Will it alarm Mexico and make her sue for peace? Will she be less disposed to continue the struggle when we inform her in advance that she shall lose nothing by its continuance?

I will not suffer myself to believe that we shall ever want men or money to prosecute successfully this war. Without money and without clothes, the sons of revolutionary fathers will march at the bidding of their country, to battle for her honor and defend her rights. Nor will I shrink back at the frightful spectre of fanaticism, nor yield a right, to escape its foulest machinations. No, sir; the God that guided and shielded the country in its fearful struggle for independence, is still our God. Many a paltry, time-serving politician, who estimates his selfish purposes higher than the constitution of his country, will be dead, and many others will be driven from the councils of the nation, shrouded with that black and bloody mantle with which they threatened to obscure the bright prospects of their country. I shall oppose every proposition by which the progress of the war may be checked by unnecessary or mischievous anticipation.

But I must say to those gentlemen who flatter themselves that now or hereafter the South will suffer herself to be degraded to preserve friendly relations with the North, that they make a sad miscalculation. I know the South, and the feelings of her generous people. They will lay no burdens upon other sections of the Union. They will require no sacrifices—make no exactions. They love the Union, and will labor to preserve it, so long as it can be preserved consistently with honor. But with all their devotion to the Union, there is not a man, woman, or child among them, but would sooner see the bright, sunny South, riven by an earthquake from the continent, and floating like an iceberg upon the ocean, than see her sons submit to outrage and degradation.

This fair land of ours should be the peaceful patrimony of a band of brothers. The South earnestly and honestly desires to preserve and strengthen the golden chain that binds us together; and when its links shall be severed by the ruthless folly of fanaticism, the blow will not be given by a Southern arm, while she will receive its infliction with unflinching firmness and unfeigned regret.

THURSDAY, February 18.

Three Million Bill.

The Senate, as in Committee of the Whole, resumed the consideration of the bill making an appropriation of three millions of dollars, for the purpose of bringing the war with Mexico to a conclusion.

Mr. BUTLER, of South Carolina, said: We are in a war; and now to examine into its origin is unwise, impolitic, and I cannot see any good that is to be attained by it. I am not disposed to go beyond its declaration, for declaration it is. This Government, in the most solemn manner, put at the disposal of the President ten millions of dollars and fifty thousand troops. They put the sword in his hand, and demanded him to use it. After this, what are we to do? That brings up the plain and practical question which seems to be involved in the bill on your table. What does that bill propose? I intend to speak directly to that before I pass to the other topics of greater importance, though, perhaps, not ultimately affecting the decision of the question. What, then, is it? It is a measure purporting to be for the purpose of obtaining a speedy, honorable, and, I hope, a safe peace. Well, so I regard the subject in one aspect. Looking at it only as it concerns our relations with a hostile Government, I would have very little difficulty on the subject. It is only in the other aspect, as it respects its bearing on our own domestic institutions, that it really becomes most formidable. But if this be a measure for peace, to take the alternative presented by my honorable friend from Maryland, (Mr. JOHNSON,) I would much prefer to "buy"—if you choose to use the word—an honorable peace, made voluntarily by the people of Mexico, rather than have any peace extorted from them at the duress of the cannon or the point of the bayonet. I do not know that it would be a subject of reproach, but it would be an event very much to be deplored if our army were to penetrate into the heart of Mexico, and there undertake to dictate terms to the people, by making them pass under the yoke. It would be unfortunate, so far as regards the peace itself. You might have hands to sign it. You might find those who under the dictation of your armies, would, perhaps, put their hands to the paper. But what people on earth, pretending to be identified with their soil—who had mingled the sweat of their brow with the very soil on which they lived—could keep such a peace with any other than Punic hearts? It would be no peace. It would be a peace only so long as the people could not break it with impunity. I am far, therefore, from desiring such a result.

And another thing I would say on this occasion: let the young adventurers of this nation—active, restless, and enterprising as they are—once look upon the fair fields of Mexico, and it will be as vain to attempt to restrain them as to restrain the young eagles from returning to the carnage of willing and submissive victims. If you ever dictate such a peace as that, with arms in your hands, within the palaces of Mexico, you are sowing the seeds of eternal strife between the two republics. It is impossible, sir, to relieve a people compelled to submit to such a peace from the abiding mortification, from which they would be continually attempting to relieve themselves. I desire no such result. I have always regarded patriotism as being somehow mystically associated with the love of soil, as well as the institutions of a people. I have always regarded that as one of the most beautiful passages in history, in which Bernadotte, whilst he felt it his duty as a sovereign to oppose Napoleon, and for that purpose exerted all his powers in conjunction with others, yet when they approached the frontiers of France, he paused and refused to invade his native soil! You cannot separate that feeling from any people. I would not wish, sir, to see any people on earth divested of that feeling. Least of all should I desire to see any act of a republic like ours tending to eradicate from the hearts of any people such a sacred national sentiment. In this point of view, therefore, I should regard it as a great misfortune, if it should become necessary to carry on our offensive operations so far that we could, by humiliation—by mere terror of our arms—force and extort from Mexico such a peace as the hearts of her people could not willingly observe.

But there is the other alternative, and I take that of my honorable friend from Maryland. Suppose a peace were presented to Mexico directly, in such terms as these: "We are engaged in war. You owe our citizens money. They have just claims against you. Thus far you have been unable to pay them. Having appealed to the arbitrament of the sword, we insist upon their adjustment." Mexico replies that she has no resources; that exhausted by this protracted war, she is unable to respond to the demand. "Very well!" we might reply; "if you cannot do that, we have this simple proposition to make: We will not only assume the debts due to our own citizens, but more than that, we are willing to give, in advance, three millions of dollars, in consideration that you will cede such territory as you can honestly and fairly—in looking at your own policy—spare, without interfering with the integrity of your country." Now, sir, it is a difficult proposition. We are speaking of this all on one side. We do not know that Mexico is going to consider it; but I am very much inclined to think, that if this money had been placed at the disposal of the President last session, we would have done more than all our armies have effected. Not by bribery. I do not mean that it should have been used for the prostituting purpose of corrupting generals and magistrates; but simply to tell a necessitous people: "You are exhausted. You have not money to pay your troops. But here, in consideration of some territory that you might spare, we are willing to advance to you three millions of dollars, and assume all the responsibility you owe our citizens in the adjustment of their claims." I believe, sir, that if you had said that, it would have had more effect than all the war measures that you have adopted, and I for one would have much preferred it. A spontaneous peace, coming from a people, made with their own consent, and without coercion, is not only more becoming as regards our national policy; but, in my opinion, would be founded in wisdom, and would be much more permanent than any other.

I know other suggestions have been made; other counsels may be followed: but I am inclined to believe that they are dangerous, and that the consequences will be found to be fatal only when it is too late to avert them. Yes, I am inclined to think that every day this war is protracted, its mischiefs will increase. If the peace had been concluded only a few months after the brilliant battles on the Rio Grande, on the 8th and 9th of May, it might have been well for us. And, indeed, it was supposed that when this Government placed at the disposal of the President ten millions of dollars and fifty thousand men—not a doubt was entertained in my part of the country, at least—that we would have a speedy and an honorable peace. We have been mistaken. We will be still more mistaken if we suppose we can conquer a peace by subjugating a people, by invading their soil, and taking their cities! As far, therefore, as that is concerned, I would be very much averse to it. I would be willing to make this experiment, and I hope it will be conceded. But I will be asked, "What territory do you want?" But for the mischievous suggestions which have come up in some of your resolutions there—I say it with all sincerity, and from the bottom of my heart, before God—I would have been much better satisfied if the territory had fallen on the northern side of the line of 36° 30′. I say this much, sir, with no purpose or desire to agitate that question; but when I am told—and in the resolutions of New York told—in the most imposing language, that this war is waged and must be prosecuted with a view to the acquisition of territory, not only to and beyond the degree I have mentioned, but *any* territory; and that, when acquired, the people whom I represent are to participate in none of the fruits of conquest—none of the fruits of victory—that all the fruits are to be like the apple of discord; why, do you suppose that we can submit to any such arrangement as that? Do you suppose that, having excited us, under the institutions of this republic, to a belief that we are equal, and that our posterity will be equal in all respects, we are told, sir, in the most insulting manner, that we are to be degraded in a political and social point of view? I say it, and I say it here, so far as it regards all the objects of life—position, empire, wealth, every thing—all would be nothing to me, if I found that I had lived with those who would regard me as an inferior in any point of view. I ask for existence for no other purpose but the enjoyment of this proud feeling of equality. Having excited it, having been taught to prize it, is it to be supposed that I am to forfeit it in this way?

Well, that is what is proposed. So far as regards this peace, if we are to have any territory at all—and it presents this singular and very imposing predicament, we go to war, putting at their disposal fifty or a hundred millions of dollars, which are expended at last under the authority of this Government. The bones of our soldiers are bleaching upon the fields of Mexico, or entombed in her soil. Thousands perish in this war. Peace is declared, and there is no indemnity or compensation. No; the only remuneration you will have will be soldiers coming upon their crutches, asking you for pensions for the balance of their lives; and yet I would rather expend all that money, and incur all these hazards, and subject myself to all these calamities, than I would see the fraternity formed under the union of this Federal constitution broken up. I have associations with the old thirteen States. I have seen and rejoiced in the blessings of our Union. I am admonished on all hands that that Union ought to be preserved. I would give every thing to preserve it, except liberty itself. But if we are to have territory, I see no other mode of preserving this Union than by giving up every thing. When I see the accumulation of resolutions here, making the current of public opinion stronger and deeper every day, I have very little confidence in any compromise by which the calamity may be sought to be averted. You cannot avert it by compromise. It is beyond you. It will come upon you; and I hope, when it does come, the Union will be found stronger than those who are willing, with their criminal casuistry, to sport with it under party banners. I think it will prove stronger. In my opinion, it is getting stronger every day, so far as regards the original States. And why? Your intercourse is more frequent—more profitable—better regulated—not only intercourse with those adjacent to each other, but what is distance now? What is the distance between Charleston and New York, between Detroit, and any part of the West, and New Orleans? Why, it ceases almost by the improvement of these modern days; and while we are rebuked every day by the inducements to continue in this Union, it is one of the objects, which it seems to me, political—if I should not use exact terms, I hope I shall be excused—political aspirants, with criminal indifference to the consequences, are sporting with every movement. When you look to the future, can you not behold the time when the grandchildren of those now living in Massachusetts, with an enterprise characteristic of all the Northern States, will be found at the South, and as you think of such a painful issue as the shedding of kindred blood in a contest of this kind, are you not forcibly admonished of the duty to consult the spirit of compromise in which this constitution originated, and which pervades that instrument throughout? If we could all but worship on the altar of justice and good faith, erected by our ancestors, I would trust every one of the questions which have been brought up here to New York, Pennsylvania, or Massachusetts.

We must deal with this subject as we find it; and I am very much afraid that the treaty —if there be a treaty made—will include some of the territory in such a manner as will bring up this question unavoidably. It would be odious, sir, to reduce it to 36° 30′, merely to announce a proposition. I would contend for the ninth part of a hair, if for nothing else but to assert my rights. I am one of those that proclaim that I would rather not have any territory at all—I would quit this war, with all its calamities and losses—rather than incur the dreadful consequences predicted, so far as regards our institutions hereafter. We cannot look to peace, without seeing dangers far more appalling than the war itself. I do not want any of the territory. I am free to say, *per se* —if I may be permitted to use the phrase—I do not want any territory. We have enough for our population—more, perhaps, than we can fill up in the next century. But there is one feature in this case which must be considered, in relation to other countries, and especially the great maritime nations of the earth. I do not want any territory as room for our population. But if Mexico would consent—and I would much rather have it by her consent—to dispose of some territory on the Pacific, by which we might have some incidental advantage for our navy on that ocean—for in that respect it is the great highway of nations, and ours should have as many advantages as any other nation.—I say, if we could get the port spoken of, (San Francisco,) with such territory as might be along with it, I would rejoice, and rejoice that it fell on the other side of the line, because it would have shown a reference, *bona fide*, to our own policy in relation to the nations of the earth, that might be really attributed to it. But when you come, sir, and undertake to acquire more territory, and define it in such a way as to bring up this question, I cannot accord to any recognition of these odious distinctions. I can indicate no path. I know not but the plan indicated by my honorable colleague, so far as it regards the mode of carrying on the war, is very good. But so far as regards the ultimate acquisition of territory, I have my doubts. I would leave that to a treaty, and if made, *bona fide*, in the exercise of the judgment of this responsible body, for the purpose of making a treaty in good faith for the whole nation, without reference to sectional benefits, I would rejoice at it. I have no objections to it thus far; but I am afraid that we will thus subject one which cannot be avoided.

But you ask what will I do? I am willing to give this money, but not with any of the qualifications or amendments offered here. I am willing to give it with a fair understanding, that it will be used for the purpose of terminating this war. There must be judgment exercised in this matter. We must trust it to somebody. The President is the responsible person, who must necessarily commence and carry on this negotiation. I am not going to say whether he is fit or unfit; I have no right to say so. I have always entertained habitual respect for those who fill the highest offices of Government, and will not be guilty of the indecorum of giving any opinion of my own. I am indebted to the President for many of his measures. The South is indebted to him. The constancy, intrepidity, and firmness, which the President displayed at the last session of Congress, during the discussion of the great measure of free trade, have laid the South under a lasting debt of gratitude to him. I have none of the feelings in relation to political influences, which may be brought to bear upon this subject, that I have seen manifested on this floor. Mr. President, we are certainly in a difficult position. If we quit the war, it will be apparently with dishonor. If we go on it must end in mischief. The truth is, we are like the shepherd who has got the wolf by the ears! It is hazardous to let go—it is worse to hold on. [A laugh.] What to do I can scarcely tell; I can do no more than offer my suggestions; I shall take refuge in the wisdom, the moderation, the firmness of Senators upon this floor—and I hope to hear them all—when I come to give my final vote; and I appeal to them. I have no vanity; and so far as regards party feeling, none at all. I have no aspirations. I shall not profit by the triumphs of any one party in the United States. I have no higher ambition than with fidelity to represent in part the State of South Carolina.

FRIDAY, February 19.

Mr. Calhoun's Slavery Resolutions.

Mr. CALHOUN rose and said: Mr. President, I rise to offer a set of resolutions in reference to the various resolutions from the State Legislatures upon the subject of what they call the extension of slavery, and the proviso attached to the House bill, called the three million bill. What I propose before I send my resolutions to the table, is to make a few explanatory remarks.

Mr. President, it was solemnly asserted on this floor, some time ago, that all parties in the non-slaveholding States had come to a fixed and solemn determination upon two propositions. One was, that there should be no further admission of any States into this Union which permitted by their constitution the existence of slavery; and the other was, that slavery shall not hereafter exist in any of the Territories of the United States; the effect of which would be to give to the non-slaveholding States the monopoly of the public domain, to the entire exclusion of the slaveholding States. Since that declaration was made, Mr. President, we have abundant proof that there was a satisfactory foundation for it. We have received already solemn resolutions passed by seven of the non-slaveholding States—one-half of the number already in the Union, Iowa not being counted—using the strongest possible language to that effect; and no doubt in a short space of time similar resolutions will be received from all of the non-slaveholding States. But we need not go beyond the walls of Congress. The subject has been agitated in the other House, and they have sent you up a bill "prohibiting the extension of slavery" (using their own language) "to any territory which may be acquired by the United States hereafter." At the same time, two resolutions which have been moved to extend the compromise line from the Rocky Mountains to the Pacific, during the present session, have been rejected by a decided majority.

Sir, there is no mistaking the signs of the times; and it is high time that the Southern States, the slaveholding States, should inquire what is now their relative strength in this Union, and what it will be if this determination should be carried into effect hereafter. Sir, already we are in a minority—I use the word "we," for brevity sake —already we are in a minority in the other House, in the electoral college, and, I may say, in every department of this Government, except at present in the Senate of the United States: here, for the present, we have an equality. Of the twenty-eight States, fourteen are non-slaveholding and fourteen are slaveholding, counting Delaware, which is doubtful, as one of the non-slaveholding States. But this equality of strength exists only in the Senate. One of the clerks, at my request, has furnished me with a statement of what is the relative strength of the two descriptions of States, in the other House of Congress, and in the electoral college. There are two hundred and twenty-eight representatives, including Iowa, which is already represented there. Of these, one hundred and thirty-eight are from the non-slaveholding States, and ninety from what are called the slave States, giving a majority in the aggregate to the former of forty-eight. In the electoral college there are one hundred and sixty-eight votes belonging to the non-slaveholding States, and one hundred and eighteen to the slaveholding, giving a majority of fifty to the non-slaveholding.

We, Mr. President, have at present only one position in the Government, by which we may make any resistance to this aggressive policy which has been declared against the South, or any other that the non-slaveholding States may choose to take. And this equality in this body is of the most transient character. Already Iowa is a State; but, owing to some domestic difficulties, is not yet represented in this body. When she appears here, there will be an addition of two Senators to the representatives here of the non-slaveholding States. Already Wisconsin has passed the initiatory stage, and will be here at next session. This will add two more, making a clear majority of four in this body on the side of the non-slaveholding States, who will thus be enabled to sway every branch of this Government at their will and pleasure. But, sir, if this aggressive policy be followed—if the determination of the non-slaveholding States is to be adhered to hereafter, and we are to be entirely excluded from the territories which we already possess, or may possess—if this is to be the fixed policy of the Government, I ask, what will be our situation hereafter?

Sir, there is ample space for twelve or fifteen of the largest description of States in the Territories belonging to the United States. Already a law is in course of passage through the other House creating one north of Wisconsin. There is ample room for another north of Iowa; and another north of that; and then that large region extending on this side of the Rocky Mountains, from 49 degrees down to the Texan line, which may be set down fairly as an area of twelve and a half degrees of latitude—that extended region of itself is susceptible of having six, seven, or eight large States. To this, add Oregon, which extends from 49 to 42 degrees, which will give four more; and I make a very moderate calculation when I say that, in addition to Iowa and Wisconsin, twelve more States upon the territory already ours—without reference to any acquisitions from Mexico—may be, and will be, shortly added to these United States. How will we then stand? There will be but fourteen on the part of the South—we are to be fixed, limited, and forever—and twenty-eight on the part of the non-slaveholding States! Twenty-eight! Double our number! And with the same disproportion in the other House and in the electoral college! The Government, sir, will be entirely in the hands of the non-slaveholding States—overwhelmingly.

Sir, if this state of things is to go on; if this determination, so solemnly made, is to be persisted in—where shall we stand, as far as this Federal Government of ours is concerned?

We shall be at the entire mercy of the non-slaveholding States. Can we look to their justice and regard for our interests? Now, I ask, can we rely on that? Ought we to trust our safety and prosperity to their mercy and sense of justice? These are the solemn questions which I put to this and the other side of the chamber.

Sir, can we find any hope by looking to the past? If we are to look to that—I will not go into the details—we will see from the beginning of this Government to the present day, as far as pecuniary resources are concerned—as far as the disbursement of revenue is involved, it will be found that we have been a portion of the community which has substantially supported this Government, without receiving any thing like a remuneration from it. But why look to the past—why should I go beyond this very measure itself? Why go beyond this determination on the part of the non-slaveholding States, that there shall be no further addition to the slaveholding States, to prove what our condition will be?

Sir, what is the entire amount of this policy? I will not say that it is so designed. I will not say from what cause it originated. I will not say whether blind fanaticism on one side, whether a hostile feeling to slavery entertained by many not fanatical on the other, has produced it; or whether it has been the work of men, who, looking to political power, have considered the agitation of this question as the most effectual mode of obtaining the spoils of this Government. I look to the fact itself. It is a policy now openly avowed as one to be persisted in. It is a scheme, Mr. President, which aims to monopolize the powers of this Government, and to obtain sole possession of its territories.

Now, I ask, is there any remedy? Does the constitution afford any remedy? And if not, is there any hope? These, Mr. President, are solemn questions—not only to us, but, let me say to gentlemen from the non-slaveholding States, to them. Sir, the day that the balance between the two sections of the country—the slaveholding States and the non-slaveholding States—is destroyed, is a day that will not be far removed from political revolution, anarchy, civil war, and wide-spread disaster. The balance of this system is in the slaveholding States. They are the conservative portion—always have been the conservative portion—always will be the conservative portion; and with a due balance on their part may, for generations to come, uphold this glorious Union of ours. But if this scheme should be carried out—if we are to be reduced to a handful—if we are to become a mere ball to play the presidential game with—to count something in the Baltimore caucus—if this is to be the result—woe, woe, I say to this Union!

Now, sir, I put again the solemn question—Does the constitution afford any remedy? Is there any provision in it by which this aggressive policy—boldly avowed, as if perfectly consistent with our institutions and the safety and prosperity of the United States!—may be confronted? Is this a policy consistent with the constitution? No, Mr. President, no! It is, in all its features, daringly opposed to the constitution. What is it? Ours is a Federal Constitution. The States are its constituents, and not the people. The twenty-eight States—the twenty-nine States (including Iowa)—stand under this Government as twenty-nine individuals, or as twenty-nine millions of individuals would stand to a consolidated power. It did not look to the prosperity of individuals, as such. No, sir; it was made for higher ends, it was formed that every State as a constituent member of this great Union of ours, should enjoy all its advantages, natural and acquired, with greater security, and enjoy them more perfectly. The whole system is based on justice and equality—perfect equality between the members of this republic. Now can that be consistent with equality which will make this public domain a monopoly on one side—which, in its consequences, would place the whole power in one section of the Union, to be wielded against the other sections of the Union? Is that equality?

How, then, do we stand in reference to this territorial question—this public domain of ours? Why, sir, what is it? It is the common property of the States of this Union. They are called "the territories of the United States." And what are the "United States" but the States united? Sir, these territories are the property of the States united; held jointly for their common use. And is it consistent with justice, is it consistent with equality, that any portion of the partners, outnumbering another portion, shall oust them of this common property of theirs—shall pass any law which shall proscribe the citizens of other portions of the Union from emigrating with their property to the Territories of the United States? Would that be consistent, can it be consistent with the idea of a common property, held jointly for the common benefit of all? Would it be so considered in private life? Would it not be considered the most flagrant outrage in the world, one which any court of equity would restrain by injunction—which any court of law in the world would overrule?

Mr. President, not only is that proposition grossly inconsistent with the constitution, but the other, which undertakes to say that no State shall be admitted into this Union which shall not prohibit by its constitution the existence of slaves, is equally a great outrage against the Constitution of the United States. Sir, I hold it to be a fundamental principle of our political system, that the people have a right to establish what government they may think proper for themselves; that every State about to become a member of this Union has a right to form its own government as it pleases; and that, in order to be admitted, there is but one qualification, and that is, that the government shall be republican. There is no express provision to that effect, but it results from that important sanction which guarantees to every State in this Union a republican form of government. Now, sir, what is proposed? It is proposed, from a vague, indefinite, erroneous, and most dangerous conception of private individual liberty, to overrule this great common liberty which the people have of framing their own constitution! Sir, the right of self-government on the part of individuals is not near so easily to be established by any course of reasoning as the right of a community or State to self-government. And yet, sir, there are men of such delicate feeling on the subject of liberty—men who cannot possibly bear what they call slavery in one section of the country —(although not so much slavery, as an institution indispensable for the good of both races) —men so squeamish on this point, that they are ready to strike down the higher right of a community to govern themselves, in order to maintain the absolute right of individuals in every possible condition to govern themselves!

Mr. President, the resolutions that I intend to offer, present, in general terms, these great truths. I propose to present them to the Senate; I propose to have a vote upon them; and I trust there is no gentleman here who will refuse it. It is manly—it is right that such a vote should be given. It is due to our constituents that we should insist upon it; and I, as one, will insist upon it that the sense of this body shall be taken; the body which represents the States in their capacity as communities, and the members of which are to be their special guardians. It is due to them, sir, that there should be a fair expression of what is the sense of this body. Upon that expression much depends. It is the only stand which we can make under the constitution. It is the only position we can take, that will uphold us with any thing like independence—which will give us any chance at all to maintain an equality in this Union, on those great principles to which I have referred. Overrule these principles, and we are nothing! Preserve them, and we will ever be a respectable portion of the Union.

Sir, here let me say a word as to the compromise line. I have always considered it as a great error—highly injurious to the South, because it surrendered, for mere temporary purposes, those high principles of the constitution upon which I think we ought to stand. I am against any compromise line. Yet I would have been willing to acquiesce in a continuance of the Missouri compromise, in order to preserve, under the present trying circumstances, the peace of the Union. One of the resolutions in the House, to that effect, was offered at my suggestion. I said to a friend there, "Let us not be disturbers of this Union. Abhorrent to my feelings as is that compromise line, let it be adhered to in good faith; and if the other portions of the Union are willing to stand by it, let us not refuse to stand by it. It has kept peace for some time, and in the present circumstances, perhaps it would be better to be continued as it is." But it was voted down by an overwhelming majority. It was renewed by a gentleman from a non-slaveholding State, and again voted down by an overwhelming majority.

I see my way in the constitution. I cannot in a compromise. A compromise is but an act of Congress. It may be overruled at any time. It gives us no security. But the constitution is stable. It is a rock. On it we can stand. It is a firm and stable ground, on which we can better stand in opposition to fanaticism, than on the shifting sands of compromise.

Let us be done with compromises. Let us go back and stand upon the constitution!

Well, sir, what if the decision of this body shall deny to us this high constitutional right, not the less clear because deduced from the whole body of the instrument and the nature of the subject to which it relates? What, then, is the question? I will not undertake to decide. It is a question for our constituents—the slaveholding States. A solemn and a great question. If the decision should be adverse, I trust and do believe that they will take under solemn consideration what they ought to do. I give no advice. It would be hazardous and dangerous for me to do so. But I may speak as an individual member of that section of the Union. There I drew my first breath. There are all my hopes. There is my family and connections. I am a planter—a cotton planter. I am a southern man and a slaveholder; a kind and a merciful one, I trust—and none the worse for being a slaveholder. I say, for one, I would rather meet any extremity upon earth, than give up one inch of our equality—one inch of what belongs to us as members of this great republic. What! acknowledge inferiority! The surrender of life is nothing to sinking down into acknowledgment of inferiority.

I have examined this subject largely—widely. I think I see the future if we do not stand up as we ought. In my humble opinion, in that case, the condition of Ireland is prosperous and happy—the condition of Hindostan is prosperous and happy—the condition of Jamaica is prosperous and happy, to what the Southern States will be if they should not now stand up manfully in defence of their rights.

Mr. President, I desire that the resolutions which I now send to the table be read.

[The resolutions were read as follows:]

Resolved, That the territories of the United States belong to the several States composing this Union, and are held by them as their joint and common property.

Resolved, That Congress, as the joint agent and representative of the States of this Union, has no right to make any law, or do any act whatsoever, that shall directly, or by its effects, make any discrimination between the States of this Union, by which any of them shall be deprived of its full and equal right in any territory of the United States acquired or to be acquired.

Resolved, That the enactment of any law which should directly, or by its effects, deprive the citizens of any of the States of this Union from emigrating, with their property, into any of the territories of the United States, will make such discrimination, and would, therefore, be a violation of the constitution, and the rights of the States from which such citizens emigrated, and in derogation of that perfect equality which belongs to them as members of this Union, and would tend directly to subvert the Union itself.

Resolved, That it is a fundamental principle in our political creed, that a people, in forming a constitution, have the unconditional right to form and adopt the government which they may think best calculated to secure their liberty, prosperity, and happiness; and that, in conformity thereto, no other condition is imposed by the Federal Constitution on a State, in order to be admitted into this Union, except that its constitution shall be republican; and that the imposition of any other by Congress would not only be in violation of the constitution, but in direct conflict with the principle on which our political system rests.

I move that the resolutions be printed. I shall move that they be taken up to-morrow; and I do trust that the Senate will give them early attention, and an early vote upon the subject.

Mr. BENTON then rose and said: Mr. President, we have some business to transact. There is something yet to be done to give effect to the ten regiment bill, and other important measures require our attention. Now, if anybody thinks that I am going to lay aside the necessary business of the session to vote on such a string of abstractions, he is greatly mistaken.

Mr. CALHOUN. The Senator says he cannot take up abstractions. The constitution is an abstraction. Propriety is an abstraction. All the great rules of life are abstractions. The Declaration of Independence was made on an abstraction; and when I hear a man declare that he is against abstract truth in a case of this kind, I am prepared to know what his course will be! I certainly supposed that the Senator from Missouri, the representative of a slaveholding State, would have supported these resolutions. I moved them in good faith, under a solemn conviction of what was due to those whom I represent, and due the whole South and the whole Union. I have as little desire as any Senator to obstruct public business. All I want is a decision, and a decision before the three million bill is decided. If the Senator from Missouri wants to-morrow morning, very well. The resolutions can be taken up on Monday.

Mr. BENTON. I will pursue my own course when the time comes. I know what are abstractions, and what are not. I know what is business, and what is not. I am for going on with the business of the session; and I say, I shall not vote for abstractions years ahead, to the exclusion of business. The Senator from South Carolina says he calculated on my support. He is mistaken. He knows very well from my whole course in public life, that I never would leave public business to take up firebrands to set the world on fire.

Mr. CALHOUN. The Senator does not at all comprehend me. I expressed a hope that he would be found ready to support the principles presented in my resolutions.

Mr. BENTON. I shall be found in the right place. I am on the side of my country and the Union.

The resolutions were then ordered to be printed.

WEDNESDAY, February 24.

Mr. Calhoun's Slavery Resolutions.

Mr. CALHOUN rose to give notice that to-morrow, if the Senate was sufficiently full, he should call up the resolutions he submitted some days since, during the morning hour, or at some other hour, if opportunity offered.

Mr. WEBSTER observed that he should probably adopt the same course in relation to the resolutions he had submitted, and perhaps it would not be improper that both should be before the Senate at the same time. It was not his purpose, when he offered the resolutions, to have addressed the Senate until the pending measure (the three million bill) had been disposed of; but the discussion had been so protracted that, should the resolutions of the Senator from South Carolina be taken up, he (Mr. W.) should follow the example thus set him, and call up his own as follow:

Resolved, That the war now existing with Mexico ought not to be prosecuted for the acquisition of territory to form new States to be adopted into the Union.

Resolved, That it ought to be signified to the Government of Mexico, that the Government of the United States does not desire to dismember the republic of Mexico, and is ready to treat with the Government of that republic for peace, for a liberal adjustment of boundaries, and for just indemnities due by either Government to the citizens of the other.

[Mr. Calhoun never called for the consideration of his resolutions, consequently Mr. Webster never called up his; nor was any further notice of either taken in the Senate.]

The Three Million Bill.

On motion by Mr. SEVIER, the Senate then resumed the consideration, as in Committee of the Whole, of the bill making further appropriation for bringing the existing war with Mexico to a speedy and honorable conclusion.

Mr. BENTON said—

Mr. PRESIDENT: The Senator from South Carolina (Mr. CALHOUN) has boldly made the issue as to the authorship of this war, and as boldly thrown the blame of it upon the present Administration. On the contrary, I believe himself to be the author of it, and will give a part of my reasons for believing so. In saying this, I do not consider the march to the Rio Grande to have been the cause of the war, any more than I consider the British march upon Concord and Lexington to have been the cause of the American Revolution, or the crossing of the Rubicon by Cæsar to have been the cause of the civil war in Rome. In all these cases, I consider the causes of war as pre-existing, and the marches as only the effect of these causes. I consider the march upon the Rio Grande as being unfortunate, and certainly should have advised against it if I had been consulted, and that without the least fear of diminishing my influence in the settlement of the Oregon question—a fear which the Senator from South Carolina says prevented him from interposing to prevent the war which he foresaw. My opinion of Mr. Polk—and experience in that very Oregon case has confirmed it—did not authorize me to conjecture that any one would lose influence with him by giving him honest opinions; so I would have advised against the march to the Rio Grande if I had been consulted. Nor do I see how any opinion adverse to the President's was to have the effect of lessening his influence in the settlement of the Oregon question. That question was settled by us, not by the President. Half the Democratic Senators went contrary to the President's opinion, and none of them lost influence with him on that account; and so I can see no possible connection between the facts of the case and the Senator's reason for not interfering to save his country from the war which, he says, he saw. His reason to me is unintelligible, incomprehensible, unconnectible with the facts of the case. But the march on the Rio Grande was not the cause of the war; but the causes of this event, like the causes of our own revolutionary war, were in progress long before hostilities broke out. The causes of this Mexican war were long anterior to this march; and, in fact, every circumstance of war then existed, except the actual collision of arms. Diplomatic intercourse had ceased; commerce was destroyed; fleets and armies confronted each other; treaties were declared to be broken: the contingency had occurred in which Mexico had denounced the existence of war; the incorporation of Texas, with a Mexican war on her hands, had produced, in legal contemplation, the *status belli* between the two countries: and all this had occurred before the march upon the Rio Grande, and before the commencement of this Administration, and had produced a state of things which it was impossible to continue, and which could only receive their solution from arms or negotiation. The march to the Rio Grande brought on the collision of arms; but, so far from being the cause of the war, it was itself the effect of these causes. The Senator from South Carolina is the author of those causes, and therefore the author of the war; and this I propose to show, at present, by evidence drawn from himself—from his public official acts—leaving all the evidence derived from other sources, from private and unofficial acts, for future production, if deemed necessary.

The Senator from South Carolina, in his efforts to throw the blame of the war upon the President, goes no further back in his search for causes than to this march upon the Rio Grande: upon the same principle, if he wrote a history of the American Revolution, he would begin at the march upon Lexington and Concord, leaving out of view the ten years work of Lord North's Administration. No, the march upon the Rio Grande was not the cause of the war: had it not been for pre-existing causes, the arrival of the American army on the Mexican frontier would have been saluted with military courtesy, according to the usage of all civilized nations, and with none so much as with the Spaniards. Complimentary visits, dinners, and fandangos, balls—not cannon balls—would have been the salutation. The causes of the war are long anterior; and I begin with the beginning, and show the Senator from South Carolina an actor from the first. In doing this, I am acting in defence of the country, for the President represents the country. The Senator from South Carolina charges the war upon the President: the whole opposition follow him: the bill under dicussion is forgotten; crimination of the President is now the object; and in that crimination, the country is injured by being made to appear the aggressor in the war. This is my justification for defending the President, and showing the truth that the Senator, in his manner of acquiring Texas, is the true cause of the war.

The cession of Texas to Spain in 1819, is the beginning point in the chain of causes which have led to this war; for unless the country had been ceded away, there could have been no quarrel with any power in getting it back. For a long time the negotiator of that treaty of cession (Mr. J. Q. Adams) bore all the blame of the loss of Texas; and his motives for giving it away were set down to hostility to the South and West, and a desire to clip the wings of the slaveholding States. At last the truth of history has vindicated itself, and has shown who was the true author of that mischief to the South and West. Mr. Adams has made a public declaration, which no one controverts, that that cession was made in conformity to the decision of Mr. Monroe's cabinet, a majority of which was slaveholding, and among them the present Senator from South Carolina, and now the only survivor of that majority. He does not contradict the statement of Mr. Adams: he, therefore, stands admitted the co-author of that mischief to the South and West with the cession of Texas involved, and to escape from which it became necessary, in the opinion of the Senator from South Carolina, to get back Texas at the expense of war with Mexico. This conduct of the Senator in giving away Texas when we had her, and then making war to get her back, is an enigma which he has never yet condescended to explain, and which, until explained, leaves him in a state of self-contradiction, which, whether it impairs his own confidence in himself or not, must have the effect of destroying the confidence of others in him, and wholly disqualifies him for the office of champion of the slaveholding States. It was the heaviest blow they had ever received, and put an end, in conjunction with the Missouri compromise, and the permanent location of the Indians west of the Mississippi, to their future growth or extension as slave States beyond the Mississippi. The compromise, which was then in full progress, and established at the next session of Congress, cut off the slave States from all territory north and west of Missouri, and south of thirty-six and a half degrees of north latitude: the treaty of 1819 ceded nearly all south of that degree, comprehending not only all Texas, but a large part of the valley of the Mississippi on the Red River and the Arkansas, to a foreign power, and brought a non-slaveholding empire to the confines of Louisiana and Arkansas: the permanent appropriation of the rest of the territory for the abode of civilized Indians, swept the little slaveholding territory west of Arkansas and lying between the compromise line and the cession line; and left the slave States without one inch of ground for their future growth. Nothing was left. Even the then Territory of Arkansas was encroached upon. A breadth of forty miles wide, and three hundred long, was cut off from her, and given to the Cherokees; and there was not as much slave territory left west of the Mississippi as a dove could have rested the sole of her foot upon. It was not merely a curtailment, but a total extinction of slaveholding territory; and done at a time when the Missouri controversy was raging, and every effort made by northern abolitionists to stop the growth of slave States. The Senator from South Carolina, in his support of the cession of Texas, and ceding a part of the valley of the Mississippi, was then the most efficient ally of the restrictionists at that time, and deprives him of the right of setting up as the champion of the slave States now. I denounced the sacrifice of Texas then, believing Mr. Adams to have been the author of it: I denounce it now, knowing the Senator from South Carolina to be its author: and for this—his flagrant recreancy to the slave interest in their hour of utmost peril—I hold him disqualified for the office of champion of the fourteen slave States, and shall certainly require him to keep out of Missouri, and to confine himself to his own bailiwick, when he comes to discuss his string of resolutions.

I come now to the direct proofs of the Senator's authorship of the war: and begin with the year 1836, and with the month of May of that year, and with the 27th day of that month, and with the first rumors of the victory of San Jacinto. The Congress of the United States was then in session: the Senator from South Carolina was then a member of this body; and, without even waiting for the official confirmation of that great event, he proposed at once the immediate recognition of the independence of Texas, and her immediate admission into this Union. He put the two propositions together—recognition and admission: and allowed us no further time for the double vote than the few days which were to intervene before the official intelligence of the victory should arrive. Here are some extracts from his speech on that occasion, and which verify what I say, and show that he was then ready to plunge the country into the Texan war with Mexico, without the slightest regard to its treaties, its commerce, its duties, or its character:

"Mr. Calhoun was of opinion that it would add more strength to the cause of Texas to wait for a few days until they received official confirmation of the victory and capture of Santa Anna, in order to obtain a more unanimous vote in favor of the recognition of Texas. * * * * He had made up his mind not only to recognize the independence of Texas, but for her admission into this Union; and if the Texans managed their affairs prudently, they would soon be called upon to decide that question. There were powerful reasons why Texas should be a part of this Union. The southern States, owning a slave population, were deeply interested in preventing that country from having the power to annoy them; and the navigating and manufacturing interests of the north and east were equally interested in making it a part of this Union. He thought they would soon be called on to decide these questions; and when they did act on it, he was for acting on both together—for recognizing the independence of Texas, and for admitting her into the Union. * * * * If events should go on as they had done, he could not but hope that before the close of the present session of Congress, they would not only acknowledge the independence of Texas, but admit her into the Union. He hoped there would be no unnecessary delay—for in such cases delays were dangerous—but that they would act with unanimity, and act promptly."

Here, then, is the proof of the fact that, ten years ago, and without a word of explanation with Mexico, or any request from Texas—without the least notice to the American people, or time for deliberation among ourselves, or any regard to existing commerce—he was for plunging us into instant war with Mexico. I say, instant war; for Mexico and Texas were then in open war; and to incorporate Texas, was to incorporate the war at the same time. All this the Senator was then for, immediately after his own gratuitous cession of Texas, and long before the invention of the London abolition plot came so opportunely to his aid. Promptness and unanimity were then his watchwords. Immediate action—action before Congress adjourned—was his demand. No delay. Delays were dangerous. We must vote, and vote unanimously and promptly. I well remember the Senator's look and attitude on that occasion—the fixedness of his look, and the magisteriality of his attitude. It was such as he often favors us with, especially when he is in a crisis, and brings forward something which ought to be instantly and unanimously rejected—as when he brought in his string of abstractions on Thursday last. So it was in 1836—prompt and unanimous action, and a look to put down opposition. But the Senate were not looked down in 1836. They promptly and unanimously refused the Senator's motion; and the crisis and the danger—good-natured souls!—immediately postponed themselves until wanted for another occasion.

The peace of the country was then saved; but it was a respite only; and the speech of the Senator from South Carolina, brief as it was, becomes momentous, as foreshadowing every thing that has subsequently taken place in relation to the admission of Texas. In this brief speech we have the shadows of all future movements, coming in procession—in advance of the events. In the significant intimation, qualified with the if——"the Texans prudently managed their affairs, they (the Senate) might soon be called upon to decide the question of admission." In that pregnant and qualified intimation, there was a visible doubt that the Texans might *not* be prudent enough to manage their own affairs, and might require help; and also a visible feeling of that paternal guardianship which afterward assumed the management of their affairs for them. In the admonitions to unanimity, there was that denunciation of any difference of opinion, which afterwards displayed itself in the ferocious hunting down of all who opposed the Texas treaty. In the reference to southern slavery, and annoyance to slave property from Texas, we have the germ of the "*self-defence*" letter, and the first glimpse of the abolition plot of John Andrews, Ashbel Smith, Lord Aberdeen—I beg pardon of Lord Aberdeen for naming him in such a connection —and the World's Convention, with which Mexico, Texas, and the United States were mystified and bamboozled in April, 1844. And, in the interests of the manufacturing and navigating states of the north and east, as connected with Texas admission, we have the text of all the communications to the agent, Murphy, and of all the letters and speeches to which the Texas question, seven years afterwards, gave rise. We have all these subsequent events here shadowed forth. And now, the wonder is, why all these things were not foreseen a little while before, when Texas was being ceded to a non-slave-holding empire! and why, after being so imminent and deadly in May, 1836, all these dangers suddenly went to sleep, and never waked up again until 1844! These are wonders; but let us not anticipate questions, and let us proceed with the narrative.

The Congress of 1836 would not admit Texas. The Senator from South Carolina became patient: the Texas question went to sleep; and for seven good years it made no disturbance. It then woke up, and with a suddenness and violence proportioned to its long repose. Mr. Tyler was then President: the Senator from South Carolina was potent under his administration, and soon became his Secretary of State. All the springs of intrigue and diplomacy were immediately set in motion to resuscitate the Texas question, and to reinvest it with all the dangers and alarms which it had worn in 1836. Passing over all the dangers of annoyance from Texas as possibly non-slave-holding, *foreseen* by the Senator in 1836, and not foreseen by him in 1819, with all the need of guardianship then foreshadowed, and all the arguments then suggested: all these immediately developed themselves, and intriguing agents traversed earth and sea, from Washington to Texas, and from London to Mexico:—passing over all this, as belonging to a class of evidence, not now to be used, I come at once to the letter of the 17th of January, from the Texan Minister to Mr. Upshur, the American Secretary of State; and the answer to that letter by Mr. Calhoun, of April 11th of the same year. They are both vital in this case; and the first is in these words:

"Sir: It is known to you that an armistice has been proclaimed between Mexico and Texas; that that armistice has been obtained through the intervention of several great powers mutually friendly; and that negotiations are now pending, having for their object a settlement of the difficulties heretofore existing between the two countries. A proposition likewise having been submitted by the President of the United States, through you, for the annexation of Texas to this country, therefore (without indicating the nature of the reply which the President of Texas may direct to be made to this proposition) I beg leave to suggest that it may be apprehended, should a treaty of annexation be concluded, Mexico may think proper to at once terminate the armistice, break off all negotiations for peace, and again threaten or commence hostilities against Texas; and that some of the other Governments who have been instrumental in obtaining their cession, if they do not throw their influence into the Mexican scale, may altogether withdraw their good offices of mediation, thus losing to Texas their friendship, and exposing her to the unrestrained menaces of Mexico. In view, then, of these things, I desire to submit, through you, to his excellency the President of the United States, this inquiry: Should the President of Texas accede to the proposition of annexation, would the President of the United States, after the signing of the treaty, and before it shall be ratified and receive the final action of the other branches of both Governments, in case Texas shall desire it, or with her consent, order such number of the military and naval forces of the United States to such necessary points or places upon the territory or borders of Texas or the Gulf of Mexico, as shall be sufficient to protect her against foreign aggression?

"This communication, as well as the reply which you may make, will be considered by me entirely confidential, not to be embraced in my regular official correspondence to my Government, but enclosed direct to the President of Texas for his information.

"With assurances of my great regard, I have the honor to be, very respectfully, your obedient servant."

This letter reveals the true state of the Texan question in January, 1844, and the conduct of all parties in relation to it. It presents Texas and Mexico, weary of the war, reposing under an armistice, and treating for peace; Great Britain and France acting the noble part of mediators, and endeavoring to make peace: our own Government secretly intriguing for annexation, acting the wicked part of mischief-makers, and trying to renew the war; and the issue of its machinations to be unsuccessful unless the United States should be involved in the renewed hostilities. That was the question; and the letter openly puts it to the American Secretary of State. The answer to that question, in my opinion, should have been, that the President of the United States did not know of the armistice and the peace negotiations at the time that he proposed to Texas to do an act which would be a perfidious violation of those sacred engagements, and bring upon herself the scourge of renewed invasion and the stigma of perfidy—that he would not have made such a proposal for the whole round world, if he had known of the armistice and the peace negotiations—that he wished success to the peacemakers, both for the sake of Mexico and Texas, and because Texas could then come into the Union without the least interruption to our friendly, commercial, and social relations with our sister republic of Mexico; and that, as to secretly lending the army and navy of the United States to Texas to fight Mexico while we were at peace with her, it would be a crime against God, and man, and our own constitution, for which heads might be brought to the block, if Presidents and their Secretaries, like constitutional Kings and Ministers, should be held capitally responsible for capital crimes. This, in my opinion, should have been the answer. But the first part of it—that of the *scienter* upon the point of the armistice and the peace negotiations—could not be given in point of fact; for the Department of State was full of communications giving that information—one of them from the agent, (Murphy,) in these words:

"The powers to be given to General Henderson are to be of the fullest and most complete character, so that no impediment shall be found requiring further or other powers, or further or other instructions. But, inasmuch as the Commissioners of Texas now in Mexico, in treaty or negotiation touching an armistice, are supposed not to have concluded their labors, and it is clear to the President of Texas that so soon as this negotiation in relation to annexation is known to the Government of Mexico, all negotiation on that and all other questions between Texas and Mexico will cease, and that the President of Mexico will instantly commence active hostilities against Texas, which Texas is wholly unprepared, by sea or land, to resist, it is understood that the Government of the United States, having invited Texas to this negotiation, will at once, and before any negotiation is set on foot, place a sufficient naval force in the Gulf to protect the coast of Texas, and hold a sufficient force of cavalry, or other description of mounted troops, on the south-western border of the United States, in readiness to protect, or aid in the protection of Texas pending the proposed negotiation for annexation. I trust my Government will at once see the propriety of this course of policy; for I found it impossible to induce this Government to enter heartily into the measure of annexation without an assurance that my Government would not fail to guard Texas against all the evils that are likely to assail Texas in consequence of her meeting and complying with the wishes of the United States."

Denial of the knowledge of the existence of the armistice, and the opening of negotiations, was, therefore, impossible. Mr. Upshur, to whom the letter of the 17th of January was addressed, gave it no answer at all. During the forty days that his life was spared, he answered not; and I mention this particular in justice to the memory of a gentleman who is no more. Mr. Nelson, the Attorney-General, his temporary successor in the Department of State, did not answer it to the Texan Minister in Washington, but he did to Mr. Murphy in Texas, in reply to his communication to the same effect with the letter. Mr. Nelson's letter is dated the 11th of March, and is in these words:

"Of the anxiety of the President to provide for the annexation of the territory of Texas to that of the United States, you have been heretofore apprised; and of his readiness, by negotiation, promptly to effectuate this desire, you are well aware. He regards the measure as one of vital importance to both parties, and as recommended by the highest considerations of a sound public policy.

"Entertaining these views, the President is gratified to perceive, in the course you have pursued in your intercourse with the authorities of Texas, the evidences of a cordial co-operation in this cherished object of his policy: but instructs me to say, that whilst approving the general tone and tenor of that intercourse, he regrets to perceive, in the pledges given by you in your communication to the Hon. Anson Jones of the 14th February, that you have suffered your zeal to carry you beyond the line of your instructions, and to commit the President to measures for which he has no constitutional authority to stipulate.

"The employment of the army or navy against a foreign power, with which the United States are at peace, is not within the competency of the President; and whilst he is not indisposed, as a measure of prudent precaution, and as preliminary to the proposed negotiation, to concentrate in the Gulf of Mexico, and on the southern borders of the United States, a naval and military force to be directed to the defence of the inhabitants and Territory of Texas *at a proper time*, he cannot permit the authorities of that Government, or yourself, to labor under the misapprehension that he has power to employ them at the period indicated by your stipulations.

"Of these impressions, Mr. Van Zandt, the chargé d'affaires of the Texan Government, has been, and General Henderson, who is daily expected here, will be fully advertised. In the mean time, the President desires that you will at once countermand your instructions to Lieutenant Davis, as far as they are in conflict with these views.

"In any emergency that may occur, care will be taken that the commanders of the naval and military forces of the United States shall be properly instructed. Your request that they may be placed under your control cannot be gratified."

This is very constitutional and proper language: and if it had not been reversed, there would have been no war with Mexico. But it was reversed. Soon after it was written, the present Senator from South Carolina took the chair of the Department of State. Mr. Pinckney Henderson, whom Mr. Murphy mentions as coming on with full powers, on the faith of the pledge he had given, arrived also, and found that pledge entirely cancelled by Mr. Tyler's answer through Mr. Nelson; and he utterly refused to treat. The new Secretary was in a strait; for time was short, and Texas must be had; and Messrs. Henderson and Van Zandt would not even begin to treat without a renewal of the pledge given by Mr. Murphy. That had been cancelled in writing, and the cancellation had gone to Texas, and had been made on high constitutional ground. The new Secretary was profuse of verbal assurances, and even permitted the Ministers to take down his words in writing, and read them over to him, as was shown by the Senator from Texas, (General HOUSTON,) when he spoke on this subject on Thursday last. But verbal assurances, or memoranda of conversations, would not do. The instructions under which the ministers acted required the pledge to be in writing, and properly signed. The then President, present Senator from Texas, who had been a lawyer in Tennessee before he went to Texas, seemed to look upon it as a case under the statute of frauds and perjuries—a sixth case added to the five enumerated in that statute—in which the promise is not valid, unless reduced to writing, and signed by the person to be charged therewith, or by some other person duly authorized by him to sign for him. The firmness of the Texan Ministers, under the instructions of President Houston, prevailed; and at last, and after long delay, the Secretary wrote, and signed the pledge which Murphy had given, and in all the amplitude of his original promise. That letter was dated on the 11th day of April, 1844, and was in these words:

"GENTLEMEN: The letter addressed by Mr. Van Zandt to the late Secretary of State, Mr. Upshur, to which you have called my attention, dated Washington, 17th January, 1844, has been laid before the President of the United States.

"In reply to it, I am directed by the President to say that the Secretary of the Navy has been instructed to order a strong naval force to concentrate in the Gulf of Mexico, to meet any emergency; and that similar orders have been issued by the Secretary of War, to move the disposable military forces on our south-western frontier, for the same purpose. Should the exigency arise to which you refer in your note to Mr. Upshur, I am further directed by the President to say, that during the pendency of the treaty of annexation, he would deem it his duty to use all the means placed within his power by the constitution to protect Texas from all foreign invasion. I have the honor to be, &c."

This is the answer given by Mr. Secretary Calhoun to the demand; and, although a little *delphic* in its specification of the *emergencies* and the *exigencies* in which our forces were to fight the Mexicans, yet, taken in connection with the terms of the letter to which it was an answer, and to which it refers, it is sufficiently explicit to show that it is a clear and absolute promise to do the thing which Murphy had promised, and which President Tyler, through the Attorney-General, (Mr. Nelson,) had refused to do, because it involved a violation of the Constitution of the United States. The promise was clear and explicit to lend the army and navy to the President of Texas, to fight the Mexicans while they were at peace with us. That was the point—at peace with us. Mr. Calhoun's assumpsit was clear and explicit to that point; for the cases in which they were to fight were to be before the ratification of the treaty by the Senate, and consequently before Texas should be in our Union, and could be constitutionally defended as a part of it. And, that no circumstance of contradiction or folly should be wanting to crown this plot of crime and imbecility, it so happened, that on the same day that our new Secretary here was giving his written assumpsit to lend the army and navy to fight Mexico while we were at peace with her, the agent Murphy was communicating to the Texan Government, in Texas, the refusal of Mr. Tyler, through Mr. Nelson, to do so, because of its unconstitutionality. Here is the letter of Mr. Murphy:

"SIR: The undersigned, chargé d'affaires of the United States near the Government of the republic of Texas, has the honor of informing Mr. Jones, that whilst his Government approves of the general tone and tenor of his intercourse with the Government of the republic of Texas, a regret is felt in perceiving that his zeal for the accomplishment of objects alike beneficial and interesting to both countries, had led him beyond the strict line of his instructions; that the President of the United States considers himself restrained by the constitution of the Union, from the employment of the army and navy against a foreign power with whom the United States are at peace; and that whilst the President of the United States is not indisposed, as a measure of prudent precaution, and as preliminary to the proposed negotiation, to concentrate in the Gulf of Mexico and on the southern borders of the United States a sufficient naval and military force, to be directed to the defence of the inhabitants and territory of Texas at a proper time, he is unwilling that the authorities of Texas should apprehend that he has power to employ this force at the period indicated in my note to you of the 14th of February last."

In conformity with the Secretary's letter of April 11th, detachments of the army and navy were immediately sent to the frontiers of Texas, and to the coast of Mexico. The Senator from South Carolina, in his colloquy with the Senator from Texas (Gen. HOUSTON) on Thursday last, seemed anxious to have it understood that these land and naval forces were not to *repel* invasions, but only to *report* them to our Government, for its report to Congress. The paper read by the Senator from Texas, consisting of our Secretary's words, taken down in his presence, and read over to him for his correction by the Texan Ministers, establishes the contrary; and shows that the repulse of the invasion was in the mean time to be made. And in fact, any other course would have been a fraud upon the promise. For, if the invasion had to be made known at Washington, and the sense of Congress taken on the question of repelling it, certainly, in the mean time, the mischief would have been done—the invasion would have been made; and, therefore, to be consistent with himself, the President in the mean time was bound to repel the invasion, without waiting to hear what Congress would say about it. And this is what he himself tells us in his two Messages to the Senate, of the 15th and 31st of May, doubtless written by his Secretary of State, and both avowing and justifying his intention to fight Mexico, in case of invasion, while the treaty of annexation was depending, without awaiting the action of Congress. Here are extracts from these Messages:

Message, 15th of May.—Extract.

"At the same time, it is due to myself that I should declare it as my opinion, that the United States having, by the treaty of annexation, acquired a title to Texas, which requires only the action of the Senate to perfect it, no other power could be permitted to invade, and, by force of arms, to possess itself of any portion of the territory of Texas, pending your deliberations upon the treaty, without placing itself in a hostile attitude to the United States, and justifying the employment of any military means at our disposal to drive back the invasion."

Message, 31st of May.—Extract.

"In my message to the Senate on the 15th of this month, I adverted to the duty which, in my judgment, the signature of the treaty for the annexation of Texas had imposed upon me, to repel any invasion of that country by a foreign power, while the treaty was under consideration in the Senate; and I transmitted reports from the Secretaries of War and of the Navy, with a copy of the orders which had been issued from those departments for the purpose of enabling me to execute that duty. In those orders, General Taylor was directed to communicate directly with the President of Texas upon the subject, and Captain Connor was instructed to communicate with the chargé d'affaires of the United States accredited to that Government. No copy of any communication which either of those officers may have made pursuant to those orders has yet been received at the departments from which they emanated."

Here are the avowals of the fact, and the reasons for it—that honor required us to fight for Texas, if we intrigued her into a war. I admit that would be a good reason between individuals, and in a case where a big bully should involve a little fellow in the fight again after he had got himself parted; but not so between nations, and under our constitution. The engagement to fight Mexico for Texas, while we were at peace with Mexico, was to make war with Mexico!—a piece of business which belonged to the Congress, and which should have been referred to them! and which, on the contrary, was concealed from them, though in session, and present! and the fact only found out after the troops had marched, and then by dint of calls from the Senate.

The proof is complete that the loan of the land and naval forces was to fight Mexico while we were at peace with her! and this becomes a great turning point in the history of this war. Without this pledge given by our Secretary of State—without his reversal of Mr. Tyler's first decision—there could have been no war! Texas and Mexico would have made peace, and then annexation would have followed of itself. The victor of San Jacinto, who had gone forth and recovered by the sword, and erected into a new republic the beautiful domain given away by our Secretary in 1819, was at the head of the Texas Government, and was successfully and honorably conducting his country to peace and acknowledged independence. If let alone, he would have accomplished his object; for he had already surmounted the great difficulty of the first step—the armistice and the commencement of peace negotiations; and under the powerful mediation of Great Britain and France, the establishment of peace was certain. A heavenly benediction rests upon the labors of the peace-maker; and what is blessed of God must succeed. At all events, it does not lie in the mouth of any man—and least of all, in the mouth of the mischief-maker—to say that the peaceful mediation would not have succeeded. It was the part of all men to have aided, and wished, and hoped for success; and had it not been for our Secretary's letter of April 11th, authentic facts warrant the assertion that Texas and Mexico would have made peace in the spring of 1844. Then Texas would have come into this Union as naturally, and as easily, and with as little offence to anybody, as Eve went into Adam's bosom in the garden of Eden. There would have been no more need for intriguing politicians to get her in, by plots and tricks, than there was for some old hag of a match-making beldame, with her arts and allurements, her philters and her potions, to get Eve into Adam's bosom. And thus, the breaking up of the peace negotiations becomes the great turning point in the problem of the Mexican war.

The pledge of the 11th April being *signed*, the treaty was *signed*, and being communicated to the Senate, it was *rejected:* and the great reason for the rejection was that the ratification of the treaty would have been WAR with Mexico! an act which the President and Senate together, no more than President Tyler and his Secretary of State together, had the power to make.

The treaty of annexation was signed, and in signing it the Secretary knew that he had made war with Mexico. No less than three formal notices were on file in the Department of State, in which the Mexican Government solemnly declared that it would consider annexation as equivalent to a declaration of war; and it was in allusion to these notices that the Secretary of State, in his notification to Mexico of the signature of the treaty, said it had been signed IN FULL VIEW OF ALL POSSIBLE CONSEQUENCES! meaning war as the consequence! At the same time, he suited the action to the word; he sent off detachments of the army and navy, and placed them under the command of President Houston, and made him the judge of the emergencies and exigencies in which they were to fight. This authority to the President of Texas was continued in full force until after the rejection of the treaty, and then only modified by placing the American diplomatic agent in Texas between President Houston and the naval and military commanders, and making him the medium of communication between a foreign President and our forces; but the forces themselves were not withdrawn. They remained on the Texan and Mexican frontier, waiting for the *exigencies* and *emergencies* in which they were to fight. During all that time a foreign President was commander-in-chief of a large detachment of the army and navy of the United States. Without a law of Congress —without a nomination from the President and confirmation by the Senate—without citizenship —without the knowledge of the American people—he was president-general of our land and sea forces, made so by the Senator from South Carolina, with authority to fight them against Mexico with whom we were at peace—an office and authority rather above that of lieutenant-general!—and we are indebted to the forbearance and prudence of President Houston for not incurring the war in 1844, which fell upon us in 1846. This is a point—this secret and lawless appointment of this president-general to make war upon Mexico, while we were at peace with her—on which I should like to hear a constitutional argument from the Senator from South Carolina, showing it to be constitutional and proper, and that of the proposed lieutenant-general unconstitutional and improper, and upon which he has erected himself into the *foreman* of the grand jury of the whole American people, and pronounced a unanimous verdict for them before he had time to hear from the ten-thousandth part of them.

The treaty was rejected by the Senate; but so apprehensive was the Senate of immediate war, that, besides keeping the detachments of the army and navy at their posts, a messenger was despatched with a deprecatory letter to Mexico, and, as report said, the offer of a large sum of money to purchase peace from her, by inducing her to treat for a boundary which would leave Texas within our limits. This was report: and I would not mention it, if the Senator was not present to contradict it, if not correct. Report at the time said from five to ten millions of dollars: from one of Mr. Shannon's letters, we may set it down at ten millions. Be it either sum, it will show that the Senator was then secretly willing to pay an immense sum to pacify Mexico, although he now declares that he does not know how he will vote in relation to the three millions responsibly asked by Mr. Polk.

The Secretary knew that he had made war with Mexico—that in accepting the gage three times laid down, he had joined an issue which that compound of Celtic and Roman blood, called Spanish, would redeem. I knew it, and said it on this floor, in secret session—for I did not then choose to say it in public—that if there was but one man of that blood in all Mexico, and he no bigger than General Tom Thumb, he would fight. Senators will recollect it. [Mr. Mangum nodded assent.]

I now come to the last act in this tragedy of errors—the alternative resolutions adopted by Congress in the last days of the session of 1844–'45, and in the last moments of Mr. Tyler's Administration. A resolve, single and absolute, for the admission of Texas as a State of this Union, had been made by the House of Representatives; it came to this body; and an alternative resolution was added, subject to the choice of the President, authorizing negotiations for the admission, and appropriating $100,-000 to defray the expenses of these negotiations. A Senator from North Carolina, not now a member of this body, but who I have the pleasure to see sitting near me, (Mr. Haywood,) knows all about that alternative resolution, and his country owes him good thanks for his labors about it. It was considered by everybody, that the choice between these resolutions belonged to the new President, who had been elected with a special view to the admission of Texas, and who was already in the city, awaiting the morning of the 4th of March to enter upon the execution of his duties, and upon whose Administration all the evils of a mistake in the choice of these resolutions were to fall. We all expected the question to be left open to the new President; and so strong was that expectation, and so strong the feeling against the decency or propriety of interference on the part of the expiring Administration, to snatch his choice out of the hands of Mr. Polk, that, on a mere suggestion of the possibility of such a proceeding, in a debate on this floor, a Senator standing in the relation personally, and politically, and locally to feel for the honor of the then Secretary of State, declared they would not have the audacity to do it. Audacity was his word: and that was the declaration of a gentleman of honor and patriotism, no longer a member of this body, but who has the respect and best wishes of all who ever knew him. I speak of Mr. McDuffie, and quote his words as heard at the time, and as since printed and published by others. Mr. McDuffie was mistaken! They did have the audacity! They did do it, or rather, HE did it, [looking at Mr. CALHOUN;] for it is incontestable that Mr. Tyler was nothing, in any thing that related to the Texas question, from the time of the arrival of his Secretary of State. His last act, in relation to Texas, was the answer which Mr. Nelson gave him through the agent, Murphy, denying his right to lend our forces to the President of Texas to fight the Mexicans while we were at peace with them: the reversal of that answer by his new Secretary was the extinction of his power over the Texas question. HE, the then Secretary of State, the present Senator from South Carolina, to whom I address myself, did it. On Sunday, the second day of March,—that day which preceded the last day of his authority—and on that day, sacred to peace—the council sat that acted on the resolutions;—and in the darkness of a night howling with the storm, and battling with the elements, as if Heaven warred upon the audacious act, (for well do I remember it,) the fatal messenger was sent off which carried the selected resolutions to Texas. The exit of the Secretary from office, and the start of the messenger from Washington, were coetaneous—twin acts—which come together, and will be remembered together. The act was then done: Texas was admitted: all the consequences of admission were incurred—and especially that consequence which Mr. de Bocanegra had denounced, and which our Secretary had accepted—WAR. The state of war was established—the *status belli* was created—and that by the operation of our own constitution, as well as by the final declaration of Mexico: for Texas then being admitted into the Union, the war with her extended to the whole Union; and the duty of protecting her, devolved upon the President of the United States. The selection of the absolute resolution exhausted our action: the alternative resolution for negotiation was defunct; the only mode of admission was the absolute one, and it made war. The war was made to Mr. Polk's hands: his Administration came into existence with the war upon its hands and under the constitutional duty to protect Texas at the expense of war with Mexico: and to that point, all events rapidly tended. The Mexican Minister, General Almonte, who had returned to Washington City after the rejection of the treaty of annexation, demanded his passports and left the United States. The land forces which had been advanced to the Sabine, were further advanced to Corpus Christi: the Mexican troops moved towards the Rio Grande: the fleet which remained at Vera Cruz, continued there: commerce died out: the citizens of each country left the other, as far as they could: angry denunciations filled the press of each country: and when a minister was sent from the United States, his reception was refused. The state of war existed legally: all the circumstances of war, except the single circumstance of bloodshed, existed at the accession of Mr. Polk; and the two countries, Mexico and the United States, stood in a relation to each other impossible to be continued. The march upon the Rio Grande brought on the conflict—made the collision of arms—but not the war. The war was prepared, organized, established by the Secretary of State, before he left the department. It was his legacy to the Democracy, and to the Polk Administration—his last gift to them, in the moment of taking a long farewell. And now he sets up for a man of peace, and throws all the blame of war upon Mr. Polk, to whom he bequeathed it.

Cicero says that Antony, flying from Rome to the camp of Cæsar in Cisalpine Gaul, was the cause of the civil war which followed—as much so as Helen was of the Trojan war. *Ut Helena Trojanis, sic iste huic reipublica causa belli—causa pestis atque exitii fuit.* He says that that flight put an end to all chance of accommodation; closed the door to all conciliation; broke up the plans of all peaceable men; and by inducing Cæsar to break up his camp in Gaul, and march across the Rubicon, lit up the flames of civil war in Italy. In like manner, I say that the flight of the winged messenger from this capital on the Sunday night before the 3d of March, despatched by the then Secretary of State, in the expiring moments of his power, and bearing his fatal choice to the capital of Texas, was the direct cause of the war with Mexico in which we are now engaged. Like the flight of Antony, it broke up the plans of all peaceable men, slammed the door upon negotiation, put an end to all chance for accommodation, broke up the camp on the Sabine, sent the troops towards Mexico, and lit up the war. Like Antony and Helen, he made the war; unlike Antony, he does not stand to it; but, copying rather the conduct of the paramour of Helen, he flies from the combat he has provoked! and, worse than Paris, he endeavors to draw along with him, in his own unhappy flight, the whole American host. Paris fled alone at the sight of Menelaus: the Senator from South Carolina urges us all to fly at the sight of Santa Anna. And, it may be, that worse than Paris again, he may refuse to return to the field. Paris went back under the keen reproach of Hector, and tried to fight.

> "For thee the soldier bleeds, the matron mourns,
> And wasteful war in all its fury burns."

Stung with this just and keen rebuke—this vivid picture of the ruin he had made—Paris returned to the field, and tried to fight: and now, it remains to be seen whether the Senator from South Carolina can do the same, on the view of the ruin which he has made: and, if not, whether he cannot, at least, cease to obstruct the arms of others—cease to labor to involve the whole army in his own unmanly retreat.

Upon the evidence now given, drawn from his public official acts alone, he stands the undisputed author and architect of that calamity. History will so write him down. Inexorable History with her pen of iron and tablets of brass, will so write him down: and two thousand years hence, and three thousand years hence, the boy at his lesson shall learn it in the book, that as Helen was the cause of the Trojan, and Antony the cause of the Roman civil war, and Lord North made the war of the Revolution, just so certainly is John C. Calhoun the author of the present war between the United States and Mexico.

I have now finished what I proposed to say, at this time, in relation to the authorship of this war. I confine myself to the official words and acts of the Senator, and rely upon them to show that he, and not Mr. Polk, is the author of this calamity. But, while thus presenting him as the author of the war, I do not believe that war was his object, but only an incident to his object; and that all his conduct in relation to the admission of Texas refers itself to the periods of our Presidential elections, and to some connection with those elections, and explains his activity and inactivity on those occasions. Thus, in May, 1836, when he was in such hot and violent haste for immediate admission, the election of that year was impending, and Mr. Van Buren the Democratic candidate; and if the Texas question could then have been brought up, he might have been shoved aside just as easily as he was afterwards in 1844. This may explain his activity in 1836. In 1840, the Senator from South Carolina was a sort of a supporter of Mr. Van Buren, and might have thought that one good turn deserves another; and so nothing was said about Texas at that election—dangerous as was the least delay four years before: and this may explain the inactivity of 1840. The election of 1844 was coming on, and the Senator from South Carolina was on the turf himself; and then the Texas question, with all its dangers and alarms, which had so accommodatingly postponed themselves for seven good years, suddenly woke up; and with an activity and vigor proportioned to its long repose. Instant admission, at all hazards, and at the expense of renewing hostilities beween Mexico and Texas, and involving the United States in them, became indispensable—necessary to our own salvation—a clear case of self-defence; and then commenced all those machinations which ended in the overthrow of Mr. Van Buren and Mr. Clay for the Presidency, and in producing the present war with Mexico; but without making the Senator President. And this may explain his activity in 1844. Now, another Presidential election is approaching; and if there is any truth in the rule which interprets certain gentlemen's declarations by their contraries, he will be a candidate again; and this may explain the reason of the production of that string of resolutions which the Senator laid upon the table last week; and upon which he has required us to vote instantly, as he did in the sudden Texas movement of 1836, and with the same magisterial look and attitude. The Texas slave question has gone by—the Florida slave question has gone by—there is no chance for it now in any of its old haunts: hence the necessity for a new theatre of agitation, even if we have to go as far as California for it, and before we have got California. And thus, all the Senator's conduct in relation to Texas, though involving his country in war, may have had no other object than to govern a Presidential election.

Our northern friends have exceeded my hopes and expectations in getting themselves and the Union safe through the Texas and Florida slave questions, and are entitled to a little repose. So far from that, they are now to be plunged into a California slave question, long before it could arise of itself, if ever. The string of resolutions laid on the table by the Senator from South Carolina is to raise a new slave question on the borders of the Pacific Ocean, which, upon his own principles, cannot soon occur, if ever. He will not take the country by conquest—only by treaty—and that treaty to be got by sitting out the Mexicans on a line of occupation. At the same time, he shows that he knows that Spanish blood is good at that game, and shows that they sat it out, and fought it out, for 800 years, against the Moors occupying half their country. By-the-by, it was only 700; but that is enough; one hundred years is no object in such a matter. The Spaniards held out 700 years against the Moors, holding half their country, and 300 against the Visigoths, occupying the half of the other half; and, what is more material, whipped them both out at the end of the time. This is a poor chance for California on the Senator's principles. His five regiments would be whipped out in a fraction of the time; but no matter; men contend more violently for nothing than for something, and if he can get up a California slave question now, it will answer all the purposes of a reality, even if the question should never arise in point of fact.

The Senator from South Carolina has been wrong in all this business, from beginning to ending—wrong in 1819, in giving away Texas—wrong in 1836, in his sudden and hot haste to get her back—wrong in all his machinations for bringing on the Texas question of 1844—wrong in breaking up the armistice and peace negotiations between Mexico and Texas—wrong in secretly sending the army and navy to fight Mexico while we were at peace with her—wrong in secretly appointing the President of Texas president-general of the army and navy of the United States, with leave to fight against a power with whom we were at peace—wrong in writing to Mexico that he took Texas in view of all possible consequences, meaning war—

wrong in secretly offering Mexico, at the same time, ten millions of dollars to hush up the war which he had created—wrong now in refusing Mr. Polk three millions to aid in getting out of the war which he made—wrong in throwing the blame of this war of his own making upon the shoulders of Mr. Polk—wrong in his retreat and occupation line of policy—wrong in expelling old Father Ritchie from the Senate, who worked so hard for him during the Texas annexation—and more wrong now than ever, in that string of resolutions which he has laid upon the table, and in which, as Sylla saw in the young Cæsar many Mariuses, so do I see in them many nullifications.

In a picture of so many and such dreadful errors, it is hard to specify the worst, or to dwell upon any one to the exclusion of the rest; but there is one feature in this picture of enormities which seems entitled to that distinction: I allude to the pledge upon which the armistice and the peace negotiations between Mexico and Texas were broken up in 1844, and those two countries put back into a state of war, and ourselves involved in the contest. The story is briefly told, and admits of no dispute. The letter of 17th January is the accusing record, from which there is no escape. Its awful words cannot be read now without freezing up the blood:

"It is known to you that an armistice exists between Mexico and Texas, and that negotiations for peace are now going on under the mediation of two powerful sovereigns, mutually friendly. If we yield to your solicitation to be annexed to the United States, under these circumstances, we shall draw upon ourselves a fresh invasion from Mexico, incur the imputation of bad faith, and lose the friendship and respect of the two great mediating powers. Now, will you, in the event of our acceding to your request, step between us and Mexico, and take the war off our hands?"

This was the letter, and the terrible question with which it concluded. Mr. Upshur, to whom it was addressed, gave it no answer. In the forty days that his life was spared, he gave it no answer. Mr. Nelson, his temporary successor, gave it an answer; and, speaking for the President of the United States, positively refused to take annexation on the awful terms proposed. This answer was sent to Texas, and put an end to all negotiation for annexation. The Senator from South Carolina came into the Department of State, procured the reversal of the President's decision, and gave the pledge to the whole extent that Texas asked it. Without, in the least, denying the knowledge of the armistice, and the negotiations for peace, and all the terrible consequences which were to result from their breach, he accepts the whole, and gives the fatal pledge which his predecessors had refused; and follows it up by sending our troops and ships to fight a people with whom we were at peace—the whole veiled by the mantle of secrecy, and pretexted by motives as unfounded as they were absurd. Now, what says morality and Christianity to this conduct? Certainly, if two individuals were engaged in strife, and two others should part them, and put them under an agreement to submit to an amicable settlement; and while the settlement was going on another man, lying behind a hedge, should secretly instigate one of the parties to break off the agreement and renew the strife, and promise to take the fight off his hands if he did: what would morality and Christianity say to this? Surely the malediction of all good men would fall upon the man who had interfered to renew the strife. And if this would be the voice of all good men in the case of mere individuals, what would it be when the strife was between nations, and when the renewal of it was to involve a third nation in the contest, and such a war as we now have with our sister republic of Mexico? This is the feature which stands out in the awful picture: this is the question which now presents itself to the moral sense of the civilized world, in judging the conduct of the Senator from South Carolina in writing that letter of the 11th of April, 1844, aggravated by now throwing upon another the blame of a war for which he then contracted.

Mr. BENTON having concluded—

Mr. CALHOUN rose and said:

One thing, Mr. President, at least, may be inferred, from the unprovoked attack of the Senator, and the great solicitude he evinced to trace the authorship of the war to me—and that is, that the war is unpopular. There can be no mistake. He felt that the tide of public sentiment had turned against it, and hence the anxiety exhibited to place its responsibility on my shoulders, and take it from those on whom it ought justly to rest. Had he supposed the opposite—had he believed that the war was necessary and unavoidable, and that its termination would be successful—I am the last man to whom he would attribute any agency in causing it. I am gratified that the Senator has furnished this evidence. It affords reasonable hope, that those who are responsible for it will exert themselves, and I hope with success, to bring it to a speedy termination.

He traces the authorship to me, because, as he asserts, I am the real author of the annexation of Texas, and that annexation is the real cause of the war. I trust, Mr. President, there will be no dispute hereafter as to who is the real author of annexation. Less than twelve months since, I had many competitors for that honor: the official organ here claimed, if my memory serves me, a large share for Mr. Polk and his Administration, and not less than half a dozen competitors from other quarters claimed to be the real authors. But now, since the war has become unpopular, they all seem to agree that I, in reality, am the author of annexation. I will not put the honor aside. I may now rightfully and indisputably claim to be the author of that great event—an event which has so much extended the domains of the Union, which has added so largely to its productive powers, which promises so greatly to extend its commerce, which has stimulated its industry, and given security to our most exposed frontier. I take pride to myself as being the author of this great event.

But the Senator objects that I so conducted the question of annexation as necessarily to lead to the war. On what does he rest this charge? He rests it on the ground that I selected the resolution as it came from the House of Representatives, as the basis of the annexation, instead of giving the Texan Government the choice between the House resolution and the amendment of the Senate originally moved by the Senator himself. He complained bitterly that the Senate resolution passed at the very heel of the session, under the expectation that it would be carried into effect by the present Administration, then just coming into power, and not by Mr. Tyler's Administration, then about to expire, had not been adopted..

He seemed to think that the then Administration had no right to act upon it, and that, undertaking to do so, was depriving its successor of some of its rights. He accused me of acting with the greatest promptness. The fact is so. The resolution, if I recollect, was signed by the late President about the first of March. I saw the importance of acting promptly, and advised the President to act without delay, that he had the constitutional right of doing so, and that I deemed it necessary that he should act in order effectually to secure the success of a measure which had originated with his Administration. His Cabinet were summoned the next day, and concurred in the opinion. That night I prepared the despatch for Mr. Donelson, our chargé in Texas, and the next day, late in the evening of the third of March, it was forwarded to him. It was my last official act of any importance as Secretary of State.

I selected the resolution of the House in preference to the amendment of which the Senator from Missouri was the author, because I clearly saw, not only that it was every way preferable, but the only certain mode by which annexation could be effected. My reasons for thinking so were fully set forth in my despatch, which may be found among the public documents accompanying the first annual Message of the present Executive. They will speak for themselves, they never have been controverted, and never can be successfully. Indeed, I never considered the Senator's amendment as expressing the deliberate sense either of the Senate or House of Representatives. It is well known that he, and a few of his friends, had the power of greatly embarrassing the passage of the resolutions of the House, if not of defeating them; and that his amendment was moved, not so much as an improvement of the resolutions as to gratify him and them. That the course I adopted did secure the annexation, and that it was indispensable for that purpose, I have high authority in my possession—that which all would admit to be the highest, if I could with propriety introduce it; and for this prompt and decided act, if for nothing else, I might claim the authorship of annexation. Now, can any thing be more absurd than the assertion that the war with Mexico resulted from selecting the House resolution, instead of the amendment of the Senator? He has ventured the bold assertion, without the shadow of an argument to sustain it. What possible difference could it make with Mexico, whether the annexation was made upon one or the other? Why should the one not be as offensive to her as the other? Indeed, I doubt much whether, even to this day, the Government of Mexico knows whether the resolution was passed with or without an alternative. Such is the baseless ground on which he has charged me with being the author of the war. I had heard, for several days past, that he had prepared to make an elaborate attack on me. Some of my friends asked, rather jestingly, if I did not expect to be annihilated. After these givings out, and such laborious preparation, I did suppose the Senator would make some show of a formidable charge; but of all the attacks I have ever witnessed, in this or any other legislative body, I have never known one so empty and ridiculous. Every one of his charges is founded either in gross error or partial statement of facts, or on some forced and absurd conclusion. I may begin with the very first that he made. He had the assurance to assert, in the presence of the Senate, that I was the first to introduce the question, who was the real author or cause of this war. Now, I appeal to every Senator, and every other individual who was present on the occasion, whether the Senator from Tennessee (Mr. Turney) did not first charge me with being the author of this war, and whether I did not limit myself to repelling this charge, by showing that it originated in the order to General Taylor, to march from Corpus Christi, and take position on the Rio del Norte? I go further, and ask, is there a Senator here ignorant of the fact, that the question of, who was the author or cause of the war, had been long before elaborately discussed in this body—in the House of Representatives, and throughout the whole country, from its declaration up to that time. In the face of all this, the Senator rises up in his place, after a long and laborious preparation, and asserts that it was I who originated the inquiry as to who was its author. This is a fair sample of the accuracy of the Senator, in his numerous allegations to show that I was the author of the war. I might go on and take them up one by one, and show that every one of his positions and deductions is equally unfounded in fact or false in conclusion. I do not deem it necessary. A large portion of his speech was but the stale repetition of what he said in the session of 1842–'43, upon the treaty which I had concluded with Texas, then under discussion in this body. All the documents now brought forward, were then before the Senate, and he went on with the same topics very elaborately, and with much more power than on the present occasion, without making any impression on the country. The country was against him then, and still remains against him, and it is in vain that he undertakes to disturb its settled conviction. It will remain ever unchanged, in spite of all that he can do. Under this conviction, I will not weary the Senate by repelling assaults then made and then repelled. The most prominent of the charges—the orders given by the Administration to place a fleet in the Gulf of Mexico, and a portion of the army on the frontier of Texas—was repelled by my then colleague, (Mr. McDuffie,) of whom he speaks so highly on this occasion. In repelling it, he said, that if the orders to which the Senator then and now objects, had not been issued, the Executive would have been guilty of great dereliction of duty.

The Florida treaty, forming another subject of attack, figured also on that occasion in connection with annexation; and what he has said now is but a repetition of what he said then. He then, as now, made me responsible for that treaty, although I was but one of six members of Mr. Monroe's Cabinet, and the youngest of its members—responsible, without advancing a particle of proof that I even gave it my support or approbation. He rests the charge on some disclaimer, as it seems, that the then Secretary of State (Mr. Adams) has, at some time, made, that he was not responsible for the treaty. The Senator may be right as to that; but how can that, by any possibility, show that I was responsible? But I am prepared to take my full share of responsibility as a member of Mr. Monroe's Cabinet, without having any particular agency in forming the treaty, or influence in inducing the Cabinet to adopt it. I then thought, and still think it a good treaty; and so thought the Senate of the United States; for, if my memory does not deceive me, it received every vote of the Senate. [A Senator: "Yes, every vote."] It then received the unanimous vote of the Senate, promptly given. Of course, if that treaty was the cause of the war with Mexico, as the Senator seems to suppose, this body is as much the author and cause of the war, as the individual on whom he is now so anxious to fix it.

I have said it is a good treaty, not without due reflection. We acquired much by it. It gave us Florida—an acquisition not only important in itself, but also in reference to the whole south-western frontier. There was, at that time, four powerful tribes of Indians, two of whom—the Creeks and the Choctaws—were contiguous to Florida, and the two others—the Chickasaws and Cherokees—were adjoining. They were the most numerous and powerful tribes in the United States, and, from their position, were exposed to be acted on and excited against us from Florida. It was important that this state of things should terminate, which could only be done by obtaining the possession of Florida.

But there were other and powerful considerations for the acquisition. We had, a short time before, extinguished the Indian title to large tracts of country in Alabama, Mississippi, and Georgia, lying upon streams and rivers which passed through Florida to the gulf—lands in a great measure valueless, without the right of navigating them to their mouths. The acquisition of Florida gave us this right, and enabled us to bring into successful cultivation a great extent of fertile lands, which have added much to the increased production of our great staple, cotton. Another important point was effected by the acquisition: It terminated a very troublesome dispute with Spain, growing out of the capture of St. Marks and Pensacola by General Jackson, in the Seminole war; and, finally, it perfected our title to Oregon, by ceding to us whatever right Spain had to that territory.

Such is the treaty on which the Senator has lavished so much of his abuse; but there were other reasons for adopting the Sabine as the boundary, and of which I was ignorant at the time the treaty was formed, and to the knowlege of which I have come within the last few years. Mr. Monroe, if I am correctly informed, in adopting that line acted under circumstances which left him little option. I am not at liberty to state them—the information I received confidentially. It is sufficient to state that he had ascertained that the Senate would not ratify a treaty with a boundary farther west. It was communicated to him by Senators of first respectability. Their reasons for refusing to ratify a treaty which would extend the boundary beyond the Sabine, I do not choose to go into, although it was communicated to me with information to which I have alluded.

But if we take out of the speech of the Senator what he has stated in relation to annexation, and the Florida treaty, in which, as I have stated, he has but repeated old and stale charges, that made not the slightest impression on the country at the time, what is there left of his present attack upon me? It is surprising that a man of his experience and sagacity should suppose that the repetition of these threadbare charges, regarded as futile when first made, should make any impression now. Indeed, I may consider myself obliged to him for repeating them, after such elaborate preparation, as it affords the most conclusive proof how exempt my course has been from any just censure during the long period of time in which he has attempted to trace it.

To make good his allegation that I am the anthor of annexation, and that annexation caused the war, he asserts that I was in favor of the annexation of Texas as far back as 1836, immediately after the battle of San Jacinto, and the capture of Santa Anna; to prove which, he read an extract from the speech which I delivered on resolutions from Mississippi, presented by her Senator, now Secretary of the Treasury, instructing the Senators to obtain an immediate recognition of the independence of Texas.

It is true that I then advocated an early recognition of the independence of Texas, and its admission into this Union; but I was not alone in that, nor did I take a leading part in the discussion; the two most prominent advocates of her cause at that time were the Senator from Mississippi, and my then colleague, (Mr. Preston;) but they were seconded by a large portion of this body at the time. The distinguished Senator from Massachusetts bore a part in the debate, and expressed his opinion in favor of recognition at an early period, and of the vast importance of the future condition of Texas to our country. I have not had time to examine the discussion; but find that I was among those who advised delay until further information could be obtained, and many were for prompt action; but the Senator from Missouri has thought proper, in the face of these facts, to hold me up as the only individual disposed for a prompt and immediate action. He has done more. He has suppressed the fact, very important to be known, that before the close of that very session, the report of the Committee on Foreign Relations, recommending that the acknowledgment of the independence of Texas, as soon as satisfactory information could be obtained that it had successfully established a Government, was adopted by the unanimous vote of the Senate, including the Senator himself, and that at the very next session her independence was recognized.

Sir, I admit, even at that early period, I saw that the incorporation of Texas into this Union, would be indispensable both to her safety and ours. I saw that it was impossible that she could stand as an independent power between us and Mexico, without becoming the scene of intrigue of foreign powers, alike destructive of the peace and security of both Texas and ourselves. I saw more: I saw the bearing of the slave question at that early stage, and that it would become an instrument in the hands of a foreign power of striking a blow at us, and that two conterminous slaveholding communities could not co-exist without one being wielded to the destruction of the other. The Senator is right. What I then said was intended to shadow forth the future, that future which actually came, when I was called, by the unanimous voice of the country, to take charge of the State Department, in reference to these very events. I saw, with General Jackson, that the golden opportunity had occurred when annexation must take place in order to avoid interminable difficulties and great disasters; and, seeing it, I did not hesitate to undertake the duty which has been assigned me, notwithstanding the difficulties, from the weakness of the Administration at that period. I succeeded, in despite of them, and that, too, without war; and all the elaborate efforts of the Senator from Missouri, never can deprive me of the credit to which I am entitled, in reference to the great question of annexation.

On a review of the whole, my course, I may say, exhibits not only some foresight in reference to it, but also some powers of averting the dangers, and securing the end which I desired.

Every measure towards the accomplishment of annexation had been consummated before the present Administration came into power. No war followed, although the act of annexation had been completed more than a year before the rupture between us and Mexico took place; nor would war have followed at all, had we acted with ordinary prudence. That Mexico was chafed, chagrined; that she threatened much, and blustered much; talked about war and even the existence of hostilities—are all true. It was, however, but talk. The strong should always permit the weak and aggrieved to talk, to bluster, and scold, without taking offence: and if we had so acted, and exercised proper skill in the management of our affairs, Mexico and ourselves would by this time have quietly and peaceably settled all difficulties, and been good friends. We have chosen to pursue the opposite course, and are in war.

Every Senator knows that I was opposed to the war; but none knows but myself the depth of that opposition. With my conceptions of its character and consequences, it was impossible for me to vote for it. When, accordingly, I was deserted by every friend on this side of the House, including my then honorable colleague among the rest, (Mr. McDuffie,) I was not shaken in the least degree in reference to my course. On the passage of the act recognizing the war, I said to many of my friends that a deed had been done from which the country would not be able to recover for a long time, if ever; and added, it has dropped a curtain between the present and the future, which to me is impenetrable; and for the first time since I have been in public life, I am unable to see the future. I also added, that it has closed the first volume of our political history under the constitution, and opened the second, and that no mortal could tell what would be written in it. These deep impressions were made upon my mind, because I saw, from the circumstances under which the war was made, a total departure from that course of policy which had governed the country from the commencement of our Government until that time; and that, too, under circumstances calculated to lead to most disastrous consequences. Since then less than a year has elapsed; but in that short period enough has already been developed to make what was then said look like prophecy.

But the Senator charges, entertaining as I did these impressions, that I did not take a stand, and arrest the march of General Taylor to the Rio del Norte. I have already stated the reasons on another occasion why I did not; and however unsatisfactory they may be to the

Senator, they are satisfactory to myself, and I doubt not they will be to the community at large. He also intimated that I ought to have communicated my views to the President. I was guilty of no neglect in that respect. I did not fail to state in the proper quarter explicitly what I thought would result from the order given to General Taylor, but I found very different views from mine entertained there. Those in power were quite as confident that the march of General Taylor to the Del Norte would not in its consequences involve war, as they were that notice without compromise in reference to the joint occupancy of Oregon would not involve war with England.

In looking back upon these matters, I have the satisfaction to feel that I fully performed my duty both here and elsewhere with reference to these important questions.

With my view of the character and consequences of the war, I have forborne much. I have suffered not a little in the estimation of my friends, both in and out of Congress, for refusing to vote for the bill recognizing the existence of a war asserted to be made by the act of Mexico. I have been urged by them to explain the reasons for my course on that occasion; but I persisted in declining to do so, because I could not see that it would be of any service to the country, while it might weaken the hands of those who are charged with the prosecution of the war. I adopted the only course which, according to my opinion, I could with propriety—to take no active or leading part in reference to the measures intended for carrying on the war, but to give a quiet and silent vote in favor of all which did not seem to me decidedly objectionable; but, in the mean time, to look out for the first favorable opportunity of presenting my views how the war should be conducted to bring it most advantageously to a successful termination. I accordingly embraced the opportunity on the discussion of the three-million bill now before the Senate, to present my views, not in the spirit of opposition, but of kindness to the Administration, reserving to myself the expression of my opinion as to the causes of the war for some suitable occasion. It seems, however, that the friends of those in power were not satisfied with this course on my part: it became an object of assault both in this Chamber and without its walls. The Senator from Tennessee immediately on my right, (Mr. TURNEY,) commenced the attack here by directly charging me with being the author of the war, and it has since been followed by the Senator from Missouri on this occasion. I have thus been forced, in self-defence, to depart from the line which I had prescribed for myself, and to enter into the question, Who is the author or the cause of the war? The responsibility is not on me, but on those who have compelled me to make the departure. Thus far I have limited what I have said strictly to self-defence, as I shall also do on the present occasion.

In looking to the causes which led to the war, I go one step further back than the Senator from Maine, (Mr. EVANS,) who discussed the subject in this aspect with great accuracy and ability. He began with Mr. Slidell's mission and negotiations. I go a step further back, to the management of the negotiation prior to that period. When this Administration came into power, there were two great questions on hand connected with our foreign relations—the Oregon and the Mexican. As different as they were in their character, and as remote as the two powers were from each other, there was an intimate connection between them which could not be overlooked in conducting the negotiation, without falling into a great and dangerous error. Such at least is my opinion. I wish to say nothing to wound the feelings of the distinguished individual who had charge of the negotiation, but it seems to me that he fell into a great error in consequence of overlooking this connection between the two subjects. To my mind it is one of the clearest of propositions, that there could be no well-founded hope of adjusting our difficulties with Mexico until the Oregon question was finally settled. Why so? The reason is obvious. Mexico knew that we had heavy claims against her, which she was little able to pay. Debtors without means are usually shy of their creditor. She could not but see that there was a chance of escaping our demands against her, provided a conflict should ensue between us and England in reference to Oregon. She could not but see more—that it might possibly afford her an opportunity of recovering either a part or the whole of Texas by an alliance with England, and availing herself of the aid of British strength and resources in waging a war against us. At all events, she would look with confidence to her being protected as an ally of England in the treaty by which the war should be terminated. Whatever objection may be made to England, she never deserts an ally in war. It seemed to me, under these circumstances, that it was a great error to suppose that the differences with Mexico could be adjusted while those with England were pending. Our true policy, then, according to my opinion, was to suspend all attempts at opening negotiation with Mexico until that question was finally settled. When that was effected, and Mexico could no longer look to the support of England in her controversy with us, she would see the folly of declining to adjust the differences between us, and enter into conflict with a power every way so vastly her superior.

There would, then, be another advantage which would greatly favor a settlement of our difficulties with Mexico. The eloquent Senator from Louisiana has truly said that Mexico, at least so far as capital is concerned, was a British colony. The immense interest which England has in the country, would have enlisted her on the side of peace, and the whole of her vast influence would have been exerted to induce Mexico to enter into a satisfactory arrangement with us. I cannot doubt that, under the influence of these powerful causes, with a little forbearance and prudence on our part, all the causes of difference between the two countries would, ere this, have been settled by a treaty satisfactory to both.

An opposite course was, however, unfortunately taken; both negotiations were pushed at the same time, and that with Mexico, with as much zeal, and as strong a pressure, as that with England. The then President of the republic of Mexico (Herrera) was friendly to the United States, and anxiously disposed, on that account, as well as others, to settle the differences with us. Acting under these feelings, he acceded to the proposition to receive a commissioner, without duly reflecting, as the events proved, on these great impediments in the minds of the Mexicans against treating with us. The result was as might have been anticipated. Paredes took advantage of the error, and hurled Herrera from power; and the effect of this premature attempt at opening negotiation, was to overthrow a friend and place an enemy in power, deeply committed against settling the differences between the two countries, and thereby—as ought to have been foreseen—greatly to increase the difficulty of any future settlement of the questions. What followed from this unfortunate step, until it ended in war between the two countries, has been so clearly traced by the Senator from Maine, as to supersede the necessity of my touching upon it.

The overlooking of the intimate connection of these two questions was not only the first link in that series of causes which finally terminated in this war, but it came near preventing the settlement of the Oregon question. Had the action of Congress, which finally led to the settlement of the Oregon question, been delayed until it was known that skirmishes had taken place between our forces and the Mexicans on the Rio Grande, (but a short period,) there is every reason to believe the Oregon question would not have been closed. I speak upon high authority,—the escape was a narrow one. Fortunately, the British Government promptly acted upon the notice, and tendered a proposition to our Minister on which the settlement was finally made, which he received and forwarded to our Government but a few days before news was received in England of the skirmishes on the Rio Grande. But while they fortunately occurred too late to prevent a settlement of the Oregon question, they unfortunately occurred too soon to preserve peace with Mexico. But if the policy which the Administration first adopted after annexation had been pursued, to occupy the frontier of Texas with our military forces to the extent of country which she held at the time of annexation, and no further, there is every reason to believe that on the settlement of the Oregon question the peace of the two countries would have been preserved.

It is true Mexico claimed the whole of Texas; but it is equally true that she recognized the difference, and showed a disposition to act upon it, between the country known as Texas proper and the country between it and the Del Norte. It is also true that we and Texas recognized the same difference, and that both regarded the boundary as unsettled, as the resolution of annexation, which provides that the boundary between Texas and Mexico shall be determined by the United States, clearly shows. It is worthy of remark in this connection, that this provision in the joint resolution is understood to have been inserted in consequence of the ground taken at the preceding session by the Senator from Missouri on the discussion of the treaty, that the Nueces was the western boundary of Texas, and that to extend that boundary to the Rio del Norte would take in part of Tamaulipas, Coahuila, and New Mexico. What, then, ought to have been the course of the Executive after annexation under this resolution? The very one which they at first pursued,—to restrict the position of our troops to the country actually occupied by Texas at the period of annexation. All beyond, as far as the Executive was concerned, ought to have been regarded as subject to the provisions of the resolutions, which authorized the Government to settle the boundary. There are but two modes of settling a disputed boundary—one by the joint consent of both parties, that is, by treaty, of which the President and the Senate are the organs; the other, by the determination of one of the parties for itself, after failing to obtain the consent of the other, and that, under our Government, can only be done by Congress. Indeed, when we speak of our Government, it is understood to mean Congress and the Executive, acting jointly—the one by passing an act or resolution, and the other by its approval. And in Congress, taken in this sense, all discretionary power under our system of Government is invested. It is only by this power that a disputed boundary can be determined by the Government for itself, and without the consent of the other party. The President had no more right to determine on his own will what the boundary was than I had, or any other Senator. Such, indeed, appeared to be the conviction of the President himself. It is only on such a supposition that we can explain his course in attempting to open a negotiation with Mexico, with a view of settling all differences between the two countries, among which the settlement of the boundary was considered a paramount question. Why negotiate, if it were not an unsettled question? Why negotiate, if the Rio del Norte—is, as it was afterwards assumed—was the clear and unquestionable boundary? And if not, upon what authority, after the attempt to open negotiation had failed, could he determine what was the boundary, viewing it as an open question? Was it not his plain duty, on such an occurrence, to submit the question to Congress, which was then in session, and in whom the right of establishing the boundary and declaring war was clearly invested? Had that course been adopted, I greatly mistake if the sense of this body would not have been decidedly opposed to taking any step which would have involved the two countries in war. Indeed, I feel a strong conviction, that if the Senate had been left free to decide on the question, not one-third of the body would have been found in favor of war. As it was, a large majority felt themselves compelled, as they believed, to vote for the bill recognizing the existence of war, in order to raise the supplies of men and money necessary to rescue the army under General Taylor, on the Del Norte, from the dangers to which it was exposed.

But to bring the matter home, the Senator himself is in no small degree responsible for the war. I intend no attack on him. I have made none, and will make none. The relations between him and myself, personal and political, have long been such, that self-respect and a sense of propriety forbid my alluding to him, except when unavoidable, and then in a courteous manner; and I now allude to his course only because it is necessary to explain mine, and the motives which governed me on the occasion.

The Senate will remember, that when the President's Message was received recommending Congress to recognize that a war existed between us and Mexico, and to raise the necessary means for its prosecution, the Senator from Mississippi, whose seat is immediately on my right, but who is now absent, (Mr. SPEIGHT,) moved to print twenty thousand copies of the Message and documents. The scene was a solemn one, and what occurred will long be remembered by the members of the body. I rose and objected; and said that we were on the eve of great events, and expressed my hope that we would proceed calmly and deliberately. I suggested that the printing of so large a number of copies would be construed into an endorsement of the Message; adding, that I was unwilling either to endorse or condemn, until the Message and documents were printed, and carefully perused by me. A debate ensued, and the Journals of the Senate will show what took place. The Senator from Missouri was the individual who made the discreet and appropriate motion to separate the recommendations of the Message into two parts, and refer that which related to recognizing the existence of war to the Committee on Foreign Relations, and that which related to the raising of men and supplies, to the Committee on Military Affairs, of which he was chairman. The latter, it was expected, would report immediate measures for the support of General Taylor. I seconded the motion, and it was carried by a large majority. I saw in it that which gave me hope, and that I should be able to effect the object I had in view, and which I will hereafter explain.

The House of Representatives acted with much more precipitancy; it passed a bill the very day the Message was received, recognizing the existence of the war, and providing means for its prosecution. It was late in the evening when it passed the House, and I am of the impression that the Senate had adjourned; and it was not reported to it that day; but be that as it may, the next day the Senator, as chairman of the Committee on Military Affairs, reported the bill to the Senate as it came from the House, with both provisions in it; directly contrary to the order of the Senate, made on his own motion, to refer the part of the Message relating to the recognition of war to the Committee on Foreign Relations. To that, and the fact that a caucus had been held of the party which agreed to sustain the report, may be traced the precipitate (to use no stronger word) action of the Senate, and the recognition of the war. It emphatically made the war. Had the order of the Senate been respected—had the Senator from Missouri, in conformity with it, and as he was in duty bound to do, moved to strike out all that related to the recognition of the war, and referred it to the Committee on Foreign Relations, and confined his report to raising the necessary means of rescuing General Taylor and his army from the pressing dangers which surrounded them, the possibility is, that the war might have been averted, and the two countries at this day have been at peace. Sir, I say possibility, because, even then, after the skirmishes between our forces had occurred, I did not despair of escaping war, if sufficient firmness and prudence were used on the part of this body. I had deeply reflected on the subject in advance, and great as were the difficulties, I still saw a gleam of hope.

The intelligence of the skirmishes on the Rio Grande was received here on Saturday. I at once saw the danger, and turned my mind to the subject. I anticipated that a Message would be received on Monday from the Executive, and formed not an incorrect opinion as to what would be its character. Casting my eyes over the whole, with a view of avoiding war, I came to the conclusion in my own mind, what course was best to effect that object. Next morning I communicated the conclusions to which I had come to two of my colleagues, who were boarding with me; I said to them, that there was but one way of escaping war, but I am not certain that it would be successful. It will, however, place us in the chapter of accidents, and thereby afford a possibility of escape. I was asked what it was, and replied, that it depended on separating the question of war from that which relates to the rescuing of General Taylor and his forces. Let the means necessary for the latter be immediately granted, but let time be taken for due and deliberate consideration of the former. Had that been done, it was my intention to throw my whole weight against the immediate declaration or recognition of war; treating what had occurred as mere hostilities between the two armies, without authority of the Congress—the war-making power of either Government.

We had not a particle of evidence then, or even now, that the Republic of Mexico had made war against the United States. Indeed, we are in the anomalous condition of the two countries being at war during and almost an entire year, without either having declared it, although the constitutions of both expressly provide that Congress shall declare war.

Instead, then, of recognizing war, I would have taken the very opposite ground—that what had occurred was mere hostilities, and not war, as the Congress of Mexico had not authorized it.

To provide for the contingency of the Congress of Mexico approving of what had occurred, and refusing to treat for the settlement of our difficulties, I would have advised the raising of ample provisional force, to be collected at some convenient and healthy point, where they could be trained during the interval, and be fully prepared to meet such decision; but even in case such decision should be made, instead of advising a formal declaration of war, I would have advised, as General Jackson recommended, giving authority to the Executive to make reprisals for seizing and holding such portion of the Mexican territory as would afford ample indemnity, to be retained until the differences between the two countries were settled; but, in the mean time, would have taken measures to repel the attacks made upon our army by the Mexican forces, and to drive them far beyond the limits of our borders.

Had this course been pursued, we should have had all the glory and reputation of the two brilliant victories at Palo Alto and Resaca de la Palma without being involved in the present indefinite and expensive war waged against Mexico. We would also have had the advantage of the chapter of accidents—of Mexico disavowing hostilities, and indemnifying our citizens—either from a sense of weakness, or of returning justice on her part, or from the influence of other powers, which have an interest in preserving peace, from their commercial or other relations with her, and thereby save a resort to arms on our part. But, at all events, failing in that, we would have avoided, by resorting to reprisals, the enormous expenses, the sacrifice of men and money, and the disasters to which the war has exposed us. I have now met, and, I trust, successfully repelled, all the charges made by the Senator from Missouri, except those relating to the Missouri compromise, and the abolition question at that period, for which I am in no ways responsible. I was not then in Congress. I filled the office of Secretary of War at the time, and had no agency or control over it. His charges are as light as air—old and stale, without even plausibility, and I have not the slightest fear of their having any weight, either here or in the community.

MONDAY, March 1.

Three Million Bill—Mr. Upham's Amendment—Ordinance of 1784 and 1787—Their Origin, and how Passed—Transcript from the Journals of the Congress of the Confederation.

Mr. UPHAM rose and moved an amendment, to come in as a second section, as follows:

SEC. 2. *And be it further enacted,* That there shall be neither slavery nor involuntary servitude in any territory which shall hereafter be acquired or be annexed to the United States, otherwise than in the punishment of crimes whereof the party shall have been duly convicted: *Provided always,* That any person escaping into the same, from whom labor or service is lawfully claimed in any one of the United States, such fugitive may be lawfully reclaimed and conveyed out of said territory to the person claiming his or her labor or service."

Mr. UPHAM sustained his amendment in substance as follows:

I will, sir, refer to the proceedings of the Congress of the Confederation in 1784. On the 9th of April, 1784, Congress took into consideration the report of a committee consisting of Mr. Jefferson, Mr. Chase of Maryland, and Mr. Howell of Rhode Island, to whom was recommitted their report of a plan for a temporary government of the western territory. The plan reported contained a clause prohibiting slavery in the territory after the year 1800. Here is the clause, and the vote upon it:

"IN CONGRESS OF THE CONFEDERATION,
"*April* 19, 1784.

"That after the year 1800 of the Christian era, there shall be neither slavery nor involuntary servitude in any of the said States, otherwise than in the punishment of crimes, whereof the party shall have been convicted to have been personally guilty." And on the question, Shall the words moved to be struck out stand? The yeas and nays being required by Mr. Howell:

New Hampshire.	Mr. Foster, ay. Mr. Blanchard, ay.	Ay.
Massachusetts...	Mr. Gerry, ay. Mr. Patridge, ay.	Ay.
Rhode Island....	Mr. Ellery, ay. Mr. Howell, ay.	Ay.
Connecticut......	Mr. Sherman, ay. Mr. Wadsworth, ay.	Ay.
New York........	Mr. De Witt, ay. Mr. Paine, ay.	Ay.
New Jersey......	Mr. Dick, ay	*
Pennsylvania.....	Mr. Mifflin, ay. Mr. Montgomery, ay. Mr. Hand, ay.	Ay.
Maryland.........	Mr. McHenry, no. Mr. Stone, no.	No.
Virginia..........	Mr. Jefferson, ay. Mr. Hardy, no Mr. Mercer, no.	No.
North Carolina..	Mr. Williamson, ay. Mr. Speight, no.	Div.

South Carolina..	Mr. Read, no. Mr. Beresford, no.	No.

"So the question was lost, and the words were stricken out."

It required the vote of seven States to carry a proposition in the affirmative, so the words were stricken out. It will be perceived, sir, by looking at the vote, that seven States voted aye, but there is an asterisk put down to the State of New Jersey, and the aye of Mr. Dick, it appears, was not counted. I do not know for what reason it was rejected, but, probably, because the whole delegation from the State was not present. Only three States voted to reject the article—Maryland, South Carolina, and Virginia. Mr. Jefferson voted to retain it, but Mr. Hardy and Mr. Mercer voted to reject it. North Carolina was divided, and her vote was lost. So the vote stands six States for retaining the article, and three for rejecting it. I have introduced these proceedings, sir, for the purpose of showing, that immediately after the peace of 1783, the people regarded slavery as a great evil, and desired to prohibit it in all the territories belonging to the Confederation..

But to proceed: In 1787, the attention of the Congress of the Confederation was again directed to the subject of slavery in the North-west Territory, and an ordinance for the government of the territory, prohibiting slavery, was reported by a committee, consisting of Mr. Carrington of Virginia, Mr. Dane of Massachusetts, Mr. R. H. Lee of Virginia, Mr. McKean of South Carolina, and Mr. Smith of New York. Here, sir, is the article prohibiting slavery, and the vote upon it:

"In Congress of the Confederation.

"13*th July*, 1787.

"According to order, the ordinance for the Government of the territory of the United States, north-west of the river Ohio, was read a third time, and passed, as follows:

* * * * * * *

"Art. 6. There shall be neither slavery nor involuntary servitude in the said territory, otherwise than in the punishment of crimes whereof the party shall have been duly convicted: *Provided always*, That any person escaping into the same, from whom labor or service is lawfully claimed in any one of the United States, such fugitive may be lawfully reclaimed, and conveyed to the person claiming his or her labor or service as aforesaid.

"*Be it ordained by the authority aforesaid*, That the resolutions of the 23d of April, 1784, relative to the subject of this ordinance, be, and the same are hereby, repealed, and declared null and void. Done, &c.

"On passing the above ordinance, the yeas and nays being required by Mr. Yates:

Massachusetts...	Mr. Holton, ay. Mr. Dane, ay.	Ay.
New York........	Mr. Smith, ay. Mr. Haring, ay. Mr. Yates, no.	Ay.
New Jersey......	Mr. Clark, ay. Mr. Scheurman, ay.	Ay.
Delaware.........	Mr. Kearny, ay. Mr. Mitchell, ay.	Ay.
Virginia...........	Mr. Gayson, ay. Mr. R. H. Lee, ay. Mr. Carrington, ay.	Ay.
North Carolina..	Mr. Blount, ay. Mr. Hawkins, ay.	Ay.
South Carolina...	Mr. Kean, ay. Mr. Huger, ay.	Ay.
Georgia...........	Mr. Few, ay. Mr. Pierce, ay.	Ay.

"So it was resolved in the affirmative."

Every State present voted to retain the article. There was but one vote against it, and that was from the State of New York. This ordinance repealed the ordinance of 1784, and forever prohibited slavery in all the territories then belonging to the Confederacy. The slave States, at that time, had no desire to see slavery established in any part of the country where it did not then exist. Universal emancipation was the wish and the prayer of the ablest and the wisest statesmen of the Confederacy.

Mr. Webster said: If my health had been better, and more time had remained to us, it was my purpose to address the Senate on the bill before it, and also on several topics with which it is connected. This purpose, under existing circumstances, I must necessarily forego. The true origin of the war with Mexico, and the motives and purposes for which it was originally commenced, however ably discussed already, are subjects not yet exhausted. I have been particularly desirous of examining the them. I am greatly deceived, Mr. President, if we shall not ere long see facts coming to the light, and circumstances found coinciding and concurring, which shall fix on the Executive Government a more definite and distinct purpose, intended to be effected with the co-operation of others, in bringing on hostilities with Mexico, than has as yet been clearly developed or fully understood.

Sir, we are in the midst of a war, not waged at home in defence of our soil, but waged a thousand miles off, and in the heart of the territories of another Government. Of that war no one yet sees the end, and no one counts the cost. It is not denied that this war is now prosecuted for the acquisition of territory; at least if any deny it, others admit it, and all know it to be true.

Under these circumstances, and plainly seeing this purpose to exist, seven or eight of the free States, comprising some of the largest, have remonstrated against the prosecution of the war for such a purpose, in language suited to express their meaning. These remonstrances come here with the distinct and precise object of dissuading us from the further prosecution of the war for the acquisition of territory by conquest. Before territory is actually obtained, and its future character fixed, they beseech us to give up an object so full of danger. One and all, they protest against the extension of slave territory; one and all, they regard it as the solemn duty of the representatives of the free States to take security in advance that no more slave States shall be added to the Union. They demand of us this pledge, this assurance, before the purchase money is paid or the bargain concluded. And yet, Mr. President, ingenuity has been taxed to its utmost; criticisms, both deep and shallow, and hypercriticisms quite incomprehensible, have all been resorted to, in the hope of showing that we do not understand the people; that their resolutions are not what they seem to be; that they do not require any immediate movement or present opposition; that they only look to some distant future, some emergencies yet to arise; that they only refer to a disposition in regard to territory, after it shall have been acquired and settled; and in one instance, I think it was said that it did not appear that any thing was required of us for fifty years to come.

But here, sir, I cannot but pause. I am arrested by the occurrences of this night which, I confess, fill me with alarm. They are ominous, portentous. Votes which have been just passed by majorities here, cannot fail to arrest public attention. Every patriotic American, every man who wishes to preserve the constitution, ought to ponder them well. I heard, sir, the honorable member from New York, (Mr. DIX,) and with a great part of his remarks I agreed; I thought they must lead to some useful result. But, then, what does he come to, after all? He is for acquiring territory under the Wilmot proviso; but, at any rate, he is for acquiring territory. He will not vote against all territory to form new States, though he is willing to say they ought not to be slave States. Other gentlemen of his party, from the Northern and Eastern States, vote in the same way and with the same view. This is called "the policy of the Northern Democracy." I so denominate the party only because it so denominates itself. A gentleman from South Carolina, (Mr. BUTLER,) if I understood him rightly, said he wanted no new territory: all he desired was equality, and no exclusion; he wished the South to be saved from any thing derogatory; and yet he does not vote against the acquisition of territory. Nor do other Senators from Southern States. They are, therefore, in general, in favor of new territory and new States being slave States. This is the policy of the Southern Democracy. Both parties agree, therefore, to carry on the war for territory, though it be not decided now whether the character of new acquired territory shall be that of freedom or of slavery. This point they are willing to leave for future agitation and future controversy. Gentlemen who are in favor of the Wilmot proviso are ready, nevertheless, to vote for this bill; though that proviso be struck out. The gentleman from New York is ready for that, and his Northern and Eastern friends, who sit round him here in the Senate, are as ready as he is. They all demand acquisition, and maintain the war for that purpose. On the other hand, the other branch of the party votes eagerly and unitedly for territory, the Wilmot proviso being rejected, because these gentlemen take it for granted, that that proviso being rejected, States formed out of Mexico will necessarily be slave States, and added to this Union as such.

Mr. President, I must be indulged here in a short retrospection. In the present posture of things and of parties, we may well look back upon the past. Within a year or two after Texas had achieved its independence, there were those who already spoke of its annexation to the United States. Against that project, I felt it to be my duty to take an early and a decided course. Having occasion to address political friends in the city of New York in March, 1837, I expressed my sentiments as fully and as strongly as I could. From those opinions I have never swerved. From the first I saw nothing, and have seen nothing, but evil and danger to arise to the country from such annexation. The prudence of Mr. Van Buren stifled the project for a time; but in the latter part of the Administration of Mr. Tyler, it was revived. Sir, the transactions and the occurrences from that time onward, till the measure was finally consummated in December, 1845, are matters of history and record. That history and that record can neither be falsified nor erased. There they stand, and must stand forever; and they proclaim to the whole world, and to all ages, that Texas was brought into this Union, slavery and all, only by means of the aid and active co-operation of those who now call themselves the "Northern Democracy" of the United States; in other words, by those who assert their own right to be regarded as nearest and dearest to the people *among* all the public men of the country. Where was the honorable member from New York, where were his Northern and Eastern friends, when Texas was pressing to get into the Union, bringing slaves and slavery with her? Where were they, I ask? Were they standing up like men against slaves and slavery? Was the annexation of a new slave State an object which "Northern Democracy" opposed, or from which it averted its eyes with horror? Sir, the gentleman from New York and his friends were consulting and assisting, aiding and abetting, the whole proceeding. Some of them were voting here as eagerly as if the salvation of the country depended on bringing in another slave State. Others of us from the North opposed it as far as we could. We remonstrated, we protested, we voted; but the "Northern Democracy" helped to out-vote us, to defeat us, to overwhelm us. And they accomplished their purpose. Nay, more. The party in the North which calls itself, by way of distinction and eminence, the "Liberty Party," opposed, with all its force, the election of the Whig candidate in 1844, when it had the power of assisting in and securing the election of that candidate, and of preventing Mr. Polk's election; and when it was clear and visible as the sun at noonday, that Mr. Polk's election would bring slaveholding Texas into the Union. No man can deny this. And in the party of this "Northern Democracy," and in this "Liberty Party," too, probably, are those, at this moment, who profess themselves ready to meet all the consequences, to stand the chance of all convulsions, to see the fountains of the great deep broken up, rather than that new slave States should be added to the Union; but who, nevertheless, will not join with us in a declaration against new States of any character, thereby shutting the door forever against the further admission of slavery.

Here, sir, is a chapter of political inconsistency which demands the consideration of the country, and is not unlikely to attract the attention of the age. If it be any thing but party attachment, carried, recklessly, to every extent, and party antipathy maddened into insanity, I know not how to describe it.

Sir, I fear we are not yet arrived at the beginning of the end. I pretend to see but little of the future, and that little gives no gratification. All I can scan is contention, strife, and agitation. Before we obtain perfect right to conquered territory, there must be a cession. A cession can only be made by treaty. No treaty can pass the Senate, till the constitution is overthrown, without the consent of two-thirds of its members. Now, who can shut his eyes to the great probability of a successful resistance to any treaty of cession, from one quarter of the Senate or another? Will the North consent to a treaty bringing in territory subject to slavery? Will the South consent to a treaty bringing in territory from which slavery is excluded? Sir, the future is full of difficulties and full of dangers. We are suffering to pass the golden opportunity for securing harmony and the stability of the constitution. We appear to me to be rushing upon perils headlong, and with our eyes all open. But I put my trust in Providence, and in that good sense and patriotism of the people, which will yet, I hope, arouse themselves before it is too late.

Mr. ARCHER said the bill had assumed the form which it bore at the last session, when he expressed himself to be favorable to its passage; and it might well be the subject of inquiry why he should not support it now. His reasons could be given in a few words. Last year, though the same phraseology was employed as in the bill now under consideration, the purpose was reputed to be to settle our boundary according to what then was assumed to be our limit, and the money was not to be employed for ulterior objects. He was opposed to the acquisition of one inch of Mexican territory beyond what was necessary to define our boundary. We should sustain and defend rather than despoil a sister republic. There were no republics but those on this continent, not one of which but required support to enable it to maintain free institutions. But if we despoil a sister republic, what sentiment did they suppose would be infused in the heart of every other republic in America? They would be induced to guard against the republic of the United States either by a military dictatorship or by a monarchy, as Paredes had attempted in Mexico, and as had been attempted in some of the South American republics. The necessity of self-preservation would drive them to such a course to secure them from being despoiled by us.

But there was another view that was just as absolutely imperative on his mind as that at which he had only just glanced. It was the introduction of the slave question, which would come up with the acquisition of new territory. Had they, he inquired, become absolutely insane with this rabid appetite for territorial acquisition? What was the superficial extent of the United States? Had gentlemen passed their minds over it? Did any man suppose that there would be no difficulty in carrying out this problem of a free Government without further acquisition, as our population increased? The House of Representatives, now with two hundred and twenty-eight members, found it necessary to adopt the "one-hour rule" in debate; but when we become a population of one hundred millions, as it had been calculated we soon should, it would be necessary to adopt a "minute rule," and then every thing would be done out of doors—nothing more than the mere forms of deliberation remaining; and we shall become the most corrupt Government ever seen in the world. And did any man doubt, if they passed this appropriation, that the struggle on the question of slavery would come? Let honorable Senators read the resolutions which have already been presented from eight or nine States of this Union, expressing their inflexible purpose to exclude slavery from all territory that may hereafter be acquired. And he had information that resolutions had passed one branch of the Legislature of Virginia, and were expected to pass the other, in which language was used which showed that the people of his State were prepared for resistance to the determination of the free States. It was evident, then, that the passage of this bill would minister to the dissensions of the States, and if they were to subscribe a paper, declaring their purpose to be to produce such a calamity, it would not be more apparent than by the passage of this bill. It was lamentable to think of the consequences to result, which would be either the overthrow of this Union, or the infusion into the veins of the body politic a poison that would make it unworthy of preservation.

The question was then taken, and it resulted thus:

YEAS.—Messrs. Allen, Ashley, Atchison, Atherton, Bagby, Benton, Breese, Bright, Butler, Calhoun, Cass, Chalmers, Colquitt, Dickinson, Dix, Fairfield, Hannegan, Houston, Johnson of Louisiana, Lewis, Mason,

Niles, Rusk, Sevier, Soulé, Sturgeon, Turney, Westcott, and Yulee—29.

NAYS.—Messrs. Archer, Badger, Berrien, Cameron, Cilley, John M. Clayton, Corwin, Crittenden, Davis, Dayton, Evans, Greene, Huntington, Jarnagin, Johnson of Maryland, Mangum, Miller, Morehead, Pearce, Phelps, Simmons, Upham, Webster, and Woodbridge—24.

The bill was then read a third time and passed.

The Senate adjourned at twenty minutes past one o'clock, A. M

TUESDAY, March 2.

Personal and Explanatory—General Jackson and Senator Benton.

[After his opposition to the ratification of the Texas annexation treaty, 1844, the party chagrined by that rejection, threw all the blame of it upon Senator Benton, using General Jackson's name to call him a traitor, who had deserted to the Whigs; and accounting for it by attributing it to the loss of his senses in being blown up in the explosion of the great gun on board the steam frigate Princeton, February, 1844. Having produced one of these publications, Senator Benton read it, for the purpose of doing justice to General Jackson, and showing what was attributed to him was a heartless calumny upon him.]

Mr. BENTON said a strange scene was then presented. General Jackson was quoted against him in every form and shape directed in the letter. Traitor—Whig—Clay man—Mexican—British—deserter—enemy to the country—lost his senses since he was blown up in the explosion of the steam-frigate Princeton: such were the strings upon which they harped, and all in the service of two men, (Messrs. Tyler and Calhoun,) who were pursuing General Jackson to an infamous condemnation, when he, (Mr. B.,) almost "solitary and alone," was defending him against the combined attacks of the whole Whig phalanx and their allies from the Democracy. He had answered nothing to these hirelings. He looked forward to the day when he was to turn upon their masters, and that day has now come. He had not even made known to General Jackson the infamous use to which they had prostituted his name. If he had, he well knew the generous soul of Jackson would have revolted at their conduct. But he said nothing. Proud, erect, silent, scornful, he let the dogs bark on! trusting to the people of Missouri to bear him harmless through the attack, and to a just Providence to bring a day of retribution upon the true assailants. He had not been deceived in either dependence. The people of Missouri saved him in 1844: Providence had given a day of retaliation now in 1847. It was not until it was all over that he had said any thing to General Jackson, and then not to humiliate him, by letting *him* suppose that it was necessary for him to disavow the infamous use that had been made of his name—infamous, when those who had endeavored to destroy him, had the audacity to quote him—and to quote him falsely—against his faithful defender against their attacks. It was at the close of his life that his friend, Major William B. Lewis, carried him an affectionate message, to which he responded, on a dying bed, with the deep feeling and cordial justice which belonged to his exalted character. The words which he then spoke, faithfully preserved and transcribed, by the hand of an amanuensis, have been transferred to the heart of his old friend, where they will live while that heart beats, and which should find a place on the stone which should cover it when cold. "Tell the Colonel I thank him for his kind recollection of me in my old age and sore afflictions.—He is not only a statesmen, but a patriot, and has done his country service.—He gave my Administration efficient support, for which I am grateful.—Thank him in my name for his kind and affectionate message.*" Such were the words of Jackson! worthy of his great soul! worthy of

---

* The whole letter from Major Lewis deserves to be given, and is here inserted entire:

"FAIRFIELD, *March* 4, 1846.

"MY DEAR COLONEL: I will thank you to hand or send the enclosed to our friend John C. Rives.

"When I last saw you in Washington, it was the day before you proposed leaving for St. Louis, and, as I was making arrangements also to return to my residence in the vicinity of Nashville, you desired me, should General Jackson be living, to present to him your kindest and most affectionate regards, and to say to him, that nothing would give you so much pleasure as to be able to shake him once more by the hand. On my arrival I found him still living, thanks to a kind Providence, and he continued to live for a week after. I got to Nashville on Sunday, the first day of June last, and on Monday morning, after an early breakfast, I mounted my horse, and rode up to the Hermitage. I found the good old general sitting up in a large arm-chair, and Mr. Healy engaged in painting his likeness for Louis Philippe. Though feeble and much emaciated, yet his voice was clear and firm, and his mind as bright and vigorous as it ever was at any period of his life. I remained at the Hermitage the greater part of two days, and had much conversation with him in relation to matters appertaining to both the past and present time, and was astonished to find how perfectly he recollected every thing, particularly such as related to his Administration, from the most important, down to the smallest and most trivial matters. He inquired after many old friends, and among them yourself, desiring to know when I had seen you last, and how you were. I told him that I had seen you but a few days before I left Washington, and that you were well, and, at the same time, delivered to him your message. He was evidently much affected when I repeated what you had desired me to say to him. After a short pause, he said: 'I thank the colonel for his kind recollection of me in my old age and sore afflictions; it would give me great pleasure to see him once more, but that, I fear, is impossible, as my life is rapidly drawing to a close.' Here he again paused, and then added: 'The colonel is not only an able and distinguished statesman, but a warm and sincere patriot, and his country is under great obligations to him. I feel grateful for the able and efficient support he gave to me during the whole of my Administration, and I beg you, when next you see him, to remember me to him, and thank him, in my name, for his kind and affectionate message.' These, I believe, my dear sir, are his precise words; for, as they were spoken with much feeling and in a deep and solemn tone of voice, they made an impression on my mind that can never be effaced: and, as life is uncertain, it may never be in my power to repeat to you, in person, the remarks of the general when I delivered to him your message, or to comply with his injunction at their close, I cannot, therefore, permit this opportunity to

his great heart! worthy of his whole life! Yet it was into HIS mouth that hirelings were instructed to put the words traitor—deserter—and every opprobrious epithet, even to an impious taunt upon a providential calamity—and apply them to Benton! But God is just, and truth is powerful, and will prevail; and Jackson and Benton stand unhurt in the face of the world, while the assailants, and their employers, hide their heads.

Expulsion of Mr. Ritchie from the Floor of the Senate.

Mr. BENTON had listened with some surprise to the lecture which the Senator from Virginia had read to him. Lately, on a recent occasion, he had been absent on account of sickness, but he found that for three days consecutively the business of the Senate had been obstructed by the discussion of a resolution against Messrs. Ritchie & Heiss, or against Mr. Ritchie alone. During the whole of that time, the business of the session was thrown aside, and from the lecture which the Senator from Virginia had read to him, he should be led to suppose that that Senator was not here, or that he fought against it manfully. The Senator says nothing.

Mr. ARCHER said that he took no part in the discussion referred to until just before the decision, and then he did not occupy more than ten minutes.

Mr. BENTON continued. The Senator from Alabama (Mr. BAGBY) was here three days, ready to proceed with his remarks on an important question then pending before the Senate; but it was thrown aside by the discussion on the resolution to expel the editor of the *Union*. Now, how did the Senator from Virginia vote on that matter? How did he vote on the motions to stave off the business, and to pursue old Father Ritchie? That is the rub. If he voted to put aside the important business of the session for such a purpose, he had no right to read such a lecture as they had just heard from him. The Senator from Virginia would have to purge himself of that before he could come here as a lecturer against a waste of time. The proceedings of the three days to which he had referred, were the worst three days' work that had ever been done here. This, he supposed, would come in for the worst one day's work. The Senator from Virginia, and his friends, had spent three days to oppress a gentleman who was of the race of men such as Madison and Jefferson, and their compeers, with whom Mr. Ritchie was a contemporary and friend.

Having been reproached for consuming the time of the Senate in resisting such a motion as this, he took the opportunity to call the attention of the American people to the combination for the expulsion of Mr. Ritchie, the friend and associate of Madison and Jefferson, ignominiously from this chamber. But it was not alone against that man, who for forty years had been the champion of Democracy and of the Republican party. The war went beyond him, though he might experience the fate of Mr. Van Buren, after his rejection on this floor. He hoped the Republican party would notice the alarm given, and be true to the cause against outrage and oppression. The expulsion of Mr. Ritchie went beyond the man: it reached the cause—the sacred cause of Democracy, attacked in his person; and he saw "the sign of an omen," as a good friend of his was accustomed to say of bad signs, in this covert design to get $18,000 of public money to start a new press, the week after the editor of the Daily Union was expelled the chamber, and, as far as such a vote went, discredited and stigmatized. The two events came together—the expulsion of one, and a grab at public money for the other—in marvellous close conjunction. The two should be contemplated as a unit!

Mr. B. intimated his intention to call for the reading of the reports which had heretofore been made on the subject of employing reporters for this body.

Mr. ARCHER received in the best part the courtesies of the Senator from Missouri; but in regard to the agency he had in the resolution to which the Senator had referred, as causing a protracted debate, he begged to remark that it originated on the other side of the chamber. Mr. A. said he sat in quietude during that discussion for reasons personal to himself—not that he was not moved, but he did not wish to express any harsh opinions, if it could be avoided, on the resolution to exclude a man from the Senate chamber who had shown himself unworthy of their courtesies. He was desirous not to let his tongue utter what his heart dictated. He had no agency in bringing the resolution before the Senate, nor would he have counselled it, for he believed the article and the author were beneath the notice of the Senate. But when the question was addressed to them whether they would maintain their dignity, who could say that the expulsion which had been resolved on was not merited? The Senator from Missouri had spoken of the editor of the Union as the champion of the Republican party. Now he (Mr. A.) was as much a Republican as any man, but he was no Democrat. It was "Republican party" in Virginia, but it was "Democratic party" in Missouri; and the very last thing he wished to be called was a Democrat. The Senator from Missouri said they were waging war against Democracy. Yes, he hoped he should ever wage war against Democracy—unappeasable war—for he looked upon Democracy as the worst enemy to our Republican institutions—worse even than monarchy. He abhorred Democracy as the worst form of tyranny. If the Senator from Missouri wished to do him honor—and he knew the Senator

pass without doing so. I consider it due not only to you, but to the memory of the illustrious dead.

"With my best wishes, I beg you to believe me, my dear sir, very truly yours, W. B. LEWIS.

"To Col. THOMAS H. BENTON, *Washington*."

from Missouri had no unkind feelings towards him—he would say, there goes a fast undeviating enemy of Democracy.

Mr. BENTON replied most amicably to the courteous part of the Senator's (Mr. ARCHER's) remarks. He felicitated himself on five-and-twenty years of most agreeable personal and parliamentary intercourse with that Senator, and wished him all honor and felicity, and especially the felicity of being yet surrounded with a charming posterity, even to the third generation. He looked upon him (Mr. ARCHER) as the *beau ideal* of an old Virginia gentleman, and who would lack nothing to the felicitous termination of an honorable and courteous life but that charming family group, to enliven and adorn his hospitable parlor, and to sweeten and embellish the evening of his days, and of all which there was yet no room to despair. But that was not the point nor the rub in this case. The point was as to the loss of three days' precious time, in pursuing old Father Ritchie, to the neglect of the public business! The Senator says he did not speak ten minutes. But did he not vote ten minutes to stave off the business? That is the rub! For one thing he must return sincere thanks to the gentleman —was in harmony with his courteous character: he says he will wage *peaceable* war on the Democracy—

Mr. ARCHER. Unappeasable, not peaceable.

Mr. BENTON, [laughingly.] Ah, then they were to have an "unappeasable" war against Democracy, and a "peaceable" war against Mexico.

Mr. BUTLER rose to take no part in the colloquy between the Senators from Missouri and Virginia, but he intended to set the matter right respecting the editor of the *Union*, for he found that he was attempted to be shielded under the liberty of the press. Mr. B. then narrated the circumstances attending the expulsion of Mr. Ritchie, to whom, he said, he had been sincerely disposed to offer a safety-valve. He was anxious that the whole matter should be referred to a committee, before whom he might appear and make some explanation, or apology, or any thing that would be satisfactory to the Senate. Mr. B. had no personal feelings in the case, for they would be the last feelings he would indulge. He would, under any such circumstances, rather play the part of the sacrifice than the butcher. But it would be recollected that he was rebuked by the Senator from Virginia for desiring to take the course which he suggested. For thirty years he had pursued the course of condemning no man unheard, and if he had been placed on the committee which he proposed, as chairman, and, perhaps, according to parliamentary usage he should have been, if Mr. Ritchie had appeared before him, and shown that the article was published without his knowledge and approbation, Mr. B. would have permitted him to escape.

Mr. ARCHER. And I avowed myself of the same opinion.

Mr. BUTLER continued. He had applied to the friends of Mr. Ritchie, all round, and they repudiated the idea of such a committee. They treated it with more than indifference. They absolutely proscribed, denounced, and refused it. He really would have been satisfied if Mr. Ritchie would have done any thing that would have enabled him to escape. But if Mr. Ritchie would not do that, he would say with Juvenal, *nulla vestigia retrorsum.* Mr. Ritchie assumed to be another Cromwell, who came down to the Long Parliament, and to one said, "Sir, you are a hypocrite;" to another, "You are a traitor;" and to another, "You are a liar;" and to another, "You are not a gentleman." Mr. Ritchie, though he did not claim the right to enter the Long Parliament and say it, claimed the right to do it through his paper; and though he was admitted to this floor by courtesy, he asserted that the Senate had no jurisdiction over him. He went so far as to deny the right of this body to raise a committee to hear him, and now he was seeking refuge under the liberty of the press, and the Senator from Missouri identified him with Jefferson and Madison to give him impunity for his course. Mr. B. had no enmity against the old gentleman; but when he heard this liberty of the press spoken of in such a connection, he had felt it to be his duty to define what he meant. When this matter was first spoken of, he heard nothing of these political schemes that were now so current, nor of any invasion of the freedom of the press; and he thought the whole thing would be soon understood.

Mr. NILES said here was a struggle between two divisions of the Senate—a large majority on the one side and a determined minority on the other—on a matter which, on the face of it, was of very little importance to the republic, whether looking to the domestic policy or the relations which were disturbed by war. The Senator from Virginia, (Mr. ARCHER,) who was about to leave the Senate, appeared to consider that he had had the revision of the courtesies of the Senate. How, then, they should get along without him he was at a loss to conjecture. There was, however, some courtesy due to his brother Senators—to those who, for acting with the Senator from Missouri, he had called recreants, and charged on them the obstruction of the public business. Mr. N. had concurred with the Senator from Missouri by calling for the yeas and nays, and voting on the amendments, because he thought they were very proper. He had acted in some measure with a view to defeat this measure. And if the Senator from Missouri, and those who had acted with him in sustaining his amendments, had acted with singular pertinacity, those on the other side had been equally pertinacious in obstructing the business of the session. And was there nothing due to the strong convictions of a minority—of those who believe this measure to be wrong—who believe it to be something more than it is on its face? Were they to be told that this subject must take precedence, although it had undergone no examination, and thereby hazard all the business before them? There were important principles involved in this proposition. If there was nothing more than appeared on the face of it, it was a new and important principle to introduce into this body. What was it? Was it not the creation of new officers to this body? Was it not to take into their own hands the jurisdiction over and the direction and control of the publication of the proceedings of this body? And has this ever been done? Had it ever been considered part of the duty of the Senate of the United States? Was it not taking away a common right of the people to write and publish what they please? If they sent out reports to the people, would those reports go out as the only true account of their proceedings? To carry out that view, they should restrain even other reporters and letter-writers, and not let their proceedings be seen until they were sent in that shape in which they intended them to be seen. And was not this a great principle? He thought this looked like interfering with the liberty of speech and of the press. And further: they were creating a new branch of expenditure for the two Houses of Congress. He did not say that this objection ought to be fatal; but the subject was one of such great importance as to require more consideration than could be given to it in these hasty proceedings. But this was not all. There was more than a suspicion that there is something behind this proposition; that it was a scheme connected with political objects; that the contingent fund of the Senate was, under cover of this proposition, to be used to establish a press to support he knew not what interest. He was satisfied there was something here more deeply interesting to those who sustain it, than merely the changing of the mode of reporting their proceedings. This looked like the first step in the drama of the opening campaign, and he denounced it as such, whoever was concerned in it. He was not willing to lend the contingent fund of the Senate for such a purpose. He had heard of some such design to build up a press before.

Mr. R. JOHNSON inquired if the Senator from Connecticut meant to say that he designed to establish a political press under cover of this resolution?

Mr. NILES. Not at all. He did not suppose the Senator from Maryland knew any thing about it. But he nevertheless believed the thing was well understood by others. We are but two years from a presidential election, and there were several candidates understood to be in the field.

Mr. BUTLER. Will you name them?

Mr. NILES did not profess to know them. We should find out when the time came who they all were, and we should then find out in whose interest this paper was.

If there were any appropriation bills that it was now desired to pass, he would give way. If not, he should go on, and he should sustain the Senator from Missouri as long as his inventive genius would enable him to prepare amendments. [Mr. WEBSTER, and others: Very well, go on.] He would go on, and like a great man now no more, he would "take the responsibility."

He contended that the last few days of a session were not the proper time to bring forward such a proposition, even if it was free from suspicion. He recapitulated his objections to it, and then made some remarks in reply to the Senator from Virginia, (Mr. ARCHER,) who seemed to think that there was no republican principle in our Government.

Mr. CALHOUN rose to say that he had no agency in getting up this matter, further than his favorable opinion of it. But still, if he thought any press had any connection with it, he would be the last man to give it his vote.

Mr. R. JOHNSON gave notice of an amendment to prevent the publication of any political matter with these reports.

Mr. BENTON said that was good as far as it went; but they all knew how easily frauds might be committed and a political press established.

Mr. HANNEGAN suggested an amendment to prohibit all connection with the party press.

The question was then taken on the pending amendment, and it was negatived—yeas 17, nays 27.

Mr. BENTON moved to amend the amendment, by adding, "Nor shall any part of the money hereby voted be employed in the purchase, establishment, or support of any political newspaper, or magazine, or political periodical of any kind: and if any part of said money is so applied, it shall be deemed a fraud upon this resolution, and shall vacate the contract;" and demanded the yeas and nays thereon.

The amendment to the amendment was disagreed to, as follows:

YEAS.—Messrs. Ashley, Bagby, Benton, Bright, Cameron, Dickinson, Dix, Fairfield, Houston, Mason, Niles, Sevier, Sturgeon, Turney, and Westcott—15.

NAYS.—Messrs. Archer, Badger, Berrien, Butler, Calhoun, Chalmers, Cilley, John M. Clayton, Corwin, Crittenden, Davis, Evans, Greene, Hannegan, Huntington, Jarnagin, Johnson of Maryland, Johnson of Louisiana, Mangum, Miller, Morehead, Pearce, Simmons, Upham, Webster, Woodbridge, and Yulee—27.

The amendment as submitted by Mr. JOHNSON, of Maryland, was then agreed to.

Mr. BENTON moved to amend, by adding the following:

"*Provided*, That the resolution expelling Thomas Ritchie from the floor of the Senate be, and the same is hereby, rescinded, and that the Daily Union, and the editors thereof, be held and deemed to be on an equal footing, and have equal privileges with other editors and papers for printing the debates of the Senate, any thing in said rescinded resolution to the contrary notwithstanding."

Mr. BENTON said he offered this to produce harmony.

Mr. R. JOHNSON asked if the amendment was in order.

The VICE PRESIDENT decided that it was.

Mr. BENTON had no doubt that it was in order. The resolution giving to this Dr. Houston—why called Doctor he knew not—still less why he was borne upon our Journal with a title, when no other person ever was—not even General Jackson, whom our Journal always calls Mr.—why this Dr. Houston was thus entitled and thus recorded he knew not; but supposed the aforesaid Doctor did, as it was believed he wrote the resolution himself which the Senator from Indiana offered; but if he was correctly informed, to be critically accurate, the said title of Doctor should have a prefix to it: this said resolution directed this Doctor to furnish copies of his reports to the principal newspapers in the United States; and unless the resolution expelling Mr. Ritchie was rescinded, he might, in the opinion of this Doctor, not be a fit person to receive that distinction at his hands.

Mr. BUTLER inquired of the Senator from Missouri, as the representative of the editor of the Union, if he was to come to this floor, and repeat his slander just as he thought proper? If Mr. Ritchie would not retract his insulting remarks against Senators—*nulla vestigia retrorsum;* and thereupon, Mr. BUTLER facing round to Mr. BENTON, repeated his questions to him.

Mr. BENTON said the editor of the Union had answered for himself in his daily paper; and as for himself, (Mr. B.,) he only answered interrogatories in writing, before commissioners in chancery, or under a *dedimus potestatem,* to take depositions. But if the Senator would write down his questions, he would write down his answers; and they would make up a case for the consideration and judgment of the Senate and the people.

Mr. BUTLER. I can soon do it.

Mr. BENTON remarked that this was not a court of chancery.

Mr. BUTLER. No; it is a court of honor.

Mr. BENTON. Oh, no; we have nothing to do with honor here. It is justice only that we want—the justice of putting the organ of the Democratic party on the same footing as the other presses here. This would be done by the adoption of his amendment.

Mr. CASS said he had taken no part in this discussion. When the subject was first introduced he was in favor of it. He thought it might be a plan that might be acceptable. It was a subject in which the country had a deep interest; but suggestions had been made which induced him to doubt its propriety. He would not vote for any proposition which was subject to the objections which had been enumerated.

Mr. BENTON said this amendment was a peace offering. It was submitted to produce harmony. It was the right hand of fellowship at the winding up of an ugly debate.

Mr. WESTCOTT called for a division of the amendment. The latter part he thought perfectly unnecessary, for Mr. Ritchie had now the same privileges as were enjoyed by the press generally.

Mr. HUNTINGTON contended that it was indivisible.

After debate the amendment was disagreed to—yeas 18, nays 26.

Mr. BENTON said they were voting away this money when there was not a shilling in the contingent fund.

Mr. WEBSTER called for the third reading now.

Mr. BENTON objected.

So the third reading was postponed until to-morrow, under the parliamentary law.

HOUSE OF REPRESENTATIVES.

WEDNESDAY, March 3.

Three Million Loan Bill—The Wilmot Proviso.

The House resolved itself into Committee of the Whole on the state of the Union, (Mr. COBB in the chair,) and took up the three million bill as it passed the Senate.

Mr. WILMOT moved to add to the bill the clause generally known as the Wilmot proviso, in the following words:

"*Provided,* That there shall be neither slavery nor involuntary servitude in any territory on the continent of America, which shall hereafter be acquired by or annexed to the United States by virtue of this appropriation, or in any other manner whatever, except for crimes, whereof the party shall have been duly convicted: *Provided always,* That every person escaping into such territory from whom labor or service is lawfully claimed in any one of the United States, such fugitive may be lawfully claimed and conveyed out of said territory to the power claiming his or her labor or service."

Mr. GRAHAM moved to amend Mr. WILMOT'S proviso by striking out all after "provided," and inserting—

"If any territory be acquired by the United States from Mexico, the Missouri compromise line of 36° 30′ shall be extended direct to the Pacific Ocean; that is, slavery shall be prohibited north of that line and allowed south of it."

Disagreed to—ayes 64, noes 96.

The question recurred on the proviso moved by Mr. WILMOT, and it was agreed to—ayes 90, noes 80.

The committee then rose and reported the bill.

Mr. RATHBUN moved the previous question, which was seconded; and the main question was ordered and put, viz., "Will the House agree to the amendment reported by the Committee of the Whole?" (the Wilmot proviso.) It was decided in the negative by yeas and nays, as follows:

YEAS.—Messrs. Abbott, John Quincy Adams, Anderson, Arnold, Ashmun, Benton, Brinkerhoff, William W. Campbell, John H. Campbell, Carroll, Cathcart, Collamer, Collin, Cranston, Cummins, Darragh, Delano, De Mott, Dillingham, Dixon, Dunlap, Ellsworth, John H. Ewing, Foot, Fries, Giddings, Gordon, Grinnell, Grover, Hale, Hamlin, Hampton, Harper, Henry, Elias B. Holmes, Hough, John W. Houston, Samuel D. Hubbard, Hudson, Hungerford, Washington Hunt, James B. Hunt, Joseph R. Ingersoll, Jenkins, James H. Johnson, Kennedy, D. P. King, Preston King, Lawrence, Levin, Lewis, McClelland, Jos. J. McDowell, McGaughey, McIlvaine, Marsh, Miller, Moseley, Moulton, Niven, Norris, Perrill, Pettit, Pollock, Ramsey, Rathbun, Ripley, Ritter, Julius Rockwell, John A. Rockwell, Root, Runk, Sawtelle, Scammon, Schenck, Seaman, Severance, Truman Smith, Caleb B. Smith, Starkweather, Stewart, Strohm, Sykes, Benjamin Thompson, Thurman, Vance, Vinton, Wentworth, Wheaton, White, Williams, Wilmot, Winthrop, Wood, Wright, and Yost—97.

NAYS.—Messrs. Stephen Adams, Atkinson, Barringer, Bayley, Bedinger, Bell, James Black, James A. Black, Bowdon, Bowlin, Boyd, Brockenbrough, Brodhead, M. Brown, William G. Brown, Burt, John G. Chapman, Augustus A. Chapman, Reuben Chapman, Chase, Chipman, Cobb, Cocke, Cottrell, Crozier, Cullom, Cunningham, Daniel, Dargan, Garrett Davis, Dockery, Douglas, Edsall, Ellett, Erdman, Edwin H. Ewing, Foster, Garvin, Gentry, Giles, Graham, Harmanson, Henley, Hilliard, Isaac E. Holmes, Hopkins, George S. Houston, Edmund W. Hubard, Hunter, Charles J. Ingersoll, Joseph Johnson, Andrew Johnson, George W. Jones, Seaborn Jones, Kaufman, Thomas B. King, Leake, Leffler, La Sere, Ligon, Long, Lumpkin, McClean, McDaniel, McHenry, McKay, John P. Martin, Barkley Martin, Morris, Morse, Newton, Owen, Parrish, Payne, Pendleton, Perry, Pillsbury, Reid, Relfe, Rhett, Roberts, Russell, Sawyer, Seddon, Alexander D. Sims, Leonard H. Sims, Simpson, Robert Smith, Stanton, Strong, Thomasson, James Thompson, Jacob Thompson, Tibbatts, Towns, Tredway, Trumbo, Wick, Woodward, Woodworth, and Young—102.

So the amendment was rejected.

Mr. WILMOT moved to lay the bill upon the table; which motion was decided by—yeas 87, and nays 114.

The bill was then read a third time.

The previous question was moved and seconded, and the main question ordered to be put, viz., "Shall the bill pass?" It was decided in the affirmative, as follows:

YEAS.—Messrs. Stephen Adams, Atkinson, Bayly, Bedinger, Benton, James Black, J. A. Black, Bowdon, Bowlin, Boyd, Brockenbrough, Brodhead, William G. Brown, Burt, John H. Campbell, Cathcart, Augustus A. Chapman, Reuben Chapman, Chase, Chipman, Cobb, Collin, Cottrell, Cullom, Cummins, Cunningham, Daniel, Dargan, De Mott, Dobbin, Douglas, Dromgoole. Dunlap, Edsall, Ellett, Ellsworth, Erdman, Faran, Ficklin, Fries, Garvin, Giles, Gordon, Harmanson, Henley, Isaac E. Holmes, Hopkins, Hough, George S. Houston, Edmund W. Hubard, Hungerford, James B. Hunt, Hunter, Charles J. Ingersoll, Jenkins, James H. Johnson, Joseph Johnson, Andrew Johnson, George W. Jones, Seaborn Jones, Kaufman, Kennedy, Lawrence, Leake, Leffler, La Sere, Ligon, Lumpkin, McClean, McClelland, McCrate, McDaniel, Joseph J. McDowell, McKay, John P. Martin, Barkley Martin, Morris, Morse, Newton, Niven, Norris, Owen, Parrish, Payne, Perrill, Perry, Pillsbury, Reid, Relfe, Rhett, Ritter, Roberts, Russell, Sawtelle, Scammon, Seddon, Alexander D. Sims, Leonard H. Sims, Simpson, Robert Smith, Stanton, Starkweather, Strong, Sykes, James Thompson, Jacob Thompson, Thurman, Tibbatts, Towns, Tredway, Wick, Williams, Woodward, Woodworth, and Yost—115.

NAYS.—Messrs. Abbott, John Quincy Adams, Arnold, Ashmun, Barringer, Bell, Brinkerhoff, Milton Brown, Buffington, William W. Campbell, Carroll, John G. Chapman, Cocke, Collamer, Cranston, Crozier, Darragh, Delano, Dixon, Dockery, John H. Ewing, Edwin H. Ewing, Foot, Gentry, Giddings, Graham, Grinnell, Grover, Hale, Hamlin, Hampton, Harper, Henry, Hilliard, Hoge, Elias B. Holmes, John W. Houston, Samuel D. Hubbard, Hudson, Washington Hunt, Joseph R. Ingersoll, Daniel P. King, Preston King, Thomas Butler King, Lewis, Long, McGaughey, McHenry, McIlvaine, Marsh, Miller, Moseley, Moulton, Pendleton, Pollock, Ramsey, Ripley, Julius Rockwell, John A. Rockwell, Root, Runk, Schenck, Seaman, Severance, Truman Smith, Albert Smith, C. B. Smith, Stewart, Strohm, Thomasson, Benjamin Thompson, Trumbo, Vance, Vinton, Wentworth, Wheaton, White, Wilmot, Winthrop, Wood, Wright, and Young—81.

So the three million bill was passed.*

The Sub-Treasury.

The House resolved itself into Committee of the Whole on the state of the Union, (Mr. COBB in the chair.)

Mr. DROMGOOLE moved to take up the bill amendatory of the act to provide for the better organization of the treasury, and for the collection, safe-keeping, transfer, and disbursement, of the public revenue. Agreed to.

Mr. WINTHROP said that he could not forbear calling the attention of the House to this second section of the bill. It furnished an admirable illustration of the financial policy of the Administration. The Government was to receive from its *debtors* nothing but gold and silver, or treasury notes at par; but when it came to its *creditors*, the case was to be changed. If the Government had no gold and silver, and its notes were at a discount, the creditor was

* [And without the proviso, the fact being established that slavery was extinct in the Territories referred to under the laws and constitution of Mexico, and therefore needing no further prohibition. The real view of Mr. Calhoun with respect to the proviso, may be seen in a confidential letter to Percy Walker, Esq., of Alabama, and since come to light, and preserved in the 2d vol. of the Thirty Years' View, ch. 168.]

to be forced to take the notes at par, or to go without his payment. The coolness with which this was held out as a positive privilege to the creditor was quite amusing. If the creditor *prefers* depreciated paper to nothing, (this section provides,) he shall be permitted to receive such paper! To this complexion it had come at last. The Government was to turn banker, to become a grand dealer in paper money, and to be allowed to pay its debts in its own depreciated notes. Thus at last were accomplished the predictions that the sub-treasury system was only a Government bank in disguise, and a bank, as it now appeared, which was to be authorized to commence its career by dealing in a depreciated currency.

Mr. Seaman moved as an amendment to this bill the Senate bill of last session, to establish a branch mint of the United States in the city of New York.

Mr. Hungerford moved to amend the amendment, as follows; which was agreed to:

"*And be it further enacted,* That whenever the treasurer shall be appointed, named in the ninth section of this act, all moneys, books, and papers in the hands of the assistant treasurer in the city of New York, shall be transferred to the treasurer of the branch mint established by this act; and said branch mint shall thereafter be the place of deposit for the public moneys instead of the rooms now used in the custom-house; and the treasurer of said branch mint shall be subject to all the provisions contained in an act entitled 'An act to provide for the better organization of the treasury, and for the collection, safe-keeping, transfer, and disbursement of the public revenue,' approved August 6, 1846, which relate to the treasurer of the branch mint at New Orleans."

The question recurred on agreeing to the amendment as amended, which was agreed to.

The Committee of the Whole rose, and reported the bill.

Mr. McKay moved the previous question; and under its operation the amendments of the Committee of the Whole were concurred in.

Mr. John A. Rockwell moved to lay the bill on the table; which motion was decided in the negative: Yeas 42, nays 75.

The question recurring on the passage of the bill, it was put, and the bill was passed, and sent to the Senate for concurrence.

The title was amended by adding "and to establish a branch mint in the city of New York."

On motion of Mr. McKay, the sixteenth joint rule was suspended, on the part of the House, for the purpose of sending the foregoing bill to the Senate.

Compliment to the Speaker.

Mr. Vinton rose and said: I avail myself of the temporary absence of the Presiding Officer of the House, to make a motion which I am sure will be acceptable to us all. In testimony of the respect and good will of the House, I offer for its adoption a resolution of thanks to the Speaker. It is drawn up in the language in which other resolutions have been presented on similar occasions. I believe it has been usual to present the resolution of thanks without remark or commendation, other than what is expressed on the face of the resolution itself. But I hope I shall not be thought too far to encroach on the usage in such cases, if I say, in one word, that personally it gives me great pleasure to offer this resolution, and that the ability, fidelity, dignity, and, above all—and far better than all these—the impartiality with which the Speaker has discharged the duties of his office, richly merit what I doubt not will be accorded to him, the unanimous thanks of the House.

Mr. V. then sent to the Clerk's table a resolution, which presented the thanks of the House to the Hon. John W. Davis, for the able, dignified, and impartial manner in which he has discharged the duties as Presiding Officer of this House for the 29th Congress.

Mr. Garrett Davis and Mr. Isaac E. Holmes rose and seconded the resolution, and it was passed by a unanimous vote.

Adjournment.

Mr. Jones then moved that the House adjourn *sine die;* which motion was decided in the negative—yeas 33, nays 83.

Mr. Andrew Johnson, from the committee appointed to wait on the President to ascertain if he had any further communication to make to Congress, made a report.

Mr. Cobb then moved that the House adjourn *sine die.*

The question was put, and decided in the affirmative.

Speaker's Valedictory.

The Speaker then rose and addressed the House, as follows:

Gentlemen: By the vote just taken, you have determined that the 29th Congress shall now close its labors, and the members composing it are to be separated, many of them forever. The separation is painful to many of us: I trust it is so to all, for we met as friends. It cannot, it must not be, that we part as enemies. If, unhappily, any unkind feelings shall have been engendered within this Hall, during the excitement of debate or of social intercourse, I conjure you as a friend and brother, that within these walls they now be forever buried and forgotten.

This Congress has been one of unusual and momentous interest—passing upon questions of war and of peace—questions upon which differences of opinion must of necessity exist, and upon which it is advantageous to the Republic that differences of opinion should exist. It prevents the abuses to which majorities so often tend, and excites a vigilance, a prudence, and a care always promotive of the best interests of the commonwealth. It is trite, but true in politics, at least, that it is manly to differ, but childish to quarrel because we differ.

I have endeavored, to the best of my ability, to redeem the pledge I made you at the opening of this Congress, viz., that, in my official duties as Speaker, I should strive to know no party but the people, and no locality but the country. In how far I have failed to be thus governed, must be left to you and your constituents to determine.

I return to you, gentlemen, my sincere and heartfelt thanks for the resolution which you have adopted approbatory of my conduct as your presiding officer; and permit me to assure you that I view it not as a commonplace compliment, offered by your hands and sanctioned by your voices, without your feeling what the resolution itself expresses. The kindness and courtesy, the forbearance and liberality, with which you have always treated me, teach me that you feel what you have so kindly expressed; and, in return, I can say that, to each and every member of this body I entertain not only the kindest feelings, but there is implanted in my breast feelings of interest and attachment that shall only go out with my life.

To those gentlemen who have so kindly relieved me in the performance of the arduous duties of the chair, I am under particular and personal obligations.

And now, gentlemen, with a fervent hope that each of you may long live to enjoy the approval of your country, your consciences, and your constituents, I proceed to consummate your last official act, by pronouncing this House adjourned without day.

So the House adjourned *sine die.*

THIRTIETH CONGRESS.—FIRST SESSION.

PROCEEDINGS AND DEBATES

IN THE

SENATE AND HOUSE OF REPRESENTATIVES.*

IN SENATE.

Monday, December 6, 1847.

In conformity with the Constitution of the United States, the First Session of the Thirtieth Congress commenced this day.

The Senate was called to order at twelve o'clock, by its presiding officer, the Vice President of the United States.

All the Senators were present except Mr. Clayton, of Delaware; Mr. Pearce, of Maryland; Mr. Calhoun, of South Carolina; Mr. Bell, of Tennessee; Mr. Benton, of Missouri; Mr. Yulee, of Florida; Messrs. Davis and Webster, of Massachusetts; Messrs. Niles and Baldwin, of Connecticut; Messrs. Colquitt and Berrien, of Georgia; and Mr. Bagby, of Alabama.

* LIST OF MEMBERS OF THE SENATE.

Maine.—John Fairfield, James W. Bradbury.
New Hampshire.—Charles G. Atherton, John P. Hale.
Massachusetts.—Daniel Webster, John Davis.
Rhode Island.—Albert C. Greene, John H. Clarke.
Connecticut.—John M. Niles, Roger S. Baldwin.
Vermont.—William Upham, Samuel S. Phelps.
New York.—John A. Dix, Daniel S. Dickinson.
New Jersey.—William L. Dayton, Jacob W. Miller.
Pennsylvania.—Simon Cameron, Daniel Sturgeon.
Delaware.—John M. Clayton, Presley Spruance.
Maryland.—James A. Pearce, Reverdy Johnson.
Virginia.—James M. Mason, Robert M. T. Hunter.
North Carolina.—George E. Badger, Willie P. Mangum.
South Carolina.—Andrew P. Butler, John C. Calhoun.
Georgia.—Walter T. Colquitt, Jno. McPherson Berrien.
Kentucky.—John J. Crittenden, Joseph R. Underwood.
Tennessee.—Hopkins L. Turney, John Bell.
Ohio.—William Allen, Thomas Corwin.
Louisiana.—Henry Johnson, Solomon U. Downs.
Indiana.—Edward A. Hannegan, Jesse D. Bright.
Mississippi.—Jefferson Davis, Henry S. Foote.
Illinois.—Sidney Breese, Stephen A. Douglas.
Alabama.—Arthur P. Bagby. [Vacancy.]
Missouri.—David R. Atchison, Thomas H. Benton.
Arkansas.—Ambrose H. Sevier, Chester Ashley.
Florida.—James D. Westcott, David L. Yulee.
Michigan.—Lewis Cass, Alpheus Felch.
Texas.—Thomas S. Rusk. [Vacancy.]

* LIST OF MEMBERS OF THE HOUSE OF REPRESENTATIVES.

Maine.—Hiram Belcher, Asa W. H. Clapp, Franklin Clark, David Hammons, Ephraim K. Smart, James S. Wiley, Hezekiah Williams.

New Hampshire.—James H. Johnson, Charles H. Peaslee, Amos Tuck, James Wilson.

Rhode Island.—Robert B. Cranston, Benj. B. Thurston.

Vermont.—Jacob Collamer, William Henry, George P. Marsh, Lucius B. Peck.

Massachusetts.—Amos Abbott, John Quincy Adams, George Ashmun, Joseph Grinnell, Artemas Hale, Charles Hudson, Daniel P. King, John G. Palfrey, Julius Rockwell, Robert C. Winthrop.

Connecticut.—James Dixon, Samuel D. Hubbard, John A. Rockwell, Truman Smith.

New York.—Ausburn Birdsall, William Collins, Harmon S. Conger, William Duer, Daniel Gott, Nathan K. Hall, John M. Holley, Elias B. Holmes, Washington Hunt, David S. Jackson, Timothy Jenkins, Daniel B. St. John, Orlando Kellogg, Sidney Lawrence, William T. Lawrence, Frederick W. Lord, William B. Maclay, Dudley Marvin, Joseph Mullin, Henry C. Murphy, William Nelson, Henry Nicoll, George Petrie, Harvey Putnam, Gideon Reynolds, Robert L. Rose, David Rumsey, Eliakim Sherrill, John J. Slingerland, George A. Starkweather, Peter H. Sylvester, Frederick A. Tallmadge, Cornelius Warren, Hugh White.

New Jersey.—Joseph E. Edsall, Dudley S. Gregory, James G. Hampton, William A. Newell, John Van Dyke.

On motion of Mr. BREESE, it was

Ordered, That the Secretary acquaint the House of Representatives that a quorum of the Senate has assembled, and that the Senate is ready to proceed to business.

On motion of Mr. FAIRFIELD, it was

Ordered, That the daily hour of meeting be twelve o'clock, until otherwise ordered.

On motion of Mr. CAMERON, it was

Resolved, That each Senator be supplied, during the present session, with newspapers, as heretofore, not exceeding the cost of four daily papers.

On motion of Mr. MANGUM,

The Senate adjourned.

HOUSE OF REPRESENTATIVES.

MONDAY, December 6.

At twelve o'clock M., BENJAMIN B. FRENCH, Esq., the Clerk of the House for the last Congress, (and who by the tenor of his appointment continues to hold office until a successor is elected,) rose and said, that as the hour of twelve o'clock had arrived, he would, in pursuance of usage, call over the list of the members by States, for the purpose of ascertaining the names of those present, and whether a quorum was in attendance.

No one objecting—

The Clerk proceeded to call the roll by States, commencing with the State of Maine; when it appeared that all the members were present except Messrs. KING, of Georgia; BOWDON, of Alabama; BROWN, of Mississippi; GAINES, of Kentucky; COCKE, of Tennessee; FICKLIN, of Illinois; and PILLSBURY, of Texas.

The Clerk then announced that a quorum being present, it was competent for the members to proceed to the election of a Speaker.

Whereupon Mr. JOHN Q. ADAMS moved that the members proceed to the election of a Speaker of the House for the Thirtieth Congress, the members voting *viva voce*.

The question being put by the Clerk, it was agreed to.

Mr. DANIEL P. KING, of Massachusetts, Mr. JAMES A. BLACK, of South Carolina, and Mr. RICHARD W. THOMPSON, of Indiana, were appointed tellers.

The Clerk then proceeded to call the roll alphabetically.

Mr. WINTHROP having received a majority of the whole number of votes given, he was declared duly elected Speaker of the House of Representatives of the United States for the Thirtieth Congress, and was thereupon conducted to the Speaker's chair by Mr. MCKAY, of North Carolina, and Mr. VINTON, of Ohio.

On taking the chair, Mr. WINTHROP addressed the House as follows:

Gentlemen of the House of Representatives of the United States:

I am deeply sensible of the honor which you have conferred upon me by the vote which has just

---

Pennsylvania.—John Blanchard, Jasper E. Brady, Richard Brodhead, Charles Brown, Chester Butler, John Dickey, George N. Eckert, John W. Farrelly, John Freedley, Moses Hampton, John W. Hornbeck, Charles J. Ingersoll, Joseph R. Ingersoll, Alexander Irvin, Lewis C. Levin, Job Mann, Abraham R. McIlvaine, Henry Nes, James Pollock, Andrew Stewart, John Strohm, William Strong, James Thompson, David Wilmot.

Delaware.—John W. Houston.

Maryland.—John G. Chapman, John W. Crisfield, Alexander Evans, Thomas W. Ligon, Robert M. McLane, J. Dixon Roman.

Virginia.—Archibald Atkinson, Thomas H. Bayly, Richard L. T. Beale, Henry Bedinger, Thomas S. Bocock, John M. Botts, William G. Brown, Thomas S. Flournoy, Andrew S. Fulton, William L. Goggin, Richard K. Meade, James McDowell, John S. Pendleton, William B. Preston, Robert A. Thompson.

North Carolina.—Daniel M. Barringer, Nathaniel Boydon, Thomas L. Clingman, John R. J. Daniel, Richard S. Donnell, James J. McKay, David Outlaw, Augustine H. Shepperd, Abraham W. Venable.

South Carolina.—James A. Black, Armistead Burt, Isaac E. Holmes, Robert Barnwell Rhett, Alexander D. Sims, Richard F. Simpson, Joseph A. Woodward.

Georgia.—Howell Cobb, Hugh A. Haralson, Alfred Iverson, John W. Jones, Thomas B. King, John H. Lumpkin, Alexander H. Stephens, Robert Toombs.

Alabama.—Franklin W. Bowdon, Williamson R. W. Cobb, John Gayle, Sampson W. Harris, Henry W. Hilliard, George S. Houston, Samuel W. Inge.

Mississippi.—Albert G. Brown, Winfield S. Featherston, Jacob Thompson, Patrick W. Tompkins.

Louisiana.—John H. Harmanson, Isaac E. Morse, Emile La Sère, Bannon G. Thibodeaux.

Ohio.—Richard S. Canby, John Crowell, John D. Cummins, Rudolphus Dickinson, Daniel Duncan, Thomas O. Edwards, Nathan Evans, James J. Faran, David Fisher, George Fries, Joshua R. Giddings, William Kennon, Samuel Lahm, John K. Miller, Jonathan D. Morris, James Ritchey, Joseph M. Root, William Sawyer, Robert C. Schenck, John L. Taylor, Samuel F. Vinton.

Kentucky.—Green Adams, Linn Boyd, Aylett Buckner, Beverly L. Clark, Garnett Duncan, Richard French, John P. Gaines, Charles S. Morehead, Samuel O. Peyton, John B. Thompson.

Tennessee.—Washington Barrow, Lucien B. Chase, William M. Cocke, John H. Crozier, Meredith P. Gentry, William P. Haskill, Hugh L. W. Hill, Andrew Johnson, George W. Jones, Frederick P. Stanton, James H. Thomas.

Indiana.—Charles W. Cathcart, George G. Dunn, Elisha Embree, Thomas J. Henley, John Pettit, John L. Robinson, William Rockhill, Caleb B. Smith, Richard W. Thompson, William W. Wick.

Illinois.—John A. McClernand, Orlando B. Ficklin, Abraham Lincoln, William A. Richardson, Robert Smith, Thomas J. Turner, John Wentworth.

Missouri.—James B. Bowlin, James S. Greene, Willard P. Hall, John Jamieson, John S. Phelps.

Arkansas.—Robert W. Johnson.

Michigan.—Kingsley S. Bingham, Robert McClelland, Charles E. Stuart.

Florida.—Edward C. Cabell.

Texas.—David S. Kaufman, Timothy Pillsbury.

Iowa.—Shepherd Leffler, William Thompson.

Wisconsin T.—John H. Tweedy.

been announced, and I pray leave to express my most grateful acknowledgments to those who have thought me worthy of so distinguished a mark of their confidence.

When I remember by whom this chair has been filled in other years, and, still more, when I reflect on the constitutional character of the body before me, I cannot but feel that you have assigned me a position worthy of any man's ambition, and far above the rightful reach of my own.

I approach the discharge of its duties with a profound impression at once of their dignity and of their difficulty.

Seven years of service as a member of this branch of the National Legislature have more than sufficed to teach me that this is no place of mere formal routine or ceremonious repose. Severe labors, perplexing cares, trying responsibilities, await any one who is called to it, even under the most auspicious and favorable circumstances. How, then, can I help trembling at the task which you have imposed on me, in the existing condition of this House and of the country?

In a time of war, in a time of high political excitement, in a time of momentous national controversy, I see before me the Representatives of the People almost equally divided, not merely, as the votes this morning have already indicated, in their preference for persons, but in opinion and in principle, on many of the most important questions on which they have assembled to deliberate.

May I not reasonably claim, in advance, from you all, something more than an ordinary measure of forbearance and indulgence, for whatever of inability I may manifest, in meeting the exigencies and embarrassments which I cannot hope to escape? And may I not reasonably implore, with something more than common fervency, upon your labors and upon my own, the blessing of that Almighty Power, whose recorded attribute it is, that "He maketh men to be of one mind in a house!"

Let us enter, gentlemen, upon our work of legislation with a solemn sense of our responsibility to God and to our country. However we may be divided on questions of immediate policy, we are united by the closest ties of permanent interest and permanent obligation. We are the Representatives of twenty millions of people, bound together by common laws and a common liberty. A common flag floats daily over us, on which there is not one of us who would see a stain rest, and from which there is not one of us who would see a star struck. And we have a common constitution, to which the oaths of allegiance, which it will be my first duty to administer to you, will be only, I am persuaded, the formal expression of those sentiments of devotion which are already cherished in all our hearts.

There may be differences of opinion as to the powers which this constitution confers upon us; but the purposes for which it was created are inscribed upon its face in language which cannot be misconstrued. It was ordained and established "to form a more perfect union, establish justice, insure domestic tranquillity, provide for the common defence, promote the general welfare, and secure the blessings of liberty to ourselves and our posterity."

Union, justice, domestic tranquillity, the common defence, the general welfare, and the security of liberty for us and for those who shall come after us, are thus the great objects for which we are to exercise whatever powers have been intrusted to us. And I hazard nothing in saying that there have been few periods in our national history, when the eyes of the whole people have been turned more intently and more anxiously towards the Capitol than they are at this moment, to see what is to be done, here and now, for the vindication and promotion of these lofty ends.

Let us resolve, then, that those eyes shall at least witness on our part duties discharged with diligence, deliberations conducted with dignity, and efforts honestly and earnestly made for the peace, prosperity, and honor of the Republic.

I shall esteem it the highest privilege of my public life, if I shall be permitted to contribute any thing to these results by a faithful and impartial administration of the office which I have now accepted.

The oath of office, as required by the sixth article of the constitution, and as prescribed by the act of Congress of June 1, 1789, to wit, "That I will support the Constitution of the United States," was then administered to the Speaker by Mr. John Q. Adams.

The Speaker announced that the next act to be done in the organization of the House was to administer the oath (or affirmation) of office to the other members present, and to that end he would, therefore, direct the Clerk to call the roll by States, commencing with the State of Maine.

The roll was then called over, and the same oath (or affirmation) as stated above, was administered by the Speaker to all the other members present.

On motion of Mr. White, it was

Ordered, That a message be sent to the Senate to inform that body that a quorum of the House of Representatives has assembled, and that Robert C. Winthrop, one of the Representatives from the State of Massachusetts, has been chosen Speaker, and that the House is now ready to proceed to business; and that the Clerk do go with said message.

IN SENATE.

Tuesday, December 7.

A message was received from the House of Representatives, by Benjamin B. French, Esq., Clerk, informing the Senate that a quorum of the House had assembled; that Robert C. Winthrop, one of the Representatives from the State of Massachusetts, had been chosen Speaker; and that the House was now ready to proceed to business.

Also, that the House had passed a resolution for the appointment of a joint committee to wait on the President of the United States, and inform him that a quorum of the House had assembled, and that the House was ready to receive any communication he might be pleased to make; and that Mr. Hunt, of New York, and Mr. Cobb, of Georgia, had been appointed the committee on their part.

The Senate adjourned.

HOUSE OF REPRESENTATIVES.

Tuesday, December 7.

Several other members appeared this day, were sworn to support the Constitution of the United States, and took their seats in the House, viz:

Mr. Thomas Butler King, of Georgia;
Mr. Franklin W. Bowdon, of Alabama;
Mr. William M. Cooke, of Tennessee; and
Mr. Orlando B. Ficklin, of Illinois.

The Delegate from the Territory of Wisconsin, Mr. John H. Tweedy, also appeared, was qualified, and took his seat.

Election of Clerk.

The first business being the resolution moved yesterday by Mr. Levin, he modified the same to read as follows:

Resolved, That this House do now proceed to vote *viva voce* for Clerk.

The resolution was agreed to.

Mr. Toombs nominated Thomas Jefferson Campbell, of Tennessee.

Mr. Campbell, having received a majority of the whole number of votes given, was duly elected Clerk of the House of Representatives of the United States for the Thirtieth Congress, and accordingly presented himself, took the oath of office, and entered upon the discharge of the duties thereof.

The President's Message.

Mr. Hunt, from the joint committee on the part of the House to wait on the President of the United States, and inform him that a quorum of the two Houses of Congress had assembled, and were ready to receive any communication he might be pleased to make, stated that the committee had performed that duty, and that the President requested the committee to report that he would forthwith transmit to the House a Message in writing.

And soon the Speaker laid before the House the Annual Message from the President of the United States, which was read, as follows:

Fellow-citizens of the Senate
and of the House of Representatives:

The annual meeting of Congress is always an interesting event. The Representatives of the States and of the people come fresh from their constituents to take counsel together for the common good. After an existence of near three-fourths of a century as a free and independent Republic, the problem no longer remains to be solved, whether man is capable of self-government. The success of our admirable system is a conclusive refutation of the theories of those in other countries who maintain that "a favored few" are born to rule, and that the mass of mankind must be governed by force. Subject to no arbitrary or hereditary authority, the people are the only sovereigns recognized by our constitution. Numerous emigrants of every lineage and language, attracted by the civil and religious freedom we enjoy, and by our happy condition, annually crowd to our shores, and transfer their heart, not less than their allegiance, to the country whose dominion belongs to the people.

No country has been so much favored, or should acknowledge with deeper reverence the manifestations of the Divine protection. An all-wise Creator directed and guarded us in our infant struggle for freedom, and has constantly watched over our surprising progress, until we have become one of the great nations of the earth.

It is in a country thus favored, and under a Government in which the Executive and Legislative branches hold their authority for limited periods, alike from the people, and where all are responsible to their respective constituencies, that it is again my duty to communicate with Congress upon the state of the Union, and the present condition of public affairs.

During the past year the most gratifying proofs are presented that our country has been blessed with a wide-spread and universal prosperity. There has been no period since the Government was founded, when all the industrial pursuits of our people have been more successful or when labor in all branches of business has received a fairer or better reward. From our abundance we have been enabled to perform the pleasing duty of furnishing food for the starving millions of less favored countries. In the enjoyment of the bounties of Providence at home, such as have rarely fallen to the lot of any people, it is cause of congratulation that our intercourse with all the powers of the earth, except Mexico, continues to be of an amicable character.

It has ever been our cherished policy to cultivate peace and good-will with all nations, and this policy has been steadily pursued by me.

No change has taken place in our relations with Mexico since the adjournment of the last Congress. The war in which the United States were forced to engage with the Government of that country still continues.

I deem it unnecessary, after the full exposition of them contained in my message of the eleventh of May, 1846, and in my annual message at the commencement of the session of Congress in December last, to reiterate the serious causes of complaint which we had against Mexico before she commenced hostilities.

It is sufficient on the present occasion to say, that the wanton violation of the rights of person and property of our citizens committed by Mexico, her repeated acts of bad faith, through a long series of years, and her disregard of solemn treaties, stipulating for indemnity to our injured citizens, not only constituted ample cause of war on our part, but were of such an aggravated character as would have justified us before the whole world in resorting to this extreme remedy. With an anxious desire to avoid a rupture between the two countries, we forbore for years to assert our clear rights by force, and continued to seek redress for the wrongs we had suffered by amicable negotiation, in the hope that Mexico might yield to pacific councils and the demands of justice. In this hope we were disappointed. Our minister of peace sent to Mexico was insultingly rejected. The Mexican Government refused even to hear the terms of adjustment which he was authorized to propose; and finally, under wholly unjustifiable pretexts, involved the two countries in war, by invading the territory of the

State of Texas, striking the first blow, and shedding the blood of our citizens on our own soil.

Though the United States were the aggrieved nation, Mexico commenced the war, and we were compelled, in self-defence, to repel the invader, and to vindicate the national honor and interests by prosecuting it with vigor until we could obtain a just and honorable peace.

On learning that hostilities had been commenced by Mexico, I promptly communicated that fact, accompanied with a succinct statement of our other causes of complaint against Mexico, to Congress; and that body, by the act of the thirteenth of May, 1846, declared, that "by the act of the Republic of Mexico, a state of war exists between that Government and the United States." This act, declaring "the war to exist by the act of the Republic of Mexico," and making provision for its prosecution "to a speedy and successful termination," was passed with great unanimity by Congress, there being but two negative votes in the Senate, and but fourteen in the House of Representatives.

The existence of the war having thus been declared by Congress, it became my duty, under the constitution and the laws, to conduct and prosecute it. This duty has been performed; and though, at every stage of its progress, I have manifested a willingness to terminate it by a just peace, Mexico has refused to accede to any terms which could be accepted by the United States, consistently with the national honor and interest.

The rapid and brilliant successes of our arms, and the vast extent of the enemy's territory which had been overrun and conquered before the close of the last session of Congress, were fully known to that body. Since that time, the war has been prosecuted with increased energy, and I am gratified to state with a success which commands universal admiration. History presents no parallel of so many glorious victories achieved by any nation within so short a period. Our army, regulars and volunteers, have covered themselves with imperishable honors. Whenever and wherever our forces have encountered the enemy, though he was in vastly superior numbers, and often intrenched in fortified positions of his own selection, and of great strength, he has been defeated. Too much praise cannot be bestowed upon our officers and men, regulars and volunteers, for their gallantry, discipline, indomitable courage and perseverance, all seeking the post of danger, and vying with each other in deeds of noble daring.

While every patriot's heart must exult, and a just national pride animate every bosom, in beholding the high proofs of courage, consummate military skill, steady discipline, and humanity to the vanquished enemy, exhibited by our gallant army, the nation is called to mourn over the loss of many brave officers and soldiers who have fallen in defence of their country's honor and interests. The brave dead met their melancholy fate in a foreign land, nobly discharging their duty, and with their country's flag waving triumphantly in the face of the foe. Their patriotic deeds are justly appreciated, and will long be remembered by their grateful countrymen. The parental care of the Government they loved and served should be extended to their surviving families.

Shortly after the adjournment of the last session of Congress, the gratifying intelligence was received of the signal victory of Buena Vista, and of the fall of the city of Vera Cruz, and with it the strong castle of San Juan de Ulloa, by which it was defended. Believing that after these and other successes, so honorable to our arms and so disastrous to Mexico, the period was propitious to afford her another opportunity, if she thought proper to embrace it, to enter into negotiations for peace, a Commissioner was appointed to proceed to the headquarters of our army, with full powers to enter upon negotiations, and to conclude a just and honorable treaty of peace. He was not directed to make any new overtures of peace, but was the bearer of a despatch from the Secretary of State of the United States to the Minister of Foreign Affairs of Mexico, in reply to one received from the latter of the twenty-second of February, 1847, in which the Mexican Government was informed of his appointment, and of his presence at the headquarters of our army, and that he was invested with full powers to conclude a definitive treaty of peace, whenever the Mexican Government might signify a desire to do so. While I was unwilling to subject the United States to another indignant refusal, I was yet resolved that the evils of the war should not be protracted a day longer than might be rendered absolutely necessary by the Mexican Government.

Care was taken to give no instructions to the Commissioner which could in any way interfere with our military operations, or relax our energies in the prosecution of the war. He possessed no authority in any manner to control these operations. He was authorized to exhibit his instructions to the General in command of the army; and in the event of a treaty being concluded and ratified on the part of Mexico, he was directed to give him notice of that fact. On the happening of such contingency, and on receiving notice thereof, the General in command was instructed by the Secretary of War to suspend further active military operations until further orders. These instructions were given with a view to intermit hostilities, until the treaty thus ratified by Mexico could be transmitted to Washington, and receive the action of the Government of the United States.

The Commissioner was also directed, on reaching the army, to deliver to the General in command the despatch which he bore from the Secretary of State to the Minister of Foreign Affairs of Mexico, and, on receiving it, the General was instructed by the Secretary of War to cause it to be transmitted to the commander of the Mexican forces, with a request that it might be communicated to his Government.

The Commissioner did not reach the head-quarters of the army until after another brilliant victory had crowned our arms at Cerro Gordo.

The despatch which he bore from the Secretary of War to the General in command of the army was received by that officer, then at Jalapa, on the seventh day of May, 1847, together with the despatch from the Secretary of State to the Minister of Foreign Affairs of Mexico, having been transmitted to him from Vera Cruz. The Commissioner arrived at the headquarters of the army a few days afterwards. His presence with the army and his diplomatic character were made known to the Mexican Government, from Puebla, on the twelfth of June, 1847, by the transmission of the despatch from the Secretary of State to the Minister of Foreign Affairs of Mexico.

Many weeks elapsed after its receipt, and no overtures were made, nor was any desire expressed by the Mexican Government to enter into negotiations for peace.

Our army pursued its march upon the capital, and, as it approached it, was met by formidable resistance. Our forces first encountered the enemy, and achieved signal victories in the severely contested battles of Contreras and Churubusco. It was not until after these actions had resulted in decisive victories, and the capital of the enemy was within our power, that the Mexican Government manifested any disposition to enter into negotiations for peace; and even then, as events have proved, there is too much reason to believe they were insincere, and that in agreeing to go through the forms of negotiation, the object was to gain time to strengthen the defences of their capital, and to prepare for fresh resistance.

The General in command of the army deemed it expedient to suspend hostilities temporarily, by entering into an armistice with a view to the opening of negotiations. Commissioners were appointed on the part of Mexico to meet the Commissioner on the part of the United States. The result of the conferences which took place between these functionaries of the two Governments was a failure to conclude a treaty of peace.

The Commissioner of the United States took with him the project of a treaty already prepared, by the terms of which the indemnity required by the United States was a cession of territory.

It is well known that the only indemnity which it is in the power of Mexico to make in satisfaction of the just and long-deferred claims of our citizens against her, and the only means by which she can reimburse the United States for the expenses of the war, is a cession to the United States of a portion of her territory. Mexico has no money to pay, and no other means of making the required indemnity. If we refuse this, we can obtain nothing else. To reject indemnity, by refusing to accept a cession of territory, would be to abandon all our just demands, and to wage the war, bearing all its expenses, without a purpose or definite object.

A state of war abrogates treaties previously existing between the belligerents, and a treaty of peace puts an end to all claims for indemnity—for tortious acts committed, under the authority of one Government against the citizens or subjects of another, unless they are provided for in its stipulations. A treaty of peace which would terminate the existing war, without providing for indemnity, would enable Mexico—the acknowledged debtor, and herself the aggressor in the war—to relieve herself from her just liabilities. By such a treaty, our citizens, who hold just demands against her, would have no remedy either against Mexico or their own Government. Our duty to these citizens must forever prevent such a peace, and no treaty which does not provide ample means of discharging these demands can receive my sanction.

A treaty of peace should settle all existing differences between the two countries. If an adequate cession of territory should be made by such a treaty, the United States should release Mexico from all her liabilities, and assume their payment to our own citizens. If, instead of this, the United States were to consent to a treaty by which Mexico should again engage to pay the heavy amount of indebtedness which a just indemnity to our Government and our citizens would impose on her, it is notorious that she does not possess the means to meet such an undertaking. From such a treaty no result could be anticipated, but the same irritating disappointments which have heretofore attended the violations of similar treaty stipulations on the part of Mexico. Such a treaty would be but a temporary cessation of hostilities, without the restoration of the friendship and good understanding which should characterize the future intercourse between the two countries.

That Congress contemplated the acquisition of territorial indemnity when that body made provision for the prosecution of the war, is obvious. Congress could not have meant, when, in May, 1846, they appropriated ten millions of dollars, and authorized the President to employ the militia and naval and military forces of the United States, and to accept the services of fifty thousand volunteers, to enable him to prosecute the war, and when, at their last session, and after our army had invaded Mexico, they made additional appropriations, and authorized the raising of additional troops for the same purpose, that no indemnity was to be obtained from Mexico at the conclusion of the war; and yet it was certain, that if no Mexican territory was acquired, no indemnity could be obtained.

It is further manifest that Congress contemplated territorial indemnity, from the fact that, at their last session, an act was passed, upon the Executive recommendation, appropriating three millions of dollars with that express object. This appropriation was made "to enable the President to conclude a treaty of peace, limits, and boundaries, with the Republic of Mexico, to be used by him in the event that said treaty, when signed by the authorized agents of the two Governments, and duly ratified by Mexico, shall call for the expenditure of the same, or any part thereof." The object of asking this appropriation was distinctly stated in the several messages on the subject which I communicated to Congress. Similar appropriations made in 1803 and 1806, which were referred to, were intended to be applied in part consideration for the cession of Louisiana and the Floridas. In like manner it was anticipated, that in settling the terms of a treaty of "limits and boundaries" with Mexico, a cession of territory estimated to be of greater value than the amount of our demands against her might be obtained; and that the prompt payment of this sum—in part consideration for the territory ceded—on the conclusion of a treaty, and its ratification on her part, might be an inducement with her to make such a cession of territory as would be satisfactory to the United States. And although the failure to conclude such a treaty has rendered it unnecessary to use any part of the three millions of dollars appropriated by that act, and the entire sum remains in the Treasury, it is still applicable to that object, should the contingency occur making such application proper.

The doctrine of no territory is the doctrine of no indemnity; and if sanctioned, would be a public acknowledgment that our country was wrong, and that the war declared by Congress with extraordinary unanimity, was unjust, and should be abandoned—an admission unfounded in fact, and degrading to the national character.

The terms of the treaty proposed by the United States were not only just to Mexico, but, considering the character and amount of our claims, the unjustifiable and unprovoked commencement of hostilities by her, the expenses of the war to which we have been subjected, and the success which had attended our arms, were deemed to be of a most liberal character.

The Commissioner of the United States was authorized to agree to the establishment of the Rio Grande as the boundary, from its entrance into the Gulf to its intersection with the southern boundary of New Mexico, in north latitude, about thirty-two degrees, and to obtain a cession to the United States of the provinces of New Mexico and the Californias, and the privilege of the right of way across the isthmus of Tehuantepec. The boundary of the Rio Grande, and the cession to the United States of New Mexico and Upper California, constituted an ultimatum which our Commissioner was, under no circumstances, to yield.

That it might be manifest not only to Mexico, but to all other nations, that the United States were not disposed to take advantage of a feeble power, by insisting upon wresting from her all the other provinces, including many of her principal towns and cities, which we had conquered and held in our military occupation, but were willing to conclude a treaty in a spirit of liberality, our Commissioner was authorized to stipulate for the restoration to Mexico of all our other conquests.

As the territory to be acquired by the boundary proposed might be estimated to be of greater value than a fair equivalent for our just demands, our Commissioner was authorized to stipulate for the payment of such additional pecuniary consideration as was deemed reasonable.

The terms of a treaty proposed by the Mexican Commissioners were wholly inadmissible. They negotiated as if Mexico were the victorious, and not the vanquished party. They must have known that their ultimatum could never be accepted. It required the United States to dismember Texas, by surrendering to Mexico that part of the territory of that State lying between the Nueces and the Rio Grande, included within her limits by her laws when she was an independent Republic, and when she was annexed to the United States and admitted by Congress as one of the States of our Union. It contained no provision for the payment by Mexico of the just claims of our citizens. It required indemnity to Mexican citizens for injuries they may have sustained by our troops in the prosecution of the war. It demanded the right for Mexico to levy and collect the Mexican tariff of duties on goods imported into her ports while in our military occupation during the war, and the owners of which had paid to officers of the United States the military contributions which had been levied upon them; and it offered to cede to the United States, for a pecuniary consideration, that part of Upper California lying north of latitude thirty-seven degrees. Such were the unreasonable terms proposed by the Mexican Commissioners.

The cession to the United States by Mexico, of the provinces of New Mexico and the Californias, as proposed by the Commissioner of the United States, it was believed, would be more in accordance with the convenience and interest of both nations, than any other cession of territory which it was probable Mexico could be induced to make.

It is manifest to all who have observed the actual condition of the Mexican Government, for some years past and at present, that if these provinces should be retained by her, she could not long continue to hold and govern them. Mexico is too feeble a power to govern these provinces, lying as they do at a distance of more than a thousand miles from her capital, and, if attempted to be retained by her, they would constitute but for a short time, even nominally, a part of her dominions.

This would be especially the case with Upper California. The sagacity of powerful European nations has long since directed their attention to the commercial importance of that province, and there can be little doubt that the moment the United States shall relinquish their present occupation of it, and their claim to it as indemnity, an effort would be made by some foreign power to possess it either by conquest or by purchase. If no foreign Government should acquire it in either of these modes, an independent revolutionary government would probably be established by the inhabitants, and such foreigners as may remain in or remove to the country, as soon as it shall be known that the United States have abandoned it. Such a Government would be too feeble long to maintain its separate independent existence, and would finally become annexed to, or be a dependent colony of, some more powerful State.

Should any foreign Government attempt to possess it as a colony, or otherwise to incorporate it with itself, the principle avowed by President Monroe in 1824, and reaffirmed in my first annual message, that no foreign power shall, with our consent, be permitted to plant or establish any new colony or dominion on any part of the North American continent, must be maintained. In maintaining this principle, and in resisting its invasion by any foreign power, we might be involved in other wars more expensive and more difficult than that in which we are now engaged.

The provinces of New Mexico and the Californias are contiguous to the territories of the United States, and if brought under the government of our laws, their resources—mineral, agricultural, manufacturing, and commercial—would soon be developed.

Upper California is bounded on the north by our Oregon possessions; and if held by the United States, would soon be settled by a hardy, enterprising, and intelligent portion of our population. The bay of San Francisco, and other harbors along the Californian coast, would afford shelter for our navy, for our numerous whale ships, and other merchant vessels employed in the Pacific Ocean, and would in a short period become the marts of an extensive and profitable commerce with China, and other countries of the East.

These advantages, in which the whole commercial world would participate, would at once be secured to the United States by the cession of this territory; while it is certain that as long as it remains a part of the Mexican dominions, they can be enjoyed neither by Mexico herself nor by any other nation.

New Mexico is a frontier province, and has never been of any considerable value to Mexico. From its locality, it is naturally connected with our western settlements. The territorial limits of the State of Texas, too, as defined by her laws, before her admission into our Union, embrace all that portion of New Mexico lying east of the Rio Grande, while Mexico still claims to hold this territory as a part of her dominions. The adjustment of this question of boundary is important.

There is another consideration which induced the belief that the Mexican Government might even desire to place this province under the protection of the Government of the United States. Numerous bands of fierce and warlike savages wander over it, and upon its borders. Mexico has been, and must continue to be, too feeble to restrain them from committing depredations, robberies, and murders, not only upon the inhabitants of New Mexico itself, but upon those of the other northern States of Mexico. It would be a blessing to all these northern States to have their citizens protected against them by the power of the United States. At this moment, many Mexicans, principally females and children, are in captivity among them. If New Mexico were held and governed by the United States, we could effectually prevent these tribes from committing such outrages, and compel them to release these captives, and restore them to their families and friends.

In proposing to acquire New Mexico and the Californias, it was known that but an inconsiderable portion of the Mexican people would be transferred with them, the country embraced within these provinces being chiefly an uninhabited region.

These were the leading considerations which induced me to authorize the terms of peace which were proposed to Mexico. They were rejected; and, negotiations being at an end, hostilities were renewed. An assault was made by our gallant army upon the strongly-fortified places near the gates of the city of Mexico, and upon the city itself; and after several days of severe conflict, the Mexican forces, vastly superior in number to our own, were driven from the city, and it was occupied by our troops.

Immediately after information was received of the unfavorable result of the negotiations, believing that his continued presence with the army could be productive of no good, I determined to recall our Commissioner. A despatch to this effect was transmitted to him on the 6th of October last. The Mexican Government will be informed of his recall; and that, in the existing state of things, I shall not deem it proper to make any further overtures of peace, but shall be at all times ready to receive and consider any proposals which may be made by Mexico.

Since the liberal proposition of the United States was authorized to be made in April last, large expenditures have been incurred, and the precious blood of many of our patriotic fellow-citizens has been shed in the prosecution of the war. This consideration, and the obstinate perseverance of Mexico in protracting the war, must influence the terms of peace which it may be deemed proper hereafter to accept.

Our arms having been everywhere victorious, having subjected to our military occupation a large portion of the enemy's country, including his capital, and negotiations for peace having failed, the important questions arise, In what manner the war ought to be prosecuted? and what should be our future policy? I cannot doubt that we should secure and render available the conquests which we have already made; and that, with this view, we should hold and occupy, by our naval and military forces, all the ports, towns, cities, and provinces now in our occupation, or which may hereafter fall into our possession; that we should press forward our military operations, and levy such military contributions on the enemy as may, as far as practicable, defray the future expenses of the war.

Had the Government of Mexico acceded to the equitable and liberal terms proposed, that mode of adjustment would have been preferred. Mexico having declined to do this, and failed to offer any other terms which could be accepted by the United States, the national honor, no less than the public interests, requires that the war should be prosecuted with increased energy and power until a just and satisfactory peace can be obtained. In the mean time, as Mexico refuses all indemnity, we should adopt measures to indemnify ourselves, by appropriating permanently a portion of her territory. Early after the commencement of the war, New Mexico and the Californias were taken possession of by our forces. Our military and naval commanders were ordered to conquer and hold them, subject to be disposed of by a treaty of peace.

These provinces are now in our undisputed occupation, and have been so for many months; all resistance on the part of Mexico having ceased within their limits. I am satisfied that they should never be surrendered to Mexico. Should Congress concur with me in this opinion, and that they should be retained by the United States as indemnity, I can perceive no good reason why the civil jurisdiction and laws of the United States should not at once be extended over them. To wait for a treaty of peace, such as we are willing to make, by which our relations towards them would not be changed, cannot be good policy; whilst our own interest, and that of the people inhabiting them, require that a stable, responsible, and free government, under our authority, should, as soon as possible, be established over them. Should Congress, therefore, determine to hold these provinces, permanently, and that they shall hereafter be considered as constituent parts of our country, the early establishment of territorial governments over them will be important for the more perfect protection of persons and property; and I recommend that such territorial governments be established. It will promote peace and tranquillity among the inhabitants, by allaying all apprehensions that they may still entertain of being again subjected to the jurisdiction of Mexico. I invite the early and favorable consideration of Congress to this important subject.

Besides New Mexico and the Californias, there are other Mexican provinces which have been reduced to our possession by conquest. These other Mexican provinces are now governed by our military and naval commanders, under the general authority which is conferred upon a conqueror by the laws of war. They should continue to be held as a means of coercing Mexico to accede to just terms of peace. Civil as well as military officers are required to conduct such a government. Adequate compensation, to be drawn from contributions levied on the enemy, should be fixed by law for such officers as may be thus employed. What further provision may become necessary, and what final disposition it may be proper to make of them, must depend on the future progress of the war, and the course which Mexico may think proper hereafter to pursue.

With the views I entertain, I cannot favor the policy which has been suggested, either to withdraw our army altogether, or to retire to a designated line, and simply hold and defend it. To withdraw our army altogether from the conquests they have made by deeds of unparalleled bravery, and at the expense of so much blood and treasure, in a just war on our part, and one which, by the act of the enemy, we could not honorably have avoided, would be to degrade the nation in its own estimation and in that of the world.

To retire to a line, and simply hold and defend it, would not terminate the war. On the contrary, it would encourage Mexico to persevere, and tend to protract it indefinitely. It is not to be expected that Mexico, after refusing to establish such a line as a permanent boundary, when our victorious army are in possession of her capital, and in the heart of her country, would permit us to hold it without resistance. That she would continue the war, and in the most harassing and annoying forms, there can be no doubt. A border warfare of the most savage character, extending over a long line, would be unceasingly waged. It would require a large army to be kept constantly in the field, stationed at posts and garrisons along such a line, to protect and defend it. The enemy, relieved from the pressure of our arms on his coasts and in the populous parts of the interior, would direct his attention to this line, and, selecting an isolated post for attack, would concentrate his forces upon it. This would be a condition of affairs which the Mexicans, pursuing their favorite system of guerilla warfare, would probably prefer to any other. Were we to assume a defensive attitude on such a line, all the advantages of such a state of war would be on the side of the enemy. We could levy no contributions upon him, or in any other way make him feel the pressure of the war, but must remain inactive and await his approach, being in constant uncertainty at what point on the line, or at what time, he might make an assault. He may assemble and organize an overwhelming force in the interior, on his own side of the line, and, concealing his purpose, make a sudden assault upon some one of our posts, so distant from any other as to prevent the possibility of timely succor or reinforcements; and in this way our gallant army would be exposed to the danger of being cut off in detail; or if, by their unequalled bravery and prowess everywhere exhibited during this war, they should repulse the enemy, their numbers stationed at any one post may be too small to pursue him. If the enemy be repulsed in one attack, he would have nothing to do but to retreat to his own side of the line, and, being in no fear of a pursuing army, may reinforce himself at leisure, for another attack on the same or some other post. He may, too, cross the line between our posts, make rapid incursions into the country which we hold, murder the inhabitants, commit depredations on them, and then retreat to the interior before a sufficient force can be concentrated to pursue him. Such would probably be the harassing character of a mere defensive war on our part. If our forces, when attacked, or threatened with attack, be permitted to cross the line, drive back the enemy, and conquer him, this would be again to invade the enemy's country, after having lost all the advantages of the conquests we have already made, by having voluntarily abandoned them. To hold such a line successfully and in security, it is far from being certain that it would not require as large an army as would be necessary to hold all the conquests we have already made, and to continue the prosecution of the war in the heart of the enemy's country. It is also far from being certain that the expense of the war would be diminished by such a policy.

I am persuaded that the best means of vindicating the national honor and interest, and of bringing the war to an honorable close, will be to prosecute it with increased energy and power in the vital part of the enemy's country.

In my annual message to Congress of December last, I declared that "the war has not been waged with a view to conquest; but, having been commenced by Mexico, it has been carried into the enemy's country, and will be vigorously prosecuted there, with a view to obtain an honorable peace, and thereby secure ample indemnity for the expenses of the war, as well as to our much-injured citizens, who hold large pecuniary demands against Mexico." Such in my, judgment, continues to be our true policy—indeed, the only policy which will probably secure a permanent peace.

It has never been contemplated by me, as an object of the war, to make a permanent conquest of the Republic of Mexico, or to annihilate her separate existence as an independent nation. On the contrary, it has ever been my desire that she should maintain her nationality, and, under a good government adapted to her condition, be a free, independent, and prosperous Republic. The United States were the first among the nations to recognize her independence, and have always desired to be on terms of amity and good neighborhood with her. This she would not suffer. By her own conduct we have been compelled to engage in the present war. In its prosecution, we seek not her overthrow as a nation; but, in vindicating our national honor, we seek to obtain redress for the wrongs she has done us, and indemnity for our just demands against her. We demand an honorable peace; and that peace must bring with it indemnity for the past, and security for the future. Hitherto Mexico has refused all accommodation by which such a peace could be obtained.

Whilst our armies have advanced from victory to victory, from the commencement of the war, it has always been with the olive-branch of peace in their hands; and it has been in the power of Mexico, at every step, to arrest hostilities by accepting it.

One great obstacle to the attainment of peace has, undoubtedly, arisen from the fact that Mexico has been so long held in subjection by one faction or military usurper after another, and such has been the condition of insecurity in which their successive governments have been placed, that each has been deterred from making peace, lest, for this very cause, a rival faction might expel it from power. Such was the fate of President Herrera's administration in 1845, for being disposed even to listen to the overtures of the United States to prevent the war, as is fully confirmed by an official correspondence, which took place in the month of August last, between him and his government, a copy of which is herewith communicated. "For this cause alone, the revolution which displaced him from power was set on foot" by General Paredes. Such may be the condition of insecurity of the present Government.

There can be no doubt that the peaceable and well-disposed inhabitants of Mexico are convinced that it is the true interest of their country to conclude an honorable peace with the United States; but the apprehension of becoming the victims of some military faction or usurper may have prevented them from manifesting their feelings by any public act. The removal of any such apprehension would probably cause them to speak their sentiments freely, and to adopt the measures necessary for the restoration of peace. With a people distracted and divided by contending factions, and a Government subject to constant changes by successive revolutions, the continual successes of our arms may fail to secure a satisfactory peace. In such event, it may become proper for our commanding generals in the field to give encouragement and assurances of protection to the friends of peace in Mexico in the establishment and maintenance of a free republican Government of their own choice, able and willing to conclude a peace which would be just to them, and secure to us the indemnity we demand. This may become the only mode of obtaining such a peace. Should such be the result, the war with Mexico has forced upon us would thus be converted into an enduring blessing to herself. After finding her torn and distracted by factions, and ruled by military usurpers, we should then leave her with a republican Government, in the enjoyment of real independence and domestic peace and prosperity, performing all her relative duties in the great family of nations, and promoting her own happiness by wise laws and their faithful execution.

If, after affording this encouragement and protection, and after all the persevering and sincere efforts we have made, from the moment Mexico commenced the war, and prior to that time, to adjust our differences with her, we shall ultimately fail, then we shall have exhausted all honorable means in pursuit of peace, and must continue to occupy her country with our troops, taking the full measure of indemnity into our own hands, and must enforce the terms which our honor demands.

To act otherwise, in the existing state of things in Mexico, and to withdraw our army without a peace, would not only leave all the wrongs of which we complain unredressed, but would be the signal for new and fierce civil dissensions and new revolutions—all alike hostile to peaceful relations with the United States.

Besides, there is danger, if our troops were withdrawn before a peace was concluded, that the Mexican people, wearied with successive revolutions, and deprived of protection for their persons and property, might at length be inclined to yield to foreign influences, and to cast themselves into the arms of some European monarch for protection from the anarchy and suffering which would ensue. This for our own safety, and in pursuance of our established policy, we should be compelled to resist. We could never consent that Mexico should be thus converted into a monarchy governed by a foreign prince.

Mexico is our near neighbor, and her boundaries are conterminous with our own, through the whole extent across the North American continent, from ocean to ocean. Both politically and commercially, we have the deepest interest in her regeneration and prosperity. Indeed, it is impossible that, with any just regard to our own safety, we can ever become indifferent to her fate.

It may be that the Mexican Government and people have misconstrued or misunderstood our forbearance, and our objects, in desiring to conclude an amicable adjustment of the existing differences between the two countries. They may have supposed that we would submit to terms degrading to the nation; or they may have drawn false inferences from the supposed division of opinion in the United States on the subject of the war, and may have calculated to gain much by protracting it; and, indeed, that we might ultimately abandon it altogether, without insisting on any indemnity, territorial or otherwise. Whatever may be the false impressions under which they have acted, the adoption and prosecution of the energetic policy proposed must soon undeceive them.

In the future prosecution of the war, the enemy must be made to feel its pressure more than they have heretofore done. At its commencement, it was deemed proper to conduct it in a spirit of forbearance and liberality. With this end in view, early measures were adopted to conciliate, as far as a state of war would permit, the mass of the Mexican population; to convince them that the war was waged not against the peaceful inhabitants of Mexico, but against their faithless Government, which had commenced hostilities; to remove from their minds the false impressions which their designing and interested rulers had artfully attempted to make, that the war on our part was one of conquest; that it was a war against their religion and their churches, which were to be desecrated and overthrown; and that their rights of person and private property would be violated. To remove these false impressions, our commanders in the field were directed scrupulously to respect their religion, their churches, and their church property, which were in no manner to be violated; they were directed also to respect the rights of persons and property of all who should not take up arms against us.

Assurances to this effect were given to the Mexican people by Major-General Taylor, in a proclamation issued in pursuance of instructions from the Secretary of War, in the month of June, 1846, and again by Major-General Scott, who acted upon his own convictions of the propriety of issuing it in a proclamation of the eleventh of May, 1847.

In this spirit of liberality and conciliation, and with a view to prevent the body of the Mexican population from taking up arms against us, was the war conducted on our part. Provisions and other supplies furnished to our army by Mexican citizens, were paid for at fair and liberal prices agreed upon by the parties. After the lapse of a few months, it became apparent that these assurances, and this mild treatment, had failed to produce the desired effect upon the Mexican population. While the war had been conducted on our part according to the most humane and liberal principles observed by civilized nations, it was waged in a far different spirit on the part of Mexico. Not appreciating our forbearance, the Mexican people generally became hostile to the United States, and availed themselves of every opportunity to commit the most savage excesses upon our troops. Large numbers of the population took up arms, and, engaging in guerilla warfare, robbed and murdered in the most cruel manner individual soldiers, or small parties, whom accident or other causes had separated from the main body of our army; bands of guerrilleros and robbers infested the roads, harassed our trains, and, whenever it was in their power, cut off our supplies.

The Mexicans having thus shown themselves to be wholly incapable of appreciating our forbearance and liberality, it was deemed proper to change the manner of conducting the war, by making them feel its pressure according to the usages observed under similar circumstances by all other civilized nations.

Accordingly, as early as the twenty-second of September, 1846, instructions were given by the Secretary of War to Major-General Taylor, to "draw supplies" for our army "from the enemy, without paying for them, and to require contributions for its support," if in that way he was satisfied he could "get abundant supplies for his forces." In directing the execution of these instructions, much was necessarily left to the discretion of the commanding officer, who was best acquainted with the circumstances by which he was surrounded, the wants of the army, and the practicability of enforcing the measure.

General Taylor, on the twenty-sixth of October, 1846, replied from Monterey, that "it would have been impossible hitherto, and is so now, to sustain the army to any extent by forced contributions of money or supplies." For the reasons assigned by him, he did not adopt the policy of his instructions, but declared his readiness to do so, "should the army, in its future operations, reach a portion of the country which may be made to supply the troops with advantage." He continued to pay for the articles of supply which were drawn from the enemy's country.

Similar instructions were issued to Major-General Scott, on the third of April, 1847, who replied, from Jalapa, on the twentieth of May, 1847, that if it be expected that "the army is to support itself by forced contributions levied upon the country, we may ruin and exasperate the inhabitants, and starve ourselves." The same discretion was given to him that had been to General Taylor in this respect. General Scott, for the reasons assigned by him, also continued to pay for the articles of supply for the army which were drawn from the enemy.

After the army had reached the heart of the most wealthy portion of Mexico, it was supposed that the obstacles which had before that time prevented it, would not be such as to render impracticable the levy of forced contributions for its support; and on the first of September, and again on the sixth of October, 1847, the order was repeated in despatches addressed by the Secretary of War to General Scott, and his attention was again called to the importance of making the enemy bear the burdens of the war by requiring them to furnish the means of supporting our army; and he was directed to adopt this policy, unless, by doing so, there was danger of depriving the army of the necessary supplies. Copies of these despatches were forwarded to General Taylor for his government.

On the thirty-first of March last, I caused an order to be issued to our military and naval commanders, to levy and collect a military contribution upon all vessels and merchandise which might enter any of the ports of Mexico in our military occupation, and to apply such contributions towards defraying the expenses of the war. By virtue of the right of conquest and the laws of war, the conqueror, consulting his own safety or convenience, may either exclude foreign commerce altogether from all such ports, or permit it upon such terms and conditions as he may prescribe. Before the principal ports of Mexico were blockaded by our navy, the revenue derived from impost duties, under the laws of Mexico, was paid into the Mexican treasury. After these ports had fallen into our military possession, the blockade was raised, and commerce with them permitted upon prescribed terms and conditions. They were opened to the trade of all nations upon the payment of duties more moderate in their amount than those which had been previously levied by Mexico; and the revenue, which was formerly paid into the Mexican treasury, was directed to be collected by our military and naval officers, and applied to the use of our army and navy. Care was taken that the officers, soldiers, and sailors of our army and navy should be exempted from the operations of the order; and as the merchandise imported upon which the order operated must be consumed by Mexican citizens, the contributions exacted were, in effect, the seizure of the public revenues of Mexico, and the application of them to our own use. In directing this measure, the object was to compel the enemy to contribute, as far as practicable, towards the expenses of the war.

For the amount of contributions which have been levied in this form, I refer you to the accompanying reports of the Secretary of War and of the Secretary of the Navy, by which it appears that a sum exceeding half a million of dollars has been collected.

This amount would undoubtedly have been much larger, but for the difficulty of keeping open communications between the coast and the interior, so as to enable the owners of the merchandise imported, to transport and vend it to the inhabitants of the country. It is confidently expected that this difficulty will, to a great extent, be soon removed by our increased forces which have been sent to the field.

Measures have recently been adopted by which the internal as well as external revenues of Mexico, in all places in our military occupation, will be seized and appropriated to the use of our army and navy.

The policy of levying upon the enemy contributions in every form, consistently with the laws of nations, which it may be practicable for our military commanders to adopt, should, in my judgment, be rigidly enforced, and orders to this effect have accordingly been given. By such a policy, at the same time that our own treasury will be relieved from a heavy drain, the Mexican people will be made to feel the burden of the war, and, consulting their own interests, may be induced the more readily to require their rulers to accede to a just peace.

After the adjournment of the last session of Congress, events transpired in the prosecution of the war which, in my judgment, required a greater number of troops in the field than had been anticipated. The strength of the army was accordingly increased by "accepting" the services of all the volunteer forces authorized by the act of the thirteenth of May, 1846, without putting a construction on that act, the correctness of which was seriously questioned. The volunteer forces now in the field, with those which had been "accepted," to "serve for twelve months," and were discharged at the end of their term of service, exhaust the fifty thousand men authorized by that act. Had it been clear that a proper construction of the act warranted it, the services of an additional number would have been called for and accepted; but doubts existing upon this point, the power was not exercised.

It is deemed important that Congress should at an early period of their session, confer the authority to raise an additional regular force to serve during the war with Mexico, and to be discharged upon the conclusion and ratification of a treaty of peace. I invite the attention of Congress to the views presented by the Secretary of War in his report upon this subject.

I recommend, also, that authority be given by law to call for and accept the services of an additional number of volunteers, to be exercised at such time and to such extent as the emergencies of the service may require.

In prosecuting the war with Mexico, whilst the utmost care has been taken to avoid every just cause of complaint on the part of neutral nations, and none has been given, liberal privileges have been granted to their commerce in the ports of the enemy in our military occupation.

The difficulty with the Brazilian Government, which at one time threatened to interrupt the friendly relations between the two countries, will, I trust, be speedily adjusted. I have received information that an Envoy Extraordinary and Minister Plenipotentiary to the United States, will shortly be appointed by his Imperial Majesty; and it is hoped that he will come instructed and prepared to adjust all remaining differences between the two Governments in a manner acceptable and honorable to both. In the mean time, I have every reason to believe that nothing will occur to interrupt our amicable relations with Brazil.

It has been my constant effort to maintain and cultivate the most intimate relations of friendship with all the independent powers of South America; and this policy has been attended with the happiest results. It is true, that the settlement and payment of many just claims of American citizens against these nations have been long delayed. The peculiar position in which they have been placed, and the desire on the part of my predecessor, as well as myself, to grant them the utmost indulgence, have hitherto prevented these claims from being urged in a manner demanded by strict justice. The time has arrived when they ought to befinally adjusted and liquidated, and efforts are now making for that purpose.

It is proper to inform you that the Goverment of Peru has, in good faith, paid the first two instalments of the indemnity of thirty thousand dollars each, and the greater portion of the interest due thereon, in execution of the convention between that Government and the United States, the ratifications of which were exchanged at Lima on the thirty-first of October, 1846. The Attorney General of the United States, early in August last, completed the adjudication of the claims under this convention, and made his report thereon, in pursuance of the act of the eighth of August, 1846. The sums to which the claimants are respectively entitled, will be paid on demand at the Treasury.

I invite the early attention of Congress to the present condition of our citizens in China. Under our treaty with that power, American citizens are withdrawn from the jurisdiction, whether civil or criminal, of the Chinese Government, and placed under that of our public functionaries in that country. By these alone can our citizens be tried and punished for the commission of any crime; by these alone can questions be decided between them, involving the rights of person and property; and by these alone can contracts be enforced, into which they may have entered with the citizens or subjects of foreign powers. The merchant vessels of the United States lying in the waters of the five ports of China open to foreign commerce, are under the exclusive jurisdiction of officers of their own Government. Until Congress shall establish competent tribunals to try and punish crimes, and to exercise jurisdiction in civil cases in China, American citizens there are subject to no law whatever. Crimes may be committed with impunity, and debts may be contracted without any means to enforce their payment. Inconveniences have already resulted from the omission of Congress to legislate upon the subject, and still greater are apprehended. The British authorities in China have already complained that this Government has not provided for the punishment of crimes, or the enforcement of contracts against American citizens in that country, whilst their Government has established tribunals by which an American citizen can recover debts due from British subjects.

Accustomed as the Chinese are to summary justice, they could not be made to comprehend why criminals who are citizens of the United States should escape with impunity, in violation of treaty obligations, whilst the punishment of a Chinese, who had committed any crime against an American citizen, would be rigorously exacted. Indeed the consequences might be fatal to American citizens in China, should a flagrant crime be committed by any one of them upon a Chinese, and should trial and punishment not follow according to the requisitions of the treaty. This might disturb, if not destroy, our friendly relations with that empire, and cause an interruption of our valuable commerce.

Our treaties with the Sublime Porte, Tripoli, Tunis, Morocco, and Muscat, also require the legislation of Congress to carry them into execution, though the necessity for immediate action may not be so urgent as in regard to China.

The Secretary of State has submitted an estimate to defray the expenses of opening diplomatic relations with the Papal States. The interesting political events now in progress in these States, as well as a just regard to our commercial interests, have, in my opinion, rendered such a measure highly expedient.

Estimates have also been submitted for the outfits and salaries of chargés des affaires to the Republics of Bolivia, Gautemala, and Ecuador. The manifest importance of cultivating the most friendly relations with all the independent States upon this continent, has induced me to recommend appropriations necessary for the maintenance of these missions.

I recommend to Congress that an appropriation be made, to be paid to the Spanish Government, for the purpose of distribution among the claimants in "the Amistad case." I entertain the conviction that this is due to Spain under the treaty of the twentieth of October, 1795; and, moreover, that, from the earnest manner in which the claim continues to be urged, so long as it shall remain unsettled, it will be a source of irritation and discord between the two countries, which may prove highly prejudicial to the interests of the United States. Good policy, no less than a faithful compliance with our treaty obligations, requires that the inconsiderable appropriation demanded should be made.

A detailed statement of the condition of the finances will be presented in the annual report of the Secretary of the Treasury. The imports for the last fiscal year, ending on the thirtieth of June, 1847, were of the value of one hundred and forty-six million five hundred and forty-five thousand six hundred and thirty-eight dollars; of which the amount exported was eight million eleven thousand one hundred and fifty-eight dollars, leaving one hundred and thirty-eight million five hundred and thirty-four thousand four hundred and eighty dollars in the country for domestic use. The value of the exports for the same period was one hundred and fifty-eight million six hundred and forty-eight thousand six hundred and twenty-two dollars; of which one hundred and fifty million six hundred and thirty-seven thousand four hundred and sixty-four dollars consisted of domestic productions, and eight million eleven thousand one hundred and fifty-eight dollars of foreign articles.

The receipts into the treasury for the same period amounted to twenty-six million three hundred and forty-six thousand seven hundred and ninety dollars and thirty-seven cents, of which there was derived from customs, twenty-three million seven hundred and forty-seven thousand eight hundred and sixty-four dollars and sixty-six cents; from sales of public lands, two million four hundred and ninety-eight thousand three hundred and thirty-five dollars and twenty cents; and from incidental and miscellaneous sources, one hundred thousand five hundred and seventy dollars and fifty-one cents. The last fiscal year during which this amount was received embraced five months under the operation of the tariff act of 1842, and seven months during which the tariff act of 1846 was in force. During the five months under the act of 1842, the amount received from customs was seven million eight hundred and forty-two thousand three hundred and six dollars and ninety cents; and during the seven months under the act of 1846, the amount received was fifteen million nine hundred and five thousand five hundred and fifty-seven dollars and seventy-six cents.

The net revenue from customs during the year ending on the first of December, 1846, being the last year under the operation of the tariff act of 1842, was twenty-two million nine hundred and seventy-one thousand four hundred and three dollars and ten cents; and the net revenue from customs during the year ending on the first of December, 1847, being the first year under the operation of the tariff act of 1846, was about thirty-one million five hundred thousand dollars; being an increase of revenue for the first year under the tariff act of 1846, of more than eight million five hundred thousand dollars over that of the last year under the tariff of 1842.

The expenditures during the fiscal year ending on the thirtieth of June last, were fifty-nine million four hundred and fifty-one thousand one hundred and seventy-seven dollars and sixty-five cents; of which three million five hundred and twenty-two thousand and eighty-two dollars and thirty-seven cents was on account of payment of principal and interest of the public debt, including treasury notes redeemed and not funded. The expenditures, exclusive of payment of public debt, were fifty-five million nine hundred and twenty-nine thousand and ninety-five dollars and twenty-eight cents.

It is estimated that the receipts into the treasury for the fiscal year ending on the thirtieth of June, 1848, including the balance in the treasury on the first of July last, will amount to forty-two million eight hundred and eighty-six thousand five hundred and forty-five dollars and eighty cents, of which thirty-one million, it is estimated, will be derived from customs; three million five hundred thousand from the sale of the public lands; four hundred thousand from incidental sources, including sales made by the Solicitor of the Treasury; and six million two hundred and eighty-five thousand two hundred and ninety-four dollars and fifty-five cents from loans already authorized by law, which, together with the balance in the treasury on the first of July last, make the sum estimated.

The expenditures for the same period, if peace with Mexico shall not be concluded, and the army shall be increased as is proposed, will amount, including the necessary payments on account of principal and interest of the public debt and treasury notes, to fifty-eight million six hundred and fifteen thousand six hundred and sixty dollars and seven cents.

On the first of the present month, the amount of the public debt actually incurred, including treasury notes, was forty-five million six hundred and fifty-nine thousand six hundred and fifty-nine dollars and forty cents. The public debt due on the fourth of March, 1845, including treasury notes, was seventeen million seven hundred and eighty-eight thousand seven hundred and ninety-nine dollars and sixty-two cents; and consequently the addition made to the public debt since that time is twenty-seven million eight hundred and seventy thousand eight hundred and fifty-nine dollars and seventy-eight cents.

Of the loan of twenty-three millions, authorized by the act of the twenty-eighth of January, 1847, the sum of five millions was paid out to the public creditors, or exchanged at par for specie; the remaining eighteen millions was offered for specie to the highest bidder not below par, by an advertisement issued by the Secretary of the Treasury, and published from the ninth of February until the tenth of April, 1847, when it was awarded to the several highest bidders, at premiums varying from one-eighth of one per cent. to two per cent. above par. The premium has been paid into the treasury, and the sums awarded deposited in specie in the treasury as fast as it was required by the wants of the Government.

To meet the expenditures for the remainder of the present and for the next fiscal year, ending on the thirtieth of June, 1849, a further loan, in aid of the ordinary revenues of the Government, will be necessary. Retaining a sufficient surplus in the treasury, the loan required for the remainder of the present fiscal year will be about eighteen million five hundred thousand dollars. If the duty on tea and coffee be imposed, and the graduation of the price of the public lands shall be made at an early period of your session, as recommended, the loan for the present fiscal year may be reduced to seventeen millions of dollars. The loan may be further reduced by whatever amount of expenditures can be saved by military contributions collected in Mexico. The most vigorous measures for the augmentation of these contributions have been directed, and a very considerable sum is expected from that source. Its amount cannot, however, be calculated with any certainty. It is recommended that the loan to be made be authorized upon the same terms, and for the same time, as that which was authorized under the provisions of the act of the twenty-eighth of January, 1847.

Should the war with Mexico be continued until the thirtieth of June, 1849, it is estimated that a further loan of twenty million five hundred thousand dollars will be required for the fiscal year ending on that day, in case no duty be imposed on tea and coffee, and the public lands be not reduced and graduated in price, and no military contributions shall be collected in Mexico. If the duty on tea and coffee be imposed, and the lands be reduced and graduated in price, as proposed, the loan may be reduced to seventeen millions of dollars, and will be subject to be still further reduced by the amount of the military contributions which may be collected in Mexico. It is not proposed, however, at present, to ask Congress for authority to negotiate this loan for the next fiscal year, as it is hoped that the loan asked for the remainder of the present fiscal year, aided by military contributions which may be collected in Mexico, may be sufficient. If, contrary to my expectation, there should be a necessity for it, the fact will be communicated to Congress in time for their action during the present session. In no event will a sum exceeding six millions of dollars of this amount be needed before the meeting of the session of Congress in December, 1848.

The act of the thirtieth of July, 1846, "reducing the duties on imports," has been in force since the first of December last; and I am gratified to state, that all the beneficial effects which were anticipated from its operation have been fully realized. The public revenue derived from customs during the year ending on the first of December, 1847, exceeds by more than eight millions of dollars the amount received in the preceding year under the operation of the act of 1842, which was superseded and repealed by it. Its effects are visible in the great and almost unexampled prosperity which prevails in every branch of business.

While the repeal of the prohibitory and restrictive duties of the act of 1842, and the substitution in their place of reasonable revenue rates levied on articles imported according to their actual value, has increased the revenue and augmented our foreign trade, all the great interests of the country have been advanced and promoted.

The great and important interests of agriculture, which had been not only too much neglected, but actually taxed under the protective policy for the benefit of other interests, have been relieved of the burdens which that policy imposed on them; and our farmers and planters, under a more just and liberal commercial policy, are finding new and profitable markets abroad for their augmented products.

Our commerce is rapidly increasing, and is extending more widely the circle of international exchanges. Great as has been the increase of our imports during the past year, our exports of domestic products sold in foreign markets have been still greater.

Our navigating interest is eminently prosperous. The number of vessels built in the United States has been greater than during any preceding period of equal length. Large profits have been derived by those who have constructed as well as by those who have navigated them. Should the ratio of increase in the number of our merchant vessels be progressive, and be as great for the future as during the past year, the time is not distant when our tonnage and commercial marine will be larger than that of any other nation in the world.

Whilst the interests of agriculture, of commerce, and of navigation, have been enlarged and invigorated, it is highly gratifying to observe that our manufactures are also in a prosperous condition. None of the ruinous effects upon this interest which were apprehended by some, as the result of the operation of the revenue system established by the act of 1846, have been experienced. On the contrary, the number of manufactories, and the amount of capital invested in them, is steadily and rapidly increasing, affording gratifying proofs that American enterprise and skill employed in this branch of domestic industry, with no other advantages than those fairly and incidentally accruing from a just system of revenue duties, are abundantly able to meet successfully all competition from abroad, and still derive fair and remunerating profits.

While capital invested in manufactures is yielding adequate and fair profits under the new system, the wages of labor, whether employed in manufactures, agriculture, commerce or navigation, have been augmented. The toiling millions, whose daily labor furnishes the supply of food and raiment, and all the necessaries and comforts of life, are receiving higher wages, and more steady and permanent employment, than in any other country, or at any previous period of our own history.

So successful have been all branches of our industry, that a foreign war, which generally diminishes the resources of a nation, has in no essential degree retarded our onward progress, or checked our general prosperity.

With such gratifying evidences of prosperity, and of the successful operation of the revenue act of 1846, every consideration of public policy recommends that it shall remain unchanged. It is hoped that the system of impost duties which is established may be regarded as the permanent policy of the country, and that the great interests affected by it may not again be subject to be injuriously disturbed, as they have heretofore been, by frequent and sometimes sudden changes.

For the purpose of increasing the revenue, and without changing or modifying the rates imposed by the act of 1846 on the dutiable articles embraced by its provisions, I again recommend to your favorable consideration the expediency of levying a revenue duty on tea and coffee. The policy which exempted these articles from duty during peace, and when the revenue to be derived from them was not needed, ceases to exist when the country is engaged in war, and requires the use of all its available resources. It is a tax which would be so generally diffused among the people, that it would be felt oppressively by none, and be complained of by none. It is believed that there are not, in the list of imported articles, any which are more properly the subject of war duties than tea and coffee.

It is estimated that three millions of dollars would be derived annually by a moderate duty imposed on these articles.

Should Congress avail itself of this additional source of revenue, not only would the amount of the public loan rendered necessary by the war with Mexico be diminished to that extent, but the public credit, and the public confidence in the ability and determination of the Government to meet all its engagements promptly, would be more firmly established, and the reduced amount of the loan which it may be necessary to negotiate could probably be obtained at cheaper rates.

Congress is, therefore, called upon to determine whether it is wiser to impose the war duties recommended, or, by omitting to do so, increase the public debt annually three millions of dollars so long as loans shall be required to prosecute the war, and afterwards provide, in some other form, to pay the semi-annual interest upon it, and ultimately to extinguish the principal. If, in addition to these duties, Congress should graduate and reduce the price of such of the public lands as experience has proved will not command the price placed upon them by the Government, an additional annual income to the treasury of between half a million and a million of dollars, it is estimated, would be derived from this source. Should both measures receive the sanction of Congress, the annual amount of public debt necessary to be contracted during the continuance of the war would be reduced near four millions of dollars. The duties recommended to be levied on tea and coffee, it is proposed shall be limited in their duration to the end of the war, and until the public debt rendered necessary to be contracted by it shall be discharged. The amount of the public debt to be contracted should be limited to the lowest practicable sum, and should be extinguished as early after the conclusion of the war as the means of the treasury will permit.

With this view, it is recommended that, as soon as the war shall be over, all the surplus in the treasury, not needed for other indispensable objects, shall constitute a sinking fund, and be applied to the purchase of the funded debt, and that authority be conferred by law for that purpose.

The act of the sixth of August, 1846, "to establish a warehousing system," has been in operation more than a year, and has proved to be an important auxiliary to the tariff act of 1846, in augmenting the revenue, and extending the commerce of the country. Whilst it has tended to enlarge commerce, it has been beneficial to our manufactures, by diminishing forced sales at auction of foreign goods at low prices, to raise the duties to be advanced on them, and by checking fluctuations in the market. The system, although sanctioned by the experience of other countries was entirely new in the United States, and is susceptible of improvement in some of its provisions. The Secretary of the Treasury, upon whom was devolved large discretionary powers in carrying this measure into effect, has collected, and is now collating, the practical results of the system in other countries, where it has long been established, and will report at an early period of your session such further regulations suggested by the investigation as may render it still more effective and beneficial.

By the act to "provide for the better organization of the treasury, and for the collection, safekeeping, and disbursement of the public revenue," all banks were discontinued as fiscal agents of the Government, and the paper currency issued by them was no longer permitted to be received in payment of public dues.

The constitutional treasury created by this act went into operation on the first of January last. Under the system established by it, the public moneys have been collected, safely kept, and disbursed by the direct agency of officers of the Government in gold and silver; and transfers of large amounts have been made from points of collection to points of disbursement, without loss to the treasury, or injury or inconvenience to the trade of the country.

While the fiscal operations of the Government have been conducted with regularity and ease, under this system, it has had a salutary effect in checking and preventing an undue inflation of the paper currency issued by the banks which exist under State charters. Requiring, as it does, all dues to the Government to be paid in gold and silver, its effect is to restrain excessive issues of bank paper by the banks disproportioned to the specie in their vaults, for the reason that they are at all times liable to be called on by the holders of their notes for their redemption, in order to obtain specie for the payment of duties and other public dues. The banks, therefore, must keep their business within prudent limits, and be always in a condition to meet such calls, or run the hazard of being compelled to suspend specie payments, and be thereby discredited. The amount of specie imported into the United States during the last fiscal year was twenty-four million one hundred and twenty-one thousand two hundred and eighty-nine dollars; of which there was retained in the country twenty-two million two hundred and seventy-six thousand one hundred and seventy dollars. Had the former financial system prevailed, and the public moneys been placed on deposit in banks, nearly the whole of this amount would have gone into their vaults, not to be thrown into circulation by them, but to be withheld from the hands of the people as a currency, and made the basis of new and enormous issues of bank paper. A large proportion of the specie imported has been paid into the treasury for public dues; and after having been, to a great extent, recoined at the mint, has been paid out to the public creditors, and gone into circulation as a currency among the people. The amount of gold and silver coin now in circulation in the country is larger than at any former period.

The financial system established by the constitutional treasury has been, thus far, eminently successful in its operations; and I recommend an adherence to all its essential provisions, and especially to that vital provision which wholly separates the Government from all connection with banks, and excludes bank paper from all revenue receipts.

In some of its details, not involving its general principles, the system is defective, and will require modification. These defects, and such amendments as are deemed important, were set forth in the last annual report of the Secretary of the Treasury. These amendments are again recommended to the early and favorable consideration of Congress.

During the past year, the coinage at the mint and its branches has exceeded twenty millions of dollars. This has consisted chiefly in converting the coins of foreign countries into American coin.

The largest amount of foreign coin imported has been received at New York; and if a branch mint were established at that city, all the foreign coin received at that port could at once be converted into our own coin, without the expense, risk, and delay of transporting it to the mint for that purpose, and the amount recoined would be much larger.

Experience has proved that foreign coin, and especially foreign gold coin, will not circulate extensively as a currency among the people. The important measure of extending our specie circulation, both of gold and silver, and of diffusing it among the people, can only be effected by converting such foreign coin into American coin. I repeat the recommendation contained in my last annual message for the establishment of a branch of the mint of the United States at the city of New York.

All the public lands which have been surveyed and were ready for market have been proclaimed for sale during the past year. The quantity offered and to be offered for sale, under proclamations issued since the first of January last, amounts to nine million one hundred and thirty-eight thousand five hundred and thirty-one acres. The prosperity of the western States and Territories in which these lands lie will be advanced by their speedy sale. By withholding them from market, their growth and increase of population would be retarded, while thousands of our enterprising and meritorious frontier population would be deprived of the opportunity of securing freeholds for themselves and their families. But in addition to the general considerations which rendered the early sale of these lands proper, it was a leading object at this time to derive as large a sum as possible from this source, and thus diminish, by that amount, the public loan rendered necessary by the existence of a foreign war.

It is estimated that not less than ten millions of acres of the public lands will be surveyed, and be in a condition to be proclaimed for sale during the year 1848.

In my last annual message I presented the reasons which, in my judgment, rendered it proper to graduate and reduce the price of such of the public lands as have remained unsold for long periods after they had been offered for sale at public auction.

Many millions of acres of public lands lying within the limits of several of the western States have been offered in the market, and been subject to sale at private entry for more than twenty years, and large quantities for more than thirty years, at the lowest price prescribed by the existing laws, and it has been found that they will not command that price. They must remain unsold and uncultivated for an indefinite period, unless the price demanded for them by the Government shall be reduced. No satisfactory reason is perceived why they should be longer held at rates above their real value. At the present period, an additional reason exists for adopting the measure recommended. When the country is engaged in a foreign war, and we must necessarily resort to loans, it would seem to be the dictate of wisdom that we should avail ourselves of all our resources, and thus limit the amount of the public indebtedness to the lowest possible sum.

I recommend that the existing laws on the subject of preëmption rights be amended and modified so as to operate prospectively, and to embrace all who may settle upon the public lands and make improvements upon them before they are surveyed, as well as afterwards, in all cases where such settlements may be made after the Indian title shall have been extinguished.

If the right of preëmption be thus extended, it will embrace a large and meritorious class of our citizens. It will increase the number of small freeholders upon our borders, who will be enabled thereby to educate their children and otherwise improve their condition, while they will be found at all times, as they have ever proved themselves to be, in the hour of danger to their country, among our hardiest and best volunteer soldiers, ever ready to tender their services in cases of emergency, and among the last to leave the field as long as an enemy remains to be encountered. Such a policy will also impress these patriotic pioneer emigrants with deeper feelings of gratitude for the parental care of their Government, when they find their dearest interests secured to them by the permanent laws of the land, and that they are no longer in danger of losing their homes and hard-earned improvements by being brought into competition with a more wealthy class of purchasers at the land sales.

The attention of Congress was invited, at their last and the preceding session, to the importance of establishing a Territorial Government over our possessions in Oregon; and it is to be regretted that there was no legislation on the subject. Our citizens who inhabit that distant region of country are still left without the protection of our laws, or any regularly organized government. Before the question of limits and boundaries of the Territory of Oregon was definitely settled, from the necessity of their condition, the inhabitants had established a temporary government of their own. Besides the want of legal authority for continuing such a government, it is wholly inadequate to protect them in their rights of person and property, or to secure to them the enjoyment of the privileges of other citizens, to which they are entitled under the Constitution of the United States. They should have the right of suffrage, be represented in a Territorial Legislature, and by a delegate in Congress, and possess all the rights and privileges which citizens of other portions of the Territories of the United States have heretofore enjoyed, or may now enjoy.

Our judicial system, revenue laws, laws regulating trade and intercourse with the Indian tribes, and the protection of our laws generally, should be extended over them.

In addition to the inhabitants in that Territory who had previously emigrated to it, large numbers of our citizens have followed them during the present year; and it is not doubted that during the next and subsequent years their numbers will be greatly increased.

Congress, at its last session, established post-routes leading to Oregon, and between different points within that territory, and authorized the establishment of post-offices at "Astoria and such other places on the coasts of the Pacific, within the territory of the United States, as the public interests may require." Post-offices have accordingly been established, deputy postmasters appointed, and provision made for the transportation of the mails.

The preservation of peace with the Indian tribes residing west of the Rocky Mountains, will render it proper that authority should be given by law for the appointment of an adequate number of Indian agents to reside among them.

I recommend that a Surveyor-General's office be established in that territory, and that the public lands be surveyed and brought into market at an early period.

I recommend, also, that grants, upon liberal terms, of limited quantities of the public lands, be made to all citizens of the United States who have emigrated, or may hereafter within a prescribed period emigrate to Oregon, and settle upon them. These hardy and adventurous citizens, who have encountered the dangers and privations of a long and toilsome journey, and have at length found an abiding-place for themselves and their families upon the utmost verge of our western limits, should be secured in the homes which they have improved by their labor.

I refer you to the accompanying report of the Secretary of War for a detailed account of the operations of the various branches of the public service connected with the department under his charge. The duties devolving on this department have been unusually onerous and responsible during the past year, and have been discharged with ability and success.

Pacific relations continue to exist with the various Indian tribes, and most of them manifest a strong friendship for the United States. Some depredations were committed during the past year upon our trains transporting supplies for the army, on the road between the western border of Missouri and Santa Fé. These depredations, which are supposed to have been committed by bands from the region of New Mexico, have been arrested by the presence of a military force, ordered out for that purpose. Some outrages have been perpetrated by a portion of the north-western bands upon the weaker and comparatively defenceless neighboring tribes. Prompt measures were taken to prevent such occurrences in future.

Between one and two thousand Indians, belonging to several tribes, have been removed during the year from the east of the Mississippi to the country allotted to them west of that river, as their permanent home; and arrangements have been made for others to follow.

Since the treaty of 1846 with the Cherokees, the feuds among them appear to have subsided, and they have become more united and contented than they have been for many years past. The commissioners, appointed in pursuance of the act of June 27th, 1846, to settle claims arising under the treaty of 1835–'36 with that tribe, have executed their duties; and after a patient investigation, and a full and fair examination of all the cases brought before them, closed their labors in the month of July last. This is the fourth board of commissioners which has been organized under this treaty. Ample opportunity has been afforded to all those interested to bring forward their claims. No doubt is entertained that impartial justice has been done by the late board, and that all valid claims embraced by the treaty have been considered and allowed. This result, and the final settlement to be made with this tribe, under the treaty of 1846, which will be completed and laid before you during your session, will adjust all questions of controversy between them and the United States, and produce a state of relations with them simple, well-defined, and satisfactory.

Under the discretionary authority conferred by the act of the 3d of March last, the annuities due to the various tribes have been paid during the present year to the heads of families instead of to their chiefs, or such persons as they might designate, as required by the laws previously existing. This mode of payment has given general satisfaction to the great body of the Indians. Justice has been done to them, and they are grateful to the Government for it. A few chiefs and interested persons may object to this mode of payment, but it is believed to be the only mode of preventing fraud and imposition from being practised upon the great body of common Indians, constituting a majority of all the tribes.

It is gratifying to perceive that a number of the tribes have recently manifested an increased interest in the establishment of schools among them, and are making rapid advances in agriculture—some of them producing a sufficient quantity of food for their support, and in some cases a surplus to dispose of to their neighbors. The comforts by which those who have received even a very limited education, and have engaged in agriculture, are surrounded, tend gradually to draw off their less civilized brethren from the precarious means of subsistence by the chase, to habits of labor and civilization.

The accompanying report of the Secretary of the Navy presents a satisfactory and gratifying account of the condition and operations of the naval service during the past year. Our commerce has been pursued with increased activity, and with safety and success, in every quarter of the globe, under the protection of our flag, which the navy has caused to be respected in the most distant seas.

In the Gulf of Mexico, and in the Pacific, the officers and men of our squadrons have displayed distinguished gallantry, and performed valuable services. In the early stages of the war with Mexico, her ports on both coasts were blockaded, and more recently many of them have been captured and held by the navy. When acting in co-operation with the land forces, the naval officers and men have performed gallant and distinguished services on land as well as on water, and deserve the high commendation of the country.

While other maritime powers are adding to their navies large numbers of war steamers, it was a wise policy on our part to make similar additions to our navy. The four war steamers authorized by the act of the 3d of March, 1847, are in course of construction.

In addition to the four war steamers authorized

by this act, the Secretary of the Navy has, in pursuance of its provisions, entered into contracts for the construction of five steamers, to be employed in the transportation of the United States mail "from New York to New Orleans, touching at Charleston, Savannah, and Havana, and from Havana to Chagres;" for three steamers to be employed in like manner from Panama to Oregon, "so as to connect with the mail from Havana to Chagres, across the isthmus;" and for five steamers to be employed in like manner from New York to Liverpool. These steamers will be the property of the contractors, but are to be built under the superintendence and direction of a naval constructor in the employ of the Navy Department, and to be so constructed as to render them convertible at the least possible expense into war steamers of the first class.

A prescribed number of naval officers, as well as a Post-Office agent, are to be on board of them, and authority is reserved to the Navy Department at all times to "exercise control over said steamships," and to "have the right" "to take them for the exclusive use and service of the United States," "upon making proper compensation to the contractors therefor."

Whilst these steamships will be employed in transporting the mails of the United States coastwise, and to foreign countries, upon an annual compensation to be paid to the owners, they will be always ready, upon an emergency requiring it, to be converted into war steamers; and the right reserved to take them for public use, will add greatly to the efficiency and strength of this description of our naval force. To the steamers thus authorized under contracts made by the Secretary of the Navy, should be added five other steamers authorized under contracts made in pursuance of law by the Postmaster-General, making an addition, in the whole, of eighteen war steamers, subject to be taken for public use. As further contracts for the transportation of the mail to foreign countries may be authorized by Congress, this number may be enlarged indefinitely.

The enlightened policy by which a rapid communication of the various distant parts of the globe is established, by means of American-built sea steamers, would find an ample reward in the increase of our commerce, and in making our country and its resources more favorably known abroad; but the national advantage is still greater, of having our naval officers made familiar with steam navigation; and of having the privilege of taking the ships already equipped for immediate service at a moment's notice; and will be cheaply purchased by the compensation to be paid for the transportation of the mail in them over and above the postages received.

A just national pride, no less than our commercial interests, would seem to favor the policy of augmenting the number of this description of vessels. They can be built in our country cheaper and in greater numbers than in any other in the world.

I refer you to the accompanying report of the Postmaster-General for a detailed and satisfactory account of the condition and operations of that department during the past year. It is gratifying to find that, within so short a period after the reduction in the rates of postage, and notwithstanding the great increase of mail service, the revenue received for the year will be sufficient to defray all the expenses, and that no further aid will be required from the treasury for that purpose.

The first of the American mail steamers authorized by the act of the 3d of March, 1845, was completed and entered upon the service on the 1st of June last, and is now on her third voyage to Bremen and other intermediate ports. The other vessels authorized under the provisions of that act are in course of construction, and will be put upon the line as soon as completed. Contracts have also been made for the transportation of the mail in a steamer from Charleston to Havana.

A reciprocal and satisfactory postal arrangement has been made by the Postmaster-General with the authorities of Bremen, and no difficulty is apprehended in making similar arrangements with all other powers with which we may have communications by mail steamers, except with Great Britain.

On the arrival of the first of the American steamers, bound to Bremen, at Southampton, in the month of June last, the British post-office directed the collection of discriminating postages on all letters and other mailable matter, which she took out to Great Britain, or which went into the British post-office on their way to France and other parts of Europe. The effect of the order of the British post-office is, to subject all letters and other matter transported by American steamers to double postage, one postage having been previously paid on them to the United States, while letters transported in British steamers are subject to pay but a single postage. This measure was adopted with the avowed object of protecting the British line of mail steamers now running between Boston and Liverpool, and, if permitted to continue, must speedily put an end to the transportation of all letters and other matter by American steamers, and give to British steamers a monopoly of the business. A just and fair reciprocity is all that we desire, and on this we must insist. By our laws, no such discrimination is made against British steamers bringing letters into our ports, but all letters arriving in the United States are subject to the same rate of postage, whether brought in British or American vessels. I refer you to the report of the Postmaster-General for a full statement of the facts of the case, and of the steps taken by him to correct this inequality. He has exerted all the power conferred upon him by the existing laws.

The Minister of the United States at London has brought the subject to the attention of the British Government, and is now engaged in negotiations for the purpose of adjusting reciprocal postal arrangements, which shall be equally just to both countries. Should he fail in concluding such arrangements, and should Great Britain insist on enforcing the unequal and unjust measure she has adopted, it will become necessary to confer additional powers on the Postmaster-General, in order to enable him to meet the emergency, and to put our own steamers on an equal footing with British steamers engaged in transporting the mail between the two countries; and I recommend that such powers be conferred.

In view of the existing state of our country, I trust it may not be inappropriate, in closing this communication, to call to mind the words of wisdom and admonition of the first and most illustrious of my predecessors, in his Farewell Address to his countrymen.

That greatest and best of men, who served his country so long, and loved it so much, foresaw, with "serious concern," the danger to our Union "of characterizing parties by geographical discriminations—*Northern* and *Southern*, *Atlantic* and *Western*—whence designing men may endeavor to excite a belief that there is a real difference of local interests and views," and warned his countrymen against it.

So deep and solemn was his conviction of the importance of the Union, and of preserving harmony between its different parts, that he declared to his countrymen in that address, "it is of infinite moment that you should properly estimate the immense value of your national Union to your collective and individual happiness; that you should cherish a cordial, habitual, and immovable attachment to it; accustoming yourselves to think and to speak of it as a palladium of your political safety and prosperity; watching for its preservation with jealous anxiety; discountenancing whatever may suggest even a suspicion that it can in any event be abandoned; and indignantly frowning upon the first dawning of every attempt to alienate any portion of our country from the rest, or to enfeeble the sacred ties which now link together the various parts."

After the lapse of half a century, these admonitions of Washington fall upon us with all the force of truth. It *is* difficult to estimate the "immense value" of our glorious Union of confederated States, to which we are so much indebted for our growth in population and wealth, and for all that constitutes us a great and a happy nation. How unimportant are all our differences of opinion upon minor questions of public policy, compared with its preservation; and how scrupulously should we avoid all agitating topics which may tend to distract and divide us into contending parties, separated by geographical lines, whereby it may be weakened or endangered.

Invoking the blessing of the Almighty Ruler of the Universe upon your deliberations, it will be my highest duty, no less than my sincere pleasure, to co-operate with you in all measures which may tend to promote the honor and enduring welfare of our common country.

JAMES K. POLK.

Washington, *December*, 1847.

The Message having been read—

Mr. Brodhead offered the following resolution:

Resolved, That the message of the President of the United States be referred to a Committee of the Whole on the state of the Union, and that 10,000 copies without, and 15,000 copies with the accompanying documents, be printed for the use of this House.

Monday, December 13.

Death of Senator Huntington.

A message was received from the Senate announcing the decease of the Hon. Jabez W. Huntington; when

Mr. John A. Rockwell, of Connecticut, rose and said—

Mr. Speaker: The melancholy duty has been assigned me to propose the usual tribute of respect to the memory of my deceased friend and colleague in the Senate, the Hon. Jabez W. Huntington, whose death has just been announced. He died at his residence, at Norwich, on the 2d of November last, after an illness of a few days, at the age of fifty-nine.

I know not, sir, in what terms to discharge this duty, nor upon which most to dwell, the value of his public services or upon the purity and integrity of his private character.

He was long in public life. After having filled important offices in his own State, in the year 1829 he was chosen a member of this House, and so continued until May, 1834, when he was elected a Judge of the Supreme Court of Connecticut, which office he resigned when elected, in 1840, to the Senate of the United States, and that high office he has now resigned to render an account of his stewardship to the Almighty Ruler of the Universe.

How faithfully he discharged the duties of these offices, of his incredible labors, his inextinguishable ardor, his admirable intellect, his earnest and fervid argument, there are many before me who will bear testimony.

He was, by profession, a lawyer; and, from a long personal knowledge, I can bear testimony that he was a most thorough, learned, and accurate lawyer, belonging to the very highest rank in his profession in his own State, and with an accumulation of legal knowledge rarely equalled. The reported decisions of our State bear witness to his ability as a Judge of the highest court of the State.

While in Congress no man worked harder or more faithfully in the discharge of his public duties, and few had acquired as ample and valuable a store of political knowledge. He was also eminently practical, and knew well how to apply to the best advantage his profound and various learning. So devoted was he in the discharge of his trust, so unceasingly was he employed, that his health fell a sacrifice to his earnest zeal in the public service.

I am aware, Mr. Speaker, that the description which I have given is of a ripe and accomplished statesman, and such was the deceased. He was more, sir. He was a man of pure character, of unyielding, unsuspected honesty; a consistent, decided Christian in his profession and practice.

The Senate and country, and his own State especially, will feel the loss of a public man of such rare endowments. That State has thus been called upon again, and for the third time within comparatively a short period, to mourn the loss of a Senator in Congress.

I invade not the sanctity of private sorrow; I would not open afresh the wounds of the family of my deceased friend, nor mock their grief by the ordinary topics of consolation. Their thoughts dwell not now on his high station, his great talents, or important public services. They think of his private virtues, of his Christian life; and their consolation is, that, at the hour of death, in the full possession of his reason up to the latest moment, he calmly, humbly, but most confidently, committed his immortal interests to the Saviour whom he trusted.

May I not hope, sir, that these repeated signals of our mortality may check somewhat the turbulence of angry passions, and lead us all to the adoption of such a course in the discussion and decision of the important questions before us, as will stand the test of that tribunal before which some of our number will probably appear during the session upon which we have entered?

Mr. Rockwell concluded by offering the following resolutions; which were read, and unanimously agreed to:

Resolved, That this House has heard with deep sensibility the announcement of the death of the Hon. Jabez W. Huntington, a Senator in Congress from the State of Connecticut.

Resolved, That, as a testimony of respect for the memory of the deceased, the members and officers of this House wear the usual badge of mourning for thirty days.

Resolved, That the proceedings of this House in relation to the death of the Hon. Jabez W. Huntington be communicated to the family of the deceased by the Clerk.

Resolved, That this House, as a further mark of respect for his memory, do now adjourn.

The House accordingly adjourned.

Tuesday, December 14.

Election of Chaplain.

Mr. Pollock moved that the House proceed to the election of Chaplain. Agreed to.

The Rev. Mr. Gurley, having received a majority of all the votes given, was declared duly elected Chaplain for the present session of Congress.

Wednesday, December 15.

Veto of the River and Harbor Bill.

The Speaker laid before the House a Message from the President of the United States, as follows:

To the House of Representatives:

On the last day of the last session of Congress, a bill, entitled "An act to provide for continuing certain works in the Territory of Wisconsin, and for other purposes," which had passed both Houses, was presented to me for my approval. I entertained insuperable objections to its becoming a law; but the short period of the session which remained afforded me no sufficient opportunity to prepare my objections, and communicate them, with the bill, to the House of Representatives, in which it originated. For this reason, the bill was retained; and I deem it proper now to state my objections to it.

Although, from the title of the bill, it would seem that its main object was to make provision for continuing certain works already commenced in the Territory of Wisconsin, it appears, on examination of its provisions, that it contains only a single appropriation of six thousand dollars to be applied within that Territory, while it appropriates more than half a million of dollars for the improvement of numerous harbors and rivers lying within the limits and jurisdiction of several of the States of the Union.

At the preceding session of Congress, it became my duty to return, with my objections, to the House in which it originated, a bill making similar appropriations, and involving like principles; and the views then expressed remain unchanged.

The circumstances under which this heavy expenditure of public money was proposed, were of imposing weight in determining upon its expediency. Congress had recognized the existence of war with Mexico, and, to prosecute it to "a speedy and successful termination," had made appropriations exceeding our ordinary revenues. To meet the emergency, and provide for the expenses of the Government, a loan of twenty-three millions of dollars was authorized at the same session, which has since been negotiated. The practical effect of this bill, had it become a law, would have been to add the whole amount appropriated by it to the national debt. It would, in fact, have made necessary an additional loan to that amount, as effectually as if in terms it had required the Secretary of the Treasury to borrow the money therein appropriated. The main question in that aspect is, whether it is wise, while all the means and credit of the Government are needed to bring the existing war to an honorable close, to impair the one and endanger the other, by borrowing money to be expended in a system of internal improvements, capable of an expansion sufficient to swallow up the revenues not only of our own country, but of the civilized world? It is to be apprehended that, by entering upon such a career at this moment, confidence, at home and abroad, in the wisdom and prudence of the Government, would be so far impaired as to make it difficult, without an immediate resort to heavy taxation, to maintain the public credit, and to preserve the honor of the nation and the glory of our arms in prosecuting the existing war to a successful conclusion. Had this bill become a law, it is easy to foresee that largely increased demands upon the treasury would have been made at each succeeding session of Congress, for the improvement of numerous other harbors, bays, inlets, and rivers, of equal importance with those embraced by its provisions. Many millions would probably have been added to the necessary amount of the war debt, the annual interest on which must also have been borrowed, and, finally, a permanent national debt been fastened on the country and entailed on posterity.

The policy of embarking the Federal Government in a general system of internal improvements had its origin but little more than twenty years ago. In a very few years the applications to Congress for appropriations in furtherance of such objects exceeded two hundred millions of dollars. In this alarming crisis, President Jackson refused to approve and sign the Maysville road bill, the Wabash River bill, and other bills of similar character. His interposition put a check upon the new policy of throwing the cost of local improvements upon the national treasury, preserved the revenues of the nation for their legitimate objects, by which he was enabled to extinguish the then existing public debt, and to present to an admiring world the unprecedented spectacle, in modern times, of a nation free from debt, and advancing to greatness with unequalled strides, under a Government which was content to act within its appropriate sphere in protecting the States and individuals in their own chosen career of improvement and of enterprise. Although the bill under consideration proposes no appropriation for a road or canal, it is not easy to perceive the difference in principle, or mischievous tendency, between appropriations for making roads and digging canals, and appropriations to deepen rivers and improve harbors. All are alike within the limits and jurisdiction of the States, and rivers and harbors alone open an abyss of expenditure sufficient to swallow up the wealth of the nation, and load it with a debt which may fetter its energies and tax its industry for ages to come.

The experience of several of the States, as well as that of the United States, during the period that Congress exercised the power of appropriating the public money for internal improvements, is full of eloquent warnings. It seems impossible, in the nature of the subject as connected with local representation, that the several objects presented for improvement shall be weighed according to their respective merits, and appropriations confined to those whose importance would justify a tax on the whole community to effect their accomplishment.

In some of the States, systems of internal improvements have been projected, consisting of roads, and canals, many of which, taken separately, were not of sufficient public importance to justify a tax on the entire population of the State to effect their construction; and yet, by a combination of local interests, operating on a majority of the legislature, the whole have been authorized, and the States plunged into heavy debts. To an extent so ruinous has this system of legislation been carried in some portions of the Union, that the people have found it necessary to their own safety and prosperity, to forbid their legislatures, by constitutional restrictions, to contract public debts for such purposes without their immediate consent.

If the abuse of power has been so fatal in the States where the systems of taxation are direct, and the representatives responsible at short periods, to small masses of constituents, how much greater danger of abuse is to be apprehended in the General Government, whose revenues are raised by indirect taxation, and whose functionaries are responsible to the people in larger masses and for longer terms?

Regarding only objects of improvement of the nature of those embraced in this bill, how inexhaustible we shall find them. Let the imagination run along our coast, from the river St. Croix to the Rio Grande, and trace every river emptying into the Atlantic and Gulf of Mexico to its source; let it coast along our lakes, and ascend all their tributaries; let it pass to Oregon, and explore all its bays, inlets, and streams; and then let it raise the curtain of the future, and contemplate the extent of this Republic, and the objects of improvement it will embrace, as it advances to its high destiny, and the mind will be startled at the immensity and danger of the power which the principle of this bill involves.

Already our Confederacy consists of twenty-nine States. Other States may at no distant period be expected to be formed on the west of our present settlements. We own an extensive country in Oregon, stretching many hundreds of miles from east to west, and seven degrees of latitude from south to north. By the admission of Texas into the Union, we have recently added many hundreds of miles to our sea-coast. In all this vast country, bordering on the Atlantic and Pacific, there are many thousands of bays, inlets, and rivers, equally entitled to appropriations for their improvement with the objects embraced in this bill.

We have seen in our States that the interests of individuals or neighborhoods, combining against the general interests, have involved their governments in debts and bankruptcy; and when the system prevailed in the General Government, and was checked by President Jackson, it had begun to be considered the highest merit in a member of Congress, to be able to procure appropriations of public money to be expended within his district or State, whatever might be the object. We should be blind to the experience of the past if we did not see abundant evidences that, if this system of expenditure is to be indulged in, combinations of individuals and local interests will be found strong enough to control legislation, absorb the revenues of the country, and plunge the Government into a hopeless indebtedness.

What is denominated a harbor by this system, does not necessarily mean a bay, inlet, or arm of the sea on the ocean or on our lake shores, on the margin of which may exist a commercial city or town engaged in foreign or domestic trade; but is made to embrace waters where there is not only no such city or town, but no commerce of any kind. By it a bay or sheet of shoal water is called a *harbor*, and appropriations demanded from Congress to deepen it, with a view to draw commerce to it, or to enable individuals to build up a town or city on its margin, upon speculation, and for their own private advantage.

What is denominated a river, which may be improved, in the system, is equally undefined in its meaning. It may be the Mississippi, or it may be the smallest and most obscure and unimportant stream bearing the name of river which is to be found in any State in the Union.

Such a system is subject, moreover, to be perverted to the accomplishment of the worst of political purposes. During the few years it was in full operation, and which immediately preceded the veto of President Jackson of the Maysville Road bill, instances were numerous of public men seeking to gain popular favor, by holding out to the people interested in particular localities, the promise of large disbursements of public money. Numerous reconnoissances and surveys were made during that period for roads and canals through many parts of the Union, and the people in the vicinity of each were led to believe that their property would be enhanced in value, and they themselves be enriched by the large expenditures which they were promised by the advocates of the system should be made from the Federal treasury in their neighborhood. Whole sections of the country were thus sought to be influenced, and the system was fast becoming one not only of profuse and wasteful expenditure, but a potent political engine.

If the power to improve a harbor be admitted, it is not easy to perceive how the power to deepen every inlet on the ocean or the lakes, and make harbors where there are none, can be denied. If the power to clear out or deepen the channel of rivers near their mouths be admitted, it is not easy to perceive how the power to improve them to their fountain head, and make them navigable to their sources, can be denied. Where shall the exercise of the power, if it be assumed, stop? Has Congress the power, when an inlet is deep enough to admit a schooner, to deepen it still more so, that it will admit ships of heavy burden? and has it not the power, when an inlet will admit a boat, to make it deep enough to admit a schooner? May it improve rivers deep enough already to float ships and steamboats? and has it no power to improve those which are navigable only for flat-boats and barges? May the General Government exercise power and jurisdiction over the soil of a State consisting of rocks and sand-bars in the beds of its rivers? and may it not excavate a canal around its waterfalls or across its lands for precisely the same object?

Giving to the subject the most serious and candid consideration of which my mind is capable, I cannot perceive any intermediate grounds. The power to improve harbors and rivers for purposes of navigation, by deepening or clearing out, by dams and sluices, by locking or canalling, must be admitted without any other limitation than the discretion of Congress, or it must be denied altogether. If it be admitted, how broad and how susceptible of enormous abuses is the power thus vested in the General Government! There is not an inlet of the ocean or the lakes, not a river, creek, or streamlet within the States, which is not brought for this purpose within the power and jurisdiction of the General Government.

Speculation, disguised under the cloak of public good, will call on Congress to deepen shallow inlets, that it may build up new cities on their shores, or to make streams navigable which Nature has closed by bars and rapids, that it may sell at a profit its lands upon their banks. To enrich neighborhoods by spending within them the moneys of the nation, will be the aim and boast of those who prize their local interests above the good of the nation, and millions upon millions will be abstracted by tariffs and taxes from the earnings of the whole people, to foster speculation and subserve the objects of private ambition.

Such a system could not be administered with any approach to equality among the several States and sections of the Union. There is no equality among them in the objects of expenditure, and, if the funds were distributed according to the merits of those objects, some would be enriched at the expense of their neighbors. But a greater practical evil would be found in the art and industry by which appropriations would be sought and obtained. The most artful and industrious would be the most successful; the true interests of the country would be lost sight of in an annual scramble for the contents of the treasury; and the member of Congress who could procure the largest appropriations to be expended in his district, would claim the reward of victory from his enriched constituents. The necessary consequence would be, sectional discontents and heartburnings, increased taxation, and a national debt, never to be extinguished.

In view of these portentous consequences, I cannot but think that this course of legislation should be arrested, even were there nothing to forbid it in the fundamental laws of our Union. This conclusion is fortified by the fact, that the constitution itself indicates a process by which harbors and rivers within the States may be improved—a process not susceptible of the abuses necessarily to flow from the assumption of the power to improve them by the General Government; just in its operation, and actually practised upon, without complaint or interruption, during more than thirty years from the organization of the present Government.

IN SENATE.

THURSDAY, December 16.

Death of Senator Speight.

Mr. FOOTE rose and addressed the Senate as follows:

Mr. President: A few days since, we were called upon to assume the customary badges of mournful respect in honor of a deceased Senator from Connecticut; and now, whilst the sentiment of fraternal grief is yet warm in our bosoms, and the tokens of sorrowing affection are still visible upon our persons, it has become necessary that I should give renewed pain to the sensibilities of Senators by passing in review before them another dispensation of Divine Providence, which, since the last annual assemblage in this Hall, has deprived the National Lgislature of an upright and efficient member, the State of Mississippi of a faithful and approved political agent, and myself of a most worthy and esteemed colleague. The Hon. JESSE SPEIGHT died at his own residence, in the State of Mississippi, on Saturday, the first day of May last, after a long and painful illness, which came upon him here, whilst arduously engaged in the extraordinary labors of the last Congress, and which continued to oppress him sorely for several months, until at last he sunk into that grave where now quietly repose all that was mortal of the patriot, the philanthropist, and the statesman. I shall not attempt, on this occasion, to deliver a formal and elaborate eulogy upon my lamented friend, feeling that I shall best display the real respect which I entertain for the well-known republican simplicity of his own tastes, by confining myself to concise and unostentious delineation of his life and character.

JESSE SPEIGHT was born in the county of Greene, and State of North Carolina, a few years anterior to the close of the last century, where he continued uninterruptedly to reside, until his removal to the State of Mississippi, in the year 1837. Prior to his migration from the State of his nativity, he had officiated as a member of her Legislature, and had likewise supplied material aid in the reformation of her organic law, as a prominent member of the convention which assembled for that purpose in the year 1837. Before leaving North Carolina, he had represented one of the congressional districts of that ancient Commonwealth in the other wing of this Capitol for four consecutive terms, closing on the 3d of March, 1837; and I am assured that his whole political conduct at that critical period of our national history was eminently creditable to himself and satisfactory to his constituents. After his removal to the West, he successively represented a most intelligent and patriotic constituency, first in one branch of our State Legislature, and then in the other, and presiding over both, at different times, with such distinguished success as greatly to elevate his character as a public man, and multiply the number of his admirers. From the presidency of the Mississippi Senate, he was elected to a seat upon this floor, where he acted under the daily and hourly inspection of those in whose presence I now speak; and I trust that I shall not be deemed by any Senator who hears me at all extravagant, when I assert, that my lamented colleague, whilst connected with this body, gave constant evidence of his possessing a sound, acute, and practical intellect; habits of persevering industry seldom surpassed; inflexible honesty of purpose; a magnanimity of soul, which held him ever in readiness for the performance of generous and noble deeds, and which equally saved him, at all times, from the least participancy in aught that could be recognized as little, or sordid, or illiberal. He was blessed with unusual sweetness and uniformity of temper; and the unceremonious cordiality of his manners rendered his society particularly agreeable and attractive. In domestic life, he was strikingly amiable and exemplary; and his untimely decease has brought sorrow and disappointment to kind and innocent hearts, which his living presence never failed to inspire with sentiments of buoyant hope and elastic gladness of spirit.

Mr. F. concluded by offering the following resolutions; which were unanimously adopted:

Resolved, unanimously, That the Senate, from a desire to exhibit a profound respect for the memory of the Hon. Jesse Speight, late a member thereof, will go into mourning by wearing crape on the left arm for thirty days.

Resolved, That, as an additional mark of respect for the memory of the Hon. Jesse Speight, the Senate do now adjourn.

Ordered, That the Secretary inform the House of Representatives thereof.

Whereupon the Senate adjourned.

HOUSE OF REPRESENTATIVES.

Thursday, December 16.

Death of Senator Speight.

A message was received from the Senate, notifying the House of the death of Mr. Senator Speight,

When Mr. Jacob Thompson rose and said:

Mr. Speaker: The message just received from the Senate announces the melancholy fact, that since the adjournment of that body last spring, another of its members has fallen asleep to wake no more. The Hon. Jesse Speight, late a Senator from the State of Mississippi, is no longer numbered with the living. Death has been moving amidst our ranks, and has thrown his sable mantle over one of the most distinguished of the country. Elevated station, personal virtues, the affection of family and friends, the confidence of constituents, and the active and zealous discharge of all the duties of life, could not shield him from a submission to that law which governs our race, that "it is appointed unto men once to die."

General Speight, my late colleague and friend, was no ordinary man, passing over the stage of life unnoticed, and leaving, when the curtain falls, no recollection behind him to distinguish him among the millions who had gone before him. The features of his character were striking and peculiar. His superior stature singled him out among his fellow-men, and commanded universal respect. This advantage of person, united with a strong natural mind, an unyielding integrity, and a benignant heart, was the key to that unvaried success which attended him in all his aspirations throughout his whole career. And to the records of his country we must turn to learn the history of his life.

He was born in the State of North Carolina. Without the advantages of fortune, and with a deficient early education, he first appeared in public life in the Legislature of the State; and in a short time he obtained the highest legislative honors, by being elected Speaker of the State Senate. From this position, in 1829, he came to the House of Representatives of the United States, in which capacity he served his country with great zeal, industry, and fidelity, for six years. In 1835 he was elected a delegate to the Convention then called in the State of North Carolina for the revisal of her constitution. There the extension of the right of suffrage and religious toleration became the leading topics of discussion, in which he bore a conspicuous part as the advocate of the largest liberty of the citizen, in the freedom of conscience, and in the exercise of political power.

Thus having been honored by the State of his nativity, and having served her people with fidelity and efficiency, it was a difficult and severe trial to sever the ties which bound him to his constituents. But, prompted by a desire to provide for his own household, and invited by the prolific soil, the genial climate and rich productions of Mississippi, he became a citizen of that State in 1837. But in this land of his adoption he soon found himself surrounded by ardent friends, who were eager to do him honor; and in 1839 he was elected to the Legislature, and became the Speaker of the House of Representatives. In 1841 he was returned to the State Senate, and was elected the President of that body. In this office he continued until, in 1844, he was elected to the Senate of the United States—a position second in dignity and importance, and in the public consideration, only to the Chief Executive of this Government. He took his seat in that body in March, 1845; and that industry, zeal, fidelity, talent, and practical good judgment, which had ever marked his course as a public man, were here exhibited. In the active discharge of his duties in this station the hand of disease was laid upon him. But his strong frame and robust constitution apparently triumphed over the first assaults of the enemy; and, after weeks of patient suffering, he so far recovered as to return to his residence in Mississippi, where, surrounded by an affectionate family and sympathizing friends, he obeyed his final summons on the 1st of May, 1847.

An "aching void" has been left in the large circle which revolved around him as its centre, and which can be filled or satisfied by naught that I can say, or that this House may do.

As a friend, he was frank, sincere, and confiding; as an enemy, ready to pardon and forget; as a presiding officer in a deliberative body, he had no superior; as a public servant, he was true, industrious, and untiring.

But he is gone to that undiscovered country to which we are all fast hastening. On our way thither, while we cherish his virtues, we can but honor his memory.

Mr. T. concluded by moving the following resolutions:

Resolved, That this House has heard with deep sensibility the announcement of the death of the Hon. JESSE SPEIGHT, a Senator in Congress from the State of Mississippi.

Resolved, That, as a testimony of respect for the memory of the deceased, the members and officers of this House will wear the usual badge of mourning for thirty days.

Resolved, That the proceedings of this House in relation to the death of the Hon. JESSE SPEIGHT, be communicated to his family by the Clerk.

Resolved, That, as a further mark of respect, this House do now adjourn.

The House accordingly adjourned.

FRIDAY, December 17.

Death of Mr. Dromgoole.

Mr. MEADE, of Virginia, rose and said:

Mr. Speaker: In obedience to an honored custom, I rise to bring to the notice of this House an event which has already been announced to the public—I allude to the death of the Hon. GEORGE C. DROMGOOLE, of Virginia, a late member of this House. He died on the 27th day of April last, at his residence in the county of Brunswick, a few days after he had received intelligence of his re-election to Congress. His loss would have been sensibly felt at any period of his public life; but at this time, when, amidst the violence of party, his moderation, wisdom, and great experience in public affairs, are so much needed, the whole country must deplore the sad event.

General DROMGOOLE commenced his political life at an early age. But a few years elapsed after he became eligible to a seat in the Legislature of Virginia, before he was called upon by his native county to represent it in that body. Since then, with but two short intervals, he has continued in the public service. The reputation he acquired as a member of the House of Delegates, soon attracted the attention of his district, and at the early age of thirty-three, he was chosen to deliberate with Madison, Monroe, and Marshall, and other distinguished worthies, in the only Convention which has assembled in Virginia since the adoption of her first constitution.

He was afterwards sent to the Senate of that State, over which body he presided for many years with distinguished ability, until 1835, when he was elected to the Congress of the United States.

Here his great powers of mind have been felt and acknowledged, and their influence may be traced through the records of this body.

From the commencement of his political career, he continued steadily to ascend the path to distinction, inspiring his friends and constituents with the firm assurance that wherever he had fixed the goal of his aspirations, there his political life would terminate.

It would be hypocrisy in me, and at the same time useless here, to affect to believe that Mr. DROMGOOLE was without his blemishes; but it is easy for those who knew him as his constituents did, to forget them. Had he faults, they belonged to the weakness of human flesh; few ever reached that soul, where honor, humanity, and truth, dwelt together and worshipped. The companions of his youth will never forget how ardent and sincere were his attachments, and how his presence would always brighten up their hearts, and wake up emotions of young sympathy and affection. The friends of his maturer years think in sadness of his warm and generous nature, his wise counsels, and steady friendship. His mind was more solid than brilliant, and its productions more fitted for use than ornament. The influence which he exercised over the feelings and opinions of others, especially his constituents, was one of his most remarkable attributes. He seldom spoke in public from impulse; hence he was always courteous to adversaries, and seldom indulged in abuse of them, but was sometimes only humorously sarcastic. The confidence of his constituents gave to his opinions the force of oracles, and against them the arguments of adversaries were hurled in vain. I have seen him in many warm political contests, and never knew him to lose the equilibrium of his temper and his perfect self-possession. His coolness, and real and unaffected confidence in his own powers and superiority, would often work his adversary into a rage, who would expend his energies in fits of desperation, and fall at last, apparently by the blows of his powerful antagonist, but in fact overcome by his own vehemence and extravagance. I have sometimes been opposed in these contests to this extraordinary man. These occasions never failed to give rise to reflections on the wonderful influence by which, apparently without much effort on his part, he controlled the action of others. Circumstances conspired, in the commencement of his public life, to give the subject of my remarks a favorable position among his fellow-men. His father, a native of Ireland, was one of the earliest settlers in this district. His was the voluntary duty to publish from his pulpit to his various congregations the Declaration of American Independence. As a minister of the Gospel, he had few equals in the powers of a strong native intellect, but few ever enjoyed to the same extent the love and affection of his people, who placed in him that implicit confidence which nothing but an irreproachable life can inspire. For more than fifty years he labored to raise his fellow-men to the same elevated platform on which he stood himself. He lived to an advanced age, exhibiting to the close of his life the rare instance of one who united in himself every human excellence. A few years only have elapsed since he left us. The sun of his evening life long lingered on the horizon, and often would the traveller turn an anxious look to the west, to see how much longer would the mellow rays of that unspotted light fall upon his path. And since it has gone down, a twilight rests over the district, by which we may trace on the tablet of every heart the character of Edward Dromgoole. The virtues of the father stood as a guarantee for the promises of the son, until his own great abilities changed doubt into assurance, and finally obtained from his country judgment for the attributes of a pure patriot and an able statesman.

I have alluded to the great weight of his opinions with his constituents. The present political position of the country had filled their minds, as it has the minds of all, with the most fearful apprehensions about the future fate of this great Confederacy. From him they expected to learn what might be the probable result of that extraordinary issue between the North and the South, about to be tried at the bar of this House. I have heard his reply to questions that would be asked him about this controversy—a reply that should sink deep in the hearts of politicians. It was, that he never doubted there still remained sense and virtue enough in the body of the people to adhere to the compact of their fathers and preserve this Union. The love of this Union was a passion with this distinguished man, and his faith in the continuance and prosperity of this Confederacy was such as no danger or crisis could shake.

The diminished majority by which he was elected to the present Congress would seem, to those at a distance, to indicate that he had lost ground with his party. No fears were ever entertained of his election, and it was well understood in his district, that numbers of his friends withheld their votes with the kind intention of merely trying the chastening effect of a small vote and seeming indifference. But few ever doubted that he was the decided favorite of his district; and had every political friend of his been impressed with the belief that his vote was necessary, I hazard nothing in saying he would have been returned by a majority of eight hundred votes.

Mr. Speaker, I am sure no one is disposed to regret the little time I have occupied in endeavoring to give a short and imperfect sketch of the life and character of this justly distinguished man. In a few days more, sir, judging from the signs of the times, this House will be torn by every passion that can conspire to destroy the wisdom of its deliberations and contribute to a country's ruin.

It may have a salutary effect, and mitigate in some measure the ferocity of the war, to pause awhile, and bend for a short space over the grave of one who, a few months ago, was himself actively engaged in the political conflicts which even then threatened the peace of the country. That voice which was then so often heard above the storm, and never unheeded, is now hushed in death. So must the passions which now disturb the bosoms of his survivors fret their brief hour, and finally subside in the silence of the grave.

What I have said, Mr. Speaker, about this gifted man, was no less due to his own high character and extraordinary qualities, in this House, of which he was so long a distinguished member, than to the deep affection and abiding confidence of his constituents, who believe that his country, like themselves, with a single tear will wash away the remembrance of his faults, while with proud and lofty emotions she may contemplate in his character that "noblest work of God, an honest man."

Mr. M. concluded by moving the following resolutions:

Resolved, That this House deeply regrets the death of the Hon. George C. Dromgoole, a late member of the House from the State of Virginia.

Resolved, That the members and officers of this House will testify their respect for the memory of the deceased by wearing the usual badge of mourning for thirty days.

Resolved, That these resolutions be communicated to the nearest relatives of the deceased.

Resolved, That, as a further mark of respect, this House do now adjourn.

The resolutions were unanimously adopted, and the House adjourned.

Monday, December 27.

Death of Senator Fairfield.

A message was received from the Senate, informing the House of the decease of the Hon. John Fairfield, a Senator from the State of Maine.

The resolutions of the Senate having been read—

Mr. HAMMONS rose and said:

Mr. Speaker: In raising my voice for the first time in this Hall, it devolves upon me to perform the most painful and melancholy duty of my life.

The Hon. JOHN FAIRFIELD, Senator from Maine, on Friday last, at twelve, meridian, was in the enjoyment of good health, with an unusual flow of spirits, surrounded with honors, and possessed of all the enjoyments that earth can afford; at a quarter before eight of the evening of the same day, he had bid adieu to time, and his pure and manly spirit had returned to Him who gave it.

Most of the morning of that day I spent with him in friendly and social converse; of the evening, in witnessing his poignant sufferings, his struggle with the King of Terrors, and in watching over his lifeless remains.

How sad, how sudden, how awful the change—a change which even now I can hardly realize!

In the meridian of his life, in the midst of his career of usefulness, and while in the full vigor of his intellect, he has fallen.

Governor FAIRFIELD was emphatically a self-made man. By his own industry and exertions he acquired an education, studied law, and at an early day took rank among the first of his profession. His fine talents and affable deportment soon arrested public attention; and he was called at an early age, from the enjoyments of private life and domestic happiness, to the performance of arduous and responsible public duties.

His public career, though not long, was brilliant. The office of Reporter of the decisions of the Supreme Court of Maine, two elections as a member of this House, four elections as the chief Executive of his native State, and two elections to the Senate of the United States—all in the brief period of about twelve years—were the rewards of his worthy and generous aspirations.

The complicated and arduous duties of all these high and honorable stations he discharged with faithfulness and distinguished ability, and to the entire satisfaction of those who had elevated him to power.

He possessed in an eminent degree all the elements of popularity, and had doubtless a stronger hold upon the affections of the people of Maine than any other man living. His popularity kept pace with his advancement, and, at the moment of his decease, I have not a doubt he possessed more numerous and devoted friends than at any former period of his life. Unshaken firmness, indomitable perseverance, and a sincerity that knew no guile, were the distinguishing traits of his character.

His whole life evinced an unwavering devotion to justice and to the great principles of popular rights.

In his death Maine has lost one of her worthiest and noblest sons—a man whom she delighted to honor; society has been bereft of one of its best and brightest ornaments; and the Senate of the United States of one of its ablest, most upright, and most useful members.

Of the loss to the partner of his bosom, and to the numerous pledges of their affection, it is vain to speak. The blow has fallen upon them with a crushing weight, which no language can portray, and which none but those who have been called to drink of the same bitter cup can conceive. May He "who tempers the wind to the shorn lamb" give them that support and consolation which no earthly power can bestow!

I will close this hasty and very imperfect sketch of my late friend's life and character by moving the adoption of the customary resolutions:

Resolved, That this House has heard with deep sensibility the announcement of the death of the Hon. JOHN FAIRFIELD, a Senator from the State of Maine.

Resolved, That, as a testimony of respect for the memory of the deceased, the members and officers of this House will wear the usual badge of mourning for thirty days.

Resolved, That the proceedings of this House in relation to the death of the Hon. JOHN FAIRFIELD be communicated to the family of the deceased by the Clerk.

Resolved, That this House will attend the funeral of the deceased in a body; and as a further mark of respect for his memory, that it do now adjourn.

The House then adjourned.

TUESDAY, December 28.

Thanks to General Scott and Army.

Mr. HUNT, by general consent, gave notice that to-morrow, or on some subsequent day, he would ask leave to introduce the following joint resolutions:

JOINT RESOLUTIONS expressive of the thanks of Congress to Major-General Winfield Scott, and the troops under his command, for their distinguished gallantry and good conduct in the campaign of 1847.

Resolved unanimously, by the Senate and House of Representatives of the United States of America in Congress assembled, That the thanks of Congress be, and they are hereby, presented to Winfield Scott, Major-General commanding in chief the army in Mexico, and through him to the officers and men of the regular and volunteer corp under him, for their uniform gallantry and good conduct, conspicuously displayed at the siege and capture of the city of Vera Cruz and castle of San Juan de Ulua, March 29, 1847; and in the successive battles of Cerro Gordo, April 18th; Contreras, San Antonio, and Churubusco, August 19th and 20th; and for the victories achieved in front of the city of Mexico, September 8th, 11th, 12th, and 13th; and the capture of the metropolis, September 14th, 1847; in which the Mexican troops, greatly superior in numbers, and with every advantage of position, were in every conflict signally defeated by the American arms.

2. *Resolved*, That the President of the United States be, and he is hereby, requested to cause to be struck a gold medal, with devices emblematical of the series of brilliant victories achieved by the army, and presented to Major-General Winfield Scott, as a testimony of the high sense entertained by Congress of his valor, skill, and judicious conduct in the memorable campaign of 1847.

3. *Resolved*, That the President of the United States be requested to cause the foregoing resolutions to be communicated to Major-General Scott in such terms as he may deem best calculated to give effect to the objects thereof.

The notice was entered on the Journal.

MONDAY, January 3, 1848.

Thanks to General Taylor—The War.

Mr. HOUSTON, of Delaware,—previous notice having been given—introduced the following joint resolution of thanks to Major-General Taylor:

Resolved by the Senate and House of Representatives of the United States of America in Congress assembled, That the thanks of Congress are due, and they are hereby tendered, to Major-General Zachary Taylor, and through him to the officers and soldiers of the regular army and of the volunteers under his command, for their indomitable valor, skill, and good conduct, conspicuously displayed on the 22d and 23d days of February last, in the battle of Buena Vista, in defeating a numerous Mexican army, consisting of four times their number, and composed of chosen troops, under their favorite commander, General Santa Anna, and thereby obtaining a victory over the enemy, which, for its signal and brilliant character, is unsurpassed in the military annals of the world.

Resolved, That the President of the United States be requested to cause to be struck a gold medal, with devices emblematical of this splendid achievement, and presented to Major-General Taylor, as a testimony of the high sense entertained by Congress of his judicious and distinguished conduct on that memorable occasion.

Resolved, That the President of the United States be requested to cause the foregoing resolutions to be communicated to Major-General Taylor in such manner as he may deem best calculated to effect the objects thereof.

FRIDAY, January 7.

The New Rule relating to Debate.

The House resolved itself into Committee of the Whole on the state of the Union, (Mr. SMITH, of Indiana, in the chair.)

The CHAIRMAN stated the pending question to be on the appeal.

Mr. SIMS, before voting on the appeal, desired to say a few words. He had found among the catalogue of rules one which provided that "no member shall occupy more than one hour in debate on any question in the House or in committee; but a member reporting the measure under consideration from a committee, may open and close the debate, provided that where debate is closed by order of the House, any member shall be allowed, in committee, five minutes to explain any amendment he may offer." That was the one-hour rule, as adopted at the present session. The 36th rule of the last Congress, which had also been adopted, provided that "no member shall speak more than once to the same question without leave of the House, unless he be the mover, proposer, or introducer of any matter pending; in which case he shall be permitted to speak in reply, but not until every member choosing to speak shall have spoken." The 133d rule provided for the suspension of the rules and orders for the purpose of going into committee and for discharging a committee from a bill. In addition to this, it was the rule as well as the practice, that debate might be closed by the previous question; and the question now was as to the interpretation which should be given to these rules, taken in connection and in harmony with each other. Under the old 36th rule, the mover was entitled to speak two hours, but he was not to speak for a second hour, until every body desiring to do so had spoken once; but what was the proviso to the new rule? It was the exclusion of a conclusion. It was intended to apply to debate closed in Committee of the Whole by order of the House, and excluded the conclusion that the preceding rule had any application to such subject. It was designed to show that the preceding rule was not to be interpreted as giving to the mover one hour to speak in addition to his opening hour, when debate was closed by order of the House. A member reporting the measure under consideration, may open and close the debate; but his right was to be operated upon by this proviso, otherwise every member who may not have spoken would also have the right to speak one hour. And if the interpretation contended for in committee were sustained, it would also prolong debate for one hour after the previous question had been ordered. After sustaining this position by argument and illustration, he concluded with the expression of a hope that the decision of the chairman would be reversed.

Mr. GREEN, Mr. STUART, of Michigan, Mr. C. J. INGERSOLL, Mr. GENTRY, Mr. RHETT, and Mr. STANTON, also participated in the discussion of the merits of the question involved in the appeal; on which the vote was taken by tellers, and sustained the decision of the Chair by 101 to 73.

So the committee decided that a mover is entitled to speak one hour, or the residue of an hour partly occupied, after the time fixed by an order of the House to terminate debate.

THURSDAY, January 13.

Return of Santa Anna to Mexico.

The SPEAKER laid before the House the following Message from the President of the United States:

WASHINGTON, *January* 12, 1848.

To the House of Representatives of the United States:

I have carefully considered the resolution of the House of Representatives of the 4th instant, requesting the President to communicate to that House "any instructions which may have been given to any of the officers of the army or navy of the United States, or other persons, in regard to the return of President General Lopez de Santa Anna, or any other Mexican, to the Republic of Mexico prior or subsequent to the order of the President or Secretary of War, issued in January, 1846, for the march of the army from the Nueces River, across the 'stupendous deserts' which intervene, to the Rio Grande; that the date of all such instructions, orders, and correspondence be set forth, together with the instructions and orders issued to Mr. Slidell at any time prior or subsequent to his departure for Mexico as Minister Plenipotentiary of the United States to that Republic," requesting the President also to "communicate all the orders and correspondence of the Government in relation to the return of General Paredes."

I transmit herewith reports from the Secretary of State, the Secretary of War, and the Secretary of the Navy, with the documents accompanying the same, which contain all the information in the possession of the Executive which it is deemed compatible with the public interests to communicate.

For further information relating to the return of Santa Anna to Mexico, I refer you to my annual message of December 8, 1846. The facts and considerations stated in that message induced the order of the Secretary of the Navy to the commander of our squadron in the Gulf of Mexico, a copy of which is herewith communicated. This order was issued simultaneously with the order to blockade the coasts of Mexico, both bearing date the 13th of May, 1846, the day on which the existence of the war with Mexico was recognized by Congress. It was issued solely upon the views of policy presented in that message, and without any understanding on the subject, direct or indirect, with Santa Anna or any other person.

General Paredes evaded the vigilance of our combined forces by land and sea, and made his way back to Mexico from the exile into which he had been driven, landing at Vera Cruz after that city and the castle of San Juan de Ulua were in our military occupation, as will appear from the accompanying reports and documents.

The resolution calls for the "instructions and orders issued by Mr. Slidell, at any time prior or subsequent to his departure for Mexico, as Minister Plenipotentiary of the United States to that Republic." The customary and usual reservation contained in calls of either House of Congress upon the Executive for information relating to our intercourse with foreign nations, has been omitted in the resolution before me. The call of the house is unconditional. It is, that the information requested be communicated, and thereby be made public, whether, in the opinion of the Executive, who is charged by the constitution with the duty of conducting negotiations with foreign powers, such information, when disclosed, would be prejudicial to the public interest or not. It has been a subject of serious deliberation with me, whether I could, consistently with my constitutional duty, and my sense of the public interests involved and to be affected by it, violate an important principle, always heretofore held sacred by my predecessors, as I should do by a compliance with the request of the House. President Washington, in a message to the House of Representatives of the 30th of March, 1796, declined to comply with a request contained in a resolution of that body, to lay before them a "copy of the instructions to the Minister of the United States who negotiated the treaty with the King of Great Britain," "together with the correspondence and other documents relative to the said treaty, excepting such of the said papers as any existing negotiations may render improper to be disclosed." In assigning his reasons for declining to comply with the call, he declared that "the nature of foreign negotiations requires caution, and their success must often depend on secrecy; and, even when brought to a conclusion, a full disclosure of all the measures, demands, and eventual concessions which may have been proposed or contemplated, would be extremely impolitic; for this might have a pernicious influence in future negotiations, or produce immediate inconveniences, perhaps danger and mischief, in relation to other powers. The necessity of such caution and secrecy was one cogent reason for vesting the power of making treaties in the President, with the advice and consent of the Senate—the principle on which that body was formed confining it to a small number of members. To admit, then, a right in the House of Representatives to demand, and to have, as a matter of course, all the papers respecting a negotiation with a foreign power, would be to establish a dangerous precedent." In that case, the instructions and documents called for, related to a treaty which had been concluded and ratified by the President and the Senate, and the negotiations in relation to it had been terminated. There was an express reservation, too, "excepting" from the call all such papers as related to "any existing negotiations" which it might be improper to disclose. In that case, President Washington deemed it to be a violation of an important principle, the establishment of a "dangerous precedent," and prejudicial to the public interests, to comply with the call of the House. Without deeming it to be necessary on the present occasion to examine or decide upon the other reasons assigned by him for his refusal to communicate the information requested by the House, the one which is herein recited is in my judgment conclusive in the case under consideration.

Indeed, the objections to complying with the request of the House contained in the resolution before me, are much stronger than those which existed in the case of the resolution in 1796. This resolution calls for the "instructions and orders" to the Minister of the United States to Mexico, which relate to negotiations which have not been terminated, and which may be resumed. The information called for, respects negotiations which the United States offered to open with Mexico immediately preceding the commencement of the ex-

isting war. The instructions given to the Minister of the United States relate to the differences between the two countries out of which the war grew, and the terms of adjustment which we were prepared to offer to Mexico in our anxiety to prevent the war. These differences still remain unsettled, and to comply with the call of the House would be to make public, through that channel, and to communicate to Mexico, now a public enemy engaged in war, information which could not fail to produce serious embarrassment in any future negotiation between the two countries. I have heretofore communicated to Congress all the correspondence of the Minister of the United States to Mexico, which, in the existing state of our relations with that Republic, can, in my judgment, be at this time communicated without serious injury to the public interest.

Entertaining this conviction, and with a sincere desire to furnish any information which may be in possession of the Executive Department, and which either House of Congress may at any time request, I regard it to be my constitutional right and my solemn duty, under the circumstances of this case, to decline a compliance with the request of the House contained in their resolution.

JAMES K. POLK.

Mr. Adams rose, and spoke briefly as follows:

Mr. Speaker: The state of my voice is such that it is not in my power to make to this House the observations which I should otherwise have felt it my duty to make upon this case. I will state, sir, that the reason why I felt it my duty to take this course is, that I consider it a novel thing, and a thing affecting the rights of this House, and of the constituency of this House—the people of the United States. It denies, sir, as I understand it, the power, the constitutional power of this House to call for that information. I believe it is the first time in the history of this Union that it has been denied. In the case to which the President refers, when a call was made upon President Washington, there was (as the Message now states) an exception for cases which he might think not proper to be inquired into at the time.

Now, sir, the President has not added what was the action of the House upon that; and the action of the House was in direct opposition to the resistance of President Washington to their call. The House formally declared—and I wish the Journal might be looked to to see—the House formally declared, against President Washington, their right to call for such information. That was their action; and, as far as I know—although the very memory of Washington, by everybody in this country, at this time, (and by none more than myself,) is reverenced next to worship—the President was wrong in that particular instance, and went too far to deny the power of the House; and as to his reasons, I never thought they were sufficient in that case. And I have always been of the opinion, and most assuredly that has been the opinion of the Democratic party, to which I do not profess to belong, [a laugh,] they have unanimously disapproved of that act of President Washington, as interfering with the rights of this House, and of their constituents, the people of the United States.

I say I cannot enter into an argument upon this subject, but I consider it of such importance, that I am certainly indisposed to lay this Message upon the table. I desire it may be printed; that it may go to the whole country; that it may be decided upon by the people as well as by this House. I think this House ought to sustain, in the strongest manner, their right to call for information upon questions in which war and peace are concerned. They ought to maintain their right, and maintain it in a very distinct manner, against this assertion on the part of the President of the United States. Now, I should be perfectly satisfied to refer the Message to the Committee on Foreign Affairs, whatever my feelings may be in respect to their firmness in resisting this claim set up on the part of the President of the United States. If the Committee on Foreign Affairs will take it, and will examine the Constitution of the United States, its principles, the history of the administration of the Government from that time to the present, and will make a report upon it, I shall be satisfied. As to a Select Committee, I shall be perfectly satisfied that a Select Committee should be appointed by the Speaker, instead of referring it to the Committee on Foreign Affairs. And, as a mark of respect to the President of the United States, I should go for a Select Committee, provided that I am not to be a member of it myself.

I therefore myself, in the first place, hope that a Select Committee, of which I shall not be a member, will be appointed; and if that is not in conformity with the opinion of a majority of this House, that it shall be referred to the Committee on Foreign Affairs. All the Messages of the President are usually referred.

I should say much more, sir, if I had the power.

Mr. King, of Georgia, said he did not propose to discuss this question, or to say five words upon it at this time. He hoped the suggestion of the venerable gentleman from Massachusetts (Mr. Adams) would prevail, and that a Select Committee would be appointed, and the honorable gentleman be made the chairman thereof.

Mr. K. rose to make the motion to refer the Message to a Select Committee, if it had not been already made by the gentleman from Massachusetts.

IN SENATE.

Friday, January 21.

The Journal having been read—

Ordered, That when the Senate adjourns, it adjourn to meet on Monday.

Death of the Hon. John W. Hornbeck.

A message was received from the House of Representatives, communicating the death of the Hon. J. W. Hornbeck, a Representative in that body from Pennsylvania, and the proceedings thereupon.

Mr. Cameron then rose and addressed the Chair as follows:

It is my duty, Mr. President, to detain the Senate for a moment before I move the customary resolutions which here mark the death of one of our number.

John W. Hornbeck, a member of the House of Representatives from the State of Pennsylvania, died at his residence, in the county of Lehigh, a few days since.

It was not my fortune to have been acquainted with him; but from those who knew him well, I learned that he was a native of New Jersey; that he graduated at Union College, in New York; and that he settled, about sixteen years since, at Allentown, Pennsylvania, where he studied law, and where he was, till the time of his death, a respected and successful member of the bar.

He was a man of learning and of ability, of quiet and unobtrusive but of social habits, and of a disposition so kind and benevolent—so willing to serve others rather than himself, that he won the esteem and love of all who came within his circle. Honorable, high-minded, and generous, he commanded the respect of all, and died, as he had lived, without an enemy.

His election was a tribute to his private virtues. Living in a district opposed to him in politics, he was elected by a decided majority over a man of sterling worth and high character.

At the meeting of Congress, he came here to fulfil his trust; but the disease which had marked him for its victim made such rapid inroads upon his constitution, that he was compelled to leave his seat the first week of the session. He returned to his home, where he died in the midst of his family and friends. Those whom he had cherished and protected were around him to smooth his pillow in the last struggle between time and eternity; and he died, as the good man can only die, calmly relying upon the mercy of his Redeemer. Whilst we mourn his early death, we should rejoice that his life was so pure as to warrant the hope that he has only exchanged mortality for a happy immortality.

It only remains for me to submit the following resolutions:

Resolved, That the Senate has received with deep sensibility the message from the House of Representatives announcing the death of the Hon. John W. Hornbeck, a Representative from the State of Pennsylvania.

Resolved, That the members of the Senate, from a sincere desire of showing every mark of respect to the memory of the deceased, will wear the usual badge of mourning for thirty days.

Resolved, That as a further testimony of respect for the memory of the deceased, the Senate do now adjourn.

The resolutions were unanimously agreed to, And the Senate adjourned.

HOUSE OF REPRESENTATIVES.

Monday, February 7.

Thanks to General Scott, etc.

Mr. Hunt asked the consent of the House to introduce the following joint resolutions, of which previous notice had been given:

JOINT RESOLUTIONS expressive of the thanks of Congress to Major-General Winfield Scott and the troops under his command, for their distinguished gallantry and good conduct in the campaign of 1847.

Resolved unanimously by the Senate and House of Representatives of the United States of America, in Congress assembled, That the thanks of Congress be, and they are hereby, presented to Winfield Scott, Major-General commanding in chief the army in Mexico, and through him to the officers and men of the regular and volunteer corps under him, for their uniform gallantry and good conduct, conspicuously displayed at the siege and capture of the city of Vera Cruz and castle of San Juan de Ulua, March 29, 1847; and in the successive battles of Cerro Gordo, April 18; Contreras, San Antonio, and Churubusco, August 19th and 20th; and for the victories achieved in front of the city of Mexico, September 8th, 11th, 12th, and 13th; and the capture of the metropolis, September 14th, 1847; in which the Mexican troops, greatly superior in numbers, and with every advantage of position, were in every conflict signally defeated by the American arms.

2. *Resolved,* That the President of the United States be, and he is hereby, requested to cause to be struck a gold medal, with devices emblematical of the series of brilliant victories achieved by the army, and presented to Major-General Winfield Scott, as a testimony of the high sense entertained by Congress of his valor, skill, and judicious conduct in the memorable campaign of 1847.

3. *Resolved,* That the President of the United States be requested to cause the foregoing resolutions to be communicated to Major-General Scott in such terms as he may deem best calculated to give effect to the object thereof.

The House then seconded the demand for the previous question, and the main question was ordered to be now put.

The roll was then called, and—

Mr. Haskell rose when his name was called and desired to explain, that while voting with great pleasure for these resolutions, he did not wish to be understood as voting for himself. Having been an officer on the occasions referred to, he was placed in a delicate position; but with this explanation he gladly gave his vote in the affimrative.

The question on the passage of the resolution was decided in the affirmative—yeas 197, nay 1.

So the resolution was adopted.

Thanks to General Taylor, etc.

Mr. Stephens, the rules having been suspended for the purpose, introduced the following joint resolutions:

Resolved by the Senate and House of Representatives of the United States of America, in Congress assembled, That the thanks of Congress are due, and they are hereby tendered, to Major-General Zachary Taylor, and, through him, to the officers and soldiers of the regular army and of the volunteers under his command, for their indomitable valor, skill, and good conduct, conspicuously displayed on the twenty-second and twenty-third days of February last, in the battle of Buena Vista, in defeating a Mexican army of more than four times their number, consisting of chosen troops, under their favorite commander, General Santa Anna, and thereby obtaining a victory over the enemy, which, for its signal and brilliant character, is unsurpassed in the military annals of the world.

Resolved, That the President of the United States be requested to cause to be struck a gold medal, with devices emblematical of this splendid achievement, and presented to Major-General Zachary Taylor, as a testimony of the high sense entertained by Congress of his judicious and distinguished conduct on that memorable occasion.

Resolved, That the President of the United States be requested to cause the foregoing resolutions to be communicated to Major-General Taylor in such terms as he may deem best calculated to give effect to the object thereof.

The resolutions were read a first and second time.

Mr. Stephens moved the previous question on their engrossment and third reading, which was seconded; and, under its operation, the resolutions were ordered to be engrossed and read a third time; and, being engrossed, they were accordingly read a third time and passed —yeas 181, nay 1.

Monday, February 14.

Refunding of Money by the States.

Mr. Murphy offered the following preamble and resolution, which were agreed to:

Whereas, by an act entitled "An act to regulate the deposits of the public money," approved June 23, 1836, the surplus in the Treasury of the United States, on the 1st of January, 1837, reserving five millions of dollars, was directed to be deposited by the Secretary of the Treasury with the several States, on receiving certificates of deposits thereof signed by their treasurers, or other competent authorities, and expressing the usual and legal obligations, and pledging the faith of the State for the safe-keeping and repayment thereof, and for paying the said moneys and every part thereof from time to time, whenever the same should be required by the Secretary of the Treasury for defraying any wants of the public treasury: in pursuance of which act, the sum of $28,101,644 91 was deposited with the several States:

And whereas, the moneys so deposited are required for the purpose of defraying the wants of the public treasury, and sound policy dictates the propriety of avoiding a large public debt, which otherwise must accrue: Therefore,

Be it Resolved, That it be referred to the Committee of Ways and Means, to inquire into the expediency of requiring the Secretary of the Treasury to call for the repayment of the moneys of the United States deposited with the States, according to the pledged faith of the States, in the manner designated by the said act of June 23, 1836.

IN SENATE.

Wednesday, February 16.

Thanks to General Scott, etc.

The Senate proceeded to the consideration of the joint resolution from the House of Representatives, expressive of thanks to General Winfield Scott, and the troops under his command, for their distinguished gallantry and services.

The resolution having had its third reading, the question was put on its passage; when—

Mr. Hale demanded the yeas and nays; and the vote was as follows:

Yeas.—Messrs. Allen, Ashley, Atchison, Badger, Bagby, Benton, Berrien, Bradbury, Bright, Butler, Calhoun, Cass, Clayton, Corwin, Crittenden, Davis of Massachusetts, Davis of Mississippi, Dayton, Dickinson, Dix, Downs, Felch, Foote, Hannegan, Houston, Hunter, Johnson of Maryland, Johnson of Louisiana, Johnson of Georgia, Mangum, Mason, Miller, Moor, Niles, Rusk, Sevier, Spruance, Sturgeon, Turney, Upham, Westcott, and Yulee—42.

Nay.—Mr. Hale—1.

Thanks to General Taylor.

The Senate then proceeded to consider the joint resolution from the House of thanks to Major-General Taylor.

The resolution having been read—

Mr. Crittenden said: I rise to inquire whether the resolution is now in a state to admit of amendment. I feel quite strongly that some little modification of the language of the resolution will be an improvement of it. When before the military committee, some exception was taken to the form of the resolution; but I am one who is not at all scrupulous about the language used on such occasions, when compliment is intended, and so, rather than disturb the resolution, we thought it best to report it back to the Senate just as it was sent to us. But upon reconsideration of the matter, I think it proper to move to amend the resolution by striking out the word "indomitable," and "thereby obtaining a victory over the enemy, which, for its signal and brilliant character, is unsurpassed in the military annals of the world."

Mr. Davis, of Massachusetts, called for a reading of the resolution as proposed to be amended.

The resolution, as amended, was then read, and the amendment was agreed to.

The question was then put, and decided as follows:

Yeas.—Messrs. Allen, Ashley, Atchison, Atherton, Badger, Bagby, Bell, Benton, Berrien, Bradbury, Breese, Bright, Butler, Calhoun, Cameron, Cass, Clarke, Clayton, Corwin, Crittenden, Davis of Massachusetts, Davis of Mississippi, Dayton, Dickinson, Dix, Downs, Felch, Foote, Greene, Houston, Hunter, Johnson of Maryland, Johnson of Louisiana, Johnson of Georgia, Mangum, Mason, Miller, Moor, Niles, Rusk, Sevier, Spruance, Sturgeon, Turney, Upham, Westcott, and Yulee—47

Nay.—Mr. Hale—1.

It being near three o'clock when the resolutions were disposed of, the special order was postponed, and the Senate proceeded to the consideration of executive business; and, after some time spent therein, adjourned.

Monday, February 21.

Heirs of John Paul Jones.

The Senate proceeded to consider the amendments made by the House of Representatives to the bill for the relief of the heirs of John Paul Jones.

The amendment having been read—

Mr. Davis, of Massachusetts, moved that the bill be referred to the committee.

Mr. Hannegan said that the bill did not originate in the committee this year, and in the peculiar circumstances of the case, was passed without reference, having passed both Houses last session, and failed to become a law in consequence of being accidentally lost in the lobby on the way to the President for his signature. Owing to the courtesy, not to say a sense of justice of the Senate, it was passed this session without being subjected to the usual form of reference to a committee. The claim itself had undergone a strict investigation on these occasions. Twice had it been the subject of a favorable report, and it had again passed the House by a large vote in its favor. The amendments were entirely immaterial, being merely verbal. There was only one that had any substance, and that made an exception against the heirs of Captain Landais, who have received their share of the original claim. He hoped that the Senator from Massachusetts would withdraw his motion, in order that he might be enabled to move the concurrence of the Senate in the amendments of the House.

Mr. Davis was quite aware that this bill had received the action of the Senate in the form in which it passed at the last session. Still he was not able to understand the bearing of the amendments which had been read. He could not determine, without some examination, whether they were important or not; therefore, without entertaining any hostile feeling to the bill, or any desire to delay its final passage, he believed that it had better be examined by a committee; at least, that was his impression, although if the Senate thought otherwise, he should not insist on his motion.

Mr. Hannegan then rose, but yielded to

Mr. Benton, who inquired if the motion was withdrawn.

Mr. Davis replied in the negative, and added, that it would not be, unless the general sense of the Senate opposed it.

Mr. Benton then said that it would not be withdrawn by the unanimous sense of the Senate, for he would object to the withdrawal of the motion. This was a case seventy years old—approaching very close to that—and within the last two or three sessions had had at least a rapid passage through the two Houses. Now he was told by old Senators, when he came there, that he should distrust any thing that went rapidly and unanimously, and their philosophical reasoning was, that the human mind was so various in its conclusions, that if any case was fully stated and presented in all its bearings, there would be difference of opinion in regard to it, and that, therefore, when a case passed rapidly through a legislative body, the presumption was that it had not been fully stated and attentively examined. He was not in his seat when this bill was called up and passed through the Senate, without the observance of the usual forms. Had he been in his place upon that occasion, he should have moved that it be subjected to all those forms which the wisdom of legislators had provided for the protection of the public interests, and for insuring sound and wholesome legislation. Now, with respect to the merits of this claim, he knew nothing. But he did know one thing: that our ancestors, the men of the Revolution, were just men. He doubted neither their justice nor their patriotism. They were also wise men. The men of the Revolution constituted a body of men rarely seen on the face of the earth—rarely equalled in the justice, wisdom, and moderation of all their doings. They who lived during the Revolution, and were cognizant of all that occurred during that period, soon after that event—each State within itself, and the General Government by assuming an amount perhaps exceeding all just demands against it—settled every just claim upon them, and they settled precisely as every man settles who is just, and at the same time, poor. They settled all accounts against them, and, if they could not pay, they gave their notes. Certificates were given in every case in which they thought that any thing was due; and his reading led him to say, that in the general assumpsit which took place about the year '94, an amount over and above what was due was assumed and allowed for the purpose of covering every thing which generosity even, not to speak of justice, demanded. That was his understanding of the closing up of the affairs of the Revolution, and with that understanding, he looked with extreme suspicion upon any claim that was now presented. In the first place, such a claim was nothing less than an impeachment of the integrity of the men of that day; if not of their integrity, at all events, of their knowledge of their own transactions; and assumed that they of the third generation knew the transactions of their grandfathers better than they did at the time when these transactions took place! He asked what would become of Senators, if, at the end of sixty or seventy years, their children should be called upon to pay any demand which might be then brought up against their ancestors? How would Senators meet a claim presented against them for transactions sixty or seventy years ago, on the part of their grandfathers? There must be some end to this business. Every generation was charged with the management of its own business. He did not say that they should have exactly a statute of limitation, but he said that that principle must go into the affairs of the whole community, otherwise nothing public or private, nothing between man and man, or nation and nation, could ever be regarded as settled. It was a just principle that they who lived at the time, and were cognizant of the transaction, were the proper persons to settle the case. There was great danger in posterity attempting to open transactions which had been passed upon by preceding generations. He hoped that the bill would be referred and examined, and that it would be subjected to every form which the wisdom of legislators had devised for the purpose of protecting the public interests and securing sound and wholesome legislation.

Mr. Cass said he hoped the bill would be passed over informally, in order that the special order might be taken up.

Several Senators. "Question."

The question was then taken on the motion to refer the bill to the committee, and it was agreed to—ayes 25.

Illness of John Quincy Adams.

Mr. Benton rose, and with great feeling, said: I am called on to make a painful announcement to the Senate. I have just been informed that the House of Representatives has this instant adjourned under the most afflicting circumstances. A calamitous visitation has fallen on one of its oldest and most valuable members—one who has been President of the United States, and whose character has inspired the highest respect and esteem. Mr. Adams has just sunk down in his chair, and has been carried into an adjoining room, and may be at this moment passing from the earth, under the roof that covers us, and almost in our presence. In these circumstances the whole Senate will feel alike, and feel wholly unable to attend to any business. I therefore move the immediate adjournment of the Senate.

The motion was unanimously agreed to; and

The Senate adjourned.

HOUSE OF REPRESENTATIVES.

Tuesday, February 22.

The House met at twelve o'clock, the usual hour, and it was marked with deep solemnity and sadness. The Rev. H. Slicer, the Congressional Chaplain, performed the duty of his office with unusual impressiveness, and tenderly and delicately alluded to the venerable sage who lay in an adjoining room, unconscious of all earthly concerns, on the verge of eternity.

The Speaker then rose and said, he deemed it proper to state to the House from the chair that his venerable colleague, John Quincy Adams, was still in a state of unconsciousness in the Speaker's room, and, in the opinion of his medical advisers, was rapidly sinking.

Mr. Burt moved that the House do now adjourn.

Mr. Giddings suggested that the Journal of yesterday should state the cause of its early adjournment.

The Speaker acquiesced, and directed the Clerk to record the melancholy circumstance.

The House then adjourned.

IN SENATE.

Tuesday, February 22.

The Journal having beeen read—

Mr. Davis, of Massachusetts, rose and said that he was informed the House of Representatives had met and instantly adjourned, in consequence of the continued and dangerous illness of Mr. Adams, who still lay within these walls in a very perilous condition. Mr. Adams, he said, had attained to a great age, and had been eminently distinguished among the illustrious men of the country; and he hoped, under the circumstances which existed, the motion he was about to make would meet with the approbation of the Senate. It seemed to him that the anxieties of the moment, as well as veneration for one who has so long been an important co-laborer in our councils, in a measure unfitted us for deliberation.

Mr. D. then moved that the Senate do now adjourn.

The question being put, it was decided in the affirmative, *nemine dissentiente;* and

The Senate adjourned.

HOUSE OF REPRESENTATIVES.

Wednesday, February 23.

After an appropriate prayer by the Rev. Mr. Slicer, the Journal of yesterday was read and approved.

The House then, on motion of Mr. Barrington, adjourned.

Thursday, February 24.

Honors to Mr. Adams.

The House met at the usual hour, and was opened by prayer by the Chaplain. A full attendance of members and a crowded audience attested the deep interest of the occasion which called the two Houses to offer public testimonials of their profound respect for the memory of the Hon. JOHN QUINCY ADAMS, who breathed his last on yesterday evening, and whose mortal remains yet lie within the walls of the Capitol.

The SPEAKER (the Hon. R. C. WINTHROP) rose, and in a feeling and affecting manner addressed the House as follows:

Gentlemen of the House of Representatives of the United States:

It has been thought fit that the Chair should announce officially to this House an event already known to the members individually, and which has filled all our hearts with sadness.

A seat on this floor has been vacated, towards which our eyes have been accustomed to turn with no common interest.

A voice has been hushed forever in this Hall, to which all ears have been wont to listen with profound reverence.

A venerable form has faded from our sight, around which we have daily clustered with an affectionate regard.

A name has been stricken from the roll of the living statesmen of our land, which has been associated for more than half a century with the highest civil service, and the loftiest civil renown.

On Monday, the 21st instant, JOHN QUINCY ADAMS sunk in his seat, in presence of us all, by a sudden illness, from which he never recovered; and he died in the Speaker's room at a quarter past seven o'clock last evening, with the officers of the House and the delegation of his own Massachusetts around him.

Whatever advanced age, long experience, great ability, vast learning, accumulated public honors, a spotless private character, and a firm religious faith, could do to render any one an object of interest, respect, and admiration, they had done for this distinguished person; and interest, respect, and admiration are but feeble terms to express the feelings with which the members of this House and the people of the country have long regarded him.

After a life of eighty years, devoted from its earliest maturity to the public service, he has at length gone to his rest. He has been privileged to die at his post; to fall while in the discharge of his duties; to expire beneath the roof of the Capitol; and to have his last scene associated forever in history with the birthday of that illustrious Patriot, whose just discernment brought him first into the service of his country.

The close of such a life, under such circumstances, is not an event for unmingled emotions. We cannot find it in our hearts to regret, that he died as he has died. He himself could have desired no other end. "This is the end of earth," were his last words, uttered on the day on which he fell. But we might almost hear him exclaiming, as he left us—in a language hardly less familiar to him than his native tongue—"*Hoc est, nimirum, magis feliciter de vitâ migrare, quam mori.*"

It is for others to suggest what honors shall be paid to his memory. No acts of ours are necessary to his fame. But it may be due to ourselves and to the country, that the national sense of his character and services should be fitly commemorated.

When the SPEAKER concluded—

Mr. HUDSON, of Massachusetts, rose and addressed the House as follows:

Mr. Speaker: I rise, with no ordinary emotions, to perform a painful duty, which has been assigned me by my colleagues, growing out of an event which has recently occurred in the midst of us, the announcement of which has just been made by the Chair. My late venerable colleague is no more! A great and good man has fallen! He has been stricken down in the midst of us, while in the discharge of his public duties. One whose public services are coeval with the establishment of our Government—one who has come down to us from past generations, and of whom it might almost be said that he was living in the midst of posterity, an example to us and to those who come after us—has ceased from his labors, and gone to his reward. The peculiar circumstances of his death are known to every member of this House, and are calculated to make a deep and lasting impression. They weigh so heavily upon my own mind and feelings, that I am almost inclined to believe that *silence* is the most appropriate token of our grief, and the most suitable tribute to his memory.

JOHN QUINCY ADAMS was born on the 11th day of July, 1767, in that part of Braintree, Massachusetts, which was subsequently incorporated into a town by the name of Quincy, and hence was in the eighty-first year of his age. In 1778, when he was but eleven years of age, he accompanied his father, John Adams, to France, who was sent with Benjamin Franklin and Arthur Lee, as Commissioners to the Court of Versailles. After remaining in France about eighteen months, during which time he applied himself closely to the study of the French and Latin languages, he returned to his own country in August, 1779. In November of the same year, his father was again despatched to Europe for the discharge of diplomatic services, and took his son John Quincy with him. At Paris he was put to school; and when, in 1780, John Adams removed to Holland, his son enjoyed the advantages of the public school at Amsterdam, and afterwards of the University at Leyden. Francis Dana, who accompanied John Adams, as Secretary to the Embassy, received in 1781 the appointment of Minister Plenipotentiary to Russia, and took John Quincy Adams, then fourteen years of age, with him as his private secretary. Here he remained till October, 1782, when he left Mr. Dana at St. Petersburgh, and returned through Sweden, Denmark, Hamburg, and Bremen, to Holland, where he remained some months, till his father took him to Paris, at the time of the signing of the treaty of peace in 1783. From that time till 1785, he was with his father in England, Holland, and France; during the whole of which period he was a close student.

At the age of eighteen, at his own request, his father permitted him to return to Massachusetts, where he entered Harvard University, and was graduated in 1787 with distinguished honors. Soon after leaving college, he entered the office of the celebrated Theophilus Parsons, afterwards Chief Justice of Massachusetts, where he remained the usual period of three years in the study of the law, when he entered the profession, and established himself at Boston.

In 1794, General Washington appointed him Resident Minister to the United Netherlands. From that period till 1801 he was in Europe, employed in diplomatic business, and as a public minister in Holland, England, and Prussia. Just as General Washington was retiring from office, he appointed Mr. Adams Minister Plenipotentiary to the Court of Portugal. While on his way to Lisbon he received a new commission, changing his destination to Berlin. During his residence of about three years and a half at Berlin, he concluded an important commercial treaty with Prussia—thus accomplishing the object of his mission. He was recalled near the close of his father's administration, and arrived in his native country in September, 1801.

In 1802 he was chosen by the Boston district to the Senate of Massachusetts, and soon after was elected by the Legislature a Senator in Congress for six years from March 3, 1803. Here he remained in the Senate of the United States until 1808, when he resigned. While in the Senate he received the appointment of Professor of Rhetoric in Harvard University, an office which he filled with distinguished ability.

In 1809 he was appointed by President Madison Envoy Extraordinary and Minister Plenipotentiary to the Court of Russia, where he rendered the most important services to his country. By his influence with that Court, he induced Russia to offer her mediation between Great Britain and the United States in the war of 1812; and, when the proper time had arrived, he was placed by President Madison at the head of five distinguished commissioners to negotiate a treaty of peace, which was concluded at Ghent in 1814. Mr. Adams was then associated with Mr. Clay and Mr. Gallatin to negotiate a commercial convention with Great Britain, and was forthwith appointed Minister Plenipotentiary to the Court of St. James. While in Europe in 1811, he received the appointment of Associate Justice of the Supreme Court of the United States, which he declined.

After remaining in England till the close of President Madison's administration, he was called home, and placed by President Monroe at the head of the Department of State, where he remained eight years.

In 1825 he was chosen by the House of Representatives President of the United States for the term of four years. On leaving the Presidency in 1829, he returned to his native place in Massachusetts, and in 1831 he was elected a member of this House, and by the free suffrages of the people has been continued in that office to the day of his death.

This is but a hasty and imperfect enumeration of the public stations which have been filled by my late lamented colleague. Of the manner in which he has discharged these public trusts it is not necessary for me to speak. Suffice it to say, that his long eventful life has been devoted to the public service, and the ability and fidelity with which he has discharged every duty are known and acknowledged throughout the nation. His fame is so blended with his country's history that it will live when all the frail monuments of art shall have crumbled into dust. By his death the country has lost a pure patriot, science an ardent votary, and the cause of human freedom a devoted friend.

But it is not as a public man merely that we are to contemplate Mr. Adams. In the private walks of life, "where tired dissimulation drops the mask," and man appears as he really is, we find in him all those silent and social virtues which adorn the character. His ardent love of justice, his inflexible regard for truth, his stern devotion to the cause of civil and religious liberty, were blended with meekness, sobriety, and charity. But the crowning glory of his character was his devotion to the cause of his Redeemer.

To that cause he was publicly dedicated on the second day of his earthly existence, and throughout a long life he manifested a firm belief in Divine revelation, and a calm trust in that Being who rules among the nations, and spreads the mantle of his love over his dependent children. But he is gone. The places that have known him will now know him no more forever. This instance of mortality, at once so peculiar and so painful, admonishes us of the uncertainty of life, and teaches us so to number our days, that we may apply our hearts unto wisdom.

We tender to his afflicted family our heartfelt sympathy, and assure them that a nation's tears will be mingled with theirs. And while we look for consolation to the wisdom and goodness of an overruling Providence, we would affectionately commend them to that gracious Being who has revealed himself as the father of the fatherless and the widow's God and friend.

Mr. Hudson concluded by offering the following resolutions:

Resolved, That this House has heard with the deepest sensibility of the death in this Capitol of John Quincy Adams, a member of the House from the State of Massachusetts.

Resolved, That, as a testimony of respect for the memory of this distinguished statesman, the officers and members of the House will wear the usual badge of mourning, and attend the funeral in this Hall on Saturday next, at twelve o'clock.

Resolved, That a committee be appointed to superintend the funeral solemnities.

Resolved, That the proceedings of this House in relation to the death of John Quincy Adams be communicated to the family of the deceased by the Clerk.

Resolved, That this House, as a further mark of respect for the memory of the deceased, do adjourn to Saturday next, the day appointed for the funeral.

Before the question was stated on these resolutions—

Mr. Holmes, of South Carolina, rose and said: Mr. Speaker, the mingled tones of sorrow, like the voice of many waters, has come unto us from a sister State—Massachusetts weeping for her honored son. The State I have the honor in part to represent, once endured, with yours, a common suffering, battled for a common cause, and rejoiced in a common triumph. Surely, then, it is meet that in this the day of your affliction we should mingle our griefs.

When a great man falls, the nation mourns; when a patriarch is removed, the people weep. Ours, my associates, is no common bereavement. The chain which linked our hearts with the gifted spirits of former times has been rudely snapped. The lips from which flowed those living and glorious truths that our fathers uttered are closed in death. Yes, my friends, Death has been among us! He has not entered the humble cottage of some unknown, ignoble peasant; he has knocked audibly at the palace of a nation! His footstep has been heard in the Hall of a State! He has cloven down his victim in the midst of the councils of a people! He has borne in triumph from among you the gravest, wisest, most reverend head! Ah! he has taken him as a trophy who was once chief over many States, adorned with virtue, and learning, and truth; he has borne at his chariot wheels a renowned one of the earth!

There was no incident in the birth, the life, the death, of Mr. Adams, not intimately woven with the history of the land. Born in the night of his country's tribulation, he heard the first murmurs of discontent; he saw the first efforts for deliverance. Whilst yet a little child, he listened with eagerness to the whispers of freedom as they breathed from the lips of her almost inspired apostles; he caught the fire that was then kindled; his eye beamed with the first ray; he watched the day-spring from on high; and long before he departed from earth, it was graciously vouchsafed unto him to behold the effulgence of her noontide glory.

His father saw the promise of the son, and early led him by the hand to drink of the very fountains of light and liberty itself. His youthful thoughts were kindled with the idealism of a republic, whose living form and features he was destined to behold visibly. Removed at an early age to a distant country, he there, under the eye of his father, was instructed in the rigid lore of a Franklin, as I have heard him say. His intellect was expanded by the conversations, and invigorated by the acute disquisitions, of the Academicians, whose fiery zeal, even at that early period, was waking up the mind of France to deeper thoughts, bolder inquiries, and more matured reflection—to result ultimately, as we all know, in terrific action. Returning to this country, he entered into the cool cloisters of the college; passed through the various stages to acquire that discipline of mind which intense study can alone impart; and thence, as he was about to emerge, appeared those buds of promise which soon blossomed into those blushing honors he afterwards wore so thick around him. His was not the dreamy life of the schools; but he leapt into the arena of activity, to run a career of glorious emulation with the gifted spirits of the earth. He saw the efforts to place his country on a deep and stable foundation, where it now rests. He had seen the colonies emerge into States, and the States cemented into Union, and realized, in the formation of this confederated republic, all that his ardent hopes had pictured out in the recesses of schools. Young as he then was, he contributed, by the energy of his mind and the vigor of his pen, to support the administration of Washington, who, we have just been told, transferred him at an early age to a foreign court; scarcely initiated into its diplomacy before his services were required for another and a more extended sphere. Passing from that, he returned to his own country, and was placed by the suffrages of his State in the chamber of the other end of this Capitol; and there, the activity of his mind, the freedom of his thought, the independence of his action, rendered him to his constituents for the time being unacceptable, by uniting him to the policy of Mr. Jefferson. He retired from the halls of Congress; but he went to no ignoble ease. Wearied with the toils, heated with the contests, covered with the dust of politics, he withdrew to the classic groves of Cambridge, and there he bathed his weary mind in the pure stream of intellectual rest. Purified, refreshed, invigorated, he came forth, after severe study and devout prayer, to do his country service. He was sent immediately to Russia, as has been stated, not to repose amidst the luxuries of courts, or in rich saloons amidst the glitter of lights and the swell of voluptuous music, but to watch the swell and play of those shadowy billows with which all Europe heaved beneath the throes of the great heart of France.

Mr. Adams saw and felt that the pulse of freedom day by day beat feebler and feebler throughout the continent. He counselled the ministers of Russia. He was one of those that stimulated them to wake from their torpor, and he had the satisfaction to behold, from the frozen regions of the north, those mighty hordes pour out upon the sunny nations of the south to give deliverance to people, states, and powers. His own country demanded his services, and he became, with Gallatin and Clay, a mediator of that peace between two nations which we trust shall exist forever, while the only contests shall be those of good will on earth and mutual brotherhood.

He went—as his father had gone after the first war of the Revolution—upon the termination of the second war, to the Court of St. James. He remained not long before another sphere was opened to him. As Secretary of State for eight years, he fulfilled the arduous duties incident to that high post in a country just emerging from conflict. To the highest office of the people he was quickly raised; and how in that sphere he moved—with what ease, ability, and grace—we all know, and history will record. He crushed no heart beneath the rude grasp of proscription; he left no heritage of widows' cries or orphans' tears.

He disrobed himself with dignity of the vestures of office, not to retire to the shades of Quincy, but, in the maturity of his intellect, in the vigor of his thought, to leap into this arena, and to continue, as he had begun, a disciple, an ardent devotee at the temple of his country's freedom. How in this department he ministered to his country's wants we all know and have witnessed. How often we have crowded into that aisle, and clustered around that now vacant desk, to listen to the counsels of wisdom as they fell from the lips of the venerable sage, we can all remember, for it was but of yesterday. But what a change! How wondrous! how sudden! 'Tis like a vision of the night. That form which we beheld but a few days since, is now cold in death!

But the last Sabbath, and in this Hall, he worshipped with others. Now his spirit mingles with the noble army of martyrs and the just made perfect in the eternal adoration of the living God! With him "this is the end of earth." He sleeps the sleep that knows no waking. He is gone—and forever! The sun that ushers in the morn of the next holy day, while it gilds the lofty dome of the Capitol, shall rest with soft and mellow light upon the consecrated spot beneath whose turf forever lies the Patriot Father and the Patriot Sage!

Mr. Vinton rose and addressed the House:

Mr. Speaker, (said he,) when the messenger of death enters this Hall and bids one of us come away, it is our custom to commit exclusively to some colleague of the departed member the solemn ceremony of its announcement. Usage requires no more. But the venerable man whom the destroying angel smote down in our very presence—the book of whose great life is now written and finished —stood out far beyond the rest of us, upon a broader and higher elevation. It is true he was the son of Massachusetts, and to her belongs the proud honor of having given him birth. But he was more than the son of Massachusetts; he did not belong to her alone; he offered himself to his country, and she made him her property. His fame, his wisdom, and his works, were all his country's. These are his rich and common legacy to us all. It is therefore that we of the great national brotherhood claim the precious privilege to cluster close around the children of Massachusetts—to take part with them in this sad solemnity—to sympathize with them, and along with them— to give utterance to our sorrow, to our reverence, to our veneration for the departed dead, and to our deep affliction in this great national bereavement. I did not rise—I dare not attempt one word of eulogy upon the illustrious dead—nor dare I venture to portray his exalted character as a statesman, or the bright virtues of his private life. I know how incompetent I am to the performance of such a task. I trust that in due time, and on some fitting occasion, this will be done by some one of the great and gifted intellects of Massachusetts. But still I hope to be permitted to say that no man has heretofore died, when a member of this body, who will fill so large a space in his country's history, or who has stamped so deeply his impress on her institutions. The solemnity of the occasion forbids, perhaps the period has not yet arrived, for the expression of an unbiased opinion respecting the effect of this on his country's welfare. But when time shall have numbered with the dead us who were actors with him upon this great drama of life; when the partialities of his friends and the prejudices of his enemies, if any he have left behind, shall have been buried in one common grave, he and the work of his great life may be safely trusted to the truthful historian, and to the judgment of an impartial posterity. To this great and just ordeal, he, with all the renowned and mighty of the earth who have gone before him, must come at last. And to its verdict, those of us who knew him best, and were most devoted to him, are most willing to commit him, and all that he achieved. The time, the place, and the manner of his death, all conspire to excite the profoundest sensation everywhere, as it has done in this Hall; and especially to teach us "what shadows we are, and what shadows we pursue;" to teach us how vain and valueless are all our struggles and contests here for distinction or for power; and, above all, that no human greatness, no fame, no honor, no high attainment, no divine exaltation of intellect, can aught avail us to avoid the dread sentence of God upon poor mortal man: "Dust thou art, and unto dust thou shalt return."

Mr. James McDowell, of Virginia, then rose and said: Such, for half a century, Mr. Speaker, has been the eminent position of Mr. Adams in the eyes of his countrymen; his participation in the highest honors which it was theirs to give; his intimate association with controlling events in their national annals, and with the formation of that public opinion which brought them about; such the veneration and almost universal homage entertained for his intellect and virtues; and such, in all respects, his great relations to this entire Union, and to the daily thought of its growing millions,—that on this sad occasion the language of all its parts will be that of lamentation and of tribute. It is not for Massachusetts to mourn alone over a solitary and exclusive bereavement. It is not for her to feel alone a solitary and exclusive sorrow. No, sir; no! Her sister Commonwealths gather to her side in this hour of her affliction, and, intertwining their arms with hers, they bend together over the bier of her illustrious son—feeling as she feels, and weeping as she weeps, over a sage, a patriot, and a statesman gone! It was in these great characteristics of individual and of public man, that his country reverenced that son when living, and such, with a painful sense of her common loss, will she deplore him now that he is dead.

Born in our revolutionary day, and brought up in early and cherished intimacy with the fathers and founders of the Republic, he was a living bond of connection between the present and the past—the venerable representative of the memories of another age, and the zealous, watchful, and powerful one of the expectations, interests, and progressive knowledge of his own.

There he sat, with his intense eye upon every thing that passed, the picturesque and rare old man, unapproachable by all others in the unity of his character and in the thousandfold anxieties which centred upon him. No human being ever entered this Hall without turning habitually and with heartfelt deference first to him, and few ever left it without pausing as they went to pour out their blessings upon that spirit of consecration to the country which brought and which kept him there.

Standing upon the extreme boundary of human life, and disdaining all the relaxations and exemptions of age, his outer framework only was crumbling away. The glorious engine within still worked on unhurt, uninjured, amid all the dilapidations around it, and worked on with its wonted and its iron power, until the blow was sent from above which crushed it into fragments before us. And however appalling that blow, and however profoundly it smote upon our own feelings as we beheld its extinguishing effect upon his, where else could it have fallen so fitly upon him? Where else could he have been relieved from the yoke of his labors so well as in the field where he bore them? Where else would he himself have been so willing to have yielded up his life, as upon the post of duty and by the side of that very altar to which he had devoted it? Where but in the Capitol of his country, to which all the throbbings and hopes of his heart had been given, would the dying patriot be so willing that those hopes and throbbings should cease? And where but from this mansion-house of liberty on earth, could this dying Christian more fitly go to his mansion-house of eternal liberty on high?

But kindling to the imagination and soothing even to the feelings as is the death of Mr. ADAMS, with all the accessories and associations of this spot around him, how infinitely deeper is the interest which is given to it by the conviction that he was willing and ready to meet it? He was happily spared, by the preservation of his rich faculties to the last, from becoming a melancholy spectacle of dotard and drivelling old age. He was still more happily spared, by the just and wise and truthful use of those faculties, from becoming the melancholy and revolting spectacle of irreverent and wicked old age. None knew better or felt more deeply than he that

"'Tis not the whole of life to live,
Nor all of death to die;"

and hence for long years his life has been a continuous and beautiful illustration of the great truth, that whilst the fear of man is the consummation of all folly, the fear of God is the beginning of all wisdom. To such an one, "composure" amid the perils of death, and when "the last of earth has come," is a supporting power frequently and divinely given; and, if it has not been permitted to him, as to a prophet of old, to be spared the bitterness of death, and to go to the heaven that he looked for, and that he loved, in a chariot of fire, yet to the eye of human faith his access to the same abode has been as speedy and as safe. Instead of wearing away under the waste of disease, and passing through all the woes and weaknesses which dissolving nature generally undergoes, a blow of brief but mortal agony strikes him at once into the tomb, and thus his spirit, instantly freed, goes right up to the parent fountain from which it came. The messenger calls, the soul is in heaven.

At this moment of fresh affliction, whilst standing in the very presence of death, it is not meet to go into any special review of the labors or opinions of the departed. Whatever may be thought of those politically, posterity will never deny to him the possession of great talents, actuated by great virtues, and directed with boldness, honesty, an earnest purpose, for an unequalled length of time, to whatever, in his judgment, was best for the interests, honor, and perpetuity of his country. This is the lesson taught by his life. That which is taught by his death calls upon us all, with solemn, appealing cry, "Be ye also ready, for ye know not the hour when the Son of Man cometh!"

Mr. NEWALL rose and moved the following as an additional resolution:

Resolved, That the seat in this Hall just vacated by the death of the late JOHN QUINCY ADAMS, be unoccupied for thirty days, and that it, together with the Hall, remain clothed with the symbol of mourning during that time.

Mr. Tallmadge, of New York, rose and said: Mr. Speaker, I do not rise to present an eulogium upon the character of the deceased, but I am confident that every manifestation of respect for the memory of the illustrious dead will meet with a cordial response from every member of this House. In compliance with the suggestions of several members, and in accordance with my own feelings, I ask leave to introduce the following additional resolution:

Resolved, That the Speaker appoint one member of this House from each State or Territory, as a committee to escort the remains of our venerable friend, the honorable John Quincy Adams, to the place designated by his friends for his interment.*

All the above resolutions were unanimously agreed to.

Mr. Vinton then moved that the Speaker's announcement of the death of the Hon. John Quincy Adams be entered on the Journal. This was also agreed to unanimously, and then the House adjourned to Saturday.

IN SENATE.

Thursday, February 24.

Death of Hon. J. Q. Adams.

A message was received from the House of Representatives announcing the death of the Hon. John Quincy Adams, a member of that body, who expired on Wednesday evening, the 23d instant, in the Capitol, and the proceedings of the House of Representatives thereupon.

The message having been read—

Mr. Davis, of Massachusetts, rose, and thus addressed that body:

Mr. President: By the recent affliction of my colleague, a painful duty devolves upon me. The message just delivered from the House, proves that the hand of God has been again among us. A great and good man has gone from our midst. If, in speaking of John Quincy Adams, I can give utterance to the language of my own heart, I am confident I shall meet with a response from the Senate.

He was born in the then Province of Massachusetts, while she was girding herself for the great revolutionary struggle which was then before her. His parentage is too well known to need even an allusion; yet I may be pardoned if I say, that his father seemed born to aid in the establishment of our free Government, and his mother was a suitable companion and co-laborer of such a patriot. The cradle hymns of the child were the songs of liberty. The power and competence of man for self-government were the topics which he most frequently heard discussed by the wise men of the day, and the inspiration thus caught gave form and pressure to his after life. Thus early imbued with the love of free institutions, educated by his father for the service of his country, and early led by Washington to its altar, he has stood before the world as one of its eminent statesmen. He has occupied, in turn, almost every place of honor which the country could give him, and for more than half a century has been thus identified with its history. Under any circumstances, I should feel myself unequal to the task of rendering justice to his memory; but, with the debilitating effect of bad health still upon me, I can only, with extreme brevity, touch upon some of the most prominent features of his life.

While yet a young man, he was, in May, 1794, appointed Minister Resident to the States General of the United Netherlands. In May, 1796, two years after, he was appointed Minister Plenipotentiary at Lisbon, in Portugal. These honors were conferred on him by George Washington, with the advice and consent of the Senate.

In May, 1797, he was appointed Minister Plenipotentiary to the King of Prussia. In March, 1798, and probably while at Berlin, he was appointed a commissioner with full powers to negotiate a treaty of amity and commerce with Sweden.

After his return to the United States, he was elected by the Legislature of Massachusetts a Senator, and discharged the duties of that station in this chamber from the 4th of March, 1803, until June, 1808, when, differing from his colleague and from his State upon a great political question, he resigned his seat. In June, 1809, he was nominated and appointed Minister Plenipotentiary to the Court of St. Petersburgh.

While at that court, in February, 1811, he was appointed an Associate Justice of the Supreme Court of the United States, to fill a vacancy occasioned by the death of Judge Cushing, but never took his seat upon the Bench.

In May, 1813, he, with Messrs. Gallatin and Bayard, was nominated Envoy Extraordinary and Minister Plenipotentiary to negotiate a treaty of peace with Great Britain, under the mediation of Russia, and a treaty of commerce with Russia. From causes which it is unnecessary to notice, nothing was accomplished under this appointment. But afterwards, in January, 1814, he, with Messrs. Gallatin, Bayard, Clay, and Russell, were appointed Ministers Plenipotentiary and Extraordinary to negotiate a treaty of peace and a treaty of commerce with Great Britain. This mission succeeded in effecting a

---

* The Speaker appointed the following gentlemen to compose the said committee:

Mr. Tallmadge, of N. Y.	Mr. Hammons, of Me.
Mr. Wilson, of N. H.	Mr. Collamer, of Vt.
Mr. Ashmun, of Mass.	Mr. Thurston, of R. I.
Mr. J. A. Rockwell, of Conn.	Mr. Newell, of N. J.
Mr. McIlvaine, of Penn.	Mr. J. W. Houston, of Del.
Mr. Ligon, of Md.	Mr. Meade, of Va.
Mr. Barringer, of N. C.	Mr. Holmes, of S. C.
Mr. Lumpkin, of Ga.	Mr. Hilliard, of Ala.
Mr. A. G. Brown, of Miss.	Mr. Morse, of La.
Mr. Schenck, of Ohio.	Mr. French, of Ky.
Mr. Gentry, of Tenn.	Mr. C. B. Smith, of Ind.
Mr. Wentworth, of Ill.	Mr. Phelps, of Mo.
Mr. R. W. Johnson, of Ark.	Mr. C. E. Stuart, of Mich.
Mr. Cabell, of Florida.	Mr. Kaufman, of Texas.
Mr. W. Thompson, of Iowa.	Mr. Tweedy, of W. T.

pacification, and the name of Mr. ADAMS is subscribed to the treaty of Ghent.

After this eventful crisis in our public affairs, he was, in February, 1815, selected by Mr. Madison to represent the country and protect its interests at the Court of St. James, and he remained there as Envoy Extraordinary and Minister Plenipotentiary until Mr. Monroe became President of the United States.

On the 5th of March, 1817, at the commencement of the new administration, he was appointed Secretary of State, and continued in the office while that gentleman was at the head of the administration.

In 1825 he was elected his successor, and discharged the duties of President for one term, ending on the 3d of March, 1829.

Here followed a brief period of repose from public service, and Mr. ADAMS retired to the family mansion at Quincy, but was elected a member of the House of Representatives from the district in which he lived, at the next election which occurred after his return to it, and took his seat in December, 1831: he retained it by successive elections to the day of his death.

I have not ventured on this occasion beyond a bare enumeration of the high places of trust and confidence which have been conferred upon the deceased. The service covers a period of more than half a century; and what language can I employ which will portray more forcibly the great merits of the deceased, the confidence reposed in him by the public, or the ability with which he discharged the duties devolved upon him, than by this simple narration of recorded facts? An ambitious man could not desire a more emphatic eulogy.

Mr. ADAMS, however, was not merely a statesman, but a ripe, accomplished scholar, who, during a life of remarkably well-directed industry, made those great acquirements which adorned his character, and gave to it the manly strength of wisdom and intelligence.

As a statesman and patriot, he will rank among the illustrious men of an age prolific in great names, and greatly distinguished for its progress in civilization. The productions of his pen are proofs of a vigorous mind, imbued with a profound knowledge of what it investigates, and of a memory which was singularly retentive and capacious.

But his character is not made up of those conspicuous qualities alone. He will be remembered for the virtues of private life—for his elevated moral example—for his integrity —for his devotion to his duties as a Christian, as a neighbor, and as the head of a family. In all these relations, few persons have set a more steadfast or brighter example, and few have descended to the grave where the broken ties of social and domestic affection have been more sincerely lamented. Great as may be the loss to the public of one so gifted and wise, it is by the family that his death will be most deeply felt. His aged and beloved partner, who has so long shared the honors of his career, and to whom all who know her are bound by the ties of friendship, will believe that we share her grief, mourn her bereavement, and sympathize with her in her affliction.

It is believed to have been the earliest wish of his heart to die, like Chatham, in the midst of his labors. It was a sublime thought, that where he had toiled in the house of the nation, in hours of the day devoted to its service, the stroke of death should reach him, and there sever the ties of love and patriotism which bound him to earth. He fell in his seat, attacked by paralysis, of which he had before been a victim. To describe the scene which ensued would be impossible. It was more than the spontaneous gush of feeling which all such events call forth, so much to the honor of our nature. It was the expression of reverence for his moral worth; of admiration for his great intellectual endowments, and of veneration for his age and public services. All gathered round the sufferer, and the strong sympathy and deep feeling which manifested itself showed that the business of the House (which was instantly adjourned) was forgotten amid the distressing anxieties of the moment. He was soon removed to the apartment of the Speaker, where he remained surrounded by afflicted friends till the weary clay resigned its immortal spirit. "This is the end of earth." Brief but emphatic words. They were among the last uttered by the dying Christian.

Thus has closed the life of one whose purity, patriotism, talents, and learning, have seldom been seriously questioned. To say that he had faults, would only be declaring that he was human. Let him who is exempt from error venture to point them out. In this long career of public life, it would be strange if the venerable man had not met with many who have differed from him in sentiment, or who have condemned his acts. If there be such, let the mantle of oblivion be thrown over each unkind thought. Let not the grave of the old man eloquent be desecrated by unfriendly remembrances, but let us yield our homage to his many virtues, and let it be our prayer that we may so perform our duties here, that if summoned in a like sudden and appalling manner, we may not be found unprepared or unable to utter his words, "I am composed."

Mr. President, with this imperfect sketch of the character and service of a great man, I leave the subject in the hands of the Senate by moving the resolutions which I sent to the Chair:

Resolved, That the Senate has received with deep sensibility the message from the House of Representatives announcing the death of the honorable JOHN QUINCY ADAMS, a representative from the State of Massachusetts.

Resolved, That in token of respect for the memory of the deceased, the Senate will attend his funeral at the hour appointed by the House of Representatives, and will wear the usual badge of mourning for thirty days.

Resolved, That, as a further mark of respect for the memory of the deceased, the Senate do now adjourn until Saturday next, to the time appointed for the funeral.

The resolutions having been read—

Mr. Benton, of Missouri, addressed the Senate as follows:

Mr. President: The voice of his native State has been heard, through one of the Senators of Massachusetts, announcing the death of her aged and most distinguished son. The voice of the other Senator from Massachusetts is not heard, nor is his presence seen. A domestic calamity, known to us all, and felt by us all, confines him to the chamber of private grief, while the Senate is occupied with the public manifestations of a respect and sorrow which a national loss inspires. In the absence of that Senator, and as the member of this body longest here, it is not unfitting or unbecoming in me to second the motion which has been made for extending the last honors of the Senate to him who, forty-five years ago, was a member of this body, who, at the time of his death, was among the oldest members of the House of Representatives, and who, putting the years of his service together, was the oldest of all the members of the American Government.

The eulogium of Mr. Adams is made in the facts of his life, which the Senator from Massachusetts (Mr. Davis) has so strikingly stated, that, from early manhood to octogenarian age, he has been constantly and most honorably employed in the public service. For a period of more than fifty years, from the time of his first appointment as minister abroad under Washington, to his last election to the House of Representatives by the people of his native district, he has been constantly retained in the public service, and that, not by the favor of a sovereign, or by hereditary title, but by the elections and appointments of republican government. This fact makes the eulogy of the illustrious deceased. For what, except a union of all the qualities which command the esteem and confidence of man, could have insured a public service so long, by appointments free and popular, and from sources so various and exalted? Minister many times abroad; member of this body; member of the House of Representatives; cabinet minister; President of the United States; such has been the galaxy of his splendid appointments. And what but moral excellence the most perfect; intellectual ability the most eminent; fidelity the most unwavering; service the most useful, would have commanded such a succession of appointments so exalted, and from sources so various and so eminent? Nothing less could have commanded such a series of appointments; and accordingly we see the union of all these great qualities in him who has received them.

In this long career of public service, Mr. Adams was distinguished not only by faithful attention to all the great duties of his stations, but to all their less and minor duties. He was not the Salaminian galley, to be launched only on extraordinary occasions, but he was the ready vessel, always launched when the duties of his station required it, be the occasion great or small. As President, as Cabinet Minister, as Minister abroad, he examined all questions that came before him, and examined all, in all their parts, in all the minutiæ of their detail, as well as in all the vastness of their comprehension. As Senator, and as a member of the House of Representatives, the obscure committee room was as much the witness of his laborious application to the drudgery of legislation as the halls of the two Houses were to the every-ready speech, replete with knowledge, which instructed all hearers, enlightened all subjects, and gave dignity and ornament to debate.

In the observance of all the proprieties of life, Mr. Adams was a most noble and impressive example. He cultivated the minor as well as the greater virtues. Wherever his presence could give aid and countenance to what was useful and honorable to man, there he was. In the exercises of the school and of the college—in the meritorious meetings of the agricultural, mechanical, and commercial societies—in attendance upon Divine worship—he gave the punctual attendance rarely seen but in those who are free from the weight of public cares.

Punctual to every duty, death found him at the post of duty; and where else could it have found him, at any stage of his career, for the fifty years of his illustrious public life? From the time of his first appointment by Washington to his last election by the people of his native town, where could death have found him but at the post of duty? At that post, in the fulness of age, in the ripeness of renown, crowned with honors, surrounded by his family, his friends, and admirers, and in the very presence of the national representation, he has been gathered to his fathers, leaving behind him the memory of public services which are the history of his country for half a century, and the example of a life, public and private, which should be the study and the model of the generations of his countrymen.

When Mr. B. concluded, the resolutions were unanimously adopted, and the Senate adjourned to Saturday.

HOUSE OF REPRESENTATIVES.

Saturday, February 26.

Obsequies of John Quincy Adams.

Pursuant to the resolve of both Houses of Congress, this day was set apart for rendering to the remains of the deceased patriot and statesman, the Hon. John Quincy Adams, the last human tribute.*

* At an early hour men in uniform might be seen hastening to their respective places of parade, while numerous groups of citizens and strangers were flocking from all directions toward the Capitol.

The SPEAKER having taken the chair, the Journal of Thursday was read. Soon after, the Senate entered, preceded by their presiding officer. He took his seat on the left of the Speaker. As the Senators passed up the centre aisle and took their seats, the Speaker and members of the House rose, and continued standing until they had taken the seats assigned them. Soon after, the President of the United States entered the Hall, and was received by all in like manner, while he took his seat on the right of the Speaker. The members of the Cabinet occupied seats in front of the Senators, and opposite to the Foreign Ministers. The Judges of the Supreme Court, preceded by their officers, passed up to seats on the right of the Clerk's desk. The relatives of the deceased were next conducted to a position reserved for them on the extreme left. Next entered the members of the Legislature of Maryland, preceded by the officers and chaplain of that body—the Legislature, sitting at Annapolis, having passed resolutions to attend the funeral. Next entered the corporate authorities of Washington, headed by their respective officers, who were conducted to places by the officers of the House. At length came the body, escorted by the Committee of Arrangements, and followed by the delegation of Massachusetts as mourners. The Speaker, the President of the Senate, the officers of both Houses, the members of the Committee of Arrangements, the pall-bearers, and attendant physicians wore white scarfs. The whole assemblage being thus at length completed, the deep silence of expectation pervaded the Hall. Not a rude sound, and scarce a sound of any kind, was to be heard among the waiting thousands who crowded the galleries and lobbies in every spot where a human being could find room to stand.

The Chaplain of the House, the Rev. Mr. GURLEY, then rose and read an appropriate portion of Holy Writ, and addressed the throne of Heavenly Grace in a meek and devout prayer.

He then read a hymn which had been selected for the occasion, and which was sung with admirable skill and impressive effect by the choir. As the wailing notes swelled and sank away in melancholy cadence, their placid, stilling, and solemnizing effect was obvious to the eye, in the countenances of the listening auditory, and prepared them for the address which followed, from these words in Job, "And thine age shall be clearer than the noonday: thou shalt shine forth, thou shalt be as the morning: and thou shalt be secure, because there is hope." —(Chapter xi. 17.)

The address was followed by a closing hymn and the Apostolic benediction, when the funeral procession began to be formed, the corpse was borne out of the Hall, the several public bodies fell into their place, passing in succession along the broad aisle and through the north door into the Rotundo, and so out on the eastern portico, and down the great flight of steps to the open area in front, where carriages were in waiting to receive them.

The procession then moved in the following order, to the Congressional Burying Ground, where the body was deposited, but in a few days is to be removed to Quincy:

Military escort of Cavalry and Infantry, of Washington and Alexandria.

Band.

The Chaplains of both Houses of Congress.

Physicians who attended the deceased.

Committee of Arrangements.

Pall-Bearers:

Hon. J. J. McKay, N. C.	The Corpse*	Hon. Truman Smith, Con.
Hon. Linn Boyd, Ken.		Hon. J. R. Ingersoll, Penn.
Hon. J. C. Calhoun, S. C.		Hon. T. H. Benton, Mo.
Chief Justice R. B. Taney,		Hon. Justice J. McLean,
General George Gibson,		Com. Charles Morris,
Hon. W. W. Seaton,		Hon. Thos. H. Crawford.

By a judicious arrangement, the doors of that vast building were thrown open to the gathering multitudes, while those of the Hall of the House of Representatives, where the funeral ceremonies were to take place, were closed to all but the members and officers of the House. The ladies' gallery was rapidly filled up, all gentlemen without distinction being peremptorily excluded. A certain portion of the semi-circular gallery (usually occupied throughout by gentlemen only) was partitioned off for the accommodation of a very large choir of singers, selected from those of the several churches of the city.

The Hall was shrouded in black, and presented a very solemn appearance. This part of the arrangements was executed with great taste and judgment by the officers of the House, under the suggestions and kind supervision of a distinguished lady. The figure of History, especially, (whose graceful form surmounts the clock, holding in her hands a tablet and a pen,) was robed with consummate taste and judgment, the black drapery covering her entire person, with the exception of the arm holding the recording pen, whose alabaster whiteness, in strong contrast with the surrounding stole, had a fine effect; heightened as it was by the attitude of the head, which, turning towards one side, happened to have its countenance in the very direction where stood the vacant seat of Mr. ADAMS, as if in the act of recording the solemn circumstances of his death. That seat, by order of the House, was draped in the deepest mourning, and, by the fact of its vacancy, recalled every beholder to the blow which had there fallen, like a thunderbolt from a cloudless sky. The portraits of WASHINGTON and of LAFAYETTE, on either hand of the chair, were covered over with thin crape, casting a melancholy dimness over the features, without entirely concealing them, the frames being covered with a deeper black. The effect of this, too, was very fine, most truly representing what would have been the feeling of both those distinguished men, if alive to witness the solemn scene; for WASHINGTON gave the deceased his first commission, and LAFAYETTE embraced him in his arms when taking his last adieu of America.

The members gradually arrived and filled up their seats in the Hall, a portion, however, being reserved for the Senate.

The space in the central area, in front of the Clerk's table, was furnished with seats for the Judges, the Cabinet, the Diplomatic Corps, and the Committee of Arrangements, consisting of one member from each State of the Union; while, in its centre, stood a table, covered with a black velvet pall, to support the corpse.

Officers of the Army and Navy, as they entered the Hall, had seats assigned them next in the rear of the Foreign Ministers. By an unfortunate omission, no seats were reserved for the Clergy; but as a number of them arrived, not only from the city, but from Baltimore, Alexandria, and several from Massachusetts, they were conducted by the officers of the House to favorable positions.

The members of the Diplomatic Body arrived severally, from time to time, and not in a body: some of them manifested their respect for the solemn occasion, and for the presence of the assembled authorities of the nation, by appearing in their full official dresses, with their respective orders and decorations, while others seem to have deemed it more appropriate to appear in simple black. The contrast could not but strike the eye.—*National Intelligencer.*

* The coffin was covered with black velvet and ornament-

Mr. J. F. Harvey, Conductor of the Car.
The family and friends of the deceased.
The Senators and Representatives from the State of Massachusetts, as mourners.
The Sergeant-at-Arms of the House.
The House of Representatives of the United States, preceded by their Speaker and Clerk.
The other officers of the House of Representatives.
The Sergeant-at-Arms of the Senate.
The Senate, preceded by their President and Secretary.
The other officers of the Senate.
The President of the United States.
The Heads of Departments.
The Judges of the Supreme Court of the United States, and its officers.
The Judges of the Circuit and District Courts of the District of Columbia, and its officers.
The Diplomatic Corps.
The Comptrollers, Auditors, and other Heads of Bureaus of the several Departments of the Government, with their officers.
Officers of the Army and Navy at the seat of Government.
Members of Maryland Legislature.
The Corporations of Washington and Alexandria.
The Columbia Typographical Society.
Officers and students of Georgetown College.
Officers and students of Columbia College.
Literary Institutions.
Fire Companies of the District.
Odd Fellows.
Citizens and Strangers.

The whole proceeding was conducted with great decorum and dignity, and the universal interest excited among people of all classes to witness it, shows the deep hold the event itself had taken on the public mind.

Monday, February 28.

Mrs. Adams.

Mr. C. J. Ingersoll rose, and asked the unanimous consent of the House to complete the honors which they had bestowed upon its late most illustrious member, by giving to his widow the same mark of national respect which had been conferred by law upon Mrs. Madison and Mrs. Harrison, to wit, that of sending and receiving through the mail all letters and papers free of postage.

He sent up to the Clerk's table the bill which he had prepared, aad he trusted there would be no objection to its immediate passage.

The bill was read as follows:

Be it enacted, &c., That all letters and packets carried to and from Louisa Catharine Adams, widow of the late John Quincy Adams, be conveyed free of postage during her natural life.

Mr. Sawyer suggested to Mr. Ingersoll, that upon Mrs. Madison had been conferred the privilege of this Hall, and that the same mark of respect should be extended to Mrs. Adams.

Mr. C. J. Ingersoll. That cannot be done by act of Congress. In the case referred to, the privilege was granted by a simple resolution of the House. This is a law of Congress.

The bill, by unanimous consent, received its second reading.

And then, having been ordered to be engrossed and read a third time now—

The bill was read a third time, and passed.

Mr. Adams.

Mr. Ashmun, on leave, offered the following resolution:

Resolved, That the Committee of Arrangements be directed to cause to be published, in pamphlet form, and in such manner as may seem to them appropriate, for the use of the House, twenty thousand copies of the addresses made by the Speaker and the members of this House, and of the addresses made to the Senate, together with the discourse of the Rev. Mr. Gurley, upon the occasion of the death of the Hon. John Quincy Adams.

Prohibition of Slavery.

Mr. Putnam moved the following preamble and resolution:

Whereas, in the settlement of the difficulties pending between this country and Mexico, territory may be acquired in which slavery does not now exist; and whereas Congress, in the organization of a Territorial Government at an early period of our political history, established a principle worthy of imitation in all future time, forbidding the existence of slavery in a free territory: Therefore,

Resolved, That in any territory which may be acquired from Mexico, over which shall be established Territorial Governments, slavery or involuntary servitude, except as a punishment for crime, whereof the party shall have been duly convicted, should be forever prohibited; and that, in any act or resolution establishing such Governments, a fundamental provision ought to be inserted to that effect.

Mr. Brodhead moved to lay the resolution on the table.

The result was announced—yeas 105, nays 92.

So the resolution was laid on the table.

Tuesday, February 29.

Business of the Supreme Court.

Mr. J. R. Ingersoll, from the Committee on the Judiciary, reported a bill supplemental to the act entitled "An act concerning the Supreme Court of the United States," approved June 17, 1844.

Mr. I. said, that in reporting this bill, he would offer a brief explanation, and ask either

---

ed with silver lace. The silver breastplate presented the following inscription:

John Quincy Adams,
Born
An Inhabitant of Massachusetts, July 11, 1767.
Died
A Citizen of the United States,
In the Capitol of Washington,
February 23, 1848;
Having served his Country for Half a Century,
And
Enjoyed its Highest Honors.

that it should be put upon its passage, if there were no objection, or, if objection should be made to that course, that it should be made the special order for an early day. The object of the bill is to relieve the Supreme Court from a great accumulation of business. Without some such provision, a crying evil will be without a remedy. It is known that the judiciary system of the United States, although in itself a good one, has probably been outgrown by the great expansiveness of the country. New States have come in rapid succession into the Union. The prospect of multiplied sovereignties in the future is as striking as the history of them in the past. With them new questions arise, and new litigation is the necessary consequence. Points are presented of extreme intricacy as well as novelty. Time is necessary for the consideration of them. The already burdened state of the docket amounts to a denial of justice. Its condition, unless speedily relieved, will become a reproach, not to the learned court, but to the whole country, and especially to Congress, which alone holds in its hand the power of present relief, and, when it shall become necessary, of eventual remedy.

In 1837 every case on the docket was called, and all but twenty-nine only were left unargued. Since that time there has been a state of accumulation which has defied the efforts of learning and ability. On the 7th of January, 1848, there were one hundred and ninety-eight cases for argument. Of these twenty-nine have been decided; seventeen have been argued and are under consideration; three have been partly argued, and will be taken up again. The Court at this moment is listening to an argument in No. 39. The session will close next week, and it is scarcely possible that further progress will be made in the docket.

What may be the best permanent system, in the event of a change, must be a subject of grave consideration. Fortunately that does not require immediate action. Different plans have been suggested. Considerable difference of opinion exists respecting them. It is surmised that even upon the bench there is not a concurrence of opinion. All that is now required can now be done. An entire devotion of the attention of the court to their appellate duties for a season may be reconciled to the uninterrupted progress of business in the circuits. This bill contemplates a relief of the judges from circuit court duties for two years. It enables them to give all their labor and abilities to the accumulated and accumulating business of the Supreme Court.

It is known that the judges are already relieved from a necessity of attending alternate sessions in their circuits. No sort of effect has been produced by this provision, which has existed in vain for five years. The reason for its failure is obvious. The annual term is now of three months' duration. Probably no set of men can apply all the energies of the most capacious and practised intellects uninterruptedly to such great and responsible duties as are here involved beyond that period; an occasional interval of rest or of study and reflection is indispensable. The term is already too long; attention and energy, however vigorous at the commencement, are seen to flag and falter towards the close. Let them adjourn when they are exhausted, and let them meet again after longer or shorter intervals, prepared to devote new and refreshed spirits to their high and honorable duties. When the loud demands of the country shall have been complied with, and the wheels of justice shall no longer be clogged and virtually arrested, and when, besides, an experiment shall have been fairly made which will shed useful light upon inquiries into a proper permanent arrangement, then it will be time to mature a system which may last for ages.

It was proposed by Mr. VINTON and others to make it the special order of the day for next Tuesday, by general consent.

WEDNESDAY, March 1.

Communication from Mrs. Adams.

The SPEAKER laid before the House the following communication:

WASHINGTON, *February* 29, 1848.

SIR: The resolutions in honor of my dear deceased husband, passed by the illustrious assembly over which you preside, and of which he at the moment of his death was a member, have been duly communicated to me.

Penetrated with grief at this distressing event of my life; mourning the loss of one who has been at once my example and my support through the trials of half a century, permit me, nevertheless, to express through you my deepest gratitude for the signal manner in which the public regard has been voluntarily manifested by your honorable body, and the consolation derived to me and mine from the reflection, that the unwearied efforts of an old public servant have not, even in this world, proved without their reward in the generous appreciation of them by his country.

With great respect, I remain, sir, your obedient servant,

LOUISA CATHARINE ADAMS.

To the Hon. ROBERT C. WINTHROP,
Speaker of the House of Representatives of the U. S.

IN SENATE.

MONDAY, April 3.

Message from the President—French Revolution of February, 1848—Overthrow of the Monarchy—Flight of the Royal Family—Establishment of the Republic.

The following Message was received from the President of the United States:

WASHINGTON, *April* 3, 1848.

To the Senate and House of Representatives of the United States:

I communicate to Congress, for their information, a copy of a despatch, with the accompanying documents, received at the Department of State from the Envoy Extraordinary and Minister Plenipotentiary of the United States at Paris, giving official information of the overthrow of the French monarchy, and the establishment in its stead of a provisional Government, based on republican principles.

This great event occurred suddenly, and was accomplished almost without bloodshed. The world has seldom witnessed a more interesting and sublime spectacle than the peaceful rising of the French people, resolved to secure for themselves enlarged liberty, and to assert in the majesty of their strength the great truth that, in this enlightened age, man is capable of governing himself.

The prompt recognition of the new Government by the representative of the United States at the French Court, meets my full and unqualified approbation; and he has been authorized, in a suitable manner, to make known this fact to the constituted authorities of the French Republic.

Called upon to act on a sudden emergency, which could not have been anticipated by his instructions, he judged rightly of the feelings and sentiments of his Government and of his countrymen, when, in advance of the diplomatic representatives of other countries, he was the first to recognize, so far as it was in his power, the free Government established by the French people.

The policy of the United States has ever been that of non-intervention in the domestic affairs of other countries, leaving to each to establish the form of Government of its own choice. While this wise policy will be maintained towards France, now suddenly transformed from a monarchy into a republic, all our sympathies are naturally enlisted on the side of a great people, who, imitating our example, have resolved to be free. That such sympathy should exist on the part of the people of the United States with the friends of free government in every part of the world, and especially in France, is not remarkable. We can never forget that France was an early friend in our eventful revolution, and generously aided us in shaking off a foreign yoke, and becoming a free and independent people.

We have enjoyed the blessings of our system of well-regulated self-government for near three-fourths of a century, and can properly appreciate its value. Our ardent and sincere congratulations are extended to the patriotic people of France, upon their noble and thus far successful efforts to found for their future government liberal institutions similar to our own.

It is not doubted that, under the benign influence of free institutions, the enlightened statesmen of republican France will find it to be for her interest and paramount glory, to cultivate with the United States the most liberal principles of international intercourse and commercial reciprocity, whereby the prosperity and happiness of both nations will be promoted.

JAMES K. POLK.

[No. 17.] Legation of the United States,
Paris, March 4, 1848.

Sir: Scarcely had my despatch of the 24th February been folded up, when events the most momentous quickly succeeded each other. Numerous barricades had risen up in the streets; civil war continued; the people were victorious; the palace of the Tuileries was carried; the King abdicated, and fled with all the royal family, and the monarchy was overthrown. All this happened in the course of the day—Thursday.

The confusion and tumult caused in the Chamber of Deputies by these events, led to the hasty and violent close of its sitting on that day. All attempts to establish a regency, with the Count de Paris as successor to the throne, failed. His mother, the Duchess of Orleans, with the young Prince himself, went to the Chamber, but soon had to make their escape. All order, all deliberation had come to an end. The ministerial members were driven out by the people, who had entered the Chamber, many of them armed, and, with menacing gesticulations, usurping the seats. In the sequel, a portion of them, with some of the opposition members, hurried to the Hotel de Ville to form a provisional Government, under voices to that effect, uttered and echoed at the close of the boisterous sitting.

At the Hotel de Ville as a rallying-point, a provisional Government was formed on the evening of Thursday, the 24th, and proclaimed on the following morning. The proclamation declared that the provisional Government desired a republic, subject to the ratification of the French people.

The persons composing the provisional Government are Messieurs Dupont, (de l'Eure,) Lamartine, Cremieux, Ledru Rollin, Garnier Pages, Marie, and Arago.

The secretaries of the Government are—Messrs. Armand Marrast, Ferdinand Flocon, Louis Blanc, and M. Albert.

The first four names of the provisional Government were of the Chamber of Deputies, a body no longer existing any more than the Chamber of Peers; the whole fabric of the late Government having been shattered to pieces.

Some accounts state that all the names composing the provisional Government, were given out from the tribune of the Chamber of Deputies before its dissolution; but there is difficulty in coming at the precise fact, such was the consternation in the Chamber when it broke up.

The provisional Government immediately announced, as formed by its own decree, a provisional cabinet, that the functions of administration might not stop.

I abstain at this juncture from presenting more of the names of the provisional cabinet than those of M. Dupont, (de l'Eure,) as President of the Council; and M. de Lamartine, as Minister of Foreign Affairs; these two posts being severed again, after having been united in M. Guizot, who, and all his associates in the late ministry, have fled.

Of a revolution so total and sudden, I am not now to speak. The journals of the world are still teeming with it. Nor can I yet speak of the acts of the new Government, except to say that they have been characterized so far by moderation and magnanimity, in the midst of triumphs of a nature to have intoxicated minds less pure and firm than happily are believed to be possessed by its leading members.

I pass to what, foremost of all at present, I am bound to report to you—namely, the part which, as representing the United States, I have taken under the new duties that encompassed me.

On Saturday, the 26th, I received an intimation, earnestly given, that my personal presence at the Hotel de Ville, to cheer and felicitate the provisional

Government, would be acceptable. The intimation was not officially sent, but I believed it to be true.

I asked a short interval for reflection.

Before the day was out, I imparted my determination to take the step.

Monday morning, the 28th, was the time appointed for it; and accordingly I repaired to the Hotel de Ville, the Secretary of Legation accompanying me.

To the provisional Government there assembled, I delivered the address, a copy of which is enclosed.

It was cordially received, and M. Arago, on the part of the members, replied to it.

He remarked that they heard without surprise, but with lively pleasure, what I said; France expected it from an ally to whom she now drew so close by the proclamation of the republic. He thanked me, in the name of the Provisional Government, for the wishes I expressed for the greatness and prosperity of France; and in alluding to the words it had called up from General Washington's address in 1796, on receiving the French colors, he expressed a confidence that they would be not merely a desire, but a reality.

M. Dupont, (de l'Eure,) as President of the Provisional Government, then advanced, and, taking me by the hand, said, "The French people grasps that of the American nation."

Here the ceremony ended. In coming away, three of the members of the Government conducted us out of the building; the guard presented arms, and cries went up of "*Vive la Republique des Etats Unis!*" Major Poussin, a French officer, who accompanied General Bernard to the United States, and who, from his attachment to our country, was naturalized there, also attended me.

On Sunday, the 27th, I received the note of that day's date from M. Lamartine, as Provisional Minister of Foreign Affairs, which announced to me, in official form, the existence of the new Government. I answered it on Monday. Copies of the note and answer are enclosed.

The Provisional Government published my answer the morning after its reception. My address of Monday has also appeared in the newspapers—not, however, in its exact form. I had written it out, to guard against inaccuracies on an occasion so grave, and left the paper in the hands of the Provisional Government; a transcript of which you now have.

This succinct narrative will accurately apprise the President of what I have done. I shall anxiously await his judgment upon it all. The events were as new as momentous. They had transcended all expectation. In recognizing the new state of things, as far as I could without your instructions, and in doing it promptly and solemnly, I had the deep conviction that I was stepping forth in aid of the great cause of order in France and beyond France, and that I was acting in the spirit of my Government and country, the interpreter of whose voice it fell upon me suddenly to become. If I erred, I must hope that the motives which swayed me will be my shield. The Provisional Government needed all the moral support attainable, after a revolutionary hurricane which shook society to its base, and left every thing at first portentous and trembling. In such an exigency, hours, moments were important; and the United States are felt as a power in the world, under the blow that has been struck.

I am not unaware that the course I have pursued departs from diplomatic usage, and separates me, for the time being, from the European diplomatic corps accredited, like myself, to the late Government of France, all the members of which will probably wait instructions before adopting any steps of recognition. Having acted under a sense of independent duty in the emergency, I am, however, not the less aware that the diplomatic corps represents countries in friendly relation with the United States, and that it will hence be as much my duty as inclination to go on maintaining that amicable footing with its members, ever dictated by reciprocal good-will among the representatives of friendly powers, whatever different forms of Government they may represent.

I have the honor, &c.,

RICHARD RUSH.

Hon. JAMES BUCHANAN, *Secretary of State.*

To the Members of the Provisional Government of the French Republic:

GENTLEMEN: As the representative of the United States, charged with the interests and rights of my country and of American citizens now in France, and too far off to wait instructions, I seize this early opportunity of tendering to you my felicitations, not doubting the sanction of my Government to the step I thus take in advance. Nor can I avoid the occasion of saying that the memory of the ancient alliance and friendship between France and the United States, is ever fresh and grateful with us, and that I am of nothing more sure than that the voice of my country will be universal and loud for the prosperity, happiness, and glory of France under the institutions she has announced, subject to ratification by the national will. All will ardently hope that through her wisdom the results may be beneficial to mankind, of which the magnanimous bearing of her people in the late events affords so auspicious a promise. It is under such institutions that the United States have for seventy years enjoyed constant prosperity, with a Government of uniform stability; and whilst they invariably leave to other nations the choice of their own forms, without interference in any way, they would naturally rejoice in beholding this great nation flourish under institutions which have secured for themselves the blessings of social order and public liberty.

Allow me, then, gentlemen, using the words of the great and good Washington, the immortal founder of my country, on an occasion which the present recalls, to signalize this address to you, by mingling my felicitations with a fervent aspiration that "THE FRIENDSHIP OF THE TWO REPUBLICS MAY BE COMMENSURATE WITH THEIR EXISTENCE."

PARIS, *le* 27 *Février*, 1848.

MONSIEUR: J'ai l'honneur de vous informer que le gouvernement provisoire de la république Française m'a confié le portefeuille des Affaires Etrangères. La forme républicaine du nouveau gouvernement n'a changé ni la place de la France en Europe, ni ses dispositions loyales et sincères à maintenir ses rapports de bonne harmonie avec les Puissances qui voudront, comme elle, l'indépendance des nations et la paix du monde.

Ce sera un bonheur pour moi, Monsieur, de concourir pas tous les moyens en mon pouvoir à cet accord des peuples dans leur dignité réciproque, et à rappeler à l'Europe que le principe de paix et le principe de liberté sont nés e même jour en France. Recevez, &c., LAMARTINE.

Monsieur Rush, Ministre Plénipotentiaire des Etats Unis à Paris.

Legation of the United States.
Paris, February 28, 1848.

Sir: I have the honor to acknowledge your note of yesterday, informing me that the Provisional Government of the French Republic has confided the department of Foreign Affairs to your hands. The choice, sir, I will dare to say, will be regarded by the world as a favorable first step in the new order of things; and I shall have great satisfaction in transmitting to my Government, by the earliest opportunity, a copy of your communication, not doubting its cordial reception. In the mean time, sir, I will be ready, under your permission, to transact with you whatever business may appertain to my country, or American citizens in France.

The United States, having learned from their own experience the value of free institutions, will naturally anticipate from similar institutions in France, administered with the wisdom and moderation of which the enlarged and beneficent principles announced in your note are the auspicious harbingers, nothing but the best results to the interests and well-being of both countries.

I pray you to accept these early assurances of the very high consideration with which I have the honor to be, sir, your most obedient servant,
RICHARD RUSH.

To his Excellency M. de Lamartine, Minister of Foreign Affairs, &c., &c., &c.

Mr. Hannegan moved that the Message and accompanying documents be referred to the Committee on Foreign Relations, and printed for the use of the Senate.

Mr. Allen said he could see no necessity for a reference of the Message. It asked for no action on the part of Congress, and consequently required no investigation by a committee.

Mr. Hannegan replied that he had made the motion because it was usual, and certainly the most respectful course to be pursued when an Executive Message was received.

Mr. Allen expressed a hope that the reference would not have the effect of delaying the action of the Senate on the joint resolutions which he had the honor to submit.

Mr. Hannegan said he had no intention to delay action on the resolutions of the Senator from Ohio, and he was not aware that the reference would have such effect.

The Message was then referred.

HOUSE OF REPRESENTATIVES.

Tuesday, April 4.

Death of the Representative James A. Black, of South Carolina.

Mr. Sims rose and said: Mr. Speaker, it is with no ordinary emotions that I now rise to announce to the House that death, whose presence has so oft and so recently called us to mourn during the progress of this session of Congress, has again demanded a victim of our number. James Augustus Black, a Representative from the State of South Carolina, is no more. He expired in this city on yesterday night, at twenty-five minutes after eleven o'clock, amidst the delegation of his State, with his family around him, without a murmur, and without a groan.

In a most extraordinary degree, through a protracted illness of seventeen days, he preserved his composure of mind, his consciousness, and constancy of purpose. At no moment did he complain. Though conscious, day by day and hour by hour, that death pursued him, and, at the final struggle, that dissolution was inevitable, he quailed not and murmured not; and at the hour that I have indicated, he breathed out his soul as composedly as the infant sinks into the softest slumber. Such were the last scenes in the life of my friend and colleague.

Mr. Speaker, under any circumstances death is a solemn occurrence; but there are concomitants that render its approach less afflictive, because more expected and appropriate than in other circumstances. When the soldier dies on the battle-field, he falls beneath the law of the occasion and propriety; and when old age sinks to rest, human destiny has been appropriately fulfilled, and man finds his end at the proper period. It is natural and appropriate, and fills us with a pleasing melancholy rather than with poignant grief, because, like the falling of the autumnal leaf, the creature perishes beneath the decree of his Creator in the proper season. But when, in the midst of life, unexpectedly, in the midst of years and acts of usefulness, one is cut down; when there is no premonitory event or circumstance to announce the destroyer's approach; when he comes upon us thus unexpectedly, the visitation is always felt with more peculiar force and regret.

Such was the fall of my friend. But a few days ago he was among us, in life and health, in the constant and assiduous performance of his duties here as a Representative. One day, thus engaged with his accustomed usefulness and ability; the next, his friends find him stricken down by the violence of disease, which, from the first, announced with a certainty which all the untiring efforts of his skilful professional attendance could not avert, that the victim was marked, and that not a ray of hope could cheer a friend or inquirer who sought to know the progress and ultimate result of his disease. His friends, his immediate family at a distance, though stricken down so unexpectedly, there were two circumstances of benevolence in the providence of God: the one, to which I have already referred, of preserving his intellect unclouded to the last, and the other of protracting his sweet resignation and patience, and his existence, until, from the distant South, his wife and child and affectionate brother were enabled to minister the last consolations of affection and tenderness around his dying bed.

There are many incidents in the life of my friend that, at the proper time, it would be pleasant and proper to dwell upon. I come not now to gather from the acts of usefulness with which his life, from earliest manhood to its close, was filled, to bind up flowers with which to deck his grave. Now is not the time to adorn his open grave, waiting for the reception of his lifeless form; and naught but the tears of affection and the weeping regrets of friends are the becoming garniture of its desolation.

I stop not, therefore, to announce, that in early manhood, at the age of eighteen, impelled by that patriotism which animated him to the last, he stepped forward in 1812 to join the army of his country. He entered the service as a lieutenant, and at the close of the war, resigning the commission of captain, which at that time he held, he retired to private life. After that he was constantly engaged in useful employments until, some few years since, he was called from the sphere of usefulness in other walks of life to take a seat upon this floor, as a Representative from the Pinckney district in South Carolina. How he performed his duties here; how he has illustrated, in the most eminent manner, the true character of a Representative; how he has shown respect to the opinions of his constituents, and discharged his duty by keeping them constantly informed by communications of the progress and state of public business here; how he has ever responded to the impulses of patriotism, which had grown into fixed principles of action in him, throughout his whole public career here, all who now hear me will bear cheerful testimony. He loved the people; not with a demagogue's love, but with a soul-stirring, divine impulse, springing from that fundamental maxim of his creed, that all men are brothers, and all men are equal, and that the people are capable of self-government. These were the fixed principles of his life; and his whole public career was but a practical embodiment and illustration of these principles.

My friend was not regularly educated; but with a strong natural intellect, with a power of reflection and observation seldom equalled, passing a busy and eventful life, he had supplied, in all the essential elements, the want of education in the amount of information that he had amassed, and those treasures from personal observation that he had collected.

One or two more remarks, and I have done. There are those who believe that the success of a public man in popular elections, is no evidence either of virtue in the constituent, or of influence or aptitude for the appointment in the representative. This is a great mistake. One who, without other circumstances than mere merit, can fasten and retain the public confidence, has a charm of excellence about him, an undefinable fascination of character and qualifications, which, although acquaintances individually may not discover it, yet constitutes a kind of divine and political electricity, which, without explanation, works its mighty power in this universe of election and popular right, and under the appointment of God, and by the common sense of the people, carries forward the great system of the government. My friend possessed this power. No man living ever had more of it; no one saw why. Other men were superior to him in attainments, superior to him in accomplishments, superior to him in wealth, seemingly superior to him in every advantage that would have a tendency to bind man to man, and bestow political or social influence; yet not a man breathed in this Congress, or elsewhere, within the whole circle of his acquaintance, who had the power in a greater degree than the deceased, to bind as with hooks of steel to himself, all who knew him or called him friend. Among his immediate constituency, his position was peculiar and lovely. The great Senator of New York, without wealth, represented the character of a Roman merely from merit, distinguished and useful. So my friend was poor, though useful and popular. This I speak in praise of him: it is his highest eulogy. He had no adventitious influences of wealth, of position, to bind him to his people; nothing but his principle of devotion to truth and to popular right, that attached them to him.

In all his life, he did his duty well; and in his death, there is nothing, now that that event is past, to regret. He was happy in his death, in that he passed quietly, as I have already noticed, through the dark valley and shadow.

I will not now attempt even to imagine, much less to speak words of consolation to the grief of the widow and the orphan. Time alone, under the persuasive influences of Christian faith, can give comfort here. Commending his family to those consolations, I ask the adoption of the following resolutions:

Resolved, That this House has heard with deep emotion the annunciation of the death of the Hon. JAMES A. BLACK, a member from the State of South Carolina.

Resolved, That this House tenders to the relatives of the deceased the expression of its sympathy, on this affecting event, and as a testimony of respect for the memory of the deceased, the members and officers of the House will go into mourning by wearing crape on the left arm for thirty days.

Resolved, That the members and officers of the House will attend the funeral of the Hon. JAMES A. BLACK, deceased, on to-morrow, at 12½ o'clock, P. M.

Resolved, That a committee be appointed for superintending the funeral of the deceased.

Ordered, That a message be sent to the Senate to notify that body of the death of the Hon. JAMES A. BLACK, late one of the Representatives from the State of South Carolina; that his funeral will take place from the hall of the House on to-morrow, at 12½ o'clock, P. M.; and that the Senate be invited to attend the same.

Resolved, That, as a further mark of respect for the memory of the deceased, this House do now adjourn.

And then the House adjourned.

IN SENATE.

Tuesday, April 4.

Death of the Representative James A. Black, of South Carolina.

A message was received from the House of Representatives, announcing the death of the Hon. James Augustus Black, of the State of South Carolina; when

Mr. Butler rose, and addressed the Senate as follows:

The death which has just been communicated by the resolutions from the House of Representatives, is an event well calculated to arrest attention, and inspire serious reflection. This is the fourth death that has occurred among us during this session—a period of four months—and the ninth occasion upon which we have been called on to go in mourning for the loss of a member belonging to the thirtieth Congress. These are circumstances that are giving to our session a melancholy celebrity.

My late colleague, the Hon. James Augustus Black, was seized on the 16th of the last month with a violent congestive chill, which terminated in an obstinate and incurable pneumonia, of which he died, at his lodgings in this city, last night, at twenty-five minutes after eleven o'clock. Before he was taken ill, he had the prospect of many days before him. With a robust constitution, he was in the enjoyment of vigorous health, neither of which had been impaired by previous disease. His last sickness was violent, painful, and protracted, but it was borne with a sustaining fortitude, worthy of a man and a Christian.

Our departed friend was born of respectable parents, in Abbeville district, South Carolina, and at the time of his death he was in the 57th year of his age. The deceased entered the army in 1812, at the age of eighteen, with the commission of lieutenant, and was promoted to the grade of captain before the close of the war.

Captain Black had not, I believe, any opportunity of distinction on the field of battle. But he left the service with the reputation of an excellent officer, having made a strong and favorable impression on the minds of his associates and military comrades. His keen sagacity, penetrating observation of men, his prompt judgment and untiring industry, associated with cordiality and frankness of manner, were qualities that well fitted him for military command. Upon one occasion, while he was stationed near St. Mary's, the intrepidity of his benevolence and courage was put to a test called for by a signal exertion to save life. By one of those sudden floods which occur in that part of the country, the hedges, causeways, and houses were submerged and swept away, destroying many lives and property. Captain Black, with much peril to himself, found a gentleman, than a young midshipman, now a captain in the navy, insensible and exhausted, floating on the wreck of a vessel. This gentleman, on hearing of the illness of Mr. Black, repaired to his bedside, and, inspired by the utmost delicacy of gratitude and friendship, ministered to his wants, with the tenderness almost of a woman.

On the close of the war, Captain Black retired to private life, and engaged in business with characteristic energy and industry. Prior to his election as member of Congress, he filled several situations of trust and responsibility. He possessed in an eminent degree the self-reliance of a self-made man, with the peculiarities of deportment and character that made him a popular favorite. From the period of his return to the twenty-eighth Congress, others have enjoyed better opportunities than myself of forming an estimate of his public career. But the deep and even affectionate anxiety manifested during his illness, and the profound sensation which his death occasioned amongst those who were particularly associated with him, are honorable commentaries upon his private virtues and his public worth.

At an early period, Mr. Black became a disciple of the old republican doctrines, and he ever afterwards maintained them with unflinching firmness and uniform consistency. He has been sustained during his public career by the unshaken confidence of an intelligent, numerous, and wealthy constituency.

A few days before he died, he gave expression to his unshrinking faith in the hopes and consolations of the Christian religion. He retained throughout his painful illness the possession of his mental faculties, and one remark which he made is worthy of record, as it affords at once matter of consolation and admiration. He said that a death-bed was not the place to prepare for death, and that he had not deferred till the last moment the solemn considerations connected with his spiritual welfare. He professed a confident adherence to the Christian faith, and expressed the hope, that through its efficacy, he should enjoy a happy existence hereafter. A few days before his death, I approached his bedside, and endeavored to cheer and encourage him. "This is indeed a great trial," he said, "but I will try and meet it as becomes a Carolinian!" Afterwards he said, "I have only one request to make: let my bones rest in the soil of my native land!"

This is not a fitting occasion on which to speak of the domestic relations of my departed colleague. Into that sacred private circle in which the virtues of the husband and the father were displayed, it is not for us to enter. It is consolatory that his wife, son, and brother, reached his dying bed in time to receive an affectionate recognition; and that he left this earthly scene with a firm hope of happiness beyond the grave, leaving behind him an unsullied name, and the reputation of a good and upright man.

Mr. B. concluded by offering the usual resolutions, incident to such mournful occasions, which were adopted, and

The Senate adjourned.

Thursday, April 6.

French Revolution.

Mr. Allen moved to postpone the previous orders, and to proceed to the consideration of the joint resolution submitted by him relating to the revolution in France.

At the request of Mr. Hannegan, who promised to renew it, the motion was withdrawn.

Mr. Hannegan, from the Committee on Foreign Relations, to whom the Message of the President was referred, reported the following series of resolutions:

JOINT RESOLUTION tendering the congratulations of the United States to the people of France.

Resolved, &c. That, in the name and on behalf of the American people, the congratulations of this Government are hereby tendered to the French people upon the recent change in their form of Government, and their successful efforts thus far to found for their country institutions similar to our own.

Be it further resolved, That the moderation, humanity, regard for order, and veneration for Christianity manifested by the French people in the accomplishment of their freedom, inspire the confident hope that their deliberations in the organization of the new Government will be so directed, under Providence, as to insure the liberty, the true glory, and the enduring happiness of a great and enlightened nation.

Be it further resolved, That Congress fully approves the conduct of our Minister, Richard Rush, in his prompt recognition of the Provisional Government of France.

And be it further resolved, That the President of the United States be, and he is hereby, requested to transmit these resolutions to the American Minister at Paris, with instructions to present them to the supreme authorities of the French Republic.

The resolutions having been read,

Mr. Hannegan moved to take up all the resolutions for consideration; which was agreed to.

The question being on the amendment moved by Mr. Hale—

Mr. Mangum moved to strike out all the original resolutions submitted by the Senator from Ohio, and insert the resolutions reported by the Committee on Foreign Relations.

Mr. Allen asked for a division of the question. His resolution was intended to give a general expression of the feeling of one nation to another. If we were to adopt individual opinions as to particular acts, we should never agree on any general form of resolution. It would be necessary to construct a resolution embracing a detail of all the French had done. To avoid that difficulty he had condensed his views into a single sentence, so as to make it most clear and simple.

To go into details in order to give a reason for every thing we do, is to place ourselves rather in the attitude of advisers than congratulators. He thought it best to embody a general expression in a few sentences, as the only way to obtain a general and prompt expression of the feelings of the Senate. He should prefer his own resolution, on account of its plainness and simplicity.

Mr. Niles said his objection to the resolutions was not because of any particular phraseology, but because we state in them what is not the fact. We go beyond what has actually been done. We say a Government has been overthrown and liberty consolidated. He presumed consolidating liberty meant providing a guarantee for the security of liberty. This had not been done. The Government established was merely temporary; it had not yet been properly elected. It may, indeed, be presumed that public opinion sanctions it. The results have not yet been obtained; so that we go beyond the pale of history. He preferred the resolutions reported by the Committee on Foreign Relations, although they did not exactly harmonize with his views.

Mr. Hannegan then addressed the Senate in support of the resolutions reported by him. He expressed his fervent desire that the revolution which had so well commenced would be carried through without the shedding of a drop of human blood. He explained to his friend from Ohio that he did not propose to interfere with his resolutions, as he would show by his vote. But he preferred the resolutions reported by the committee. He went for the spirit of the resolutions. The resolutions he had reported were merely an embodiment of the public sentiment, an echo of the opinions of every man in the country, of every laborer round the Capitol. He referred to the action of our Government in the revolution of 1789, when Louis XVI. communicated to General Washington the fact that he had signed the constitution pressed on him by the National Convention. General Washington communicated that information to Congress, and Congress replied by resolutions. Here, then, was something like a precedent. He disliked the word. But if we had no exact precedent, it was because the event itself was without precedent.

He had heard suggestions from the distinguished Senators from South Carolina and Connecticut that it was too early to adopt these resolutions. So he had himself thought at first. But reflection had led him to think differently, and as he could see no ill consequences likely to result from the passage of the resolutions, he would vote for immediate action. When liberty and humanity had been laid in a common grave, monarchs had exchanged congratulations; and now, when new-born France stretches out her hand, and invites us by her infant smiles, shall we hesitate to cheer and sustain her? If there was any thing in these resolutions at war with the usage of nations, or against the courtesy of international intercourse, he would pause before he gave his sanction to the resolutions. But he saw nothing of the kind in them. It was not impossible that before the present sun may set, we may have information that every Government of Europe has recognized the act of the French people. He complimented our minister on his promptitude; said he had trembled lest Mr. Rush should have proved derelict, in which case he could not have safely returned home; and quoted language imputed by a correspondent to M. Lamartine, that two things which had occurred had given him peculiar delight—the advances of the nuncio of the Pope and of the minister of the United States.

He briefly adverted to the manner in which the revolution had been accomplished; and expressed his entire confidence in the discretion and sagacity of the French people for the support of those brilliant intellects to whom their destinies had for the present been intrusted. The spirit of liberty was now afoot, traversing the whole world, and he anticipated the general emancipation of the human race from thraldom and tyranny. All this was to be traced to our example, and we had some reason to be proud of the laurels which our fathers had gained in the cause of freedom.

He was authorized to say that if any of these resolutions should pass before midnight, they would be forwarded by express to go by the Cambria, which sails on Saturday from the United States. He would now say that he would not stop here; but, if the acts of the Convention—to assemble on the 20th instant—should realize the hopes we indulge, he would send out such an embassy as had never before gone from our shores to congratulate and fraternize with the French people.

Mr. Allen then expressed his gratification at the manner in which the Senator from Indiana had referred to his (Mr. A.'s) course in offering his resolutions. He went on to remark on the debate which took place on the question of sending a chargé to Rome, and to some observations which had fallen from him in the warmth of discussion, in which he had expressed a hope that Congress would, before the termination of the session, pass a resolution congratulating the French people. In conformity with that suggestion, he had felt himself called on to offer the resolutions. He did not think there could be any objection to congratulating France, but there might very probably, and very properly, be differences as to the exact form in which the resolutions should be clothed.

Mr. Downs said, he should be satisfied with either of the resolutions which were before the Senate; but he was compelled to say a few words on the subject of the revolution itself, in consequence of what fallen from him on a previous day. He went on to advocate the cause of the French people up to this time, and to distinguish the progress of this revolution from that of the old revolution, referring to the error committed by the leaders in the latter in setting up the Goddess of Reason, and throwing off all allegiance to a superintending Providence. In the present revolution, morality and liberty went hand in hand, and some dignitaries of the church had eloquently sustained the cause of freedom. He stated that France asked no aid from us further than our cheering and sustaining voice; and we ought to cheer and support her in her cause, for our own sake as well as for hers. It would strengthen our own system. And if France should hereafter need advice, we shall stand in a position to enable us to offer it with effect. He read extracts from letters which had come into his hands from Paris, in order to show that the revolution was passing off quietly and without any disasters.

Mr. Dayton said he would have been much better satisfied, if the Senator from Ohio had consented to let these resolutions lie over until the first or second Monday in May. He thought that if the laborers round the Capitol were shaking hands with each other, the Senate within was engaged pretty much in the same way. This might do well enough for us as individuals, but it did not become us as a legislative body. If we are to congratulate a people on consolidating liberty, we should first be sure that liberty is consolidated, or perhaps when we send them out, the return may be *non est.* It was said that it was right to offer congratulations when a child was born. True; but he would wait until it was born. France had not yet been delivered—she may miscarry. He referred to the haste with which results were achieved, by a mere stroke of a pen—the emancipation of a hundred thousand slaves, without providing any recompense for the owners—the redemption of pledges from the pawnbrokers—the conversion of the Tuileries into a hospital. All these were done by a set of intelligent men, who were only a *quasi* Government, and might be displaced as rapidly as they were elevated. It becomes us to do things decently and in order, and he thought a month's delay could not diminish the value of the congratulations. It would give him great pleasure to vote for the resolutions after we have had time to ascertain the result.

Mr. Johnson, of Georgia, objected to delay. He did not think that a month would be sufficient to enable us to know the precise result of the great movement which had taken place. It might require the lapse of a year before the French can have matured their system of government. It occupied much time before our constitution was matured, and it had only grown with our growth, and strengthened with our strength. And still our Government is yet considered by foreign nations as merely an experiment. We could not, therefore, reasonably expect that a month would enable us to come to a more correct judgment than we can now arrive at. He had doubts at first, but they had been dispelled by the Message from the President.

He said he should give his vote in favor of the resolutions reported from the Committee on Foreign Relations. He did not object to the word "consolidate" in the resolutions of the Senator from Ohio, but he objected to a statement which went beyond the fact, when it indicated that the French people had succeeded. He would not congratulate them on their *success*, but he was willing to say *success so far*. They had only decreed a Republic, but the Republic had not yet been established. He read a long extract, to prove that the French people had acted with great moderation throughout the whole movement hitherto, and that under the whole of the decrees of the new Government there lay the elements of public liberty. A movement in favor of public freedom anywhere would call forth the sympathy of our citizens, but a movement in France produced recollections and associations of a peculiar nature, calculated to excite in us the warmest sympathies.

Mr. PHELPS said he agreed with his countrymen in rejoicing at every advance of human liberty; but he was opposed to any hasty action of Congress, for the purpose of congratulating the French people, until we have knowledge of the events which must occur before it is consummated.

Mr. HOUSTON said he desired to make some remarks, and as the hour was late, he moved that the Senate adjourn.

Mr. HANNEGAN requested the Senator from Texas to withdraw his motion. It was desirable to pass the resolutions to-night, in order that they may be transmitted by the Cambria, which will sail at twelve o'clock on Saturday. If the vote was not taken this evening, there was no probability that the resolutions would be again acted on before the assembling of the French Convention on the 20th. He had an understanding with the Senator from Kentucky, by which he was pledged to assist in disposing of the judiciary bill to-morrow and Saturday, and next week he had promised to aid in having the California bill acted on. So that he hoped the motion would be withdrawn.

Mr. HOUSTON said the delay of a day could be of no great importance. The President's Message would go out by the Cambria, and this would satisfy France as to the disposition of our Government to sympathize with her.

Mr. HANNEGAN asked for the yeas and nays on the motion; and they were ordered, when

Mr. HOUSTON withdrew the motion.

After a few remarks from Mr. CRITTENDEN, Mr. BUTLER, and Mr. DAVIS of Mississippi, the question was put on the passage of the resolutions, and decided as follows:

YEAS.—Messrs. Allen, Ashley, Atchison, Atherton, Bell, Bradbury, Breese, Butler, Cass, Clarke, Crittenden, Davis of Mississippi, Dickinson, Dix, Douglas, Downs, Felch, Foote, Hale, Hannegan, Houston, Johnson of Maryland, Johnson of Georgia, Lewis, Mason, Moor, Niles, Rusk, Spruance, Turney, Underwood, and Westcott—32.

NAYS.—None.

The following are the resolutions as passed:

Resolved, &c., That in the name and behalf of the American people, the congratulations of Congress are hereby tendered to the people of France, upon the success of their recent efforts to consolidate the principles of liberty in a republican form of Government.

And be it further resolved, That the President of the United States be, and he is hereby, requested to transmit this resolution to the American Minister at Paris, with instructions to present it to the French Government.

At half-past six o'clock, the Senate adjourned.

FRIDAY, April 7.

Supreme Court Bill.

On motion of Mr. CRITTENDEN, the Senate postponed the previous orders, and proceeded to the consideration of the bill concerning the Supreme Court of the United States.

The bill was then considered as in Committee of the Whole.

Mr. BUTLER said he was a member of the Judiciary Committee, and felt it to be his duty to say that the bill received the assent of only a majority of the committee. The greatest objection he had heard against it was that advanced by the Senator from Missouri, who asserted that it was intended to cut loose the Supreme Court of the United States from the States. He would say he, for one, in supporting the bill, entertained no such intention. The accumulated cases before the Supreme Court rendered some measure of this kind necessary, judgments being suspended for three or four years, because of the impossibility of reaching them. He went on to show that no harm could arise from passing the bill, while much would be prevented by passing it.

Mr. WESTCOTT said he was one of the minority of the committee who had voted against the bill, and he had seen no reason since to change his views. He opposed the bill partly for the reasons so cogently urged by the Senator from Missouri, and partly because he thought the delay in deciding on cases before the Supreme Court could, in all cases, be remedied by the parties or by the court. The passage of the bill he regarded as dangerous to the system. The present system worked very well, and he did not wish to see it changed.

Mr. ASHLEY also regarded the bill as dangerous, and he could not, therefore, give it his support. He stated that an opinion prevailed even among the judges themselves, that it was unconstitutional for Congress to compel the judges to peform circuit duties. He looked back into the early history of our Judiciary, and expressed his belief that the judges of the Supreme Court performed harder duties than are performed now. He expressed his conviction that from the year 1789 to this time, every movement for the relief of the judges of the Supreme Court had emanated from the judges themselves. If he was mistaken in this fact, it was after the closest examination he had been able to give to the subject. The law of 1793, which gave relief to the court, continued in force until 1802. They had been accustomed to meet on the first Monday in February; subsequently the time was changed to the first Monday in January, and latterly to the first Monday in December. Other reliefs have been given, yet the docket had been gradually on the increase; so that the lengthening of the time has not had the effect of diminishing the business, which has fallen in arrear. During the last term about forty-one cases were disposed of, comparing very unfavorably with the number of cases in the State courts, where there is as much talent and legal ability as in the Supreme Court. One-third of the appeals came from Louisiana and Arkansas, yet we do not hear from these States a single application for this bill. It has emanated from the Supreme Court itself.

Mr. Dayton. I desire to make a very few remarks on this bill. Of course I do not propose to follow the chairman of the committee from whom this bill came, through all his objections. We considered them in committee, and did not regard them as militating against the merits of the bill, which lie within a much narrower compass than that which has been assumed by the honorable Senator from Arkansas. It is proper, in the first place, to look to the evil which this measure is designed to remedy. There are now upon the list, as I am informed by the Senator from Kentucky, (Mr. Crittenden,) one hundred and sixty-four cases undisposed of; fifty-two cases having been disposed of at the last session of the court. Assuming, then, that the same progress shall be made at future sessions of the court, it will require three or four years to dispose of the calendar, while if the present measure of relief be granted, you can dispose substantially of the aggregate of the calendar in a single year—rubbing out old scores, and giving the court a new docket. Such is the present state of the calendar of the Supreme Court, and such is the object sought to be attained by the bill now before the Senate.

Now, what are the objections urged against the passage of the bill? Why, first, it is objected that the bill originates with the judges, and that every other bill relative to the Supreme Court, from 1789 to this hour, originated with them, or through their instrumentality. Now, who are properly to be supposed to be most familiar with the business of the court, and most anxious for its prompt despatch? Sir, we are not to assume that the judges of the Supreme Court of the United States are any other than high-minded, upright, and honorable men, desirous of discharging with fidelity and efficiency the high functions imposed upon them by law. It is surely no more than just to those gentlemen, to give them that degree of credit. The court is, then, the very source from which such a measure should emanate with propriety, because it is a source that acts with light and knowledge. And, pray, whence does that very bill which the Senator from Arkansas now proposes as the bill upon which Congress ought to act, emanate? From a majority of the judges of that court; and permit me to say, that from consideration of the measure in committee, I am satisfied, that if adopted, it will produce the very evil which the Senator, and those who think with him, deprecate so much—the separation of the court from the State judicatures, and its continual session here as a central, absolute power. That is the measure of all others most likely to produce the result which the Senator dreads. But I refrain from any remark on that bill till it comes before us. At present, we have to deal with this temporary law. It provides for the evil. It applies a remedy suggested by the court itself. Is there any thing really in the objection, that the design is to undermine the present system, and obtain for the court the power of sitting here continually, cutting itself altogether loose from the States? I appeal to the intelligence, to the knowledge of members of the Senate, as to the character of the judges presiding in that court, and ask whether it is possible that such a design can be entertained by them? Those most deeply interested in that court come here and say, "Our docket is encumbered by upwards of one hundred and sixty cases. A case coming up now cannot be reached within several years. We ask of you only to allow a prolongation of the term, from three months to one year. We ask no additional remuneration—no additional privileges. We ask only the privilege of laboring continuously for one year, for the purpose of disposing of all the cases on the docket." Such is the appeal and request of the court; and now gentlemen object, that this merely covers a design to undermine the present system, and establish a court that is to live here for all time to come, independent of the States. Permit me to ask the Senate with all respect, to look at the case as it really exists. There are one hundred and sixty cases on the docket, and the court, with no disposition in the world to get rid of labor, ask only, that instead of being compelled to adjourn at the end of three months, they may be allowed to labor till the end of the year. One might reasonably imagine, that this was a case in which any impeachment of the motives of the court was utterly impossible.

Mr. Allen. I have a very few words to say

on this subject. The United States Supreme Court has a jurisdiction, both as regards territory and subject-matter, greater than any other judicial tribunal in the world. Every thing, therefore, which relates to the organization of that court, becomes a matter of the gravest importance, and is entitled to the most serious consideration. The judges of the court are elected by the Executive. They are appointed for life. In that respect, the organization of this court is not in harmony with the balance of the political system of this country. It has about it no one single feature by which it is connected either with the States of this Union, or with the people of these States, except it be the circuit feature, which gives the members of the court a direct intercourse and communication with the States and the people of this Confederacy. It is in that circuit feature that the strength of this tribunal consists; and the day that that feature ceases to exist in its organization, will the public opinion of this country move upon the subject, and never cease its action, till the tribunal itself is entirely reorganized. If, therefore, I was ever so much disposed to attack this tribunal, and to break it down, the thing that I would first do, would be to encourage the concentration of the tribunal permanently at the Capitol of the United States, and its total withdrawal from any communication with the States and people of the Union. I say this to those who may lay a greater estimate upon this tribunal than I do, that if they do not want it to be passed through the burning crucible of the public will, and recast in all its elements *de novo*, they had better let this circuit feature remain untouched.

It is proposed here to relieve the judges of this court from circuit duties for one year. For it is a bill of relief from the labor and expense of travel. It is a bill of relief and repose. But it is limited to one year. Now, I have observed, and all who have seen as much of legislation as I have must also have observed, that when you commence legislating by instalment, you never end. You commence in this case by giving this court one year's relief; and the next year, the same reason existing for a repetition of the act, the precedent of the previous year is pleaded as an additional argument for an extension of the relief one year longer. It is the grant of an exemption from the labor and expense of travel, to the judges of the court; and the same force which is now brought to bear in favor of this bill, through the instrumentality of the present contact of Congress with the judges of the court, will be brought to bear with added strength next session; all the reasons that are now urged being poured forth, with the additional one that Congress once did the act. Now, though I have no idea that the gentlemen who advocate this bill intend any such thing—as I do not suppose that there are any members of this body who would vote for the permanent concentration of this court here—yet I am convinced that that result will inevitably follow from the adoption of this measure. You commence this business of relief from circuit duty—I care not what the excuse may be, it is the commencement of a system of relief from circuit duty, freeing them from the labor and expense of travel—and when you commence it, the same reason applying the next year for the continuance of it, the same motives which induce us to pass this bill now being equally influential then, the bill will be renewed, and so on *ad infinitum*. I view this measure, then, as simply a bill to change the judicial system of the United States; though not so designed, yet in its consequences tending to that point inevitably. Viewing the matter in that light, it next becomes a subject of inquiry, what will be the effect upon our political organization? What will be the effect of the existence of a fixed, central tribunal, seated in this Capitol, composed of men who hold their places for life, cut off from all communication with the States and the people of the States—a Washington City star chamber, under the influences which act upon the capital where the political powers of the nation are all concentrated temporarily? When that kind of a spectacle is presented to the people of the United States, how long will it stand? If it stood twenty-five years, it would become the prevailing power of the Government. Power is a thing which generates itself, which enlarges itself, which contains within itself the means of its own expansion, sustenance, and support. It wants nothing but time to gratify the cravings of its ambition. Whether it be judicial or not, duration is all that it wants to make itself permanent over any other power that is fleeting and transitory. This local power, if it were permitted to stand twenty-five years, would render the whole constitution a perfect nullity. In less than ten years it would take the place of your Attorney General in all the decisions of the Executive upon law questions, and thereby connect itself with the administrative portion of the Government. The idea would be perfectly natural that the Executive would connect itself with the judiciary, would consult its members, would employ its influence; and thus the two would mutually strengthen each other, and engross the powers and energies of the Government more and more in one spot in Washington City.

Besides, the permanence and existence of the court here would give it large influence over our deliberations in these Halls. The very fact that nine men armed with great power, having great reputation and beyond the reach of popular control, being permanently located here for their lifetime, would render them objects of adulation and importunity and court for men at a distance, who wished to achieve illicit objects in this Capitol. It would become a cabal. These results would flow inevitably, if it were not for the fact that such a power would call down upon it the curses of the nation too soon to allow it to take hold and mature itself.

Mr. Crittenden. I intend to occupy the attention of the Senate only for a few moments. I regret that gentlemen have chosen this occasion, so important in itself, for the purpose of debating questions and principles which, according to my judgment, are not included in the subject under our consideration. To what purpose is it to debate the question as to the political character of the Supreme Court of the United States—to debate the question whether it was best to appoint the judges in the manner prescribed for in our constitution, or to change that constitution, and make them elective? Where is the necessity of inquiring into the nature and extent of the jurisdiction of the court? Where the propriety, on this occasion, of inquiring into the individual or collective competency of the judges? In no one of any of these particulars, in no regard to any principle or question involved in it as a system, does this bill touch the subject. It takes the court as it stands—as it is legally and constitutionally established—without change or alteration of its jurisdiction, and simply proposes —what? That, because of an inconvenient accumulation of business in the Supreme Court of the United States, rendering it impossible for the court to dispose of the business before it in less than two or three years, a remedy should be applied, by which this evil may be obviated. And what is the remedy? This bill simply proposes to authorize the judges of the Supreme Court to hold a second term in the course of the year besides that to which they are now limited, for the purpose of despatching this accumulated business. Now, what principle is involved in this beyond the simple question of providing a remedy which all admit? Sir, if I understand all the arguments that have any application to this subject, gentlemen would have no objection to this measure if they did not apprehend that it was intended as a wedge, or the commencement, as they express it, of another system, having for its object the suspension of the judges of the Supreme Court from all duty in the circuit courts, confining them to the duties belonging to the Supreme Court. Gentlemen imagine this, and therefore refuse to apply the proposed remedy for an acknowledged evil. They do not suppose that the evil is so great but that it may be borne. So it may. And gentlemen speak of the danger of the remedy. Let us examine it. The bill provides for a single year. According to existing laws, the next term of the Supreme Court will commence on the first Monday in December next. We are now in the first week in April. Four months of the year have then expired. The three corresponding months of the next year will be occupied by the court in the transaction of its business, so that the whole peril of the proposed measure lies within the compass of eight months. But, forsooth, if we indulge the Supreme Court—for gentlemen seem to regard it as an indulgence —by granting them permission to come here and despatch the business of the court in that period, great danger is to arise—a new system is to grow up—a new principle is to be evolved which is to relieve the judges of the Supreme Court from all other duties except those belonging to the Supreme Court, and other serious political consequences will result! I do not apprehend any such thing. The bill itself seems to guard against any such consequences by its limitation to one year. It is proposed solely as a particular remedy for a particular case. But are not those consequences in our own hands? Are gentlemen afraid that they themselves will do this wrong? There is not a Senator here, so far as I can judge from the opinions that I have heard expressed, who is willing to change the present system so far as to separate the judges from the circuit court and limit them to the Supreme Court. I am glad to believe that there is not a single Senator who entertains that opinion. When the Senate, then, have the issue and consequences in their own hands, I ask, what solid ground there is for any apprehension? Is there any danger that the Senator from Arkansas will be even in these revolutionary times so perfectly revolutionized in his opinions as to come back prepared to reverse all his opinions which he has expressed here to-day? Here is an evil which we can correct. This bill proposes to correct it. The only objection is, that the remedy proposed is one out of which dangerous consequences may hereafter grow; and we have no security for ourselves that that will not be the case. Why, sir, we are afraid of ourselves! If I believed that ever so remotely or possibly this measure could be perverted to such an object as gentlemen seem to apprehend, I would be one of the last to vote for it. But I do not desire to go into this subject. I desire rather to have this bill voted upon than any thing elese. If the Senate be against it, let it go.

Mr. Benton. I always regret, sir, when debate takes a personal turn; and when the intentions or wishes or motives of Senators become the subject of remark, the discussion may be regarded as having become personal. In the little I have said and the little I may say, I leave out of view entirely the intentions of every Senator. I impute to no one a design to separate the Supreme Court of the United States from the States, but I reason from the nature and effect of things. The effect of this measure will be that separation, and it is perfectly immaterial what are the intentions of Senators, or what obligations they may impose upon themselves never to do this again. If a Senator says he will vote this once and never vote it again, certainly he will do what he says; but it is altogether a personal matter; it depends upon his life—upon his coming here—upon this Senate continuing in time to come, to be exactly what it is to-day. The moment we go into the intention of Senators in regard to our legislation, we fall into the absurdity that the Senate is not only permanent as a body, but permanent in its constituent members —that they are always to sit here, and that having done the thing once they will not do it again. But we are to have successors, and God knows there have been examples enough to show that successors are not at all bound by any resolves of those who preceded them. As reasonable men we would be bound on a recurrence of the evil that now exists to apply the same remedy. That is the point of view in which I regard this question; and while I am ready to admit that every Senator will redeem his pledge and vote against it, I must say that it is only by virtue of his pledge he will be bound, because if this divorce of the Supreme Court from their duties in the States is an appropriate remedy for a surcharged docket now, it must be the remedy in all time to come. Just so often as there is a surcharged docket, this will be the remedy if we agree to it now. Here lies the difficulty. The danger is in admitting this to be the appropriate remedy, thereby making it the remedy in any case which is to occur hereafter, until it become habitual, just as habitual as to pass the bill every year. Thus the application of this remedy will become a matter of course, till at last there will be a general law to divorce the Supreme Court from the States forever.

For myself, I look upon this one-year plan as the application for the wood which is to make the handle to the axe. Grant but a little bit of wood, and the whole forest will be cut down. Begin with these yearly instalments of relief, and where will you end? Fortified, strengthened, stimulated by this encouragement, that best of all argument, precedent, will be urged, and the separation of the Supreme Court from the States will be inevitable. That there is a great evil I do not dispute, all admit it. The docket its locked up, and the court cannot meet and despatch cases as they arise. The question is, What is the appropriate remedy? In the first place, I say that the remedy we propose to apply is a greater evil than the evil itself; and, secondly, that it is no remedy. The docket will be as it is at present, for we know that if we pass this bill, the appeals must be more numerous than heretofore. I desire time for deliberation in order that the attention of the Judiciary Committee may be directed to the subject. I recollect very well that some years ago a judge of the Supreme Court told me that he could get on very well if it were not for the business of this district; that there is very little limitation with respect to the cases arising here; that the counsel and the parties all live here, and that the court is blocked up with the business of the District of Columbia, which there is no reason in the world to bring before it. It seems to me that there might be some additional limitations imposed which would diminish the number of appeals; but I have not examined this subject for the purpose of ascertaining the appropriate remedy. I can only express the belief that the evil may be remedied without falling into a far greater evil than the one of which we wish to get rid. I am in favor of a remedy ample and complete, or none at all. I am against the application of a little half-way remedy—a temporary instalment remedy—for I believe it will be like all other instalment remedies, renewed until it become habitual.

The judges have separated—they have gone away—some of them are near the discharge of their duties in the circuit. I think it will be best in all the circumstances, to recommit the bill, and as we have a long session before us, devote time and consideration to the subject; which may result in the application of a permanent and safe remedy, relieving us from the necessity of recurring year after year to a species of remedy, which, after all, does not meet the case, and produces a greater evil than that which it was designed to remove.

Mr. Badger. I feel great reluctance in rising to say any thing on this bill. I see around me friends who are anxious for its passage, gentlemen whose wishes I delight to promote, and for whose deliberate judgment I entertain the highest respect. But I am deeply impressed with the conviction that the measure now proposed for the action of the Senate is mischievous in its tendency. Without reference to the motives and considerations which have induced its introduction into Congress, and before I make two or three observations on the merits of the measure, as some gentlemen who have spoken on this subject have stated views in reference to this court in which I did not concur, permit me to say, that I am, in every sense of the term, a friend of that court. I regard that institution as one of the wisest provisions of the great charter of our liberties which our ancestors devised and transmitted to us. I am not opposed to the independent tenure of office by which the judges occupy their seats on that bench. I look upon that as the very provision of the Constitution of the United States which renders the court not only in the highest sense valuable, but which alone renders it safe; and I should look with horror upon a tribunal of last resort, vested with such high powers, if its members held their office by the tenure of Executive caprice or popular passion and prejudice. Neither am I opposed to this bill on the ground that it may have been suggested by the judges, and is intended to afford them relief. I shall always feel myself prompt and ready to afford any relief to the gentlemen who occupy a place upon that bench, provided it be in my judgment consistent with the public welfare; and other things being equal, it would be to me a strong recommendation of a measure that it was calculated to afford relief, and manifest a generous consideration on the part of Congress for those high functionaries, upon the efficient discharge of whose duties every thing which is in the highest degree valuable to us as American citizens, in my opinion, greatly depends. Still, I am opposed to this bill. I am opposed to it because I am a friend to the court. I am opposed to it because I believe it to be the commencement of a system by which the moral influence and power of that court will ultimately be overthrown; and it will remain either an incubus upon our institutions, pressing them with a weight injurious to the community, or perhaps producing such a state of things in the public mind as ultimately to destroy the institution itself, or overthrow that independent tenure of office which to me is its highest recommendation.

I think that, in view of the past legislation of Congress, and of the consideration suggested by the Senator from Missouri, there is every reason to believe that at the next session of Congress the necessity for further relaxation will not only not be removed or diminished, but will be increased, and more strongly urged as a reason for a continuance of relief. If appeals be so numerous now, when the circuits below do have occasionally two judges for the purpose of hearing and deciding important causes, what may we expect when, for a whole year, the determination of every cause, important or unimportant, involving, whatever amount of property, or whatever perplexing questions, will be thrown, by the necessity of the case, on a single judge? I think that in every important cause there will be a writ of error or appeal to the Supreme Court; and that twelve months hereafter you will have just as much reason, nay, greater reason, for the passage of a special law.

Then, as I apprehend, if Congress act consistently, applying this remedy from year to year, *toties quoties*, it must come to this, that we shall have these gentlemen as judges of the Supreme Court of appeals, not mingling with the ordinary transactions of business—not accustomed to the "forensic *strepitus*" in the courts below—not seeing the rules of evidence practically applied to the cases before them—not enlightened upon the laws of the several States, which they have finally to administer here, by the discussions of able and learned counsel in the courts below—not seen by the people of the United States—not known and recognized by them—not touching them as it were in the administration of their high office—not felt, and understood, and realized as part and parcel of this great popular Government; but sitting here alone—becoming philosophical and speculative in their inquiries as to law—becoming necessarily more and more dim as to the nature of the law of the various States, from want of familiar and daily connection with them—unseen, final arbiters of justice, issuing their decrees as it were from a secret chamber—moving invisibly amongst us, as far as the whole community is concerned; and, in my judgment, losing in fact the ability to discharge their duties as well as that responsive confidence of the people, which adds so essentially to the sanction of all the acts of the officers of Government.

During a session of upwards of ninety days the court decided, as the Senator from Arkansas informs us, about forty cases.

Mr. Crittenden. Upwards of fifty cases.

My friend from Kentucky says, from the statement of the clerk, upwards of fifty cases have been decided. I imagine that the two statements are quite reconcilable. The clerk puts down all the cases that have gone off the docket; several cases being involved in one opinion, and some merely docketed and dismissed. Why were not there more cases disposed of? We are all somewhat familiar with the manner in which cases are argued in that court. Now, Lord Bacon has informed us in one of his essays—and no man understood better, theoretically, than he the duties of a judge, whatever might have been his practical discharge of those duties—that one of the offices of a judge was, "to moderate length, repetition, and impertinence of speech," using the latter term of course in its original and appropriate signification, not as meaning insolence, but irrelevancy. Now, has that remedy been applied by the court? Has the court taken upon itself the responsibility which it ought to have exercised, in order to prevent a waste of the public time by those who happen to gain the ear of the court a little earlier, in debate, indulging in idle and frivolous discussion, felt by the court themselves to be totally immaterial to the decision of the cause? Has the court been careful to prevent discussion of questions which might be regarded as axiomatic in this country—dissertations or scholastic essays, like those delivered to young men prosecuting their studies in a lawyer's office, in the expectation of obtaining a license? It is quite familiar to us all, that in a case which attracted some attention, one of the learned counsel occupied an entire day for the purpose of demonstrating this very difficult proposition in America, that the people are sovereign; and then pursued his argument on the second day by endeavoring to make out the extremely difficult conclusion from the first proposition, that being sovereign, they had a right to frame their own constitution! Well, now, if the court sit quietly while gentlemen, from whatever motive, either to gain distinction from an exhibition of their polemical powers, capacity for didactic discussion, or any other reason, occupy the attention of the court with such discussions, what hope, what expectation can be entertained, that this bill will supply any remedy for the evil of a surcharged docket?

I have no doubt, if the court had met on the 1st of December, with the resolute purpose of confining the argument of counsel to the questions on record, and refusing to listen to any discussion of any points which the court considered to be clear and settled, that instead of deciding forty cases, the court might have decided one hundred and forty. Gentlemen around me know, that we belong to a profession exceedingly discursive, and that when we have looked into a subject, and imagine that we can make a display, we are very apt to occupy time without consideration of the just claims of those who are to come after us.

Mr. Phelps. I regard this judicial system which has been in operation some fifty years, and with a very slight interruption ever since the organization of the Government, as the best that can be devised for the General Government and for the people. I deprecate as much as the Senator from North Carolina, or any other gentleman on this floor, the separation of the judges of the Supreme Court from their circuit duties. The consideration that the separation of the judges of the Supreme Court from their circuit duties would operate very much to the prejudice of the country, is not to be overlooked. I have had my fears, however, that this system, admirable as it is, would have to be abandoned; and that apprehension has been founded upon the fact, that in the first place, the judges have not time to attend to their circuit duties; and that, in the second place, the docket of the Supreme Court had become so loaded, that the business of the court cannot be despatched—the very evil which I apprehended as likely to grow out of the extension of our territory, and the utter impracticability of having the duties of the circuit court discharged by such a number of judges as would be proper to be congregated here. If you increase the number of the judges of the Supreme Court with a view to enable them to discharge all the duties of the circuit courts, you have a court too numerous. On the other hand, they cannot, if they be limited to their present number, discharge the duties of the circuit courts. What is to be done? Some remedy must be applied. In my humble judgment, we have this alternative before us: we must either afford temporary relief, or abandon the system altogether. This is the issue presented. Well, not being disposed to abandon the system—preferring to retain it, and for the very considerations suggested by other Senators—I desire to apply some remedy to relieve the court from the accumulation of business here. In my judgment, if an extra session of this court can dispose of this accumulation of business, the court can attend in future to the ordinary discharge of its duties. If this be not done, what is the result? Why, if the docket of this court is allowed to accumulate and increase from year to year, and the community becomes satisfied that the business of the court cannot be despatched, we are driven irresistibly to the very measure which gentlemen deprecate—the separation of the court from the States. In these circumstances there is but one alternative—we must either change the system, or we must adopt some temporary measure of relief. I am decidedly of opinion that we should resort to some measure of temporary relief, and preserve the system. It is really a choice of evils, and I prefer that course which looks to temporary relief, rather than that which must result in an entire change of the system. As to the recommendation of the Senator from North Carolina, I have only to say, that it is easy to talk on this floor about the manner in which the judges should discharge their duties. I confine myself to the subject before us, and allow the judges to go on in their own way.

Mr. Foote. Until the debate occurred to which we have just listened, I confess that I was decidedly favorable to the passage of this bill. But some objections to its becoming a law have been preferred which are too cogent to be resisted; and I shall, contrary to my first inclinations, vote against it. The merits of the bill have been so fully debated, that nothing which I could now say would aid the Senate in coming to a wise decision concerning it. I shall, therefore, content myself with responding to a single suggestion which has just fallen from the Senator from Vermont. That gentleman seems to be particularly horrified at certain animadversions in which honorable Senators have indulged touching the conduct of those who preside in the Supreme Court of the Union. He appears to be of opinion that we ought not, under any circumstances, to find fault with the action of a co-ordinate department of the Government, and especially with the judicial department. The Senator may or may not be right in the general doctrine which he asserts; and yet it is most evident to me, that if any one of the three departments of Government decreed by the constitution to be separate and independent of each other, should be allowed to interfere with the action of another in any case, the exception to the general rule should be admitted in favor, either of the Legislative or Executive, in preference to the Judiciary. Nor do I imagine that there will be much difference of opinion as to the correctness of this proposition among Senators who attach sufficient importance to the fact, that the judges of the Supreme Court are appointed (not elected, either by the people or otherwise) for life, and are only responsible to the country through the medium of impeachment—a proceeding long since ascertained to be wholly inefficient for the purpose of punishing an unworthy judicial functionary. The occasion is not such as to allow of my objecting in form to the mode in which the members of the Supreme Court of the Union are appointed to their high stations, or to their peculiar tenure of office, which induced Mr. Jefferson to declare this tribunal to be a solecism in our system.

Mr. Downs. I confess I agree with the Senator from North Carolina, that much of the evil that we complain of might be remedied by the court itself, still I think it is necessary that the bill should pass. It is not an act for the relief of the court, but for the relief of those who are engaged in litigation before that court—for the relief of the people of the United States. It is said that if this measure be not adopted, another measure will be brought forward that will remedy the evil. I shall be happy to see a remedy applied, and I see an opportunity now for the adoption of a remedy. There is in my State a large amount of property in litigation. A case was carried to the Supreme Court before the act of 1844 was passed, involving some hundred thousand acres of land, and it still remains undecided; how many years more it will take, I do not know. The delay has become positively intolerable. But if the court could be allowed to sit through the year, the docket might be cleared off, and we should then have time to adopt such measures as may be necessary to prevent a recurrence of the evil.

Mr. Calhoun. I rise simply to state, in a very few words, the reasons that will govern me, in giving my vote on this occasion. It must be admitted, on all sides, that this is intended to be only a temporary measure, and that the present system ought to be continued. I believe this is the general impression; such is mine, very strongly. This bill is presented on the ground, that the cases upon the docket have so accumulated, that it requires an extraordinary law—to relieve the judges from their circuit duties for one year—in order to clear them off. Well, what possible assurance have we, that at the end of the year the same reason will not exist for enacting such a law for the next year? It appears to me that we are inverting the order of things. The first object should be to adopt some measure that would prevent the accumulation of cases in future, and then some measure for disposing of those which now exist. But proceeding as we are, it appears to me it will be tantamount—without intending it to be so—to a permanent change in the circuit system. Now, I believe there are very few Senators prepared for this; I believe the judges themselves are not. We have ample time during the remaining part of the session—it will probably last three months, yet I should be very glad to think it would terminate in three—surely this will furnish ample opportunity to the Judiciary Committee, or if that committee be overloaded with business, to a Select Committee to take the subject into consideration, and propose some measure that will prove an effectual remedy for the evil that is complained of.

Mr. Dayton. The Judiciary Committees in both Houses have had the subject under consideration. A bill has been reported, and is now before the House of Representatives; but any bill that is passed should be a bill calculated to sweep away the accumulations of the cases with which the docket of the Supreme Court is now lengthened. They must be disposed of irrespective of any bill for the regulation of the Judiciary hereafter.

Mr. Calhoun. I was not aware that there was a bill before the House relating to this subject; but that being the case, it is a reason why this bill should lie upon the table until that bill passes. Let us apply first the general remedy, and then adopt any additional measure that may be necessary. Being strongly desirous that the system should not be changed, and fearing that this bill if adopted will change it, I feel myself compelled to vote against it.

The question was then taken on the engrossment of the bill, and decided as follows:

Yeas.—Messrs. Bell, Breese, Butler, Crittenden, Dayton, Downs, Greene, Hannegan, Johnson of Maryland, Mangum, Mason, Miller, Pearce, Phelps. Rusk, Underwood, and Upham—17.

Nays.—Messrs. Allen, Ashley, Badger, Bagby, Benton, Calhoun, Davis of Mississippi, Dickinson, Dix, Douglas, Felch, Foote, Hale, Houston, Lewis, Niles, Spruance, Turney, and Westcott—19.

HOUSE OF REPRESENTATIVES.

Monday, April 10.

French Revolution.

Mr. Stewart, of Pennsylvania, said he hoped the House would this morning, by common consent, take up and dispose of the joint resolutions from the Senate tendering the congratulations of the American to the French people. It would take but little time, he said, to dispose of them.

The resolutions were taken up, and read the first time by their title.

Mr. Thompson, of Pennsylvania, moved the previous question.

Mr. Ashmun said the resolutions had not been read. He called for their reading before any action was taken upon them.

The Speaker said, the resolutions having been read the first time, the previous question, being moved, would apply to the second reading.

The previous question was seconded, and, under its operation, the resolutions were read a second time by their title.

The question being on the third reading—

Mr. Holmes, of South Carolina, called for the reading of the entire resolutions; which were read for information, as follows:

Resolved, &c., That in the name and behalf of the American people, the congratulations of Congress are hereby tendered to the people of France upon the success of their recent efforts to consolidate the principles of liberty in a republican form of Government.

And be it further resolved, That the Pesident of the United States be, and he is hereby, requested to transmit this resolution to the American Minister at Paris, with instructions to present it to the French Government.

Mr. Ashmun confessed that he objected to the resolutions of the gentleman from Ohio the other day; and he hesitated to concur in the proceedings contemplated this day, because France has not yet achieved republican liberty. They had been told that a republican government had been formed in France; that it had been already achieved, and was now existing. The President of the United States, in his

Message to Congress, had announced the fact, "that France had been suddenly transformed into a republic." The President must have singular ideas of what constitutes a republican government. Indeed, his conduct as the Executive of our own Union, in his frequent usurpation of power, gave room to doubt whether he well understood the true spirit of republicanism. But how was the present government of France established? Where was the charter of that Government? Where was its constitution? Everybody who had read the proceedings in France knew that the present Government was formed by the introduction of a mob into the Chamber of Deputies. In the midst of turbulence, a soldier took a bayonet, and, piercing a piece of paper with names upon it, held it up, and, with a shout, the names on that paper were proclaimed to be the Government. Such was the history of the transaction. That was the charter of France at the present moment. It was a bayonet government. It was not a government established by the exercise of constitutional liberty. The power of France was exercised by a few gentlemen; but where was the charter to limit their power? It did not exist. On the contrary, the papers of this morning brought the intelligence, in a document issued by the Minister of the Interior, that those few individuals were sovereign and independent, and that their own discretion was the limit of their power. In such a case, then, might it not be that the same power which constituted them the Government of France might turn them out, and put others in their place? He denied, then, that France had achieved republican liberty. It was nothing less than an arbitrary despotism at present. It was true that yesterday, (Sunday,) the 9th of April, was appointed for the election of nine hundred French delegates; and if they have succeeded, we may look forward to the organization of a national legislature; but, until that has been done, he confessed that, individually, he had no sanguine hopes of the result.

The question then recurred on the third reading of the resolutions; which was agreed to without a division.

Mr. COBB, of Georgia, moved the previous question on the final passage of the resolutions; which was seconded, and the main question was ordered to be now put.

Mr. STEWART, of Pennsylvania, called for the yeas and nays; which were ordered, and resulted as follows:

YEAS.—Messrs. Adams, Ashmun, Atkinson, Barringer, Barrow, Bayly, Beale, Bedinger, Bingham, Birdsall, Blanchard, Bocock, Botts, Bowdon, Bowlin, Boyd, Brady, Bridges, Brodhead, William G. Brown, Charles Brown, Albert G. Brown, Buckner, Burt, Cabell, Canby, Cathcart, Chase, Franklin Clark, Beverly L. Clark, Howell Cobb, W. R. W. Cobb, Cocke, Collins, Crisfield, Crowell, Crozier, Cummins, Dickey, Dickinson, Dixon, Duer, Daniel Duncan, Garnett Duncan, Eckert, Edsall, Edwards, Embree, Nathan Evans, Faran, Farrelly, Featherston, Ficklin, Freedley, French, Fries, Fulton, Gentry, Giddings, Goggin, Gott, Green, Gregory, Hale, Nathan K. Hall, Hammons, James G. Hampton, Haralson, Harmanson, Harris, Haskell, Henley, Hill, Hilliard, Elias B. Holmes, George S. Houston, Hubbard, Hudson, Hunt, Inge, Irvin, Iverson, Jackson, Jameson, Jenkins, Andrew Johnson, James H. Johnson, R. W. Johnson, George W. Jones, John W. Jones, Kaufman, Kellogg, Kennon, Thomas B. King, La Sère, Sidney Lawrence, Leffler, Lincoln, Lord, Maclay, McClelland, McClernand, McDowell, McIlvaine, McKay, McLane, Mann, Marsh, Marvin, Mead, Miller, Morehead, Morris, Morse, Murphy, Nelson, Nes, Newall, Nicoll, Palfrey, Peaslee, Peck, Pendleton, Petrie, Pettit, Peyton, Phelps, Pollock, Preston, Richardson, Richey, Robinson, Rockhill, Julius Rockwell, John A. Rockwell, Rumsey, St. John, Sawyer, Shepperd, Sherrill, Silvester, Simpson, Sims, Smart, Caleb B. Smith, Robert Smith, Stanton, Starkweather, Andrew Stewart, Charles E. Stuart, Strohm, Strong, Tallmadge, Taylor, Thibodeaux, Thomas, James Thompson, Jacob Thompson, Richard W. Thompson, John B. Thompson, William Thompson, Thurston, Tompkins, Tuck, Turner, Venable, Warren, Wentworth, Wick, Wiley, Williams, Wilmot, and Woodward—174.

NAYS.—Messrs. Cranston and Root—2.

So the joint resolutions of the Senate were concurred in and finally passed.

IN SENATE.

MONDAY, April 10.

California Claims.

On motion of Mr. CASS, the Senate proceeded to consider the bill for ascertaining and paying certain claims in California.

The bill being under consideration, as in Committee of the Whole—

Mr. BENTON rose and addressed the Senate as follows:

Mr. President: These claims grow out of the conquest of California, and are supported by a mass of depositions taken by the Military Committee of the Senate, and printed by its order. These depositions constitute a document of eighty pages, and are full of material, valuable to the public history of the country, as well as to the private rights of the claimants. The Senate, on the application of the committee, have ordered twenty thousand extra copies of this document to be printed—a fact which sufficiently announces its public and national importance; for no extras, much less twenty thousand, are ever printed of merely private papers. It requires a public interest to be concerned before such a thing can be done; and that is eminently the case in the present instance. These depositions concern public history; and no one can understand the history of the United States, as connected with the conquest of California, without understanding them.

The conquest of California was commenced, and its first act finished, before the existence of the Mexican war was known in that country;

and this fact standing out incontestably among the events of the times, and presenting a presumptive case of aggression against the United States, very naturally attracted the attention of the committee, and commanded their most searching and thorough examination. The result is before the Senate, in the depositions referred to, and may be examined in detail by every Senator. For myself, I propose only to make a brief, connected story from their ample contents, to rebut in the first place an injurious presumption, and to exhibit afterwards in lucid order the summary of events which gave rise to these California claims, and show that they ought to be paid.

In the month of May, 1845, Mr. Fremont, then a brevet captain of engineers, set out on his third expedition of geographical and scientific exploration in the Great West. War had not then broken out between the United States and Mexico; but affairs were critical between them, and Mr. Fremont was determined, by no act of his, to increase the difficulties, or to give any cause of complaint to the Mexican Government. His line of observation would lead him to the Pacific Ocean through a Mexican province—through the desert parts first, and the settled parts afterwards, of the Alta California. Approaching the settled parts of the province at the commencement of winter, he left his equipment of sixty men and two hundred horses on the frontier, and proceeded alone to Monterey, to make known to the Governor the object of his coming, and his desire to pass the winter, for the refreshment of his men and horses, in the uninhabited parts of the valley of San Joaquin. The permission was granted, but soon revoked, under the pretext that Mr. Fremont had come into California, not to pursue science, but to excite the American settlers to revolt against the Mexican Government. Upon this pretext troops were raised, and marched to attack him. Having notice of their approach, he took a position on the mountain, hoisted the flag of the United States, and determined, with his sixty brave men, to defend themselves to the last extremity. Waiting there four days, and not being attacked, he quit his position, descended from the mountain, and set out for Oregon, that he might give no further pretext for complaint by remaining in California.

The United States consul at Monterey, Mr. O. Larkin, gave official information of these events to the Secretary of State, (Mr. Buchanan,) and from these I will read what is necessary to verify the statements which I have made:

"Captain J. C. Frémont, of the United States army, arrived at this United States consular-house in Monterey, on the 27th of January, 1846. Being very anxious to join his party of fifty men at the second place of rendezvous, without the settlement, they having missed the first place by mistake, he remained but two days, in which time, with myself, he visited the commandant-general, prefecto, alcalde, and Colonel Alvarado, informing them that he was surveying the nearest route from the United States to the Pacific Ocean. This information, and that his men were not United States soldiers, was, also, by myself, officially given to the prefecto. Having obtained funds and supplies from myself, he returned to his camp; it being well known in Monterey that he was to return when he collected his men. Some fifteen or twenty days after this, Captain Frémont, with his party, encamped at a vacant rancho belonging to Captain Fisher, (about ninety miles from here,) to recruit his men and animals. From there he proceeded towards Santa Cruz, making short journeys. On the 3d of March he encamped on the rancho of Mr. E. P. Hartwell, where he received letters from the general and prefecto, ordering him out of the country, and to obey the order without any pretext whatever, or immediate measures would be taken to compel him to do so. This not corresponding with assurances received at Monterey, it was not answered, *and he gave orders to hoist the United States flag the next morning, as the only protection his men were to look to.* From the 7th to the 10th of March, they fortified their camp with a breastwork of logs. Encamped on a high hill, which commanded a view of the surrounding country, they could see, with the use of spy-glasses, the general and his troops, numbering about two hundred men, at their camp, in the mission of St. John's, preparing their cannon. On the 9th instant I sent duplicate letters—one by an American, who lost his papers, and the other by a Californian—to Captain Frémont, informing him of the movements of the Californians. The Californian courier returned to the consulate in about nine or ten hours, bringing a letter from Captain Frémont, having travelled in that time sixty miles. He reported being well treated by Captain Frémont and his men; *and that two thousand of his countrymen would not be sufficient to compel him to leave the country, although his party was so small.*"—*Letter, 27th March*, 1846.

"Captain Frémont was well received in this place, and to the last day we heard of him, by the natives individually, who sold him provisions, and liked his presence. During his encampment thirty or forty miles from here, despatches were received by the commandant, General José Castro, a native of Monterey, from Mexico, ordering him to drive Captain Frémont out of this department; which order, with one hundred and seventy or two hundred men present, and over one hundred more daily expected, he pretended to execute. Captain Frémont left his camp a few hours after he received the undersigned's letter of the 9th of March, (not from fright of General Castro,) as he had been preparing the week before to travel. It is supposed he has gone to Santa Barbara, where an American was sent by the undersigned in February, with funds and provisions for his use.

"The undersigned has not supposed, during the whole affair, that General Castro wished to go after Captain Frémont, and was very confident that, with all California, he would not have attacked him, even had he been sure of destroying the whole party, as five times their number could have taken their place before the expected battle. Captain Frémont received verbal applications from English and Americans to join his party, and could have mustered as many men as the natives. He was careful not to do so. Although he discharged five or six of his men, he took no others in their place." —*Letter*, *April* 3, 1846.

This is the official history of the first difficulty with the Californian authorities, and presents the conduct of Mr. Fremont in the most unexceptionable point of view: halting his command upon the frontier; going alone to Monterey; asking and obtaining permission to winter in an uninhabited valley; only raising the flag of the United States when in danger of being attacked; leaving the country as soon as the danger was over; and refusing to receive any of the American settlers into his service, (even to supply the place of discharged men,) that there might be no room for misconstruction of his conduct, or for false accusations against the settlers.

The hoisting of the United States flag on this occasion is the only act which requires a word of explanation or of justification. It was complained of as an act of aggression: it was no such thing, but an act of self-protection and of self-defence. It was an appeal to their country, and a proper appeal for an American officer to make when in danger of being unjustly attacked. Mr. Fremont, in his reply to the consul's communication, in a brief note written in pencil, and in view of the enemy, gave the reason for the act which justified it, and exalted it into an act of devotion and heroism. It was in these words:

"I this moment received your letters, and without waiting to read them, acknowledge the receipt which the courier requires immediately. I am making myself as strong as possible, in the intention that if we are unjustly attacked, we will fight to extremity, and refuse quarter, trusting to our country to avenge our death. No one has reached our camp, and from the heights we are able to see troops (with the glass) mustering at St. John's, and preparing cannon. I thank you for your kindness and good wishes, and would write more at length as to my intentions, did I not fear that my letter would be intercepted. We have in nowise done wrong to the people or the authorities of the country, and if we are hemmed in and assaulted here, we will die, every man of us, under the flag of our country.

"Very truly yours, J. C. FREMONT.

"P. S. I am encamped on the top of the Sierra, at the head waters of a stream which strikes the road to Monterey, opposite the house of Don Joaquin Gomez.

"J. C. F.

"THOMAS O. LARKIN, Esq.,
"*Consul for the United States, Monterey.*"

Such was the reason for raising the flag. It was raised at the approach of danger: it was taken down when danger disappeared. It was well and nobly done, and worthy of our admiration—sixty of our countrymen, three thousand miles from home, in sight of the Pacific Ocean, appealing to the flag of their country, unfurling it on the mountain-top, and determined to die under it before they would submit to unjust aggression.

Turning his back on California, and looking to Oregon as the field of his further labors, Mr. Fremont determined to explore a new route to the Wah-lah-math settlements and the tide-water region of the Columbia, through the wild and elevated region of the Tlamath Lakes. A romantic interest attaches to this region from the grandeur of its features, its lofty mountains, and snow-clad peaks, and from the formidable character of its warlike inhabitants. In the first week of May he was at the north end of the great Tlamath Lake, and in Oregon, the lake being passed near its south end by the parallel of forty-two degrees. On the 8th day of that month a strange sight presented itself—two men riding up and penetrating a region which few ever approached without paying toll of life and blood. They proved to be two of Mr. Fremont's old *voyageurs*, and quickly told their story. They were part of a guard of six men conducting a United States officer who was on his trail with despatches from Washington, and whom they had left two days back while they came on to give notice of his approach, and to ask that assistance might be sent him. They themselves had only escaped the Indians by the swiftness of their horses. It was a case in which no time was to be lost or mistake to be made. Mr. Fremont determined to go himself; and taking ten picked men, four of them Delaware Indians, he took down the western shore of the lake on the morning of the 9th, (the direction the officer was to come,) and made a ride of sixty miles without a halt. But to meet men, and not to miss them, was the difficult point in that trackless region. It was not the case of a high-road where all travellers must meet in passing each other: at intervals, there were places—defiles or camping grounds—where both parties must pass; and, watching for these, he came to one in the afternoon, and decided in his own mind that, if the party was not killed, it must be there that night. He halted and encamped; and, as the sun was going down, had the inexpressible satisfaction to see the four men approaching. The officer proved to be Lieutenant Gillespie, of the United States marines, who had been despatched from Washington the November previous, to make his way by Vera Cruz, Mexico, and Mazatlan, to Monterey, in Upper California, deliver despatches to the United States consul there, and then find Mr. Fremont, wherever he should be. His despatches for Mr. Fremont were only a letter of introduction from the Secretary of State, (Mr. Buchanan,) and some letters and slips of papers from Senator Benton and his family, and some verbal communications from the Secretary of State. The depositions taken by the committee show the nature of these verbal communications, which were, in substance, that he should watch and counteract any foreign schemes in California, and conciliate the good will of the inhabitants towards the United States. Upon this intimation of the Government's wishes, Mr. Fremont turned back from Oregon, in the edge of which he then was, and returned to California.

This is the letter of introduction; and I think it right to show it, and to read it, lest any one should suppose it to be of more importance than it is:

"Washington, *November* 3, 1845.

"My dear Sir: The bearer hereof, Mr. Archibald H. Gillespie, is about to visit the north-west coast of America, on business, and has requested me to give him a letter of introduction to you. This I do with pleasure, because he is a gentleman of worth and respectability, and is worthy of your regard. I do not deem it probable that he will fall in with you, but, if he should, allow me to speak for him your friendly attention. He will be able to communicate to you information of the health of Mrs. Frémont and of Colonel Benton and his family.

"From your friend, very respectfully,

"JAMES BUCHANAN.

"J. C. Fremont, Esq., *Oregon.*"

This is the letter, and of itself it signified nothing; but it accredited the bearer, and gave the stamp of authority to what he communicated, and upon this Mr. Fremont acted; for it was not to be supposed that Lieutenant Gillespie had been sent so far, and through so many dangers, merely to deliver him that letter on the shores of the Tlamath Lake. Mr. Gillespie, in his testimony, has explained all the reasons of the mystery of this letter, and of the verbal communications, and shown that they were precautions to avoid detection in his perilous journey through Mexico in the fall of 1845.

This is not the time or the occasion, Mr. President, to show amidst what dangers and hardships scientific discovery was pursued by Mr. Fremont in these remote and unexplored regions. The time may come for telling these things. But the events of a week on the shores of the great Tlamath Lake, sketched with the brevity which the occasion requires, may give a glimpse of these hardships and dangers, and of the courage and fidelity with which he was supported by his men.

The night he met Mr. Gillespie presented one of those scenes to which he was so often exposed, and which nothing but the highest degree of vigilance and courage could prevent from being fatal. The camping-ground was on the western side of the lake, the horses picketed with long halters on its shore to feed on the grass, and the men (fourteen in number) sleeping by threes at different fires; for, though in May, the elevation of the place and the proximity of snow-clad mountains made the night intensely cold. His feelings joyfully excited by hearing from home, (the first word of intelligence he had received since leaving the United States, a year before,) Mr. Fremont sat up by a large fire, reading his letters and papers, and watching over the safety of his camp while the men slept. Towards midnight, he heard a movement among the horses, indicative of alarm and some danger. Horses, and especially mules, become extremely sensitive to danger under long travelling and camping in the wilderness, and manifest their alarm at the approach of any thing strange. Taking a six-barrelled pistol in his hand, and without waking the camp, he went down among them. The moon shone brightly—he could see nothing. Encouraged by his presence, the horses became quiet—poor dumb creatures, that could not tell what they had seen—and he returned to the camp, supposing it was only some beast of the forest, some wolf or bear prowling for food, that had disturbed them. He returned to the camp-fire; Lieutenant Gillespie woke up, talked with him awhile, and then laid down again. Finally, nature had her course with Mr. Fremont himself. Excited spirits gave way to exhausted strength. The day's ride and the night's excitement demanded the reparation of repose. He laid down to sleep, and without waking up a man to watch, relying upon the loneliness of the place and the long ride of the day as a security against the proximity of danger. It was the second time in twenty thousand miles of wilderness explorations that his camp had slept without a guard; the first was in his second expedition, and on an island in the Great Salt Lake, and when the surrounding waters of the lake itself constituted a guard. The whole camp was then asleep. A cry from Carson roused it. In his sleep he heard a groan—it was the groan of a man receiving the tomahawk in his brains. All sprung to their feet. The savages were in the camp; the hatchet and the winged arrow were at work. Basil Lajeunesse, a brave and faithful young Frenchman, the follower of Fremont in all his expeditions, was dead; and Iowa was dead; a brave Delaware Indian, one of those who had accompanied Mr. Fremont from Missouri was dying—it was his groan which awoke Carson. Another of the Delawares was a target for arrows, from which no rifle could save him—could only avenge him. The savages had waited till the moon was in the trees, casting long shadows over the camp: then approaching from the dark side, with their objects between themselves and the light, they used only the hatchet and the formidable bow, whose arrow went to its mark without a flash or a sound to show whence it came. All advantages were on the side of the savages; but the camp was saved, the wounded protected from massacre, and the dead from mutilation. In the morning, Lieutenant Gillespie recognized, in the person of one of the slain assailants, the Tlamath chief who, the morning before, had given him a salmon in token of friendship, and who had followed him all day to kill and rob his party at night—a design in which they would certainly have been successful had it not been for the promptitude and decision of Mr. Fremont's movement. Mr. Fremont himself would have been killed when he went to the horses, had it not been that they counted upon the destruction of the whole camp, and feared to alarm it by killing one before the general massacre.

It was on the 9th of May—a day immortalized by American arms at Resaca de la Palma—that this fierce and bloody work took place.

The morning of the 10th of May was one of gloom in the camp. The evening sun of the 9th had set upon it full of life and joy at a happy meeting: the same sun rose upon it in the morning stained with blood, ghastly with the dead and wounded, and imposing mournful duties on the survivors. The wounded were to be carried, the dead to be buried, and so buried as to be hid and secured from discovery and violation. They were carried ten miles, and every precaution taken to secure them from the wolf and the savage; for men, in these remote and solitary dangers, become brothers, and defend each other living and dead.

The return route lay along the shores of the lake, and during the day the distant canoes of the savages could be seen upon it, evidently watching the progress of the party, and meditating a night attack. All precautions, at the night encampment, were taken for security—horses and men enclosed in a breastwork of great trees, cut down for the purpose, and half the camp constantly on the watch. At leaving in the morning an ambuscade was planted—and two of the Tlamaths were killed by the men in ambush. At night the main camp, at the north end of the lake, was reached. It was strongly fortified, and could not be attacked; but its whole neighborhood was infested, and scouts and patrols were necessary to protect every moment. In one of these excursions the Californian horse, so noted for his spirit and docility, showed what he would do at the bid of his master. Carson's rifle had missed fire at ten feet distant. The Tlamath bow, arrow on the string, was bending to the pull. All the rifles in the party could not have saved him. A horse and his rider did it. Mr. Fremont touched his horse; he sprang upon the savage, and the hatchet of a Delaware completed the deliverance of Carson.

It was in the midst of such dangers as these that science was pursued by Mr. Fremont, that the telescope was carried to read the heavens, the barometer to measure the elevations of the earth, the thermometer to measure the temperature of the air, the pencil to sketch the grandeur of mountains and to paint the beauty of flowers, the pen to write down whatever was new or strange or useful in the works of nature; it was in the midst of such dangers as these, and in the wildest regions of the Farthest West, that Mr. Fremont was pursuing science, and shunning war, when the arrival of Lieutenant Gillespie turned him back into California, and engaged him in the operations which gave rise to the bill which now claims the attention of the Senate.

Mr. Fremont turned back to California, and arrived in the valley of the Sacramento at a most critical and exciting time. Three great operations, fatal to American interests, were then going on, and past remedy, if not arrested at once. These were the massacre of the Americans, and the destruction of their settlements in the valley of the Sacramento, the subjection of California to British protection, and the transfer of the public domain to British subjects, and all with a view to anticipate the events of a Mexican war, and to shelter California from the just reclamations of the United States.

The American settlers came to the camp of Mr. Fremont, in the valley of the Sacramento, laid all these dangers before him, and implored him to place himself at their head, and save them from destruction. General Castro was then in march upon them; the Indians were excited to burn their wheat-fields and to attack their families. Juntas were in session to transfer the country to Great Britain; the public domain was passing away in large grants to British subjects; a British fleet was expected on the coast; the British vice-consul, Forbes, and the emissary priest, Macnamara, ruling and conducting every thing, and all their plans so far advanced as to render the least delay fatal. It was then the beginning of June. War existed between the United States and Mexico, but that was not known in California. Mr. Fremont had left the two countries at peace when he set out upon his expedition, and was determined to do nothing to disturb their relations; he had even left California to avoid giving offence; and to return and take up arms in so short a time, was apparently to discredit his own previous conduct as well as to implicate his Government. He felt all the responsibilities of his position; but the actual approach of Castro and the immediate danger of the settlers left him no alternative. He determined to put himself at the head of the people, and to save the country. To repulse Castro was not sufficient. To overturn the Mexican Government in California, and to establish its INDEPENDENCE was the bold resolve, and the only one adequate to the emergency. That resolve was taken, and executed with a celerity that gave it a romantic success. The American settlers rushed to his camp; brought their arms, horses, and ammunition; were formed into a battalion, and obeyed with zeal and alacrity the orders they received. In thirty days all the northern part of California was freed from Mexican authority; independence proclaimed; the flag of independence (the bear flag) adopted; Castro flying to the south; the American settlers saved from destruction; and the British party in California counteracted and broken up in all their schemes.

The effects of this decisive and rapid movement can only be conceived from a careful perusal of the depositions. From them it will be seen that the deep-laid plans, conducted by the British vice-consul, Forbes, and the emissary priest, Macnamara, were going on, to shelter California under the British crown, and to vest its domain in British subjects; that every thing was verging to a crisis, and a British fleet expected upon the coast, when this rapid and successful movement broke up all these designs. And when Admiral Seymour arrived on the 16th of July, instead of an invitation from the California junta to take the country under British protection, and an invitation from the grantees of principalities to take British interests under his protection, he found the American flag flying over Monterey, Fremont and his riflemen encamped over the town, the British party extinct, and the Americans triumphant. The effect which the appearance of this daring body of Western riflemen produced upon the minds both of the British and American naval officers, is well stated by Lieutenant Minor in his deposition, and, in justice to those men as well as to the truth of history, deserves to be read here. He says:

"The undersigned was on duty on shore when Captain Frémont arrived with his force at Monterey from the north. The undersigned believes that the appearance of this body of men, and the well-known character of its commander, not only made a strong impression upon the British admiral and officers, but an equally impressive and more happy one upon those of the American navy then in Monterey. For himself, the undersigned can say, that, after he had seen Captain Frémont's command, all his doubts regarding the conquest of California were removed."

This is the testimony of a disinterested witness; one who himself, in the subsequent operations in California, rendered good service on land, there being no chance for him on the water. It shows that the timely and successful movement of the California battalion, and its sudden appearance at Monterey, simultaneously with the arrival of the American and British fleets, was the turning point in the fate of California. It showed the country was in arms to resist instead of asking British protection; and it encouraged the navy to believe that the whole country could be conquered: for, without a land force, the naval forces could only have operated along the coast.

And here a great fact presents itself—one which these depositions have consecrated to history, and which belongs to the chapter of events which determine the fate of countries. It is the fact that Fremont's operations determined the action of Commodore Sloat, and induced him to take possession of Monterey, contrary to his intention when he anchored before that town; and thereby anticipated Admiral Seymour, frustrated his designs, whatever they were, and induced him to leave Monterey as suddenly and as mysteriously as he had arrived. The depositions establish this fact, and some reference to their contents will prove what I say; and, first, of the effect of these operations in deciding the action of Commodore Sloat. It is in proof that he entered the Bay of Monterey as a friend, on the 2d of July, offering to salute the town, which the authorities declined, on the ground that they had no powder to return it, but probably because the British admiral was expected. On the 5th of July, the operations of Fremont were heard of, and on the 7th, Commodore Sloat took the town. The testimony of the naval officers (Messrs. Minor and Wilson) and the Commodore's own correspondence (pages 70 and 73), show circumstantially that his action was induced by hearing of these operations; and the testimony of Messrs. Fremont and Gillespie pointedly prove it. Mr. Fremont says:

"I came down to Monterey with my command, upon the request of Commodore Sloat, to co-operate with him; and immediately on my arrival waited upon him, in company with Lieutenant Gillespie, on board the frigate Savannah. Commodore Sloat appeared uneasy at the great responsibility he had assumed. He informed me that he had applied to Lieutenat Gillespie, whom he knew to be an agent of the Government, for his authority, but that he had declined to give it. He then inquired to know under what instructions I had acted in taking up arms against the Mexican authorities. I informed him that I had acted solely on my own responsibility, and without any authority from the Government to justify hostilities. Commodore Sloat appeared greatly disturbed with this information, and gave me distinctly to understand, that in raising the flag at Monterey he had acted upon the faith of our operations in the north. Commodore Sloat soon relinquished the command to Commodore Stockton, who determined to prosecute hostilities to the complete conquest of California."

Captain Gillespie says:

"In reply to the above question of the honorable committee, I beg leave to state, that an interview between Commodore Sloat, Captain Frémont, and myself, held on board of the United States frigate, Savannah, lying in the harbor of Monterey, in July, 1846, Commodore Sloat manifested a feeling of dissatisfaction that Captain Frémont and myself had not reported ourselves and the force under our command to him, and said, addressing both, as near as I can recollect: 'I do not know by what authority you are acting. I can do nothing. Mr. Gillespie has told me nothing; he came to Mazatlan, and I sent him to Monterey; but I know nothing. I want to know by what authority you are acting.' Captain Fremont replied, 'he had acted upon his own authority, and not from orders of the Government.' Commodore Sloat then expressed much surprise and distress, and, and said, 'I have acted upon the faith of your operations in the north.'"

Coincident with these statements is the letter of Commodore Sloat, of the 6th of July, to Commander Montgomery, of the Portsmouth, then in the Bay of St. Francisco, who had sent down a launch with the news of Fremont's successes. The letter is dated from the flag-ship Savannah, Bay of Monterey, July 6, 1847:

"Since I wrote you last evening I have determined to hoist the flag of the United States at this place to-morrow, as I would prefer being sacrificed for doing too much than too little. * * If you consider that you have sufficient force, or if Fremont will join you, you will hoist the flag of the United States at Yarba Buena, or any other proper place, and take possession, in the name of the United States, of the fort, and that portion of the country."

This settles the great fact that Mr. Fremont's operations determined the action of Commodore Sloat—induced him to change his mind after he had been four days at Monterey—encouraged him to take the town, and to send out orders to hoist the United States flag at other places. On the 16th, Admiral Seymour, in the Collingwood, of 80 guns, arrived; the frigate Juno was previously on the coast: the largest squadron that the British Government had ever had in the Pacific Ocean was then there; and all the evidence combines to show that the object of this squadron was to watch Commodore Sloat, to follow him wherever he went, to anticipate him in getting to Monterey, and to be in readiness to take California under the British flag, and to do what the protection of British interests might require him to do. This is well and fully shown by the testimony. Lieutenant Minor says:

"The undersigned, being in command of the southern district of California, during the latter part of 1846, was informed by Pedro C. Carrillo, (and he believes the information thus obtained is founded on facts,) that he, the said Carrillo, was a member of a junta that assembled at Santa Barbará, in June, 1846, for the purpose of declaring the independence of California, and of asking the protection of the United States or Great Britain; that the junta was represented by all of the inhabited portions of California; that a majority of the same were for claiming the protection of England; that their resolves would probably have been executed, had it not been for the war and their fears of an armed force, then on the north side of the bay of San Francisco, under the command of Captain Frémont. The undersigned has understood from other sources entitled to confidence, that a majority of the people of California desired the protection of England; the opinion he thus formed was strengthened by the fact that an English frigate (the Juno) had, about the time the junta met, landed an English subject named Macnamara, at Santa Barbara, of whom it was said that he had obtained a grant from the Mexican Government of a large and fertile portion of California, embracing the whole valley of the San Joaquin, from its source to its mouth—a valley, as the undersigned believes, comprising one-third of the richest portion of California. The undersigned believes that the British squadron in the Pacific, commanded by Rear Admiral Sir George T. Seymour, composed then of a larger force than they ever had upon that ocean, were employed in closely watching the movements of the American commodore. Being aware of this fact, Commodore Sloat, when he heard of the first battle on the Rio Grande, got under way in the frigate Savannah, then anchored off Mazatlan, for the ostensible purpose of proceeding to California; an English vessel of war weighed soon after the Savannah, and stood in the direction of San Blas, where it was known the admiral was. After cruising in the Gulf two days, the Commodore returned to his anchorage off Mazatlan, when another English ship got under way, and stood in the direction of San Blas. The undersigned believes that this manœuvre of Commodore Sloat was intended for the deception of the English admiral. On the 8th of June, 1846, the Savannah again made sail, and, after a passage of twenty-three days, during which a press of canvas was carried, she arrived at the port of Monterey, in Upper California. The Collingwood, of eighty guns, the flag-ship of Admiral Seymour, entered the harbor on the 15th July, and the undersigned believes that the Admiral was disappointed when he saw the American flag flying on shore."

Midshipman Wilson says:

"On the sixteenth of the same month (July) Admiral Seymour, who had been following us for several months previous, arrived and anchored in his flag-ship, the Collingwood, (80.)

"Upon his vessel appearing in sight, Commodore Sloat sent orders, I understood, to the commanders of the different vessels comprising our squadron, to be in readiness, in case the Admiral should be entering with hostile intentions, or an order to that effect, leaving the impression on the minds of his officers, that Admiral Seymour must have intended to have prevented our squadron from taking possession of California. Although such had been our impression previously, and, but for the timely movements of Colonel Frémont and his party in the north, thereby influencing the Commodore in his movements, such I fear would have been the result."

This testimony, as to the presumed designs of the British admiral, is fully corroborated by all that was going on in California itself, while Admiral Seymour was watching and following Commodore Sloat on the coast of California. During all that time *júntas* were held, under the management of the British vice-consul, Forbes, to place the country under British protection; the public domain was passing away to British subjects; the arrival of a British fleet in the course of the summer to take possession of California was confidently foretold; and, as a preliminary to this measure, the expulsion and destruction of the Americans was resolved upon, the *banda* or proclamation for their expulsion actually issued, and troops raised and Indians excited for their destruction. The expected arrival of the British fleet connected itself with all these operations; and all these would have been successful had it not been for the success of Mr. Fremont and the people, and so says all the testimony. There is too much of it to read; and, besides, a part of this labor has been anticipated, and well performed, in the luminous and statesmanlike observations of the Senator from New York, (Mr. Dix,) in what he presented to the Senate a few days ago in favor of this bill, and in his expositions of British designs upon this continent. He read some passages from the depositions which show these designs in California. I will now read more for the same purpose, and especially to show that a British interest was to be created, to claim his protection as soon as the admiral arrived, and the Americans to be expelled or destroyed to prevent their opposition:

Captain Gillespie's deposition.—Extract.

"Having joined Lieutenant-Colonel Frémont upon the 9th of May, 1846, upon the northern end of the Tlamath lake, I returned with him to the valley of the Sacramento, and arrived at the settlement upon the 24th of the same month. We could obtain no news from below; so soon, however, as it became known to the settlers that Captain Frémont had returned, they came to the camp, bringing us the information that the Indians of the valley were leaving their ranchos or wigwams and flying to the mountains. In some places, they had shown a very hostile feeling, and certainly had been aroused by some foreign emissary. Remaining at Lawson's two days, we proceeded down the valley, and on arriving at Neal and Dutton's, upon Deer creek, the reports we had received were confirmed, the Indians in that section having taken to the mountains, and had killed an Indian boy in the employ of Mr. Dutton because he had refused to follow them. On the day the camp remained at this place, the settlers, old and young, men and women, came to Captain Frémont, begging him to take part against the Indians, and to give them protection.

"About June 30th, I learned that the junta which was to have assembled at Santa Barbara upon the 15th of June, and which had been planned and arranged by and through the agency of Mr. Forbes, the British vice-consul, and an Irish Catholic priest by the name of Macnamara, had been prevented from assembling in consequence of the rising of the settlers. This junta was proposed for the purpose of asking the protection of England, and of giving an immense tract of land in the valley of the San Joaquin for the settlement of ten thousand Irishmen, to be brought to California under the direction of Macnamara. All this intrigue of British agents was broken up by the timely and prompt operations of the settlers, under the direction of Captain Frémont."

Captain Hensley's deposition.—Extract.

"I am a resident in California, where I have resided since the autumn of 1843. In the month of May, 1846, I went to San Francisco, where I met with General Vallejo, one of the most prominent and influential men in Upper California. I understood from him that he had recently attended a convention, composed of General Castro, himself, and five others, delegates from the different districts in California, at which the proposition had been made and debated to separate from Mexico, and establish a government in California, under the protection of some foreign power, believed by us to be England; but, as the General positively stated, the majority was not in favor of placing the country under the protection of the United States, though he himself was. General Vallejo was of course guarded in conversing on so dangerous a subject as this was at that time; but the above is the substance of his remarks, as understood by myself and others who heard them.

"About this time I heard that Captain Frémont had returned from the northward, and was then in the upper part of the Sacramento valley. I immediately repaired to his camp, where I informed him of all that I had learned respecting the condition of the country, and the designs of the leading men among the Californians, giving it as my opinion that the American residents would have to leave the country or fight for their homes; at the same time saying I was sure we would not leave the country.

"Captain Frémont resolved to join the Americans for their safety, and to overthrow the Mexican forces in that province.

"The 4th of July was duly celebrated, and on the 5th we organized the 'California battalion,' adopting the 'grizzly bear' as our emblem, requesting Captain Frémont to take command of the battalion, and of all the forces and resources of the country, which command he accepted. As soon as it was known that Captain Frémont had accepted the command, the Californian population seemed to become well pleased with the change in affairs, and brought in their property and means of warfare, which they placed at Frémont's disposal. He restored to them and to the American settlers all the horses which had been previously captured or pressed into the service by the Americans, retaining only a number sufficient for the actual wants of the service. He then set out with the battalion in pursuit of Castro, by way of the Sacramento, sending me with a small party to communicate with Dr. Marsh. When I arrived at Marsh's, I learned that war had been declared between the United States and Mexico, and that Commodore Sloat had arrived at Monterey and raised the American flag. Returning with this intelligence, I found that Captain Frémont had already learned it, and was on his way to Monterey. I followed and joined him at the mission of San Juan, near Monterey."

Captain Chile's statement.—Extract.

"I know that General Vallejo left Sonoma for the purpose of attending a general council at Monterey, about the time the Irish priest, Macnamara, arrived in California, and a short time before the revolution in that country; and I recollect hearing that the English consul, Mr. Forbes, accompanied him to the Puebla de los Angeles, for the purpose of seeing the Governor in relation to obtaining a grant of land, upon which it was said a colony of British subjects was to be established.

"The revolution, to the best of my knowledge, put an entire stop to such grants and sales."

Captain Owen's deposition.—Extract.

"The settlers made many applications for help to Captain Frémont, on the ground that they were American citizens. We went down and camped at the Buttes, about sixty miles above Suter's. There was a good deal of correspondence between the settlers and our camp, and as the danger seemed near at hand, and there was no other way to get out of it, it was finally agreed to join the settlers and fight the Californians. In this way the revolution began. The settlers were driven to it in self-defence. But I do not think that it would have taken place, or that they could have been united together without the aid and protection of Captain Frémont. They had not confidence enough in their own strength to undertake the war without support. Captain Frémont's party was strong and well armed, and went together like one man. The strength of this party and the name of Captain Frémont as a United States officer, gave confidence, and kept the people together both during the revolution and the war afterwards."

Lieutenant Loker's deposition.—Extract.

"About the time Castro was raising men to drive Colonel Frémont out of the country, I was staying at Suter's Fort, in the Sacramento valley; there was also a considerable number of American settlers around and near the fort, and Castro's movements created a good deal of excitement, so much so that many of them wanted to go to Frémont's assistance immediately, and would have gone had not the Colonel and his party arrived on the American fork. After he had left for the Tlamath lake there was a good deal of talk about England taking possession of the country, and many foreigners of the highest standing in the country asserted that they knew that England had a mortgage on it; and that a British man-of-war was on the north-west coast, and would be down in the course of the summer to take possession of California. Soon after Colonel Frémont left, Major Gillespie arrived, started after, and brought him back; then commenced the revolution, which had he not countenanced and aided, I know not what would have been the consequences to the American settlers, (women and children included;) for, just before his return, there was a meeting of the principal men of the country at Monterey; they there thought it advisable to order all foreigners to leave the country, and published a *banda* to that effect, ordering all foreigners to leave the country by a certain day, or force would be used to compel them to leave; women and children were included in the banishment; and Colonel Frémont returning in the country about that time, and finding the men in the valley much excited, and the alarm of the women, could not have acted otherwise than he did."

Dr. Baldwin's deposition.—Extract.

"I again entered Mexico (city) on the 14th of September, 1847, and remained there until the 1st of November; during that time I made the acquaintance of the priest Macnamara, and, from sources entitled to credit, I was informed that he had, under the auspices of the British legation, projected a plan to colonize California with emigrants from Ireland. His project had met the approbation of the Mexican Government, and he went to California to perfect his plans. In the mean time it was ascertained that the ulterior views of Macnamara were to promote the interest of the British Government, and not the Mexican Government. A fierce opposition was contemplated by the republican members of Congress when he should return with his matured plans from California; this resistance became unnecessary in consequence of the conquest of California by the arms of the United States. Macnamara lived in the family of either the British consul or chargé d'affaires in Mexico."

This is a part—a small part only—of the depositions which establish the great points which I have mentioned, that there was a plan in progress at the time of Mr. Fremont's return from the Tlamath Lake, to place California under British protection—to transfer the public domain to British subjects, and to expel or destroy all the American settlers; and that this plan was frustrated by the heroic determination of Mr. Fremont to put himself at the head of the people, and to overturn the Mexican Government in California. But it is not all the proof which shows the British desire to possess California, and especially the magnificent Bay of San Francisco. The desire is no new passion with that power. From the time of the great navigator, Captain Cook, her eyes have been fixed on the north-west coast of America. Three times, within half a century, have British national vessels surveyed that coast, and especially the Bay of San Francisco. Vancouver, Beechey, and Belcher, have each surveyed it, and the bay itself, with all the particularity of the survey of a British harbor. Here is a chart of this bay made by Beechey in 1828, published at the Royal Hydrographic Bureau, exhibiting the most commodious and capacious harbor upon the face of the earth, large enough to hold all the navies of the world, an easy and defensible entrance from the sea, opening out forty miles to the right and left, sheltered from every wind, receiving two handsome rivers, draining a basin of five hundred miles of fertile valleys and picturesque mountains, a healthy and delightful climate, and backed at the distance of one hundred and twenty miles by the lofty ridge of the *Sierra Nevada*, crowned with eternal snow. Upon this bay Great Britain has had her eye fixed for half a century; and, in June, 1846, at the moment of Mr. Fremont's return from the Tlamath Lake, all her long-deferred and cherished inclinations seemed to be on the point of realization. The revolt of the settlers frustrated this ripened hope, in the apparent moment of fruition, and placed the coveted prize under the flag of the United States.

This finishes the first act of the conquest of California. It finishes the revolutionary movement in favor of independence, and brings Mr. Fremont and his victorious battalion to Monterey—their flag of independence exchanged for that of the United States—themselves uniting with the naval forces, and turning over all the fruits of their successful enterprise to the Government of the United States.

The committee, appreciating at its full value all the importance of this revolutionary movement, both as it concerns nations and individuals, and the truth of history, have instituted into it a most searching examination; and the result is what I have stated, and what the document of evidence proves. And their opinion was unanimous, that although this movement was made without the authority or knowledge of the Government, and without the knowledge that war existed at the time between the United States and Mexico, yet such being the fact, and the United States having received all the benefits of the movement, they are bound in honor and in conscience to pay all its expenses.

Commodore Sloat returned to the United States; Commodore Stockton succeeded to the command; and here commenced his connection with the conquest of California. He proposed to complete the conquest by pursuing Castro to the south, and taking the "*City of the Angels.*" But the aid of a land force was indispensable to this enterprise; and here the American settlers again showed their courage and patriotism. Commodore Stockton applied to Fremont and Gillespie to join with their battalion—to serve under him, and obey his orders. They agreed to do so, both men and officers, and this was fully sworn by Commodore Stockton before the late court-martial. On receiving the command from Commodore Sloat, he says:

"I immediately sent to Major Frémont to inform him of what had occurred, and to let him know that if he and Lieutenant Gillespie, with the volunteers who were with them, would volunteer to serve under my command, so long as I might be in possession of California and desired their services, I would form a battalion by appointing him (Captain Frémont) major, and Lieutenant Gillespie captain, and all the other necessary officers. This was all done in the course of the day and the next morning, when they were ordered to embark on board the United States ship Cyane, to be landed at San Diego. These men were not of the kind of *personnel* which sometimes compose regular armies; they were principally free American citizens who had settled in California; they were men of respectability, of influence, and of property; they were no ordinary men, because, when told that I had offered them as pay ten dollars a month, they said (as I was told) that they would not accept that pay; that it would not pay their expenses; but that they would volunteer to serve under my command without (fixed) compensation."

Thus the men of the battalion passed into the service of the United States without a stipulation for fixed compensation, but with the full expectation that justice would be done them. Mr. Fremont, actuated wholly by public and patriotic considerations, took command under Commodore Stockton. His influence carried along with him the whole of the battalion. He gave up his independent position; became subordinate to Commodore Stockton; carried with him the men of the country, and insured the complete conquest of the country; for, without land forces, the conquest could not have been accomplished.

This was the last of July. Leaving their horses on shore, the men immediately went on board the Cyane, sailed down the coast five hundred miles to San Diego, and marched for Los Angeles, distant one hundred and fifty miles. This city (the capital of the Californias) was taken early in August; and with its capture the conquest of California was complete. But the conquest was to be preserved. The orders to the naval officers were to conquer, hold, and govern California; and to do that, the service of land forces was further wanted. The seamen and marines were wanted on board the vessels; no troops of the United States were there. The further services of Fremont's battalion became indispensable. They demanded twenty-five dollars a month, (which is very near the amount allowed by law to mounted men,) and only remained in service upon condition of receiving it. So testifies Captain Hensley, an officer of the battalion, and a gentleman of character and intelligence, who was examined before the committee. He says:

"I was present when the California battalion was mustered into the service of the United States, and the men then positively refused to serve for eleven dollars per month. They remained in the service without any rate of pay being specified, until, in August, 1846, at the City of Angels, Colonel Frémont ordered me to inquire of my company at what rate of pay they would consent to remain in the service. They unanimously demanded twenty-five dollars per month, and refused to remain any longer in service unless that amount was promised them. I considered the rate of pay demanded by the men as reasonable for that country, and under all the circumstances."

Upon these terms they remained in service to garrison the country.

But a new and more arduous service was required from the California battalion. In the fall of 1846, an insurrection broke out in Southern California, and the battalion was called upon to join in its suppression. Most of them had returned to the north. Another campaign to the south was required, and many recruits necessary to complete its strength. A body of emigrants had just arrived from the United States, and stopped in the valley of the Sacramento. Leaving their families slightly provided with shelter and subsistence, above two hundred of them joined Mr. Fremont for this new expedition of near seven hundred miles distance. At first it was attempted from the San Francisco Bay by sea. Baffled in that attempt, after twenty days' contest with adverse winds, a return to Monterey, and an overland march to Los Angeles, became unavoidable. It was the beginning of winter—the cold rains already set in—a country of defiles and mountains, and in a state of insurrection, to be traversed—and every thing to be procured, and without money. In a few weeks all was ready—cannon mounted, beef-cattle procured, six hundred horses collected. It was a march of extraordinary hardship, as well as requiring military skill. Every day many horses perished of hunger and cold, and on Christmas day above a hundred died on the Santa Barbara Mountain in a storm of wind and rain black with the tempest from the Pacific Ocean. The march required skill; but it was with something more than a soldier's eye that Mr. Fremont felt it to be his duty to survey the field before him. He knew that the Californians against whom he was going were themselves revolutionists—successful insurgents against Mexican authority—and conscious that they must come either under the American or British flag. Conciliation was his policy. To gain over these people by mildness and justice, instead of crushing them by arms, became his object; and to the attainment of this object all his military movements became subordinate and subservient.

San Luis Obispo, a focus of insurrection, the seat of a commandant, and distant one hundred and fifty miles, was to be taken and passed. He conceived the design of a secret march—a surprise—a capture without bloodshed—and the seizure of the insurgent chiefs: and he accomplished that design. The secret march was made—the town surprised—and the arrests effected—and effected with the quiet and order of so many civil arrests in one of our peaceful cities. Don Jesus Pico, and some thirty others, were taken. Then an event occurred which gave a decisive turn to the character of the war, and insured its peaceful and happy conclusion. Don Jesus Pico was particularly obnoxious to the Americans. He had broken his parole—been active in the insurrection—and had sent out expeditions in which Captain Borrows and some brave men had been killed. He was placed before a court-martial, condemned, and ordered to be shot. Mr. Fremont pardoned him, and in that act consummated his policy of conciliation, prevented further resistance to his march, and prepared the way for the capitulation of Couenga. Don Jesus was connected with all the principal families by blood and by marriage. He was cousin to Don Andres Pico, a principal chief of the insurrection at Los Angeles. He attached himself to Mr. Fremont, took the side of peace and conciliation, went with him in his march, and contributed to quiet the towns through which they had to pass. The people remained in their houses, offered no resistance, and received no harm. A corps of observation, which hung upon his march, yielded the maritime pass of the *Punto Gordo* without resistance, and galloped about without giving or receiving any serious attack. The main body of the insurgents at Los Angeles, hearing of his approach, and that he had passed Santa Barbara, marched out to meet him; then, changing their minds, they turned back to the south, and fought the actions of the 8th and 9th of January with Commodore Stockton. Repulsed, but not routed, (for Commodore Stockton's command was all on foot, and the insurgents all mounted,) they turned again to meet Mr. Fremont, and took post in the pass of San Fernando. They undertook to defend the pass, which being turned by the riflemen, they fell back into the plain of Couenga, famous as a battle-field in the strifes of California. Mr. Fremont sent them a message. They agreed to meet him. He went out alone to see them, attended only by Don Jesus Pico, (who had attached himself to him for life and for death since his pardon,) and had an interview with Don Andres Pico and other chiefs. They agreed to capitulate to him, and to nobody but him, declaring that they would take to the mountains "*and die like wild beasts*" before they would submit to any one but him. The terms were agreed upon, and they were conformable to the law of nations, and to the law of common sense and justice. The insurgents gave up their cannon and public arms, retired to their homes, promised submission to the American authority, and aid in preserving order, and in return were to receive protection, and not to be required to take the oath of allegiance to the United States until a definitive treaty of peace with Mexico should fix their political condition. These terms, agreed upon in person, were reduced to form by commissioners appointed on each side, approved by the respective commanders-in-chief, (Commodore Stockton and Don Andres Pico,) and the war not only terminated and peace established, but the fruits of peace acquired and enjoyed.

This was the conclusion of the war, and was so related by the United States consul at Monterey, (Mr. O. Larkin,) who was a prisoner in the hands of the insurgents at the time of Mr. Fremont's approach to Los Angeles. He says:

"On the 3d or 4th of January, news reached the Puebla that Colonel Frémont was south of Santa Barbara, marching to meet the Californian forces. The latter had mustered all they could, to the number of 400 to 500, and encamped two or three days at the mission of San Fernando, awaiting the arrival of the riflemen, and appeared very anxious to have a fight. Information now reached General Flores that Commodore Stockton, with 600 men from San Diego, would soon be in his vicinity. He immediately ordered all the Mexicans and Californians to leave San Fernando, and march to the opposite side of the Puebla to meet the marine forces. * * * * * * *

"On the 13th of January, the capitulation of Couenga was signed. * * * *

"The war in California is now over, as far as the Californians are concerned, *and if their manners and customs are tolerated, and common protection afforded them, they will gradually fall into the new order of affairs.* They have had, in different parts, nine hundred men under arms, every man with good horses and a lance, most of them with swords, pistols, rifles, or carbines, every one of them countrymen, to aid them either by choice or force; a perfect knowledge of every hill and valley; yet they did not succeed, and have found their losses in horses and waste of time so great, as to prefer peace for the future, under a guarantee of good treatment."

The capitulation of Couenga was the happy conclusion of the war, and is so testified by many witnesses. Midshipman Wilson, a captain in the California battalion, says:

"We had frequent skirmishes with parties of the enemy until the *capitulation of Couenga*, which acted almost magically in restoring peace and tranquillity to the country; and but for that capitulation, so beneficial in its results, my impression is that the Californians would have carried on a system of guerilla warfare, by which many lives and much property would have been sacrificed."

Colonel Russell, who was chief staff officer in the battalion, and one of the commissioners for making the capitulation, says:

"At the capitulation of Don Andres Pico to Colonel Frémont, he and other Californians boldly declared their determination never to submit to any other officer than him, and on the terms granted in the capitulation of Couenga, of which I was one of the negotiators.

"I hesitate not to give it as my decided opinion that the *capitulation of Couenga* on the 13th of January, 1847, was the main cause of saving the country from a bloody, vexatious, predatory warfare, that would necessarily have been protracted for a considerable length of time.

"I remained at Los Angeles over two months after the capitulation, and became well acquainted, and conversed much with the families in that part of the country, and from all I could learn, the good results of that treaty in preventing a guerilla warfare was fully confirmed."

This was the conclusion of the war, and the restoration of peace and its fruits. The capitulation of Couenga was the pacification and the reconciliation of California. It was the last act in the drama of the conquest, and, like the first movement in the valley of the Sacramento, was done upon the responsibility of Mr. Fremont alone. From the day it was signed peace and good-will prevailed in the country. Travelling and living became as secure as in any part of the United States. Mr. Fremont could have gone back alone, without arms or guards, upon the line of his march from Los Angeles to Monterey, without interruption from the people, except in the manifestations of their gratitude and affection. He did go back upon it in that extraordinary ride with Don Jesus Pico, and was greeted everywhere by the hospitalities of the people. He afterwards lived two months as governor in the capital of California, like any governor would live in the capital of one of our States, without guards or sentries, or any semblance of military protection, the battalion being sent off ten miles to keep it out of the town.

And thus the same men who began the war finished it. The California battalion, formed out of the American settlers on the Sacramento and the men of the topographical party, (reinforced afterwards by later emigrants from the United States,) finished on the plains of Couenga the movement which had commenced at Sonoma, and in the same spirit of justice, moderation, and patriotism. In conjunction with the sailors and marines, they had twice conquered California before the United States troops arrived in the country. They did it without aid from the United States—without quartermasters, commissaries, and paymasters to carry, feed, and pay them. The fruits of all their labors have been received by the United States, and the bill rendered is only seven hundred thousand dollars—a fraction only of the amount paid to those who arrived after the work was done. It should have been provided for in one of the public bills. It is an appropriation, and of a public nature, and of the most sacred nature. It should at least have had a place in that "*deficiency*" bill of fourteen millions which lately passed Congress; for what can be more deficient than nonpayment, for almost two years, for such extraordinary services? Even if this bill is passed at once, and with the least possible delay from legislative forms, it will still be almost half a year before the claimants can begin to touch their pay.

The bill is carefully drawn, both with a view to public and to private justice. It is intended to settle up and pay up at once all just claims, and to close the door forever upon all false ones. A commission acquainted with the subject, familiar with every transaction, is to go to California, visit every district in which claims originated, call all before them, allow the good, reject the bad, and bar all that are not presented to them. In this way, and in this alone, can justice be done to all parties, just claimants saved from the depredations of agents and speculators, the United States saved from paying false accounts, and California prevented from becoming a mine for the production of false claims for half a century to come. The great and main facts, that services have been rendered, that the United States have received the benefit of these services, and that they have not been paid for, are established by the depositions; the mode of settlement, and the detail of payment, is directed by the bill.

Tuesday, April 11.

California Claims.

On motion of Mr. Cass, the Senate resumed the consideration of the bill for ascertaining and paying certain claims in California.

Mr. Dayton then occupied the floor, premising that he did not propose to discuss the merits of the bill, but to go at large into the subject of the war in Mexico, with which it was connected. He apologized for taking this course now, regretting that circumstances connected with his personal concerns had prevented him from addressing the Senate earlier in the session. He believed we had now reached a point at which we may exercise the right of self-judgment. We had made an armistice, and there is in existence a paper called, or miscalled, a treaty, and we may now pause and inquire what we are likely to gain by this war. Indemnity for the past probably means the hundred millions we have paid for the expenses of the war; and security for the future must imply the twenty millions we are to pay for territory.

His remarks now were rendered necessary, in consequence of the course which had been taken by the Senator from Massachusetts, (now absent from his seat,) who had stated to the country his course on the subject of the treaty, and the reasons on which he founded it. That Senator, in throwing off all responsibility from himself, had thrown a heavier responsibility on other Senators who had taken a different course. He therefore felt himself bound to say something, at this time, in defence of his own course.

He then replied to some of the points taken by the Senator from Massachusetts, for the purpose of explaining his own course in voting for the treaty, as he avowed he had done. He designated the treaty as bad enough, but it remained for those who had insisted on the unconstitutionality of the war, and who had yet voted against the treaty, to make the propriety of their course clear to the world. He felt, that during the whole of the war, we had been obliged to act on alternatives; and in this position he felt himself when called to vote on the treaty. He did not desire territory, but he was sure, that under this Administration, there was no hope of obtaining a peace without an accession of territory. The Senator from Massachusetts was willing to put the question to the people as to the accession of territory; but this was not merely putting it off until the next spring, but was, after all, but an uncertain test. The cry of "new territory" he regarded as likely to produce a powerful effect at the next fall elections; and he regretted that the Senator from Massachusetts had urged on the Whig party to make the question of "no territory" the issue at those elections. From this course he (Mr. D.) would appeal to the whole Whig party. He preferred peace at this moment, even with territory, to a remote peace even without territory. If the question of no territory was to be made the test, there would be an end of the Whig party before the end of the year. It would find an early grave, and all its conservative glory would be buried with it. Its enemies might then inscribe on its tomb, "*Hic jacet;*" and they could truly add—

> It never said a foolish thing,
> And never did a wise one.

On the description given by the Senator from Massachusetts of the population of California he made some observations, for the purpose of showing by inference, that if it was a correct delineation, there was no reason to have any apprehensions on the subject of members from that quarter being admitted to seats in the two Houses of Congress.

The fact that the line of thirty-two, established by the treaty, excludes all territory which is favorable for the employment of slaves, was to him a very strong inducement to vote in favor of it. If a slave should follow his master from one of our Southern States into California, he could not carry with him any part of the municipal law by which he had been governed in the State which he had quitted; and, by the laws of California, he would stand forth a man, unfettered, and subjected to none of the slave regulations. He disclaimed any alliance with abolitionists, and enlarged a little on the misunderstanding between the South and the North on the exciting topic of slavery.

In his conclusion, he expressed a doubt as to what may be the effect of the revolution of France on the feelings of the Mexicans. But he warned every one not to be deceived into the belief that the revolution had reached its termination, or had even advanced sufficiently to disclose what would be its result. A king may be stricken down, but a wealthy, elevated, proud population, would not be likely to yield and abandon all their wealth and influence without a struggle. He concluded with expressing his hope, that whatever convulsions might shake surrounding nations, the independence, happiness, and prosperity of our own Republic would remain unshaken and progressive.

WEDNESDAY, April 12.

California Claims.

The Senate resumed the consideration of the bill for ascertaining and paying certain claims in California.

The bill being under consideration as in Committee of the Whole—

Mr. MASON rose, and said he would confine himself in his remarks to the bill before the Senate, and the matters which are properly connected with it. Adverting to the charge which had been made against the United States of commencing a war of aggression against a sister Republic, he expressed regret that such a charge should have been made, not only by the press, but on the floor of legislation, as he looked on it as the only dark spot which would appear on the page of the present day. He asserted that the accusation was unsustainable by fact; that it would be denied by the records of Congress; and that history would establish the truth. The war was just in its conception, and the manner in which it had been conducted reflected honor on our country.

The California claims became interesting, not merely on the historical grounds set forth by the Senator from Missouri, but because they were based on services performed without the sanction of Government; and it was proper that the grounds on which they were to be allowed ought to be placed clearly before the country. The Committee on Military Affairs had reported fully on the subject, and the claims had been explained by Colonel Fremont himself. Some part of the services had been accidental in their occurrence, before the commencement of the war. The officer in command was fully justified in the course he took. He then repeated briefly the history of the expedition under Lieutenant Colonel Fremont; glanced at the condition of California, and the danger which menaced her freedom from British influences, which were actively at work; reading from printed reports and correspondence in corroboration and illustration of his statements. He also referred to the difficulties which Colonel Fremont had to contend against, in consequence of the dissatisfaction of the inhabitants of California, and the necessity of guarding against and suppressing internal insurrections. He particularly dwelt on the fact that the events of a hostile character on the part of Colonel Fremont, which took place before the war had properly commenced, were unauthorized by our Government, and consequently that the Administration could not be properly held responsible for them.

The claims amounted to $700,000; and he thought Congress was bound to pay them. But he did not wish to see a board constituted, as this was in the bill itself, as he regarded this as a usurpation of the appointing power by the Senate, which was, in his opinion, an unjustifiable encroachment.

For the purpose of amendment he moved to recommit the bill, with the following instructions: "so to amend the bill as to provide that a board consisting of two competent persons as commissioners, shall be appointed by the President, by and with the advice and consent of the Senate, with power to examine into and determine the claims and demands arising out of the late military operations in California in the bill mentioned."

Mr. Cass said, as he did not see the Senator from North Carolina, who desired to speak on the bill, in his seat, he would move that, by general consent, the bill be passed over informally.

Mr. Rusk here made a movement; when—

Mr. Cass said that he did not know that the Senator from Texas intended to speak. In that case he would withdraw his motion.

Mr. Rusk said he wished to say a few words, but he was not anxious to go on at the present moment; any other time would suit him as well.

Mr. Mangum renewed the request that the bill be, by general consent, informally passed over; which was agreed to.

The Senate then proceeded to the consideration of Executive business. After some time, the doors were reopened, and

The Senate adjourned.

HOUSE OF REPRESENTATIVES.

Thursday, April 13.

Mr. Horace Mann, of Massachusetts, elected to supply the vacancy occasioned by the death of the Hon. John Quincy Adams, appeared this day, was qualified according to law, and took his seat in the House.

IN SENATE.

Monday, April 17.

California Claims.

On motion of Mr. Badger, the Senate proceeded to the consideration of the bill relating to California claims, the question pending being to recommit the bill with instructions.

Mr. Badger suggested to the Senator from Virginia, to modify his motion to recommit, by the omission of the instructions, so as to leave the committee at discretion to put the clause in the bill into such a shape as would meet the acquiescence of the Senate.

Mr. Mason replied, that he had received a similar suggestion from other friends; and that he would, therefore, withdraw so much of his amendment as related to instructions to the committee.

The motion to recommit was then agreed to.

Friday, April 28.

The Late John Quincy Adams.

Mr. Hale submitted the following resolution for consideration:

Resolved, That the Secretary of the Senate procure, for the use of the Senate, 5,000 copies of the addresses made by the Speaker and members of the House of Representatives, and of the addresses made to the Senate, together with the discourse of the Rev. Mr. Gurley, upon the occasion of the death of the Hon. John Quincy Adams, provided they can be obtained upon the same terms that 20,000 copies of the same were furnished to the House of Representatives.

HOUSE OF REPRESENTATIVES.

Saturday, April 29.

Yucatan.

The Speaker also laid before the House the following Message, this day received from the President of the United States:

To the Senate and
House of Representatives of the United States:

I submit, for the consideration of Congress, several communications received at the Department of State from Mr. *Justo Sierra*, Commissioner of Yucatan, and also a communication from the Governor of that State, representing the condition of extreme suffering to which their country has been reduced by an insurrection of the Indians within its limits, and asking the aid of the United States.

The communications present a case of human suffering and misery which cannot fail to excite the sympathies of all civilized nations. From these and other sources of information, it appears that the Indians of Yucatan are waging a war of extermination against the white race. In this cruel war they spare neither age nor sex, but put to death indiscriminately all who fall within their power. The inhabitants, panic-stricken, and destitute of arms, are flying before their savage pursuers towards the coast; and their expulsion from their country, or their extermination, would seem to be inevitable, unless they can obtain assistance from abroad.

In this condition they have, through their constituted authorities, implored the aid of this Government to save them from destruction, offering, in case this should be granted, to transfer the "dominion and sovereignty of the peninsula" to the United States. Similar appeals for aid and protection have been made "to the Spanish and the English Governments."

Whilst it is not my purpose to recommend the adoption of any measure, with a view to the acquisition of the "dominion and sovereignty" over Yucatan, yet, according to our established policy, we could not consent to a transfer of this "dominion and sovereignty" either to Spain, Great Britain, or any other European power. In the language of President Monroe, in his message of December, 1823, "we should consider any attempt on their part to extend their system to any portion of this hemisphere as dangerous to our peace and safety." In my annual message of December, 1845, I declare that, "near a quarter of a century ago, the principle was distinctly announced to the world, in the annual message of one of my predecessors, that the 'American continents, by the free and independent condition which they have assumed and maintained, are henceforth not to be considered as subjects for future colonization by any European power.'" "This principle will apply with greatly increased force, should any European power attempt to establish any new colony in North America. In the existing circumstances of the world, the present is deemed a proper occasion to reiterate and reaffirm the principle avowed by Mr. Monroe, and to state my cordial concurrence in its wisdom and sound policy. The reassertion of this principle, especially in reference to North America, is at this day but the promulgation of a policy which no European power should cherish the disposition to resist. Existing rights of every European nation should be respected; but it is due alike to our safety and our interests that the efficient protection of our laws should be extended over our whole territorial limits, and that it should be distinctly announced to the world, as our settled policy, that no future European colony or dominion shall, with our consent, be planted or established on any part of the American continent."

Our own security requires that the established policy thus announced should guide our conduct, and this applies with great force to the peninsula of Yucatan. It is situated in the Gulf of Mexico, on the North American continent; and from its vicinity to Cuba, to the capes of Florida, to New Orleans, and indeed to our whole south-western coast, it would be dangerous to our peace and security if it should become a colony of any European nation.

We have now authentic information, that if the aid asked from the United States be not granted, such aid will probably be obtained from some European power, which may hereafter assert a claim to "dominion and sovereignty" over Yucatan.

Our existing relations with Yucatan are of a peculiar character, as will be perceived from the note of the Secretary of State to her Commissioner, dated on the 24th of December last; a copy of which is herewith transmitted. Yucatan has never declared her independence, and we treat her as a State of the Mexican Republic. For this reason we have never officially received her Commissioner; but whilst this is the case, we have, to a considerable extent, recognized her as a neutral in our war with Mexico. Whilst still considering Yucatan as a portion of Mexico, if we had troops to spare for this purpose, I would deem it proper, during the continuance of the war with Mexico, to occupy and hold military possession of her territory, and to defend the white inhabitants against the incursions of the Indians, in the same way that we have employed our troops in other States of the Mexican Republic in our possession, in repelling the attacks of savages upon the inhabitants, who have maintained their neutrality in the war. But, unfortunately, we cannot at the present, without serious danger, withdraw our forces from other portions of the Mexican territory now in our occupation, and send them to Yucatan. All that can be done, under existing circumstances, is to employ our naval forces in the Gulf, not required at other points, to afford them relief. But it is not to be expected that any adequate protection can thus be afforded, as the operations of such naval forces must of necessity be confined to the coast.

I have considered it proper to communicate the information contained in the accompanying correspondence, and I submit to the wisdom of Congress to adopt such measures as, in their judgment, may be expedient to prevent Yucatan from becoming a colony of any European power, which, in no event, could be permitted by the United States; and at the same time to rescue the white race from extermination or expulsion from their country.

JAMES K. POLK.

WASHINGTON, *April* 29, 1848.

Mr. ROCKWELL, of Massachusetts, moved that the Message and accompanying documents be referred to the Committee on Territories.

[Many voices: Refer it to the Committee on Foreign Affairs.]

He said it was perfectly evident that this was one of the most interesting messages that could possibly be communicated by the President of the United States to Congress. He did not know that the Committee on Territories was the most proper committee to which the reference could be made: he did not know, for he had no time to consider, whether that committee, or the Committee on Foreign Affairs, or a select committee, was the most appropriate committee. But he deemed the occasion appropriate to make some remarks to this House on the policy of this Government towards its territories. It was manifest, that while the Congress of the United States was occupied in the various matters which had for some weeks engrossed its attention, there was lying before them, demanding their grave consideration, in relation to several of the States in Mexico, matters of more important interest to the existence, to the duration of this Republic, than could be found in any of the other relations of this Government. He proposed, if it was in order on this occasion, to make some remarks upon the general policy of this Government towards any territories which might be expected to be acquired from the Republic of Mexico by treaty of peace or otherwise.

Mr. COBB, of Georgia, inquired if such a course of remark would be in order?

The SPEAKER, remarking that he could not decide whether remarks were in order until they were submitted, said that a general speech on the subject of territories already embraced within the limits of the United States, under a treaty which was understood to have been ratified by the Senate, would hardly apply to the question of aiding a people of another territory.

Mr. Rockwell said he understood that the message of the President of the United States certainly contemplated, when viewed in some aspects, the annexation of the territory of Yucatan; [cries of "No, no;"] and the question would arise upon that message, in what manner the Government should proceed in relation to any acquisition from the Republic of Mexico in any manner.

Mr. Cobb made the point of order, that the gentleman from Massachusetts having very properly notified the House that it was his intention to enlarge his remarks to cover the whole ground in relation to territories already annexed, this discussion was irrelevant, and not in order, on the motion to refer the message just received. And he submitted to the Chair, and to the gentleman from Massachusetts, that if the House intended to take any order whatever on the message, it was certainly unwise to enter upon a general debate; for the discussion must necessarily be prolonged, and would eventuate in preventing any action. The message ought to be referred at once to the proper committee, which he thought was the Committee on Foreign Affairs; let the committee report, and then the House could go into a discussion of the merits of the question, which would then be in order. At present, it seemed that the only legitimate discussion would be as to the propriety of referring and printing the document, and not the whole subject in relation to our territories. He made this point of order, and he trusted it would be acquiesced in by the gentleman from Massachusetts.

The Speaker stated, that being in the House, and not in Committee of the Whole on the state of the Union, the rules of the House must apply, and no remarks would be in order which did not apply to Yucatan, its condition, and the message of the President of the United States. In Committee of the Whole, a wider range of debate was allowed.

Mr. Cobb called for the enforcement of the decision.

IN SENATE.

Saturday, April 29.

After the customary prayer—

On motion of Mr. Hannegan, the reading of the Journal was dispensed with.

A message was received from the President of the United States, relative to affairs in Yucatan. [See House proceedings for the message.]

There were sundry documents accompanying the message. The message having been read—

Mr. Hannegan moved that the message and documents be referred to the Committee on Foreign Relations, and that they be printed.

Mr. Calhoun. Before that question is put, I rise to express my regret that the President should place this recommendation on any other ground than that of humanity. If I heard the message aright, he asserts the principle as deduced from Mr. Monroe's declaration, that when the people of any portion of this continent is placed in the condition in which Yucatan is, and either party should be compelled to apply to us for protection, we should interpose and protect them, to prevent the interference of England, or some other foreign power. A broad and dangerous principle, truly. It goes far beyond Mr. Monroe's declaration. It is difficult to say what limits can be fixed to it, or to what it would carry us, if reduced to practice. I take this early opportunity—for experience has brought me to strike at once on the introduction of an objectionable measure—to express my surprise and regret, that the President should seize such an occasion as this to recommend the occupation of Yucatan by our army, or a portion of it, if it could be spared from Mexico. It is startling. Who can tell to what it will lead, and where it will end? How strange to recommend it at such a time, on the ground, if we did not occupy it, some other power might. In the present condition of Europe, there is no more probability that England, or any other power there, would seize on Yucatan, than that I, as an individual, would. Who can suppose, engrossed as she is, and all other powers in that quarter of the globe are, with questions connected with their existence, that they could, for a moment, entertain a idea of the kind? England has enough to attend to at home. Who can tell what may be her condition? The supposition of the possibility of such a step on her part seems to me strange and unaccountable. I did hope that the experience of the Mexican war—that precipitate and rash measure, which has cost the country so dearly in blood and treasure—would have taught the Administration moderation and caution, and induced them to shun any course of policy calculated to plunge the country in a similar cost and sacrifice. Who can form an estimate of the expenditure, the sacrifice of life, and the difficulties to which the adoption of the President's recommendation in this case would lead? The condition of Europe ought to admonish us against taking it.

What are the causes which have led to its present upheaving, and the reeling to and fro of all her Governments? What are those which are assigned for the overthrow of the French monarchy, and the danger that threatens the British with the same fate? Among the prominent is the heavy burdens imposed on the people, which have crushed them to the earth, and which has been continually increasing. It is charged that the onerous burdens imposed on the people of France by the mighty wars of Napoleon, instead of being diminished, were actually increased under the Government of its late monarch, and that those imposed on the people of England to resist his gigantic power, are as great as they were at the end of the mighty contest between the two powers, allowance being made for the depreciation of the currency. Are we not fairly liable to the same charge? Has there been any alleviation of the burden imposed on our people by the payment of the debts of the Revolution, or the war of 1812? Are our expenses less that they were in the war of 1812, allowing for the depreciation of the currency during that conflict? Those who have not attended to the subject, would be surprised, on comparing the expenses of the Government now with what it was during Mr. Monroe's administration. It terminated in 1825, twenty-three years ago. The average expenditure of that administration did not exceed $10,000,000 annually, deducting the payment of the principal and interest of the public debt. It is difficult to say what it is now; it will probably be not less than $30,000,000. It is true, our population has increased, but it has probably not more than doubled, while our expenses have increased threefold. And yet, heedless of consequences, it is proposed to adopt a course of policy, before we have extricated ourselves from the burden and losses of the Mexican war, which may lead to expenses and sacrifices of which no one can form even a conjecture. I am willing, on the score of humanity, to go as far as we can with safety and propriety, in this case. How far that is, I am not prepared to say; but I cannot possibly support the course of policy recommended by the President, as I understand the message. I am not certain as to what he intends; but be it such as I suppose or not, I cannot but regret that he should mix up what ought to be an appeal purely to our humanity with the considerations he has. The case of Yucatan is indeed an awful one. In the midst of our sympathy, we may derive instruction from it. The people of Yucatan, after they threw off the Spanish yoke, acting on the idea that all men are qualified to enjoy the blessing of liberty, and ought of right to possess it, liberated the large mass of their population, consisting of aborigines in a state of ignorance and subjection, and raised them to a level with themselves, by making them citizens. The result is such as we this day witness. They were too ignorant to appreciate liberty, or exercise the rights it conferred; and instead of gratitude, they have turned round and murdered thse who conferred it on them, and laid waste and devasted the country. Such are the fruits of a misguided, misjudging philanthropy, combined with erroneous political notions, which are so prevalent at the present time in more enlightened and civilized countries, but which, whenever reduced to practice, must lead to disastrous consequences.

Mr. FOOTE. I rise for the purpose of urging on the honorable Senator from Indiana, whose official station as chairman of the Committee on Foreign Affairs, seems to indicate the peculiar propriety of a suitable response to what has fallen from the honorable Senator from South Carolina, being offered by him. The unhappy condition of one of our most worthy associates in this body, so pathetically alluded to by the Senator from Indiana, might well prevent a long debate at the present moment. But, yielding to none in sympathy for my suffering friend and his distressed family, I feel bound to insist, that at least a few remarks should be made by some Senator in defence of the Executive message, so pointedly and, as I think, unjustly assailed, by the Senator from South Carolina. The speech of the Senator from South Carolina going out without any reply, is well calculated to engender prejudice and diffuse error, as I am sure, in relation to a great question, involving most deeply the honor and welfare of the Republic, and which, in several of its bearings, is one of peculiar delicacy to the present condition of our country and the civilized world. I hope the honorable Senator from Indiana will consent to say something at once in defence of the message. If he will not, as he seems unwilling to do, I feel bound to say, before I yield the floor, what I am convinced will be justified by the reading of the document in question, when it shall have been examined, that it has been most surprisingly misunderstood by the Senator from South Carolina, who, "taking the question at the first pop," as he styles it, has entirely failed to interpret the language of the message. It is an approximation to his usual accuracy in such matters. I have read the message at the Clerk's table, and feel authorized to insist, that had the distinguished Senator from South Carolina done himself and the country the justice to examine it before he indulged in the harsh strictures to which we have listened, he never would have uttered two-thirds of what we have heard from him on the present occasion. I solemnly invoke a complete suspension of the public judgment in regard to the message until it shall have been printed and dispassionately examined.

Mr. HANNEGAN. I feel as much anxiety to reply to what has fallen from the Senator from South Carolina as the Senator from Mississippi can do; but from the fact I have stated, I feel a disinclination to do so at present.

On motion, the Senate adjourned.

HOUSE OF REPRESENTATIVES.

MONDAY, May 1.

Death of Senator Ashley, of Arkansas.

A message was received from the Senate, announcing the decease of the Hon. CHESTER ASHLEY, and the proceedings of the Senate having been read—

Mr. JOHNSON, of Arkansas, rose and addressed the House as follows:

Mr. SPEAKER: The message just received from the Senate announces to this House the melancholy intelligence that death has again visited the halls of our National Council. The Hon. Chester Ashley, late a Senator of the State of Arkansas, is no more.

He is the second Senator, in the brief existence of Arkansas as a State of this Union, who has died, in the maturity of years which promised wisdom and usefulness, in the full vigor of a sound constitution, and the enjoyment of a general good health that promised long life.

He died, sir, on Saturday last, the 29th of April, at two o'clock in the afternoon, after a short but painfully afflicting illness. Conscious of his approaching dissolution, he made the fullest preparation. Granted to him, as it was, to enjoy the full possession of his intellect to the latest moment, but with a heart full of solicitude for his bereaved family, he died reconciled with God and the world, calm and resigned. He died in the midst of friends that were attached to him, and his family that worshipped him. Blessed with the kind offices of a Christian ministry, he was calmed in the hour of his last sleep with the elevated thoughts, the pure and soothing consolations of the Christian religion. He died, sir, whilst yet at the summit of a just ambition, whilst yet in the enjoyment of the proudest honors to which an American and a patriot could aspire. Happy, sir, are these circumstances; few can be favored with a death like this.

He was born in Westfield, Massachusetts, and, when less than a year old, was taken with his father and family, who removed to Hudson, New York. He was educated to the legal profession, and, at the age of twenty-seven, emigrated to Illinois.

He afterwards married in Missouri, and in 1819, removed to and settled in the then Territory of Arkansas. Urged by a spirit of enterprise, sustained alone by a firm and active intellect, he fixed his habitation in a region whose boundaries were unexplored, whose lands were an unbroken wilderness, whose limits were filled with strange and savage tribes, and of which legend and tradition could tell but little. There, sir, without wealth, acquaintance, or resources, at opening manhood, near thirty years ago, he cast his lot. He closed his life, sir, a Senator of this great American Union.

Poor at the outset of his life in Arkansas, upon his profession alone he depended for the support of himself and family. Of a mind active and powerful, he acquired distinction early as a sound lawyer and an able advocate. Devoted to his profession, studious and energetic, for many years previous to his abandonment of his practice, he ranked unrivalled as the first and ablest member of the bar. The history of a professional life, its privations, trials, and dangers in a frontier country, however interesting in a thousand incidents, however eminent for success, is scarcely an object of general interest. Sufficient is it to say, a quarter of a century of uninterrupted devotion, the attainment through it of pecuniary independence, and the ultimate accumulation of wealth, marked his professional career.

He was energetic by nature, sound in judgment, deliberate in action, and distinguished for accomplished manners and unyielding purpose. His habits were frugal, temperate, and marked by no excess.

He was elected to the United States Senate in the fall of 1844, to fill the vacancy of the lamented Fulton, who died under like sudden, painful, and afflicting circumstances.

Upon his entrance into the Halls of the Senate, he was placed at once in a position conspicuous for its importance, and which required of its occupant a high order of talent and great experience. That position he continued to occupy. The acceptable manner in which he discharged the duties of that position, as chairman of the Committee on the Judiciary, is too well known to this House and the country, to require any comment.

He was re-elected for the full term, in 1846, after a most excited and protracted contest. For his success in that instance, he was not less indebted to his own strong will, his habits of labor, his energy, and admitted ability, than to the ardent devotion of his friends; and there is not one who then opposed him, whose heart does not reject, at the knowledge of this grief, the transient acrimony of that hour.

A human being, his were the virtues, the passions, and incident difficulties of humanity. To the deep grief of his many friends, and to the utter desolation of his family, he is lost. The scene of his happiness and his brightest virtues was the domestic circle; the temple in which he worshipped was made up of their unchanging affection, their trusting and confiding love. Truly has this circle been riven to the centre, and this temple cast down. The light which guided and cheered has gone out for them, and who is there that does not sympathize with griefs heartrending, with griefs so deep, and so well-founded! No language of mine could adequately portray them; but none there are that would not alleviate them, none so poor of heart as do not sympathize.

In the annunciation of this event, so afflicting to so many, I have discharged a painful duty which I owe to this House, to my State, and to the memory of an eminent representative of her rights, her interests, and her dignity. I could never have anticipated it, and I pray God that a like task, so intimately connected with the sorrows of others, may never again become my lot.

Mr. J. concluded by moving the following resolutions:

Resolved, That this House has heard, with deep sensibility, the announcement of the death of the Hon. Chester Ashley, a Senator in Congress from the State of Arkansas.

Resolved, That, as a testimony of respect for the

memory of the deceased, the members and officers of this House will wear the usual badge of mourning for thirty days.

Resolved, That the proceedings of this House in relation to the death of the Hon. Chester Ashley, be communicated to the family of the deceased by the Clerk.

Resolved, That this House will attend the funeral of the deceased in a body; and, as a further mark of respect for his memory, that it do now adjourn until twelve o'clock to-morrow.

The question was stated on agreeing to the resolutions; when—

Mr. White, of New York, rose and addressed the House as follows:

Mr. Speaker: May I be permitted in a few words to express upon this occasion my sorrow and grief at the sudden departure forever of our esteemed and worthy friend? Three winters have we lodged at the same house and fed at the same table; three winters and more have we been in daily social and familiar intercourse, and never, upon any occasion, or at any time, have I observed for a single moment an impertinent or angry remark—a discourteous, unkind, or ungentlemanly action.

Of his early life I know but little; but it must have been a life of industry, sobriety, prudence, and economy, to have placed him where he was when stricken down by the arrow of death. The artificer of his own fame and fortune, which were all that the moderated ambition of man could desire, though they could not avert the relentless assaults of the destroyer, yet offer a bright and glowing picture to the young men of our country to imitate his virtues if they would obtain the honors.

What a solemn warning to us all! On Saturday, one week before his death, Mr. Ashley, with his family and a party of friends, visited that hallowed and beautiful spot where repose the earthly remains of the immortal Washington. No member of this House has better assurances of seeing many days and years return than did this Senator upon that occasion: in the enjoyment of perfect health, buoyant and elastic spirits, most cheerful and even gay, having for the time laid aside his *toga virilis senatoris*, and entering with the light joyousness of youth into the social scenes and circles of the day, added much to the pleasure and happiness of the party by the radiation of joys from his own heart. But where is he now? In the cold embrace of that stern monarch who has so often visited these halls, that well may we cry for mercy, and implore the protection of Almighty God to save us from the grasp of this destroying angel. With these often-repeated and solemn warnings, who among us can claim one day or one hour as his own? Shall these calls pass unheard and unheeded? Shall we still pursue the shadow? or, rather, shall we, like sane and sober men, accountable to God and our country, apply ourselves with diligence and zeal to the duties before us as legislators, as men, and as Christians?

The resolutions were then unanimously adopted, and the House adjourned until twelve o'clock to-morrow.

IN SENATE.

Monday, May 1.

Death of Senator Ashley, of Arkansas.

As soon as the Journal was read,

Mr. Borland, of Arkansas, announced the death of his colleague, the Hon. Chester Ashley, as follows:

Mr. President: My official introduction into this Chamber has been marked with calamity, and overcast with gloom. The first of its public duties that has devolved upon me is of deep solemnity, and its performance is undertaken with feelings of oppressive sadness.

Just one week ago, a venerable form—in the fulness of life, and the seeming vigor of perfect health—rose in his place, and, in a voice well known and respected here, announced my position in this assembly. That form will not rise again in this presence; for it now lies lifeless and cold as a clod of the valley. That voice will be heard no more within these walls; for it is hushed in death. In return for the kind courtesy of presenting me, as his colleague, to this company of honorable Senators, I pay but the poor and painful tribute of making known his final separation. The last act of his public life was my introduction; the first of mine must be his obituary.

Chester Ashley, a Senator from the State of Arkansas, is no more. He breathed his last at his lodgings in this city, on Saturday last, the 29th of April, at fifteen minutes before two o'clock, in the afternoon. On Sunday of last week, he felicitated himself upon the perfection of his health. Soon after breakfast, the next morning, he complained of slight indisposition; but so slight as hardly to command a second thought. At the usual hour he proceeded to his place in this Chamber. When the Journal had been read, he did me the favor to present my credentials, as his colleague. A few minutes after, his indisposition increased; he had the sensation of chilliness, and, leaving the Capitol, returned to his lodgings. That evening I found him deeply jaundiced, and in the delirium of fever. This latter symptom had usually marked even his slightest indisposition—as is very common with individuals of large brain and sanguine temperament. His family, however, thought him not seriously ill—certainly not in danger. But on Thursday morning he had grown evidently worse, and a distinguished physician of the city was called to see him. His condition was found to be such even then, as to afford little hope of his recovery. Another eminent practitioner was consulted, and the same opinion given.

On Friday morning I was invited to make

a third party in the professional consultation. But there was no ground for hope. An intense and extensive inflammation had seized upon the bowels, and, in my opinion, upon the liver also; and was of that type, occasionally encountered, which, setting at naught the highest science and the best directed efforts of human skill, runs, almost from the very outset, steadily and rapidly into a fatal termination. I had seen similar cases before; and I am particularly reminded by it of that of the late Senator Fulton, who was, alike in station, in disease, and in death, the predecessor of him whose loss we now deplore.

Colonel Ashley was a native of New England. He was born at Westfield, in Massachusetts, on the 1st day of June, 1790; and, consequently, at the time of his death, was in the 58th year of his age. When an infant of only three months, he was carried by his parents, who removed to the town of Hudson, in New York. He grew up, engaged in the practice of the law, and resided there about twenty-seven years; then migrated to Illinois, where he remained about two years; and subsequently visiting the territory, of what is now the State of Arkansas, in 1819, determined to make his residence at Little Rock, then a mere landing on the southern bank, some three hundred miles above the mouth of the Arkansas River. Soon afterwards he married in Missouri, and removed, with his young family, to his home in the wilderness.

At that period, a settlement in what was truly "the far West," was no trivial undertaking. It required a high degree of enterprise to encounter the privations, hardships, and perils of frontier life—now so much talked about, but then actually endured. An uncommon share of mental forecast would alone suffice to ascertain a point in so wide a range, which must become the centre of important operations, from which settlement and civilization must radiate, and then throw back an accumulated interest. A firmness, fixedness, singleness of purpose, true to its object as the needle to the pole, was alone capable of abiding the full development of the little cloud of improvement, then no bigger than a man's hand, which was, within a quarter of a century, to cover with its golden drapery the whole horizon. Yet many a New England boy —many a stripling, from anywhere this side the mountains, impelled by the irrepressible spirit of progress, guided by a judgment so clear in its preceptions, and so rapid in its combinations, as to seem intuitive, and sustained by a will as potent as the lever of Archimedes, has exhibited all the high qualities I have mentioned; and that, too, in the construction of imperishable monuments—not monuments like the towering pyramids of Egypt, barren of utility as the wastes of sand they overlook—nor like the huge walls of the Roman coliseum, within which human beings were wont to be degraded to the cruel level of wild beasts; but of monuments of a purer order, of a loftier structure, of more comprehensive proportions —dedicated to the higher sentiments of the human heart, and adapted to the true wants of human society—monuments made up of the wilderness reclaimed and converted into cultivated fields; of the towns, with their bristling spires, which crowd our thoroughfares; of the teeming commerce of our "inland seas;" and, above all, of the millions of freemen who sleep securely under their own roof-trees, and stand in conscious sovereignty upon the fertile soil of their own broad acres. In a word—the noble aggregate of these monuments is before the world, in the peerless prosperity of "the great West." I have selected the New England boy, the cis-montane strippling, as the type of a class. And of that class it would be difficult to find a more characteristic representative than the individual of whom I am here to speak, whether we regard the vigor, the perseverance, or the success of his exertions.

At the age of twenty-nine years, without patrimony, without resources of any kind, except those he possessed in his acute and comprehensive intellect, his high purpose, and indomitable will, but recently married to a woman of congenial spirit, he landed at Little Rock, and entered upon the practice of the law, which was necessarily restricted then, and for several years afterwards, almost exclusively to cases before the territorial courts, involving the titles to land, and personal violence among a border population. In attending to these cases, of which, on account of his high intelligence and untiring industry, he soon obtained a large proportion, he was frequently required to traverse, as his circuit, the whole country which now forms the State of Arkansas, and portions of that included in Missouri. Even for one who participated in them, it would be difficult to depict the scenes incident to professional life, in times and under circumstances when the law was administered almost without books, the courts often held in the open air, the leathern thong serving the place of prison walls, and the ready rifle that of the jailer's key. Then the land had no roads, the streams no bridges, the country, for many miles between certain points of settlement, was unmarked by human habitations. Through all this, the course of the young lawyer was onward and upward—undismayed, unchecked by difficulties, which seemed, indeed, but to excite to still greater activity the strong energies of his nature. Storing his mind from books whenever the means were within his reach, he was ever improving his powers by those exercises among men, and in the practical affairs of life, which qualify the man of business to be useful to his fellows, while giving due attention to his own interests. But it is not necessary that I should follow up in detail the steps of him I would represent. It is of results, and not the particular means of their accomplishment, I have to speak. And if the results attained by my deceased colleague may be the measure of his worth, then, in the success of his exertions, he has established a reputation for wisdom and sagacity which might satisfy the ambition of any man. Devoting himself assiduously to the business of his profession, he suffered not the contagious example of political aspiring to lure him from the high and holy purpose of making provision for the wants and comforts of the interesting family he was gathering around him. Until the frosts of more than fifty winters had bleached his locks, we find him in the walks of private life, with unflagging industry and unabating vigor raising upon the foundations he had already laid the superstructure of affluence for his children. He was at length successful; and, as if Providence—ever propitious to those who are laborious in useful pursuits—had been watching his career, so soon as he had completed the provision for his own household, a station of high public trust—the station he held in this Chamber—was presented to his acceptance.

Although he had long enjoyed a high character for ability, and ever felt a deep interest in the public welfare, it was not until the month of April, 1844, that Colonel ASHLEY entered actively into the political movements of the country. At that time, a warm party contest was commencing, and his talents were called into the service upon the Democratic electoral ticket of Arkansas. Well and nobly did he justify the confidence and fulfil the expectations which had induced his selection. With an activity rarely witnessed in one of his years, he traversed the whole State, through the heats and rains of summer; with zeal and power he advocated the principles, and urged upon the people the measures of his political faith; and while all confessed his fidelity and efficiency in the cause he espoused, even those who most suffered from the blows he dealt so fast and forcibly, were the last to be offended at the manner of their infliction. He accomplished one achievement in that canvass, which stands unparalleled, I apprehend, in the annals of political controversy. He actually converted from the "error of his ways" one of the electors on the opposing party ticket—caused him to withdraw from the contest, and enjoyed the satisfaction of knowing that, in the autumn election, he voted for the Democratic electors. From this, some idea may be formed of the character of his services. *Ex pede Herculem!* In the month of August of that year, the excellent, the estimable Fulton died. Almost all eyes were at once turned to the accomplished elector as his successor. So, when the General Assembly of the State convened in November, the popular expectation was realized, and Colonel ASHLEY was elected to a seat in this body to fill the unexpired term, without any regular opposition, and by an almost unanimous vote. In 1846 he was re-elected to the same high station for six years from the 4th day of last March. From these demonstrations, an estimate may be formed of the place he occupied in the hearts of his people—of the standing he had at home, in the Territory of which he had been among the earliest pioneers—in the State he had helped to found, and with whose growth he had grown, and with whose strength he had strengthened. Of his standing and his reputation here, I am not competent to speak from personal observation. To those whom I address, he was better known. But if I may judge from the distinguished position you assigned him, even as a new member, in the business of this body, it is certain that he fully sustained the reputation for ability with which he came here. And from those indications which never deceive, for they are of the heart, so abundantly furnished by the anxious throng of his brother Senators about his deathbed—by the quivering lips and tearful eyes of hosts of friends—by the touching solemnity of this Chamber—I gather testimonials to his heart's goodness; laurels for the crown of his private worth, of far more real value than those which may be commanded by the brightest corruscations of mere intellect—far more enduring than "the bubble reputation" snatched from the cannon's mouth.

If to be great a man must perform with ability his public trusts, so to be good he must sustain worthily his private relations. In my opinion, no man can be wholly unhappy who is surrounded with an amiable family, nor can he be otherwise than good if he devote himself with fidelity to the happiness of that family. I am aware, sir, that I am approaching a sacred subject—fitter for discussion in narrower and less public walls than these. But I merely allude to it in illustration of the finest feature in the human character—I mean domestic affection—a feature strikingly predominant in the otherwise strongly marked character of my deceased colleague. Many who now hear me have noticed and admired, as all must respect, this endearing characteristic. It distinguished him at home, wherever he was known. But if he loved his family, he was loved by them in return. If his investment of the heart's best treasures in this noblest of institutions, sanctioned of Heaven and known among men, was munificent, he was not without reward—well and punctually was he repaid with usury. Even had business disappointed or ambition failed him, he had this rich resource, which no power on earth could destroy. The tide of domestic affection and happiness at home, like the fabled Pactolus, rolled its golden sands, in attractive beauty and unfailing abundance, along his pathway of life.

But, sir, if the strong cords of pious sympathy, which bind the members of a family together, confer the truest happiness upon those within the charmed circle, the severance, and, above all, the sudden and unexpected severance of those cords, is productive of the hardest agony the heart can know. That this is so, I have but to refer to that scene which I have but recently left. But who shall describe that? Surely I shall not attempt it. Sir, though I am comparatively but a young man, my pursuits in life and my own sad experience have made me familiar with scenes of suffering, too often with death. As a duty, I have trained myself to look upon the sufferings, even the dissolution of my own sex, not with coldness of heart, I trust, but with some degree of composure. But the sight of a woman's sorrows—and of such sorrows as I have had to witness within the last few days—has, I confess, unmanned me—has made me a very child in feeling; and in its manifestations I have seen the strong man, full of life and hope, suddenly cut down—not afraid to die, but unwilling to leave those he loved so tenderly. His agony was touching. I bowed my heart in humility before that Power who has created, and who may destroy all things, while I confessed the emptiness of earth and the fleeting vanity of all human pursuits. But, sir, it was the heart-breaking of that noble and devoted wife, who, for more than a quarter of a century, had spread the balm of her affection about his heart, and smiled away his cares, while she leaned upon him for that support and protection which was never withheld—it was the utter prostration of that lovely daughter, who, like an angel of grace, hung about his pillow, endeavoring to repay his early and never-failing care, with those offices of affection which the heart of woman alone knows when to offer, as her hand alone can apply;—it was these things, sir, which overcame me—under these my heart has sunk. From the scene of these occurrences I have come here to speak of their subject. No wonder, then, I am unable to do him justice; no wonder that language fails to do the bidding of my own full heart, and falls far short of your desires.

But, sir, gloomy as the picture we contemplate undoubtedly is, it is not entirely without relief. Deep as its shades confessedly are, the light is not wholly excluded. Our friend has died, and his loss has brought agony to the hearts of survivors; but, as he lived not without usefulness, so he has died not without hope. He gave abundant and heart-cheering evidence, in that hour when deception is never practised, and self-delusion rarely indulged—on his death-bed, and when he knew he must die—in that solemn and soul-trying hour, he gave abundant and heart-cheering evidence that he was a *patriot* and a *Christian*. It has been my fortune to stand by many beds of death, in the retirement of domestic privacy, surrounded by all the endearing associations of home and friends. I have seen brave men die upon the field of battle, when nerved by all the appliances of enthusiasm—the clash of arms and the shouts of victory. But I can say with perfect truth, that never have I seen any man meet death (although unwillingly) with more calm courage or pious resignation. Among his last words, addressed to his family, with great self-possession, and in tones of emphatic sincerity, were these—and they are worthy of remembrance: "Pray for the welfare of our country, and prepare to meet me in Heaven."

Mr. President, my relations toward all of the three Senators from Arkansas have been peculiar. Though not yet five years a resident of that State, it has been my fortune to succeed one of them upon this floor—to have attended, as a friend and medical adviser, in the dying hours of the other two; and, in reference to the last, to pronounce his eulogy. Sad have been these latter relations; and strange are the mutations which they mark upon the calendar of human affairs! May Heaven grant me strength to sustain the responsible duties to which I have succeeded.

Mr. Borland concluded by offering the following resolutions:

Resolved, That the Senate has heard with deep sensibility the announcement of the death of the Hon. Chester Ashley, a Senator from the State of Arkansas.

Resolved, That, as a testimony of respect for the memory of the deceased, the members and officers of the Senate wear the usual badge of mourning for thirty days.

Resolved, That the proceedings of the Senate in relation to the death of the Hon. Chester Ashley be communicated to the family of the deceased by the Secretary.

Resolved, That the Senate will attend the funeral of the deceased in a body; and, as a further mark of respect for his memory, that it do now adjourn.

Mr. Breese then addressed the Senate to the following effect:

Mr. President: In rising to second the motion of the honorable Senator who has just made the solemn announcement of the death of one of our honored associates—an event alike startling and sudden—I may be permitted, I hope, without intrusion, to add a few words to the beautiful eulogium he has so feelingly pronounced. I fear, in so doing, I shall disturb the harmony of its language whilst it is yet vibrating on the ear, and interrupt that generous flow of feeling it has so universally inspired. Yet, sir, there are circumstances in the life of the deceased, and of him who now addresses you, to which it may not be improper, on this mournful occasion, to advert, and which prompt me to offer a slight tribute to his memory. It is, sir, thirty years since we met for the first time in the then far-off wilderness of the West, he my senior by many years, then a practising lawyer, I a student, preparing for that honorable profession, both buoyant with hope, with a bright and promising world before us, and both entering it with an ardor and a determination to win a name. Professional business in the winter of 1819–'20, called the deceased temporarily, as he thought, to Arkansas, from which he did not return. Common report, which reached the friends he had left in Illinois, told them of the high standing he had acquired at the bar of that State; and that he had, by a proper exercise of his talents, amassed a large fortune. I never saw him again until I met him here as an associate in this Chamber, at the second session of the twenty-eighth Congress. Our acquaintance was at once renewed, and we had much to speak of the varied yet similar fortunes a quarter of a century had achieved for us. In the next Congress we were appointed on two of the most important committees of this body; we lived together at the same house, and an intimacy was established, mutually cordial and sincere. Knowing him as I did, Mr. President, I may be permitted to say, that to every task to which he was called he brought to its accomplishment untiring industry, great research, and an unflagging zeal seldom surpassed. His talents were of no common order, for he was never found unprepared upon any subject submitted to his charge; and, with six years service still before him, who knows to what high honors he might have attained? The character of his mind was investigating; and, aided by a pleasing manner, always courteous, and often energetic, he was enabled to make his views well understood by the Senate, and to produce a marked effect, upon its deliberations. As a public man, sir, he was valuable, and gave certain promise of great usefulness and distinction.

In his disposition, the deceased was eminently social. His suavity of manner, his unruffled temper, his freedom from irritation by all those little annoyances that disturb the pathway of our lives, was a common remark to those who were intimately associated with him. But it was in the family circle he shone most conspicuous, as a husband, as a father, as one connected with those delicate relations of life in which humanity is exhibited in its most captivating form. In all of these, sir, he was a model and an example, lavishing all the tenderness of his nature upon those dear objects of his love, who returned it with the most sincere and devoted affection, and to whom it was permitted to receive his last sigh at that dread moment which must come upon us all. How terrible is this blow to them, who, but a few days ago, were all joy and gladness, now sobbing in anguish over his inanimate remains, conscious—painfully conscious—they are never more to feel the pulsations of that heart which beat alone in love for them; and as they take their lonely way back to their home, how agonizing will be the thought that they have parted forever with the idol of their hearts—their protector, their father, their dearest friend—and that his place at their once happy board is to be vacant forever.

How quick, Mr. President, is the passage from the Senate to the grave! How fleeting and transitory the hopes and promises of this life! And how full of warning should be this sad event, so sudden and so startling, prompting us to recur often to the injunction, "Be ye also ready," for no one of us can tell at what moment that awful summons may break upon our ear; no one can tell when the dread messenger may appear.

> "Leaves have their time to fall,
> And flowers to wither, at the north wind's breath,
> And stars to set; but all,
> Thou hast all seasons for thine own, O Death!"

The resolutions having been unanimously adopted—

The Senate adjourned.

FRIDAY, May 5.

Aid for Yucatan.

The special order being the bill to enable the President to take temporary military occupation of Yucatan, and the bill being under consideration as in Committee of the Whole—

Mr. HANNEGAN then rose and addressed the Senate, at some considerable length, and with no little animation, in favor of the bill as reported by the committee. When the bill was first reported he did not anticipate any opposition, but since it had become apparent that there would be, he should confine himself to the remarks made by the Senator from South Carolina, (Mr. CALHOUN,) and endeavor, as far as was in his power, to answer, and he hoped successfully, all his objections. Mr. H. then proceeded, with his usual fervor, to reply to the objections of Mr. CALHOUN *seriatim*, as derived from the remarks of that gentleman, on the introduction of the bill. He (Mr. H.) could not discover, after the closest and most rigid scrutiny, any of those hidden dangers in the message that had been suggested by the Senator from South Carolina, but not designated; but he did discover that Yucatan appealed to this country, urging it, by every tie of humanity that binds man to man, to save her from destruction, or that in two short months she must cease to exist—that the whole white population must be swept from the face of the earth. The committee had reported a bill strictly in accordance with the message, proposing to allow force enough to drive back the savage hordes from their murderous assaults upon the innocent and unoffending inhabitants; this was all the bill proposed, and neither the President nor any one else had ever dreamed of any thing but temporary military occupation. He would not pretend to say that a state of things might not arise which would oblige us to hold the country permanently, and he should not, in his opinion, be acting fairly or candidly, if he avowed that under no circumstances would he consent to a permanent occupation; that, however, was his private opinion. Already had we seen that one of the most formidable powers of the earth was hastening with race-horse speed to seize the Isthmus; and although the Senator from South Carolina had said that England in her present condition could no more seize Yucatan than he could, they had the most authentic information that she had seized Honduras and the Mosquito country, and had been advancing her troops upon Yucatan, under the guise of taking care of British interests. England never had enough to do at home to prevent her from accomplishing any mighty designs which she had in anticipation. Had they not seen in the late troubles in Europe, where thrones had been demolished "as by the stroke of the enchanter's wand," England had remained firm and immovable? Does any one suppose that her settlement near Yucatan was brought about by any hope of gain to her citizens from a miserable traffic in dye-woods? If they did, they were mistaken. That nation was looking to secure the great route by the Isthmus to the Pacific, which would give her the control of the trade of the East. Let her get possession of Yucatan, and what would be the effect on southern interests? Look to the map, and see that Yucatan shakes hands almost with Cuba; let her then obtain Yucatan, and he had no more doubt that she would get possession of Cuba than he had that the trees would sprout and the flowers blossom in the spring; indeed, at this very hour had they possession of information that England was endeavoring to obtain that fertile island, and that once effected, the Gulf of Mexico would become a *mare clausum*. Cuba was said to be the key, and with Yucatan she would have both lock and key, and control the whole outlet of the vast Mississippi; and were they to fold their arms quietly, and see Yucatan and Cuba fall into the arms of England?

Mr. Clayton took the ground that the President had merely suggested the employment of the troops so long as the Mexican war should continue, and not an hour longer. The President, therefore, could not be regarded as responsible for this bill, which went beyond his suggestion, inasmuch as it proposed a temporary occupation, and the word temporary meant just so long as might be convenient. He viewed the bill as incompatible with our treaty stipulations with Mexico, which provided that we should withdraw our troops within a designated line. After the ratification of this treaty, Mexico may think proper to resume her sovereignty over Yucatan. Can Mexico be made to believe that we are only actuated by motives of humanity, and that our real object is not to scatter our treaty stipulations to the winds? It should also be recollected that we have concluded an armistice with Mexico. Now, will not that armistice be violated the moment we send fresh troops into Mexico?*

* To understand this reference to the "*Armistice and Treaty*" then pending with Mexico, and the ill effect it might have upon them, it is necessary to remember that peace negotiations had commenced in Mexico, (accompanied by an armistice,) for the termination of the war; and that these negotiations were proceeding successfully.

Mr. Davis, of Mississippi, said that the President had proposed nothing beyond the temporary occupation of Yucatan. Whenever a proper time came, he was ready to take his stand against the intervention of European powers. But that did not enter into this question. Yucatan was a part of Mexico, and he was willing, on the ground of humanity, to respond to the request of Yucatan for aid in her present difficulty and distress. He said, that whenever the two great salient points should be endangered by England, whenever Yucatan and Cuba should be attempted by her, he would step forward to oppose her.

Mr. D. then moved to strike out all after the word "authorized" in the fourth line, down to the same word in the second line of the second section, and to insert, after the word "duty," in the fifth line, the following words: "To answer the exigent demand for the immediate presence of a portion of our army in Yucatan."

So that the bill, if amended, would read:

Be it enacted, &c., That the President of the United States be, and he is hereby, authorized and empowered to accept the services of an equal number of volunteer troops to supply the place of such as may be withdrawn from their present duty, to answer to the exigent demand for the immediate presence of a portion of our army in Yucatan: *Provided*, Their services shall be required; the same to be raised for services during the war with Mexico, agreeably to the provisions of the act of May thirteenth, eighteen hundred and forty-six, and March third, eighteen hundred and forty-seven.

Mr. Hannegan. Where, then, would be the authority for the President to take possession of and to occupy Yucatan?

Mr. Davis, of Mississippi. He would derive his authority from the declaration of war with Mexico. It is on the ground of our war with Mexico that he wished to place this measure.

Mr. Crittenden said the amendment completely changed the character of the bill, making it merely an authority to raise an additional force for the war in Mexico. He referred to the difficulty which the chairman of the Military Committee had found in marching along at the head of his twenty thousand volunteers. He had been daily giving the word, "forward, march!" but not a step had they advanced. This amendment cut loose the bill from the suggestion of the President. If the treaty should be ratified, these troops would not be required. What, then, would become of the people of Yucatan? Besides, the object of raising troops for the war with Mexico is to put down an enemy. How was this object to be effected by lending aid to Yucatan, who is our enemy? He thought the armistice also stood in the way. The civil war in Yucatan was raging at the time the armistice was made, and probably, had it been intended to exclude Yucatan, it would have been done in express language. The chairman of the Committee on Foreign Relations, he presumed, regarded this measure as distinct from the war in Mexico.

If so, he could only regard it as a violation of the principle of intervention which we laid down for the observance of all other nations. Other nations would be induced to create slight pretexts, on which they would justify themselves in following our example. This might lead to a slumbering and protracted war everywhere. It would add to the number of the unjust wars which had agitated the world.

Mr. DAVIS, of Mississippi, made a brief explanation in reference to the terms of the armistice, which, in his view, excluded the wild Indians and bodies of troops which were acting without authority.

Mr. FOOTE thought that the President was in a most unfortunate predicament, as he seemed to have failed to obtain the acquiescence of either party, and went on to address the Senate until the hour of adjournment, near four o'clock.

The Senate adjourned to Monday.

MONDAY, May 8.

Special Order—Yucatan.

The Senate proceeded to the consideration of the bill to enable the President of the United States to take temporary military occupation of Yucatan; the question pending being on the amendment moved by Mr. DAVIS, of Mississippi, as a substitute for the original bill.

A discursive colloquial discussion went on for some time, having little relation to the bill, in which Messrs. JOHNSON of Maryland, HOUSTON, HANNEGAN, DAVIS of Mississippi, CALHOUN, CRITTENDEN, WESTCOTT, CASS, and FOOTE, took part; when a motion was made to adjourn, but was withdrawn; and

Mr. JOHNSON, of Maryland, submitted the following resolution, which was considered and agreed to:

Resolved, That the President be requested to communicate to the Senate all the information in his possession in relation to the condition of Yucatan, and which he had before him when his recent message relative to that country was sent to Congress, and also any information which he may since have obtained as to its present condition.

The Senate then adjourned.

TUESDAY, May 9.

Yucatan.

The Senate resumed the consideration of the bill to enable the President to take temporary military occupation of Yucatan.

Mr. LEWIS said he desired to offer an amendment to the amendment of the Senator from Mississippi, (Mr. DAVIS.) The amendment was in the shape of a preamble, to go at the head of the bill, and a proviso to be inserted at the close. He thought, that to put the bill on the ground of humanity alone, would be carrying them further than he was disposed to go. They could not, and ought not, to become the champions of the whole human race; he thought the true base to place it on was, that Mexico owed Yucatan protection, and as she was no longer able, from the fact of our having superseded her military power, that we were bound to treat the invasion of Yucatan as other Mexican invasions. If the amendment prevails, it will read—

Whereas an extraordinary war is now being waged by the Indian upon the white population of Yucatan, which, if not arrested, threatens the extinction of the white race; and whereas Yucatan, as one of the States of Mexico, is entitled to the protection of the Mexican Government; and whereas, by reason of the existing war, the authority of the Mexican Government has been to a great extent suppressed within the limits of Mexico, and the military authority of the United States substituted in its stead; and whereas to such substitution is to be mainly attributed the impunity which is now given to cruelty and outrage on the part of the insurgents, justice and good faith to Yucatan, as well as the existing armistice with Mexico, require, as in the case of other Indian invasions of Mexican territory during the war, that the United States, having superseded the power of Mexico, should assume the protection of Yucatan until Mexico shall be in a condition to reassume the same. Therefore—

Be it enacted, &c., That the President of the United States be, and he is hereby, authorized and empowered to accept the services of an equal number of volunteer troops to supply the place of such as may be withdrawn from their present duty to answer to the exigent demand for the immediate presence of a portion of our army in Yucatan: *Provided*, Their services shall be required; the same to be raised for service during the war with Mexico, agreeably to the provisions of the act of May thirteenth, eighteen hundred and forty-six, and March third, eighteen hundred and forty-seven; and provided, further, that nothing herein contained shall be so construed as to require that the protection hereby afforded to the people of Yucatan should be withdrawn, until Mexico is in a situation to resume the same; and provided, further, that no warrant is hereby intended to be given for the permanent occupation or annexation of the territory of Yucatan to the United States.

Mr. DAVIS, of Mississippi, accepted the modification without hesitation; when—

Mr. NILES rose and addressed the Senate to a late hour against any interference with the internal concerns of other nations, and urging caution and prudence in all our relations with other countries. It was after four when Mr. N. closed his remarks.

Mr. CASS took the floor; when—

Mr. BREESE moved to go into Executive session; but the Senate refused the motion, and adjourned.

WEDNESDAY, May 10.

Occupation of Yucatan.

The Senate resumed the consideration of the bill to enable the President to take temporary military occupation of Yucatan.

Mr. Cass then rose to address the Senate, and began by referring to the remarks of the Senator from Connecticut, as to the great delay in the Executive department, in relation to the case of Yucatan. He stated that this delay was caused by the desire to obtain all necessary information on the subject. As soon as this was obtained, the facts were communicated to the Senate for its prompt and energetic action.

He stated that the question involved matters concerning our own security. The declaration of Mr. Monroe, and the doctrines expressed by Mr. Polk two years ago, contemplated no interference with European settlements on this continent. They merely looked to a prevention of the reduction of any of the free States of America to European dependence.

He glanced back to the discovery of America, and the establishment of the colonial governments; to subsequent changes of domination, which rendered this country for centuries a battle-field for European ambition to fight in. Thence he came down to the revolutions which agitated Europe, and applauded the wisdom and patriotism of Mr. Monroe in seizing the proper opportunity to publish his declaration against any further interference on the part of Europe.

To other points in the remarks of the Senator from Connecticut he made brief replies. He then contended that the policy of our country was not to interfere with other powers, but to prevent other powers from interfering with us. We are bound to act promptly and vigorously, when we see any evidence of a desire on the part of Europen powers to interfere with us. The war with Mexico—"rash and precipitate" as it had been called—had placed us in a position to enforce the policy laid down by Mr. Monroe. If we had not obtained a foot of land in Mexico, the war would be worth all that it has cost us, in the glory which it has shed around our country. No European power will now venture an interference with us.

The position of Yucatan, between us and the advancing Indians, is one of peculiar interest to us. Her condition calls on us for our deepest sympathy. England holds the key of the Mediterranean. She has stretched her powerful arm so as to touch every cape and headland on every ocean.

Mr. Crittenden asked how near a ship of war could approach any harbor of Yucatan?

Mr. Cass said the power of steam would be able to carry any naval armament to the coast.

Mr. Crittenden asked how near a steam-frigate could approach?

Mr. Cass disclaimed any particular knowledge on this subject. The Senator from Connecticut had supposed England had reached the highest point of elevation, and that she was approaching her decline. He would not pretend to give an opinion on this point. But he believed that although great reforms, which he believed were necessary, might be effected in the English system of government, it was idle to anticipate that her Government would be overthrown—that she would be destroyed. Her intelligence and her moral power would remain, and she would rise, like Antæus, stronger after every stroke. He understood there were now four companies of British artillery in the southern portion of Yucatan. How largely they may be reinforced he could not say. He did not say what course England would pursue, but it was our duty to be on our guard against any interference which may be injurious to our interests. When she lays the lion's paw on Yucatan, it will be difficult to displace it.

The value of the commerce of the Mississippi down to the Gulf of Mexico, it was impossible to estimate. Here was the great artery of the boundless and extending West, the population of which the man is now living who may see multiplied to a hundred millions. The idea of Napoleon was to have possession of the Mediterranean, but fate prevented him. England has now the command of that sea. Let England get possession of Yucatan, and she will make the gulf a *mare clausum*. The Gulf of Mexico should be American: not that America should exclusively use it in time of peace; but in case of war, we should be able to close it against hostile occupation.

With the command of Cuba, the water of the gulf is reduced to a hundred miles. While Cuba and Yucatan are held by feeble powers, having no ambition to interfere with our commercial interests, there is no danger. But let these places fall into the hands of a power like England, and the danger will be evident. He did not mean to say that she contemplated taking possession of Cuba by force, or of Yucatan by force; but if she should yield to the request of Yucatan and lend her aid, and thus acquire possession, what right shall we have to complain? England wants Cuba for commercial purposes; we want it for our very existence as a nation. In a question of so much importance as the possession of Cuba, we should resist to the last. He hoped it would be communicated to Spain that the United States would not see Cuba transferred to any other power. So long as Spain can remain at peace, and be able to retain her monarchy and power, there is nothing to be apprehended. But this condition was not likely to be permanent, and he trusted Spain would, before any change took place, perceive that it was more to her interest to dispose of Cuba by purchase than to retain it, or yield it for any other consideration. He referred to the remarks of Lord William Bentinck, in the British Parliament——

Mr. Westcott, in some explanatory remarks, insisted that Lord William Bentinck's observations on Cuba were intended to convey an intimation of a desire to abolish slavery in the southern States of the United Sates.

Mr. Calhoun replied that he did not doubt that there was a disposition in the British Government to abolish slavery all over the world. But since the debate which had been referred to, a momentous change had taken place in the opinions of British statesmen on this subject, and there was nothing to be feared from the interference of England in our institutions.

Mr. CASS resumed. He only desired to show that there were English statesmen who contemplated taking possession of Cuba, in order to shut up the Gulf of Mexico, or, as they expressed it, to cut our trade in two.

The object of this bill is to aid Yucatan. There was no more connection now between Yucatan and Mexico, than between Yucatan and China. Yucatan is independent, and may select her own government. He did not think we were precluded by the armistice, and he gave his reasons at some length. As to the character of the Indians in Yucatan, he regarded it as so low as to render that race entirely unfit to enjoy an equality of rights and privileges with the white race. The war in Yucatan was clearly a war of races—a war for physical existence, and not for moral power; and we are called on by humanity to interfere to prevent the entire extermination of the white race.

He expressed his opinion that the British agents had supplied the Indians with arms; not because the arms had the Tower stamp upon them, but because the Indians would not be likely to purchase them, and must have been supplied gratuitously. He stated, from his own knowledge, that in 1822, the British agents were in the practice of inviting the Indians on the north-western frontier to certain places, where they were gratuitously furnished with arms.

He expressed his preference for the bill in its original shape over the amendment which had been submitted.

Mr. DAVIS, of Massachusetts, obtained the floor, when, on motion of Mr. BREESE, and by common consent, the further consideration of the bill was postponed till to-morrow.

The Senate adjourned.

THURSDAY, May 11.

Occupation of Yucatan.

The Senate resumed the special order, being the bill to enable the President to take temporary military occupation of Yucatan.

Mr. DAVIS, of Massachusetts, expressed his intention not to confine himself to the question of the amendment, but to go generally into the subject under discussion.

A message was received from the President some short time ago, stating that the subject was of such great and pressing importance as to permit no delay in the action of the legislative branch. The result was the bill now before the Senate. He felt greatly obliged to the Senator from South Carolina for bringing this message so promptly to the attention of the Senate. It appeared, from what had subsequently occurred, that the ground of humanity, originally taken, had been entirely abandoned. From the candid avowal of the chairman of Foreign Relations, and of the Senator from Michigan, it would appear that we are called on to take possession of Yucatan, because it would be unsafe in the hands of any other Government. In this view, therefore, he was about to discuss the bill.

The representations made to the Senate are, that the people of Yucatan are divided, and that one portion cannot sustain itself against the majority. It is said that this is a war of races. This he denied. It was an assumption not borne out by the documents which had been laid on the tables of Senators. An officer in the navy, Mr. McKenney, estimates that about 120,000 Indians are engaged in this war. Out of at least 500,000, which is the minimum amount of the Indians, about one quarter only is engaged in the war. Therefore it is not a war of races. The mixed race, it is worthy of remark, have all joined the Indians. What wrongs have been committed to provoke the Indians to this war? He called attention to the fact, that these Indians took the field when their country was invaded by Mexico, and defeated Ampudia. They were therefore a brave people. They were then promised a remission of the capitation tax, which oppressed them severely. But this promise was violated, and thus commenced the war.

The Yucatanese, on the other hand, are represented as weak, cowardly, helpless. Our officers seem thus to consider them in their letters. Part of them deserted the army in the hour of need. Instead of being a contest of races, one of our officers describes it as a war of parties. And we are called on to assist in exterminating these Indians, who, in the time of danger, drove back the invaders of their country. He thought it unjust to charge upon these people that they are savages. They have been admitted to all the political rights of other citizens; they have a right to all the privileges which belong to the Yucatanese. They were not wanderers, living by hunting, predatory, but subsisted on the soil, made fruitful by their labor.

It is proposed to take temporary occupation of this country. What was meant by temporary occupation? We are told that it is intended to hold occupation until Mexico shall be able and willing to protect them. This was not likely to be the case; and why should we not as well strike out of these papers the word "temporary," and insert "continuous and permanent" occupation? The people of Yucatan want us to protect them against Mexico. This is what they want.

He was gratified that the Senator from Michigan had discussed this question on the true ground. It was a question of annexation. How was Texas admitted? She had for seven years maintained herself in an independent position, and was therefore in a condition to enter into any arrangement for annexing herself to what country she pleased.

That Yucatan was in a state of war with Mexico, he did not say; she perhaps held a neutral character. She had not been always consistent in her course, having at one time allied herself to Santa Anna. She is now in a state of rebellion against Mexico.

On the subject of the declaration of Mr. Monroe he made some remarks, to show that the views of Mr. Polk, at the period when the Panama mission was under consideration, were not similar to what they are now represented by his friends to be. He gave a brief history of the nominations of ministers to Panama, and the debate to which they gave rise. The object of that Congress was not to call in bayonets and swords and military array, but to wield only the moral power of united opinion. Yet it was contended that this Congress was a fearful source of danger to our country; that we ought to conform to the recommendation of the Father of his Country to avoid entangling alliances; and the resolutions submitted in the House apprehended a breach of our neutral engagements with Spain and other countries, and might involve us in the danger of war. He quoted from the speech of Mr. Polk on that occasion, to show that he was then opposed to making common cause with the republics of the South; and that self-preservation was the first law of nature. Such was the language of the President when he opposed the Panama mission.

He expressed doubts as to the effect of this measure on the treaty now pending with Mexico.* Some who were opposed to the treaty would rather rejoice at such a result as its violation would produce. An expedition to Yucatan, undertaken under an invitation from her, in which she looks to annexation with the United States as a remuneration, would be as likely to lead to war as was the annexation of Texas. We might thus, in addition to a war with England and Spain, have a renewed war with Mexico on our hands. He reminded the Senate, that when the treaty with Mexico was received at Washington, the Yucatan commissioner presented a protest against any treaty which did not include a protection for Yucatan. It is evident, therefore, that Yucatan feels a great interest in the defeat of the treaty with Mexico, and will not hesitate to adopt a course which might lead to its defeat.

He was disposed to do a great deal for humanity; but he could not bring himself to sanction a measure of such doubtful and dangerous import as this was now urged on the Senate.

Saturday, May 13.

Occupation of Yucatan.

On motion of Mr. Hannegan, the Senate proceeded to the consideration of the special order, being the bill to enable the President of the United States to take temporary military occupation of Yucatan; when

Mr. Miller rose and said, that if this bill had been placed simply on the ground of humanity, it would have met with his entire approbation. But, in the progress of the discussion, the measure had been entirely stripped of humanity, and advocated as a matter of cold, calculating policy. It was a strange proposition to require of us aid to resist an overwhelming foe, and then that we should receive pay for the same. He gave a brief historical view of the circumstances which had preceded this application, and then reviewed the correspondence which had taken place between the Secretary of State and the Yucatan commissioner. He dwelt on the fact that at the time of this application, Yucatan was a part of the territory of Mexico. The commissioner presents a deplorable picture of the condition of Yucatan—representing the white race as in danger of extermination by the Indians. But no response being given to the cry of distress, he shows a pretty accurate knowledge, if not of human nature generally, of the human nature of our country, by then calling the attention of our Government to the declaration of Mr. Monroe, and referring to our course in reference to the Greeks, &c., and by throwing out a menace of appealing to England or other European powers, in case we do not act. It was like the case of a man who, finding his house on fire, offers his neighbor a deed of the building if he will put out the fire; but, seeing that his neighbor makes no movement to save the property, he tells him, Well, if you don't take the offer, there is a man over the way who will do it, and I will go to him.

He adverted to the position taken by the chairman of Foreign Relations, that it was necessary to act to keep England out of Yucatan; so that the real object was, not to drive out the Indians, but to drive out the English. The Eagle and the Lion were to be watching to see which shall seize the victim. He put the case of the people of South Carolina, or Alabama, making an application to Great Britain. What would be thought if Great Britain were to indicate a disposition to take possession of the complaining State, without the sanction of the General Government? Would it not be regarded as an act of war? If Yucatan is not independent of Mexico, we cannot interfere without danger of war. He referred to the pending treaty, the ratification of which may be defeated by any unwise and overhasty movement on our part. Mr. Sierra, the Yucatan commissioner, had entered a protest against the treaty, but withheld his threat of calling on other powers until a subsequent period. He took exception to the style assumed by Mr. Sierra in his letter of protest—a style which would have been suitable to a sovereign prince making on some other sovereign a demand sanctioned by the laws of nations.

It had been rumored that the President him-

* The treaty of peace with Mexico had been actually concluded at the time this debate on Yucatan was going on, and was only waiting its final form in the exchange of ratifications, which took place at the city of Queretaro, a few days thereafter, to wit, on the 30th day of May, 1848.

self was not at heart in favor of the pending treaty with Mexico, and since this subject had been before the Senate, the probability of the rumor had received some strength. He adverted to the causes of the war with Mexico—to the annexation of Texas and the boundary question—to the manner in which it had been carried on, and to the anxious desire for its speedy termination which at this moment pervades the whole country. It was emphatically the duty of every man who held the peace of the country in his hands, to be particularly cautious not to do any thing which would tend to the disappointment of those hopes and desires.

If this measure were only urged in a spirit of charity, for the sole purpose of saving the white citizens of Yucatan from extermination by the Indians, we certainly should have no right to be displeased because we have been anticipated either by Spain or England. The reply of Spain, in which she declares that she will not take advantage of the present distressed condition of Yucatan to seize on her territory, he lauded as worthy of old Spain in her best days. Such an answer ought to have been ours. France had also declined in a similar manner. And as to the interference of England, he had seen no proofs of it. It did not yet appear that she had been even asked. The possession of English arms he did not regard as ground of suspicion against the English Government. England could not intefere without bringing on her war with Mexico and war with ourselves, who are now at war with Mexico. A great deal of political capital has been made out of this cry about English interference in Texas and in California, but he has yet to discover the first particle of evidence on which this cry could be justified.

He proceeded to remark on the declaration of Mr. Monroe, which was issued in opposition to the encroaching spirit of the Holy Alliance. He denied that it could be applied here without a complete perversion of the principle. We propose to do precisely what we say England and France and Spain shall not do. We desire to take possession of another State, and defend the act by appealing to the declaration of Mr. Monroe, which was issued to prevent one nation from interfering with the affairs of another. If we say to another, You shall not take Yucatan, shall we take Yucatan ourselves? Are we about to drive others away from this afflicted territory, in order that we may have all the plunder to ourselves?

If Great Britain has determined to take possession of Yucatan or any portion of it, to the detriment of our national safety, it becomes a great question between us and Great Britain. If so, we ought at once to speak out in plain language, and tell her we will oppose her, instead of trying to get ahead of the Lion, in order to be beforehand in seizing the prey. The first is the manly course. The possession of Cuba would in all probability come up under the next Administration, because, in the present state of Europe, it is not likely that Spain will long hold out.

Monday, May 15.

Message from the President—Yucatan.

A Message was received from the President of the United States, transmitting, in compliance with a resolution of the 13th instant, calling for copies of any orders to officers of our naval squadron in relation to giving aid to Yucatan, a communication from the Navy Department, containing copies of orders issued on the 8th and 12th May to Commodore Perry.

[The communication of the 8th instant directs the Commodore to allow powder to be landed at Sisal, provided the Commodore has reason to think that it will not be used against us. That of the 12th instant compliments Commodore Perry on his efforts, with his limited means, to give aid; and satisfaction that he should have visited the coast; directs the entire force of the marines at Alvarado to be sent to Laguna, with instructions to repel the Indians if they approach that point, and tells him that his force will not justify a march into the interior, and goes on to say, that "while the United States are engaged in a war with Mexico, the actual presence, without our consent, of the armed force of a neutral power, within the territory of our enemy, co-operating with any portion of the Mexican people in military operations, cannot be permitted. Such a state of things, it is hoped, will not occur. If you should have reason to believe that it will, you will communicate it without further delay, that the President may take such measures as his constitutional duty will require at his hands."]

The bill to enable the President of the United States to take temporary military occupation of Yucatan was taken up.

Mr. Calhoun rose, and referred to the ground on which the Message of the President of the United States had placed the proposition now before the Senate, to prevent Yucatan from becoming a colony of a foreign power, and to prevent also the devastation of the country and the destruction of the white inhabitants. He had placed our proposed interference on the ground of Mr. Monroe's declaration. Against all these points, against the message and report of the Committee on Foreign Relations, he had, after deep reflection, made up his mind to record his vote.

He went on to show that the declaration of Mr. Monroe was published in opposition to the designs of the Allied powers, called the Holy Alliance; and contended that the case of Yucatan could not be brought within the range of that declaration. He stated what was the conduct of the Holy Alliance, and what were their designs, and the alarm taken by England at the innovating principles laid down by them. He adverted to the information given by Mr.

Rush, and the manner in which the Cabinet acted on it. The schemes and the existence of the Holy Alliance had entirely disappeared; and, if a final blow had been necessary, it was given by the recent revolutions in Europe. A more especial declaration with regard to Spain was then agreed on, and Yucatan cannot be comprehended in it.

It had been charged that England would interfere to save the people of Yucatan; but he had seen no evidence of any thing of the kind. He had seen no proof that England had furnished arms to Yucatan; none that she intended to make a settlement in Yucatan. If England should come in, she comes without any hostile intentions against Yucatan, and we should have no right to take offence at her conduct.

He glanced at the causes which led to this declaration of Mr. Monroe; the principal of which was, the attempt of Russia to extend her settlements on the north-west coast of America, in which she was opposed by England and the United States. He gave his own version of the history of the construction of this declaration, varying in some respects from that which was given by the Senator from Indiana. The effect of this declaration was, to impose a check on the colonization schemes of England, which so offended her as to prevent her from going heartily with the United States against the claims of Russia.

He denied that there was any such principle in the declaration of Mr. Monroe, as is assumed by the Message of the President. If his views were to be received as the true construction, and they were to be carried out, we should be kept in a constant state of war. There are cases in which he would be willing to interfere. He instanced the case of Cuba. So long as that island remained in the hands of a peaceful nation like Spain, we ought to be content. But he would never consent to let Cuba go into the hands of any other European power, because the transfer would be prejudicial to our interests.

In the case of Texas, he favored annexation, because he saw clearly, in his opinion, that there might be an interference on the part of England, which would involve us in a triple war—with England, with Texas, and Mexico.

He had been asked if he would resist England in case she should attempt to relieve Yucatan, and should take possession. He was prepared to answer that he would not, and this for irresistible reasons. Yucatan was, for the greater part, worthless. The possession of her would not strengthen the facilities of England to injure us. Yucatan has no ports which could be made serviceable to her. He took a glance at the outward and inward passages into the Gulf of Mexico, to show that England, in consequence of her great naval power, had entire command of the Caribbean Sea, and could, in time of war, close the gulf against us.

In the event of our interference with Yucatan, who can fix the cost or the limitation of the war? We might defeat the Indians, but they would retire, and render it necessary that we should pursue. It would be a repetition of the Seminole war; and no one could say what would be the expense of the war, and when it could be brought to a termination. He was opposed to it also, because it involved a violation of our treaty with Mexico.

The Senate adjourned.

WEDNESDAY, May 17.

Occupation of Yucatan.

The Senate proceeded to consider the bill to enable the President of the United States to take temporary military occupation of Yucatan.

The question being on the amendment proposed by Mr. Dix—

Mr. Dix rose to explain his amendment. He stated the position of Yucatan at this moment, reduced by her helplessness to offer the surrender of her sovereignty to any nation which will aid in her rescue from the hostility of the Indians which threaten the extermination of the white inhabitants. The President had, as he was bound to do, communicated to the Senate the proposition of Yucatan to our Government. The Committee on Military Affairs had reported a bill. This being a question relative to the internal difficulties in which Yucatan is involved, becomes one of some delicacy and complexity. As we lay down the rule that interference with the domestic concerns of other nations cannot be permitted by foreign Governments, it is our duty to take care that we ourselves do not violate this rule. But there were, in the case of Yucatan, circumstances which seemed to authorize and justify some interference on our part. He proceeded to give a succinct history of the changes in Yucatan, which had resulted in her obtaining, not an entire, but a qualified independence of Mexico. He viewed her as occupying a neutral position in relation to the United States.

By the treaty with Mexico, we are restrained from any hostile act towards any part of the territory of Mexico. He did not see that we could take military occupation of Yucatan, under a rigid construction of the treaty with Mexico, without subjecting ourselves to the imputation of bad faith. He expressed a hope that the chairman of Foreign Relations would not adhere to the first section of the bill. As to the other sections of the bill, they had his entire acquiescence. The outrages which characterized the war in Yucatan shocked humanity. He pointed out the difference between his amendment and the original section. The latter supersedes the Government of Yucatan, while the former contemplates co-operation with that Government. He thought that we might properly transfer some of our troops from Mexico, for the purpose of aiding the Yucatanese in their defensive contest against the Indians. By his substitute, he defined the conditions on which an army and navy shall be employed. They are to be subordinate to the Government of Yucatan.

He did not think that this interposition would be any violation of international law. We are already in possession of one of her ports—Laguna—and this fact may be cited as a justification of our interference. If we were at peace with Mexico, this would be a very embarrassing case. It must be a very extreme case which would justify us in trampling on the political organizations of nations; but such cases he admitted might occur, in which all respect for these political organizations must yield to the higher duties which bind man to man.

To prevent a breach of international obligations, we have no right to interfere in the affairs of European countries. At the same time, he held that we had a right to take such measures as would prevent the interference of European powers in the domestic concerns of this continent. What those measures should be, he would not pretend to say. It was a question of prudence. But he did not place his support of this bill on the ground of the danger of European interference in the affairs of Yucatan.

One of the main grounds on which he placed his support of this bill was that of justice. We had taken away the means which would have enabled Mexico to assist Yucatan, and we are bound in strict justicé to do what we have prevented Mexico from doing.

He also supported the bill on the ground of humanity. We are in the full enjoyment of all the blessings and privileges of law, order, tranquillity, and uninterrupted prosperity. In Central America the picture is reversed; there, law, order, tranquillity, and prosperity, are all rent asunder—towns sacked, houses burned, and every description of ferocious outrage perpetrated. Such was the sketch—an imperfect one he admitted—but he would not attempt to fill it up with the loathsome details which truth would furnish.

Mr. CLAYTON said he would ask the Senator from New York, if he was perfectly satisfied that a war was at this moment existing between the whites and the Indians.

Mr. DIX said he was perfectly satisfied of the fact.

After a few words from Mr. DIX, by way of conclusion—

Mr. HANNEGAN then rose and said, that since this bill was under discussion yesterday, he had received intelligence that a treaty had been concluded between the Government of Yucatan and the Indians, and that the war had been brought to a close. Similar information had reached the city, in the Baltimore Sun, which had given the heads of the treaty. The terms agreed on appeared to him to be fair, and he trusted that the difficulties had been settled. In this state of things, he thought it due to the Senate to state that he should no longer feel himself called on to press the passage of this bill. No harm could result from a little delay, and it might be advisable to wait for further advices from Yucatan before any definite action took place. As we are in a state of war with Mexico, no foreign armed vessels would attempt to enter the ports of Yucatan. A force of four hundred marines had been ordered from Alvarado to Laguna, and this would suffice for the present. He would, therefore, move that the bill be informally passed over.

Mr. DIX said, that if he had been aware of these facts, he would not have troubled the Senate with the remarks which he had felt himself called on to submit.

HOUSE OF REPRESENTATIVES.

MONDAY, May 29.

Message from the President—Affairs of Oregon—Territorial Government recommended to be Established.

Mr. SMITH, of Indiana, asked the general consent of the House to offer a resolution making the bill to establish the Territorial Government of Oregon the special order of the day, immediately after the general appropriation bills (now the special order) shall have been disposed of, except on Fridays and Saturdays.

Mr. MCCLERNAND appealed to his friend from Indiana (Mr. SMITH) to modify his amendment, so as to resolve the House into Committee at once, in order that immediate action might be had upon the Oregon territorial bill. Mr. McC. had a letter from a citizen of Oregon, dated as late as the 1st of January last, which represented the country to be in a most distressing situation. The Indians had murdered a number of the whites, and an open and cruel war was waged by the Indians against them. Humanity and public duty demanded that prompt measures should be taken to give security to the persons and property of American citizens in Oregon.

The SPEAKER, by general consent, laid before the House the following Message from the President of the United States:

To the Senate and House of Representatives of the United States:

I lay before Congress the accompanying memorial and papers, which have been transmitted to me by a special messenger, employed for that purpose by the Governor and "Legislative Assembly of Oregon Territory," who constitute the temporary government which the inhabitants of that distant region of our country have, from the necessity of their condition, organized for themselves. The memorialists are citizens of the United States. They express ardent attachment to their native land, and, in their present perilous and distressed situation, they earnestly invoke the aid and protection of their Government.

They represent that "the proud and powerful tribes of Indians" residing in their vicinity, have recently raised "the war-whoop, and crimsoned their tomahawks in the blood of their citizens;" that they apprehend that "many of the powerful tribes inhabiting the upper valley of the Columbia, have formed an alliance for the purpose of carrying on hostilities against their settlements;" that the number of the white population is far inferior to that of the savages; that they are deficient in arms and money, and fear that they do not possess strength to repel the "attack of so formidable a foe, and protect their families and property from violence and rapine." They conclude their appeal to the Government of the United States for relief by declaring: "If it be at all the intention of our honored parent to spread her guardian wing over her sons and daughters in Oregon, she surely will not refuse to do it now, when they are struggling with all the ills of a weak and temporary government, and when perils are daily thickening around them and preparing to burst upon their heads. When the ensuing summer's sun shall have dispelled the snow from the mountains, we shall look with glowing hope and restless anxiety for the coming of your laws and your arms."

In my message of the 5th of August, 1846, communicating "a copy of the convention for the settlement and adjustment of the Oregon boundary," I recommended to Congress that "provision should be made by law at the earliest practicable period, for the organization of a territorial government in Oregon." In my annual message of December, 1846, and again in December, 1847, this recommendation was repeated.

The population of Oregon is believed to exceed twelve thousand souls, and it is known that it will be increased by a large number of emigrants during the present season. The facts set forth in the accompanying memorial and papers, show that the dangers to which our fellow-citizens are exposed are so imminent, that I deem it to be my duty again to impress on Congress the strong claim which the inhabitants of that distant country have to the benefit of our laws and the protection of our Government.

I therefore again invite the attention of Congress to the subject, and recommend that laws be promptly passed establishing a Territorial Government, and granting authority to raise an adequate volunteer force for the defence and protection of its inhabitants. It is believed that a regiment of mounted men, with such additional force as may be raised in Oregon, will be sufficient to afford the required protection. It is recommended that the force raised for this purpose should engage to serve for twelve months, unless sooner discharged. No doubt is entertained, with proper inducements in land bounties, such a force can be raised in a short time. Upon the expiration of their service many of them will doubtless desire to remain in the country, and settle upon the land which they may receive as bounty.

It is deemed important that provision be made for the appointment of a suitable number of Indian agents to reside among the various tribes in Oregon, and that appropriations be made to enable them to treat with these tribes, with a view to restore and preserve peace between them and the white inhabitants.

Should the laws recommended be promptly passed, the measures for their execution may be completed during the present season, and before the severity of winter will interpose obstacles in crossing the Rocky Mountains. If not promptly passed, a delay of another year will be the consequence, and may prove destructive to the white settlements in Oregon. JAMES K. POLK.

Washington, *May* 29, 1848.

Mr. Cobb, of Georgia, said the information contained in the Message of the President of the United Sates, which had just been read, had been confirmed by private letters which some gentlemen on this floor had received from citizens of Oregon. The time at which it came to them was very opportune. He was happy to hear the gentleman from Indiana (Mr. C. B. Smith) this morning introduce a resolution to make the bill for the establishment of a territorial Government in Oregon a special order, but he feared, if it was to be preceded by the appropriation bills, that some weeks would elapse before this House could take action upon it, and that it would not be reached until the arrival of a period too late for the purpose contemplated by this Message. What had they now heard? Why, that the Indian tribes were waging war against our citizens in Oregon, who called upon us for assistance; and it was our duty to respond promptly to that call, and furnish them with the means of protection. The bill to establish a territorial government in Oregon had been long before Congress, and it had been postponed again and again, until the people of that Territory had been driven to form a government for themselves, using for their protection all the power which God and Nature had given them. But they now appealed to this Government in an unusual emergency, and that appeal should be promptly responded to by this House. Immediate action should be had for the protection of our own people in one of our own Territories. He suggested, therefore, and he should make such a motion when he had an opportunity to do so, that the President's Message should be laid on the table and printed, and he should then move an amendment to the motion of the gentleman from Indiana, (Mr. C. B. Smith,) to strike out all that portion which provides for making the Oregon territorial bill the special order immediately after the general appropriation bills, and insert words to postpone the present special orders, that immediate action might be taken on the territorial bill, so as to dispose of it at the earliest practicable period.

Mr. Murphy wished to ask the gentleman from Georgia if it was necessary, in order to give protection to the people of Oregon, to organize a territorial government in that territory? Could they not act promptly, and adopt a measure to furnish them with protection? Nay, could not the Executive do it without any action of this House?

Mr. Cobb said it must be admitted that it was in the power of the Government of the United States to protect its own people without the passage of this bill, but this bill was a protection to which the people of Oregon had been entitled for two years. For more than two years they had been promised the protection of laws; and now, when such an opportunity presented itself, and the people were exposed to immediate danger, and the consequences which followed if support were withheld, why, he would ask the gentleman from New York, should they stop half way?

Mr. C. therefore moved that the Message and accompanying documents be laid on the table and printed.

Mr. VINTON said the Message now before the House, if he had heard it correctly, proposed, in the first place, to raise a military force for the protection of our people in Oregon, and in the next place, it proposed that the Congress of the United States should provide a territorial government for the Territory of Oregon. Now, there was no necessary connection between these two things. If our people were in danger, that might be good ground, of course, for raising a military force for their protection; but a bill to establish a territorial government did not contemplate any such thing as raising a military force. It would be out of place in such a bill to make an addition to the standing army.

The proposition of the gentleman from Georgia (Mr. COBB) contemplated the putting aside of the appropriation bills, for the purpose of taking up the Oregon territorial bill, giving notice of a provision which he should move to incorporate into that bill to raise a military force for Oregon. They were now about entering upon the month of June, and the great appropriation bills, which would require much time and attention in their consideration, had not yet been acted upon; and unless the House was disposed to give to them more attention than it had heretofore been its pleasure to devote to them, they would not be able to dispose of them by the first of July next, when they should enter upon the fiscal year for which these bills made provision. And after that period they would have to be acted upon by the Senate, so that the Government would not have at its command the means which these bills provided at the time they would be required. If there was an immediate necessity for raising a military force for the protection of the citizens of Oregon, he was willing that that subject should be promptly acted upon; but the general appropriation bills were of more importance than any private bill. The gentleman from Georgia, he would suggest, could accomplish his purpose by moving to make the Oregon territorial bill the special order for Fridays and Saturdays; but if they took up the territorial bill, and intended thereby to make provision for the protection of the citizens of Oregon, they would not be able to dispose of it for a month to come; and it was for that, amongst other reasons, that he was opposed to incorporating in the same bill a proposition to protect the people of Oregon, and one establishing a territorial government for that people.

Mr. HARALSON said it was important to act speedily on this Message from the President of the United States. Our citizens who were now inhabitants of Oregon, were in need of military aid to protect them against the Indian tribes, and prompt action was necessary to give them that aid. He hoped it would not be mixed up with the consideration of the Oregon territorial bill; for when that bill shall come up, it would be discussed from day to day and week to week, and hence it was important to give this Message such a direction—for instance, by referring it to the Military Committee—as would lead to the furnishing of speedy relief to those who appealed to us for protection.

How could this be done? They were separate questions; both embraced, it was true, in the Message of the President—one, however, urging the importance of the establishment of a territorial government in Oregon; and the other a specific recommendation that the President be authorized to raise a volunteer force, for the purpose of going speedily to the scene of these disturbances, and giving relief to our citizens there. He would propose, then, instead of the motion of his colleague, that the President's Message be referred to the Committee on Military Affairs, with instructions to that committee to report, and to report forthwith, if they pleased, a bill to this House, authorizing the President to raise a sufficient force to proceed forthwith to Oregon, to give our citizens there the relief they demand. Thus speedy relief would be afforded, and the House would not place themselves in the attitude of disregarding the call, and engaging in idle debate upon subjects disconnected with that relief. The two subjects were not connected with each other; the one related to the establishment of a territorial government which might tend ultimately to their security against the encroachments of the Indians; and the other proposed to raise a military force for their immediate relief.

Mr. COBB would answer his colleague's interrogatory with great pleasure, by telling him that there was not a question which could arise out of the Oregon bill, either in its present form or as it might be amended, which had not been discussed over and over again; and upon the determination of this House to act, or not to act, would depend the early decision or the postponement of the question.

Mr. VENABLE concurred fully with the gentlemen who thought they should adopt immediate action for the protection of the people of Oregon, and he took occasion to say to his friend from Vermont, that whatever might be the disposition of others, it was none of his (Mr. V.'s) to annex this amendment to the Oregon bill for the purpose of avoiding the discussion of the question to which the gentleman had referred. He wished to stand *rectus in curia* upon that question; and when it came up, he trusted an opportunity would be afforded him of giving his views in full. A more important and interesting question had never, and could never, be agitated. He was unwilling, by indirect legislation or by parliamentary manœuvre, to avoid any question; he was willing that the world should know any political opinion he held, and to give full expression to it, affect whatever individual it might.

He concurred with his friend from Georgia, (Mr. Haralson.) He would detach this question from party strife, from slavery, the Wilmot proviso, and other political questions. When the voice of distress and agony came up to us from those who had carried their wives and their little ones into that territory under the expectation of our protection, let them afford immediate relief.

His principal object in rising was to inform the people everywhere that there was no disposition, he believed, on his side of the House, and it was disclaimed on the other, to blink this great question. He was willing to discuss it; he wanted all its principles to be made as familiar as household words, let who would be injured by it. He wanted it understood. When the Oregon bill came up, he hoped that no hurry to adjourn, or any thing else, would prevent a thorough discussion and understanding of each other's views. If the platform on which he and those who thought with him stood had a bad foundation, let it be torn from them; but let it be understood that the rights of the southern portion of the Confederacy were never to be made the subject of compromise. He felt that his children were the legitimate children of the country; that they had an equal interest in the common property of the Union, and no man should say, you have no right to put your foot upon the territory of the Union. With his heart's blood he would defend that principle. In all our broad territory, whether acquired by purchase or conquest, by cession or treaty, his children and the children of his constituents had the right to put their foot and their property, and to demand that protection which the Constitution of the United States gave them. When he ceased to stand by this right, he hoped to be denounced as recreant to every high, noble, and holy feeling which should fill an American bosom.

Mr. Nicoll obtained the floor, and, after some conversation—at the suggestion of Mr. Haralson and others, having moved an amendment to the motion to print, to refer to the Committee on Military Affairs—demanded the previous question.

The demand was seconded, and the main question ordered, and being taken, the amendment and motion as amended were successively agreed to, and then the Message was referred to the Committee on Military Affairs, and printed.

IN SENATE.

Thursday, June 1.

Oregon Territorial Bill.

On motion of Mr. Bright, the Senate resumed the consideration of the bill to establish the Territorial Government of Oregon.

The question being on the amendment moved by Mr. Hale, to insert the following section:

"Sec. —. *And be it further enacted*, That the inhabitants of said Territory shall be entitled to enjoy all and singular the rights, privileges, and advantages, granted and secured to the people of the territory of the United States north-west of the river Ohio, by the articles of compact contained in the ordinance for the government of said territory, on the thirteenth day of July, seventeen hundred and eighty-seven; and shall be subject to all the conditions, and restrictions, and prohibitions in said articles of compact imposed upon the people of said territory; and the existing laws now in force in the Territory of Oregon, under the authority of the provisional government established by the people thereof, shall continue to be valid and operative therein, so far as the same be not incompatible with the principles and provisions of this act; subject, nevertheless, to be altered, modified, or repealed by the Governor and Legislative Assembly of the said Territory of Oregon; and the laws of the United States are hereby extended over, and declared to be in force in, said Territory, so far as the same or any provision thereof may be applicable."

Mr. Butler briefly explained his course in the Judiciary Committee in relation to the bill of last session, in order to show that it was only intended to make it conform to the laws of Iowa. If the bill now brought forward as the bill of last session, contains the ordinance of 1787, it was adopted by a misconception on his part. The amendment of the Senator from New Hampshire extended that ordinance to the Territory of Oregon, which was already covertly included in the clause of last session as it came from the Committee on Territories.

Mr. Bright regretted the absence of the chairman of the Committee on Territories. The bill would not have been brought up during his absence but for the recent events in Oregon, and the Message of the President on the subject. The bill is substantially the same as the bills for the admission of Wisconsin and Iowa, with the exception of the 12th section, which varies in some respects from the clause in the other bills. The laws of Oregon prohibit slavery in the Territory, and these laws will remain unless changed by the legislative authority. He objected to the proposition of the Senator from Florida to insert the 12th section of the bill of the last session, because it restricted the Legislature of Oregon too severely. If the question which has been introduced by the Senator from New Hampshire were now to be discussed, the bill could not be passed for some days, and he regretted that that Senator should have felt it his duty to offer it at this time. He would have no objection to strike out the 12th section if any substitute could be provided for it.

Mr. WESTCOTT, if he understood the section, regarded it as excluding slavery, as adopting the organic law of Iowa to that effect. Did the Senator from Indiana admit that the act of the provisional government of Oregon excluded slavery?

Mr. BRIGHT said he so admitted it.

Mr. HALE, with leave of the Senator, withdrew his amendment for the present. He had been accused of thrusting a firebrand in the Senate. He would now take it out, and see how the bill would go on without it. He would renew it hereafter or not, as he might deem best.

The question recurring on the motion of Mr. WESTCOTT—

Mr. BRIGHT, with the consent of the friends, consented to strike out the 12th section. He moved to strike it out.

Mr. HALE said if that section was stricken out he should renew his amendment. His object was to permit the bill to pass in its present shape. He asked the yeas and nays on the motion.

Mr. CALHOUN thought the striking out of the 12th section would not remove the difficulty. There are three questions involved: 1st, The power of Congress to interfere with persons emigrating with their property into the State; 2d, The power of the Territorial Government to do so; and, 3d, The power of Congress to vest such a power in the Territory. The amendment moved by the Senator from Florida was the only course. He did not wish to delay the bill. But if the matter was to be gone into, it would be the best way to separate the military authority from the residue of the bill, and act on that at present.

Mr. MILLER expressed surprise at the extent of the assumption that the people of Oregon had no right to prohibit slavery. Where was the authority to create slavery there?

Mr. DICKINSON said he was willing to strike out the 12th section, and to leave the territorial government to take care of itself. He had full confidence in the wisdom of the territorial legislature to make its own laws.

Mr. BAGBY referred to the principles laid down in the resolutions he had some time since submitted to the Senate as those which must be sustained, and should regulate the action of Congress. Congress has no more right over the territory than it has over any other property of the United States. Here we were about to erect a wall around a territory in which citizens of other States could not meet without leaving their property behind them. He differed from the Senator from South Carolina as to the twelfth section. That section was an eyesore to him, and he wished it stricken out; in which event he would vote for the bill, deeming it sufficient for its purposes as it would then stand. He protested against the monstrous doctrine advanced by the Senator from New York, (Mr. DICKINSON,) and protested also against these attempts to stir up agitation in reference to a territory into which it was generally admitted that slavery was never likely to enter.

Mr. HALE. Will the Senator allow me? I have withdrawn my firebrand, and this is a southern firebrand which is now thrown in.

Mr. BAGBY. I know he has withdrawn it, but he promises to renew it. The northern fire burns more slowly than the southern fire; and whenever the Senator from New Hampshire desires to renew it, he has wind enough to kindle a flame. He deprecated the new doctrine as to these ephemeral things called territorial governments, by which any twenty thousand settlers on the public lands might set up a government, and demand the right to enact their own laws. He contended that a power could not be delegated to a creature which the creator did not possess. If by inherent right the people could form a government, why do they come to Congress to ask the power? and to what extent could Congress confer power? Not beyond the power vested in it by the constitution.

Mr. FOOTE regretted that this discussion had been commenced and had gone on in such a strange manner. Admitting that the striking out of the twelfth section would remove his objection to the bill, still the Senator from Alabama went at length into a question which it had been the desire of many Senators, by a mutual understanding, to avoid. He was prepared to go into this question whenever it was forced upon him; but he had been stricken with a thrill of delight as he listened to the wise and patriotic suggestions of the Senator from Missouri yesterday, that we should confine our attention to the duties imposed on us. Should the resolutions submitted by the Senator from New York be taken up, he should be prepared to offer his views at length on this question. He was opposed to the agitation of this question at the present time, as it might enable an individual to whom the Abolitionists were attracted, to increase his popularity, and might also have the effect of exciting the South so as to weaken the strength of the great party to which he was attached in that section of the Union. There was a plan on foot to distract the South, which he would expose at a proper time.

Mr. HALE assured the Senator from Mississippi that his friends did not calculate on the vote of his State at the pending election. He had risen to say, that this firebrand did not come from him. He had drawn out his firebrand, but the fire had burned more brightly than before it was taken out. He regretted that Senators should now consider the ordinance of 1787 as insulting to the southern States. If that ordinance was an insult, how was it they had remained quiet under it more than half a century? With all his respect for gentlemen, and all his abhorrence to wound the feelings of any, he could not avoid saying that he felt little sympathy with those who had lived under an insult which was sixty years old before it was discovered. He charged the Senator from Alabama with introducing and arguing abstractions, while he charged him (Mr. Hale) with doing that very thing. At the risk of offending those who had sustained him at a time when sympathy was worth something and votes were worth more, he had withdrawn his amendment, and then a more pestiferous movement was made.

Mr. Butler asked if the Senator had not indicated, when he withdrew his proposition, his intention to introduce the firebrand again, as soon as he saw that one which was about to be introduced had burned out?

Mr. Hale replied. He had asked the Chair if it would be in order to offer his amendment again, if he withdrew it for the purpose of enabling the Senator from Florida to offer his? Having been informed that it would be in order, he withdrew it, stating that he might offer it, or not, as he should think proper. His intention was, if the bill was suffered to pass in the shape proposed, not to offer it again. But when he found other doctors dosing it, he determined that he would try his own medicine again. He then laid down his proposition that slaves could not be regarded as property, and quoted some judicial decisions to sustain him in this view.

In the views which he had expressed, he was happy to say that he was supported by many distinguished men from the South. Every southern gentleman regarded the existence of slavery as an evil, and was anxious to free the slaveholding States from the odium of its introduction. It was alleged by some, that the curse had its origin in the mercenary course pursued by the New England merchants, who entered into the traffic in slaves for profit; others charged all the responsibility on Great Britain. If the evil, therefore, was of that odious character that even the South shrunk from the responsibility of its introduction, with what consistency could southern Senators vote for extending it to new territories where it had never yet obtained a footing, and where it was said that it was not likely to enter? He gave southern gentlemen great credit for the open and manly manner in which they expressed their views. They met the question fairly and candidly. Every man could understand them. There was no beating about the bush among them. With such opponents it was gratifying to contend. Very different was their course to that of certain animals which had been characterized as northern men with southern principles. He invoked the attention of the Senate to the declaration of the Senator from Mississippi, that in the discussion of this great question, he was not influenced by truth, justice, and humanity; but that he was anxious to evade its full and fair discussion, from an apprehension that it would have the effect of distracting a party, and weakening that glorious ticket which was to sweep over the whole of the United States like a hurricane.

Mr. Foote begged to explain, that he had only named this as one of the consequences of the discussion of the question at this time, and he was prepared, at a proper time, to go into the proofs which had come into his possession on this point. But he had stated, as his main objection, the delay of the bill; which must be the consequence of the agitation of the subject at this time, and this, too, at a moment when our immediate action is demanded by the perilous condition of our fellow-citizens in the Territory of Oregon.

Some further discussion ensued between Mr. Hale and Mr. Foote, which partook of a personal character, and had no reference to the question legitimately before the Senate; and, pending this debate,

The Senate adjourned.

Friday, June 2.

Oregon.

On motion of Mr. Bright, the Senate resumed the consideration of the bill to establish a territorial government in Oregon.

Mr. Bright withdrew his motion to strike out the twelfth section.

Mr. Berrien renewed the motion, and asked the yeas and nays, which were ordered.

Mr. Westcott wished to ask if Senators understood the character and effect of the existing laws in Oregon. He alluded to all the laws. We were about to sanction laws which have not yet been submitted to us. There was among them a sumptuary law, prohibiting the introduction of any ardent spirits in the territory. [Mr. Hale: Good!] The Senator from New Hampshire says "good," and he will probably vote for the bill. But he would ask if the territorial government had a right to interfere with the United States system of import duties? The provisional government of Oregon was merely an assemblage of emigrants who first went there—of all nations and casts—and never was recognized as a government while we held the territory in joint occupation with Great Britain. He suggested these facts for the consideration of the Senate.

Mr. Turney was in favor of the motion when made by the Senator from Indiana, because he regarded it as intended to conciliate the North and the South. But he had withdrawn it, and it was renewed by a Southern Senator; so that it was intended now to make it a sectional question. He regarded it as a violation of the common platform agreed on by the Democratic party. He warned the Senators who advocated the retention of the section, of the dangers to which they subjected themselves by withdrawing the motion to strike it out. The party would be at sea, and there could be no union between the North and South.

Mr. Badger gave briefly his reasons for

voting to retain the twelfth section. The settlers in Oregon, for the purpose of self-defence, had established a provisional government. Congress was now called on to sanction the acts of this provisional government. Should this section be stricken out, the people of Oregon will be left in a situation in which they will have no laws which can be carried into execution. Months must elapse before the system now to be established can be made effective. We must either give temporary force to the laws now existing, or abolish them. He regarded the retention of the section as necessary to enable the people to obtain the benefits of the existing laws. He thought the inhabitants ought to have the power to establish their own municipal regulations, and that the restrictions contained in the Senate bill are sufficient to prevent any evil results.

Mr. RUSK regretted that the Senator from Indiana had consented to withdraw his motion to strike out the section, because he thought it constituted a common ground on which all might have united, and have avoided the discussion of the slavery question. He took a different view of the effect of this section from that taken by the Senator from North Carolina who had just spoken.

Mr. WESTCOTT sent to the Secretary a copy of the organic laws of Oregon, as adopted previous to the treaty of Oregon; which was read.

Mr. BUTLER said it was evident that this bill did not come to the Senate with the twelfth section in it by the consent of a full Committee on the Territories. It was sanctioned by two members of that committee, and was in direct conflict with the well-guarded and able bill reported by the Judiciary Committee. He had hoped the section would be stricken out, and that the people of Oregon might be left to make such laws as they may think proper, whether they exclude or admit slavery. He did not wish to send out a bill which could be held up by the North as a concession of the South. He was willing to give the people the right to legislate hereafter, but he was required to go further. He did not, however, admit the right of a territory to legislate in opposition to the opinions of Congress. He believed that slavery would never exist in Oregon, and therefore he would not discuss the question now. But he protested against the doctrine that any territory could frame laws in contradiction to the laws of Congress.

Mr. BADGER explained what he had said, and which (he complained) had been misunderstood or misstated, and reasserted the grounds on which he had placed his argument against striking out the section. He insisted that territories had no power to legislate independent of Congress; that they derived all their legislative authority from Congress. The people of Oregon had established a government without the authority of Congress, and it had continued by sufferance and not by right, until Congress shall establish it. By the omission of Congress, the people of Oregon have been compelled to make laws; but any of these laws—such as that assuming the right to make war, and to dispose of the public lands—as violate the powers of the General Government, are void.

Mr. RUSK referred to the fifteenth section of the act which gives to all the existing regulations the force and character of laws. He objected to the twelfth section, because it was taken up by politicians to foment discords in the country and on this floor. He did not wish to force, or to restrict slavery, in any State. But he would not go into that question now. He hoped the friends of the bill would reconsider their course.

Mr. NILES said he had always desired to avoid this subject whenever it was introduced on a mere abstraction; but now it was brought before us in a bill of a very important character to establish a form of government. He objected to the term "firebrand" being applied to the subject. The question, as far as he understood it, was, whether we should incorporate slavery in the new territory, or leave the door open, and permit slavery to insinuate and establish itself there. He understood the gist of the principle laid down by some Senators to be, that slavery was the fundamental law of every territory. If it was intended to assert that all property belongs to the Federal Government, what became of the rights of the States? And how could this ground be taken by the advocates of State rights? The constitution took no cognizance of property. Its regulation was left to the States; and if what is property in one State is not property in another, we must adopt some rule of decision which will violate the provisions of one State or another. The question is in our hands, and the majority must determine it, and the minority must submit to the decision. He was ready to act on this view.

We had been told that the Federal Government must not touch slavery, and he went with the Southern Senators in that view. It was said to be a State right, yet here it is required to be regulated by the Federal Government. He could not go for this. To introduce slavery into a territory now free was a new question, and he was not prepared to sanction it. He asked Senators if they supposed that the Northern States would send representatives here to see such a course carried out. The doctrine that the question of slavery should be left to the people of the territory to determine, (which might be very popular,) he was opposed to, because he did not recognize every assemblage of individuals as possessing the element of sovereignty.

Mr. DOWNS followed. He stated that he did not go to the full extent of the sentiments entertained and expressed by some of the Southern Senators. He had never gone the length of asserting that slavery was the fundamental law of any territory. He complained of the assertion that this question concentrated power in the South. He said that the South had never received her due portion of the benefits of the Federal Government. He did not allude to offices. The South was willing to permit the offices, which they considered as merely incidents, to be given to the North; but in commercial facilities and in the appropriations for the public benefit, the South had been left far behind the North. The South did not desire to bring on this question for debate. She understood her position too well. She knew that her position was a defensive one, and it was not for her to come forward and provoke a discussion. The vote of the South in favor of the annexation of Texas, was an act of self-defence in consequence of the repeated assaults made on her from the North. There had been no preliminary movements in the South—no meetings; all the movements were made in the North. And these movements led to the union of the South for the purpose of self-defence. On the Missouri question, the South did not move the first, nor will they make the first movement. They will expostulate with their friends in the North; they would entreat, but they would not move until they should find it necessary for self-preservation. Let us lay this question at rest; let us dig a grave and bury it, and swear on the constitution never again to disturb its repose, and every member from the South will come there and kiss the book.

Mr. Houston, for the purpose of putting an end to the discussion, moved to amend the twelfth section, in the ninth line, by inserting the following words: "or in violation of any rights by the laws or Constitution of the United States vested in or secured to the citizens of the United States, or any of them," so that the section would read as follows:

Sec. 12. *And be it further enacted*, That the inhabitants of the said Territory shall be entitled to all the rights, privileges, and immunities heretofore granted and secured to the Territory of Iowa and to its inhabitants; and the existing laws now in force in the Territory of Oregon, under the authority of the provisional government established by the people thereof, shall continue to be valid and operative therein, so far as the same be not incompatible with the provisions of this act, or in violation of any rights by the law or Constitution of the United States vested or secured to the citizens of the United States, or any of them; subject, nevertheless, to be altered, modified, or repealed, by the Governor and Legislative Assembly of the said Territory of Oregon; and the laws of the United States are hereby extended over and declared to be in force in said Territory, so far as the same, or any provision thereof, may be applicable.

The amendment was agreed to.

The question recurring on the motion to strike out the section—

Mr. Calhoun asked the Senator from Texas what was the object contemplated in his amendment; whether it was to give protection to the property of Southern gentlemen?

Mr. Houston said his object was to protect the citizens of Oregon. As to slavery, it was a question not belonging to Congress. It was the province of the Judiciary to set aside any unconstitutional act of Congress. He was not to be alarmed by any little outbreaks in this chamber. He had no idea that we were standing on the verge of a crisis—that the Union was about to be dissolved. He believed nothing of the kind. He had too much confidence in the integrity and patriotism of Senators; and that if it should fail, he would appeal to the integrity and patriotism North and South. He regretted to see the most important principles made the football of passion and bad feeling.

Mr. Calhoun made a few remarks on the applicability of the principles adopted in reference to Iowa to the Territory of Oregon.

Mr. Houston explained.

Mr. Hannegan suggested that the ordinance of 1787 could never have been operative in Iowa.

Some further explanations on the subject were made between Mr. Butler and Mr. Crittenden.

Mr. Hannegan said that every difficulty had been removed by the adoption of the amendment. He hoped the bill would now be passed, and that then, for an important reason, the Senate would go into Executive business.

Mr. Calhoun made some explanation as to the admission of Iowa.

Mr. Berrien added a few words, and moved that the Senate proceed to the consideration of Executive business.

Mr. Bright asked for the yeas and nays; which were ordered.

Mr. Upham moved that the Senate adjourn.

On motion of Mr. Hannegan, the Senate proceeded to the consideration of Executive business, and, after some time spent therein, the doors were reopened, and

The Senate adjourned.

HOUSE OF REPRESENTATIVES.

Monday, June 5.

The journal of Saturday was read and approved.

Mr. William Pitt Lynde, a Representative from the State of Wisconsin, appeared this day, was sworn to support the Constitution of the United States, and took his seat in the House.

IN SENATE.

Friday, June 23.

Territory of Oregon.

The bill to establish a Territorial Government in the Territory of Oregon was taken up for consideration as in Committee of the Whole.

Mr. Davis, of Mississippi, could not see what importance could be attached to the amendment, as the ordinance of 1787 could have no application to the Territory of Oregon, where it could never be in operation.

Mr. BADGER said *proprio vigore* the ordinance could not apply, and there would be no propriety in the amendment. But the bill conferred on Oregon all the rights, privileges, and immunities given to other Territories and States, and on reference to the subject, it appeared that the restriction of the ordinance of 1787 was operative in some of them. He desired to guard against any conclusion that the restriction should operate in Oregon.

Mr. DAVIS, of Mississippi, said, why did not the Senator from North Carolina move at once that the inhibition of slavery which is adopted as to Iowa, should not be adopted as to Oregon?

Mr. BADGER contended that his motion was to that effect, although the language was different.

Mr. JOHNSON, of Maryland, argued that the amendment was in effect a prohibition of the establishment of slavery in Oregon, whether she wills it or not. It is said that Oregon has already abolished slavery. Then what do we propose to do, but to sanction what the people of Oregon have already done? If they have excluded slavery, we only give approval of their decision, with an addition that it shall be perpetual. Slavery cannot be carried into Oregon, because it cannot be carried into Iowa, if you pass the law as it stands. It will be as perfectly excluded as if we passed the Wilmot Proviso. He opposed the amendment of his friend from Georgia. By the 6th article of the ordinance of 1787, slavery is prohibited in the Territory of Iowa, so far as regards certain sections. The amendment under consideration leaves the bill precisely as it stands. In every view he could take of it, it could have no effect. Was it the intention of the North to prohibit slavery for all time? Was it the intention of the South to say this is right? Did the North intend to say that slavery might be introduced in Oregon? He desired to see the platform established. He wished to have the question distinctly determined, so that the people might understand what was intended to be done. He assured Southern Senators, if they voted for this 12th section, they would vote the Wilmot Proviso.

Mr. FOOTE expressed his willingness to withdraw his amendment, if the Senator from North Carolina would consent to withdraw his motion.

Mr. BADGER said he would do so with the greatest pleasure, after he had made a brief explanation as to his amendment. He then briefly replied to the remarks of the Senator from Maryland, in order to show that that Senator had not examined the proposition with his usual accuracy, or that he was less fortunate than usual in his clearness of explanation. He then read an extract from documents and statutes on file, to justify himself against the attacks which had been made upon him. Different minds took different views of the subject, and it was his object to throw out something which would settle and guide them. He considered the ordinance of 1787 a dead letter in Oregon. He considered Congress as having full power and authority over the whole question, until it abandoned this power and authority to the States. He believed that slavery would never exist in Oregon, as it was not desired there by a majority of the people. He thought the matter should be left in the hands of the people of Oregon.

The amendment was then withdrawn.

Mr. BERRIEN and Mr. JOHNSON, of Maryland, mutually explained as to the effect of the 12th section of the bill.

Mr. DAVIS, of Mississippi, then sent to the Chair the following amendment, to come in at the close of the bill:

Provided, That nothing contained in this act shall be so construed as to authorize the prohibition of domestic slavery in said Territory whilst it remains in the condition of a Territory of the United States.

Mr. HALE then said he thought the proper course would be to take the question on the amendment that he had offered and withdrawn, and said he should move it when the bill came up. The following is the amendment:

That the inhabitants of said Territory shall be entitled to enjoy all and singular the rights, privileges, and advantages, granted and secured to the people of the territory of the United States, north-west of the river Ohio, by the articles of compact contained in the ordinance for the government of said territory on the 13th day of July, 1787; and shall be subject to all the conditions, and restrictions, and prohibitions in said articles of compact imposed upon the people of said territory; and the existing laws now in force in the Territory of Oregon, under the authority of the provisional government established by the people thereof, shall continue to be valid and operative therein, so far as the same be not incompatible with the principles and provisions of this act; subject, nevertheless, to be altered, modified, or repealed by the Governor and Legislative Assembly of the said Territory of Oregon; and the laws of the United States are hereby extended over, and declared to be in force in, said Territory, so far as the same, or any provision thereof, may be applicable.

MONDAY, June 26.

Territory of Oregon.

On motion of Mr. BRIGHT, the Senate proceeded to the consideration of the bill to establish a Territorial Government in Oregon.

The question being on the motion of Mr. DAVIS, of Mississippi, to amend—

Mr. DIX said he had hitherto abstained from entering into the discussion of slavery in the Territories, because he had regarded the questions heretofore presented as abstract questions. Here, however, is an act of legislation which is to establish our government over thousands of miles. It will affect the interests, the destinies of the population which will hereafter fill the valleys and crown the mountains of Oregon. The discussion now, therefore, conducted in a temperate manner, can do no harm; but out of it some light may be struck to guide us through our progress. He adverted to the different views which had been thrown out on the subject; but there was a question which, in his opinion, lay beyond all these, the determination of which may have a great effect on the settlement of the question. He referred to that of the power of Congress to regulate the government of the Territories, and all matters relating to them.

The right to regulate all matters relating to the public domain may be construed to extend over all classes occupying those public lands. He referred to the constitutional clause on this subject, of which he thought an improper construction had been given. He went into a history of the clause, dwelling on the mode in which it was introduced, and of the proposition made to amend it. The proposition was introduced by Mr. Madison, and although not adopted in that form, it was not rejected. That of Mr. Morris was favored and adopted. He also stated the proceedings in relation to the introduction of the celebrated ordinance of 1787. The coincidence of the two subjects in point of time, might, he thought, throw some light on the views of the Convention. Mr. Madison denied the legality of the ordinance; but to give a further insight into the views of Mr. Madison, he read an extract from a paper in the Federalist, of which Mr. Madison was the author. Mr. Madison, he thought, regarded the new Government about to be established under the constitution, as intended to supply defects in the Government under the Confederation; and this was made clear by Mr. Madison himself in the forty-third number of the Federalist. He referred to the condition of the North-west Territory at the time when this ordinance was passed; and it was in looking at the character of the States about to be admitted, that Mr. Madison regarded this power as of very great importance.

He proceeded to show how far this ordinance was sustained by the action of Congress, in order that the Senate might have before it the full benefit of a knowledge of the legislative precedents in its favor. From these he inferred an intention to extend the area of human liberty. Neither the framers of the ordinance nor the first Congress could have considered the prohibition of slavery as incompatible with the establishment of States out of the North-west Territory on an equal footing with the original States. The authority of the ordinance was recognized by the Supreme Court of Louisiana, as appears from a decision which he read of that court in 1830. He recited the dates of several acts on which he relied to support his views of the force of the ordinance, and to illustrate the action of Congress under its operation. He made frequent use of extracts from the several laws on the subject, and from the judicial decisions under them. Slavery existed in Louisiana when she came into the United States, and although Congress adopted no course which would interfere with the vested rights of property in that State, laws were passed restricting the importation of slaves from foreign countries. He looked at the acts by which subsequent States had been admitted, to show that Congress had exercised power over the question of slavery in the Territories until they became States.

The decisions of the Supreme Court of the United States, as to the existence of this power in Congress, he quoted from very copiously. Writers on public law concur in this construction. He insisted, that by every authority which could be quoted, the question of this power had received a similar decision. The question of power, therefore, was, in his opinion, indisputable. He would next consider whether it was expedient in all cases to exercise this power.

On the subject of the prohibition of slavery in the Territory of Oregon, the very admission, broadly made, that it was unnecessary, because slavery would never exist in that Territory, divested the question of any injurious operation. In reference to the effect of the prohibition of slavery on the slave population, he contended, that as productive surface was the great element in the multiplication of races, the extension of slavery over a larger surface tended irresistibly to the increase of slaves. So that by every step we may take in extending slave territory, we are reproducing the original responsibility of the establishment of slavery.

In reference to emigration from Europe, he stated that we had, within the last twenty-five years, received an addition of one million persons from England and Ireland; yet this drain did not diminish the population of these countries, because the reproduction was more than equal to the exhaustion. The character of the various races which flocked into our country was a subject well worthy the consideration of the philosophical statesman. He believed the only States in which the black population was on the increase, were those in which slavery existed. He referred to the depressed condition of the blacks which prevailed in New York and some other States, and laid it down as a principle which never varied, that a degraded race could never multiply. Emancipated slaves, he asserted, never multiplied.

It would not be right for us to check the tide of emigration from foreign countries. The trackless wastes of our Western Territories would be the homes of all the foreign emigrants who may flock into the country, as well as our own surplus population. As to the propriety of a policy which looked to the peopling of our country from the race most celebrated for its moral and intellectual elevation, he considered there could never be a doubt. He admitted that there was a section of the country where slave property was considered necessary, but in what he had said he had no reference to these States. He depicted the advantages which would result from the substitution of independent for slave labor, both as to individual interest and national character.

There was nothing in the soil, climate, or productiveness of Oregon, to render slave labor indispensable. But it could be profitably employed there, as in every new country, for a short time. And he asked, would it not be unwise to decline to prohibit slavery in a Territory where it could not long continue to exist, and where it must ultimately wear out in the competition with free labor? If we strike out the 12th section, we say that slavery may exist in Oregon, unless the Territorial Government shall re-enact the prohibition of it. Such he considered to be its effect. He read the section, and assumed that the part of that section which provides that the laws existing in Oregon shall continue in force, must operate as an exclusion of slavery full as effectually as if the amendment suggested by the Senator from New Hampshire (Mr. Hale) had been adopted.

He referred to the positions he laid down in the discussion of the three million bill, which he still held. The principle of these positions was, that we are bound to take a territory as we find it: if we find slavery there, we ought not to abolish it—if we find that no slavery exists there, we ought not to introduce it so long as it continues to be in the condition of a Territory; and that we have no power over the regulation of the subject as soon as the Territory becomes a State. He still maintained these views.

Mr. Calhoun said, if the discussion was to continue, he thought it would be better to continue it on this amendment. He was not now prepared to go into the debate himself; but if no other Senator was now prepared to go on, he would wish the bill to go over until to-morrow morning, when he would be prepared to deliver his views.

The motion was agreed to, and the further consideration of the bill was then postponed.

Thursday, June 29.

Oregon Bill.

On motion of Mr. Bright, the Senate proceeded to the consideration of the bill to establish a Territorial Government in Oregon.

The question being on the motion of Mr. Davis, of Mississippi, to amend the bill—

Mr. Phelps said it was not his purpose, when the debate commenced, to take any part in this debate, which he regarded as dangerous; but he had changed his purpose, in consequence of the points which had been taken by Senators. He took a view of the character of the Missouri compromise, and stated that it was now asserted, that in the teeth of this compromise, Congress has no power to exclude slavery in any of the Territories of the United States. It was now insisted that there was in Congress no power whatever to interfere in this question. Before he could give his assent to this new doctrine, he must be permitted to examine it.

He went on to say, that it was too late now to set up this objection, because it was a question settled by the legislation of the country from the adoption of the constitution to this day. The acquisition of territory brought with it the power to govern it. The power of Congress over it is unqualified and unlimited. If Congress possess the general power of legislation in relation to Territories, it has the same power as the State Governments have over their territory. If there are any restrictions on this power, he called on Senators to point out the clause in the constitution which contains them. There is no restriction, unless it be one arising from the subject itself.

He admitted that all the powers of Government are held in trust; but there is no analogy between this and a common legal trust. No two things are wider than a legislative power and a legal trust: the former involves a large amount of discretion. The analogy drawn between the Government and a corporation was well enough in principle, but it had no application in this case. He examined the character of slave property, which had its origin in domestic relations; it is merely an incident to the relation between parent and child, and a still closer incident to the relation between master and servant; it is analogous to the relation between master and apprentice; it can exist nowhere where that relation does not exist. The right of the citizen to remove his property into any other State is fully admitted; but the citizen, when he removes his property to another State, takes it there subject to the local laws of that State. Does not this hold good as to all property? This is a species of property which is not recognized everywhere as such: the citizen can remove property which is everywhere recognized as such, but he has no right to carry a peculiar kind of property, only recognized as such in his own State. If he has a right to carry this property, how is it that he can lose his title to it? It is not so as to goods and merchandise, which are recognized and respected everywhere. You may carry your property where you please, but it must be subject to the jurisdiction of the State where he selects his residence. This slave property is incident to a peculiar institution which is permitted in particular States, but is not permitted to exist in others. If you take it into those States in which it is not permitted to exist, how is it to stand against the power of local legislation?

But it is still further insisted that the South has the power to carry its property into any other State, and to hold it in defiance of local legislation. Admit this, and the power is yielded to spread slavery over any territory you may acquire; and wherever the area of freedom is to be extended, the standard of slavery must be carried with it. Against this, he must enter his protest. Before he could admit this doctrine, he must see the clause which ties up his hands.

It had been said, the constitution recognizes this description of property. The constitution speaks of persons "held to service," but it is silent as to their being property. He denied that what was incident to a domestic relation, and ceased when the institution ceased, could be regarded as property. The regulation which binds master to slave is confined to the State in which that relation exists, but cannot extend beyond it. But where did Southern Senators find the clause authorizing the extension of this institution, by the introduction of slavery, in States whose local legislation is opposed to it? The claim is asserted to introduce slavery into Oregon: he would like to know on what basis it rested. The master, when he takes his slave into a free State, emancipates him, whether he will or not. It depends not on his will, but on the local laws of the State into which he has carried his slave.

The people of Oregon having formed a temporary government, adopted a system of laws by which slavery was prohibited. This clause recognizes those laws, and the motion is to strike out the clause. If we are called on to force the institution on the Territory, it may be well to look at the consequences. If they are not adapted to the institution, the institution is not adapted to them. It is suited to a different region of country. Let us not force it on them. If they are to have it, let them introduce it themselves, when they have grown up into greater power. We should let them alone.

He disclaimed any desire to make a display by going into the thousand and one stories—some exaggerated, and others without foundation—with which the Senate was entertained yesterday. He did not intend to throw any reproach on the South because of the existence of slavery. The people of the South had received it from their ancestors. He was willing to say, as far as his narrow observation had extended, that many of the slaves were much better treated than he previously had expected. Still it was an evil—admitted to be such by many Southern gentlemen themselves; and he hoped no favor would be shown to an effort to extend the institution.

If the new ground taken, which violates the Missouri compromise, be maintained, he foresaw great difficulty and danger. The question in that case never can, never will be settled. It can only be settled by a withdrawal of the free States. He would not have meddled with this debate, but his silence was forbidden by a strong sense of duty.

HOUSE OF REPRESENTATIVES.

Thursday, July 6.

Important Message from the President—Peace with Mexico—Treaty Ratified by each Power, and Ratifications Exchanged—Terms and Conditions of the Treaty—Important Recommendations.

The Speaker laid before the House the following Message in writing from the President of the United States:

To the Senate and House of Representatives of the United States:

I lay before Congress copies of a treaty of peace, friendship, limits, and settlement, between the United States and the Mexican Republic, the ratifications of which were duly exchanged at the city of Queretaro, in Mexico, on the 30th day of May, 1848.

The war in which our country was reluctantly involved, in the necessary vindication of the national rights and honor, has been thus terminated; and I congratulate Congress, and our common constituents, upon the restoration of an honorable peace.

The extensive and valuable territories ceded by Mexico to the United States constitute indemnity for the past, and the brilliant achievements and signal successes of our arms will be a guarantee of security for the future, by convincing all nations that our rights must be respected. The results of the war with Mexico have given to the United States a national character abroad which our country never before enjoyed. Our power and our resources have become known, and are respected throughout the world; and we shall probably be saved from the necessity of engaging in another foreign war for a long series of years. It is a subject of congratulation that we have passed through a war of more than two years' duration, with the business of the country uninterrupted, with our resources unexhausted, and the public credit unimpaired.

I communicate for the information of Congress the accompanying documents and correspondence relating to the negotiation and ratification of the treaty.

Before the treaty can be fully executed on the part of the United States, legislation will be required. It will be proper to make the necessary appropriations for the payment of twelve millions of dollars, stipulated by the twelfth article to be paid to Mexico in four equal annual instalments. Three millions of dollars were appropriated by the act of March 3, 1847, and that sum was paid to the Mexican Government after the exchange of the ratifications of the treaty.

The fifth article of the treaty provides, that "in order to designate the boundary line with due precision upon authoritative maps, and to establish upon the ground landmarks which shall show the limits of both Republics, as described in the present article, the two Governments shall each appoint a commissioner and a surveyor, who, before the expiration of one year from the date of the exchange of ratifications of this treaty, shall meet at the port of San Diego, and proceed to run and mark the said boundary in its whole course to the mouth of the Rio Bravo del Norte." It will be necessary that provision should be made by law for the appointment of a commissioner and a surveyor on the part of the United States, to act in conjunction with a commissioner and surveyor to be appointed by Mexico, in executing the stipulations of this article.

It will be proper also to provide by law for the appointment of a "board of commissioners" to adjudicate and decide upon all claims of our citizens against the Mexican Government, which, by the treaty, have been assumed by the United States.

New Mexico and Upper California have been ceded by Mexico to the United States, and now constitute a part of our country. Embracing nearly ten degrees of latitude, lying adjacent to the Oregon Territory, and extending from the Pacific Ocean to the Rio Grande, a mean distance of nearly a thousand miles, it would be difficult to estimate the value of these possessions to the United States. They constitute of themselves a country large enough for a great empire, and their acquisition is second only in importance to that of Louisiana in 1803. Rich in mineral and agricultural resources, with a climate of great salubrity, they embrace the most important ports on the whole Pacific coast of the continent of North America. The possession of the ports of San Diego, Monterey, and the bay of San Francisco, will enable the United States to command the already valuable and rapidly increasing commerce of the Pacific. The number of our whale-ships alone, now employed in that sea, exceeds seven hundred, requiring more than twenty thousand seamen to navigate them; while the capital invested in this particular branch of commerce is estimated at not less than forty millions of dollars. The excellent harbors of Upper California will, under our flag, afford security and repose to our commercial marine; and American mechanics will soon furnish ready means of ship-building and repair, which are now so much wanted in that distant sea.

By the acquisition of these possessions, we are brought into immediate proximity with the west coast of America, from Cape Horn to the Russian possessions north of Oregon; with the islands of the Pacific Ocean; and, by a direct voyage in steamers, we will be in less than thirty days of Canton and other parts of China.

In this vast region, whose rich resources are soon to be developed by American energy and enterprise, great must be the augmentation of our commerce; and with it, new and profitable demands for mechanic labor in all its branches, and new and valuable markets for our manufactures and agricultural products.

While the war has been conducted with great humanity and forbearance, and with complete success on our part, the peace has been concluded on terms the most liberal and magnanimous to Mexico. In her hands the territories now ceded had remained, and, it is believed, would have continued to remain, almost unoccupied, and of little value to her or to any other nation; whilst, as a part of our Union, they will be productive of vast benefits to the United States, to the commercial world, and to the general interests of mankind.

The immediate establishment of territorial governments, and the extension of our laws over these valuable possessions, are deemed to be not only important, but indispensable to preserve order, and the due administration of justice within their limits, to afford protection to the inhabitants, and to facilitate the development of the vast resources and wealth which their acquisition has added to our country.

The war with Mexico having terminated, the power of the Executive to establish or to continue temporary civil governments over these territories, which existed under the laws of nations whilst they were regarded as conquered provinces, in our military occupation, has ceased. By their cession to the United States, Mexico has no longer any power over them; and, until Congress shall act, the inhabitants will be without any organized government. Should they be left in this condition, confusion and anarchy will be likely to prevail.

Foreign commerce to a considerable amount is now carried on in the ports of Upper California, which will require to be regulated by our laws. As soon as our system shall be extended over this commerce, a revenue of considerable amount will be at once collected, and it is not doubted that it will be annually increased. For these and other obvious reasons, I deem it my duty earnestly to recommend the action of Congress on the subject at the present session.

In organizing governments over these territories, fraught with such vast advantages to every portion of our Union, I invoke that spirit of concession, conciliation, and compromise in your deliberations, in which the constitution was framed, in which it should be administered, and which is so indispensable to preserve and perpetuate the harmony and union of the States. We should never forget that this Union of confederated States was established and cemented by kindred blood, and by the common toils, sufferings, dangers, and triumphs of all its parts, and has been the ever augmenting source of our national greatness, and of all our blessings.

There has, perhaps, been no period since the warning so impressively given to his countrymen by Washington to guard against geographical divisions and sectional parties, which appeals with greater force than the present to the patriotic, sober-minded, and reflecting of all parties and of all sections of our country. Who can calculate the value of our glorious Union? It is a model and example of free government to all the world, and is the star of hope and the haven of rest to the oppressed of every clime. By its preservation, we have been rapidly advanced as a nation to a height of strength, power, and happiness without a parallel in the history of the world. As we extend its blessings over new regions, shall we be so unwise as to endanger its existence by geographical divisions and dissensions?

With a view to encourage the early settlement of these distant possessions, I recommend that liberal grants of the public lands be secured to all our citizens who have settled, or may in a limited period settle, within their limits.

In execution of the provisions of the treaty, orders have been issued to our military and naval forces to evacuate, without delay, the Mexican provinces, cities, towns, and fortified places in our military occupation, and which are not embraced in the territories ceded to the United States. The army is already on its way to the United States. That portion of it, as well regulars as volunteers, who engaged to serve during the war with Mexico, will be discharged as soon as they can be transported or marched to convenient points in the vicinity of their homes. A part of the regular army will be employed in New Mexico and Upper California, to afford protection to the inhabitants, and to guard our interests in these territories.

The old army, as it existed before the commencement of the war with Mexico—especially if authority be given to fill up the rank and file of the several corps to the maximum number authorized during the war—it is believed, will be a sufficient force to be retained in service during a period of peace. A few additional officers in the line and staff of the army have been authorized; and these, it is believed, will be necessary in the peace establishment, and should be retained in the service. The number of the general officers may be reduced, as vacancies occur by the casualties of the service, to what it was before the war.

While the people of other countries, who live under forms of government less free than our own, have been for ages oppressed by taxation to support large standing armies in periods of peace, our experience has shown that such establishments are unnecessary in a republic. Our standing army is to be found in the bosom of society. It is composed of free citizens, who are ever ready to take up arms in the service of their country, when an emergency requires it. Our experience in the war just closed fully confirms the opinion, that such an army may be raised upon a few weeks' notice, and that our citizen-soldiers are equal to any troops in the world. No reason, therefore, is perceived why we should enlarge our land forces, and thereby subject the treasury to an annual increased charge.

Sound policy requires that we should avoid the creation of a large standing army in a period of peace. No public exigency requires it. Such armies are not only expensive and unnecessary, but may become dangerous to liberty.

Besides making the necessary legislative provisions for the execution of the treaty, and the establishment of Territorial Governments in the ceded country, we have, upon the restoration of peace, other important duties to perform. Among these, I regard none as more important than the adoption of proper measures for the speedy extinguishment of the national debt. It is against sound policy and the genius of our institutions, that a public debt should be permitted to exist a day longer than the means of the treasury will enable the Government to pay it off.

We should adhere to the wise policy laid down by President Washington, of "avoiding the accumulation of debt, not only by shunning occasions of expense, but by vigorous exertions in time of peace to discharge the debts which unavoidable wars have occasioned, not ungenerously throwing upon posterity the burden we ourselves ought to bear."

At the commencement of the present administration, the public debt amounted to $17,788,799 62. In consequence of the war with Mexico, it has been necessarily increased, and now amounts to $65,778,-450 41, including the stock and treasury notes which may yet be issued under the act of January 28, 1847, and the sixteen million loan recently negotiated under the act of March 31, 1848.

In addition to the amount of the debt, the treaty stipulates that twelve millions of dollars shall be paid to Mexico in four equal annual instalments of three millions each; the first of which will fall due on the 30th of May, 1849. The treaty also stipulates that the United States shall "assume and pay" to our own citizens "the claims already liquidated and decided against the Mexican Republic," and "all claims not heretofore decided against the Mexican Government" "to an amount not exceeding three and one-quarter millions of dollars." The "liquidated" claims of citizens of the United States against Mexico, as decided by the joint board of commissioners under the convention between the United States and Mexico, of the 11th of April, 1839, amounted to $2,026,139 68. This sum was payable in twenty equal quarterly instalments. Three of them have been paid to the claimants by the Mexican Government, and two by the United States; leaving to be paid of the principal of the liquidated amount assumed by the United States, the sum of $1,519,604 76, together with the interest thereon. These several amounts of "liquidated" and unliquidated claims assumed by the United States, it is believed, may be paid as they fall due out of the accruing revenue, without the issue of stock or the creation of any additional public debt.

I cannot too strongly recommend to Congress the importance of husbanding all our national resources, of limiting the public expenditures to necessary objects, and of applying all the surplus at any time in the treasury to the redemption of the debt. I recommend that authority be vested in the Executive by law to anticipate the period of reimbursement of such portion of the debt as may not be now redeemable, and to purchase it, at par, or at the premium which it may command in the market, in all cases in which that authority has not already been granted. A premium has been obtained by the Government on much the larger portion of the loans; and if when the Government becomes a purchaser of its own stock, it shall command a premium in the market, it will be sound policy to pay it, rather than to pay the semi-annual interest upon it. The interest upon the debt, if the outstanding treasury notes shall be funded, from the end of the last fiscal year until it shall fall due and be redeemable, will be very nearly equal to the principal, which must itself be ultimately paid.

Without changing or modifying the present tariff of duties, so great has been the increase of our commerce under its benign operation, that the revenue derived from that source and from the sales of the public lands will, it is confidently believed, enable the government to discharge annually several millions of the debt, and at the same time possess the means of meeting necessary appropriations for all other proper objects. Unless Congress shall authorize largely increased expenditures, for objects not of absolute necessity, the whole public debt existing before the Mexican war, and that created during its continuance, may be paid off, without any increase of taxation on the people, long before it will fall due.

Upon the restoration of peace, we should adopt a policy suited to a state of peace. In doing this, the earliest practicable payment of the public debt should be a cardinal principle of action. Profiting by the experience of the past, we should avoid the errors into which the country was betrayed shortly after the close of the war with Great Britain in 1815. In a few years after that period, a broad and latitudinous construction of the powers of the Federal Government unfortunately received but too much countenance. Though the country was burdened with a heavy public debt, large and in some instances unnecessary and extravagant expenditures were authorized by Congress. The consequence was, that the payment of the debt was postponed for more than twenty years; and even then, it was only accomplished by the stern will and unbending policy of President Jackson, who made its payment a leading measure of his administration. He resisted the attempts which were made to divert the public money from that great object, and apply it in wasteful and extravagant expenditures for other objects, some of them of more than doubtful constitutional authority and expediency.

If the Government of the United States shall observe a proper economy in its expenditures, and be confined in its action to the conduct of our foreign relations, and to the few general objects of its care, enumerated in the constitution, leaving all municipal and local legislation to the States, our greatness as a nation in moral and physical power, and in wealth and resources, cannot be calculated.

By pursuing this policy, oppressive measures operating unequally and unjustly upon sections and classes will be avoided; and the people, having no cause of complaint, will pursue their own interests, under the blessings of equal laws and the protection of a just and paternal Government.

By abstaining from the exercise of all powers not clearly conferred, the cement of our glorious Union, now numbering thirty States, will be strengthened as we grow in age and increase in population, and our future destiny will be without a parallel or example in the history of nations.

JAMES K. POLK.

WASHINGTON, *July* 6, 1848.

The Message having been read—

Mr. BURT moved to refer so much of it as related to making provisions for carrying into effect the treaty with Mexico, to the Committee of Ways and Means; so much as related to the army, to the Committee on Military Affairs; so much as related to the establishment of territorial governments, to the Committee on Territories; and that the Message be printed.

Mr. McKAY suggested to the gentleman to modify his motion. There was another very important part of the Message—much more important than that which referred to the appropriations necessary to carry the treaty into effect; for those would not be needed until the next session. He referred to that which proposed to authorize the President to purchase the stock of the Government, and suggested that that portion be referred also to the Committee of Ways and Means.

Mr. BURT acquiesced in the suggestion, and modified his motion accordingly.

Mr. THOMPSON, of Pennsylvania, obtained the floor, and moved the previous question on Mr. BURT's motion.

Pending this question, the House adjourned.

IN SENATE.

THURSDAY, July 6.

The Oregon Bill.

On motion of Mr. BRIGHT, the prior orders were postponed, and the Senate proceeded to the consideration of the bill to establish a Territorial Government in Oregon; when—

The question being on the amendment submitted by Mr. DAVIS, of Mississippi—

Mr. MASON addressed the Senate. He stated that the people of Oregon had undertaken to pass laws purely conventional and without authority, among which was one prohibiting slavery therein forever. No one now believes that the people of a territory belonging to the United States have the right to pass any laws which can be binding, unless by the consent of the United States Government. By the 12th section of this bill, the laws of Oregon are sanctioned, among which is this law prohibiting involuntary servitude in the Territory, or in other words, prohibiting the introduction of slavery into that Territory. It becomes us to uncover this act, and to defeat it. Our object should be to defeat the recommendation of the committee. Should this measure succeed, and slavery be prohibited, it will be in derogation of the spirit and letter of the constitution.

He referred to the prevailing disposition to make the construction of the constitution a mere struggle for power, and predicted the most calamitous results from a continuance of such a course. He went into the history of the introduction of the provision concerning slavery into the constitution, to show that in the form in which it was adopted, it was adopted by the aid of three New England States; the two-thirds vote being inserted for an equivalent.

The ordinance of 1787 was a compact formed between the United States Government and the people in possession of the North-west Territory, before the constitution was formed. The history of that ordinance is shrouded in secrecy, as the journals were not made public. But it is well known that there was much conflict. The item concerning slavery was the result of compromise. Under the Articles of Confederation, most of the States were large importers of slaves, and, having an immense territory under their control, they limited the territory within which slavery should be permitted to exist. This will account for the introduction of the slave clause in the ordinance of 1787. He recited some of the difficulties which stood in the way of the perfection of the ordinance. Some States came into the measure with difficulty, and some with a protest. He read several extracts from the papers before him, to show the various action of the States on the subject. The course of New York in 1780 he contrasted with the course of her able representative on this floor (Mr. DIX) now. Virginia never would have been a party to that compact, never would have made the cession she did, had she supposed her right to extend her population whither she would, would have been denied. Slaves form a great part of the property of the South, and are a considerable element of her political power; and he asked, by what authority was this property to be touched and interfered with by the General Government? Legislative discretion he regarded as limited by the object of the trust committed to it; and it did not extend to any interference with the question of slavery. There were States who did not regard the slave as a trust, as he was defined to be by the Senator from Vermont, but as a real property, which the owner, under the sanctions of the constitution, may take where he pleases. There are now three millions of slaves penned up in the slave States, and they are an increasing population, increasing faster than the whites. And are the slaves to be always confined within what may be deemed their prison States? He referred to the attempt to settle the manumitted slaves of John Randolph on lands purchased for that purpose in the State of Ohio, when they were forcibly driven off, to show the character of the humanity which was professed by the anti-slavery party.

That a slave was not property, but a mere incident to a domestic relation, as was asserted by the Senator from Vermont, he entirely denied. The slave was property under the construction of the common law. The first slave who landed on our shores brought his condition with him, and it was recognized by the colonial laws. That condition was, that he was the substantial property of his master—not temporarily, as in the case of master and apprentice, but for life. Writers have described him, not as an incident to a domestic relation, but as an incident to the right of conquest. What forms may be thrown round him by convention or by law, is another question. In Africa, they are either taken in battle or sold by parents; but they are in bondage—perpetual bondage; and this condition they bring with them here, and it is recognized by our laws. The first slaves were brought to Virginia in 1620, by a Dutch vessel, and were sold as merchandise; and this was done with the knowledge and permission of the British Crown. This proves that it requires no special legislation to institute slavery, but it must require a special law to abolish it. He denied the proposition that when a slave enters a free State, where there is no such domestic relation, he becomes free, on this ground, that the relation cannot be abolished without a special law. There was no law, originating under the present constitution, until 1820, which interfered with the right of the owner of a slave to carry his property with him into any of the States of the Union. Congress had never undertaken any thing more than to regulate the subject in the admission of any new territory.

Mr. Johnson, of Georgia, moved that the further consideration of the bill be passed over informally until to-morrow, which was agreed to.

Friday, July 7.

Oregon Bill.

On motion of Mr. Bright, the Senate proceeded to the consideration of the special order, being the bill to establish a territorial government in Oregon; when—

The question being on the amendment submitted by Mr. Davis, of Mississippi—

Mr. Johnson, of Georgia, said, that although the British Parliament was considered as omnipotent, still the meanest subject was protected in his property. How strange, therefore, must it appear, that the American Congress should be engaged in seriously discussing a question which affects the property of fifteen of the States of the Union! The admission of the right of Congress to prohibit slavery implies the right of Congress to establish slavery. And what would be thought if the fifteen slaveholding States were to come forward with a proposition to Congress to establish slavery in the States in which it does not now exist? Or, if it was proposed to prohibit any citizen of the free States from entering a slaveholding State with his property, would not the right of Congress to interfere be denied? He looked on the present question as a question of power, in which the numerical strength of the free States was to be arrayed against the feebleness of the South. In this condition, the South has only to say, "We stand still; we have not the power to resist." The South invokes the free States to stay their hands, and to yield obedience to the mandates of the constitution.

He referred to the restricted nature of our Government, and quoted from the authorities, to show the extent of the powers of Congress in reference to the Territories. He regarded the word "territory" in the constitution as meaning nothing more nor less than *land*. Congress had a right to protect this property, to cause surveys to be made, and to establish judicial districts and courts to try criminals who may commit offences against the property. Beyond this power, he thought, Congress could not go. Wherever the framers of the constitution intended to confer exclusive legislation, they inserted in the constitution proper terms to express that intention. The power of Congress to establish territorial governments, although it had been denied by some, he would be willing to admit, for the sake of argument. But if Congress had the power, it must use it in reference to its character as a trust—it must act as a mere agent. The territory is the property of the United States, and not of the Government of the United States. If Congress had the power to distribute the public lands among the several States, and were to do so, would it be tolerated if Congress were to give a portion of this land free, while it clogged another with the condition that no slave should be there? Yet the principle was the same in this case as in the effort to prohibit slavery in the Territories.

Gentlemen had referred to former legislation on the subject, and had brought forward precedents to throw their light on our path. He examined some of these precedents, in order to show that they did not aid the purposes of those who had brought them forward. He stated that Mr. Dane, of Massachusetts, not Mr. Jefferson, was the author of the restrictive clause in the ordinance of 1787; so that all the weight supposed to attach to it from the name of Jefferson fell to the ground. Having been adopted before the existence of the present constitution, the ordinance could not properly be quoted as a legislative precedent under our constitution. He did not doubt that any of the great States had the right to establish slavery within their limits; yet, under this ordinance of 1787, the United States could not establish slavery within their territories. Looking at the ordinance as a compromise, neither party to such compromise parted with any of its respective rights. He had carefully examined all the acts which had been relied on to prove the power of Congress over slavery, and had found that, in part, they related to the powers exercised by Congress under the clause relating to commerce. Their only connection with the subject was in relation to the traffic of slaves.

The amendment of the Senator from Mississippi brought up the question, whether Congress had the right to interfere on the question of the transfer of slaves from one Territory to another. He maintained that Congress had reserved the power of the *veto* over the laws of a Territory; so that if a Territory should pass a law excluding slaves from a Territory, it would not be valid until it had received the sanction of Congress. He held that the constitution had as effectually precluded Congress from abolishing slavery, as it had excluded the assumption of titles of nobility.

He referred to the condition of the Mexican territories, to show that the prohibition of slavery is a political law there, and read an extract from a judicial decision to prove from the laws of nations, that a political law is changed, when by conquest, or otherwise, territory is transferred from one country to another. If a Carolinian were to go into these territories with his slaves, his property in these slaves would be recognized completely there. He stated that he intended to vote for the amendment of the Senator from Mississippi.

Mr. FOOTE reminded the Senator from Georgia, that their Northern friends had stood by the interests of the South, in resisting the Wilmot proviso.

Mr. JOHNSON said he had not the least intention to say any thing which could evince unkindness to the North. He admitted there had been occasions when the North had stood forward in behalf of the South. But he did not thank the North for offering them the Wilmot proviso.

On motion of Mr. DAVIS, of Massachusetts, the further consideration of the bill was then passed over.

WEDNESDAY, July 12.

Oregon Bill.

On motion of Mr. BRIGHT, the Senate proceeded to the consideration of the special order, being the bill to establish a Territorial Government in Oregon; when—

Mr. DAVIS, of Mississippi, addressed the Senate. He commenced with a reference to the importance of the bill, the twelfth section of which discourses abolition. He denied that there was any intention to force slavery on Oregon. The South only desired to show the ground on which she has stood from the commencement of the Confederacy to this moment; and further, that she should be let alone. He stated that the Missouri compromise had obtained its validity from the consent of the States. Congress might enact laws on the subject, or make compromises; but without the consent of the States interested, they would have no validity.

As to the introduction of slavery into Oregon, no Southern Senator had ever asked it. The fact that the slave is property, which its owner may carry away with him into any part of the Union, was that which they were desirous to see recognized. The clause in the constitution relative to the regulation of commerce was a constitutional admission that the slave is property. It is because slaves are considered property that the importation of slaves from Africa has been carried on under the sanction of this clause in the constitution. The words "slave, or any other property," in the constitution, are conclusive on that point. If the existence of the slave as property be admitted, what power has Congress to interfere with it? He denied that there was any such power in Congress. What powers Congress possesses, he showed by reference to the constitution itself. Congress had no power to change the condition of slavery, or to strip the master of his right in his property. Entering a Territory with this property, the citizen has a right to its protection.

On the acquisition of Territory, the condition of slavery was not changed. The Government acquired no new power over it, but stood merely in the position of an agent for its protection. He spoke depreciatingly of the persons who had assumed in Oregon the right to make laws for the Territory, contending that they were without qualifications for the task. They were far inferior in intelligence, in morals, and in personal wealth, to the population lying south of the Oregon boundary.

As to the inviolability of the law which prevailed in a Territory when acquired, he admitted that until abrogated, the existing law or municipal regulation must remain in force within the territory itself. He denied that there was any power in Congress, or in the people of the Territory, to interrupt the slave system. He gave his views as to the motives which induced Virginia to cede the Northwestern Territory, which originated in a patriotic and generous feeling on the part of the mother State. He regarded the course pursued by the Northern States in relation to fugitive slaves as an outrage on justice, and a violation of that principle of the equality of the States which is guaranteed by the terms of that instrument. The owner of a slave, when he entered some of these States, if he took his slave with him, was either exposed to the mortification of seeing his slave seduced from his side, or seized and carried away by violence.

What remedy has been proposed by the opponents of slavery? What good have they done? They have abducted slaves, but emancipated none. Do they expect to persuade the South to give up slavery? It is probably for the political advantage of the section in which the agitation against slavery orignates. The spirit of concession exhibited by the South had failed to produce a corresponding spirit in the North. The latter still continued to assail the South as influenced only by a desire to increase the slave power, and obtain still greater political influence in the scale of States.

He insisted that the disorder and agitation which prevailed in the Southern States, was not of domestic origin, but came from New England and from Great Britain.

He asserted it to be the duty of the United States to protect the property of a slave-owner during the transit from one State to another. The resolutions of the States who favored abolition were adopted entirely with the view to obtaining additional political power, and imposed on the South the strongest obligation to rise in self-defence. He referred to the fraternal feeling which induced the Southern States to make common cause with the North in the war of the Revolution. The South had no especial cause of complaint; it was flourishing by its trade with Great Britain. But it was actuated by fraternal feeling and principle to take up arms; and now, was she to be asked to give up her domestic institutions? The South asked for no new guarantee, no new security; but she desired that the constitution should be preserved from violation.

If the spirit of the Missouri compromise was to be invoked, as was proposed by his friend from Indiana, (Mr. Bright,) he had a right to ask that the South should be placed on a basis of permanent security, so that there may hereafter be no new agitation on the subject. He was willing to go far, as far as his principles would permit, to meet the North. But if nothing would satisfy the North short of the destruction of this institution, then was the time for dissolution come; but let us separate peacefully, and with good feelings towards each other. Let not the battle-fields of our country be stained with the blood of brother fighting against brother. He trusted the danger would pass away, and that this agitation would turn out to be nothing more than a temporary struggle between politicians.

Mr. Clayton rose and said, it was very evident that the speeches on the other side were rather intended to exasperate than to conciliate the South. He viewed the amendments which had been offered as clashing with each other; but nothing had as yet transpired during this protracted debate, to show on what ground it was expected that Senators could meet. There had been no indication of any sentiment by which the Senate could be guided to any result. He stated that the Committee on Territories was now engaged in preparing a bill relative to the new Territories; but as there were but four members on that committee, the work went on slowly. He referred to the course by which a compromise of the tariff question was entered into. A committee was appointed, to which the subject was referred, and the report of that committee conciliated both parties, and brought the question to a decision. He would now desire to adopt a similar course. He moved that the subject be recommitted to a committee of eight members, to be appointed by ballot, four to be selected from the North, and four from the South, and he would go further, and say, two from each party in the South, and two from each party in the North.

If the report of that committee shall be that nothing can be effected at this session, let us do our ordinary business and go home.

Mr. Foote expressed his regret that the debate had assumed the character it had. He had been ever ready to hail the tender of the olive branch from the North whenever it was made. And he rejoiced now that this offer had been again made, and from the distinguished Senator from Delaware. He hoped it would be responded to in the same spirit. But he would not pledge himself to cease, in case of a report from the committee that nothing could be effected at this session, from using every effort in his power to call the attention of the country to the subject.

Mr. Fitzgerald asked the Senator from South Carolina to explain away an aspersion which he had—no doubt inadvertently—cast on the State of Michigan on the subject of fugitive slaves, as it appeared in his printed speech.

Mr. Calhoun replied, by reiterating the charge against Michigan in still stronger terms, designating the course of that State, in reference to fugitive slaves, as the most outrageous that had ever been perpetrated.

Mr. Corwin asked if the Supreme Court had not decided that no State could pass any law on the subject?

Mr. Butler replied, that the Supreme Court had decided, by a bare majority, that a State cannot pass a law in violation of any law of Congress. Pennsylvania made it a felony for a master to recover his fugitive slave in any other than a particular way. This, although sustained by the decision of a local court, was decided by the Supreme Court to be unconstitutional.

Mr. CALHOUN complained that a different construction had been placed on the law relative to ordinary fugitives from justice, and on that relative to fugitive slaves. This showed that the power of the United States was too inadequate to secure equal justice throughout the whole of the Union.

Mr. CORWIN referred to the course of Ohio, where a law similar to that passed in Pennsylvania became a law in Ohio, in repealing the law as soon as the Supreme Court had decided it to be unconstitutional.

Mr. CALHOUN said the decision did not touch the ordinance of 1787; it was merely a decision under the constitution. The ordinance was a previous contract, which was not touched by the constitution.

Mr. CORWIN replied that the language of the ordinance and that of the constitution were nearly the same; that the constitution adopted and reimposed the obligations of the ordinance, and that the decision of the Supréme Court embraced both.

Mr. BRIGHT asked if the motion of the Senator from Delaware was not to refer this bill and the subject of the Territories of California and New Mexico to a committee of eight members.

Mr. CLAYTON explained, that he only moved to recommit this bill and the various amendments.

Mr. DICKINSON said this was the first speck of light we have had for some time, and he hoped the motion of the Senator from Delaware would prevail.

Mr. BUTLER said if this motion should prevail, the Committee on Territories would feel itself bound to suspend its action on the bills under consideration, until the judgment of this special committee should be expressed. He believed that the principle which would be introduced in this bill would govern every other territorial bill which might be brought before Congress. Although the Senator from New Hampshire might have courage to sport with the elements of danger by which the Union itself might be overthrown, he (Mr. B.) had not the courage to sport with them. He believed it to be necessary that this question should be settled this session.

Mr. WESTCOTT said he should vote for the motion of the Senator from Delaware. He never had any fear that the Senate would attach any Wilmot proviso to this bill; or, if it did, we have a Chief Magistrate at the other end of the avenue who would put a veto on it. He had no fear, therefore, that the Senator from New Hampshire, or any of those who acted with him, would be gratified. He hoped the Committee on Territories would be discharged from the consideration of the California and New Mexico bills, and that they would be referred to this Select Committee.

Mr. BERRIEN urged the Senate to come to a vote, without further debate. He could see nothing in the motion which could be objectionable to any party; and he hoped, that on the calm comparison of opinions in the committee-room, some arrangement of a satisfactory character might be agreed on.

Mr. DOWNS spoke in favor of the proposition; and, after a few words from Mr. BALDWIN against the motion—

Mr. BRIGHT suggested a modification, to the effect that the Committee on Territories be discharged from the further consideration of so much of the President's Message as relates to New Mexico, California, and Oregon, and that the same be referred to the Select Committee of eight.

Mr. CLAYTON accepted the modification; and the question was then taken by yeas and nays, and decided in the affirmative, as follows:

YEAS.—Messrs. Atchison, Atherton, Badger, Bell, Benton, Berrien, Borland, Breese, Bright, Butler, Calhoun, Clayton, Davis of Mississippi, Dayton, Dickinson, Downs, Foote, Hannegan, Hunter, Johnson of Maryland, Johnson of Louisiana, Lewis, Mason, Metcalfe, Rusk, Sebastian, Spruance, Turney, Underwood, Westcott, and Yulee—31.

NAYS.—Messrs. Baldwin, Bradbury, Clarke, Corwin, Davis of Massachusetts, Dix, Fitzgerald, Greene, Hale, Hamlin, Miller, Niles, Upham, and Walker—14.

And at five P. M. the Senate adjourned in a state of exhaustion, after a continuous session of six hours.

THURSDAY, July 13.

Oregon Territorial Bill—Mr. Clayton's Select Committee—Members Elected by Ballot.

At twelve o'clock the Senate proceeded to ballot for chairman to the Select Committee; when Mr. CLAYTON, of Delaware, was duly elected.

The Senate then proceeded to ballot for the committee, when the remaining seven were chosen; and it was then ordered that the bill to establish the Territorial Government of Oregon, with the several amendments proposed thereto, and so much of the President's Message as relates to New Mexico and California, be referred to a Select Committee, consisting of Mr. CLAYTON, chairman; Messrs. BRIGHT, CALHOUN, CLARKE, ATCHISON, PHELPS, DICKINSON, and UNDERWOOD.

On motion of Mr. DICKINSON,

Resolved, That the committee to which was referred the President's message relating to the organization of Territorial Governments in Oregon, Upper California, and New Mexico, have the use of the anteroom during their sittings.

Tuesday, July 18.

Oregon Territorial Government—Select Committee—Bill Reported for the Organization of Territorial Government in the three Territories of Oregon, California, and New Mexico—Compromise the Basis.

Mr. Clayton, from the Select Committee on the Territories of Oregon, California, and New Mexico, reported a bill for the organization of Territorial Governments in each of them. [It appeared to be a very long bill, containing no less than thirty-seven sections.]

Mr. Clayton said the subjects referred to this committee were of infinite difficulty. The territories for which temporary civil governments were to be organized embraced an area of 1,044,492 square miles—about as large as that of one-third of all Europe, and capable of sustaining, sooner or later, the population of a mighty empire. The intrinsic difficulties necessarily belonging to such an organization, were increased by the nature and character of the population now existing there, as well as that hereafter to be introduced by the extension of the Constitution and the laws of the United States over so vast a country. The committee had entered upon the discharge of their duties, under all these embarrassments, with untiring industry, with a zealous resolution, and an indefatigable spirit, which he had never known surpassed. He felt it due, in justice to each and every one of his colleagues, to say, that amidst all their long conferences and laborious discussions on the various topics necessarily considered by them, the most conciliatory spirit had been evinced by them, each endeavoring to maintain the honor and interest, not merely of his own section of country, but that of the whole nation, and each endeavoring to yield so much as he felt could be properly and honorably conceded, without the sacrifice of what was essentially due to his own constituents, and the people of all the States. The conferences of the committee were in this spirit—attended with free and ample discussion—and, after a full interchange of views, a vote was taken on a proposition moved by the Senator from Missouri, (Mr. Atchison,) "that the spirit of the Missouri compromise be adopted to govern the settlement of all the Territories of the United States." On this question the committee divided, five for and three against the motion. The Senator from Indiana (Mr. Bright) then moved the proposition, notice of which had been previously given in the Senate, containing the *words* of the Missouri compromise. As the condition of the territory was now said to be different from that to which that compromise applied in 1820, a motion was made by the Senator from Kentucky (Mr. Underwood) to amend that proposition, by providing that "all the territory in New Mexico and California, south of the parallel of 36° 30′, shall be placed on the same footing in all respects as to slavery that existed in Louisiana while it was a territory." On this question the committee divided, four for the motion and four against it. After the failure of this motion, the question was taken on the proposition of the Senator from Kentucky, and with a like result—the committee being again equally divided.

At this stage of the proceedings all compromise appeared to be impossible. But the committee proceeded afterwards to consider a proposition to endeavor to adjust the great question, at least so far as to enable Congress to extend the laws over and provide for the administration of justice in the Territories, leaving for the present the settlement of it to the laws of population, or the adaptation of soil, climate, and all circumstances to the various kinds of labor. While it was admitted on all sides that by far the greatest portion of the Territories was properly adapted to free labor, and would necessarily be free soil forever, yet it was also with equal unanimity conceded that there was a portion of it where free labor never could be introduced, owing to the climate and the peculiar productions of that portion. It was thought that if Oregon, which no one imagines can ever be slaveholding, could be organized as the people of that Territory desired, by the temporary adoption of their present laws interdicting or prohibiting slavery till the Territorial Legislature proposed to be organized, by a popular vote, under the bill referred to us, could enact some law on the subject, most of the objections which had been urged in debate to the twelfth section, would be obviated, without any sacrifice of principle by those who urged them; and that, after thus disposing of the question, so far as relates to Oregon, the Territories of California and New Mexico could be organized in the same bill by the appointment of a governor, secretary, and judges, to compose, according to the old precedents, a temporary Legislature for each of these Territories, but without the power to legislate on the subject of slavery; thus placing that question beyond the power of the Territorial Legislature, and resting the right to introduce or prohibit slavery in these two Territories on the constitution, as the same should be expounded by the judges, with a right of appeal to the Supreme Court of the United States. It was thought that by this means Congress would avoid the decision of this distracting question, leaving it to be settled by the silent operation of the constitution itself; and that in case Congress should refuse to touch the subject, the country would be slaveholding only where, by the laws of Nature, slave labor was effective, and free labor could not maintain itself. On the other hand, in case Congress should hereafter choose to adopt the compromise line of 36° 30′, (north of which, I suppose, it is not expected that slave labor can be introduced,) or any other rule of settlement, it will be free to act as, to its wisdom and patriotism, shall seem fit.

After many conflicts of opinion, these views

thus generally expressed, were substantially agreed upon with great unanimity, all the members of the committee agreeing to make the report, and but two of them (one from the North and the other from the South) disapproving any of the material features as they understand it. By order of the committee, I have prepared a bill in accordance with these views. It contains some important amendments to the Oregon bill, particularly so far as it corrects the defective description of the boundaries in that bill.

I do not expect, sir, that this or any other proposition which the wit of man can possibly suggest, will prevent agitation on this subject, which is now daily spreading through the country, and, I fear, dividing it into geographical parties. If the Missouri compromise of 36° 30′ should be adopted, the agitators would immediately raise the standard of repeal, and agitate as fiercely as ever. We know that, sir. They will agitate after the passage of any bill. But this bill resolves the whole question between the North and South into a constitutional and a judicial question. It only asks of men of all sections to stand by the constitution, and suffer that to settle the difference by its own tranquil operation. If the constitution settles the question either way, let those who rail at the decision vent their indignation against their ancestors who adopted it. We offer no bill to introduce slavery by Congressional enactment into any free territory. If, as the South contends, the constitution gives the right to carry their slaves there, they will maintain that right. If, as the North contends, the constitution confers no such right, they will vindicate their claim. And Oregon will be at once organized as a Territory, with power to elect their own Legislature—a power which the committee think cannot now, with any propriety, be conferred upon the population of the two other territories.

I now, sir, have the honor to report, as an amendment and a substitute for the bill referred to the Select Committee, "A bill to establish the Territorial Governments of Oregon, California, and New Mexico." The committee, with all becoming modesty, desire to say that they do not view their work as perfect; but it is the very best which, under all the embarrassing circumstances of their position, they have been able to propose. To the Senate they appeal for assistance to correct any errors into which they may have inadvertently fallen. But it is the honest opinion of a large majority of the committee, that by the passage of this bill the safety of the Union will be placed beyond the reach of agitation, and that the question, and the only question, which now threatens to endanger it, may be, not immediately but ultimately, put at rest forever.

The bill was then read a first time and unanimously ordered to be printed.

On motion, the Senate adjourned.

Wednesday, July 19.

The Compromise.

Mr. Clayton rose and said: There may possibly be some misapprehension in regard to a portion of the remarks made by me yesterday, in introducing the bill for the organization of Territorial Governments in Oregon, New Mexico, and California, and I desire to correct it, if any such exist. The Select Committee desired, and in that desire I fully concur, that the bill should speak for itself, and that it should be regarded as the exponent of their views and opinions. It was not my purpose to submit the remarks which I made yesterday in lieu of a report; nor were they to be regarded as tantamount to a report. The bill, I repeat, is to speak for itself. It fully reveals the sentiments of the committee, and for that very reason a formal report was deemed unnecessary. I do not know that it is now necessary for me to say any thing more than to add, that a large majority of the committee decidedly expressed the wish that this measure might become a law, with the expectation and design that it would prove to be an adjustment of the great question now in controversy between the North and the South. I shall, if there be no objection, call up the bill to-morrow, and then every member of the committee will have an opportunity of expressing his views upon the subject—an opportunity of which I design to avail myself.

Mr. Calhoun. I am exceedingly gratified by the explanation of the Senator from Delaware. Had it not been made, it might have been supposed in some quarters that the whole committee had concurred in all the particular views which he for himself had expressed. I agree with him in testifying that it was the unanimous understanding of the committee that the bill should speak for itself; and I may add, that it was also understood by me that this was to be a permanent, and not a temporary settlement of the whole question.

Mr. King inquired whether the remarks of the honorable Senator from Delaware had been regarded in the light of a report from the committee, and were so recorded on the Journal by the Secretary?

The Vice-President replied in the negative.

Here the explanations ended.

HOUSE OF REPRESENTATIVES.

Saturday, July 22.

Vattemare's Franking Privilege.

The Senate bill to facilitate international exchanges was read a first and second time.

Mr. Goggin moved that it be put upon its passage.

Mr. Cobb, of Georgia, moved to lay the bill on the table. He thought they had gone quite far enough in this matter. He did not think it right and proper that the bill should pass, and he therefore would move to lay it on the table.

Mr. Goggin remonstrated: the bill had passed the Senate by a unanimous vote; he hoped the gentleman from Georgia would consent to withdraw his motion, and let it be referred to the Committee on the Post Office and Post Roads.

But Mr. Cobb refused; and the question was about to be put, when—

Mr. Root asked leave to say a word. If the gentleman would withdraw his motion for a few moments, Mr. R., if he insisted on that condition, would promise to renew it.

Mr. Cobb assenting—

Mr. Root expressed his hope that the bill would be suffered to pass. He had just learned from a member of the Committee on the Library, that the amount to be taken from the post-office revenue by this bill would be very small. That gentleman was a good judge of what the system would require; and certainly, if gentlemen were not disposed to repeal all our previous legislation on that subject, this bill ought to pass. If the system of exchange was wrong, let it be repealed; but if gentlemen were not prepared to retrace their steps, and undo all they had done, they should suffer this small bill to become a law. It was a fact that the Government was remitting the duty on all the astronomical instruments imported for the use of the observatory; on the same principle the duty on these articles of international exchange ought to be relinquished. The bill was so carefully guarded, that it was impossible the privilege could be abused: it merely provided a convenience for carrying into execution the laws already passed on the same subject. He now, though with great reluctance, complied with his promise, by renewing the motion to lay the bill upon the table.

The question being put, there appeared a majority against laying it on the table.

Mr. Ficklin demanded the yeas and nays, which, being ordered and taken, stood—yeas 79, nays 95.

So the bill was not laid upon the table.

It was then, on motion of Mr. Goggin, referred to the Committee on the Post Office and Post Roads.

IN SENATE.

Monday, July 24.

Territorial Bill.

On motion of Mr. Clayton, the Senate resumed the consideration of the bill to establish Territorial Governments in Oregon, California, and New Mexico.

Mr. Clarke being entitled to the floor, gave way for a moment, and

Mr. Hale moved to amend the bill in the fifth section, by striking out the words "free white," so as it shall read, "that every male inhabitant above the age of twenty-one years," &c.

Mr. Clarke stated that he regretted that he had been appointed a member of the committee, because the condition of his health, and other circumstances, rendered it peculiarly inconvenient for him to attend. But while he was out of the Senate chamber he was elected a member, and he was subsequently induced by his friends to forego his intention to ask to be excused. His health would not now permit him to address the Senate at any length, even if he could be assured of the propriety of taking up the time of this body, which he was not. He stated that the bill now reported received the sanction of six out of the eight members of the committee, two of the members (of whom he was one) objecting to it. His views, and the views of his State, (Rhode Island,) were decidedly against the introduction of slavery into a free State, and against the extension of slavery to any territory which we may have acquired by conquest. He intended to move again in the Senate the amendment which he had unsuccessfully proposed in committee. As far as he understood the opinion of the committee, it was that the Territory of Oregon was in every sense a free Territory. On looking over the bill, he found that this principle did not seem to be sufficiently carried out in the construction of the bill. He stated that it was his intention to move an amendment to the sixth section of the bill; the closing paragraph is: "All the laws passed by the Legislative Assembly shall be submitted to the Congress of the United States, and if disapproved, shall be null and of no effect." To this he moved to add a proviso, that no law on the subject of slavery shall be in force until it shall have received the approval of Congress.

The adoption of this proviso would satisfy his mind that slavery would never be permitted to exist in the Territory of Oregon. He thought that by the adoption of this proviso, the bill would be rendered acceptable to all parts of the Union. Some doubts having existed as to the fact whether slavery existed in Mexico at the time when the Territories of California and New Mexico came into our possession, he had found a decree published by President Herrera, in which he declares that slavery is abolished in Mexico, and all who were then slaves should become free, which he sent to the Secretary to be read, as also a subsequent act confirming the decree. This fact he proposed to embody in an amendment which he would submit to the 26th section of the bill. It was urged in committee, that on the Territories of California and New Mexico coming into the possession of the United States, every owner of a slave would have a right to bring his property into the Territories. To this it was objected, that this being a constitutional question, it should be referred to the supreme court of the Territory, with an appeal to the Supreme Court of the United States. To this effect he also proposed to submit an amendment in the 24th section of the bill. He then referred to the importance of this measure at a moment when the public opinion throughout the Union was so violently agitated on the question of slavery. The resolutions of the Legislature of Rhode Island required of him to vote against the introduction of slavery into any free State. As the bill was now constructed he could not give his assent to it. He had reserved the right in committee to move an amendment to the bill.

Mr. Miller rose to state his objections to the bill: he objected to this triple alliance of two new Territories, scarcely a month old, with the Territory of Oregon. Oregon is a native-born Territory, and why was she to find herself, at her outset, brought into such a connection? He understood the character of the people of Oregon, who were mostly emigrants from our own States; but he did not understand the character of the people of California and New Mexico. He was prepared to give his assent to a government for the former, but he was not now prepared to give a government to the others. He desired more information on the subject, before he could consider himself prepared to give his vote. There was a sort of understanding that Texas and Oregon should be admitted together—Oregon as a free, Texas as a slave State. Texas was admitted, and Oregon was kept knocking at our doors until arrangements could be matured for admitting her on the same footing. He then proceeded to the consideration of the bill itself, which had been reported as a compromise. He showed the reasons which convinced his mind that it was, in fact, no such compromise as had been expected. He referred to the debate which had already taken place, on the power of Congress to abolish slavery, in which it was strenuously denied by the Senators from the Southern States; yet, in this bill there was an assumption of the power, in the clause prohibiting the passage of any law which abolishes slavery. Believing in this power, he was not opposed to its exercise, but he was opposed to its admission for the benefit of one part of the Union, and not of the other: it was all on one side. He had prepared an amendment providing that the laws now in existence in the Territories shall continue in force. As to the inhibition of the Territorial Legislatures in Mexico to pass any laws respecting slavery, what did it mean but a prohibition of the passing of any laws abolishing slavery? Slavery will, of course, go to California and New Mexico, as there is no law there to prevent it. If a person takes his slave there, and his property is taken, and he appeals to the Supreme Court, the court will probably decide, that as Congress has passed no law prohibiting slavery there, slavery may exist there. And while the question remains undecided, the slave will stand on the same footing with his master—under the protection of the constitution—and strife and bloodshed may ensue. He alluded to the difficulty which would stand in the way of any slave who desired to bring his case, by a writ of habeas corpus, before a judicial tribunal for decision: he illustrated this by the case of the agent of the State of Massachusetts, who was sent to Charleston, South Carolina, for the purpose of testing the constitutionality of the law where he could have no lawyer to aid him, and was himself imprisoned, and then compelled to leave the State.

Mr. Breese. If the Senator from New Jersey will allow me, I will ask him if the question of servitude could not be brought before the Supreme Court of the United States, very readily, by an action, by the slave, of assault and battery and false imprisonment? In the State which he (Mr. B.) had the honor in part to represent, the question of freedom or slavery could not be tried on the return to a writ of habeas corpus. If the party holding the petitioner for the writ, returned upon it that he was held as a slave, the question cannot be tried by the judge, but the party is driven to his suit at law to try his right to freedom. Such a suit would bring up the question fairly, and without the intervention of a jury. The person claimed as a slave brings his action, and there never has been found any difficulty in obtaining the aid of counsel, even in slave States, for such purpose. The master pleads to the action, that true it is he holds the plaintiff in his custody, as he has a right to do, for he is his slave. The slave replies, setting forth the fact that California, on its cession to the United States, was free; that slavery did not exist there, and that it is not recognized by the Constitution of the United States or any act of Congress; and that by virtue of that constitution he is free. The defendant demurs, and the question of law arising thereon is decided by the court, and if the decision be *against* the slave, the Supreme Court of the United States have jurisdiction under the 25th section of the Judiciary act of 1789, because a decision has been pronounced against a right claimed under the constitution. If the Senator will look to the case of Menard *vs.* Aspasia, in 5th Peters' Rep., he will find such to be the opinion of the Supreme Court. He would further say to the Senator, that in all his observation and experience in cases of this sort, and they have not been inconsiderable, he has discovered that the courts of the slave States have been more liberal in their adjudications upon the question of slavery than the courts of some of the free States. The courts of one of them (Illinois) had uniformly decided cases against the right of freedom claimed by persons held in bondage under a modified form of servitude, recognized by its old constitution. In precisely similar cases, the courts of Kentucky and Missouri, to which States such persons had been taken, decided in favor of the right to freedom. And it is a remarkable fact, that in all cases in those States, and he believed in other slave States, where there was any doubt about the right to hold the person in slavery, the decision has been invariably against the right.

Mr. Miller resumed, stating that in different States in the Union public opinion operated strongly to bias the course of law. But he protested against legislating for California and New Mexico in such a loose manner as to leave open a field for perpetual strife between the master and the slave, or between the slave-owner and any philanthropic individual who may journey into these distant regions for the purpose of instructing the slave in his own rights. This question was a political one. The South regarded it as such, contending that this question must be settled, or the Union would be dissolved. He denied that even a decision of the Supreme Court would satisfy the party against whose wishes it militated. The decision of the Supreme Court, in the case of the United States Bank, was not satisfactory to the opposite party; and no better result could be anticipated in this case.

He was willing to vote for a bill which prohibited slavery in any Territory which was free at the time of the passage of the bill. If slavery existed in a Territory at the time of its acquisition by the United States, he would leave it to the people to determine whether it should continue. He would not vote for its abolition there. He had not voted against the continuance of slavery when Texas was admitted into the Union, because it had previously been in existence there. For whose benefit should we now extend slavery in California and New Mexico, where it has already been abolished? Great Britain had introduced slavery in this country, and what was the general tone of public opinion on this subject? Was it not termed a curse which had been entailed on us by Great Britain? And shall we extend this curse to the Territories over which we extend our protection?

The South asserted that it had a greater interest in the question than the North. This he denied. He denied that the South had any exclusive privilege to carry her slaves to the Territories for sale. The North had an equal right to enjoy the profit of such a traffic, and had therefore as great an interest in the question as the South. Slavery does not exist now on the Pacific, and by his vote it should never be permitted there.

As to California and New Mexico, he would not charge the South with having plunged the country in war for the purpose of obtaining additional slave territory, because the South had been opposed to the acquisition of this new territory. But he put it to the South, whether this extension of our territory did not hold out the strongest temptations to the spreading this institution into countries where it has not heretofore existed?

The proper way to settle the question was by the legislative authority. The people would not rebel against the law; and he was not disposed to surrender the power of Congress over the subject.

Mr. Phelps rose and vindicated his own course, as he judged from present appearances that he was the only representative of the opinion he entertained from the entire North. This was not a pleasant situation. He accepted the position he occupied with great reluctance. But when he went into it, he did not go there as the mere representative of one State, but for the purpose of conciliating and harmonizing the Union. He had not anticipated the severe, unreasonable opposition he had encountered. He had said he could justify himself to the country, and he was confident he could vindicate himself to his immediate constituents. He was not to be driven out of the Senate by the opposition which had risen up. His friend from Connecticut (Mr. Baldwin) had taken an objection to the bill on the ground of what lawyers call a special demurrer, because the committee had pinned the three Territories together in one bill.

Mr. Baldwin explained that his was more than a technical objection.

Mr. Phelps resumed. The bill had been presented to the country as an odious measure. It had been grossly misrepresented in the newspapers, and he feared Senators had taken their impressions more from these paragraphs than from an examination of the bill. The main opposition came from his own section of country. If he stood alone, he must stand on his own legs, and trust to his own intelligence for his defence. He had, a short time since, addressed the Senate, and given his views in a manner which could not be misunderstood. He was opposed to the extension of slavery to any Territory which is subject to our legislative control.

What was the condition in which California and New Mexico have come under our care? Slavery has been abolished there. Such is the state in which we receive them. By the laws of nations, the laws of all conquered countries remain until changed by the conqueror. If these laws are to be retained, there is an express law containing a prohibition of slavery, and this will continue until we shall change it. He insisted that there was nothing in the bill to warrant the belief that it could ever carry slavery into these Territories. The Senators from New Hampshire, (Mr. Hale,) and from Maine, (Mr. Hamlin,) who had addressed the Senate, went over precisely the same ground which he had travelled. There was no difference between them; and all that surprised him was, that after following the same path, they had, just at the close, shot off entirely in a new direction. He had determined never to suffer himself to yield to momentary impulses, which might mislead him as they had misled others. He would rather follow the dictates of his deliberate judgment.

He replied to the objections made to the phraseology that the laws of Oregon shall continue in force until modified, altered, or rejected, contending that there was nothing in this clause to excite alarm. It was to be expected that the new legislature would re-enact the prohibition of slavery, if they made any new law; and if not, the present law would remain in force. He believed, from the spirit he had witnessed in the committee, that the South would make no objection to the continuance of this restriction in Oregon. Why, then, should the North endeavor to disturb this harmony of sentiment by its criticism on the bill? The provision contained in the bill relative to the existing laws in Oregon, and the power of the legislature to change or continue them, he considered as being an effectual prohibition of slavery in the Territory, without the assent of Congress. As to the judicial authority, he would only say that the constitution ought to be expounded by those constitutionally appointed for that purpose. The President, who was not elected by his vote, he might distrust. But as to the Supreme Court, whether they differed from him in political views or not, he had yet to learn that they had, in any single instance, forfeited the confidence of the country. He could repose in their decision with entire submission, whether it was for or against him.

He said he was well aware of the effect which this question was intended to have on the country. It was intended for political purposes. It was well enough to go into this to a certain extent, but it would be dangerous to explode all at once. Popular excitement was not to be trifled with. The wheel of revolution was going round, and we know not who is to be the last victim. We had, a short time since, congratulated a foreign nation on its success thus far in throwing off an odious tyranny. An individual who had spent his life over his books was thrown to the head of the Provisional Government, and the next turn of the wheel has thrown him off into disgrace. There is but one power that can control these things, and that power is not human. We have now a new political church, a sort of city of refuge, to which political criminals may resort for safety. But he had no fear of the result. He trusted to the intelligence of the people.

He had thus expressed his views on the subject, because he considered himself as implicated. If there was cowardice in the bill, he had no fear on the subject. He would rather attach the term to the weathercock of popular impulse, to him who fears to do a wise act, lest he should offend some transient caprice. If there were any to whom responsibility should attach, it was to those who voted for the annexation of Texas, out of which grew the Mexican war. The Senator from Connecticut (Mr. NILES) had given the casting vote on the question of the annexation of Texas, and he was responsible for all the difficulties which had grown out of it. That Senator had thrown the most offensive epithets on this bill and its originators, and he was bound to come forward and aid in a compromise. If (said Mr. P.) my old coat and jacket are to be stuffed with straw and burnt in effigy, I would prefer that the Senator from Connecticut should take my position, and let his coat and jacket take the place of mine.

Mr. FITZGERALD followed in some remarks, to show that his vote on this question ought not to be received as compromising General Cass, or as prejudicing his election. All this had been alleged as likely to be the effect of his course. He had seen General Cass since his departure from Washington, but he had never exchanged a word with him on this subject. He had been left free by his friends to act on his own responsibility. Although he was a personal and political friend of General Cass, he would not shrink from any responsibility he might incur. If all which has been said against General Cass in the newspapers be true, he has sins enough of his own to answer for, without being responsible for his (Mr. F.'s) acts. He voted against the appointment of this committee, because he was desirous that the Oregon bill should be disposed of, as was due to the citizens of that Territory. He was delighted, however, to see the rainbow of peace exhibiting itself, after the clouds which had threatened us. He had strong objections to parts of the bill; yet, if he thought it would produce harmony and peace, he would vote for it although it would be his last act, and he should thereafter be plunged in disgrace. But he feared, from what he had heard, that its friends were doomed to disappointment. There was a political storm raging in the North, the effects of which no one could foresee. It threatened to come upon us like a whirlwind, and who can tell where it may be stayed? He alone was responsible for his own acts. He would give another reason why he voted against the raising of the committee. He was not in very good humor at that time, because he had heard imputations thrown on Northern States, and, among others, upon the State represented by him, on the subject of fugitive slaves. There were many cases of fugitives who had not been reclaimed. When he lived in Indiana, there were bands of thieves—horse-stealers as well as negro-stealers—roaming through that State and Kentucky, but he never thought of charging these offences upon the States in which they existed. He did not desire to be considered as committed to the support of this bill, in its present shape.

Mr. CORWIN rose to state his objections to the bill, to the examination of which he had devoted himself, with a sincere desire to obtain a complete and elementary knowledge of the bill. He did not apprehend any of those awful results from this bill which had been felt by some. He did not dread a dissolution of the Union. If he did, he should not regard a seat on this floor as worth having. He did not even apprehend all that had been apprehended from that dreadful name—the Wilmot proviso—that raw-head-and-bloody-bones which had been so often invoked to raise our fears. The paternity of that proviso seemed to have been lost sight of. It seemed to have been forgotten that it was penned by the same hand which drew up our Declaration of Independence. It was from the hand of Jefferson himself; and great was the revolution which must have taken place when the new opinions we now hear are promulgated around us. It would be very unpleasant to him to say any thing to wound the feelings of those who had so meritoriously united to produce this bill. But he could not see that pressing emergency for its passage, to which every other consideration must give way. He did not see why Oregon, which had hitherto taken care of herself, could not go on a little longer; and he would be willing to let these foreign provinces take care of themselves for another twelvemonth. We had a Message from the President, which had rarely been adverted to. Persons had been employed to ascertain the geography of the Mexican provinces; and, after all, they had been obliged to apply to the Executive to know where they are. We are told that Texas claims to the banks of the Rio Grande, and in that case she will take some three-fourths of the territory comprehended under the name of New Mexico. It would be well to obtain some information on this point before we proceed to establish a government for this new territory.

He asserted his belief, that if the Senators from the South believed that, if an appeal to the Supreme Court in cases under this bill, the decision would be against them, they would never vote for this bill. So if the Senator from Vermont thought the decision would be against him, he would vote against it. He regarded slavery as a local institution, which could not be carried into any other State, the laws of which prohibited it. He would not, if we conquered the hottest climate on the earth, where the white man could not work—he would not vote to establish slavery there, unless it had previously existed there; and in saying this, he followed in the track of General Washington, who entertained that opinion to the day of his death, and of Thomas Jefferson.

He wished some Senator would inform him whether slavery at this moment exists in Mexico, and whether it is hereditary or not?

Mr. Hannegan. Peon slavery exists now in California. The creditor may sell his debtor as a slave for all time, with all his property.

Mr. Corwin had heard the same from other sources, and he therefore must believe it to be so. How, then, can a case be made out for the Supreme Court, in which it will not be decided that slavery in some form does not exist? If a man shall be taken as a slave, because he owes another five dollars, and sold into perpetual slavery, shall we permit such a law to remain in force? You have made the land red with blood under the pretence that you have gone thither to give freedom to the captive. You have shown, as he had always anticipated, that this was all hypocrisy, and that you now desire to fasten the iron heel, not only of peon slavery, but of negro slavery, upon them. He protested against this course of hypocrisy and murder and cruelty, transcending in horror the bloody code of Draco.

He stated that all the leading men of the State of Virginia—all that galaxy from which she derived the splendor of her high character—were opposed to the extension of slavery; and among these, he instanced Mr. Jefferson as the most prominent. He went on to show, that if there were fanatics in the North, there were also fanatics in the South; and that the latter were by far the most dangerous; for, if the former went into the slaveholding States to carry thither these principles, they were at least the principles of human freedom. The efforts of the Southern fanatics were directed to the extension of slavery over a broader surface of territory, and its introduction into lands which had never before been tainted by the breath of a slave.

About six o'clock Mr. Corwin concluded, having occupied the floor nearly three hours.

Mr. Underwood rose to speak, but there were cries of "Adjourn, adjourn!" and "No, no; dispose of the bill!" when Mr. U. moved that the Senate adjourn.

Mr. Berrien demanded the yeas and nays, which were ordered, and resulted—yeas 29, nays 25.

And the Senate adjourned.

Tuesday, July 25.

Territorial Bill.

Mr. Clayton moved to proceed to the consideration of the bill to establish Territorial Governments in Oregon, New Mexico, and California.

Mr. Underwood said, that when he went into the committee, he did not doubt the power of Congress over the subject of the government of Territories. Without it, officers in the employ of the public could not be protected in the performance of their duties. Congress had always exercised the power to legislate on the subject. On going into the committee, his first object was, to effect a compromise on the basis of the Missouri line, amended so as to adapt it to the new Territories. In this he had failed. He then explained his proposition at length. With some few restrictions, he proposed to leave the legislative bodies free to act on all subjects. He thought this would have been satisfactory everywhere. The people of the Territories would have been gradually trained for admission into the Union. A free choice was left to them to choose the institutions of the South or of the North. Why should either section of our country, North or South, interpose to prevent it? Why should they, who are strangers to the peculiar institutions which prevail, tell the people where they are, what is best for their interests? He regarded it as our true policy to let slavery alone. Climate and population are continuing to drive slavery further and further to the south, to the latitude where free labor could not flourish. He read a number of extracts from a pamphlet in his hands, showing, that in the first stage after the introduction of slavery, the increase of slaves is great; in the second stage, the white population increases in an equal ratio with the slaves; and in the third stage, the slave race diminishes rapidly. All this proved the assertion, that climate and population would banish slavery from the northern latitudes. He recommended these facts to the consideration of abolitionists, and entreated them to suffer the conviction to enter their minds, that their truest policy was to leave the institution to take the course to which climate and population impelled it.

The policy of the North was calculated to let the slaves in the South loose on society; and the effect of this state of things would be, the neglect of cultivation, and distress and starvation among the slaves themselves. He had been always opposed to the rule of the House which prohibits the discussion of the subject. It would please him better to let free discussion go on, so that the South may be able to hear what it is that the North intend, or ask.

Mr. BUTLER rose and adverted to the importance of the issue now presented. Fifteen States are contending for the enlargement of their power, while fifteen others are struggling only, as he believed, for what were their rights. The discussion had worn a calm and temperate character until yesterday, when the Senator from Ohio poured forth from his full mind, arguments and statements which had forever banished from his breast the hope of a successful termination of the efforts at compromise. That Senator had asserted it as his honest opinion, that it was no matter what course was adopted in this Senate, the course of public opinion could not be arrested or turned aside. He insisted that the South had fulfilled all its obligations in relation to the existing compact between the North and South. He vindicated Virginia against the insinuations which had been poured out upon her, and stated that she had been unjustly and unnaturally aspersed by those who benefited by her liberality when she made the cession of the North-west Territory. They who had profited by her bounty, now turned upon her and insulted her.

If it was a question how much the non-slaveholding States had gained from the labor of the slaveholding States, the figures of rhetoric would soon give way before the figures of arithmetic. He asked, if the forefathers of the South, when they gave their consent to the constitution, had supposed that they were giving to the North authority for the unlimited expansion of their political power, while they were imposing on the South the Procrustean process, by which she was always to be clipped and kept within narrow fetters, would they have ever given their consent to the instrument?

He commented severely on the course of the Eastern States in refusing to give up the fugitive slaves from the South. He referred to the statement which had been made in debate, that the compromise in the Convention was the result of a bargain, and expressed his deep regret at the degradation which was imposed on him and on the whole South by this bargain. He complained that the South had degenerated, and been impoverished for the benefit of the North; and that all this had been effected out of the power which the South had surrendered to the North in the Convention. He feared it was a destiny from which she was no longer able to free herself. But he would still resist; and would not trust to any Presidential vetoes—either to the veto of Mr. Cass, or the veto of General Taylor. He would resist as far as he was able.

He referred to the history of the Oregon bill for the purpose of showing that the South had uniformly exhibited a strong disposition to make concessions, but that they had not been met in a kindred spirit. He felt sure, that if the power was to be conferred on the Legislatures of California and New Mexico to enact laws on the subject, composed of all classes and colors of character, the decisions would be uniformly adverse to the interests of the South. He was opposed to this power being given to these foreign bodies. Congress has the power to exercise sovereignty over the Territories, and in this power is included the regulation of the affairs of the Territories, with certain restrictions.

He was not disposed to indulge in declamation, or to stand here as a modern declaimer. He had not aided to carry slavery into Oregon; he was not responsible for the spread of it. He had admired the oratory of the Senator from Ohio, which he characterized as equally beautiful and *ad captandum;* but he charged that the love of power was at the bottom of it. He ridiculed the moral tone of the Senator's speech, and related an anecdote of a party of clergymen at a religious revival, who were called to dine on venison, when, after the blessing had been asked, one whispered to the clergyman, that Pequod had killed the deer on Sunday. What was to be done? The minister told his brethren that the venison had been killed on Sunday: Could they eat it? Why, you have asked a blessing, I believe! Yes. Well, then, that will partly consecrate the venison; so we may eat the meat, and then give Pequod thirty-nine lashes. This was morality! and such was the morality of the North in its treatment of the South.

He resisted the assertion that slaves on board a ship, if driven by stress of weather out to sea, became free, which he understood to have been made by the Senator from Connecticut, [Mr. BALDWIN.]

Mr. Baldwin explained what he had said, in order to correct any misapprehension.

Mr. Butler said, if any one took his slaves from a ship, and the captain was a foreigner, he should think himself entitled by the constitution to demand a declaration of war. He did not regard the authorities which had been produced as conclusive, because the cases were not sufficiently analogous to the cases which he had assumed. If he could find any other practical bill which protected the South, he would be willing to take it; but he saw no probability of obtaining a better one than this.

Mr. Foote rose and said, he would not have taken any part in this discussion, but for something which had fallen in debate. Humble as he was, he found himself between two opposing fires. He had been assailed in New England, and he had also been attacked as more dangerous than an abolitionist in the leading paper published in Charleston, South Carolina —the Charleston Mercury. And he had been told by the Senator from New Hampshire that he was so considered here. He had therefore thought it was a proper opportunity for him to make some few remarks, in order that his true position should no longer be misunderstood. He would not go into declamation, neither would he go into any history of the slave-trade, which had been already given with sufficient ability by others. He did not hold himself responsible for the introduction of slavery, nor had he ever entertained any extraordinary affection for slave-dealers from any section of the Union.

He referred to the argument of the Senator from South Carolina, (Mr. Calhoun,) that the introduction of a new Territory, acquired by conquest, into the Union, although slavery may have been abolished there previously, carried slavery with it. To this his heart assented, but his judgment could not yet assent to it. He was still in doubt. He feared that the argument of the Senator from Vermont had not been answered, and that it could not be met in this Senate; and that it could not be met in the Supreme Court; and that the decision of that court, as it is now constituted, would be against the South. And then, said he, where are we? He laid it down that the northern men were the shrewdest men in the Union. He had travelled over every part of the Union to the Rio Grande, and had found Yankees everywhere; and he had never found one who was not anxious to own a slave. And they were the most rigid of masters—they were masters indeed. As soon as a Yankee could command four hundred dollars, he laid it out in a slave, because he knew that he laid out his money to advantage. Living in a cotton-growing country, he knew that a slave was the most valuable property he could possess. He admired the Yankees very much. He had never desired to hang them all. And if he had, as had been charged against him, ever used such an expression in the heat of the moment, he would now retract it. He was perfectly satisfied that the Yankees would never vote for the abolition of slavery, if they could gain any profit by continuing it.

He was not pleased with the bill, but he did not say he would not vote for it. He represented the sunny South, and the generous influences which governed that region would have their effect on his course. He was willing to admit these new States immediately, as he believed that they would become cotton-growing and slave States. Next to that, he was disposed to take the Missouri compromise, as proposed to be amended, by leaving the people below 36° 30′ to take their own course. Thirdly, he was in favor of the Missouri compromise, as proposed to be amended by the Senator from Kentucky, (Mr. Underwood.) This he preferred to the present compromise.

Mr. Baldwin and Mr. Berrien made some explanations.

Mr. Johnson, of Maryland, rose to address the Senate, and, after proceeding for a short time, yielded the floor, about 7 o'clock; and

Mr. Mangum moved that the Senate adjourn.

Mr. Berrien called for the yeas and nays on this motion, and they were ordered.

The question was then taken, and decided in the affirmative, as follows:

Yeas.—Messrs. Atchison, Badger, Baldwin, Bell, Benton, Berrien, Bradbury, Butler, Calhoun, Clarke, Clayton, Corwin, Davis of Massachusetts, Dix, Dodge, Greene, Hamlin, Johnson of Maryland, Johnson of Louisiana, Lewis, Mangum, Metcalfe, Niles, Phelps, Spruance, Underwood, Upham, Walker, Westcott, and Yulee—30.

Nays.—Messrs. Allen, Borland, Breese, Bright, Davis of Mississippi, Dickinson, Douglas, Felch, Fitzgerald, Foote, Hannegan, Houston, Hunter, Johnson of Georgia, King, Mason, Rusk, Sebastian, and Turney—19.

The Senate then adjourned.

HOUSE OF REPRESENTATIVES.

Wednesday, July 26.

Territory of Oregon.

The bill to establish a Territorial Government in Oregon was then taken up.

Mr. Wallace, who was entitled to the floor, addressed the committee in a constitutional argument against the power of Congress to impair the right of property in slaves, and exposing the agitations of northern abolitionists as a species of madness, incompatible with any just sense of patriotic duty.

Mr. Crowell followed, in a general speech on the subject of slavery in the District of Columbia.

Mr. C. having concluded—

Mr. Iverson obtained the floor, and spoke on the general subject of slavery, alleging the insecurity of trusting to northern compromises; contending that both the Whig candidates were unsound on this question, and arguing the hopelessness of the cause of the South in the event of their success.

IN SENATE.

WEDNESDAY, July 26.

Oregon, Californian and New Mexican Territorial Bill.

Mr. CLAYTON moved that the Senate resume the consideration of the Territorial bill; and the motion being agreed to, the Senate resumed the debate on the bill.

The question pending being on the motion of Mr. HALE, to strike from the fifth section the words "free white"—

Mr. JOHNSON, of Maryland, who had the floor, yielded for a moment, and—

Mr. WALKER gave notice of an amendment which he proposed to offer to the sixth section, which was, to strike out the words "nor shall the lands or other property of non-residents be taxed higher than the lands or other property of residents."

Mr. JOHNSON resumed, in explanation of certain amendments which he intended to offer, and in illustration of his views generally on the subject. He was not disposed to vote for the bill, unless he could be perfectly satisfied that the cases of appeal could be brought to the Supreme Court. The first twenty sections of the bill relate to the Territory of Oregon, the next seven refer to California, and the remaining nine concern New Mexico. He drew a distinction between the Territory of Oregon and the other Territories, as to the character of their population. Oregon was already a portion of the old confederacy, peopled by citizens either natives of the United States, or well acquainted with the laws and customs of the country. He went on to remark on the provisions in the bill for the government of these different Territories, legislative and judicial. The powers of these departments he thought sufficient for the purpose. The writ of habeas corpus being a common law writ, it may be issued by any of the judges.

It was owing to the differences of opinion in the Senate as to the existence of the power in Congress to control the question of slavery, that the subject was referred to the special committee, with a view to a compromise. It became necessary to report a bill embracing all the Territories, which had met with the disapproval of a portion of the Senate. It was to quiet the agitation which shakes the country to its centre, that the question was referred to a committee to prepare a compromise.

If a stranger was now to come among us and to be told that we had three millions of slaves in our midst, and that this question which now agitates the Senate, was as to the propriety of uniting in a reference of all the difficulties arising out of such a condition of things to our common constitution, he would be struck aghast at the idea that there were some who were opposed to the proposition. He (Mr. J.) thought the step taken, the wisest that could have been selected. He had intended, however, had he not been anticipated by the Senator from Indiana, (Mr. BRIGHT,) to submit an amendment adopting the line of the Missouri compromise.

He glanced at the course taken by the Senators who had spoken in opposition to the bill, and stated that the tone in which their opinions were given proved that they were honest, and ready to support their sentiments to the death, and that it was insulting to the South, although any intention to insult was distinctly disavowed. The stand which the North had taken from the first was too insulting to the South to permit any prospect of union; and it was in this state of things that the committee was appointed and the bill reported, this being the only mode in which they could hope for any extrication from this difficulty. He made a sharp criticism on the language he attributed to the Senator from Ohio, (Mr. CORWIN,) that a majority of the Supreme Court coming from the South, would be likely to vote one way.

Mr. CORWIN explained this expression attributed to him, which he disavowed in its offensive sense, and expressed his high respect for the members of that tribunal.

Mr. JOHNSON resumed, asserting that this appeal to the Supreme Court was the only amicable mode of adjusting a question which threatened the honor and the interests of the South. He did not speak as a slave owner; he did not hold a slave, and he never expected to hold one. The few he once had came to him by inheritance, and he had long since manumitted them. He was glad he had done so then, for the interference of the abolitionists would have prevented him from doing it now. He cared not what effect this movement might have upon the political prospects of either of the candidates for the Presidency, so that an amicable and permanent adjustment of the controversy on this subject might be produced. There was no way so likely to be satisfactory as the reference of the matter to the Supreme Court. Excitable as southern men are reputed to be, they had on this question acted with a moderation which proved that their character had been misunderstood. They were mostly slaveholders, and they had sat in silence while one Senator had charged them with being Hotspurs in human flesh; while the Senator from Ohio had said that the institution of slavery had its origin in blood, and rapine, and robbery. That Senator had gone so far as to say that if the slaveholders were not damned, it would be not because they did not merit it, but that God in his mercy would pardon them for their ignorance, because they knew not what they did.

Mr. CORWIN said he was satisfied that he

had used no such expression. He had spoken at great disadvantage, but his memory held no such language.

Mr. Johnson persisted that language of this kind, or something very like it, had been used. It struck his ear too painfully for him to mistake.

Mr. Berrien said the words, as they struck his ear, were to the effect that slaveholders would be punished but for their ignorance—they knew not what they did.

Mr. Corwin said he might have used some such expression as to slave-dealers, but certainly not to slaveholders.

Mr. Berrien expressed himself perfectly satisfied.

Mr. Johnson rejoiced that the painful impression had been removed from his mind. He then proceeded to show, that from the character of the Supreme Court, he was sure the compromise in this particular would be acquiesced in by the country. He adduced the fact, that while statesmen, politicians were found differing on a subject, the Supreme Court was unanimous. On the subject of the right of a State to levy duties on imports and tonnage, advocated by the Senator from South Carolina, there could be no doubt that the decision of the Supreme Court would be unanimous against him. On the question of the constitutionality of the United States Bank, while Congress was deciding one way, the court was unanimously the other way. The members of the Supreme Court were not politicians. They were born in a different atmosphere, and they addressed themselves to different hearers. Politicians were always differing and disputing—one taking this side of a question, and another taking an opposite view, all equally honest. How desirable, then, in a case of such importance as this, to call in a third party, rather than that we should be driven to despair—above all, to bloodshed. We are ready to yield enough; do not ask for more. It ought not to be expected that the South shall surrender all that is dear to her, and do the bidding of the North. Ten thousand times rather would her children yield their lives. They are willing to adopt the appeal to the Supreme Court, and if the decision of that court be against them, they will be satisfied.

He was not the advocate of slavery itself; he never had been so. He would rejoice to see the institution at an end; and it was with sincere regret he admitted that it was the agitation which had been stirred up in the North which had alone prevented the friends of freedom from emancipating the slaves in Maryland. He alluded to Connecticut, from which State the compromise was opposed, as having scarcely become a free State.

Mr. Baldwin stated that there had been but a very few slaves there.

Mr. Johnson. Connecticut, then, only sinned a little. As he understood it, they kept them until they became too old for use, and died out. The Senator from Connecticut might then have a little charity for Maryland.

Mr. Baldwin said he had a great deal.

Mr. Johnson said, a great deal, indeed. She would take all, and allow nothing to the other side. So, in Ohio, where free negroes were treated as slaves.

[A sort of colloquial debate took place, in which Mr. Baldwin, Mr. Dix, Mr. Johnson, Mr. Douglas, and Mr. Dayton, took part, which could only be partially heard.]

Mr. Johnson resumed. The Senator from Ohio had complained that California was three thousand miles from Washington, and no slave could find means to employ a lawyer to carry up his case. He would reply to this, that there could not be found in the whole southern bar a lawyer who would not gratuitously give his services to a black man, to free him from slavery, where there was a reasonable ground for the application. He also referred to the readiness of judges to decide in favor of the slave. And he believed that if this bill should pass, there would be always found at the southern bar members who would be ready to sue out the freedom of slaves who were entitled to it. The question whether a slave owner is entitled to carry his slaves into the Territory, will be decided on the first appeal; and that will decide the matter in every future case which can arise. The question rises above party and sectional considerations. It assumes the character, and dignity, and importance of a national one.

Mr. Badger then obtained the floor, and commenced with an expression of his sincere regret that the Senator who had charge of this bill, should have started with an assertion that it was to be pressed through the Senate in hot haste. Instead of invoking the fullest examination of the bill, and of allowing Senators freely to discuss it, the question was pressed on an exhausted Senate. Every motion to adjourn was constantly resisted. Even on the first day of the introduction of the bill, his friend from Delaware had voted against adjournment, the yeas and nays having been demanded. And on Monday evening, when his friend from Kentucky desired to address the Senate, and moved an adjournment, the same course was pursued.

Mr. Clayton reminded the Senator from North Carolina that he had last night suggested an adjournment, and voted for it, to enable the Senator from Maryland to address the Senate.

Mr. Badger replied that this was a different matter. The Senator from Maryland was about to speak in defence of the bill, and this may be the reason for the readiness of his friend from Delaware to adjourn. He repeated that every effort had been made to press this question on an exhausted Senate. He knew no reason for thus pressing a question of such importance. There was plenty of time before us. He was as desirous as any Senator to go home and see his children; but when a question of real magnitude was before the Senate, he was willing to sit here until full and ample time had been given for its examination—say three weeks, or a month, or more. As circumstances now stood, he should go at some length into the reasons he had to assign for the vote he was about to give.

He regarded this bill as a complete surrender of the rights of the South; and on this point he expanded his views to much extent. He then referred to the course taken by one of his distinguished colleagues from North Carolina in the House, in which that gentleman had charged him (Mr. B.) with having made a speech which he had not made, and which speech that gentleman had, with great industry, circulated through the State of North Carolina, for the purpose of keeping him (Mr. B.) in the minds of his constituents. He went on to set that matter right, for the purpose of correcting the false impression made by that speech. He then went into a history and definition of the powers granted to Congress by the constitution, among which he included that of governing the territory ceded to us. That power included either the introduction or the abolition of slavery in the territories ceded to us. The power of acquiring territory has been sustained by the decision of the Supreme Court; and the acquisition of territory carries with it the power to govern the territory, and the power to govern includes the power to regulate slavery.

In the course of his remarks, Mr. BADGER made copious references to authorities, which he quoted at length to sustain his positions. He did not see why a time may not come when we shall be obliged to hold territory, like England, in China, or some other country; and if we maintain that we have a right to introduce negro slavery there, we shall be obliged to show some authority beyond our own wishes. We have as great a right to acquire territory as any nation or republic in the world, and the only restraint on our rule is that which arises from our own convictions as to what is right and proper. It is supposed by some that we have a right to acquire territory only for the purpose of colonizing our slaves; but he held that we had as much right to acquire it for a perpetuity. The provisions in the constitution which had been frequently referred to, were intended merely to limit our powers with reference to the States of the Union; but in relation to territories acquired by conquest or cession, the arm of the Government is not shortened by these restrictions.

When the Missouri compromise bill came to the Senate from the House, it contained a provision excluding slavery from the South. It was amended in the Senate without a division, and a provision was introduced containing a restriction on slavery in the North and the West.

Mr. CALHOUN said he had always the impression that Mr. Pinkney (who had been alluded to) was an abolitionist. He had addressed a meeting in Hagarstown in favor of abolitionism.

Mr. BADGER said he had a paper before him which rebuked that charge. Had he been an abolitionist, he would not have voted as he did on the Missouri compromise. If the Senator from South Carolina referred to Mr. Pinkney's course to impugn his authority, he referred to it for no purpose.

Mr. CALHOUN said he had merely referred to it as a fact.

Mr. BADGER said, it was, as a fact, deserving of record. He, as a representative of one of the southern States, was called on, with his colleague, to give up all the rights and interests of the South. He believed negro slavery would be as effectually excluded by this bill as if the Wilmot proviso, or any other bill, had passed. He had a respect for the Supreme Court, but he was not willing to leave the decision of the question to a court, so large a portion of which were opposed to slavery.

Mr. BUTLER asked the Senator, if he could point out a mode which would be effectual, in case this mode of appeal should fail?

Mr. BADGER said, he thought he could very readily do so; but he desired now to go on with his argument. He would willingly vote for this bill, could he be assured that it would be productive of peace and tranquillity throughout the country. He would go home to his constituents, one of the Old Thirteen, and throw himself confidently before them, and appeal to their generous patriotism. But, believing that it can only be productive of new agitation, he could not reconcile it to his views of propriety to vote for it. He believed that North Carolina would sustain him in the adoption of his own views.

Opinions are various in the Senate with reference to the bill. Some were willing to take it up as it is; others were opposed to it. He thought that the question ought to be settled. If the climate was suited to the productions of the South, he thought it ought to be filled with a population from the South.

It was not intended to introduce slavery in the North. We are called on to legislate on a great fact. We live in the midst of three millions of slaves. In the employment of these, no man will use them where they are unproductive of profit.

He stated the changes which Moses made in the Jewish laws, and that he was compelled to adapt his code to the position and prejudices of the people who were to be regulated by them. He advised us to adopt the same wise policy, and to rely on the blessing of God upon our success.

He concluded with asserting that he would be glad to be convinced of the futility of his arguments, to be satisfied that he entertained wrong views; but while he felt the conviction that this bill surrendered the views of the

South, he could not vote for it. Like his friend from Maryland, he would willingly see his candidate for the Presidency defeated, rather than that this question should not be settled. Much as he believed that the interests of the country were connected with the success of that candidate, he would be willing to postpone all the advantages to be obtained for his success, rather than that the settlement of this question should not take place.

Mr. Butler spoke nearly three hours, but the confusion was too great in the gallery to allow his argument to be heard.

Mr. Dix then obtained the floor, and commenced with a defence of the State of New York against the charge which had been made against her of refusing to surrender fugitives from justice, claimed under requisition from the State of Virginia. He alleged that this was not the act of the State, but of the Governor. He read the resolutions adopted by the Legislature, of which he was a member, which condemned the course of the Governor. He defended New York against attacks which had been levelled against her, and pointed the attention of the Senate to several bright pages in her political history. Of her social character, her love and patronage of the arts, her system of education, and all her great works of internal improvement, it was unnecessary for him to speak. Her blood was mingled with that of the sons of the Palmetto State on the fields of Mexico; and the recollection of this union in death ought to make the Senator from South Carolina more reluctant to cast reproach on New York.

Mr. Dix closed his speech at half-past seven P. M.

Mr. Dayton then rose to address the Senate in opposition to the bill, but had not proceeded far with his remarks when he gave way to—

Mr. Mangum, who moved an adjournment.

Mr. Dayton expressed his willingness to proceed. He did not desire an adjournment upon his account.

The question being taken by yeas and nays, the motion was decided in the negative.

Mr. Dayton resumed, and concluded his remarks.

Mr. Upham followed upon the same side.

Mr. Bell also opposed the bill.

Mr. Berrien delivered an argument in support of the bill.

Mr. Bradbury followed in opposition to the bill.

Mr. Underwood, at one o'clock, A. M., moved an adjournment; which was disagreed to by yeas and nays.

Mr. Borland addressed the Senate at considerable length.

Mr. Berrien followed in an earnest defence of the bill; when—

Mr. Baldwin moved that the Senate adjourn; which was decided in the negative.

Mr. Niles addressed the Senate for some half hour. There being only one Senator present in his seat, he moved that the Senate adjourn.

It was then two A. M., but instantly Senators rose from sofas and various parts of the lobby, and the yeas and nays were demanded, and the motion was disagreed to.

Mr. Niles then proceeded very coolly in his remarks until he closed.

The debate was further continued by Messrs. Atchison, Dickinson, Bright, Calhoun, and others, when the Senate proceeded to vote on the amendments.

Mr. Baldwin moved to amend the bill in the twenty-sixth section, by inserting after the word "slavery," in line 10, the following:

Or to repeal the laws which were in force in said Territory, when forming part of the Republic of Mexico, prohibiting slavery or involuntary slavery therein, or any law securing the personal liberty of all the inhabitants thereof, but such laws, so far as they may not be inconsistent with the Constitution of the United States, shall be and remain in force until repealed by Congress.

Mr. B. made some remarks in favor of this amendment.

The question was then taken, and the amendment was disagreed to.

Mr. Clarke moved to amend the bill in the 26th section, after the word "slavery," by adding:

It being understood and declared that, at the time of the cession of the Territories of New Mexico and California by Mexico to the United States, slavery and involuntary servitude had been abolished by the laws of Mexico, and did not exist therein; and that the laws now in said Territory shall be and remain in full force until territorial legislatures shall be formed by Congress, with authority to change or repeal the same.

This amendment was also disagreed to.

Mr. Hale moved to amend the twelfth section, which provides that the existing laws in Oregon shall continue to be valid for *three months* after the first meeting of the Legislature, by striking out the words "three months;" and on this motion he asked for the yeas and nays, which were ordered.

The question being taken, it was decided as follows:

Yeas.—Messrs. Allen, Atherton, Baldwin, Benton, Bradbury, Clarke, Corwin, Davis of Massachusetts, Dayton, Dix, Dodge, Felch, Fitzgerald, Greene, Hale, Hamlin, Miller, Niles, Spruance, Upham, and Walker—21.

Nays.—Messrs. Atchison, Badger, Bell, Berrien, Borland, Breese, Bright, Butler, Calhoun, Clayton, Davis of Mississippi, Dickinson, Douglas, Downs, Foote, Hannegan, Houston, Hunter, Johnson of Maryland, Johnson of Louisiana, Johnson of Georgia, King, Lewis, Mangum, Mason, Metcalfe, Rusk, Sebastian, Sturgeon, Turney, Underwood, Westcott, and Yulee—33.

Mr. Baldwin moved to amend the bill by adding the following as the 37th section:

And be it further enacted, That it shall be the

duty of the attorneys for said Territories, respectively, on the complaint of any person held in involuntary servitude therein, to make application in his behalf, in due form of law, to the court next thereafter to be holden in said Territory, for a writ of habeas corpus, to be directed to the person so holding such applicant in service, as aforesaid, and to pursue all needful measures in his behalf; and if the decision of such court shall be adverse to such application, or if, in the return of the writ, relief shall be denied to the applicant on the ground that he is a slave held in servitude in said Territory, said attorney shall cause an appeal to be taken therefrom; and the record of all the proceedings in the case to be transmitted to the Supreme Court of the United States, as speedily as may be; and to give notice thereof to the Attorney General of the United States, who shall prosecute the same before said court, who shall proceed to hear and determine the same at the first term thereof.

The question on this amendment was decided in the negative.

Mr. HALE modified his motion so as to stand thus: Strike out a "free white" from fifth section, and insert next after the word "act," in the fourth line, the words, "and qualified to vote by the existing laws, now in force in the Territory of Oregon under the authority of the Provisional Government established by the people thereof."

The question being taken on this amendment, it was decided as follows:

YEAS.—Messrs. Baldwin, Benton, Clarke, Davis of Massachusetts, Greene, Hale, and Upham—7.

NAYS.—Messrs. Allen, Atchison, Atherton, Badger, Bell, Berrien, Borland, Bradbury, Breese, Bright, Butler, Calhoun, Clayton, Corwin, Davis of Mississippi, Dayton, Dickinson, Dix, Dodge, Douglas, Downs, Felch, Fitzgerald, Foote, Hamlin, Hannegan, Houston, Hunter, Johnson of Maryland, Johnson of Georgia, King, Lewis, Mason, Metcalfe, Miller, Niles, Rusk, Sebastian, Sturgeon, Turney, Underwood, Walker, Westcott, and Yulee—44.

Mr. CLARKE moved to amend the bill by adding at the close of the sixth section the following words:

Provided, however, That no law repealing the act of the Provisional Government of said Territory prohibiting slavery or involuntary servitude therein, shall be valid until the same shall be approved by Congress.

On this amendment the yeas and nays were ordered, and the question being taken on the motion, it was decided as follows:

YEAS.—Messrs. Allen, Baldwin, Benton, Bradbury, Clarke, Corwin, Davis of Massachusetts, Dayton, Dix, Dodge, Felch, Fitzgerald, Greene, Hale, Hamlin, Miller, Niles, Upham, and Walker—19.

NAYS.—Messrs. Atkinson, Atherton, Badger, Bell, Berrien, Borland, Breese, Bright, Butler, Calhoun, Clayton, Davis of Mississippi, Dickinson, Douglas, Downs, Foote, Hannegan, Houston, Hunter, Johnson of Maryland, Johnson of Georgia, King, Lewis, Mason, Metcalfe, Phelps, Rusk, Sebastian, Sturgeon, Turney, Underwood, Westcott, and Yulee—33.

Mr. DAVIS, of Massachusetts, moved to amend the 12th section, by inserting the following words:

That so much of the 6th article of the ordinance of the 13th of July, 1787, as is contained in the following words, to wit, "There shall be neither slavery nor involuntary servitude in the said Territory otherwise than in the punishment of crimes, whereof the party shall have been duly convicted," shall be and remain in force within the Territory of Oregon."

On this motion the yeas and nays were ordered, and the question being taken on the amendment, it was decided as follows:

YEAS.—Messrs. Allen, Atherton, Baldwin, Benton, Bradbury, Clarke, Corwin, Davis of Massachusetts, Dayton, Dix, Dodge, Felch, Fitzgerald, Greene, Hale, Hamlin, Miller, Niles, Spruance, Upham, and Walker—21.

NAYS.—Messrs. Atchison, Badger, Bell, Berrien, Borland, Breese, Bright, Butler, Calhoun, Clayton, Davis of Mississippi, Dickinson, Douglas, Downs, Foote, Hannegan, Houston, Hunter, Johnson of Maryland, Johnson of Louisiana, Johnson of Georgia, King, Lewis, Mangum, Mason, Metcalfe, Rusk, Sebastian, Sturgeon, Turney, Underwood, Westcott, and Yulee—33.

Mr. JOHNSON, of Maryland, moved to amend the bill in the 24th and 31st sections, by inserting the following words after the words which empower the Legislature to pass any law:

Except only that, in all cases involving title to lands, the said writs of error or appeals shall be allowed and decided by the said supreme court, without regard to the value of the matter, property, or title in controversy. And except, also, that a writ of error or appeal shall also be allowed to the Supreme Court of the United States from the decision of the said supreme court created by this act, or any judge thereof, or of the district courts created by this act, or of any judge thereof, upon any writ of habeas corpus involving the question of personal freedom.

The question, after some remarks from Messrs. BRIGHT, BORLAND, and DICKINSON, was taken by yeas and nays, and decided as follows:

YEAS.—Messrs. Allen, Atherton, Badger, Berrien, Bradbury, Clarke, Clayton, Corwin, Davis of Massachusetts, Dayton, Dix, Dodge, Felch, Fitzgerald, Greene, Hale, Hamlin, Houston, Johnson of Maryland, Johnson of Louisiana, King, Mangum, Metcalfe, Miller, Niles, Phelps, Rusk, Spruance, Sturgeon, Upham, and Walker—31.

NAYS.—Messrs. Atchison, Benton, Borland, Bright, Butler, Calhoun, Davis of Mississippi, Dickinson, Downs, Foote, Hannegan, Hunter, Johnson of Georgia, Lewis, Mason, Sebastian, Turney, Westcott, and Yulee—19.

The bill was then reported to the Senate.

The question was then taken on the engrossment of the bill; and, the yeas and nays being ordered, it was decided as follows:

YEAS.—Messrs. Atchison, Atherton, Benton, Berrien, Borland, Breese, Bright, Butler, Calhoun,

Clayton, Davis of Mississippi, Dickinson, Douglas, Downs, Foote, Hannegan, Houston, Hunter, Johnson of Maryland, Johnson of Louisiana, Johnson of Georgia, King, Lewis, Mangum, Mason, Phelps, Rusk, Sebastian, Spruance, Sturgeon, Turney, Westcott, and Yulee—33.

Nays.—Messrs. Allen, Badger, Baldwin, Bell, Bradbury, Clarke, Corwin, Davis of Massachusetts, Dayton, Dix, Dodge, Felch, Fitzgerald, Greene, Hale, Hamlin, Metcalfe, Miller, Niles, Underwood, Upham, and Walker—22.

[Mr. Pearce, of Maryland, we happen to know, remained until a late hour of the night in the Senate, but was obliged, through fatigue and indisposition, to leave the Senate some time before midnight.]

The bill was then read a third time, and passed.

And at seven minutes before 8 A. M., (Thursday morning,) after a continuous session of twenty-one hours, the Senate adjourned till Friday.

The bill is set out in full in the Senate Debates of the day, (July 26, 1848,) and besides the principal features of it as presented in the progress of discussion, contained a brief section which was not adverted to at the time, but requires to be known to show the whole character of the bill. It was the last section but one, and was in these words:

"Sec. 35. And be it further enacted, That the constitution and laws of the United States are hereby extended over, and declared to be in force, in said Territories of California and New Mexico, so far as the same, or any provision thereof, may be applicable."

HOUSE OF REPRESENTATIVES.

Friday, July 28.

*The Oregon Bill.**

The Oregon bill having been taken up—

Mr. Adams, of Kentucky, who had the floor from a preceding day, addressed the committee mainly on the question of slavery in the Territory, over which he believed Congress had control, and incidentally in reply to positions assumed by his colleagues heretofore.

Mr. Collins followed in favor of the doctrine of the proviso.

Mr. Dunn then addressed the committee in a speech upon general politics.

Mr. Hall, of Missouri, followed Mr. Dunn in a speech urging Congress to act immediately on the bill to establish the Territorial Government of Oregon.

Mr. Mullin then got the floor, and the committee rose and reported progress.

Monday, July 31.

Oregon Territorial Bill.

On motion of Mr. Wentworth, the House resolved itself into Committee of the Whole on the state of the Union, (Mr. Morehead, of Kentucky, in the chair,) and resumed the consideration of the bill to establish the Territorial Government of Oregon.

The debate having been closed—

Mr. Smith, of Indiana, proposed to avail himself of the privilege given to him by the rules to make some remarks on this bill. The question involved in the bill had been discussed on almost every bill before the House for some time, and they should now show by their votes whether any principle had been recognized by the House or not. He did trust, however, whatever might be the decision of the House of Representatives and the Senate on this controverted question of slavery, that Congress would give a Territorial Government to Oregon before the adjournment. And he protested against the attempt which had been made to unite the fate of the Territory of Oregon with the newly-acquired territory from Mexico. He protested against identifying the fate and the interests of Oregon with the fate and interests of New Mexico and California. There was no reason why the people of Oregon should be compelled to remain without a government until they could settle the question growing out of the new territory. Why, we had as yet barely acquired New Mexico and California. They were not yet part and parcel of this Union, because the treaty by which Mexico ceded them to us had not yet been carried out. We had made no appropriation as yet for that purpose. No legislative act had been done by Congress to consummate and carry out the stipulations of the treaty, and he repeated that it would be unjust to compel the people of Oregon to unite their fate with the people of Mew Mexico and California.

Mr. Cobb, of Georgia, inquired, if the gentleman from Indiana, as the chairman of the Committee on the Territories, was not instructed by his committee to report bills to establish Territorial Governments in New Mexico and California?

Mr. Smith replied, that he had separate bills for that purpose. He desired them to be considered separately. He was opposed to uniting them in one bill, inasmuch as they presented different questions, which should be separately acted upon.

Mr. Cobb was aware of that; but he understood the gentleman from Indiana to say, that we had not yet so acquired those Territories as to enable us to establish governments in them.

Mr. Smith said, they were not part of this

---

* This was a bill for Oregon—a separate bill for that Territory alone—originating in the House, and now taken up for consideration. The bill from the Senate, for the three Territories, had been laid upon the table, without any proceeding having been had upon it—which might be considered, and was, the end of it, as it could not be got up without a two-third vote. The House proceeded with its own bill—perfected it—passed it—and sent it to the Senate for concurrence. There, of course, it became the bill on which the Senate acted.

Union as Oregon was, nor would be, without further legislation, of which the bills he had ready to report were part. Congress must first pass a bill to carry out the treaty, before they would be properly part of this Union.

Mr. COBB asked, then, what authority they had to establish Territorial Governments by the bills which the gentleman from Indiana was desirous to report?

Mr. SMITH supposed that all necessary enactments would be made for that purpose, and these bills were a part of the necessary legislation. Now, suppose they never should appropriate money to pay for these Territories, would they be ours then? It was not necessary, however, to consume time on that point. What he desired to do now was, to look at the past legislation of Congress on this question. They found gentlemen telling them that they ought not to create a government for Oregon which would restrict slavery, for that they had no power to do so. Now, why was there this sensitiveness on the part of gentlemen? Why, they had been legislating on this question ever since he had had a seat on this floor. During the first Congress of which he was a member, a bill was passed by this House by a large majority, creating a Territorial Government for Oregon, which contained a provision which was a prohibition of slavery. He desired to refer to one or two things which occurred when this bill passed. He would quote from the Journal of the 2d session of the 28th Congress, of the date of the 3d February, 1845, page 318:

"The question being, first, 'Will the House agree to the amendments to the said bill reported from the Committee of the Whole House on the state of the Union?' when a division of the said amendments being called for, the first of the said amendments was read, and agreed to; and the second of said amendments was then read, as follows: And at the end of the sixth section the following: '*Provided, however*, That there shall neither be slavery nor involuntary servitude in the said Territory, otherwise than in the punishment of crimes, whereof the party shall have been duly convicted.' And the question being put, 'Will the House agree thereto?' it was decided in the affirmative: Yeas 129, nays 69."

The bill, with that provision in it, was subsequently passed by 140 yeas to 59 noes. Only fifty-nine! and they were not all southern gentlemen either. Most of the opposition which that bill met grew out of other questions. It was thought by some that they could not organize a Territorial Government in Oregon while the convention with Great Britain for the joint occupation of that Territory remained unrescinded; but he found that a good many of his Democratic friends, who were now so very sensitive on the subject, then voted with him (Mr. S.) and his friends in favor of that bill containing that proviso.

Mr. SMITH trusted that this bill would be considered and acted upon on its own merits, without connecting it with New Mexico or California. Mr. S. was, however, for excluding slavery from all the Territories.

Ever since the foundation of this Government, our policy had been to restrict slavery wherever it could be done. The Missouri compromise was an act restricting the extent of slavery; but this Government had never passed any act, at any time, to advance the extent of slavery one foot.

Mr. VINTON asked whether the Legislature of Texas had passed any law prohibiting the carrying of slaves beyond the line of 36° 30′?

Mr. KAUFMAN replied that the resolutions of annexation did not require that it should. No gentleman could fairly charge Texas with bad faith when she had made the very words of the annexation resolutions a part and parcel of her constitution. Does not the gentleman contend that the annexation resolutions forbid slaves from going north of 36° 30′ in Texas? And would a law of the Texas Legislature be more binding than her constitution?

Mr. SMITH (resuming) said that gentlemen might plead as they would, but they well knew that the word of promise might have been kept to the ear, but was broken to the sense. All he knew about it was, that the compromise was understood by all to be, that there should no slavery exist north of 36° 30′. If Texas meant to observe and carry out that compromise in good faith, ought she not to have passed a law rendering it impossible that slavery should have any existence north of that line? Yet it did exist there. Slaves were at this hour held in Texas north of that line; and they would continue to be held there till doomsday; for Texas declared that slavery should not be interfered with either north or south of the line.

Mr. STEPHENS said that the resolutions of annexation had been incorporated into the constitution of Texas and formed a part of it.

Mr. SMITH. Does the gentleman mean to say that slaves cannot now be held to the north of 36° 30′?

Mr. STEPHENS. They cannot.

Mr. SMITH went on to say that Congress were now asked to take a new position, to adopt an entirely new course, and extend slavery into territory now free. It amounted to this, that the Congress of the United States, representing free as well as slave States, should engage in the business of extending slavery. Had this ever yet been done? Never. Congress had acted in the restriction of slavery, never in its extension. They were now called on to establish it. Had Congress any power to establish it? Would gentlemen's zeal in favor of their institution carry them so far as to say that it had? It had never been attempted before. To do what was now asked would be virtually to establish slavery in all the States as well as all the Territories of the Union. He would ask his friend from Illinois (Mr. MCCLERNAND) whether he was willing to stand up in his own Legislature, and vote that one-half of the State of Illinois should be given up to the presence of slavery? He knew he would not; yet he was for establishing it up to a certain line in the Territories of the Pacific.

Mr. McClernand said the gentleman from Indiana misrepresented him. All he proposed was, that the States south of 36° 30′ should determine the question of slavery for themselves. He said nothing in his amendment which he had proposed about slavery in the Territories.

Mr. Smith said that everybody knew, that in selecting a region wherein to settle for life, men were always greatly influenced by a knowledge of the laws and customs that prevailed there, and this was especially true of slavery and slave laws. If, indeed, Congress was passive on the subject, that would be another affair; but in that case slavery would not exist in the Territories, because it did not exist here now, and was prohibited by law. But gentlemen were not satisfied with this; they wanted Congress to establish it there. It was contended that a southern man had a right to go into those Territories with all his property. Well, if he had a right, therefore, to carry his slave there, then, by the same reasoning, he had a right to come with his slaves into Indiana; for the constitution gave him equal rights with the people of all the States into which he went. A citizen of Pennsylvania had a right to go there with his property, and could not a citizen of South Carolina go with his? Had Indiana a right to exclude a citizen of New York from coming there with his cows and oxen?

Mr. Holmes said, Yes, she had.

Mr. Smith said, a State had no right to prevent the citizen of another State from coming there, and bringing his property with him. But the whole error lay in maintaining that slaves were property. He admitted that people of all the States were permitted to come with that which was recognized as property by the constitution, by the laws of nature, and by the laws of God; they might bring their horses, and their cattle, and their goods; but this did not prove they had a right to come there with slaves. A man's horse was his property, and he had a right to come there with his horse; and he had a right, too, to kill his horse, if he pleased; he might shoot him through the head upon the highway; because a horse was recognized as property by the laws of all civilized nations. But he could not kill his slave; he could not beat out his brains or shoot him down on the highway. Why? Because he was not property. There existed, indeed, a peculiar relation between master and slave, but that relation was created wholly by positive statute. Let him suppose a case. Gentlemen said a man had a right to go into the Territories with his slaves, because in the slave States these were regarded as property, so recognized by law. Now, suppose the laws of South Carolina recognized the right of a man to marry two wives, or many wives, at the same time; suppose bigamy or polygamy to be permitted by the laws of South Carolina, would it be maintained that a man might go into the Territories, and live there with half a dozen wives at once? He would have no more right to do this than to go there and hold his slaves. Both institutions existed only by positive municipal law; and municipal regulations extended no further than the jurisdiction did which established them.

Mr. S. having closed his remarks—

The question was stated on striking out the first section of the bill, viz:

"That, from and after the passage of this act, all that part of the territory of the United States which lies west of the summit of the Rocky Mountains, known as the Territory of Oregon, shall be organized into and constitute a temporary Government by the name of the Territory of Oregon: *Provided*, That nothing in this act contained shall be construed to impair the rights of person or property now pertaining to the Indians in said Territory, so long as such rights shall remain unextinguished by treaty between the United States and such Indians, or to affect the authority of the Government of the United States to make any regulation respecting such Indians, their lands, property, or other rights, by treaty, law, or otherwise, which it would have been competent to the Government to make if this act had never passed: *And provided further*, That nothing in this act contained shall be construed to inhibit the Government of the United States from dividing said Territory into two or more Territories, in such manner and at such times as Congress shall deem convenient and proper, or from attaching any portion of said Territory to any other State or Territory of the United States."

Pending this amendment the committee rose, and the House adjourned.

IN SENATE.

Monday, July 31.

Territorial Governments.

Mr. Benton offered a bill providing a government for the Territories of Oregon, New Mexico, and California, which, he was understood to say, was copied from the act of 1804, relating to Louisiana, in effect that the people should be governed according to the existing laws, until others were made. He desired that it might be printed, and laid on the table; and, if nothing better be offered in the mean time by anybody else, he should call it up for consideration.

Mr. Hannegan said: On Saturday last, Mr. President, I gave notice to the Senate that I would to-day introduce a bill providing for the organization of Territorial Governments in Oregon, California, and New Mexico. In connection with some of my friends, I have given to this subject all the attention in my power, under a feeling of the deepest anxiety, and I have become satisfied, that after the ordeal through which the question has already passed—after the searching investigation to which it was subjected by the select committee appointed by the Senate—a committee so remarkable, so pre-eminent, I might well say, for intellect, for wisdom, and for patriotism—it is in vain for any individual to attempt its adjustment. I believe that when the proposition which emanated from that committee, representing every section of the Union, and representing the two great parties of the country, has failed, there is no hope left to us of a final adjustment of the question at this time. I regret it deeply. From various quarters of the country, appeals to me have been made, with various motives; and it has been urged upon me that it is most expedient to leave this question open, because that course would promote the prospects of the election of a favorite candidate for the Presidency—my favorite, sir. But I am incapable of regarding this subject in that aspect. Perish the prospects of any living man, be he whom he may, and mine own first, sooner than leave open, from such considerations as those, a question so momentous, so agitating and exciting! No, sir; I cannot look at the subject in that light. I can look at it only with a view to the best interests of my country. I believe the question should be settled, and settled promptly.

I think, sir, that the events of the present day are full of admonition to us, and I fear that the admonition is not sufficiently heeded. When Christendom looks at the debates which have taken place here, and at the other end of the Capitol, they will believe us to be on the verge of disunion and civil war. At the very same moment that we are standing out before Europe as the bright exemplar, illuminating and arousing makind to a consciousness of the value of rational and regulated liberty, we present this humiliating spectacle of internal dissension! Why, sir, it was but the other day, as I have been informed through the correspondence of one of our diplomatic agents, that in the great German Parliament, assembled for the purpose of uniting in one great confederacy the Germanic States, on an allusion being made to the United States of America, that august assemblage, composed of men cold and phlegmatic as you have been ever taught to regard them, rose simultaneously in token of respect, and burst forth into loud and long protracted shouts, at the bare mention of our name! Yet, here we are, in relation to a question which should excite no feeling, which involves no interest upon one side, and only serves to assail an interest upon the other, sending forth to the world a picture that borders upon the horrors of that which has recently startled men in France. Gentlemen talk of disunion as coolly as we talk about our ordinary appropriation bills! Disunion! It is moral treason to breathe the word! Disunion! As was well said the other day by the venerable Senator from Kentucky, whose whole life has been one continued career of patriotism, how can you dismember us, when Kentucky stretches her arms across the Ohio, to Ohio, Indiana, and Illinois? You can never dismember us! We will hold the Union together with hooks of steel. We cannot separate! Yet, we may go and familiarize the public mind with the thought of disunion and civil war, until you do indeed light up the torch of the incendiary. It has become already familiar "as a household word." All this may go on, till at last we behold the gleaming sword of brother arrayed against brother, and our streams and rivers running red with blood; but you can never, on this or any other question, dismember the Union!

I have said, sir, that I hold it moral treason to talk of disunion or civil war here! What! talk of disunion at this hour, when from the central heaven, beams all over Christendom the star of our Republic—not the less brilliant, because, like the fire-fly, its light is mellow and mild—when our principles are scattered broadcast throughout the European world—when the German Parliament offers its enthusiastic homage at the mere mention of our country's name! Is it at such a period that we send words of excitement and discord abroad, to make those who are struggling to imitate our example, doubt the capacity of man for self-government!

HOUSE OF REPRESENTATIVES.

TUESDAY, August 1.

Oregon.

On motion of Mr. SMITH, of Indiana, the House resolved itself into Committee of the Whole on the state of the Union, (Mr. MOREHEAD, of Kentucky, in the chair,) and resumed the consideration of the bill to establish the Territorial Government of Oregon.

The question pending when the committee rose yesterday, was on agreeing to the amendment moved by Mr. ROCKWELL, of Connecticut, to the first section, to confirm to the missionaries at the several stations land not exceeding in quantity in each case 640 acres.

The question was now put, and the amendment was agreed to.

The question was then put on striking out the first section, and it was rejected.

Mr. KAUFMAN moved to insert a new section, to come in between the second and third sections, which was ruled out of order.

Mr. BOYD. Mr. Chairman, be good enough to state the precise point.

The CHAIRMAN. The bill before the committee is a bill to provide a Territorial Government for the Territory of Oregon, and the proposition of the gentleman from Texas is to organize Territorial Governments for New Mexico and California. The Chair rules the amendment out of order; and the question is, Shall the decision of the Chair stand as the judgment of the committee?

Mr. Cobb, of Georgia, called for tellers, and they were ordered, and reported 88 in the affirmative, and 60 in the negative. The decision of the Chair was therefore sustained.

Wednesday, August 2.

Message from the President—Mexican Negotiations—Declines, for the present, to Communicate the Instructions, to the United States Ministers, Messrs. Ambrose H. Sevier and Nathan Clifford, because Incompatible with the Interest of the United States.

The Speaker laid before the House the following Message:

To the House of Representatives of the United States:

In answer to the resolution of the House of Representatives of the 17th instant, requesting the President "to communicate (if not inconsistent with the public interest) copies of all instructions given to the Hon. Ambrose H. Sevier and Nathan Clifford, commissioners appointed to conduct negotiations for the treaty lately concluded between the United States and the Republic of Mexico," I have to state, that in my opinion it would be "inconsistent with the public interest" to give publicity to these instructions at the present time. I avail myself of this occasion to observe, that as a general rule, applicable to all our important negotiations with foreign powers, it could not fail to be prejudicial to the public interest to publish the instructions to our ministers until some time had elapsed after the conclusion of such negotiations. In the present case, the object of the mission of our commissioners to Mexico has been accomplished. The treaty, as amended by the Senate of the United States, has been ratified, the ratifications have been exchanged, and the treaty has been proclaimed as the supreme law of the land. No contingency occurred which made it either necessary or proper for our commissioners to enter upon any negotiations with the Mexican Government, further than to urge upon that Government the ratification of the treaty in its amended form.

JAMES K. POLK.

Washington, *July* 29, 1848.

Oregon Territorial Government.

On motion of Mr. Smith, of Indiana, the House resumed the consideration of the bill to establish the Territorial Government of Oregon, and the amendments thereto reported by the Committee of the Whole, on which the previous question had been seconded, and the main question ordered.

The question being on agreeing to the said amendments, they were severally read and agreed to without division, except the two following, on which separate votes were taken, viz:

On concurring with the Committee of the Whole in striking out in the second section the words, "and shall approve of all laws passed by the Legislative Assembly before they shall take effect." [The effect of this amendment is to deprive the Governor of the power of approval

or disapproval of the laws passed by the Legislature.]

The vote on agreeing to this amendment resulted—yeas 132, nays 63.

So the amendment was concurred in.

The other amendment was on agreeing with the Committee of the Whole in striking out that part of the 12th section which extends the ordinance of 1787 over the Oregon Territory, which is in the following words:

"That the inhabitants of said Territory shall be entitled to enjoy all and singular the rights, privileges, and immunities granted and secured to the people of the territory of the United States north-west of the river Ohio, by the articles of compact contained in the ordinance for the Government of said territory, on the thirteenth day of July, seventeen hundred and eighty-seven; [and shall be subject to all the conditions, and restrictions, and prohibitions in said articles of compact imposed upon the people of said territory,] and."

On agreeing to this amendment, the yeas and nays were taken, and resulted as follows:

Yeas.—Messrs. Barringer, Bayly, Beale, Birdsall, Bocock, Botts, Bowdon, Bowlin, Boyd, Brodhead, Wm. G. Brown, Albert G. Brown, Burt, Cabell, Chapman, Chase, Beverly L. Clarke, Clingman, Howell Cobb, Williamson R. W. Cobb, Cocke, Crisfield, Crozier, Daniel, Garnett Duncan, Alexander Evans, Featherston, Ficklin, Flournoy, French, Fulton, Gayle, Gentry, Goggin, Green, Willard P. Hall, Haralson, Harmanson, Harris, Haskell, Hill, Hilliard, Isaac E. Holmes, George S. Houston, Inge, Charles J. Ingersoll, Iverson, Jameson, Andrew Johnson, Robert W. Johnson, George W. Jones, John W. Jones, Kaufman, Kennon, Thomas Butler King, La Sère, Ligon, Lumpkin, McClernand, McDowell, McKay, McLane, Miller, Outlaw, Pendleton, Phelps, Pillsbury, Preston, Rhett, Richardson, Robinson, Roman, Sawyer, Shepperd, Simpson, Sims, Stanton, Stephens, Thibodeaux, Thomas, Jacob Thompson, Robert A. Thompson, Tompkins, Toombs, Venable, Wallace, Wick, and Woodward—88.

Nays.—Messrs. Abbott, Adams, Ashmun, Bingham, Blanchard, Brady, Butler, Canby, Cathcart, Franklin Clark, Collamer, Collins, Conger, Cranston, Crowell, Cummins, Darling, Dickey, Dickinson, Dixon, Duer, Daniel Duncan, Dunn, Eckert, Edwards, Embree, Nathan Evans, Faran, Farrelly, Fisher, Freedley, Fries, Giddings, Gott, Gregory, Grinnell, Hale, Nathan K. Hall, Hammons, Jas. G. Hampton, Moses Hampton, Henley, Henry, Elias B. Holmes, John W. Houston, Hubbard, Hudson, Hunt, Joseph R. Ingersoll, Jenkins, Kellogg, Daniel P. King, Lahm, William T. Lawrence, Sidney Lawrence, Lincoln, Lord, Lynde, Maclay, McClelland, McIlvaine, Job Mann, Horace Mann, Marsh, Marvin, Morris, Mullin, Nelson, Newell, Nicoll, Palfrey, Peaslee, Peck, Petrie, Pettit, Pollock, Putnam, Reynolds, Richey, Rockhill, Julius Rockwell, John A. Rockwell, Rose, Root, Rumsey, St. John, Schenck, Sherrill, Silvester, Slingerland, Smart, Caleb B. Smith, Robert Smith, Truman Smith, Starkweather, Andrew Stewart, Charles E. Stuart, Strohm, Tallmadge, Taylor, James Thompson, Richard W. Thompson, Wm. Thompson, Thurston, Turner, Tuck, Van Dyke, Vinton, Warren, Wentworth, White, Wiley, Williams, and Wilmot—114.

So the House refused to concur with the committee in striking out.

The amendments having all been acted on—

The bill was ordered to be engrossed, and being engrossed, was read a third time, and, under the operation of the previous question, was passed by yeas and nays—yeas 129, nays 71.

IN SENATE.

Thursday, August 3.

Oregon

The bill received from the House of Representatives to establish a Territorial Government in Oregon, was read a first and second time; when

Mr. Clayton rose, and referred to the fact that a bill for the establishment of Territorial Governments in Oregon, California, and New Mexico, had passed the Senate, and was sent to the House for concurrence. Of the fate of that bill, no official communication has yet been made to the Senate. But we have now a bill from the House for the establishment of a Territorial Government in Oregon. Public rumor informs us that the Senate bill to which he had referred, was at once, and without even the courtesy of a reading, laid on the table; so that, by the rules of the House, it cannot be taken up again without a vote of two-thirds in its favor. Now, as to this bill just received, he was disposed to treat it with proper respect, and to vote for its reference to the appropriate committee.

He had desired to make some remarks on the bill which went from the Senate, because the character of the bill, and the course of the Select Committee, seemed to be greatly misunderstood. On the one side, it was asserted that the North had lost all her rights; while on the other, it was contended, with as much boldness, that the South had given up its rights. If both the North and South have lost their rights, who has got them? He went into a view of the bill, as the best answer he could give to these contradictory complaints; and stated, that it was the best measure that could have been suggested for the settlement of this dangerous and difficult question. He was sure that it secured the right of appeal, and that in referring it to the Supreme Court, it adopted the very best course, because the people, being law abiding, would submit to the decision of that court, which occupied the highest place in their confidence.

In the committee, the South had offered a number of propositions, all of which were rejected. The South then called on the North to propose something; but the North declined to offer any. It was then, by a lucky accident, that the principle of the compromise bill suggested itself, and that bill was prepared and reported. No sooner was it reported, than it began to provoke opposition from every quarter. The bill had been called a cowardly bill—a dodging, evasive measure. He had foretold that no bill which could be reported would abate the agitation throughout the country. But he would ask the North, What have you done? The members of the committee favorable to the bill had assumed the responsibility of offering a bill to the Senate. Is any one else ready to assume any responsibility? It appeared not. The bill had been assailed from every quarter, but no one had the courage to present any counter-proposition.

He then proceeded to reply, in detail, to the attacks made on the bill by various Senators, charging on the Senator from New York, (Mr. Dix,) that his argument against the bill was controverted by the fact that he had given a casting vote for the annexation of Texas. He thought it impossible to settle this question on any geographical line. He did not believe that members would come back here next session in better temper, and more disposed to settle the question. He believed that the country was getting into an alarming condition. But he would not cease to hope. Although he stood, like the man in the almanac, pierced through with a thousand arrows, he would never cease in his endeavors to bring this question to a settlement. He might fail now; but he would renew his efforts hereafter. He would rely on the constitutional mode of settling the question by the Supreme Court. In this dark and gloomy hour, that was the dial-plate which glittered through, and which he trusted would guide us to a safe and harmonious result. He moved to refer the bill to the Committee on Territories.

Mr. Downs said, that he had suggested a division of the Territory of Oregon into two Governments, the one embracing that part below thirty-six degrees, and the other above. He would now give notice of his intention to move an amendment, which he sent to the Chair, and which he asked to have printed, embracing the principle of the Missouri compromise.

Mr. Badger rose to address the Senate.

Mr. King said, there was no question before the Senate.

Mr. Dickinson. The question of reference is not debatable.

Mr. Yulee. If the Senator from North Carolina will give way, I will make a motion to permit him to proceed.

Mr. Foote hoped no friend of the compromise would interpose an objection to the freest discussion. He insisted that the Senator from North Carolina should proceed, as the Senator from Delaware had been permitted to do.

Mr. Badger said he desired no permission. He would, for the sake of having an opportunity to say a few words, move that the bill be indefinitely postponed. He then gave, briefly, some of the reasons which had brought him to the conclusion that the bill had surrendered the rights of the South.

Mr. Clayton made a few remarks in reply.

Mr. Badger withdrew his motion to postpone.

The Chair decided that the Senator had no right to withdraw his motion, without the consent of the Senate.

Mr. Badger appealed from the decision of the Chair.

The appeal was laid on the table.

Mr. Phelps expressed a hope that the bill would be referred to a proper committee. He desired a free discussion, until the country should wake up and understand the merits of the bill. He was prepared to meet the responsibility of the position he had assumed; he was willing to meet his constituents and to defend his course, and he had no apprehension about the result. He was deeply indebted to his friend from North Carolina, (Mr. Badger,) who had completely vindicated his (Mr. P.'s) course, when he said that the bill surrendered all the rights of the South. In that case, (said Mr. P.,) I can no longer be charged with surrendering the rights of the North. He desired the bill to go to a committee, to look into this and other statements which had been made here and elsewhere. He had hoped he had sufficiently explained his course, but it was not so: every breeze from the North assailed him and the bill.

The committee who had charge of the bill were sent there to perform certain duties. These duties were not to go to fisticuffs in the committee-room for sectional objects. He had a duty to his country to perform, and not a mere duty to a section. If any objected to the bill, let them submit such proposition as in their judgments could extricate us from the embarrassment in which we are placed.

Mr. Mangum moved that the Senator from North Carolina have leave to withdraw his motion for indefinite postponement.

Mr. Badger said he did not wish for leave.

Mr. Mangum withdrew the motion.

The question was then taken by yeas and nays, on the motion of indefinite postponement, and decided—yea 1, nays 47.

Mr. Foote, when his name was called, stated, by permission of the Senate, that he should vote in the negative, not because he intended to commit himself in support of the bill, (for he knew nothing of its character,) but simply because he was of opinion that every bill from the House of Representatives ought to be received and treated with due consideration and respect.

The bill was then referred to the Committee on Territories.

Monday, August 7.

Oregon.

On motion of Mr. Douglas, the Senate proceeded to the consideration of the bill to establish the Territorial Government of Oregon.

The bill being before the Senate as in Committee of the Whole, and the question being on the amendments reported by the Committee on the Territories—

The first amendment was the introduction of the following proviso to the sixth section: "That no act of the Territorial Legislature shall become a law until approved by the Governor."

Mr. Davis, of Mississippi, moved to amend the amendment by adding the words, "of the Territory, or, if disapproved by said Governor, until specifically submitted to and approved by the Congress of the United States."

The amendment to the amendment was agreed to.

Mr. Douglas explained, that the absolute veto power was embraced in all the Territorial Governments.

Mr. Hale suggested an amendment, making it the duty of the Governor to transmit any bill which did not become a law, to Congress, as follows: "And it shall be the duty of the Governor to transmit copies of any acts disapproved by him to Congress."

Mr. Turney moved to add, "and his reasons for disapproval."

Mr. Hale accepted the addition as a modification of his amendment, and then withdrew his amendment.

The question recurred on the amendment of Mr. Davis, of Mississippi; which was agreed to.

Mr. Hale renewed his motion to amend, and again withdrew it.

The amendment, as amended, was then agreed to.

Mr. Hale moved to insert his amendment in the third section, as follows: "And it shall be the duty of said Governor, immediately after the session of the Legislature, to transmit copies of any acts from which he may have withheld his approval, together with his reasons for such disapproval."

The amendment was agreed to.

The second amendment of the committee being under consideration, as follows: At the beginning of the 14th section insert: "Inasmuch as the said Territory is north of the parallel of thirty-six degrees and thirty minutes of north latitude, usually known as the Missouri compromise"—

Mr. Underwood moved to strike out "thirty-six degrees and thirty minutes," and insert "forty-two;" and to strike out the words "usually known as the Missouri compromise."

Mr. Douglas suggested, that the better mode would be, to take the question on the amendment altogether.

Mr. Underwood thought, that the amendment, as reported, left the disputed question of slavery open, to be renewed in the California bill, and it was his desire to make the language so plain as to preclude the reopening of this debate.

Mr. Butler said, he was a passive member

of the committee, intending to vote against this whole section, the reasons for which he should give hereafter.

Mr. NILES expressed astonishment that the Committee on the Territories should have reported an amendment which had nothing to do with the subject-matter of this bill, as it is well known that all of Oregon lies north of 36° 30′. He was at a loss to understand the reason for such a provision. Was it intended to refer to some other subject which might come up for legislation hereafter? If it was intended for any thing, it must be to exercise influence over legislative action in the other Territories. He was entirely opposed to this mode of legislation. If it was a re-enactment of the compromise bill, he thought it better, after our failure to legislate in that form, to leave it alone. Perhaps it was to ease off the feelings of certain Senators here, and to enable them to justify their votes. He did not wish to see any thing go abroad which might be construed into a compromise, when compromise is not intended.

Mr. DOUGLAS explained that the amendment was reported with the unanimous desire of the committee, that no Senator's vote on the bill should be understood as committing him in the great question.

Mr. HALE said he should vote against the amendment, and, whatever the vote on the amendment, he should vote for the bill. But he desired it to be distinctly understood, that he did not by such vote commit himself in the slightest degree as to his future course.

Mr. MASON charged the language reported in the amendment as unintelligible. He attributed to the committee the design to evade the slavery question. He referred to the state of public opinion abroad, and to the convention about to be assembled at Buffalo, for the choice of a standard-bearer. But one god was to be worshipped there, and that god was power—the power to trample down the constitution of the country. He referred to the recent decision of Virginia not to regard any law of the United States which should prevent her citizens from carrying their slaves into any of the Territories. He and his constituents were willing to be bound by the principle of the compromise; but it was not to be expected that they would go one single step beyond it. It would be to expect them to submit to insult.

Mr. DAYTON replied to the threats held out by the Senator from Virginia, that if she was to be forced another step, she would proclaim nullification. He repudiated for the Whig party this question as the great issue to be tried at the coming election. The questions of free soil and slavery were not the great questions of the Whig party. They constituted too narrow a ledge for that party to stand on. Nor would it be generally understood that this was the great issue with the Democratic party. As to the amendment, whatever may be the understanding with which it was adopted in the committee, Senators would have to stand on their recorded votes. He did not see how the amendment could be sustained.

Mr. JOHNSON, of Maryland, said, that it being evident the bill could not be disposed of to-day, he would therefore move that its further consideration be postponed until to-morrow.

Mr. BUTLER said he had no objection to the postponement, provided it did not interfere with his remarks which he was about to make. He desired to be heard on this bill before the vote was taken on it.

The motion to postpone was then agreed to.

TUESDAY, August 8.

Message from the President—French Republic—Decree of National Assembly—Thanks to the Congress of the United States for its Congratulations on the Establishment of the Republic.

The following Message was received from the President of the United States:

To the Senate and House of Representatives of the United States:

It affords me satisfaction to communicate herewith, for the information of Congress, copies of a decree adopted by the National Assembly of France, in response to the resolution of the Congress of the United States, passed on the 13th April last, tendering the congratulations of the American to the French people, upon the success of their recent efforts to consolidate the principles of liberty in a republican form of Government.

JAMES K. POLK.

WASHINGTON, *August* 8, 1848.

FRENCH REPUBLIC.

Liberty, Equality, Fraternity!

NATIONAL ASSEMBLY.

The National Assembly has unanimously adopted the decree of the following tenor:

ARTICLE 1. In the name of the French people, the National Assembly, profoundly touched by the sentiments which dictated the resolution of the Congress of the United States, on the 13th April, offers to the American people the thanks of the Republic and the expression of its fraternal amity.

ARTICLE 2. The Commissioner of Executive power is charged to transmit the present decree to the French legation at Washington, with the order to present it to the American Government.

Decreed, after deliberation in public session at Paris, on the 25th May, 1848.

Signed by the President and Secretaries, Buchez Peupin, Leon Robert, F. De George, T. Lacrosse, Emile Pêan, Edmund Lafayette.

A true copy for transmission:

The President and Secretaries. Signed: Marie, F. Bérard, Emile Pêan, Edmund Lafayette, L. Robert des Ardennes.

The Minister of Foreign Affairs:

JULES BASTIDE.

On motion of Mr. ALLEN, it was ordered that the foregoing Message and decree be entered on the Journal.

THURSDAY, August 10.

Oregon.

The Senate resumed the consideration of the bill to establish a Territorial Government in Oregon.

The question being on the motion of Mr. UNDERWOOD, to strike out, in page seventeen, line one, the words, "thirty-six degrees and thirty minutes," and inserting "forty-two;" and also the words, "usually known as the Missouri compromise"—

Mr. WEBSTER addressed the Senate. He admitted the propriety of the establishment of a Territorial Government in Oregon, and he was willing to vote for this bill as it came from the House. If amended as now proposed, he would not be able to vote for it. He recited the words of the section, and said, the amendment proposed gave a reason for the application of the principle of the ordinance of 1787 to the Territory of Oregon. When a single reason was given for any act, it was intended to be inferred that there were no other reasons. The Territory of Oregon was above the line of the Missouri compromise. His objection to slavery was irrespective of lines and points of latitude: it took in the whole country, and the whole question. He was opposed to it in every shape, and in every qualification; and was against any compromise of the question.

As to California and New Mexico, he said it was easy to foresee to what the acquisition of this Territory would lead. He wished it were as easy to see that there would be a harmonious conclusion of the matter. He congratulated himelf that he had taken no part in the late war, except to oppose its commencement with all his might, and at the close to oppose the treaty with all his might. He believed the war itself to be a calamity. He looked on the treaty by which it had been concluded as a calamity; and he greatly feared that the treaty would turn out to be the most permanent calamity.

Mr. BUTLER contended that the establishment of governments in the Territories of California and New Mexico, ought to have been embraced in this Oregon bill. He disapproved of this policy of giving especial protection to the Territories north of the Missouri line of compromise, and giving to the North all that valuable portion of the Union. The resolutions of the State of Virginia, which were referred to the other day by a Senator from that State, (Mr. MASON,) had been responded to by all the Southern States of the Union. He thought States should never pass resolutions until they were sure that the citizens would sustain them. He would tell the Senate that his advice to his constituents would be, to go to these new Territories with arms in their hands; to go as armed communities, and take possession of the lands which they had helped to acquire, and see who would attempt to dispossess them. Would the military force of the United States shoot down the ploughman at his plough? So help him God, he would so advise his constituents, to take with them their property there, and settle at all hazards. He was willing, had the compromise bill passed, to bow to it, and if the decision of the Supreme Court should have been adverse to his opinions, he would submit to it. But that bill had been not only rejected by the House of Representatives, but it had been treated with so little respect, that he felt it due to himelf and to the South to let their position be well understood. He was opposed to the bill.

He had always opposed a war of conquest and aggrandizement, for he had foreseen that our triumphs would turn out to be apples of discord from which serious evils would result. He should now take his position, and let Congress make what laws they may, he would advise his constituents to assert their rights with arms in their hands, and take possession of the land. The subtleties and sophisms of the laws of nations would be feeble barriers to the spirit which would show itself in the South. He would go home and tell his constituents these views, and he trusted he had not so much infirmity as to shrink from carrying them into effect. Times and circumstances had changed the character of this bill for the establishment of a Territory in Oregon from what it was two years ago. Then it was comparatively innocent; now he regarded it as a masked battery, from behind which the institutions of the South were to be assailed with a firm determination to subdue them. The South would not fear a contest. She was ready to meet her opponents in a fair and open manner, but she would rise indignant against these covert attacks. He was ready to embark in the boat with his State, and to trust it to the care of Heaven. So beautifully are the elements of our Government arranged, that they scarcely require the agency of man to secure their harmonious and permanent progress. But the act of man could pervert and destroy these tendencies, and produce discord and confusion.

Mr. DOUGLAS, desiring to have the bill placed in a proper shape, would not make any remarks in this stage.

Mr. UNDERWOOD withdrew his proposition to amend, as he perceived the sense of the Senate was against it.

The question then recurring on the amendment as reported by the Committee—

Mr. CALHOUN said he should vote against the amendment, because he regarded it as ambiguous, and he was against all ambiguity. Again, he opposed it because the North could not be more determined to exclude the South than he was to resist such exclusion. He would be as firm in maintaining his ground as Northern Senators were in maintaining theirs. A majority would always be able to carry their views; but here a minority, aided by a few from the majority, attempted to impose on the South restrictions which could not be submitted to.

This question, in his opinion, would never heal itself; that it must go through, and that the sooner it is met the better. He believed the question would never heal or be terminated here. In the body politic, as well as in the natural body, there are diseases which, if not timely checked, must end fatally. There is an impression here that slavery is sinful. This was not rashly asserted by him, as he had resided some time in New England, and had then become convinced that it would lead to serious evils. How it came up here, he would not now stop to examine. This Government has assumed a consolidating tendency, and this had produced a perversion of feeling and of policy, of which the course now pursued in relation to the South is one of the effects. The country is now agitated throughout; and there are political circumstances which will prevent this excitement from dying out. The conviction of the sinfulness of slavery in the North will keep this excitement from subsiding.

He then adverted to the influence of this question on the pending Presidential election, and the effects it must exert on the vote of the South. Each party will try to keep this question separate, to keep the people in the dark, and to suppress the discussion of it, lest it might result in injury. He intimated that the South must naturally incline to yield to the North; and touched upon the suggestions made by the Southern delegations as to the course to be pursued to put down abolition. A difference of opinion arising between the members, the course adopted by the House in the reception of abolition petitions, had led to constant discord and uproar, while in the Senate only one petition on the subject had ever been presented there without the question of reception being called.

He referred to the insurrection of the slaves in the West India Islands; and the same spirit, though suppressed, exists here. He dreaded the result which would follow, if the same spirit which now animated the North should continue to grow and spread. He feared that the effect of this growing spirit was felt in this Senate, where the compromise bill was introduced and passed; yet, when it was rejected in the House, and this bill relating to Oregon came here, not one of those Northern Senators who were friendly to that compromise, ventured to move an amendment by attaching the compromise bill to this Oregon bill. He referred to the positions taken by the South and the North on the slave question. The latter had been unable to meet the arguments of the Southern Senators, and turned out of the direct course to discuss the question of the extension of territory, which was not connected with the subject, and was not advocated by a single representative from his State. He would now tell the people of the South, that they can never settle this qestion until they take it into their own hands. It was unnecessary for him to assert now his regard for the Union. His whole life was sufficiently known. His time, his mind, and all his energies had been given to it; and he made a solemn appeal to the Senate, not, by their own hands, to destroy this glorious fabric of our constitution. He believed, if the great struggle should come, the calamity will not fall the heaviest on the South. In the North the divisions were so numerous as to keep the people distracted and disunited, while in the South all are united. He admitted that the South was poor in comparison with the North; but if slavery had impoverished the South, had it impoverished the North? Slavery had benefited all mankind—all countries but the South. Slavery, like the waters of the Nile, had spread its fertilizing influence over all the world. It had benefited all but the Southern planter, who had been the tutor, the friend, as well as the master, of the slave, and had raised him up to civilization. And the South had made great concessions to the North for the purpose of cementing the Union.

Mr. MANGUM said he should vote for the amendment, because he regarded it as a modification; but whether it prevailed or not, he should vote against the bill.

Mr. NILES said the whole course of the South had in view the extension of slavery. He denied that the South had been weakened, and compelled to make concessions to the North. The compromise bill was no concession of the South, even in the opinions of Southern men themselves, and certainly it was not so in the general estimation of the country. He complained that the Senator from South Carolina had traced the present crisis to a wrong cause, when he attributed it to the abolitionists of the North. The real fact is, that it springs from the opposition made by the free States to the Southern policy of extending the institution of slavery over the new Territories. This is resisted by the free States, and they are prepared to resist it to the last. They think the slave power strong enough, and they will oppose every effort to extend slavery over the continent. The movement of the North was forced upon them, by the attempt to mix up this slavery question with the politics of the country. It had been given out by the South, that no candidate for the Presidency should be supported there who did not pledge himself against the Wilmot proviso. Now, when this course was taken, it was incumbent on the North to make a counteracting movement.

Mr. BUTLER said the South did not take this course until ten of the Northern States had pledged themselves in an opposite manner.

Mr. NILES admitted that this was true. But here was the distinction: the Northern States merely asserted their opinions as a principle, while the South follow up their pledge by an awful threat of nullification if their wishes are not complied with. The Senator from South

Carolina had spoken of his attachment to the Union, and declared he would make a struggle to preserve it; and then he said they must take the matter in their own hands—meaning the slaveholders. They were to take charge of the Union. He preferred doing it in the usual way, through the legitimate medium, and this he presumed would be the general impression. He had no fears for the Union. It has strength enough to resist any collisions. The question, if not settled by Congress, will finally settle itself. He would vote against the proposition.

Mr. Webster and Mr. Niles mutually explained on the subject of the existence of slavery in Texas at the time of annexation.

Mr. Metcalfe then expressed his intention to vote for the bill, whether it contained the compromise or not. He stated, that like the Senator from Massachusetts, he had been opposed to the war, and if he did not oppose the treaty, forsooth, it was because it was the best we could do—bad enough, it is true—but there was no alternative. He thought it would now be the best thing we could do, if we could give back the whole of this new territory, and take again our fifteen or eighteen millions which we have to pay for it. Kentucky, while she stretched out one arm to the North, would not withdraw her other hand from the South. She thought the South was now in the right; but he believed that the North would, in the hour of need, act generously; and that the Union would not be endangered. The honorable Senator, who had uttered once the noble sentiment —"Union now and forever"—would himself stand by the South in the time of need; and he did not believe that the South would take the matter into their hands. He said the sons of the South came into Kentucky and stole away their daughters and cousins, and Kentucky sent her boys, by way of retaliation, to steal the Southern girls; and while this game was fairly played, it was idle to talk of disunion.

Mr. Johnson, of Maryland, made some remarks in reply to what had fallen from the Senator from Massachusetts, in the course of which he stated, that if the North had come to a fixed determination to prevent the South by legislation from carrying their slaves into the new Territories, the States could remain together no longer. This he stated, not as his individual opinion, but as the sentiment of the South. He believed in the existence of the power in Congress to pass a law to prohibit slavery, and if such a law were presented from the Supreme Court for a decision on its constitutionality, it would be in favor of the law. As a judicial question, the decision would be against the protection of the South.

In reference to the annexation of Texas, he stated that it was advocated by Senators from the northern States as advantageous to the North, on account of the market which it would open for their maufactures; and he adverted to the fact that some of the Senators had been induced to vote for it by the promise of the President, that he would act upon the alternative proposition.

He had voted for the compromise bill, because he thought it the only mode of settling the question.

Mr. Webster said he only spoke for himself; he did not speak for the North. He did not know what the North is, or where the North is. He had been among the earliest to oppose acquisition of foreign territory. He referred to the maxim of Lord Bacon—that the best way to avoid any domestic disputes or difficulties, was to avoid the occasion for them; and said, that in accordance with this maxim, he (Mr. W.) had always opposed the acquisition of foreign territory. There were wiser heads than Lord Bacon's now. There are persons who will provoke occasions, or certainly will meet them, and adopt circumstances, as they may arise. He then referred to the course of the remarks of the Senator from South Carolina, and went on to show that there was no constitutional authority for the acquisition of foreign territory, and that no one had pretended to show any constitutional warrant for the power exercised by Congress, without the consent of the States, to make laws for Territories which never came within the contemplation of the constitution or its framers. He enumerated the difficulties in which this acquisition of territory had plunged us. He was not apprehensive of any disunion. He never contemplated its possibility. He was not one of those who accustom themselves to speak of such a contingency. An earthquake may come, a volcano may burst forth; but human foresight can do nothing to prevent such calamities. So the dissolution of the Union is among those possible calamities; but what could human wisdom do to further, in advance of it, the happiness of the human race? He believed there was a disposition everywhere to support the Union, and that five out of six of our citizens would be glad to give back the new Territories we have acquired.

Mr. Berrien made a few remarks, for the purpose of inducing the Senator from Massachusetts to review his legal opinion as to the absence of all power in the constitution for the acquisition of foreign territory. He assigned the reasons which induced him to differ from these opinions.

Mr. Foote said he rose for the purpose of putting an end to the debate. He saw no probability of proper deliberation being given to this bill at this late period of the session. Several amendments had been offered, among them, one of his own, and several Senators were very anxious to be heard on this subject. He did not see any possibility of deciding the question at this session. He admitted the pressing occasion for the establishment of a government in Oregon; but he thought, that as it was so short an interval until the next session, no great injury could result from the delay. He moved to lay the bill on the table, but withdrew it, on the pledge that it would be renewed by

Mr. Johnson, of Georgia, who said that the South honestly held the opinion that Congress has no power to prohibit slavery. He believed the contrary opinion was entertained with equal honesty in the North. If the North, having the majority, insist on exercising the power, what can follow but the degradation of the South, or the dissolution of the Union? The only remedy was a just and honorable compromise. If the Missouri compromise was offered to the South, in the spirit in which it was offered in 1820, she would accept it. He desired to know from the chairman of the Committee on Territories whether the Missouri compromise in the bill was tendered in the spirit in which it was offered in 1820?

Mr. Douglas replied in the affirmative. He made a few remarks in explanation of his own course. He gave his own opinion in the affirmative, but said that was not the understanding of the committee.

Mr. Foote renewed his motion to lay the bill on the table.

The Senate then took a recess until half-past five o'clock.

Night Session.

Oregon.

The question pending when the Senate took a recess was the motion of Mr. Foote to lay the Oregon bill on the table. The question was then taken by yeas and nays, and decided in the negative: yeas 15, nays 36.

A debate then ensued, which was kept up with great spirit until near 10 o'clock, in which Messrs. Hunter, King, Foote, Douglas, Mason, Webster, Berrien, Walker, Butler, Calhoun, Bright, Dickinson, Metcalfe, Underwood, Davis of Mississippi, Hannegan, and others participated.

The question was then taken on the amendment of the Committee on the Territories to insert the words: "That inasmuch as the said Territory is north of the parallel of 36° 30′ of north latitude, usually known as the Missouri compromise," &c., with the understanding that in case the above amendment of the committee should be voted down, the question should be taken on the amendment sent to the Chair by Mr. Douglas, embracing the Missouri compromise.

The yeas and nays having been called, the question was decided in the negative—yeas 2, nays 52.

The question was then taken on the amendment embracing the Missouri compromise, and it was decided as follows:

Yeas.—Messrs. Atchison, Badger, Bell, Benton, Berrien, Borland, Bright, Butler, Calhoun, Cameron, Davis of Mississippi, Dickinson, Douglas, Downs, Fitzgerald, Foote, Hannegan, Houston, Hunter, Johnson of Maryland, Johnson of Louisiana, Johnson of Georgia, King, Lewis, Mangum, Mason, Metcalfe, Pearce, Sabastian, Spruance, Sturgeon, Turney, and Underwood—33.

Nays.—Messrs. Allen, Atherton, Baldwin, Bradbury, Breese, Clarke, Corwin, Davis of Massachusetts, Dayton, Dix, Dodge, Felch, Greene, Hale, Hamlin, Miller, Niles, Phelps, Upham, Walker, and Webster—21.

The question was about to be taken on the engrossment, when—

Mr. Davis, of Mississippi, moved to strike out all after the enacting clause, and insert the bill which had passed the Senate and been laid on the table by the House; but, on the urgent appeal of Messrs. Berrien, Metcalfe, and other Senators round him, he withdrew it.

And the question was taken on the engrossment, and decided in the affirmative, as follows:

Yeas.—Messrs. Atchison, Badger, Bell, Benton, Berrien, Borland, Breese, Bright, Butler, Cameron, Clayton, Davis of Mississippi, Dickinson, Douglas, Downs, Fitzgerald, Hannegan, Houston, Hunter, Johnson of Maryland, Johnson of Louisiana, Johnson of Georgia, King, Lewis, Mangum, Mason, Metcalfe, Pearce, Sebastian, Spruance, Sturgeon, Turney, and Underwood—33.

Nays.—Messrs. Allen, Atherton, Baldwin, Bradbury, Calhoun, Clarke, Corwin, Davis of Massachusetts, Dayton, Dix, Dodge, Felch, Greene, Hale, Hamlin, Miller, Niles, Phelps, Upham, Walker, Webster, and Westcott—22.

The bill was then read a third time, and passed.

The Senate adjourned.

HOUSE OF REPRESENTATIVES.

Friday, August 11.

Oregon Bill.

The House proceeded to the consideration of the amendments of the Senate to the bill of the House to establish the Territorial Government of Oregon.

Mr. Smith, of Indiana, moved that the House do not concur in the amendments of the Senate, and on that motion demanded the previous question.

Mr. Kaufman inquired of the Speaker if a division could be had, so as to vote on the amendments separately?

The Speaker replied, that after the previous question had been seconded, the question would then come up on concurrence in the amendments separately, if a division was called by any member.

The Speaker announced the question upon seconding the demand for the previous question; and requested the House to come to order, and gentlemen to take their seats.

The previous question was seconded, and the main question was ordered, being first on Mr. Smith's motion to non-concur in the Senate's amendments.

A division being called for by various gentlemen—

The question was announced on non-concurring in the first amendment, which makes it the duty of the Governor of the Territory to transmit to each House of Congress copies of any bills he may veto, with his reasons therefor, immediately after such session of the Territorial Legislature.

Mr. White asked the yeas and nays, which were ordered.

The question was then taken on concurring in the Senate's first amendment, (stated above,) and decided in the negative: Yeas 92, nays 106.

So the House refused to concur in the first amendment.

The second amendment next came up, which directly confers the veto power on the Governor of the Territory, and provides that in such cases the bill shall not become a law, unless approved by Congress.

This amendment was non-concurred in without a division.

The third amendment of the Senate inserts, after the enacting clause of the 14th section, the following:

That the line of thirty-six degrees thirty minutes of north latitude, known as the Missouri compromise line, as defined by the eighth section of an act entitled "An act to authorize the people of the Missouri Territory to form a constitution and State Government, and for the admission of such State into the Union on an equal footing with the original States, and to prohibit slavery in certain Territories," approved March 6th, 1820, be, and the same is hereby, declared to extend to the Pacific Ocean; and the said eighth section, together with the compromise therein effected, is hereby revived, and declared to be in full force and binding for the future organization of the Territories of the United States, in the same sense and with the same understanding with which it was originally adopted, and.

The vote on concurring in this amendment was taken by yeas and nays, and resulted as follows:

Yeas.—Messrs. Adams, Atkinson, Barringer, Barrow, Bayly, Beale, Bedinger, Birdsall, Bocock, Botts, Bowden, Bowlin, Boyd, Boydon, Brodhead, Charles Brown, Albert G. Brown, Buckner, Burt, Cabell, Chapman, Chase, Beverly L. Clarke, Clingman, Howell Cobb, Williamson R. W. Cobb, Cocke, Crozier, Daniel, Donnell, Garrett Duncan, Alexander Evans, Featherston, Flournoy, French, Fulton, Gayle, Goggin, Greene, Willard P. Hall, Haralson, Harmanson, Harris, Haskell, Hill, Hilliard, Isaac E. Holmes, George S. Houston, Charles J. Ingersoll, Iverson, Andrew Johnson, Robert W. Johnson, George W. Jones, John W. Jones, Kaufman, Thos. Butler King, Ligon, Lumpkin, McDowell, McKay, McLane, Meade, Morehead, Outlaw, Pendleton, Phelps, Pillsbury, Preston, Rhett, Roman, Shepperd, Stanley, Stephens, Thomas, Jacob Thompson, John B. Thompson, Robert A. Thompson, Tompkins, Toombs, Venable, Wallace, and Woodward—82.

Nays.—Messrs. Abbott, Ashmun, Bingham, Blanchard, Brady, Butler, Canby, Cathcart, Franklin Clark, Collamer, Collins, Conger, Cranston, Crowell, Cummins, Darling, Dickey, Dickinson, Dixon, Duer, Daniel Duncan, Dunn, Eckert, Edsall, Edwards, Embree, Nathan Evans, Faran, Farrelly, Ficklin, Fisher, Freedley, Fries, Gott, Gregory, Grinnell, Hale, Nathan K. Hall, Hammons, James G. Hampton, Moses Hampton, Henley, Henry, Elias B. Holmes, John W. Houston, Hubbard, Hudson, Hunt, Joseph R. Ingersoll, Irvin, Jenkins, Kellogg, Kennon, Daniel P. King, William T. Lawrence, Sidney Lawrence, Lincoln, Lord, Lynde, Maclay, McClelland, McClernand, McIlvaine, Job Mann, Horace Mann, Marsh, Marvin, Miller, Morris, Mullin, Murphy, Nelson, Nes, Newell, Nicoll, Palfrey, Peaslee, Peck, Petrie, Pettit, Pollock, Putnam, Reynolds, Richey, Robinson, Rockhill, John A. Rockwell, Rose, Root, Rumsey, St. John, Sawyer, Schenck, Sherrill, Silvester, Slingerland, Smart, Caleb B. Smith, Robert Smith, Truman Smith, Starkweather, Andrew Stewart, Charles E. Stuart, Strohm, Strong, Tallmadge, Taylor, James Thompson, Richard W. Thompson, William Thompson, Thurston, Tuck, Turner, Van Dyke, Vinton, Warren, Wentworth, White, Wick, Williams, and Wilmot—121.

Mr. Smith, of Indiana, moved to reconsider this vote, and moved to lay that motion on the table; which latter motion was agreed to.

It was ordered that the Senate be informed of the action of the House on said amendments.

IN SENATE.

Saturday, August 12.

The Oregon Bill.

The bill to establish a Territorial Government in Oregon, as amended by the House of Representatives, was taken up.

The amendments having been read—

Mr. Douglas moved the appointment of a committee of conference.

Mr. Benton rose to make a motion which would supersede the other motion. He moved that the Senate recede from its amendment.

Mr. Mason moved to lay the bill and amendments on the table, and asked for the yeas and nays; which were ordered.

The question was then taken and decided in the negative—yeas 18, nays 32.

Mr. Benton renewed his motion to recede. This question had been a long time before the Senate. He had patiently waited with an anxious desire to adopt some measure of conciliation. From the first he had been opposed to clogging Oregon with California. He wishen to see Oregon go through by herself. When the subject was referred to a select committee of eight, a bill had been brought in, constructed for the purpose of conciliating different feelings. He had not approved of that bill; but he had always determined to vote for it. He had not impeded its progress by interposing a single word. He gave his vote for it, while he disapproved of it at the same time. Then there came up the adjustment on the parallel line of 36° 30′. He was extremely reluctant to go for that measure. Oregon was four hundred miles distant from the nearest, and nearly a thousand miles from the remotest point of California; and there was no rule which applied equally to both. Still he had voted for that bill, in order to put an end to the question; and on similar grounds he had given his vote for the Oregon bill. That bill had been sent to the House, and had been returned from the House, with the Missouri compromise stricken out. He thought he had now done enough to secure conciliation and compromise. He had done enough when he consented to attach California to Oregon. Oregon was now in a deplorable condition. A few years ago we were ready to fight all the world to get possession of her; and now we are just as willing to throw her away as we were then to risk every thing for her possession. She is left without a government, without laws, while at this moment she is engaged in a war with the Indians. There were twelve thousand or fifteen thousand persons settled there, who had claims on our protection. She was three thousand miles from the metropolitan seat of government. And yet, although she had set up a provisional government for herself, and this provisional government had taken on itself the enactment of laws, it is left to the will of every individual to determine for himself whether he will obey those laws or not. She has now reached a point beyond which she can exist no longer. She can work along no further, no longer. The war hereafter will not be between whites and Indians; it will be a conflict between whites and whites. It will become necessary that every dispute shall be settled by a resort to arms. And can this Senate satisfy itself that it will have performed its duty, while it sits with folded arms, and declines to do any thing? It is a duty, a solemn obligation, enforced by the awful solemnity of our oaths, which we cannot avoid without a violation of that duty. If we refrain from extending the protection of this Government to the people of Oregon, we violate these obligations. He held it to be our bounden duty to provide a government for Oregon; and he would not, so far as he was able, permit the bill to establish that government, by putting a weight of extraneous matter on it, to sink it down.

The CHAIR announced its decision, that the motion to recede takes precedence of the motion to insist and to ask for a committee of conference.

Mr. BERRIEN would not call in question the decision of the Chair. He made an appeal to the Senate not to let this last opportunity for conciliation pass away. He hoped the motion to recede would not prevail. The question involved the interests of the people of Oregon; and more than that, the harmony of the people of the United States. If this measure should not prevail, it will be taken as evidence that the Government will hereafter rule the South with a rod of iron. He hoped a committee of conference would be granted, in order that gentlemen might compare opinions, in the hope of coming to some satisfactory conclusion. He trusted that this course would be pursued, in order that southern representatives might carry home the gratifying information that Congress were disposed to consult the feelings of their constituents. It was suggested by the Senator from Missouri, that the appointment of a committee of conference would be to transfer the power of Congress to a committee. He contended that if the establishment of a government in Oregon was impeded, it was by fastening on it this proviso in relation to a Territory where it is not needed. Does any man believe that slavery will ever exist in Oregon? And if not, how did the attaching of California to the bill clog and bear it down? He designated more in detail the position in which southern Senators were placed. He complimented the Senator from Massachusetts (Mr. WEBSTER) on the statesmanlike ground on which he had placed his opposition. In his course there was no demagogism, no free-soil fallacy. But he regarded the view of that Senator as to the three-fifths provision as incorrect; and he went at some length into an explanation of his own opinions as to the intent of that provision, and concluded with a renewed appeal to the Senate not to recede.

Mr. CALHOUN expressed his apprehension that there was a fixed majority in this Senate and in the House, opposed to any further trial at conciliation. Still he hoped the Senate would preserve a correct position, and vote for the appointment of a committee of conference. He might say, without any self-flattery, that he had all along foreseen this result. Let those who opposed the views of the South lay their cause before the country, and defend it as they could. The great strife between the North and the South is ended. The North is determined to exclude the property of the slaveholder, and of course the slaveholder himself, from its territory. On this point there seems to be no division in the North. In the South, he regretted to say, there was some division of sentiment. The effect of this determination of the North was to convert all the southern population into slaves; and he would never consent to entail that disgrace on his posterity. He denounced any southern man who would not take the same course. Gentlemen were greatly mistaken, if they supposed the Presidential question in the South would override this more important one. The separation of the North and the South is completed. The South has now a most solemn obligation to perform—to herself—to the constitution—to the Union. She is bound to come to a decision not to permit this to go on any further, but to show that, dearly as she prizes the Union, there are questions which she regards as of greater importance than the Union. She is bound to fulfil her obligations as she may best understand them. This is not a question of territorial government, but a question involving the continuance of the Union. Perhaps it was better that this question should come to an end, in order that some new point should be taken.

He had given what he deemed a clear constitutional vote on the compromise bill, (Mr. Clayton's.) He had also voted for the introduction of the Missouri compromise into this bill; although he could not constitutionally vote for the bill, which he regarded as artificial. Gentlemen may do with this bill as they please. If they will not give now what the South asks as a compromise, she will, at the next session, demand all, and will not be satisfied with any thing less.

Mr. Bell said, he was a southern Senator, and deeply involved in southern interests; but he must have greatly mistaken his true course if the arguments to which he had listened were correct. There were wiser heads than his; but still, in the vote which he should give, he must conform to his own judgment. He believed that the Senator from South Carolina, and those who concurred with him, had placed the South in a wrong position, when they assumed that, by the decision of this question, the die would be cast, and the issue must now be made which involves the dissolution of the Union. He contended that this issue was prematurely made when it was made on the Oregon bill. If we are to quarrel with the North, let us be sure that in all respects our ground of dispute is tenable for us. The vote of the House has been cited here as evidence that this issue could no longer be avoided. He came to no such conclusion. He knew and felt the influence of too many sympathies with the North. Until a vote of Congress should, on the subject of the southern Territories, actually separate the Union, he never would believe that such a vote could be given. As to this question, he had voted against laying this bill on the table, and against its postponement, because he desired to give his southern friends an opportunity of having a committee of conference, from which he expected nothing favorable.

Mr. Westcott and Mr. Downs explained their votes on the question to lay the subject on the table.

Mr. Bell resumed. He would vote against receding, and would then vote to insist, although he did not expect any good from a conference. He desired to see the Oregon bill passed, even without this restriction; and he could not use it as a means of attack on gentlemen. Whether he could vote for it himself was doubtful, regarding as he did the feelings of the friends with whom he was associated. He controverted the doctrine, that even if the whole country, North and South, was opposed to slavery, Congress had no power to legislate on the subject. He thought the Missouri compromise had settled that point. He repeated, in conclusion, his conviction that the making up of the issue at this time was premature. When the whole question as to the Territories of California and New Mexico should come up, it would be time enough to tender the issue.

Mr. Houston wished to make his position known, not only on this continent, but that it should be blazoned forth to the world. He believed that the crisis so much spoken of had come. Texas was peculiarly situated. The line of 36° 30′ divides her territory. North of that, slavery is prohibited; south of it, slavery may or may not exist, as she may select. Texas had entered the Union on this condition, and she was willing to adhere to that condition. He did not see that this bill affected the interests of Texas in any way. The extension in Oregon of the line to 42° could not affect the southern States. We stood on the frontier, and he saw nothing in whatever legislation might take place in reference to territory north of 42° which could concern his State. He reminded the Senate that thirteen Senators from the northern States had voted for the admission of Texas as she came in. And he was ready to vote for the admission of Oregon, even with the prohibition of slavery attached to it, as it could never affect the southern Territories. He might vote against receding, because he hoped something better might be obtained. As to the southern Territories, the Government of California is not now before us. He remembered the cry of disunion and nullification when the high tariff was imposed. That cry reached him in the wilderness, an exile from kindred, and friends, and sections; but it rung in his ears, and wounded his heart. But now he was in the midst of such a cry, and he was bound to act as a man conscious of the solemn responsibilities imposed on him. He had heard the menaces and cries of disunion until he had become familiar with them, and they had now ceased to produce alarm in his bosom. He had no fear of the dissolution of the Union, when he recollected how it had been established, and how it had been defended. It could not be the interest of the North to destroy the South, notwithstanding the papers signed by old men, and old women, and pretty little girls, praying for abolition, got up in the very small coteries—these could not ruffle the Union. The intelligent and manly spirits of the North would rise up to defend the Union. He wished no separation of the States. He had too much confidence in the North to fear any injury from that section. And he thought the South—and he was a southern man—should make some sacrifice for the purpose of reconciliation with the North. As to the Presidential elections, he hoped they would always continue, and that the Republic would long exist; but he did not dread the influence which these questions would exercise on legislation. Oregon cannot obtain protection and good government, except from Congress; and he hoped these would be extended to her.

Mr. JOHNSON, of Georgia, rose and addressed the Senate in reply to the Senator from Texas, declaring that the South could not with any propriety rely on the magnanimity of the North. He also took exception to the course of the Senator from Tennessee, (Mr. BELL,) who, as a southern man, looked forward to the day when the South would be saved by northern generosity. He would not dwell on the incendiary publications which had been circulated, as blood in the human body, through every vein and artery. But this, with numerous other acts of notoriety, might be quoted to show the character of northern generosity. He went into a view of the course which had been pursued in reference to the Oregon question.

The South had only asked us to keep off legislative action on this subject. They asked only that the question should be submitted to the Supreme Court, to be decided upon in conformity with the constitution. But the compromise based on this principle had been laid on the table by the other House—rejected without any of that courtesy and magnanimity of which the Senators from Missouri and Texas had promised to us.

Mr. DAVIS, of Mississippi, rose, and took the floor in continuance of the debate; and, as the hour for the recess had nearly arrived, he moved that the Senate go into Executive session; which was agreed to.

EVENING SESSION.

Oregon.

The Senate resumed the consideration of the bill to establish a Territorial Government in Oregon.

Mr. WEBSTER (Mr. JOHNSON yielding the floor) said he was not inclined to prolong this debate, and he was equally disinclined to introduce into it any new excitement and warmth. As a question of parliamentary proceeding, he understood the House had sent to the Senate a bill concerning Oregon, no part of which had been objected to, and no part had been stricken out. An amendment had been made, which, as the Senator from Missouri had justly stated, had nothing to do with Oregon. It was an amendment proper enough in itself, but which had no bearing at all on Oregon. The successive section says that the ordinance of 1787 shall be applicable to Oregon. The amendment had been added to the bill by a majority of the Senate. And if the majority of the Senate think any thing can be gained by sending the bill to a second committee of conference, it is perfectly parliamentary for them to do so. But as he had voted against the amendment, it was natural that he should vote for the easiest mode of getting rid of it; that is, by receding. The gentleman from Georgia (Mr. BERRIEN) had not overstated the importance of this amendment. If wrong had been done, it should be fairly presented to the world; and if it shall not meet its approbation, we have only to submit quietly to the rebuke. He perfectly acquiesced in the opinion, that this was a fit subject to be presented to the judgment of the civilized world.

The ordinance of 1787 refers to the existence of a particular kind of slaves not known in Europe, or in any civilized countries. Although slavery as attached to the South exists in other countries, he knew not that slaves transferable as chattels, to be separated from the glebe, were to be found but in America, and in the colonies of America. He remembered when this was regarded as an evil fixed on us by the mother country, and it must be considered as an entailment. He referred to the original introduction of slavery in the South, and assumed that no one, as far as he could gather from the acts and debates in Congress, had contemplated any extension of it to new territory. In the Convention, and in the first Congress, it was conceded that slavery was a State institution, and that Congress had no power over it. He was of this opinion, and he would countenance no efforts to produce excitement by the introduction of these questions.

The framers of the constitution never contemplated the acquisition of foreign territory. Since that period, new Territories have been acquired by purchase or conquest. Five slave States have been since admitted, sending ten Senators to this Chamber. But not one free State has been admitted. [Several voices: "Iowa."] Is Iowa admitted? Her Senators are not here. That would be one to five. This fact shows that we have not disfavored slavery. As already there have been five States created out of these new Territories, he did not deem it his duty to go any further. As the Senator from Georgia desires to leave the question to the decision of the civilized world, and as he acquiesced in that course, how would it then stand? The Southern Senators say we deprive them of the right to go into these newly acquired Territories with their property. We certainly do not prevent them from going into these Territories with what is in general law called property. But these States have by their local laws created a property in persons, and they cannot carry these local laws with them. Slavery is created and exists by a local law, which is limited to a certain section; and it is asked that Congress shall establish a local law in other Territories, to enable southern Senators to carry their particular law with them. No man can be held as a slave, except the local law shall accompany him. The slave is held to be free, until evidence shall be presented to prove that he is a slave. There is a belief prevailing, that slave labor and free labor cannot exist together. He had a letter of Mr. Mason, in which it is stated that slave labor will expel free labor. This was not a universal rule, as there was useful free labor in parts of Virginia and Tennessee.

He was not willing to extend the area of slavery, or to increase the slave representation in the other House. He thought enough had been yielded when twenty representatives from slave States, elected by three-fifths, were in the House of Representatives. When the constitution was adopted, no one looked for any accession of new States. Looking to the new circumstances—the acquisition of so much new territory—he thought it his duty to take his stand, and to say that he would never vote to extend the area of slavery.

Mr. Johnson, of Georgia, then resumed his remarks, and continued until a late hour.

Mr. Johnson, of Maryland, followed, and spoke for near an hour; when—

Mr. Houston rose and addressed the Senate at very considerable length, chiefly in reply to Mr. Johnson, of Georgia, and others. In the course of his remarks he paid a beautiful compliment to Mr. Clay, declaring that he deserved to have a statue erected in the rotundo for his stand in relation to the Missouri compromise.

At this point of his speech there was an involuntary burst of feeling from the galleries and lobby, both of which were densely crowded, that could not be suppressed.

Mr. King rose to express his astonishment at such proceedings. Long as he had been connected with Congress, he had never, in the course of his political life, witnessed such a scene. Had the United States Senate become a theatre, wherein the speakers were to be applauded or hissed? He trusted he might never again witness such conduct. He gave notice that if there were any more such exhibitions, he should feel compelled to have the galleries cleared.

Mr. Dickinson hoped no further notice would be taken of it, as it was evidently one of those involuntary bursts of feeling which, however much they were to be condemned, could not at all times be suppressed. He was convinced there would be no more of it, and hoped the Senator from Texas would proceed.

Mr. Mason said, if there were any repetitions of that character, if no other Senator moved to clear the galleries, he would do so himself. Mr. M. manifested some warmth.

Mr. Phelps rose, and turning towards Mr. King, remarked, the Senator from Alabama says that he never witnessed such a scene in this Capitol before; if that Senator has not, I have: and was about to proceed, when the Chair requested the Senator from Texas to proceed.

Mr. Houston then concluded his remarks.

Mr. Turney moved that the Senate adjourn, and desired to have the hour entered on the Journal. [It was then past midnight.]

On this question the yeas and nays were demanded, and the result was as follows:

Yeas.—Messrs. Atchison, Berrien, Borland, Butler, Calhoun, Davis of Mississippi, Downs, Hannegan, Johnson of Maryland, King, Lewis, Mangum, Mason, Rusk, Sebastian, Turney, Westcott, and Yulee—18.

Nays.—Messrs. Allen, Atherton, Badger, Baldwin, Bell, Benton, Bradbury, Breese, Bright, Clarke, Corwin, Davis of Massachusetts, Dayton, Dickinson, Dix, Dodge, Douglas, Felch, Fitzgerald, Greene, Hale, Hamlin, Houston, Johnson of Louisiana, Metcalfe, Miller, Niles, Phelps, Spruance, Underwood, Upham, and Walker—32.

Mr. Butler desired to make a motion, and moved that the Senate galleries be cleared, in order to go into Executive session.

There was some time spent in discussing points of order, in which Messrs. Berrien, Benton, Breese, Hale, Davis of Massachusetts, and others participated.

Mr. Bell spoke at some length as to what might appear the object of such a motion at that particular juncture.

[The scene was more than usually exciting at one time.]

The Chair ruled the motion of Mr. Butler out of order, from which an appeal was taken; and the result was, that the Chair was sustained—Yeas 36, nays 11.

Mr. Badger then addressed the Senate in favor of a committee of conference being appointed.

Mr. Metcalfe spoke at great length, insisting that a committee of conference between the two Houses might be able to accommodate the matter satisfactorily.

Mr. Foote spoke for near half an hour, endeavoring to get Mr. Benton to withdraw his motion to recede.

Mr. Benton playfully observed, that he always had an objection to retreating. One of his earliest recollections was the old Roman maxim, *non retrahit pedem;* and, if the object of the gentleman's speech was to induce him to draw back his foot, he might have saved himself the trouble.

Mr. Foote again rose to speak.

Mr. Walker made a point of order. The rule said that no Senator could speak more than twice on any one subject, whereas the gentleman from Mississippi had spoken some half dozen times at least.

[Several voices: "Oh, let the gentleman proceed; we will listen to him with the greatest pleasure."]

Mr. Foote then went on very coolly, declaring his ability to speak two entire days and nights without any very great inconvenience to himself.

The debate was continued until after nine o'clock, A. M. Sunday, and was closed in a speech by Mr. Foote.

The question being put on the motion of Mr. Benton, to recede from all the amendments, a division of the question was called for, and it was ordered that the question be taken separately on each amendment.

Upon the question to recede from the first amendment, giving the veto power to the Governor, the yeas and nays were ordered, and it was determined in the affirmative—yeas 31, nays 23.

Upon the question to recede from the second amendment, relating to the same subject, it was determined in the affirmative without a division.

Upon the question to recede from the third amendment, being the section extending the line of the *Missouri compromise* to the Pacific Ocean, the yeas and nays were ordered, and it was determined in the affirmative, as follows:

Yeas.—Messrs. Allen, Baldwin, Benton, Bradbury, Breese, Bright, Cameron, Clarke, Corwin, Davis of Massachusetts, Dayton, Dickinson, Dix, Dodge, Douglas, Felch, Fitzgerald, Greene, Hale, Hamlin, Hannegan, Houston, Miller, Niles, Phelps, Spruance, Upham, Walker, and Webster—29.

Nays.—Messrs. Atchison, Badger, Bell, Berrien, Borland, Butler, Calhoun, Davis of Mississippi, Downs, Foote, Hunter, Johnson of Maryland, Johnson of Louisiana, Johnson of Georgia, Lewis, Mangum, Mason, Metcalfe, Pearce, Rusk, Sebastian, Turney, Underwood, Westcott, and Yulee—25.

[Mr. Atherton was present, but did not vote, having, as it is understood, paired off with Mr. King, who had been compelled to leave from exhaustion. Messrs. Clayton and Sturgeon were also absent, the former being still detained at home by the indisposition of a member of his family.]

The remaining amendments were separately receded from without a division, and the bill stands passed in the precise form in which it came from the House of Representatives.

HOUSE OF REPRESENTATIVES.

Monday, August 14.

Oregon Territorial Government.

Mr. Robinson, from the Committee on Enrolled Bills, reported that the committee had examined the bill to establish a Territorial Government for Oregon, and found it correctly enrolled.

He moved to suspend the seventeenth joint rule, which forbids bills being presented to the President on the last day of the session, so as to permit the Oregon bill, and all other bills which had passed, or might pass, to be sent to the President; and on that motion he demanded the previous question.

Mr. Bayly moved that the House adjourn.

Mr. Rhett demanded the yeas and nays on the motion.

The Speaker decided that the motion to adjourn was not in order. The two Houses, by a joint resolution, had fixed twelve o'clock today as the time for the adjournment *sine die.* By the Constitution of the United States, neither House, without the consent of the other, could adjourn for more than three days. If the motion to adjourn were received and agreed to, the House would stand adjourned until the first Monday in December. The motion was not, therefore, in order.

Special Message from the President—Oregon Territorial Act—Reasons for Approving the Act—Harmony and Stability of the Union, Overruling Consideration—Impressive Appeal to the People to preserve forever inviolate the Missouri and the Texas Compromises.

Mr. Cobb, of Georgia, called for the reading of the President's Message just received, (and which, it was understood, had reference to his approval of the Oregon Territorial bill.)

[The following is the Message:

To the House of Representatives of the United States:

When the President has given his official sanction to a bill which has passed Congress, usage requires that he shall notify the House in which it originated of that fact. The mode of giving this notification has been by an oral message delivered by his private secretary.

Having this day approved and signed an act entitled "An act to establish the Territorial Government of Oregon," I deem it proper, under the existing circumstances, to communicate the fact in a more solemn form.

The deeply interesting and protracted discussions which have taken place in both Houses of Congress, and the absorbing interest which the subject has excited throughout the country, justify, in my judgment, this departure from the form of notice observed in other cases.

In this communication with a co-ordinate branch of the Government, made proper by the considerations referred to, I shall frankly, and without reserve, express the reasons which have constrained me not to withhold my signature from the bill to establish a Government over Oregon, even though the two Territories of New Mexico and California are to be left, for the present, without Governments. None doubt that it is proper to establish a Government in Oregon. Indeed, it has been too long delayed. I have made repeated recommendations to Congress to this effect. The petitions of the people of that distant region have been presented to the Government, and ought not to be disregarded. To give to them a regularly organized Government and the protection of our laws, which as citizens of the United States they claim, is a high duty on our part, and one which we are bound to perform, unless there be controlling reasons to prevent it.

In the progress of all Governments, questions of such transcendent importance occasionally arise, as to cast in the shade all those of a mere party character. But one such question can now be agitated in this country; and this may endanger our glorious Union, the source of our greatness and all our political blessings. This question is slavery. With the slaveholding States this does not embrace merely the rights of property, however valuable; but it ascends far higher, and involves the domestic peace and security of every family.

The fathers of the constitution—the wise and patriotic men who laid the foundation of our institutions—foreseeing the danger from this quarter, acted in a spirit of compromise and mutual concession on this dangerous and delicate subject;

and their wisdom ought to be the guide of their successors. Whilst they left to the States exclusively the question of domestic slavery within their respective limits, they provided that slaves who might escape into other States not recognizing the institution of slavery, shall "be delivered up on the claim of the party to whom such service or labor may be due."

Upon this foundation the matter rested until the Missouri question arose.

In December, 1819, application was made to Congress by the people of the Missouri Territory for admission into the Union as a State. The discussion upon the subject in Congress involved the question of slavery, and was prosecuted with such violence as to produce excitements alarming to every patriot in the Union. But the good genius of conciliation which presided at the birth of our institutions finally prevailed, and the Missouri compromise was adopted. The eighth section of the act of Congress of the 6th of March, 1820, "to authorize the people of the Missouri Territory to form a constitution and State Government," &c., provides: "That, in all that territory ceded by France to the United States, under the name of Louisiana, which lies north of thirty-six degrees and thirty minutes north latitude, not included within the limits of the States contemplated by this act, slavery and involuntary servitude, otherwise than in the punishment of crimes, whereof the parties shall have been duly convicted, shall be, and is hereby, forever prohibited: *Provided, always,* That any person escaping into the same, from whom labor or service is lawfully claimed, in any State or Territory of the United States, such fugitive may be lawfully reclaimed, and conveyed to the person claiming his or her labor or services aforesaid."

This compromise had the effect of calming the troubled waves, and restoring peace and good-will throughout the States of the Union.

The Missouri question had excited intense agitation of the public mind, and threatened to divide the country into geographical parties, alienating the feelings of attachment which each portion of our Union should bear to every other. The compromise allayed the excitement, tranquillized the popular mind, and restored confidence and fraternal feeling. Its authors were hailed as public benefactors.

I do not doubt that a similar adjustment of the questions which now agitate the public mind would produce the same happy results. If the legislation of Congress on the subject of the other Territories shall not be adopted in a spirit of conciliation and compromise, it is impossible that the country can be satisfied, or that the most disastrous consequences shall fail to ensue.

When Texas was admitted into the Union, the same spirit of compromise which guided our predecessors in the admission of Missouri, a quarter of a century before, prevailed without any serious opposition. The "joint resolution for annexing Texas to the United States," approved March the first, one thousand eight hundred and forty-five, provides that "such States as may be formed out of that portion of said territory lying south of thirty-six degrees thirty minutes north latitude, commonly known as the Missouri compromise line, shall be admitted into the Union with or without slavery, as the people of each State asking admission may desire. And in such State or States as shall be formed out of said territory north of the Missouri compromise line, slavery or involuntary servitude (except for crime) shall be prohibited."

The Territory of Oregon lies far north of thirty-six degrees thirty minutes, the Missouri and Texas compromise line. Its southern boundary is the parallel of forty-two, leaving the intermediate distance to be three hundred and thirty geographical miles.

And it is because the provisions of this bill are not inconsistent with the terms of the Missouri compromise, if extended from the Rio Grande to the Pacific Ocean, that I have not felt at liberty to withhold my sanction. Had it embraced territories south of that compromise, the question presented for my consideration would have been of a far different character, and my action upon it must have corresponded with my convictions.

Ought we now to disturb the Missouri and Texas compromises? Ought we, at this late day, in attempting to annul what has been so long established and acquiesced in, to excite sectional divisions and jealousies; to alienate the people of different portions of the Union from each other, and to endanger the existence of the Union itself?

From the adoption of the Federal Constitution, during a period of sixty years, our progress as a nation has been without example in the annals of history. Under the protection of a bountiful Providence, we have advanced with giant strides in the career of wealth and prosperity. We have enjoyed the blessings of freedom to a greater extent than any other people, ancient or modern, under a Government which has preserved order, and secured to every citizen life, liberty, and property. We have now become an example for imitation to the whole world. The friends of freedom in every clime point with admiration to our institutions. Shall we, then, at the moment when the people of Europe are devoting all their energies in the attempt to assimilate their institutions to our own, peril all our blessings by despising the lessons of experience, and refusing to tread in the footsteps which our fathers have trodden? And for what cause would we endanger our glorious Union? The Missouri compromise contains a prohibition of slavery throughout all that vast region extending twelve and a half degrees along the Pacific, from the parallel of thirty-six degrees thirty minutes to that of forty-nine degrees, and east from that ocean to and beyond the summit of the Rocky Mountains. Why, then, should our institutions be endangered, because it is proposed to submit to the people of the remainder of our newly acquired territory lying south of thirty-six degrees thirty minutes, embracing less than four degrees of latitude, the question whether, in the language of the Texas compromise, they "shall be admitted (as a State) into the Union with or without slavery?" Is this a question to be pushed to such extremities by excited partisans on the one side or the other, in regard to our newly-acquired distant possessions on the Pacific, as to endanger the union of thirty glorious States which constitute our Confederacy? I have an abiding confidence that the sober reflection and sound patriotism of the people of all the States will bring them to the conclusion that the dictate of wisdom is to follow the example of those who have gone before us, and settle this dangerous question on the Missouri compromise, or some other equitable compromise, which would respect the rights of all, and prove satisfactory to the different portions of the Union.

Holding as a sacred trust the Executive authority for the whole Union, and bound to guard the rights of all, I should be constrained, by a sense of duty, to withhold my official sanction from any measure which would conflict with these important objects.

I cannot more appropriately close this message than by quoting from the Farewell Address of the Father of his Country. His warning voice can never be heard in vain by the American people. If the spirit of prophecy had distinctly presented to his view, more than a half-century ago, the present distracted condition of his country, the language which he then employed could not have been more appropriate than it is to the present occasion. He declared:

"The unity of Government which constitutes you one people, is also now dear to you. It is justly so; for it is a main pillar, in the edifice of your real independence, the support of your tranquillity at home, your peace abroad, of your safety, of your prosperity, of that very liberty which you so highly prize. But, as it is easy to foresee that, from different causes, and from different quarters, much pains will be taken, many artifices employed, to weaken in your minds the conviction of this truth —as this is the point in your political fortress against which the batteries of internal and external enemies will be the most constantly and actively (though often covertly and insidiously) directed—it is of infinite moment that you should properly estimate the immense value of your national union to your collective and individual happiness; that you should cherish a cordial, habitual, and immovable attachment to it; accustoming yourselves to think and to speak of it as a palladium of your political safety and prosperity; watching for its preservation with jealous anxiety; discountenancing whatever may suggest even a suspicion that it can in any event be abandoned; and indignantly frowning upon the first dawning of every attempt to alienate any portion of our country from the rest, or to enfeeble the sacred ties which now link together the various parts.

"For this you have every inducement of sympathy and interest. Citizens by birth or choice of a common country, that country has a right to concentrate your affection. The name of AMERICAN, which belongs to you in your national capacity, must always exalt the just pride of patriotism more than any appellation derived from local discriminations. With slight shades of difference, you have the same religion, manners, habits, and political principles. You have, in a common cause, fought and triumphed together. The independence and liberty you possess are the work of joint councils and joint efforts, of common dangers, sufferings, and success.

"With such powerful and obvious motives to union, affecting all parts of our country, while experience shall not have demonstrated its impracticability, there will always be reason to distrust the patriotism of those who, in any quarter, may endeavor to weaken its bands.

"In contemplating the causes which may disturb our Union, it occurs as matter of serious concern, that any ground should have been furnished for characterizing parties by geographical discriminations—*Northern* and *Southern*, *Atlantic* and *Western;* whence designing men may endeavor to excite a belief that there is a real difference of local interests and views. One of the expedients of party to acquire influence within particular districts, is to misrepresent the opinions and aims of other districts. You cannot shield yourselves too much against the jealousies and heart-burnings which spring from these misrepresentations. They tend to render alien to each other those who ought to be bound together by fraternal affection."

JAMES K. POLK.

WASHINGTON, *August* 14, 1848.

[This Message, requiring no action on the part of the House, and being merely justificatory and explanatory, had fulfilled its mission when it had been read at the clerk's table; and the act itself had become law in receiving his sanction.]

Mr. BURT moved to lay the resolution on the table, and on that motion he demanded the yeas and nays.

The yeas and nays were ordered, and being taken, resulted: Yeas 72, nays 77.

So the House refused to lay the resolution on the table.

The question recurred on the adoption of the resolution.

[It now wanted but twelve minutes to twelve o'clock.]

Mr. BURT and other gentlemen demanded the yeas and nays.

The SPEAKER stated that another call of the yeas and nays would more than exhaust all the time which was left. If the yeas and nays were ordered, it would be his duty to arrest the call and adjourn the House at twelve o'clock.

Mr. HOUSTON of Alabama, asked the general consent that the President's Message be printed.

Objections were made, unless gentlemen on Mr. HOUSTON's side would withdraw the demand for the yeas and nays. [Increased confusion.]

Mr. HUNT moved to reconsider the vote by which the yeas and nays had been ordered. He appealed to gentlemen not to persist in killing the little time that remained.

Mr. JONES of Tennessee demanded the yeas and nays on the motion to reconsider.

The yeas and nays were refused, and the motion to reconsider the demand for the yeas and nays was agreed to.

At two minutes to twelve, Mr. STANTON made another unsuccessful appeal to have the Message laid before the House.

The Clerk still progressed with the call, and having reached the name of Mr. RICHARDSON—

The Speaker's hammer fell, and

The SPEAKER rose, and said that the Senate and House of Representatives, by joint resolution, having directed the President of the Senate and the Speaker of the House of Representatives, to adjourn their respective Houses on the 14th day of August at twelve o'clock, M., and that day and that hour having now arrived, the Chair declares that this House stands adjourned *sine die.*

THIRTIETH CONGRESS.—SECOND SESSION.

PROCEEDINGS AND DEBATES

IN THE

SENATE AND HOUSE OF REPRESENTATIVES.

IN SENATE.

MONDAY, December 4, 1848.

At twelve o'clock, the Senate was called to order by Mr. ATCHISON; and forty-one Senators appearing in their seats,

On motion of Mr. BREESE,

Ordered, That the Secretary acquaint the House of Representatives that a quorum of the Senate has assembled, and that the Senate is ready to proceed to business.

On motion of Mr. BRADBURY,

Ordered, That the daily hour of meeting of the Senate be twelve o'clock, meridian, until otherwise ordered.

New Territories.

Mr. DOUGLAS gave notice that he should to-morrow, or at some early day, ask leave to introduce the following bills:

A bill to establish the Territory of Minnesota.

A bill to establish the Territory of Nebraska.

A bill to establish the Territory of New Mexico.

New State.

A bill for the introduction of California as a State of the Union.

The Senate adjourned.

HOUSE OF REPRESENTATIVES.

MONDAY, December 4.

At twelve o'clock, M., the House was called to order by the Speaker, Hon. ROBERT C. WINTHROP, and the roll having been called by the Clerk, THOMAS J. CAMPBELL, Esq., it appeared

that 178 gentlemen had answered to their names.

Two new members, elected to supply vacancies which occurred at the last session in the representation from the State of New York, appeared, were qualified according to law, and took their seats, viz: Mr. ESBOND BLACKMAR, elected to supply the vacancy occasioned by the death of the Hon. JOHN M. HOLLEY; and Mr. HORACE GREELEY, elected in the place of DAVID S. JACKSON, Esq., whose seat, being contested at the last session by James Monroe, Esq., was declared vacant by the House.

IN SENATE.

TUESDAY, December 5.

The VICE PRESIDENT assumed the chair.

The following Message was received from the President of the United States, by Mr. J. KNOX WALKER, his Secretary, and was read:

Fellow-citizens of the Senate
and of the House of Representatives:

Under the benignant Providence of Almighty God, the representatives of the States and of the people are again brought together to deliberate for the public good. The gratitude of the nation to the sovereign Arbiter of all human events, should be commensurate with the boundless blessings which we enjoy.

Peace, plenty, and contentment reign throughout our borders, and our beloved country presents a sublime moral spectacle to the world.

The troubled and unsettled condition of some of the principal European Powers has had a necessary tendency to check and embarrass trade, and to depress prices throughout all commercial nations; but notwithstanding these causes, the United States, with their abundant products, have felt their effects less severely than any other country, and all our great interests are still prosperous and successful.

In reviewing the great events of the past year, and contrasting the agitated and disturbed state of other countries with our own tranquil and happy condition, we may congratulate ourselves that we are the most favored people on the face of the earth. While the people of other countries are struggling to establish free institutions, under which man may govern himself, we are in the actual enjoyment of them—a rich inheritance from our fathers. While enlightened nations of Europe are convulsed and distracted by civil war or intestine strife, we settle all our political controversies by the peaceful exercise of the rights of freemen at the ballot-box. The great republican maxim so deeply engraven on the hearts of our people, that the will of the majority—constitutionally expressed—shall prevail, is our sure safeguard against force and violence. It is a subject of just pride, that our fame and character as a nation continue rapidly to advance in the estimation of the civilized world. To our wise and free institutions it is to be attributed, that while other nations have achieved glory at the price of the suffering, distress, and impoverishment of their people, we have won our honorable position in the midst of an uninterrupted prosperity, and of an increasing individual comfort and happiness. I am happy to inform you that our relations with all nations are friendly and pacific. Advantageous treaties of commerce have been concluded, within the last four years, with New Granada, Peru, the Two Sicilies, Belgium, Hanover, Oldenburg, and Mecklenburg-Schwerin. Pursuing our example, the restrictive system of Great Britain, our principal foreign customer, has been relaxed; a more liberal commercial policy has been adopted by other enlightened nations, and our trade has been greatly enlarged and extended. Our country stands higher in the respect of the world than at any former period. To continue to occupy this proud position, it is only necessary to preserve peace, and faithfully adhere to the great and fundamental principle of our foreign policy of non-interference in the domestic concerns of other nations. We recognize in all nations the rights which we enjoy ourselves, to change and reform their political institutions, according to their own will and pleasure. Hence we do not look behind existing governments, capable of maintaining their own authority. We recognize all such actual governments, not only from the dictates of true policy, but from a sacred regard for the independence of nations.

While this is our settled policy, it does not follow that we can ever be indifferent spectators of the progress of liberal principles. The Government and people of the United States hailed with enthusiasm and delight the establishment of the French Republic, as we now hail the efforts in progress to unite the States of Germany in a confederation, similar in many respects to our own Federal Union. If the great and enlightened German States, occupying, as they do, a central and commanding position in Europe, shall succeed in establishing such a Confederated Government, securing at the same time to the citizens of each State, local governments adapted to the peculiar condition of each, with unrestricted trade and intercourse with each other, it will be an important era in the history of human events. Whilst it will consolidate and strengthen the power of Germany, it must essentially promote the cause of peace, commerce, civilization, and constitutional liberty throughout the world.

With all the governments on this continent our relations, it is believed, are now on a more friendly and satisfactory footing than they have ever been at any former period.

Since the exchange of ratifications of the treaty of peace with Mexico, our intercourse with the Government of that Republic has been of the most friendly character. The Envoy Extraordinary and Minister Plenipotentiary of the United States to Mexico has been received and accredited; and a diplomatic representative from Mexico of similar rank has been received and accredited by this Government. The amicable relations between the two countries which had been suspended have been happily restored, and are destined, I trust, to be long preserved. The two Republics, both situated on this continent, and with conterminous territories, have every motive of sympathy and of interest to bind them together in perpetual amity.

This gratifying condition of our foreign relations renders it unnecessary for me to call your attention more specifically to them.

It has been my constant aim and desire to cultivate peace and commerce with all nations. Tranquillity at home, and peaceful relations abroad, constitute the true permanent policy of our country. War, the scourge of nations, sometimes becomes inevitable, but is always to be avoided when it can be done consistently with the rights and honor of the nation.

One of the most important results of the war into which we were recently forced with a neighboring nation, is the demonstration it has afforded of the military strength of our country. Before the late war with Mexico, European and other foreign powers entertained imperfect and erroneous views of our physical strength as a nation, and of our ability to prosecute war, and especially a war waged out of our own country. They saw that our standing army on the peace establishment did not exceed ten thousand men. Accustomed themselves to maintain in peace large standing armies for the protection of thrones against their own subjects, as well as against foreign enemies, they had not conceived that it was possible for a nation without such an army, well disciplined and of long service, to wage war successfully. They held in low repute our militia, and were far from regarding them as an effective force, unless it might be for temporary defensive operations when invaded on our own soil. The events of the late war with Mexico have not only undeceived them, but have removed erroneous impressions which prevailed to some extent even among a portion of our own countrymen. That war has demonstrated, that upon the breaking out of hostilities not anticipated, and for which no previous preparation had been made, a volunteer army of citizen-soldiers equal to veteran troops, and in numbers equal to any emergency, can in a short period be brought into the field. Unlike what would have occurred in any other country, we were under no necessity of resorting to draughts or conscriptions. On the contrary, such was the number of volunteers who patriotically tendered their services, that the chief difficulty was in making selections, and determining who should be disappointed and compelled to remain at home. Our citizen-soldiers are unlike those drawn from the population of any other country. They are composed indiscriminately of all professions and pursuits: of farmers, lawyers, physicians, merchants, manufacturers, mechanics, and laborers; and this, not only among the officers, but the private soldiers in the ranks. Our citizen-soldiers are unlike those of any other country in other respects. They are armed, and have been accustomed, from their youth up, to handle and use fire-arms; and a large proportion of them, especially in the western and more newly settled States, are expert marksmen. They are men who have a reputation to maintain at home by their good conduct in the field. They are intelligent, and there is an individuality of character which is found in the ranks of no other army. In battle, each private man, as well as every officer, fights not only for his country, but for glory and distinction among his fellow-citizens when he shall return to civil life.

The war with Mexico has demonstrated not only the ability of the Government to organize a numerous army upon a sudden call, but also to provide it with all the munitions and necessary supplies with despatch, convenience, and ease, and to direct its operations with efficiency. The strength of our institutions has not only been displayed in the valor and skill of our troops engaged in active service in the field, but in the organization of those executive branches which were charged with the general direction and conduct of the war. While too great praise cannot be bestowed upon the officers and men who fought our battles, it would be unjust to withhold from those officers necessarily stationed at home, who were charged with the duty of furnishing the army, in proper time, and at proper places, with all the munitions of war and other supplies so necessary to make it efficient, the commendation to which they are entitled. The credit due to this class of our officers is the greater, when it is considered that no army in ancient or modern times was ever better appointed or provided than our army in Mexico. Operating in an enemy's country, removed two thousand miles from the seat of the Federal Government, its different corps spread over a vast extent of territory, hundreds and even thousands of miles apart from each other, nothing short of the untiring vigilance and extraordinary energy of these officers could have enabled them to provide the army at all points, and in proper season, with all that was required for the most efficient service.

It is but an act of justice to declare, that the officers in charge of the several executive bureaus, all under the immediate eye and supervision of the Secrêtary of War, performed their respective duties with ability, energy, and efficiency. They have reaped less of the glory of the war, not having been personally exposed to its perils in battle, than their companions in arms; but without their forecast, efficient aid, and co-operation, those in the field would not have been provided with the ample means they possessed of achieving for themselves and their country the unfading honors which they have won for both.

When all these facts are considered, it may cease to be a matter of so much amazement abroad how it happened that our noble army in Mexico, regulars and volunteers, were victorious upon every battle-field, however fearful the odds against them.

The war with Mexico has thus fully developed the capacity of republican Governments to prosecute successfully a just and necessary foreign war with all the vigor usually attributed to more arbitrary forms of government. It has been usual for writers on public law to impute to republics a want of that unity, concentration of purpose, and vigor of execution, which are generally admitted to belong to the monarchical and aristocratic forms; and this feature of popular government has been supposed to display itself more particularly in the conduct of a war carried on in an enemy's territory. The war with Great Britain in 1812, was to a great extent confined within our own limits, and shed but little light on this subject. But the war which we have just closed by an honorable peace, evinces beyond all doubt that a popular representative Government is equal to an emergency which is likely to arise in the affairs of a nation.

The war with Mexico has developed most strikingly and conspicuously another feature in our institutions. It is, that without cost to the Government or danger to our liberties, we have, in the bosom of our society of freemen, available in a just and necessary war, virtually a standing army of two millions of armed citizen-soldiers, such as fought the battles of Mexico.

But our military strength does not consist alone in our capacity for extended and successful operations on land. The navy is an important arm of the national defence. If the services of the navy were not so brilliant as those of the army in the late war with Mexico, it was because they had no enemy to meet on their own element. While the army had opportunity of performing more conspicuous service, the navy largely participated in the conduct of the war. Both branches of the service performed their whole duty to the country. For the able and gallant services of the officers and men of the navy—acting independently as well as in co-operation with our troops—in the conquest of the Californias, the capture of Vera Cruz, and the seizure and occupation of other important positions on the Gulf and Pacific coasts, the highest praise is due. Their vigilance, energy, and skill rendered the most effective service in excluding munitions of war and other supplies from the enemy, while they secured a safe entrance for abundant supplies for our own army. Our extended commerce was nowhere interrupted; and for this immunity from the evils of war, the country is indebted to the navy.

High praise is due to the officers of the several executive bureaus, navy-yards, and stations connected with the service, all under the immediate direction of the Secretary of the Navy, for the industry, foresight, and energy with which every thing was directed and furnished to give efficiency to that branch of the service. The same vigilance existed in directing the operations of the navy, as of the army. There was concert of action and of purpose between the heads of the two arms of the service. By the orders which were from time to time issued, our vessels of war on the Pacific and the Gulf of Mexico were stationed in proper time and in proper positions to co-operate efficiently with the army. By this means their combined power was brought to bear successfully on the enemy.

The great results which have been developed and brought to light by this war, will be of immeasurable importance in the future progress of our country. They will tend powerfully to preserve us from foreign collisions, and to enable us to pursue uninterruptedly our cherished policy of "peace with all nations, entangling alliances with none."

Occupying, as we do, a more commanding position among nations than at any former period, our duties and our responsibilities to ourselves and to posterity are correspondingly increased. This will be the more obvious when we consider the vast additions which have been recently made to our territorial possessions, and their great importance and value.

Within less than four years the annexation of Texas to the Union has been consummated; all conflicting title to the Oregon Territory south of the forty-ninth degree of north latitude, being all that was insisted on by any of my predecessors, has been adjusted; and New Mexico and Upper California have been acquired by treaty. The area of these several Territories, according to a report carefully prepared by the Commissioner of the General Land Office, from the most authentic information in his possession, and which is herewith transmitted, contains one million one hundred and ninety-three thousand and sixty-one square miles, or seven hundred and sixty-three million five hundred and fifty-nine thousand and forty acres; while the area of the remaining twenty-nine States, and the territory not yet organized into States east of the Rocky Mountains, contains two million fifty-nine thousand five hundred and thirteen square miles, or thirteen hundred and eighteen million one hundred and twenty-six thousand and fifty-eight acres. These estimates show that the territories recently acquired, and over which our exclusive jurisdiction and dominion have been extended, constitute a country more than half as large as all that which was held by the United States before their acquisition. If Oregon be excluded from the estimate, there will still remain within the limits of Texas, New Mexico, and California, eight hundred and fifty-one thousand five hundred and ninety-eight square miles, or five hundred and forty-five million twelve thousand seven hundred and twenty acres; being an addition equal to more than one-third of all the territory owned by the United States before their acquisition; and, including Oregon, nearly as great an extent of territory as the whole of Europe, Russia only excepted. The Mississippi, so lately the frontier of our country, is now only its centre. With the addition of the late acquisitions, the United States are now estimated to be nearly as large as the whole of Europe. It is estimated by the superintendent of the coast survey, in the accompanying report, that the extent of the sea-coast of Texas on the Gulf of Mexico is upwards of four hundred miles; of the coast of Upper California, on the Pacific, of nine hundred and seventy miles; and of Oregon, including the Straits of Fuca, of six hundred and fifty miles; making the whole extent of sea-coast on the Pacific one thousand six hundred and twenty miles, and the whole extent on both the Pacific and the Gulf of Mexico two thousand and twenty miles. The length of the coast on the Atlantic, from the northern limits of the United States, around the Capes of Florida to the Sabine, on the eastern boundary of Texas, is estimated to be three thousand one hundred miles; so that the addition of sea-coast, including Oregon, is very nearly two-thirds as great as all we possessed before; and, excluding Oregon, is an addition of one thousand three hundred and seventy miles; being nearly equal to one-half of the extent of coast which we possessed before these acquisitions. We have now three great maritime fronts—on the Atlantic, the Gulf of Mexico, and the Pacific—making in the whole an extent of sea-coast exceeding five thousand miles. This is the extent of the sea-coast of the United States, not including bays, sounds, and small irregularities of the main shore, and of the sea islands. If these be included, the length of the shore line of coast, as estimated by the superintendent of the coast survey, in his report, would be thirty-three thousand and sixty-three miles.

It would be difficult to calculate the value of these immense additions to our territorial possessions. Texas, lying contiguous to the western boundary of Louisiana, embracing within its limits a part of the navigable tributary waters of the Mississippi, and an extensive sea-coast, could not long have remained in the hands of a foreign power, without endangering the peace of our south-western frontier. Her products in the vicinity of the tributaries of the Mississippi must have sought a market through these streams, running into and through our territory; and the danger of irritation and collision of interests between Texas as a foreign State and ourselves, would have been imminent, while the embarrassments in the commercial intercourse between them must have been constant and unavoidable. Had Texas fallen into the hands, or under the influence and control of a strong maritime or military foreign power, as she might have done, these dangers would have been still greater. They have been avoided by her voluntary and peaceful annexation to the United States. Texas, from her position, was a natural and almost indispensable part of our territories. Fortunately, she has been restored to our country, and now constitutes one of the States of our Confederacy, "upon an equal footing with the original States." The salubrity of climate, the fertility of soil, peculiarly adapted to the production of some of our most valuable staple commodities, and her commercial advantages, must soon make her one of our most populous States.

New Mexico, though situated in the interior, and without a sea-coast, is known to contain much fertile land, to abound in rich mines of the precious metals, and to be capable of sustaining a large population. From its position, it is the intermediate and connecting territory between our settlements and our possessions in Texas, and those on the Pacific coast.

Upper California, irrespective of the vast mineral wealth recently developed there, holds at this day, in point of value and importance to the rest of the Union, the same relation that Louisiana did, when that fine territory was acquired from France forty-five years ago. Extending nearly ten degrees of latitude along the Pacific, and embracing the only safe and commodious harbors on that coast for many hundred miles, with a temperate climate, and an extensive interior of fertile lands, it is scarcely possible to estimate its wealth until it shall be brought under the government of our laws, and its resources fully developed. From its position, it must command a rich commerce of China, of Asia, of the islands of the Pacific, of Western Mexico, of Central America, the South

American States, and of the Russian possessions bordering on that ocean. A great emporium will doubtless speedily arise on the Californian coast, which may be destined to rival in importance New Orleans itself. The depôt of the vast commerce which must exist on the Pacific will probably be at some point on the bay of San Francisco, and will occupy the same relation to the whole western coast of that ocean, as New Orleans does to the valley of the Mississippi and the Gulf of Mexico. To this depôt our numerous whale ships will resort with their cargoes, to trade, refit, and obtain supplies. This of itself will largely contribute to build up a city, which would soon become the centre of a great and rapidly increasing commerce. Situated on a safe harbor, sufficiently capacious for all the navies as well as the marine of the world, and convenient to excellent timber for ship-building, owned by the United States, it must become our great western naval depôt.

It was known that mines of the precious metals existed to a considerable extent in California at the time of its acquisition. Recent discoveries render it probable that these mines are more extensive and valuable than was anticipated. The accounts of the abundance of gold in that territory are of such an extraordinary character, as would scarcely command belief, were they not corroborated by the authentic reports of officers in the public service, who have visited the mineral district, and derived the facts which they detail from personal observation. Reluctant to credit the reports in general circulation as to the quantity of gold, the officer commanding our forces in California visited the mineral district in July last, for the purpose of obtaining accurate information on the subject. His report to the War Department of the result of his examination, and the facts obtained on the spot, is herewith laid before Congress. When he visited the country, there were about four thousand persons engaged in collecting gold. There is every reason to believe that the number of persons so employed has since been augmented. The explorations already made warrant the belief that the supply is very large, and that gold is found in various places in an extensive district of country.

Information received from officers of the navy, and other sources, though not so full and minute, confirm the accounts of the commander of our military force in California. It appears, also, from these reports, that mines of quicksilver are found in the vicinity of the gold region. One of them is now being worked, and is believed to be among the most productive in the world.

The effects produced by the discovery of these rich mineral deposits, and the success which has attended the labors of those who have resorted to them, have produced a surprising change in the state of affairs in California. Labor commands a most exorbitant price, and all other pursuits but that of searching for the precious metals are abandoned. Nearly the whole of the male population of the country have gone to the gold district. Ships arriving on the coast are deserted by their crews, and their voyages suspended for want of sailors. Our commanding officer there entertains apprehensions that soldiers cannot be kept in the public service without a large increase of pay. Desertions in his command have become frequent, and he recommends that those who shall withstand the strong temptation, and remain faithful, should be rewarded.

This abundance of gold, and the all-engrossing pursuit of it, have already caused in California an unprecedented rise in the price of the necessaries of life.

That we may the more speedily and fully avail ourselves of the undeveloped wealth of these mines, it is deemed of vast importance that a branch of the mint of the United States be authorized to be established, at your present session, in California. Among other signal advantages which would result from such an establishment would be that of raising the gold to its par value in that Territory. A branch mint of the United States at the great commercial depôt on the west coast, would convert into our own coin not only the gold derived from our own rich mines, but also the bullion and specie which our commerce may bring from the whole west coast of Central and South America. The west coast of America, and the adjacent interior, embrace the richest and best mines of Mexico, New Granada, Central America, Chili, and Peru. The bullion and specie drawn from these countries, and especially from those of Western Mexico and Peru, to an amount in value of many millions of dollars, are now annually diverted and carried by the ships of Great Britain to her own ports, to be recoined or used to sustain her National Bank, and thus contribute to increase her ability to command so much of the commerce of the world. If a branch mint be established at the great commercial point upon that coast, a vast amount of bullion and specie would flow thither to be recoined, and pass thence to New Orleans, New York, and other Atlantic cities. The amount of our constitutional currency at home would be greatly increased, while its circulation abroad would be promoted. It is well known to our merchants trading to China and the west coast of America, that great inconvenience and loss are experienced from the fact that our coins are not current at their par value in those countries.

The powers of Europe, far removed from the west coast of America by the Atlantic Ocean which intervenes, and by a tedious and dangerous navigation around the southern cape of the continent of America, can never successfully compete with the United States in the rich and extensive commerce which is opened to us at so much less cost by the acquisition of California.

The vast importance and commercial advantages of California have heretofore remained undeveloped by the Government of the country of which it constituted a part. Now that this fine province is a part of our country, all the States of the Union, some more immediately and directly than others, are deeply interested in the speedy development of its wealth and resources. No section of our country is more interested, or will be more benefited, than the commercial, navigating, and manufacturing interests of the eastern States. Our planting and farming interests in every part of the Union will be greatly benefited by it. As our commerce and navigation are enlarged and extended, our exports of agricultural products and of manufactures will be increased; and in the new markets thus opened, they cannot fail to command remunerating and profitable prices.

The acquisition of California and New Mexico, the settlement of the Oregon boundary, and the annexation of Texas, extending to the Rio Grande, are results which, combined, are of greater consequence, and will add more to the strength and wealth of the nation, than any which have preceded them since the adoption of the constitution.

But to effect these great results, not only California, but New Mexico, must be brought under the control of regularly organized governments. The existing condition of California, and of that part of New Mexico lying west of the Rio Grande, and without the limits of Texas, imperiously demand that Congress should, at its present session, organize territorial governments over them.

Upon the exchange of ratifications of the treaty of peace with Mexico on the thirtieth of May last, the temporary governments which had been established over New Mexico and California by our military and naval commanders, by virtue of the rights of war, ceased to derive any obligatory force from that source of authority; and having been ceded to the United States, all government and control over them under the authority of Mexico had ceased to exist. Impressed with the necessity of establishing territorial governments over them, I recommended the subject to the favorable consideration of Congress in my message communicating the ratified treaty of peace, on the sixth of July last, and invoked their action at that session. Congress adjourned without making any provision for their government. The inhabitants, by the transfer of their country, had become entitled to the benefits of our laws and constitution, and yet were left without any regularly organized government. Since that time, the very limited power possessed by the Executive has been exercised to preserve and protect them from the inevitable consequences of a state of anarchy. The only government which remained was that established by the military authority during the war. Regarding this to be a *de facto* government, and that by the presumed consent of the inhabitants it might be continued temporarily, they were advised to conform and submit to it for the short intervening period before Congress would again assemble, and could legislate on the subject. The views entertained by the Executive on this point are contained in a communication of the Secretary of State, dated the seventh of October last, which was forwarded for publication to California and New Mexico, a copy of which is herewith transmitted.

The small military force of the regular army, which was serving within the limits of the acquired territories at the close of the war, was retained in them, and additional forces have been ordered there for the protection of the inhabitants, and to preserve and secure the rights and interests of the United States.

No revenue has been or could be collected at the ports of California, because Congress failed to authorize the establishment of custom-houses, or the appointment of officers for that purpose.

The Secretary of the Treasury, by a circular letter addressed to collectors of the customs on the seventh day of October last, a copy of which is herewith transmitted, exercised all the power with which he was invested by law.

In pursuance of the act of the fourteenth of August last, extending the benefit of our post-office laws to the people of California, the Postmaster General has appointed two agents, who have proceeded, the one to California, and the other to Oregon, with authority to make the necessary arrangements for carrying its provisions into effect.

The monthly line of mail steamers from Panama to Astoria has been required to "stop and deliver and take mails at San Diego, Monterey, and San Francisco." These mail steamers, connected by the isthmus of Panama with the line of mail steamers on the Atlantic between New York and Chagres, will establish a regular mail communication with California.

It is our solemn duty to provide, with the least practicable delay, for New Mexico and California, regularly organized territorial governments. The causes of the failure to do this at the last session of Congress are well known, and deeply to be regretted. With the opening prospects of increased prosperity and national greatness which the acquisition of these rich and extensive territorial possessions affords, how irrational it would be to forego or to reject these advantages, by the agitation of a domestic question which is coeval with the existence of our Government itself, and to endanger by internal strifes, geographical divisions, and heated contests for political power, or for any other cause, the harmony of the glorious Union of our confederated States, that Union which binds us together as one people, and which for sixty years has been our shield and protection against every danger! In the eyes of the world and of posterity, how trivial and insignificant will be all our internal divisions and struggles, compared with the preservation of this Union of the States in all its vigor and with all its countless blessings! No patriot would foment and excite geographical and sectional divisions. No lover of his country would deliberately calculate the value of the Union. Future generations would look in amazement upon the folly of such a course. Other nations at the present day would look upon it with astonishment; and such of them as desire to maintain and perpetuate thrones and monarchical or aristocratical principles will view it with exultation and delight, because in it they will see the elements of faction, which they hope must ultimately overturn our system. Ours is the great example of a prosperous and free self-governed Republic, commanding the admiration and the imitation of all the lovers of freedom throughout the world. How solemn, therefore, is the duty, how impressive the call upon us and upon all parts of our country, to cultivate a patriotic spirit of harmony, of good-fellowship, of compromise and mutual concession, in the administration of the incomparable system of government formed by our fathers in the midst of almost insuperable difficulties, and transmitted to us, with the injunction that we should enjoy its blessings, and hand it down unimpaired to those who may come after us!

In view of the high and responsible duties which we owe to ourselves and to mankind, I trust you may be able, at your present session, to approach the adjustment of the only domestic question which seriously threatens, or probably can ever threaten, to disturb the harmony and successful operation of our system.

The immensely valuable possessions New Mexico and California are already inhabited by a considerble population. Attracted by their great fertility, their mineral wealth, their commercial advantages, and the salubrity of the climate, emigrants from the older States, in great numbers, are already preparing to seek new homes in these inviting regions.

Shall the dissimilarity of the domestic institutions in the different States prevent us from providing for them suitable governments? These institutions existed at the adoption of the constitution, but the obstacles which they interposed were overcome by that spirit of compromise which is now invoked. In a conflict of opinions or of interests, real or imaginary, between different sections of our country, neither can justly demand all which it might desire to obtain. Each, in the true spirit of our institutions, should concede something to the other.

Our gallant forces in the Mexican war, by whose patriotism and unparalleled deeds of arms we obtained these possessions as an indemnity for our just demands against Mexico, were composed of citizens who belonged to no one State or section of our Union. They were men from slaveholding and non-slaveholding States, from the North and the South, from the East and the West. They were all companions-in-arms and fellow-citizens of the same common country, engaged in the same common cause. When prosecuting that war, they were brethren and friends, and shared alike with each other, common toils, dangers, and sufferings. Now, when their work is ended, when peace is restored, and they return again to their homes, put off the habiliments of war, take their places in society, and resume their pursuits in civil life, surely a spirit of harmony and concession, and of equal regard for the rights of all, and of all sections of the Union, ought to prevail in providing governments for the acquired territories—the fruits of their common service. The whole people of the United States, and of every State, contributed to defray the expenses of that war; and it would not be just for any one section to exclude another from all participation in the acquired territory. This would not be in consonance with the just system of government which the framers of the constitution adopted.

The question is believed to be rather abstract than practical, whether slavery ever can or would exist in any portion of the acquired territory, even if it were left to the option of the slaveholding States themselves. From the nature of the climate and productions, in much the larger portion of it, it is certain it could never exist; and in the remainder, the probabilities are, it would not. But however this may be, the question, involving, as it does, a principle of equality of rights of the separate and several States, as equal co-partners in the Confederacy, should not be disregarded.

In organizing governments over these Territories, no duty imposed on Congress by the constitution requires that they should legislate on the subject of slavery, while their power to do so is not only seriously questioned, but denied by many of the soundest expounders of that instrument. Whether Congress shall legislate or not, the people of the acquired Territories, when assembled in convention to form State constitutions, will possess the sole and exclusive power to determine for themselves whether slavery shall or shall not exist within their limits. If Congress shall abstain from interfering with the question, the people of these Territories will be left free to adjust it as they may think proper when they apply for admission as States into the Union. No enactment of Congress could restrain the people of any of the sovereign States of the Union, old or new, north or south, slaveholding or non-slaveholding, from determining the character of their own domestic institutions as they may deem wise and proper. Any and all of the States possess this right, and Congress cannot deprive them of it. The people of Georgia might, if they chose, so alter their constitution as to abolish slavery within its limits; and the people of Vermont might so alter their constitution as to admit slavery within its limits. Both States would possess the right; though, as all know, it is not probable that either would exert it.

It is fortunate for the peace and harmony of the Union that this question is in its nature temporary, and can only continue for the brief period which will intervene before California and New Mexico may be admitted as States into the Union. From the tide of population now flowing into them, it is highly probable that this will soon occur.

Considering the several States and the citizens of the several States as equals, and entitled to equal rights under the constitution, if this were an original question, it might well be insisted on that the principle of non-interference is the true doctrine, and that Congress could not, in the absence of any express grant of power, interfere with their relative rights. Upon a great emergency, however, and under menacing dangers to the Union, the Missouri compromise line in respect to slavery was adopted. The same line was extended further west in the acquisition of Texas. After an acquiescence of nearly thirty years in the principle of compromise recognized and established by these acts, and to avoid the danger to the Union which might follow if it were now disregarded, I have heretofore expressed the opinion that that line of compromise should be extended on the parallel of thirty-six degrees thirty minutes from the western boundary of Texas, where it now terminates, to the Pacific Ocean. This is the middle ground of compromise, upon which the different sections of the Union may meet, as they have heretofore met. If this be done, it is confidently believed a large majority of the people of every section of the country, however widely their abstract opinions on the subject of slavery may differ, would cheerfully and patriotically acquiesce in it, and peace and harmony would again fill our borders.

The restriction north of the line was only yielded to in the case of Missouri and Texas upon a principle of compromise, made necessary for the sake of preserving the harmony, and possibly the existence of the Union.

It was upon these considerations that, at the close of your last session, I gave my sanction to the principle of the Missouri compromise line, by approving and signing the bill to establish "the Territorial Government of Oregon." From a sincere desire to preserve the harmony of the Union, and in deference for the acts of my predecessors, I felt constrained to yield my acquiescence to the extent to which they had gone in compromising this delicate and dangerous question. But if Congress shall now reverse the decision by which the Missouri compromise was effected, and shall propose to extend the restriction over the whole territory, south as well as north of the parallel of thirty-six degrees, thirty minutes, it will cease to be a compromise, and must be regarded as an original question.

If Congress, instead of observing the course of non-interference, leaving the adoption of their own domestic institutions to the people who may inhabit these Territories; or if, instead of extending the Missouri compromise line to the Pacific, shall prefer to submit the legal and constitutional questions which may arise to the decision of the judicial tribunals, as was proposed in a bill which passed the Senate at your last session, an adjustment may be effected in this mode. If the whole subject be referred to the Judiciary, all parts of the Union should cheerfully acquiesce in the final decision of the tribunal created by the constitution for the settlement of all questions which may arise under the constitution, treaties, and laws of the United States.

Congress is earnestly invoked, for the sake of the Union, its harmony, and our continued prosperity as a nation, to adjust at its present session this, the only dangerous question which lies in our path—if not in some one of the modes suggested, in some other which may be satisfactory.

In anticipation of the establishment of regular governments over the acquired territories, a joint commission of officers of the army and navy has been ordered to proceed to the coast of California and Oregon, for the purpose of making *reconnoissances*, and a report as to the proper sites for the erection of fortifications or other defensive works on land, and of suitable situations for naval stations. The information which may be expected from a scientific and skilful examination of the whole face of the coast will be eminently useful to Congress, when they come to consider the propriety of making appropriations for these great national objects. Proper defences on land will be necessary for the security and protection of our possessions; and the establishment of navy-yards, and a dock for the repair and construction of vessels, will be important alike to our navy and commercial marine. Without such establishments, every vessel, whether of the navy or of the merchant service, requiring repair, must at great expense, come round Cape Horn to one of our Atlantic yards for that purpose. With such establishments, vessels, it is believed, may be built or repaired as cheaply in California as upon the Atlantic coast. They would give employment to many of our enterprising ship-builders and mechanics, and greatly facilitate and enlarge our commerce in the Pacific.

As it is ascertained that mines of gold, silver, copper, and quicksilver exist in New Mexico and California, and that nearly all the lands where they are found belong to the United States, it is deemed important to the public interests, that provision be made for a geological and mineralogical examination of these regions. Measures should be adopted to preserve the mineral lands, especially such as contain the precious metals, for the use of the United States; or if brought into the market, to separate them from the farming lands, and dispose of them in such a manner as to secure a large return of money to the treasury, and at the same time lead to the development of their wealth by individual proprietors and purchasers. To do this, it will be necessary to provide for an immediate survey and location of the lots. If Congress should deem it proper to dispose of the mineral lands, they should be sold in small quantities, and at a fixed minimum price.

I recommend that surveyor generals' offices be authorized to be established in New Mexico and California, and provision made for surveying and bringing the public lands into market at the earliest practicable period. In disposing of these lands, I recommend that the right of pre-emption be secured, and liberal grants made to the early emigrants who have settled or may settle upon them.

It will be important to extend our revenue laws over these territories, and especially over California, at an early period. There is already a considerable commerce with California; and until ports of entry shall be established and collectors appointed, no revenue can be received.

If these and other necessary and proper measures be adopted for the development of the wealth and resources of New Mexico and California, and regular territorial governments be established over them, such will probably be the rapid enlargement of our commerce and navigation, and such the addition to the national wealth, that the present generation may live to witness the controlling commercial and monetary power of the world transferred from London and other European emporiums to the city of New York.

The apprehensions which were entertained by some of our statesmen, in the earlier periods of the Government, that our system was incapable of operating with sufficient energy and success over largely extended territorial limits, and that if this were attempted, it would fall to pieces by its own weakness, have been dissipated by our experience. By the division of power between the States and Federal Government, the latter is found to operate with as much energy in the extremes as in the centre. It is as efficient in the remotest of the thirty States which now compose the Union, as it was in the thirteen States which formed our constitution. Indeed, it may well be doubted, whether, if our present population had been confined within the limits of the original thirteen States, the tendencies to centralization and consolidation would not have been such as to have encroached upon the essential reserved rights of the States, and thus to have made the Federal Government a widely different one, practically, from what it is in theory, and was intended to be by its framers. So far from entertaining apprehensions of the safety of our system by the extension of our territory, the belief is confidently entertained, that each new State gives strength and an additional guarantee for the preservation of the Union itself.

In pursuance of the provisions of the thirteenth article of the treaty of peace, friendship, limits, and settlement, with the Republic of Mexico, and of the act of July the twenty-ninth, 1848, claims of our citizens which had been "already liquidated and decided against the Mexican Republic," amounting, with the interest thereon, to two million twenty-three thousand eight hundred and thirty-two dollars and fifty-one cents, have been liquidated and paid. There remain to be paid of these claims, seventy-four thousand one hundred and nine-two dollars and twenty-six cents.

Congress, at its last session, having made no provisions for executing the fifteenth article of the treaty, by which the United States assume to make satisfaction for the "unliquidated claims" of our citizens against Mexico, to "an amount not exceeding three and a quarter millions of dollars," the subject is again recommended to your favorable consideration.

The exchange of ratifications of the treaty with Mexico took place on the thirtieth of May, 1848. Within one year after that time, the commissioner and surveyor which each Government stipulates to appoint, are required to meet "at the port of San Diego, and proceed to run and mark the said boundary in its whole course to the mouth of the Rio Bravo del

Norte." It will be seen from this provision, that the period within which a commissioner and surveyor of the respective Governments are to meet at San Diego, will expire on the thirtieth of May, 1849. Congress, at the close of its last session, made an appropriation for "the expenses of running and marking the boundary line" between the two countries, but did not fix the amount of salary which should be paid to the commissioner and surveyor to be appointed on the part of the United States. It is desirable that the amount of compensation which they shall receive should be prescribed by law, and not left, as at present, to Executive discretion.

Measures were adopted at the earliest practicable period to organize the "Territorial Government of Oregon," as authorized by the act of the fourteenth of August last. The Governor and Marshal of the Territory, accompanied by a small military escort, left the frontier of Missouri in September last, and took the southern route, by the way of Santa Fé and the river Gila, to California, with the intention of proceeding thence in one of our vessels of war to their destination. The Governor was fully advised of the great importance of his early arrival in the country, and it is confidently believed he may reach Oregon in the latter part of the present month, or early in the next. The other officers for the Territory have proceeded by sea.

In the month of May last, I communicated information to Congress that an Indian war had broken out in Oregon, and recommended that authority be given to raise an adequate number of volunteers to proceed, without delay, to the assistance of our fellow-citizens in that Territory. The authority to raise such a force not having been granted by Congress, as soon as their services could be dispensed with in Mexico, orders were issued to the regiment of mounted riflemen to proceed to Jefferson Barracks, in Missouri, and to prepare to march to Oregon as soon as the necessary provision could be made. Shortly before it was ready to march, it was arrested by the provision of the act passed by Congress on the last day of the last session, which directed that all the non-commissioned officers, musicians, and privates of that regiment, who had been in service in Mexico, should, upon their application, be entitled to be discharged. The effect of this provision was to disband the rank and file of the regiment; and before their places could be filled by recruits, the season had so far advanced that it was impracticable for it to proceed until the opening of the next spring.

In the month of October last, the accompanying communication was received from the Governor of the temporary government of Oregon, giving information of the continuance of the Indian disturbances, and of the destitution and defenceless condition of the inhabitants. Orders were immediately transmitted to the commander of our squadron in the Pacific, to despatch to their assistance a part of the naval forces on that station, to furnish them with arms and ammunition, and to continue to give them such aid and protection as the navy could afford, until the army could reach the country.

It is the policy of humanity, and one which has always been pursued by the United States, to cultivate the good-will of the aboriginal tribes of this continent, and to restrain them from making war, and indulging in excesses, by mild means, rather than by force. That this could have been done with the tribes in Oregon, had that Territory been brought under the government of our laws at an earlier period, and had suitable measures been adopted by Congress, such as now exist in our intercourse with the other Indian tribes within our limits, cannot be doubted. Indeed, the immediate and only cause of the existing hostility of the Indians of Oregon, is represented to have been the long delay of the United States in making to them some trifling compensation, in such articles as they wanted, for the country now occupied by our emigrants, which the Indians claimed, and over which they formerly roamed. This compensation had been promised to them by the temporary government established in Oregon, but its fulfilment had been postponed from time to time, for nearly two years, whilst those who made it had been anxiously waiting for Congress to establish a territorial government over the country. The Indians became at length distrustful of their good faith, and sought redress by plunder and massacre, which finally led to the present difficulties. A few thousand dollars in suitable presents, as a compensation for the country which had been taken possession of by our citizens, would have satisfied the Indians, and have prevented the war. A small amount properly distributed, it is confidently believed, would soon restore quiet. In this Indian war, our fellow-citizens of Oregon have been compelled to take the field in their own defence, have performed valuable military services, and been subjected to expenses which have fallen heavily upon them. Justice demands that provision should be made by Congress to compensate them for their services, and to refund to them the necessary expenses which they have incurred.

I repeat the recommendation heretofore made to Congress, that provision be made for the appointment of a suitable number of Indian agents to reside among the tribes of Oregon, and that a small sum be appropriated to enable these agents to cultivate friendly relations with them. If this be done, the presence of a small military force will be all that is necessary to keep them in check, and preserve peace.

I recommend that similar provision be made as regards the tribes inhabiting northern Texas, New Mexico, California, and the extensive region lying between our settlements in Missouri and these possessions, as the most effective means of preserving peace upon our borders, and within the recently-acquired territories.

The Secretary of the Treasury will present in his annual report a highly satisfactory statement of the condition of the finances.

The imports for the fiscal year ending on the thirtieth of June last, were of the value of one hundred and fifty-four million nine hundred and seventy-seven thousand eight hundred and seventy-six dollars; of which the amount exported was twenty-one million one hundred and twenty-eight thousand and ten dollars, leaving one hundred and thirty-three million eight hundred and forty-nine thousand eight hundred and sixty-six dollars in the country for domestic use.

The value of the exports for the same period was one hundred and fifty-four million thirty-two thousand one hundred and thirty-one dollars, consisting of domestic productions, amounting to one hundred and thirty-two million nine hundred and four thousand one hundred and twenty-one dollars, and twenty-one million one hundred and twenty-eight thousand and ten dollars of foreign articles.

The receipts into the treasury for the same period, exclusive of loans, amounted to thirty-five million four hundred and thirty-six thousand seven hundred and fifty dollars and fifty-nine cents; of which there was derived from customs thirty-one million seven hundred and fifty-seven thousand and seventy dollars and ninety-six cents; from sales of public lands, three million three hundred and twenty-eight thousand six hundred and forty-two dollars and fifty-six cents; and from miscellaneous and incidental sources, three hundred and fifty-one thousand and thirty-seven dollars and seven cents.

It will be perceived that the revenue from customs for the last fiscal year, exceeded by seven hundred and fifty-seven thousand and seventy dollars and ninety-six cents the estimate of the Secretary of the Treasury in his last annual report; and that the aggregate receipts during the same period from customs, lands, and miscellaneous sources, also exceeded the estimate by the sum of five hundred and thirty-six thousand seven hundred and fifty dollars and fifty-nine cents—indicating, however, a very near approach in the estimate to the actual result.

The expenditures during the fiscal year ending on the thirtieth of June last, including those for the war, and exclusive of payments of principal and interest for the public debt, were forty-two million eight hundred and eleven thousand nine hundred and seventy dollars and three cents.

It is estimated that the receipts into the treasury for the fiscal year ending on the thirtieth of June, 1849, including the balance in the treasury on the first of July last, will amount to the sum of fifty-seven million forty-eight thousand nine hundred and sixty-nine dollars and ninety cents; of which thirty-two millions of dollars, it is estimated, will be derived from customs; three millions of dollars from the sales of the public lands; and one million two hundred thousand dollars from miscellaneous and incidental sources, including the premium upon the loan, and the amount paid and to be paid into the treasury on account of military contributions in Mexico, and the sales of arms and vessels and other public property, rendered unnecessary for the use of the Government by the termination of the war; and twenty million six hundred and ninety-five thousand four hundred and thirty-five dollars and thirty cents from loans already negotiated, including treasury notes funded, which, together with the balance in the treasury on the first of July last, make the sum estimated.

The expenditures for the same period, including the necessary payment on account of the principal and interest of the public debt, and the principal and interest of the first instalment due to Mexico on the thirtieth of May next, and other expenditures growing out of the war, to be paid during the present year, will amount, including the reimbursement of treasury notes, to the sum of fifty-four million one hundred and ninety-five thousand two hundred and seventy-five dollars and six cents; leaving an estimated balance in the treasury on the first of July, 1849, of two million eight hundred and fifty-three thousand six hundred and ninety-four dollars and eighty-four cents.

The Secretary of the Treasury will present, as required by law, the estimate of the receipts and expenditures for the next fiscal year. The expenditures as estimated for that year, are thirty-three million two hundred and thirteen thousand one hundred and fifty-two dollars and seventy-three cents, including three million seven hundred and ninety-nine thousand one hundred and two dollars and eighteen cents for the interest on the public debt, and three million five hundred and forty thousand dollars for the principal and interest due to Mexico, on the thirtieth of May, 1850, leaving the sum of twenty-five million eight hundred and seventy-four thousand and fifty dollars and thirty-five cents; which, it is believed, will be ample for the ordinary peace expenditures.

The operations of the tariff act of 1846 have been such during the past year as fully to meet the public expectation, and to confirm the opinion heretofore expressed of the wisdom of the change in our revenue system which was effected by it. The receipts under it into the treasury for the first fiscal year after its enactment, exceeded by the sum of five million forty-four thousand four hundred and three dollars and nine cents, the amount collected during the last fiscal year under the tariff act of 1842, ending the thirtieth of June, 1846. The total revenue realized from the commencement of its operation, on the first of December, 1846, until the close of the last quarter, on the thirtieth of September last, being twenty-two months, was fifty-six million six hundred and fifty-four thousand five hundred and sixty-three dollars and seventy-nine cents—being a much larger sum than was ever before received from duties during any equal period under the tariff acts of 1824, 1828, 1832, and 1842. Whilst by the repeal of highly protective and prohibitory duties the revenue has been increased, the taxes on the people have been diminished. They have been relieved from the heavy amounts with which they were burdened under former laws in the form of increased prices or bounties paid to favored classes and pursuits.

The predictions which were made, that the tariff act of 1846 would reduce the amount of revenue below that collected under the act of 1842, and would prostrate the business and destroy the prosperity of the country, have not been verified. With an increased and increasing revenue, the finances are in a highly flourishing condition. Agriculture, commerce, and navigation, are prosperous; the prices of manufactured fabrics, and of other products, are much less injuriously affected than was to have been anticipated, from the unprecedented revulsions which, during the last and the present year, have overwhelmed the industry, and paralyzed the credit and commerce of so many great and enlightened nations of Europe.

Severe commercial revulsions abroad have always heretofore operated to depress, and often to effect disastrously, almost every branch of American industry. The temporary depression of a portion of our manufacturing interests is the effect of foreign causes, and is far less severe than has prevailed on all former similar occasions.

It is believed that, looking to the great aggregate of all our interests, the whole country was never more prosperous than at the present period, and never more rapidly advancing in wealth and population. Neither the foreign war in which we have been involved, nor the loans which have absorbed so large a portion of our capital, nor the commercial revulsion in Great Britain in 1847, nor the paralysis of credit and commerce throughout Europe in 1848, have affected injuriously to any considerable extent any of the great interests of the country, or arrested our onward march to greatness, wealth, and power.

Had the disturbances in Europe not occurred, our commerce would undoubtedly have been still more extended, and would have added still more to the national wealth and public prosperity. But notwithstanding these disturbances, the operations of the revenue system established by the tariff act of 1846 have been so generally beneficial to the Government and the business of the country, that no change in its provisions is demanded by a wise public policy, and none is recommended.

The operations of the constitutional treasury established by the act of the sixth of August, 1846, in the receipt, custody, and disbursement of the public money, have continued to be successful. Under the system the public finances have been carried through a foreign war, involving the necessity of loans and extraordinary expenditures, and requiring distant transfers and disbursements, without embarrassment, and no loss has occurred of any of the public money deposited under its provisions. Whilst it has proved to be safe and useful to the Government, its effects have been most beneficial upon the business of the country. It has tended powerfully to secure an exemption from that inflation and fluctuation of the paper currency, so injurious to domestic industry, and rendering so uncertain the rewards of labor, and it is believed has largely contributed to preserve the whole country from a serious commercial revulsion, such as often occurred under the bank deposit system. In the year 1847, there was a revulsion in the business of Great Britain of great extent and intensity, which was followed by failures in that kingdom unprecedented in number and amount of losses. This is believed to be the first instance when such disastrous bankruptcies, occurring in a country with which we have such extensive commerce, produced little or no injurious effect upon our trade or currency. We remained but little affected in our money market, and our business and industry were still prosperous and progressive.

During the present year, nearly the whole continent of Europe has been convulsed by civil war and revolutions, attended by numerous bankruptcies, by an unprecedented fall in their public securities, and an almost universal paralysis of commerce and industry; and yet, although our trade and the prices of our products must have been somewhat unfavorably affected by these causes, we have escaped a revulsion, our money market is comparatively easy, and public and private credit have advanced and improved.

It is confidently believed that we have been saved from their effect by the salutary operation of the constitutional treasury. It is certain, that if the twenty-four millions of specie imported into the country during the fiscal year ending on the thirtieth of June, 1847, had gone into the banks, as to a great extent it must have done, it would, in the absence of this system, have been made the basis of augmented bank paper issues, probably to an amount not less than sixty or seventy millions of dollars, producing, as an inevitable consequence of an inflated currency, extravagant prices for a time, and wild speculation, which must have been followed, on the reflux to Europe, the succeeding year, of so much of that specie, by the prostration of the business of the country, the suspension of the banks, and most extensive bankruptcies. Occurring, as this would have done, at a period when the country was engaged in a foreign war; when considerable loans of specie were required for distant disbursements, and when the banks, the fiscal agents of the Government, and the depositories of its money, were suspended, the public credit must have sunk, and many millions of dollars, as was the case during the war of 1812, must have been sacrificed in discounts upon loans, and upon the depreciated paper currency which the Government would have been compelled to use.

Under the operations of the constitutional treasury, not a dollar has been lost by the depreciation of the currency. The loans required to prosecute the war with Mexico were negotiated by the Secretary of the Treasury above par, realizing a large premium to the Government. The restraining effect of the system upon the tendencies to excessive paper issues by banks, has saved the Government from heavy losses, and thousands of our business men from bankruptcy and ruin. The wisdom of the system has been tested, by the experience of the last two years; and it is the dictate of sound policy that it should remain undisturbed. The modifications in some of the details of this measure, involving none of its essential principles, heretofore recommended, are again presented for your favorable consideration.

In my message of the sixth of July last, transmitting to Congress the ratified treaty of peace with Mexico, I recommended the adoption of measures for the speedy payment of the public debt. In reiterating that recommendation, I refer you to the considerations presented in that message in its support. The public debt, including that authorized to be negotiated, in pursuance of existing laws, and including treasury notes, amounted at that time to sixty-five million seven hundred and seventy-eight thousand four hundred and fifty dollars and forty-one cents.

Funded stock of the United States, amounting to about half a million of dollars, has been purchased, as authorized by law, since that period, and the public debt has thus been reduced, the details of which will be presented in the annual report of the Secretary of the Treasury.

The estimates of expenditures for the next fiscal year, submitted by the Secretary of the Treasury, it is believed will be ample for all necessary purposes. If the appropriations made by Congress shall not exceed the amount estimated, the means in the treasury will be sufficient to defray all the expenses of the Government; to pay off the next instalment of three millions of dollars to Mexico, which will fall due on the thirtieth of May next; and still a considerable surplus will remain, which should be applied to the further purchase of the public stock and reduction of the debt. Should enlarged appropriations be made, the necessary consequence will be to postpone the payment of the debt. Though our debt, as compared with that of most other nations, is small, it is our true policy, and in harmony with the genius of our institutions, that we would present to the world the rare spectacle of a great republic, possessing vast resources and wealth, wholly exempt from public indebtedness. This would add still more to our strength, and give to us a still more commanding position among the nations of the earth.

The public expenditures should be economical, and be confined to such necessary objects as are clearly within the powers of Congress. All such as are not absolutely demanded should be postponed, and the payment of the public debt at the earliest practicable period should be a cardinal principle of our public policy.

For the reason assigned in my last annual message, I repeat the recommendation that a branch of the mint of the United States be established at the city of New York. The importance of this measure is greatly increased by the acquisition of the rich mines of the precious metals in New Mexico and California, and especially in the latter.

I repeat the recommendation heretofore made, in favor of the graduation and reduction of the price of such of the public lands as have been long offered in the market, and have remained unsold, and in favor of extending the rights of preëmption to actual settlers on the unsurveyed as well as the surveyed lands.

The condition and operations of the army, and the state of other branches of the public service, under the supervision of the War Department, are satisfactorily presented in the accompanying report of the Secretary of War.

On the return of peace, our forces were withdrawn from Mexico, and the volunteers, and that portion of the regular army engaged for the war, were disbanded. Orders have been issued for stationing the forces of our permanent establishment at various positions in our extended country where troops may be required. Owing to the remoteness of some of these positions, the detachments have not yet reached their destination. Notwithstanding the extension of the limits of our country and the forces required in the new territories, it is confidently believed that our present military establishment is sufficient for all exigencies, so long as our peaceful relations remain undisturbed.

Of the amount of military contributions collected in Mexico, the sum of seven hundred and sixty-nine thousand six hundred and fifty dollars was applied towards the payment of the first instalment due under the treaty with Mexico. The further sum of three hundred and forty-six thousand three hundred and sixty-nine dollars and thirty cents has been paid into the treasury, and unexpended balances still remain in the hands of disbursing officers and those who were engaged in the collection of these moneys. After the proclamation of peace, no further disbursements were made of any unexpended moneys arising from this source. The balances on hand were directed to be paid into the treasury, and individual claims on the fund will remain unadjusted until Congress shall authorize their settlement and payment. These claims are not considerable in number or amount.

I recommend to your favorable consideration the suggestions of the Secretary of War and the Secretary of the Navy in regard to legislation on this subject.

Our Indian relations are presented in a most favorable view in the report from the War Department. The wisdom of our policy in regard to the tribes within our limits, is clearly manifested by their improved and rapidly improving condition.

A most important treaty with the Menomonies has been recently negotiated by the Commissioner of Indian Affairs in person, by which all their land in the State of Wisconsin—being about four millions of acres—has been ceded to the United States. This treaty will be submitted to the Senate for ratification at an early period of your present session.

Within the last four years, eight important treaties have been negotiated with different Indian tribes, and at a cost of one million eight hundred and forty-two thousand dollars; Indian lands to the amount of more than eighteen million five hundred thousand acres, have been ceded to the United States; and provision has been made for settling in the country west of the Mississippi the tribes which occupied this large extent of the public domain. The title to all the Indian lands within the several states of our Union, with the exception of a few small reservations, is now extinguished, and a vast region opened for settlement and cultivation.

The accompanying report of the Secretary of the Navy gives a satisfactory exhibit of the operations and condition of that branch of the public service.

A number of small vessels, suitable for entering the mouths of rivers, were judiciously purchased during the war, and gave great efficiency to the squadron in the Gulf of Mexico. On the return of peace, when no longer valuable for naval purposes, and liable to constant deterioration, they were sold, and the money placed in the treasury.

The number of men in the naval service, authorized by law during the war, has been reduced by discharges below the maximum fixed for the peace establishment. Adequate squadrons are maintained in the several quarters of the globe, where experience has shown their services may be most usefully employed; and the naval service was never in a condition of higher discipline or greater efficiency.

I invite attention to the recommendation of the Secretary of the Navy on the subject of the marine corps. The reduction of the corps at the end of the war, required that four officers of each of the three lower grades should be dropped from the rolls. A board of officers made the selection; and those designated were necessarily dismissed, but without any alleged fault. I concur in opinion with the Secretary, that the service would be improved by reducing the number of landsmen, and increasing the marines. Such a measure would justify an increase of the number of officers to the extent of the reduction by dismissal, and still the corps would have fewer officers than a corresponding number of men in the army.

The contracts for the transportation of the mail in steamships convertible into war-steamers, promise to realize all the benefits to our commerce and to the navy which were anticipated. The first steamer thus secured to the Government was launched in January, 1847. There are now seven; and in another year there will, probably, be not less than seventeen afloat. While this great national advantage is secured, our social and commercial intercourse is increased and promoted with Germany, Great Britain, and other parts of Europe, with all the countries on the west coast of our continent, especially with Oregon and California, and between the northern and southern sections of the United States. Considerable revenue may be expected from postages; but the connected line from New York to Chagres, and thence across the isthmus to Oregon, cannot fail to exert a beneficial influence, not now to be estimated, on the interests of the manufactures, commerce, navigation, and currency of the United States. As an important part of the system, I recommend to your favorable consideration the establishment of the proposed line of steamers between New Orleans and Vera Cruz. It promises the most happy results in cementing friendship between the two Republics, and in extending reciprocal benefits to the trade and manufactures of both.

The report of the Postmaster-General will make known to you the operations of that department for the past year.

It is gratifying to find the revenues of the department, under the rates of postage now established by law, so rapidly increasing. The gross amount of postages during the last fiscal year amounted to four million three hundred and seventy-one thousand and seventy-seven dollars, exceeding the annual average received for the nine years immediately preceding the passage of the act of the third of March, 1845, by the sum of six thousand four hundred and fifty-three dollars, and exceeding the amount received for the year ending the thirtieth of June, 1847, by the sum of four hundred and twenty-five thousand one hundred and eighty-four dollars.

The expenditures for the year, excluding the sum of ninety-four thousand six hundred and seventy-two dollars, allowed by Congress, at its last session, to individual claimants, and including the sum of one hundred thousand five hundred dollars paid for the services of the line of steamers between Bremen and New York, amounted to four million one hundred and ninety-eight thousand eight hundred and forty-five dollars, which is less than the annual average for the nine years previous to the act of 1845, by three hundred thousand seven hundred and forty-eight dollars.

The mail routes, on the thirtieth day of June last, were one hundred and sixty-three thousand two hundred and eight miles in extent—being an increase during the last year of nine thousand three hundred and ninety miles. The mails were transported over them, during the same time, forty-one million twelve thousand five hundred and seventy-nine miles; making an increase of transportation for the year of two millions one hundred and twenty-four thousand six hundred and eighty miles, whilst the expense was less than that of the previous year by four thousand two hundred and thirty-five dollars.

The increase in the mail transportation within the last three years has been five millions three hundred and seventy-eight thousand three hundred and ten miles, whilst the expenses were reduced four hundred and fifty-six thousand seven hundred and thirty-eight dollars—making an increase of service at the rate of fifteen per cent., and a reduction in the expenses of more than fifteen per cent.

During the past year, there have been employed under contracts with the Post Office Department, two ocean steamers in conveying the mails monthly between New York and Bremen, and one, since October last, performing semi-monthly service between Charleston and Havana; and a contract has been made for the transportion of the Pacific mails across the isthmus from Chagres to Panama.

Under the authority given to the Secretary of the Navy, three ocean steamers have been constructed and sent to the Pacific, and are expected to enter upon the mail service between Panama and Oregon, and the intermediate ports, on the first January next, and a fourth has been engaged by him for the service between Havana and Chagres; so that a regular monthly mail line will be kept up after that time between the United States and our territories on the Pacific.

Notwithstanding this great increase in the mail service, should the revenue continue to increase the present year as it did in the last, there will be received near four hundred and fifty thousand dollars more than the expenditures.

These considerations have satisfied the Postmaster-General that, with certain modifications of the act of 1845, the revenue may be still further increased, and a reduction of postages made to a uniform rate of five cents, without an interference with the principle, which has been constantly and properly enforced, of making that department sustain itself.

A well-digested cheap postage system is the best means of diffusing intelligence among the people, and is of so much importance in a country so extensive as that of the United States, that I recommend to your favorable consideration the suggestions of the Postmaster-General for its improvement.

Nothing can retard the onward progress of our country, and prevent us from assuming and maintaining the first rank among nations, but a disregard of the experience of the past, and a recurrence to an unwise public policy. We have just closed a foreign war by an honorable peace—a war rendered necessary and unavoidable in vindication of the national rights and honor. The present condition of the country is similar in some respects to that which existed immediately after the close of the war with Great Britain in 1815, and the occasion is deemed to be a proper one to take a retrospect of the measures of public policy which followed that war. There was at that period of our history a departure from our early policy. The enlargement of the powers of the Federal Government by *construction*, which obtained, was not warranted by any just interpretation of the constitution. A few years after the close of that war, a series of measures was adopted which, united and combined, constituted what was termed by their authors and advocates the "American system."

The introduction of a new policy was for a time favored by the condition of the country; by the heavy debt which had been contracted during the war; by the depression of the public credit; by the deranged state of the finances and the currency; and by the commercial and pecuniary embarrassment which extensively prevailed. These were not the only causes which led to its establishment. The events of the war with Great Britain, and the embarrassments which had attended its prosecution, had left on the minds of many of our statesmen the impression that our Government was not strong enough, and that to wield its resources successfully in great emergencies, and especially in war, more power should be concentrated in its hands. This increased power they did not seek to obtain by the legitimate and prescribed mode—an amendment of the constitution—but by *construction.* They saw governments in the Old World based upon different orders of society, and so constituted as to throw the whole power of nations into the hands of a few, who taxed and controlled the many without responsibility or restraint. In that arrangement they conceived the strength of nations in war consisted. There was also something fascinating in the ease, luxury, and display of the higher orders, who drew their wealth from the toil of the laboring millions. The authors of the system drew their ideas of political economy from what they had witnessed in Europe, and particularly in Great Britain. They had viewed the enormous wealth concentrated in few hands, and had seen the splendor of the overgrown establishments of an aristocracy which was upheld by the restrictive policy. They forgot to look down upon the poorer classes of the English population, upon whose daily and yearly labor the great establishments they so much admired were sustained and supported. They failed to perceive that the scantily-fed and half-clad operatives were not only in abject poverty, but were bound in chains of oppressive servitude for the benefit of favored classes, who were the exclusive objects of the care of the Government.

It was not possible to reconstruct society in the United States upon the European plan. Here there was a written constitution, by which orders and titles were not recognized or tolerated. A system of measures was therefore devised, calculated, if not intended, to withdraw power gradually and silently from the States and the mass of the people, and by *construction* to approximate our Government to the European models, substituting an aristocracy of wealth for that of orders and titles.

Without reflecting upon the dissimilarity of our institutions, and of the condition of our people and those of Europe, they conceived the vain idea of building up in the United States a system similar to that which they admired abroad. Great Britain had a national bank of large capital, in whose hands was concentrated the controlling monetary and financial power of the nation; an institution wielding almost kingly power, and exerting vast influence upon all the operations of trade, and upon the policy of the government itself. Great Britain had an enormous public debt, and it had become a part of her policy to regard this as a "public blessing." Great Britain had also a restrictive policy, which placed fetters and burdens on trade, and trammelled the productive industry of the mass of the nation. By her combined system of policy, the landlords and other property-holders were protected and enriched by the enormous taxes which were levied upon the labor of the country for their advantage.

Imitating this foreign policy, the first step in establishing the new system in the United States was the creation of a national bank. Not foreseeing the dangerous power and countless evils which such an institution might entail on the country, nor perceiving the connection which it was designed to form between the bank and the other branches of the miscalled "American system," but feeling the embarrassments of the treasury, and of the business of the country, consequent upon the war, some of our statesmen who had held different and sounder views were induced to yield their scruples, and, indeed, settled convictions of its unconstitutionality, and to give it their sanction, as an expedient which they vainly hoped might produce relief. It was a most unfortunate error, as the subsequent history and final catastrophe of that dangerous and corrupt institution have abundantly proved. The bank, with its numerous branches, ramified into the States, soon brought many of the active political and commercial men in different sections of the country into the relation of debtors to it, and dependents upon it for pecuniary favors; thus diffusing throughout the mass of society a great number of individuals of power and influence to give tone to public opinion, and to act in concert in cases of emergency. The corrupt power of such a political engine is no longer a matter of speculation, having been displayed in numerous instances, but most signally in the political struggles of 1832–'3–'4, in opposition to the public will represented by a fearless and patriotic President.

But the bank was but one branch of the new system. A public debt of more than one hundred and twenty millions of dollars existed; and it is not to be disguised, that many of the authors of the new system did not regard its speedy payment as essential to the public propriety, but looked upon its continuance as no national evil. Whilst the debt existed, it furnished aliment to the national bank, and rendered increased taxation necessary to the amount of the interest, exceeding seven millions of dollars annually.

This operated in harmony with the next branch of the new system, which was a high protective tariff. This was to afford bounties to favored classes and particular pursuits, at the expense of all others. A proposition to tax the whole people for the purpose of enriching a few, was too monstrous to be openly made. The scheme was, therefore, veiled under the plausible but delusive pretext of a measure to protect "home industry;" and many of our people were, for a time, led to believe that a tax which in the main fell upon labor, was for the benefit of the laborer who paid it. This branch of the system involved a partnership between the Government and the favored classes—the former receiving the proceeds of the tax imposed on articles imported, and the latter the increased price of similar articles produced at home, caused by such tax. It is obvious that the portion to be received by the favored classes would, as a general rule, be increased in proportion to the increase of the rates of tax imposed, and diminished as those rates were reduced to the revenue standard required by the wants of the Government. The rates required to produce a sufficient revenue for the ordinary expenditures of Government, for necessary purposes, were not likely to give to the private partners in this scheme profits sufficient to satisfy their cupidity; and hence a variety of expedients and pretexts were resorted to for the purpose of enlarging the expenditures, and thereby creating a necessity for keeping up a high protective tariff. The effect of this policy was to interpose artificial restrictions upon the natural course of the business and trade of the country, and to advance the interests of large capitalists and monopolists, at the expense of the great mass of the people, who were taxed to increase their wealth.

Another branch of this system was a comprehensive scheme of internal improvements, capable of indefinite enlargement, and sufficient to swallow up as many millions annually as could be exacted from the foreign commerce of the country. This was a convenient and necessary adjunct of the protective tariff. It was to be the great absorbent of any surplus which might at any time accumulate in the treasury, and of the taxes levied on the people, not for necessary revenue purposes, but for the avowed object of affording protection to the favored classes.

Auxiliary to the same end, if it was not an essential part of the system itself, was the scheme which, at a later period, obtained, for distributing the proceeds of the sales of the public lands among the States. Other expedients were devised to take money out of the treasury, and prevent its coming in from any other source than the protective tariff. The authors and supporters of the system were the advocates of the largest expenditures, whether for necessary or useful purposes or not, because the larger the expenditures the greater was the pretext for high taxes in the form of protective duties.

These several measures were sustained by popular names and plausible arguments, by which thousands were deluded. The bank was represented to be an indispensable fiscal agent for the Government; was to equalize exchanges, and to regulate and furnish a sound currency, always and everywhere of uniform value. The protective tariff was to give employment to "American labor" at advanced prices; was to protect "home industry," and furnish a steady market for the farmer. Internal improvements were to bring trade into every neighborhood, and enhance the value of every man's property. The distribution of the land money was to enrich the States, finish their public works, plant schools throughout their borders, and relieve them from taxation. But the fact, that for every dollar taken out of the treasury for these objects a much larger sum was transferred from the pockets of the people to the favored classes, was carefully concealed, as was also the tendency, if not the ultimate design of the system, to build up an aristocracy of wealth, to control the masses of society; and monopolize the political power of the country.

The several branches of this system were so intimately blended together, that in their operation each sustained and strengthened the others. Their joint operation was, to add new burdens of taxation, and to encourage a largely increased and wasteful expenditure of public money. It was the interest of the bank that the revenue collected and the disbursements made by the Government should be large, because, being the depository of the public money, the larger the amount, the greater would be the bank profits by its use. It was the interest of the favored classes, who were enriched by the protective tariff, to have the rates of that protection as high as possible; for the higher those rates, the greater would be their advantage. It was the interest of the people of all those sections and localities who expected to be benefited by expenditures for internal improvements, that the amount collected should be as large as possible, to the end that the sum disbursed might also be the larger. The States being the beneficiaries in the distribution of the land money, had an interest in having the rates of tax imposed by the protective tariff large enough to yield a sufficient revenue from that source to meet the wants of the Government, without disturbing or taking from them the land fund; so that each of the branches constituting the system had a common interest in swelling the public expenditures. They had a direct interest in maintaining the public debt unpaid, and increasing its amount, because this would produce an annual increased drain upon the treasury, to the amount of the interest, and render augmented taxes necessary. The operation and necessary effect of the whole system were, to encourage large and extravagant expenditures, and thereby to increase the public patronage, and maintain a rich and splendid government at the expense of a taxed and impoverished people.

It is manifest that this scheme of enlarged taxation and expenditures, had it continued to prevail, must soon have converted the Government of the Union, intended by its framers to be a plain, cheap, and simple confederation of States, united together for common protection, and charged with a few specific duties, relating chiefly to our foreign affairs, into a consolidated empire, depriving the States of their reserved rights, and the people of their just power and control in the administration of their Government. In this manner the whole form and character of the Government would be changed, not by an amendment of the constitution, but by resorting to an unwarrantable and unauthorized construction of that instrument.

The indirect mode of levying the taxes by a duty on imports, prevents the mass of the people from readily perceiving the amount they pay, and has enabled the few, who are thus enriched, and who seek to wield the political power of the country, to deceive and delude them. Were the taxes collected by a direct levy upon the people, as is the case in the States, this could not occur.

The whole system was resisted from its inception by many of our ablest statesmen, some of whom doubted its constitutionality and its expediency, while others believed it was, in all its branches, a flagrant and dangerous infraction of the constitution.

That a national bank, a protective tariff, levied not to raise the revenue needed, but for protection merely, internal improvements, and the distribution of the proceeds of the sales of the public lands, are measures without the warrant of the constitution, would, upon the maturest consideration, seem to be clear. It is remarkable that no one of these measures, involving such momentous consequences, is authorized by any express grant of power in the constitution. No one of them is "incident to, as being necessary and proper for the execution of, the specific powers" granted by the constitution. The authority under which it has been attempted to justify each of them is derived from inferences and constructions of the constitution, which its letter and its whole object and design do not warrant. Is it to be conceived that such immense powers would have been left by the framers of the constitution to mere inferences and doubtful constructions? Had it been intended to confer them on the Federal Government, it is but reasonable to conclude that it would have been done by plain and unequivocal grants. This was not done; but the whole structure of which the "American system" consisted, was reared on no other or better foundation than forced implications and inferences of power, which its authors assumed might be deduced by construction from the constitution.

But it has been urged that the National Bank, which constituted so essential a branch of this combined system of measures, was not a new measure, and that its constitutionality had been previously sanctioned, because a bank had been chartered in 1791, and had received the official signature of President Washington. A few facts will show the just weight to which this precedent should be entitled as bearing upon the question of constitutionality.

Great division of opinion upon the subject existed in Congress. It is well known that President Washington entertained serious doubts both as to the constitutionality and expediency of the measure; and while the bill was before him for his official approval or disapproval, so great were these doubts, that he required "the opinion in writing" of the members of his cabinet to aid him in arriving at a decision. His cabinet gave their opinion, and were divided upon the subject—General Hamilton being in favor of, and Mr. Jefferson and Mr. Randolph being opposed to the constitutionality and expediency of the bank. It is well known, also, that President Washington retained the bill from Monday, the fourteenth, when it was presented to him, until Friday, the twenty-fifth of February—being the last moment permitted him by the constitution to deliberate, when he finally yielded to it his reluctant assent, and gave it his signature. It is certain that as late as the twenty-third of February—being the ninth day after the bill was presented to him—he had arrived at no satisfactory conclusion; for on that day he addressed a note to General Hamilton, in which he informed him that "this bill was presented to me by the joint committee of Congress at 12 o'clock on Monday, the fourteenth instant;" and he requested his opinion, "to what precise period, by legal interpretation of the constitution, can the President retain it in his possession, before it becomes a law by the lapse of ten days." If the proper construction was, that the day on which the bill was presented to the President, and the day on which his action was had upon it, were both to be counted inclusive, then the time allowed him, within which it would be competent for him to return it to the House, in which it originated, with his objections, would expire on Thursday, the twenty-fourth of February. General Hamilton on the same day returned an answer, in which he states: "I give it as my opinion that you have ten days exclusive of that on which the bill was delivered to you, and Sundays; hence, in the present case, if it is returned on Friday, it will be in time." By this construction, which the President adopted, he gained another day for deliberation, and it was not until the twenty-fifth of February that he signed the bill; thus affording conclusive proof that he had at last obtained his own consent to sign it not without great and almost insuperable difficulty. Additional light has been recently shed upon the serious doubts which he had on the subject, amounting at one time to a conviction that it was his duty to withhold his approval from the bill. This is found among the manuscript papers of Mr. Madison, authorized to be purchased for the use of the Government by an act of the last session of Congress, and now for the first time accessible to the public. From these papers, it appears that President Washington, while he yet held the bank bill in his hands, actually requested Mr. Madison, at that time a member of the House of Representatives, to prepare the draught of a veto message for him. Mr. Madison, at his request, did prepare the draught of such a message, and sent it to him on the twenty-first of February, 1791. A copy of this original draught, in Mr. Madison's own handwriting, was carefully preserved by him, and is among the papers lately purchased by Congress. It is preceded by a note, written on the same sheet, which is also in Mr. Madison's handwriting, and is as follows:

"February 21st, 1791. Copy of a paper made out and sent to the President at his request, to be ready in case his judgment should finally decide against the bill for incorporating a national bank, the bill being then before him."

Among the objections assigned in this paper to the bill, and which were submitted for the consideration of the President, are the following:

"I object to the bill, because it is an essential principle of the Government that powers not delegated by the constitution cannot be rightfully exercised; because the power proposed by the bill to be exercised is not expressly delegated, and because I cannot satisfy myself that it results from any express power by fair and safe rules of interpretation."

The weight of the precedent of the bank of 1791, and the sanction of the great name of Washington which has been so often invoked in its support, are greatly weakened by the development of these facts. The experiment of that bank satisfied the country that it ought not to be continued, and at the end of twenty years Congress refused to recharter it. It would have been fortunate for the country, and saved thousands from bankruptcy and ruin, had our public men of 1816 resisted the temporary pressure of the times upon our financial and pecuniary interests, and refused to charter the second bank. Of this the country became abundantly satisfied, and at the close of its twenty years' duration, as in the case of the first bank, it also ceased to exist. Under the repeated blows of President Jackson, it reeled and fell, and a subsequent attempt to charter a similar institution was arrested by the veto of President Tyler.

Mr. Madison, in yielding his signature to the charter of 1816, did so upon the ground of the respect due to precedents; and, as he subsequently declared, "the Bank of the United States, though, on the original question, held to be unconstitutional, received the Executive signature."

It is probable that neither the bank of 1791, nor that of 1816, would have been chartered but for the embarrassments of the Government in its finances, the derangement of the currency, and the pecuniary pressure which existed—the first the consequence of the war of the Revolution, and the second the consequence of the war of 1812. Both were resorted to in the delusive hope that they would restore public credit, and afford relief to the Government, and to the business of the country.

Those of our public men who opposed the whole "American system," at its commencement, and throughout its progress, foresaw and predicted that it was fraught with incalculable mischiefs, and must result in serious injury to the best interests of the country. For a series of years their wise counsels were unheeded, and the system was established. It was soon apparent that its practical operation was unequal and unjust upon different portions of the country, and upon the people engaged in different pursuits. All were equally entitled to the favor and protection of the Government. It fostered and elevated the money-power, and enriched the favored few by taxing labor, and at the expense of the many. Its effect was to "make the rich richer, and the poor poorer." Its tendency was to create distinctions in society based on wealth, and to give to the favored classes undue control and sway in our Government. It was an organized money-power, which resisted the popular will, and sought to shape and control the public policy.

Under the pernicious workings of this combined system of measures, the country witnessed alternate seasons of temporary apparent prosperity; of sudden and disastrous commercial revulsions; of unprecedented fluctuation of prices, and depression of the great interests of agriculture, navigation, and commerce; of general pecuniary suffering, and of final bankruptcy of thousands. After a severe struggle of more than a quarter of a century, the system was overthrown.

The bank has been succeeded by a practical system of finance, conducted and controlled solely by the Government. The constitutional currency has been restored; the public credit maintained unimpaired, even in a period of foreign war; and the whole country has become satisfied that banks, national or State, are not necessary as fiscal agents of the Government. Revenue duties have taken the place of the protective tariff. The distribution of the money derived from the sale of the public lands has been abandoned, and the corrupting system of internal improvements, it is hoped, has been effectually checked.

It is not doubted, that if this whole train of measures designed to take wealth from the many, and bestow it upon the few, were to prevail, the effect would be to change the entire character of the Government. One only danger remains. It is the seductions of that branch of the system, which consists in internal improvements, holding out, as it does, inducements to the people of particular sections and localities to embark the Government in them without stopping to calculate the inevitable consequences. This branch of the system is so intimately combined and linked with the others, that as surely as an effect is produced by an adequate cause, if it be resuscitated and revived, and firmly established, it requires no sagacity to foresee that it will necessarily and speedily draw after it the re-establishment of a national bank, the revival of a protective tariff, the distribution of the land money, and not only the postponement to the distant future of the payment of the present national debt, but its annual increase.

I entertain the solemn conviction, that if the internal improvement branch of the "American system" be not firmly resisted at this time, the whole series of measures composing it will be speedily re-established, and the country be thrown back from its present high state of prosperity, which the existing policy has produced, and be destined again to witness all the evils, commercial revulsions, depression of prices, and pecuniary embarrassments, through which we have passed during the last twenty-five years.

To guard against consequences so ruinous, is an object of high national importance, involving, in my judgment, the continued prosperity of the country.

I have felt it to be an imperative obligation to withhold my constitutional sanction from two bills which had passed the two Houses of Congress, involving the principle of the internal improvement branch of the "American system," and conflicting in their provisions with the views here expressed.

This power, conferred upon the President by the constitution, I have on three occasions, during my administration of the Executive department of the Government, deemed it my duty to exercise; and on this last occasion of making to Congress an annual communication "of the state of the Union," it is not deemed inappropriate to review the principles and considerations which have governed my action. I deem this the more necessary, because, after the lapse of nearly sixty years since the adoption of the constitution, the propriety of the exercise of this undoubted constitutional power by the President, has for the first time been drawn seriously in question by a portion of my fellow-citizens.

The constitution provides that "every bill which shall have passed the House of Representatives and the Senate shall, before it becomes a law, be presented to the President of the United States: if he approve, he *shall* sign it; but if not, he *shall* return it, with his objections, to that House in which it shall have originated, who shall enter the objections at large on their Journal, and proceed to reconsider it."

The preservation of the constitution from infraction is the President's highest duty. He is bound to discharge that duty, at whatever hazard of incurring the displeasure of those who may differ with him in opinion. He is bound to discharge it, as well by his obligations to the people who have clothed him with his exalted trust, as by his oath of office, which he may not disregard. Nor are the obligations of the President in any degree lessened by the prevalence of views different from his own in one or both houses of Congress. It is not alone hasty and inconsiderate legislation that he is required to check; but if at any time Congress shall, after apparently full deliberation, resolve on measures which he deems subversive of the constitution, or of the vital interests of the country, it is his solemn duty to stand in the breach and resist them. The President is bound to approve, or disapprove, every bill which passes Congress and is presented to him for his signature. The constitution makes this his duty, and he cannot escape it if he would. He has no election. In deciding upon any bill presented to him, he must exercise his own best judgment. If he cannot approve, the constitution commands him to return the bill to the House in which it originated, with his objections; and if he fail to do this within ten days, (Sundays excepted,) it shall become a law without his signature. Right or wrong, he may be overruled by a vote of two-thirds of each House; and, in that event, the bill becomes a law without his sanction. If his objections be not thus overruled, the subject is only postponed, and is referred to the States and the people for their consideration and decision. The President's power is negative, merely, and not affirmative. He can enact no law. The only effect, therefore, of his withholding his approval of a bill passed by Congress, is to suffer the existing laws to remain unchanged, and the delay occasioned is only that required to enable the States and the people to consider, and act upon the subject in the election of public agents who will carry out their wishes and instructions. Any attempt to coerce the President to yield his sanction to measures which he cannot approve, would be a violation of the spirit of the constitution, palpable and flagrant; and if successful, would break down the independence of the Executive department, and make the President, elected by the people, and clothed by the constitutution with power to defend their rights, the mere instrument of a majority of Congress. A surrender, on his part, of the powers with which the constitution has invested his office, would effect a practical alteration of that instrument, without resorting to the prescribed process of amendment.

With the motives or considerations which may induce Congress to pass any bill, the President can have nothing to do. He must presume them to be as pure as his own, and look only to the practical effect of their measures when compared with the constitution or the public good.

But it has been urged by those who object to the exercise of this undoubted constitutional power, that it assails the representative principle and the capacity of the people to govern themselves; that there is greater safety in a numerous representative body, than in the single Executive created by the constitution, and that the Executive veto is a "one-man power," despotic in its character. To expose the fallacy of this objection, it is only necessary to consider the frame and true character of our system. Ours is not a consolidated empire, but a confederated Union. The States, before the adoption of the constitution, were co-ordinate, co-equal, and separate independent sovereignties, and by its adoption they did not lose that character. They clothed the Federal Government with certain powers, and reserved all others, including their own sovereignty, to themselves. They guarded their own rights, as States, and the rights of the people, by the very limitations which they incorporated into the Federal constitution, whereby the different departments of the General Government were checks upon each other. That the majority should govern, is a general principle, controverted by none; but they must govern according to the constitution, and not according to an undefined and unrestrained discretion, whereby they may oppress the minority.

The people of the United States are not blind to the fact that they may be temporarily misled, and that their representatives, legislative and executive, may be mistaken or influenced in their action by improper motives. They have therefore interposed between themselves and the laws which may be passed by their public agents, various representations, such as Assemblies, Senates, and Governors in their several States; a House of Representatives, a Senate, and a President of the United States. The people can by their own direct agency make no law; nor can the House of Representatives immediately elected by them; nor can the Senate; nor can both together, without the concurrence of the President, or a vote of two-thirds of both House.

Happily for themselves, the people, in framing our admirable system of Government, were conscious of the infirmities of their representatives; and, in delegating to them the power of legislation, they have fenced them around with checks, to guard against the effects of hasty action, of error, of combination, and of possible corruption. Error, selfishness, and faction have often sought to rend asunder this web of checks, and subject the Government to the control of fanatic and sinister influences; but these efforts have only satisfied the people of the wisdom of the checks which they have imposed, and of the necessity of preserving them unimpaired.

The true theory of our system is not to govern by the acts or decrees of any one set of representatives. The constitution interposes checks upon all branches of the Government, in order to give time for error to be corrected, and delusion to pass away; but if the people settle down into a firm conviction different from that of their representatives, they give effect to their opinions by changing their public servants. The checks which the people imposed on their public servants in the adoption of the constitution, are the best evidence of their capacity for self-government. They know that the men whom they elect to public stations are of like infirmities and passions with themselves, and not to be trusted without being restricted by co-ordinate authorities and constitutional limitations. Who that has witnessed the legislation of Congress for the last thirty years will say, that he knows of no instance in which measures not demanded by the public good, have been carried? Who will deny that, in the State governments, by combinations of individuals and sections, in derogation of the general interest, banks have been chartered, systems of internal improvement adopted, and debts entailed upon the people, repressing their growth, and impairing their energies for years to come?

After so much experience, it cannot be said that absolute unchecked power is safe in the hands of any one set of representatives, or that the capacity of the people for self-government, which is admitted in its broadest extent, is a conclusive argument to prove the prudence, wisdom, and integrity of their representatives.

The people, by the constitution, have commanded the President, as much as they have commanded the legislative branch of the Government, to execute their will. They have said to him in the constitution, which they require he shall take a solemn oath to support, that if Congress pass any bill which he cannot approve, "he shall return it to the House in which it originated, with his objections." In withholding from it his approval and signature, he is executing the will of the people constitutionally expressed, as much as the Congress that passed it. No bill is presumed to be in accordance with the popular will until it shall have passed through all the branches of the Government required by the constitution to make it a law. A bill which passes the House of Representatives may be rejected by the Senate; and so a bill passed by the Senate may be rejected by the House. In each case the respective Houses exercise the veto power on the other.

Congress, and each House of Congress, hold under the constitution a check upon the President, and he, by the power of the qualified veto, a check upon Congress. When the President recommends measures to Congress, he avows, in the most solemn form, his opinions, gives his voice in their favor, and pledges himself in advance to approve them if passed by Congress. If he acts without due consideration, or has been influenced by improper or corrupt motives—or if from any other cause Congress, or either House of Congress, shall differ with him in opinion, they exercise *their veto* upon his recommendations, and reject them; and there is no appeal from their decision, but to the people at the ballot-box. These are proper checks upon the Executive, wisely interposed by the constitution. None will be found to object to them, or to wish them removed. It is equally important that the constitutional checks of the executive upon the legislative branch should be preserved.

If it be said that the Representatives in the popular branch of Congress are chosen directly by the people, it is answered, the people elect the President. If both Houses represent the States and the people, so does the President. The President represents in the executive department the whole people of the United States, as each member of the legislative department represents portions of them.

The doctrine of restriction upon legislative and executive power, while a well-settled public opinion is enabled within a reasonable time to accomplish its ends, has made our country what it is, and has opened to us a career of glory and happiness to which all other nations have been strangers.

In the exercise of the power of the veto, the President is responsible not only to an enlightened public opinion, but to the people of the whole Union, who elected him, as the representatives in the legislative branches, who differ with him in opinion, are responsible to the people of particular States, or districts, who compose their respective constituencies. To deny to the President the exercise of this power, would be to repeal that provision of the constitution which confers it upon him. To charge that its exercise unduly controls the legislative will, is to complain of the constitution itself.

If the Presidential veto be objected to upon the ground that it checks and thwarts the public will, upon the same principle the equality of representation of the States in the Senate should be stricken out of the constitution. The vote of a Senator from Delaware has equal weight in deciding upon the most important measures with the vote of a Senator from New York; and yet the one represents a State containing, according to the existing apportionment of representatives in the House of Representatives, but one thirty-fourth part of the population of the other. By the constitutional composition of the Senate, a majority of that body from the smaller States represents less than one-fourth of the people of the Union. There are thirty States; and, under the existing apportionment of representatives, there are two hundred and thirty members in the House of Representatives. Sixteen of the smaller States are represented in that House by but fifty members; and yet the Senators from these States constitute a majority of the Senate. So that the President may recommend a measure to Congress, and it may receive the sanction and approval of more than three-fourths of the House of Representatives, and of all the Senators from the large States, containing more than three-fourths of the whole population of the United States; and yet the measure may be defeated by the votes of the Senators from the smaller States. None, it is presumed, can be found ready to change the organization of the Senate on this account, or to strike that body practically out of existence, by requiring that its action shall be conformed to the will of the more numerous branch.

Upon the same principle that the veto of the President should be practically abolished, the power of the Vice President to give the casting vote upon an equal division of the Senate, should be abolished also. The Vice President exercises the veto power as effectually by rejecting a bill by his casting vote, as the President does by refusing to approve and sign it. This power has been exercised by the Vice President in a few instances, the most important of which was the rejection of the bill to re-charter the Bank of the United States in 1811. It may happen that a bill may be passed by a large majority of the House of Representatives, and may be supported by the Senators from the larger States, and the Vice President may reject it by giving his vote with the Senators from the smaller States; and yet none, it is presumed, are prepared to deny to him the exercise of this power under the constitution.

But it is, in point of fact, untrue that an act passed by Congress is conclusive evidence that it is an emanation of the popular will. A majority of the whole number elected to each house of Congress constitutes a quorum, and a majority of that quorum is competent to pass laws. It might happen that a quorum of the House of Representatives, consisting of a single member more than half of the whole number elected to that House, might pass a bill by a majority of a single vote, and in that case a fraction more than one-fourth of the people of the United States would be represented by those who voted for it. It might happen that the same bill might be passed by a majority of one, of a quorum of the Senate, composed of Senators, from the fifteen smaller States, and a single Senator from a sixteenth State, and if the Senators voting for it happened to be from the eight of the smallest of these States, it would be passed by the votes of Senators from States having but fourteen Representatives in the House of Representatives, and containing less than one-sixteenth of the whole population of the United States. This extreme case is stated to illustrate the fact, that the mere passage of a bill by Congress is no conclusive evidence that those who passed it represent the majority of the people of the United States, or truly reflect their will. If such an extreme case is not likely to happen, cases that approximate it are of constant occurrence. It is believed that not a single law has been passed since the adoption of the constitution, upon which all the members elected to both Houses have been present and voted. Many of the most important acts which have passed Congress have been carried by a close vote in thin Houses. Many instances of this might be given. Indeed, our experience proves that many of the most important acts of Congress are postponed to the last days, and often the last hours of a session, when they are disposed of in haste, and by Houses but little exceeding the number necessary to form a quorum.

Besides, in most of the States the members of the House of Representatives are chosen by pluralities, and not by majorities of all the voters in their respective districts; and it may happen that a majority of that House may be returned by a less aggregate vote of the people than that received by the minority.

If the principle insisted on be sound, then the constitution should be so changed, that no bill shall become a law unless it is voted for by members representing in each House a majority of the whole people of the United States. We must remodel our whole system, strike down and abolish not only the salutary checks lodged in the Executive branch, but must strike out and abolish those lodged in the Senate also, and thus practically invest the whole power of the Government in a majority of a single assembly—a majority uncontrolled and absolute, and which may become despotic. To conform to this doctrine of the right of majorities to rule, independent of the checks and limitations of the constitution, we must revolutionize our whole system. We must destroy the constitutional compact by which the several States agreed to form a Federal Union, and rush into consolidation, which must end in monarchy or despotism. No one advocates such a proposition; and yet the doctrine maintained, if carried out, must lead to this result.

One great object of the constitution, in conferring upon the President a qualified negative upon the legislation of Congress, was to protect minorities from injustice and oppression by majorities. The equality of their representation in the Senate, and the veto power of the President, are the constitutional guarantees which the smaller States have that their rights will be respected. Without these guarantees, all their interests would be at the mercy of majorities in Congress representing the larger States. To the smaller and weaker States, therefore, the preservation of this power, and its exercise upon proper occasions demanding it, is of vital importance. They ratified the constitution, and entered into the Union, securing to themselves an equal representation with the larger States in the Senate; and they agreed to be bound by all laws passed by Congress, upon the express condition, and none other, that they should be approved by the President, or passed, his objections to the contrary notwithstanding, by a vote of two-thirds of both Houses. Upon this condition, they have a right to insist, as a part of the compact to which they gave their assent.

A bill might be passed by Congress against the will of the whole people of a particular State, and against the votes of its Senators and all its Representatives. However prejudicial it might be to the interests of such State, it would be bound by it if the President shall approve it, or it should be passed by a vote of two-thirds of both Houses; but it has a right to demand that the President shall exercise his constitutional power and arrest it, if his judgment is against it. If he surrender this power, or fail to exercise it in a case where he cannot approve, it would make his formal approval a mere mockery, and would be itself a violation of the constitution, and the dissenting State would become bound by a law which had not been passed according to the sanctions of the constitution.

The objection to the exercise of the *veto* power is founded upon an idea respecting the popular will, which, if carried out, would annihilate State sovereignty, and substitute for the present Federal Government a consolidation, directed by a supposed numerical majority. A revolution of the Government would be silently effected, and the States would be subjected to laws to which they had never given their constitutional consent.

The Supreme Court of the United States is invested with the power to declare, and has declared, acts of Congress passed with the concurrence of the Senate, the House of Representatives, and the approval of the President, to be unconstitutional and void; and yet none, it is presumed, can be found, who will be disposed to strip this highest judicial tribunal under the constitution of this acknowledged power—a power, necessary alike to its independence and the rights of individuals.

For the same reason that the Executive veto should, according to the doctrine maintained, be rendered nugatory, and be practically expunged from the constitution, this power of the court should also be rendered nugatory and be expunged, because it restrains the legislative and executive will, and because the exercise of such a power by the court may be regarded as being in conflict with the capacity of the people to govern themselves. Indeed, there is more reason for striking this power of the court from the constitution than there is that of the qualified veto of the President; because the decision of the court is final, and can never be reversed, even though both Houses of Congress and the President should be unanimous in opposition to it; whereas the veto of the President may be overruled by a vote of two-thirds of both Houses of Congress, or by the people at the polls.

It is obvious that to preserve the system established by the constitution, each of the co-ordinate branches of the Government—the executive, legislative, and judicial—must be left in the exercise of its appropriate powers. If the executive or the judicial branch be deprived of powers conferred upon either as checks on the legislative, the preponderance of the latter will become disproportionate and absorbing, and the others impotent for the accomplishment of the great objects for which they were established. Organized as they are by the constitution, they work together harmoniously for the public good. If the Executive and the Judiciary shall be deprived of the constitutional powers invested in them, and of their due proportions, the equilibrium of the system must be destroyed, and consolidation, with the most pernicious results, must ensue—a consolidation of unchecked, despotic power, exercised by majorities of the legislative branch.

The executive, legislative, and judicial, each constitutes a separate co-ordinate department of the Government; and each is independent of the others. In the performance of their respective duties under the constitution, neither can, in its legitimate action, control the others. They each act upon their several responsibilities in their respective spheres; but if the doctrines now maintained be correct, the executive must become practically subordinate to the legislative, and the judiciary must become subordinate to both the legislative and the executive; and thus the whole power of the Government would be merged in a single department. Whenever, if ever, this shall occur, our glorious system of well-regulated self-government will crumble into ruins—to be succeeded, first by anarchy, and finally by monarchy or despotism. I am far from believing that this doctrine is the sentiment of the American people; and during the short period which remains in which it will be my duty to administer the Executive Department, it will be my aim to maintain its independence, and discharge its duties, without infringing upon the powers or duties of either of the other departments of the Government.

The power of the Executive veto was exercised by the first and most illustrious of my predecessors, and by four of his successors who preceded me in the administration of the Government, and, it is believed, in no instance, prejudicially to the public interests. It has never been, and there is but little danger that it ever can be abused. No President will ever desire, unnecessarily, to place his opinion in opposition to that of Congress. He must always exercise the power reluctantly, and only in cases where his convictions make it a matter of stern duty, which he cannot escape. Indeed, there is more danger that the President, from the repugnance he must always feel to come in collision with Congress, may fail to exercise it in cases where the preservation of the constitution from infraction, or the public good, may demand it, than that he will ever exercise it unnecessarily or wantonly.

During the period I have administered the Executive Department of the Government, great and important questions of public policy, foreign and domestic, have arisen, upon which it was my duty to act. It may indeed be truly said, that my administration has fallen upon eventful times. I have felt most sensibly the weight of the high responsibilities devolved upon me. With no other object than the public good, the enduring fame, and permanent prosperity of my country, I have pursued the convictions of my own best judgment. The impartial arbitrament of enlightened public opinion, present and future, will determine how far the public policy I have maintained, and the measures I have from time to time recommended, may have tended to advance or retard the public prosperity at home, and to elevate or depress the estimate of our national character abroad.

Invoking the blessings of the Almighty upon your deliberations at your present important session, my ardent hope is, that in a spirit of harmony and concord, you may be guided to wise results, and such as may redound to the happiness, the honor, and the glory of our beloved country.

JAMES K. POLK.

WASHINGTON, *December* 5, 1848.

Mr. ATHERTON moved that five thousand copies of the Message, and two thousand copies of the Message and accompanying documents, in addition to the usual number, be printed for the use of the Senate.

The Senate then adjourned.

HOUSE OF REPRESENTATIVES.

TUESDAY, December 5.

President's Message.

A communication in writing was received from the President of the United States, by J. KNOX WALKER, his Private Secretary; which was read.

[See Senate report for the Message.]

IN SENATE.

THURSDAY, December 7.

Mr. BORLAND, of Arkansas, and Mr. RUSK, of Texas, appeared in their seats to-day.

The Journal having been read,

On motion, it was ordered, that when the Senate adjourns, it adjourn to meet on Monday.

Death of Hon. Dixon H. Lewis.

Mr. KING then rose, and addressed the Senate as follows:

I rise, Mr. President, to call the attention of this honorable body to an afflictive dispensation of Providence, which has deprived the Senate of the United States of one of its most esteemed and honored members, the country of a talented and useful citizen, and the State of Alabama of a vigilant and faithful representative.

On the 25th day of October last, and in the 47th year of his age, DIXON H. LEWIS, a Senator from the State of Alabama, breathed his last in the city of New York. Although far from his home, he was surrounded by anxious and devoted friends. The amiable and affectionate partner of his bosom watched over him with that tender care which none but woman could bestow; and nothing was omitted which, it was believed, could contribute to his recovery, allay his sufferings, or soothe his dying moments. His immortal spirit calmly passed away without a struggle, and his lifeless body alone remained to his bereaved family and sorrowing friends.

Then it was, Mr. President, that the Mayor and Common Council of the city of New York, actuated by that liberal spirit which has ever characterized the emporium of our country, desirous of showing the high respect in which they held that distinguished individual for his many private virtues and useful public services, asked and obtained permission to take upon itself the necessary arrangements for his funeral. They were of a public character, and conducted in such a manner as could not fail to be most gratifying to the family and friends of the deceased.

His body reposes in the beautiful grounds of Greenwood, in the identical spot, as I am informed, where he once expressed a wish to be interred, should it so happen that his earthly career should be terminated while in its vicinity. Providence so ordered it; and I avail myself of this occasion to tender to the Mayor and Common Council of the city of New York, the gratitude of the State of Alabama, for the distinguished respect paid to the memory of one of her most honored and cherished sons.

Mr. LEWIS, Mr. President, was a native of the State of Georgia. He received his education at the College of South Carolina, where, by his social qualities, he endeared himself to his associates; while his scholastic attainments furnished evidence that he was possessed of talents of a superior order, and pointed him out as one destined to acquire reputation in whatever pursuit he might engage.

On the completion of his collegiate course, Mr. LEWIS moved to the State of Alabama, became a student in a law office, and by close application, soon qualified himself for the bar. He obtained a license to practise in the several courts of the State. His professional career was short, but he had obtained a reputable standing; and had he continued to pursue the profession, he must soon have become eminent as a lawyer. The inclination, however, of Mr. LEWIS, immediately led him to engage in politics. He became a candidate for the State Legislature, and the people of the county in which he resided, elected him with great unanimity as one of its members. Although quite a young man, he very soon acquired a commanding influence with the members of the House in which he served.

Mr. LEWIS was what is termed a State-rights man, a strict constructionist; and, while a member of the Legislature, rendered himself conspicuous by an able advocacy of resolutions denying to Congress the power to establish a national bank, to impose a tariff for protection, or to execute works of internal improvement. His opinions were in accordance with those of a large majority of the people of Alabama; in the year 1829, as I believe, he was elected by the Congressional district in which he resided to represent them in the Congress of the United States. He continued, without intermission, to serve in the House of Representatives until the spring of the year 1844, commanding, by his talents, firmness, and urbanity, the respect and confidence of its members.

In 1844 a vacancy was produced in the Senate of the United States by my resignation, and Mr. LEWIS was appointed by the Governor of Alabama to fill the vacancy. On the meeting of the State Legislature, the selection of the Governor was approved, and Mr. LEWIS was elected, without opposition, for the unexpired term. Again was he chosen, at the session of the Legislature of the last winter, for the full term of six years.

Few, Mr. President, very few of the distinguished men of our country have, for so long a period, maintained their position in the councils of the nation, and have more firmly adhered to the principles they professed, than my late lamented colleague. Most of the Senators present have served with him, and to them I can fearlessly appeal to bear testimony to the high esteem in which he was held by his brother Senators, and to the zeal and ability with which he discharged the various duties which devolved upon him.

But it is not my purpose to pronounce a eulogy on the life and public services of DIXON H. LEWIS. They are known and properly appreciated by his countrymen; and nothing which I could say would add to his well-earned reputation, or cause his loss to be more deeply lamented. He has gone from among us; and the places which knew him shall know him no more forever.

It only remains for me, Mr. President, to submit the following resolutions for the adoption of the Senate:

Resolved, unanimously, That the Senate, from a sincere desire of showing every mark of respect due to the memory of the Hon. DIXON H. LEWIS, deceased, late a member thereof, will go into mourning by wearing crape on the left arm for thirty days.

Resolved, unanimously, That, as an additional mark of respect for the memory of the Hon. DIXON H. LEWIS, the Senate do now adjourn.

The resolutions being under consideration—

Mr. DIX said:

I rise, Mr. President, to second the resolutions offered by the honorable Senator from Alabama, (Mr. KING.)

When the career of his lamented colleague was suddenly terminated in the city of New York, I chanced to be there, and I was the only one of his associates on this floor who had the opportunity of following him to his final resting-place. It seemed to me for this reason that I might appropriately speak of his last illness; of the honors paid to his memory; and for the satisfaction of distant friends, of the spot where his remains repose. Of his talents, his patriotism, his public services, the kindly feeling which he carried into his intercourse with others, the purity of his private character, his stern integrity, and his fidelity to all the obligations of life, I need say nothing. On this subject the honorable Senator who moved the resolutions has left little to be said. But I cannot forbear to add, that all my intercourse with him in this body strongly impressed me with his liberality as a gentleman, his uprightness as a man, and his conscientiousness as a legislator.

Mr. LEWIS arrived at New York on the 9th of October, unwell, though not, as was supposed, seriously so. He accompanied a friend, shortly after his arrival, on an excursion through the city, and passed nearly an entire day in the examination of various objects of interest. On several succeeding days he was out again. But he soon afterwards became indisposed a second time; from this moment his strength rapidly declined, and on the 25th of October his connection with the things of earth was dissolved forever.

The Mayor of the city, on receiving the mournful intelligence, called the Common Council together, and it was immediately resolved, with one accord, to give his remains a public burial. I will not dwell on the funeral ceremonies performed at the City Hall, the words of eloquence spoken over him, or the extended procession moving through streets thronged with the population of the city. Suffice to say, the former Mayors of New York, members of Congress, State and city authorities, public societies, citizens, all united in paying the honors due to him as one of the representatives of a sovereign State in this body, cut off at a distance from those by whom these tributes of respect would otherwise have been rendered.

Thus attended, his remains were consigned to the earth, in one of the rural cemeteries, which the principal cities of New York and some of the neighboring States have, within a few years, set apart for the reception of their dead—places selected for their natural beauty, and adorned with all that art could devise, or taste suggest. Greenwood, where our departed associate lies, is one of the most beautiful of these receptacles for the dead. It is on Long Island, four miles from New York, and contains near two hundred acres, covered with forest trees, and in its season with luxuriant vegetation, swelling into hills and sinking into valleys and dells; where all that could offend the eye has given way to embellishments in harmony with "the religion of the place." There is nothing in which the spirit of improvement has manifested itself in a purer sentiment and taste. Our ancient burying-grounds were too often bare and unsheltered fields, on which settlement had encroached, and robbed them of their only fitness—solitude. Sometimes they had become unsightly enclosures, in the heart of busy towns, with the tide of population sweeping by, and the noisy conflict of life perpetually breaking the silence of the scene.

Turning from these exposed and neglected repositories to the rural cemeteries, the mind is relieved, and elevated by the contrast. It was a noble conception—worthy of our endowments and our destinies—to make the cities of the dead more attractive in their external aspect than the cities of the living.

Among the surest of our instincts is the desire that our own remains, and those of our kindred, may rest amid scenes of rural beauty in undisturbed repose. Nature herself associates quietude and stillness with sleep—whether it be the sleep of life or of death. It is her voice which speaks within us, when we ask that our last resting-place may be chosen apart from the turbulent haunts of men. It is said (with what truth I do not know) that Mr. LEWIS, when he first visited Greenwood, intimated a wish, if he should die in the neighorhood, that his remains might be deposited there. I have before me a letter from one of his most intimate friends in New York, who says: "A year ago he visited Greenwood, and was enchanted with it. He often referred to this visit, and spoke of the cemetery as above all others suited to be the last resting-place of men. It was, therefore, with melancholy pleasure that we selected it for him."

It is satisfactory to reflect, that he rests in the spot which so often called forth expressions of his admiration, and to believe that his own wishes, in this respect, could not have been better fulfilled. Near the principal entrance into these consecrated grounds, on a slight elevation, overlooking some of the most varied and beautiful scenery they contain, reposes all that was mortal of our deceased associate and friend. And if I might express the feeling of the community, by whom his remains were given back to the dust from which they came, it would be responsive to his own—that they may rest where, in the order of Providence, the thread of his life was severed—among those whose mournful privilege it was to enshrine them with the ashes of their own kindred. If this feeling shall be gratified, his family, his friends, the State he represented here, may be assured that he will lie among us —not as a stranger, but as one of ourselves—children alike of a common Union, and heirs of a common prosperity and fame.

Mr. DICKINSON said: With no ordinary emotion, Mr. President, I rise to unite in lamenting the dispensation which has deprived a sovereign State of an able and faithful representative, and the Senate of a courteous and honorable member; and to second, with my whole heart, the glowing and eloquent tribute which has just been paid to the memory of a valued friend by his late colleague. The deceased was amongst my earliest and most intimate acquaintances here. Our seats were adjoining, and we had much opportunity for free and friendly conversation. I found him kind, frank, and sincere; a ready and able counsellor; firm and decided in his opinions, yet yielding and conciliatory, and regardful of the opinions and motives of those with whom he differed. With an intuitive perception and a mind of uncommon vigor, he grasped the most intricate subjects; and, though he seldom spoke publicly, he gave evidence in his intercourse of the mature strength of the statesman and the cultivated taste of the scholar. Though he finished his earthly course in a State distant from his own, he died at home, for his home was the Union. He was surrounded by kind and sympathizing friends and skilful professional attendants, and the companion of his joys and sorrows stood by his bedside to smooth his dying pillow, and close his eyes in death. He expired in a city where his public services and private virtues were properly appreciated, and where the public authorities did honor to themselves and their State by paying becoming respect to his memory. His mortal remains were interred at Greenwood, whose fadeless verdure aptly illustrates the immortality to which his deathless spirit has flown, and where we are often admonished, by seats made vacant in our midst, we must soon be prepared to follow.

The resolutions were then agreed to, and

The Senate adjourned.

HOUSE OF REPRESENTATIVES.

THURSDAY, December 7.

The Journal of yesterday was read and approved.

Death of Hon. Dixon H. Lewis.

A message was here received from the Senate, informing the House of the death, during the recess of Congress, of the Hon. DIXON H. LEWIS, Senator from the State of Alabama.

The message having been read—

Mr. HARRIS, of Alabama, rose and addressed the House as follows:

Mr. Speaker, the communication just made by the Senate to the House, notifies us officially that a seat upon its floor is no longer filled by its accustomed occupant!—that DIXON H. LEWIS, another Senator of this great confederated republic, has passed from the council chambers of earth to the unseen, mysterious, and solemn realities of another state of existence. Days, yea weeks, have passed away since the unwelcome event was first heralded to the nation at large. We have all accustomed ourselves to contemplate the unalterable fact, free from that shock to the sensibilities of our nature which every generous bosom first feels when a good and a great man is called from his country, his family, and his friends. Perhaps the assuasive influence of time may have even partially relumed with returning cheerfulness the happy domestic circle, rendered lonely and desolate by his taking away. She, the companion of his youthful days; the mother of his children; his faithful, constant friend, even to the gates of death; she who bends lowest beside his bier; even she may have learned to school her wrung sensibilities to the hard lessons of Christian resignation! Heaven grant that it may be so!

But still, Mr. Speaker, the long and uninterrupted continuance in the councils of the country of this distinguished statesman, the relations of intimacy and friendship in which he stood to many on this floor, and of official responsibility and co-operation in which he stood to all, render peculiarly fit the melancholy task of pausing in the midst of other duties, briefly to contemplate the character of a great man, who was with us but yesterday, and with whom *we* may be to-morrow.

DIXON H. LEWIS was born in the county of Hancock, in the State of Georgia. At an early period of his life he emigrated with his father to the State of Alabama, then a new State, and destined to prove the cherishing friend of his unfolding talents and his manly virtues. At a premature age, he exhibited traits of that mental vigor and power of discrimination, which, in after years, developed and strengthened by exercise in the practical business of life, placed him among the profoundest statesmen of his country. His education was completed at South Carolina College, and there, within the walls of his *alma mater*, the first intellectual triumphs of the embryo statesman were achieved. In the emulous conflicts of scholastic rivalry, his were competitors whose ascendency would have reflected no discredit upon any from whom they might have snatched the palm. In the catalogue of names constituting the class in which Mr. LEWIS gradated, are an unprecedented number of those who have held high and prominent positions before the country; many of whom have graced with their presence the halls of this Capitol, and adorned other stations of equal responsibility in the States to which they respectively belonged. And yet among these stood, *primus inter pares*, the distinguished Senator whose death we deplore. Emerging from the shades of the academy crowned with its highest honors, and with a mind well stored with the rich endowments of classic lore, he entered upon the more rugged arena of practical life. And here the promise of his schoolboy days was not disappointed. Competition paused to admire his rapid and early ascendency to the head of his profession as a lawyer. He continued, however, but a short time at the bar. His active and excitable mind panted for a more enlarged and congenial range of thought than could be supplied by the dry details of the law. He stepped upon the theatre of politics, and there performed his part till the curtain of death concealed him from our eyes.

Perhaps no circumstance connected with the history of this eminent citizen is so demonstrative of his true worth, as the long uninterrupted career of public honor it was his fortune to enjoy. Scarce had he passed the boundary which separates youth from manhood, when, in eighteen hundred and twenty-six, the voice of the people placed him in the Legislature of his State. He took at once, and by common consent, a position in that body to which mere pretension or mediocrity would have aspired in vain. And be it spoken to his honor, as a consistent and far-sighted statesman, that at that period, twenty-two years ago, he impressed upon the archives of the State the evidence of those principles of public action from which, to the day of his death, he never departed. From the councils of the State he was transferred to this branch of Congress, and was removed hence only to be promoted to an office of still higher dignity in the other end of the Capitol. On this floor, he sat as a representative for eighteen consecutive years; in the Senate for two; and had been elected in December last for an additional full senatorial term, under circumstances which went far to show how strong the confidence his talents and fidelity had inspired. It was at a time like this, with the highest honor his State could bestow, newly conferred upon him, with a bright career of honor and usefulness before him, that the inexorable tyrant summoned him away.

DIXON H. LEWIS, whether we regard the physical, the mental, or the moral man, was cast in no ordinary mould. The more than usual proportions which distinguished him physically, but typified the large and comprehensive grasp of intellect which was his, and which directed the impulses of a heart which beat in unison with all that was generous or elevated in man. There was nothing grovelling in his nature. The attainment of "noble ends by noble means," was the highest reward to which his virtuous ambition aspired. From all expedients of doubtful propriety he shrunk with instinctive timidity. But, governed as he was in all the relations of life, by well-considered and fixed principles, he always moved forward to the performance of a known duty with a heart that knew no quailing. Hence, amid all the fluctuations of opinion to which the public mind has been subjected, since he became connected with the political history of his own times, his last recorded acts are in perfect consistence with his first. His nature was essentially democratic. His sympathies were ever with the masses. Hence his uniform opposition to every species of partial legislation, and his strenuous advocacy of whatever respected the greatest good of the greatest number. A more critical review of his public life than would be suited to the present occasion, would exhibit him as prominently connected with every great measure of progress and reform which has marked the last twenty years of our public history.

But his race on earth is ended. He will be missed from the councils of his country, so long adorned by his virtues and enlightened by his wisdom; from the social throng, once enlivened by the flow of his generous heart; but most of all, from that magic circle where cluster the hallowed affections of home, and where he formed the idol of every heart.

Unlike the patriarch statesman who fell before our eyes, full of years as well as of honors, his earthly sojourn was comparatively brief.

Forty-six years only served to fill the measure of his allotment in time. His sun of earthly existence was but at its meridian when the midnight of death was tolled; the summer of his life but half gone, when the sickle was put in, and the harvest gathered!

> The hand of the reaper
>   Takes the ears that are hoary;
> But the voice of the weeper
>   Wails manhood in glory.

Mr. HARRIS concluded by offering the following resolutions, which were read, as follows:

Resolved, That the House of Representatives has received with deep sensibility the message from the Senate announcing the death of the Hon. DIXON H. LEWIS, a Senator from the State of Alabama.

Resolved, That the members and officers of this House, from a sincere desire of manifesting their respect for the memory of the deceased, will wear the usual badge of mourning for thirty days.

Resolved, That the proceedings of this House, in relation to the death of the Hon. DIXON H. LEWIS, be communicated to his family by the Clerk.

Resolved, That, as a further mark of respect for the memory of the deceased, the House do now adjourn.

Before the question was put on the above resolutions—

On motion of Mr. HILLIARD, it was

Ordered, That when the House adjourns, it adjourn to meet on Monday next.

The question was then put on the foregoing resolutions, and they were unanimously adopted.

And the House accordingly adjourned to Monday, at twelve o'clock.

IN SENATE.

MONDAY, December 11.

Messrs. CLAYTON of Delaware, YULEE of Florida, and JOHNSON of Georgia, appeared in their seats.

The VICE PRESIDENT laid before the Senate a communication from the Navy Department, enclosing reports from the officers of the First and Second Comptrollers, in compliance with the act of May, 1820.

Mr. KING presented the credentials of BENJAMIN FITZPATRICK, appointed a Senator from the State of Alabama, to fill the vacancy caused by the death of the Hon. DIXON H. LEWIS.

The credentials having been read, Mr. FITZPATRICK was duly qualified, and took his seat.

Mr. FELCH presented the credentials of SOLON BORLAND, elected a Senator from the State of Arkansas, to fill the vacancy created by the resignation of the Hon. AMBROSE H. SEVIER.

The credentials having been read, Mr. BORLAND was qualified, and took his seat.

Chaplain.

On motion of Mr. KING, the Senate proceeded to the election of a Chaplain.

The Senators proceeded to ballot, and on the first ballot, the numbers appeared as follows:

Total number of votes	47
Necessary to a choice	24
For Mr. Slicer	28
Mr. Henshaw	6
Mr. Smith	9
Mr. Dewey	4
Blank	1

So the Rev. Mr. Slicer was re-elected Chaplain.

The Senate adjourned.

THURSDAY, December 14.

Death of Hon. A. D. Sims.

A message from the House of Representatives was received by Mr. CAMPBELL, their Clerk, announcing that the House had received information of the death of the Hon. A. D. SIMS, late a Representative from the State of South Carolina, and communicating the proceedings of the House thereupon.

The message having been read—

Mr. BUTLER rose and said:

Mr. PRESIDENT: My late colleague, the Hon. ALEXANDER DROMGOOLE SIMS, whose death has been announced by the message just read, took his seat in the House of Representatives, for the first time, in the Twenty-ninth Congress. A few days before his sudden death, which took place on the 16th of last month, at Kingstree, South Carolina, he learned that he had been returned for the third time, by the same district to Congress. These marks of popular favor were honorable evidence that he had won and retained the confidence of an intelligent constituency.

Mr. SIMS was born in Brunswick county, in Virginia, on the 12th of June, 1803. His highly respectable parents, though in moderate circumstances, belonged to that class of persons who placed a high value on the advantages of a liberal education; and two of their sons attained eminence and distinction, and by their success in life, made a worthy requital for the sacrifices of their parents.

The deceased, of whom I am speaking, if not a scholar in the highest import of that term, was a gentleman of excellent intellect, and of various and elegant literary attainments. His brother (late a professor of Alabama University) was an eminent divine and ripe scholar. My colleague, after passing through his ordinary academic course, became a student in the North Carolina University, and continued in that institution until his junior year, when, perhaps attracted by the high reputation of Dr. Nott, for whose character he seemed to have entertained a pious veneration, he joined one of the higher classes in Union College in the State of New York, and was graduated in that institution in 1823, leaving behind him a high reputation for capacity and attainments, especially in those branches of learning comprehending the tasteful pursuits of literature and the philosophy of the human mind.

On his return from college he studied law in the office of his uncle, (the late General DROMGOOLE,) and, for one or two years after his admission to the bar, he practised in the courts of Virginia. His success not being equal to his expectation or the aspirations of his ambition—for he was an ambitious man—he removed, in 1826, to Darlington district, South Carolina, and took charge of an academy. In this situation he was eminently useful, and laid the foundation of many enduring friendships, to which he may perhaps have been indebted for his subsequent success in life. Some of his pupils are now citizens of distinction, and bear testimony to the excellence of their teacher and preceptor, and perhaps the highest and most honorable movements he has left behind him, are the intelligent citizens who acknowledge with gratitude the instructions derived from him.

Mr. SIMS was admitted to the bar of South Carolina in the year 1829, and soon acquired a lucrative practice. As a counsellor, solicitor, and advocate, I can speak of him with unfeigned pleasure. Ha was engaged in the most important causes on his circuit, and was always equal to them. In the Supreme Court, some of his arguments are marked by research, learning, and ability.

His ambition aspired rather more to political distinction than to forensic reputation, and before he entered upon the responsible duties of public life, he took an active part in popular meetings in the exciting politics of the time. In 1840 he was returned a member of the Legislature of South Carolina. His efforts here enhanced his reputation among his constituents and fellow-citizens, and he was transferred to the Congress of the United States.

His career in that body is better known to others present than to myself. Judging from a notice taken of him in a late book of biographical sketches, he has acquired something like a historical reputation. In early life he was thoroughly schooled in the doctrines of the Republican party, and throughout his political career he adhered to them with consistency and firmness.

Mr. SIMS possessed in a very high degree what is implied in the term address. He was a pleasing speaker, a man of frank and conciliatory manners, and of kind and tolerant disposition.

The triumph of his late success, and his sudden death, were brought in instructive proximity with each other, and are mournful commentaries on the mutability of human life, and the nothingness of human ambition.

If he had faults, Mr. President, (and who of us is without them?—"the heart knoweth its own bitterness,") let them sleep with him in the grave, the common lot and the rebuking leveler of mankind.

Mr. President, I offer the following resolutions:

Resolved, unanimously, That the Senate has heard with deep sensibility of the sudden death of the Hon. ALEXANDER D. SIMS, a Representative from the State of South Carolina.

Resolved, unanimously, That the members of the Senate, from a sincere desire of showing every mark of respect to the memory of the deceased, will wear the usual badge of mourning for thirty days.

Resolved, unanimously, That, as a further mark of respect for the memory of the deceased, the Senate do now adjourn.

Agreed to, and the Senate adjourned.

HOUSE OF REPRESENTATIVES.

THURSDAY, December 14.

SAMUEL A. BRIDGES, from the State of Pennsylvania, appeared this day and took his seat.

Death of Hon. Alexander Dromgoole Sims.

Mr. WALLACE rose and said:

Mr. SPEAKER: I rise, sir, to call the attention of this honorable body to an afflictive dispensation of Divine Providence, which has deprived this House of one of its most useful members, and the State of South Carolina of a much valued and honored citizen.

On the 16th day of November last, in the forty-sixth year of his age, my colleague, the honorable ALEXANDER DROMGOOLE SIMS, breathed his last, in the village of Kingstree, Williamsburg district, in the State of South Carolina. He died, surrounded by devoted friends, in the midst of the people he so ably and faithfully represented on this floor.

The approach of death, even when his fatal

dart is pointed at the aged and infirm, to the reflecting mind, is always terrible; but it is calculated to impress our minds with feelings of far more than ordinary solemnity, when the blow falls upon the young, or when a brother, in all the pride of his strength, in the full vigor of health and manhood, full of hope and of promise, is stricken down before our eyes, and his connection with the things of this world forever dissolved.

A few days only has passed since my honorable colleague filled that seat (pointing to Mr. SIMS's seat on the floor of the House) with distinguished honor to himself and his country. He was in the prime of life, in the full enjoyment of health, and apparently with a long and honorable career of usefulness and distinction in the path of life before him. But when most unlooked for by himself or his friends, "the silver cord was loosed, the pitcher broken at the fountain," and he now calmly sleeps, undisturbed and unshaken by the rude blasts of life, "in the narrow house appointed for all living."

This awful dispensation of Divine Providence is of consequence not only to the dead, to the immortal destiny of our departed friend, but is full of instruction and admonition to the living also. It most forcibly reminds us of the frail and uncertain tenure of human life, the vanity and nothingness of all human ambition and human pursuits, and that, of a truth, "in the midst of life we are in death."

Mr. SIMS was a native of Virginia, and was born in Brunswick county, in that State, in the year 1803. At the age of twenty-three, he graduated at Union College, in the State of New York. After the close of his collegiate course, he read law with his friend and relative General Dromgoole, at one time a distinguished member of this honorable body from the State of Virginia.

In 1826, he removed to Darlington district, in the State of South Carolina; and in 1829, was admitted to the practice of law in the courts of that State, where he soon rose to eminence in his profession, in the practice of which he continued until the year 1840, when he was returned a member of the General Assembly for Darlington, in which service he continued until elected to Congress, in 1844. And his constituency, among the most intelligent in the State, have pronounced their approval of his course as a member of this honorable body, by re-electing him *twice* to the same responsible position, his last election having transpired but a few days before his death.

Mr. SIMS was a statesman of the State-rights school, and his public life—at all times distinguished by much ability, the strictest integrity, and a conscientious discharge of every duty—was in strict conformity to the doctrines of the true republican faith.

Of our departed friend it may be truly said, he was a faithful friend and a true patriot—the honest man and the worthy citizen. But it has pleased an all-wise Providence to remove him hence; and while we bow with humble resignation to the will of Him who holds the destinies of nations as well as individuals in his hand, we, at the same time, cannot but feel that the loss of a citizen of such distinguished public worth and ability is indeed a public calamity.

In order, Mr. Speaker, that suitable and appropriate honors may be paid to the memory of the distinguished dead, I move, sir, the following resolutions:

Resolved, unanimously, That this House, from a sincere desire of showing every mark of respect due to the memory of the Hon. ALEXANDER D. SIMS, deceased, late a member of this body, will go into mourning by wearing crape on the left arm for thirty days.

Resolved, unanimously, That, as a further mark of respect to the memory of the Hon. ALEXANDER D. SIMS, this House do now adjourn.

And the House adjourned until to-morrow at twelve o'clock.

IN SENATE.

MONDAY, December 18.

Railroad across the Isthmus.

Mr. BENTON moved that the Senate proceed to the consideration of the special order, being the bill to make compensation for the transportation of troops and supplies, for a limited time, over the Isthmus of Panama; which motion was agreed to.

Mr. BENTON then said: Mr. President, the object of that bill has been very fully set forth by the petition of the memorialists, which was laid before the Senate several days since, and which has been printed by order of the Senate for the use of its members, and reprinted in the newspapers in this city, and many newspapers throughout the country.

The object which the petition so fully, and yet so briefly and clearly points out, needs nothing at all from me to enhance it in the estimation of this body or the country. It is vain, sir, for me to enlarge upon the subject. This great object, favored by all persons and circumstances and considerations, needs no commendation from me.

The bill, Mr. President, puts it into the hands of the Secretary of the Navy to contract with those petitioners for a limited time, and for a sum not exceeding a certain amount.

The conclusion of this contract is put into the hands of the Secretary of the Navy, because in his hands alone is the great business of the mail steamers plying between our possessions on the Atlantic and our possessions on the Pacific side of North America. These mail steamers are designed, to a certain extent, to become auxiliary and subservient to the naval operations of the United States, liable to become a part of its naval force, and on that account they are not under the control of the Postmaster-General, to whom their immediate supervision would seem to belong.

Nor does this bill command the Secretary of War—to whom, also, might be referred the approval of such contracts with propriety—to conclude it. The Secretary of the Navy is the person to whom the bill refers the conclusion of the contract, because he already has in his hands the great business of controlling the Steamships which carry mails between the eastern and western extremes of our possessions, and it only lacks, sir, that a link be completed which lies between the Atlantic and Pacific Oceans, to perfect the communication between the two sides of our continent.

The bill also provides for the transportation of naval as well as military stores; therefore, it very appropriately refers the completion of the contract to the Secretary of the Navy.

The persons, Mr. President, named in the bill, and who, if the bill passes, are those with whom the contract will be made, are persons who, in my opinion, are entitled to the most favorable consideration. They are, in the first place, persons who are acquainted practically with what they undertake to do. One of the petitioners, Mr. Stephens, is known throughout the reading world for his travels in a part of South America, which lies near the country over which this road is to run. Besides being known as a traveller in all this region, he has visited the isthmus in company with two engineers, to ascertain for himself, not merely the practicability, but the cost of the work; and, though necessarily aided by the surveys which have been made heretofore under the contracts of different governments, he has nevertheless examined every inch of ground himself, accompanied by skilful engineers, who have made their own report of the route. He has knowledge upon the subject, and without knowledge of the subject, it is in vain for anybody to undertake it.

The company who apply for this privilege have another recommendation—that of capital to accomplish it. They then, sir, have another recommendation, which is, an interest in the completion of the work. They are the contractors for the transportation of the mails on the other side of the isthmus. They have already put afloat three steamers of the first class, which have cost them six hundred thousand dollars. These steamers are now passing around to commence the business of transportation on the other side of the isthmus. They have, then, a great sum already embarked in this business, and they have a direct interest in making successful the large amount of money which they have invested on the other side. They who undertake to carry "persons and things" from the other side of the isthmus are those who, above all others, are the most interested in having the means of accomplishing, in the shortest possible time, the transit across the isthmus of the "persons and things" in the transportation of which their success depends. They have a direct interest in their money already invested, and they have an interest in the success of their enterprise.

They have another reason, Mr. President, why they should have this grant from us. They already have it from the Government which owns the country—from the Government of New Granada—and are at this time in possession of the privilege of opening this road.

I will read to the Senate the letter of General Herran, Minister from New Granada to this Government, procured by these three gentlemen, Messrs. Aspinwall, Stephens, and Chauncey. It is dated—

LEGATION OF NEW GRANADA,
Washington, Dec. 18, 1848.

GENTLEMEN: I have had various conferences with Mr. John L. Stephens, as representative of the association which you have formed, and with powers sufficient to solicit the privilege of constructing a railroad in the Isthmus of Panama, under the conditions which, in the name of my Government, I have proposed to him. From these conferences it has resulted that Mr. Stephens has given me sufficient guarantees, besides those which are expressed in the privilege conceded to Matthew Klein, under date of the 8th of June, 1847, to insure the execution of this work, [this is a very material statement, sir,] and that your association binds itself to fulfil the conditions which I have proposed in favor of New Granada, besides those which are set forth in the privilege.

In virtue of this agreement, I declare that you are in possession of the privilege conceded by the Government of New Granada for the construction of a railroad over the Isthmus of Panama.

I am, your very obedient servant,
P. A. HERRAN.

Messrs. W. H. ASPINWALL, JNO. STEPHENS, and HENRY CHAUNCEY.

This letter is in Spanish, sir, and I give it a literal translation as I go on. The last sentence is perhaps the most essential of all. "In virtue of this agreement I declare that you are in possession of the privilege conceded by the Government of New Granada for the construction of a railroad over the Isthmus of Panama."

So, that, Mr. President, besides securing to these applicants this contract heretofore, as stated by them in their petition, the Minister of New Granada has now, on this day, given them an official letter declaring that they are in possession of it. And it is probable that the Minister himself may be within the sound of my voice when I make this declaration, that he has, on this day, and for the purpose for which it is now used, declared that these persons are in possession of the privilege granted by that Government. Let it be known that this day the parties are in possession.

I deem it fortunate, Mr. President, that, after the delays which have taken place for more than three centuries, in executing some easy and practicable communication between these two great oceans, the time has arrived now when the great work can be accomplished. Two Governments, both in the New World, republics, and friendly to each other, have entered into a treaty for the purpose of securing the execution of this work. An article has been inserted in the treaty, unanimously agreed to on the part of the American Senate, by which, sir, we acquire an interest, an invaluable interest, in the use of that work, provided we use the right secured to us of opening the way across the isthmus.

This is done by two Republics—powers of the New World—acting together in making this treaty, and taking into their own hands as appropriate, the great work which is to carry into effect the great idea of Columbus, in proposing to go west in order to arrive at the east. It is now in our power to accomplish it. The petitioners undertake to do it within three years; and that undertaking is made by an actual view, an actual examination by engineers of the whole work to be accomplished. Their contract with the Government of New Granada gives them eight years in which to do this work. The privilege of which they alone are now in possession expires after eight years, and does not expire for eight years; but, actuated by their own interests, as well as anxious to comply with the universal desire to facilitate the intercourse between the two great oceans, these petitioners are ready to accomplish this work within less than half the time.

This is as desirable to us, to the Government of this country, and to all who have yet to traverse the two oceans, as it is to them. Their interest requires it, and our convenience, and the successful carrying on of our own business requires it also. In the case of this company—informed as they are—acquainted as they are with the work which they have to do, and in possession of the necessary capital to accomplish it—already having six hundred thousand dollars invested in the line, which is on the other side of the Isthmus, and deeply interested in the returns which they have themselves to get from capital already laid out—we have every possible human guarantee that these gentlemen will have the work accomplished within the time which they name. Then, Mr. President, it is a subject of congratulation, a subject of rejoicing, that the United States of America, one of the first powers in the world, shall be the first to carry out the great idea of Columbus of going west to obtain the east. Other plans may follow, sir. There is one contemplated across the Isthmus of Tehuantepec by an English company. Let it go on. Let it succeed. Let there be as many as possible. But, sir, when that work is accomplished, it is still a British work. It is none of ours. It is not guaranteed to us by treaties. We will have to take our chance along with other nations.

We may also, sir, in time, perhaps before long, accomplish the great idea of Mr. Jefferson in sending Lewis and Clarke to the Pacific Ocean, the great object of which was to examine into the practicability of opening a communication between the two sides of the continent. We may have an American road yet to the Pacific Ocean: but that must be a work of time. The work across the Isthmus of Tehuantepec may be called a foreign work, as it concerns us. This across the Isthmus of Darien may be considered an American work, and that will be completed immediately. I hope, then, that the Senators may see that every interest and every feeling that belongs to the Americans—for I appropriate that term by way of distinction to the first power in the New World—should make us anxious to accomplish this work, and to do it at once. Great will be the pride of all America to be the first to accomplish this work, and to accomplish it under circumstances which will give it a national character with respect to ourselves.

Mr. BREESE. Mr. President, I do not rise at this time for the purpose of discussing the merits of this important enterprise. I shall leave that for some other and more auspicious time. But I rise to express my hope that the honorable Senator from Missouri will not attempt to precipitate action upon this bill, nor attempt to get a vote of the Senate upon it to-day, nor this week, but that he will give us ample time and abundant opportunity to consider it fully in all its details, and in its whole scope. I rise, sir, merely to state to the Senate that I have received information, upon which I can implicitly rely, that a far more beneficial proposition than this presented by the Committee on Military Affairs, will very soon be offered for the consideration of the Senate.

Sir, this is a vast matter, and a vast undertaking which these individuals, the memorialists to this Government, are about to attempt, and for which they are to receive the sanction, patronage, and funds of the Government. If I understand any thing about it, this road will be about fifty miles in length, which, at a cost of fifty thousand dollars per mile, would amount to a little more than two millions of dollars. And now, sir, by this bill the Government proposes to pay to them, for twenty years, six millions of dollars for transportation of all kinds, leaving a profit of four millions, without counting the tolls levied on that portion of the commerce of the world that may pass over the route.

The Senator says we have obtained the right to pass across the isthmus by treaty with New Granada, and that that right will be gone unless we exercise it. What is that right designated by the 35th article of the treaty? It is nothing more than a right of way guaranteed to us, and we are not subjected to the condition of constructing a road in order to secure the privileges guaranteed by this right of way.

I hope the attention of the Senate will be called to this matter, and to the vast sum of money proposed to be paid to these gentlemen; and that Senators will bear in mind that a proposition much more favorable will be presented to them. The Senate, therefore, should not act hastily upon this subject, but give us all time to look into it, and to make up our minds fully in regard to it.

HOUSE OF REPRESENTATIVES.

WEDNESDAY, December 20.

Territorial Government.

Mr. SMITH, of Indiana, from the Committee on the Territories, reported a bill to establish the Territorial Government of Upper California, which was read and committed.

IN SENATE.

FRIDAY, January 5, 1849.

Purchase of Cuba.

The following resolution, offered by Mr. MILLER, December 18, was taken up for consideration:

Resolved, That the President of the United States be requested to inform the Senate whether any, and what negotiations or correspondence have taken place between this Government and the Government of Spain, or between any persons acting under the direction or authority of either Government, in relation to the purchase of Cuba by the United States; and that he communicate to the Senate copies of such negotiations or correspondence, so far as the same may be communicated consistently with the public interest.

Opposition being manifested—

Mr. MILLER called for the yeas and nays on the adoption of the resolution, but the call was not sustained..

Mr. RUSK moved to lay the resolution on the table, but withdrew the motion.

Several SENATORS called for the yeas and nays on this motion.

Mr. MILLER rose to offer some explanations concerning the resolution; when—

Mr. DICKINSON said the question was not now debatable.

Mr. MILLER. I hope that the Senator who moved to lay the resolution on the table will withdraw his motion, in order to allow me an opportunity to say a few words in explanation.

Mr. RUSK. I have no objections, so far as the subject is under my control, to allow the gentleman from New Jersey to offer any explanations he may be pleased to make. For one, I do not believe that any such negotiations or correspondence have been entered into by the two Governments named in the resolution; and the only authority for entertaining any such belief, on the part of any one, is a few vague rumors which have been circulated in some of the newspapers.

Mr. MILLER. I would state to the Senate that this resolution is in the ordinary form of resolutions of inquiry of this nature. The answer to the resolution is submitted to the discretion of the President. If he thinks it inconsistent with the public interest to give the information asked for, he may decline to furnish it.

When the resolution was called up a few days since, the Senator from Georgia (Mr. BERRIEN) suggested to the Senate that it was not strictly in order to present a resolution of this kind in open Senate, but that it should be made the subject of executive session. Since that time I have been looking into the precedents of this kind, and I find abundance of them, which authorized the presentation of this resolution in open Senate.

Resolutions requiring information from the President in regard to correspondence between this Union and other nations might, perhaps, develop matters which it would be more proper to deliberate and act upon in executive session. But in the cases of the negotiations between this Government and Mexico, and in the negotiations with regard to the annexation of Texas, and the negotiations between this Government and Great Britain in relation to the Territory of Oregon, resolutions of this kind were offered and received in open Senate. Therefore the resolution is not subject to any objection of that character.

Again: I consider that the subject matter of this resolution is not of the ordinary character. This matter of purchasing foreign nations, people, and territories, is not of the ordinary character of the negotiations between nations. Hence I deemed it proper to offer this resolution, for the purpose of informing the country whether any negotiations of this kind have been carried on between this and the Spanish Government.

My impression at the time I offered the resolution was, and still is, that if any such negotiations between the two nations are in progress, the country ought to be informed of the fact: the country should know it before the object of the negotiation is consummated; and it was for this purpose that I presented the resolution.

Mr. RUSK. I wish simply to ask the honorable Senator from New Jersey, if he entertains any suspicion that such negotiations or correspondence are or have been in progress?

Mr. MILLER. Since the honorable Senator from Texas has propounded the question, I must say that I have such suspicions. I know very well, sir, that the pretty general impression of the country is, that something of the kind has been going on, and my only object in offering the resolution was to elicit the truth, and quiet the public mind.

Mr. FOOTE. From the manner in which this subject has been introduced by the Senator from New Jersey, I feel myself authorized to propound an inquiry to him, which he may answer or not, at his pleasure and discretion. I wish to know whether, in the event of his ascertaining that any correspondence or negotiations in reference to this subject have actually taken place, he is prepared to assume an attitude hostile to the annexation of Cuba to this country, and whether he is or is not prepared to act upon the subject? If he is not prepared to act, then I think there is no necessity for this resolution. If, however, the Senator from New Jersey, in the event of such a correspondence or negotiation having actually occurred, or being in progress, intends to throw obstacles in the way, for the purpose of preventing its consummation, there is some reason for his resolution; but if he intends to remain inactive, and is resolved that no action shall follow after the information shall be obtained, I must repeat that I see not the slightest reason whatever for the passage of the resolution.

Mr. Dickinson. I renew the motion to lay the resolution on the table.

Mr. Miller. I hope the honorable Senator from New York will withdraw his motion for a moment, in order that I may reply to the question of the Senator from Mississippi.

Mr. Dickinson. I will withdraw my motion if the Senator from New Jersey will renew it after he has made his reply.

Mr. Miller. I would not like to renew the motion to lay the resolution on the table myself, but I have no doubt others will do it. The gentleman can renew it himself.

Mr. Dickinson. I will withdraw my motion for the present.

Mr. Miller. Mr. President, perhaps it would be wise in me to reserve my answer to the question of the Senator from Mississippi till the facts of the case are laid before the country. But I have no desire to conceal my opinions or intentions in regard to this matter. My own opinion is made up upon this subject, and I do not hesitate to say that I shall be opposed to the annexation of Cuba to this country, at all times and under all circumstances.

Mr. Foote. I would simply state, that if such be the determination of the honorable Senator from New Jersey, he will find himself in an awkward position in less than four months, for the President elect is decidedly in favor of the annexation of Cuba, and has so declared himself.

Mr. Dickinson renewed his motion to lay the resolution on the table.

Mr. Hale called for the yeas and nays, which were ordered, and decided in the affirmative—yeas 23, nays 19.

So the resolution was laid on the table.

Tuesday, January 9.

Admission of California.

Mr. Berrien, from the Committee on the Judiciary, to whom was referred the bill for the admission of California into the Union as a State, reported the same back without amendment, and submitted a report in writing.

The report was read by the Secretary.

Wednesday, January 17.

Reduced Rates of Postage.

Mr. Niles moved to postpone the prior orders of the day, with a view to take up the bill to reduce the rates of postage and for other purposes.

The motion having been agreed to, the bill was taken up and considered as in Committee of the Whole.

The bill was read by sections.

Mr. Niles. The question is upon the amendments offered by the committee. The committee have had these amendments under consideration since they were printed; and in consequence of the treaty with Great Britain, they have deemed it necessary to alter some parts of the section relating to foreign letter postage. I have to offer an amendment as a substitute for the fourth section, adopting the rules prescribed in the treaty with England—which we are bound by that treaty to adopt—with respect to our postal connections with her; and which rules, from the consideration of having uniformity in the matter, they have concluded to adopt in relation to the postal arrangements with all other foreign countries.

Mr. Niles. Mr. President, I presume the Senate would obtain a very correct idea of the section and the amendment offered as a substitute from their reading; but, perhaps a few words of explanation will not be amiss. By the recent treaty with England, we have established the rate of steam postage on all letters conveyed in her mails into that country, or in any mails of Great Britain and the United States, at sixteen cents; with the additional provision, also, that the inland postage of letters for England through the United States shall be five cents, and the inland postage of our letters through Great Britain three cents—making twenty-four cents, as the combined postage on letters going in our steamers or their steamers. Well, sir, as we were under the necessity of adopting these rates in our intercourse with Great Britain, we thought it best to make the rule applicable to all other countries, and therefore fixed the uniform rate of postage upon all other foreign letters conveyed in our mails at twenty-one cents; this rate to prevail with Great Britain or any other foreign country with whom we have established mail lines. This amount of twenty-one cents is uniform in its application to other countries, so that a person can send a letter from Liverpool, Bremen, or any other part of the Continent, at precisely the same rate of postage as it is received at New York. The same rate applies in regard to letters received from foreign countries, it being deemed necessary by the committee to preserve as much uniformity as possible; it making, therefore, no difference between letters received at New York from abroad, and those which may be received at any distant part of the country, fixing the English postage in all cases at five cents.

The section provides further, in regard to letters not conveyed in the foreign mails of the United States, where we cannot control the postage, except the English postage, that the same principle shall obtain, fixing the rate of postage on letters thus conveyed at five cents. This is the whole charge we impose on them. They of course will be subjected to the rate of foreign postage, sixteen cents in British mails—the only country that has any mail line established permanently to the United States.

A further provision is made in this section with regard to letters conveyed in private vessels that do not carry regular public mails. The section is limited to letters that are actually posted in the United States. Thus they are received by such vessels, and when they come into our ports go to the post office; and the provision is, that those that come from such vessels to the post office, or go from the post office to such vessels, pay five cents postage, including inland postage; so that in all parts of the United States the postage may be the same. As this section covers the whole of the arrangements for foreign postage, there is also a provision in regard to postage on pamphlets, magazines, and newspapers, though the postage upon this description of mailable matter has also been controlled by the treaty with England. The treaty fixes the rate of postage on a newspaper by its weight; the English rate of postage upon a newspaper being one penny English currency, while we have adopted two cents. This is a very low postage, and the committee had some doubts whether the sum would cover the English postage as well as the steam postage; but, considering that the bill proposes to reduce the newspaper postage at home to one cent and to half a cent, they thought it on the whole best to preserve uniformity, and that it would be better to let the rate stand at two cents, including the steam postage as well as inland. So that newspapers as well as letters can be received throughout the United States at uniform rates of two cents; the same to those going out of the country.

In respect to pamphlets, the custom of the English postal system is a singular one. They adopt a low rate for the first ounce, a higher rate for the second, and so progress upwards. We have adopted their rule in part. We propose the rate of two cents—a sum to which we are confined in the treaty as far as England is concerned—for the first ounce, including English postage, and we increase the postage on such mail matter as pamphlets and magazines, according to weight. We propose to advance the postage as the weight increases, but not to continue the principle of progression as the English law does. We merely propose to double the charge upon all exceeding the first rate. The first rate is two ounces. The English mail carries two ounces for one penny. Our old law fixed the rate at two and a half cents, and one cent for every succeeding ounce. I think we have had very good reasons for making these changes, particularly in regard to letters. With regard to these pamphlets, which are an important item in the communication between the two countries, this provision of the bill, I think, is very liberal—about what it ought to be. It fixes the first rate of two ounces at two cents, all beyond that at two cents the ounce; and this in the progression is considerably below the English rate of postage for similar matter. The first rate, as I have said, of this class of matter is two ounces, which is subject to one penny postage in England, and which we have been bound by the treaty not to increase. The first rate of two ounces is two cents, and an additional two cents for all beyond that.

Mr. DAYTON. Mr. President, it is certainly very desirable that this bill should be acted upon, and acted upon promptly. But it is still more desirable that it should be acted upon intelligibly. Now, if I understand the amendment offered by the Senator from Connecticut, and that portion of his remarks I have been able to hear, it seems to me that, in reference to the subject of foreign postage, it is an entirely new bill, regulating the whole subject matter of foreign postage as applied to letters, newspapers, periodicals, and every thing of that description; and likewise as affecting the question of franking, this amendment is a most important one. It has just been offered, and I am perfectly satisfied that Senators have not been able to give it a satisfactory examination; and, for one, I would much prefer that the bill and amendments offered by the Senator from Connecticut should be laid upon the table, and printed by the Senate for the use of its members.

Mr. NILES was understood to say that he thought Senators had had time to consider the whole subject. He thought that if Senators had paid a little attention to the amendment when it was read, and to his subsequent explanation of it, they would have been able to understand the subject very well; but he presumed that, on account of the noise which prevailed in the Chamber, some Senators had not been able to hear the amendment and his remarks upon it very distinctly. He did not know when they would have a more favorable opportunity to consider the subject than the present. The whole matter had been before the country for some time, and the bill with the original amendments had been printed in all the newspapers, and he presumed they had been read and discussed by Senators and the people generally. The amendment which he had just offered was one which he presumed would not attract much attention here, although one of very great use to the country. The original amendments proposed by the committee had been printed, but the amendment which he had just presented did not come from the committee, and he did not propose to have it printed at all. He did not wish to embarrass the committee, and he thought it his duty to offer the amendment in the Senate, in order that they might decide upon it as they might deem best.

In regard to the section that had just been read, and upon which he had made a few remarks, he would say, that although it had been considerably altered from that reported from the committee, it was much the same thing in substance as the corresponding section that had been printed. The alterations which had been made, had been rendered necessary by the late treaty in regard to postal arrangements which have been entered into between this country and Great Britain. In the section reported by the committee, he would remark, the foreign postage had been stated at twenty-one cents. That was the sea postage, and it left the inland postage in this country and other countries to be regulated by the laws here and the laws there. But an arrangement having been made between this country and Great Britain in relation to the inland as well as the sea postage upon letters passing between the two countries, it had been thought best that all foreign postage rates should be made uniform, and in consequence the amendment to establish the uniform rate of twenty-one cents upon all letters sent to or received from foreign countries had been proposed.

Mr. WESTCOTT. I would inquire of the Chair whether the amendments that were reported by the Post Office Committee last week have been adopted?

The VICE PRESIDENT. These amendments have not been adopted. The question of their adoption is now pending, and also upon the amendment offered by the Senator from Connecticut.

Mr. NILES. Mr. President, I would say to my friend from New Jersey, (Mr. DAYTON,) and others, that I desire to get the action of the Senate upon the amendments, and, if they are adopted, I shall not object to the postponement of the bill in order to have it printed as amended.

This is a subject which every one must see depends very much upon the arrangement and perfection of its details. We had the subject under consideration nearly the whole of last session, and it has been discussed and debated in full; and, as the merits of the whole bill depend upon the details, I would like to get these amendments acted upon, as the committee wish to get the bill and amendments before the Senate in a connected form, and that has been my sole object to-day.

Mr. PEARCE. Mr. President, there are some amendments to this bill to which I shall be opposed; but the particular amendment under consideration seems to me to be entirely proper. That amendment relates to the postage of letters sent by sea, and has received the approbation of the whole Postage Committee. I believe the Senator from Connecticut has explained that, by the postal arrangements with Great Britain, certain rates of postage have been imposed upon letters sent or received by the British mail steamers, or by our own mail steamers, to and from Great Britain. The only object of the amendment proposed by the Senator from Connecticut, is to equalize the rates of postage upon all letters sent by sea. It is manifest and proper that we should not have one rate of postage where letters or papers are sent to or received from Great Britain, and another rate upon letters and papers which come from or are sent to other countries beyond the sea. The only object of this amendment is to equalize the rates of postage in all such cases. It seems to me that this is very proper, and cannot be liable to any manner of objection. The Senator from New Jersey cannot, I think, object to the amendments being acted upon in committee, and then printed for the use of the Senate.

Mr. DAYTON, (interposing.) I have no objection to that.

The amendment to the amenament was agreed to.

HOUSE OF REPRESENTATIVES.

THURSDAY, January 18.

The Question as to the Territory of Wisconsin.

Mr. MULLIN moved to add, at the end of line 491, an appropriation of the same amount ($10,500) for the same officers, &c., of the Territory of Wisconsin, as is included in the bill for the Territory of Oregon.

Mr. HALL, of Missouri, (on a *pro-forma* amendment to the amendment,) said it appeared to him that this was the most extraordinary effort which had ever been made to organize a territorial government. A proposition had been before the Senate since the early part of the last session of Congress, to organize the Territory of Nebraska, and both Houses of Congress had refused to pass such a bill. But here was an effort made to introduce into the civil and diplomatic appropriation bill an item, which, *per se*, established a territorial government over Minnesota. Now, was it proper to introduce a proposition of this kind into a general appropriation bill? Gentlemen could not relieve themselves of the difficulty by saying that the Territory of Wisconsin existed by law; and on the contrary, he thought it was absolutely certain that no such territorial government did exist. Congress had authorized the people of Wisconsin to come into the Union as a State; they had come in; and Minnesota, the part which had been stricken from the former Territory of Wisconsin, he apprehended, could not be called a Territory, without a law of Congress declaring it to be a Territory.

He conceived that this was nothing more nor less than an attempt to establish a territorial government in an indirect way. He would inquire why a territorial government could be established in this manner over the Territory of Minnesota, any more than territorial governments could be established over the Territories of Nebraska, California, or New Mexico? If bills were necessary to establish territorial governments over these, why was not a bill equally necessary to establish such a government over Minnesota? If Minnesota required to have a territorial government, let a bill be introduced and passed, in the usual form, for that purpose; but let them not attempt to sneak a government through in this bill.

Mr. SCHENCK moved to amend the amendment by including a similar provision for the Territory of Iowa.

He said when the State of Iowa was admitted into the Union, there had been left without the State a much larger territory—a territory three or four times as large as that portion of the former Territory of Wisconsin, which had been left out of the State of Wisconsin. If a Territory was to be erected in this manner; if by admitting a Delegate they drew in a Territory, the example should be followed up by providing also for a much larger piece of Iowa, and now recognizing and providing for it as the Territory of Iowa. Congress would then have two Territories on its hands, without all the trouble of requiring the Committee on Territories to report bills, and those bills to pass both Houses, and be approved by the President, establishing territorial governments, and without the necessity of discussion upon the Wilmot proviso and other vexed questions. A very compendious way of doing the work! It was true, it looked rather preposterous—if any thing done by Congress could be considered preposterous. He meant this with the most perfect respect. He did not think this House could do any thing at which gentlemen ought to be surprised.

It had been attempted in this indirect way to admit one Territory (of Wisconsin.) Now, he desired gentlemen to show the difference between the Territory of Iowa and the Territory of Wisconsin. One had organized a State government by the vote of its people; so had the other. In the case of Wisconsin, a small piece of the Territory of Wisconsin was left out of the State; and in the case of Iowa, a piece much larger had been left out. If the one piece was now to be considered the Territory of Wisconsin, so also should the other be considered the Territory of Iowa. He hoped, inasmuch as the House had admitted a Delegate from Wisconsin, they would go on and provide all the necessary appropriations for the support of the territorial government, and that they would make the same provision for Iowa, in anticipation of thir holding a convention and sending a Delegate. He did this to save the consistency of the House; and following up the amendment of the gentleman from New York, he moved to add Iowa.

Mr. MULLIN modified his amendment by accepting Mr. SCHENCK's amendment thereto.

The question was therefore on an amendment making provision for the expenses of the territorial governments of Wisconsin and Iowa.

Mr. VAN DYKE moved to amend the amendment by striking out "Iowa."

It was no time now (he said) to argue the question whether the Delegate had been properly admitted from Wisconsin, as the gentleman from North Carolina (Mr. BOYDEN) was disposed to do. He denied—it was not true that there was any law of Congress embracing that whole territory as a State. The law of Congress which admitted Wisconsin as a State embraced but a portion of what was once, by the law of Congress, the Territory of Wisconsin. But, was it true that there was no such Territory as Wisconsin? There was a law upon our statute book creating the Territory of Wisconsin, and its limits were given. There was also a law upon the statute book carving out from that same Territory of Wisconsin a State, but leaving the balance of the Territory as it stood before. But the act of Congress which carved out that portion of the Territory and made it a State, did not repeal in words or effect the law by which the old territorial government was given to the Territory of Wisconsin. Congress had admitted about half of that Territory as a State, and it was claimed that, in consequence, the former law was annulled; and that, too, without any repealing words—without any antagonism. If this were true, the people residing in that portion of the Territory were outlawed; society was there reduced to its original elements; there were no judges, no sheriffs, no judicial tribunals, and all the laws which Congress had ever given them as a Territory had been abrogated and destroyed, simply because Congress had erected a State out of a portion of that Territory.

The question was taken on Mr. VAN DYKE's amendment to the amendment, and it was rejected.

The question was taken, and the amendment as amended was rejected.

IN SENATE.

FRIDAY, January 19.

Territory of Minnesota.

Mr. DOUGLAS moved that the Senate proceed to the consideration of the bill establishing the Territory of Minnesota.

The VICE PRESIDENT. The Senate will now proceed to the consideration of the bill asked for by the Senator from Illinois.

Mr. KING. I have not examined the facts connected with this bill to determine satisfactorily to myself what number of citizens of the United States are contained within the limits of the country now proposed to be organized into a Territory. Perhaps the Senator from Illinois can inform me in relation to this matter.

Mr. Douglas. In answer to that question, I would state that my impression is, that there are now somewhere between eight and ten thousand people scattered in various parts of the Territory, though aggregated into compact settlements. There are more than the usual number of inhabitants necessary for the establishment of a territorial government.

Mr. King. I am not willing, sir, to throw any obstacle in the way of establishing the laws of the United States over all our people, wherever they may be, provided they are so contiguous to each other that the laws can easily operate upon them. But if a few individuals are located here and there, and scattered over an immense tract of country, the Senator will perceive at once—as the Senator from Illinois himself must be aware—that it will be almost an impossibility to establish and carry into execution a territorial government.

Mr. Westcott. I would state to the Senator from Alabama that, a day or two since, I had a very interesting conversation with the delegate from Minnesota in relation to this very subject. Contiguous to the falls of St. Anthony, I understand there are about six thousand people located within about one hundred square miles of the territory. This settlement polls some twelve hundred votes, and this delegate with whom I had the conversation was elected as such by that settlement. There are two or three other settlements, as the Senator from Illinois has just stated, compact in their nature. This delegate has impressed upon my mind the great necessity of having a territorial government for Minnesota by a variety of reasons. Emigrants are crowding rapidly into the Territory, and the inhabitants are building mills of a very important character. They are absolutely making improvements on the rivers, and preparing to make a dam along the side of one of the larger streams. There is no law to affect the action of individuals in this respect; and in fact ever since Wisconsin was admitted into the Union, there have been no laws of any description to regulate the affairs of the inhabitants. I am told there are some forty lawyers practising there, which is a favorable sign as to the resources and extent of the settlement. I am fully satisfied of the necessity for an immediate organization of a government over them.

Mr. Dodge, of Iowa. The establishment of this territorial government in Minnesota is a matter of deep interest not only to the inhabitants of that Territory, but to those of my State. There is no existing government or laws now in that Territory. Their establishment has been put off from time to time, without reason or justice, for a long time past. A bill similar to the one presented by the Senator from Illinois almost unanimously passed the House of Representatives at the last session of Congress. Ever since the adoption of a State constitution by Wisconsin, this Territory has been without laws. Whole counties that were once a portion of Wisconsin are now without any law whatever. The public mind has looked anxiously to this session of Congress with the expectation of the establishment of a territorial government. I trust that no opposition will be made to a measure that has been so long pending in both Houses of Congress.

Mr. Butler. Mr. President, as I understand this matter, part of the territory now called Minnesota formed or constituted a part of the Territory of Wisconsin. The eastern boundary of the territory of Minnesota, separating it from Wisconsin, runs down from the western point of Lake Superior to the St. Croix River. That river, therefore, forms a very valuable and important medium of communication between the settlers in this territory and the more easterly portions of this country, and in that part of the territory I understand there are many inhabitants. They have hitherto been under the protection of the laws of the Territory of Wisconsin, but since the admission of that Territory into the Union as a State, these settlers have been left without any such protection.

All that part of the territory called Minnesota lying beyond the line which I have indicated, and extending to the Mississippi, falls under the ordinance of 1787. It is impossible for Congress now to retrocede it, or to compel Wisconsin to take it back. The inhabitants of this territory are now without the protection of law, and they call for such protection perhaps as much as any other portion of the Union similarly situated. About fourteen hundred of the inhabitants are settled upon that portion of the territory formerly embraced within the limits of Wisconsin. Beyond the Mississippi, I believe, there is another settlement upon very good land.

Mr. Douglas, (in his seat.) There are two settlements beyond the Mississippi.

Mr. Butler. Very well; there are two settlements, then. I understand the population is increasing very rapidly, and their judicial matters are becoming more and more complicated every day, and require a political jurisdiction of some kind to be established at once. If there are ten thousand inhabitants in that territory, they certainly demand at least an ordinary territorial government.

Mr. King. I wish the honorable Senator from Iowa to understand that my object was not to oppose the establishment of a territorial government over this country, provided there are a sufficient number of inhabitants in that country to render the establishment of such a form of government over them proper and expedient. I have thought, however, that the movement made to establish such a government there was rather premature; but the statement of my honorable friend from Illinois (Mr. Douglas) that there are some ten thousand inhabitants in that country, and that they are distributed in compact settlements, although distant from each other, has obviated my objections to the immediate establishment of a territorial government over them.

I think, however, the remarks of my honorable friend from South Carolina, in regard to having yielded so large a portion of the territory originally belonging to that section of the country, from which five States were to be made, and five only, for the purpose of forming a new and additional State, is an evidence of the liberality of that section of the country in which I live. I am not disposed to oppose the formation of any such States, if of reasonable dimensions, although their formation might be supposed to operate in some degree against what is supposed to be the particular interests of my section of the country. I wish the same feeling actuated other quarters of this Union, in regard to the establishment of territorial governments over sections of the country, where there are at this time ten times as many inhabitants as Minnesota now contains. But such is not the case, and I deeply regret it.

Mr. DODGE, of Iowa. Mr. President, I wish to say a few words in reply to my friend from Alabama. We know the Senator from Alabama. We know him well, as one of our best friends. We know him as an enlightened and liberal statesman, who soars above all the petty and sectional prejudices which have well-nigh plunged our country into a civil war. As regards the feelings to which the Senator has referred, entertained in some sections of this Union in relation to the organization of territorial governments over certain Territories, belonging to this country, I can say, for one, that I shall be found voting on all occasions in favor of the organization of governments in our new Territories, being willing to risk the small popularity which I now enjoy in the promotion of what I may consider the general good of this whole country. As to this matter of boundary, I will state that Wisconsin would have gladly retained all that portion of the territory embaced in the ordinance of 1787, which was at first assigned to her. That portion of her territory was not set off because it was the choice of her people, but because the Congress of the United States dismembered her territory, and curtailed her limits. I am sorry that the views of the Senator from Alabama with regard to Iowa and Wisconsin did not prevail at that time. If we have obtained too much elbow room it is not our fault, and if injustice has been done to Wisconsin by curtailing her limits, I hope the same injustice will not be done to Minnesota by cutting off that portion of her territory which was originally embraced in the ordinance of 1787, and thus curtail her just limits and restrict her boundaries.

Mr. BADGER. Mr. President, I would inquire of the honorable Senator who reported this bill, what its provisions are? I would like to know if it is similar to other territorial bills that have been extended to the inhabitants of other sections of our country. I think this is clearly a case calling for a territorial government, but I would like to know how many officers it is proposed to give to these ten thousand people.

Mr. DOUGLAS. It strikes me that the provisions of this bill are the same as those of the bill by which a territorial government was extended to Wisconsin when she had not so many inhabitants as Minnesota now has. It provides for precisely the same form of government as was extended to Iowa when she had not so many inhabitants as Minnesota, and precisely the same government as was extended to Oregon when she had about the same number of inhabitants that Minnesota now has, to wit: a territorial government with a small legislative body, a governor, a district attorney and judges, a marshal, and other necessary officers. The bill provides for the simplest form of a territorial government, and does not contain a single peculiar provision.

The bill was ordered to its engrossment, read a third time, by unanimous consent, and passed.

WEDNESDAY, January 24.

Admission of California.

Mr. DOUGLAS moved to postpone the previous orders, and to take up the bill for the admission of California into the Union as a State.

Mr. NILES. If we take up this bill, we must necessarily postpone the bill that was up the other day relating to the reduction of postage, and which was made the special order prior to this bill. And we all know that if we take up this bill, and enter upon the debate, it will probably consume the whole of the session, and will preclude the opportunity of acting upon the bill to which I have referred. I feel it my duty, therefore, to take the sense of the Senate upon the motion to take up the bill.

Mr. DOUGLAS. I trust that the honorable Senator will allow the bill to be taken up at this time. It has been before the Senate since the first week of the session, and has been postponed from time to time, with the general understanding that it should be acted upon at an early day. I do not think that it is going to occupy so much tine as the Senator imagines. I do not think it is going to take up a great deal of time. I hope at least that the Senator will allow it to be taken up, that we may ascertian whether it is likely that much time will be required for its discussion, and if that be the case, it can from time to time give place to other business, and among the rest to the bill which the Senator has named. I hope that my motion to take up the bill will prevail.

The question being put, a division was called for; and no quorum voting—

Mr. NILES demanded the yeas and nays.

They were not ordered.

The question was again put, and, upon a division, it was decided in the affirmative: ayes 25, noes 11.

The bill was accordingly taken up for consideration as in Committee of the Whole.

Mr. DOUGLAS. I laid upon the Secretary's table the other day a substitute which I proposed to offer for the original bill. I now ask that the substitute be read, and that the vote be taken upon making the substitution of the one for the other, with the understanding that the substitute will be open for amendment as an original bill.

The bill proposed to be substituted was read by the Secretary.

The question being taken, the substitute was agreed to.

Mr. BUTLER. The only difficulty that I have upon the subject is this: I am willing to take up the bill as an original bill, but it seems to me that it would be highly proper that it should go to a committee, to be reported upon in the same manner as all original bills. If there was a reason for sending the original bill to a committee, I think the same reason exists why this should be referred either to the Committee on Territories or to the Judiciary Committee.

The VICE PRESIDENT. To which committee does the Senator propose that the bill shall be referred?

Mr. BUTLER. It seems to me it ought to go to the Judiciary Committee, the bill being for the admission of a new State into the Union.

Mr. DOUGLAS moved to refer the bill and proposed amendments to a select committee.

The VICE PRESIDENT. The first motion properly before the Senate is the one made by the Senator from South Carolina, (Mr. BUTLER,) to refer the bill to the Committee on the Judiciary.

Mr. BUTLER. I am opposed to the reference of this bill to a select committee; however, if gentlemen insist upon putting that motion, I will withdraw mine and give place to it.

The VICE PRESIDENT. The question before the Senate is upon the reference of this bill and proposed amendments to a select committee.

The motion was then put and carried.

Mr. FOOTE. I wish simply to ask the unanimous consent of the Senate, if it is not entirely out of order, to be allowed to refer an amendment to this California bill, which I shall prepare, to the select committee to whose charge the bill and proposed amendments have been given.

Leave was granted accordingly.

The VICE PRESIDENT appointed the following gentlemen as the special committee: Messrs. DOUGLAS, JOHNSON of Mayland, JONES of Iowa, CLAYTON of Delaware, DAVIS of Mississippi, BADGER of North Carolina, and NILES of Connecticut.

MONDAY, January 29.

Admission of California as a State.

Mr. DOUGLAS, from the Select Committee to which was referred the bill for the admission of California into the Union as a State, reported the following amendment thereto, viz:

Strike out all after the enacting clause, and insert the following:

That Congress doth consent that the portion of the territory of the United States which is included within the following limits, to wit: beginning in the Pacific Ocean on the parallel of forty-two degrees of north latitude; thence east on said parallel to the dividing ridge which separates the waters flowing into the Colorado River from those which flow into the Great Basin; thence along said dividing ridge to the point where it was crossed by Lieutenant Colonel John C. Frémont, in eighteen hundred and forty-four, as shown on the map of his exploration; thence south-westwardly along the line of said exploration, as shown on the map of said Frémont's surveys, published by order of the Senate in eighteen hundred and forty-eight, to its intersection with the one hundred and seventeenth meridian of west longitude; thence in a direct line to the intersection of the Sierra Nevada Mountains with those of the west range; thence due west to the Pacific Ocean; thence along the coast, including the adjacent islands, to the place of beginning, shall be set apart as the territory of one State, and, upon the fulfilment of the conditions hereinafter contained, the same is hereby declared to be one of the States of this Union, by the name and style of the State of California, upon an equal footing with the original States in all respects whatsoever, with the unconditional reservation to the United States of all right of property in the public domain, and other property ceded to the United States by the treaty of peace concluded with the Republic of Mexico, February second, eighteen hundred and forty-eight, free from taxes, or assessments of any kind by said State, and also the power of disposing of the same, including the right of adjusting all claims and titles to lands derived from foreign Governments, in such manner as Congress shall prescribe.

SEC. 2. *And be it further enacted*, That the acting governor of the Territory of California, so soon as he shall have been furnished with a copy of this act, to the end that the people may have an opportunity of establishing for themselves a constitution and republican form of Government for said State, shall immediately proceed to lay off the country embraced within the limits of the proposed State, into convenient districts for the election of delegates to a convention, for the purpose of forming a State constitution, and shall designate the time and place of holding the election in each district; appoint the officers to conduct the same, and prescribe the mode of making the returns thereof; and shall apportion the delegates, fifty in all, among the several districts, as near as may be, according to the number of legal voters in each; and he shall also designate the time and place for the assembling of said convention. Every white male citizen of the United States, including those who shall have become such under the provisions of the said treaty with Mexico, being actual residents of the proposed State, and having attained the age of twenty-one years, shall be entitled to vote at said election.

SEC. 3. *And be it further enacted*, That so soon as said constitution and State Government shall have been established, and the President of the United States officially notified thereof, he shall issue his proclamation declaring the said State of California to be one of the States of this Union, upon an equal footing with the original States in all respects whatever.

SEC. 4. *And be it further enacted*, That the laws of the United States, so far as they are not locally inapplicable, are hereby extended to and declared to be in force in said State, and until the next general census, the said State shall be entitled to one representative in the Congress of the United States.

SEC. 5. *And be it further enacted*, That Congress doth consent that the portion of the territory of the United States which is bounded as follows, to wit: on the north by the forty-second parallel of north latitude, on the east by the summit of the Rocky Mountains and the State of Texas, on the south by the Republic of Mexico, and on the west by the proposed State of California and the Pacific Ocean, including the islands adjacent to the shore, shall become one of the States of this Union, by the name and style of the State of New Mexico, or such other name as the people thereof shall, in their constitution, adopt, upon an equal footing with the original States in all respects whatsoever, so soon as it shall contain the proper number of inhabitants, and they shall establish for themselves a constitution and republican form of State Government, the United States reserving to themselves all rights of property in the public domain, and other property ceded to the United States by the treaty concluded with the Republic of Mexico, on the second day of February, eighteen hundred and forty-eight, free from taxes and assessments of any kind by said State, and also the power of disposing of the same, including the right of adjudicating all claims and titles to lands derived from any foreign Government, in such manner as Congress shall prescribe.

SEC. 6. *And be it further enacted*, That the laws of the United States, so far as they are not locally inapplicable, are hereby extended to and declared to be in force in the country embraced within the limits of the said State of New Mexico.

SEC. 7. *And be it further enacted*, That the sum of one hundred thousand dollars, of any moneys in the treasury not otherwise appropriated, be, and the same is hereby, appropriated for the purpose of carrying into effect the provisions of this act.

WEDNESDAY, January 31.

Railroad across the Isthmus of Panama.

The Senate resumed, as in Committee of the Whole, the consideration of the bill making compensation for the transportation of the naval and military stores across the Isthmus of Panama.

Mr. UNDERWOOD. Mr. President, in order to test the sense of the Senate upon the subject, I move to strike out the words "mails of the United States" in the ninth and tenth lines of the first section of the amendment; and I would state to the Senator from Illinois, that retaining the words which I propose to strike out can have no good effect whatever, and may lead to mischief.

Mr. DOUGLAS. I will state to the Senate that my idea upon that point is this: If these words be stricken out, we shall have to pay for carrying the mails in addition to the sum now proposed; whereas, if they be left in, we shall not have to pay any thing in addition to the sum proposed in my amendment for carrying the mails. The only difference, therefore, is that, if this motion prevails, we shall have to pay more money than we would if the amendment proposed by the Senator from Kentucky should be rejected.

Mr. UNDERWOOD. The effect of my amendment, if it prevails, will be this: According to the principle of the law which I have just read, this entire subject of the transportation of the mails of the United States is to be regulated by the Governments of the two countries, and not by the company. We must make an arrangement with the Government of New Granada in regard to this matter. If we do not do it, then, sir, the company which constructs the railroad will be compelled to do it; and if you retain the provision which I propose to strike out, you will impose upon them the obligation to make an arrangement for carrying our mails, when the Government of New Granada says it shall be regulated by treaties with foreign nations. By retaining this provision, you will throw the duty of making this arrangement upon the company, when the very face of the charter itself shows that the Government of New Granada have retained the right to make the arrangement with our Government. I think it best to leave this point, where the charter places it, to be settled by the two Governments, and, therefore, to test the sense of the Senate, I move to strike out that provision.

Mr. BENTON. Mr. President, I understand that the mails of the United States are to be carried across the isthmus over this road by a special agent, without the intervention of any post office whatsoever—taken across like any other freight. That is the manner in which the mails are now carried across, and it is expected that all freight will go exactly in the same way. It is for our own security that we have inserted the word "mails," to prevent the company from exacting any thing from us for carrying them in addition to the sum mentioned in the bill. We are perfectly satisfied if they go across in the same way in which the British mails go across the isthmus. The Government of New Granada is satisfied with the same, and it is therefore my opinion that there is no necessity for striking out the words which the Senator from Kentucky has read. And his conclusion is precisely the reverse of the conclusion at which I would arrive. He thinks that the striking out would do no harm, if it does no good; my conclusion is, that the staying in would do no harm. So that we have come to directly contradictory conclusions. I think that our best course is to leave the words where they are. It will be time enough to settle this question with New Granada when it arises with that Government. But there is no expectation that the question will ever be raised. It is for our own security that we have inserted the word "mails," as they do not come under the head of munitions of war or the other articles specified in the bill.

The question on the amendment proposed by Mr. UNDERWOOD was then taken, and the amendment was rejected.

Mr. ALLEN. It is very obvious, sir, that if it be the will of the Senate to pass this bill, embracing, as it does, an object of such magnitude, and promising to bring with it so many consequences, the Senate ought to go into a critical examination, not only of the general principle upon which it stands, but of the measure itself, in all of its details. This, sir, will be a matter of some labor, and will consume much of the time of the Senate, because many questions, relating to the details of this thing, must be made in the various propositions to amend. We are now, sir, past the middle of this short session, and, although I am not aware that we have any very extraordinary business demanding, for any extraordinary reasons, our prompt attention, still I think it would be a useless waste of time to enter into the discussion of all the questions arising upon the details of this measure, until we know something about the temper of the Senate towards the measure itself. Undoubtedly the proposition submitted by the Senator from Mississippi is founded in solid reason. If I comprehend the proposition, it is this: that the Government of the United States shall pay no more for the transportation of its men and property across the isthmus than other people pay for the transportation of their bodies and their property. The defect in the proposition is, that it anticipates the use of this road, and engages the Government to employ the road to transport its men and arms and munitions of war, when it would be quite time to do so after the road is completed. But, sir, I go not now into this matter—I will not enter into the details of this discussion. I will not, for instance, go into a discussion of that part of the bill in which the rate of transportation is fixed at eight dollars per ton over a road to be some thirty-odd miles long, whilst at the same time vessels are freighted at Boston for Canton, to run over a line of eighteen thousand miles for fifteen dollars a ton. I do not choose to go into these details; but, in order to try the temper of the Senate in regard to this measure, and to let us see whether it is worth our while to spend day in and day out in debating its details, I move, sir, that the bill be indefinitely postponed, and I ask for the yeas and nays on that motion.

The yeas and nays were ordered.

Mr. WEBSTER. I should regret, sir, that a measure which I regard as exceedingly important, should be disposed of by indefinite postponement. I had hoped that the measure might be allowed to proceed until its details were arranged, so that they might be satisfactory to the Senate, and I rise merely to express my opinion in favor of the measure, generally, concurring in it, especially for the reasons assigned by the honorable Senator from Missouri. I think the circumstances of the country call for the adoption of this particular measure. I do not mean to say, sir, that there may not be several modes of establishing a communication with the Pacific coast that are equally desirable. I am willing to say, on the other hand, that I have regarded the subject of a communication across from the Atlantic to the Pacific, by way of Tehuantepec, as preferable, on account of its being nearer to our ports on the Gulf; and I will add, that if the proposition for a railroad were now before us, connecting the two oceans by that route, and the proposition had advanced so far that we could pronounce it to be practicable, I should give it my most hearty support. I do not think the view which has been adopted by the Senator from Connecticut is entirely correct, that the present exigency for a channel of communication will be a very short one. I do not apprehend that there will cease to be an occasion for a great deal of intercourse between the Atlantic and Pacific, and between our own Territories on either side of the continent. I think the progress of things is onward; and, let the speculations and operations in the gold mines go forward more or less rapidly, I think an intercourse is now to be opened for general purposes of trade and commerce between the Atlantic and Pacific. I have not devoted my attention to the particular provisions or details of this measure. I am not in possession of such estimates as enable me to say whether the limitations so called in the bill now on your table, or the limitation which will be in the same bill if the motion of the Senator from Connecticut prevail, is the best limitation. The bill proposes to authorize the Secretary of the Navy to contract for the transportation of these goods and merchandise, munitions of war, and troops across the isthmus, and to pay for this transportation an annual sum. The bill limits that sum at two hundred and fifty thousand dollars. The Senator from Connecticut moves to substitute one hundred and fifty thousand. Without more information than I have upon this point, I cannot say which would be the proper sum. I understand that the parties who have undertaken the construction of the road, estimate the cost of its construction at four or five millions of dollars; and they have founded their opinion upon the cost commonly attending the construction of roads in the United States, economically conducted, making, of course, proper allowance for the necessarily augmented cost of a work to be done so far from the resources which are to supply the means. It is known, too, sir, that a very great reduction for wear and tear is made from the receipts of all railroads, so that the general estimates of income, by reference to any ordinary rule of computation, not allowing for the wear of the road, would be very inadequate to represent the actual state of things that will arise when the road has been completed.

Now, it is evident, sir, that this proposed road will shorten the distance between the ports of the United States on the Atlantic, and the ports of the United States on the Pacific. It is a nearer route by not less than ten thousand miles of sailing—I believe certainly not less than nine thousand. It will shorten the communication in point of time more than one-half, and whatever shortens the time diminishes the cost. If troops are to be conveyed, they are under pay while at sea; if munitions of war or merchandise are to be transported, they ought to reach their distination within as short a time as possible; and in every point of view in which we can make an estimate of this matter, we must all, I think, see that a great, a very great, I am not prepared to say how great, saving will inure to the United States by adopting the shortest route.

Mr. CLAYTON. I have long had this object of establishing a passage, either by railroad or canal, across the isthmus, in view. In 1835, I had the honor to offer to the Senate of the United States a resolution for instituting a mission to the Governments of Central America and New Granada, for the purpose of paving the way for cutting a canal across the isthmus. The resolution was adopted, after considerable discussion, by the Senate, I believe without a dissenting vote, at least so it would appear from the Journal. The resolution was to this effect:

"*Resolved*, That the President of the United States be respectfully requested to consider the expediency of opening negotiations with the Governments of other nations, and particularly the Governments of Central America and New Granada, for the purpose of effectually protecting, by suitable treaty stipulations with them, such individuals or companies as may undertake to open a communication between the Atlantic and Pacific Oceans, by the construction of a ship canal across the Isthmus which connects North and South America, and of securing forever, by such stipulations, the free and equal right of navigating such canal to all such nations, on the payment of such reasonable tolls as may be established, to compensate the capitalists who may engage in such undertaking, and complete the work."

In pursuance of the suggestion herein contained, the President of the United States sent a chargé d'affaires to the Republics of Central America and New Granada, but the enterprise fell through, as I think, on account of the incompetency of the minister sent, and nothing was done in furtherance of my proposition, or for the accomplishment of the different projects which were suggested at the time for making either canal or railroad across the isthmus.

We are now in the middle of the nineteenth century, and I think, with deference to those gentlemen who have expressed their views in regard to this subject, that it is a disgrace to the age in which we live, and to the country in which we live, that as yet no passage, by either railroad or canal, has been obtained from ocean to ocean, either by Tehuantepec or Panama. Here is a proposition now before us, for expending some two or three millions of dollars to save us nine thousand miles of ship navigation, and the most dangerous navigation in the world. The question is, whether these two or three millions of dollars shall be expended for such a purpose? And on this occasion, as well as on former occasions on which this subject has been presented, we have been met with the objection that there are other and better routes; one of which is by railroad from the Mississippi to the Pacific, the other at Tehuantepec. On this subject I think and feel disposed to act very much like the Senator from Massachusetts. If I could obtain a railroad or canal across the Isthmus of Tehuantepec, I would prefer it, and for reasons which I think will readily suggest themselves to any one who will look at the map. It is a vastly better route for our own country; but I cannot disguise from myself the fact that either of these routes is calculated to throw the control of the commerce that is conducted through these channels into the lap of the United States, for I hold that no other country can compete with the United States successfully upon either of these routes.

This is to be an American road. It will have that character abroad, do what you may. American citizens are intrusted with the construction of it. Well, if this work is to be, and be called an American work, I desire that it should be a road worthy of the American name; and in my opinion the American Government should, within its constitutional sphere, aid as far as it can individual enterprise in making a road worthy of the American character. I do not want a road attempted there by individuals, and carried on by piecemeal, commencing with a railroad of a few miles, and perhaps ending for some years to come with a plank or a mule road. I desire that the improvement should go on continuously, and in the shortest practicable time. And now allow me one general remark in regard to the sum to be expended. I would aid, as far as the constitutional power of the Government will enable us to do it, in making a road from the Mississippi River to the Pacific, or a road across the Isthmus of Tehuantepec, as I design to aid in the construction of the road proposed by this bill, and whatever the cost of a passage by canal or railroad across to the Pacific on either isthmus may be, whether two millions, two and a half millions, six millions, twenty millions, or even fifty millions. I say, sir, that the wit of man cannot find any other mode of expending the same amount of money as much for the benefit of this country and of the whole human family. And I repeat that I do think, that in the middle of the nineteenth century, it is a disgrace to the Government that nothing has yet been attempted with success to save our commerce the dangerous navigation of nine thousand miles around the cape. I take the proposition now before us, because it is practicable. I would not delay the work from year to year, and from day to day. If we can, by expending the sum of two and a half millions of dollars, or less, accomplish so great an object, I say, for one, that I am willing to authorize the expenditure.

Mr. DAVIS, of Mississippi. I agree with the Senator from Delaware in a part of what he has said, and differ very widely with him in relation to other portions of his remarks. I think, if there is any ground for mortification in regard to this matter, it is that this Republic, the mother of the republics of the American continent, does not contemplate the transportation of the property of the Government and of the citizens of the Republic within her own limits; that she does not construct for herself, if she have the constitutional power to undertake such a work at all, a road from the valley of the Mississippi to the western limit of the territorial possessions of the United States. If I were to contemplate the idea of constructing a road, either through the instrumentality of the Government exclusively, or by advances of money made to contractors for that purpose, I should make the line of road pass through the territory of the United States. Such a road I would regard as more advantageous to the interests of this country and its citizens. I would consider it preferable in a commercial point of view, and still more so upon political considerations, that our citizens and their property, instead of being separated from the country in their transit from one portion of the United States to the other, should be kept within our own limits; and that the connection with our remote possessions should be as direct as possible. It is not that I have any want of confidence in the attachment of any American citizen to the Government of the United States; for I have an abiding confidence in that attachment. I believe that it is not to be broken off, however widely they may be separated from the Government. But, if any thing is calculated to invite or lead to a forgetfulness of that attachment, it would be for our citizens to find themselves on the shores of the Pacific a powerful people, having an extensive commerce with Asia, without any communication with the United States, and with the legislature sitting here to fix the laws governing their intercourse, both domestic and foreign. If that people are to be bound permanently to this Union, if it is to be made their interest in all time to come to remain a portion of the United States, then I say it is necessary that a ready and accessible means of communication should be afforded them; and the links of communication must be continuous; towns, villages, and hamlets, must extend along the line of communication, from the seat of the General Government until we stand upon the shores of the Pacific. This must be our ulterior object, and all other measures in reference to this subject must be considered as temporary expedients only.

I am not willing to see this Government permanently coupled with any work outside of the United States, and if we are to have any connection whatever with this proposed Panama road, let it be temporary, and let it be in dollars paid for heads and tons conveyed, and let them bear the charge of making the road. I am not willing to pay any stipulated sum to this company in prospect, or when they have perfected the work, other than that which they may receive upon a contract for carrying public stores or for carrying persons, when they are in readiness to perform such work. It is with this view that I have presented the amendment. And adopting the bill in that form, we shall be equally ready to avail ourselves of the road across Tehuantepec, if one be constructed there. I believe that the route proposed will be subject to interruptions from foreign countries, especially in time of war. I believe with the Senator from Delaware, that the Tehuantepec route would connect itself more intimately with the interests of the United States; but there are other considerations which should not be lost sight of. We have no right of way, and the time must be remote when a road will be constructed there, unless the Government of the United States expend a large sum of money in the construction of a road through the Republic of Mexico. Notwithstanding the amusing definition which the honorable gentleman gave of the name of Tehuantepec—and which, I suppose, was given by him more in jest than seriously—I will tell him that, although there are north-west winds sometimes prevailing along that coast, such as he has described, rendering the approach of vessels extremely hazardous, yet there are deep indentations in the coast where vessels may safely enter, the force of the waves being broken by the jutting head-lands which extend for a considerable distance into the sea. So far, then, as those two routes are concerned, the advantage is decidedly in favor of Tehuantepec. But it is not my purpose to enter into this question at all. We have nothing to do with one or the other of them; they are foreign routes; we neither propose to determine the route nor to build the roads; but if they are built, and their services are afforded to us at reasonable rates, then let us avail ourselves of them, whether the road be through Tehuantepec or Panama. I therefore say again, that I am opposed to any proposition to expend even the hundredth part of the sum stated by the Senator from Delaware in the construction of a road. I wish to confine the expenditure of any money for the establishment of a communication with the Pacific within our own country, taking such a course as will lead in a direct line through the valley of the Mississippi to the Pacific. Wherever the passage of the mountains may be most advantageously made, let the road be there constructed, and let us look finally to the accomplishment of a direct passage across the continent, within the limits of the United States, from one sea to the other.

FRIDAY, February 2.

Admission of Califonia.

Mr. DOUGLAS moved that the prior orders be postponed, and that the Senate proceed to the consideration of the bill for the admission of California as a State into the Union.

Mr. NILES thought that if the bill was called up now, it would be debated at length, and consume much time. He said there was a bill, of which he had the care—the postage reform bill—which he was very desirous to have acted upon as speedily as possible. The postage bill, he said, had been twice up for consideration, and he would like to have it taken up, and disposed of to-day. He would therefore move to take up the postage bill, if the Senator from Illinois would withdraw his motion.

The question was taken on Mr. DOUGLAS's motion, and negatived on a division—18 voting in the affirmative, and 23 in the negative.

The question being taken on the motion of Mr. NILES, it was agreed to.

MONDAY, February 5.

Virginia Resolutions—Slavery—Wilmot Proviso—Rights of the States in the acquired Territories—Duty to themselves if these rights denied.

Mr. HUNTER presented the following resolutions, passed by the Legislature of Virginia:

Whereas the institution of slavery was fully discussed in the Convention which formed the Constitution of the United States, and the rights of slaveholders recognized and protected by the provisions of that instrument, and without the compromises then solemnly entered into, the union of the States never could have been formed; and whereas the General Assembly of Virginia, regarding what is known as the "Wilmot proviso" as in palpable disregard of the compromises of the constitution, did, on the 8th day of March, 1847, adopt a series of resolutions, distinctly indicating the course which the State of Virginia would pursue in the event of its passage by the Congress of the United States, as applicable to territory to be acquired from Mexico; and whereas the present General Assembly have seen with deep concern a disposition manifested by the House of Representatives of the United States to violate the principles embodied in said resolutions, and to make still further aggressions upon the rights of the Southern States; under these circumstances, this General Assembly deem the occasion fit to reaffirm said resolutions, and most respectfully, but most earnestly, to call the attention of all those who are attached to the union of the States to the serious and inevitable consequences which must follow such action upon the part of the General Government: Be it therefore,

I. *Resolved by the General Assembly of Virginia,* That, after the fullest re-examination and reconsideration of the resolutions adopted on the 8th of March, 1847, by this body, we do consider said resolutions as founded in truth, consonant with the constitution, and conducive to its preservation, and therefore we feel it to be our indispensable duty to adhere to and reaffirm them, as follows:

"*Resolutions relative to the prohibition by the Congress of the United States of slavery in any territory to be acquired by conquest or treaty.*—[Adopted March 8, 1847.]

"1. *Be it resolved, unanimously, by the General Assembly of Virginia,* That the Government of the United States has no control, directly or indirectly, mediately or immediately, over the institution of slavery, so as to impair the rights of the slaveholder; and that, in taking any such control, it transcends the limits of its legitimate functions, by destroying the internal organization of the sovereignties who created it.

"2. *Resolved, unanimously,* That all territory which may be acquired by the arms of the United States, or yielded by treaty with any foreign power, belongs to the several States of this Union, as their joint and common property, in which each and all have equal rights; and that the enactment, by the Federal Government, of any law which should directly, or by its effects, prevent the citizens of any State from emigrating, with their property, of whatever description, into such territory, would make a discrimination unwarranted by and in violation of the compromises of the constitution, and the rights of the States from which such citizens emigrated, and in derogation of that perfect equality that belongs to the several States as members of this Union, and would tend directly to subvert the Union itself.

"3. *Resolved,* That if, in disregard alike of the spirit and principles of the act of Congress on the admission of the State of Missouri into the Union, generally known as the Missouri compromise, and of every consideration of justice, of constitutional right, and of fraternal feeling, the fearful issue shall be forced upon the country which must result from the adoption and attempted enforcement of the Wilmot Proviso, as an act of the General Government, the people of Virginia can have no difficulty in choosing between the only alternatives that will then remain—of abject submission to aggression and outrage on the one hand, or determined resistance on the other, at all hazards and to the last extremity.

"4. *Resolved, unanimously,* That the General Assembly holds it to be the duty of every man, in every section of this Confederacy (if the Union is dear to him), to oppose the passage of any law, for whatever purpose, by which territory to be acquired may be subject to such a restriction.

"5. *Resolved, unanimously,* That the passage of the above-mentioned proviso makes it the duty of every slaveholding State, and of all the citizens thereof, as they value their dearest privileges, their sovereignty, their independence, their rights of property, to take firm, united, and concerted action in this emergency."

II. *Resolved,* That we regard the passage of a law by the Congress of the United States, abolishing slavery or the slave trade in the District of Columbia, as a direct attack upon the institutions of the Southern States, to be resisted at every hazard.

III. *Resolved*, That in the event of the passage by Congress of the "Wilmot Proviso," or any law abolishing slavery or the slave trade in the District of Columbia, the Governor of this Commonwealth is requested immediately to convene the Legislature of this State (if it shall have adjourned) to consider of the mode and measure of redress.

IV. *Resolved*, That the Governor of this Commonwealth be requested to send a copy of these resolutions to each of the States of this Union, and also to our Senators and Representatives in Congress.

Mr. Hunter, in presenting the above resolutions, said, I present to you a series of resolutions recently passed by the General Assembly of Virginia in relation to the subject of slavery. Some two years since, that State felt it to be her duty, under the circumstances which surrounded her, to declare her opinions as to the right of Congress to prohibit slavery in territory to be acquired either by conquest or treaty. These resolutions denied the power of Congress "to control, directly or indirectly," the institution of slavery, so as to impair the rights of the slaveholder; they declared that the territory to be acquired by the United States from any foreign power would be the common property of the States, and that any Federal legislation which directly or indirectly prevented the citizens of any of the States from emigrating to it with their property, of whatever description, would violate the constitution and the rights of the States, would derogate from that perfect equality which belongs to the States of this Confederacy, and tend to subvert the Union itself; they proclaimed that if the Wilmot Proviso should be adopted, in disregard of the spirit and principles of the Missouri compromise, and of every consideration of right, justice, and fraternal feeling, the people of Virginia could have no difficulty in choosing between the only alternatives that would then remain—of abject submission to aggression and outrage on the one hand, or determined resistance on the other, at all hazards and to the last extremity. They declared it to be the duty of every man from every section of this Confederacy, if he loves the Union, to oppose the passage of such a law; and, in the event of its enactment, they warned the slaveholding States, and every citizen thereof, that it would be their duty, as they valued their dearest privileges, their sovereignty, their independence, and their rights of property, to take firm, united, and concerted action in that emergency. Such were the resolutions unanimously adopted by the General Assembly of Virginia in 1847. Since that period, there have been two general elections by the people; and again, at the present session of the Legislature, these resolutions have been solemnly reaffirmed, with the addition of another, made necessary by the progress of events. That resolution declares it to be the opinion of the General Assembly, that any "law abolishing slavery or the slave trade in the District of Columbia would be a direct attack upon the institutions of the southern States, to be resisted at every hazard."

The adoption of these resolutions, Mr. President, was perhaps due from the State, not only to the rights of her own citizens, but to the Union, which she has ever sought to cherish and preserve. If she entertained these opinions, it was her duty to warn her sister States of her feelings and intentions in the most solemn form known to her proceedings.

To manifest the sincerity of her desire to promote concord, she approaches her confederates not only in the spirit, but in the very language of compromise, and submits to their consideration the fearful alternatives between which she must choose if she cannot be permitted to retain her position of equality in this Union, even by the sacrifice of a portion of her rights and interests. It was once—it may be, perhaps, still—within the range of possibility, that such a course on the part of all the southern States might induce a pause in the progress of what we feel to be aggression and insult, however differently it may have been intended. At any rate, it is due from Virginia to make every effort to save both the Union and the indispensable rights of her people. It is due from her, because no State has contributed more than she did to make and maintain the Union as it now exists. In almost every battle of the Revolution—from the Heights of Abraham to the plains of Georgia—from what was then the remote north-west—from Kaskaskia and Vincennes to Jersey and the Carolinas—her blood was poured; and, to the extent of her means, her treasure was as freely expended.

She not only sacrificed to make, but also to maintain, the union of the States. To secure harmony and promote fraternal feelings, she ceded away her north-western territory, and submitted to conditions which gave, forever, the preponderance of political power to the non-slaveholding States—so little was she jealous of their progress, or doubtful of their disposition at all times to do her justice. Under all circumstances, and at all times, she has manifested her attachment to the Union. She has reared her sons to cherish and revere it as, originally, it was formed. It has ever been as a household word with us—sacred for its domestic associations, and which never passed the lips that it did not stir the heart.

Sir, we have been taught to believe that our constitution, if administered truly, and in a spirit of justice and fraternal feeling, contained more securities for human happiness and the liberty of the citizen than any other instrument ever devised by the art of man. But the Union which we love is a confederacy of equals. The constitution which we cherish makes no invidious distinction between States or citizens, but distributes equally its blessings and its burdens.

Such is the Union and such is the constitution which the blood of our fathers was shed to procure; and shall their sons so far fail in reverence to it, as to agree to the subversion of the very principle which lies at the foundation of the structure? Sir, this cannot, ought not to be. The South cannot consent to be made the Jamaica or even the Ireland of this Confederacy, without an effort to prevent it. It would not be for the glory or even for the interest of the non-slaveholding States to force us to such extremities if they could. Sir, they can have no interest in forcing us to extremities; and I believe that they would pause in that progress which is inevitably leading to such a result, if they understood fully how we think and feel on this subject. Alas! sir, that it should be so; but we have ceased to study and consider the feelings and opinions of each other in the true spirit of fraternal affection.

HOUSE OF REPRESENTATIVES.

THURSDAY, February 8.

The Treaty with Mexico.

The question was put on the motion of Mr. HOUSTON, of Alabama, that the House proceed to the consideration of business on the Speaker's table.

And the motion having been agreed to—

The SPEAKER laid before the House the following message, in writing, from the President of the United States:

To the House of Representatives of the United States:

In reply to the resolutions of the House of Representatives of the fifth instant, I communicate herewith a report from the Secretary of State, accompanied with all the documents and correspondence relating to the treaty of peace concluded between the United States and Mexico at Guadalupe Hidalgo, on the second of February, 1848, and to the amendments of the Senate thereto, as requested by the House in the said resolutions.

Amongst the documents transmitted will be found a copy of the instructions given to the commissioners of the United States who took to Mexico the treaty, as amended by the Senate, and ratified by the President of the United States. In my message to the House of Representatives of the twenty-ninth of July, 1848, I gave as my reason for declining to furnish these instructions, in compliance with a resolution of the House, that, "in my opinion it would be inconsistent with the public interests to give publicity to them at the present time." Although it may still be doubted, whether giving them publicity in our own country, and, as a necessary consequence, in Mexico, may not have a prejudicial influence on our public interests, yet, as they have been again called for by the House, and called for in connection with other documents, to the correct understanding of which they are indispensable, I have deemed it my duty to transmit them.

I still entertain the opinion, expressed in the message referred to, "that, as a general rule, applicable to all our important negotiations with foreign powers, it could not fail to be prejudicial to the public interests to publish the instructions to our ministers, until some time had elapsed after the conclusion of such negotiations."

In these instructions of the 18th of March, 1848, it will be perceived "that the task was assigned to the commissioners of the United States of consummating the treaty of peace, which was signed at Guadalupe Hidalgo, on the second day of February last, between the United States and the Mexican Republic; and which, on the tenth of March last, was ratified by the Senate, with amendments."

They were informed "that this brief statement will indicate to you clearly the line of your duty. You are not sent to Mexico for the purpose of negotiating any new treaty, or of changing in any particular the ratified treaty which you will bear with you. None of the amendments adopted by the Senate can be rejected or modified, except by the authority of that body. Your whole duty will, then, consist in using every honorable effort to obtain from the Mexican Government a ratification of the treaty in the form in which it has been ratified by the Senate, and this with the least practicable delay." "For this purpose, it may, and most probably will, become necessary that you should explain to the Mexican Minister for Foreign Affairs, or to the authorized agents of the Mexican Government, the reasons which have influenced the Senate in adopting these several amendments to the treaty. This duty you will perform, as much as possible, by personal conferences. Diplomatic notes are to be avoided, unless in case of necessity. These might lead to endless discussions and indefinite delay. Besides, they could not have any practical result, as your mission is confined to procuring a ratification from the Mexican Government of the treaty as it came from the Senate, and does not extend to the slightest modification in any of its provisions."

The commissioners were sent to Mexico to procure the ratification of the treaty as *amended* by the *Senate.* Their instructions confined them to this point. It was proper that the amendments to the treaty adopted by the United States, should be explained to the Mexican Government, and explanations were made by the Secretary of State, in his letter of the 18th of March, 1848, to the Mexican Minister of Foreign Affairs, under my direction. This despatch was communicated to Congress with my message of the 6th of July last, communicating the treaty of peace, and published by their order. This despatch was transmitted by our commissioners from the city of Mexico to the Mexican Government, then at Queretaro, on the 17th of April, 1848, and its receipt acknowledged on the 19th of the same month. During the whole time that the treaty, as amended, was before the Congress of Mexico, these explanations of the Secretary of State, and these alone, were before them.

The President of Mexico, on these explanations, on the 8th day of May, 1848, submitted the amended treaty to the Mexican Congress, and on the 25th of May that Congress approved the treaty as amended without modification or alteration. The final action of the Mexican Congress had taken place before the commissioners of the United States had been officially received by the Mexican authorities, or held any conference with them, or had any other communication on the subject of the treaty, except to transmit the letter of the Secretary of State.

In their despatch transmitted to Congress with my message of the 6th of July last, communicating the treaty of peace, dated "City of Queretaro, May 25, 1848, nine o'clock, P. M." the commissioners say: "We have the satisfaction to inform you that we reached this city this afternoon at about five o'clock, and that the treaty, as amended by the Senate of the United States, passed the Mexican Senate about the hour of our arrival by a vote of 33 to 5. It having previously passed the House of Deputies, nothing now remains but to exchange the ratifications of the treaty."

On the next day, (the 26th of May,) the commissioners were for the first time presented to the President of the Republic, and their credentials placed in his hands. On this occasion the commissioners delivered an address to the President of Mexico, and he replied. In their despatch of the 30th of May, the commissioners say: "We enclose a copy of our address to the President, and also a copy of his reply. Several conferences afterwards took place between Messrs. Rosa, Cuevas, Couto, and ourselves, which it is not thought necessary to recapitulate, as we enclose a copy of the protocol, which contains the substance of the conversations. We have now the satisfaction to announce that the exchange of ratifications was effected to-day." This despatch was communicated with my message of the 6th of July last, and published by order of Congress.

The treaty, as amended by the Senate of the United States, with the accompanying papers, and the evidence that in that form it had been ratified by Mexico, was received at Washington on the 4th day of July, 1848, and immediately proclaimed as the supreme law of the land. On the 6th of July I communicated to Congress the ratified treaty, with such accompanying documents as were deemed material to a full understanding of the subject, to the end that Congress might adopt the legislation necessary and proper to carry the treaty into effect. Neither the address of the commissioners, nor the reply of the President of Mexico on the occasion of their presentation, nor the memorandum of conversations embraced in a paper called the Protocol, nor the correspondence now sent, were communicated, because they were not regarded as in any way material; and in this I conformed to the practice of our Government. It rarely, if ever, happens that all the correspondence, and especially the instructions to our ministers, is communicated. Copies of these papers are now transmitted, as being within the resolutions of the House, calling for all such "correspondence as appertains to said treaty."

When these papers were received at Washington, peace had been restored, the first instalment of three millions paid to Mexico, the blockades were raised, the city of Mexico evacuated, and our troops on their return home. The war was at an end, and the treaty as ratified by the United States was binding on both parties, and already executed in a great degree. In this condition of things, it was not competent for the President alone, or for the President and Senate, or for the President, Senate, and House of Representatives combined, to abrogate the treaty, to annul the peace, and restore a state of war, except by a solemn declaration of war.

Had the protocol varied the treaty as amended by the Senate of the United States, it would have had no binding effect.

It was obvious that the commissioners of the United States did not regard the protocol as in any degree a part of the treaty, nor as modifying or altering the treaty as amended by the Senate. They communicated it as the substance of conversations held after the Mexican Congress had ratified the treaty, and they knew that the approval of the Mexican Congress was as essential to the validity of a treaty in all its parts, as the advice and consent of the Senate of the United States. They knew, too, that they had no authority to alter or modify the treaty in the form in which it had been ratified by the United States, but that if failing to procure the ratification of the Mexican Government, otherwise than with amendments, their duty, imposed by express instructions, was to ask of Mexico to send without delay a commissioner to Washington to exchange ratifications here, if the amendments of the treaty proposed by Mexico, on being submitted, should be adopted by the Senate of the United States.

I was equally well satisfied that the Government of Mexico had agreed to the treaty as amended by the Senate of the United States, and did not regard the protocol as modifying, enlarging, or diminishing its terms or effect.

The President of that Republic, in submitting the amended treaty to the Mexican Congress, in his message on the 8th day of May, 1848, said: "If the treaty could have been submitted to your deliberation precisely as it came from the hands of the plenipotentiaries, my satisfaction at seeing the war at last brought to an end would not have been lessened, as it this day is, in consequence of the modifications introduced into it by the Senate of the United States, and which have received the sanction of the President." "At present it is sufficient for us to say to you, that if, in the opinion of the Government, justice had not been evinced on the part of the Senate and Government of the United States, in introducing such modifications, it is presumed, on the other hand, that they are not of such importance that they should set aside the treaty. I believe, on the contrary, that it ought to be ratified upon the same terms in which it has already received the sanction of the American Government. My opinion is also greatly strengthened by the fact that a new negotiation is neither expected nor considered possible; much less could another be brought forward upon a basis more favorable for the Republic."

The deliberations of the Mexican Congress, with no explanation before that body from the United States except the letter of the Secretary of State, resulted in the ratification of the treaty as recommended by the President of that Republic, in the form in which it had been amended and ratified by the United States. The conversations embodied in the paper called a protocol, took place after the action of the Mexican Congress was complete; and there is no reason to suppose that the Government of Mexico ever submitted the protocol to the Congress, or ever treated it or regarded it as in any sense a new negotiation, or as operating any modification or change of the amended treaty. If such had been its effect, it was a nullity until approved by the Mexican Congress; and such approval was never made or intimated to the United States. In the final consummation of the ratification of the treaty by the President of Mexico, no reference is made to it. On the contrary, this ratification, which was delivered to the commissioners of the United States, and is now in the State Department, contains a full and explicit recognition of the amendments of the Senate just as they had been communicated to that Government by the Secretary of State, and been afterwards approved by the Mexican Congress. It declares, that, "having seen and examined the said treaty, and the modifications made by the Senate of the United States of America, and having given an account thereof to the general Congress, conformably to the requirement in the 14th paragraph of the 110th article of the Federal Constitution of these United States, that body has thought proper to approve of the said treaty with the modifications thereto, in all their parts: and in consequence thereof, exerting the power granted to me by the constitution, I accept, ratify, and confirm the said treaty with its modifications, and promise, in the name of the Mexican Republic, to fulfil and observe it, and cause it to be fulfilled and observed."

Upon an examination of this protocol, when it was received with the ratified treaty, I did not regard it as material, or as in any way attempting to modify or change the treaty, as it had been amended by the Senate of the United States.

The first explanation which it contains is, "that the American Government, by suppressing the ninth article of the treaty of Guadalupe, and substituting the third article of the treaty of Louisiana, did not intend to diminish, in any way, what was agreed upon by the aforesaid article (ninth) in favor of the inhabitants of the territories ceded by Mexico. Its understanding is, that all of that agreement is contained in the third article of the treaty of Louisiana. In consequence, all the privileges and guarantees, civil, political, and religious, which would have been possessed by the inhabitants of the ceded territories, if the ninth article of the treaty had been retained, will be enjoyed by them without any difference under the article which has been substituted."

The ninth article of the original treaty stipulated for the incorporation of the Mexican inhabitants of the ceded territories, and their admission into the Union, "as soon as possible, according to the principles of the Federal Constitution, to the enjoyment of all the rights of citizens of the United States." It provided also that in the mean time they should be maintained "in the enjoyment of their liberty, their property, and the civil rights now vested in them, according to the Mexican laws." It secured to them similar political rights with the inhabitants of the other territories of the United States, and at least equal to the inhabitants of Louisiana and Florida, when they were in a territorial condition. It then proceeded to guarantee that ecclesiastical and religious corporations should be protected in the discharge of the offices of their ministry, and the enjoyment of their property of every kind, whether individual or corporate; and finally, that there should be a free communication between the Catholics of the ceded territories and their ecclesiastical authorities, "even although such authorities should reside within the limits of the Mexican Republic, as defined by this treaty."

The ninth article of the treaty as adopted by the Senate, is much more comprehensive in its terms, and explicit in its meaning, and it clearly embraces, in comparatively few words, all the guarantees inserted in the original article. It is as follows: "Mexicans who, in the territories aforesaid, shall not preserve the character of citizens of the Mexican Republic, conformably with what is stipulated in the preceding article, shall be incorporated into the Union of the United States, and be admitted, at the proper time, (to be judged of by the Congress of the United States,) to the enjoyment of all the rights of citizens of the United States, according to the principles of the constitution, and in the mean time shall be maintained and protected in the free enjoyment of their liberty and property, and secured in the free exercise of their religion without restriction." This article, which was substantially copied from the Louisiana treaty, provides equally with the original article for the admission of these inhabitants into the Union; and, in the mean time, whilst they shall remain in a territorial state, by one sweeping provision declares that they "shall be maintained and protected in the free enjoyment of their liberty and property, and secured in the free exercise of their religion without restriction."

This guarantee embraces every kind of property, whether held by ecclesiastics or laymen, whether belonging to corporations or individuals. It secures to these inhabitants the free exercise of their religion without restriction, whether they choose to place themselves under the spiritual authority of pastors resident within the Mexican Republic or the ceded territories. It was, it is presumed, to place this construction beyond all question, that the Senate superadded the words, "without restriction," to the religious guarantee contained in the corresponding article of the Louisiana treaty. Congress itself does not possess the power, under the constitution, to make any law prohibiting the free exercise of religion. If the ninth article of the treaty, whether in its original or amended form, had been entirely omitted in the treaty, all the rights and privileges which either of them confers would have been secured to the inhabitants of the ceded territories by the Constitution and laws of the United States.

The protocol asserts that "the American Government, by suppressing the tenth article of the treaty of Gaudalupe, did not, in any way, intend to annul the grants of land made by Mexico in the ceded territories;" that "these grants, notwithstanding the suppression of the article of the treaty, preserve the legal value which they may possess; and the grantees may cause their legitimate titles to be acknowledged before the American tribunals;" and then proceeds to state, that "conformably to the law of the United States, legitimate titles to every description of property, personal and real, existing in the ceded territories, are those which were legitimate titles under the Mexican law in California and New Mexico up to the thirteenth of May, 1846; and in Texas, up to the second of March, 1836." The former was the date of the declaration of war against Mexico, and the latter that of the declaration of independence by Texas.

The objection to the tenth article of the original

treaty was, not that it protected legitimate titles which our laws would have equally protected without it, but that it most unjustly attempted to resuscitate grants which had become a mere nullity, by allowing the grantees the same period after the exchange of the ratifications of the treaty to which they had been originally entitled after the date of their grants, for the purpose of performing the conditions on which they had been made. In submitting the treaty to the Senate, I had recommended the rejection of this article. That portion of it in regard to lands in Texas did not receive a single vote in the Senate. This information was communicated by the letter of the Secretary of State to the Minister for Foreign Affairs of Mexico, and was in possession of the Mexican Government during the whole period the treaty was before the Mexican Congress, and the article itself was reprobated in that letter in the strongest terms. Besides, our commissioners to Mexico had been instructed, that "neither the President nor the Senate of the United States can ever consent to ratify any treaty containing the 10th article of the treaty of Gaudalupe Hidalgo in favor of grantees of land in Texas or elsewhere." And again: Should the Mexican government persist in retaining this article, then all prospect of immediate peace is ended; and of this you may give them an absolute assurance."

On this point the language of the protocol is free from ambiguity; but if it were otherwise, is there any individual, American or Mexican, who would place such a construction upon it as to convert it into a vain attempt to revive this article, which had been so often and solemnly condemned? Surely no person could for one moment suppose that either the commissioners of the United States, or the Mexican Minister for Foreign Affairs, ever entertained the purpose of thus setting at naught the deliberate decision of the President and Senate, which had been communicated to the Mexican Government with the assurance that their abandonment of this obnoxious article was essential to the restoration of peace.

But the meaning of the protocol is plain. It is simply that the nullification of this article was not intended to destroy valid legitimate titles to land which existed and were in full force independently of the provisions and without the aid of this article. Notwithstanding it has been expunged from the treaty, these grants were to "preserve the legal value which they may possess." The refusal to revive grants which had become extinct, was not to invalidate those which were in full force and vigor. That such was the clear understanding of the Senate of the United States, and this in perfect accordance with the protocol, is manifest from the fact, that whilst they struck from the treaty this unjust article, they at the same time sanctioned and ratified the last paragraph of the eighth article of the treaty, which declares that, "In the said territories property of every kind, now belonging to Mexicans not established there, shall be inviolably respected. The present owners, the heirs of these, and all Mexicans who may hereafter acquire said property by contract, shall enjoy with respect to it guarantees equally ample as if the same belonged to citizens of the United States."

Without any stipulation in the treaty to this effect, all such valid titles under the Mexican Government would have been protected under the Constitution and laws of the United States.

The third and last explanation contained in the protocol is, that "the Government of the United States, by suppressing the concluding paragraph of article twelfth of the treaty, did not intend to deprive the Mexican Republic of the free and unrestrained faculty of ceding, conveying, or transferring, at any time, (as it may judge best,) the sum of twelve millions of dollars, which the same Government of the United States is to deliver in the places designated by the amended article."

The concluding paragraph, or rather sentence, of the original twelfth article thus suppressed by the Senate, is in the following language: "Certificates, in proper form, for the said instalments respectively, in such sums as shall be desired by the Mexican Government, and transferable by it, shall be delivered to the said Government by that of the United States."

From this bare statement of facts, the meaning of the protocol is obvious. Although the Senate had declined to create a Government stock for the twelve millions of dollars, and issue transferable certificates for the amount, in such sums as the Mexican Government might desire, yet they could not have intended thereby to deprive that Government of the faculty which every creditor possesses of transferring for his own benefit the obligation of his debtor, whatever this may be worth, according to his will and pleasure.

It cannot be doubted that the twelfth article of the treaty, as it now stands, contains a positive obligation, "in consideration of the extension acquired by the boundaries of the United States," to pay to the Mexican Republic twelve millions of dollars, in four equal annual instalments of three millions each. This obligation may be assigned by the Mexican Government to any person whatever; but the assignee, in such case, would stand in no better condition than that Government. The amendment of the Senate, prohibiting the issue of a government transferable stock for the amount, produces this effect, and no more.

The protocol contains nothing from which it can be inferred that the assignee could rightfully demand the payment of the money in case the consideration should fail, which is stated on the face of the obligation.

With this view of the whole protocol, and considering that the explanations which it contained, were in accordance with the treaty, I did not deem it necessary to take any action upon the subject. Had it varied from the terms of the treaty as amended by the Senate, although it would even then have been a nullity in itself, yet duty might have required that I should make this fact known to the Mexican Government. This not being the case, I treated it in the same manner I would have done had these explanations been made verbally by the commissioners to the Mexican Minister for Foreign Affairs, and communicated in a despatch to the State Department.

JAMES K. POLK.

WASHINGTON, *February* 8, 1849.

The Message having been read—

Mr. JOHNSON, of Arkansas, said that he had no doubt the whole House would desire an opportunity to look into this Message. He would therefore move that it be laid on the table and printed.

The question was taken on the motion of Mr. Johnson, and decided in the affirmative.

IN SENATE.

WEDNESDAY, February 14.

President and Vice President elect—Counting the Electoral Vote.

The Journal having been read—

A message was received from the House of Representatives by Mr. CAMPBELL, their Clerk, as follows:

Mr. PRESIDENT: I am directed to inform the Senate that the House of Representatives is now ready to receive the Senate, to count the votes for President and Vice President.

Mr. BADGER, at the request of the Senator from Ohio, (Mr. ALLEN,) moved the reconsideration of the vote by which the Senate bill, granting a right of way across the public lands, and to dispose of said land in aid of the several States, for the construction of railroads and canals, was yesterday passed.

The bill having been sent to the House of Representatives—

Mr. BADGER moved that the Secretary be directed to request the return of the bill from the House.

The motion, after some remarks from Mr. BADGER, Mr. ALLEN, Mr. KING, Mr. BREESE, and Mr. BERRIEN, was agreed to.

Counting the votes.

In compliance with the invitation from the House, the Senate then proceeded to the House of Representatives.

On the return of the Senate—

Mr. DAVIS, of Mississippi, from the committee appointed on the part of the Senate, jointly with the committee appointed on the part of the House of Representatives, to ascertain and report a mode of examining the votes for President and Vice President of the United States, and of notifying the persons elected of their election, reported that the committee had performed that duty, and had instructed him to submit the following resolution:

Resolved, That a committee of one member of the Senate be appointed by that body to join a committee of two members of the House of Representatives, to be appointed by that body, to wait on General Zachary Taylor, of Louisiana, and inform him that he has been duly elected President of the United States for four years, commencing with the fourth day of March, 1849; and also to wait on Millard Fillmore, of New York, and inform him that he has been duly elected Vice President of the United States for four years, commencing with the fourth day of March, 1849.

The resolution having been concurred in—

The Senate adjourned.

HOUSE OF REPRESENTATIVES.

WEDNESDAY, February 14.

The Journal of yesterday was read and approved.

Counting the Votes of Electors for President and Vice President.

Mr. BARROW rose and said, that he had a motion which he had reduced to writing, and which he desired to offer. It was read for information, as follows.

Resolved, That the Clerk inform the Senate that the House is now ready to receive that body, for the purpose of proceeding to open and count the votes of the electors for President and Vice President of the United States.

The resolution was adopted.

The Clerk having delivered the message to the Senate, informing them that the House was in waiting for the purpose of counting the votes for President and Vice President—

The Senate attended in the Hall of the House.

The Senate, preceded by the Hon. GEORGE M. DALLAS, Vice President of the United States, and its officers, entered the Hall.

The Senators took the seats prepared for them in the circle in front of the Speaker's chair.

The Vice President took the seat of the Presiding Officer, the Speaker of the House of Representatives being seated at his left hand.

The Sergeants-at-Arms of the two Houses were on the lower platform, at the right and left.

The Hon. JEFFERSON DAVIS, the Teller on the part of the Senate, took a seat at the Clerk's desk, supported by the Hon. WASHINGTON BARROW and ROBERT McCLELLAND, Tellers on the part of the House of Representatives, who were assisted by the Secretary of the Senate and the Clerk of the House.

When thus organized, the two branches of Congress in joint assembly, and the aisles and galleries densely crowded with ladies and citizens, the Hall presented an imposing appearance.

The VICE PRESIDENT then rose and said: In obedience to law, the Senate and House of Representatives have assembled, on the present occasion, so that I may fulfil the duty enjoined upon me by the constitution, by opening, in their presence, the sealed certificates of the lists of persons voted for, by the Electors in the respective States, as President and Vice President, cause the votes to be counted, and have the persons to fill those offices ascertained and declared, agreeably to the constitution.

The VICE PRESIDENT then opened the certificate of the electors of the State of Maine, and said: I now open and present to the Tellers chosen by the two Houses the certificate transmitted by the Electors of the State of Maine, that the votes therein recorded may be counted.

Mr. JEFFERSON DAVIS proceeded to read the certificate, and the vote reported was registered by the tellers in duplicate lists.

The same form was observed with the certificates from the States of New Hampshire, Massachuetts, Rhode Island, Connecticut, Vermont, New York, New Jersey, Pennsylvania, and Delaware.

The certificates from the States of Maryland, Virginia, North Carolina, South Carolina, Georgia, Kentucky, Tennessee, Ohio, Louisiana, and Mississippi, were severally presented in succession in like manner, and read by Mr. Barrow.

Those from Indiana, Illinois, Alabama, Missouri, Arkansas, Michigan, Florida, Texas, Iowa, and Wisconsin, were read by Mr. McClelland. The Tellers having read, counted, and registered the votes of the Electors of the thirty States, and compared their duplicate lists, delivered the same to the Vice President.

The Vice President then rose and read the report of the Tellers. The result was as follows:

List of Votes for President and Vice President of the United States for four years, commencing March 4, 1849.

	STATES.	For President.		For V. President.	
		Taylor.	Cass.	Fillmore.	Butler.
1	Maine*	......	9	......	9
2	New Hampshire	......	6	......	6
3	Massachusetts	12	......	12	–
4	Rhode Island	4	......	4	–
5	Connecticut	6	......	6	–
6	Vermont	6	......	6	–
7	New York	36	......	36	–
8	New Jersey	7	......	7	–
9	Pennsylvania	26	......	26	–
10	Delaware	3	......	3	–
11	Maryland	8	......	8	–
12	Virginia	......	17	......	17
13	North Carolina	11	......	11	–
14	South Carolina	......	9	......	9
15	Georgia	10	......	10	–
16	Kentucky	12	......	12	–
17	Tennessee	13	......	13	–
18	Ohio	......	23	......	23
19	Louisiana	6	......	6	–
20	Mississippi	......	6	......	6
21	Indiana	......	12	......	12
22	Illinois	......	9	......	9
23	Alabama	......	9	......	9
24	Missouri	......	7	......	7
25	Arkansas	......	3	......	3
26	Michigan	......	5	......	5
27	Florida	3	......	3	–
28	Texas	......	4	......	4
29	Iowa	......	4	......	4
30	Wisconsin	......	4	......	4
		163	127	163	127

The Vice President of the United States then, in pursuance of the resolution adopted by the Senate and House of Representatives on the 7th instant, announced the state of the votes to the Houses of Congress in joint meeting, as follows:

That the whole number of electors appointed to vote for President and Vice President of the United States is 290; of which number 146 make a majority.

The State of the vote for President of the United States, as delivered by the tellers, is—

For Zachary Taylor, of Louisiana . . . 163
For Lewis Cass, of Michigan 127

And the state of the vote for Vice President of the United States, as delivered by the tellers, is—

For Millard Fillmore, of New York . 163
For William O. Butler, of Kentucky . 127

That Zachary Taylor, of Louisiana, had received a majority of the whole number of votes of the electors chosen in the several States to vote for President of the United States; and that Millard Fillmore, of New York, had received a majority of the whole number of the votes of the electors chosen in the several States to vote forVice President of the United States.

And thereupon,

The Vice President of the United States declared that Zachary Taylor, of the State of Louisiana, is duly elected President of the United States for the term of four years, to commence on the fourth day of March 1849; and that Millard Fillmore, of the State of New York, is duly elected Vice President of the United States for the term of four years, to commence on the fourth day of March, 1849.

The joint meeting of the two Houses of Congress was then dissolved, and the Senate returned to its Chamber.

Mr. Barrow, from the Joint Committee appointed on the part of the House of Representatives, to ascertain and report a mode of examining the votes for President and Vice Pesident of the United States, and of notifying the persons elected of their election, reported the following resolution; which was read, and unanimously agreed to:

Resolved, That a committee of two members be appointed on the part of the House of Representatives, to join a committee of one member on the part of of the Senate, to wait upon Zachary Taylor, of Louisiana, and inform him that he has been duly elected President of the United States for four years, to commence on the fourth day of March, 1849; and also to wait on Millard Fillmore, of New York, and inform him that he has been duly elected Vice President of the United States for four years, to commence on the 4th day of March, 1849.

And then the House adjourned.

Monday, February 19.

Territorial Governments—California and New Mexico.

Mr. Smith, of Indiana, moved to suspend the rules, to enable him to offer the following resolution:

* After the returns from the State of Maine had been read, Mr. Stephens rose and suggested that the reading at length of the returns from each State in detail be dispensed with.

The Vice President stated that no motion was in order, and no other mode of proceeding could be adopted but that pointed out by the Constitution of the United States, but that the tellers might abridge the reports so far as to give merely the results of the electoral ballotings of each State.

Resolved, That the bills reported from the Committee on Territories to organize Territorial Governments in California and New Mexico, be made the special order immediately after the bill now under consideration of the Committee of the Whole House on the state of the Union, entitled "A bill to provide for carrying into execution in part the 12th article of the treaty of Mexico," shall be disposed of, such special order to continue from day to day until said bills shall be disposed of; and all previous special orders shall be postponed until such bills shall be finally acted upon.

The question beng taken, the rules were suspended—two-thirds voting in the affirmative.

The resolution was adopted.

IN SENATE.

TUESDAY, February 20.

General Appropriation Bill—Mr. Walker's Amendment—Proposal to amend the Bill by adding a Section to extend certain Laws of Congress to the New Territories—Further Proposal to modify the Section and extend the Constitution of the United States to the Territories.

The Senate, as in Committee of the Whole, resumed the consideration of the bill making appropriations for the civil and diplomatic expenses of the Government for the year ending June 30, 1850; the question pending being upon the amendment submitted yesterday by Mr. WALKER, in the following words:

SEC. —. *And be it further enacted*, That all and singular the several acts of Congress respecting the registering, recording, enrolling, or licensing ships or vessels, and the entry and clearance thereof, and the foreign and coasting trade and fisheries, and all the acts respecting the imposing and collecting of duties on imports, and all acts respecting trade and intercourse with the Indian tribes, and all acts respecting the public lands, of a public and general character, and the provisions whereof can be made to apply to the territory west of the Rio del Norte, acquired from Mexico by the treaty of the second day of February, eighteen hundred and forty-eight, be, and the same are hereby, extended over and to, and made in full force and efficacy in all said territory; and the President of the United States may prescribe and adopt such rules, regulations, and measures consistent with and in conformity to those laws, for the enforcement of the same, as may be necessary in said territory; and may prescribe and establish, temporarily, such divisions, districts, ports, offices, and all arrangements proper to enable said laws to be executed; and appoint and commission such officers as may be necessary to administer such laws in said territories; said officers to receive such compensation as the President may prescribe, not exceeding double the compensation heretofore paid to similar officers of the United States, or its Territories, for like services; and to enable the same to be done, the sum of one hundred thousand dollars be appropriated, out of any money in the treasury not otherwise appropriated.

Mr. WALKER, being entitled to the floor, said: To the amendment which I offered yesterday, I shall now propose some modifications by the consent of the Senate. Before doing so, I wish to remark, that after consultation with many friends, and particularly with the Senator from Mississippi, (Mr. FOOTE,) who had given notice of his intention to offer a somewhat similar amendment, I have come to the conclusion, so far as the amendment is concerned, to extend its provisions, and to extend them in such a manner as I think will be beneficial to the objects which are sought to be obtained. The amendment, sir, as I first introduced it, it will be perceived, proposed merely to extend certain laws, which related directly or indirectly to the revenue system of the United States, to the territories acquired by treaty with Mexico. From the accounts, sir, which we have from that interesting section of our country, there is a great degree of disorder and distraction prevailing among the people. If, then, the members of the Congress of the United States can, upon any subject, look with an eye to their duties as statesmen, it occurs to me that they will seriously consider the propriety of endeavoring, as far as in their power lies, to amend that condition of things.

Mr. ATHERTON. If the Senator from Wisconsin will pardon me one moment—I understand the Senator to modify the amendment which he submitted. Has that modification been presented?

Mr. WALKER. I am about to present it.

Mr. ATHERTON. If the modification is similar to it, I would raise the question of order, whether the amendment be in order?

Mr. FOOTE said, if the Senator from New Hampshire would allow him, he trusted that he would not at present offer any obstacle to the amendment. The amendment was, in substance, similar to the one he had proposed to present.

Mr. ATHERTON felt it to be his duty to take the opinion of the Presiding Officer, as to whether the modification was in order; it was well to have it decided before they went into the discussion of the subject.

The VICE PRESIDENT. Will the Senator from New Hampshire state the grounds of his objection?

Mr. ATHERTON said his objection was, that the amendment was not germane to the purposes of the appropriation bill. It was carrying into effect the laws of the United States in a territory where these laws at present had no existence. The object of it was, so far as he understood it, to extend the laws of the United States over the Territories of the United States, or the creating of a government for the Territories of the United States. They might just as well, it seemed to him, introduce a clause into the appropriation bill creating a State government as one creating a territorial government; and he felt it to be his duty to take exception to that course.

The Vice President decided that the objection was not a sufficient ground for rejecting the amendment.

Mr. Walker (resuming the floor) said: I was remarking, sir, that from the exciting condition of things in California and New Mexico, the duty devolved upon Congress of remedying this state of things, as far as it is in their power. To that end, sir, the extension or modification of the amendment which I offered, when the bill was last up, is extended. And I will here read it, that what few remarks I propose to make may be understood. Some of the alterations are merely verbal; others are substántial.

Mr. W. read his amendment as modified, as follows:

Sec. —. *And be it further enacted*, That the [Constitution of the United States and] all and singular the several acts of Congress respecting the registering and recording, enrolling or licensing ships or vessels, and the entry and clearance thereof, and the foreign and coasting trade and fisheries, and all the acts respecting the imposing and collecting of duties on imports, and all acts respecting trade and intercourse with the Indian tribes, and all acts respecting the public lands of a public and general character, and the provisions whereof [are suitable and proper to be applied] to the territory west of the Rio del Norte, acquired from Mexico by the treaty of the 2d of February, 1848, be, and the same are hereby, extended over and [given] full force and efficacy in all said territory; and the President of the United States [be, and he is hereby, authorized to prescribe and establish all proper and useful rules and regulations (in conformity with the Constitution of the United States) for the enforcement of said laws, in said Territory, and for the preservation of order and tranquillity, and for the establishment of justice therein, and from time to time to modify or change the said rules and regulations in such manner as may seem to him discreet and proper] and may prescribe and establish temporarily such divisions, districts, ports, offices and arrangements [for the execution of] said laws, and appoint and commission such officers as may be necessary to administer such laws in said Territory [for such term or terms as he may prescribe, whose authority shall continue until otherwise provided by Congress;] said officers to receive such compensation as the President may prescribe, not exceeding double the compensation heretofore paid to similar officers of the United States, or its Territories, for like services; and to enable the same to be done, the sum of "two" hundred thousand dollars be appropiated, out of any money in the Treasury not otherwise appropriated.

The words changed or introduced in the modification are within brackets.

Mr. W. then continued: It will be seen, sir, that the provisions of this amendment do not relate merely to the extension of the revenue laws over the Territories of New Mexico and California, but, in fact, to the placing of the power somewhere by which the order and stability of these Territories may be regulated, and that the evils that now exist may be to some extent mitigated. This power, under the exigency of the case, the amendment proposes to give to the President of the United States, under the restrictions and limitations provided in the amendment. I have looked, sir, with much interest to the result of the action of Congress with regard to our newly acquired territories. Still, I could not deem it my duty to take any prominent stand with reference to the bill already reported by the Senator from Illinois, to provide for the organization of governments for those territories. That Senator has done, it seems to me, all that could have been done. He has introduced bills for the establishment of a government there; he has urged them with great zeal, eloquence, and force. He has presented them to Congress and to the country. The present Congress is drawing to a close, and the probability is, that this bill for the establishment of a government in California and New Mexico cannot be reached, or if reached, it cannot be passed. In this state of the case, sir, this civil and diplomatic bill being before us, I have felt that it would not be immodest on my part, or trespassing upon the time of the Senate, to propose this amendment. Should it be adopted, the interests of the United States would be, to a considerable extent, protected in her relations with that territory. To a great extent the power can be exercised by the properly-constituted authorities of the land to preserve the peace, good order, and interests of those territories. It will be seen—and it is but candid to admit the fact—that this amendment, going to the extent it does, will leave the people of these territories yet to take the initiative steps in such municipal government and municipal regulations as they may deem proper for their welfare and security. The amendment does not provide any thing upon the subject. It is silent concerning all municipal regulations, and leaves the people of that territory to adopt such as they may deem necessary for themselves.

From the State which I have the honor to represent, many intelligent and enterprising men have gone to these territories. Many more are going. From the State whence you come, Mr. President, there are many others who are moving westward to those newly-acquired territories. There is, perhaps, not a Senator upon this floor who does not know of many freinds and neighbors who have gone, or who are about to go to settle there. We must, then, all feel interested in establishing a government of some kind; we must all feel that a government is necessary—that it is our duty, if not on their account, upon account of old associations, old friendships, and old ties, to extend some protection and some government to these people.

Taking these views, sir, I again repeat, that I have looked with much solicitude to what should be the action of Congress upon this subject. There are questions which have heretofore been agitated, and there may be others which may arise in this discussion. But, sir, if my voice can have any weight—if my opinions are worthy to be heard, I would speak in terms of admonition to those who are disposed to agitate these subjects. I would suggest to them at least to be modestly silent, and, if possible, give the amendment their support. Let us have some kind of unity upon this important matter, and extend to these Territories that degree of protection which duty to ourselves, to our neighbors, and to our nation would seem to demand. I shall feel exceedingly gratified to know that our high duty to the country has been discharged by the Congress of the United States, if not by the passage of this amendment, by adopting something of the kind by which a government, to some extent, shall be extended to that Territory.

At present I shall not make any further observations. I have offered this amendment with, I believe, good motives; such as I hope to be governed by in my future action while I have the honor to sit here. Others may misconstrue my motives; but whatever construction may be put upon them I care not, so long as I feel assured that those motives are pure, and that I have used my humble efforts in discharging the obligations I owe to my country and to that far-off Territory.

Mr. BELL and Mr. DAYTON respectively offered amendments to Mr. WALKER's proposition, which, after debate, were both rejected.

SATURDAY, February 24.

General Appropriation Bill—Mr. Walker's modified Amendment, to extend the Constitution by Law to the Territories.

[The debate upon this proposition was so important in the eyes of the speakers, that each one, to avoid all misapprehension, revised and corrected his own remarks, reserving them for that purpose, for publication among the prepared speeches in the appendix. From that appendix, under the proper dates, this abridgment is now made.]

Mr. WEBSTER said: Mr. President, it is of importance that we should seek to have clear ideas and correct notions of the question which this amendment of the member from Wisconsin has presented to us; and especially that we should seek to get some conception of what is meant by the proposition, in a law, to "extend the Constitution of the United States to the Territories." Why, sir, the thing is utterly impossible. All the legislation in the world, in this general form, could not accomplish it. There is no cause for the operation of the legislative power in such a manner as that. The constitution—what is it? We extend the constitution of the United States by law to a territory! What is the constitution of the United States? Is not its very first principle that all within its influence and comprehension shall be represented in the Legislature which it establishes, with not only a right of debate and a right to vote in both Houses of Congress, but a right to partake in the choice of the President and Vice President? And can we by law extend these rights, or any of them, to a Territory of the United States? Everybody will see that it is altogether impracticable. Well, sir, the amendment goes on, and says that the revenue laws shall, so far as they are suitable, be applied in the Territories. Now, with respect to that qualification, made by the honorable member from Wisconsin, I shall like to know if he understands it as I suppose he does. Does the expression "as far as suitable" apply to the constitution or the revenue laws, or both?

Mr. WALKER. It was not the proposition to extend the constitution beyond the limits to which it was applicable.

Mr. WEBSTER. It comes to this, then, that the constitution is to be extended as far as practicable; but how far that is, is to be decided by the President of the United States, and therefore he is to have absolute and despotic power. He is the judge of what is suitable and what is unsuitable, and what he thinks is suitable is suitable, and what he thinks unsuitable is unsuitable. He is "*omnis in hoc;*" and what is this but to say, in general terms, that the President of the United States shall govern this territory as he sees fit till Congress makes further provision? Now, if the gentleman will be kind enough to tell me what principle of the constitution he supposes suitable, what discrimination he can draw between suitable and unsuitable, which he proposes to follow, I shall be instructed. Let me say that in this general sense there is no such thing as extending the constitution. The constitution is extended over the United States and over nothing else, and can extend over nothing else. It cannot be extended over any thing except over the old States and the new States that shall come in hereafter, when they do come in. There is a want of accuracy of ideas in this respect that is quite remarkable among eminent gentlemen, and especially professional and judicial gentlemen. It seems to be taken for granted that the right of trial by jury, the *habeas corpus*, and every principle designed to protect personal liberty, is extended by force of the constitution itself over every new Territory. That proposition cannot be maintained at all. How do you arrive at it by any reasoning or deduction? It can only be arrived at by the loosest of all possible constructions. It is said this must be so, else the right of the *habeas corpus* would be lost. Undoubtedly these rights must be conferred by law before they can be enjoyed in a Territory.

Sir, if the hopes of some gentlemen were realized, and Cuba were to become a possession of the United States by cession, does any body suppose that the *habeas corpus* and the trial by jury would be established in it by the mere act of cession? Why more than election laws and the political franchises, or popular franchises? Sir, the whole authority of Congress on this subject is embraced in that very short provision, that Congress shall have power to make all needful rules and regulations respecting the *territories* of the United States. The word is *Territories;* for it is quite evident that the compromises of the constitution looked to no new acquisitions to form new Territories. But as they had been acquired from time to time, new Territories have been regarded as coming under that general provision for making rules for *Territories.* We have never had a *Territory* governed as the United States are governed. The Legislature and the Judiciary of Territories have always been established by a law of Congress. I do not say that while we sit here to make laws for these Territories, we are not bound by every one of those great principles which are intended as general securities for public liberty. But they do not exist in Territories till introduced by the authority of Congress. These principles do not, *proprio vigore*, apply to any one of the Territories of the United States, because that Territory, while a Territory, does not become a part, and is no part of the United States.

Mr. CALHOUN. I rise, not to detain the Senate to any considerable extent, but to make a few remarks upon the proposition first advanced by the Senator from New Jersey, fully endorsed by the Senator from New Hampshire, and partly endorsed by the Senator from Massachusetts, *that the Constitution of the United States does not extend to the territories.* That is the point. I am very happy, sir, to hear this proposition thus asserted, for it will have the effect of narrowing very greatly the controversy between the North and the South, as it regards the slavery question in connection with the territories. It is an implied admission on the part of those gentlemen that, if the constitution does extend to the territories, the South will be protected in the enjoyment of its property—that it will be under the shield of the constitution. You can put no other interpretation upon the proposition which the gentlemen have made, that the constitution does not extend to the territories.

Then the simple question is, does the constitution extend to the territories, or does it not extend to them? Why, the constitution interprets itself. It pronounces itself to be the supreme law of the land.

Mr. WEBSTER. What land?

Mr. CALHOUN. The land; the Territories of the United States are a part of the land. It is the supreme law, not within the limits of the States of this Union merely, but wherever our flag waves—wherever our authority goes, the constitution in part goes, not all its provisions certainly, but all its suitable provisions. Why, can we have any authority beyond the constitution? I put the question solemnly to gentlemen: if the constitution does not go there, how are we to have any authority or jurisdiction whatever? Is not Congress the creature of the constitution? does it not hold its existence upon the tenure of the continuance of the constitution; and would it not be annihilated upon the destruction of that instrument, and the consequent dissolution of this confederacy? And shall we, the creature of the constitution, pretend that we have any authority beyond the reach of the constitution? Sir, we were told a few days since, that the courts of the United States had made a decision that the constitution did not extend to the territories without an act of Congress. I confess that I was incredulous, and I am still incredulous that any tribunal pretending to have a knowledge of our system of government, as the courts of the United States ought to have, could have pronounced such a monstrous judgment. I am inclined to think that it is an error which has been unjustly attributed to them; but if they have made such a decision as that, I for one say, that it ought not and never can be respected. The territories belong to us; they are ours; that is to say, they are the property of the thirty States of the Union; and we, as the representatives of those thirty States, have the right to exercise all that authority and jurisdiction which ownership carries with it.

Sir, there are some questions that do not admit of lengthened discussion. This is one of them. The mere statement is sufficient to carry conviction with it. And I am rejoiced to hear gentlemen acknowledge that, if the constitution is there, we are under its shield. The South wants no higher ground to stand upon. The gentlemen have put us upon high ground by the admission that their only means of putting their claims above ours is, to deny the existence of the constitution in California and New Mexico. The Senator from Massachusetts, I say, in part, endorsed the proposition. He qualified it, however, by saying that all the fundamental principles of that instrument must be regarded as having application to the Territories. Now, is there a more fundamental principle than that the States of which this Federal Union is composed, have a community of interest in all that belongs to the Union in its federative character? And that the territory of the United States belongs to the Union in that capacity is declared by the constitution, and that there shall be, in all respects, perfect equality among all the members of the confederacy. There is no principle more distinctly set forth than that there shall be no discrimination in favor of one section over another, and that the constitution shall have no half-way operation in regard to one portion of the Union, while it shall have full force and effect in regard to another portion.

I will not dwell upon this. I will only listen, if gentlemen choose to go on, in order to discover by what ingenuity they can make out their case. It is a mere assumption to say that the constitution does not extend to the territories. Let the gentlemen prove their assumption. I hold the course of the whole of this debate to be triumphant to us. We are placed upon higher ground; we have a narrower question to defend; and it will be understood by the community that we are nonsuited only by a denial of the existence of the constitution in the territories.

Mr. WEBSTER. The honorable Senator from South Carolina alludes to some decision of the United States courts as affirming that the Constitution of the United States does not extend to the Territories, and he says that with regard to——

Mr. CALHOUN. I hope the gentleman will state my position exactly right. I said I was told a few days since that they had so decided, but that I was incredulous of the fact.

Mr. WEBSTER. I can remove the gentleman's incredulity very easily, for I can assure him that the same thing has been decided by the United States courts over and over again for the last thirty years.

Mr. CALHOUN. I would be glad to hear the gentleman mention a case in which such a decision was given.

Mr. WEBSTER. Upon a few moments' consideration I could mention a number of cases. The constitution, as the gentleman contends, extends over the Territories. How does it get there? I am surprised to hear a gentleman so distinguished as a strict constructionist affirming that the Constitution of the United States extends to the Territories without showing us any clause in the constitution in any way leading to that result; and to hear the gentleman maintaining that position without showing us any way in which such a result could be inferred, increases my surprise.

One idea further upon this branch of the subject. The Constitution of the United States extending over the Territories and no other law existing there! Why, I beg to know how any Government could proceed, without any other authority existing there than such as is created by the Constitution of the United States? Does the Constitution of the United States settle titles to land? Does it regulate the rights of property? Does it fix the relations of parent and child, guardian and ward? The Constitution of the United States establishes what the gentleman calls a confederation for certain great purposes, leaving all the great mass of laws which is to govern society to derive their existence from State enactments. That is the just view of the state of things under the constitution. And a State or a Territory that has no law but such as it derives from the Constitution of the United States, must be entirely without any State or Territorial Government. The honorable Senator from South Carolina, conversant with the subject as he must be, from his long experience in different branches of the Government, must know that the Congress of the United States have established principles in regard to the Territories, that are utterly repugnant to the constitution. The Constitution of the United States has provided for them an independent judiciary; for the judge of every court of the United States holds his office upon the tenure of good behavior. Will the gentleman say that in any court established in the Territories the judge holds his office in that way? He holds it for a term of years, and is removable at executive discretion. How did we govern Louisiana before it was a State? Did the writ of *habeas corpus* exist in Louisiana during its Territorial existence? Or the right to trial by jury? Who ever heard of trial by jury there before the law creating the Territorial Government gave the right to trial by jury? No one. And I do not believe that there is any new light now to be thrown upon the history of the proceedings of this Government in relation to that matter. When new territory has been acquired it has always been subject to the laws of Congress, to such law as Congress thought proper to pass for its immediate government, for its government during its territorial existence, during the preparatory state in which it was to remain until it was ready to come into the Union as one of the family of States.

The honorable Senator from South Carolina argues that the constitution declares itself to be the law of the land, and that, therefore, it must extend over the Territories. "The land," I take it, means the land over which the constitution is established, or, in other words, it means the States united under the constitution. But does not the gentleman see at once that that argument would prove a great deal too much? The constitution no more says that the constitution itself shall be the supreme law of the land, than it says that the laws of Congress shall be the supreme law of the land. It declares that the constitution and the laws of Congress passed under it shall be the supreme law of the land.

Mr. CALHOUN. The laws of Congress made in pursuance of its provisions.

Mr. WEBSTER. Well, I suppose the revenue laws are made in pursuance of its provisions; but, according to the gentleman's reasoning, the constitution extends over the Territories as the supreme law, and no legislation on the subject is necessary. This would be tantamount to saying that the moment territory is attached to the United States, all the laws of the United States, as well as the Constitution of the United States, become the governing will of men's conduct, and of the rights of property, because they are declared to be the law of the land—the laws of Congress being the supreme law as well as the Constitution of the United States. Sir, this is a course of reasoning that cannot be maintained. The Crown of England often makes conquests of territory. Who ever heard it contended that the constitution of England, or the supreme power of Parliament, because it is the law of the land, extended over the territory thus acquired, until made to do so by a special act of Parliament? The whole history of colonial conquests shows entirely the reverse. Until provision is made by act of Parliament for a civil government, the territory is held as a military acquisition. It is subject to the control of Parliament, and Parliament may make all laws that they deem proper and necessary to be made for its goverment; but until such provision is made, the territory is not under the dominion of English law. And it is exactly upon the same principle that territories coming to belong to the United States by acquisition or by session, as we have no *jus coloniæ*, remain to be made subject to the operation of our supreme law by an enactment of Congress.

Mr. CALHOUN. I shall be extremely brief in noticing the arguments of the honorable Senator from Massachusetts, and I trust decisive. His first objection is, as I understand it, that I show no authority by which the constitution of the United States is extended to the Territories. How does Congress get any power over the Territories?

Mr. WEBSTER. It is granted in the constitution in so many words: the power to make laws for the government of the Territories.

Mr. CALHOUN. Well, then, the proposition that the constitution does not extend to the Territories is false to that extent. How else does Congress obtain the legislative power over the Territories? And yet the honorable Senator says I assign no reason for it. I assigned the strongest reason. If the constitution does not extend there, you have no right to legislate or to do any act in reference to the Territories.

Well, as to the next point. The honorable Senator states that he was surprised to hear from a strict constructionist the proposition that the constitution extends itself to the Territories. I certainly never contended that the constitution was of itself sufficient for the government of Territories without the intervention of legislative enactments. It requires human agency everywhere; it cannot extend itself within the limits of any State, in the sense of which the gentleman speaks of it. It is, nevertheless, the supreme law, in obedience to which, and in conformity with which, all legislative enactments must be made. And the proposition that the Constitution of the United States extends to the Territories so far as it is applicable to them, is so clear a proposition that even the Senator from Massachusetts, with his profound talent, cannot disprove it. I will put the case of some of the negative provisions of the constitution. Congress shall make no law concerning religion, nor create titles of nobility. Can you establish titles of nobility in California? If not, if all the negative provisions extend to the Territories, why not the positive? I do not think it necessary to dwell any longer upon this point.

Mr. WEBSTER. The precise question is, whether a Territory, while it remains in a territorial state, is a part of the United States? I maintain it is not. And there is no stronger proof of what has been the idea of the government in this respect than that to which I have alluded, and which has drawn the honorable member's attention. Now, let us see how it stands. The judicial power of the United States is declared by the constitution to be "vested in one Supreme Court and in such inferior courts as Congress shall from time to time ordain and establish." The whole judicial power, therefore, of the United States is in these courts. And the constitution declares that "all the judges of these courts shall hold their offices during good behavior." Then the gentleman must admit that the legislation of Congress heretofore has not been altogether in error; that these territorial courts do not constitute a part of the judicial power of the United States, because the whole judicial power of the United States is to be vested in one Supreme Court, and such inferior courts as Congress shall establish, and the judges of all these courts are to have a life tenure under the law; and we do not give such tenure, nor never did, to the judges of these territorial courts. That has gone on the presumption and true idea, I suppose, that the territories are not even part of the United States, but are subject to their legislation. Well, where do they get this power of legislation? Why, I have already stated that the constitution says "the Congress shall have power to dispose of, and make all needful rules and regulations respecting, the territory or other property belonging to the United States;" and it is under that clause, and that clause only, that the legislation of Congress in respect to the Territories has been conducted. And it is apparent from our history that no other provision was intended for territorial government, inasmuch as it is highly probable, I think certain, that no acquisition of foreign territory was ever contemplated.

And again: there is another remarkable instance. The honorable gentleman, and his friends who act with him on these subjects, hold that the power of internal improvement within the United States does not belong to Congress. They deny that we can pass any law for internal improvements within any State of this Union, while they all admit that the moment we get out of the State into a Territory, we can make just as much improvement as we choose. There is not an honorable gentleman on that side of the chamber who has not, time and again, voted money out of the public treasury for internal improvements out of the Union, in Territories, under the conception that, under that provision of the constitution to which I have referred, they do not constitute any portion of the Union—that they are not parts of the Union.

Sir, there is no end to illustrations that might be brought upon this subject; our history is full of them. Our history is uniform in its course. It began with the acquisition of Louisiana. It went on after Florida became a part of the Union. In all cases, under all circumstances, by every proceeding of Congress on the subject, and by all judicature on the subject, it has been held that Territories belonging to the United States were to be governed by a constitution of their own, framed by a convention, and in approving that constitution the legislation of Congress was not necessarily confined to those principles that bind it when it is exercised in passing laws for the United States itself. But, sir, I take leave of the subject.

Mr. CALHOUN. Mr. President, a few words. First, as to the judiciary. If Congress has decided the judiciary of the Territories to be part of the judiciary of the United States, Congress has decided wrong. It may be that it is a part of the judiciary of the United States, though I do not think so.

Mr. WEBSTER, (in his seat.) Nor I.

Mr. CALHOUN. Again: the honorable gentleman from Massachusetts says that the Territories are not a part of the United States—are not of the United States. I had supposed that all the Territories were a part of the United States. They are called so.

Mr. WEBSTER, (in his seat.) Never.

Mr. CALHOUN. At all events, they belong to the United States.

Mr. WEBSTER, (still in his seat.) That is another thing. The colonies of England belong to England, but they are not a part of England.

Mr. CALHOUN. Whatever belongs to the United States, they have authority over, and England has authority over whatever belongs to her. We can have no authority over any thing that does not belong to the United States, I care not in what light it may be placed.

But, sir, as to the other point raised by the Senator—internal improvements. The Senator says there is not a member on this side of the chamber, but what has voted to appropriate money out of the public treasury for internal improvements in the Territories. I know that a very large portion of the gentlemen on this side have voted to appropriate money out of the public treasury for improvements in Territories, upon the principle of ownership; that the land in the Territories in which improvements are made has an increased value in proportion to the sums appropriated, and the appropriations have, in every case, been given in alternate sections. But many gentlemen here have even utterly denied our right to make them under that form. But that question comes under another category altogether. It comes under the category whether we have a right to appropriate funds out of the common treasury at all for internal improvements.

Sir, I repeat it, that the proposition that the Constitution of the United States extends to the Territories is so plain a one, and its opposite—I say it with all respect—is so absurd a one, that the strongest intellect cannot maintain it. And I repeat, that the gentlemen acknowledge, by implication, if not more than that, that the extension of the Constitution of the United States to the Territories would be a shield to the South upon the question in controversy between us and them. I hold it to be a most important concession. It narrows the ground of controversy between us. We then cannot be deprived of our equal participation in those Territories without being deprived of the advantages and rights which the constitution gives us.

Mr. DAYTON. Mr. President, I desire to make a single remark in answer to an observation of the honorable Senator from South Carolina, (Mr. CALHOUN,) so often repeated, to wit: That this opposition to the extension of the constitution to the Territories of California and New Mexico, is an implied admission of the right of the South to carry slavery there, provided the constitution gets there. Now, sir, a matter is admitted by implication only when it is not expressly denied. When I first assumed this position, I assumed it with the express allegation that, with the constitution or without the constitution there, the laws of California stand, and, as they do stand, I do not believe that any one has a right to carry slavery there; but as the southern view of this question differed from mine, and inasmuch as my sole purpose in bringing forward this amendment was to afford present protection to the inhabitants of California against disorder and anarchy, I was unwilling to do any thing which, in the view of any section of this confederacy, could alter existing rights upon the subject of slavery. And now I have been taken to task by my friend from South Carolina—for I take pleasure in calling him such—for the assertion of a principle like this: "That I fear to extend the constitution to the Territories; that I dislike to give to the South the benefit of the constitution." I would give to the South every benefit to which the constitution itself entitles them; but when they ask me to extend that constitution to a region of country where I believe it does not belong, and when they tell me in the same breath, that it will give to them rights that they do not conceive that they now have, then, I beg to stop; I beg to say I will go no further. I am disposed to give law to California, but I am not disposed to alter the condition of parties upon the slave question in that country, at this period; and, entertaining that opinion, I am bold enough to express it; and, feeble as I am, I think able to maintain its propriety.

Now, sir, I have, in reference to this matter, taken no ground which has not been fully and amply sustained by the Senator from Massachusetts, (Mr. WEBSTER.) The Senator from South Carolina (Mr. CALHOUN) says that I have been endorsed in full by the Senator from New Hampshire, (Mr. HALE,) and in part by the

Senator from Massachusetts. I have been endorsed in full by both. I have at no time qualified my original proposition. My original proposition was based upon the amendment of the Senator from Wisconsin, (Mr. WALKER,) and that amendment was, that the Constitution of the United States be extended to these Territories; and my position was, that you could not extend the constitution thither. I did not say that you could not enact a law giving them (the people of California) the benefit of trial by jury, or *habeas corpus*, or any other of the commonplace principles which protect men in the enjoyment of civil liberty. I said you could not in this way, speaking upon this amendment, extend the Constitution of the United States over California. That was my original proposition. The Senators who have advocated the amendment of the Senator from Wisconsin, contend that you can, upon this amendment, extend the Constitution of the United States there. Why, the Senator from South Carolina does not pretend that you can extend that part of it which is a league, a compact. How much of it, then, as the amendment stands, are you to extend? The whole, or a part of it?

But, sir, it is no part of my purpose further to consume the time of the Senate. I answered only upon this proposition, because I did not wish the legal position which I originally took upon the question before the Senate to be misstated and misunderstood.

Mr. BADGER moved that the Senate adjourn.

The motion was rejected, on a division—ayes 20, noes 23.

Mr. DOUGLAS. Mr. President, I have not many words to say on the question which has been occupying the attention of the Senate. Whether Congress has, or has not, the power to extend the constitution over California, I shall vote for the proposition to extend the constitution over that country. I believe we have the power to extend it, in all parts, over that country. I believe, furthermore, that we have the same power to extend the constitution over a country that we have to bring a country inside of it. I believe that the effect of extending the constitution over it will be to make California a State of this Union, giving them two Senators and a Representative in the Congress of the United States, and authorizing them to form a constitution and State government as they please. And, believing that, I am in favor of the amendment of the Senator from Wisconsin. It extends the revenue laws thither. It extends the judiciary, the land laws, the Indian laws, and all other general laws of Congress over it. And by extending the Constitution of the United States over it, as a constitution, in so many words, it erects it into a State, with the right of representation in the Union. And I am sorry that the Senator from Massachusetts (Mr. WEBSTER) is not now in his seat, to say whether or not that will not be the legal effect of it. It is true, that that State would be in a *quasi* condition, inchoate, until it organized a State government, until it elected its Legislature, and that Legislature elected its Senators; but the moment that be done, it will be a State of this Union, with the right of representation here. And it would be a State with all its laws complete. That would be the most summary mode by which this question could be disposed of. I do not think it is the best mode. I think if we are going to make a State, we had better do so by passing a bill purporting to be a State bill, authorizing them to form a constitution, and that in due form, by prescribing who may be legal voters, and by prescribing a mode by which they may agree upon the time and place of forming that constitution. Such, I think, would be the proper course of proceeding, and I entertain not a doubt that Congress has power to do this, although I express it with great deference to the opinions entertained by the members of the Committee on the Judiciary upon this subject.

I do not think that the Senator from New Jersey has treated the proposition for admitting California as a State with quite that liberality —I will not say fairness—that he ought to have done, especially with reference to the only proposition now pending for her admission as a State. He speaks of the bill as proposing to *create* a State. I am going into no metaphysical discussion as to this question of power to create a State. I do not think that the bill that I have proposed does create a State. I do not believe that the Senator from New Jersey would think so, if he would examine it. The bill proposes that the people of California be authorized to erect for themselves a constitution and State government, and that, when they shall erect a State for themselves, they shall be a State of this Union. The bill does not raise any such question as that of creating a State. The only question raised is simply that authorizing the people resident in that country to assemble in a convention, composed of delegates elected in the usual manner, to form a constitution and State government, and, when that shall have been done, to admit them into the Union on an equal footing with the other States in all respects whatsoever. I would ask the Senator from New Jersey, if Congress has not the power to give that assent, how can you get them into the Union? And if he calls that the creation of a State, then he is denying the right which was exercised by Congress, in every case in which a State has come into this Union. It is true that the original bill upon which the committee made their report did provide that "California shall be a State of the Union;" but that contemplated that the government therein was to be erected by the people thereof, and not by the Congress of the United States, as I declared then, in answer to a member of that committee, in discussion here. It was no proposition to create a State whatever. It was merely the consent of

Congress that that people might form a constitution and State government, and nothing more.

But, sir, the proposition for the admission of California into this Union as a State, is precisely in accordance with all legislation upon this subject from the foundation of the Government, wherever there has been any prior legislation of Government on the subject. "Congress doth consent that it shall be erected into a State." These people erect themselves into a State, and become a State from the day when that shall have been accomplished. Sir, I do not deem it necessary to say more upon this question of the power of Congress to create a State.

MONDAY, February 26.

General Appropriation Bill—The New Territories.

The question being upon the amendments offered respectively by Mr. WALKER and Mr. DAYTON, relating to the new Territories obtained by the treaty with Mexico—

Mr. DOWNS said: Mr. President, I know that but very little time is left, and that the Senate has much to do, and that, consequently, there is no time to enter into any thing like a general discussion of this subject. I shall, therefore, offer a few remarks on two points only. The first is the position assumed by the honorable Senator from New Jersey, (Mr. DAYTON,) that the Constitution of the United States either does not extend, *proprio vigore*, to the new Territories, or that it is incompetent for Congress to extend it thither.

I shall not enter into a discussion of the subject, as it has been already pretty extensively discussed. I wish only to express my astonishment at the extraordinary position assumed by the honorable Senator from New Jersey. It seems to me that it totally changes the position heretofore assumed by that Senator, and others from his section, on this slave question. Why, sir, we have been discussing here, during the last session, about what rights the southern section of the United States, or the people of that section, have in the new Territories under the Constitution of the United States. The Senator from New Jersey entered into that discussion as fully and as ably as any Senator on this floor. Various views of the operation of the constitution in those Territories were presented. Everybody seemed to consider that the constitution must necessarily extend there. I say, that after all this, I cannot but express my astonishment that the Senator has brought forward a new light upon that subject, and has now found out that all our discussions heretofore have been absurdities; that all that was said at the last session about the operation of the Constitution of the United States in those Territories was useless, because we have no power to extend the constitution at all.

I am astonished, Mr. President, on another ground. I have heard the suggestion frequently made—and I lament that the suggestion was ever made—that it is not by the mass of the people of the North, but only by certain fanatics there, that the constitution was sought to be amended, so as to strike out of it that provision which guarantees the institution of slavery in the South. I must congratulate those fanatics, and those who support them, that a new light has beamed on this subject; that it is not necessary to amend the constitution, in order to deprive it of that operation in favor of the South so far as it regards the new Territories; that it is only necessary to adopt this new construction of the extent of the operations of the constitution, and the rights of the South are at once swept away, so far as the Territories are concerned.

I am astonished at this suggestion for another reason. We of the South are frequently taunted with a disregard of the constitution and want of attachment to the Union, which charges are utterly without foundation. We have been told, that however objectionable the institution of slavery might be, yet, so far as it was guaranteed by the constitution, we should have it to the fullest extent. Now, however, I regret to see one of the leading men of the North—still more I regret to see two, yea perhaps more—take the ground, in connection with this subject, that we shall not have the full extent of the provisions of the constitution. But, sir, while I regret that such a position has been taken on this subject, I rejoice at it on one account. I wish it to be recorded, that it may stand in judgment against these gentlemen hereafter. I consider the ground which they have taken on this subject, and the particular reason which the honorable gentleman from New Jersey has given for his objection, as a retraction of what was said by gentlemen at the last session as to the operation of the constitution in those Territories. I understand the principal ground of objection of the honorable Senator from New Jersey to be, that the extension of the constitution over those Territories would give to the South rights which they could not otherwise possess. As I do not wish to mistake or to misrepresent him, I will quote his own language, as published in the papers. He says:

"In the third place, and more especially, it is objectionable, because it assumes to extend, by present enactments, the Constitution of the United States over the Territories of California and New Mexico.

"Now, sir, in the first place, this is objectionable because of its changing the present condition of things in reference to the question of carrying slaves into these Territories."

There are other clauses in the same paragraph which I will not read. The Senator then objects to extending the constitution over California, because it changes the state of things there; because it changes the issue; because it places those who hold southern views on a different footing. Mr. President, I am glad, because it is an implied admission that we were right and they were wrong in the discussion here last session, and that we have a right under the constitution to remove with our slaves to California and New Mexico. But has the Senator considered the ultimate and inevitable consequences of the doctrine which he advocates? I should like to know from that Senator, if the Constitution of the United States does not extend to those Territories, by what kind of authority we go there? What authority have we over them? What right has Congress at all, either in the Territories or elsewhere, except under the constitution? What right has the Senator himself to a seat here except under it? Can we exercise any authority with regard to that Territory, unless it is brought within the control of the constitution? If the constitution does not extend over it, pray what does extend over it? I have understood that our treaties made in accordance with the Constitution of the United States, and the constitution itself, were the supreme law of the land. If we have no constitution there, we have no law nor right there. What right have we to hold that country as our property, unless the constitution has operation there? None, sir, none whatever. If the constitution, if the treaty made under the authority of the constitution, does not extend there, there is no law there; and if this be true, then it is declarative that we have no more right to that country than to any foreign country. I regret to hear such a declaration, for I consider it, coming from the very high authority that it does, as an annunciation that we have no right to that Territory; that every foreigner — Frenchman, Englishman, South American, or any one else—has as much right as we have to go there, and carry off the gold with which it abounds. If we have no greater right under the constitution, I cannot see that we have any at all. But I will not dwell upon the subject.

It seems to me that the Senator could not have been very positive in his own conviction on the subject, for, in the succeeding part of the same speech, he assumes a position which is utterly in conflict with the idea that no constitution or constitutional law exists there. In speaking of the difficultes which the South would encounter in taking their slaves thither—which, I think was a very unnecessary caution—he describes the process by which, if slaves are taken there, a *habeas corpus* would be sued out and the slaves released, and depicted the consequences that would ensue if the South should attempt to resist the process. Now, I would like to have the honorable Senator tell me how a *habeas corpus* could be issued in California, unless the Constitution of the United States be in operation there. I do not understand that there is any such right in operation now under the laws of the Mexican Government, and I cannot see how it could be extended thither, unless the Constitution of the United States be in operation there. But I will not dwell on this point. My principal object was to consider another branch of the Senator's argument, and that is, upon the subject of the competency of Congress to admit States into this Union without their having framed a constitution and organized a State government.

I feel myself called on, anxious as I am to avoid trespassing upon the time of the Senate, to offer some remarks upon this subject, from the constant allusion that has been made on all sides to the action of the Committee on the Judiciary on it, and the misunderstanding which prevails in some quarters in regard to the position which I, as the minority of that committee, hold upon this subject. I think it is clear, and that it can be demonstrated, and I wish it to be so understood, that it is competent for Congress to admit a State into the Union before it has formed a constitution and State government. And I will say that the speech of the honorable Senator from New Jersey seems to admit that Congress has this power. He says: "Now, sir, permit me to say, as to this mode of admitting a State, if within the letter, it is in my judgment against the spirit and intent of the constitution." He seems to admit, then, that it is within the letter, but against the spirit of the constitution. Again he says: "But, sir, there are other objections to admitting this country as a State, aside from these constitutional or legal difficulties. This matter of admitting a State into the Union is a matter, to a great extent, of *discretion*." He puts discretion in italics; "and in this case it is expressly made by the treaty with Mexico matter of discretion."

Mr. President, I understand from this, that the honorable Senator from New Jersey abandons the ground taken by the committee, that it was not "competent" for Congress to admit California as a State, and puts it on the ground of "expediency" alone. That is a very different question, and I do not intend to take up the time of the Senate in discussing it. Although the majority of the committee went upon the point that it was not competent for Congress to admit a State until she had formed a constitution and State government, yet from the resolution which was the result of their investigations, it appears that they came to the same conclusion that I did—namely, that it was a question of expediency. Incompetency is left out of the question. For at the close of their report, they offer the following resolution:

"*Resolved*, that it is *inexpedient* to pass the bill entitled 'A bill for the admission of California into the Union as a State.'"

So the committee seems to have come back to the question of expediency. I think, then, it is clear that it is competent for Congress to admit a State under such circumstances.

The expediency of this act is another question.

There are some other of the remarks of the gentleman upon this branch of the subject which require notice. He says:

"Again: why should we overstep that system of legislation which we have acted upon heretofore on all and every occasion? First, a temporary government; then the lowest grade of territorial government; then the second in degree; then admitting the Territory into the Union as a State."

Mr. President, although this general statement may be correct in many cases, it is not correct in detail. There has been no uniform practice which has been adopted in every case. The Senator says, "First, in every case, a temporary government." This is a mistake; there was no temporary government, in the sense the Senator understands it—that is, authorized by Congress—in Vermont, and in some other cases. And it is not a fact that in any case a territorial government was established and the State admitted after she had formed a constitution. In the act authorizing Louisiana to form a constitution, it was provided that she should submit her constitution to Congress, and if it was not disapproved during the next session of Congress, she should be a State in the Union. Congress did approve of it; but if this had not been done, Louisiana would have been in the Union under the previous act.

Mr. DAYTON, (interposing.) The honorable gentleman will please recollect that I applied that remark altogether to the States acquired from foreign governments, and not to States constructed from our original territory, or from parts of other States.

Mr. DOWNS. Perhaps the gentleman did confine his remarks to that class of cases; but, for my part, I cannot see the least difference between the two. I consider that when any territory is acquired from a foreign country it becomes a part of the United States. We have the same control over it as we have over territory transferred by a State. The question of power is the same in both cases. The question of expediency may be very different. It may not be expedient to bring a new people into the Union at once, whereas it may be expedient to give the people of a State formed from some other State instant admission into the Union. In the case of a foreign country, you must obtain the consent of the foreign government, and in the case of a State we must obtain the consent of the State government. And whenever that consent is gained, all difference as to power ceases to exist. In the case of Kentucky, we could not act until we obtained the consent of Virginia; and in the case of Louisiana, we could not act until we obtained the consent of the foreign power to which she belonged; but the moment that consent was obtained, all difference as to the power of Congress to admit those Territories into the Union as States ceased. But it is not a fact that the course laid down by the Senator from New Jersey has been followed in every instance of the acquisition of foreign country. It was not adopted in the case of Texas. Texas had no preliminary government of that kind. She had a government of her own.

Now, Mr. President, the gentleman has admitted at last that Kentucky is an exception. That is a question that was much mooted at the time this question was first brought before the Senate. The gentleman now admits that Kentucky was brought into the Union before she had formed a State constitution. The facts are so clear that it cannot be doubted. But the gentleman says that the case of Kentucky is no rule on this subject, because it has not been followed in other cases; that it is no precedent. And he says, in direct and strong language, that "it is one which the conduct of the Government for fifty years has repudiated. It stands alone."

Mr. President, however high the authority of the gentleman on this subject may be, and however disposed he may be to repudiate the precedent of Kentucky, I now present to the Senate an authority, which I think the Senator from New Jersey will not repudiate when he shall come to reflect upon it. It is not an idea of my own, it is the authority of the Father of his Country. The very opinion which has been advanced upon this subject by the minority of the committee, has been sanctioned by the very highest authority, by Washington himself, in a case very similar to this. In 1790, when this question was opening in Kentucky, when Virginia had given her consent that Kentucky should form a separate State, but when there was no State government there, no organization of any kind, except the convention which assembled to decide whether they would agree to accept the terms of Virginia or not—that convention did assemble merely for the purpose of expressing the opinion of the people of that district that they would become a State—when, having obtained the consent of Virginia, they sent a memorial to Congress and to the President of the United States, (Washington,) requesting that this proceeding might be sanctioned, and that they might be permitted to come into the Union as a State. On that occasion, and under these circumstances, Washington, in his annual address to Congress, used the following language:

"Since your last session I have received communications by which it appears that the district of Kentucky, at present a part of Virginia, has concurred in certain propositions contained in a law of that State, in consequence of which the district is to become a distinct member of the Union, in case the requisite sanction of Congress be added. For this sanction application is now made. I shall cause the papers in this very important transaction to be laid before you. The liberality and harmony with which it has been conducted, will be found to do great honor to both the parties; and the sentiments of warm attachment to the Union and its present government expressed by our fellow-citizens of Kentucky, cannot fail to add an affectionate concern for their particular welfare to the great national impressions under which you will decide on the case submitted to you."

This is the authority of one whose opinions are not often doubted, and whose authority is seldom questioned, that, in a case not stronger than the one now before us, it is not only competent for Congress to admit a State into the Union, but he recommended it on high national considerations, as well as peculiar considerations applicable to that country. This case is analogous, in many respects, to that of Kentucky. The settlement of Kentucky at that time was the first step the United States were making west of the Alleghany mountains. The great national considerations then connected with it were very similar to those now applicable to California—the great emigration to that country, the settlement of that mighty region. I shall not dwell on this point; but, if it were necessary to go through all the cases of the admission of States into the Union, Senators would find that there has been no uniformity upon the subject. Perhaps there have been more cases where Territories have been first organized as Territories and then admitted into the Union, than any other, but there has been no rule upon the subject whatever.

I do not wish the honorable Senator from New Jersey, or anybody, to suppose that by the admission of a State, I understand the creation of a State. I have taken no such ground. It is only necessary that Congress should give their consent, and that they can do before the constitution is formed, as well as after it. But the Senator seems to think that there will be great difficulty in admitting a State at once. It was not the idea or intention of those who advanced the opinion that a State could be admitted, that she could be brought into the Union by Congress and put into full operation at once. On the contrary, they expressly disclaimed all such idea and intention. She cannot be brought in at once. She must have a State organization before she can elect her Senators and Representatives, and until they are elected she cannot be practically in the Union. The position I assumed was, that the consent of Congress might be given before her constitution and State government were formed; and in the very bill which the minority of the committee reported, provision was made that Congress should, in the first instance, give their consent to the formation of a constitution and State government, and that, when they had formed their constitution and government, they should be admitted. It provided nothing but what was usual in such cases.

Mr. President, before leaving this subject, I would state that, notwithstanding the doubts which gentlemen have; notwithstanding the aversion they may have to giving the people of California a government at the present session, I think that that people will form a constitution and present it here; that it will become proper for Congress to act upon it, and I think they will act upon it. I will not enter further into the question of expediency.

I believe that the ground taken by Senators, concerning the character and number of the population of California, is altogether wrong. I believe that the population of that country in a year hence, will astonish the Senator from New Jersey himself. I believe that it will turn out that his calculations have been the furthest from correctness of any calculations he ever made. There is already a large population in that country. The number is rapidly increasing, and the desire to go there is increasing every day. I have seen no calculation that I think comes up to the number that will pour into that country during the next year; and whether we give them a government or not, I believe they will form their own laws and constitution. Perhaps they have done so already. I believe they will send their Senators and Representatives here, and they will demand to be admitted notwithstanding the difficulties of Senators.

Mr. President, I have done all that I have desired. I have said all that I have wished to say upon this subject on this occasion. I think I have shown that the position assumed by myself, namely, that it is competent for Congress to admit California into this Union as a State, is correct. As in all other cases, the question of expediency is for Congress to decide. And I wish it to be distinctly and clearly known everywhere, that those who object to this amendment, do so on the ground that it throws the broad shield of the constitution over the rights of the southern section of this Confederacy in those Territories.

Mr. BERRIEN said: Sir, having been called to the floor, I avail myself of the occasion to state the view which I entertain of the amendment offered by the Senator from New Jersey; and, sincerely and anxiously disposed to see this agitating question brought to a termination, my first impression was, that I would be enabled to sustain that amendment with certain modifications, which I proposed to that Senator. I suggested to him the propriety of extending the time of the operation of the provision, so as to relieve us from the necessity of a certain recurrence to these same agitating questions at the next session of Congress, in which he acquiesced. But I proposed to the Senator another modification, which it was not his pleasure to adopt, and which it is not in my power to offer to the Senate now, because we have attained the last stage to which we can proceed by way of amendment. That refusal makes it impossible for me to sustain the Senator's amendment. My objection to it, without the modification which I proposed, is that, in my judgment, it makes us assume the exercise of a power beyond the Constitution of the United States, or neglect an obligation which the constitution imposes. If it be said that our legislation, in regard to Florida and Louisiana, has gone to the whole extent which the amendment of the Senator from New Jersey proposes, I answer, that the action of Congress in those cases was, in my opinion, not well considered; that it was, in my judgment, a species of legislation which is more honored in the breach than in the observance. A statement of the modification which I suggested to the Senator from New Jersey, will explain my view of this matter. He proposes to adopt the laws of the Mexican Republic as they existed in the Territories of New Mexico and California anterior to the cession of those Territories to us. I suggested to him this modification, to insert the words "so far as the same are consistent with the Constitution of the United States." The Senator refuses to accept this modification, and, therefore, I decline to support his amendment.

This, sir, leads to a very brief consideration of the question which was discussed here the other day. That question is, whether the constitution operates within the Territories of the United States, and if it does, then in what manner? Does it so operate by its own force, or by the legislation of Congress? When the honorable Senator from Massachusetts (who I believe is called to other duties to-day) suggested to us the propriety of having an accurate apprehension of the terms of a proposition, I presumed, from the brief observations which I had submitted upon the subject, that I was probably included in the remark. I accept the admonition, sir. It is certainly important to have a clear conception of the terms in which a proposition is stated. But there is another admonition which is equally important. It is, that we should not only have a clear conception of the term in which a proposition is expressed, but that we should also make some reasonable estimate of the value of the proposition itself. The naked question which was discussed the other day, whether the constitution operates within the Territory of the United States of itself, or by and through the legislation of Congress, is itself, in my judgment, comparatively valueless in this discussion. If I were not averse to employ the language of paradox, I would say that those who occupy the opposite sides of this proposition, are both right and both wrong—that the constitution does and does not extend to the Territories. It is certainly true, as was said by the Senator from Massachusetts, that it does not operate in the Territories *proprio vigore*, as a whole, in its totality. Whether you adopt one mode of considering this instrument or another, whether you describe it as a compact between confederated States, or as an act of the people of the States of the Union, by which they ordained and established a government, still it is evident, that as a totality it cannot operate by its own force in the Territories of the United States. The great object of the constitution was the formation of a system of government; and so far as its provisions relate to that object, they do not extend to the Territories of the United States. That object we seek to accomplish, when, under the authority of the constitution, we are about to organize a government for these Territories.

But it was not the sole object of the constitution to ordain and establish a government for the thirteen States, by whose delegates the constitution was formed. It was also intended to establish certain great principles by which that government was to be regulated. It contained, moreover, and especially in the amendments, certain principles of public liberty, certain safeguards of individual right, which are capable of being extended to the Territories of the United States. When, therefore, it is said that the constitution does not so extend, the answer is, Yes, that is true; as a whole, it does not operate there: and when, on the other hand, it is said that the constitution does extend to the Territories, the answer is, Yes, that also is true; there are portions of it which do, and must of necessity, operate in the Territories of the United States. By what authority are we about to organize a government over those Territories? We are told that it is under the provision of the constitution which gives us power to make needful rules and regulations for the government of the territory or other property of the United States. Now, I doubt, sir, whether that is the true source of our authority. I think it too limited. I think the object of these rules and regulations is clearly indicated by the expressions "to *dispose of*" and make rules respecting "the territory or *other property* of the United States." The Territories are therein obviously considered as *property*, and not as the *habitations of freemen*, whose municipal regulations are to be prescribed by Congress or adopted by themselves. But I do find a power derived from the constitution to organize a government for the Territories, which, though not expressed, is still as distinct as though it was given in terms. Since, by the constitution, we have power to do that, which must or may result in the acquisition of territory, we must also have power to do whatever is required to be done for the government of such territory. I hold that the power is given to Congress as clearly as though it were expressed in language. Then, sir, whether it results from the clause which has been referred to, or whether it is deduced as an incident from the war or treaty-making power, it is still a power derived from the constitution, and is to be exercised in conformity to it. Whether you trace it to one or the other of these sources, when you are legislating for the establishment of a government in a Territory of the United States, do you not bring the Constitution of the United States to operate within that Territory? Is not the mere act of establishing a government, the sole authority to do which you derive from the Constitution of the United States, the evidence of the fact that the constitution *quoad hoc* does extend to that Territory? What other powers have you than those which you derive from the constitution?

But, sir, the concession which has been made upon this point goes further. It is said by the Senator from Massachusetts that, although the constitution does not operate as a whole in the Territories—does not operate at all in the Territories—yet it operates upon us, and that we are bound to regulate ourselves by the principles of the constitution in organizing a government for the Territories. The honorable Senator will not, and does not say, that while legislating for the Territories, we are not bound by every one of the great principles of public liberty which were incorporated in the constitution. Then, sir, to what does this argument amount? Of what importance is the question whether the constitution operates in the Territories by its own intrinsic force, or by an act of legislation which our constitutional duty makes it obligatory upon us to perform? I have, I confess, sir, been somewhat surprised in the course of this discussion. It began with the declaration, which has been reiterated in its progress, that it had been solemnly and repeatedly decided by the Supreme Court of the United States that the constitution did not extend to the Territories. Mr. President, I am willing to admit that some of the decisions of that tribunal may have escaped my recollection; but I can hardly persuade myself that a series of decisions, which it is repeatedly asserted have been made at various times for the last thirty years, on a question so important, could have been entirely forgotten. In answer to the assertion that there have been such decisions, I therefore only say, *non mi recordo.* I know the case to which Senators have referred, that of an *American Insurance Company* against *Canter;* but it is very certain that that case decides no such proposition. The Constitution of the United States was referred to in that case for the purpose of showing that admiralty jurisdiction was vested in the courts of the United States, and the argument was, that jurisdiction could not be exercised by the local judiciary of the Territory. Now, sir, this decision only proves that it was competent for the local judicial authorities to hold jurisdiction of a case in admiralty. *Arguendo,* it was said that, under one or the other of these sources of authority to which I have before referred, Congress has a right to establish a government. The court did not decide to which it should be referred. That question was left open. But, having decided the right of Congress to establish a territorial government in Florida, the court proceeded further to declare, that the same authority had the right to vest the jurisdiction of such a case in the tribunals which might be constituted by the territorial legislature so created. They have decided nothing, therefore, in regard to the question whether the constitution operates in the Territories, and, except by inference, that the particular provision of the constitution vesting admiralty jurisdiction in the courts of the United States does not apply to the Territories; that the judicial power exercised by the territorial courts is not part of the judicial power of the United States, but is derived from grant by Congress to the territorial legislature. They illustrate this proposition, by referring to the difference of the tenure of office between the judicial officers of the United States and those in the Territories. They say that all judicial power which is conferred by the constitution, is vested in the Supreme Court and such inferior courts as Congress may from time to time ordain or establish; and that by the constitution the tenure of office of all these judges is during good behavior, while that of the territorial judges is only for a term of years.

The decision, then, amounts to this, and is limited to this, that the judicial power granted under the constitution, to be exercised within the limits of the United States, is not the judicial power which is established by Congress within the Territories; that the right of determining this question by the judicial power which rests on the authority of Congress to make a Territory, was not a portion of the judicial power established by the constitution to be exercised within the limits of the United States. Now, I suppose there can be nothing more clear than this; but it is very far from establishing the proposition that no part of the constitution can operate in the Territories, by its own force or by legislative act. The whole extent of the decision is simply that the judicial power conferred by the constitution is to be exercised within the limits of the United States, and does not of necessity extend to the Territories.

But here is a proposition by this amendment to put in force the laws of the Mexican Republic, without regard to the constitution and laws of the United States. I ask for a modification of the amendment, which shall provide that these laws shall be allowed to operate in subordination to the Constitution of the United States. It is said, that on the acquisition of territory by the United States, the laws of the pre-existing Government must continue in force until they are repealed by this Government. Now, sir, I confess I am unwilling that the citizens of the United States who may be in that Territory should be subjected unlimitedly to the authority of those laws, of laws enacted by the Mexican Government. There are laws there which conflict with the rights of individuals as freemen, and I am not willing that these shall continue to operate without restraint upon American citizens.

But, in the next place, it is said that this is in the discretion of the President of the United States, and that he will enforce those laws only which conform to the Constitution of the United States. I answer, that it is the duty of every department of this Government to bear its own burdens; and when we send from these Halls an act giving a government to a Territory, we must impose the limitations which the constitution requires. If the Senator from New Jersey had been disposed to accept this modification, "so far as they may be consistent with the Constitution of the United States," we should have a guarantee for our citizens, and I would have been disposed to acquiesce in the proposition thus modified. His refusal forbids me to do so.

Mr. President, it is said that it is impossible to distinguish between those provisions of the constitution which are suitable and proper to be observed in the Territories, and those which are not. Let me suggest to you what I suppose to be a very plain and broad line of discrimination between these two classes of constitutional provisions. I suppose that, considering the constitution as an ordination and establishment, by the people of the United States, of a system of government, all those provisions which relate alone to that object, are to be limited in their operations to the States over which that government was to be established. But I suppose, also, that leaving those provisions *en masse*, there is another class which affects private rights, the liberty of the citizen, which applies to citizens of the United States wherever they may be found within the limits of its authority; and if it be true that these provisions cannot operate without the legislation of Congress in a Territory for which we are providing a system of government, it serves only to render more imperative our obligation to make the necessary enactment.

A citizen of the United States does not lose his character of citizen of the United States by removing into a Territory of the United States. He ceases to be a citizen of the individual State from which he removes, and he becomes a citizen of the Territory to which he goes, but he retains his character of a citizen of the United States. That is his birthright, or it has been granted to him in conformity to the law of Congress. I will ask, sir, did the citizens of the North-western Territory lose their character of citizens of the Confederacy when that Territory was transferred by Virginia to the Confederation? They were citizens of Virginia, as well as of the Confederacy, and when the lands on which they dwelt were transferred by Virginia to the Confederacy, were they denationalized, and divested by this act of their rights as citizens of the Confederacy? It may be said that the privilege of the writ of *habeas corpus* does not by force of the constitution extend to a Territory, that it can only be availed of under the authority of a government which is created by Congress. Sir, if this be so, can there be any more cogent reason for such legislation by Congress as will secure to the citizen of a Territory the benefit of its provisions? It is conceded that we have the power to do so; nay, that we are bound to do so, by the admission which is made in this argument, that we would be wanting in the performance of our duty, if, in organizing a government for a Territory, we failed to observe with religious scrupulousness the great, free, liberal, and conservative principles of the constitution. Surely, the privilege of *habeas corpus* is one of these; and if we have the power, and obligation is upon us, how can we fail to exercise the power in fulfilment of the obligation? I am not aware that this proposition can be stated more plainly.

I object, then, to the amendment of the Senator from New Jersey, because it does not throw around a citizen of these Territories the panoply of the constitution, but subjects him to the dominion of foreign law, to be enforced by Executive discretion; and I will vote for the amendment of the Senator from Wisconsin, if he will accept as a modification an amendment which shall limit the enactment by which the constitution is to be extended to these Territories, to such of its provisions as can be applied to the condition of a Territory of the United States.

Mr. DAYTON. I have no purpose to enter again into the discussion of any question connected with this matter. I have no purpose, therefore, to answer the arguments of my friend from Georgia, further than by the simple interrogatory, which may be addressed to him and all others who adopt the same line of argument. He says that the principles of the constitution to which he refers already extend to and cover the Territories. If so, I beg to know why you want any special act of legislation to carry them there? I think, sir, that it will puzzle those gentlemen who contend for this position to answer this question.

Mr. UNDERWOOD. It is of very great importance, in my estimation, that the new legal question which has been started, and which brings me to my feet on this occasion, should be clearly understood. I hope the Senate will give me their attention, and to compensate that favor, I will promise to be very brief. I never heard, until the Senator from Massachusetts (Mr. WEBSTER) on yesterday expressed the opinion, that the constitution in its provisions did not extend to the Territories of the United States, and I listened with profound attention to what he said, and also to what was advanced by the Senator from South Carolina, (Mr. CALHOUN.) It is the great respect which I have for all the opinions of the distinguished Senator from Massachusetts upon constitutional questions, and the difference which exists between him and myself upon this question, which induces me to occupy the time of the Senate. I think all has not been said on the subject which can be properly said, and I wish to supply what I regard to be an omission in a very few words. I hold that the laws of Congress are, like the laws of all other civilized communities, either general or special; that they either extend over the whole territory of the United States, or over localities which may be designated by law. Now, sir, if you look at the acts of every civilized community, you will find that the laws passed by the legislative power operate in that way, and you will find that the constitutional provisions under our system act in the same way. You have an express constitutional provision respecting the District of Columbia. You have exclusive jurisdiction within the District. You have powers there which do not extend to the Territories belonging to the United States, and the people of the States. Our powers under the constitution in relation to this District are local and not general. I hold that all the principles and provisions of the Constitution of the United States which are general, like the provisions which are not limited, which are not local, extend just as well over the Territories of the United States as they do over the different States of this Union, and that they have precisely the same effect in the Territories as they have in the States. It may require legislation to carry out constitutional power. The constitutional power may be inefficient, it may be worthless, it may amount to nothing, until Congress passes a law to execute and carry the power into operation. To illustrate: all your judicial power is to be vested in the judiciary, but until you pass laws by which the judiciary is to be organized, courts held, and offices provided, the investiture of the judicial power in respect to the States as well as the Territories is a dead letter. It requires the action of Congress. And so, sir, as to many other powers of the Government. They have what may be termed a latent efficacy, but it cannot operate until, like the power which propels the engine, you have prepared the machinery upon which the power acts. I think that this proposition is just as clear, and that it can be demonstrated by argument, as that two and two make four, and I will proceed now to prove it.

The constitution says that it is the supreme law of *the land*. What land? The *whole* land, constituting part and parcel of the United States, is the obvious answer. Upon what principle can we restrict the operation of the constitution to less than the whole? I shall not repeat the arguments that have been used upon this subject. I will leave it where the learned Senator from South Carolina left it, in the interesting discussion which took place between him and the Senator from Massachusetts. But the constitution does not stop there. In the next clause it goes on to say that the judges and officers of every State in the Union, and every officer belonging to the United States Government, without qualification or limitation, shall take an oath "to support the constitution." You have officers in the Territories; you have had them from the foundation of the Government, and you cannot govern a Territory without executive and judicial officers. All of them are required to take an oath or affirmation which obliges them to support the constitution when they come to administer their respective duties. After taking this oath, they are perjured in the eye of Heaven if they intentionally disregard the provisions of the constitution. How can they support the constitution unless by respecting and enforcing its principles and provisions? The learned Senator from Massachusetts says, and says most appropriately and forcibly, that the principles of the constitution are obligatory upon us even while legislating for the Territories. That is true, I admit, in its fullest force; but if it is obligatory upon us while legislating for the Territories, it is impossible that it will not be equally obligatory upon the officers who are appointed to administer the laws in those Territories?

Mr. WEBSTER. I never said it was not obligatory upon them. What I said was, that in making laws for these Territories, it was the high duty of Congress to regard those great principles in the constitution intended for the security of personal liberty and for the security of property.

Mr. UNDERWOOD. The gentleman's sentiments were quoted a short time ago, while he was absent, by a Senator near me, who understood them precisely as I did; but I am happy to hear this qualification of the position which I understood the gentleman to take. I did think that the gentleman was right when he said that, in legislating for the Territories, we were bound by the principles of the constitution. Certain is it, that we are so bound or we are not. If there is no such obligation imposed upon us, then we may legislate adverse to these principles, and contradictory to them, in making laws for our Territories. If the gentleman intends to be understood that we ought to respect the principles of the constitution in legislating for the Territories, but may violate them with impunity and without judicial check, his position is so much the worse, so much the more dangerous to be advanced, coming, as it does, from the great constitutional lawyer of the United States. I say that we are bound, in legislating for the Territories, as well as for the States, scrupulously to observe every principle and provision of the constitution, for we have taken an oath to support it. If we, through inadvertence or design, violate it, then the executive and judicial dapartments, whether in the States or Territories, and who are called upon to apply and enforce our acts upon the people, are bound by their oaths to disregard every thing condemned by the constitution. Let me put a case, by way of illustration. Ours is a Protestant country in the main, while New Mexico and California are Catholic countries. Suppose we provide by our legislation that nobody shall be appointed to an office there who professes the Catholic religion. What do we do by an act of this sort?

Mr. Webster. We violate the constitution, which says that no religious test shall ever be required as a qualification to an office.

Mr. Underwood. I put the case to show how the constitution might be violated, and how we may violate our oaths. But this is not all. The constitution defines what treason is; and if you will look at the legislative act to provide for the punishment of certain crimes against the United States, you will find that treason is likewise defined in it. When that act of Congress was passed, we had a Territory north-west of the Ohio River. I have made a hasty examination to see whether I could find the criminal code of the United States extended by express words to the Territory north-west of the Ohio. I found no such enactment. Well, if the criminal code of the United States was not by express provision extended to the Territory north-west of the Ohio, how did it get there? Under the new doctrine it has not reached there yet, unless it went at the different times at which the portions of that Territory have been admitted into the Union as States; and, in that case, there is still a portion of the territory at the head of the Mississippi which the criminal code has not yet reached. Is that true, sir? No, sir. How does it go there? It goes there, because it is a part of the general law of the land. It goes there, because it is a part, as far as treason is concerned, of the constitution of the land. It gets there in that way, most clearly. Sir, this may be, and is, a most important doctrine. Suppose the people of California, having been incorporated into the United States by treaty, are guilty of treason; suppose they act so as to forfeit their lives, under the act for the punishment of crimes, adopted in 1789, in reference to treason: are they to be punished; or does it require express legislation now to extend the criminal code there before you can reach them? These are very important inquiries. I deny that it requires an express act to extend our criminal code; but that that code, made for the whole people of the United States without restriction, being general in its provisions, extends everywhere over the whole territory of the United States, unless there is some express limitation in it. Under the idea that the Congress of the United States may legislate in violation of the constitution, or contrary to the constitution, let me present a case to test the principle. Suppose we now pass a law for the punishment of treason in California, and provide for conviction upon the testimony of one witness. A man is brought up before a California judge to be tried; here is the act of Congress, stating that conviction may take place upon the testimony of one witness; here is a judge who has sworn to support, in other words, to carry out the principles of the constitution, by the provisions of which the conviction can only take place upon the testimony of two witnesses. Which shall prevail? If there is no constitutional authority in California, and your law is the sole rule of action on the part of the officers of your Government, of course you will convict upon the testimony of one witness. But how is it possible to do that in the face of the constitution, which the judge has sworn to support? Where you have an officer, the constitutional provision requiring him to take an oath to support the constitution prevails; and where you administer that oath, the oath carries with it the obligation to sustain every principle of the constitution which has operation, and which the officer may be required to act under; and thus it goes into operation in every Territory just as soon as you have officers and a government in that Territory.

It does seem to me, sir, that this question, which I have made in reference to the duties of officers of the Government under the constitution, growing out of their oath of office, ought to be considered as making the case so plain, that it is impossible to resist the idea of applying all the principles of the constitution, so far as they are suitable to be applied, to the Territories. But I think you have legislated upon this very idea which I have now advanced. You had a territorial government under the old confederation north-west of the Ohio. The constitution operated differently from the law under which the old territorial government operated; in other words, the law by which your territorial government north-west of the Ohio operated, was in many of its provisions contradictory to the provisions of the Constitution of the United States; and upon the adoption of the constitution and the going into operation of the Federal Government, so far as the organization of the North-west Territory was concerned, Congress produced a conformity at the first session, by enacting that henceforth that portion of the ordinance of 1787 which provided for the appointment of officers by Congress should be repealed, and thereafter they shall be appointed in accordance with the Constitution of the United States. Before the constitution was adopted, the judges and other officers were appointed by Congress. After the adoption of the constitution, that could not be done. There was, therefore, a conflict between the constitution and the organic law of the Territory. All that Congress did was to modify the territorial law, and to provide that the officers should be appointed in conformity with the provisions of the constitution, and should make their reports to the President of the United States, which before they had been required to make to Congress. But if you look at the laws, you will not find any declaration or enactment which carries the constitution and laws of the United States to the Territories. Now, sir, the omission to extend the constitution and general laws to the Territories in express words, shows, as I conceive, at that early period of the history of the country, that it was unnecessary in the opinion of Congress to do so; but that they went, without any legislation, by their intrinsic power; and must have gone there in the way I have stated, because you required every officer who discharged any public function in the Territory to take an oath to support the constitution. An oath to support a thing which had no validity—no operation! Sir, is it not—I hardly know what term to apply—absurd? no, I will not say absurd—queer, that you should require from your officer an oath to support a thing which had no existence, validity, or operation—nothing to do with his action as an officer? This does seem to me to be the strangest thing in the world.

Mr Webster. Will the gentleman consider that this oath is to be taken under the territorial law, in pursuance of the constitution, and never before a territorial government has been formed? The gentleman may designate it by any adjective he pleases; the whole basis of his argument is fallacious, because the oath is to be taken when the act of Congress points out the government.

Mr. Underwood. Mr. President, if the oath of a territorial officer is thus limited, it means less than the oath according to the constitution imports. I deny that laws can limit and restrain it in this way. Do these officers, when they take the oath prescribed by the constitution, swear, I will execute my duties as Congress and the organic law in this Territory shall prescribe them, and I shall only look to Congress as dictating to me the manner in which I shall discharge my duties? No, sir. The gentleman's suggestion now is a restriction. I deny that there can be any such restriction. The oath to be administered is, that he will support the Constitution of the United States, not partially and in a limited sense, but wherever it can operate upon his official duties. That is the nature of the oath, as I conceive, without limitation and without restriction. Well, as to my honorable friend's illustrations that were given the other day, I admit, with him, that there may be no law relating to descents; there may be no law in the Territories regulating the rights of property, the titles to estates; or there may be laws in California and New Mexico at this time, of Spanish origin, which may be wholly inconsistent with the principles of our Government—may be wholly inconsistent with what the Congress of the United States or the American people may desire. I admit there can be no new law enforced there without a legislative change, unless the old law is abrogated by the conflict with the constitution. I admit, that upon the principles of international law, the code existing there at the time we acquired the territory remains until it is our pleasure to change it. But how does the constitution operate upon territory which we have acquired, and in which there are no people? How does it operate in the construction of society *ab ovo*, if I may be permitted the expression? When we permit people to go into such territory, they have no law regulating descents, or regulating any one of their civil rights. It requires an act of Congress, therefore, to regulate descents and conveyances, to give titles to land, and to provide for all the other great interests of the new colony or society. How does this concession, then—which I think perfectly correct—how does the concession operate against the position I have assumed, that all the principles of the constitution which can have an operation in the Territories, go there of their own intrinsic force? I conceive it does not touch the position. You have no right in a State to make any of those regulations to which the Senator from Massachusetts refers. It belongs to the State to make them, and this only proves what I advanced in the outset. Your power may be dormant, inactive, inefficient, until you bring it into operation by legislative enactments. But you have got a treaty which operates, I presume, in California and New Mexico. How does that treaty operate there? I say, in virtue of this constitution; and but for the constitution the treaty could have no effect. The treaty operates, so far as our title to these Territories is concerned, according to the decisions of the Supreme Court, upon one of two grounds: either by conquest, where, by the war power, you have annexed the country, or by treaty, where you have acquired the Territories by contract. We have acquired these Territories under both these titles, but it is in virtue of the provisions of the constitution that you are allowed to acquire territory in either way. The constitution, therefore, operates so far as to make California and New Mexico a part of this country. To that extent, most undoubtedly, it operates, without being carried there by any legislative act of Congress. Can that be denied? Why, any one that would deny this, must deny that we have any title to the country at all. The treaty only operates in virtue of the higher operation of the constitution.

One idea more. According to the principles of international law, when one people conquers another people, the conquered people lose, so to speak, their allegiance to their former masters, and are bound by a new description of allegiance to the new master, the conqueror. Well, when we have acquired, by treaty or by conquest, a territory with people in it, the allegiance which bound them to their old master being broken, and the allegiance which binds them to the new being fixed, I ask you, sir, if they are not in the condition to be traitors to the country if they commit treason against it? And, if so, whether the principles of the constitution and the criminal law not being expressly extended there, do not operate as well in that territory as in any part of the United States? If they be not, then there can be no offences against the United States perpetrated or punished; there can be no traitors punished; the criminal code is a dead letter, and nothing operates unless it be the treaty. Sir, I cannot conceive that any doctrine of this sort can be maintained, unless the decision of the Supreme Court can be produced showing that the extension of the provisions of the constitution to newly-acquired territory requires a special act of Congress. I have seen no such decision; and, unless such can be produced, it is clear to my mind that the doctrine is fallacious.

One or two words more, and I have done. Mr. President, I regret, as much as it is possible for any man to regret, that we are wasting day after day upon a question of this sort, growing out of the institution of slavery in the South, and the hostility towards it in the North, operating most injuriously upon all the legislation of this body, and especially when we endeavor to form governments for these Territories. Sir, it is a sad spectacle in the face of the American people. But it has been so, is so now, and will be so in time to come, unless we take the proper means to put the question at rest forever. There is, in my humble judgment, but one way of settling it harmoniously; and if the Congress of the United States would adopt that, it does seem to me it would give peace and tranquillity to all sensible men. We should leave it to the people of the Territory to settle for themselves. What objection can there be to this? I was astonished when acting in the committtee of eight at the last session, when the proposition was made, to find but one man besides myself on that committee voting for it, and that was the Senator from New York, (Mr. DICKINSON.) What is the proposition of the Senator from Tennessee and of the Senator from Illinois? It is to let them form a State government and admit them as a State; and in this way they will regulate and settle this question for themselves. Sir, can they settle the question any better if they do form a State government for themselves, than they can if you leave it to them to settle it in their territorial legislature? It does seem to me altogether out of the question for us to be gravely debating here about allowing them to form a State constitution, and of admitting them into the Union—a thing to which I am altogether opposed: it does seem to me altogether out of the question to propose settling the question in that way, while, at the same time, we are refusing to allow them to settle it for themselves by the instrumentality of territorial legislation. There is some magic, I suppose, about a State constitution; and if they do not settle it by that magic wand, it is not to be settled at all. It does seem to me that upon so plain a proposition there ought not to be two opinions. I am afraid, seeing that it can be so easily settled, if you will only consent to let the people settle it for themselves—I am afraid that political agitators, party influences, party hopes, ulterior views of personal elevation ambition, and wickedness, more than humanity and virtue, are at the bottom of this difficulty, opposing the great interest of the mass of the American people, ninety-nine hundredths of whom have no interest in the question at all. Sir, it astonishes me to see the quintessence of the wisdom of a great nation like ours, assembled in the two halls of Congress, gravely debating and arguing that State legislation is the only way of settling the question, or of leaving it to the people to be settled, when you can as easily leave it to them to be settled by a territorial government. Sir, I have known some men in the course of my life, who never could do any thing except in a particular way of their own, a way that was not appreciated by ordinary honest minds. With this class of men to whom I allude there must always be some *hocus pocus* in all their actions, otherwise nothing could be done well and to their liking.

Mr. DOWNS. I will remind the gentleman of what he has perhaps forgotten, that the very purpose for which these amendments were offered, was to effect the object which the Senator from Kentucky desires. If we could have a territorial bill passed, there would have been no necessity for these propositions. It was not through any desire to introduce into legislation what the Senator calls *hocus pocus*, but it was to effect an object which could not be secured in any other way.

Mr. UNDERWOOD. I beg the Senator's pardon; I did not intend any thing personal towards any human being. I know that the object of these amendments, the avowed object, is to get a government for the Territories in such way as to settle the question, so that Congress may have done with it. The tendency of my remarks is to show the danger, the impolicy, I had almost said the wickedness, of refusing to allow the question of slavery in the new Territories to be settled by the people of the Territories for themselves. What is the North contending for, when they refuse to let us of the South, with their aid, pass a bill by which this matter shall be conceded to the people of the Territories? I will tell you what they are contending for: they are just saying in this very refusal, to the people of California and New Mexico, You shall not have the power to mould your institutions; you shall not have the power to make the institutions of Kentucky, of Tennessee, or any of the southern States, the model for your own, but you shall adopt for your fundamental principles of government what we choose to dictate to you. Your essential elements of prosperity shall not be judged of by yourselves; you shall be dictated to by us. If it does not amount to this, it amounts to nothing. Well, if you dictate and prescribe to these people a positive rule by which you compel them to base their institutions upon those of the free States, and refuse them the liberty to base their institutions upon the model of the slaveholding States, I ask gentlemen if it can be done without, to that extent, casting a reflection upon the slaveholding States? I know my honorable friend from New Jersey (Mr. DAYTON) said, God forbid that any thing that he should do or say should operate so as to wound the feelings of the people of the South; but must he not perceive that just as soon as Congress says to the people of these Territories, You shall be deprived of the power of modelling your institutions on the basis of those of the southern States, and you shall model them upon the basis of the institutions of the free States,—to that extent Congress reflects on, and stigmatizes the people of one portion of the Union and their institutions, and to that extent eulogizes the people of another portion of the United States and their institutions, as being the model of all that is right and proper, and worthy of imitation?

Now, you can avoid all this, and the people of the North, by avoiding it, can just accomplish what they desire; for no southern man that I know of—very few, I believe, at least—expect that slavery will go to that country, from its character, its soil, its productions, its climate, and the pursuits of the people. But, sir, if the people themselves desire the institution of slavery, should they be deprived of the privilege of asking Kentuckians, or the people of any other southern State, to come there with their slaves? That is the question. If you say they shall not exercise their own volition and judgment, but that they shall submit to your dictation, to that extent you violate republican principles, and undermine the very foundations upon which all our institutions rest. You say to a people, you may establish for yourselves a government, but you shall not have the privilege of making it such as you wish it to be; you shall make it according to our dictation. And you do this, sir, when, if the people of the Territories had the power, and in its exercise were to establish southern institutions, they would not thereby introduce a single additional slave into the United States! Nobody claims the right of introducing slaves from Africa, or any foreign country. Why, then, restrict the people of these Territories in the exercise of their judgment in regard to their own interest? Why tie their hands, and say that they shall not do that which they think best? To do it is despotism, practised in the name of liberty. Sir, I am done with this subject. I gave my views at length during the last session of Congress, and I should not have said a word now but for the new question which has been started in the course of this debate. I am one of those who do not believe —and have so expressed the opinion here at the last session—that the operation of the Constitution of the United States within the Territories of New Mexico and California will, *per se*, or of its own vitality, of its own intrinsic force, establish slavery or tolerate the holding of slaves there, by abolishing the Mexican laws as they existed when we acquired those Territories. But if I am mistaken in that; if the southern view—for so I call it, being upon this particular in a minority among the southern members of this body—if the southern view upon this question be correct, how are my northern friends acting upon this subject? They are unfaithful, as I conceive, in their course of action, to the constitution which they are sworn to support. They are bound to extend that glorious instrument over every part of the country, whether it be a Territory or a State; and as they have annexed those Territories, and made them a part of the United States, I hold it to be their bounden duty to extend the constitution over them, if it is not already operative in them. If they do not do it, they will have violated, in substance, the compromises of the constitution in reference to slavery, provided the southern opinion be correct. To refuse to extend the shield of the constitution because it might protect the institution of slavery, is just as bad as to refuse to comply with those provisions which require the surrender of fugitive slaves. It is another mode of doing the same thing.

PRESIDING OFFICER. The hour for taking a recess has arrived.

Mr. UNDERWOOD. Well, sir, I shall say no more. After the recess any gentleman who chooses may have possession of the floor.

On the reassembling of the Senate the debate was continued, as follows:

Mr. HUNTER. I have a question to propose to the honorable Senator from New Jersey (Mr. DAYTON) before the question is taken upon his amendment as amended, which I will briefly state. The amendment, as originally introduced, provides for all "the military, civil, and judicial powers exercised by the officers of the *existing* Government." This morning he modified his amendment so as to read, "powers exercised by the officers of the *Mexican* Government," &c.

I rise for the purpose of ascertaining what are his sentiments, and what those of gentlemen here professing to be willing to compromise this question in relation to this modification which the Senator has made. I had no share in preparing this amendment; but, once offered, I determined, if there was any possibility of settling the question that has been so long pending, so as to give a government to our recently acquired Territories without sacrificing the rights of my constituents, to aid in bringing about the result. I suppose the scheme of the Senator from New Jersey for compromise was based on the principle of leaving undecided, or in abeyance, the question as to whether slavery can or cannot exist in the Territories acquired from Mexico. It is known that there are two parties in relation to this question: one maintaining that all the laws of the conquered country remain in force, and amongst them the Mexican law prohibiting slavery; the other party assert that only so much of the laws remain in force as are not inconsistent with the fundamental privileges of the States and the citizens of those States; in other words, not inconsistent with the Constitution of the United States. I do not propose to argue the question whether these laws are, to the extent claimed, repealed or not in those Territories, being of the same mind as the Senator from Massachusetts, (Mr. Webster,) and not desirous of introducing any topic that would engender heats or promote excitement. I simply desire to ascertain upon what principle gentlemen are willing to compromise, in order to see if there is a possibility of settling the question, for a time at least. For one, I am willing to compromise, provided the question I referred to be left unsettled. I examined this amendment before the modification was introduced, and I did think it left the question at issue undecided and in abeyance. I confess the Senator's speech accompanying the introduction of the amendment, was of a character that did not at all accord with the views I entertained of his proposition; but, at the same time, perceiving that the amendment would mean what it purported to mean, the tone of his commentary did not vary my judgment and decision as to the course I might pursue in voting on the amendment. But the modification introduced this morning puts a different face on the matter, because in it the Mexican laws are especially alluded to, and their existence re-affirmed; and this, in my estimation, destroys effectually what I understood to be his scheme of compromise. He stated that it made no difference whether the word "Mexican" or the word "existing" was embodied in the amendment. Why, sir, in our view of the question, it makes all the difference in the world; for we believe that none of the existing laws in Mexico can remain in force which are at all inconsistent with the constitution or the rights of the States; and, as I have before stated, some of those laws are, in my opinion, inconsistent with our rights and with the constitution. If he strikes out the word "existing," and inserts the word "Mexican," I would inquire if by such a course he intends to reaffirm the Mexican laws in relation to slavery? If he does, I put it to the honorable Senator whether it would not be more candid to introduce the Wilmot proviso at once; and, if he does not, so to shape the amendment as to leave the question in abeyance? We shall then, without deciding the question or committing either party, establish, if I may so call it, for the time being, a temporary military government, which may enable us to preserve public peace and tranquillity, protect public and private property in the Territories, and secure the citizens now residing, and those who will soon be there, against anarchy and violence; and these objects may perhaps all be accomplished, by enforcing so much of the existing Mexican law as shall not be inconsisent with the constitution and the rights of the States. I shall be prepared, sir, to accept any compromise based upon that principle. If I am asked to reaffirm the validity of the Mexican laws, to which I have alluded, I ask why not at once introduce the Wilmot proviso? Would not the introduction of that provision be more direct, and in fact the very thing that perhaps the gentleman intends by his modification? If that be his meaning, then this amendment as modified is no compromise at all; and I must confess that I have a suspicion that such was the meaning of the speech he delivered in support of his proposition. As I before said, it is not my purpose to go into the question in dispute between us. I wish, if I can, to do all in my power to promote some scheme of compromise, in order that this vexed question of the Territories may be settled, and that they may have a government suitable to their protection and necessary to their prosperity. The only mode in which this object can be effected is, by leaving this question, as to the existence of the Mexican law prohibiting slavery, undecided and in abeyance. I do not speak now of the amendment offered by the Senator from Wisconsin, (Mr. Walker.) I prefer that to the one before us, because it leaves these regulations of the Territories to the President of the United States, so far only as his regulation may not be inconsistent with the constitution, and, therefore, is more limited than that of the Senator from New Jersey. Sir, I am prepared to meet the Senator from New Jersey and gentlemen from the North in a spirit of compromise on this question; and if they will present a proposition which does not sacrifice the rights of that section of the Union which I in part represent, I am ready to accede to it. But it is too much to ask of me to agree to the enactment of this Mexican law abrogating slavery. If we are to reaffirm that law—which I presume is the design of the Senator from New Jersey in his modification—we might, as I said before, as well adopt the Wilmot proviso at once. I wish to know whether it is his object, in presenting this modification, to reaffirm that law?

There is another question, also, to which I would like a reply. I understood him to state that the Constitution of the United States does not extend over these Territories. Now, we all know that there are certain privileges given to the Catholic church, by the Mexican law existing in those Territories when conquered, which are totally inconsistent with the provisions of our constitution. I would inquire whether he proposes by his modified amendment to reaffirm the Mexican laws which give these privileges to the Catholic church, at the same time that he enacts that which abrogates the institution of slavery?

Mr. Dayton. I hoped to have been relieved, not for my own sake, but that of the Senate, from further addressing it upon this subject; but the question propounded by my honorable friend from Virginia, (Mr. Hunter,) requires an answer at my hands, which answer I have not the slightest difficulty in making. When I introduced this proposition, it was not as a scheme of compromise at all; I introduced it because it was an established precedent, acted on heretofore under precisely the same circumstances, and had been found to answer our purpose. I preferred it, therefore, to any new precedent, crouched in different phraseology, and carrying with it I know not what. That was my purpose in introducing this amendment, which is a copy *verbatim et literatim* of the law for the government of Florida—saving only, that in that law for the government of Florida, we extended all those laws of the Federal Government over that Territory which forbids the importation of free persons of color. The Senator from Virginia knows why I strike that portion of the act out of my amendment.

Mr. Hunter. It was certainly not at my request; I had no objection to it.

Mr. Foote, (in his seat.) It was at my request.

Mr. Dayton. It was with a view to meet in good feeling the wishes of Senators on the other side of the Chamber, that I acceded to their suggestions in this respect; I myself did not consider it of any importance, as it applied only to the foreign slave trade, which is piracy now by law. The amendment, with that exception, was, I believe, a precise copy of the original Florida act, with the additional item of an appropriation to carry it into effect. Having offered the amendment, and discussed its merits at some length, the Senator at my right, (Mr. Berrien,)—for whose legal attainments and judicial knowledge I have the greatest respect—suggested, as did other southern Senators, that the terms of the amendment might be so construed as to refer to the species of temporary military government recently established in California, the Secretary of State having communicated the fact in an official document that the late military government should be considered the government *de facto;* and the modifications made to the amendment this morning were modifications made to relieve from any doubt on that subject, and are in the handwriting of the Senator from Georgia. Thus I would inform my honorable friend from Virginia, that these modifications of which he complains, in my amendment, were made at the suggestion of southern gentlemen; I not having been applied to by any northern men upon the subject. They were modifications made to meet the feelings and views of southern Senators, and not to further my own particular designs or views; because, as far as my understanding of the modifications proposed was concerned, I considered that they would make no material difference in its general character. There is no government, according to my understanding of the subject, existing now in California—that is to say, no American government—and when we speak of the existing government there, we speak of a government existing there at the time of the cession, just as you spoke of an existing government in Florida when you passed a similar law, some time after the cession. But, to relieve the amendment from any doubt upon that matter, I agreed to strike out the word "existing," and insert the word "Mexican."

Mr. Hunter. The Senator from New Jersey has not answered the precise point of my objection.

Mr. Dayton. I am coming to it.

Mr. Hunter. I stated that the word "existing" meant so much of the law remaining after California was ceded as was not inconsistent with our constitution, but that he reaffirms by this amendment the law in relation to negro slavery; it is sacrificing the principle which the South have hitherto, and will in future maintain, and which affects her dearest interests.

Mr. Dayton. I was answering the Senator, not all at once, in a single sentence, but categorically. He conceives that the change of the word "existing" into "Mexican" affects the character of the whole amendment, and invalidates the rights of the South. Now, if such be his opinion, I can only say to him, restore the amendment to its original form; I have not the slightest objection. I desire to subserve no purpose of my own in these modifications. In my understanding of the matter, the amendment as modified will not reaffirm the Mexican laws; it was with no such design that I accepted the modification relating to them. By this amendment we do not enact or re-enact, annul or disannul; we simply let things remain as they are, directing only that the officers who may be appointed shall exercise the powers heretofore exercised, and govern the country accordingly.

As to the extension of the Wilmot proviso by this modification, or dreaming that it was equivalent to an incorporation of that proviso, neither of those ideas entered into my mind for a moment. I would most cheerfully assent to any suggestion which might carry out the views of gentlemen on the different sides of this Chamber, who are desirous simply of giving a government to this country calculated to suppress anarchy and disorder—neither committing one party nor the other, asking no advantage from the South, nor feeling disposed to yield any advantage to them. That was my sole purpose in offering my amendment.

Mr. Hunter. I did not wish to interrupt the Senator in his remarks; I simply wish to state that I did not rise before for the purpose of entering into any contest, or of creating the occasion for one. My sincere desire is to compromise this question; and I wished to ascertain the feelings of northern gentlemen, to see if there was any possibility of effecting that end. I am willing to enter into such a compromise, provided it is based upon the principle that we leave this question undecided and in abeyance, and only adopt such laws as may be necessary in order to preserve the people of these Territories from anarchy and violence. I am anxious to secure the country from internal disorders and civil war—evils with which, by late accounts, it appears threatened. My remarks were prompted by a serious desire to effect that end, if possible; and now, after hearing the statement made by the Senator from New Jersey, I am willing to vote for his amendment, provided it be so modified as to attain the end which I have suggested, and no other. That is to say, I should be willing to vote for it so modified, if the proposition of the Senator from Wisconsin, which I prefer, should fail.

Mr. BERRIEN. The reference which the Senator from New Jersey has just made to me, renders it necessary that I should say a few words in relation to the modification of this amendment. It is very true that I suggested to that Senator the fact, that by an official communication made to the Senate, containing a letter from the Secretary of State, it appeared that there was an existing government in California. It was, therefore, suggested to him that the expression of "existing laws" might be construed to have reference to laws which, as in Oregon, may have been enacted by the existing government, and these it was not the purpose of Congress to carry into effect. It was therefore proposed to him to insert in lieu of it the word "Mexican." Thus far the statement of the Senator is correct, but it stops short of the most important fact; it omits the statement of a fact which would have obviated the difficulty of the Senator from Virginia.

The statement of the Senator from New Jersey is confined to a part, and does not embrace the whole modification suggested to him, and that it was made to depend upon his acceptance of it as a whole. It was proposed to him to insert after the word "Mexican," the words "not inconsistent with the Constitution of the United States;" and these words are in my handwriting, upon the paper of which the Senator has spoken, which contains the proposed modifications.

Mr. HUNTER, (in his seat.) That would have been perfectly satisfactory.

Mr. BERRIEN. The Senator from New Jersey declined to receive this modification, and it was that refusal which induced me to offer the considerations I presented to-day upon the subject under discussion.

I desire that Senators from New Jersey and Virginia will both understand me, as not having proposed to re-establish, or continue in force, the Mexican laws on the subject of slavery. I do not recognize the proposition, so often and so confidently asserted, that the laws existing in conquered or ceded territories remain in force until they are specifically repealed; and I am not disposed to re-enact them, as this amendment proposes to do. I suppose that the laws of the conquered territory, in so far as they affect the relations of individual citizens, remain in force until they are repealed by an act of specific or of general legislation, which shall extend the authority of the conquering nation over it. Recurring to the proposition which I have before stated to the Senate, I desire now to say that I am ready to maintain it before whatever tribunal it shall arise. I hope to be able to maintain that the Mexican laws which affect the relations of a people to their Government, do not remain in force, within the principle of the decision which is invoked for their support. It is not necessary that I should enter into any further discussion of this matter. I barely desired to correct myself, from the possible apprehension that I could have suggested an amendment that could have the effect spoken of.

Mr. WESTCOTT. Mr. President, I have no idea that the amendment of the Senator from Wisconsin (Mr. WALKER) touches, or was intended in any wise to touch or interfere with, the question of slavery in those Territories. Indeed, I know it was not so intended. The amendment leaves the question where it found it. The issue of slavery or no slavery in these Territories, which the Senator from Connecticut (Mr. NILES) says he is ready, and which he seems anxious to meet, is not involved. I am not so eager for that contest. I do not see how that Senator, or how any patriotic man can be. One reason that I favor this amendment is, because it leaves that question to be settled hereafter. If Congress is to attempt to settle it by legislation, it is best to postpone the decision of it to a more auspicious period. By so doing, time is given to the true friends of the country and of the Union in all sections, to exert themselves to promote conciliation and harmony. Who does not see at this time that the portents are ominous of discord and danger? This is not a propitious moment for calm and cool deliberation on this subject. The public mind is heated in both sections. Politicians, especially, are excited. We are just over a closely contested Presidential election, and in which this question was a prominent and exciting topic of discussion. Give time and opportunity for all to cool. If it is to come, at least put the evil day afar off. Avoid it. Shun it. Postpone it. Give time for reason and patriotism to resume their sway. This is the only effect of the first amendment. It does not give the President power to take slavery into the Territories if it is not there, nor to exclude it if it is there. It passes by the question entirely. The President is given no authority in relation to it. He cannot, under this law, change the condition of things with respect to slavery in anywise. If he should attempt it, he would do wrong. This is the compromise, and the only compromise, the first amendment offers, and it is offered to both sides and to all sides. It is impartial. The Senator from Connecticut rejects it. He is armed, ready for the quarrel. Senators are now called upon to decide which course is the best. I repeat, the vital question in issue is left untouched—its decision is postponed. Neither party is prejudiced. Sir, I am willing to bear my full share of all the censure of the Senator from Connecticut cast upon this amendment and those in anywise instrumental in its being proposed.

The Senator from Wisconsin (Mr. Walker) did me the honor to show me the amendment he intended to offer soon after he had prepared it, and also to give that consideration to some suggestions I made as to induce him to embody some of them in his draught; and subsequently the honorable Senator from Mississippi (Mr. Foote) consulted me with respect to the draughting of the proposition he made, and most of which is now added to or incorporated in the first amendment. The original draught of the amendment of the Senator from Wisconsin was confined to the extension of the revenue laws, and I believe the land laws, to the Territories, and the appointment of officers under them. The including of all other general laws, and the authority to make rules and regulations, I regarded as the most important matter. I have listened to all the objections urged against the propositions of the Senators from Wisconsin and Mississippi, and my judgment as to their wisdom, patriotism, and wise policy, has been confirmed.

Sir, I do not hesitate, as a southern Senator, to say here in my place that I regard the postponement of the decision of this slavery question at this session, as much more propitious to the perpetuity of this Union than its decision *in any way* could be *at this session*, if such decision could be made. I advocate this amendment distinctly on that ground. A decision by Congress, even if in favor of the South, at this session, I have apprehensions would not be peaceably acquiesced in, in the present state of excited feeling on this subject in the other sections. The public mind is, I fear, diseased with respect to it. Such decision now would be used by fanatics and demagogues, who are the enemies of the South, to carry out their unpatriotic, if not treasonable designs. They would, by such decision at this time, I fear, be able to excite prejudice, and mislead the people, and the ball might rebound. It would not be a settlement of the question, but would occasion renewed and more violent agitation. Sir, I believe it would be the part of true wisdom and patriotism not to decide, or to attempt to decide this question at this session, even if we could decide it. I would advise the South in all sincerity, that if they had the power at this session to organize these territorial governments, and expressly repudiate the Wilmot proviso in the law establishing the governments, it would still be the part of wisdom to postpone such decision. Give all time to cool. It is not a propitious time either to decide upon the Wilmot proviso, or to further discuss it. No man would be more gratified in his inmost heart to see this question properly and forever settled according to the constitution. No man can have felt more deeply than I have, and do, its momentous character. Its decision now, either way, is, I fear, fraught with imminent peril to our institutions. I have heretofore said, sir, that the interposition of the illegal action of Congress, now or hereafter, on this subject, would be, as it should be, resisted by the South. How can the flame that will burst forth from the South be stifled? Who will attempt it? But with respect to the North, I hope, if time is given, and if opportunity is afforded for the influence of patriotic citizens in those sections that I know are attached to the constitution and Union to be exerted, I believe the present feeling hostile to the South will subside. I will not despair of the Republic when the virtuous and patriotic can be aroused to protect it. Sir, I repeat, if the South had the ascendency at this time, I fear the exercise of its power, even in defence of its constitutional rights on this subject, would be but the signal for renewed and still more rancorous hostility to the South by the demagogues and fanatics who have fanned the flame of discord to its present fierceness. They must, if time is given, in a brief period sink to their true position. But, sir, who has any hope that this question can be decided this session, however desirable it may be? I have none. I reiterate again, (to impress it upon Senators,) that I do not desire this slavery question decided now, for I should not have confidence that such decision would be final; and that I, therefore, approve of this amendment because it leaves it undecided. I appeal to Senators on all sides and of all parties to sustain it: because it avoids such decision, because it postpones a dangerous crisis, which, I trust under Providence, may be, if time is afforded, passed through without harm to my country and institutions. I vote for this amendment expressly because I am anxious to give this perilous topic the go-by. My opinions are known. When the issue forced upon us arrives, I am prepared to act; but I confess I shrink with apprehension from the near approach of a crisis, upon the issues of which may depend the perpetuity of this Union. I would not accelerate the coming of that crisis, but I would give some chance for the storm to be averted. I do not desire to witness the conflict that is to occur if this amendment, or some similar proposition, be not adopted. Others may. I cannot. I envy no man who does.

The question was then taken on Mr. Dayton's amendment to Mr. Walker's amendment, in the following words:

"That until other provision for the government of the Territories recently acquired from Mexico, under the late treaty with that Government, (dated second February, eighteen hundred and forty-eight,) shall be made by Congress, all the military, civil, and judicial powers heretofore exercised by the officers of the Mexican Government in the same Territories, shall be vested in such person or persons, and shall be exercised in such manner, as the President of the United States shall direct, for the maintaining the inhabitants of said Territories in the free enjoyment of their liberty, property, and religion; and the laws of the United States, relating to the revenue and its collection, shall be extended to said Territories. And the President of the United States shall be, and he is hereby, authorized, within the term aforesaid, to establish such districts for the collection of the revenue, and during the recess of Congress appoint such officers, whose commissions shall expire at the end of the next session of Congress, to enforce the said laws, as to him shall seem expedient; said officers to receive such compensation as the President may prescribe, not exceeding double the compensation heretofore paid to similar officers of the United States or its Territories, for like service; and to enable the same to be done, the sum of two hundred thousand dollars be appropriated out of any money in the treasury not otherwise appropriated."

The yeas and nays being called for, and ordered, they resulted as follows:

YEAS.—Messrs. Allen, Atherton, Cameron, Dayton, Dodge of Wisconsin, Dodge of Iowa, Hamlin, and Mangum—8.

NAYS.—Messrs. Atchison, Badger, Baldwin, Bell, Berrien, Borland, Bradbury, Bright, Butler, Clarke, Corwin, Davis of Massachusetts, Davis of Mississippi, Dickinson, Dix, Douglas, Downs, Felch, Fitzgerald, Fitzpatrick, Foote, Greene, Hale, Hannegan, Houston, Hunter, Johnson of Maryland, Johnson of Louisiana, Johnson of Georgia, Jones, King, Mason, Miller, Niles, Phelps, Rusk, Sebastian, Spruance, Sturgeon, Turney, Underwood, Upham, Wales, Walker, Webster, Westcott, and Yulee—47.

The question then recurring on Mr. WALKER's amendment,

Mr. BERRIEN offered a modification of the amendment, which Mr. WALKER accepted, so that the amendment now reads as follows:

"SEC. —. *And be it further enacted,* That the Constitution of the United States, in so far as its provisions can be applied to the condition of a Territory, and all and singular the several acts of Congress respecting the registering, recording, enrolling, or licensing ships or vessels, and the entry and clearance thereof, and the foreign and coasting trade and fisheries, and all the acts respecting the imposing and collecting of duties on imports, and all acts respecting trade and intercourse with the Indian tribes, and all acts respecting the public lands, or the survey or sale thereof, and all and singular the other acts of Congress of a public and general character, and the provisions whereof are suitable and proper to be applied to the territory west of the Rio del Norte, acquired from Mexico by the treaty of the second day of February, eighteen hundred and forty-eight, be, and the same are hereby, extended over and given full force and efficacy in all said territory; and the President of the United States be, and he is hereby, authorized to prescribe and establish all proper and needful rules and regulations (in conformity with the Constitution of the United States), for the enforcement of the provisions of the constitution hereinbefore referred to of said laws in said territory, and for the preservation of order and tranquillity, and the establishment of justice therein; and from time to time to modify or change the said rules and regulations, in such manner as may seem to him discreet and proper, and may prescribe and establish, temporarily, such divisions, districts, ports, offices, and arrangements proper for the execution of said laws, and appoint and commission such officers as may be necessary to administer such laws in said territory, for such term or terms as he may prescribe, whose authority shall continue until otherwise provided by Congress; said officers to receive such compensation as the President may prescribe, not exceeding double the compensation heretofore paid to similar officers of the United States or its Territories for like services; and to enable the same to be done, the sum of two hundred thousand dollars be appropriated, out of any money in the treasury not otherwise appropriated."

Mr. UNDERWOOD moved to amend the amendment, by striking out the words "west of the Rio Grande," and inserting the word "territory" in the place of the word "territories."

Mr. HOUSTON. Mr. President, it is not my intention to inflict a speech upon the Senate at this advanced stage of the session. I have merely risen to state my objection to any amendment of the character of that proposed by the honorable gentleman from Kentucky. I presume that the passage of the amendment brought forward by the honorable gentleman from Wisconsin, will not entirely close the question to which the amendment of the honorable gentleman from Kentucky obviously points; and if that Senator should, at any future time, see proper to raise that question, we who represent Texas on this floor, will be prepared, I am satisfied, to show that the Rio Grande is the western boundary of Texas; that she owns every foot of land up to the eastern bank of that river. As the amendment now stands, it certainly does not invade the rights of the Territories proposed, or the State proposed, or of the United States. Nor was it in any such spirit, or with any such design, that that amendment was suggested and framed. It was suggested and framed with a disposition not only to allay all feeling in the other House, but with a disposition, at least on the part of the gentleman who introduced it, without consultation, to accord to Texas that portion of territory which she has ever claimed from the very inception of her existence. And I presume that no one who has any regard for the rights of Texas, will leave that, so far as it affects her, an open question.

With these remarks, Mr. President, I will take leave of the subject, only adding that I shall vote for no amendment which may seem even to menace the rights of the State which I have the honor in part to represent.

Mr. RUSK. Mr. President, I would not willingly trespass upon the patience of the Senate at so late an hour, but I must beg their indulgence while I say a few words upon a subject upon which I feel constrained to speak.

I regret exceedingly that the honorable Senator from Kentucky, (Mr. UNDERWOOD), should have taken this occasion to offer an amendment of this sort, to raise a question which, if it is likely to be acted upon against the rights of the State of Texas, will, in all probability, consume the remainder of the time allotted to us for the passage of this bill.

Mr. President, the rights of Texas are well-founded. There are but two claimants to the territory east of the Rio Grande. There is but one regularly-organized claim to it, and that is the claim of the State of Texas; she has a regular claim. There is a different claim, however, started here—not by the Government, nor by a single constituted authority of the United States—for the purpose of appropriating it to the United States. This claim has only been set up here incidentally. The President of the United States, and the Government of the United States, have always and uniformly recognized the rights of Texas.

Then, sir, it is due to Texas, according to the terms of the joint resolution by which she was adopted into this Confederacy, if this Government is disposed to keep her faith to Texas, that this question should be settled here as between Texas and the Government of the United States, and not slighted over as between Texas and a Territory, or a State which is hereafter to come into the Union. Under such circumstances, I do not apprehend that the amendment of the honorable Senator from Kentucky will be allowed to pass. I have stood here ever since I had the honor to take a seat in this body, ready upon any and all occasions to defend the rights of Texas, and shall hereafter, whenever this question may be presented, be found ready still to defend them.

Mr. Webster. Mr. President, I do not mean to say whether Texas has a just claim to the extent stated by her representatives or not. It is far from my purpose, on this occasion, to give any vote which shall have a bearing, one way or the other, on that question. I shall not, certainly, vote for the amendment of the honorable member from Wisconsin, (Mr. Walker,) because it implies the right of Texas to the country east of the Rio Grande. Nor shall I vote for the amendment of the honorable member from Kentucky, (Mr. Underwood,) because it purports, or may be implied to deny that right. Sir, are we now prepared, on an inappropriate, incongruous, alien proposition, to amend a bill for the civil and diplomatic service of the Government, to go into that great question—the boundary of Texas? Far be it from me to give any vote on any such collateral question as this, touching that great and important interest. I shall vote against the amendment of the honorable member from Kentucky; I shall vote against the amendment of the honorable member from Wisconsin, "*nequi teneo, nequi refellor*." This is no occasion to settle a question so important to one of the States of this Union, and so important to the whole Union itself.

Mr. Underwood. Mr. President, I do not intend to detain the Senate by an argument. I rise for the purpose of stating the object which I had in view in offering the amendment. This amendment, if it has any effect at all, will strengthen the proposition before the Senate. Do Senators expect that this question of settling the boundaries of the State of Texas can be acted upon by the other branch of Congress? If we pass the amendment, as it now stands, will it not be an expression of the opinion that the Rio Grande is the true boundary of Texas? Unquestionably it will have that effect. It will have the effect of embarrassing this measure if it gets to the other branch of Congress.

I am not at all surprised that the gentleman from Massachusetts (Mr. Webster) will not vote for my amendment, because, if it prevails, it will make the proposition stronger, as he has already notified us that he would not vote for any such proposition in any shape. I desire to give a government to California without any embarrassment in relation to the boundary of Texas. I will not further detain the Senate.

Mr. Underwood's amendment was not agreed to.

The question then recurred on the original amendment of Mr. Walker, as modified by Mr. Berrien, and resulted as follows:

Yeas.—Messrs. Atchison, Bell, Berrien, Borland, Butler, Davis of Mississippi, Dickinson, Dodge of Iowa, Douglas, Downs, Fitzgerald, Fitzpatrick, Foote, Hannegan, Houston, Hunter, Johnson of Louisiana, Johnson of Georgia, King, Mangum, Mason, Rusk, Sebastian, Sturgeon, Turney, Underwood, Walker, Westcott, and Yulee—29.

Nays.—Messrs. Allen, Atherton, Badger, Baldwin, Bradbury, Bright, Cameron, Clarke, Corwin, Davis of Massachusetts, Dayton, Dix, Dodge of Wisconsin, Felch, Greene, Hale, Hamlin, Johnson of Maryland, Jones, Miller, Niles, Pearce, Phelps, Spruance, Upham, Wales, and Webster—27.

So Mr. Walker's amendment was adopted, the Senate sitting as in Committee of the Whole.

Friday, March 2.

Retirement of the Vice President.

The Vice President arose, and addressed the Senate as follows:

Gentlemen of the Senate: The close of my official term being near at hand, I conform to an established and convenient practice, by withdrawing from the deliberations of this body, and thus creating the occasion for the choice of a temporary President.

It is impossible for me, however, to do this, without begging you, each and all, to accept my thanks for the courtesy and respect by which you have lightened the burden of my service in your Chamber.

The elevated principle and dignified tone which mark the proceedings of the Senate; the frank and yet forbearing temper of its discussions; the mutual manifestations of conciliatory deference, so just and appropriate among the delegates of independent States; and the consequent calmness and precision of its legislative action, have attracted to it a very large share of veneration and confidence. Four years of experience convince me that this confidence is not misplaced. It is true, that such an assembly, constantly handling topics of the widest bearing, of the highest and deepest concern to diversified constituencies, cannot avoid being occasionally disturbed by conflicting sentiments of patriotic duty, or by sudden impulses of feeling. But these transient disturbances are too intimately and obviously associated with representative fidelity, with unquestionable freedom of debate, and with a quick sense of public honor, to be subject to entire repression by the strictest rules of order. They are, indeed, rare, passing over the scene like flashes which do but startle, and then cease, and which serve only to exhibit in stronger relief the grave decorum of its general conduct. Long, forever, may this character be maintained in the Senate, strengthening, as it cannot fail to strengthen, the attachment of the American people to their admirable constitution of government.

You will, I trust, pardon me if I protract, for an instant, these parting words, in order to utter one or two sentiments, derived solely from my position as an agent of the nation.

A *right* to vote upon any question pending before this body, when its members are equally divided, is given to the Vice President by the constitution; and the *duty* to exercise that right is imposed upon him by an express rule of the Senate.

Although it so happened that equal divisions have occurred, during my official term, with unusual frequency—not less than *thirty* times—and although no one can be insensible to the signal responsibility of giving to this or the other scale, on such contingencies, the final preponderance, I am not aware of having faltered in casting my suffrage as, in my conscience, I believe the people of the United States, and especially that vast majority of them whose judgments and affections cling with ever-renewing conviction and devotion to the harmony and duration of the Union, would have prescribed. Of the cardinal duties of American functionaries, I have deemed *that* to be the foremost, which consists in practically upholding and exemplifying the beneficence, independent social organization, equality, and fraternity, so distinctly and directly inculcated in the constitution. Nor, Senators, is any man fit to participate in the government of great societies, with elements combined as ours are, who hesitates about disobliging the few who have access to or surround him, for the sake of the many whom he can never see. In these reflections lies the simple and safe rule of truly patriotic action. I am far from the self-flattery of supposing that the deciding votes so often, and sometimes so suddenly, required at my hands, conformed unerringly to this rule; but I cannot repress the hope that time and trial will prove them to have been as positively right as I am absolutely certain they were rightly intended.

My draught, gentlemen, on your generous indulgence, is a heavy one, when I ask you to forget or overlook the many imperfections with which the duties of the chair have been discharged. Its labors, occasionally more arduous and anxious, are always more absorbing than is generally supposed; and I undertook them with an oppressive consciousness of inexperience. Now that I am finally relieved from the burden, let me say that I shall take back to the private pursuits whence I was unexpectedly called, the most grateful recollections of your kindness, and an ardent wish that your toils to advance the prosperity of a country, beloved by us all, may be rewarded by the purest public favor, and by prolonged lives of happiness and honor.

Vice President Pro Tem.

On motion by Mr. BENTON,

Mr. ATCHISON was then appointed President of the Senate *pro tem.*

Mr. ATCHISON said, on taking the chair—

SENATORS: I cannot refrain from returning to you my heartfelt thanks for the repeated honors you have conferred on me; and I can only renew the pledge that I made when this honor was first conferred on me—that I will endeavor to discharge the duties of the station faithfully and impartially.

Mr. WEBSTER rose and said: Mr. President, we have witnessed, sir, the retirement from the chair of the Vice President of the United States, who has presided over the deliberations of this body for four years. It has happened to me to have been a member of the Senate from the time when he took his seat as its presiding officer, and it gives me great pleasure, sir, to perform the duty which I now rise to discharge, by offering a resolution, appropriate I hope the Senate will think, to this occasion. I propose a resolution, gravely and most respectfully tendering the thanks of this body to the Vice President of the United States, for the ability and impartiality with which he has presided over its deliberations during the time he has filled the chair.

Mr. W., in conclusion, submitted the following resolution:

Resolved, unanimously, That the thanks of the Senate are due, and are hereby tendered, to George M. Dallas, Vice President of the United States and President of the Senate, for the dignity and impartiality with which he has presided over its deliberations.

The question being taken upon the resolution, it was agreed to.

On motion by Mr. BENTON,

Ordered, That the Secretary of the Senate inform the House of Representatives that the Hon. D. R. Atchison has been appointed President of the Senate *pro tem.*

Credentials of Hon. James Shields.

Mr. DOUGLAS presented the credentials of the Hon. JAMES SHIELDS, elected a Senator from the State of Illinois, for six years from the 4th inst., in the place of the Hon. S. BREESE; which were read.

Mr. WALKER rose and said, in justice to General SHIELDS, in justice to the Senate of the United States, in justice to the people, and all concerned—and he disavowed any other purpose—he would move to refer these credentials to the Committee on the Judiciary. He would embody in a resolution instructions to the committee, if he had time to prepare it, to inquire into the eligibility of General SHIELDS. He wished that questions, which have lately to some extent excited an interest among the members of the Senate and the people of the United States, might be inquired into.

Mr. Mangum thought the motion premature. The proper time to make such a motion would be when General Shields presented himself to take the oath of office. But, beyond that, the present body should not decide a question which properly devolved on the Senate as it would be constituted in a few days.

Mr. Walker appreciated the suggestion, and withdrew his motion.

HOUSE OF REPRESENTATIVES.

Friday, March 2.

General Appropriation Bill—The New Territories.

The House resolved itself into Committee of the Whole on the State of the Union, (Mr. Stephens, of Georgia, in the chair,) and proceeded to the consideration of the amendments to the bill making appropriations for the civil and diplomatic expenses of the Government.

The recommendations of the Committee of Ways and Means, with reference to the amendments of the Senate, were concurred in without a division, with the exception of those subsequently noticed.

The following amendment of the Senate came up:

"Sec. —. *And be it further enacted*, That the Constitution of the United States, in so far as the provisions of the same be applicable to the condition of a Territory of the United States, and all and singular the several acts of Congress respecting the registering, recording, enrolling or licensing ships or vessels, and the entry and clearance thereof, and the foreign and coasting trade and fisheries, and all the acts respecting the imposing and collecting of duties on imports, and all acts respecting trade and intercourse with the Indian tribes, and all acts respecting the public lands, or the survey or sale thereof, and all and singular the other acts of Congress of a public and general character, and the provisions whereof are suitable and proper to be applied to the territory west of the Rio del Norte, acquired from Mexico by the treaty of the 2d February, 1848, be, and the same are hereby, extended over and given full force and efficacy in all said territory; and the President of the United States be, and he is hereby authorized to prescribe and establish all proper and needful rules and regulations, in conformity with the Constitution of the United States, for the enforcement of the provisions of the constitution herinbefore referred to, and of said laws in said territory, and for the preservation of order and tranquillity, and to the establishment of justice therein, and from time to time to modify or change the said rules and regulations in such manner as may seem to him discreet and proper, and to establish temporarily such divisions, districts, ports, officers, and all arrangements for the execution of said laws, and appoint and commission such officers as may be necessary to administer such laws in said territory, for such term or terms as he may prescribe, whose authority shall continue until otherwise provided by Congress; said officers to received such compensation as the President may prescribe, not exceeding double the compensation heretofore paid to similar officers of the United States or its Territories for like services; and to enable the same to be done, the sum of $200,000 be appropriated, out of any money in the treasury not otherwise appropriated."

This amendment the Committee of Ways and Means of the House had moved to amend, as follows:

"That the President of the United States be, and he is hereby, authorized to hold possession of and occupy all the territories ceded by Mexico to the United States by the treaty of the 2d day of February, 1848; and that he be authorized for that purpose, and in order to maintain the authority of the United States and to preserve peace and order in said territories, to employ such parts of the army and navy of the United States as he may deem necessary.

"*And be it further enacted*, That until six months after the expiration of the next session of Congress, unless Congress shall sooner provide for the government of said territories, the existing laws thereof shall be maintained and observed; and that the civil and judicial authorities heretofore exercised in said territories shall be vested in, and exercised by, such person or persons as the President of the United States shall appoint and direct, to the end that the inhabitants of said territories may be protected in the full and free enjoyment of their liberty, property, and religion; and all existing laws of the United States in force in relation to the public lands of the United States, and in relation to their intercourse with the Indian tribes, shall be deemed, so far as practicable, applicable to said territories: *Provided, nevertheless*, That martial law shall not be proclaimed or declared in said territories, or in either of them, nor any military court established, except ordinary courts-martial for the trial of persons belonging to the army and navy of the United States: *And provided, also*, That all existing laws of the United States relative to trial by jury in criminal cases, the issuing writs of *habeas corpus*, and the proceedings thereupon, are hereby declared to apply to and to be in force in said territories; and any decision upon any writ of *habeas corpus* ordering the discharge or detention of any person, shall be subject to be reviewed in the Supreme Court of the United States, under such regulations as shall be prescribed by that tribunal.

"*And be it further enacted*, That the sum of $200,000 be, and the same is hereby, appropriated for the purpose of carrying the provisions of this act into effect, to be paid out of any moneys in the treasury not otherwise appropriated."

And the question being on the amendment of the committee to the amendment of the Senate.

Mr. Schenck moved to amend the amendment of the Senate by striking out, in the twelfth and thirteenth lines, the words "west of the Rio Del Norte."

Mr. S. would ask, he said, that the rule of the House might be observed. He wished the Clerk to read the amendment of the Senate as it now stood, to state the words proposed to be stricken out, and then to state the amendment of the Senate as it would read if the words were stricken out.

The Clerk did so.

Mr. Schenck asked for tellers, who were appointed, (Messrs. Schenck and Harmanson.)

And the question on the amendment was then taken, and decided in the affirmative—ayes 93, noes 81.

So the amendment was agreed to.

The Slave Trade.

Mr. Sidney Lawrence moved to amend the amendment of the Senate, by adding thereto the following proviso:

That nothing in this act shall be so construed as to extend any law relating to the coastwise slave trade to California and New Mexico.

The amendment was agreed to.

The question then recurred upon agreeing to the substitute of the Committee of Ways and Means, which was read.

Mr. Grinnell called for the reading of the Senate amendment as amended, which was read.

The question was then taken by tellers, (Messrs. Root and Meade,) who reported—yeas 17; the noes were not counted.

So the amendment of the Committee of Ways and Means was rejected.

The question now come up on agreeing to that amendment of the Senate, to wit, that which extends the constitution and laws of the United States over the new Territories.

The yeas and nays were asked, and ordered; and being taken, resultsd as follows:

Yeas.—Messrs. Adams, Atkinson, Barringer, Barrow, Bayly, Beale, Bedinger, Birdsall, Bocock, Botts, Bowdon, Bowlin, Boyd, Boyden, Bridges, Brodhead, Charles Brown, Albert G. Brown, Buckner, Burt, Cabell, Chapman, B. L. Clarke, Clingman, Howell Cobb, Williamson R. W. Cobb, Cocke, Crisfield, Crozier, Daniel, Donnell, Garnett Duncan, Alexander Evans, Featherston, Ficklin, Flournoy, French, Fulton, Gaines, Gayle, Gentry, Goggin, Green, Willard P. Hall, Haralson, Harmanson, Harris, Haskell, Hill, Hilliard, Isaac E. Holmes, George S. Houston, John W. Houston, Inge, C. J. Ingersoll, Iverson, Jameson, Andrew Johnson, R. W. Johnson, George W. Jones, John W. Jones, Kaufman, Kennon, Thomas B. King, La Sère, Leffler, Levin, Ligon, Lumpkin, McClernand, McDowell, McKay, McLane, McQueen, Meade, Morehead, Morse, Outlaw, Pendleton, Peyton, Phelps, Pilsbury, Preston, Rhett, Richardson, Roman, Sawyer, Shepperd, Simpson, Stanton, Stephens, Thibodaux, Thomas, Jacob Thompson, John B. Thompson, Robert A. Thompson, Tompkins, Toombs, Venable, Williams, and Woodward—100.

Nays.—Messrs. Abbott, Ashmun, Belcher, Bingham, Blackmar, Brady, Butler, Canby, Cathcart, Collamer, Collins, Conger, Cranston, Crowell, Cummins, Darling, Dickey, Dixon, Duer, Dunn, Eckert, Edsall, Edwards, Embree, Nathan Evans, Faran, Farrelly, Fisher, Freedley, Fries, Giddings, Gott, Greeley, Gregory, Grinnell, Hale, N. K. Hall, Hammons, Jas. G. Hampton, Henley, Henry, Elias B. Holmes, Hubbard, Hudson, Hunt, Jenkins, James H. Johnson, Kellogg, Daniel P. King, Lahm, William T. Lawrence, Sidney Lawrence, Lincoln, Lord, Lynde, McClelland, McIlvaine, Job Mann, Horace Mann, Marsh, Marvin, Miller, Morris, Mullin, Murphy, Nelson, Nes, Newell, Nicoll, Palfrey, Peaslee, Peck, Petrie, Pettit, Pollock, Putnam, Reynolds, Richey, Robinson, Julius Rockwell, John A. Rockwell, Rose, Root, Rumsey, St. John, Schenck, Sherrill, Silvester, Slingerland, Smart, Caleb B. Smith, Robert Smith, Truman Smith, Starkweather, Andrew Stewart, Charles E. Stuart, Strohm, Strong, Tallmadge, Taylor, James Thompson, Richard W. Thompson, Wm. Thompson, Thurston, Tuck, Turner, Van Dyke, Vinton, Warren, Wentworth, White, Wick, Wiley, Wilmot, and Wilson—114.

So the amendment was rejected.

Mr. Pettit moved a reconsideration of the vote, and that that motion be laid on the table.

And the question having been taken, and decided in the affirmative—

The motion to reconsider was laid on the table.

The action of the Committee of the Whole on the state of the Union, upon the other amendments, not particularly specified, was concurred in.

IN SENATE.

Saturday, March 3.

Department of the Interior.

Mr. Hunter, from the Committee on Finance, to which was referred the bill from the House of Representatives to establish the Home Department, and to provide for the Treasury Department an Assistant Secretary of the Treasury, and a Commissioner of the Customs, reported it with amendments.

Mr. Underwood moved to take up the bill to establish a Home Department.

The motion to take up the bill was agreed to, and the Senate proceeded, as in Committee of the Whole, to its consideration.

Mr. Hunter said, the Committee on Finance proposed to amend the bill by striking out the provisions for a Commissioner of Customs, and an Assistant Secretary of the Treasury, together with so much of the 14th section as proposed to transfer clerks to that commissioner. The committee saw no sufficient reason for creating these new offices, and as provisions already existed for performing the duties proposed to be assigned to them, by persons other than the Secretary of the Treasury, they did not see how his labors were to be lessened by the proposed change, nor was it shown to them that the public business would thus be dispatched with more facility.

Mr. Davis. A large portion of the labors of the Secretary of the Treasury are a mechanical discharge of duties which cannot be discharged under the present organization, but which will be discharged by the Commissioner of Customs and the Assistant Secretary of the

Treasury, by the authority in the bill. It is only by giving them the powers which belong to such an organization, that they will be enabled to relieve the Secretary of the Treasury from these mere manual labors. The transfer of the duties is a concomitant of such an organization.

Mr. ALLEN. I am opposed to this bill; nor do I think we shall have time, during the few hours that remain of this session, to go into the business of creating a new department and new bureaus. This is a bill which will be followed by another bill the next session of Congress, requiring a hundred additional clerks, notwithstanding there are now twice that number. Besides, we propose to make a Cabinet officer the very last day of this Administration. We are assuming that those who are to succeed us require more advisers than we have had; we are doing that thing which they ought to do, if they think it is required. When a new Administration comes in, if they think there is a necessity existing for this department, doubtless they will recommend it to Congress at the next session, when it can be fully considered. I am utterly opposed to taking upon ourselves the responsibility of this augmentation of patronage, and consequent expense to the people. The Government has got along in peace and war with our present departments. They have got along most triumphantly; and I never heard till to-day, that the Secretary of the Treasury was incapable of performing all the duties of his office, and that it was necessary to add another member to the Cabinet. Sir, there are two things that never go back: one, the increase of officers, the other, the increase of their salaries. We never decrease offices; we never decrease salaries. And if we begin by this division of the Treasury Department into two departments, it will not be five years before we shall be told that there are causes for augmenting the other departments. If there had been a proposition merely to create an Under Secretary of the Treasury, or to have created a Commissioner of Customs, one or both, there would have been some plausibility in the thing. But here is a proposal to transfer a very large part of the duties of the Secretary entirely from the Secretary of the Treasury, to a new Secretary of a Home Department; and, after having diminished his labors one-half, then we are to create two new bureaus. Now, at the close of a war, with a national debt on our hands, and with a bill pending, as I understand, for issuing treasury notes, which is but another form of borrowing some five or six millions of dollars, I do not think it is right to augment the offices of Government. Every one knows, who has any experience in public affairs, that if the tendency of things in our Government shall continue, the present tariff will not suffice to keep the Government on foot, much less to supply the funds for the gradual extinction of the national debt. There must be retrenchment, or perpetual loans and perpetual debt. The custom-house cannot yield enough to meet the demands now made upon the public treasury, nor can a tariff be made high enough to yield a revenue to meet these demands. The issuing of treasury notes will become the permanent policy of the country, if retrenchment be not resorted to. I made some allusion the other day to adding up these figures. I know, and every one knows, that there is less attention paid to the expenditures of the Government than perhaps at any period of our history; and every one knows where the fault is, and that this tendency is hourly increasing; but this is not the time to discuss this matter further.

Mr. DAVIS, of Mississippi. As usual, I agree very well with the Senator from Ohio, that it is very improper to increase the powers of the Federal Government beyond what they must necessarily be. But here, sir, the vast increase of patronage amounts to an addition of three officers and two clerks, I believe. This is all that is added. There is a division of the Treasury Department, merely to expedite the business, and relieve it from manual and mechanical labor. The new officers would perform duties which are now performed by the Treasury Department, and also the duties now performed by some other departments. The questions coming up under the custom laws, which are now referred to the Comptroller of the Treasury, will be decided by the Commissioner of Customs. They are sometimes at present detained from sixty to ninety days, and then go to the Secretary of the Treasury himself. If a Commissioner of Customs is appointed, all these questions growing out of custom laws will be decided promptly by him, and thus a large benefit will be conferred on men engaged in commerce, and the revenue of the country, as these questions involve the revenue of the country as well as the commercial interests of individuals.

With this brief answer to the Senator from Ohio, I will only say that I do not intend to defend this bill, because I believe it has been before the Senate so long as to need no further defence or explanation. I leave it to the Senate, to be debated by those who shall think proper to debate it.

Mr. WEBSTER. Sir, I am in favor of this bill, and I have no objection to the amendments. I am rather inclined to concur in them, and upon the whole, I am of the opinion that it is now most expedient, if the Senate approve of the general object of the bill, to take it and pass it. As far back as the time of Mr. Monroe, and up to this time, persons most skilled and of the most experience in the administration of this Government, have recommended the creation of some other department, and to make some further distribution of the duties. Gentlemen can remember what Mr. Monroe, and, I believe, earlier, what Mr. Madison said on that subject. I believe it is true that the business of the Government has outgrown the means of performing the duties of it. It is said, but not very conclusively, that we create offices from time to time, and make additions to salaries of existing offices. Well, the country is increasing; the business of the Government is increasing; there is a great deal more work to be done. I do not know one bureau, one department, one clerkship in the administration of this Government that may now be considered a sinecure. I am persuaded that a great portion of the officers in the Treasury Department are over-worked, as well as in the War and other Departments. This bill may not be perfect; it may require further consideration. I wish there was more time to consider it now. But the popular branch of the Legislature has passed it. It is here. It is my opinion that there is a general sense in the country that some such provision is necessary. I see nothing incongruous in separating the business of the Land Office from the Treasury Department, because, in the first place, the business of the land office is enough of itself to occupy the attention of one man. I agree that, so far as the revenue of the country results from the receipts from the public lands, if there were no other object, it might be well that they should continue under the same administration. But for all essential purposes it is the same. The proceeds of the public lands are brought into view by the Secretary of the Treasury. And they will be hereafter, as heretofore, included in every estimate of the public income. I see no inconvenience, but it will relieve the head of the Treasury Department from acting and deciding upon these very numerous and very important land questions that arise for his decision. I will not say any thing of the importance of the Indian Department, now attached to the Department of War; I will not say any thing of certain portions of the duties now assigned to the Department of State, such as the Patent Office, which are quite abundant to supply work enough for the most intelligent and most diligent man in the country. I believe this to be the case, and I entirely concur with what has been said by the member from Mississippi. I shall, for myself, be content to vote for the bill as it is. The subject will be open for revision hereafter, and nothing will be established but what Congress may revise.

Mr. NILES. This is not a bill properly before us for legislation. It is not a proper subject of legislation. You cannot create a new department by the legislation of Congress. The departments of this Government grow not out of the jurisdiction, but the duties of the Government. The necessity of the performance of new duties would lead to the necessity of having new officers to perform those duties. If we were to have an internal revenue, or a direct tax, or any other mode of raising revenue within the country, it might require a new department relating to this internal revenue, and it might include the internal trade and the agricultural interests and statistics of the country, and be connected with all the industrial pursuits of the country. The departments grow out of the nature of the public duties. The Department of State is connected with our foreign relations, or with the business of the nation as a confederated State. The Department of the Treasury is connected with the revenue of the country. The Department of War is connected with the military establishment of the country, and the Department of the Navy with the naval establishment of the country. Then we have an Attorney-General, who is the law officer of the Government; the Postmaster-General, who is connected with the mail service of the country. Now, can you, by law, create a new department where there are no additional public duties to be discharged? Why, sir, it is not a new department; it is a new Cabinet officer. What are his appropriate duties. He has no appropriate duties by this bill; and the very fact that the bill provides for this high officer but one clerk, proves that he has no duties whatever as the head of a department. It cannot be called a department. This is only a bureau. The officer is to have supervision in case of appeal, but he has no independent judicial department.

It is important, it is said, that this new officer should be appointed, in order to relieve the Treasury Department. But, as I understand the bill, there are various other duties given to this new officer. One of the bureaus of that department is given to him, it is true; but he has also taken a bureau from almost every other department. He has taken a bureau from the War Department, and from the State Department, and so of others. He has taken the Patent bureau, the Public Land bureau, and a number of other bureaus, thrown together without appropriate connection, and placed under this new officer, and called a department. And what is the advantage of making a separation of these bureaus from the departments to which they are now attached? Why, sir, it is known that they are substantially independent of the departments. They discharge their own appropriate duties; and the cases of appeal are not very numerous, nor very troublesome. They are merely to settle some general principle. All the detail of the ordinary business of the bureau may be considered as independent of the department. This is the case already with most of the bureaus of the Treasury Department. The accounting bureaus are independent by law, and ought to be. They merely bring general principles before the proper head of the department. Questions of law are referred to the law officer of the Government. Those cases where appeal is made to the head of the department, or the Attorney-General, are very few, and are not very troublesome.

Now, I see no appropriate duties for this new officer—none at all. What, then, is the necessity of creating an additional officer of this kind, who will have no appropriate duties —a mere officer to be placed at the head of the several bureaus which are now brought together without reason?

Mr. MASON said: What is it that it is proposed to do by this bill? Because it seemed necessary, from the nature of our State relations, of our State governments, of our people with their federated governments, that some matters of domestic interest should be managed by the Federal Government, it is now proposed to take advantage of that, and to organize a separate department, to include all those powers, and to absorb hereafter as much power as those who hold the reins of Government shall see fit to place in their hands. The Patent Office, the whole subject connected with patents, by the constitution, is vested in the Federal Government. What is it but a mere subordinate affair, though a matter of some interest, that is connected with this branch of the service? It has less reference to the great powers of the Government which are to be managed for the benefit of the whole people, but it could not well be managed by the States, and was vested in the General Government. It is a purely subordinate matter. Then there is the Indian Bureau, comprising our relations with the Indians, which were necessarily vested in the Federal Government. What does that amount to? These Indian tribes are decreasing in number every day; and they are driven further to the west, till, I apprehend, they will be driven to the very verge of the Pacific. How do our relations with them stand in comparison with those great departments of the Government which were carved out of the original power of managing our foreign relations? They are purely subordinate. Then the public lands must be left to the control of the General Government. That, too, is a purely subordinate department, entirely so. It is indeed a source of revenue, and at one time was a source of large revenue, but it was still subordinate.

Mr. President, these three subordinate bureaus have been heretofore assigned to their appropriate departments. The Patent Office has been under the supervision of the State Department, the Indian Bureau under the supervision of the War Department, and the Land Office under the supervision of the Treasury Department. But now it is said that these three subordinate bureaus devolve so much labor on the heads of those departments that they cannot properly attend to their duties; and, therefore, you must constitute out of them a separate department to enter into the organization of the Government, with a view to provide for this difficulty. Why, sir, if any of these departments are overworked, if they find it impossible to perform all the labor devolved upon them, what will be easier—unless there be a design to create a new department for the purpose of increasing the Federal patronage—than to give each of these bureaus an assistant, with the right of appeal to the head of the bureau? That is all that is wanted to obviate the difficulty.

It cannot be expected or supposed that the Secretary would go into the details of the individual cases; he can do no more than to settle principles. If an assistant is given in the Land Office, Patent Office, or Indian Bureau, he may relieve the heads of departments of much of their labor, and the power of appeal will give individuals equal justice. We all know very well, that in the general arrangement of these bureaus, the heads of the Patent Office, the Land Office, and the Bureau of Indian Affairs, must necessarily be men of superior intelligence, gentlemen of integrity, and conversant with all the affairs of the business over which they are placed. The chances are largely in favor of your finding in these bureaus men just as capable of attending to these duties as in the heads of departments themselves. There can be no question, that if the object is merely to provide means of doing the work, it can be better, far better done by keeping the offices, as they now are, separate, and, to a certain extent, independent, giving an assistant to each, subject to appeal to the head of the bureau. Why, sir, the heads of the departments are not only statesmen, but politicians, a great many of them, and necessarily so. They administer the Government honestly, I have no doubt, and correctly, within the sphere of their appropriate and regular duties. But they do more. They are managing the great political machinery of Government out of doors. Their minds are, to some extent, engrossed by matters of public interest, and to some extent, by matters of personal interest, which utterly preclude the possibility of their going into the details of all these minor subjects. I am against any interference in this matter, and especially at this juncture.

Mr. CALHOUN. I am aware of the impatience of the Senate to dispose of the subject; and I do not intend to detain them beyond what I deem it my duty to say on this occasion. This is a very important bill, and I exceedingly regret that I am so imperfectly acquainted with the principles upon which it has been urged at this time. I have no further opportunity to know its contents than by hearing it read, and hearing this discussion, and there has been so much noise that the greater part of what has been read and said has escaped my ear. I also regret exceedingly that there is so short a period to consider this bill, because I have noticed, as the result of my experience, that a measure, however important, is scarcely ever urged or opposed to any purpose at this late period of a session. Sir, is it fair to urge a bill of this magnitude upon the country at this time? I concur entirely with what was said by the Senator from Virginia, (Mr. MASON.) Bills of a character similar to this have been urged upon Congress, I believe, from the very first administration of General Washington, repeated at intervals by several Administrations, but never acted upon by Congress. There were never any considerable efforts made to carry them through. This I consider the strongest possible evidence against the propriety of such a measure. Why has Congress never carried out the suggestion of those eminent men who administered the affairs of this Government in the early days of this Confederacy? Why has Congress never acted in accordance with those suggestions and recommendations? Because they have felt it their duty, under a deep sense of the obligations imposed upon them by the constitution, to resist all attempts that have ever been made heretofore to embark in such a policy.

Mr. President, there is something ominous in the expression, "The Secretary of the Interior." This Government, as has been well said by the Senator from Virginia, was made to take charge of the exterior relations of the States. And if there had been no exterior relations the Federal Government would never have existed—the exterior relations with foreign countries, and the exterior relations of States with States, and that only carried to a very limited extent. Sir, the name "Interior Department" itself indicates a great change in the public mind. What has been the cause? We are told that the business of Government now has become such that the existing departments are overloaded, and that it requires a new department to be constituted. Is the fact so? What evidence have we of that fact? Has there been a committee appointed to call upon the several departments, or any of them, or upon the President of the United States, to ascertain whether that is the case? I understand not. We have but a communication from a single department; and upon that authority alone, at this last stage of the session, when we have but a few hours left to consider the importance of this bill, it is urged upon us. Sir, there is something striking, in the fact that this measure comes recommended from an outgoing Administration, and is supported here mainly by the friends of the incoming Administration, professing opposite political principles. That fact is very remarkable. The vote recently taken exhibited that remarkable state of things.

If the departments are overcharged, what has been the cause? Has it not resulted from the overaction of our Government? Is it not a strong admonition to us to retrace many of our steps, instead of forming new machinery to give a new impulse to that overaction? and a very powerful impulse this measure will give. But suppose that this overburden of business has not been the result of overaction, is there no other way of remedying it? May it not be corrected in a much more simple and safe form, by following the policy which has been already adopted in at least one of the departments—the Post-office Department—that of having an assistant, two or three of them, if necessary? Why not adopt the same machinery here instead of creating a new department, and bringing under its control half a dozen different branches of the public business having no connection with each other? I lay it down as a rule, founded on some experience, that it is far better that large masses of business, in their nature analogous to one another, should be under a common head, instead of being divided off. All that belongs to the revenue, directly or indirectly, ought to be under the charge of the Secretary of the Treasury; all that belongs to the War Department should be under the charge of the Secretary of War, and so on.

Mr. President, I understand that this bill proposes to make it a portion of the duty of this department to take charge of our Indian affairs. Who does not see that the Indian affairs are immediately connected with the War Department? Who does not see that the preservation of peace and harmony on our frontier, both between ourselves and the Indians, and between the Indian tribes themselves, depends upon the action of the War department? In my judgment, the Indian affairs are so intimately connected with the War Department that they cannot be separated without producing mischievous consequences.

The next feature of this bill is, as I understand it, that it provides for the creation of the office of Commissioner of Customs——

Mr. HUNTER, (interposing.) I would inform the honorable Senator that the new bureau of Commissioner of Customs is put under the charge of the Secretary of the Treasury.

Mr. CALHOUN. Then I will pass that over and go to the Land Office. The Land Office is put under this new department. Who does not see that there is a far more intimate relation between the duties of the Land Office and the duties of the Treasury Department, than between them and the duties of a department like this that is proposed to be established? The proceeds of the sales of the public lands, being a branch of the revenue, ought to be under the control of the Treasury Department. Does not every man see that every thing relating to the revenue ought to be under the control of a common head? It now appears, that after taking away that important branch from the Treasury Department, that department is to have new bureaus created for it, in addition to what it had before, thus adding machinery to machinery, and every addition to this machinery, giving a new impulse to that overaction of the Government which causes the necessity for these additions.

Well, sir, what is the next branch of business that is conferred upon this new department? The Patent Office. I admit that there is not a very intimate relation between the Patent Office and the State Department, which now has charge of it. But now I put a question to gentlemen who advocate this bill. The Patent Office is already charged with the subject of agriculture, making long annual reports, and very expensive ones. Is it intended to transfer that with the Patent Office to this Home Department? Is agriculture to go over to this new department, with the Patent Office? for, as the bill now stands, that is the practical operation of it.

Mr. Davis, of Mississippi, (interposing.) If the Senator wishes me to answer, I would say that it is one of the blessings to be derived from the contemplated organization, that instead of extending, as has been done for several years, the interference of the Federal Government in the agriculture of the country, by throwing it as one office into a new department, the head of that department will not have to build his reputation upon it. And for that reason the arrangement proposed by the bill is considered preferable to the present arrangement.

Mr. Calhoun. I am obliged to the Senator for expressing his views so distinctly. There is no power so strong as that of this Patent Office. Congress has struggled, but in vain, for years to limit this power. It has gone on increasing from year to year, until it has become a great overshadowing institution.

There is another large branch of business growing up connected with the legislation of Congress—the Smithsonian Institution. The Government is the trustee of that institution. The Government controls the Board of Trustees, and I venture to say that five years will not pass before the Smithsonian Institution will go into the Home Department. There is no end to these additions. Even the penitentiary of the District is placed under its control. Every thing upon the face of God's earth will go into the Home Department,—Indian Affairs, Patent Office, Land Office, Public Buildings, all, all thrown together without the slightest connection. This thing ought not to be. This is a monstrous bill. It is ominous. It will turn over the whole interior affairs of the country to this department; and it is one of the greatest steps that ever has been made in my time to absorb all the remaining powers of the States.

Sir, it is time to stop. Ours is a Federal Government. The States are the constituents of the Federal Government. It is a created, and it is a supervisory power. We are, step by step, concentrating and consolidating this power, until finally we will take the last and final step, and conduct all the business under the name of the "Department of the Interior." Sir, I cannot believe that if this bill had been earlier taken up, if there had been eight or ten days' deliberate discussion on it, it would receive the sanction of this Senate, or that it would have received the sanction of so many friends who, upon the general questions of the country, have always stood by the constitution and maintained the rights of the States. But, Mr. President, I know the disposition of the Senate, and I yield the floor.

Mr. Hunter. I took the floor, Mr. President, for the purpose of replying to an argument which seems to have some weight here; much more weight, I think, than is due to it. It is said that the Secretary of the Treasury will be unable to discharge all the duties of his office, unless we adopt some measure of this kind; that it will be impossible for him to undergo the labor that will be required of him, unless he shall be relieved from some of the duties of his office. Now, I ask, to what extent will this bill relieve the Secretary of the Treasury? It will be found, upon an examination of it, that the greater portion of the business of this Minister of the Interior is to be transferred, not from the Treasury, but from the other departments of the Government. First, he is to have charge of the Indian affairs, which is a transfer from the War Department, to which, as was stated by the Senator from South Carolina, it very properly belongs, inasmuch as they involve matters of war and peace with the Indian tribes. The next subject to be transferred to the Minister of the Interior is that of Patents, which is taken from the State Department. The only subject transferred from the Treasury Department is the control of the public lands, so far as relates to the right to decide in certain cases of appeal from the Land Office, and the general supervision of the public property in land. Now, in relation to this, one of two things must exist. If the Secretary of the Treasury is to be relieved from all the business connected with the public lands, then it must follow that the Minister of the Interior is to make the collections and disbursements of the income from that office. But that is not the business which is to be given to him, for, if it were, what would result? That we should have two Treasuries: one under the Secretary of the Treasury, as at present, for the receipt and disbursement of the income derived from customs; the other under the Secretary of the Interior, for the management and disbursement of the income derived from the public lands. In what manner would the affairs of this Government be administered, if we should thus disturb the harmony and unity of the Treasury Department? Well, then, if it is not intended by this bill, as I believe it is not, to transfer the collection of revenue from public lands to this Minister of the Interior, how is it that we relieve the Secretary of the Treasury, by its enactment? Why, we relieve him only of the decision of appeals from the Commissioner of Public Lands, and from a species of general supervision of the public property in lands. If I understand it, the purpose is to transfer only the power of deciding certain judicial cases arising in the Land Office, together with the supervision of the public lands, as a source of revenue; that is, to commit to his discretion the manner in which they shall be brought into the market. Now, this last duty manifestly belongs to the Secretary of the Treasury, who ought to control and manage the receipt of public revenue from whatever source derived. It is a mistake to suppose that this is a measure for the relief of the Treasury Department. It relieves the War Department to a far greater extent, taking from it as it does, the Indian affairs and also the Pensions. It relieves the State Department to a greater extent, in taking from it the Patent Office and its concerns. It relieves the Secretary of the Treasury from very little; and from that of which he might be relieved by merely increasing the power of the Commissioner of the Land Office. If I have succeeded in what I intended, I think I have shown that this bill, so far as the public lands are concerned, affords no relief to the Secretary of the Treasury, which could not very properly be given to him by increasing to a small extent the power of the Commissioner of the Land Office; and that all beyond giving the Commissioner the power of appeal, is improper to be given to any other than the head of the Treasury Department. The control of the mode of bringing the public lands into market, as a source of revenue, manifestly belongs to him. As a proof of this, we find that this very bill still leaves to the Secretary of the Treasury the control of the whole machinery for collecting and disbursing the proceeds from the sales of the public lands. Why not leave to his discretion, then, the mode in which they are to be brought into market?

But it is said that the Department is to find great relief in the appointment of an Assistant Secretary of the Treasury. This assistance is more fallacious, if possible, than the other which I have just been combating. What portion of the labors of the Secretary is he to take? Allow me to read the power that is given to him. He is to examine all letters, contracts, and warrants prepared for the signature of the Secretary of the Treasury, and to perform certain duties now discharged by clerks. What duty is here imposed upon him which is not already performed by some of the clerks of the department? It is not proposed to take from the Secretary the labor of signing these warrants; and it could not be taken from him without disarranging the whole machinery of the Treasury Department, and disturbing the system of checks and balances depending on the fact of his having to sign these warrants. This, then, relieves him of nothing. Nothing is transferred from him which might not easily be performed by the chief clerk in that department, and by enlarging the duties of the Commissioner of the Land Office in regard to appeals. And why not do this? We might as well as to create an additional department of the Government. Who can doubt that the creation of an additional department will bring with it a long train of new officials and much additional patronage?

Mr. President, if I had no other objection to this bill, I should vote against it at this late period of the session, because we have not had time to examine and mature it, and because such a bill would stand in the way hereafter of a proper reform of the Treasury Department. Sir, in my opinion, that reform will not be found to consist in multiplying departments and bureaus, and in increasing patronage. No, sir, the labors of that Secretary are to be lessened and the department itself reformed, not by increasing its officers, but by introducing a better system of bookkeeping, and a more judicious arrangement of the duties of the offices which already exist. The officers should be so classed and the accounts so arranged that each in its sphere should contribute to present the process of receipt and disbursement, not in detached portions, but as one whole, whose parts could be traced in minute detail through all the offices which stated the particulars from which the general results were derived. In other words, the reform of method in this department will be found here, as it has been found elsewhere, to consist in introducing fully and completely the system of bookkeeping by double entry. The forms of public accounts should be so prescribed, and the officers so classified in conformity to that arrangement, that each should perform a part, and but a single part, in ascending from minute details to the simple and general results of the ledger, with the same accuracy of balance-sheet and the same periodical rests which distinguish a well-kept private counting-house. A system approximating to this degree of excellence has been matured in France, and might be created here, if we were to take the proper pains, and guide ourselves by the lights of experience. If such a reform were once adopted here, I believe that a Secretary of fair financial ability could discharge all the duties now imposed upon the Department of the Treasury without being overtasked. I know, sir, that the Senator from Mississippi has admonished us that the labors of the Department, with the duties now imposed upon it, must break down any Secretary who undertakes them. They are great, I know, far greater than they need be, if the proper system were introduced, and the proper degree of responsibility enforced. But the remedy proposed in this bill does not even touch the evil. It is the system of accounts, and mode in which they are kept, which produces confusion and embarrassment. Why, sir, I was surprised to find that money derived from customs was often not transferred by warrant to the books of the Treasury Department for months after its receipt, and that revenue stated in Treasury reports as the receipt of one year was often in part the product of another. Sir, I could go further into this matter of the mode in which the public accounts are kept if there were time for it.

After an extended debate, the bill was reported to the Senate without amendment, ordered to a third reading, and read a third time.

The question being stated upon the passage of the bill, the yeas and nays were demanded and ordered, and being taken, resulted as follows:

Yeas.—Messrs. Badger, Baldwin, Bell, Berrien, Breese, Clarke, Corwin, Davis of Masschusetts,

Davis of Mississippi, Dayton, Dodge of Iowa, Douglas, Downs, Fitzgerald, Foote, Greene, Hale, Houston, Johnson of Maryland, Johnson of Louisiana, Jones, Mangum, Metcalfe, Miller, Pearce, Spruance, Underwood, Upham, Wales, Walker, and Webster—31.

NAYS.—Messrs. Allen, Atchison, Atherton, Benton, Borland, Bradbury, Bright, Butler, Calhoun, Cameron, Dickinson, Dix, Felch, Fitzpatrick, Hamlin, Hunter, King, Mason, Niles, Phelps, Rusk, Sebastian, Sturgeon, Turney, and Yulee—25.

So the bill was passed.

General Appropriation Bill.

Mr. ATHERTON, from the committee of conference on the part of the Senate on the disagreeing votes of the two Houses on the bill making appropriations for the civil and diplomatic expenses of the Government for the year ending June 30, 1850, and for other purposes, reported "that they have met the committee of conference on the part of the House of Representatives, and, after full and free conference, they could come to no agreement."

A message was received from the House of Representatives announcing that said House had concurred in the 53d amendment of the Senate to the bill making appropriation for the civil and diplomatic expenses of the Government for the year ending June 30, 1850, with an amendment, in which they asked the concurrence of the Senate; and that they had receded from their disagreement to the other amendments of the Senate.

The 53d amendment referred to was the provision relative to a government for California.

The Senate proceeded to consider the amendment of the House of Representatives.

Mr. WEBSTER moved that the Senate concur; and upon that question he asked the yeas and nays.

Mr. UNDERWOOD. I hope that the pending amendment will not prevail. If this amendment is to be adopted as a whole, allow me to comment very briefly upon both. The first section provides as follows:

"That the President of the United States be, and he hereby is, authorized to hold possession of and occupy the Territories of California and New Mexico, ceded by Mexico to the United States by the treaty of the 2d day of February, 1848, and that he be authorized, for that purpose, and in order to maintain the authority of the United States, and preserve peace and order in said Territories, to employ such parts of the army and navy of the United States as he may deem necessary."

That is the first clause. The whole of it amounts to this: that the President may use portions of the army and navy to hold possession of the country. Now, who can object to that? No one; all agree there. The next clause is:

"That, until the expiration of the next session of Congress, unless Congress shall sooner provide for the Government of said Territories, the existing laws thereof shall be maintained and observed; and that the civil and judicial authorities heretofore exercised in said Territories shall be vested in and exercised by such person or persons as the President of the United States shall appoint and direct, to the end that the inhabitants of said Territories may be protected in the full and free enjoyment of their liberty, property, and religion; *Provided, nevertheless,* That martial law shall not be proclaimed or declared in said Territories, or either of them, nor any military court established or instituted, except ordinary courts-martial for the trial of persons belonging to the army and navy of the United States."

Now, I have already expressed an opinion that the constitution goes there without any enactment at all. I think the proposition is as clear as any thing can possibly be. But there are gentlemen on this floor who dispute it. Then, if it be a debatable and disputable matter, this secures it. Here is the act which carries it there. If it goes there without any legislation, as some gentlemen contend, it does not require this provision. If it does not go there of itself, here is the very thing we want. Here is the legislation to carry it there. Who is there, then, that can object to the first section of the bill? By it we have got two things: we have got the right to occupy the country with our army and navy, and we have got the right to have the constitution administered.

Mr. FOOTE. We have got both now.

Mr. UNDERWOOD. I say we have got both now. But some of our associates dispute it; and if they are willing to give us a special enactment for it, I have no objection. So much for the first section. Then as to the second. I prefer retaining it to striking it out. I apprehend that some gentlemen suppose that the code of Spanish law, without legislation by us, is to prevail in that country always; and that they object on that ground to this section. Now, if there be any objection of that sort, it is wholly untenable because it is temporary; the words are "until the 4th day of July, 1850, unless Congress sooner provide for the government of the Territories." Well, now, sir, you must have officers to administer your laws there upon the principles of the constitution; and if you strike out the whole section, where will you get the authority to appoint them? It is this second section which provides the authority. And when they are appointed, what follows? In the third section it is provided that "to the end that the inhabitants may be protected," &c.; and here follows another provision, "that martial law shall not be proclaimed," &c. Now, in the second section, the proviso introduces a valuable provision; the second section provides for the appointment of officers who are to execute the laws; and the second section continues the Mexican code in force until July, 1850, unless Congress shall sooner provide.

Mr. FOOTE. I cannot permit the views of the honorable Senator from Kentucky, for whose judgment I have great respect, to pass without a proper response. And I will ask him to send me the amendment which he holds in his hand, for examination. As I was proceeding to say, some time ago, the first proposition of the amendment, is an absurdity, and is unnecessary. It is a matter already provided for. And what is that? Why, that the Government of the United States shall take possession of California and New Mexico. Is it not a fact that we are now in possession? Is it true? I thought it was a part of our history, and not the least creditable part of our history, that these Territories are now in our possession. It is provided that the President shall be authorized to "hold and occupy"—those are the terms—"the territory ceded by Mexico." Do we not occupy the Territories now? Certainly they are occupied, either actually or constructively, by this Government. Sir, is not the President authorized to hold possession? Is there any Senator who dares to take up the contrary position? Why, sir, we have conquered the country: we have occupied the country: we still hold possession of it, against all the powers of the earth. And I ask of any American Senator here if he presumes to assert, in the presence of such a body of men as is here assembled, that we are not now in possession? If gentlemen have any doubt on the subject, I can show them that the President of the United States considers himself as having conquered the country; as being in possession; as being entitled to hold possession; as being bound by every obligation to hold possession in all time to come. Why, then, insert this provision? It is useless.

Mr. DAVIS, of Mississippi. I now move that the Senate disagree to the amendment of the House; and I add to it another motion that the Senate appoint a Committee of Conference; and I will state why I make these motions. It is in order that the whole subject, relating to California, may be stricken out; and that, at this last moment of the session, we may proceed to pass the civil and diplomatic appropriation bill.

Mr. DOUGLAS. That is the last of all propositions that I can consent to. I would rather see the civil and diplomatic appropriation bill fail, than to see the proposition for a government for California fail. Between the two evils, it does not take me an instant to choose which I would prefer. I have supported every form of bill on which we have been able to vote, in order to give a government to California. I am prepared to do it yet, as far as I can do it, consistently with the principles which I hold to be essential. But I cannot consent now to abandon the whole thing; to leave the people of California without a government, merely for the sake of getting a little money for our own office-holders. And, sir, for what shall the people of California be thrown off? For what shall they be exposed to all the horrors of anarchy and of bloodshed, of murder, and of rapine? For what, sir? Merely because there is a technical difference between the amendment of the House and that of the Senate. I, sir, am for concurring. Let us clinch the nail while we can. What is the difference between the two propositions? There is not a shadow of difference; not a particle of substantial difference. There is not a lawyer in the Senate who can show that there is a particle of legal difference. It is simply a quarrel between the Senate's amendment and the amendment of the House; it is merely a controversy for triumph. Yes, sir, the Senate's amendment does continue the existing laws of the Territory. And the Supreme Court has decided the question.

Mr. DAVIS, of Mississippi. I am sure the Senator from Illinois does not wish to misrepresent me; therefore I take it for granted he has misunderstood my purpose. Sir, my purpose was to do that which it was in our power to perform, instead of wasting the last moments of the session in attempting to do that which we cannot accomplish. And, as to the bloodshed, murder, and robbery, I tell the Senator that California is filling with American citizens, who carry with them their protection wherever they go. The elements of government are formed in the breast of every American citizen.

Mr. DOUGLAS. I cannot say I am glad to hear the explanation of the Senator from Mississippi, for the explanation goes to show that the people of California are to be abandoned. He argues that they are capable of taking care of themselves, and that they need no aid from the Government. He ought to have made that argument against the proposition of the Senate. It is an argument against a territorial bill. It is an argument against all legislation. For that reason it is that I am alarmed, lest the people of California shall be abandoned, and no law provided for their protection.

Mr. HUNTER. I rise to offer an amendment, which perhaps will enable us to compromise this difficulty. If, in the second section, we adopt, after "the existing laws," the words, "so far as may be consistent with the Constitution of the United States," so as to enact the existing laws only to that extent, I think it probable that we shall all agree. As I understand, the Senator from Massachusetts and other Senators here wish to compromise on the principle of leaving this great question undecided, or of leaving it, if it has to be decided, to the Supreme Court of the United States.

Mr. WEBSTER. I hope the Senator will allow me to interrupt him. I feel an intense desire that this debate shall be terminated. And I put it to the candor of gentlemen whether it is worth while to send the bill back to the House at this hour of the night for such a purpose, when there is in the bill itself a provision that the Constitution of the United States is to be extended to the Territory? There is this provision in the amendment of the Senator from Wisconsin, although I do not think such a provision at all necessary; for, if the Constitution of the United States goes there, it goes, as has been argued on all sides of the Senate, as the supreme law of the land. Of course everybody knows that the laws of a conquered country exist until the laws of the conquering country are established. Now, I put it to the Senator from Virginia whether it is worth while to send back this bill for the purpose of making a provision which is wholly nugatory?

Mr. Hunter. I have no desire to prolong the debate. My most earnest desire is that the difficulty shall be adjusted. The Senator from Massachusetts says, that according to his construction of the amendment, it does extend the Constitution of the United States to the Territory. I do not rise for the purpose of arguing the matter; but there are gentlemen on this side who doubt the correctness of that construction. They believe it is an enactment of all the Mexican laws, without restriction or modification. Well, now, if the Senator from Massachusetts is willing that only so much of the Mexican laws as are consistent with the constitution and laws of this country shall be adopted, why not agree to this amendment?

Mr. Webster. I am unwilling that the bill should be sent back to the House. If the gentleman is willing to run the risk of losing the bill, let him take it on his responsibility.

Mr. Hunter. I am willing to take the responsibility. If we agree to the amendment, I have no doubt the House will agree to it, and especially if the Senator from Massachusetts is right in his construction of the amendment. If our object is compromise, and we do not desire to give an undue advantage—and I say it in all sincerity, for I am willing to compromise on this basis—leave the question to itself; leave it undecided; and, if it be brought up, let it be decided by the Supreme Court of the United States. Now, I ask if this is not fair? I am willing to do this, and I understand that the Senator from Massachusetts is also willing.

Mr. Webster. It is undecided now.

Mr. Hunter. The Senator from Massachusetts says it is undecided now. Well, if he believes so, why not introduce the amendment, which will test the question on this side of the Chamber as well as on that? Sir, I seek no advantage over the North, and I am sure they do not wish to obtain any advantage over us. The Senator says he would not endanger the bill by sending it to the House. I do not believe it would endanger it. I believe the House will take the same view that the Senator from Massachusetts does; and, if so, they will adopt the amendment. But, if it will endanger the passage of the bill, it can only be on the ground that the House mean to re-enact the Mexican law, which excludes slavery; and, if it does re-enact that law, I would be willing to lose the bill sooner than agree to it. Yes, I will take the responsibility of losing the bill, so far as my vote is concerned, and giving occasion for an extra session of Congress, sooner than any law which prohibits slavery in California shall be adopted. The Senator from Massachusetts says that the understanding in all quarters is, that the existing laws in that Territory will remain in force until we supersede them. Then why not say they shall be in force so far as not inconsistent with the constitution? I do not rise here for the purpose of arguing the question. My object is compromise; my desire is to settle the difficulty. And I think it would be the part of wisdom if gentlemen on the other side would agree to this amendment. If they will not agree to it, I cannot vote for the original amendment, and shall not vote for it, whatever may be the consequences—whether we lose the bill and give occasion for a called session or not.

Mr. Westcott. I am not in favor of the amendment which has been adopted by the House, nor will the proposed amendment by the Senator from Virginia at all reconcile me to do it; and, if it is adopted by the Senate, it will not induce me to acquiesce in what is represented as a compromise. If I am incorrect in what I now state, I request Senators who are in favor of the amendment to correct me. Sir, the primary objection which will exist, as well after the proposition of the Senator from Virginia is adopted as now, is this: there is no provision in the amendment that has been adopted by the House extending to California and New Mexico the revenue laws of this country, the land laws, the laws for the punishment of crimes and misdemeanors against the United States, nor any solitary provision on the subject. If I am mistaken I desire to be corrected. There is nothing, I say, that will extend the acts of Congress relating to the revenue and to the public lands to California. Now, I ask, if this amendment be adopted, what measure the President can adopt to protect the property of the United States there? In a territory which is so much alluded to as a valuable acquisition to this country, how are we to protect the gold mines? how are we to collect a revenue? The laws that were in force anterior to the execution of the treaty have ceased to exist; are we to adopt their laws in relation to duties on imports, in relation to titles to lands? Sir, this, it appears to me, will be the effect of the amendment of the House if adopted.

Mr. Foote. If the Senator will allow me—

Mr. Westcott. I have the floor.

Mr. Foote. I know that. I rise to a point of order. I understand that the Congress of the United States has arrived at the point of adjournment. Let those take the consequences upon themselves who have dared to resist a reasonable proposition. I insist that the Congress of the United States is now bound to adjourn. We have no right to sit here at all.

The Vice President decided that the Senator from Florida was in order.

Mr. Westcott. This is an objection which is radical with me, and which, if I am not incorrect, I have observed will not be cured by the amendments of the Senator from Virginia. Sir, with respect to that amendment, I do not think it will place this question in the aspect in which the gentleman thinks it will place it, and, therefore, it does not affect my objection. With respect to the slavery question, I have been anxious that it should be set at rest; and it was only for that reason that I was willing to advocate the insertion of what did seem to me to be incongruous in an appropriation bill, a provision for the government of California. It was, I say, for the purpose of preserving the peace and harmony of the country that I was induced to support the proposition; but I look to the country to sanction the course that I took. Sir, I have no idea that the people of this country, if this distracting question could have been silenced, would ever have failed to sustain the Senator from Wisconsin. On the contrary, the plaudits of the country, for having restored harmony, would have followed his efforts, I have no doubt.

Mr. YULEE. There is a strong conviction upon my mind that we have no right to proceed with legislation; and, if a portion of the Senate think otherwise, in order to test the sense of the Senate, I will move that the Senate now adjourn *sine die.*

Mr. DAVIS, of Mississippi, moved that there be a call of the Senate.

Mr. YULEE. I made my motion as the best means of reaching the decision of the Senate upon the rightfulness of our continuing our session after 12 o'clock.

Mr. TURNEY. I desire that the Secretary shall note the hour upon the journal.

[It was then twenty minutes past 2 o'clock A. M.]

Mr. WEBSTER. What is the question?

The VICE PRESIDENT. The question is upon the motion to adjourn *sine die.*

Mr. WEBSTER. I protest against it. We have no right to adjourn without the consent of the other House.

Mr. MASON. The amendment that was sent to the House provided a government for California. It provided for the appointment of civil officers, and extended the constitution and laws of this country over the territory. The House struck out the whole amendment, and sent us one back providing, in the first clause, for a military occupation of the country, and in the second, re-enacting the laws of Mexico, and directing them to be enforced. Now, the motion I have made is, to strike out the second section, for the purpose of avoiding the enactment of Mexican laws, and of leaving the country to be governed by military authority.

Mr. BERRIEN. I desire to make one more effort to preserve this bill, if it be possible. And, if I can have the attention of Senators for a moment, I will very briefly explain my views in relation to this motion of the Senator from Virginia. The bill had been truly described by the Senator to be, in its first section, a legislative provision for the establishment of what will amount to a military government; and by its second section, re-enacting the laws of Mexico. It is said, that, forasmuch as the provisions of the constitution, or as the constitution, as far as it is applicable, is extended to California and New Mexico, these Mexican laws are controlled by its provisions, and, therefore, no apprehension is to be entertained of any mischief that can rise from the adoption of that section. Now, sir, if it be true, that, by force of extending the provisions of the constitution to those Territories, the Mexican laws will be subjected to their control, and can only operate in subordination to the constitution; if gentlemen are sincere in the expression of that opinion, and entertain at the same time the belief of a conflict between the constitution and these Mexican laws, why should we go through the useless legislation of re-enacting every existing law in Mexico, when, in consequence of the extension of the constitution, by another clause, they can have no operation?

Mr. MASON. I comprehend the suggestion of the Senator from Georgia, and accept his modification.

Mr. BERRIEN. I propose, then, instead of a motion to strike out the second section, to submit a motion to strike out these words: "The existing laws thereof shall be retained and observed." Mr. President, the advocates of the amendment maintain this proposition, that the laws of a conquered or ceded territory continue to be of force until they are repealed. We propose to repeal no law of the territory, either of New Mexico or of California. If gentlemen, then, confide in the opinion which they express, that the law of nations does that which they ask us to do by positive enactment, they will vote for the amendment. I ask, then, whether, believing that the laws of a conquered country do remain in force, so far as they regulate the relations between individual and individual, and so far as they do not conflict with the political law of the conquering country—I take that to be the proposition that is laid down in the case which is so often referred to in this discussion—if gentlemen are satisfied of the correctness of the opinion they have advanced, where is the utility of the re-enactment of these Mexican laws? It is an act of supererogation.

Mr. WEBSTER. A few words. In the first place as to the point of order: I do not see how we can now strike out that portion of the bill relating to California. The House having acted upon it, if any thing is to be done, it must be by a committee of conference. So much for the suggestion of the Senator from Florida. Then I have to say to the Senator from South Carolina that he is quite mistaken if he supposes that I intend to rely on his support. Far from it. But it will be remembered here and hereafter—let the issue of this great question be whatever it may—that from the first I have done what that gentleman did not do, resist the introduction of the provision relating to California into this annual appropriation bill.

Mr. Butler. I resisted it from the beginning.

Mr. Foote. The motion is unparliamentary.

Mr. Webster. I do not deny that it is unparliamentary. But is every thing that we do prudent, is every thing discreet, is every thing worthy of us? We hold the destinies of this Republic in our hands. Parliamentary? No, sir, I cannot say it was parliamentary. I cannot say that if you had a bill under consideration for abolishing flogging in the navy, you might not introduce an amendment declaring war with Great Britain. But there is a question of prudence. And I say, that when we are engaged upon a question of making appropriations for the annual disbursements of this Government, it is not usual, it is not wise, it does not become us, to introduce a subject so disputatious as that its further progress may endanger the passage of the measure before us. That is the main reason why I voted against the proposition of the Senator from Wisconsin. And the only reason why I did not offer a proposition of my own was, that I thought it would be better not to send the bill again to the House. I have gone through this fire, and I will come out of it; and there will be no smoke upon my garments. Let the matter end as it will, I have resisted the introduction of this subject; but it was forced upon us. It went to the House; and now we are reaping the consequences. We cannot now get rid of it. There is no motion, that would be in accordance with parliamentary usage, by which we can strike out altogether that on which the House have acted. It is out of our power. We must act upon things as they are. And these things exist in their present state by the votes of the two Houses. We may amend the amendment, but we cannot strike it out.

And now a few words for the Senator from Georgia, to whom I always listen with the greatest pleasure. The question between him and me is a practical question. There is no theory in it. There is no difference as to fundamental principles. It is a practical question, which arises here on Sabbath morning, the fourth of March. I do not say it is a great or very important question. But it affects a point upon which the Government has not been affected during the sixty years of its duration. It is, whether Congress will withhold the means that are necessary for carrying on the operations of the Government, whether they will withhold the means necessary for its preservation. That is the question. It cannot be blinked, and it shall not, God willing, and I living. That is the question, and I leave gentlemen to act with the same independence with which I claim to act myself. I shall stay here until the question is settled.

Now let me say a word upon the proposition of the Senator from Georgia—a patriotic Senator, a learned lawyer, a man of talent and character, to whom I never listened without respect. Well, what does he say? He says, and says truly, that, by the law of nations, the laws existing in these conquered Territories continue to be in force until the conquering power sees proper to withdraw them. Nothing is more clear than that. Every jurisconsult in the world knows that. Well, then, what does this bill propose to do? It proposes, I do not say unnecessarily, but it proposes to affirm what the Senator from Georgia says is already the law of nations. That is all. Well, will the case stand differently? It will stand differently in this respect only, that those laws only will be in force which are not repugnant to the Constitution of the United States. I have yielded to the proposition of the Senator from Wisconsin, so far as to let it have what force it could in giving to the people of the Territories a continuance of the laws that already exist until we make new ones. But it is admitted that we may make a nugatory and unnecessary affirmance of the law of nations. There can be no harm in it, however. It comes now to this practical question, at this hour in the morning, on the fourth of March, whether we shall, with the known difference between the two Houses, send the bill back with an amendment which does not alter the state of the case at all? That is the question. It does not alter the state of the case at all; and no lawyer, least of all so good a lawyer as my honorable friend from Georgia, can show where it alters it at all. He says the laws will remain until altered by our legislation, in obedience to the law of nations. Well, I say the affirmance of this law cannot be wrong. It may be unnecessary. But shall we, on that account, send the bill back to the House of Representatives? I speak before grave men, sir; I wish to prejudge nothing. And this leads to a single remark on another proposition of my honorable friend. He say he wishes to leave this state of things to be decided by the supreme judicial tribunal of the country. Do we not all know that we have got to act upon the subject legislatively? Do we propose to leave this subject open for a series of years, until some sort of process, unknown to me, some sort of bill, can get into the Supreme Court, upon which a decision may be had in relation to it? I tell you, sir, my opinion has been, and is, that what we now do is temporary, because we have no time to perfect a system of territorial government. This is a short session, and we are at the end of it. And we propose by this bill that the Mexican laws shall exist? How long? The Senator from Georgia says until repealed. We propose to shorten their duration. We propose to fix a time beyond which they shall not continue. Otherwise, if we did not act at all, they would exist forever. Now, I put it to the Senator from Georgia—and there is no difference of opinion between us as to the law of nations—but I put it to him, whether, as a practical measure, it is worth while to send this bill back to the House to accomplish nothing? Sir, I shall detain the Senate no longer.

Mr. BERRIEN. Sir, the honorable Senator says, that taking what he supposes to be my statement of the law of nations, in that particular he entirely agrees with me. But he does not state the whole proposition. I did state, in the hearing of the Senate, that the laws of a conquered country remained in force until they were repealed by the conquering power. But I did also say—what the Senator did not—that that principle does not apply to all the laws. I said that those laws which regulate the relations between individuals remain in force, notwithstanding that the supreme authority is that of the conquering power.

Mr. WEBSTER. The Senator is quite right in that. The reason that I did not advert to it was, because, in the subject before us, we did not propose to touch any thing beyond the political regulations of the Territories.

Mr. BERRIEN. The honorable Senator has not touched the question. The question is, whether a law regulating slavery is not a question to be settled by the supreme judicial tribunal? There is no question as to whether it does, or not, exist under our organic law as a basis of representation, and subject to taxation.

Mr. WEBSTER. Where?

Mr. BERRIEN. In the Constitution of the United States.

Mr. WEBSTER. But in what locality?

Mr. BERRIEN. Everywhere, where the constitution extends.

Mr. WEBSTER. In Massachusetts?

Mr. BERRIEN. Yes, in Massachusetts, and only not now in Massachusetts because Massachusetts, in the exercise of her sovereign authority, has abolished the institution. But slavery was recognized by the constitution as existing in the several States of the Union, and was made a basis of representation and taxation. Then the question is, whether that which is made the basis of taxation and representation is not a law political; whether it is not a law affecting commerce, the relations of individuals; or whether it is a law affecting the relations of the people and their government? The principle of the law of nations, as laid down everywhere, is this: The law which affects the relations of individuals exists, notwithstanding a change of sovereignty. The law which affects the relation of people to the sovereign at once ceases. Well, now, we have no sovereign except the people, who form the government; and all the laws which affect the relations between the people and the government at once cease. And the simple inquiry is, whether slavery, as recognized by the Constitution of the United States, does affect the relationship which exists between the people of the United States and the Government? And the question will be made clearly applicable to any territory which may be acquired by the United States, whether it be annexed to the United States as territory, or whether it be incorporated into the Union as States—the relations which exist between the people and this Government, or between the people and the political laws, which cannot exist after a transfer of Mexican authority. But that is not the only question between the Senator from Massachusetts and myself. He stated a portion of my argument without stating the modification. It is not, therefore, a mere nugatory provision to re-enact the laws of Mexico. The Senator proposes not merely to re-enact the private laws, the laws which affect the relation between individual and individual, but, by a general sweeping enactment, he re-enacts those laws which, under the principle embraced in the law of nations, would cease to have vitality.

A message was here received from the House of Representatives announcing that they were ready to adjourn. (Quarter-past three o'clock, A. M.)

Mr. CASS. As I am among those who believe that the term of this session has expired, and that it is incompetent for us now to do business, I cannot vote upon any motion. I have sat here as a mere looker on. I merely desire to explain why I took no part in the proceedings.

Mr. BERRIEN. Upon the motion before the Senate I ask for the yeas and nays.

They were ordered.

Mr. BRADBURY. I shall vote against the amendment offered by the Senator from Georgia, (Mr. BERRIEN,) as I am satisfied that if it is adopted, or any other amendment, excepting one to strike out the entire clause relating to territorial governments, and the bill is again returned to the House at this late hour, it will defeat it. I am not willing to do any thing that will defeat this bill. It is a most important appropriation bill, and I will take upon myself no share of the responsibility of defeating it. I feared this result when the attempt was first made to ingraft upon it the incongruous proposition to give the President the power to govern our Territories; and believing, also, that by entertaining the proposition we were losing all chance to pass, at this session, suitable territorial bills, I opposed the amendment of the Senator from Wisconsin (Mr. WALKER) at the outset. The House has rejected it, and sent back another proposition less objectionable in its character. The responsibility is now on those who began this course of ingrafting incongruous amendments on appropriation bills. If they send back this bill at this late hour, with the amendment of the Senator from Georgia, the bill will be lost, and they must take the responsibility of the loss.

The question being put upon the amendment, and the yeas and nays having been ordered—

Mr. BORLAND. I ask to be excused from voting, for the reasons which have been so clearly expressed by the Senator from Michigan and the Senator from Florida.

The yeas and nays being then taken, resulted as follows:

YEAS.—Messrs. Atchison, Bell, Berrien, Butler,

Cameron, Davis of Mississippi, Dickinson, Downs, Fitzpatrick, Foote, Houston, Hunter, Johnson of Georgia, King, Mangum, Mason, Rusk, Sebastian, Turney, Westcott, and Yulee—21.

NAYS.—Messrs. Atherton, Baldwin, Bradbury, Bright, Clarke, Corwin, Davis of Massachusetts, Dayton, Dix, Dodge of Iowa, Douglas, Felch, Greene, Hale, Hamlin, Johnson of Maryland, Jones, Metcalfe, Miller, Niles, Pearce, Spruance, Underwood, Upham, Wales, Walker, and Webster—27.

So the amendment was rejected.

Mr. FOOTE. I move that the Senate of the United States do now adjourn. It is nearly four o'clock.

The yeas and nays were then taken, and resulted as follows:

YEAS.—Messrs. Fitzpatrick, Hale, Hunter, Johnson of Georgia, Mason, Niles, and Yulee—7.

NAYS.—Messrs. Atchison, Atherton, Baldwin, Bell, Berrien, Bradbury, Bright, Butler, Cameron, Clarke, Corwin, Davis of Massachusetts, Davis of Mississippi, Dayton, Dodge of Iowa, Douglas, Downs, Greene, Houston, Johnson of Maryland, Jones, Mangum, Metcalfe, Miller, Pearce, Rusk, Spruance, Sturgeon, Underwood, Upham, Wales, Walker, and Webster—33.

So the Senate refused to adjourn.

Mr. WEBSTER. The motion first in order is to concur in the amendment of the House; and I ask whether, if this motion be rejected, we cannot then vote to recede from our own amendment?

Mr. KING. There can be no question but that the Senate has power, at this time, to recede from their amendment to the bill; and, if they do so recede, the amendment of the House falls as a matter of course, and it strips the bill of the whole matter relating to California. We have done that very thing this night, on the motion of the Senator from New Hampshire, in relation to treasury notes. There can be no doubt about it. The practice has been uniform. In order that bills may not be defeated, one or the other House recedes.

Mr. BRIGHT. The Senator from Alabama is perfectly correct in regard to the parliamentary law. What is the effect of our receding from the amendment? It will be that the bill, when stripped of the proposition relating to California, will become a law without being sent back to the other House.

Mr. WEBSTER. Allow me to say to the Senator from Indiana that that is not the question, and cannot 'be. Two or three hours ago, on the coming in of this question, I moved that the Senate agree to the amendment of the House. The Vice President decided that that proposition might be superseded by a motion to amend. But no proposition can now be in order to recede. We have got to dispose of the amendment of the House, and, therefore, I insist, with as much confidence as becomes me, that you now put the question, Does the Senate agree to the amendment of the House?

The debate was continued by Messrs. FOOTE, TURNEY, UNDERWOOD, and others.

Mr. WEBSTER. I am disposed to make one more effort to dispose of this subject; that is, some time between this and twelve o'clock to-morrow. I have been of opinion that all this matter about California was wrong. I will not pursue it. But I am willing to take this course: I am willing now to withdraw my motion to concur, though I do not do it at this moment until I state what my view is. I am willing to withdraw my motion to agree to the amendment of the House, if gentlemen will then move to recede from the Senate's amendment, and let the bill pass as a mere appropriation bill.

Mr. ATHERTON. Mr. President——

Mr. BERRIEN. Will the Senator permit me—

Mr. ATHERTON. I wish to say one word. I was about to endeavor to get the floor to make the same suggestion which has been made by the Senator from Massachusetts. I have had on myself some responsibility as it regards this bill. I feared at the time of the introduction of the amendment, and so stated, that it would endanger the passage of the bill. I objected to the amendment, and resisted it on that ground. I feel that, so far as my own action is concerned, I am clear of responsibility in this respect, and I find no fault with gentlemen who thought otherwise. With regard to the Indian appropriation bill, the House offered an amendment to the amendment of the Senate. The Committee of Conference were unable to agree. I made a motion that the Senate disagree to the amendment of the House to the amendment of the Senate. I made it in that form. The question was put and carried, and the bill was passed. The amendment of the Senate and the amendment of the House to that amendment being thus disposed of, the bill was passed. Now, I hope the Senator from Massachusetts, if he varies his motion, will put it in this form: that the Senate disagree to the amendment of the House and recede from their own amendment.

The VICE PRESIDENT. Do I understand the Senator from New Hampshire as making that motion?

Mr. ATHERTON. I will make the motion.

Mr. WEBSTER. If the Chair says that the question can be entertained, I will yield the floor.

The VICE PRESIDENT. It can be entertained.

Mr. DOUGLAS. In the first place, Mr. President, the two motions cannot be put together; I object to their being so put; and I renew the motion to concur; which, I apprehend, has precedence, whether proposed first or last.

Mr. BRIGHT. I wish to make one remark. The Senator from Massachusetts moved that the Senate concur in the amendment of the House, and I followed that motion by another, that the Senate recede from its amendment. The Chair decided that the motion to concur must be put first. And if the Senator from Massachusetts withdraw his motion, then, as a matter of course, my motion follows.

Mr. DOUGLAS. I wish now to understand

whether a motion to recede takes precedence of a motion to concur.

The VICE PRESIDENT. The motion to recede being first made takes precedence.

Mr. DOUGLAS. Well, I hope the Senate will not recede. I hope we shall proceed, and give some sort of government to California. We can do that if we adhere, or if we concur. I am willing to do either. And in either way we get a government for California. But I can never vote to recede, and thereby abandon the country.

Mr. BUTLER. What is California in comparison with thirty States?

The question being taken on the motion to recede, it was decided in the affirmative, by yeas and nays, as follows:

YEAS.—Messrs. Atchison, Atherton, Baldwin, Bell, Berrien, Bradbury, Bright, Butler, Cameron, Clarke, Corwin, Davis of Massachusetts, Davis of Mississippi, Dayton, Dickinson, Dix, Downs, Felch, Fitzpatrick, Greene, Hale, Hannegan, Houston, Hunter, Johnson of Maryland, Johnson of Georgia, Jones, Mangum, Mason, Miller, Niles, Pearce, Rusk, Spruance, Turney, Upham, Wales, and Webster—38.

NAYS.—Messrs. Dodge of Iowa, Douglas, Metcalfe, Sturgeon, Underwood, Walker, and Westcott —7.

So the Senate having receded from their amendment, the bill was passed.

Message from the House of Representatives.

The following message was received from the House of Representatives, by Mr. CAMPBELL, their Clerk:

"Mr. President: I am directed to inform the Senate that the House of Representatives, having no business before it, is, if the Senate have no communication to make to it, now ready to adjourn."

Thanks to the President pro tem.

Mr. MANGUM submitted the following resolution, which was considered by unanimous consent, and agreed to:

Resolved unanimously, That the thanks of the Senate are due, and are hereby tendered, to the Hon. Mr. ATCHISON, for the ability, dignity, and impartiality with which he has performed the duties of President of the Senate *pro tempore.*

Adjournment sine die.

Mr. DODGE, from the committee appointed on the part of the Senate, jointly with the committee appointed on the part of the House of Representatives, to wait on the President of the United States, and notify him that the two Houses, having finished the legislation before them, are ready, if he has no further communication to make, to adjourn, reported that they had performed the duty assigned them, and that the President replied that he had no further communication to make.

On motion, it was

Ordered, That a message be sent to the House of Representatives to inform the House that the Senate, having finished the business before them, are about to adjourn.

Whereupon, at seven o'clock A. M. of Sunday, March 4, the Senate adjourned *sine die.*

HOUSE OF REPRESENTATIVES.

SATURDAY, March 3.

Mr. GREELEY offered the following resolution, which was read twice:

JOINT RESOLUTION concerning the future appellation or name of our Federal Union.

Whereas our common country is known among the nations of the earth only as "the United States of America," a designation at once inconveniently cumbrous and palpably indefinite, since the term "United States" is common to other political Confederations, even on this continent, and is very likely to be adopted by or applied to others in the course of not many years:

And whereas that transcendent genius and true hero, by whose life-long devotion and daring this continent was added to the domain of civilization and Christianity, was treated in his earlier life with neglect and contumely as a visionary and a charlatan, in his latter years with monstrous ingratitude and wrong as a usurper and tyrant, while, by an amazing fatality, mankind have since conspired to perpetuate the injustice of his age by bestowing on the continent so discovered by Columbus the name of a mere follower in his footsteps, without a shadow of just pretence to the discovery of the New World: Therefore,

Resolved, That this Union of States will hereafter be known and officially designated by the name or appellation COLUMBIA, in grateful acknowledgment of our obligations to, and in tardy atonement for the injustice hitherto suffered by, the great discoverer of this continent.

Thanks to the Speaker.

The Chair being now occupied by Mr. COBB, of Georgia—

Mr. McDOWELL submitted the following resolution:

Resolved, That the thanks of this House are due and are hereby presented to the Hon. ROBERT C. WINTHROP, for the able, impartial, and dignified manner in which he has discharged the duties of Speaker during the present Congress.

So the resolution was adopted.

Civil and Diplomatic Appropriations.

Mr. VINTON, from the Committee of Conference appointed on the part of the House to meet a similar committee on the part of the Senate on the subject of the disagreeing votes of the two Houses on the bill making appropriations for the civil and diplomatic expenses of the Government, said, that the committee had had the same under consideration, and had been unable to come to any agreement. He asked, therefore, that the committee on the part of the House might be discharged.

The SPEAKER said that if the House refused

to insist on its disagreement, they might recede. If they receded, the amendment would then be open to amendment, precisely as it was before the original disagreement. The question would then be restored to the precise condition in which it was before the House disagreed to the Senate's amendments.

Mr. McClernand moved that the House recede from its disagreement to the amendment of the Senate; and he demanded the previous question, and the yeas and nays on his motion.

The previous question was seconded, and the main question was ordered, (being upon the motion to recede.)

Mr. Pettit asked the yeas and nays; which were ordered, and being taken, were: yeas 110, nays 107.

So the House voted to recede.

Mr. Morehead, who said that it was apparent to the House that it was indispensably necessary that they should do something in relation to this particular subject, that was contested by the different sections of the country. He had been the most of this day engaged upon the Committee of Conference between the two Houses, and he had endeavored faithfully and honestly to hit upon some common ground on which they could adjust this question. He thought he had attained that object. He desired to offer an amendment striking out that part of the Senate's amendment in relation to "west of the Rio Grande," and to insert a proviso, which he understood would be satisfactory to those most deeply and vitally interested—at least a portion of them—to the effect that nothing in this act should affect in any way the question of the boundary of the State of Texas.

He moved this amendment, and asked the previous question.

The amendment was sent up to the Chair, and read as follows:

Strike out "west of the Rio Grande," and add: *Provided*, That nothing in this act shall affect in any way the question of the boundary of the State of Texas.

The question was taken by tellers, (Messrs. Wentworth and Morehead,) and decided in the affirmative—ayes 106, noes 101.

So there was a second to the previous question.

And the question "Shall the main question be now taken?" was put and decided in the affirmative—yeas 110, nays 101.

So the main question was ordered.

The Speaker stated that the question was on agreeing to the Senate's amendment, proposed by the gentleman from Kentucky.

A conversation arose, participated in by several gentlemen, upon points of order. An appeal was taken by Mr. Cobb, of Georgia, from the Speaker's decision as to the pending question, but was subsequently withdrawn.

Mr. Wentworth asked the yeas and nays, which were ordered.

The question was taken and decided in the affirmative—yeas 187, nays 19.

So the amendment of Mr. Morehead to the Senate's amendment was agreed to.

Mr. Thompson, (his right to the floor having been sustained by the Speaker,) remarking that he intended to detain the House but a very few moments, proceeded to say, that he had labored with great assiduity to effect a settlement, by compromise, of this difficult question, that had been exciting so much, and which was, perhaps, now threatening, the integrity and safety of the union of these States. He now addressed himself to northern men and to southern men; and if he knew himself, he had no sectional feelings in what he had to say. The true substantial question now presented to the consideration of the House was this: to the civil and diplomatic appropriation bill the Senate had made an amendment providing for the establishment of a government in California, in which there were certain provisions, which provisions were found embraced in several statutory laws of the United States. Two amendments had been ordered in the Senate, and the third had been reported by the Committee of Ways and Means of the House of Representatives. Neither of these amendments had been adopted; and it was perfectly manifest, that unless something was done by way of compromise, they would leave this Hall at twelve o'clock to-night under a state of excitement that would pervade all parts of the Union.

He proposed a substitute for the amendment of the Senate, which (after a statement of its provisions) he sent up to the Clerk's table, where it was read, as follows:

That the President of the United States be, and he hereby is authorized to hold possession of and occupy the territories ceded by Mexico to the United States by the treaty of the 2d of February, eighteen hundred and forty-eight; and that he be, and hereby is, authorized for that purpose, and in order to maintain the authority of the United States, and preserve peace and order, in said territories, to employ such parts of the army and navy of the United States as he may deem necessary, and that the Constitution of the United States, so far as the same is applicable, be extended over said territories.

Sec. 2. *And be it further enacted, &c.*, That until the fourth day of July, eighteen hundred and fifty, unless Congress shall sooner provide for the Government of said territories, the existing laws thereof shall be retained and observed, and that the civil and judicial authority heretofore exercised in said territories shall be vested in, and exercised by, such person or persons as the President of the United States shall appoint and direct, to the end that the inhabitants of said territories may be protected in the full and free enjoyment of their liberty, property, and religion: *Provided nevertheless*, That martial law shall not be proclaimed or declared in said territories, or either of them, nor any military court established or instituted, except ordinary courts-martial for the trial of persons belonging to the army and navy of the United States; and the imprisonment of any citizen of said territories for debt is hereby forbidden.

SEC. 3. *And be it further enacted, &c.*, That to enable the President to carry into execution the provisions of this act, the sum of two hundred thousand dollars is hereby appropriated, out of any money in the treasury not otherwise appropriated.

The yeas and nays were asked and ordered, and being taken, were—yeas 111, nays 105.

So the amendment was agreed to.

The question then recurred on agreeing to the amendment of the Senate as amended.

The yeas and nays were asked and ordered; and being taken, were—yeas 110, nays 104.

So the House agreed to the amendment of the Senate as amended.

On motion of Mr. VINTON, the House receded from all its disagreements to the other amendments of the Senate to the said bill.

Mr. COCKE moved a reconsideration of the motion, and that that motion be laid on the table.

Ordered accordingly.

A message was received from the President, by J. KNOX WALKER, Esq., his Private Secretary, notifying the House that he had approved and signed the civil and diplomatic appropriation bill, and the bill extending the revenue laws of the United States over Upper California.

Adjournment.

Mr. ROCKWELL, of Connecticut, from the Joint Committee appointed to wait upon the President, reported that the committee had performed that duty, and that the President had stated that he had no further communication to make to Congress.

Mr. KAUFMAN (at seven o'clock on Sunday morning) moved that the House adjourn *sine die;* which motion was agreed to.

The SPEAKER then rose, and addressed the House as follows:

Gentlemen of the House of Representatives:

The hour has arrived which terminates our relations to the country, and our relations to each other, as members of the Thirtieth Congress; and you have already pronounced the word which puts an end at once to my vocation and to your own.

But neither the usage of the occasion, nor my own feelings, will allow me to leave the Chair, without a word of acknowledgment, and a word of farewell to those with whom I have been so long associated, and by whom I have been so highly honored.

Certainly, gentlemen, I should subject myself to a charge of great ingratitude, were I not to thank you for the resolution in reference to my official services, which you have placed upon the records within a few hours past.

Such a resolution, I need not say, is the most precious testimonial which any presiding officer can receive, and affords the richest remuneration for any labor which it may have cost.

It did not require, however, this formal tribute at your hands, to furnish me with an occasion of grateful acknowledgment to you all. I am deeply sensible, that no intentions however honest, and no efforts however earnest, could have carried me safely and successfully through with the duties which have been imposed upon me, had I not been seconded and sustained, from first to last, by your kind co-operation and friendly forbearance.

I beg you, then, to receive my most hearty thanks, not merely for so generous an appreciation of my services, but for the uniform courtesy and confidence which you have manifested towards me during my whole official term, and by which you have done so much to lighten the labors and relieve the responsibilities which are inseparable from the Chair of this House.

I can honestly say, gentlemen, that I have endeavored, to the best of my ability, to fulfil the pledges with which I entered upon this arduous station, and to discharge its complicated and difficult duties without partiality and without prejudice. Nor am I conscious of having given just cause of imputation or offence to any member of the House. If there be one, however, towards whom I have seemed, at any moment, to exhibit any thing of injustice or any thing of impatience, I freely offer him the only reparation in my power, in this public expression of my sincere regret.

We have been associated, gentlemen, during a most eventful period in the history of our country and of the world. It would be difficult to designate another era in the modern annals of mankind, which has been signalized by so rapid a succession of startling political changes.

Let us rejoice that while the powers of the earth have almost everywhere else been shaken, that while more than one of the mightiest monarchies and stateliest empires of Europe have tottered or have fallen, our own American Republic has stood firm.

Let us rejoice at the evidence which has thus been furnished to the friends of liberty throughout the world, of the inherent stability of institutions which are founded on the rock of a written constitution, and which are sustained by the will of a free and intelligent people.

And let us hope and trust—as I, for one, most fervently and confidently do—that, by the blessing of God upon prudent, conciliatory, and patriotic counsels, every cause of domestic dissension and fraternal discord may be speedily done away, and that the States and the people, whose Representatives we are, may be bound together forever in a firm, cordial, and indissoluble union.

Offering once more to you all my most grateful acknowledgments of your kindness, and my best wishes for your individual health and happiness, I proceed to the performance of the only duty which remains to me, by announcing, as I now do,

That the House of Representatives of the United States stands adjourned, *sine die.*

THIRTY-FIRST CONGRESS.—FIRST SESSION.

BEGUN AT THE CITY OF WASHINGTON, DECEMBER 3, 1849.

PROCEEDINGS AND DEBATES

IN THE

SENATE AND HOUSE OF REPRESENTATIVES.*

IN SENATE.

Monday, December 3, 1849.

The First Session of the Thirty-First Congress commenced this day, conformably to the Constitution of the United States, at the Capitol, in the city of Washington.

Forty-one Senators appeared in their seats.

The Hon. Millard Fillmore, Vice President of the United States and President of the Senate, took the chair.

Mr. Underwood presented the credentials of the Hon. Henry Clay, elected a Senator by the Legislature of Kentucky for the term of

* LIST OF MEMBERS OF THE SENATE.

Maine.—Hannibal Hamlin, James W. Bradbury.
New Hampshire.—John P. Hale, Moses Norris, Jr.
Massachusetts.—Daniel Webster, John Davis.
Rhode Island.—Albert C. Greene, John H. Clarke.
Connecticut.—Roger S. Baldwin, Truman Smith.
Vermont.—Samuel S. Phelps, William Upham.
New York.—Daniel S. Dickinson, William H. Seward.
New Jersey.—William L. Dayton, Jacob W. Miller.
Pennsylvania.—Daniel Sturgeon, James Cooper.
Delaware.—John Wales, Presley Spruance.
Maryland.—David Stewart, James A. Pearce.
Virginia.—James M. Mason, Robert M. T. Hunter.
North Carolina.—Willie P. Mangum, George E. Badger.
South Carolina.—John C. Calhoun, Arthur P. Butler.
Georgia.—John M. Berrien, William C. Dawson.
Kentucky.—Joseph R. Underwood, Henry Clay.
Tennessee.—Hopkins L. Turney, John Bell.
Ohio.—Thomas Corwin, Salmon P. Chase.
Louisiana.—Solomon W. Downs, Pierre Soulé.
Indiana.—Jesse D. Bright, James Whitcomb.
Mississippi.—Jefferson Davis, Henry S. Foote.
Illinois.—Stephen A. Douglas, James Shields.
Alabama.—Jeremiah Clemens, William R. King.
Missouri.—Thomas H. Benton, David R. Atchison.
Arkansas.—William K. Sebastian, Solon Borland.
Florida.—David L. Yulee, Jackson Morton.
Michigan.—Lewis Cass, Alpheus Felch.
Texas.—Thomas J. Rusk, Sam Houston.
Wisconsin.—Henry Dodge, Isaac P. Walker.
Iowa.—George W. Jones, Augustus C. Dodge.

LIST OF MEMBERS OF THE HOUSE OF REPRESENTATIVES.

Maine.—Thomas J. D. Fuller, Elbridge Gerry, Rufus K. Goodenow, Nathaniel S. Littlefield, John Otis, Cullen Sawtelle, Charles Stetson.

New Hampshire.—Harry Hibbard, Charles H. Peaslee, Amos Tuck, James Wilson.

Vermont.—William Hebard, William Henry, James Meacham, Lucius B. Peck.

Massachusetts.—Charles Allen, George Ashmun, James H. Duncan, Orin Fowler, Joseph Grinnell, Daniel P. King, Horace Mann, Julius Rockwell, Robert C. Winthrop—vacancy.

Rhode Island.—Nathan F. Dixon, George G. King.

Connecticut.—Walter Booth, Thomas B. Butler, Chauncey F. Cleveland, Loren P. Waldo.

New York.—Henry P. Alexander, George R. Andrews, Henry Bennett, David A. Bokee, George Briggs, James Brooks, Lorenzo Burrows, Charles E. Clarke, Harmon S. Conger, William Duer, Daniel Gott, Herman D. Gould, Ransom Halloway, William T. Jackson, John A. King, Preston King, Orsamus B. Matteson, Thomas McKissock, William Nelson, J. Phillips Phœnix, Harvey Putnam, Gideon Reynolds, Elijah Risley, Robert L. Rose, David Rumsey, Jr., William A. Sackett, Abraham M. Schermerhorn, John L. Schoolcraft, Peter H. Silvester, Elbridge G. Spaulding, John R. Thurman, Walter Underhill, Hiram Walden, Hugh White.

New Jersey.—Andrew K. Hay, James G. King, William A. Newell, John Van Dyke, Isaac Wildrick.

Pennsylvania.—Chester Butler, Samuel Calvin, Joseph Casey, Joseph R. Chandler, Jesse C. Dickey, Milo M.

six years, commencing the fourth day of March, 1849; which were read, and the oath prescribed by law was administered to Mr. CLAY, and he took his seat in the Senate.

Mr. MANGUM presented the credentials of the Hon. JAMES SHIELDS, of Illinois, elected a Senator by the Legislature of Illinois for the term of six years, commencing on the fourth day of March, 1849; which were read, and the oath prescribed by law was administered to Mr. SHIELDS, and he took his seat in the Senate.

On motion of Mr. STURGEON, ordered that the Secretary of the Senate acquaint the House of Representatives that a quorum of the Senate has assembled, and that the Senate is ready to proceed to business.

Mr. DODGE, of Iowa, submitted the following resolution, which was considered by unanimous consent, and agreed to:

Resolved, That each Senator be supplied during the present session with newspapers, as heretofore, not exceeding the cost of four daily newspapers.

On motion of Mr. MANGUM, the Sentate adjourned.

HOUSE OF REPRESENTATIVES.

MONDAY, December 3.

Pursuant to the provision of the Constitution of the United States, which declares that "Congress shall assemble at least once in every year, and such meeting shall be on the first Monday in December, unless they shall, by law, appoint a different day," the House of Representatives assembled this day.

Precisely at the hour of twelve, meridian, the House was called to order by THOMAS J. CAMPBELL, Esq., Clerk of the House of Representatives of the 30th Congress. And, agreeably to usage, the Clerk proceeded to call the roll of Members in the order of the States and Territories. Before doing so, he stated that, in discharging this duty, he should call the names of such members as, from *prima facie* evidence before him, he was satisfied had been elected.

The roll having been called, it appeared that 223 Members had answered to their names.

The CLERK having announced that a majority of the whole number of Members elected had answered to their names,

Mr. BOYD moved that the House do now proceed to the election of Speaker, *viva voce*.

No objection having been made—

The House proceeded to the election of a Speaker.

The CLERK announced the following Members as tellers to count the vote: Mr. HILLIARD, of Alabama; Mr. STRONG, of Pennsylvania; Mr. DUER, of New York; Mr. MILLER, of Ohio.

The roll having been called in alphabetical order, the following was declared to be the result of the ballot:

Dimmick, John Freedley, Alfred Gilmore, Moses Hampton, John W. Howe, Lewis C. Levin, Job Mann, James X. McLanahan, Henry D. Moore, Henry Nes, Andrew J. Ogle, Charles W. Pitman, Robert R. Reed, John Robbins, Jr., Thomas Ross, Thaddeus Stevens, William Strong, James Thompson, David Wilmot.

Delaware.—John W. Houston.

Maryland.—Richard I. Bowie, Alexander Evans, William T. Hamilton, Edward Hammond, John B. Kerr, Robert M. McLane.

Virginia.—Thomas H. Averett, Thomas H. Baly, James M. H. Beale, Thomas S. Bocock, Henry A. Edmundson, Thomas S. Haymond, Alexander R. Halladay, James McDowell, Fayette McMullen, Richard K. Meade, John S. Millson, Jeremiah Morton, Richard Parker, Paulus Powell, James A. Seddon.

North Carolina.—William S. Ashe, Joseph P. Caldwell, Thomas L. Clingman, John R. J. Daniel, Edmund Deberry, David Outlaw, Augustine H. Shepperd, Edward Stanly, Abraham W. Venable.

South Carolina.—Armistead Burt, William F. Colcock, Isaac E. Holmes, John McQueen, James L. Orr, Daniel Wallace, Joseph A. Woodward.

Georgia.—Howell Cobb, Thomas C. Hackett, Hugh A. Haralson, Thomas Butler King, Allen F. Owen, Alexander H. Stephens, Robert Toombs, Marshall J. Wellborn.

Alabama.—Albert J. Alston, Franklin W. Bowdon, Williamson R. W. Cobb, Sampson W. Harris, Henry W. Hilliard, David Hubbard, Samuel W. Inge.

Mississippi.—Albert G. Brown, Winfield S. Featherston, William McWillie, Jacob Thompson.

Louisiana.—Charles M. Conrad, John H. Harmanson, Emile La Sère, Isaac E. Morse.

Ohio.—Joseph Cable, Lewis D. Campbell, David K. Cartter, Moses B. Corwin, John Crowell, David T. Disney, Nathan Evans, Joshua R. Giddings, Moses Hoagland, William F. Hunter, John K. Miller, Jonathan D. Morris, Edson B. Olds, Emery D. Potter, Joseph M. Root, Robert C. Schenck, Charles Sweetser, John L. Taylor, Samuel F. Vinton, William A. Whittlesey, Amos E. Wood.

Kentucky.—Linn Boyd, Daniel Breck, George A. Caldwell, James L. Johnson, Humphrey Marshall, John C. Mason, Finis E. McLean, Charles S. Morehead, Richard H. Stanton, John B. Thompson.

Tennessee.—Josiah M. Anderson, Andrew Ewing, Meredith P. Gentry, Isham G. Harris, Andrew Johnson, George W. Jones, John H. Savage, Frederick P. Stanton, James H. Thomas, Albert G. Watkins, Christopher H. Williams.

Indiana.—Nathaniel Albertson, William J. Brown, Cyrus L. Dunham, Graham N. Fitch, Willis A. Gorman, Andrew J. Harlan, George W. Julian, Joseph E. McDonald, Edward W. McGaughey, John L. Robinson.

Illinois.—Edward D. Baker, William H. Bissell, Thomas L. Harris, John A. McClernand, William A. Richardson, John Wentworth, Timothy R. Young.

Missouri.—William V. N. Bay, James B. Bowlin, James S. Green, Willard P. Hall, John S. Phelps.

Arkansas.—Robert W. Johnson.

Michigan.—Kinsley S. Bingham, Alexander W. Buel, William Sprague.

Florida.—E. Carrington Cabell.

Texas.—Volney E. Howard, David S. Kaufman.

Iowa.—Shepherd Leffler, William Thompson.

Wisconsin.—Orsamus Cole, James D. Doty, Charles Durkee.

Oregon.—S. R. Thurston.

Minnesota.—Henry H. Sibley.

Mr. Cobb, of Georgia, received	103
Mr. Winthrop, of Massachusetts	96
Mr. David Wilmot, of Pennsylvania	8
Mr. Meredith P. Gentry, of Tennessee	6
Mr. Horace Mann, of Massachusetts	2
Mr. James Thompson, of Pennsylvania	1
Mr. Chauncey F. Cleveland, of Conn.	1
Mr. James A. Seddon, of Virginia	1
Mr. James L. Orr, of South Carolina	1
Mr. David T. Disney, of Ohio	1
Mr. Joseph M. Root, of Ohio	1
	221

No gentleman having received a majority of the whole number, the House again proceeded to vote.

The roll was then called a second time, when the tellers reported that the whole number of votes given was 221; necessary to a choice 111; of which—

Mr. Cobb, of Georgia, received	102
Mr. Winthrop	96
Mr. Wilmot	8
Mr. Gentry	6
Mr. Horace Mann	2
Mr. James Thompson	1
Mr. Cleveland	1
Mr. Seddon	1
Mr. Disney	1
Mr. Durkee	1
Mr. F. P. Stanton	1
Mr. Woodward	1
No choice.	221

The roll was then called a third time, when the tellers reported that the whole number of votes given was 221; necessary to a choice 111; of which—

Mr. Cobb, of Georgia, received	102
Mr. Winthrop	96
Mr. Wilmot	7
Mr. Gentry	6
Mr. Cleveland	2
Mr. Horace Mann	2
Mr. James Thompson	1
Mr. Potter	1
Mr. Meade	1
Mr. Seddon	1
Mr. Tuck	1
Mr. F. P. Stanton	1
No choice.	221

The House then again proceeded to vote for Speaker.

The roll was then called a fourth time, when the tellers reported that the whole number of votes given was 221; necessary to a choice 111; of which—

Mr. Cobb, of Georgia, received	102
Mr. Winthrop	96
Mr. Cleveland	2
Mr. Wilmot	7
Mr. Gentry	6
Mr. Horace Mann	2
Mr. Seddon	2
Mr. James Thompson	1
Mr. Potter	1
Mr. Booth	1
Mr. Frederick P. Stanton	1
No choice.	221

Tuesday, December 4.

At 12 o'clock, M., the House was called to order by Thomas J. Campbell, Esq, Clerk of the House of Representatives of the 30th Congress.

The Journal of yesterday was read and approved.

Vote for Speaker.

Mr. Boyd, of Kentucky, moved that the House do now proceed to ballot for Speaker.

(Several Voices: Vote—not ballot.)

Mr. White said he would like to understand that question.

Mr. Boyd said he intended, of course, that the House should vote, according to usage, *viva voce.*

The question was then taken, and decided in the affirmative, without a division.

So the House again proceeded to vote for Speaker.

Mr. Hilliard, of Alabama; Mr. Strong, of Pennsylvania; Mr. Duer, of New York; and Mr. Miller, of Ohio, resumed their seats at the Clerk's table as tellers to count the vote.

The roll was called for the fifth time, when the tellers reported that the whole number of votes given in was 224; necessary to a choice 113; of which—

Mr. Cobb, of Georgia, received	102
Mr. Winthrop	96
Mr. Wilmot	10
Mr. Gentry	6
Mr. Mann, of Massachusetts	2
Mr. Richardson	2
Mr. Cleveland	1
Mr. Potter	1
Mr. Haralson	1
Mr. Stanton, of Tennessee	1
Mr. Thompson, of Pennsylvania	1
Mr. Root	1
	224

No gentleman having received a majority of the whole number, the House again proceeded to vote.

The roll was then called a sixth time, when the tellers reported that the whole number of votes given in was 224; necessary to a choice 113; of which—

Mr. Cobb, of Georgia, received	101
Mr. Winthrop	97
Mr. Wilmot	9
Mr. Gentry	6

Mr. Mann, of Massachusetts	3
Mr. Potter	2
Mr. Richardson	2
Mr. Thompson, of Pennsylvania	1
Mr. Cleveland	1
Mr. Stanton, of Tennessee	1
Mr. Julian	1
No choice.	224

The roll was then called a seventh time, when the tellers reported that the whole number of votes given in was 224; necessary to a choice 113; of which—

Mr. Cobb, of Georgia, received	100
Mr. Winthrop	97
Mr. Wilmot	9
Mr. Gentry	6
Mr. Potter	3
Mr. Richardson	3
Mr. Mann, of Massachusetts	2
Mr. Boyd	1
Mr. Allen	1
Mr. Stanton, of Tennessee	1
Mr. Cleveland	1
No choice.	224

The roll was then called the eighth time, when the tellers reported that the whole number of votes given was 224; necessary to a choice 113; of which—

Mr. Cobb, of Georgia, received	99
Mr. Winthrop	97
Mr. Wilmot	9
Mr. Gentry	6
Mr. Potter	4
Mr. Mann, of Massachusetts	2
Mr. Richardson	2
Mr. Boyd	1
Mr. Bayly	1
Mr. Cleveland	1
Mr. Howe	1
Mr. Stanton, of Tennessee	1
No choice.	224

No gentleman having received a majority of the whole number, the House again proceeded to vote.

The roll was then called a ninth time, when the tellers reported that the whole number of votes given in was 224; necessary to a choice 113; of which—

Mr. Cobb, of Georgia, received	100
Mr. Winthrop	97
Mr. Wilmot	8
Mr. Gentry	6
Mr. Potter	4
Mr. Mann, of Massachusetts	2
Mr. Richardson	2
Mr. Cleveland	1
Mr. Durkee	1
Mr. Stanton, of Tennessee	1
Mr. Boyd	1
Mr. Johnson, of Arkansas	1
No choice.	224

The House then again proceeded to vote for Speaker.

The roll was then called a tenth time, when the tellers reported that the whole number of votes given in was 224; necessary to a choice 113; of which—

Mr. Cobb, of Georgia, received	99
Mr. Winthrop	97
Mr. Wilmot	9
Mr. Gentry	6
Mr. Potter	4
Mr. Richardson	3
Mr. Mann, of Massachusetts	2
Mr. Stanton, of Tennessee	2
Mr. Cleveland	1
Mr. Durkee	1
	224

There was no choice.

And then, on motion by Mr. JOHNSON, of Arkansas, the House adjourned until 12 o'clock to-morrow.

IN SENATE.

WEDNESDAY, December 5.

Mr. MANGUM. I have in my hand a resolution which I will send to the Secretary's table, in order that it may be read, and I hope that it will be, by unanimous consent, acted upon immediately. It proposes to give aid to the President of this body in the discharge of the multifarious duties devolving upon him. I will remark that it is not without precedent. During the whole period that Colonel Richard M. Johnson filled the office of Vice President and President of this body, he was allowed a clerk, and the office was not dispensed with until a President *pro tempore* was elected. Indeed, it was not until I had the honor to discharge the duties of that office that the employment of a clerk was deemed unnecessary. I will remark, in addition, that the Vice President is suffering from an affection of the eyes, which renders it impossible for him to read or write by candlelight.

The resolution was read as follows:

Resolved, That the Vice President be authorized to employ a clerk during the present session, and that such clerk be paid the same rate of compensation as heretofore paid to persons employed in that capacity.

The resolution was agreed to.

HOUSE OF REPRESENTATIVES.

WEDNESDAY, December 5.

The House was called to order at twelve o'clock.

The Journal of yesterday was read and approved.

Vote for Speaker.

On motion of Mr. BOYD, the House again proceeded to vote for Speaker.

Mr. Hilliard, of Alabama; Mr. Strong, of Pennsylvania; Mr. Duer, of New York; and Mr. Miller, of Ohio, resumed their seats at the desk, to act as tellers to count the vote.

The House then again proceeded to vote for Speaker.

The roll was then called the eleventh time, when the tellers reported that the whole number of votes given in was 223; necessary to a choice 112; of which—

Mr. Cobb, of Georgia, received	98
Mr. Winthrop	97
Mr. Root	7
Mr. Gentry	5
Mr. Potter	4
Mr. Richardson	4
Mr. Cleveland	2
Mr. Mann, of Massachusetts	2
Mr. Stanton, of Tennessee	1
Mr. King, of New York	1
Mr. Allen	1
Mr. Venable	1
	223

No gentleman having received a majority of the whole number, the House again proceeded to vote.

The roll was then called a twelfth time, when the tellers reported that the whole number of votes given in was 223; necessary to a choice 112; of which—

Mr. Cobb, of Georgia, received	97
Mr. Winthrop	97
Mr. Root	7
Mr. Gentry	5
Mr. Potter	5
Mr. Richardson	4
Mr. Mann, of Massachusetts	2
Mr. Cleveland	2
Mr. Harmanson	1
Mr. Stanton, of Tennessee	1
Mr. Allen	1
Mr. Booth	1
	223

No gentleman having received a majority of the whole number, the House again proceeded to vote.

The roll was then called a thirteenth time, when the tellers reported that the whole number of votes given in was 223; necessary to a choice 112; of which—

Mr. Winthrop received	98
Mr. Cobb, of Georgia	93
Mr. Potter	9
Mr. Root	7
Mr. Richardson	6
Mr. Gentry	5
Mr. Cleveland	2
Mr. Allen	1
Mr. Harris, of Alabama	1
Mr. Mann, of Massachusetts	1
No choice.	223

The roll was then called the fourteenth time, when the tellers reported that the whole number of votes given was 223; necessary to a choice 112; of which—

Mr. Winthrop received	99
Mr. Cobb, of Georgia	89
Mr. Potter	10
Mr. Richardson	8
Mr. Root	7
Mr. Gentry	5
Mr. Cleveland	3
Mr. Allen	1
Mr. Kaufman	1
No choice.	223

On motion of Mr. Thompson, of Mississippi, the House then adjourned until to-morrow at 12 o'clock.

IN SENATE.

Thursday, December 6.

Mr. Calhoun presented the credentials of the Hon. Jeremiah Clemens, elected a Senator by the Legislature of the State of Alabama, to supply the vacancy occasioned by the decease of the Hon. Dixon H. Lewis; which were read, and the oath prescribed by law was administered to him, and he took his seat in the Senate.

HOUSE OF REPRESENTATIVES.

Thursday, December 6.

The House was called to order at 12 o'clock, by Thomas J. Campbell, Esq., Clerk of the late House of Representatives.

The Journal of yesterday was read and approved.

Vote for Speaker.

On motion of Mr. Wentworth, the House again proceeded to vote for Speaker.

Messrs. Hilliard of Alabama, Strong of Pennsylvania, Duer of New York, and Miller of Ohio, resumed their seats at the Clerk's table, as tellers, to count the vote.

The roll was then called a fifteenth time, when the tellers reported that the whole number of votes given in was 225; necessary to a choice 113; of which—

Mr. Winthrop received	101
Mr. Cobb, of Georgia	89
Mr. Potter	10
Mr. Richardson	9
Mr. Tuck	7
Mr. Gentry	5
Mr. Cleveland	2
Mr. Allen	1
Mr. Bocock	1
No choice.	225

The roll was then called for the sixteenth time, when the tellers reported that the whole number of votes given in was 225; necessary to a choice 113; of which—

Mr. Winthrop received	100
Mr. Cobb, of Georgia	73
Mr. Richardson	19
Mr. Potter	16
Mr. Tuck	8
Mr. Gentry	5
Mr. Cleveland	2
Mr. Daniel	1
Mr. Root	1
No choice.	225

The roll was then called the seventeenth time, when the tellers reported that the whole number of votes given was 225; necessary to a choice 113; of which—

Mr. Winthrop received	100
Mr. Cobb, of Georgia	66
Mr. Richardson	25
Mr. Potter	17
Mr. Tuck	8
Mr. Gentry	5
Mr. McClernand	1
Mr. Cleveland	1
Mr. Allen	1
Mr. Burt	1
No choice.	225

The roll was called the eighteenth time, when the tellers reported that the whole number of votes given in was 225; necessary to a choice 113; of which—

Mr. Winthrop received	100
Mr. Cobb, of Georgia	63
Mr. Richardson	26
Mr. Potter	18
Mr. Tuck	9
Mr. Gentry	5
Mr. Cleveland	1
Mr. Wellborn	1
Mr. McClernand	1
Mr. Preston King	1
	225

There was no choice;

When, on motion of Mr. LEVIN, the House adjourned till to-morrow, at 12 o'clock.

FRIDAY, December 7.

Vote for Speaker.

The House again proceeded to vote for Speaker.

Messrs. HILLIARD of Alabama, STRONG of Pennsylvania, DUER of New York, and MILLER of Ohio, resumed their seats at the Clerk's table as tellers to count the vote.

The roll was then called the nineteenth time, when the tellers reported that the whole number of votes given was 225; necessary to a choice 113; of which—

Mr. Winthrop received	101
Mr. Cobb, of Georgia	63
Mr. Richardson	29
Mr. Potter	15
Mr. Wilmot	8
Mr. Gentry	5
Mr. Stanton, of Tennessee	1
Mr. Bowdon	1
Mr. McClernand	1
Mr. Booth	1
No choice.	225

The roll was called for the twentieth time, when the tellers reported that the whole number of votes given in was 225; necessary to a choice 113; of which—

Mr. Winthrop received	102
Mr. Cobb, of Georgia	62
Mr. Richardson	28
Mr. Potter	18
Mr. Wilmot	7
Mr. Gentry	5
Mr. Featherston	1
Mr. McClernand	1
Mr. Booth	1
No choice.	225

The roll was called the twenty-first time, when the tellers reported that the whole number of votes given in was 225; necessary to a choice 113; of which—

Mr. Winthrop received	102
Mr. Cobb, of Georgia	66
Mr. Richardson	23
Mr. Potter	19
Mr. Wilmot	7
Mr. Gentry	5
Mr. Hall	1
Mr. McClernand	1
Mr. Booth	1
No choice.	225

The roll was then called the twenty-second time, when the tellers reported that the whole number of votes given was 225; necessary to a choice 113; of which—

Mr. Winthrop received	102
Mr. Cobb, of Georgia	65
Mr. Richardson	23
Mr. Potter	18
Mr. Wilmot	7
Mr. Gentry	5
Mr. Strong	2
Mr. Morse	1
Mr. McClernand	1
Mr. Booth	1
No choice.	225

The House adjourned until to-morrow at 12 o'clock.

IN SENATE.

Saturday, December 8.

The Senate met at 12 o'clock, pursuant to adjournment.

Mr. Pearce presented the credentials of the Hon. David Stewart, appointed a Senator by the Governor of the State of Maryland, to fill the vacancy created by the resignation of the Hon. Reverdy Johnson; which were read, and the oath prescribed by law was submitted to Mr. Stewart, and he took his seat in the Senate.

After a brief interval, there being no business before the Senate—

On motion, the Senate adjourned.

HOUSE OF REPRESENTATIVES.

Saturday, December 8.

Vote for Speaker.

On motion by Mr. Wentworth, the House again proceeded to vote for Speaker, *viva voce.*

Messrs. Hilliard of Alabama, Strong of Pennsylvania, Duer of New York, and Miller of Ohio, resumed their seats at the Clerk's table, as tellers, to count the vote.

The roll was then called the twenty-third time, when the tellers reported that the whole number of votes given was 225; necessary to a choice 113; of which—

Mr. Winthrop received	102
Mr. Cobb, of Georgia	31
Mr. Potter	29
Mr. Richardson	23
Mr. Wilmot	7
Mr. Miller	5
Mr. Strong	5
Mr. Gentry	4
Mr. Bayly	3
Mr. McDowell	3
Mr. Boyd	3
Mr. Disney	2
Mr. McClernand	2
Mr. Meade	2
Mr. Thomas	1
Mr. Thompson, of Pennsylvania	1
Mr. Inge	1
Mr. Booth	1
No choice.	225

The roll was then called the twenty-fourth time, when the tellers reported that the whole number of votes given was 224; necessary to a choice 113; of which—

Mr. Winthrop received	102
Mr. Potter	40
Mr. Cobb, of Georgia	16
Mr. Richardson	16
Mr. Boyd	14
Mr. Miller	8
Mr. Wilmot	7
Mr. Strong	5
Mr. Gentry	5
Mr. Bayly	3
Mr. Meade	2
Mr. McDowell	2
Mr. Disney	1
Mr. Thomas	1
Mr. Green	1
Mr. McClernand	1
Mr. Booth	1
No choice.	225

The roll was then called a twenty-fifth time, when the tellers reported that the whole number of votes given was 225; necessary to a choice 113; of which—

Mr. Winthrop received	102
Mr. Potter	48
Mr. Boyd	22
Mr. Richardson	12
Mr. Cobb, of Georgia	9
Mr. Miller	8
Mr. Wilmot	8
Mr. Gentry	5
Mr. McClernand	2
Mr. Bayly	2
Mr. Booth	1
Mr. Brown, of Indiana	1
Mr. Inge	1
Mr. McDowell	1
Mr. Meade	1
Mr. Thomas	1
Mr. Wallace	1
No choice.	225

Mr. Haralson rose and said, that as this was Saturday, and as there was little or no probability that a Speaker could be elected to-day, he would move that the House adjourn until Monday, at 12 o'clock, M. (Cries of "Agreed"—"No"—"Another vote.") Tellers on the motion were asked and refused.

And the question was then taken and decided in the negative.

So the House refused to adjourn.

The roll was called for the twenty-sixth time, when the tellers reported that the whole number of votes given in was 225; necessary to a choice 113; of which—

Mr. Winthrop received	102
Mr. Potter	61
Mr. Boyd	22
Mr. Cobb, of Georgia	7
Mr. Wilmot	7
Mr. Richardson	6
Mr. Miller	6
Mr. Gentry	5
Mr. Bayly	2
Mr. La Sère	1
Mr. Harris, of Alabama	1
Mr. Stanton, of Tennessee	1
Mr. Thomas	1
Mr. McClernand	1
Mr. Meade	1
Mr. Booth	1
No choice.	225

On motion of Mr. Wentworth, the House then again proceeded to vote for Speaker.

The roll was then called the twenty-seventh time, when the tellers reported that the whole number of votes given was 225; necessary to a choice 113; of which—

Mr. Winthrop received	102
Mr. Potter	70
Mr. Boyd	17
Mr. Wilmot	7
Mr. Cobb, of Georgia	6
Mr. Gentry	5
Mr. Miller	5
Mr. Richardson	5
Mr. Bayly	2
Mr. Booth	1
Mr. Hackett	1
Mr. Meade	1
Mr. Thomas	1
Mr. Thompson, of Mississippi	1
Mr. Woodward	1
No choice.	225

The roll was then called the twenty-eighth time, when the tellers reported that the whole number of votes given in was 224; necessary to a choice 113; of which—

Mr. Winthrop received	101
Mr. Potter	76
Mr. Boyd	14
Mr. Wilmot	7
Mr. Cobb, of Georgia	5
Mr. Gentry	5
Mr. Richardson	4
Mr. Miller	3
Mr. Bayly	2
Mr. Green	1
Mr. Brown, of Mississippi	1
Mr. Woodward	1
Mr. McClernand	1
Mr. Thompson, of Pennsylvania	1
Mr. Meade	1
Mr. Booth	1
	224

Mr. Holmes moved that the House adjourn until Monday, at 12 o'clock, M.

Tellers were ordered and appointed—Messrs. Peck of Vermont, and Hampton of Pennsylvania.

The question was taken and decided in the affirmative—ayes 118, noes not counted.

So the House adjourned until Monday, at 12 o'clock, M.

IN SENATE.

Monday, December 10.

The Journal having been read—

Mr. Seward asked leave to withdraw from the files of the Senate the papers of Barclay, Livingston and others, with a view to their being submitted to the House of Representatives; which was granted.

After an interval of some time, and there being no business before the Senate, on motion—

The Senate adjourned.

HOUSE OF REPRESENTATIVES.

Monday, December 10.

The Journal of Saturday was read and approved.

Vote for Speaker.

On motion of Mr. Wentworth, the House again proceeded to vote for Speaker.

Messrs. Hilliard of Alabama, Strong of Pennsylvania, Duer of New York, and Miller of Ohio, resumed their seats at the Clerk's table as tellers to count the votes.

The roll was then called the twenty-ninth time, when the tellers reported that the whole number of votes given was 224; necessary to a choice 113; of which—

Mr. Winthrop received	102
Mr. Potter	76
Mr. Green	10
Mr. Wilmot	6
Mr. Boyd	5
Mr. Cobb, of Georgia	5
Mr. Gentry	5
Mr. Miller	3
Mr. Brown, of Indiana	2
Mr. Richardson	1
Mr. McWillie	1
Mr. Stanton, of Tennessee	1
Mr. Durkee	1
Mr. Bowdon	1
Mr. McLane, of Maryland	1
Mr. Harris, of Alabama	1
Mr. Meade	1
Mr. Bayly	1
Mr. Kaufman	1
No choice.	224

The roll was then called the thirtieth time, when the tellers reported that the whole number of votes given was 224; necessary to a choice 113; of which—

Mr. Winthrop received	102
Mr. Potter	77
Mr. Green	12
Mr. Wilmot	6
Mr. Gentry	5
Mr. Cobb, of Georgia	5
Mr. Boyd	4
Mr. Miller	4
Mr. William J. Brown	2
Mr. Kaufman	1
Mr. Richardson	1
Mr. McQueen	1
Mr. Frederick P. Stanton	1
Mr. Meade	1
Mr. Bayly	1
Mr. Durkee	1
No choice.	224

The roll was then called the thirty-first time, when the tellers reported that the whole number of votes given was 224; necessary to a choice 113; of which—

Mr. Winthrop received	101
Mr. Potter	78
Mr. Green	10
Mr. Wilmot	6
Mr. Boyd	5
Mr. Gentry	5
Mr. Howell Cobb	5
Mr. Miller	3
Mr. Bayly	2
Mr. William J. Brown	2
Mr. Horace Mann	1
Mr. Kaufman	1
Mr. Durkee	1
Mr. Colcock	1
Mr. Frederick P. Stanton	1
Mr. Sampson W. Harris	1
Mr. Meade	1
No choice.	224

Mr. Morse rose and said that he held in his hand a resolution which he offered after consultation with a very few friends on his side of the House, none of whom, unfortunately, agreed with him in opinion, but which, in his judgment, was calculated to terminate what was now beginning to be a ridiculous course of action on the part of this House.

The resolution was read by the Clerk, as follows:

Whereas, the Hon. Howell Cobb, of Georgia, and Robert C. Winthrop, of Massachusetts, have each received more than one hundred votes, on a large number of ballots:

Be it resolved, That the Clerk of the House be required to place the names of Howell Cobb and Robert C. Winthrop in a box, and the first name drawn out by one of the pages shall be Speaker of the Thirty-First Congress.

The country looked at this House, and expected to see it organized. There were, it was well known, a few individuals who had obstinately been voting against either of the candidates which had been brought forward, and would continue to vote against either of the candidates who might be brought forward by the two great parties of this country. This would forever prevent an organization of the House, upon the plan under which they were now proceeding. It was due to the legislation of this country that one or the other of these two great parties should have the control of the organization of this body. Those members who differed from the great body of the House, who could not find an acceptable man in either of the great parties, still persisted in preventing the organization. He desired to see this contest terminated. The House had indicated, by a large number of votings, that the two gentlemen selected by their respective parties each commanded almost a majority of the House. Both these gentlemen, (without intending any invidious distinction,) it was admitted, were as well qualified to discharge the functions of Speaker as any gentlemen who could be selected from this House.

If he could see, in the future, any hope of electing a Speaker, he would not have offered this proposition to refer the decision of the question to chance. But circumstances being as they were, he proposed that the names of Robert C. Winthrop and Howell Cobb—each of whom had received more than one hundred votes upon a large number of votings—should be placed in a box, and that one of the pages should draw out a name, and the gentleman whose name was first drawn should be Speaker of the House. He knew that there might, and probably would be, objections made to this proposition, and that it might seem wrong to gentlemen that so important a matter should be left to the decision of chance. But graver questions than this had been decided in the same way. He desired, as far as he could, to clear himself and the House of the ridiculous attitude of spending day after day in further voting, without the least hope of coming to a successful result.

Mr. Brown, of Mississippi, moved to lay the resolution on the table.

The first question being on this motion—

Mr. Root said he regretted that they should be in so unfortunate a predicament; that the great body of the House should have been struggling so long to organize, and have been defeated in all their efforts by a few obstinate members; for that was about the situation in which they now were, according to the representation of the gentleman from Louisiana, (Mr. Morse.) Two hundred and twenty gentlemen, perfectly well disposed to organize the House, and proceed with the business of the country—constituting the two great parties, to one of which, it was claimed, the Speaker certainly belonged—had (to use the expression of the gentleman from Louisiana, which he, Mr. R., would not use on his own account) brought themselves to a ridiculous situation! Now, if there was one thing in this matter more ridiculous than another, it was that this confession should have been made by any gentleman representing either of these great parties. That two hundred and twenty gentlemen, well-disposed, patriotic, intelligent men, belonging to the two great parties—to one of which, it was said, belonged the organization of the House—could not of themselves organize, but had to get up a gambling resolution, a lottery, (a laugh,) in which there were just as many blanks as prizes, (renewed laughter,) have a drawing, and call upon one of their little pages (if he understood the resolution correctly) to intervene and help these two great parties out of the difficulty, (laughter.)

The gentleman from Louisiana had said they were in a ridiculous situation. He (Mr. R.) would never have said that. He did not see any thing ridiculous in the proceedings of this

House, or meeting, or whatever they may call their assemblage. They had been characterized by great order and decorum. But he believed they would deserve to be characterized as a ridiculous assemblage, if they resorted to such means to get a Speaker as was proposed by the gentleman from Louisiana. Now, he did not feel authorized to give advice to either of the two great parties; but as he was willing to take it, he might perhaps offer a little—that was, for each to stand up and die *game*. Let me tell these two great parties that they have not got us into a Philadelphia Convention nor into a Baltimore Convention; there is no yelling a man down here yet.

(A voice: Nor into a Buffalo Convention.)

No, (said Mr. R.,) nor into a Buffalo Convention. If you had, you would have had a Speaker long ago—as good a one as you will get after all your labors.

They had heard (he proceeded to say) something from the gentleman from North Carolina, (Mr. VENABLE,) who had said that both parties were patriotic in their efforts to elect a Speaker and organize the House, and that if half a dozen individuals saw fit to take the responsibility of defeating the organization of the House, why! the blame would be on them, (a laugh,) and that they would be called to an account by their constituents. That was the very accountability he (Mr. R.) courted. Let every gentleman look to his own constituents, if he pleased, or to the authority which controlled him. Gentlemen needed not be at the trouble of reminding him of what he owed to his constituents, they and he would arrange that. This was not the first time he had belonged to a small party. It was not the first time he had heard the majority of the House denouncing a few men who did not act with them. In the days of the Mexican war there were *fourteen* who were denounced as "traitors," because they did not see fit to vote with the majority of the House.

They settled that matter with their constituents; he (Mr. R.) did, and he was *here;* while some gentlemen who had denounced him as a "traitor," had endeared themselves so much to their constituents that they kept them at home. He concluded by remarking that he hoped they would have action upon this resolution in a direct form, so that the vote might go to the country, and the position of gentlemen, on all sides, be distinctly understood. He thanked the *Clerk* for his attention, saying he believed he was about the *only one* who had heard him, (merriment.)

Mr. WOODWARD said: The remarks that have just fallen from the gentleman from Louisiana (Mr. MORSE) entitle me, if they do not make it my duty, to be heard on the subject he has introduced.

I belong to no faction on this floor. I am connected with no set of men organized to run a particular candidate. I have indicated no man who I insist on having elected, as others have. I have voted for several gentlemen, as many I believe from free States as from slave States; and am ready to vote for others. For the nominee of what is called the Democratic caucus, I confess I have not voted; and if I could with propriety assign my reason for not so voting, it may be that there are not ten men upon this floor who would not justify me. But, sir, how shall I defend that vote? Shall I make a personal attack on the nominee? That I could not do without violating all those proprieties which I have been educated to observe, and which I hope I shall never cease to regard. And I reprobate the course of the gentleman from North Carolina, (Mr. VENABLE,) as I do that of the gentleman from Louisiana, (Mr. MORSE,) in making issues against gentlemen, which they cannot meet, without going into the discussion of the political conduct of candidates. How do you know what justification I might be able to make for not voting for the nominee of a majority of what is called the Democratic party? If it were lawful to make such a question here, I believe I could convince more members than have voted for both the party nominees, that I am justifiable in voting against him. I disagree with those gentlemen who would destroy the individuality of Representatives and convert them into mere machines, to be moved by party caucuses. The candidate of a caucus is always a compromise candidate; I cannot compromise with such politicians as have been engaged in making the nomination in question.

The gentleman appears to think that we ought to vote as a majority may dictate. Sir, what right has the majority to control my vote? I consent that the majority must decide questions; their vote must prevail against that of the minority; but the minority has as perfect a right to an independent vote as the majority. My right to vote is as perfect as that of all the members on this floor; and if I thought myself right, I would vote against all the people in the United States, and would interfere with no rights of theirs in doing so.

I say, I have no candidate of my own, but am ready to vote for any unobjectionable one. Between the two candidates of caucus, my vote never would have decided the question; no candidate has ever been so nearly elected, that my vote would have produced an election.

Whenever the numerical relations of two candidates are such that I can decide the case between them, my purpose has been to do so. But as matters have stood, my vote for either would have been a mere complimentary one, or in subservience to the authority of caucus. And I never can give a complimentary vote to either nominee, nor shall I recognize the authority of caucus to dictate a vote I could not justify myself in giving.

In alluding to objections against the gentleman from Georgia, (Mr. Cobb,) nothing of a personal nature is meant, nor any thing reflecting on his character as a man.

Mr. Morse said, before the vote was taken, he desired to say one single word in reply to the remarks of the gentleman from Ohio, (Mr. Root.) That gentleman had the peculiar faculty, whenever he rose, of putting the House in a good mood; but he (Mr. M.) confessed he thought ridicule and laughter no very valid answer to the arguments in favor of the resolution he had had the honor to introduce.

One week had elapsed, and they were further from an organization than they were the day they took their seats. It was no answer to tell him that it was a "gambling" transaction. The House had the right to elect the manner of selecting their Speaker; and when a plan was presented which afforded to every gentleman the opportunity of saying whether one of two gentlemen avowedly competent to discharge the duties—gentlemen of known experience, and who had commanded larger votes than any other two gentlemen on this floor probably could command—should fill the chair, ridicule would not divert him from the support of what he believed would be a fair, open, correct manner of giving to this body an organization, and relieving the two great parties of the country from the ridicule (he used the expression) which had been brought upon them by a few individuals. He did not charge the Whig or the Democratic party with being the cause of disorganization. Other persons were responsible. Both these parties had shown themselves to be honest, serious in their endeavors to give to this body an organization, and proceed with the public business; and if they did not succeed, it would be from no failure on their part to present, and, as long as was reasonable, to stand by, two men who were qualified in every respect to fill the chair. He was not invading the right of the gentleman from South Carolina, who thought he had the right to vote upon all great questions, and that every Representative from every Congressional district had the right to be heard. They would be heard if this resolution were adopted. They had the right to change the manner of voting, and to arrive at the sense of the House in any way which the majority saw fit. They might insert the name of a candidate for Speaker in a resolution, as they had before done in the case of Mr. French, who was made Clerk in that way, and in other cases, and all gentlemen would have the right to vote upon the question. If the honorable gentleman from South Carolina did not like the nominee of the Whig party, he could vote against their resolution; and if he did not like the nominee of his own party, he could also vote against such a resolution.

It was a question which appealed to the common sense of this body. Would they sit here and allow a few gentlemen to defeat all their attempts at an organization, until the public press should cry shame upon the Representatives of the people? He trusted not. He trusted that gentlemen would be satisfied with the result of this resolution, which would be to give them one of two gentlemen, either of whom was well qualified to fill the chair. Gentlemen had told the House that they would sit here and vote for months before they would change their position. If there were any probability of their changing their votes so as to result in an election, he would be in favor of continuing to vote; but gentlemen knew they would not get a Speaker which belonged to one of the two great parties. He trusted gentlemen would reflect, and so vote as to extricate the House from the ridiculous position in which they were now placed.

Mr. Brown, of Mississippi, hoped that this discussion would be brought to an end. The House had been entertained with a comedy from the gentleman from Ohio, (Mr. Root,) with something like a tragedy from the gentleman from South Carolina, (Mr. Woodward,) and an afterpiece from the gentleman from Louisiana, (Mr. Morse.) He hoped now that the play would be brought to a close. He trusted that the question would not further be discussed, but that the vote would now be taken on his motion to lay on the table.

Mr. Root. What will the gentleman from Mississippi gain by laying the resolution on the table?

Mr. Brown. We will then have another vote.

Mr. Root. We shall gain nothing. If laid upon the table, the House can take it up again at any time.

The question was then taken, and decided in the affirmative without a division.

So the resolution was laid on the table.

Mr. Wentworth now moved that the House proceed to the election of Speaker, *viva voce.*

Mr. Bowie sent to the Clerk's table the following resolutions, which were read for information:

Resolved, That the organization of this House cannot longer be suspended, without jeopardizing the confidence of the people in their Representatives, and exciting their just apprehensions that the spirit of party has triumphed over the deliberate reason of this assembly.

Resolved, That each party, and every member of each party in this House, is under the most solemn obligations to cultivate a spirit of conciliation and self-sacrifice, and give up to their country their personal and party predilections.

Resolved, That a committee of —— be elected, by ballot, who shall recommend to this House suitable persons, to fill the offices of the Speaker and Clerk of this House, and that the committee report by 12 o'clock, to-morrow.

The resolutions having been read—

Mr. Wentworth insisted on his motion, and the question thereon having been taken and decided in the affirmative—

The House decided that it would proceed to the election of Speaker, *viva voce.*

Mr. POTTER rose, and was understood to say that he felt highly flattered by the vote which had been given to him. Conceiving, however, that the majority did not lean in that direction, and not desiring to embarrass the action of the House, he hoped his friends would make no further use of his name.

The roll was called for the thirty-second time, when the tellers reported that the whole number of votes given in was 224; necessary to a choice 113; of which—

Mr. Winthrop received	101
Mr. W. J. Brown	53
Mr. Boyd	15
Mr. Disney	13
Mr. H. Cobb	10
Mr. Wilmot	6
Mr. Gentry	5
Mr. Green	5
Mr. Strong	3
Mr. Miller	3
Mr. James Thompson	3
Mr. McClernand	1
Mr. Horace Mann	1
Mr. Meade	1
Mr. F. P. Stanton	1
Mr. A. G. Brown	1
Mr. Potter	1
Mr. Durkee	1
No choice.	224

Mr. HOLMES, of South Carolina, moved that the House adjourn.

Mr. HALL, of Missouri, asked the yeas and nays; which were refused.

Tellers were asked and appointed, (Messrs. CABELL, of Florida, and BOWLIN.)

The question was then taken, and decided in the negative—ayes, 92, noes 100.

So the House refused to adjourn.

Mr. SWEETSER rose and offered the following resolution:

Whereas this House has balloted seven days for Speaker without an election, it is manifest that, from present indications, no organization can now be hoped for: Therefore,

Resolved, That, the Senate concurring, this House stand adjourned until the 1st day of January, 1850, at twelve o'clock.

TUESDAY, December 11.

The Journal of yesterday was read and approved.

Vote for Speaker.

On motion of Mr. WENTWORTH, the House proceeded to vote for Speaker, *viva voce.*

Messrs. HILLIARD of Alabama, STRONG of Pennsylvania, DUER of New York, and MILLER of Ohio, resumed their seats at the Clerk's table as tellers to count the vote.

The roll was then called the thirty-third time, when the tellers reported that the whole number of votes given in was 224; necessary to a choice 113; of which—

Mr. Winthrop received	101
Mr. William J. Brown	80
Mr. Boyd	15
Mr. Disney	8
Mr. Wilmot	5
Mr. Gentry	5
Mr. Howell Cobb	5
Mr. Horace Mann	1
Mr. Frederick P. Stanton	1
Mr. Bayly	1
Mr. Meade	1
Mr. Durkee	1
No choice.	224

The roll was then called the thirty-fourth time, when the tellers reported that the whole number of votes given was 224; necessary to a choice 113; of which—

Mr. Winthrop received	101
Mr. Brown, of Indiana	84
Mr. Boyd	12
Mr. Disney	7
Mr. Wilmot	5
Mr. Gentry	5
Mr. Cobb, of Georgia,	5
Mr. Mann, of Massachusetts	1
Mr. Stanton, of Tennessee	1
Mr. Bayly	1
Mr. Meade	1
Mr. Durkee	1
No choice.	224

The roll was then called the thirty-fifth time, when the tellers reported that the whole number of votes given was 224; necessary to a choice 113; of which—

Mr. Winthrop received	101
Mr. William J. Brown	88
Mr. Boyd	12
Mr. Wilmot	5
Mr. Morehead	5
Mr. Howell Cobb	5
Mr. Disney	4
Mr. Horace Mann	1
Mr. Frederick P. Stanton	1
Mr. Meade	1
Mr. Durkee	1
No choice.	224

The roll was called for the thirty-sixth time, when the tellers reported that the whole number of votes given in was 224; necessary to a choice 113; of which—

Mr. Winthrop received	101
Mr. Brown, of Indiana	97
Mr. Boyd	7
Mr. Morehead	5
Mr. Wilmot	5
Mr. Cobb, of Georgia	4

Mr. Durkee	1
Mr. McDowell	1
Mr. Meade	1
Mr. Mann, of Massachusetts	1
Mr. Stanton, of Tennessee	1
No choice.	224

The roll was then called the thirty-seventh time, when the tellers reported that the whole number of votes given was 224; necessary to a choice 113; of which—

Mr. W. J. Brown received	107
Mr. Winthrop	101
Mr. Wilmot	6
Mr. Morehead	5
Mr. Horace Mann	1
Mr. Boyd	1
Mr. F. P. Stanton	1
Mr. Durkee	1
Mr. McDowell	1
No choice.	224

The roll was called for the thirty-eighth time, when the tellers reported that the whole number of votes given in was 225; necessary to a choice 113; of which—

Mr. Brown, of Indiana, received	109
Mr. Winthrop	100
Mr. Wilmot	6
Mr. Morehead	5
Mr. Mann, of Massachuestts	1
Mr. Boyd	1
Mr. Durkee	1
Mr. Vinton	1
Mr. McDowell	1
No choice.	225

The roll was then called the thirty-ninth time, when the tellers reported that the whole number of votes given was 226; necessary to a choice 114; of which—

Mr. William J. Brown received	109
Mr. Winthrop	101
Mr. Wilmot	7
Mr. Morehead	5
Mr. Boyd	1
Mr. Durkee	1
Mr. Vinton	1
Mr. McDowell	1
No choice.	226

Mr. Thompson, of Kentucky, moved that the House adjourn until to-morrow, at 12 o'clock.

Mr. Winthrop rose and said he desired to say to the members here assembled that it was well known to many of his friends, and, he believed, to the great majority of those who had thus far honored him with their support, that he should have withdrawn his name long ago from this protracted contest if they had allowed him to do so. He had repeatedly expressed to them his personal desire not to stand in the way of a satisfactory organization of the House, or indeed of any organization, believing that the highest interests of the country, that the peace and safety of the Union, demanded that an organization of some sort should be effected without delay. But as he had seen his friends continuing to persist in the idea that his name was at their control, and not under his own, he had, therefore, allowed the contest to go on, as it had gone on, until this moment. He now begged leave to say publicly, as he had heretofore often said privately, that nothing could give him greater pain than to imagine for an instant that he had stood in the way of any organization of this House which might be effected, and much more in the way of any organization which could be effected by his friends. He desired to say to them all that, while he thanked them cordially for the devoted support which they had given him, it would afford him the utmost satisfaction if they could concentrate their efforts on some other candidate; and he should most cordially unite with them on any other candidate whom they might adopt.

Mr. Thompson, remarking that he knew it was not in order to debate the motion to adjourn, said that he had from the very beginning voted for the gentleman from Massachusetts as candidate for Speaker, and should continue so to do. He regretted that the gentleman should see fit to withdraw his name. He (Mr. T.) would prefer him to any other gentleman in this body, for his known ability and experience. But if the gentleman insisted upon withdrawing his name as one of the nominees, those gentlemen who had supported him wanted time to deliberate and concertmeasures. As a matter of justice and equity, therefore, he moved that the House adjourn; and he asked the yeas and nays on the motion.

The question then recurred on the demand of Mr. Thompson for the yeas and nays on his motion to adjourn, and they were ordered.

And the question was then taken, and decided in the negative—yeas 110, nays 114.

So the House refused to adjourn.

Mr. Cobb, of Alabama, moved that the House proceed to vote for Speaker.

Mr. Hall moved to amend the motion of the gentleman from Alabama, (Mr. Cobb,) by substituting a resolution that William J. Brown, of Indiana, be declared the duly elected Speaker of this House.

Mr. Meade submitted that the motion of the gentleman from Alabama (Mr. Cobb) was out of order, because the election of Speaker was the regular business before the House unless that business were superseded by some other.

Mr. Baker, amid great confusion, moved that the House adjourn.

Mr. Stanton, of Tennessee, on the other side of the House, submitted a similar motion, remarking that he believed a motion to adjourn was always in order.

The Clerk thereupon put the question on that motion; and the motion having prevailed, the House, at a late hour,

Adjourned.

Wednesday, December 12.

Election of Speaker.

The Journal of yesterday was read and approved.

On motion of Mr. Kaufman, the House proceeded to vote for Speaker, *viva voce.*

Messrs. Hilliard of Alabama, Strong of Pennsylvania, Duer of New York, and Miller of Ohio, resumed their seats at the Clerk's table as tellers to count the vote.

The roll was then called the fortieth time, when the tellers reported that the whole number of votes given in was 226; necessary to a choice 114; of which—

Mr. William J. Brown received	112
Mr. Duer	26
Mr. Stanly	18
Mr. Morehead	17
Mr. Winthrop	17
Mr. McGaughey	13
Mr. Horace Mann	5
Mr. Julian	3
Mr. Boyd	3
Mr. Vinton	2
Mr. Chandler	2
Mr. Thaddeus Stevens	2
Mr. Rockwell	1
Mr. Outlaw	1
Mr. Conrad	1
Mr. Bowdon	1
Mr. Holmes	1
Mr. Daniel P. King	1
No choice.	226

Thursday, December 13.

Election of Speaker.

The Journal of yesterday was read and approved.

Mr. Brown, of Mississippi, rose and said, that he would ask leave of the House to offer the resolution which he would send to the Clerk's desk.

The resolution was read, as follows:

Resolved, That Howell Cobb, of Georgia, is hereby chosen Speaker of the House of Representatives of the Thirty-first Congress.

Mr. Brown remarked, that he had been induced to offer this resolution without any consultation with his political friends, and without having given the remotest intimation to his friend from Georgia (Mr. Cobb) of his intention of so doing, as he was sure if he had intimated his intention to the gentleman, he would have been denied the privilege of making this motion. He was sincerely desirous of seeing an end put to the protracted votings for Speaker. They had been engaged in this unprofitable business for nine days, and they were now just where they commenced on the first morning of the session. Not only were they without a Speaker, but without a candidate for Speaker. It was well known that the political party to which he belonged had a majority in this House—impracticable, it was true—but still a majority; and although they had heretofore failed to concentrate upon any candidate in sufficient force to elect him, still they had approximated nearer that point than their opponents had. There was a little portion of the Democratic party who refused to vote with the great majority of the party; but not only was there a like portion of the Whig Free Soilers who refused to vote with the large body of their party, but a portion of the southern Whigs who also refused to act with their party. Under these circumstances it must be apparent to every one, that unless something else were done than to continue as they were now doing, no choice at all of Speaker could be effected.

If we exclude the Free Soilers on both sides, the Democrats have a majority over the Whigs. If you count them on both sides, dividing them according to their party predilections, we still have a majority of one, and this if all the seats were occupied; but it is the misfortune of the Whigs to have four absentees—Mr. King of Georgia, Mr. Gentry of Tennessee, Mr. Julian of Indiana, and Mr. Palfrey of Massachusetts, who had failed of his election. This gives us the advantage by five votes. We all know, if you exclude the Free-Soilers entirely, counting them on neither side, our majority is not thereby diminished, but is increased by two or three votes.

He did not intend to demand that a vote should be taken upon the resolution. His object in introducing it had been that he might have an opportunity, on his own responsibility alone, to call upon the Whigs, if they were desirous of organizing the House, to unite with them to accomplish that object. They being in a minority, could better do it than to ask them (the Democrats) to come over to them. If no gentleman desired to discuss the resolution he would now withdraw it.

The House proceeded to vote, *viva voce*, for the election of Speaker.

Messrs. Hilliard of Alabama, Strong of Pennsylvania, Duer of New York, and Miller of Ohio, resumed their seats at the Clerk's table, as tellers to count the votes.

The roll was then called the forty-first time, when the tellers reported that the whole number of votes given was 224; necessary to a choice 113; of which—

Mr. Winthrop received	59
Mr. H. Cobb	40
Mr. Boyd	26
Mr. Potter	24
Mr. Stanly	21
Mr. Morehead	10
Mr. Bayly	6
Mr. Wilmot	4
Mr. Thaddeus Stevens	4
Mr. McGaughey	3
Mr. R. M. McLane	2
Mr. Schenck	2
Mr. McDowell	2
Mr. Gorman	2
Mr. Hilliard	2
Mr. McClernand	2
Mr. Julian	2
Mr. Outlaw	1
Mr. Marshall	1
Mr. Burt	1
Mr. Breck	1
Mr. Frederick P. Stanton	1
Mr. Strong	1
Mr. Conrad	1
Mr. Andrew Johnson	1
Mr. Ashmun	1
Mr. McLanahan	1
Mr. Disney	1
Mr. Root	1
Mr. Bingham	1
No choice.	224

Whereupon, on motion of Mr. Houston, at a late hour—

The House adjourned until to-morrow, at 12 o'clock.

Friday, December 14.

The Speakership—Debate Terminated.

Mr. Dimmick, of Pennsylvania, now rose and offered the following resolution, which was read:

Resolved, That this House shall proceed to the election of a Speaker, and continue its efforts to effect such an election, without debate from any member of this House, until an election is effected.

Mr. Woodward said that he desired to make a single observation. The proposition which he had introduced was perfectly consistent with every resolution that had been offered. They might adopt it, and adopt every resolution which had been before the House. This one might follow.

The question was then taken on the resolution of Mr. Dimmick, and was decided in the affirmative by an overwhelming "aye."

So the resolution was adopted.

(The annunciation was greeted with strong marks of approbation.)

The call of the roll was then again demanded from every part of the Hall.

And the House again proceeded to vote for Speaker *viva voce*.

Messrs. Hilliard of Alabama, Strong of Pennsylvania, Duer of New York, and Miller of Ohio, resumed their seats at the Clerk's table as tellers, to count the votes.

The roll was then called the forty-second time, when the tellers reported that the whole number of votes given was 225; necessary to a choice 113; of which—

Mr. Boyd received	51
Mr. Winthrop	36
Mr. Stanly	30
Mr. Potter	24
Mr. Howell Cobb	18
Mr. Thaddeus Stevens	11
Mr. Morehead	9
Mr. Robert M. McLane	8
Mr. Wilmot	6
Mr. Duer	5
Mr. Hilliard	3
Mr. McGaughey	3
Mr. Outlaw	2
Mr. McDowell	2
Mr. Marshall	2
Mr. Disney	2
Mr. Julian	2
Mr. Vinton	2
Mr. Gorman	1
Mr. Toombs	1
Mr. Frederick P. Stanton	1
Mr. Newell	1
Mr. Tuck	1
Mr. Baker	1
Mr. Fuller	1
Mr. McClernand	1
Mr. Durkee	1
No choice.	225

The roll was then called the forty-third time, when the tellers reported that the whole number of votes given was 225; necessary to a choice 113; of which—

Mr. Boyd received	68
Mr. Stanly	40
Mr. Winthrop	25
Mr. Potter	24
Mr. Stevens, of Pennsylvania	13
Mr. Morehead	10
Mr. McLane, of Maryland	7
Mr. Wilmot	6
Mr. Cobb, of Georgia	6
Mr. Duer	5
Mr. Conrad	3
Mr. Outlaw	3
Mr. Hilliard	2
Mr. Baker	2
Mr. Julian	2
Mr. Newell	1
Mr. McDowell	1
Mr. McGaughey	1
Mr. Robinson	1
Mr. Marshall	1
Mr. Stanton, of Tennessee	1
Mr. Vinton	1
Mr. McClernand	1
Mr. Durkee	1
No choice.	225

The roll was then called the forty-fourth time, when the tellers reported that the whole number of votes given was 223; necessary to a choice 112; of which—

Mr. Boyd received	82
Mr. Stanly	49
Mr. Winthrop	27
Mr. Potter	22
Mr. Stevens, of Pennsylvania	12
Mr. Wilmot	6
Mr. Morehead	6
Mr. Duer	3
Mr. Strong	2
Mr. Julian	2
Mr. Outlaw	2
Mr. Hilliard	1
Mr. Cobb, of Georgia	1
Mr. Schenck	1
Mr. McGaughey	1
Mr. Robinson	1
Mr. Baker	1
Mr. Stanton, of Tennessee	1
Mr. Mann, of Massachusetts	1
Mr. McClernand	1
Mr. Durkee	1
No choice.	223

The House adjourned until to-morrow, at 12 o'clock.

IN SENATE.

SATURDAY, December 15.

The Hon. SAM HOUSTON, Senator from the State of Texas, appeared in his seat in the Senate.

HOUSE OF REPRESENTATIVES.

SATURDAY, December 15.

The Speakership.

Mr. PRESTON KING rose and said, he would state to the House that if the Democratic party desired to organize the House, by the choice of a Democratic Speaker, they could do so by supporting WILLIAM STRONG, the Representative of the Berks district, in Pennsylvania. If the Democratic party would vote for Mr. STRONG, he could be elected.

The House then proceeded to vote, *viva voce*, for Speaker.

Messrs. HILLIARD of Alabama, STRONG of Pennsylvania, DUER of New York, and MILLER of Ohio, resumed their seats at the Clerk's table as tellers to count the votes.

The roll was then called the forty-fifth time, when the tellers reported that the whole number of votes given was 226; necessary to a choice 114, of which—

Mr. Boyd received	82
Mr. Stanly	55
Mr. Thaddeus Stevens	24
Mr. Potter	22
Mr. Winthrop	20
Mr. Morehead	8
Mr. William Strong	3
Mr. Schenck	1
Mr. Outlaw	1
Mr. Howell Cobb	1
Mr. Robinson	1
Mr. James Thompson	1
Mr. Frederick P. Stanton	1
Mr. Kaufman	1
Mr. Baker	1
Mr. Disney	1
Mr. Duer	1
Mr. McClernand	1
Mr. Tuck	1
No choice.	226

The roll was called the forty-sixth time, when the tellers reported that the whole number of votes given in was 226; necessary to a choice 114; of which—

Mr. Boyd received	85
Mr. Stanly	67
Mr. Thaddeus Stevens	23
Mr. Potter	17
Mr. Winthrop	14
Mr. Morehead	5
Mr. Strong	5
Mr. Disney	3
Mr. Howell Cobb	1
Mr. Outlaw	1
Mr. Robinson	1
Mr. James Thompson	1
Mr. Tuck	1
Mr. Duer	1
Mr. Featherston	1
No choice.	226

The roll was then called the forty-seventh time, when the tellers reported that the whole number of votes given was 225; necessary to a choice 113; of which—

Mr. Boyd received	86
Mr. Stanly	66
Mr. Thaddeus Stevens	27
Mr. Potter	18
Mr. Winthrop	10
Mr. Morehead	4
Mr. Disney	3
Mr. Strong	2
Mr. Howell Cobb	1
Mr. Williams	1
Mr. Outlaw	1
Mr. Robinson	1
Mr. Jacob Thompson	1
Mr. Conrad	1
Mr. Duer	1
Mr. James G. King	1
Mr. James Thompson	1
No choice.	225

Mr. HOLMES, of South Carolina, rose and was understood to say that he did not think there were two members in the House who did not see the importance of adjourning for the purpose of conference. Therefore, with a view to give the interval between this and the Sabbath day to that object, he would move that the House do now adjourn until Monday, at 12 o'clock.

Tellers were demanded.

Mr. Holmes withdrew the motion.

Mr. Richardson renewed it.

Tellers were asked and ordered, and Messrs. Johnson of Arkansas, and Clingman of North Carolina, were appointed.

And the question having been put, the affirmative votes stood 114—a majority of the whole number present.

So the House adjourned until Monday, at 12 o'clock.

Monday, *December* 17.

The Speakership.

Mr. Stanly rose and said: Before the Clerk proceeds to call the roll I desire to trespass on the attention of the House a moment.

I rise respectfully to request those gentlemen who have voted for me to discontinue doing so. I desire to repeat what I stated the other day, that I do not feel able (in the presence of others so much better qualified to discharge the duties of the Chair) to undertake them, even supposing I could be elected. It is due to the House and to the country that another person should be elected. And as I am unwilling to trespass upon the House in violation of the rule some days ago adopted forbidding debate, I will only beg leave to say, that one of my colleagues has said that North Carolina would be found willing and ready to act as she had been in 1775, when the Mecklenburg declaration was made. I wish to say, that I have no doubt North Carolina will be ready to act. She will be found in favor of the Union—opposed to faction and disorganization, no matter from what quarter they may come. Her voice in 1849 will be as it was in 1775, when she heard of the battle of Lexington. She declared in her Mecklenburg resolutions, her determination to throw off the yoke of English oppression, and she said, as I say now, "The cause of Boston is the cause of all." The people of North Carolina will always be found on the side of Law, Order, and the Union.

(The close of these remarks was greeted with applause.)

The House then proceeded to vote, *viva voce*, for Speaker.

The roll was then called for the forty-eighth time, when the tellers reported that the whole number of votes given in was 223; necessary to a choice 112; of which—

Mr. Boyd received	86
Mr. Winthrop	70
Mr. Stevens, of Pennsylvania	18
Mr. Potter	17
Mr. Morehead	16
Mr. Disney	4
Mr. Stanly	3
Mr. Strong	3
Mr. Outlaw	2
Mr. Robinson	1
Mr. Cobb, of Georgia	1
Mr. Conrad	1
Mr. Chandler	1
No choice.	223

The roll was then called the forty-ninth time, when the tellers reported that the whole number of votes given was 223; necessary to a choice 112; of which—

Mr. Boyd received	87
Mr. Winthrop	72
Mr. Morehead	22
Mr. Potter	14
Mr. Thaddeus Stevens	11
Mr. Disney	5
Mr. Strong	4
Mr. Conrad	2
Mr. Robinson	1
Mr. Outlaw	1
Mr. Howell Cobb	1
Mr. Chandler	1
Mr. Stanly	1
Mr. Julian	1
No choice.	223

The roll was called for the fiftieth time, when the tellers reported that the whole number of votes given in was 221; necessary to a choice, 111; of which—

Mr. Boyd received	87
Mr. Winthrop	75
Mr. Morehead	18
Mr. Potter	15
Mr. Stevens, of Pennsylvania	9
Mr. Strong	3
Mr. Disney	3
Mr. Outlaw	2
Mr. Conrad	2
Mr. Cobb, of Georgia	1
Mr. Vinton	1
Mr. Robinson	1
Mr. Julian	1
Mr. Stanly	1
Mr. White	1
Mr. McLane, of Maryland	1
No choice.	221

The roll was called the fifty-first time, when the tellers reported that the whole number of votes given in was 222; necessary to a choice 112; of which—

Mr. Boyd received	87
Mr. Winthrop	57
Mr. White	16
Mr. Morehead	14
Mr. Potter	13
Mr. T. Stevens	6
Mr. King, of New Jersey	5
Mr. Conrad	4

Mr. Strong	4
Mr. Disney	4
Mr. Schenck	3
Mr. Julian	2
Mr. Stanly	2
Mr. H. Cobb	1
Mr. R. M. McLane	1
Mr. Hilliard	1
Mr. Robinson	1
Mr. McLanahan	1
	—
No choice.	222

TUESDAY, December 18.

The Speakership.

Mr. KAUFMAN obtained the floor.

He said that he held in his hand a resolution which he desired to present to the consideration of the House. He would, in the first instance, ask the unanimous consent of the House to preface the resolution with a very few remarks. That courtesy had been extended yesterday to the gentleman from Kentucky, (Mr. THOMPSON,) and he (Mr. K.) was satisfied that it would not now be refused to him.

No objection having been made, Mr. K. proceeded with his remarks.

The resolution, he said, which he wished to offer for the consideration of the House, for the great purpose, as he conceived, of conducing to its organization, and of allaying the excitement which prevailed in every section of the Union, by reason of the state of things now existing here, was substantially the same as that which he had offered yesterday with this exception, that the resolution which he was now about to offer provided that it should not commence to take effect until to-morrow. He would read it.

Mr. K. then read the resolution, which was in the following words:

Resolved, That if on to-morrow no member have a majority of all the votes cast for Speaker on the first vote, then, on the second vote on to-morrow, if any member shall receive only one less than a majority of the whole number of votes, he shall be declared elected; but if no member be elected Speaker on said second vote, than on the third next vote, if any member shall receive only two less than a majority, he shall be declared elected, and so on, requiring one vote less to elect for every ballot taken, until a choice of Speaker is made.

The resolution having been read—

Mr. K. proceeded to remark, that before he referred more particularly to the resolution, he would state, in a word, what was the objection which he entertained to the resolution which had been introduced yesterday by the gentleman from Kentucky, (Mr. THOMPSON.) He (Mr. K.) conceived that it would be more satisfactory to the people of the country, that, whatever was done, should be done—

Mr. BROWN, of Mississippi, interposed, and said that he had risen to a point of order. It would be recollected by the House that a resolution had been adopted several days ago, by which all debate was prohibited.

The CLERK said it was true that such a resolution had been adopted; but that the gentleman from Texas (Mr. KAUFMAN) had obtained the unanimous consent of the House to explain his resolution.

Mr. KAUFMAN said he had distinctly asked the courtesy of the House to preface his resolution with a few remarks. The consent of the House had been given, and he hoped that no gentleman would take exception to his proceeding.

Mr. BROWN said he certainly had not understood that the gentleman from Texas (Mr. KAUFMAN) had obtained the unanimous consent of the House to make his remarks. If he (Mr. B.) had understood that to be the proposition, he, for one, would have objected to it. He objected to the resolution, and he objected to any debate upon it.

The CLERK announced the question upon laying the whole subject upon the table.

(Loud cries of "Question!")

The question was taken and decided in the affirmative.

So the whole subject was laid on the table.

(Cries of "Call the roll!")

Mr. STRONG, of Pennsylvania, said he had been acting as one of the tellers without intermission for thirteen days. He thought, therefore, he was entitled to an honorable discharge, and he asked that another person might be substituted in his place.

The CLERK invited the following gentlemen to take their seats as tellers, to respite those who had been acting, viz: Messrs. VAN DYKE of New Jersey, HARRIS of Alabama, HENRY of Vermont, and GORMAN of Indiana.

The CLERK was proceeding to call the roll, when—

Mr. MCGAUGHEY rose, and announced to the House his intention not to give his vote upon the call of the roll to-day. His reason for this course would be found in the fact that one of his colleagues on the Democratic side (Mr. MCDONALD) had met with an accident, which rendered it inconvenient for him to attend the House to-day. His colleague would attend, if it should be necessary for him to do so. If that necessity should not arise, he would not be present, and he (Mr.McG.) should decline to vote.

The roll was then called the fifty-second time, when the tellers reported that the whole number of votes given was 223; necessary to a choice 112; of which—

Mr. Winthrop received	95
Mr. Boyd	66
Mr. McClernand	13
Mr. Potter	11
Mr. Disney	9
Mr. Cobb, of Georgia	7
Mr. Julian	7
Mr. Morehead	4
Mr. Stevens, of Pennsylvania	3
Mr. Robinson	2

Mr. McLane, of Maryland 1
Mr. Clingman. 1
Mr. Outlaw 1
Mr. McLanahan 1
Mr. Baker 1
Mr. Cabell, of Florida 1

No choice. 223

The roll was then called the fifty-third time, when the tellers reported that the whole number of votes given was 223; necessary to a choice 112; of which—

Mr. Winthrop received 97
Mr. Boyd 57
Mr. McClernand 18
Mr. Potter 10
Mr. Disney 9
Mr. Howell Cobb 8
Mr. Julian. 7
Mr. Morehead 4
Mr. Robinson 3
Mr. Robert M. McLane 2
Mr. Thaddeus Stevens 2
Mr. Outlaw 1
Mr. E. C. Cabell 1
Mr. Baker 1
Mr. A. H. Stephens 1

No choice. 223

Mr. Savage sent to the Clerk's table the following resolution, which was read:

Resolved, That if the House fail to elect a Speaker during the present day, it will, upon its meeting to-morrow, apply to its proceedings, as far as practicable, the principle embodied in the 12th article of the Amendments to the Constitution of the United States, prescribing the mode of electing a President and Vice President.

Resolved, That the House will upon the calling of the roll, cast its vote for Speaker; and if no person shall have a majority of all the votes, then from the persons having the highest number, (not exceeding three in the list of those voted for,) the House shall proceed to choose its Speaker; and if the three persons on the last vote should be voted for, and neither of them should have a majority of all the votes, then the House shall choose its Speaker, by another vote, from the two highest on the list.

The resolution having been read—

The question was taken on the adoption thereof, and decided in the negative without a division.

So the resolution was rejected.

The roll was then called a fifty-fourth time, when the tellers reported that the whole number of votes given in was 222; necessary to a choice 112; of which—

Mr. Winthrop received 97
Mr. Boyd 51
Mr. McClernand 23
Mr. Cobb, of Georgia 11
Mr. Potter 8
Mr. Disney 8
Mr. Morehead 5

Mr. Strong 4
Mr. Julian. 4
Mr. Robinson 3
Mr. Stevens, of Pennsylvania . . 2
Mr. Outlaw 1
Mr. McLane, of Maryland . . . 1
Mr. Hilliard 1
Mr. Duer 1
Mr. Miller 1
Mr. McLanahan 1

No choice. 222

Mr. Holmes moved that the House do now adjourn.

(Cries of "Go on with the roll!")

Tellers were demanded on the motion of Mr. Holmes, and were refused.

Mr. Holmes withdrew the motion.

The roll was then called the fifty-fifth time, when the tellers reported that the whole number of votes given was 222; necessary to a choice 112; of which—

Mr. Winthrop received 97
Mr. Boyd 47
Mr. McClernand 26
Mr. Strong 16
Mr. Cobb, of Georgia. 16
Mr. Morehead 5
Mr. Disney 4
Mr. Julian 3
Mr. Hilliard 2
Mr. Thaddeus Stevens 2
Mr. Robinson 2
Mr. Outlaw 1
Mr. McLanahan. 1

No choice. 222

Mr. Johnson of Arkansas moved that the House do now adjourn.

The question was taken, and decided in the affirmative without a division.

So the House adjourned until to-morrow, at 12 o'clock.

Wednesday, December 19.

The House was called to order at 12 o'clock by Thomas J. Campbell, Esq.

The Clerk was proceeding to read the journal——

Rev. Theobald Mathew.

Mr. Baker rose and said, that he held in his hand a resolution which he desired to offer, and which, he was sure, would receive the unanimous assent of this House. He would send it to the Clerk's table to be read.

The resolution was then read by the Clerk in the following words:

Resolved, That the Rev. Father Mathew be respectfully invited to take a seat upon the floor of this House.

Mr. Giddings asked that the resolution might be again read; and the resolution having been read accordingly—

The question thereon was taken and decided in the affirmative.

So the resolution was adopted.

The Doorkeeper of the late House of Representatives, ROBERT E. HORNER, Esq., was directed to see the order of the House executed.

Thereupon, the Rev. THEOBALD MATHEW was conducted to a seat within the bar.

The Speakership.

The House then again proceeded to vote *viva voce* for the election of Speaker.

Messrs. HARRIS of Alabama, HENRY, GORMAN, and NEWELL, resumed their seats at the Clerk's table as tellers to count the votes.

The roll was then called the fifty-sixth time, when the tellers reported that the whole number of votes given was 224; necessary to a choice 113; of which—

Mr. Winthrop received	84
Mr. Boyd	37
Mr. McClernand	35
Mr. Strong	17
Mr. Cobb, of Georgia	15
Mr. King, of New Jersey	5
Mr. Julian	4
Mr. McDowell	4
Mr. Morehead	4
Mr. Baker	3
Mr. Conrad	2
Mr. Stevens, of Pennsylvania	2
Mr. Bissell	2
Mr. Hilliard	1
Mr. Cabell, of Florida	1
Mr. Robinson	1
Mr. Clingman	1
Mr. La Sère	1
Mr. Wilmot	1
Mr. John A. King	1
Mr. Miller	1
Mr. Stanly	1
Mr. McGaughey	1
No choice.	224

The roll was called for the fifty-seventh time, when the tellers reported that the whole number of votes given in was 223; necessary to a choice, 112; of which—

Mr. Winthrop received	88
Mr. McClernand	40
Mr. Boyd	33
Mr. Strong	17
Mr. Cobb, of Georgia	13
Mr. King, of New Jersey	5
Mr. McDowell	5
Mr. Julian	4
Mr. Morehead	4
Mr. Hilliard	2
Mr. Conrad	2
Mr. Stevens, of Pennsylvania	2
Mr. Bissell	2
Mr. Venable	1
Mr. Wilmot	1
Mr. Miller	1
Mr. Clingman	1
Mr. McGaughey	1
Mr. Levin	1
No choice.	223

The roll was then called the fifty-eighth time, when the tellers reported that the whole number of votes given was 224; necessary to a choice 113; of which—

Mr. Winthrop received	86
Mr. McClernand	46
Mr. Boyd	32
Mr. Strong	17
Mr. Howell Cobb	10
Mr. Julian	5
Mr. McDowell	5
Mr. James G. King.	4
Mr. Morehead	4
Mr. Thaddeus Stevens	2
Mr. Williams	2
Mr. Hilliard	1
Mr. Wilson	1
Mr. Alexander H. Stephens	1
Mr. E. C. Cabell	1
Mr. La Sère	1
Mr. Wilmot	1
Mr. Miller	1
Mr. Conrad	1
Mr. Bissell	1
Mr. McGaughey	1
Mr. Marshall	1
No choice.	224

On motion of Mr. Vinton,
The House adjourned.

THURSDAY, December 20.

The Speakership.

The House proceeded to vote *viva voce* for the election of Speaker.

Messrs. VENABLE of North Carolina, HENRY of Vermont, GORMAN of Indiana, and NEWELL of New Jersey, resumed their seats at the Clerk's table as tellers to count the vote.

The roll was then called the fifty-ninth time, when the tellers reported that the whole number of votes given was 218; necessary to a choice 110; of which—

Mr. Stanly received	75
Mr. McClernand	50
Mr. Boyd	28
Mr. Strong	15
Mr. Winthrop	13
Mr. Wilmot	7
Mr. Miller	6
Mr. E. C. Cabell	6
Mr. Schenck	3
Mr. H. Cobb	2
Mr. McDowell	2
Mr. T. Stevens	2
Mr. Bowie	1
Mr. R. McLane	1
Mr. Morehead	1

Mr. Beale	1
Mr. Potter	1
Mr. Conrad	1
Mr. R. W. Johnson	1
Mr. McGaughey	1
Mr. Carter	1
No choice.	218

Saturday, December 22.

Election of Speaker—Mr. Stanton's Resolution.

Mr. Stanton, of Tennessee, now rose and called for the reading of the proposition which he had submitted.

The proposition having been read in the words following:

Resolved, That the House will proceed immediately to the election of a Speaker, *viva voce;* and if, after the roll shall have been called three times, no member shall have received a majority of the whole number of votes, the roll shall again be called, and the member who shall then receive the largest number of votes, provided it be a majority of a quorum, shall be declared to be chosen Speaker:

Mr. Holmes moved that it be laid upon the table.

And the question, "Shall these propositions be laid upon the table?" was then taken and decided in the negative—yeas 94, nays 124.

So the House decided that the two propositions should not be laid on the table.

The question then recurred on the original proposition of Mr. Stanton.

The Clerk proceeded with the call of the roll, which having been completed the vote was announced—yeas 113, nays 106.

So the original proposition of Mr. Stanton was adopted.

Election of Speaker Consummated.

There was now a general demand over the House that the roll be called.

Mr. Stanly rose and said: Mr. Clerk, with the permission of the House, I wish to make a statement relating to myself. After the adoption of this resolution—which I earnestly hope will lead to an organization—I presume, of course, it is desirable that the members of each party should vote for their respective favorites. The other side have their favorite, and we have ours, and all who wish an organization will vote for some gentleman of whose election we can have a reasonable hope. I most respectfully but earnestly express the wish that no gentleman will vote for me, but that they will all, for the sake of their country, give their votes for him who is decidedly the favorite of the Whig party, as I shall.

The House again proceeded to vote *vica voce* for the election of Speaker.

Messrs. Venable of North Carolina, Henry of Vermont, and Van Dyke of New Jersey, resumed their seats at the Clerk's table as tellers to count the votes.

The roll was called for the sixtieth time, when the tellers reported that the whole number of votes given was 217; necessary to a choice 109; of which—

Mr. Howell Cobb received	95
Mr. Winthrop	90
Mr. Wilmot	9
Mr. Morehead	4
Mr. Strong	4
Mr. E. C. Cabell	4
Mr. McGaughey	3
Mr. Potter	3
Mr. Boyd	3
Mr. Bowie	1
Mr. Durkee	1
No choice.	217

The roll was called the sixty-first time, when the tellers reported that the whole number of votes given in was 220; necessary to a choice 111; of which—

Mr. Cobb, of Georgia, received	96
Mr. Winthrop	92
Mr. Wilmot	9
Mr. Morehead	4
Mr. Strong	4
Mr. McGaughey	3
Mr. Potter	3
Mr. Boyd	3
Mr. Cabell, of Florida	2
Mr. Stephens, of Georgia	1
Mr. Toombs	1
Mr. Durkee	1
Mr. Vinton	1
No choice.	220

The roll was called the sixty-second time, when the tellers reported that the whole number of votes given was 221; necessary to a choice 111; of which—

Mr. H. Cobb received	97
Mr. Winthrop	97
Mr. Wilmot	9
Mr. Strong	4
Mr. Morehead	4
Mr. Potter	3
Mr. Boyd	3
Mr. E. C. Cabell	2
Mr. Durkee	1
Mr. A. H. Stephens	1
No choice.	221

The House had now reached the contingency contemplated in the proposition of Mr. Stanton. It had exhausted the three votings therein provided for, without a result, and had arrived at that point where, in fulfilment of the agreement entered into between the two parties, a Speaker was to be elected by a plurality vote.

The most intense interest was manifested in every part of the Hall.

The roll was called the sixty-third and last time; Mr. Venable, of North Carolina, one of the tellers, checking the votes, and announcing, in a distinct and audible voice, as a vote was added to the name of Mr. WINTHROP or Mr. COBB, the aggregate number of votes which either had received.

(When the name of Mr. J. CABLE was called, that gentleman rose and said: Under protest, I vote for HOWELL COBB.)

(When the name of Mr. HARLAN was called, Mr. H. rose, and was understood to say that from conversations he had heard on this floor, from personal conversations, and from a knowledge of the qualifications of the two gentlemen he inclined to the belief that, as it was now reduced to a certainty that one of the two would be elected, it would be safe for him to cast his vote for HOWELL COBB. He therefore did so.)

The roll was called for the sixty-third time when the tellers reported that the whole number of votes given in was 221; of which—

Mr. H. Cobb received	102
Mr. Winthrop	99
Mr. Wilmot	8
Mr. Morehead	4
Mr. Strong	3
Mr. A. H. Stephens	1
Mr. Colcock	1
Mr. Durkee	1
Mr. Potter	1
Mr. Boyd	1
	221

The aggregate result was now announced by Mr. VAN DYKE on the part of the tellers—who added, that HOWELL COBB having received 102 votes, had received the largest number cast for any gentleman for whom votes had been given.

Mr. STANLY rose and said: I have risen to offer a resolution to consummate the work of organization, which I trust in God is now so near its completion. I, therefore, send to the Clerk's table this resolution.

The resolution of Mr. STANLY was then read in the following words:

Resolved, That the Hon. HOWELL COBB, a Representative from the State of Georgia, be declared duly elected Speaker of the House for the Thirty-first Congress.

The resolution having been read—

Mr. ROOT said, I desire the question to be taken by yeas and nays.

Mr. STANLY. Well, sir; agreed.

The CLERK stated the question to be on ordering the yeas and nays.

(Great confusion in the Hall.)

The CLERK put the question, and declared that the yeas and nays had been ordered by the House.

The CLERK proceeded to call the roll, and one or two members had answered to their names, when—

Mr. SCHENCK interposed with the remark, I say that HOWELL COBB is *now* the Speaker of this House by its own order and action, without any resolution.

(Great disorder, and cries "Go on with the roll.")

The call of the roll having been at length completed, the vote was announced, yeas 149, nays 34.

So the resolution was adopted.

The CLERK then read the resolution, and requested Mr. WINTHROP of Massachusetts and Mr. McDOWELL of Virginia to conduct the Speaker to the chair.

The two gentlemen designated proceeded to discharge this duty, Mr. WINTHROP approaching Mr. COBB with much good humor, and shaking hands cordially with him.

Mr. COBB was thereupon conducted to the chair and took his seat.

After a moment's pause, the Speaker rose and addressed the House as follows:

Gentlemen of the House of Representatives:

It would be useless to disguise the fact that I feel deeply embarrassed in taking this chair under the circumstances attending my election.

I am conscious of the difficulties by which this position is surrounded at the present time.

The peculiar organization of this body, as exhibited in our proceedings since we first met—the nature and character of the various important and exciting questions of public policy which will engage our attention during the present session of Congress—conspire to render the duties of the office peculiarly embarrassing, onerous, and responsible.

I may be permitted, therefore, to ask in advance your generous aid and support in the effort I shall make, firmly, faithfully, and impartially, to discharge its duties.

The country has been looking with anxiety to our efforts to effect an organization. The people will continue to regard with intense interest every step we take in our legislative course. Our duties will be laborious, our responsibilities great. Let us, then, in view of these considerations, invoke, in the discharge of these duties, a patriotism as broad as the Union, and as comprehensive as the nature and character of her various interests and institutions. Guided by this spirit, under the blessing of Heaven, our action will result in the continued prosperity of our common country.

Accept, gentlemen, my grateful acknowledgments for the honor you have confered on me in selecting me as your presiding officer during the present Congress.

President's Message.

Mr. VINTON. Mr. Speaker, the annual communication from the Executive has so long been delayed that the country, as a matter of course, is very desirous of knowing what it is. For the purpose, therefore, of preparing the way for offering the customary resolution informing the Senate that this House is organized, and the President that both Houses are organized, and ready to receive any communication from him, I move that the Chair now proceed to swear in the members of this House.

The Speaker. That will be done without the necessity for a motion.

The Clerk. Mr. Linn Boyd, a Representative from Kentucky, and the oldest consecutive member of the House, will please administer the oath of office to the Speaker elect.

The Speaker accordingly descended from his seat, and took the oath to support the Constitution of the United States, administered by Mr. Boyd.

And the House adjourned.

Monday, December 24.

The Message.

A Message in writing was received from the President of the United States by the hands of Col. W. W. S. Bliss, his Private Secretary.

The Speaker said if there was no objection the Chair would lay the message before the House.

No objection having been made, the Message was read, as follows:

Fellow-Citizens of the Senate and House of Representatives:

Sixty years have elapsed since the establishment of this Government, and the Congress of the United States again assembles, to legislate for an empire of freemen. The predictions of evil prophets, who formerly pretended to foretell the downfall of our institutions, are now remembered only to be derided, and the United States of America, at this moment, present to the world the most stable and permanent government on earth.

Such is the result of the labors of those who have gone before us. Upon Congress will eminently depend the future maintenance of our system of free government, and the transmission of it, unimpaired, to posterity.

We are at peace with all the nations of the world, and seek to maintain our cherished relations of unity with them. During the past year we have been blessed, by a kind Providence, with an abundance of the fruits of the earth; and, although the destroying angel, for a time, visited extensive portions of our territory with the ravages of a dreadful pestilence, yet the Almighty has at length deigned to stay his hand, and to restore the inestimable blessing of general health to a people who have acknowledged his power, deprecated his wrath, and implored his merciful protection.

While enjoying the benefits of amicable intercourse with foreign nations, we have not been insensible to the distractions and wars which have prevailed in other quarters of the world. It is a proper theme of thanksgiving to Him who rules the destinies of nations, that we have been able to maintain, amidst all these contests, an independent and neutral position towards all belligerent Powers.

Our relations with Great Britain are of the most friendly character. In consequence of the recent alteration of the British navigation acts, British vessels, from British and other foreign ports, will, (under our existing laws,) after the first day of January next, be admitted to entry in our ports, with cargoes of the growth, manufacture, or production of any part of the world, on the same terms, as to duties, imposts, and charges, as vessels of the United States with their cargoes, and our vessels will be admitted to the same advantages in British ports, entering therein on the same terms as British vessels. Should no order in council disturb this legislative arrangement, the late act of the British Parliament, by which Great Britain is brought within the terms proposed by the act of Congress of the 1st of March, 1817, it is hoped, will be productive of benefit to both countries.

A slight interruption of diplomatic intercourse, which occurred between this Government and France, I am happy to say has been terminated, and our minister there has been received. It is, therefore, unnecessary to refer now to the circumstances which led to that interruption. I need not express to you the sincere satisfaction with which we shall welcome the arrival of another Envoy Extraordinary and Minister Plenipotentiary from a sister republic, to which we have so long been, and still remain, bound by the strongest ties of amity.

Shortly after I had entered upon the discharge of the Executive duties, I was apprised that a war steamer, belonging to the German Empire, was being fitted out in the harbor of New York, with the aid of some of our naval officers, rendered under the permission of the late Secretary of the Navy. This permission was granted during an armistice between that empire and the Kingdon of Denmark, which had been engaged in the Schleswig-Holstein war. Apprehensive that this act of intervention on our part, might be viewed as a violation of our neutral obligations, incurred by the treaty with Denmark, and of the provisions of the act of Congress of the 20th of April, 1818, I directed that no further aid should be rendered by any agent or officer of the Navy, and I instructed the Secretary of State to apprise the Minister of the German Empire accredited to this Government, of my determination to execute the law of the United States, and to maintain the faith of treaties with all nations. The correspondence which ensued between the Department of State and the Minister of the German Empire, is herewith laid before you. The execution of the law and the observance of the treaty were deemed by me to be due to the honor of the country, as well as to the sacred obligations of the constitution. I shall not fail to pursue the same course, should a similar case arise, with any other nation. Having avowed the opinion, on taking the oath of office, that, in disputes between conflicting foreign governments, it is our interest, not less than our duty, to remain strictly neutral, I shall not abandon it. You will perceive, from the correspondence submitted to you, in connection with this subject, that the course adopted in this case has been properly regarded by the belligerent Powers interested in the matter.

Although a Minister of the United States to the German Empire was appointed by my predecessor, in August, 1848, and has for a long time been in attendance at Frankfort-on-the-Main, and although a minister appointed to represent that empire was received and accredited here, yet no such government as that of the German Empire has been definitively constituted. But Mr. Donelson, our representative at Frankfort, remained there several months, in the expectation that a union of the German States, under one constitution or form of government, might at length be organized. It is believed, by those well acquainted with the existing relations between Prussia and the States of Germany, that no such union can be permanently established without her coöperation. In the event of the formation of such a union, and the organization of a central Power in Germany, of which she should form a part, it would become necessary to withdraw our Minister at Berlin; but while Prussia exists as an independent kingdom, and diplomatic relations are maintained with her, there can be no necessity for the continuance of the mission to Frankfort. I have, therefore, recalled Mr. Donelson, and directed the archives of the legation, at Frankfort, to be transferred to the American legation at Berlin.

Having been apprised that a considerable number of adventurers were engaged in fitting out a military expedition, within the United States, against a foreign country, and believing, from the best information I could obtain, that it was destined to invade the Island of Cuba, I deemed it due to the friendly relations existing between the United States and Spain; to the treaty between the two nations; to the laws of the United States; and, above all, to the American honor, to exert the lawful authority of this Government in suppressing the expedition and preventing the invasion. To this end, I issued a proclamation, enjoining it upon the officers of the United States, civil and military, to use all lawful means within their power. A copy of that proclamation is herewith submitted. The expedition has been suppressed. So long as the act of Congress of the 20th April, 1818, which owes its existence to the law of nations and to the policy of Washington himself, shall remain on our statute book, I hold it to be the duty of the Executive faithfully to obey its injunctions.

While this expedition was in progress, I was informed that a foreigner, who claimed our protection, had been clandestinely, and, as was supposed, forcibly, carried off in a vessel from New Orleans to the Island of Cuba. I immediately caused such steps to be taken as I thought necessary, in case the information I had received should prove correct, to vindicate the honor of the country, and the right of every person seeking an asylum on our soil to the protection of our laws. The person alleged to have been abducted was promptly restored, and the circumstances of the case are now about to undergo investigation before a judicial tribunal. I would respectfully suggest that, although the crime charged to have been committed in this case is held odious, as being in conflict with our opinions on the subject of national sovereignty and personal freedom, there is no prohibition of it, or punishment for it, provided in any act of Congress. The expediency of supplying this defect in our criminal code is, therefore, recommended to your consideration.

I have scrupulously avoided any interference in the wars and contentions which have recently distracted Europe.

During the late conflict between Austria and Hungary, there seemed to be a prospect that the latter might become an independent nation. However faint that prospect at the time appeared, I thought it my duty, in accordance with the general sentiment of the American people, who deeply sympathized with the Magyar patriots, to stand prepared, upon the contingency of the establishment by her of a permanent government, to be the first to welcome independent Hungary into the family of nations. For this purpose, I invested an agent, then in Europe, with power to declare our willingness promptly to recognize her independence in the event of her ability to sustain it. The powerful intervention of Russia in the contest extinguished the hopes of the struggling Magyars. The United States did not at any time interfere in the contest; but the feelings of the nation were strongly enlisted in the cause, and by the sufferings of a brave people, who had made a gallant though unsuccessful effort to be free.

Our claims upon Portugal have been, during the past year, prosecuted with renewed vigor, and it has been my object to employ every effort of honorable diplomacy to procure their adjustment. Our late Chargé d'Affaires at Lisbon, the Hon. George W. Hopkins, made able and energetic, but unsuccessful efforts to settle these unpleasant matters of controversy, and to obtain indemnity for the wrongs which were the subjects of complaint. Our present Chargé d'Affaires at that court will also bring to the prosecution of these claims ability and zeal. The revolutionary and distracted condition of Portugal in past times has been represented as one of the leading causes of her delay in indemnifying our suffering citizens. But I must now say it is a matter of profound regret that these claims have not yet been settled. The omission of Portugal to do justice to the American claimants has now assumed a character so grave and serious that I shall shortly make it the subject of a special message to Congress, with a view to such ultimate action as its wisdom and patriotism may suggest.

With Russia, Austria, Prussia, Sweden, Denmark, Belgium, the Netherlands, and the Italian States, we still maintain our accustomed amicable relations.

During the recent revolutions in the Papal States, our Chargé d'Affaires at Rome has been unable to present his letter of credence, which, indeed, he was directed by my predecessor to withhold until he should receive further orders. Such was the unsettled condition of things in those States that it was not deemed expedient to give him any instructions on the subject of presenting his credential letter different from those with which he had been furnished by the late Administration, until the 25th of June last; when, in consequence of the want of accurate information of the exact state of things at that distance from us, he was instructed to exercise his own discretion in presenting himself to the then existing Government, if in his judgment sufficiently stable; or, if not, to await further events. Since that period Rome has undergone another revolution, and he abides the establishment of a government sufficiently permanent to justify him in opening diplomatic intercourse with it.

With the Republic of Mexico, it is our true policy to cultivate the most friendly relations. Since the ratification of the treaty of Guadalupe Hidalgo, nothing has occurred of a serious character to disturb them. A faithful observance of the treaty, and a sincere respect for her rights, cannot fail to secure the lasting confidence and friendship of that Republic. The message of my predecessor to the House of Representatives, of the 8th of February last, communicating, in compliance with a resolution of that body, a copy of a paper called a Protocol, signed at Queretaro on the 30th of May, 1848, by the Commissioners of the United States and the Minister of Foreign Affairs of the Mexican Government, having been a subject of correspondence between the Department of State and the Envoy Extraordinary and Minister Plenipotentiary of that Republic accredited to this Government, a transcript of that correspondence is herewith submitted.

The Commissioner on the part of the United States for making the boundary between the two Republics, though delayed in reaching San Diego by unforeseen obstacles, arrived at that place within a short period after the time required by the treaty, and was there joined by the Commissioner on the part of Mexico. They entered upon their duties; and, at the date of the latest intelligence from that quarter, some progress had been made in the survey. The expenses incident to the organization of the commission, and to its conveyance to the point where its operations were to begin, have so much reduced the fund appropriated by Congress, that a further sum, to cover the charges which must be incurred during the present fiscal year, will be necessary. The great length of frontier along which the boundary extends, the nature of the adjacent territory, and the difficulty of obtaining supplies, except at or near the extremes of the line, render it also indispensable that a liberal provision should be made to meet the necessary charges during the fiscal year ending on the 30th of June, 1851. I accordingly recommend this subject to your attention.

In the adjustment of the claims of American citizens on Mexico provided for by the late treaty, the employment of counsel, on the part of the Government, may become important for the purpose of assisting the Commissioners in protecting the interests of the United States. I recommend this subject to the early and favorable consideration of Congress.

Complaints have been made in regard to the inefficiency of the means provided by the Government of New Granada for transporting the United States mail across the Isthmus of Panama, pursuant to our Postal Convention with that Republic, of the 6th of March, 1854. Our Chargé d'Affaires at Bogota has been directed to make such representations to the Government of New Granada as will, it is hoped, lead to a prompt removal of this cause of complaint.

The sanguinary civil war with which the Republic of Venezuela has for some time past been ravaged, has been brought to a close. In its progress, the rights of some of our citizens, resident or trading there, have been violated. The restoration of order will afford to the Venezuelan Government an opportunity to examine and redress those grievances, and others of long standing, which our representatives at Caraccas have hitherto ineffectually urged upon the attention of that Government.

The extension of the coast of the United States on the Pacific, and the unexampled rapidity with which the inhabitants of California especially are increasing in numbers, have imparted new consequence to our relations with the other countries whose territories border upon that ocean. It is probable that the intercourse between those countries and our possessions in that quarter, particularly with the Republic of Chili, will become extensive and mutually advantageous in proportion as California and Oregon shall increase in population and wealth. It is desirable, therefore, that this Government should do every thing in its power to foster and strengthen its relations with those States, and that the spirit of amity between us should be mutual and cordial.

I recommend the observance of the same course towards all other American States. The United States stand as the great American power, to which, as the natural ally and friend, they will always be disposed first to look for mediation and assistance, in the event of any collision between them and any European nation. As such, we may often kindly mediate in their behalf, without entangling ourselves in foreign wars or unnecessary controversies. Whenever the faith of our treaties with any of them shall require our interference, we must necessarily interpose.

A convention has been negotiated with Brazil, providing for the satisfaction of American claims on that Government, and it will be submitted to the Senate. Since the last session of Congress, we have received an Envoy Extraordinary and Minister Plenipotentiary from the Empire, and our relations with it are founded upon the most amicable understanding.

Your attention is earnestly invited to an amendment of our existing laws relating to the African slave trade, with a view to the effectual suppression of that barbarous traffic. It is not to be denied that this trade is still, in part, carried on by means of vessels built in the United States, and owned or navigated by some of our citizens. The correspondence between the Department of State and the Minister and Consul of the United States at Rio de Janeiro, which has, from time to time, been laid before Congress, represents that it is a customary device to evade the penalties of our laws by means of sea-letters. Vessels sold in Brazil, when provided with such papers by the Consul, instead of returning to the United States for a new register, proceed at once to the coast of Africa, for the purpose of obtaining cargoes of slaves. Much additional information, of the same character, has recently been transmitted to the Department of State. It has not been considered the policy of our laws to subject an American citizen, who, in a foreign country, purchases a vessel built in the United States, to the inconvenience of sending her home for a new register, before permitting her to proceed on a voyage. Any alteration of the laws, which might have a tendency to impede the free transfer of property in vessels between our citizens, or the free navigation of those vessels between different parts of the world, when employed in lawful commerce, should be well and cautiously considered; but I trust that your wisdom will devise a method by which our general policy, in this respect, may be preserved, and at the same time the abuse of our flag, by means of sea-letters, in the manner indicated, may be prevented.

Having ascertained that there is no prospect of the reunion of the five States of Central America, which formerly composed the republic of that name, we have separately negotiated with some of them treaties of amity and commerce, which will be laid before the Senate.

A contract having been concluded with the State of Nicaragua, by a company composed of American citizens, for the purpose of constructing a ship-canal through the territory of that State, to connect the Atlantic and Pacific Oceans, I have directed the negotiation of a treaty with Nicaragua, pledging both Governments to protect those who shall engage in and perfect the work. All other nations are invited by the State of Nicaragua to enter into the same treaty stipulations with her; and the benefit to be derived by each from such an arrangement will be the protection of this great inter-oceanic communication against any power which might seek to obstruct it, or to monopolize its advantages. All States entering into such a treaty will enjoy the right of passage through the canal on payment of the same tolls.

The work, if constructed under these guarantees, will become a bond of peace instead of a subject of contention and strife between the nations of the earth. Should the great maritime States of Europe consent to this arrangement, (and we have no reason to suppose that a proposition so fair and honorable will be opposed by any,) the energies of their people and ours will co-operate in promoting the success of the enterprise. I do not recommend any appropriation from the National Treasury for this purpose, nor do I believe that such an appropriation is necessary. Private enterprise, if properly protected, will complete the work, should it prove to be feasible. The parties who have procured the charter from Nicaragua, for its construction, desire no assistance from this Government beyond its protection; and they profess that, having examined the proposed line of communication, they will be ready to commence the undertaking whenever that protection shall be extended to them. Should there appear to be reason, on examining the whole evidence, to entertain a serious doubt of the practicability of constructing such a canal, that doubt could be speedily solved by an actual exploration of the route.

Should such a work be constructed, under the common protection of all nations, for equal benefits to all, it would be neither just nor expedient that any great maritime State should command the communication. The territory through which the canal may be opened ought to be freed from the claim of any foreign power. No such power should occupy a position that would enable it hereafter to exercise so controlling an influence over the commerce of the world, or to obstruct a highway which ought to be dedicated to the common uses of mankind.

The routes across the Isthmus, at Tehuantepec and Panama, are also worthy of our serious consideration. They did not fail to engage the attention of my predecessor. The negotiator of the treaty of Guadalupe Hidalgo was instructed to offer a very large sum of money for the right of transit across the Isthmus of Tehuantepec. The Mexican Government did not accede to the proposition for the purchase of the right of way, probably because it had already contracted with private individuals for the construction of a passage from the Guasacualco river to Tehuantepec. I shall not renew any proposition to purchase, for money, a right which ought to be equally secured to all nations, on payment of a reasonable toll to the owners of the improvement, who would, doubtless, be well contented with that compensation and the guarantees of the maritime States of the world, in separate treaties negotiated with Mexico, binding her and them to protect those who should construct the work. Such guarantees would do more to secure the completion of the communication through the territory of Mexico than any other reasonable consideration that could be offered; and as Mexico herself would be the greatest gainer by the opening of this communication between the Gulf and the Pacific Ocean, it is presumed that she would not hesitate to yield her aid, in the manner proposed, to accomplish an improvement so important to her own best interests.

We have reason to hope that the proposed railroad across the Isthmus of Panama will be successfully constructed, under the protection of the late treaty with New Granada, ratified and exchanged by my predecessor, on the 10th of June, 1848, which guarantees the perfect neutrality of the Isthmus, and the rights of sovereignty and property of New Granada over that territory, "with a view that the free transit from ocean to ocean may not be interrupted or embarrassed" during the existence of the treaty. It is our policy to encourage every practicable route across the Isthmus, which connects North and South America, either by railroad or canal, which the energy and enterprise of our citizens may induce them to complete; and I consider it obligatory upon me to adopt that policy, especially in consequence of the absolute necessity of facilitating intercourse with our possession on the Pacific.

The position of the Sandwich Islands, with reference to the territory of the United States on the Pacific; the success of our persevering and benevolent citizens, who have repaired to that remote quarter in christianizing the natives, and inducing them to adopt a system of government and laws suited to their capacity and wants; and the use made by our numerous whale-ships of the harbors of the islands, as places of resort for obtaining refreshments and repairs,—all combine to render their destiny peculiarly interesting to us. It is our duty to encourage the authorities of those islands in their efforts to improve and elevate the moral condition of the inhabitants; and we should make reasonable allowances for the difficulties inseparable from this task. We desire that the islands may maintain their independence, and that other nations should concur with us in this sentiment. We could, in no event, be indifferent to their passing under the dominion of any other Power. The principal commercial States have in this a common interest, and it is to be hoped that no one of them will attempt to interpose obstacles to the entire independence of the islands.

The receipts into the Treasury for the fiscal year ending on the 30th of June last were, in cash, forty-eight million eight hundred and thirty thousand ninety-seven dollars and fifty cents, ($48,830,097 50,) and in Treasury notes funded, ten million eight hundred and thirty-three thousand dollars, ($10,833,000,) making an aggregate of fifty-nine million six hundred and sixty-three thousand ninety-seven dollars and fifty cents, ($59,663,097 50;) and the expenditures for the same time were, in cash, forty-six million seven hundred and ninety-eight thousand six hundred and sixty-seven dollars and eighty-two cents, ($46,798,667 82;) and in Treasury notes funded, ten million eight hundred and thirty-three thousand dollars, ($10,833,000,) making an aggregate of fifty-seven million six hundred and thirty-one thousand six hundred and sixty-seven dollars and eighty-two cents, ($57,631,667 82.)

The accounts and estimates which will be submitted to Congress in the report of the Secretary of the Treasury, show that there will probably be a deficit, occasioned by the expenses of the Mexican war and treaty, on the 1st day of July next, of five million eight hundred and twenty-eight thousand one hundred and twenty-two dollars and sixty-six cents, ($5,828,121 66,) and on the 1st day of July, 1851, of ten million five hundred and forty-seven thousand and ninety-two dollars and seventy-three cents, ($10,547,092 73,) making in the whole a probable deficit to be provided for, of sixteen million three hundred and seventy-five thousand two hundred and fourteen dollars and thirty-nine cents, ($16,375,214 39.) The extraordinary expenses of the war with Mexico, and the purchase of California and New Mexico, exceed in amount this deficit, together with the loans heretofore made for those objects. I, therefore, recommend that authority be given to borrow whatever sum may be necessary to cover that deficit. I recommend the observance of strict economy in the appropriation and expenditure of the public money.

I recommend a revision of the existing tariff, and its adjustment on a basis which may augment the revenue. I do not doubt the right or duty of Congress to encourage domestic industry, which is the great source of national as well as individual wealth and prosperity. I look to the wisdom and patriotism of Congress for the adoption of a system which may place home labor at last on a sure and permanent footing, and, by due encouragement of manufactures, give a new and increased stimulus to agriculture, and promote the development of our vast resources and the extension of our commerce. Believing that to the attainment of these ends (as well as the necessary augmentation to the revenue and the prevention of frauds) a system of specific duties is best adapted, I strongly recommend to Congress the adoption of that system, fixing the duties at rates high enough to afford substantial and sufficient encouragement to our own industry, and, at the same time, so adjusted as to insure stability.

The question of the continuance of the Subtreasury system is respectfully submitted to the wisdom of Congress. If continued, important modifications of it appear to be indispensable.

For further details and views of the above, and other matters connected with commerce, the finances and revenue, I refer to the report of the Secretary of the Treasury.

No direct aid has been given by the General Government to the improvement of agriculture, except by the expenditure of small sums for the collection and publication of agricultural statistics, and for some chemical analyses, which have been, thus far, paid for out of the patent fund. This aid is, in my opinion, wholly inadequate. To give to this leading branch of American industry the encouragement which it merits, I respectfully recommend the establishment of an Agricultural Bureau, to be connected with the Department of the Interior. To elevate the social condition of the agriculturist, to increase his prosperity and to extend his means of usefulness to his country, by multiplying his sources of information, should be the study of every statesman, and a primary object with every legislator.

No civil government having been provided by Congress for California, the people of that Territory, impelled by the necessities of their political condition, recently met in convention, for the purpose of forming a constitution and State government, which the latest advices give me reason to suppose has been accomplished; and it is believed they will shortly apply for the admission of California into the Union as a sovereign State. Should such be the case, and should their constitution be conformable to the requisitions of the Constitution of the United States, I recommend their application to the favorable consideration of Congress.

The people of New Mexico will also, it is believed, at no very distant period present themselves for admission into the Union. Preparatory to the admission of California and New Mexico, the people of each will have instituted for themselves a republican form of government, "laying its foundations in such principles, and organizing its powers in such form, as to them shall seem most likely to effect their safety and happiness."

By awaiting their action, all causes of uneasiness may be avoided, and confidence and kind feeling preserved. With the view of maintaining the harmony and tranquillity so dear to all, we should abstain from the introduction of those exciting topics of a sectional character which have hitherto produced painful apprehensions in the public mind; and I repeat the solemn warning of the first and most illustrious of my predecessors against furnishing "any ground for characterizing parties by geographical discriminations."

A Collector has been appointed at San Francisco, under the act of Congress extending the revenue laws over California; and measures have been taken to organize the custom-houses at that and the other ports mentioned in that act, at the earliest period practicable. The Collector proceeded overland, and advices have not yet been received of his arrival at San Francisco. Meanwhile, it is understood that the customs have continued to be collected there by officers acting under the military authority, as they were during the administration of my predecessor. It will, I think, be expedient to confirm the collections thus made, and direct the avails (after such allowances as Congress may think fit to authorize) to be expended within the Territory, or to be paid into the Treasury, for the purpose of meeting appropriations for the improvement of its rivers and harbors.

A party, engaged on the coast survey, was despatched to Oregon in January last. According to the latest advices, they had not left California; and directions have been given to them, as soon as they shall have fixed on the sites of the two light-houses and the buoys authorized to be constructed and placed in Oregon, to proceed without delay to make reconnoissances of the most important points on the coast of California, and especially to examine and determine on sites for light-houses on that coast, the speedy erection of which is urgently demanded by our rapidly increasing commerce.

I have transferred the Indian Agencies from Upper Missouri and Council Bluffs to Santa Fé and Salt Lake, and have caused to be appointed subagents in the valley of the Gila, the Sacramento and San Joaquin rivers. Still further legal provisions will be necessary for the effective and successful extension of our system of Indian intercourse over the new Territories.

I recommend the establishment of a branch mint in California, as it will, in my opinion, afford important facilities to those engaged in mining, as well as to the Government in the disposition of the mineral lands.

I also recommend that commissions be organized by Congress to examine and decide upon the validity of the present subsisting land titles in California and New Mexico; and that provision be made for the establishment of offices of Surveyor General in New Mexico, California, and Oregon, and for the surveying and bringing into market the public lands in those Territories. Those lands, remote in position and difficult of access, ought to be disposed of on terms liberal to all, but especially favorable to the early emigrants.

In order that the situation and character of the principal mineral deposits in California may be ascertained, I recommend that a geological and mineralogical exploration be connected with the linear surveys, and that the mineral lands be divided into small lots suitable for mining, and be disposed of, by sale or lease, so as to give our citizens an opportunity for procuring a permanent right of property in the soil. This would seem to be as important to the success of mining as of agricultural pursuits.

The great mineral wealth of California, and the advantages which its ports and harbors and those of Oregon afford to commerce, especially with the islands of the Pacific and Indian Oceans, and the populous regions of Eastern Asia, make it certain that there will arise in a few years large and prosperous communities on our western coast. It, therefore, becomes important that a line of communication, the best and most expeditious which the nature of the country will admit, should be opened within the territory of the United States, from the navigable waters of the Atlantic or the Gulf of Mexico to the Pacific. Opinion, as elicited and expressed by two large and respectable conventions, lately assembled at St. Louis and Memphis, points to a railroad as that which, if practicable, will best meet the wishes and wants of the country. But while this, if in successful operation, would be a work of great national importance, and of a value to the country which it would be difficult to estimate, it ought also to be regarded as an undertaking of vast magnitude and expense, and one which must, if it be indeed practicable, encounter many difficulties in its construction and use. Therefore, to avoid failure and disappointment; to enable Congress to judge whether, in the condition of the country through which it must pass, the work be feasible; and, if it be found so, whether it should be undertaken as a national improvement or left to individual enterprise; and, in the latter alternative, what aid, if any, ought to be extended to it by the Government, I recommend, as a preliminary measure, a careful reconnoissance of the several proposed routes by a scientific corps, and a report as to the practicability of making such a road, with an estimate of the cost of its construction and support.

For further views on these and other matters connected with the duties of the Home Department, I refer you to the report of the Secretary of the Interior.

I recommend early appropriations for continuing the river and harbor improvements which have been already begun, and also for the construction of those for which estimates have been made, as well as for examinations and estimates preparatory to the commencement of such others as the wants of the country, and especially the advance of our population over new districts, and the extension of commerce, may render necessary. An estimate of the amount which can be advantageously expended within the next fiscal year, under the direction of the Bureau of Topographical Engineers, accompanies the report of the Secretary of War, to which I respectfully invite the attention of Congress.

The cession of territory made by the late treaty with Mexico has greatly extended our exposed frontier, and rendered its defence more difficult. That treaty has also brought us under obligations to Mexico, to comply with which a military force is requisite. But our military establishment is not materially changed, as to is efficiency, from the condition in which it stood before the commencement of the Mexican war. Some addition to it will, therefore, be necessary; and I recommend to the favorable consideration of Congress an increase of the several corps of the army at our distant western posts, as proposed in the accompanying report of the Secretary of War.

Great embarrassment has resulted from the effect upon rank in the army, heretofore given to brevet and staff commissions. The views of the Secretary of War on this subject are deemed important, and if carried into effect will, it is believed, promote the harmony of the service. The plan proposed for retiring disabled officers, and providing an asylum for such of the rank and file as from age, wounds, and other infirmities occasioned by service, have become unfit to perform their respective duties, is recommended as a means of increasing the efficiency of the army, and as an act of justice due from a grateful country to the faithful soldier.

The accompanying report of the Secretary of the Navy presents a full and satisfactory account of the condition and operations of the naval service during the past year. Our citizens engaged in the legitimate pursuits of commerce have enjoyed its benefits. Wherever our national vessels have gone, they have been received with respect, our officers have been treated with kindness and courtesy, and they have on all occasions pursued a course of strict neutrality, in accordance with the policy of our Government.

The naval force at present in commission is as large as is admissible, with the number of men authorized by Congress to be employed.

I invite your attention to the recommendation of the Secretary of the Navy on the subject of a reorganization of the Navy, in its various grades of officers, and the establishing of a retired list for such of the officers as are disqualified for active and effective service. Should Congress adopt some such measure as is recommended, it will greatly increase the efficiency of the Navy, and reduce its expenditures.

I also ask your attention to the views expressed by him in reference to the employment of war-steamers, and in regard to the contracts for the transportation of the United States mails and the operation of the system upon the prosperity of the Navy.

By an act of Congress passed August 14, 1848, provision was made for extending post office and mail accommodations to California and Oregon. Exertions have been made to execute that law; but the limited provisions of the act, the inadequacy of the means it authorizes, the ill adaptation of our post office laws to the situation of that country, and the measure of compensation for services allowed by those laws, compared with the prices of labor and rents in California, render those exertions, in a great degree, ineffectual. More particular and efficient provision by law is required on this subject.

The act of 1845, reducing postage, has now, by its operation during four years, produced results fully showing that the income from such reduced postage is sufficient to sustain the whole expense of the service of the Post Office Department, not including the cost of transportation in mail steamers on the lines from New York to Chagres, and from Panama to Astoria, which have not been considered by Congress as properly belonging to the mail service.

It is submitted to the wisdom of Congress whether a further reduction of postage should not now be made, more particularly on the letter correspondence. This should be relieved from the unjust burden of transporting and delivering the franked matter of Congress, for which public service provision should be made from the Treasury. I confidently believe that a change may safely be made, reducing all single-letter postage to the uniform rate of five cents, regardless of distance, without thereby imposing any greater tax on the Treasury than would constitute a very moderate compensation for this public service; and I, therefore, respectfully recommend such a reduction. Should Congress prefer to abolish the franking privilege thereby, it seems probable that no demand on the Treasury would result from the proposed reduction of postage. Whether any further diminution should now be made, or the result of the reduction to five cents, which I have recommended, should be first tested, is submitted to your decision.

Since the commencement of the last session of Congress a postal treaty with Great Britain has been received and ratified, and such regulations have been formed by the Post Office Departments of the two countries, in pursuance of that treaty, as to carry its provisions into full operation. The attempt to extend this same arrangement, through England, to France, has not been equally successful; but the purpose has not been abandoned.

For a particular statement of the condition of the Post Office Department, and other matters connected with that branch of the public service, I refer you to the report of the Postmaster General.

By the act of 3d March, 1849, a Board was constituted to make arrangements for taking the seventh census, composed of the Secretary of State, the Attorney General, and the Postmaster General, and it was made the duty of this Board "to prepare and cause to be printed such forms and schedules as might be necessary for the full enumeration of the inhabitants of the United States; and also proper forms and schedules for collecting, in statistical tables, under proper heads, such information as to mines, agriculture, commerce, manufactures, education, and other topics, as would exhibit a full view of the pursuits, industry, education, and resources of the country." The duties enjoined upon the Census Board thus established having been performed, it now rests with Congress to enact a law for carrying into effect the provision of the Constitution which requires an actual enumeration of the people of the United States within the ensuing year.

Among the duties assigned by the Constitution to the General Government is one of local and limited application, but not on that account the less obligatory. I allude to the trust committed to Congress, as the exclusive legislator and sole guardian of the interests of the District of Columbia. I beg to commend these interests to your kind attention. As the National Metropolis, the City of Washington must be an object of general interest; and, founded as it was under the auspices of him whose immortal name it bears, its claims to the fostering care of Congress present themselves with additional strength. Whatever can attribute to its prosperity must enlist the feelings of its constitutional guardians, and command their favorable consideration.

Our Government is one of limited powers, and its successful administration eminently depends on the confinement of each of its coördinate branches within its own appropriate sphere. The first section of the Constitution ordains that "all legislative powers therein granted shall be vested in a Congress of the United States, which shall consist of a Senate and House of Representatives." The Executive has authority to recommend (not to dictate) measures to Congress. Having performed that duty, the Executive department of the Government cannot rightfully control the decision of Congress on any subject of legislation, until that decision shall have been officially submitted to the President for approval. The check provided by the Constitution, in the clause conferring the qualified veto, will never be exercised by me, except in the cases contemplated by the fathers of the Republic. I view it as an extreme measure, to be resorted to only in extraordinary cases—as where it may become necessary to defend the Executive against the encroachments of the legislative power, or to prevent hasty and inconsiderate or unconstitutional legislation. By cautiously confining this remedy within the sphere prescribed to it in the contemporaneous expositions of the framers of the Constitution, the will of the people, legitimately expressed on all subjects of legislation, through their constitutional organs, the Senators and Representatives of the United States, will have its full effect. As indispensable to the preservation of our system of self-government, the independence of the Representatives of the States and the people is guaranteed by the Constitution; and they owe no responsibility to any human power but their constituents. By holding the Representative responsible only to the People, and exempting him from all other influences, we elevate the character of the constituent and quicken his sense of responsibility to his country. It is under these circumstances only that the elector can feel that, in the choice of the law-maker, he is himself truly a component part of the sovereign power of the nation. With equal care we should study to defend the rights of the Executive and Judicial departments. Our Government can only be preserved in its purity by the suppression and entire elimination of every claim or tendency of one coördinate branch to encroachment upon another. With the strict observance of this rule and the other injunctions of the Constitution; with a sedulous inculcation of that respect and love for the union of the States which our fathers cherished and enjoined upon their children; and with the aid of that overruling Providence which has so long and so kindly guarded our liberties and institutions, we may reasonably expect to transmit them with their innumerable blessings to the remotest posterity.

But attachment to the Union of the States should be habitually fostered in every American heart. For more than half a century, during which kingdoms and empires have fallen, this Union has stood unshaken. The patriots who formed it have long since descended to the grave; yet still it remains, the proudest monument to their memory, and the object of affection and admiration with every one worthy to bear the American name. In my judgment its dissolution would be the greatest of calamities, and to avert that should be the study of every American. Upon its preservation must depend our own happiness and that of countless generations to come. Whatever dangers may threaten it, I shall stand by it and maintain it in its integrity, to the full extent of the obligations imposed and the power conferred upon me by the Constitution. Z. TAYLOR.

Washington, *December 4th*, 1849.

The message having been read—

Mr. Toombs rose and moved the adoption of a resolution, that the message be referred to the Committee of the Whole on the state of the Union; and that fifteen thousand copies extra, with the accompanying documents, be printed.

IN SENATE.

Thursday, January 3, 1850.

Missouri Resolutions on Slavery.

Mr. Atchison presented resolutions passed by the General Assembly of the State of Missouri, on the subject of slavery, and he asked that they be read and printed. They are as follows:

Resolved, by the General Assembly of the State of Missouri, 1st. That the Federal Constitution was the result of a compromise between the conflicting interests of the States which formed it, and in no part of that instrument is to be found any delegation of power to Congress to legislate on the subject of slavery, excepting some special provisions having in view the prospective abolition of the African slave trade, and for the recovery of fugitive slaves. Any attempt, therefore, on the part of Congress, to legislate on the subject so as to affect the institution of slavery in the States, in the District of Columbia, or in the Territories, is, to say the least, a violation of the principle upon which that instrument was founded.

2d. That the Territories acquired by the blood and treasure of the whole nation ought to be governed for the common benefit of the citizens of all the States; and any organization of the territorial governments excluding the citizens of any part of the Union from removing to such Territories with their property would be an exercise of power by Congress inconsistent with the spirit upon which our federal compact was based, insulting to the sovereignty and dignity of the States thus affected, calculated to alienate one portion of the Union from another, and tending ultimately to disunion.

3d. That this General Assembly regard the conduct of the northern States on the subject of slavery as releasing the slaveholding States from all further adherence to the basis of compromise fixed on by the act of Congress of the 6th of March, 1820, even if such act ever did impose any obligation upon the slaveholding States, and authorizes them to insist on their rights under the Constitution; but, for the sake of harmony, and for the preservation of our Federal Union, they will still sanction the application of the principle of the Missouri compromise to the recent territorial acquisitions, if by such concession future aggression upon the equal rights of the States may be arrested, and the spirit of anti-slavery fanaticism be extinguished.

4th. The right to prohibit slavery in any Territory belongs exclusively to the people thereof, and can only be exercised by them in forming their constitution for a State government, or in their sovereign capacity as an independent State.

5th. That in the event of the passage of any act conflicting with the principles herein expressed, Missouri will be found in hearty coöperation with the slaveholding States in such measures as may be deemed necessary for our mutual protection against the encroachments of northern fanaticism.

6th. That our Senators in Congress be instructed, and our Representatives be requested, to act in conformity with the foregoing resolutions.

Resolved by the House of Representatives, (the Senate concurring therein,) That the Secretary of State be required to transmit a copy of the resolutions passed at this session of the General Assembly on the subject of slavery to the Executive of each of the States of the Union, with the request that the same be laid before each of their respective Legislatures, and also a copy to each of our Senators and Representatives in Congress.

[*Approved March 10th*, 1849.

The resolutions having been read by the Secretary—

Mr. Benton. This is the proper time for me to say, what I believe to be the fact, that these resolutions do not represent the sentiments of the people of Missouri. They are a law-abiding and a Union-loving people, and have no idea of entering into combinations to resist or intimidate the legislation of Congress. The General Assembly has mistaken the sentiment of the State in adopting these resolutions; and many members who voted for them, and the Governor who signed them, have since disavowed and repudiated them.

I do not discuss these resolutions at this time. That discussion is no part of my present object. I speak of the pledge which they contain, and call it a mistake; and say, that whatever may be the wishes or the opinions of the people of Missouri on the subject of the extension or non-extension of slavery to the Territories, they have no idea of resisting any act of Congress on the subject. They abide the law, when it comes, be it what it may, subject to the decision of the ballot-box and the judiciary.

I concur with the people of Missouri in this view of their duty, and believe it to be the only course consistent with the terms and intention of our Constitution, and the only one which can save this Union from the fate of all the confederacies which have successively appeared and disappeared in the history of nations. Anarchy among the members, and not tyranny in the head, has been the rock on which all such confederacies have split. The authors of our present form of government knew the danger of this rock, and they endeavored to provide against it. They formed a Union—not a league—a Federal Legislature to act upon persons, not upon States; and they provided peaceful remedies for all the questions which could arise between the people and the Government. They provided a Federal judiciary to execute the Federal laws when found to be constitutional, and popular elections to repeal them when found to be bad. They formed a government in which that law and the popular will, and not the sword, was to decide questions; and they looked upon the first resort to the sword for the decision of such questions as the death of the Union.

The old Confederation was a league, with a legislature acting upon sovereignties, without power to enforce its decrees, and without union except at the will of the parties. It was powerless for government, and a rope of sand for union. It was to escape from that helpless and tottering government that the present Constitution was formed; and no less than ten numbers of the Federalist—from the tenth to the twentieth—were devoted to the defects of the old system, and the necessity of the new one. I will read some extracts from these numbers, the joint product of Hamilton and Madison, to show the difference between the league which we abandoned and the Union which we formed—the dangers of the former and the benefits of the latter—that it may be seen that the resolutions of the General Assembly of Missouri, if carried out to their conclusions, carry back this Union to the league of the Confederation—make it a rope of sand, and the sword the arbiter between the federal head and its members.

Mr. B. then read as follows:

"The great and radical vice, in the structure of the existing Confederation, is in the principle of legislation for States or Governments, in their corporate or collective capacities, and as contradistinguished from the individuals of which they consist. Though this principle does not run through all the powers delegated to the Union, yet it pervades and governs those on which the efficacy of the rest depends. The consequence of this is, that, though in theory constitutionally binding on the members of the Union, yet in practice they are mere recommendations, which the States observe or disregard at their option. Government implies the power of making laws. It is essential to the idea of a law that it be attended with a sanction, or, in other words, a penalty or punishment for disobedience. This penalty, whatever it may be, can only be inflicted in two ways—by the agency of the courts and ministers of justice, or by military force; by the coercion of the magistracy, or by the coercion of arms. The first kind can evidently apply only to man; the last kind must of necessity be employed against bodies politic, or communities, or States. It is evident there is no process of a court by which their observance of the laws can, in the last resort, be enforced. Sentences may be denounced against them for violations of their duty; but these sentences can only be carried into execution by the sword. In an association where the general authority is confined to the collective bodies of the communities that compose it, every breach of the laws must involve a state of war, and military execution must become the only instrument of civil obedience. Such a state of things can certainly not deserve the name of government, nor would any prudent man choose to commit his happiness to it."

Of the certain destruction of the Union when the sword is once drawn between the members of a Union and their head, they speak thus:

"When the sword is once drawn, the passions of men observe no bounds of moderation. The suggestions of wounded pride, the instigations of irritated resentment, would be apt to carry the States, against which the arms of the Union were exerted, to any extremes necessary to avenge the affront, or to avoid the disgrace of submission. The first war of this kind would probably terminate in a dissolution of the Union."

Of the advantage and facility of the working of the Federal system, and its peaceful, efficient, and harmonious operation—if the Federal laws are made to operate upon citizens, and not upon States—they speak in these terms:

"But if the execution of the laws of the National Government should not require the intervention of the State Legislatures; if they were to pass into immediate operation upon the citizens themselves, the particular governments could not interrupt their progress without an open and violent exertion of unconstitutional power. They would be obliged to act, and in such manner as would leave no doubt that they had encroached on the national rights. An experiment of this nature would always be hazardous in the face of a constitution in any degree competent to its own defence, and of a people enlightened enough to distinguish between a legal exercise and an illegal usurpation of authority. The success of it would require not merely a factious majority in the Legislature, but the concurrence of the courts of justice, and of the body of the people. If the judges were not embarked in a conspiracy with the Legislature, they would pronounce the resolutions of such a majority to be contrary to the supreme law of the land, unconstitutional and void. If the people were not tainted with the spirit of their State representatives, they, as the natural guardians of the Constitution, would throw their weight into the national scale, and give it a decided preponderance in the contest."

Of the ruinous effects of these civil wars among the members of a Republican Confederacy, and their disastrous influence upon the cause of civil liberty itself throughout the world, they thus speak:

"It is impossible to read the history of the petty republics of Greece and Italy, without feeling sensations of disgust and horror at the distractions with which they were continually agitated, and at the rapid succession of revolutions by which they were kept continually vibrating between the extremes of tyranny and anarchy. From the disorders which disfigure the annals of those republics, the advocates of despotism have drawn arguments, not only against the forms of republican government, but against the very principles of civil liberty. They have decreed all free government as inconsistent with the order of society, and have indulged themselves in malicious exultation over its friends and partisans."

And again they say:

"It must carry its agency to the persons of the citizens. It must stand in need of no intermediate legislation; but must itself be empowered to employ the arm of the ordinary magistrate to execute its own resolutions. The majesty of the national authority must be manifested through the medium of the courts of justice."

After reading these extracts, Mr. B. said: It was to get rid of the evils of the old Confederation that the present Union was formed; and, having formed it, they who formed it undertook to make it perpetual, and for that purpose had recourse to all the sanctions held sacred among men—commands, prohibitions, oaths. The States were forbid to form compacts or agreements with each other; the constitution and the laws made in pursuance of it, were declared to be the supreme law of the land; and all authorities, State and Federal, legislative, executive, and judicial, were to be sworn to support it. The resolutions which have been read contradict all this, and the General Assembly mistook their own powers as much as they mistook the sentiments of the people of Missouri when they adopted them.

This is all that I shall say at present. I make no objection to the reception or printing of these resolutions. My only object, at present, is to make and save the two points: *first*, that the General Assembly mistook the sentiments of the people of Missouri in adopting these resolutions; *secondly*, that they mistook their own powers in doing so.

Mr. ATCHISON. As no objection has been taken to the printing of the resolutions, I have but one word to say; and that is merely to express an opinion that the people of the State of Missouri, when the time arrives, will prove to all mankind that every sentiment contained in these resolutions from first to last will be sustained by them.

The question then being taken upon the motion to print, it was agreed to.

HOUSE OF REPRESENTATIVES.

MONDAY, January 7.

Officers of the House—Clerk.

The SPEAKER. The regular business is the execution of the order heretofore adopted by the House, in relation to the election of officers. The gentlemen appointed as tellers on a former occasion are requested to resume their seats at the Clerk's table.

Thereupon, Messrs. THOMPSON of Pennsylvania, CROWELL of Ohio, WHITE of New York, and HARALSON of Georgia, resumed their seats at the Clerk's table.

The roll was then called; when the tellers reported that 220 votes had been given; necessary to a choice 111; of which—

Mr. John W. Forney received	107
Mr. Thomas J. Campbell	94
Mr. C. W. Phileo	6
Mr. Nathan Sargent	3
Mr. Solomon Foot	3
Mr. Benjamin B. French	2
Mr. John H. C. Mudd	2
Mr. D. W. C. Clark	2
Mr. P. B. Prindle	1
No choice.	220

The roll was called the fourth time; the tellers reported that 219 votes had been given in; necessary to a choice 110; of which—

Mr. Forney received	107
Mr. Campbell	95
Mr. Phileo	6
Mr. Foot	5
Mr. Sargent	3
Mr. French	2
Mr. Clark	1
No choice.	219

Mr. MARSHALL rose and asked the unanimous consent of the House to introduce a resolution.

The resolution was read for information, as follows:

Resolved, That THOMAS J. CAMPBELL, who is now performing *ex gratia* the duties of Clerk, should be sworn by the Speaker, to act *pro tempore* as Clerk of this House, and that he be sworn accordingly.

The resolution having been read,

The roll was called the fifth time. The tellers reported that 220 votes had been given in; necessary to a choice 111; of which—

Mr. Forney received	106
Mr. Campbell	102
Mr. Phileo	4
Mr. French	2
Mr. Sargent	2
Mr. Prindle	2
Mr. Clark	1
Mr. Gouverneur	1
No choice.	220

The roll was then again called—being the sixth time. The tellers reported that 219 votes had been given in; necessary to a choice 110; of which—

Mr. Forney received	106
Mr. Campbell	72
Mr. Foot	25
Mr. Prindle	6
Mr. French	4

Mr. Phileo 4
Mr. Sargent 2

No choice. 219

The roll was again called, being the seventh time. The tellers reported that 220 votes had been given in; necessary to a choice 111; of which—

Mr. Forney received 107
Mr. Foot 91
Mr. Campbell 14
Mr. Phileo 4
Mr. French 2
Mr. Gouverneur 1
Mr. Prindle 1

No choice. 220

Tuesday, January 8.

The Journal of yesterday was read and approved.

Mr. Gentry, of Tennessee, appeared, was qualified, and took his seat.

Officers of the House—Clerk.

The Speaker. The regular business is the execution of the order heretofore adopted by the House, in relation to the election of officers. The gentlemen appointed as tellers on a former occasion are requested to resume their seats at the Clerk's table.

The roll was then called—being the eighth time; when the tellers reported that 221 votes had been given; necessary to a choice 111; of which—

Mr. John W. Forney received . . 106
Mr. Solomon Foot 94
Mr. Thomas J. Campbell . . . 13
Mr. C. W. Phileo 4
Mr. M. St. Clair Clarke . . . 2
Mr. Benjamin B. French . . . 1
Mr. P. B. Prindle 1

No choice. 221

The roll was then called the ninth time. The tellers reported that 219 votes had been given in, necessary to a choice 110; of which—

Mr. Forney received 105
Mr. Foot 93
Mr. Campbell 13
Mr. Phileo 5
Mr. French 1
Mr. Gouverneur 1
Mr. M. St. Clair Clarke 1

No choice. 219

The roll was then called the tenth time. The tellers reported that 216 votes had been give in; necessary to a choice 109; of which—

Mr. Forney received 104
Mr. Foot 93
Mr. Campbell 13
Mr. Phileo 4
Mr. Gouverneur 1
Mr. M. St. Clair Clarke . . . 1

No choice. 216

Wednesday, January 9.

Officers of the House—Clerk.

The House again proceeded to vote for the election of a Clerk.

The roll was then called.

The tellers reported that 219 votes had been given; necessary to a choice 110; of which—

Mr. John W. Forney received . . 106
Mr. Solomon Foot 104
Mr. C. W. Phileo 4
Mr. M. St. Clair Clarke . . . 3
Mr. Benjamin B. French . . . 1
Mr. S. L. Gouverneur 1

No choice. 219

The roll was then again called for the twelfth time. The tellers reported that 220 votes had been given; necessary to a choice 111; of which—

Mr. Forney received 105
Mr. Foot 103
Mr. M. St. Clair Clarke 5
Mr. Phileo 4
Mr. French 3

No choice. 220

The roll was then called the thirteenth time. The tellers reported that 220 votes had been given in; necessary to a choice 111; of which—

Mr. Forney received 104
Mr. Foot 103
Mr. Campbell 13
Mr. M. St. Clair Clarke . . . 5
Mr. Phileo 4

No choice. 220

The roll was again called—being the fourteenth time. The tellers reported that 217 votes had been given in; necessary to a choice 109; of which—

Mr. Forney received 103
Mr. Foot 98
Mr. Clarke 7
Mr. French 4
Mr. Phileo 4
Mr. Prindle 1

No choice. 217

Thursday, January 10.

The roll was called the fifteenth time. The tellers reported that 215 votes had been given in; necessary to a choice 108; of which—

Mr. J. W. Forney received . . . 102
Mr. S. Foot 103
Mr. C. W. Phileo 4
Mr. M. St. Clair Clarke . . . 3
Mr. B. B. French 3

No choice. 215

Re-Nomination of Mr. Campbell.

Mr. WILLIAMS rose and re-nominated Thomas Jefferson Campbell, Clerk of the late House of Representatives.

The roll was then again called—being the sixteenth time. The tellers reported that 216 votes had been given in; necessary to a choice, 109; of which—

Mr. Forney received 96
Mr. Prindle 63
Mr. Campbell 32
Mr. French 11
Mr. Fisher 7
Mr. Phileo 4
Mr. Foot 2
Mr. John Smith 1

No choice. 216

The roll was called the seventeenth time. The tellers reported that 218 votes had been given; necessary to a choice 110; of which—

Mr. Forney received 93
Mr. Prindle 63
Mr. Campbell 29
Mr. French 18
Mr. Fisher 9
Mr. Phileo 3
Mr. Foot 2
Mr. Gouverneur 1

No choice. 218

FRIDAY, January 11.

Election of Clerk.

The roll was called the eighteenth time. The tellers reported that 213 votes had been given in; necessary to a choice 107; of which—

Mr. Campbell received 96
Mr. Forney 93
Mr. French 18
Mr. Foot 3
Mr. Prindle 2
Mr. Gouverneur 1

No choice. 213

The roll was again called—being the nineteenth time. The tellers reported that 218 votes had been given in; necessary to a choice 110; of which—

Mr. Campbell received 103
Mr. Forney 97
Mr. French 13
Mr. Foot 3
Mr. Prindle 2

No choice. 218

The roll was again called, for the twentieth time. The tellers reported that 221 votes had been given in; necessary to a choice 111; of which—

Mr. Campbell received 112
Mr. Forney 95
Mr. French 11
Mr. Foot 2
Mr. Prindle 1

221

Messrs. ORR, WALLACE, CROWELL, and EWING, changed their votes before the result was announced, remarking that they did so with a view to put an end to this protracted controversy. Other members also changed their votes.

Mr. CAMPBELL having received a majority of all the votes, was declared to be duly elected Clerk of this House for the Thirty-first Congress.

There was some applause, which was promptly checked by the SPEAKER.

Mr. CAMPBELL was then sworn.

Mr. WOOD said, he was extremely gratified that the southern Democrats had shown their true principles and position in the result of the last ballot; that he felt relieved; and that a dissolution of all political connection between the northern and southern Democracy ought to take place.

MONDAY, January 21.

California and New Mexico.

The SPEAKER then laid before the House the following message:

WASHINGTON, *January* 21, 1850.

To the House of Representatives of the United States:

I transmit to the House of Representatives, in answer to a resolution of that body, passed on the 31st of December last, the accompanying reports of heads of Departments, which contain all the official information in the possession of the Executive asked for by the resolution.

On coming into office I found the military commandant of the department of California exercising the functions of civil governor in that Territory, and left, as I was, to act under the treaty of Guadalupe Hidalgo without the aid of any legislative provision establishing a Government in that Territory, I thought it best not to disturb that arrangement, made under my predecessor, until Congress should take some action on that subject. I therefore did not interfere with the powers of the military commandant, who continued to exercise the functions of civil governor, as before; but I made no such appointment, conferred no such authority, and have allowed no increased compensation to the commandant for his services.

With a view to the faithful execution of the treaty, so far as lay in the power of the Executive, and to enable Congress to act at the present session, with as full knowledge and as little difficulty as possible on all matters of interest in these Territories, I sent the Hon. Thomas Butler King as bearer of despatches to California, and certain officers to California and New Mexico, whose duties are particularly defined in the accompanying letters of instruction addressed to them severally by the proper Departments.

I did not hesitate to express to the people of those Territories my desire that each Territory should, if prepared to comply with the requisitions of the Constitution of the United States, form a plan of a State constitution, and submit the same to Congress, with a prayer for admission into the Union as a State, but I did not anticipate, suggest, or authorize, the establishment of any such government without the assent of Congress, nor did I authorize any Government agent or officer to interfere with or exercise any influence or control over the election of Delegates, or over any Convention, in making or modifying their domestic institutions, or any of the provisions of their proposed constitution. On the contrary, the instructions given by my orders were, that all measures of domestic policy adopted by the people of California, must originate solely with themselves; that while the Executive of the United States was desirous to protect them in the formation of any Government republican in its character, to be at the proper time submitted to Congress, yet it was to be distinctly understood that the plan of such a Government must at the same time be the result of their own deliberate choice, and originate with themselves, without the interference of the Executive.

I am unable to give any information as to laws passed by any supposed Government in California, or of any census taken in either of the territories mentioned in the resolution, as I have no information on those subjects.

As already stated, I have not disturbed the arrangements which I found had existed under my predecessor.

In advising an early application by the people of these Territories for admission as States, I was actuated principally by an earnest desire to afford to the wisdom and patriotism of Congress the opportunity of avoiding occasions of bitter and angry dissensions among the people of the United States.

Under the constitution, every State has the right of establishing, and from time to time, altering its municipal laws and domestic institutions, independently of every other State and of the General Government, subject only to the prohibitions and guarantees expressly set forth in the Constitution of the United States. The subjects thus left exclusively to the respective States, were not designed or expected to become topics of national agitation. Still, as under the constitution, Congress has power to make all needful rules and regulations respecting the Territories of the United States, every new acquisition of Territory has led to discussions on the question, whether the system of involuntary servitude which prevails in many of the States should or should not be prohibited in that Territory. The periods of excitement from this cause, which have heretofore occurred, have been safely passed; but during the interval, of whatever length, which may elapse before the admission of the Territories ceded by Mexico as States, it appears probable that similar excitement will prevail to an undue extent.

Under these circumstances I thought, and still think, that it was my duty to endeavor to put it in the power of Congress, by the admission of California and New Mexico as States, to remove all occasion for the unnecessary agitation of the public mind.

It is understood that the people of the western part of California have formed a plan of a State constitution and will soon submit the same to the judgment of Congress and apply for admission as a State. This course on their part, though in accordance with, was not adopted exclusively in consequence of any expression of my wishes, inasmuch as measures tending to this end had been promoted by the officers sent there by my predecessor, and were already in active progress of execution before any communication from me reached California. If the proposed constitution shall, when submitted to Congress, be found to be in compliance with the requisitions of the Constitution of the United States, I earnestly recommend that it may receive the sanction of Congress.

The part of California not included in the proposed State of that name, is believed to be uninhabited, except in a settlement of our countrymen in the vicinity of Salt Lake.

A claim has been advanced by the State of Texas to a very large portion of the most populous district of the Territory commonly designated by the name of New Mexico. If the people of New Mexico had formed a plan of a State Government for that Territory as ceded by the treaty of Guadalupe Hidalgo, and had been admitted by Congress as a State, our constitution would have afforded the means of obtaining an adjustment of the question of boundary with Texas by a judicial decision. At present, however, no judicial tribunal has the power of deciding that question, and it remains for Congress to devise some mode for its adjustment. Meanwhile I submit to Congress the question, whether it would be expedient before such adjustment to establish a Territorial Government, which, by including the district so claimed, would practically decide the question adversely to the State of Texas, or by excluding it, would decide it in her favor. In my opinion such a course would not be expedient, especially as the people of this Territory still enjoy the benefit and protection of their municipal laws, originally derived from Mexico, and have a military force stationed there to protect them against the Indians. It is undoubtedly true that the property, lives, liberties, and religion of the people of New Mexico are better protected than they ever were before the treaty of cession.

Should Congress, when California shall present herself for incorporation into the Union, annex a condition to her admission as a State affecting her domestic institutions contrary to the wishes of her people, and even compel her temporarily to comply with it, yet the State could change her constitution at any time after admission, when to her it should seem expedient. Any attempt to deny to the people of the State the right of self-government in a matter which peculiarly affects themselves will infallibly be regarded by them as an invasion of their rights; and, upon the principles laid down in our own Declaration of Independence, they will certainly be sustained by the great mass of the American people. To assert that they are a conquered people, and must as a State submit to the will of their conquerors, in this regard, will meet with no cordial response among American freemen. Great numbers of them are native citizens of the United States, and not inferior to the rest of our countrymen in intelligence and patriotism; and no language of menace to restrain them in the exercise of an undoubted right, substantially guaranteed to them by the treaty of cession itself, shall ever be uttered by me, or encouraged and sustained by persons acting under my authority. It is to be expected that in the residue of the territory ceded to us by Mexico the people residing there will, at the time of their incorporation into the Union as a State, settle all questions of domestic policy to suit themselves.

No material inconvenience will result from the want, for a short period, of a Government established by Congress over that part of the Territory which lies eastward of the new State of California; and the reasons for my opinion that New Mexico will at no very distant period ask for admission into the Union are founded on unofficial information, which I suppose is common to all who have cared to make inquiries on that subject.

Seeing, then, that the question, which now excites such painful sensations in the country, will in the end certainly be settled by the silent effect of causes independent of the action of Congress, I again submit to your wisdom the policy recommended in my annual message of awaiting the salutary operation of those causes, believing that we shall thus avoid the creation of geographical parties, and secure the harmony of feeling so necessary to the beneficial action of our political system. Connected, as the Union is, with the remembrance of past happiness, the sense of present blessings, and the hope of future peace and prosperity, every dictate of wisdom, every feeling of duty, and every emotion of patriotism, tend to inspire fidelity and devotion to it, and admonish us cautiously to avoid any unnecessary controversy which can either endanger it or impair its strength, the chief element of which is to be found in the regard and affection of the people for each other.

Z. TAYLOR.

The message having been read—

Mr. VENABLE moved that it be referred, with the accompanying documents, to the Committee on the Territories.

WEDNESDAY, January 23.

President's Message—California.

On the motion of Mr. VENABLE, the House resumed the consideration of the special message of the President; the pending question being on the motion of Mr. VENABLE, to refer to the Committee on Territories, and print.

Mr. CLINGMAN, who was entitled to the floor, waived his right.

Mr. SEDDON addressed the House on the subject of the President's communication in reply to the resolutions submitted by Mr. VENABLE; at the close of which, there was some applause, which was checked by the SPEAKER.

Mr. SEDDON having concluded—

Mr. MCCLERNAND moved to amend the motion of Mr. VENABLE, so as to refer the message to the Committee of the Whole on the state of the Union, and print; and upon that motion he demanded the previous question.

Pending this question—

On motion of Mr. STANLY, the House adjourned.

IN SENATE.

TUESDAY, January 29.

The Slavery Question—Mr. Clay's Compromise Resolutions—His Eight Resolutions, covering all the Points of the Question, with his Introductory and Explanatory Speech.

Mr. CLAY. Mr. President, I hold in my hand a series of resolutions which I desire to submit to the consideration of this body. Taken together, in combination, they propose an amicable arrangement of all questions in controversy between the free and the slave States, growing out of the subject of slavery. It is not my intention, Mr. President, at this time, to enter into a full and elaborate discussion of each of these resolutions, taken separately, or the whole of them combined together, as composing a system of measures; but I desire to present a few observations upon each resolution, with the purpose, chiefly, of exposing it fairly and fully before the Senate and before the country; and I may add, with the indulgence of the Senate, towards the conclusion, some general observations upon the state of the country and the condition of the question to which the resolutions relate. Whether they shall or shall not meet with the approbation and concurrence of the Senate—as I most ardently hope they may; as I most sincerely believe they ought—I trust that at least some portion of the long time which I have devoted, with care and deliberation, to the preparation of these resolutions, and to the presentation of this great national scheme of compromise and harmony, will be employed by each Senator before he pronounces against the proposition embraced in these resolutions. The resolutions, sir, are all preceded by a short preamble, to which of course I attach no very great importance. The preamble and first resolution are as follows:

It being desirable for the peace, concord, and harmony of the union of these States to settle and adjust amicably all existing questions of controversy between them arising out of the institution of slavery, upon a fair, equitable, and just basis: Therefore

1st. *Resolved*, That California, with suitable boundaries, ought, upon her application, to be admitted as one of the States of this Union, without the imposition by Congress of any restriction in respect to the exclusion or introduction of slavery within those boundaries.

Mr. President, it must be acknowledged that there has been some irregularity in the movements which have terminated in the adoption of a constitution by California, and in the expression of her wish—not yet formally communicated to Congress it is true, but which may be anticipated in a few days—to be admitted into the Union as a State. There has been some irregularity in the manner in which they have framed that constitution. It was not preceded by any act of Congress authorizing the convention and designating the boundaries of the proposed State, according to all the early practice of this Government, according to all the cases of the admission of new States into this Union, which occurred prior, I think, to that of Michigan. Michigan, if I am not mistaken, was the first State which, unbidden, unauthorized by any previous act of Congress, undertook to form for herself a constitution, and to knock at the door of Congress for admission into the Union. I recollect that at the time when Michigan thus presented herself, I was opposed, in consequence of that deviation from the early practice of the Government, to the admission. The majority determined otherwise, and it must be in candor admitted by all men, that California has much more reason to do what she has done, unsanctioned and unauthorized by a previous act of Congress, than Michigan had to do what she did.

Sir, notwithstanding the irregularity of the admission of Michigan into the Union, it has been a happy event. She forms now one of the bright stars of this glorious Confederacy. She has sent here to mingle in our councils Senators and Representatives—men eminently distinguished, with whom we may all associate with pride, with pleasure, and with satisfaction. And I trust that if California—irregular as her previous action may have been in the adoption of a constitution, but more justifiable than was the action of Michigan—if she also shall be admitted, as is proposed by this first resolution, with suitable limits, that she too will make her contribution of wisdom, of patriotism, and of good feeling to this body, in order to conduct the affairs of this great and boundless empire.

The resolution proposes her admission when she applies for it. There is no intention on my part to anticipate such an application, but I thought it right to present this resolution as a part of the general plan which I propose for the adjustment of these unhappy difficulties.

The second resolution, sir, is as follows:

2d. *Resolved*, That as slavery does not exist by law, and is not likely to be introduced into any of the territory acquired by the United States from the Republic of Mexico, it is inexpedient for Congress to provide by law, either for its introduction into or exclusion from any part of the said territory; and that appropriate Territorial Governments ought to be established by Congress in all of the said territory, not assigned as the boundaries of the proposed State of California, without the adoption of any restriction or condition on the subject of slavery.

This resolution, sir, proposes, in the first instance, a declaration of two truths—one of law and the other of fact. The truth of law which it declares is, that there does not exist, at this time, slavery within any portion of the territory acquired by the United States from Mexico. When I say, sir, that it is a truth, I speak my own solemn and deliberate conviction. I am aware that some gentlemen have held a different doctrine; but I persuade myself that they themselves, when they come to review the whole ground, will see sufficient reasons for a change, or at least a modification of their opinions; but that, at all events, if they adhere to that doctrine, they will be found to compose a very small minority of the whole mass of the people of the United States.

The next truth which the resolution asserts is, that slavery is not likely to be introduced into any portion of that territory. That is a matter of fact; and all the evidence upon which the fact rests is perhaps as accessible to other Senators as it is to me; but I must say that from all I have heard or read, from the testimony of all the witnesses I have seen and conversed with, from all that has transpired and is transpiring, I do believe that not within one foot of the territory acquired by us from Mexico will slavery ever be planted, and I believe it could not be done even by the force and power of public authority.

Sir, facts are daily occurring to justify me in this opinion. Sir, what has occurred? And upon that subject, and indeed upon this whole subject, I invite Senators from the free States especially to consider what has occurred even since the last session—even since the commencement of this session—since they left their respective constituencies without an opportunity of consulting with them upon the great and momentous fact; the fact that California herself, of which it was asserted and predicted that she never would establish slavery within her limits when she came to be admitted as a State; that California herself, embracing, of all other portions of the country acquired by us from Mexico, that country into which it would have been most likely that slavery should have been introduced; that California herself has met in convention, and by a unanimous vote, embracing in that body slaveholders from the State of Mississippi, as well as from other parts, who concurred in the resolution—that California by a unanimous vote has declared against the introduction of slavery within her limits. I think, then, that taking this leading fact in connection with all the evidence we have from other sources on the subject, I am warranted in the conclusion which constitutes the second truth which I have stated in this resolution, that slavery is "not likely to be introduced into any of the territory acquired by us from Mexico."

Sir, the latter part of that resolution asserts that it is the duty of Congress to establish appropriate territorial governments within all the country acquired from Mexico, exclusive of

California, not embracing in the acts by which these governments shall be constituted either a prohibition or an admission of slavery.

Sir, much as I am disposed to defer to high authority—anxious as I really am to find myself in a position that would enable me to coöperate heartily with the other departments of the Government in conducting the affairs of this great people, I must say that I cannot, without a dereliction of duty, consent to an abandonment of them without government, leaving them to all those scenes of disorder, confusion, and anarchy which I apprehend, in respect of some of them, there is too much reason to anticipate will arise. It is the duty, the solemn—I was going to add the most sacred duty—of Congress to legislate for their government if they can, and at all events to legislate for them, and to give them the benefit of law, and order, and security.

The next resolutions are the third and fourth, which, having an immediate connection with each other, should be read and considered together. They are as follows:

3d. *Resolved*, That the western boundary of the State of Texas ought to be fixed on the Rio del Norte, commencing one marine league from its mouth, and running up that river to the southern line of New Mexico; thence with that line eastwardly, and so continuing in the same direction to the line established between the United States and Spain, excluding any portion of New Mexico, whether lying on the east or west of that river.

4th. *Resolved*, That it be proposed to the State of Texas that the United States will provide for the payment of all that portion of the legitimate and *bona fide* public debt of that State, contracted prior to its annexation to the United States, and for which the duties on foreign imports were pledged by the said State to its creditors not exceeding the sum of $——— in consideration of the said duties so pledged having been no longer applicable to that object after the said annexation, but having thenceforward become payable to the United States; and upon the condition also that the said State of Texas shall, by some solemn and authentic act of her Legislature, or of a convention, relinquish to the United States any claim which it has to any part of New Mexico.

Mr. President, I do not mean now, I do not know that I shall at any time—it is a very complex subject, and one not free from difficulty—go into the question of what are the true limits of Texas. My own opinion is, I must say, without intending by the remark to go into any argument, that Texas has not a good title to any portion of what is called New Mexico. And yet, sir, I am free to admit that, looking at the grounds which her representatives assumed, first in the war with Santa Anna in 1836, then at what transpired between Mr. Trist and the Mexican negotiators when the treaty of peace was negotiated, and then the fact that the United States have acquired all the country which Texas claimed as constituting a portion of her territory; looking at all these facts, but without attaching to them, either together or separately, the same degree of force which gentlemen who think that Texas has a right to New Mexico do, I must say that there is plausibility, to say the least of it, in the pretensions that she sets up to New Mexico. I do not think they constitute or demonstrate the existence of a good title, but a plausible one. Well, then, sir, what do I propose? Without entering into any inquiry whether the Nueces or the Rio Grande was the true boundary of Texas, I propose by the first of these two resolutions, that its western limits shall be fixed on the Rio del Norte—extending west from the Sabine to the mouth of the Rio del Norte—and that it shall follow up the Bravo, or the Rio del Norte, to where it strikes the southern line of New Mexico, and then diverging from that line, follow on in that direction until it reaches the line as fixed by the United States and Spain by their treaty of 1819; and thus embracing a vast country abundantly competent to form two or three States—a country which I think the highest ambition of her greatest men ought to be satisfied with as a State and member of this Union.

But, sir, the second of these resolutions makes a proposition to the State of Texas upon which I desire to say a few words. It proposes that the Government of the United States will provide for the payment of all that portion of the debt of Texas for which the duties received upon imports from foreign countries was pledged by Texas at a time when she had authority to make pledges. How much it will amount to I have endeavored to ascertain, but all the means requisite to the ascertainment of the sum have not been received, and it is not very essential at this time, because it is the principle and not the amount that is most worthy of consideration. Now, sir, the ground upon which I base this liability on the part of the United States to pay a specified portion of the debt of Texas is not new to me. It is one which I have again and again announced to be an opinion entertained by me. I think it is founded upon principles of truth and eternal justice. Texas being an independent Power, recognized as such by all the great powers of the earth, invited loans to be made to her to enable her to prosecute the then existing war between her and Mexico. She told those whom she invited to make these loans that "if you make them, the duties on foreign imports shall be sacredly pledged for the reimbursement of the loans." The loans were made. The money was received, and expended in the establishment of her liberty and her independence. After all this, she annexed herself to the United States, who thenceforward acquired the right to the identical pledge which she had made to the public creditor to satisfy the loan of money which he had advanced to her. The United States became the owners of that pledge and the recipient of all the duties payable in the ports of Texas.

Now, sir, I do say that, in my humble judgment, if there be honor, or justice, or truth amongst men, we do owe to the creditors who thus advanced their money upon that pledge the reimbursement of the money, at all events to the extent that the pledged fund would have reimbursed it, if it had never been appropriated by us to our use. We must recollect, sir, that in relation to that pledge, and to the loan made in virtue and on the faith of it, there were three parties bound—I mean after annexation: the United States, Texas, and the creditor of Texas, who had advanced his money on the faith of a solemn pledge made by Texas.

Texas and the United States might do what they thought proper; but in justice they could do nothing to deprive the creditor of a full reliance upon the pledge upon the faith of which he had advanced his money. Sir, it is impossible now to ascertain how much would have been received from that source of revenue by the State of Texas if she had remained independent. It would be most unjust to go there now and examine at Galveston and her other ports to ascertain how much she now receives by her foreign imports; because, by being incorporated into this Union, all her supplies which formerly were received from foreign countries, and subject—many of them at least—to import duties, are now received by the coasting trade, instead of being received from other countries, as they would have been if she remained independent. Considering the extent of her territory, and the rapid manner in which her population is increasing, and is likely to increase, it is probable that in the course of a few years there might have been such an amount received at the various ports of Texas—she remaining independent—as would have been adequate to the extinction of the debt to which I have referred.

But, sir, it is not merely in the discharge of what I consider to be a valid and legitimate obligation resting upon the United States to discharge the specified duty, it is not upon that condition alone that this payment is proposed to be made; it is also upon the further condition that Texas shall relinquish to the United States any claim that she has to any portion of New Mexico. Now, sir, although, as I believe, she has not a valid title to any portion of New Mexico, she has a claim; and for the sake of that general quiet and harmony, for the sake of that accommodation which ought to be as much the object of legislation as it is of individuals in their transactions in private life, we may do now what an individual in analogous circumstances might do, give something for the relinquishment of a claim, although it should not be well founded, for the sake of peace. It is therefore proposed—and this resolution does propose—that we shall pay the amount of the debt contracted by Texas prior to its annexation to the United States, in consideration of our reception of the duties applicable to the extinction of that debt; and that Texas shall also, in consideration of a sum to be advanced, relinquish any claim which she has to any portion of New Mexico.

The fifth resolution, sir, and the sixth, like the third and fourth, are somewhat connected together. They are as follows:

5th. *Resolved,* That it is inexpedient to abolish slavery in the District of Columbia, whilst that institution continues to exist in the State of Maryland, without the consent of that State without the consent of the people of the District, and without just compensation to the owners of slaves within the District.

6th. *But Resolved,* That it is expedient to prohibit within the District the slave-trade, in slaves brought into it from States or places beyond the limits of the District, either to be sold therein as merchandise, or to be transported to other markets without the District of Columbia.

The first of these resolutions, Mr. President, in somewhat different language, asserts substantially no other principle than that which was asserted by the Senate of the United States twelve years ago, upon resolutions which I then offered, and which passed—at least the particular resolution passed—by a majority of four-fifths of the Senate. I allude to the resolution presented by me in 1838. I shall not enlarge on that resolution; it speaks for itself; it declares that the institution of slavery should not be abolished in the District of Columbia without the concurrence of three conditions; first, the assent of Maryland; second, the assent of the people within the District; and third, compensation to the owners of the slaves within the District for their property.

The next resolution proposed deserves a passing remark. It is that the slave trade within the District ought to be abolished, prohibited. I do not mean by that the alienation and transfer of slaves from the inhabitants within this District—the sale by one neighbor to another of a slave which the one owns and the other wants, that a husband may perhaps be put along with his wife, or a wife with her husband. I do not mean to touch at all the question of the right of property in slaves amongst persons living within the District; but the slave trade to which I refer was, I think, pronounced an abomination more than forty years ago, by one of the most gifted and distinguished sons of Virginia, the late Mr. Randolph. And who is there who is not shocked at its enormity? Sir, it is a great mistake at the North, if they suppose that gentlemen living in the slave States look upon one who is a regular trader in slaves with any particular favor or kindness. They are often—sometimes unjustly, perhaps—excluded from social intercourse. I have known some memorable instances of this sort. But, then, what is this trade? It is a good deal limited since the retrocession of the portion of the District formerly belonging to Virginia. There are Alexandria, Richmond, Petersburg, and Norfolk, south of the Potomac, and Baltimore, Annapolis, and perhaps other ports, north of the Potomac. Let the slave-dealer, who chooses to collect his slaves in Virginia and Maryland, go to these places; let him not come here and establish his jails and put on his chains, and sometimes shock the sensibilities of our nature by a long train of slaves passing through that avenue leading from this Capitol to the house of the Chief Magistrate of one of the most glorious Republics that ever existed. Why should he not do it? Sir, I am sure I speak the sentiments of every Southern man, and every man coming from the slave States, when I say let it terminate, and that it is an abomination; that there is no occasion for it; it ought no longer to be tolerated.

The seventh resolution relates to a subject embraced in a bill now under consideration by the Senate. It is as follows:

7th. *Resolved*, That more effectual provisions ought to be made by law, according to the requirement of the constitution, for the restitution and delivery of persons bound to service or labor in any State who may escape into any other State or Territory in the Union.

Sir, that is so evident, and has been so clearly shown by the debate which has already taken place on the subject, that I have not now occasion to add another word.

The last resolution of the series of eight is as follows:

And 8th. *Resolved*, That Congress has no power to prohibit or obstruct the trade in slaves between the slaveholding States; but that the admission or exclusion of slaves brought from one into another of them, depends exclusively upon their own particular laws.

It is obvious that no legislation is necessary or intended to follow that resolution. It merely asserts a truth, established by the highest authority of law in this country, and in conformity with that decision I trust there will be one universal acquiescence.

I should not have thought it necessary to embrace in that resolution the declaration which is embraced in it, but that I thought it might be useful in treating of the whole subject, and in accordance with the practice of our British and American ancestors, occasionally to resort to great fundamental principles, and bring them freshly and manifestly before our eyes, from time to time, to avoid their being violated upon any occasion.

Mr. President, you have before you the whole series of resolutions, the whole scheme of arrangement and accommodation of these distracting questions, which I have to offer, after having bestowed on these subjects the most anxious, intensely anxious, consideration ever since I have been in this body. How far it may prove acceptable to both or either of the parties on these great questions, it is not for me to say. I think it ought to be acceptable to both. There is no sacrifice of any principle, proposed in any of them, by either party. The plan is founded upon mutual forbearance, originating in a spirit of conciliation and concession; not of principles, but of matters of feeling. At the North, sir, I know that from feeling, by many at least cherished as being dictated by considerations of humanity and philanthropy, there exists a sentiment adverse to the institution of slavery.

Sir, I might, I think—although I believe this project contains about an equal amount of concession and forbearance on both sides—have asked from the free States of the North a more liberal and extensive concession than should be asked from the slave States. And why, sir? With you, gentlemen Senators of the free States, what is it? An abstraction, a sentiment —a sentiment, if you please, of humanity and philanthropy—a noble sentiment, when directed rightly, with no sinister or party purposes; an atrocious sentiment—a detestable sentiment—or rather the abuse of it—when directed to the accomplishment of unworthy purposes. I said that I might ask from you larger and more expansive concessions than from the slave States. And why? You are numerically more powerful than the slave States. Not that there is any difference—for upon that subject I cannot go along with the ardent expression of feeling by some of my friends coming from the same class of States from which I come—not that there is any difference in valor, in prowess, in noble and patriotic daring, whenever it is required for the safety and salvation of the country, between the people of one class of States and those of the other. You are in point of numbers, however, greater; and greatness and magnanimity should ever be allied together.

But there are other reasons why concession upon such a subject as this should be more liberal, more expansive, coming from the free than from the slave States. It is, as I remarked, a sentiment, a sentiment of humanity and philanthropy on your side. Aye, sir, and when a sentiment of that kind is honestly and earnestly cherished, with a disposition to make sacrifices to enforce it, it is a noble and beautiful sentiment; but, sir, when the sacrifice is not to be made by those who cherish that sentiment and inculcate it, but by another people, in whose situation it is impossible, from their position, to sympathize and to share all and every thing that belongs to them, I must say to you, Senators from the free States, it is a totally different question. On your side it is a sentiment without sacrifice, a sentiment without danger, a sentiment without hazard, without peril, without loss. But how is it on the other side, to which, as I have said, a greater amount of concession ought to be made in any scheme of compromise?

In the first place, sir, there is a vast and incalculable amount of property to be sacrificed, and to be sacrificed, not by your sharing in the common burdens, but exclusive of you. And this is not all. The social intercourse, habit, safety, property, life, every thing, is at hazard in a greater or less degree in the slave States.

Sir, look at that storm which is now raging before you, beating in all its rage pitilessly on your family. They are in the South. But where are your families, where are your people, Senators from the free States? They are safely housed, enjoying all the blessings of domestic comfort, peace, and quiet in the bosom of their own families.

Behold, Mr. President, that dwelling-house now wrapped in flames. Listen, sir, to the rafters and beams which fall in succession, amid the crash; and the flames ascending higher and higher as they tumble down. Behold those women and children who are flying from the calamitous scene, and with their shrieks and lamentations imploring the aid of high Heaven. Whose house is that? Whose wives and children are they? Yours in the free States? No. You are looking on in safety and security, whilst the conflagration which I have described is raging in the slave States, and produced, not intentionally by you, but produced from the inevitable tendency of the measures which you have adopted, and which others have carried far beyond what you have wished.

In the one scale, then, we behold sentiment, sentiment, sentiment, alone; in the other property, the social fabric, life, and all that makes life desirable and happy.

But, sir, I find myself engaged much beyond what I intended, when I came this morning from my lodgings, in the exposition with which I intended these resolutions should go forth to the consideration of the world. I cannot omit, however, before I conclude, relating an incident, a thrilling incident, which occurred prior to my leaving my lodgings this morning.

A man came to my room—the same at whose instance a few days ago I presented a memorial calling upon Congress for the purchase of Mount Vernon for the use of the public—and, without being at all aware of what purpose I entertained in the discharge of my public duty to-day, he said to me: "Mr. Clay, I heard you make a remark the other day which induces me to suppose that a precious relic in my possession would be acceptable to you." He then drew out of his pocket, and presented to me, the object which I now hold in my hand. And what, Mr. President, do you suppose it is? It is a fragment of the coffin of Washington—a fragment of that coffin in which now repose in silence, in sleep, and speechless, all the earthly remains of the venerated Father of his Country. Was it portentous that it should have been thus presented to me? Was it a sad presage of what might happen to that fabric which Washington's virtue, patriotism, and valor established? No, sir, no. It was a warning voice, coming from the grave to the Congress now in session to beware, to pause, to reflect before they lend themselves to any purposes which shall destroy that Union which was cemented by his exertions and example. Sir, I hope an impression may be made on your mind such as that which was made on mine by the reception of this precious relic.

And, in conclusion, I now ask every Senator, I entreat you, gentlemen, in fairness and candor, to examine the plan of accommodation which this series of resolutions proposes, and not to pronounce against them until convinced after a thorough examination. I move that the resolutions be read and received.

The resolutions were then read as follows:

It being desirable for the peace, concord, and harmony of the Union of these States, to settle and adjust amicably all existing questions of controversy between them, arising out of the institution of slavery, upon a fair, equitable, and just basis: Therefore,

1st. *Resolved*, That California, with suitable boundaries, ought upon her application to be admitted as one of the States of this Union, without the imposition by Congress of any restriction in respect to the exclusion or introduction of slavery within those boundaries.

2d. *Resolved*, That as slavery does not exist by law, and is not likely to be introduced into any of the territory acquired by the United States from the Republic of Mexico, it is inexpedient for Congress to provide by law either for its introduction into or exclusion from any part of the said territory; and that appropriate Territorial Governments ought to be established by Congress in all of the said territory, not assigned as the boundaries of the proposed State of California, without the adoption of any restriction or condition on the subject of slavery.

3d. *Resolved*, That the western boundary of the State of Texas ought to be fixed on the Rio del Norte, commencing one marine league from its mouth, and running up that river to the southern line of New Mexico; thence with that line eastwardly, and so continuing in the same direction to the line as established between the United States and Spain, excluding any portion of New Mexico, whether lying on the east or west of that river.

4th. *Resolved*, That it be proposed to the State of Texas that the United States will provide for the payment of all that portion of the legitimate and *bona fide* public debt of that State contracted prior to its annexation to the United States and for which the duties on foreign imports were pledged by the said State to its creditors, not exceeding the sum of $———, in consideration of the said duties so pledged having been no longer applicable to that object after the said annexation, but having henceforward become payable to the United States; and upon the condition also that the said State of Texas shall, by some solemn and authentic act of her Legislature, or of a convention, relinquish to the United States any claim which it has to any part of New Mexico.

5th. *Resolved*, That it is inexpedient to abolish slavery, in the District of Columbia, whilst that institution continues to exist in the State of Maryland, without the consent of that State, without the consent of the people of the District, and without just compensation to the owners of slaves within the District.

6th. *But Resolved*, That it is expedient to prohibit within the District the slave-trade, in slaves brought into it from States or places beyond the limits of the District, either to be sold therein as merchandise, or to be transported to other markets without the District of Columbia.

7th. *Resolved*, That more effectual provision ought to be made by law, according to the requirement of the constitution, for the restitution and delivery of persons bound to service or labor in any State, who may escape into any other State or Territory in the Union.

And 8th. *Resolved*, That Congress has no power to prohibit or obstruct the trade in slaves between the slaveholding States; but that the admission or exclusion of slaves brought from one into another of them, depends exclusively upon their own particular laws.

Mr. CLAY. I had intended to propose that we should now fix upon some convenient day for the discussion of these resolutions. I shall be satisfied with any early day which the Senate in their pleasure may decide upon. I would propose Monday or Tuesday of the next week.

Mr. FOOTE. Mr. President, I wish it were in my power to act in accordance with the request of the honorable Senator from Kentucky, (Mr. CLAY,) who seems so strongly to deprecate debate, at the present moment, upon the resolutions introduced by him, and who has so strongly urged us to deliberate well and dispassionately upon these resolutions before we take ground against them. But indeed, sir, I feel it impossible to remain altogether silent without more or less subjecting myself to misconstruction, and exposing to serious danger principles which I hold to be indispensable to the safety of the southern States of the Confederacy, and to the integrity of the Union itself. I know well that the honorable Senator's intentions are pure and patriotic—that he designs only the safety and happiness of the whole republic; and yet I do verily believe that if the resolutions now introduced by him shall be adopted, accompanied by the remarks which he has just uttered in our hearing, without any response, or even suggestion of objection from any southern Senator, a presumption of *acquiescence* might arise which would be deeply detrimental to a cause which I hold dearer than life itself. I do not propose to discuss these resolutions *in extenso;* I will not thus far interfere with the wishes of the honorable Senator from Kentucky; but a few remarks by way of *protest*, I must be allowed at once to put in. These, though, will be as brief as possible. In offering such remarks, I find myself somewhat embarrassed, in consequence of never having had an opportunity of reading the resolutions of the honorable Senator, and only having heard them read by him in the course of his comments upon them. If I misconstrue their import in any particular it will not be matter of surprise to any one, or constitute just ground of complaint against me.

If I understand the resolutions properly, they are objectionable, as it seems to me: 1. Because they only assert that it is not *expedient* that Congress should abolish slavery in the District of Columbia; thus allowing the implication to arise that Congress has power to legislate on the subject of slavery in the District, which may hereafter be exercised if it should become expedient to do so; whereas, I hold that Congress has, under the Constitution, no such legislative power at all, and any attempt thus to legislate would be a gross fraud upon all the States of the Union.

2. The resolutions of the honorable Senator assert that slavery does not now exist by law in the territories recently acquired from Mexico; whereas I am of opinion that the treaty with the Mexican republic carried the constitution, *with all its guarantees*, to all the territory obtained by treaty, and secured the privilege to every southern slaveholder to enter any part of it, attended by his slave property, and to enjoy the same therein free from all molestation or hindrance whatsoever.

3. Whether slavery is or is not likely to be introduced into these territories, or into any one of them, is a proposition too uncertain, in my judgment, to be at present positively affirmed; and I am unwilling to make a solemn legislative declaration on the point. *Let the future provide the appropriate solution of this interesting question.*

4. Considering, as I have several times heretofore formally declared, the title of Texas to all the territory embraced in her boundaries as laid down in her law of 1836, full, complete, and undeniable, I am unwilling to say any thing, by resolution or otherwise, which may in the least degree draw that title into question, as I think is done by one of the resolutions of the honorable Senator from Kentucky.

5. I am, upon constitutional and other grounds, wholly opposed to the principle of *assuming State debts*, which I understand to be embodied in one of the resolutions of the honorable Senator from Kentucky. If Texan soil is to be bought, (and with certain appropriate *safeguards*, I am decidedly in favor of it,) let us pay to the sovereign State of Texas the value thereof in money, to be used by her as she pleases. It will be, as I think, more delicate and respectful to let her provide for the management of this matter, which is strictly *domestic* in its character, in such manner as she may choose—presuming that she will act wisely, justly, and honorably towards all to whom she may be indebted.

6. As to the abolition of the *slave trade* in the District of Columbia, I see no particular objection to it, provided it is done in a delicate and judicious manner, and is not a concession to menaces or demands of factionists and fanatics. If other questions can be adjusted, this one will, perhaps, occasion but little difficulty.

7. The resolutions which provide for the restoration of fugitives from labor or service, and for the establishment of territorial governments free from all restriction on the subject of slavery, have my hearty approval. The last resolution—which asserts that Congress has no power to prohibit the trade in slaves from State to State—I equally approve.

8. If all other questions connected with the subject of slavery can be satisfactorily adjusted, I see no objection to admitting all California above the line of 36 degrees and 30 minutes into the Union; provided another new slave State can be laid off within the present limits of Texas, so as to keep up the present *equiponderance* between the slave and the free States of the Union;

and provided, further, all this is done by way of *compromise*, and in order to save the Union, (as dear to me as to any man living.)

Having thus frankly stated my objections to the honorable Senator's resolutions, and having stated also wherein I approve them, I shall cease to occupy the attention of the Senate.

Mr. Mason. It is with much reluctance at any time that I trespass on the time of the Senate after the hour of actual business has arrived, but I do not feel myself at liberty, standing as I do upon this question, to allow the resolutions offered by the Senator from Kentucky to pass unnoticed on my part, lest it should possibly be considered that the State which I represent in part is prepared, I would almost say to any extent, to respond to the spirit of these resolutions. Sir, I regret deeply that, in the earnest and honest desire which I have no doubt the Senator entertains to have these disturbing questions composed, he has felt it his duty, representing one of the slaveholding States, to offer such a proposition. I would go with him who went furthest, but within the limits of strict duty, in adjusting these unhappy differences; but I do not feel at liberty to move one step towards such a compromise, if constitutional right is invaded in the slightest degree.

Sir, so far as I have read these resolutions, there is but one proposition to which I can give a hearty assent, and that is the resolution which proposes to organize Territorial governments at once in these Territories, without a declaration one way or the other as to their domestic institutions. But there is another which I deeply regret to see introduced into this Senate by a Senator from a slaveholding State; it is that which assumes that slavery now does not exist by law in those countries. I understand one of these propositions to declare that by law slavery is now abolished in New Mexico and California. That was the very proposition advanced by the non-slaveholding States at the last session, combated and disproved, as I thought, by gentlemen from the slaveholding States, and which the compromise bill was framed to test. So far I regarded the question of law as disposed of, and it was clearly and satisfactorily shown to be against the spirit of the resolution of the Senator from Kentucky. If the contrary is true, I presume the Senator from Kentucky would declare that if a law is now valid in the Territories abolishing slavery, that it could not be introduced there even if a law was passed creating the institution or repealing the statutes already existing; a doctrine never assented to, so far as I know, until now, by any Senator representing one of the slaveholding States. Sir, I hold the very opposite, and with such confidence that at the last session I was willing and did vote for a bill to test this question in the Supreme Court. Yet this resolution assumes the other doctrine to be true, and our assent is challenged to it as a proposition in law.

I do not mean to detain the Senate by any discussion, but I deemed it to be my duty to enter a decided protest on the part of Virginia against such doctrines. They concede the whole question at once, that our people shall not go into the new Territories and take their property with them; a doctrine to which I never will assent, and for which, sir, no law can be found. There are other portions of the resolutions, for which, if they could be separated, I should be very willing to vote. That respecting fugitive slaves, and that respecting the organization of governments in these Territories, I should be willing to vote for, and I am happy to declare the gratification I experience at finding the Senator from Kentucky, differing so much on this subject from the Executive message recently laid before the Senate. I beg not to be understood as having spoken in any spirit of unkindness towards the Senator from Kentucky, for whom I entertain the warmest and most profound respect; but I cannot but express also my regret that he has felt it to be his duty, standing as he does before this people, and representing the people he does, to introduce into this body resolutions of this kind.

Mr. Davis, of Mississippi. I do not rise to continue the discussion, but, as it has been made an historical question as to what the position of the Senate was twelve years ago, and as with great regret I see this, the conservative branch of the Government, tending towards that fanaticism which seems to prevail with the majority in the United States, I wish to read from the journals of that date the resolutions then adopted, and to show that they went further than the honorable Senator from Kentucky has stated. I take it for granted, from the date to which the honorable Senator has alluded, he means the resolutions introduced by the honorable Senator from South Carolina, (Mr. Calhoun,) not now in his seat, and to which the Senator from Kentucky proposed certain amendments. Of the resolutions introduced by the Senator from South Carolina, I will read the fifth in the series, that to which the honorable Senator from Kentucky must have alluded. It is in these words:

"*Resolved*, That the intermeddling of any State, or States, or their citizens, to abolish slavery in the District, or any of the Territories, on the ground or under the pretext that it is immoral or sinful, or the passage of any act or measure of Congress with that view, would be a direct and dangerous attack on the institutions of all the slaveholding States."

Such is the general form of the proposition. It was variously modified, but never, in my opinion, improved. On the 27th, the fifth resolution being again under consideration, Mr. Clay, of Kentucky, moved to amend the amendment by striking out all after the word "resolved," and insert:

"That the interference, by the citizens of any of the States, with a view to the abolition of slavery in this District, is endangering the rights and security of the people of the District; and that any act or measure of Congress designed to abolish slavery in this District would be a violation of the faith implied in the cessions by the States of Virginia and Maryland; a just cause of alarm to the the people of the slaveholding States, and have a direct and inevitable tendency to disturb and endanger the Union.

"*And resolved*, That it would be highly inexpedient to abolish slavery within any district of country set apart for the Indian tribes, where it now exists, or in Florida, the only Territory of the United States in which it now exists, because of the serious alarm and just apprehensions which would be thereby excited in the States sustaining that domestic institution; because the people of that Territory have not asked it to be done, and, when admitted into the Union, will be exclusively entitled to decide that question for themselves; because it would be in violation of the stipulations of the treaty between the United States and Spain, of the 22d of February, 1819; and also because it would be in violation of a solemn compromise, made at a memorable and critical period in the history of this country, by which, whilst slavery was prohibited north, it was admitted south, of the line of thirty-six degrees and thirty minutes north latitude."

But this resolution was not finally adopted. Upon the motion of Mr. BUCHANAN to amend said amendment, by striking out the second clause thereof, commencing with the word "resolved," it was determined in the affirmative, and finally the resolution which here follows was substituted in place of the second clause:

"That the interference, by the citizens of any of the States, with a view to the abolition of slavery in this District, is endangering the rights and security of the people of the District; and that any act or measure of Congress, designed to abolish slavery in this District, would be a violation of the faith implied in the cessions by the States of Virginia and Maryland; a just cause of alarm to the people of the slaveholding States, and have a direct and inevitable tendency to disturb and endanger the Union."

This was the form in which the resolution was finally adopted, passing by a vote of thirty-six to eight. Here, then, was fully and broadly asserted the danger resulting from the interference in the question of slavery in the District of Columbia, as trenching upon the rights of the slaveholding States. Twelve years only have elapsed, yet this brief period has swept away even the remembrance of principles then deemed sacred and necessary to secure the safety of the Union. Now an honorable and distinguished Senator, to whom the country has been induced to look for something that would heal the existing dissensions, instead of raising new barriers against encroachment, dashes down those heretofore erected, and augments the existing danger. A representative from one of the slaveholding States raises his voice for the first time in disregard of this admitted right.

But, sir, we are called on to receive this as a measure of compromise! Is a measure in which we of the minority are to receive nothing, a measure of compromise? I look upon it as but a modest mode of taking that, the claim to which has been more boldly asserted by others; and that I may be understood upon this question, and that my position may go forth to the country in the same columns that convey the sentiments of the Senator from Kentucky, I here assert that never will I take less than the Missouri compromise line extended to the Pacific Ocean, with the specific recognition of the right to hold slaves in the territory below that line; and that, before such territories are admitted into the Union as States, slaves may be taken there from any of the United States at the option of their owners. I can never consent to give additional power to a majority to commit further aggressions upon the minority in this Union; and will never consent to any proposition which will have such a tendency, without a full guarantee or counteracting measure is connected with it. I forbear commenting at any further length upon the propositions embraced in the resolutions at this time.

Mr. CLAY. I am extremely sorry that this premature, and—allow me to say—in my opinion unnecessary discussion has taken place. Whenever the Senator who has just resumed his seat chooses to meet me in argument at a proper time, I pledge myself to show him that there is not the slightest discrepancy in my course in 1838 and now.

Mr. DAVIS. of Mississippi. Now is the time.

Mr. CLAY. I choose not to give way now.

Mr. DAVIS, of Mississippi. The Senator asked me to name my time; and I say now.

Mr. CLAY. Not until I am done. I am reminded of my coming from a slave State. I tell the Senator from Mississippi, and I tell the Senator from Virginia, that I know my duty, and that I mean to express the opinions that I entertain, fearless of all mankind.

But, sir, in regard to this resolution of 1838, I regret extremely this premature discussion. I think it would have been better for the whole Senate if it had been deferred. And I trust the gentlemen on the other side will excuse me for saying that it would have been better for themselves if they had forborne to enter into the discussion until the question came regularly up. But, sir, as I do not choose that what I consider a mistaken representation of my sentiments in 1838 should go out, I will simply state what they were then, and what they are now.

Sir, there is not a word in that resolution that implies that any faith was pledged to the States, other than to Virginia and to Maryland, that Congress would not abolish slavery in this District. The resolution says that the agitation of the question of abolition by people living out of the District is, in its tendency, dangerous to the Slave States; and that the abolition of slavery in the District of Columbia would be just cause of alarm, not merely to Virginia and Maryland, but to all the slave States. And why? What was it that Abolitionists then proposed? It was abolition without compensation; it was to take the slaves without paying for them. And would it not in that form have been a just cause of alarm to the other States of the Union owning property of that description? The assertion, therefore, of opinion which I made then was, that, by the nature and object of the cession of the ten-miles-square by Virginia and Maryland, it could not have been anticipated by either of those States that the power conveyed to the General Government over the ten-miles-square would be so exercised as to abolish slavery within those States respectively; and, further, that, slavery continuing in Virginia and Maryland, if such an abolition were to take place in the District of Columbia, and without compensation to the slaveholder, it would be, as it undoubtedly would have been, a just cause of alarm to the owners of that description of property, wherever situated. Now, sir, that was my doctrine in 1838, and that is my doctrine still.

Sir, I do not regard the mere phraseology of the resolution. I will not substitute the word "unconstitutional" for the word "inexpedient," for I do not believe it to be unconstitutional. I cannot believe it. If a power to legislate in all cases whatever he granted to Congress, does it not comprehend the power to legislate on the subject of slavery as well as upon all other subjects? The power is there; but there is an implied faith connected with the power, resulting from the circumstances to which I have referred, imposing on Congress the obligation not to exercise the power as long as slavery in Virginia and Maryland exists. And, now that Virginia has separated from the District, such abolition may not take place without the consent of the people of the District and of Maryland, and also without, what I contended for in 1838, compensation to the owners of the slaves for their property thus liberated.

I am extremely sorry to hear the Senator from Mississippi say that he requires, first, the extension of the Missouri compromise line to the Pacific, and also that he is not satisfied with that, but requires, if I understood him correctly, a positive provision for the admission of slavery south of that line. And now, sir, coming from a slave State, as I do, I owe it to myself, I owe it to truth, I owe it to the subject, to say that no earthly power could induce me to vote for a specific measure for the introduction of slavery where it had not before existed, either south or north of that line. Coming as I do from a slave State, it is my solemn, deliberate and well-matured determination that no power, no earthly power, shall compel me to vote for the positive introduction of slavery either south or north of that line. Sir, while you reproach, and justly too, our British ancestors for the introduction of this institution upon the continent of America, I am, for one, unwilling, that the posterity of the present inhabitants of California and of New Mexico shall reproach us for doing just what we reproach Great Britain for doing to us. If the citizens of those Territories choose to establish slavery, and if they come here with constitutions establishing slavery, I am for admitting them with such provisions in their constitutions; but then it will be their own work, and not ours, and their posterity will have to reproach them, and not us, for forming constitutions allowing the institution of slavery to exist among them. These are my views, sir, and I choose to express them; and I care not how extensively or universally they are known. The honorable Senator from Virginia has expressed his opinion that slavery exists in these Territories, and I have no doubt that opinion is sincerely and honestly entertained by him; and I would say, with equal sincerity and honesty, that I believe that slavery nowhere exists within any portion of the territory acquired by us from Mexico. He holds a directly contrary opinion to mine, as he has a perfect right to do; and we will not quarrel about that difference of opinion.

But, sir, I sincerely regret, as I have before stated, a discussion upon these resolutions at this time; or I could show, and at a proper time would show, that the proposition which I make of leaving the subject unacted upon with regard to slavery—without any declaration either for or against it—leaving the question entirely open—I say I could show that it is a much better proposition, as far as the interests of the South are concerned, than that of extending the Missouri line to the Pacific, unless you should couple with it that which the Senator from Mississippi knows to be impossible, a declaration or provision for the introduction of slavery south of that line.

Mr. Davis. The Senator from Mississippi knows that.

Mr. Clay. And I say, sir, in my place, that I consider it is much better for the South that the whole subject should be open on both sides of an imaginary line—for instance, the line of 36° 30′—than that slavery should be interdicted positively north of 36° 30′, with freedom to introduce or establish slavery south of that line according to the will of the people; and the proposition that I have made is infinitely better for the South than the proposition which the Senator has suggested, unless he could persuade Congress to adopt his proposition to declare positively and absolutely the right to introduce slavery south of that line. Now, all this I could have shown, and would have shown, if necessary in the progress of the argument, if Senators had not entered into a discussion, and committed themselves upon the question—if they had chosen to wait and give a full and fair consideration to these resolutions —to view them as a system, and to view them independently of each other. But they have chosen to anticipate the argument, and I could not remain silent in justice to myself.

Mr. Davis, of Mississippi. The Senator from Kentucky rose with an announcement that he wanted to know my time for meeting him in argument, and I have told him that my time is now. Several times has he regretted this premature discussion; but pray, sir, who introduced it? The Senator submitted his resolutions, discussed them *seriatim*, and then concluded with a set speech. Are we to understand that all this was done without intending to influence opinion? Was it a mere volley of blank cartridges that he was firing, in order that he might come up under cover of the smoke, and make a charge upon us before we saw him? Why, sir, at the door of any other man might lie the charge of entering prematurely upon this discussion more properly than at mine. He it was who began the discussion, and I was the last to engage in it. But he announces as his conviction, as his determined purpose, to resist the introduction of slavery into any part of California. Sir, his opinions may have been very deliberately formed. He may have been all the time making up those determinations, that he has been preparing these resolutions; for certainly no language of mine can have produced the determination of the Senator. I have not proposed to compel slaveholders to take their slaves to California, nor to revive the African slave trade. Neither was the construction warranted by my having used the word upon which he hangs his argument. I did not use the word "introduction," nor suggest the idea of compulsion. The Senator has set up his own cob-house, to show how skilfully he could knock it down. It is no fabric of mine. We maintain that it is the right of the people of the South to carry this species of property to any portion of the Territories of the United States; that it rests under the constitution, upon the same basis as other property; but, when speaking of a compromise, it was the ultimatum I announced. It is strange that the Senator from Kentucky should be so much surprised; it certainly was not a new question with him, nor with his colleague, with whom, on a former occasion, a similar proposition originated. It is a partial recognition of a right we claim to be co-extensive with the Territories of the United States; but which we are willing, in a spirit of compromise, and in compliance with the past acquiescence of the States, to restrict by the parallel of 36° 30′ north.

Now, this is conceding a great deal. If the line were established upon any great principle arising from climate or productions, it would be different; then the line would not extend upon the same parallel of latitude. If it were a line of temperature, then, as the isothermal line bends upward, it would go north of that parallel of latitude. It is out of respect to the past, and from anxious desire peaceably to adjust a most vexatious and dangerous question, that we agree to adopt this arbitrary line. And this compromise, upon which most of his fame rests, originated under like circumstances, with the Senator who now with such settled purpose declares his opposition to a fair application of its principle to the present case. Then all the Territory involved, that of Missouri was slave territory; the compromise act prohibited slavery in a part of the territory. Now, according to the position of the Senator, slavery is excluded from the whole territory of California and New Mexico. What, then, would the application of the spirit of the Missouri compromise require? Clearly that in running the line the question should be put at rest by declaring that below said line slavery should be permitted. It is common property of the States, and if it be proposed to make a division of it, fairness and future peace require that the rights and conditions of each part should be prescribed. Less than this would but narrow the ground and preserve the controversy. And unless that compromise was founded in fraud, we expect its application in this case, where all is disputed, express provisions on both sides of the line. We cannot agree to leave the question open, especially after what has been said to-day. It is the effect and not the form which I consider it my duty to examine. What matters it whether it be under cover of the acts of the Mexican Government, or by the operation of Congressional law, that slavery is excluded? The effect is the same, under the rule the Senator from Kentucky adopts, as would result from an act of prohibition by the Congress of the United States. I can only say that whenever the Senator chooses to make his argument, I shall be ready to meet it.

Mr. CLAY. I propose that these resolutions be made the order of the day for Tuesday next.

The resolutions were then made the special order of the day for Tuesday next.

HOUSE OF REPRESENTATIVES.

TUESDAY, February 5.

Obituary.

Mr. HAYMOND arose and addressed the House as follows:

Mr. SPEAKER: I have risen for the purpose of announcing to this House the death of the honorable ALEXANDER NEWMAN, a member elect to a seat in this Congress from the fifteenth Congressional district of Virginia, which district I have the honor to represent.

Mr. NEWMAN, while on a visit to Pittsburg in July last, fell a victim to the terrible scourge of Asiatic cholera, which has stricken down so many of our people in the valley of the Mississippi and Ohio rivers during the past year, and closed his mortal career in a few hours after he was taken ill. He left, sir, I am informed, a young and numerous family of children that looked to him for protection and support.

Mr. NEWMAN was a native of Virginia, and was born in 1806, in the vicinity of Orange.

I knew him well and favorably from the time he entered public life until the day of his decease. He was a gentleman of warm and of ardent feelings, firm and steadfast in his political opinions, kind and courteous in his social relations. When quite young, and shortly after he was married, Mr. Newman removed to and settled in the county of Marshall. In 1836 he was first elected a member of the Legislature of his native State from that county; which he continued to represent for several years, and until he was elected by his district to represent them in the State Senate; in which several stations he so conducted himself as to secure the support and confidence of his constituents. In June, 1845, he was appointed postmaster for the city of Wheeling, which position he continued to occupy until March, 1849, when he resigned, and became a candidate for a seat on this floor. He was elected over a talented and distinguished gentleman, and would at this time be occupying the seat which I now occupy, if he had not been stricken down in the prime of life.

Mr. Haymond offered the following resolutions of condolence, which were agreed to:

Resolved, That this House, having heard with deep regret of the death of the Hon. Alexander Newman, a member elect of this body from the fifteenth Congressional District of Virginia, will, as a mark of respect for his memory, wear crape on the left arm for thirty days.

Resolved, That this resolution be forwarded to his family.

Resolved, As a further mark of respect, that this House do now adjourn.

And so the House adjourned.

IN SENATE.

Tuesday, February 5.

Mr. Clay's Compromise Resolutions.

Mr. Mangum moved that the Senate proceed to the consideration of the special order.

The Senate accordingly, as in Committee of the Whole, proceeded to the consideration of the resolutions submitted by Mr. Clay, on the 29th ultimo, proposing an amicable arrangement of all questions in controversy between the Free and the Slave States, growing out of the subject of slavery.

Mr. Clay addressed the Senate at great length in suppport and defence of his resolutions. Before he had concluded he gave way for a motion to adjourn.

Thursday, February 7.

Mr. Clay's Compromise.

The Senate proceeded to the consideration of the special order, being the resolutions submitted by the Senator from Kentucky, (Mr. Clay.) Mr. Clay resumed and concluded his argument in their support.

Thursday, February 14.

Constitution of California.

The Vice President laid before the Senate the following message, transmitted by the President of the United States:

To the Senate of the United States:

I transmit herewith to the Senate, for the information of that body, an authenticated copy of the "Constitution of the State of California," received by me from the Hon. William M. Gwin.

Z. TAYLOR.

Washington, *February* 13, 1850.

Mr. Douglas. Mr. President, I move to refer the message, and accompanying papers to the Committee on Territories.

Mr. Benton. It had been my expectation, sir, that the honorable Senator from Kentucky (Mr. Clay) would make a motion for a select committee on the President's message which has just come in. I think, sir, that it is an appropriate occasion for such a committee, and that the honorable Senator from Kentucky is the appropriate person to make the motion. I wait, sir, to see if he will, in obedience to a sense of public duty, make that motion.

Mr. Clay. Mr. President, after the motion which has been made by the honorable Senator from Illinois, it would not be in order to propose a reference to a select committee.

Mr. Douglas. I will, with the permission of the Senate, state to the honorable Senator from Kentucky, that if it is his wish to submit that motion, I will waive my own.

The motion to refer the documents to the Committee on Territories was then withdrawn.

Mr. Clay. I am very sensible, indeed, of the courtesy of the honorable Senator from Illinois. It was not my purpose to make the motion to refer this subject to a select committee. The honorable Senator from Missouri (Mr. Benton) and myself had some little conversation on the subject a day or two ago, in the course of which he kindly expressed a wish that I would make such a motion; but I told him, I think, that my personal feelings were such that I had no desire to take the lead upon the subject; but I added that, if it were the pleasure of the Senate to direct me to act in conjunction with any select committee on the subject, especially as it had had the kindness heretofore to exonerate me from the duty of acting on its standing committees, I should feel myself bound most cheerfully to obey that wish; but at the same time that I could not, in accordance with my present feelings, make the motion myself.

Mr. Foote. I move, sir, that the subject lie upon the table for the present.

Mr. Douglas. I hope it will not take that course, but that it may go to some committee.

Mr. Foote. The reason why I wish the subject to lie over is, that I hold in my hand a resolution which I propose to offer and which embraces this whole subject. I would have offered it to-day only I thought that the attention of the Senate would have been called to other matters more pressing.

The motion to postpone was rejected by a vote of 20 to 18.

Mr. DOUGLAS. I now move that the message be referred to the Committee on Territories.

Mr. BENTON. Mr. President, I but pursue a course according to the early precedents and the early action of the Senate. I have in my hand a memorandum of the admission of all the States which have been admitted into this Union from Vermont to Iowa. The course which was followed in the admission of the whole of them down to Wisconsin, was to refer the applications for the admission of new States, together with the President's message by which they were usually communicated, to committees named by the Senate. The first precedent which I find upon this subject relates to the admission of Vermont. "In the House of Representatives, on the 9th of February, 1791, a message was received from the President of the United States communicating authentic documents, asking, with the consent of the State of New York, that Vermont be admitted into the Union." That message and accompanying documents were referred to three members. I find—

"*February 12th*, bill for admission of Vermont, received from the Senate."

"In the Senate of the United States, 9th February, 1791, a message was received from the President of the United States.

"*Ordered*, That the message from the President of the United States of this date, with the papers accompanying it, be referred to Messrs. King, Monroe, Ellsworth, Langdon, and Hawkins, to consider and report what is proper to be done thereon."

These are the early precedents, sir, on which I think we may act.

I think the present is an appropriate occasion for referring the President's message to a committee specially appointed by the Senate for that purpose, and I will therefore submit a motion that the Senator from Kentucky be chairman of such a committee by order of the Senate. If the Senator himself does not feel justified by his personal feelings in coming forward on this occasion—though I believe if he yielded to a sense of public duty he would feel that the country looks to him on this occasion—but if he does not feel himself at liberty from personal considerations, I, sir, will make the motion, and now move that it be referred to a select committee of which the Senator from Kentucky is to be chairman—the rest to be appointed by the Senate.

The VICE PRESIDENT. It is moved that this message be referred to a select committee, to be appointed by the Senate, of which the Senator from Kentucky (Mr. CLAY) is to be chairman. The Chair is in doubt whether this can be done under the rules, unless by unanimous consent.

Mr. FOOTE. I object to that motion. I wish it to be understood, however, that I have no objection to the honorable Senator from Kentucky at all; but I hold in my hand a resolution which I intended to offer during the day, the object of which is to permit this particular subject, with all the questions now before the Senate on the subject of slavery, together with all bills, to be referred to a special committee of fifteen members of the Senate, to be chosen by ballot. For one, sir, I am unwilling that the different portions of this subject shall be divided. I am anxious that a special committee shall be raised by ballot to consider the whole question in all its bearings, which are so well known that it is unnecessary for me to explain them. It is on that account, and not because I have not the most exalted respect for the honorable Senator from Kentucky, that I object to the motion.

Mr. DOUGLAS. I rise merely to state that I submitted the motion in obedience to what I considered my duty, to refer this message and the constitution accompanying it to the Committee on Territories, to which all the other bills in relation to the same subject have been referred; and I wish to state further, that if it is the desire of the Senate, in the present attitude of affairs, to raise a select committee as proposed, I will interpose no objection. On the contrary, I will be entirely willing, not only that this should go there, but that all the other bills and resolutions on this subject which have been referred to the Committee on Territories shall be reported back and sent there too.

I merely wish to state that, in making the motion, I have no desire and no feeling on the subject, and I hope the Senate will take that course which they think is due to the subject to take, without reference to any feelings of delicacy.

Mr. FOOTE. I am not desirous to submit my motion at the present moment, especially as the time is come for taking up the order of the day; and it is not, in my opinion, seemly that we should continue this debate under present circumstances. I move, therefore, that the further consideration of this subject be postponed until to-morrow morning.

Mr. MILLER. I would suggest to the honorable Senator from Mississippi whether it would not be better to order the constitution to be printed.

Mr. FOOTE. Certainly; include that in my motion.

The further consideration of the subject was then postponed and the message and accompanying documents were ordered to be printed.

The Compromise.

The Senate proceeded to the consideration of the special order, being the series of resolutions introduced by Mr. CLAY.

Mr. DAVIS, of Mississippi, addressed the Senate for an hour and a half, and then gave way.

Appointment of a Select Committee.

Mr. FOOTE submitted the following resolution:

Resolved, That the message of the President this day received, on the subject of admitting California as a State into the Union, with the accompanying documents, be referred to a special committee of fifteen, to be chosen by ballot, whose duty it shall be to consider the same, and also to take into consideration the various propositions now before the Senate relating to the same subject, in connection with the question of domestic slavery, in all its various bearings, and to report, if they find it practicable to do so, a plan for the definitive settlement of the present unhappy controversy, and rescue from impending perils the sacred Union itself.

On motion, the Senate adjourned.

Monday, February 18.

Mr. Calhoun resumed his seat this morning for the first time since his severe indisposition.

The Compromise.

The Senate resumed the consideration of the special order, being a series of resolutions offered by Mr. Clay.

Mr. Downs addressed the Senate for upwards of two hours, and without concluding, gave way for a motion to adjourn.

The Senate adjourned.

Tuesday, February 19.

The Compromise.

The Senate proceeded to the consideration of the special order, being a series of resolutions some time since submitted by Mr. Clay.

Mr. Downs resumed and concluded the speech which he commenced yesterday.

Mr. Miller next obtained the floor; but as it was too late to proceed to-day, and as the Senator from Alabama was entitled to the floor on another object—the reference of the President's message accompanying the constitution of the State of California—he moved that the further consideration of this subject be postponed to Thursday next; which was agreed to.

On motion, the Senate then proceeded to the consideration of Executive business; and, after some time, the doors were reopened, and

The Senate adjourned.

Thursday, February 21.

The Compromise.

The Senate resumed the consideration of the resolutions some time since offered by Mr. Clay.

Mr. Miller resumed and concluded the speech which he commenced on Thursday last.

Mr. Rusk. As there is a special order for to-morrow, I will move that these resolutions be postponed until Wednesday.

Mr. Walker. I would ask if it is the intention of the honorable Senator to address the Senate upon the resolutions on that day?

Mr. Rusk. That is my object.

The motion was agreed to, and the resolutions were accordingly postponed until Wednesday.

Committee to Prepare a Compromise.

Mr. Foote. I now ask permission, sir, to renew the motion which I made this morning for the appointment of a committee of thirteen, with certain instructions, for the purpose of maturing a scheme of compromise for the adjustment of all pending questions growing out of the subject of slavery. I will state that the resolution which I have presented for this purpose has been carefully drawn; and that it will not interfere in the least degree with the propositions that have been or may be submitted by any other gentleman. If this resolution be adopted and the questions referred, the resolutions of the Senator from Kentucky will still be before the Senate, as the motion of the Senator from Missouri to refer the President's message in relation to the admission of California to the Committee on Territories, will also be for consideration. My object is not to interfere with debate, but to let it go on for a few days, and in the mean time I hope the committee will be accorded by the Senate. I have an abiding and entire confidence that the thirteen gentlemen selected to serve upon that committee will arrange some scheme for the permanent adjustment of those questions that now agitate the country. And, sir, if this be not speedily done, much more serious consequences than those which we have yet realized will inevitably ensue. I do hope that under the circumstances, honorable Senators, if they have not very good reasons for voting against my resolution, will sustain it.

Mr. Clemens. How will this committee be constituted?

Mr. Foote. The motion is to select by ballot six Senators from the slaveholding and six from the free States; and the thirteenth member to be chosen by the twelve thus elected; and the duty of the committee is prescribed in the paper which I have submitted to the Senate.

Wednesday, February 27.

The Compromise.

The Senate resumed the consideration of the resolutions submitted by Mr. Clay, in relation to the adjustment of the questions in controversy between the States of the Union arising out of the institution of slavery.

Mr. Benton. Mr. President: It has been affirmed and denied on this floor that slavery was abolished in Mexico. I am one of those who affirm its abolition; and I propose now to read some passages from Mexican law, for the purpose of supporting my opinion. In doing this, I shall have recourse to authentic law publications in Mexico, and shall produce the laws on which I rely, both in the original language and in an English translation. I begin with the decree of the President Guerrera in 1829, and read from a book which was printed in the city of Mexico in the year 1838, and which is the eleventh volume of the laws of Mexico, officially published under the orders of the Supreme Government. I will read the title-page to show its authentic and official character. This is it:

"Recopilacion de leyes, decretos, bandos, reglamentos, circulares, y providencias de los supremos poderes y otras autoridades de la republica Mexicana. Formada de orden del Supremo Gobierno por al lic. Basilio Jose Arrillaga."

In English this title reads thus:

"Collection of laws, decrees, proclamations, regulations, circulars, and official orders of the supreme powers, and other authorities of the Mexican Republic, made by order of the Supreme Government by the lawyer Basilio José Arrillaga."

From this title it will be seen that this volume, from which I propose to read the decree of 1829, is not only authentic and official, but that it is the work of a lawyer acting under the orders of the Supreme Government, and supposed to know what were and what were not the laws of his country. With this exposition of the character of the work, and its title to credit, I proceed to read the decree. It stands thus on page 213, under the month of September, 1829:

"*Dia* 15.—*Decreto del Gobierno en virtud de facultades estraordinarias.*

"*Abolicion de la esclavitud en la república.*—1°. Queda abolida la esclavitud en la republica. 2°. Son por consiguiente libres los que hasta hoy se habian considerado como esclavos. 3°. Cuando las circunstancias del erario lo permitan, se indemnizará á los propietarios de esclavos en los terminos que dispusieren las leyes. (*Se circulo el mismo dia por la secretaría de relaciones, y se publico en bando de* 16.)"

In English:

"*Day* 15.—*Decree of the Government in virtue of extraordinary powers.*

"*Abolition of slavery in the republic.*—1. Slavery is abolished in the republic. 2. Consequently those are free who until now have been considered as slaves. 3. When the circumstances of the treasury permit it, the owners of slaves shall be indemnified in the manner prescribed by the laws. (*Circulated the same day from the Department of Relations, and published in the proclamation of the* 16*th.*)"

This is the decree of Guerrera, the validity of which has been disputed, and not without reason, if nothing further had been done. It was a decree, and not a law; and a decree upon a legislative subject. It was an executive decree upon a matter of legislation, and its validity was questioned at the time. Two years afterwards (that is to say, in the year 1831) the General Congress occupied itself with reviewing all the acts of the President Guerrera in virtue of the extraordinary powers conferred upon him, and on the 15th of February of that year passed a law in relation to them. This law classified the whole of these acts, annulled some classes, confirmed others, and reserved some for the future revision of the General Congress. This latter class appears to have comprehended the decree of the 15th September, 1829, in relation to the abolition of slavery, and was in these words:

"9. Todas las leyes, decretos, reglamentos, ordenes y providencias que en virtud de las citadas facultades extraordinarias expidió el gobierno, y son del resorte del poder legislativo, se sujetan á la calificacion del Congreso General, quedando desde ahora sin valor, hasta su revision por las camaras."—p. 38.

In English: "9. All the laws, decrees, regulations, orders, and instructions issued by the Government in virtue of its extraordinary powers, and which are of legislative cognizance, will be subject to the qualification of the General Congress, remaining from this time without force until their revision by the chambers."

This act is cautiously drawn. It does not annul the decree of the 15th of September; it does not confirm it; it admits its validity up to that time, but suspends it until the General Congress should act upon it. This action took place—took place in April, 1837—and I will now read the act which was then passed. It is in the same authentic collection of the laws of Mexico—Arrillaga's collection—from which I have already read, and is volume thirteenth of that collection. At page 270 of this volume, under date of April 5th, 1837, we find this act of the General Congress:

"*Dia* 5.—*Queda abolida la esclavitud en la republica sin excepcion alguna.*

"1°. Queda abolida, sin excepcion alguna, la esclavitud en toda la republica. 2°. Los dueños de esclavos manumitidos por la presente ley, ó por el decreto de 15 de Setiembre de 1829, (*Recopilacion de ese mes, p.* 213,) seran indemnizados del interes de ellos, estimandose este por la calificacion que se haga de sus calidades personales; a cuyo efecto se nombrará un perito por el comisario general, ó quien haga sus veces, y otro por el dueño; y en caso de discordia un tercero, que nombrará el alcalde constitucional respectivo, sin que pueda interponerse recurso alguno de esta determinacion. La indemnizacion de que habla este articulo, no tendrá lugar respecto de los colonos de Texas que hayan tomado parte en la revolucion de aquel departamiento." (*Se circulo en el mismo dia por el ministerio del interior y se publicó en bando de* 7.)

IN ENGLISH: "*Day* 5.—*Slavery is abolished in the Republic, without any exception.*

"1. Slavery is abolished, without any exception, in the whole Republic. 2. The masters of slaves manumitted by the present law, or by the decree of the 15th of September, 1829, (Recopilacion of that month, p. 213,) shall be indemnified for their value, (*del interes de ellos,*) according to the estimate which shall be made of their personal qualities; to which effect there shall be named a competent person (*un perito*) by the commissary general, or whoever occupies his place, and another by the master; and in case of disagreement a third, who shall be named by the respective constitutional alcalde, without any recourse from this determination. The indemnification of which this article speaks, shall not have operation with respect to those colonists of Texas, who may have taken part in the revolution of that department. (*Circulated the same day by the Minister of the Interior, and published in proclamation of the 7th.*)"

This act of the General Congress is a full confirmation of the Presidential decree of September, 1829, and that without reference to the meaning of the verb "*queda*," twice used, and which signifies literally "*remains.*" The literal translation would be, "*slavery remains abolished*," &c., which would imply that it had been abolished before. I translate it idiomatically, and as equivalent to "*is;*" but consider it of no importance here, as the law expressly confirms the abolition decree of Guerrera.

Thus far we have a decree, disputed, abolishing slavery in Mexico, and a law, not disputable, confirming that decree; and here I might stop; but the case requires me to go on, and I produce other law, and still higher than that which I have quoted. I allude to the Constitution of the Republic of Mexico of the year 1843. I have a copy of the Mexican constitution of that year—an authentic copy—printed under the license which the law requires. For, to avoid errors in the editions of that fundamental law, it is forbid, by law, to be reprinted except by the permission of the Supreme Government or of the General Congress. This copy was printed in the city of Mexico the 12th day of June, 1843—the day of the signature and promulgation of the constitution—and bears its authorization upon its title page. I consider it authentic, and produce it as such; and in article 9, title 2, of this constitution, and under the head which treats of the rights of the inhabitants of the Republic, and at the head of the enumeration of those rights, stands this declaration:

"1. Ninguno es esclavo en el territorio de la nacion, y el que se introduzca se considerarà en la clase de libre, quedando bajo la proteccion de las leyes."

In English: "1. No one is slave in the territory of the nation, and any introducted shall be considered free, and shall be under the protection of the laws."

This is the declaration of the Constitution of Mexico, and applies both to the present and the future. It declares that there are no slaves in the territory of the nation, and if any are brought in they shall be free. This is surely enough—enough to satisfy all minds, that slavery has been abolished in Mexico, and that there is not the least ground for fearing, or hoping, that it can ever exist in California or New Mexico by virtue of Mexican law. It is enough, I think; but I have more authority yet, and will produce it, though a work of supererogation. For this is a case to multiply authorities until doubt is extinguished—to heap up and pile up—to put Pelion upon Ossa—until all beneath is crushed into atoms and expunged from view. Behold this formidable quarto! [holding up a large book.] It is a Spanish law dictionary, printed in Madrid, reprinted in Mexico, gone through several editions in each country, and authority in both. It is the law dictionary of *Escriche* in Spain, and of *San Miguel* in Mexico; and here is one, and there is the other. The Spanish edition is full upon the subject of *slaves* and *slavery:* the Mexican reprint of the same work (1837) omits the definitions, and says, under the head "*esclavitud*," it is not necessary to occupy a couple of columns with slavery and the slave trade—that the trade was abolished by treaty with Great Britain, and slavery itself by the laws of the republic—and then speaks of Guerrera's decree of 1829, and of the confirmatory act of 1837, in these words:

"El decreto de 15 de Setiembre de 1829, dió libertad á los esclavos que ya existen en la república, bajo indemnizacion à sus duenos ó poseedores para que no apareciese atacada la propiedad: y últimamente en Abril de 1837, se ha publicada nueva ley sobre abolicion de la esclavitud."

In English: "The decree of the 15th of September, 1829, gave liberty to the slaves then in the republic, with indemnity to their owners or possessors, that property might not seem to be attacked: and finally, in April, 1837, a new law had been published on the abolition of slavery."

This is the historical account of the abolition of slavery in Mexico. The reprint was in the year 1837, and therefore could not mention the constitutional declaration of 1843. The law dictionary of *Escriche*, and its reprint with notes and additions by *San Miguel*, to adapt it to the Mexican jurisprudence, are of as high authority in Spain, and in the American States of Spanish origin, as the law dictionary of *Jacob* is with us.

I quote no more upon this head. I think every one must see that slavery was abolished throughout the Mexican territory before the cession of California and New Mexico to the United States, and that slavery cannot exist there now by virtue of Mexican law. This is as far as I propose to go upon that point at present. I limit myself to showing its abolishment, by Mexican law, before we acquired the countries; and that is enough, in my opinion, to show the Wilmot proviso, in relation to these countries, to be a thing of nothing—an empty provision—a cloud without rain—unless it be a rain of blood.

But there is another view of this point which I mean to touch, and that is, to show that African slavery never did exist in Mexico in the form that it now exists in any State of this Union; that there were differences in the Mexican law while it existed, and that to such a degree that it nearly prevented slavery in Mexico; and that, if that law was now in full force in New Mexico and California, not a single slaveholder in any State of this Union would carry a slave there except to set him free. These differences went to the facilities and the rights of manumission, and arose from the opposite policy of the two countries; in the United States to discourage emancipation, in Mexico to promote it. To show these differences I will read from Humboldt's essay on New Spain, and from the law dictionary of *Escriche*. I use Humboldt first, and read from the Paris, quarto edition, of 1808:

"D'ailleurs, les esclaves, qui heureusement se trouvent en très-petit nombre au Mexique, y sont, comme dans toutes les possessions espagnoles, un peu plus protégé par les lois que les nègres qui habitent les colonies des autres nations européenes. Ces lois sont toujours interprétées en faveur de la liberté. Le Gouvernement désire voir augmenter le nombre des affranchis. Un esclave qui par son industrie, s'est procuré quelque argent, peut forcer son maître de l'affranchir en lui payant la somme modique de 1,500 ou 2,000 livres. La liberté ne sauroit être refusée au nègre sous prétexte qu'il a couté le triple en l'acherant, ou qu'il possède un talent particulier pour exercer un métier lucratif. Un esclave qui a été cruellement maltraité, acquiert par la même son affranchisement d'après la loi, si toutesfois le juge embrasse la cause de l'opprimé. On concoit que cette loi bienfaisante doit être bien souvent éludée. J'ai vu cependant à Mexique même, au mois de juillet, 1803, l'example de deux négresses à qui le magistrat qui fait les fonctions *d'alcalde du corte*, donna la liberté, parceque leur maîtresse, une dame native des îles, les avoit couvertes de blesseures faites avec des ciseaux, des épingles et des canifs."—*Page* 133–'4.

"Le royaume de la Nouvelle Espagne est, de toutes les colonies des Européens sous la zone torride, celle dans la quelle il y a le moins de nègres. On peut presque dire qu'il n'y a point d'esclaves. On parcourt toute la ville de Mexico sans trouver un visage noir. Le service d'aucune maison ne s'y fait avec des esclaves. Sous ce point de vue surtout, le Mexique offre un contraste bien grand avec la Havane, avec Lima et Caraccas."—*Page* 130.

In English: "Moreover, the slaves, who happily find themselves in very small number in Mexico, are there, as in all the Spanish possessions, a little more protected by the laws than the negroes who inhabit the colonies of other European nations. The laws are always interpreted in favor of liberty. The Government desires to see the number of enfranchised augmented. A slave who, by his industry, may have procured money, can compel his master to enfranchise him by paying him the moderate sum of 1,500 or 2,000 livres.* Liberty cannot be refused a negro under the pretext that he cost the triple in purchasing him, or that he possesses a special talent for exercising a lucrative trade. A slave who has been cruelly maltreated acquires thereby his enfranchisement according to the law, provided always the judge embraces the cause of the oppressed. One may conceive that this beneficent law is often eluded. I saw, nevertheless, in Mexico itself, in the month of July, 1803, the example of two negresses to whom the magistrate who exercised the functions of *alcalde of the court*, gave their liberty, because their mistress, a native woman of the islands, had covered them with wounds made with scissors, pins, and knives."—*Page* 133–'4.

"The kingdom of New Spain is, of all the colonies of the Europeans under the torrid zone, that in which there are the fewest negroes; one may almost say that there are no slaves. One may go all over the city of Mexico without meeting a black face. No house is there served with slaves. Under this point of view, above all, Mexico offers a great contrast with Havana, with Lima, and Caraccas."—*Page* 130.

I will now read from *Escriche*, who, as a law writer, is more full and precise, and shows such a multitude of cases in which a slave could easily obtain or actually force his freedom, that, under such laws, in a country where slaves were of any value, no man would or could hold them. I read from the dictionary, under the words, *Esclavo*, *Esclavitud:*

"El señor hace suyo todo cuanto ganan y adquieren por cualquier titulo sus esclavos; y si los pusiere al frente de tienda, nave ú otro cualquiera establecimiento, queda obligado á guardar y cumplir los contratos que hicieren, como si él mismo hubiese intervenido en ellos."—*Ley* 7, *tit.* 21, *Part.* 4.

"El señor que fuere mayor de catorce años puede dar libertad á su esclavo en testamento; y el que fuere mayor de veinte puede darsela en instrumento, ó ante el juez, ó bien ante amigos, con asistencia de cinco testigos; mas el minor de veinte y mayor de diez y siete puede darla ante el juez con otorgamiento de su curador, á su hijo habido en esclava, á su padre, madre, hermano y maestro, á su nodriga, á la persona que le hubiere criado, á la que hubiese criado el mismo, y á su hermano de leche, al siervo que le hubiese librado de muerte ó de deshonra, al que quisiere hacer administrador extrajudicial de sus cosas siendo de diez y siete años, y á la esclava con quien tratare de casarse."—*Ley* 1, *tit.* 22, *Part.* 4.

"Si dos ó mas señores tuvieren un esclavo, puede libertarlo cualquiera de ellos, dando á los otros el justo precio de la parte que á cada uno correspondiente; y aun puede comprarlo un tercero con objeto de darle libertad."—*Ley* 2, *tit.* 22, *Part.* 4.

"Merece la libertad el esclavo en los cuatro casos siguientes: 1°. Si delatase al raptor ó forzador de muger virgen: 2°. Si descubriese al que hace moneda falsa: 3°. Si descubriese al gefe militar que abandonó su puesto: 4°. Si acusare al homicida de su señor, ó vengare su muerte, ó descubriere traicion contra al rey ó el reino. En los tres primeros casos debe el rey dar el precio de esclavo á su dueño."—*Ley* 3, *tit.* 23, *Part.* 4.

"Si el dueño prostituyere públicamente á su esclava, queda esta libre por el mismo hecho, y no puede aquel recobrar ni tener deréchо alguno sobre ella."—*Ley* 4, *tit.* 22, *Part.* 4.

"Adquiere par fin libertad el esclavo, por el matrimonio que contrajere con persona libre, ó por las órdenes sagradas que recibiere, con noticia y consentimiento de su señor; como tambien por la prescripcion, cuando con buena fé se tratare como libre por diez años en la tierra donde mora su señor ó por veinte en otra, ó sin buena fé por espacio de treinta."—*Leyes* 5, 6, *and* 7, *tit.* 22, *Part.* 4.

In English: "The master makes his own whatever his slaves gain and acquire, by whatever title; and if he puts them at the head of a shop, stall, or

* $300 to $400.

other establishment whatsoever, he shall be obliged to attend to and fulfil all contracts they may make, as if himself had entered into them."—*Law* 7, *tit.* 21, *Part* 4.

"The master who may be above the age of fourteen years may liberate his slave by testament; and he who may be above the age of twenty, may liberate him by instrument, or before the judge, or even before friends, with the aid of five witnesses; moreover, the minor of twenty and over sixteen, may give liberty, with consent of his guardian, to his child had by a slave woman, to his father, mother, brother, and teacher, or to his nurse, or to the person who shall have brought him up, or whom he shall have brought up, and to his foster-brother, to the servant who may have saved him from death or from dishonor, to him whom he may wish to make extrajudicial administrator of his goods, being of seventeen years, and to the slave woman with whom he may propose to marry."—*Law* 1, *tit.* 22, *Part* 4.

"If two or more masters have a slave, either of them may liberate him, giving to the others the just price which belongs to each; and even a third party may purchase him for the purpose of setting him free."—*Law* 2, *tit.* 22, *Part* 4.

"The slave shall deserve his liberty in the four following cases: 1. If he shall inform on the ravisher or forcer of a virgin woman; 2. If he discovers the maker of false money; 3. If he shall discover a military chief who abandons his post; 4. If he shall inform on the murderer of his master, or shall avenge his death, or discover treason against the king or the kingdom. In the three first cases the king shall give the price of the slave to his master."—*Law* 3, *tit.* 22, *Part* 4.

"If the master publicly prostitutes his slave woman, she is thereby freed, and he cannot recover her, or have any right over her."—*Law* 4, *tit.* 22, *Part* 4.

"Finally, a slave will acquire his liberty by contracting matrimony with a freed person, or by receiving sacred orders, with the knowledge and consent of his master; as likewise by prescription, when in good faith he shall be called a free man for ten years in the country where his master lives, or for twenty years in another, or without good faith for the space of thirty."—*Laws* 5, 6, 7, *tit.* 22, *Part* 4.

I conclude this exposition of Mexican law in relation to slavery by producing the definition of that word in Spanish law. For this purpose, I quote from the same law dictionary, *Escriche*, where we find it thus: "*Esclavitud: El estado de un hombre que es propiedad de otro contra el derecho natural.*" In English: "*Slavery: the condition of a man who is the property of another against natural right.*" I quote this definition for the purpose of showing that, under the laws of Spain, in force in Mexico, slavery was held to be against natural right—therefore not derived from nature, or divine law, but founded in municipal law, and only existing by positive enactment—and, by consequence, that no argument in favor of slavery in New Mexico or California as an institution of divine origin, or of any origin in any place, independent of positive law, can derive any countenance from Spanish law. Further than this I do not go at present. I limit myself to the three points, which, I believe, I have established: *first*, that slavery was abolished in California and New Mexico before we acquired those countries; *secondly*, that, even if not abolished, no person would carry a slave to these countries to be held under such law; *thirdly*, that no slavery can hereafter exist in either of those countries, except by virtue of positive law, yet to be passed. The practical application which I make of this exposition of law is, that the proviso of which we have heard so much is of no force whatever—unnecessary in any point of view—and of no more effect, if passed, than a piece of blank paper pasted on the statute book.

Mr. Rusk then addressed the Senate for an hour mainly on the subject of the boundary of Texas, and then gave way for a motion to adjourn; and the Senate adjourned.

Monday, March 4.

The Compromise.

The Senate proceeded to the consideration of the special order, being the resolutions submitted by Mr. Clay, upon which this day had been assigned to the Senator from South Carolina, (Mr. Calhoun.)

Mr. Calhoun. As much indisposed as I have been, Mr. President and Senators, I have felt it to be my duty to express to you my sentiments upon the great question which has agitated the country and occupied your attention. And I am under peculiar obligations to the Senate for the very courteous manner in which they have afforded me an opportunity of being heard to-day.

I had hoped that it would have been in my power during the last week to have delivered my views in relation to this all-engrossing subject, but I was prevented from doing so by being attacked by a cold which is at this time so prevalent and which has retarded the recovery of my strength.

Acting under the advice of my friends, and apprehending that it might not be in my power to deliver my sentiments before the termination of the debate, I have reduced to writing what I intended to say. And, without further remark, I will ask the favor of my friend, the Senator behind me to read it.

Mr. Mason. It affords me great pleasure to comply with the request of the honorable Senator, and to read his remarks.

The honorable gentleman then read Mr. Calhoun's remarks as follows:

Mr. Calhoun. I have, Senators, believed from the first that the agitation of the subject of slavery would, if not prevented by some timely and effective measure, end in disunion. Entertaining this opinion, I have on all proper occasions, endeavored to call the attention of each of the two great parties which divide the country to adopt some measure to prevent so great a disaster, but without success. The agitation has been permitted to proceed, with almost no attempt to resist it, until it has reached a period when it can no longer be disguised or denied that the Union is in danger. You have thus had forced upon you the greatest and the gravest question that can ever come under your consideration: How can the Union be preserved?

To give a satisfactory answer to this mighty question, it is indispensable to have an accurate and thorough knowledge of the nature and the character of the cause by which the Union is endangered. Without such knowledge it is impossible to pronounce, with any certainty, by what measure it can be saved; just as it would be impossible for a physician to pronounce, in the case of some dangerous disease, with any certainty, by what remedy the patient could be saved, without familiar knowledge of the nature and character of the cause of the disease. The first question, then, presented for consideration, in the investigation I propose to make, in order to obtain such knowledge, is: What is it that has endangered the Union?

To this question there can be but one answer: that the immediate cause is the almost universal discontent which pervades all the States composing the southern section of the Union. This widely-extended discontent is not of recent origin. It commenced with the agitation of the slavery question, and has been increasing ever since. The next question going one step further back, is: What has caused this widely-diffused and almost universal discontent?

It is a great mistake to suppose, as is by some, that it originated with demagogues, who excited the discontent with the intention of aiding their personal advancement, or with the disappointed ambition of certain politicians, who resorted to it as the means of retrieving their fortunes. On the contrary all the great political influences of the section were arrayed against excitement, and exerted to the utmost to keep the people quiet. The great mass of the people of the South were divided, as in the other section, into Whigs and Democrats. The leaders and the presses of both parties in the South were very solicitous to prevent excitement and to preserve quiet; because it was seen that the effects of the former would necessarily tend to weaken, if not destroy the political ties which united them with their respective parties in the other section. Those who know the strength of party ties will readily appreciate the immense force which this cause exerted against agitation and in favor of preserving quiet. But as great as it was, it was not sufficiently so to prevent the wide-spread discontent which now pervades the section. No, some cause far deeper and more powerful than the one supposed must exist to account for discontent so wide and deep. The question then recurs: What is the cause of this discontent? It will be found in the belief of the people of the southern States as prevalent as the discontent itself, that they cannot remain as things now are consistently with honor and safety in the Union. The next question to be considered is: What has caused this belief?

One of the causes is, undoubtedly, to be traced to the long-continued agitation of the slave question on the part of the North, and the many aggressions which they have made on the rights of the South during the time. I will not enumerate them at present, as it will be done hereafter, in its proper place.

There is another, lying back of it, with which this is intimately connected, that may be regarded as the great and primary cause. That is to be found in the fact that the equilibrium between the two sections of the Government as it stood when the constitution was ratified and the Government put in action, has been destroyed. At that time there was nearly a perfect equilibrium between the two, which afforded ample means to each to protect itself against the aggression of the other, but, as it now stands, one section has the exclusive power of controlling the Government, which leaves the other without any adequate means of protecting itself against its encroachment and oppression. To place this subject distinctly before you, I have, Senators, prepared a brief statistical statement, showing the relative weight of the two sections in the Government under the first census of 1790 and the last census of 1840.

According to the former, the population of the United States, including Vermont, Kentucky, and Tennessee, which then were in their incipient condition of becoming States, but were not actually admitted, amounted to 3,929,827. Of this number the northern States had 1,977,899, and the southern 1,952,072, making a difference of only 25,827 in favor of the former States. The number of States, including Vermont, Kentucky, and Tennessee, was sixteen, of which eight, including Vermont, belonged to the northern section, and eight, including Kentucky and Tennessee, to the southern; making an equal division of the States between the two sections under the first census. There was a small preponderance in the House of Representatives, and in the electoral college, in favor of the northern, owing to the fact, that, according to the provisions of the constitution, in estimating Federal numbers, five slaves count but three; but it was too small to affect sensibly the perfect equilibrium which, with that exception, existed at the time. Such was the equality of the two sections when the States composing them agreed to enter into a Federal Union. Since then the equilibrium between them has been greatly disturbed.

According to the last census the aggregate population of the United States amounted to 17,063,357, of which the northern section contained 9,728,920 and the southern 7,334,437, making a difference, in round numbers, of

2,400,000. The number of States had increased from sixteen to twenty-six, making an addition of ten States. In the mean time the position of Delaware had become doubtful as to which section she properly belongs. Considering her as neutral, the northern States will have thirteen, and the southern States twelve; making a difference in the Senate of two Senators in favor of the former. According to the apportionment under the census of 1840, there were 223 members of the House of Representatives, of which the northern States had 135 and the southern States (considering Delaware as neutral) 87; making a difference in favor of the former in the House of Representatives of 48. The difference in the Senate of two members, added to this, gives to the North in the electoral college a majority of 50. Since the census of 1840 four States have been added to the Union; Iowa, Wisconsin, Florida, and Texas. They leave the difference in the Senate as it stood when the census was taken, but add two to the side of the North in the House, making the present majority in the House in its favor 50, and in the electoral college 52.

The result of the whole is to give the northern section a predominance in every part of the Government, and thereby concentrate in it the two elements which constitute the Federal Government—a majority of States and a majority of their population, estimated in federal numbers. Whatever section concentrates the two in itself possesses the control of the entire Government.

But we are just at the close of the sixth decade, and the commencement of the seventh. The census is to be taken this year, which must add greatly to the decided preponderance of the North in the House of Representatives and in the electoral college. The prospect is, also, that a great increase will be added to its present preponderance in the Senate during the period of the decade, by the addition of new States. Two Territories, Oregon and Minnesota, are already in progress, and strenuous efforts are making to bring in three additional States from the territory recently conquered from Mexico; which, if successful, will add three other States in a short time to the northern section, making five States; and increasing the present number of its States from fifteen to twenty, and of its Senators from thirty to forty. On the contrary, there is not a single territory in progress in the southern section, and no certainty that any additional State will be added to it during the decade. The prospect, then, is, that the two sections in the Senate, should the efforts now made to exclude the South from the newly-acquired territories succeed, will stand, before the end of the decade, twenty northern States to twelve southern, (considering Delaware as neutral,) and forty northern Senators to twenty-four southern. This great increase of Senators added to the great increase of members of the House of Representatives and the electoral college on the part of the North, which must take place under the next decade, will effectually and irretrievably destroy the equilibrium which existed when the Government commenced.

Had this destruction been the operation of time, without the interference of Government, the South would have had no reason to complain; but such was not the fact. It was caused by the legislation of this Government, which was appointed as the common agent of all, and charged with the protection of the interests of and security of all. The legislation by which it has been effected may be classed under three heads. The first is, that series of acts by which the South has been excluded from the common territory belonging to all of the States, as the members of the Federal Union, and which have had the effect of extending vastly the portion allotted to the Northern section, and restricting within narrow limits the portion left the South; the next consists in adopting a system of revenue and disbursements, by which an undue proportion of the burden of taxation has been imposed upon the South and an undue proportion of its proceeds appropriated to the North; and the last is a system of political measures by which the original character of the Government has been radically changed. I propose to bestow upon each of these, in the order they stand, a few remarks with the view of showing that it is owing to the action of this Government that the equilibrium between the two sections has been destroyed, and the whole powers of the system centred in a sectional majority.

The first of the series of acts by which the South was deprived of its due share of the territories, originated with the Confederacy, which preceded the existence of this Government. It is to be found in the provision of the ordinance of 1787. Its effect was to exclude the South entirely from that vast and fertile region which lies between the Ohio and the Mississippi Rivers, now embracing five States and one Territory. The next of the series is the Missouri compromise, which excluded the South from that large portion of Louisiana which lies north of 36° 30′, excepting what is included in the State of Missouri. The last of the series excluded the South from the whole of the Oregon Territory. All these, in the slang of the day, were what are called slave territories, and not free soil; that is, territories belonging to slaveholding powers, and open to the emigration of masters with their slaves. By these several acts, the South was excluded from 1,238,025 square miles, an extent of country considerably exceeding the entire valley of the Mississippi. To the South was left the portion of the Territory of Louisiana lying south of 36° 30′, and the portion north of it included in the State of Missouri; the portion lying south of 36° 30′, including the States of Louisiana and Arkansas; and the territory lying west of the latter and south of 36° 30′, called the

Indian country. These, with the Territory of Florida, now the State, makes in the whole 283,503 square miles. To this must be added the territory acquired with Texas. If the whole should be added to the southern section, it would make an increase of 325,520, which would make the whole left to the South 609,023. But a large part of Texas is still in contest between the two sections, which leaves it uncertain what will be the real extent of the portion of territory that may be left to the South.

I have not included the territory recently acquired by the treaty with Mexico. The North is making the most strenuous efforts to appropriate the whole to herself, by excluding the South from every foot of it. If she should succeed it will add to that from which the South has already been excluded 526,078 square miles, and would increase the whole which the North has appropriated to herself to 1,764,023, not including the portion that she may succeed in excluding us from in Texas. To sum up the whole, the United States, since they declared their independence, have acquired 2,373,046 square miles of territory, from which the North will have excluded the South, if she should succeed in monopolizing the newly acquiring territories, from about three-fourths of the whole, leaving to the South but about one-fourth.

Such is the first and great cause that has destroyed the equilibrium between the two sections in the Government.

The next is the system of revenue and disbursements which has been adopted by the Government. It is well known that the Government has derived its revenue mainly from duties on imports. I shall not undertake to show that such duties must necessarily fall mainly on the exporting States, and that the South, as the great exporting portion of the Union, has in reality paid vastly more than her due proportion of the revenue; because I deem it unnecessary, as the subject has on so many occasions been fully discussed. Nor shall I, for the same reason, undertake to show that a far greater portion of the revenue has been disbursed at the North than its due share, and that the joint effect of these causes has been to transfer a vast amount from South to North, which, under an equal system of revenue and disbursements, would not have been lost to her. If to this be added, that many of the duties were imposed, not for revenue, but for protection; that is, intended to put money, not in the treasury, but directly into the pockets of the manufacturers, some conception may be formed of the immense amount which, in the long course of sixty years, has been transferred from South to North. There are no data by which it can be estimated with any certainty; but it is safe to say that it amounts to hundreds of millions of dollars. Under the most moderate estimate, it would be sufficient to add greatly to the wealth of the North, and thus greatly increase her population by attracting emigration from all quarters to that section.

This, combined with the great primary cause, amply explains why the North has acquired a preponderance over every department of the Government by its disproportionate increase of population and States. The former, as has been shown, has increased in fifty years 2,400,000 over that of the South. This increase of population during so long a period, is satisfactorily accounted for by the number of emigrants, and the increase of their descendants, which have been attracted to the northern section from Europe and the South, in conseqence of the advantages derived from the causes assigned. If they had not existed; if the South had retained all the capital which has been extracted from her by the fiscal action of the Government; and, if it had not been excluded by the ordinance of '87 and the Missouri compromise from the region lying between the Ohio and the Mississippi Rivers, and between the Mississippi and the Rocky Mountains north of 36° 30′, it scarcely admits of a doubt that it would have divided the emigration with the North, and by retaining her own people, would have at least equalled the North in population under the census of 1840, and probably under that about to be taken. She would also, if she had retained her equal rights in those territories, have maintained an equality in the number of States with the North, and have preserved the equilibrium between the two sections that existed at the commencement of the Government. The loss then of the equilibrium is to be attributed to the action of this Government.

But while these measures were destroying the equilibrium between the two sections, the action of the Government was leading to a radical change in its character, by concentrating all the power of the system in itself. The occasion will not permit me to trace the measures by which this great change has been consummated. If it did, it would not be difficult to show that the process commenced at an early period of the Government; that it proceeded, almost without interruption, step by step, until it absorbed virtually its entire powers. But, without going through the whole process to establish the fact, it may be done satisfactorily by a very short statement.

That the Government claims, and practically maintains, the right to decide in the last resort as to the extent of its powers, will scarcely be denied by any one conversant with the political history of the country. That it also claims the right to resort to force to maintain whatever power she claims, against all opposition, is equally certain. Indeed it is apparent, from what we daily hear, that this has become the prevailing and fixed opinion of a great majority of the community. Now, I ask, what limitation can possibly be placed upon the powers of a Government claiming and exercising such rights? And, if none can be, how can the separate governments of the States maintain and protect the powers reserved to them by the constitution, or the people of the several States maintain those which are reserved to them, and among others, the sovereign powers by which they ordained and established not only their separate State constitutions, and Governments, but also the constitution and Government of the United States? But, if they have no constitutional means of maintaining them against the right claimed by this Government, it necessarily follows that they hold them at its pleasure and discretion, and that all the powers of the system are in reality concentrated in it. It also follows that the character of the Government has been changed, in consequence, from a Federal Republic, as it originally came from the hands of its framers, and that it has been changed into a great national consolidated Democracy. It has indeed, at present, all the characteristics of the latter, and not one of the former, although it still retains its outward form.

The result of the whole of these causes combined is, that the North has acquired a decided ascendency over every department of this Government, and through it a control over all the powers of the system. A single section, governed by the will of the numerical majority, has now, in fact, the control of the Government and the entire powers of the system. What was once a constitutional Federal Republic is now converted, in reality, into one as absolute as that of the autocrat of Russia, and as despotic in its tendency as any absolute Government that ever existed.

As, then, the North has the absolute control over the Government, it is manifest that on all questions between it and the South, where there is a diversity of interests, the interests of the latter will be sacrificed to the former, however oppressive the effects may be, as the South possesses no means by which it can resist through the action of the Government. But if there was no question of vital importance to the South in reference to which there was a diversity of views between the two sections, this state of things might be endured without the hazard of destruction to the South. But such is not the fact. There is a question of vital importance to the southern section, in reference to which the views and feelings of the two sections are as opposite and hostile as they can possibly be.

I refer to the relation between the two races in the southern section, which constitutes a vital portion of her social organization. Every portion of the North entertains views and feelings more or less hostile to it. Those most opposed and hostile regard it as a sin, and consider themselves under the most sacred obligation to use every effort to destroy it. Indeed to the extent that they conceive they have the power, they regard themselves as implicated in the sin, and responsible for suppressing it by the use of all and every means. Those less opposed and hostile, regard it as a crime—an offence against humanity, as they call it; and although not so fanatical, feel themselves bound to use all efforts to effect the same object; while those who are least opposed and hostile, regard it as a blot and a stain on the character of what they call the nation, and feel themselves accordingly bound to give it no countenance or support. On the contrary, the southern section regards the relation as one which cannot be destroyed without subjecting the two races to the greatest calamity, and the section to poverty, desolation, and wretchedness; and accordingly they feel bound by every consideration of interest and safety to defend it.

This hostile feeling on the part of the North towards the social organization of the South long lay dormant, but it only required some cause to act on those who felt most intensely that they were responsible for its continuance to call it into action. The increasing power of this Government, and of the control of the northern section over all its departments, furnished the cause. It was this which made an impression on the minds of many that there was little or no restraint to prevent the Government from doing whatever it might choose to do. This was sufficient of itself to put the most fanatical portion of the North in action for the purpose of destroying the existing relation between the two races in the South.

The first organized movement towards it commenced in 1835. Then, for the first time, societies were organized, presses established, lecturers sent forth to excite the people of the North, and incendiary publications scattered over the whole South through the mail. The South was thoroughly aroused. Meetings were held everywhere, and resolutions adopted, calling upon the North to apply a remedy to arrest the threatened evil, and pledging themselves to adopt measures for their own protection if it was not arrested. At the meeting of Congress, petitions poured in from the North, calling upon Congress to abolish slavery in the District of Columbia, and to prohibit what they called the internal slave trade between the States, announcing at the same time that their ultimate object was to abolish slavery, not only in the District, but in the States and throughout the Union. At this period the number engaged in the agitation was small, and possessed little or no personal influence.

Neither party in Congress had, at that time, any sympathy with them or their cause. The members of each party presented their petitions with great reluctance. Nevertheless, as small and contemptible as the party then was, both of the great parties at the North dreaded them. They felt that, though small, they were organized in reference to a subject which had a great and commanding influence over the northern mind. Each party on that account feared to oppose their petitions lest the opposite party should take advantage of the one who might do so by favoring their petitions. The effect was, that both united in insisting that the petitions should be received, and that Congress should take jurisdiction of the subject for which they prayed. To justify their course, they took the extraordinary ground that Congress was bound to receive petitions on every subject, however objectionable it might be, and whether they had or had not jurisdiction over the subject. These views prevailed in the House of Represenatives, and partially in the Senate, and thus the party succeeded in their first movements in gaining what they proposed—a position in Congress from which agitation could be extended over the whole Union. This was the commencement of the agitation, which has ever since continued, and which, as is now acknowledged, has endangered the Union itself.

As for myself, I believed, at that early period, if the party who got up the petitions should succeed in getting Congress to take jurisdiction, that agitation would follow, and that it would, in the end, if not arrested, destroy the Union. I then so expressed myself in debate, and called upon both parties to take grounds against assuming jurisdiction, but in vain. Had my voice been heeded, and had Congress refused to take jurisdiction, by the united votes of all parties, the agitation which followed would have been prevented, and the fanatical zeal that gives impulse to the agitation, and which has brought us to our present perilous condition, would have become extinguished from the want of something to feed the flame. *That* was the time for the North to show her devotion to the Union; but unfortunately both of the great parties of that section were so intent on obtaining or retaining party ascendency, that all other considerations were overlooked or forgotten.

What has since followed are but the natural consequences. With the success of their first movement, this small fanatical party began to acquire strength; and with that to become an object of courtship to both the great parties. The necessary consequence was a further increase of power, and a gradual tainting of the opinions of both of the other parties with their doctrines until the infection has extended over both; and the great masses of the population of the North who, whatever may be their opinion of the original abolition party, which still preserves its distinctive organization, hardly ever fail, when it comes to acting, to co-operate in carrying out their measures. With the increase of their influence, they extended the sphere of their action. In a short time after the commencement of their first movement, they had acquired sufficient influence to induce the Legislatures of most of the northern States to pass acts which in effect abrogated the provision of the constitution that provides for the delivery up of fugitive slaves. Not long after petitions followed to abolish slavery in forts, magazines, and dock-yards, and all other places where Congress had exclusive power of legislation. This was followed by petitions and resolutions of Legislatures of the northern States and popular meetings, to exclude the southern States from all territories acquired or to be acquired, and to prevent the admission of any State hereafter into the Union which, by its constitution, does not prohibit slavery. And Congress is invoked to do all this expressly with the view to the final abolition of slavery in the States. That has been avowed to be the ultimate object from the beginning of the agitation until the present time; and yet the great body of both parties of the North, with the full knowledge of the fact, although disavowing the abolitionists, have co-operated with them in almost all their measures.

Such is a brief history of the agitation, as far as it has yet advanced. Now, I ask Senators, what is there to prevent its further progress, until it fulfils the ultimate end proposed, unless some decisive measure should be adopted to prevent it? Has any one of the causes, which has added to its increase from its original small and contemptible beginning until it has attained its present magnitude, diminished in force? Is the original cause of the movement, that slavery is a sin, and ought to be suppressed, weaker now than at the commencement? Or is the Abolition party less numerous or influential, or have they less influence over, or control over the two great parties of the North in elections? Or has the South greater means of influencing or controlling the movements of this Government now than it had when the agitation commenced? To all these questions but one answer can be given: no, no, no! The very reverse is true. Instead of being weaker, all the elements in favor of agitation are stronger now than they were in 1835, when it first commenced, while all the elements of influence on the part of the South are weaker. Unless something decisive is done, I again ask what is to stop this agitation, before the great and final object at which it aims —the abolition of slavery in the States—is consummated? Is it, then, not certain, that if something decisive is not now done to arrest it, the South will be forced to choose between abolition and secession? Indeed, as events are now moving, it will not require the South to secede to dissolve the Union. Agitation will of itself effect it, of which its past history furnishes abundant proof, as I shall next proceed to show.

It is a great mistake to suppose that disunion can be effected by a single blow. The cords which bind these States together in one common Union are far too numerous and powerful for that. Disunion must be the work of time. It is only through a long process, and successively, that the cords can be snapped, until the whole fabric falls asunder. Already the agitation of the slavery question has snapped some of the most important, and has greatly weakened all the others, as I shall proceed to show.

The cords that bind the States together are not only many, but various in character. Some are spiritual or ecclesiastical; some political; others social. Some appertain to the benefit conferred by the Union, and others to the feeling of duty and obligation.

The strongest of those of a spiritual and ecclesiastical nature consisted in the unity of the great religious denominations, all of which originally embraced the whole Union. All these denominations, with the exception, perhaps, of the Catholics, were organized very much upon the principle of our political institutions; beginning with smaller meetings corresponding with the political divisions of the country, their organization terminated in one great central assemblage, corresponding very much with the character of Congress. At these meetings the principal clergymen and lay members of the respective denominations from all parts of the Union met to transact business relating to their common concerns. It was not confined to what appertained to the doctrines and discipline of the respective denominations, but extended to plans for disseminating the Bible, establishing missionaries, distributing tracts, and of establishing presses for the publication of tracts, newspapers, and periodicals, with a view of diffusing religious information, and for the support of the doctrines and creeds of the denomination. All this combined, contributed greatly to strengthen the bonds of the Union. The strong ties which held each denomination together formed a strong cord to hold the whole Union together; but, as powerful as they were, they have not been able to resist the explosive effect of slavery agitation.

The first of these cords which snapped, under its explosive force, was that of the powerful Methodist Episcopal Church. The numerous and strong ties which held it together are all broke, and its unity gone. They now form separate churches, and, instead of that feeling of attachment and devotion to the interests of the whole church which was formerly left, they are now arrayed into two hostile bodies, engaged in litigation about what was formerly their common property.

The next cord that snapped was that of the Baptists, one of the largest and most respectable of the denominations. That of the Presbyterian is not entirely snapped, but some of its strands have given away. That of the Episcopal Church is the only one of the four great Protestant denominations which remains unbroken and entire.

The strongest cord of a political character consists of the many and strong ties that have held together the two great parties, which have, with some modifications, existed from the beginning of the Government. They both extended to every portion of the Union, and strongly contributed to hold all its parts together. But this powerful cord has fared no better than the spiritual. It resisted for a long time the explosive tendency of the agitation, but has finally snapped under its force—if not entirely, in a great measure. Nor is there one of the remaining cords which has not been greatly weakened. To this extent the Union has already been destroyed by agitation, in the only way it can be, by snapping asunder and weakening the cords which bind it together.

If the agitation goes on, the same force, acting with increased intensity, as has been shown, will finally snap every cord, when nothing will be left to hold the States together except force. But surely that can, with no propriety of language, be called a union, when the only means by which the weaker is held connected with the stronger portion is *force*. It may, indeed, keep them connected; but the connection will partake much more of the character of subjugation, on the part of the weaker to the stronger, than the union of free, independent, and sovereign States, in one confederation, as they stood in the early stages of the Government, and which only is worthy of the sacred name of union.

Having now, Senators, explained what it is that endangers the Union, and traced it to its cause, and explained its nature and character, the question again recurs, How can the Union be saved? To this I answer, there is but one way by which it can be, and that is, by adopting such measures as will satisfy the States belonging to the southern section that they can remain in the Union consistently with their honor and their safety. There is, again, only one way by which that can be effected, and that is, by removing the causes by which this belief has been produced. Do *that*, and discontent will cease, harmony and kind feelings between the sections be restored, and every apprehension of danger to the Union removed. The question then is, By what can this be done? But, before I undertake to answer this question, I propose to show by what the Union cannot be saved.

It cannot, then, be saved by eulogies on the Union, however splendid or numerous. The cry of "Union, Union, the glorious Union!" can no more prevent disunion than the cry of "Health, health, glorious health!" on the part of the physician can save a patient lying dangerously ill. So long as the Union, instead of being regarded as a protector, is regarded in the opposite character, by not much less than a majority of the States, it will be in vain to attempt to conciliate them by pronouncing eulogies on it.

Besides, this cry of Union comes commonly from those whom we cannot believe to be sincere; it usually comes from our assailants. But we cannot believe them to be sincere; for, if they loved the Union, they would necessarily be devoted to the constitution. It made the Union, and to destroy the constitution would be to destroy the Union. But the only reliable and certain evidence of devotion to the constitution is to abstain, on the one hand, from violating it, and to repel, on the other, all attempts to violate it. It is only by faithfully performing these high duties that the constitution can be preserved, and with it the Union.

But how stands the profession of devotion to the Union by our assailants, when brought to this test? Have they abstained from violating the constitution? Let the many acts passed by the northern States to set aside and annul the clause of the constitution providing for the delivery up of fugitive slaves answer. I cite this, not that it is the only instance, (for there are many others,) but because the violation in this particular is too notorious and palpable to be denied. Again, have they stood forth faithfully to repel violations of the constitution? Let their course in reference to the agitation of the slavery question, which was commenced and has been carried on for fifteen years, avowedly for the purpose of abolishing slavery in the States—an object all acknowledged to be unconstitutional—answer. Let them show a single instance, during this long period, in which they have denounced the agitators or their attempts to effect what is admitted to be unconstitutional, or a single measure which they have brought forward for that purpose. How can we, with all these facts before us, believe that they are sincere in their profession of devotion to the Union, or avoid believing their profession is but intended to increase the vigor of their assaults and to weaken the force of our resistance?

Nor can we regard the profession of devotion to the Union, on the part of those who are not our assailants, as sincere, when they pronounce eulogies upon the Union, evidently with the intent of charging us with disunion, without uttering one word of denunciation against our assailants. If friends of the Union, their course should be to unite with us in repelling these assaults, and denouncing the authors as enemies of the Union. Why they avoid this, and pursue the course they do, it is for them to explain.

Nor can the Union be saved by invoking the name of the illustrious Southerner whose mortal remains repose on the western bank of the Potomac. He was one of us—a slaveholder and a planter. We have studied his history, and find nothing in it to justify submission to wrong. On the contrary, his great fame rests on the solid foundation that, while he was careful to avoid doing wrong to others, he was prompt and decided in repelling wrong. I trust that, in this respect, we profited by his example.

Nor can we find any thing in his history to deter us from seceding from the Union, should it fail to fulfil the objects for which it was instituted, by being permanently and hopelessly converted into the means of oppressing instead of protecting us. On the contrary, we find much in his example to encourage us, should we be forced to the extremity of deciding between submission and disunion.

There existed then, as well as now, a Union —that between a parent country and her then colonies. It was a union that had much to endear it to the people of the colonies. Under its protecting and superintending care the colonies were planted and grew up and prospered, through a long course of years, until they became populous and wealthy. Its benefits were not limited to them. Their extensive agricultural and other productions gave birth to a flourishing commerce, which richly rewarded the parent country for the trouble and expense of establishing and protecting them. Washington was born and grew up to manhood under that Union. He acquired his early distinction in its service, and there is every reason to believe that he was devotedly attached to it. But his devotion was a rational one. He was attached to it, not as an end, but as a means to an end. When it failed to fulfil its end, and, instead of affording protection, was converted into the means of oppressing the colonies, he did not hesitate to draw his sword, and head the great movement by which that union was forever severed, and the independence of these States established. This was the great and crowning glory of his life, which has spread his fame over the whole globe, and will transmit it to the latest posterity.

Nor can the plan proposed by the distinguished Senator from Kentucky, nor that of the Administration, save the Union. I shall pass by, without remark, the plan proposed by the Senator, and proceed directly to the consideration of that of the Administration. I, however, assure the distinguished and able Senator, that in taking this course, no disrespect whatever is intended to him or his plan. I have adopted it, because so many Senators of distinguished abilities, who were present when he delivered his speech, and explained his plan, and who were fully capable to do justice to the side they support, have replied to him.

The plan of the Administration cannot save the Union, because it can have no effect whatever towards satisfying the States composing the southern section of the Union that they can, consistently with safety and honor, remain in the Union. It is, in fact, but a modification of the Wilmot proviso. It proposes to effect the same object, to exclude the South from all territory acquired by the Mexican treaty. It is well known that the South is united against the Wilmot proviso, and has committed itself by solemn resolutions, to resist should it be adopted. Its opposition *is not to the name*, but that which it *proposes to effect*. That the southern States hold to be unconstitutional, unjust, inconsistent with their equality as members of the common Union, and calculated to destroy irretrievably the equilibrium between the two sections. These objections equally apply to what, for brevity, I will call the Executive proviso. There is a difference between it and the Wilmot, except in the mode of effecting the object, and in that respect I must say that the latter is much the least objectionable. It goes to its object openly, boldly, and distinctly. It claims for Congress unlimited power over the territories, and proposes to assert it over the territories acquired from Mexico, by a positive prohibition of slavery. Not so the Executive proviso. It takes an indirect course, and in order to elude the Wilmot proviso, and thereby avoid encountering the united and determined resistance of the South, it denies, by implication, the authority of Congress to legislate for the territories, and claims the right as belonging exclusively to the inhabitants of the territories. But to effect the object of excluding the South, it takes care, in the mean time, to let in emigrants freely from the northern States, and all other quarters, except from the South, which it takes special care to exclude by holding up to them the danger of having their slaves liberated under the Mexican laws. The necessary consequence is to exclude the South from that territory, just as effectually as would the Wilmot proviso. The only difference in this respect is, that what one proposes to effect directly and openly, the other proposes to effect indirectly and covertly.

But the Executive proviso is more objectionable than the Wilmot, in another and more important particular. The latter, to effect its object, inflicts a dangerous wound upon the constitution, by depriving the southern States, as joint partners and owners of the territories, of their rights in them; but it inflicts no greater wound than is absolutely necessary to effect its object. The former, on the contrary, while it inflicts the same wound, inflicts others equally great, and, if possible, greater, as I shall next proceed to explain.

In claiming the right for the inhabitant, instead of Congress, to legislate for the territories, in the Executive proviso, it assumes that the sovereignty over the territories is vested in the former; or, to express it in the language used in a resolution offered by one of the Senators from Texas, (General Houston, now absent,) they have "the same inherent right of self-government as the people in the States." The assumption is utterly unfounded, unconstitutional, without example, and contrary to the entire practice of the Government, from its commencement to the present time, as I shall proceed to show.

The recent movement of individuals in California to form a constitution and a State Government, and to appoint Senators and Representatives, is the first fruit of this monstrous assumption. If the individuals who made this movement had gone into California as adventurers, and if, as such, they had conquered the territory and established their independence, the sovereignty of the country would have been vested in them, as a separate and independent community. In that case, they would have had the right to form a constitution, and to establish a government for themselves; and if, afterwards, they thought proper to apply to Congress for admission into the Union as a sovereign and independent State, all this would have been regular, and according to established principles. But such is not the case. It was the United States who conquered California, and finally acquired it by treaty. The sovereignty, of course, is vested in them, and not in the individuals who have attempted to form a constitution and a State, without their consent. All this is clear, beyond controversy, unless it can be shown that they have since lost or been divested of their sovereignty.

Nor is it less clear, that the power of legislating over the acquired territory is vested in Congress, and not, as is assumed, in the inhabitants of the territories. None can deny that the Government of the United States have the power to acquire territories, either by war or treaty; but if the power to acquire exists, it belongs to Congress to carry it into execution. On this point there can be no doubt, for the constitution expressly provides that Congress shall have power, "to make all laws which shall be necessary and proper to carry into execution the foregoing powers," (those vested in Congress,) "and all other powers vested by this constitution in *the Government* of the United States, or in *any department* or *office* thereof." It matters not, then, where the power is vested; for, if vested at all in the Government of the United States, or any of its departments or officers, the power of carrying it into execution is clearly vested in Congress. But this important proviso, while it gives to Congress the power of legislating over territories, imposes important restrictions on its exercise, by restricting Congress to passing laws necessary and proper for carrying the power into execution. The prohibition extends, not only to all laws not suitable or appropriate to the object of the power, but also to all that are unjust, unequal, or unfair; for all such laws would be unnecessary and improper, and, therefore, unconstitutional.

Having now established beyond controversy, that the sovereignty over the territories is vested in the United States—that is, in the several States composing the Union—and that the power of legislating over them is expressly vested in Congress, it follows that the individuals in California who have undertaken to form a constitution and a State, and to exercise the power of legislating without the consent of Congress, have usurped the sovereignty of the State and the authority of Congress, and have acted in open defiance of them both. In other words, what they have done, is revolutionary and rebellious in its character, anarchical in its tendency, and calculated to lead to the most dangerous consequences. Had they acted from premeditation and design, it would have been, in fact, actual rebellion; but such is not the case. The blame lies much less upon them than upon those who have induced them to take a course so unconstitutional and dangerous. They have been led into it by language held here, and the course pursued by the Executive branch of the Government.

I have not seen the answer of the Executive to the calls made by the two Houses of Congress for information as to the course which it took, or the part which it acted in reference to what was done in California. I understand the answers have not yet been printed. But there is enough known to justify the assertion that those who profess to represent and act under the authority of the Executive, have advised, aided, and encouraged the movement, which terminated in forming what they call a constitution and a State. Gen. Riley, who professed to act as civil governor, called the convention, determined on the number and distribution of the delegates, appointed the time and place of its meeting, was present during the session, and gave its proceedings his approbation and sanction. If he acted without authority, he ought to have been tried or at least reprimanded and disavowed. Neither having been done, the presumption is that his course has been approved. This of itself is sufficient to identify the Executive with his acts and to make it responsible for them. I touch not the question whether Gen. Riley was appointed or received the instructions under which he professed to act from the present Executive or its predecessor. If from the former, it would implicate the preceding as well as the present Administration. If not, the responsibility rests exclusively on the present.

It is manifest from this statement that the Executive Department has undertaken to perform acts preparatory to the meeting of the individuals to form their so-called constitution and government, which appertain exclusively to Congress. Indeed, they are identical in many respects with the provisions adopted by Congress, when it gives permission to a territory to form a constitution and government in order to be admitted as a State into the Union.

Having now shown that the assumption upon which the Executive and the individuals in California acted throughout this whole affair is unfounded, unconstitutional, and dangerous, it remains to make a few remarks in order to show that what has been done is contrary to the entire practice of the government from its commencement to the present time.

From its commencement until the time that Michigan was admitted, the practice was uniform. Territorial Governments were first organized by Congress. The Government of the United States appointed the governors, judges, secretaries, marshals, and other officers, and the inhabitants of the territory were represented by legislative bodies, whose acts were subject to the revision of Congress. This state of things continued until the government of a territory applied to Congress to permit its inhabitants to form a constitution and government preparatory to admission into the Union. The preliminary act to giving permission was, to ascertain whether the inhabitants were sufficiently numerous to authorize them to be formed into a State. This was done by taking a census. That being done, and the number proving sufficient, permission was granted. The act granting it fixed all the preliminaries —the time and place of holding the Convention; the qualification of the voters; establishment of its boundaries, and all other measures necessary to be settled previous to admission. The act giving permission necessarily withdraws the sovereignty of the United States, and leaves the inhabitants of the incipient State as free to form their constitution and government as were the original States of the Union after they had declared their independence. At this stage, the inhabitants of the territory became for the first time a people, in legal and constitutional language. Prior to this, they were, by the old acts of Congress, called inhabitants, and not people. All this is perfectly consistent with the sovereignty of the United States, with the powers of Congress, and with the right of a people to self-government.

Michigan was the first case in which there was any departure from the uniform rule of acting. Hers was a very slight departure from established usage. The ordinance of 1787 secured to her the right of becoming a State when she should have 60,000 inhabitants. Owing to some neglect, Congress delayed taking the census. In the mean time her population increased until it clearly exceeded more than twice the number which entitled her to admission. At this stage she formed a constitution and government without the census being taken by the United States, and Congress waived the omission, as there was no doubt she had more than a sufficient number to entitle her to admission. She was not admitted at the first session she applied, owing to some difficulty respecting the boundary between her and Ohio. The great irregularity, as to her admission, took place at the next session, but on a point which can have no possible connection with the case of California.

The irregularities in all other cases that have since occurred are of a similar nature. In all there existed territorial governments established by Congress, with officers appointed by the United States. In all the territorial government took the lead in calling conventions and fixing the preliminaries preparatory to the formation of a constitution and admission into the Union. They all recognized the sovereignty of the United States and the authority of Congress over the Territories; and wherever there was any departure from established usage, it was done on the presumed consent of Congress, and not in defiance of its authority, or the sovereignty of the United States over the Territories. In this respect California stands alone, without usage, or a single example to cover her case.

It belongs now, Senators, for you to decide

what part you will act in reference to this unprecedented transaction. The Executive has laid the paper purporting to be the Constitution of California before you, and asks you to admit her into the Union as a State; and the question is, Will you or will you not admit her? It is a grave question, and there rests upon you a heavy responsibility. Much, very much will depend upon your decision. If you admit her, you endorse and give your sanction to all that has been done. Are you prepared to do so? Are you prepared to surrender your power of legislation for the territories—a power expressly vested in Congress by the constitution, as has been fully established? Can you, consistently with your oath to support the constitution, surrender the power? Are you prepared to admit that the inhabitants of the territories possess the sovereignty over them, and that any number, more or less, may claim any extent of territory they please, may form a constitution and government, and erect it into a State, without asking your permission? Are you prepared to surrender the sovereignty of the United States over whatever territory may be hereafter acquired, to the first adventurers who may rush into it? Are you prepared to surrender virtually to the Executive department all the powers which you have heretofore exercised over the territories? If not, how can you, consistently with your duty and your oaths to support the constitution, give your assent to the admission of California as a State, under a pretended constitution and government? Again, can you believe that the project of a constitution which they have adopted has the least validity? Can you believe that there is such a State in reality as the State of California? No, there is no such State. It has no legal or constitutional existence. It has no validity, and can have none without your sanction. How, then, can you admit it as *a State*, when, according to the provision of the Constitution, your power is limited to admitting new *States?* To be admitted, it must be a State, an existing State, independent of your sanction, before you can admit it. When you give your permission to the inhabitants of a territory to form a constitution and a State, the constitution and State they form derive their authority from the people, and not from you. The State before admitted is actually a State, and does not become so by the *act of admission*, as would be the case with California, should you admit her contrary to constitutional provisions and established usage heretofore.

The Senators on the other side of the chamber must permit me to make a few remarks in this connection particularly applicable to them, with the exception of a few Senators from the South, sitting on that side of the chamber. When the Oregon question was before this body not two years since, you took (if I mistake not) universally the ground that Congress had the sole and absolute power of legislating for the territories. How then can you now, after the short interval which has elapsed, abandon the ground which you took, and thereby virtually admit that the power of legislating, instead of being in Congress, is in the inhabitants of the territories? How can you justify and sanction by your votes the acts of the Executive, which are in direct derogation of what you then contended for? But to approach still nearer to the present time, how can you, after condemning, little more than a year since, the grounds taken by the party which you defeated at the last election, wheel round and support by your votes the grounds which, as explained recently on this floor by the candidate of the party in the last election, are identical with those on which the Executive has acted in reference to California? What are we to understand by all this? Must we conclude that there is no sincerity, no faith in the acts and declarations of public men, and that all is mere acting or hollow profession? Or are we to conclude that the exclusion of the South from the territory acquired from Mexico is an object of so paramount a character in your estimation, that right, justice, constitution, and consistency must all yield when they stand in the way of our exclusion?

But, it may be asked, what is to be done with California should she not be admitted? I answer, remand her back to the territorial condition, as was done in the case of Tennessee, in the early stage of the Government. Congress, in her case, had established a territorial government in the usual form, with a governor, judges, and other officers appointed by the United States. She was entitled under the deed of cession to be admitted into the Union as a State as soon as she had sixty thousand inhabitants. The territorial government, believing it had that number, took a census, by which it appeared it exceeded it. She then formed a constitution, and applied for admission. Congress refused to admit her, on the ground that the census should be taken by the United States, and that Congress had not determined whether the territory should be formed into one or two States, as it was authorized to do under the cession. She returned quietly to her territorial condition. An act was passed to take a census by the United States, containing a provision that the territory should form one State. All afterwards was regularly conducted, and the territory admitted as a State in due form. The irregularities in the case of California are immeasurably greater, and offer much stronger reasons for pursuing the same course. But, it may be said, California may not submit. That is not probable; but if she should not, when she refuses it will then be time for us to decide what is to be done.

Having now shown what cannot save the Union, I return to the question with which I commenced, How can the Union be saved?

There is but one way by which it can with any certainty; and that is, by a full and final settlement, on the principle of justice, of all the questions at issue between the two sections. The South asks for justice, simple justice, and less she ought not to take. She has no compromise to offer but the constitution, and no concession or surrender to make. She has already surrendered so much that she has little left to surrender. Such a settlement would go to the root of the evil, and remove all cause of discontent, by satisfying the South she could remain honorably and safely in the Union, and thereby restore the harmony and fraternal feelings between the sections which existed anterior to the Missouri agitation. Nothing else can, with any certainty, finally and forever settle the questions at issue, terminate agitation, and save the Union.

But can this be done? Yes, easily; not by the weaker party, for it can of itself do nothing —not even protect itself—but by the stronger. The North has only to will it to accomplish it —to do justice by conceding to the South an equal right in the acquired territory, and to do her duty by causing the stipulations relative to fugitive slaves to be faithfully fulfilled—to cease the agitation of the slave question, and to provide for the insertion of a provision in the Constitution, by an amendment, which will restore to the South in substance the power she possessed of protecting herself, before the equilibrium between the sections was destroyed by the action of this Government. There will be no difficulty in devising such a provision—one that will protect the South, and which at the same time will improve and strengthen the Government, instead of impairing and weakening it.

But will the North agree to do this? It is for her to answer this question. But, I will say, she cannot refuse, if she has half the love of the Union which she professes to have, or without justly exposing herself to the charge that her love of power and aggrandizement is far greater than her love of the Union. At all events, the responsibility of saving the Union rests on the North, and not the South. The South cannot save it by any act of hers, and the North may save it without any sacrifice whatever, unless to do justice, and to perform her duties under the Constitution, should be regarded by her as a sacrifice.

It is time, Senators, that there should be an open and manly avowal on all sides, as to what is intended to be done. If the question is not now settled, it is uncertain whether it ever can hereafter be; and we, as the representatives of the States of this Union, regarded as governments, should come to a distinct understanding as to our respective views, in order to ascertain whether the great questions at issue can be settled or not. If you, who represent the stronger portion, cannot agree to settle them on the broad principle of justice and duty, say so; and let the States we both represent agree to separate and part in peace. If you are unwilling we should part in peace, tell us so, and we shall know what to do, when you reduce the question to submission or resistance. If you remain silent, you will compel us to infer by your acts what you intend. In that case, California will become the test question. If you admit her, under all the difficulties that oppose her admission, you compel us to infer that you intend to exclude us from the whole of the acquired territories, with the intention of destroying irretrievably the equilibrium between the two sections. We would be blind not to perceive, in that case, that your real objects are power and aggrandizement, and infatuated not to act accordingly.

I have now, Senators, done my duty in expressing my opinions fully, freely, and candidly, on this solemn occasion. In doing so, I have been governed by the motives which have governed me in all the stages of the agitation of the slavery question since its commencement. I have exerted myself, during the whole period, to arrest it, with the intention of saving the Union, if it could be done; and, if it could not, to save the section where it has pleased Providence to cast my lot, and which I sincerely believe has justice and the constitution on its side. Having faithfully done my duty to the best of my ability, both to the Union and my section, throughout this agitation, I shall have the consolation, let what will come, that I am free from all responsibility.

The reading of Mr. CALHOUN's views having been concluded—

Mr. WALKER rose, but yielded to—

Mr. WEBSTER. I hope, sir, that, by rising at the conclusion of the speech which has just been read in our hearing, it may not be inferred that I have any purpose of going into an answer or reply to that speech. I wish, in the first place, only to say that it gives me very sincere pleasure to see the honorable member from Carolina able to be in his place to-day, and to take part in these deliberations; and, sir, there is not a man in the country who will feel more satisfaction than myself when he shall be so far restored to health as to participate in these debates in the accustomed manner. I have had the pleasure of that gentleman's acquaintance for thirty years; and my prayer to-day is, that he will yet have an opportunity to perform much public service for the benefit of all portions of the country.

But I wish to say, sir, that I desire as soon as there may be an opportunity, to say to the Senate what I propose to say on this question; at the same time I do not desire to do an act of discourtesy to other gentlemen, who have manifested a disposition to speak. There is an honorable member over the way, from Maine, who, I believe, has once or twice given way to others; I believe, also, the honorable member from Wisconsin, to whose kindness I owe this opportunity of addressing the Chair, has, by a sort of assent, the right to be heard before this debate passes into other hands; and, while I am willing to yield to their prior claims, I wish to say that as soon as may be—perhaps as early as Wednesday or Thursday next—I shall be very glad to have an opportunity to address the Senate.

Mr. Walker. I shall have a great deal of pleasure at any time in yielding any title that I may have to the floor to the Senator from Massachusetts. The Senator from Maine, I believe, has the floor for to-morrow on the subject of the President's message accompanying the constitution of California. I should propose to occupy it on Wednesday; but, if the Senator from Massachusetts has any desire whatever to address the Senate on that day, I will, while up, if he will give me an intimation to that effect, move to postpone the consideration of the resolutions to that day for his benefit.

Mr. Webster. I am very much obliged to the honorable member; but Thursday will suit me as well.

Mr. Walker. I will move, then, that the further consideration of the resolutions be postponed until Wednesday—preferring, however, to give way to the Senator from Massachusetts if he desires it.

Wednesday, March 6.

Claims for slaves deported.

Mr. Hunter submitted the following resolution:

Resolved, That the Secretary of State be directed to communicate to the Senate such information as may be found on the records and on the files of the Department of State, concerning the correspondence and negotiation with Great Britain on the subject of the claims of American citizens for slaves, the property of those citizens, deported from the United States by the officers of the British Government, in violation of the 7th article of the definitive treaty of peace of the 3d of September, 1783, together with copies of such letters and documents as may be calculated to exhibit the latest proceedings on the subject, and the fact whether further application for indemnity from the British Government was ever made by the Government of the United States, after the ratification of the treaty of 1794, between the United States and Great Britain.

Mr. Hunter. As this is merely a resolution of inquiry, I hope there will be no objection on the part of the Senate to consider it now.

Mr. King. I do not exactly understand the object of the resolution which has just been offered by my friend from Virginia. I presume that subject was definitely settled under the auspices of the treaty with Russia, by which there was a settlement of all claims for compensation for slaves taken during the late war with Great Britain.

Mr. Hunter. If the Senator will allow me, I can explain this matter in a very few words. This resolution relates to slaves taken contrary to the stipulations of the treaty of peace entered into in the year 1783 between this country and Great Britain. It was a subject of negotiation between the two countries. These negotiations were probably abandoned after the ratification of Jay's treaty, and the neglect to secure indemnity was one of the chief points of objection to that treaty. The claim of indemnity for these slaves, stands pretty much on the same footing as the claims for indemnity for French spoliations, and I think it will so turn out, when we get the correspondence and all the facts. I wish to obtain the correspondence for that purpose.

Mr. King. I have no objection.

The question was then taken on the adoption of the resolution, and it was agreed to.

The Compromise.

The Senate resumed the consideration of the special order, viz: Mr. Clay's series of resolutions.

Mr. Walker, who was entitled to the floor, addressed the Senate for upward of two hours.

Mr. Seward. If the honorable Senator is not particularly desirous of continuing his remarks at this time, I would propose, as it is now late, that the subject be postponed.

Mr. Walker. In consequence of the interruptions that have taken place, I shall not be able to conclude to-day.

Mr. Dawson. The honorable Senator has been subjected to so many interruptions, that it is proper, if he will consent to yield for an adjournment, that he should have another day.

Thursday, March 7.

The Compromise.

The Vice President. The resolutious submitted by the Senator from Kentucky, were made the special order of the day at 12 o'clock. On this subject the Senator from Wisconsin, (Mr. Walker), has the floor.

Mr. Walker. Mr. President, this vast audience has not assembled to hear me, and there is but one man, in my opinion, who can assemble such an audience. They expect to hear him, and I feel it to be my duty, as well as my pleasure, to give the floor, therefore, to the Senator from Massachusetts. I understand it is immaterial to him upon which of these questions he speaks, and, therefore, I will not move to postpone the special order.

Mr. Webster. I beg to express my obligations to my friend from Wisconsin, (Mr. Walker,) as well as to my friend from New York, (Mr. Seward,) for their courtesy in allowing me to address the Senate this morning.

Mr. President, I wish to speak to-day, not as a Massachusetts man, nor as a northern man, but as an American, and a member of the Senate of the United States. It is fortunate that there is a Senate of the United States; a body not yet moved from its propriety, not lost to a just sense of its own dignity, and its own high responsibilities, and a body to which the country looks with confidence, for wise, moderate, patriotic, and healing counsels. It is not to be denied that we live in the midst of strong agitations, and surrounded by very considerable dangers to our institutions of government. The imprisoned winds are let loose. The East, the West, the North, and the stormy South, all combine to throw the whole ocean into commotion, to toss its billows to the skies, and to disclose its profoundest depths. I do not expect, Mr. President, to hold, or to be fit to hold, the helm in this combat of the political elements; but I have a duty to perform, and I mean to perform it with fidelity—not without a sense of the surrounding dangers, but not without hope. I have a part to act, not for my own security or safety, for I am looking out for no fragment upon which to float away from the wreck, if wreck there must be, but for the good of the whole, and the preservation of the whole; and there is that which will keep me to my duty during this struggle, whether the sun and the stars shall appear, or shall not appear, for many days. I speak to-day for the preservation of the Union. "Hear me for my cause." I speak to-day, out of a solicitous and anxious heart, for the restoration to the country of that quiet and that harmony which make the blessings of this Union so rich and so dear to us all. These are the topics that I propose to myself to discuss; these are the motives, and the sole motives, that influence me in the wish to communicate my opinions to the Senate and the country; and if I can do any thing, however little, for the promotion of these ends, I shall have accomplished all that I desire.

Mr. President, it may not be amiss to recur very briefly to the events which, equally sudden and extraordinary, have brought the political condition of the country to what it now is. In May, 1846, the United States declared war against Mexico. Her armies, then on the frontiers, entered the provinces of that Republic, met and defeated all her troops, penetrated her mountain passes, and occupied her capital. The marine force of the United States took possession of her forts and her towns on the Atlantic and on the Pacific. In less than two years a treaty was negotiated, by which Mexico ceded to the United States a vast territory, extending seven or eight hundred miles along the shores of the Pacific—reaching back over the mountains, and across the desert, until it joined the frontier of the State of Texas. It so happened, that, in the distracted and feeble state of the Mexican Government, before the declaration of war by the United States against Mexico had become known in California, that the people of California—under the lead of American officers, perhaps, generally—overthrew the existing Provincial Government of California, the Mexican authorities, and run up an independent flag. When the news arrived at San Francisco, that war had been declared by the United States against Mexico, this independent flag was pulled down, and the stars and stripes of this Union hoisted in its stead. So, sir, before the war was over, the powers of the United States, military and naval, had possession of San Francisco and Upper California, and a great rush of emigrants, from various parts of the world, took place into California, in 1846 and 1847. But now, behold another wonder.

In January of 1848, the Mormons, it is said, or some of them, made a discovery of an extraordinarily rich mine of gold; or, rather, of a very great quantity of gold, hardly fit to be called a mine, for it was spread near the surface—on the lower part of the south or American branch of the Sacramento. They seem to have attempted to conceal their discovery for some time; but soon another discovery, perhaps of greater importance, was made, of gold in another part of the American branch of the Sacramento, and near Sutter's fort, as it is called. The fame of these discoveries spread far and wide. They excited more and more the spirit of emigration toward California, which had already been excited; and persons crowded in hundreds, and flocked toward the Bay of San Francisco. This, as I have said, took place in the winter and spring of 1848. The digging commenced in the spring of that year; and from that time to this, the work of searching for gold has been prosecuted with a success not heretofore known in the history of this globe. We all know, sir, how incredulous the American public was at the accounts which reached us at first of these discoveries; but we all know that these acounts received, and continue to receive, daily confirmation; and down to the present moment, I suppose the assurances are as strong, after the experience of these several months, of mines of gold, apparently inexhaustible, in the regions near San Francisco, in California, as they were at any period of the earlier dates of the accounts. It so happened, sir, that although in the time of peace it became a very important subject for legislative consideration and legislative decision, to provide a proper territorial government for California, yet, differences of opinion in the counsels of the Government prevented the establishment of any such territorial government for California, at the last session of Congress. Under this state of things, the inhabitants of San Francisco and California—then amounting to a great number of people—in the summer of last year, thought it to be their duty to establish a local government. Under the proclamation of General Riley, the people chose delegates to a convention. That convention met at Monterey. They formed a constitution for the State of California, and it was adopted by the people of California in their primary assemblages. Desirous of immediate connection with the United States, its Senators were appointed and Representatives chosen, who have come hither, bringing with them the authentic constitution of the State of California; and they now present themselves, asking in behalf of their State, that the State may be admitted into this Union as one of the United States. This constitution, sir, contains an express prohibition against slavery or involuntary servitude in the State of California. It is said, and I suppose truly, that of the members who composed that convention, some sixteen were natives, and had been residents of the slaveholding States, and about twenty-two were from the non-slaveholding States, and the remaining ten members were either native Californians, or old settlers in that country. This prohibition against slavery, it is said, was inserted with entire unanimity.

Mr. Hale. Will the Senator give way until order is restored?

The Vice President. The Sergeant-at-Arms will see that order is restored, and no more persons admitted to the floor.

Mr. Cass. I trust the scene of the other day will not be repeated. The Sergeant-at-Arms must display more energy in suppressing this disorder.

Mr. Hale. The noise is outside of the door.

Mr. Webster. And it is this circumstance, sir, the prohibition of slavery by that convention, which was contributed to raise—I do not say it has wholly raised—the dispute as to the propriety of the admission of California into the Union under this constitution. It is not to be denied, Mr. President—nobody thinks of denying that, whatever reasons were assigned at the commencement of the late war with Mexico, it was prosecuted for the purpose of the acquisition of territory, and under the alleged argument that the cession of territory was the only form in which proper compensation could be made to the United States, by Mexico, for the various claims and demands which the people of this country had against that Government. At any rate, it will be found that President Polk's message at the commencement of the session of December, 1847, avowed, that the war was to be prosecuted until some acquisition of territory was made. And, as the acquisition was to be south of the line of the United States, in warm climates and countries, it was naturally, I suppose, expected by the South, that whatever acquisitions were made in that region, would be added to the slaveholding portion of the United States. Events have turned out as was not expected, and that expectation has not been realized; and therefore some degree of disappointment and surprise has resulted, of course. In other words, it is obvious that the question which has so long harassed the country, and at times very seriously alarmed the minds of wise and good men, has come upon us for a fresh discussion—the question of slavery in these United States.

Now, sir, I propose—perhaps at the expense of detail and consequent detention of the Senate—to review, historically, this question of slavery, which—partly in consequence of its own merits, and partly, perhaps mostly, in the manner it is discussed, in one and the other portion of the country—has been a source of so much alienation and unkind feeling between the different portions of the Union. We all know, sir, that slavery has existed in the world from time immemorial. There was slavery, in the earliest periods of history, in the Oriental nations. There was slavery among the Jews—the theocratic government of that people made no injunction against it. There was slavery among the Greeks; and the ingenious philosophy of the Greeks found, or sought to find, a justification for it, exactly upon the grounds which have been assumed, for such a justification, in this country; that is, a natural and original difference among the races of mankind—the inferiority of the black or colored race, to the white. The Greeks justified their system of slavery upon that ground precisely. They held the African, and in some parts, the Asiatic tribes, to be inferior to the white race; but they did not show, I think, by any close process of logic, that, if this were true, the more intelligent and the stronger, had therefore a right to subjugate the weaker.

The more manly philosophy and jurisprudence of the Romans, placed the justification of slavery on entirely different grounds.

The Roman jurists, from the first, and down to the fall of the empire, admitted that slavery was against the natural law, by which, as they maintained, all men, of whatsoever clime, color, or capacity, were equal; but they justified slavery—first, upon the ground and authority of the law of nations—arguing, and arguing truly, that at that day the conventional law of nations admitted, that captives in war, whose lives, according to the notions of the times, were at the absolute disposal of the captors, might, in exchange for exemption from death, be made slaves for life, and that such servitude might descend to their posterity. The jurists of Rome also maintained that, by the civil law, there might be servitude—slavery, personal and hereditary—first, by the voluntary act of an individual who might sell himself into slavery; second, by his being received into a state of slavery, by his creditors, in satisfaction of a debt; and, thirdly, by being placed in a state of servitude, or slavery, for crime. At the introduction of Christianity into the world, the Roman world was full of slaves, and I suppose there is to be found no injunction against that relation between man and man in the teachings by the Gospel of Jesus Christ, or by any of his Apostles. The object of the instruction, imparted to mankind, by the founder of Christianity, was to touch the hearts, purify the soul, and improve the lives of individual men. That object went directly to the first fountain of all political and all social relations of the human race—the individual heart and mind of man.

Now, sir, upon the general nature, and character, and influence of slavery, there exists a wide difference between the northern portion of this country and the southern. It is said, on the one side, that if not the subject of any injunction or direct prohibition in the New Testament, slavery is a wrong; that it is founded merely in the right of the strongest; and that it is an oppression, like all unjust wars—like all those conflicts by which a mighty nation subjects a weaker nation to their will; and that slavery, in its nature, whatever may be said of it in the modifications which have taken place, is not in fact according to the meek spirit of the Gospel. It is not kindly affectioned. It does not "seek another's and not its own." It does not "let the oppressed go free." These are sentiments that are cherished, and recently with greatly augmented force, among the people of the northern States. It has taken hold of the religious sentiment of that part of the country, as it has more or less taken hold of the religious feelings of a considerable portion of mankind. The South, upon the other side, having been accustomed to this relation between the two races all their lives, from their birth; having been taught in general to treat the subjects of this bondage with care and kindness—and I believe, in general, feeling for them great care and kindness—have yet not taken this view of the subject which I have mentioned. There are thousands of religious men, with consciences as tender as any of their brethren at the North, who do not see the unlawfulness of slavery, and there are more thousands, perhaps, that, whatsoever they may think of it in its origin, and as a matter depending upon natural right, yet take things as they are, and, finding slavery to be an established relation of the society where they live, can see no way in which—let their opinions on the abstract question be what they may—it is in the power of the present generation to relieve themselves from this relation. And, in this respect, candor obliges me to say, that I believe they are just as conscientious, many of them—and of the religious people, all of them—as they are in the North, in holding different opinions.

Why, sir, the honorable Senator from South Carolina, the other day, alluded to the great separation of that great religious community, the Methodist Episcopal Church. That separation was brought about by differences of opinion upon this peculiar subject of slavery. I felt great concern, as that dispute went on, about the result; and I was in hopes that the difference of opinion might be adjusted, because I looked upon that religious denomination as one of the great props of religion and morals, throughout the whole country, from Maine to Georgia. The result was against my wishes and against my hopes. I have read all their proceedings, and all their arguments, but I have never yet been able to come to the conclusion, that there was any real ground for that separation; in other words, that no good could be produced by that separation. Sir, when a question of this kind takes hold of the religious sentiments of mankind, and comes to be discussed in religious assemblies of the clergy and laity, there is always to be expected, or always to be feared, a great degree of excitement. It is in the nature of man, manifested by his whole history, that religious disputes are apt to become warm, and men's strength of conviction is proportionate to their views of the magnitude of the questions. In all such disputes, there will sometimes be men found with whom every thing is absolute—absolutely wrong, or absolutely right. They see the right clearly; they think others ought to do it, and they are disposed to establish a broad line of distinction between what they think right, and what they hold to be wrong. And they are not seldom willing to establish that line upon their own convictions of the truth and the justice of their own opinions, but they are willing to mark and guard that line, by placing along it a series of dogmas, as lines of boundary are marked by posts and stones. There are men, who, with clear perceptions, as they think, of their own duty, do not see how too hot a pursuit of one duty may involve them in the violation of another, or how too warm an embracement of one truth may lead to a disregard of other truths equally important. As I heard it stated strongly, not many days ago, these persons are disposed to mount upon some duty as a war-horse, and to drive furiously on, and upon, and over all other duties, that may stand in the way. There are men, who, in times of that sort, and disputes of that sort, are of opinion, that human duties may be ascertained with the precision of mathematics. They deal with morals as with mathematics, and they think what is right may be distinguished from what is wrong with the precision of an algebraic equation. They have, therefore, none too much charity toward others who differ with them. They are apt, too, to think that nothing is good but what is perfect, and that there are no compromises or modifications to be made in submission to difference of opinion, or in deference to other men's judgment. If their perspicacious vision enables them to detect a spot on the face of the sun, they think that a good reason why the sun should be struck down from heaven. They prefer the chance of running into utter darkness, to living in heavenly light, if that heavenly light be not absolutely without any imperfection. There are impatient men—too impatient always to give heed to the admission of St. Paul, "that we are not to do evil that good may come"—too impatient to wait for the slow progress of moral causes in the improvement of mankind. They do not remember that the doctrines and the miracles of Jesus Christ have in eighteen hundred years, converted only a small portion of the human race; and among the nations that are converted to Christianity, they forget how many vices and crimes, public and private, still prevail, and that many of them—public crimes especially, which are offences against the Christian religion—pass without exciting particular regret or indignation. Thus wars are waged, and unjust wars. I do not deny that there may be just wars. There certainly are; but it was the remark of an eminent person, not many years ago, on the other side of the Atlantic, that it was one of the greatest reproaches to human nature, that wars were sometimes necessary. The defence of nations sometimes causes a war against the injustice of other nations.

Now, sir, in this state of sentiment, upon the general nature of slavery, lies the cause of a great portion of those unhappy divisions, exasperations, and reproaches, which find vent and support in different parts of the Union. Slavery does exist in the United States. It did exist in the States, before the adoption of this constitution, and at that time.

And now let us consider, sir, for a moment, what was the state of sentiment, North and South, in regard to slavery at the time this constitution was adopted. A remarkable change has taken place since, but what did the wise and great men of all parts of the country think of slavery? In what estimation did they hold it in 1787, when this constitution was adopted? Now, it will be found, sir, if we will carry ourselves by historical research back to that day, and ascertain men's opinions by authentic records still existing among us, that there was no great diversity of opinion between the North and the South upon the subject of slavery; and it will be found that both parts of the country held it equally an evil—a moral and political evil. It will not be found, that either at the North or at the South, there was much, though there was some, invective against slavery as inhuman and cruel. The great ground of objection to it was political; that it weakened the social fabric; that, taking the place of free labor, society was less strong and labor was less productive; and, therefore, we find, from all the eminent men of the time, the clearest expression of their opinion that slavery was an evil. And they ascribed it, not without truth, and not without some acerbity of temper and force of language, to the injurious policy of the mother country, who, to favor the navigator, had entailed these evils upon the colonies. I need hardly refer, sir, to the publications of the day. They are matters of history on the record. The eminent men, the most eminent men, and nearly all the conspicuous men of the South, held the same sentiments, that slavery was an evil, a blight, a blast, a mildew, a scourge, and a curse. There are no terms of reprobation of slavery so vehement in the North of that day as in the South. The North was not so much excited against it as the South, and the reason is, I suppose, because there was much less at the North; and the people did not see, or think they saw, the evils so prominently as they were seen, or thought to be seen, at the South.

Then, sir, when this constitution was framed, this was the light in which the Convention viewed it. The Convention reflected the judgment and sentiments of the great men of the South. A member of the other house, whom I have not the honor to know, in a recent speech, has collected extracts from these public documents. They prove the truth of what I am saying, and the question then was, how to deal with it, and how to deal with it as an evil? Well, they came to this general result. They thought that slavery could not be continued in the country if the importation of slaves were made to cease, and therefore they provided, that after a certain period, the importation might be prevented by the act of the new Government. Twenty years was proposed by some gentleman—a northern gentleman, I think—and many of the southern gentlemen opposed it as being too long. Mr. Madison, especially, was something warm against it. He said it would bring too much of this mischief into the country to allow the importation of slaves for such a period, because we must take along with us, in the whole of this discussion, when we are considering the sentiments and opinions in which this constitutional provision originated, that the conviction of all men was, that if the importation of slaves ceased, the white race would multiply faster than the black race, and that slavery would therefore gradually wear out and expire. It may not be improper here to allude to that—I had almost said celebrated—opinion of Mr. Madison. You observe, sir, that the term slave, or slavery, is not used in the constitution. The constitution does not require that "fugitive slaves" shall be delivered up. It requires that "persons bound to service in one State, and escaping into another, shall be delivered up." Mr. Madison opposed the introduction of the term slave, or slavery, into the constitution; for he said he did not wish to see it recognized by the constitution of the United States of America, that there could be property in men. Now, sir, all this took place at the Convention in 1787; but connected with this—concurrent and contemporaneous—is another important consideration, not sufficiently attended to. The Convention for framing this Constitution, assembled in Philadelphia in May, and sat until September, 1787. During all that time, the Congress of the United States was in session at New York. It was a matter of design, as we know, that the Convention should not assemble in the same city where Congress was holding its sessions. Almost all the public men of the country, therefore, of distinction and eminence, were in one or the other of these two assemblies; and I think it happened in some instances, that the same gentlemen were members of both. If I mistake not, such was the case of Mr. Rufus King, then a member of Congress from Massachusetts, at the same time a member of the Convention to frame the constitution from that State. Now, it was in the summer of 1787, the very time when the Convention in Philadelphia was framing this constitution, that the Congress in New York was framing the ordinance of 1787. They passed that ordinance on the 13th of July, 1787, at New York, the very month—perhaps the very day—on which these questions about the importation of slaves, and the character of slavery, were debated in the Convention at Philadelphia. And, so far as we can now learn, there was a perfect concurrence of opinion between these respective bodies; and it resulted in this ordinance of 1787, excluding slavery, as applied to all the territory over which the Congress of the United States had jurisdiction, and that was, all the territory north-west of the Ohio. Three years before, Virginia and other States had made a cession of that great territory to the United States. And a most magnificent act it was. I never reflect upon it without a disposition to do honor and justice—and justice would be the highest honor—to Virginia for that act of cession of her north-western territory. I will say, sir, it is one of her fairest claims to the respect and gratitude of the United States, and that perhaps it is only second to that other claim, which attaches to her: that in her counsels, and from the intelligence and patriotism of her leading statesmen, proceeded the first idea, put into practice, for the formation of a general Constitution of the United States. Now, sir, the ordinance of 1787 applied thus to the whole territory over which the Congress of the United States had jurisdiction. It was adopted nearly three years before the Constitution of the United States went into operation; because the ordinance took effect immediately on its passage, while the Constitution of the United States, having been framed, was to be sent to the States to be adopted by their conventions; and then a Government had to be organized under it. This ordinance, then, was in operation and force when the constitution was adopted, and this Government put in motion, in April, 1789.

Mr. President, three things are quite clear as historical truths. One is, that there was an expectation that on the ceasing of the importation of slaves from Africa, slavery would begin to run out. That was hoped and expected. Another is, that as far as there was any power in Congress to prevent the spread of slavery in the United States, that power was executed in the most absolute manner and to the fullest extent. An honorable member, whose health does not allow him to be here to-day——

A SENATOR. He is here. (Referring to Mr. CALHOUN.)

Mr. WEBSTER. I am very happy to hear that he is—may he long be in health and the enjoyment of it to serve his country—said the other day, that he considered this as the first in the series of measures calculated to enfeeble the South, and deprive them of their just participation in the benefits and privileges of this Government. He says, very properly, that it was done under the old Confederation, and before this constitution went into effect; but, my present purpose is, only to say, Mr. President, that it was done with the entire and unanimous concurrence of the whole South. Why, there it stands! The vote of every State in the Union was unanimous in favor of the ordinance, with the exception of a single individual vote, and that individual was a northern man. But, sir, the ordinance abolishing or rather prohibiting slavery north-west of the Ohio, has the hand and seal of every southern member in Congress.

This was the state of things, sir, and this the state of opinion under which those two very important matters were arranged, and those two important things done; that is, the establishment of the constitution, with a recognition of slavery as it existed in the States, and the establishment of the ordinance prohibiting, to the full extent of all territory owned by the United States, the introduction of slavery into those territories. And here, sir, we may pause. We may reflect for a moment upon the entire coincidence and concurrence of sentiment between the North and the South, upon this question, at the period of the adoption of the constitution. But opinions, sir, have changed—greatly changed—changed North and changed South. Slavery is not regarded in the South now as it was then. I see an honorable member of this body paying me the honor of listening to my remarks; he brings to me, sir, freshly and vividly, the sentiments of his great ancestor, so much distinguished in his day and generation, so worthy to be succeeded by so worthy a grandson, with all the sentiments he expressed in the Convention in Philadelphia, on this subject.

Here we may pause. There was unanimity of sentiment, if not a general concurrence of sentiment, running through the whole community, and especially entertained by the eminent men of all portions of the country, in regard to this subject. But soon a change began at the North and the South, and a severance of opinion soon showed itself—the North growing much more warm and strong against slavery, and the South growing much more warm and strong in its support. Sir, there is no generation of mankind whose opinions are not subject to be influenced by what appears to them to be their present, and emergent, and exigent interest. I impute to the South no particularly interested view, in the change which has come over her. I impute to her certainly no dishonest view. All that has happened has been natural. It has followed those causes which always influence the human mind and operate upon it. What, then, have been the causes which have created so new a feeling in favor of slavery in the South—which have changed the whole nomenclature of the South on the subject—and from being thought of and described in the terms I have mentioned, but will not repeat, it has now become an institution, a cherished institution there; no evil, no scourge, but a great religious, social, and moral blessing, as I think I have heard it latterly described? I suppose this, sir, is owing to the sudden uprising and rapid growth of the cotton plantations of the South. So far as any motive of honor, justice, and general judgment could act, it was the cotton interest that gave a new desire to promote slavery, to spread it, and to use its labor. I again say that this is produced by the causes, which we must always expect to produce like effects—their whole interests became connected with it. If we look back to the history of the commerce of this country, at the early commencement of this Government, what were our exports? Cotton was hardly, or but to a very limited extent, known. The tables will show that the exports of cotton for the years 1790 and '91, were hardly more than forty or fifty thousand dollars a year. It has gone on increasing rapidly until it may now be, perhaps, in a season of great product and high prices, a hundred millions of dollars. Then there was more of wax, more of indigo, more of rice, more of almost every thing exported from the South, than of cotton. I think I have heard it said, when Mr. Jefferson negotiated the treaty of 1794 with England, he did not know that cotton was exported at all from the United States; and I have heard it said, that after the treaty, which gave to the United States the right to carry their own commodities to England in their own ships, the custom-house in London refused to admit cotton, upon an allegation that it could not be an American production, there being, as they supposed, no cotton raised in America. They would hardly think so now!

Well, sir, we know what follows. The age of cotton became a golden age for our southern brethren. It gratified their desire for improvement and accumulation, at the same time that it excited it. The desire grew by what it fed upon, and there soon came to be an eagerness for other territory—a new area or new areas for the cultivation of the cotton crop; and measures were brought about, somewhat rapidly, one after another, under the lead of southern men at the head of the Government—they having a majority in both branches of the Government—to accomplish their ends. The honorable member from Carolina observed, that there has been a majority all along in favor of the North. If that be true, sir, the North acted either very liberally and kindly, or very weakly; for they never exercised that majority five times in the history of the Government. Never. Whether they were out-generalled, or whether it was owing to other causes, I shall not stop to consider, but no man acquainted with the history of the country can deny, that the general lead in the politics of the country, for three-fourths of the period that has elapsed since the adoption of the constitution, has been a southern lead. In 1802, in pursuit of the idea of opening a new cotton region, the United States obtained a cession from Georgia of the whole of her western territory, now embracing the rich and growing State of Alabama. In 1803 Louisiana was purchased from France, out of which the States of Louisiana, Arkansas, and Missouri have been framed, as slaveholding States. In 1819 the cession of Florida was made, bringing another cession of slaveholding property and territory. Sir, the honorable member from South Carolina thought he saw in certain operations of the Government, such as the manner of collecting the revenue, and the tendency of those measures to promote emigration into the country, what accounts for the more rapid growth of the North than the South. He thinks they were not the operation of time, but of the system of government established under this constitution. That is a matter of opinion. To a certain extent, it may be so; but it does seem to me, that if any operation of the Government could be shown in any degree to have promoted the population, and growth, and wealth of the North, it is much more sure that there are sundry important and distinct operations of the Government, about which no man can doubt, tending to promote, and which absolutely have promoted, the increase of the slave interest, and the slave territory, of the South. Allow me to say, that it was not time that brought in Louisiana; it was the act of men. It was not time that brought in Florida; it was the act of men. And lastly, sir, to complete those acts of men, who have contributed so much to enlarge the area and the sphere of the institution of slavery, Texas—great, and vast, and illimitable Texas—was added to the Union, as a slave State, in 1845; and that, sir, pretty much closed the whole chapter and settled the whole account. That closed the whole chapter—that settled the whole account—because the annexation of Texas, upon the conditions and under the guarantees upon which she was admitted, did not leave an acre of land, capable of being cultivated by slave labor, between this Capitol and the Rio Grande, or the Nueces, or whatever is the proper boundary of Texas—not an acre, not one. From that moment, the whole country from here to the western boundary of Texas, was fixed, pledged, fastened, decided to be slave territory forever, by the solemn guarantees of law. And I now say, sir, as the proposition upon which I stand this day, and upon the truth and firmness of which I intend to act until it is overthrown, that there is not, at this moment, within the United States, or any territory of the United States, a single foot of land, the character of which, in regard to its being free-soil territory or slave territory, is not fixed by some law, and some irrepealable law, beyond the power of the action of this Government. Now, is it not so with respect to Texas? Why, it is most manifestly so. The honorable Senator from South Carolina, at the time of the admission of Texas, held an important post in the Executive Department of the Government; he was Secretary of State. Another eminent person, of great activity and adroitness in affairs—I mean the late Secretary of the Treasury, (Mr. Walker)—was a leading member of this body, and took the lead in the business of annexation; and I must say that they did their business faithfully; there was no botch in it. They rounded it off, and made as close joiner-work as ever was put together. Resolutions of annexation were brought into Congress fitly joined together—compact, firm, efficient, conclusive, upon the great object which they had in view.

Allow me to read one of these resolutions. It is the third clause of the second section of the resolution of the 1st March, 1845, for the admission of Texas. That clause reads in these words:

"New States, of convenient size, not exceeding four in number, in addition to said State of Texas, and having sufficient population, may hereafter, by the consent of said State, be formed out of the territory thereof, which shall be entitled to admission under the provisions of the Federal Constitution. And such States as may be formed out of that portion of said territory lying south of 30° 30′ north latitude, commonly known as the Missouri compromise line, shall be admitted into the Union, with or without slavery, as the people of each State, asking admission, may desire; and in such State or States as shall be formed out of said territory north of said Missouri compromise line, slavery or involuntary servitude (except for crime) shall be prohibited."

Now what is here stipulated, enacted, secured? It is, that all Texas south of 36° 30′, which is nearly the whole of it, shall be admitted into the Union as a slave State—it was a slave State, and therefore came in as a slave State—and that new States shall be made out of it; and that such States as are formed out of that portion of Texas lying south of 36° 30′, may come in as slave States, to the number of four, in addition to the State then in existence, and admitted at that time by these resolutions. I know no mode of legislation which can strengthen that. I know no mode of recognition that can add a tittle of weight to it. I listened respectfully to the resolutions of my honorable friend from Tennessee, (Mr. BELL.) He proposed to recognize that stipulation with Texas. But any additional recognition would weaken the force of it, because it stands here on the ground of a contract for a consideration. It is a law founded on a contract with Texas, and destined to carry that contract into effect. A recognition founded on any consideration, and any contract, would not be so strong as it now stands on the face of the resolution. Now, I know no way, I candidly confess, in which this Government, acting in good faith, as I trust it always will, can relieve itself from that stipulation and pledge, by any honest course of legislation whatever. And, therefore, I say again, that so far as Texas is concerned—the whole of Texas south of 36° 30′, which I suppose embraces all the slave territory—there is no land, not an acre, the character of which is not established by law—a law which cannot be repealed without the violation of a contract.

I hope, sir, it is now apparent, that my proposition, so far as Texas is concerned, has been maintained, and the provision in this article—and it has been well suggested by my friend from Rhode Island, that that part of Texas which lies north of thirty-four degrees of north latitude, may be formed into three States—is dependent in like manner upon the consent of Texas, herself a slave State.

Well, now, sir, how came it?—how came it, that within these walls, where it is said by the honorable member from South Carolina, the free States have a majority—that this resolution of annexation, such as I have described it, found a majority in both Houses of Congress? Why, sir, it found that majority by the vast addition of northern votes added to the entire southern vote, or, at least, nearly the whole of the southern votes. It was made up of northern as well as of southern votes. In the House of Representatives it stood, I think, about eighty southern votes for the admission of Texas, and about fifty northern votes for the admission of Texas. In the Senate the vote stood for the admission of Texas twenty-seven, and twenty-five against it; and of those twenty-seven votes, constituting a majority, for the admission of Texas, in this body, no less than thirteen of them came from the free States—four of them were from New England. The whole of these thirteen Senators, from the free States—within a fraction you see of one-half of all the votes in this body for the admission of Texas, with its immeasurable extent of slave territory—were sent to this body by free-soil votes.

Sir, there is not so remarkable a chapter in our history of political events, political parties, and political men, as is afforded by this measure for the admission of Texas, with this immense territory, over which a bird cannot fly in a week. (Laughter.) Sir, New England, with some of her votes, supported this measure. Three-fourths of the votes of liberty-loving Connecticut went for it in the other House, and one-half here. There was one vote for it in Maine, but I am happy to say, not the vote of the honorable member who addressed the Senate the day before yesterday, (Mr. HAMLIN,) and who was then a Representative from Maine in the other House; but there was a vote or two from Maine—ay, and there was one vote for it in Massachusetts, the gentleman then representing and now living in the district, in which the prevalence of free-soil sentiment for a couple of years or so, has defeated the choice of any member to represent it in Congress. Sir, that body of northern and eastern men, who gave those votes at that time, are now seen taking upon themselves, in the nomenclature of politics, the appellation of the northern Democracy. They undertook to wield the destinies of this empire—if I may call a republic an empire—and their policy was, and they persisted in it, to bring into this country all the territory they could. They did it under pledges—absolute pledges to the slave interest in the case of Texas, and afterward in the case of these new conquests. My honorable friend from Georgia, in March, 1847, moved the Senate to declare that the war ought not to be prosecuted for acquisition, for conquest, for the dismemberment of Mexico. The same northern Democracy entirely voted against it. He did not get a vote from them. It suited the views, the patriotism, the elevated sentiments of the northern Democracy, to bring in a world here, among the mountains and valleys of California and New Mexico, or any other part of Mexico, and then quarrel about it—to bring it in, and then to put upon it the saving grace of the Wilmot proviso. There were two eminent and highly respectable gentlemen from the North and East, then leading gentlemen in the Senate —I refer, and I do so with entire respect, for I entertain for both of those gentlemen in general, high regard, to Mr. Dix of New York, and Mr. Niles of Connecticut—who voted for the admission of Texas. They would not have that vote any other way than as it stood; and they would have it as it did stand. I speak of the vote upon the annexation of Texas. Those two gentlemen would have the resolution of annexation just as it is, and they voted for it just as it is, and their eyes were all open to it. My honorable friend, the member who addressed us the other day, from South Carolina, was then Secretary of State. His correspondence with Mr. Murphy, the chargé d'affaires of the United States in Texas, had been published. That correspondence was all before those gentlemen, and the Secretary had the boldness and candor to avow in that correspondence, that the great object sought by the annexation of Texas was to strengthen the slave interest of this country. Why, sir, he said, in so many words——

Mr. Calhoun. Will the honorable Senator permit me to interrupt him for a moment?

Mr. Webster. Certainly.

Mr. Calhoun. I am very reluctant to interrupt the honorable gentleman; but, upon a point of so much importance, I deem it right to put myself *rectus.* I did not put it upon the ground assumed by the Senator. I put it upon this ground: that Great Britain had announced to this country, in so many words, that her object was to abolish slavery in Texas, and through Texas, to accomplish the abolishment of slavery in the United States and the world. The ground I put it on was, that it would make an exposed frontier, and, if Great Britain succeeded in her object, it would be impossible that that frontier could be secured against the aggression of the Abolitionists; and that this Government was bound, under the guarantees of the constitution, to protect us against such a state of things.

Mr. Webster. That comes, I suppose, sir, to exactly the same thing. It was, that Texas must be obtained for the security of the slave interest of the South.

Mr. Calhoun. Another view is very distinctly given.

Mr. Webster. That was the object set forth in the correspondence of a worthy gentleman not now living, who preceded the honorable member from South Carolina in that office. There repose on the files of the Department of State, as I have occasion to know, strong letters from Mr. Upsher to the United States Minister in England, and I believe there are some to the same minister from the honorable Senator himself, asserting to this extent the sentiments of this Government, that Great Britain was expected not to interfere to take Texas out of the hands of its then existing government, and make it a free country. But my argument—my suggestion is this: that those gentlemen who composed the northern Democracy, when Texas was brought into the Union, saw with all their eyes, that it was brought in as a slave country, and brought in for the purpose of being maintained, as slave territory, to the Greek Kalends. I rather think the honorable gentleman, who was then Secretary of State, might, in some of his correspondence with Mr. Murphy, have suggested that it was not expedient to say too much about this object, that it might create some alarm; but, sir, he did avow it boldly and manfully; he did not disguise his conduct.

Mr. Calhoun. Never, never.

Mr. Webster. What he means he is very apt to say.

Mr. Calhoun. Always, always.

Mr. Webster. And I honor him for it. This was in 1845. Then, in 1847, *flagrante bello* between the United States and Mexico, the proposition I have mentioned, was brought forward by my friend from Georgia—the northern Democracy voting straight ahead against it. Their remedy was to apply to the acquisitions, after they should come in, the Wilmot proviso. What follows? These two gentlemen, worthy and honorable, and influential men—and if they had not been, they could not have carried the measure—these two gentlemen, members of this body, brought in Texas, and by their votes they prevented the passage of the resolution of the honorable member from Georgia, and then they went home and took the lead in the Free-Soil party. And there they stand, sir! They leave us here, bound in honor and conscience by the resolution of annexation; they leave us here to take the odium of fulfilling the obligations, in favor of slavery, which they voted us into, or else the greater odium of violating those obligations while they are at home making rousing and capital speeches for free soil and no slavery. (Laughter.) And therefore I say, sir, that there is not a chapter in our history, respecting public measures and public men, more full of what should create surprise—more full of what does create, in my mind, extreme mortification—than that of the conduct of the northern Democracy.

Mr. President, sometimes, when a man is found in a new relation to things around him, and to other men, he says that the world has changed, and that he has not changed. I believe, sir, that our self-respect leads us often to make this declaration in regard to ourselves, when it is not exactly true. An individual is more apt to change, perhaps, than all the world around him is to change. But, under the present circumstances, and under the responsibility which I know I incur by what I am now stating here, I feel at liberty to recur to the various expressions and statements, made at various times, of my own opinions and resolutions respecting the admission of Texas, and all that has followed. Sir, as early as 1836, or in the earlier part of 1837, a matter of conversation and correspondence between myself and some private friends, was this project of annexing Texas to the United States; and an honorable gentleman, with whom I have had a long acquaintance, a friend of mine, now perhaps in this chamber—I mean Gen. Hamilton, of South Carolina—was knowing to that correspondence. I had voted for the recognition of Texan independence, because I believed it was an existing fact, surprising and astonishing as it was, and I wished well to the new Republic; but I manifested from the first, utter opposition to bringing her with her territory into the Union. I had occasion, sir, in 1837, to meet friends in New York, on some political occasion, and I then stated my sentiments upon the subject. It was the first time that I had occasion to advert to it; and I will ask a friend near me to do me the favor to read an extract from the speech, for the Senate may find it rather tedious to listen to the whole of it. It was delivered in Niblo's Garden in 1837.

Mr. Greene then read the following extract from the speech of the honorable Senator, to which he referred:

"Gentlemen, we all see that, by whomsoever possessed, Texas is likely to be a slaveholding country; and I frankly avow my entire unwillingness to do any thing which shall extend the slavery of the African race on this continent, or add other slaveholding States to the Union.

"When I say that I regard slavery in itself as a great moral, social, and political evil, I only use language which has been adopted by distinguished men, themselves citizens of slaveholding States.

"I shall do nothing, therefore, to favor or encourage its farther extension. We have slavery already among us. The constitution found it among us; it recognized it, and gave it solemn guarantees.

"To the full extent of these guarantees, we are all bound in honor, in justice, and by the constitution. All the stipulations contained in favor of the slaveholding States, which are already in the Union, ought to be fulfilled, and, so far as depends on me, shall be fulfilled in the fulness of their spirit, and to the exactness of their letter. Slavery, as it exists in the States, is beyond the reach of Congress. It is a concern of the States themselves. They have never submitted it to Congress, and Congress has no rightful power over it.

"I shall concur, therefore, in no act, no measure, no menace, no indication of purpose which shall interfere or threaten to interfere with the exclusive authority of the several States over the subject of slavery, as it exists within their respective limits. All this appears to me to be matter of plain and imperative duty.

"But when we come to speak of admitting new States, the subject assumes an entirely different aspect. Our rights and our duties are then both different. * * * * *

"I see, therefore, no political necessity for the annexation of Texas to the Union—no advantages to be derived from it; and objections to it of a strong, and, in my judgment, of a decisive character."

Mr. Webster. I have nothing, sir, to add to, nor to take back from, those sentiments. That, the Senate will perceive, was in 1837. The purpose of immediately annexing Texas, at that time, was abandoned or postponed; and it was not revived, with any vigor, for some years. In the mean time, it had so happened, that I had become a member of the Executive Administration, and was, for a short period, in the Department of State. The annexation of Texas had become a subject of conversation—not confidential—with the President and heads of Departments, as well as with other public men. No serious attempt was then made to bring it about. I left the Department of State in May, 1843, and shortly after I learned, though no way connected with official information, that a design had been taken up, of bringing in Texas, with her slave territory and population, into the United States. I was here, in Washington, at the time; and the persons are now here who will remember, that we had an arranged meeting for conversation upon it. I went home to Massachusetts, and proclaimed the existence of that purpose; but I could get no audience, and but little attention. Some did not believe it, and some were engaged in their own pursuits. They had gone to their farms, or to their merchandise, and it was impossible to arouse any sentiment in New England or in Massachusetts that should combine the two great political parties against this annexation; and, indeed, there was no hope of bringing the northern Democracy into that view, for the leaning was all the other way. But, sir, even with Whigs, and leading Whigs, I am ashamed to say, there was a great indifference toward the admission of Texas, with slave territory, into this Union. It went on. I was then out of Congress. The annexation resolutions passed the 1st of March, 1845. Texas complied with them; the Legislature of Texas complied with the conditions, and accepted the guarantees; for the phraseology of the language of the resolution is, that Texas is to come in "upon the conditions, and under the guarantees, herein prescribed." I happened to be returned to the Senate in March, 1845, and was here in December, 1845, when the acceptance by Texas, of the conditions proposed by Congress, were laid before us by the President; and an act, for the consummation of the connection, was laid before the two Houses. The connection was not completed. A final law, doing the deed of annexation, ultimately, had not been passed; and when it was upon its final passage here, I expressed my opposition to it, and recorded my vote in the negative; and there that vote stands, with the observations that I made upon that occasion. It happened, that between 1837 and this time, on various occasions and opportunities, I had expressed my entire opposition to the admission of slave States, or the acquisition of new slave territories, to be added to the United States. I know, sir, no change in my own sentiments, or my own purposes, in that respect. I will now, again, ask my friend from Rhode Island, to read another extract from a speech of mine, made at a Whig Convention, in Springfield, Massachusetts, in the month of September, 1847.

Mr. Greene here read the following extract:

"We hear much just now of a *panacea* for the dangers and evils of slavery and slave annexation, which they call the '*Wilmot Proviso*.' That certainly is a just sentiment, but it is not a sentiment to found any new party upon. It is not a sentiment on which Massachusetts Whigs differ. There is not a man in this hall who holds to it more firmly than I do, nor one who adheres to it more than another.

"I feel some little interest in this matter, sir. Did not I commit myself in 1838 to the whole doctrine, fully, entirely? And I must be permitted to say, that I cannot quite consent that more recent discoverers should claim the merit and take out a patent.

"I deny the priority of their invention. Allow me to say, sir, it is not their thunder. * * * *

"We are to use the first, and last, and every occasion which offers, to oppose the extension of slave power.

"But I speak of it here, as in Congress, as a political question—a question for statesmen to act upon. We must so regard it. I certainly do not mean to say that it is less important in a moral point of view—that it is not more important in many other points of view; but, as a legislator, or in any official capacity, I must look at it, consider it, and decide it, as a matter of political action."

Mr. Webster. On other occasions, in debates here, I have expressed my determination to vote for no acquisition, or cession, or annexation, North or South, East or West. My opinion has been, that we have territory enough, and that we should follow the Spartan maxim, "Improve, adorn what you have, seek no farther." I think that it was in some observations that I made here on the three million loan bill, that I avowed that sentiment. In short, sir, the sentiment has been avowed quite as often, in as many places, and before as many assemblages, as any of the humble sentiments of mine ought to be avowed.

But now that, under certain conditions, Texas is in with all her territories, as a slave State, with a solemn pledge that if she is divided into many States, those States may come in as slave States south of 36° 30′, how are we to deal with it? I know no way of honorable legislation, but, when the proper time comes for the enactment, to carry into effect all that we have stipulated to do. I do not entirely agree with my honorable friend from Tennessee, (Mr. Bell,) that, as soon as the time comes when she is entitled to another Representative, we should create a new State. The rule in regard to it I take to be this: that when we have created new States out of territories, we have generally gone upon the idea, that when there is population enough to form a State—sixty thousand, or some such thing—we would create a State; but it may be thought quite a different thing when a State is divided, and two or more States made out of it. It does not follow, in such a case, that the same rule of apportionment should be applied. That, however, is a matter for the consideration of Congress when the proper time arrives. I may not be here—I may have no vote to give on the occasion; but I wish it to be distinctly understood to-day, that according to my view of the matter, this Government is solemnly pledged by law, to create new States out of Texas, with her consent, when her population shall justify such a proceeding, and so far as such States are formed out of Texan territory lying south of 36° 30′, to let them come in as slave States. That is the meaning of the resolution which our friends, the northern Democracy, have left us to fulfil; and I, for one, mean to fulfil it, because I will not violate the faith of the Government.

Now, as to California and New Mexico, I hold slavery to be excluded from those territories by a law even superior to that which admits and sanctions it in Texas—I mean the law of nature—of physical geography—the law of the formation of the earth. That law settles forever, with a strength beyond all terms of human enactment, that slavery cannot exist in California or New Mexico. Understand me, sir—I mean slavery as we regard it; slaves in the gross, of the colored race, transferable by sale and delivery, like other property. I shall not discuss that point. I leave it to the learned gentlemen who have undertaken to discuss it; but I suppose there is no slave of that description in California now. I understand that *peonism*, a sort of penal servitude, exists there; or, rather, a voluntary sale of a man and his offspring for debt, as it is arranged and exists in some parts of California and New Mexico. But what I mean to say is, that African slavery, as we see it among us, is as utterly impossible to find itself, or to be found in Mexico, as any other natural impossibility. California and New Mexico are Asiatic in their formation and scenery. They are composed of vast ridges of mountains, of enormous height, with sometimes broken ridges and deep valleys. The sides of these mountains are barren—entirely barren—their tops capped by perennial snow. There may be in California, now made free by its constitution—and no doubt there are—some tracts of valuable land. But it is not so in New Mexico. Pray, what is the evidence which any gentleman has obtained on this subject, from information sought by himself or communicated by others? I have inquired, and read all I could, to obtain information on this subject. What is there in New Mexico that could by any possibility induce any body to go there with slaves? There are some narrow strips of tillable land on the borders of the rivers; but the rivers themselves dry up before midsummer is gone. All that the people can do is to raise some little articles—some little wheat for their tortillas—and all that by irrigation. And who expects to see a hundred black men cultivating tobacco, corn, cotton, rice, or any thing else, on lands in New Mexico, made fertile only by irrigation? I look upon it, therefore, as a fixed fact, to use an expression current to the day, that both California and New Mexico are destined to be free, so far as they are settled at all, which I believe, especially in regard to New Mexico, will be very little for a great length of time—free by the arrangement of things by the Power above us. I have therefore to say, in this respect also, that this country is fixed for freedom, to as many persons as shall ever live there, by as irrepealable and a more irrepealable law, than the law that attaches to the right of holding slaves in Texas; and I will say further, that if a resolution, or a law, were now before us, to provide a territorial government for New Mexico, I would not vote to put any prohibition into it whatever. The use of such a prohibition would be idle, as it respects any effect it would have upon the territory; and I would not take pains to reaffirm an ordinance of nature, nor to re-enact the will of God. And I would put in no Wilmot proviso, for the purpose of a taunt or a reproach. I would put into it no evidence of the votes of superior power, to wound the pride, even whether a just pride, a rational pride, or an irrational pride—to wound the pride of the gentlemen who belong to the southern States. I have no such object—no such purpose. They would think it a taunt—an indignity. They would think it to be an act taking away from them what they regard a proper equality of privilege; and whether they expect to realize any benefit from it or not, they would think it a theoretic wrong—that something more or less derogatory to their character and their rights had taken place. I propose to inflict no such wound upon any body, unless something essentially important to the country, and efficient to the preservation of liberty and freedom, is to be effected. Therefore, I repeat, sir—and I repeat it because I wish it to be understood—that I do not propose to address the Senate often on this subject. I desire to pour out all my heart in as plain a manner as possible; and I say again, that if a proposition were now here for a government for New Mexico, and it was moved to insert a provision for a prohibition of slavery, I would not vote for it.

Now, Mr. President, I have established, so far as I proposed to go into any line of observation to establish, the proposition with which I set out, and upon which I propose to stand or fall; and that is, that the whole territory of the States in the United States, or in the newly-acquired territory of the United States, has a fixed and settled character, now fixed and settled by law, which cannot be repealed in the case of Texas, without a violation of public faith, and cannot be repealed by any human power in regard to California or New Mexico; that, under one or other of these laws, every foot of territory in the States, or in the territories, has now received a fixed and decided character.

Sir, if we were now making a government for New Mexico, and any body should propose a Wilmot proviso, I should treat it exactly as Mr. Polk treated that provision for excluding slavery from Oregon. Mr. Polk was known to be in opinion decidedly averse to the Wilmot proviso; but he felt the necessity of establishing a government for the Territory of Oregon, and, though the proviso was there, he knew it would be entirely nugatory; and, since it must be entirely nugatory, since it took away no right, no describable, no estimable, no weighable, or tangible right of the South, he said he would sign the bill for the sake of enacting a law to form a Government in that territory, and let that entirely useless, and, in that connection, entirely senseless, proviso remain. For myself, I will say that we hear much of the annexation of Canada; and if there be any man, any of the Northern Democracy, or any of the Free-soil party, who suppose it necessary to insert a Wilmot proviso in a territorial government for New Mexico, that man will of course be of opinion that it is necessary to protect the everlasting snows of Canada from the foot of slavery, by the same overpowering wing of an act of Congress. Sir, wherever there is a particular good to be done—wherever there is a foot of land to be stayed back from becoming slave territory—I am ready to assert the principle of the exclusion of slavery. I am pledged to it from the year 1837; I have been pledged to it again and again; and I will perform those pledges; but I will not do a thing unnecessary, that wounds the feelings of others, or that does disgrace to my own understanding.

Mr. President, in the excited times in which we live, there is found to exist a state of crimination and recrimination between the North and the South. There are lists of grievances produced by each; and those grievances, real or supposed, alienate the minds of one portion of the country from the other, exasperate the feelings, subdue the sense of fraternal connection, and patriotic love, and mutual regard. I shall bestow a little attention, sir, upon these various grievances, produced on the one side and on the other. I begin with the complaints of the South: I will not answer, farther than I have, the general statements of the honorable Senator from South Carolina, that the North has grown upon the South in consequence of the manner of administering this Government, in the collecting of its revenues, and so forth. These are disputed topics, and I have no inclination to enter into them. But I will state these complaints, especially one complaint of the South, which has in my opinion just foundation; and that is, that there has been found at the North, among individuals and among the Legislatures of the North, a disinclination to perform, fully, their constitutional duties, in regard to the return of persons bound to service, who have escaped into the free States. In that respect, it is my judgment that the South is right, and the North is wrong. Every member of every Northern Legislature, is bound, by oath, like every other officer in the country, to support the Constitution of the United States; and this article of the constitution, which says to these States, they shall deliver up fugitives from service, is as binding in honor and conscience as any other article. No man fulfils his duty in any Legislature who sets himself to find excuses, evasions, escapes, from this constitutional obligation. I have always thought that the constitution addressed itself to the Legislatures of the States themselves, or to the States themselves. It says, that those persons escaping to other States, shall be delivered up, and I confess I have always been of the opinion, that it was an injunction upon the States themselves. When it is said that a person escaping into another State, and becoming therefore within the jurisdiction of that State, shall be delivered up, it seems to me the import of the passage is, that the State itself, in obedience to the constitution, shall cause him to be delivered up. That is my judgment. I have always entertained that opinion, and I entertain it now. But when the subject, some years ago, was before the Supreme Court of the United States, the majority of the judges held that the power to cause fugitives from service to be delivered up, was a power to be exercised under the authority of this Government. I do not know, on the whole, that it may not have been a fortunate decision. My habit is to respect the result of judicial deliberations and the solemnity of judicial decisions. But, as it now stands, the business of seeing that these fugitives are delivered up, resides in the power of Congress, and the national judicature, and my friend at the head of the Judiciary Committee has a bill on the subject now before the Senate, with some amendments to it, which I propose to support, with all its provisions, to the fullest extent. And I desire to call the attention of all sober-minded men, of all conscientious men, in the North, of all men who are not carried away by any fanatical idea, or by any false idea whatever, to their constitutional obligations. I put it to all the sober and sound minds at the North, as a question of morals and a question of conscience, What right have they, in all their legislative capacity, or any other, to endeavor to get round this constitution, to embarrass the free exercise of the rights secured by the constitution, to the persons whose slaves escape from them? None at all—none at all. Neither in the forum of conscience, nor before the face of the constitution, are they justified, in my opinion. Of course, it is a matter for their consideration. They probably, in the turmoil of the times, have not stopped to consider of this; they have followed what seemed to be the current of thought and of motives as the occasion arose, and neglected to investigate fully the real question, and to consider their constitutional obligations, as I am sure, if they did consider, they would fulfil them with alacrity. Therefore, I repeat, sir, that here is a ground of complaint against the North, well founded, which ought to be removed—which it is now in the power of the different departments of this Government to remove—which calls for the enactment of proper laws, authorizing the judicature of this Government, in the several States, to do all that is necessary for the recapture of fugitive slaves, and for the restoration of them to those who claim them. Wherever I go, and whenever I speak on the subject—and when I speak here, I desire to speak to the whole North—I say that the South has been injured in this respect, and has a right to complain; and the North has been too careless of what I think the constitution peremptorily and emphatically enjoins upon it as a duty.

Complaint has been made against certain resolutions that emanate from Legislatures at the North, and are sent here to us, not only on the subject of slavery in this District, but sometimes recommending Congress to consider the means of abolishing slavery in the States. I should be sorry to be called upon to present any resolutions here which could not be referable to any committee or any power in Congress, and, therefore, I should be unwilling to receive from the Legislature of Massachusetts any instructions to present resolutions expressive of any opinion whatever on the subject of slavery, as it exists at the present moment in the States, for two reasons; because—first, I do not consider that the Legislature of Massachusetts has any thing to do with it; and next, I do not consider that I, as her representative here, have any thing to do with it. Sir, it has become, in my opinion, quite too common; and if the Legislatures of the States do not like that opinion, they have a great deal more power to put it down, than I have to uphold it. It has become, in my opinion, quite too common a practice for the State Legislatures to present resolutions here on all subjects, and to instruct us here on all subjects. There is no public man that requires instruction more than I do, or who requires information more than I do, or desires it more heartily; but I do not like to have it come in too imperative a shape. I took notice, with pleasure, of some remarks upon this subject made the other day in the Senate of Massachusetts, by a young man of talent and character, from whom the best hopes may be entertained. I mean Mr. Hilliard. He told the Senate of Massachusetts that he would vote for no instructions whatever to be forwarded to members of Congress, nor for any resolutions to be offered, expressive of the sense of Massachusetts, as to what their members of Congress ought to do. He said that he saw no propriety in one set of public servants giving instructions and reading lectures to another set of public servants. To their own master, all of them must stand or fall, and that master is their constituents. I wish these sentiments could become more common—a great deal more common. I have never entered into the question, and never shall, about the binding force of instructions. I will, however, simply say this: if there be any matter of interest pending in this body, while I am a member of it, in which Massachusetts has an interest of her own not adverse to the general interest of the country, I shall pursue her instructions with gladness of heart, and with all the efficiency which I can bring to it. But if the question be one which affects her interest, and at the same time affects the interests of all other States, I shall no more regard her political wishes or instructions, than I would regard the wishes of a man who might appoint me an arbitrator or referee, to decide some question of important private right, and who might *instruct* me to decide in his favor. If ever there was a government upon earth, it is this Government; if ever there was a body upon earth, it is this body, which should consider itself as composed by agreement of all, appointed by some, but organized by the general consent of all, sitting here under the solemn obligations of oath and conscience, to do that which they think is best for the good of the whole.

Then, sir, there are those abolition societies, of which I am unwilling to speak, but in regard to which I have very clear notions and opinions. I do not think them useful. I think their operations for the last twenty years have produced nothing good or valuable. At the same time, I know thousands of them are honest and good men; perfectly well-meaning men. They have excited feelings; they think they must do something for the cause of liberty; and in their sphere of action, they do not see what else they can do, than to contribute to an abolition press, or an abolition society, or to pay an abolition lecturer. I do not mean to impute gross motives even to the leaders of these societies, but I am not blind to the consequences. I cannot but see what mischiefs their interference with the South has produced. And is it not plain to every man? Let any gentleman who doubts of that, recur to the debates in the Virginia House of Delegates in 1832, and he will see with what freedom a proposition, made by Mr. Randolph for the gradual abolition of slavery, was discussed in that body. Every one spoke of slavery as he thought; very ignominious and disparaging names and epithets were applied to it. The debates in the House of Delegates on that occasion, I believe, were all published. They were read by every colored man who could read, and if there were any who could not read, those debates were read to them by others. At that time Virginia was not unwilling nor afraid to discuss this question, and to let that part of her population know as much of it as they could learn. That was in 1832. As has been said by the honorable member from South Carolina, these abolition societies commenced their course of action in 1835. It is said—I do not know how true it may be—that they sent incendiary publications into the slave States; at any event, they attempted to arouse, and did arouse, a very strong feeling; in other words, they created great agitation in the North against southern slavery. Well, what was the result? The bonds of the slaves were bound more firmly than before; their rivets were more strongly fastened. Public opinion, which in Virginia had begun to be exhibited against slavery, and was opening out for the discussion of the question, drew back and shut itself up in its castle. I wish to know whether any body in Virginia can, now, talk as Mr. Randolph, Gov. McDowell, and others talked there openly, and sent their remarks to the press, in 1832. We all know the fact, and we all know the cause, and every thing that this agitating people have done, has been, not to enlarge, but to restrain, not to set free, but to bind faster, the slave population of the South. That is my judgment. Sir, as I have said, I know many abolitionists in my own neighborhood, very honest, good people, misled, as I think, by strange enthusiasm; but they wish to do something, and they are called on to contribute, and they do contribute; and it is my firm opinion this day, that within the last twenty years, as much money has been collected and paid to the abolition societies, abolition presses, and abolition lecturers, as would purchase the freedom of every slave, man, woman, and child in the State of Maryland, and send them all to Liberia. I have no doubt of it. But I have yet to learn that the benevolence of these abolition societies has at any time taken that particular turn. [Laughter.]

Again, sir, the violence of the press is complained of. The press violent! Why, sir, the press is violent everywhere. There are outrageous reproaches in the North against the South, and there are reproaches in not much better taste in the South against the North. Sir, the extremists of both parts of this country are violent; they mistake loud and violent talk for eloquence and for reason. They think that he who talks loudest, reasons the best. And this we must expect, when the press is free, as it is here—and I trust always will be—

for, with all its licentiousness, and all its evil, the entire and absolute freedom of the press is essential to the preservation of government, on the basis of a free constitution. Wherever it exists, there will be foolish paragraphs, and violent paragraphs, in the press, as there are, I am sorry to say, foolish speeches and violent speeches in both Houses of Congress. In truth, sir, I must say that, in my opinion, the vernacular tongue of the country has become greatly vitiated, depraved, and corrupted, by the style of our congressional debates. [Laughter.] And if it were possible for our debates in Congress to vitiate the principles of the people as much as they have depraved their taste, I should cry out, "God save the Republic!"

Well, in all this I see no solid grievance—no grievance presented by the South, within the redress of the Government, but the single one to which I have referred; and that is, the want of a proper regard to the injunction of the constitution, for the delivery of fugitive slaves.

There are also complaints of the North against the South. I need not go over them particularly. The first and gravest is, that the North adopted the constitution, recognizing the existence of slavery in the States, and recognizing the right, to a certain extent, of representation of the slaves in Congress, under a state of sentiment and expectation which do not now exist; and that, by events, by circumstances, by the eagerness of the South to acquire territory, and extend their slave population, the North finds itself, in regard to the influence of the South and the North, of the free States and the slave States, where it never did expect to find itself when they entered the compact of the constitution. They complain, therefore, that, instead of slavery being regarded as an evil, as it was then, an evil, which all hoped would be extinguished gradually, it is now regarded by the South as an institution to be cherished, and preserved, and extended—an institution which the South has already extended to the utmost of her power by the acquisition of new territory. Well, then, passing from that, everybody in the North reads; and everybody reads whatsoever the newspapers contain; and the newsdapers, some of them—especially those presses to which I have alluded—are careful to spread about among the people every reproachful sentiment uttered by any Southern man bearing at all against the North—every thing that is calculated to exasperate, to alienate; and there are many such things, as everybody will admit, from the South, or some portion of it, which are spread abroad among the reading people; and they do exasperate, and alienate, and produce a most mischievous effect upon the public mind at the North. Sir, I would not notice things of this sort appearing in obscure quarters; but one thing has occurred in this debate which struck me very forcibly. An honorable member from Louisiana addressed us the other day on this subject. I suppose there is not a more amiable and worthy gentleman in this chamber, nor a gentleman who would be more slow to give offence to anybody, and he did not mean in his remarks to give offence. But what did he say? Why, sir, he took pains to run a contrast between the slaves of the South and the laboring people of the North, giving the preference in all points of condition, and comfort, and happiness, to the slaves of the South. The honorable member doubtless did not suppose that he gave any offence, or did any injustice. He was merely expressing his opinion. But does he know how remarks of that sort will be received by the laboring people of the North? Why, who are the laboring people of the North? They are the North. They are the people who cultivate their own farms with their own hands—freeholders, educated men, independent men. Let me say, sir, that five-sixths of the whole property of the North, is in the hands of the laborers of the North; they cultivate their farms, they educate their children, they provide the means of independence; if they are not freeholders, they earn wages; these wages accumulate, are turned into capital, into new freeholds; and small capitalists are created. That is the case, and such the course of things, with us, among the industrious, and frugal. And what can these people think when so respectable and worthy a gentleman as the member from Louisiana, undertakes to prove that the absolute ignorance, and the abject slavery of the South, is more in conformity with the high purposes and destinies of immortal, rational, human beings, than the educated, the independent, free laborers of the North?

There is a more tangible, and irritating cause of grievance at the North. Free blacks are constantly employed in the vessels of the North, generally as cooks and stewards. When the vessel arrives, these free colored men are taken on shore, by the police or municipal authority, imprisoned, and kept in prison, till the vessel is again ready to sail. This is not only irritating, but exceedingly inconvenient in practice, and seems altogether unjustifiable, and oppressive. Mr. Hoar's mission, some time ago, to South Carolina, was a well-intended effort to remove this cause of complaint. The North thinks such imprisonment illegal, and unconstitutional; as the cases occur constantly and frequently, they think it a great grievance.

Now, sir, so far as any of these grievances have their foundation in matters of law, they can be redressed, and ought to be redressed; and so far as they have foundation in matters of opinion, in sentiment, in mutual crimination and recrimination, all that we can do is, to endeavor to allay the agitation, and cultivate a better feeling and more fraternal sentiments between the South and the North.

Mr. President, I should much prefer to have heard from every member on this floor, declarations of opinion that this Union should never be dissolved, than the declaration of opinion that in any case, under the pressure of any circumstances, such a dissolution was possible. I hear with pain, and anguish, and distress, the word secession, especially when it falls from the lips of those who are eminently patriotic, and known to the country, and known all over the world, for their political services. Secession! Peaceable secession! Sir, your eyes and mine are never destined to see that miracle. The dismemberment of this vast country without convulsion! The breaking up of the fountains of the great deep without ruffling the surface! Who is so foolish—I beg everybody's pardon—as to expect to see any such thing? Sir, he who sees these States, now revolving in harmony around a common centre, and expects to see them quit their places and fly off without convulsion, may look the next hour to see the heavenly bodies rush from their spheres, and jostle against each other in the realms of space, without producing the crush of the universe. There can be no such thing as a peaceable secession. Peaceable secession is an utter impossibility. Is the great constitution under which we live here—covering this whole country—is it to be thawed and melted away by secession, as the snows on the mountain melt under the influence of a vernal sun—disappear almost unobserved, and die off? No, sir! no, sir! I will not state what might produce the disruption of the States; but, sir, I see it as plainly as I see the sun in heaven—I see that disruption must produce such a war as I will not describe, in its twofold characters.

Peaceable secession! peaceable secession! The concurrent agreement of all the members of this great Republic to separate! A voluntary separation, with alimony on one side and on the other. Why, what would be the result? Where is the line to be drawn? What States are to secede? What is to remain American? What am I to be?—an American no longer? Where is the flag of the Republic to remain? Where is the eagle still to tower? or is he to cower, and shrink, and fall to the ground? Why, sir, our ancestors—our fathers, and our grandfathers, those of them that are yet living among us with prolonged lives—would rebuke and reproach us; and our children, and our grandchildren, would cry out, Shame upon us! if we, of this generation, should dishonor these ensigns of the power of the Government, and the harmony of the Union, which is every day felt among us with so much joy and gratitude. What is to become of the army? What is to become of the navy? What is to become of the public lands? How is each of the thirty States to defend itself? I know, although the idea has not been stated distinctly, there is to be a southern confederacy. I do not mean, when I allude to this statement, that any one seriously contemplates such a state of things. I do not mean to say that it is true, but I have heard it suggested elsewhere, that that idea has originated in a design to separate. I am sorry, sir, that it has ever been thought of, talked of, or dreamed of, in the wildest flights of human imagination. But the idea must be of a separation, including the slave States upon one side, and the free States on the other. Sir, there is not—I may express myself too strongly perhaps—but some things, some moral things, are almost as impossible, as other natural or physical things; and I hold the idea of a separation of these States—those that are free to form one government, and those that are slaveholding to form another—as a moral impossibility. We could not separate the States by any such line, if we were to draw it. We could not sit down here to-day, and draw a line of separation, that would satisfy any five men in the country. There are natural causes that would keep and tie us together, and there are social and domestic relations which we could not break, if we would, and which we should not, if we could. Sir, nobody can look over the face of this country at the present moment—nobody can see where its population is the most dense and growing—without being ready to admit, and compelled to admit, that, ere long, America will be in the valley of the Mississippi.

Well, now, sir, I beg to inquire what the wildest enthusiast has to say, on the possibility of cutting off that river, and leaving free States at its source and its branches, and slave States down near its mouth? Pray, sir—pray, sir, let me say to the people of this country, that these things are worthy of their pondering and of their consideration. Here, sir, are five millions of freemen in the free States north of the river Ohio: can anybody suppose that this population can be severed by a line that divides them from the territory of a foreign and an alien government, down somewhere, the Lord knows where, upon the lower banks of the Mississippi? What will become of Missouri? Will she join the arrondissement of the slave States? Shall the man from the Yellow Stone and the Platte be connected in the new Republic with the man who lives on the southern extremity of the Cape of Florida? Sir, I am ashamed to pursue this line of remark. I dislike it—I have an utter disgust for it. I would rather hear of natural blasts and mildews, war, pestilence, and famine, than to hear gentlemen talk of secession. To break up! to break up this great Government! to dismember this great country! to astonish Europe with an act of folly, such as Europe for two centuries has never beheld in any Government! No, sir! no, sir! There will be no secession. Gentlemen are not serious when they talk of secession.

Sir, I hear there is to be a Convention held at Nashville. I am bound to believe that if worthy gentlemen meet at Nashville in Convention, their object will be to adopt counsels conciliatory—to advise the South to forbearance and moderation, and to advise the North to forbearance and moderation, and to inculcate principles of brotherly love, and affection, and attachment to the constitution of the country, as it now is. I believe, if the Convention meet at all, it will be for this purpose; for certainly, if they meet for any purpose hostile to the Union, they have been singularly inappropriate in their selection of a place. I remember, sir, that when the treaty was concluded between France and England, at the peace of Amiens, a stern old Englishman and an orator, who disliked the terms of the peace as ignominious to England, said in the House of Commons, that if King William could know the terms of that treaty, he would turn in his coffin. Let me commend this saying of Mr. Windham, in all its emphasis and in all its force, to any persons who shall meet at Nashville for the purpose of concerting measures for the overthrow of the Union of this country, over the bones of Andrew Jackson.

Sir, I wish to make two remarks, and hasten to a conclusion. I wish to say, in regard to Texas, that if it should be hereafter at any time the pleasure of the Government of Texas to cede to the United States a portion, larger or smaller, of her territory which lies adjacent to New Mexico and north of the 34° of north latitude, to be formed into free States, for a fair equivalent in money, or in the payment of her debt, I think it an object well worthy the consideration of Congress, and I shall be happy to concur in it myself, if I should be in the public counsels of the country at the time.

I have one other remark to make: In my observations upon slavery as it has existed in the country, and as it now exists, I have expressed no opinion of the mode of its extinguishment or melioration. I will say, however, though I have nothing to propose on that subject, because I do not deem myself so competent as other gentlemen to consider it, that if any gentleman from the South shall propose a scheme of colonization to be carried on by this Government upon a large scale, for the transportation of free colored people to any colony or any place in the world, I should be quite disposed to incur almost any degree of expense to accomplish that object. Nay, sir, following an example set here more than twenty years ago by a great man, then a Senator from New York, I would return to Virginia, and through her for the benefit of the whole South, the money received from the lands and territories ceded by her to this government, for any such purpose as to relieve, in whole or in part, or in any way, to diminish or deal beneficially with, the free colored population of the Southern States. I have said that I honor Virginia for her cession of this territory. There have been received into the treasury of the United States eighty millions of dollars, the proceeds of the sales of the public lands ceded by Virginia. If the residue should be sold at the same rate, the whole aggregate will exceed two hundred millions of dollars. If Virginia and the South see fit to adopt any proposition to relieve themselves from the free people of color among them, they have my free consent that the Government shall pay them any sum of money out of its proceeds which may be adequate to the purpose.

And now, Mr. President, I draw these observations to a close. I have spoken freely, and I meant to do so. I have sought to make no display; I have sought to enliven the occasion by no animated discussion; nor have I attempted any train of elaborate argument. I have sought only to speak my sentiments, fully and at large, being desirous, once and for all, to let the Senate know, and to let the country know, the opinions and sentiments which I entertain on all these subjects. These opinions are not likely to be suddenly changed. If there be any future service that I can render to the country, consistently with these sentiments and opinions, I shall cheerfully render it. If there be not, I shall still be glad to have had an opportunity to disburden my conscience from the bottom of my heart, and to make known every political sentiment that therein exists.

And now, Mr. President, instead of speaking of the possibility or utility of secession, instead of dwelling in these caverns of darkness, instead of groping with those ideas so full of all that is horrid and horrible, let us come out into the light of day; let us enjoy the fresh air of liberty and union; let us cherish those hopes which belong to us; let us devote ourselves to those great objects that are fit for our consideration and our action; let us raise our conceptions to the magnitude and the importance of the duties that devolve upon us; let our comprehension be as broad as the country for which we act, our aspirations as high as its certain destiny; let us not be pigmies in a case that calls for men. Never did there devolve, on any generation of men, higher trusts than now devolve upon us for the preservation of this constitution, and the harmony and peace of all who are destined to live under it. Let us make our generation one of the strongest, and the brightest link, in that golden chain which is destined, I fully believe, to grapple the people of all the States to this constitution, for ages to come. It is a great popular constitutional Government, guarded by legislation, by law, by judicature, and defended by the whole affections of the people. No monarchical throne presses these States together; no iron chain of despotic power encircles them; they live and stand upon a Government popular in its form, representative in its character, founded upon principles of equality, and calculated, we hope, to last forever. In all its history, it has been beneficent; it has trodden down no man's liberty; it has crushed no State. Its daily respiration, its liberty and patriotism; its yet youthful veins are full of enterprise, courage, and honorable love of glory and renown. It has received a vast addition of territory. Large before, the country has now, by recent events, become vastly larger. This Republic now extends, with a vast breadth, across the whole continent. The two great seas of the world wash the one and the other shore. We realize, on a mighty scale, the beautiful description of the ornamental edging of the buckler of Achilles—

"Now the broad shield complete the artist crowned,
With his last hand, and poured the ocean round;
In living silver seemed the waves to roll,
And beat the buckler's verge, and bound the whole."

Mr. CALHOUN. I rise to correct what I conceive to be an error of the distinguished Senator from Massachusetts, as to the motives which induced the acquisition of Florida, Louisiana, and Texas. He attributed it to the great growth of cotton, and the desire of the southern people to get an extension of territory, with the view of cultivating it with more profit than they could in a compact and crowded settlement. Now, Mr. President, the history of these acquisitions, I think, was not correctly given. It is well known that the acquisition of Florida was the result of an Indian war. The Seminole Indians residing along the line attacked one of our fortresses; troops were ordered out; they were driven back; and, under the command of General Jackson, Pensacola and St. Marks were seized. It was these acts, and not the desire for the extended cultivation of cotton, which led to the acquisition of Florida. I admit that there had been for a long time a desire on the part of the South, and of the Administration, I believe, to acquire Florida; but it was very different from the reason assigned by the honorable Senator. There were collected together four tribes of Indians—the Creeks, the Choctaws, the Chickasaws, and the Cherokees—about thirty thousand warriors—who held connection, almost the whole of them, with the Spanish authorities in Florida, and carried on a trade perpetually with them. It was well known that a most pernicious influence was thus exercised over them; and it was the desire of preventing conflict between the Indians and ourselves in the South, as I believe, which induced the acquisition of Florida. I come now to Louisiana. We well know that the immediate cause for the acquisition of Louisiana, was the suspension of our right of deposit at New Orleans. Under a treaty with Spain we had a right to the navigation of the river as far as New Orleans, and a right to make deposits in the port of New Orleans. The Spanish authorities interrupted that right, and that interruption produced a great agitation at the West, and I may say throughout the whole United States. The gentlemen then in opposition, a highly respectable party—the old Federal party, which I have never said a word of disrespect in regard to—if I mistake not, took the lead in a desire to resort to arms to acquire that territory. Mr. Jefferson, more prudent, desired to procure it by purchase. A purchase was made, in order to remove the difficulty, and to give an outlet to the west to the ocean. That was the immediate cause of the acquisition of Louisiana. Now, sir, we come to Texas. Perhaps no gentleman had more to do with the acquisition of Texas than myself; and I aver, Mr. President, that I would have been among the very last individuals in the United States, to have made any movement at that time for the acquisition of Texas; and I go farther: if I know myself, I was incapable of acquiring any territory simply on the ground that it was to be an enlargement of slave territory. I would just as freely have acquired it if it had been on the northern as on the southern side. No, sir; very different motives actuated me. I knew at a very early period—I will not go into the history of it—the British Government had given encouragement to the abolitionists of the United States, who were represented at the World's Convention. The question of the abolition of slavery was agitated in that convention. One gentleman stated that Mr. Adams informed him, that if the British Government wished to abolish slavery in the United States, they must begin with Texas. A commission was sent from this World's Convention to the British Secretary of State, Lord Aberdeen; and it so happened, that a gentleman was present when the interview took place between Lord Aberdeen and the committee, who gave me a full account of it shortly after it occurred. Lord Aberdeen fell into the project, and gave full encouragement to the abolitionists. Well, sir, it is well known that Lord Aberdeen was a very direct, and, in my opinion, a very honest and worthy man; and when Mr. Pakenham was sent here to negotiate with regard to Oregon, and incidentally with respect to Texas, he was ordered to read a declaration to this Government, stating that the British Government was anxious to put an end to slavery all over the world, commencing at Texas. It is well known, farther, that at that very time a negotiation was going on between France and England to accomplish that object, and our Government was thrown, by stratagem, out of the negotiation; and that object was—first, to induce Mexico to acknowledge the independence of Texas upon the ground that she would abolish it. All these are matters of history; and where is the man so blind—I am sure the Senator from Massachusetts is not so blind—as not to see, that if the project of Great Britain had been successful, the whole frontier of the States of Louisiana and Arkansas, and the adjacent States, would have been exposed to the inroads of British emissaries. Sir, so far as I was concerned, I put it exclusively upon that ground. I never would run into the folly of re-annexation, which I always held to be absurd. Nor, sir, would I put it upon the ground—upon which I might well have put it—of commercial and manufacturing considerations, because those were not my motive-principles, and I chose to assign what were. So far as commerce and manufactures were concerned, I would not have moved in the matter at that early period.

The Senator objects that many northern gentlemen voted for annexation. Why, sir, it was natural that they should be desirous of fulfilling the obligations of the constitution; and besides, what man at that time doubted that the Missouri compromise line would be adopted, and that the territory would fall entirely to the South? All that northern men asked for, at that time, was the extension of that line. Their course, in my opinion, was eminently correct and patriotic.

Now, Mr. President, having made these corrections, I must go back a little farther, and correct a statement which I think the Senator has left very defective, relative to the ordinance of 1787. He states very correctly that it commenced under the old Confederation; that it was afterward confirmed by Congress; that Congress was sitting in New York at the time, while the Convention sat in Philadelphia; and that there was concert of action. I have not looked into the ordinance very recently, but my memory will serve me thus far, that Mr. Jefferson introduced his first proposition to exclude slavery in 1784. There was a vote taken upon it, and I think on that vote every southern Senator voted against it; but I am not certain of it. One thing I am certain of, that it was three years before the ordinance could pass. It was sturdily resisted, down to 1787; and when it was passed, as I had good reason to believe, it was upon a principle of compromise—first, that the ordinance should contain a provision similar to the one put in the constitution, with respect to fugitive slaves; and next, that it should be inserted in the constitution; and this was the compromise upon which the prohibition was inserted in the ordinance of 1787. We thought we had an indemnity in that, but we made a great mistake. Of what possible advantage has it been to us? Violated faith has met us on every side, and the advantage has been altogether in their favor. On the other side, it has been thrown open to a northern population to the entire exclusion of the southern. This was the leading measure which destroyed the compromise of the constitution, and then followed the Missouri compromise, which was carried mainly by northern votes, although now disavowed and not respected by them. That was the next step; and between these two causes, the equilibrium has been broken.

Having made these remarks, let me say, that I took great pleasure in listening to the declarations of the honorable Senator from Massachusetts upon several points. He puts himself upon the fulfilment of the contract of Congress, in the resolutions of Texas annexation, for the admission of the four new States provided for by those resolutions, to be formed out of the territory of Texas—all that was manly, statesmanlike, and calculated to do good, because just. He went farther: he condemned, and rightfully condemned—and in that he has shown great firmness—the course of the North relative to the stipulations of the constitution for the restoration of fugitive slaves; but permit me to say, for I desire to be candid upon all subjects, that if the Senator, together with many friends on this side of the chamber, puts his confidence in the bill which has been reported here, farther to extend the laws of Congress upon this subject, it will prove fallacious. It is impossible to execute any law of Congress, until the people of the States shall co-operate.

I heard the gentleman with great pleasure say, that he would not vote for the Wilmot proviso, for he regarded such an act as unnecessary, considering that nature had already excluded slavery. As far as the new acquisitions are concerned, I am disposed to leave them to be disposed of as the hand of nature shall determine. It is what I always have insisted upon. Leave that portion of the country more natural to a non-slaveholding population, to be filled by that description of population; and leave that portion into which slavery would naturally go, to be filled by a slaveholding population—destroying artificial lines, though perhaps they may be better than none. Mr. Jefferson spoke like a prophet, of the effect of the Missouri compromise line. I am willing to leave it for nature to settle and to organize governments for the territories, giving all free scope to enter and prepare themselves to participate in their privileges. We want, sir, nothing but justice. When the gentleman says that he is willing to leave it to nature, I understand he is willing to remove all impediments, whether real or imaginary. It is consummate folly, to assert that the Mexican law prohibiting slavery in California and New Mexico, is in force; and I have always so regarded it.

No man would feel more happy than myself, to believe that this Union, formed by our ancestors, should live forever. Looking back to the long course of *forty* years' service here, I have the consolation to believe, that I have never done one act which would weaken it—that I have done full justice to all sections. And if I have ever been exposed to the imputation of a contrary motive, it is because I have been willing to defend my section from unconstitutional encroachments. But I cannot agree with the Senator from Massachusetts, that this Union cannot be dissolved. Am I to understand him, that no degree of oppression, no outrage, no broken faith can produce the destruction of this Union? Why, sir, if that bcomes a fixed fact, it will itself become the great instrument of producing oppression, outrage, and broken faith. No, sir! the Union can be broken. Great moral causes will break it, if they go on; and it can only be preserved by justice, good faith, and a rigid adherence to the constitution.

Mr. Webster. Mr. President, a single word in reply to the honorable member from South Carolina. My distance from the honorable member, and the crowded state of the room, prevented me from hearing the whole of his remarks. I have only one or two observations to make; and, to begin, I first notice the honorable member's last remark. He asks me if I hold the breaking up of the Union, by any such thing as the voluntary secession of States, as an impossibility? I know, sir, this Union can be broken up; every Government can be; and I admit that there may be such a degree of oppression, as will warrant resistance, and a forcible severance. That is revolution—that is revolution! Of that ultimate right of revolution, I have not been speaking. I know that that law of necessity does exist. I forbear from going farther, because I do not wish to run into a discussion of the nature of this Government. The honorable member and myself have broken lances sufficiently often before on that subject.

Mr. CALHOUN. I have no desire to do it now.

Mr. WEBSTER. I presume the gentleman has not, and I have quite as little. The gentleman refers to the occasions on which these great acquisitions were made to territory on the southern side. Why, undoubtedly, wise and skilful public men, having an object to accomplish, may take advantage of occasions. Indian wars are an occasion; a fear of the occupation of Texas by the British was an occasion; but when the occasion came, under the pressure of which, or under the justification of which, the thing could be done, it was done, and done skilfully. Let me say one thing farther; and that is, that if slavery were abolished, as it was supposed to have been, throughout all Mexico, before the revolution and the establishment of the Texan Government, then if it were desirable to have possession of Texas by purchase, as a means of preventing its becoming a British possession, I suppose that object could have been secured by making it a free territory of the United States as well as a slave territory.

Sir, in my great desire not to prolong this debate, I have omitted what I intended to say upon a particular question, under the motion of the honorable Senator from Missouri, proposing an amendment to the resolution of the honorable member from Illinois; and that is, upon the propriety and expediency of admitting California, under all circumstances, just as she is. The more general subjects involved in this question, are now before the Senate, under the resolutions of the honorable member from Kentucky. I will say that I feel under great obligations to that honorable member for introducing the subject, and for the very lucid speech which he made, and which has been so much read throughout the whole country. I am also under great obligations to the honorable member from Tennessee for the light which he has shed upon this subject; and, in some respects, it will be seen that I differ very little from the leading subjects submitted by either of those honorable gentlemen.

Now, sir, when the direct question of the admission of California shall be before the Senate, I propose—but not before every other gentleman who has a wish to adress the Senate, shall have ratified that desire—to say something upon the boundaries of California, upon the Constitution of California, and upon the expediency, under all the circumstances, of admitting her with that constitution.

Mr. CALHOUN. One word, and I have done; and that word is, that notwithstanding the acquisition of the vast territory of Texas, represented by the Senator from Massachusetts, it is the fact that all that addition to our territory, made it by no means equal to what the northern States had excluded us from before that acquisition. The territory lying west, between the Mississippi and the Rocky Mountains, is three-fourths of the whole of Louisiana; and that which lies between the Mississippi and the Ohio, added to that, makes a much greater extent of territory than Florida, and Texas, and that portion of Louisiana that has fallen to our share.

Mr. WALKER moved the postponement of the farther consideration of the resolutions until to-morrow; which was agreed to.

TUESDAY, March 12.

Committee to Prepare a Compromise.

Mr. FOOTE. I hope not to interfere with any urgent business which any member of the Senate wishes to bring forward this morning, when I state that I wish to have some action upon a subject to which I have before called the attention of the Senate. I feel confident that the motion introduced some days ago, based on the resolutions of the honorable Sentor from Tennessee, can be taken up and disposed of in a very few minutes, if gentlemen will act with their accustomed cordiality on such occasions. I wish, therefore, to renew my motion, heretofore made, and which is in writing in the hands of the Clerk. With that object, I move that the Senate proceed to the consideration of the resolutions of the honorable Senator from Tennessee.

Mr. BALDWIN. I wish to inquire if that resolution was not laid upon the table?

The VICE PRESIDENT. It was submitted, and lies on the table under the rule.

Mr. BALDWIN. I understand the object of the motion made by the honorable Senator from Mississippi is, to take up these resolutions at this time, with a view of moving to refer them to a sectional committee, consisting of a certain number of members from the North and an equal number from the South, for the purpose of adjusting all the questions which have been agitated before the country, and debated in the Senate, in connection with the proposition which is pending here upon the recommendation of the President for the admission of California as a State. I am utterly opposed, sir, to taking up these resolutions for any such purpose, because they are not, in my opinion, topics which can be legitimately connected with the proposition submitted by the message of the President. What, sir, is the state of that proposition? The President has submitted to Congress the constitution prepared by the people of California, and has recommended Congress to admit California as a State. A motion has been made already to submit that message, and the consideration of the constitution accompanying it, to the Committee on the Territories, with instructions to that committee to report a bill in conformity with the recommendation of the President for the admission of California as a State. That presents, in my judgment, a question standing by itself which ought to be considered by itself, and decided upon its own merits by the Senate, irrespective of the views that may be entertained by Senators from different sections of the country in regard to other matters which have been brought into discussion before the Senate.

Sir, the people of California have come here claiming a right—a right secured to them by the treaty with Mexico, by which we acquired a title to this territory. This, sir, is their claim. By the stipulation of that treaty, they were entitled to admission into this Union, with all the privileges of members of this Union, at the proper time, to be judged of by Congress, and in the mean time were to be secured in the enjoyment of all their rights, their liberty, and their property.

Mr. King. I do not wish to interrupt the honorable Senator, but the subject-matter of the resolutions is not under consideration, and it is not in order to go into a discussion of the general matters connected with the resolutions on a mere question to take up the resolutions. When the Senate decides to take them up, we shall have the whole matter before us; and I hope we shall not engage in discussing them till that time.

Mr. Hamlin. I would inquire if this matter is in order now, and if an objection to their consideration would not cause them to lie over?

Mr. King. Not at all.

The Vice President. The Chair is of the opinion that it is not in order at this time.

Mr. Baldwin. The question lies over under the rule. A motion is made to take it up, for the purpose of moving the reference of these resolutions to a sectional committee, who are to consider all the questions referred to in these resolutions—the question of the admission of California—the question in regard to fugitive slaves—every question, in short, which has been brought into discussion before the Senate, in connection with the subject of slavery, and to report upon these in the aggregate. Now, sir, I am opposed to taking up these resolutions for any such purpose. I am opposed to taking them up at all at this time, when the question of the admission of California is presented to us on its own merits, upon the recommendation of the President, and the proposition of the honorable Senator from Missouri, to refer them to a committee, with instructions, has been the subject of debate from day to day. Now, we are called, pending the debates upon that question, to admit—what I, for one, am unwilling to admit—that this, or any other question pending before the Senate or Congress of the United States, is to be regarded as a sectional question—a question not to be decided upon the principles of compromise, settled by our fathers in the constitution.

Mr. Foote. I rise to a point of order. I insist that the honorable Senator is out of order. He is discussing the general merits of this proposition. The simple question before the Senate is, whether the resolutions shall be now taken up for consideration. A member is entitled to state any reasons in opposition to taking them up, but to go into a general discussion of the merits of all the propositions connected with the subject of slavery, is as grossly unparliamentary as any thing which I can conceive of.

Mr. Baldwin. I will waive any further remarks at present.

The Vice President. The question is on taking up these resolutions.

Mr. Hale and Mr. Chase called for the yeas and nays, and they were ordered, and being taken, resulted as follows:

Yeas.—Messrs. Atchison, Badger, Bell, Berrien, Bradbury, Cass, Clay, Clemens, Davis of Mississippi, Dawson, Dickinson, Dodge of Iowa, Downs, Foote, Hunter, Jones, King, Mangum, Mason, Morton, Pratt, Rusk, Sebastian, and Sturgeon—24.

Nays.—Messrs. Baldwin, Benton, Butler, Calhoun, Chase, Clark, Corwin, Davis of Massachusetts, Dayton, Dodge of Wisconsin, Felch, Greene, Hale, Hamlin, Phelps, Seward, Shields, Smith, Underwood, Upham, Walker, and Yulee—22.

So the resolutions were taken up for consideration and read.

Mr. Foote. I now move that these resolutions be referred to a select committee of thirteen, to consist of six members from the South and six from the North, and one to be by them chosen; and that said committee be instructed to exert themselves to mature some scheme of compromise for the adjustment of all pending questions growing out of the institution of slavery, and to report by bill or otherwise.

The Vice President. It appears to the Chair, that this motion, in part, is not in order, inasmuch as the rules prescribe how a committee shall be elected. This resolution seems to contemplate that a portion of this committee shall be elected by the Senate, and a portion by the committee itself. The Chair will read the rule, and submit himself to the guidance of the Senate:

"In the appointment of the standing committees, the Senate will proceed, by ballot, severally to appoint the chairman of each committee, and then by one ballot the other members necessary to complete the same; and a majority of the whole number of votes given shall be necessary to the choice of the chairman of a standing committee. All other committees shall be appointed by ballot, and a plurality of votes shall make a choice."

Mr. Foote. I will save further trouble on that matter, as we all understand the character of the committee. I will, therefore, withdraw that motion and will now simply move that this subject be referred to a committee of thirteen, to be appointed by ballot.

The Vice President then stated the question, as modified by Mr. Foote.

Mr. Berrien. I rise to say that I suppose the objection suggested by the Chair does not present the question of order to the consideration of the Senate, but the question as to the adoption of the resolution upon its merits.

The Vice President. The Chair begs leave to state, that the motion appears to be in conflict with the rules.

Mr. Berrien. If the resolution be taken up for consideration, it is subject to modification either by the mover or by the action of the Senate, in such way as to make it conform to the rule; and that reflection, I think, will satisfy the Chair, that the objection is not one of order under the rules, but one which may be decided by the Senate.

Mr. Clay. I hope the honorable Senator from Mississippi will persevere in his modification, which he has last suggested; for, really, I should, for one, be extremely unwilling, in the constitution of a committee, or in any other act of this body, to give them a sectional aspect of any sort. I think, therefore, that the proposition as made by the Senator from Mississippi, in the first instance, but which, he now proposes to modify, was exceptionable, whether liable to the objection named by the Chair, or not; and I am rather inclined to differ with my friend near me, (Mr. Berrien,) and to think that it is liable to the objection. While I am up, I beg leave to say a word or two; and, first, in regard to the constitution of the committee, if this proposition should be adopted as the Senator from Mississippi proposes. Sir, I had nothing to do with it. I was not consulted in relation to any member whatever to be placed on that committee. The Senator from Mississippi, in that kind and friendly manner in which intercourse with him has been generally carried on, mentioned the purpose which he had in view in proposing the appointment of a committee of thirteen, in imitation of what was done in a most memorable epoch of the country, and asked me if I would concur in such a measure. I stated to the Senator, what I wish now to state to the Senate, that I considered an amicable adjustment of all the questions which unfortunately divide and agitate this country, as of such great and paramount importance, that I will vote for any proposition, coming from any quarter, which looks to, or proposes such an adjustment. That is the object which I understand the honorable gentleman from Mississippi proposes to accomplish. I am, I must add, at the same time, however, far less sanguine than he is, that such a committee will be able to present to the Senate a scheme of adjustment and arrangement of this unhappy subject which will command the majority; still I would make the experiment, and I would make experiments day after day, and night after night, if necessary, to accomplish the great and patriotic object to which I refer. With regard to the formation of the committee, I dare say the honorable Senator from Mississippi may have consulted with other gentlemen, but I certainly was not consulted. With reference to the appearance of this subject in the newspapers, I think, that upon these grave and important matters, we ought not to allow ourselves to be too easily and lightly affected by trivial circumstances. I beg leave to state, that upon the other memorable occasion to which I have referred, I made out the committee of thirteen, and put it into the hands of the then Speaker, and he appointed every member I proposed. In reference to the second committee, the joint committee on the part of the House and an appropriate number on the part of the Senate—on all sides of the House, members came flocking around me, begging that I would make a committee to be balloted for by the House. I accordingly turned my attention to the subject, and determined on the twenty-three names, and caused them to be distributed by the officers throughout the House, and eighteen were elected at the first ballot, and the other five, who had the highest number, each having a plurality, were on my motion elected, further balloting being dispensed with. I think these little matters in the newspapers—how they get there, I do not know—our conversations in social intercourse, about the constitution of a committee, our arrangements about the disposition of the public business, and especially arrangements about the disposition of that great and momentous subject which now engages our attention, ought not to be caught at, criticized, and examined, for the purpose of injuring the great work which we all have at heart, and about which we ought all to cooperate.

Mr. Butler. I do not wish to be misunderstood, so far as regards my course on this subject. I never have said that I was opposed to such a committee, permanently, nor do I rise to say it now, or to make any strictures on the mode of organizing the committee, as suggested by the honorable Senator from Mississippi. Committees of all kinds are usually made up in the way which he has indicated. But, Mr. President, I have an objection to this committee being organized at this time, and I persevere in that objection; for I take it that if the committee is now organized as contemplated, there must be referred to it the resolutions of the Senator from Tennessee, and that of the Senator from Missouri.

Mr. Foote. Will the honorable Senator bear with me while I state, that the resolution is so worded that the resolutions of the honorable Senator from Tennessee are alone to be referred to that committee. I stated distinctly that the object was to allow the debate to go on upon the other questions; and permit me further to say, that if we can get a plan for a general adjustment—as I have no doubt we can—the debate now in progress on the various resolutions, can have further progress on the practical plan to be proposed, and can be much more profitably carried on than now.

Mr. Butler. Then I am to understand the honorable Senator as only intending to refer the resolutions of the Senator from Tennessee. He must see very readily that the other gentlemen will move to refer their resolutions to the same committee immediately. I will answer for it that they will severally make such a motion as soon as the committee is raised. The Senator from Missouri will doubtless move to refer his proposition, and there can be as little doubt that the Senator from New Hampshire will move to refer his Wilmot proviso. The committee will go there with instructions, and thus trammelled—

Mr. Foote. While I move to refer the resolutions of the honorable Senator from Tennessee, I expressly propose that this committee shall investigate the whole subject, and endeavor to propose some plan for the adjustment of the whole matter. They will consider the subject in all the bearings and aspects which it presents. I cannot see any necessity to oppose it. Certainly, if a motion were made here to refer the Wilmot proviso to a committee of compromise, it would be so absurd a proposition, that every man of sense would vote it down at once.

Mr. Butler. I shall sit down with a single remark. Though I am not ultimately opposed to the committee, I would prefer that it should be made up after the discussion. That has been my view. I would not interfere with any suggestion of this kind from any opposition to what may be supposed a satisfactory, and, I hope, an honorable adjustment of this matter; but I must be permitted to say, that when I hear the word compromise used so often, and see all the motions of compromise coming from one source—the South—not one proposed from the other portions of this Confederacy, except so far as the very honorable feeling which has been indicated by the distinguished Senator from Massachusetts—I have some little fear on the subject, and am afraid that any proposition, brought in by such a committee, would be liable to many objections, and might go forth to the public rather as a source of irritation than of pacification.

Mr. Cass. I desire to say a few words upon this subject; but as the hour for proceeding to the order of the day has arrived, and as I am unwilling to trespass upon the time of the honorable Senator from Tennessee, (Mr. Turney,) I move that the further consideration of this subject be postponed until half-past twelve o'clock to-morrow.

The question was then taken on the motion to postpone, and it was agreed to.

Wednesday, March 13.

Slavery—Select Committee.

The Vice President. The time having arrived for the special order of the day, the Senate will now proceed to the consideration of the resolutions of the Senator from Tennessee, which the Senator from Mississippi has moved to refer to a select committee of thirteen.

Mr. Berrien. As I understand the resolution now presented on the motion of the Senator from Mississippi, it does not specify the resolutions which are to be referred.

Mr. Foote. I did specify them in my motion.

The Vice President. The Senator will recollect that the resolutions of the Senator from Tennessee were under consideration when the motion was made by the Senator from Mississippi to refer them.

Mr. Baldwin. I desire to offer an amendment, as follows:

"Except the sixth resolution, which is referred to the Committee on Territories, with instructions to report a bill in conformity with said resolution."

The sixth resolution is in these words:

Resolved, That the constitution recently formed by the people of the western portion of California, and presented to Congress by the President, on the 13th day of February, 1850, be accepted, and that they be admitted into the Union as a State upon an equal footing in all respects with the original States.

Mr. Benton. Will the Senator from Connecticut yield the floor for one moment?

Mr. Baldwin. I will.

Mr. Benton. My mind has been directed to the same point as that referred to by the Senator from Connecticut. I was for proposing an amendment in the same terms, but I afterward thought, for the purpose of making all sure, and of keeping the question of the admission of California wholly unmixed with every thing that is going on here, in connection with the subject of slavery, it would be preferable to offer the amendment in this shape:

"But nothing in this resolution shall be construed to authorize the said committee to take into consideration any thing which relates to the admission of the State of California into the Union."

The Vice President. Will the Senator from Connecticut accept that amendment?

Mr. Baldwin. I accept it, sir.

The Vice President. The resolution of the Senator from Connecticut is modified as follows——

Mr. Cass. Mr. President——

Mr. Webster. Will the member from Michigan permit me to say a word or two?

Mr. Cass. Certainly.

Mr. Webster. The distinguished member from Michigan (Mr. Cass) is kind enough to allow me an opportunity of saying, that I have no desire to oppose this resolution of the honorable member from Mississippi, if anybody thinks it necessary, or would be useful. But, from what I have seen, sir, and from what we have all seen and heard, within the last month, my own persuasion is, that no benefit is likely to arise from any attempt to draw up a series of resolutions for the settlement of all the questions now in agitation. I see no hope that such a series of resolutions would pass the two Houses of Congress. At the close of my remarks on Thursday, I signified that I should take an opportunity, as early as might be convenient, consistently with the rights of others, to say what I had to say on the subject immediately embraced by the resolution of the chairman of the Committee on the Territories, (Mr. Douglas,) and the amendment proposed to it by the honorable member from Missouri, (Mr. Benton.) Upon the direct subject of the admission of California, under the circumstances, I have not a particle of doubt. I am clear in the opinion, that the true course—and the only course of proceeding efficiently—is to keep that measure separate; and I am prepared to vote for the admission of California exactly as she presents herself, with her boundaries precisely as they are; and I hope, in a very short course of observations addressed to the Senate, to show, that if the question were now here before us, and we were ourselves to prescribe boundaries for California, we could not make any boundaries for that State better than are provided for by her own constitution. In order to make out this, I propose to say something upon the nature of the country, the extent of the territory, and whatsoever else may appropriately belong to the question of the boundaries of States in that quarter of the world. In short, I incline to think it expedient—quite expedient—to proceed in that course of legislation which the President has suggested, in his message transmitting the constitution of California.

Mr. Cass. On this subject, sir, I agree precisely with what was said by the distinguished Senator from Kentucky, (Mr. Clay.) I shall vote for the reference. I should vote for almost any proposition that had the appearance of bringing this country into harmony upon this perplexing question—almost any proposition that may be submitted, that has even the appearance of such a result. I do not see any possible objection to this course. It commits no one. It is simply an instruction to a committee to inquire into what can be done.

It does not suspend the operation of the Senate at all. Its discussions, its debates, its votes, will go on, as though this question had not been submitted to a committee. It is one chance more for terminating this fearful controversy. I agree, too, with the Senator from Kentucky, in that my hopes are not strong as to any favorable result to grow out of this committee. The chances have been much diminished by the vote taken on yesterday. If that vote contained any indication of the feeling in this chamber, with regard to the committee itself, and the benefit to result from it, I am sorry to say, that I can anticipate very little good from the proposition of the Senator from Mississippi, (Mr. Foote,) relative to the resolutions prepared with great care, and submitted with great good sense and excellent good feeling such as have always distinguished the Senator from Tennessee, (Mr. Bell.) For myself, I am not prepared to say what my views will be upon this whole matter. They are not yet formed. I say, merely, that this course holds out one hope the more, and is, therefore, well worthy of adoption. So far as respects the proposition connected with Texas, I am myself prepared to consider it in a spirit of fairness and liberality. The honorable Senator from Tennessee (Mr. Bell) has said, that a doubt has been suggested with respect to the disposition of this Senate, and perhaps of the country, to carry into effect the Texas guarantees. I believed that that gentleman was wholly in error. I am sorry to find, from various indications here, that he was not. For myself, without going into the great question at all, I am prepared to say, that as long as I have a vote to give, I will faithfully carry out the spirit of the articles of annexation; and I will not look behind their guarantees. I will abide by them, and I am prepared at all times to say so.

But however this proposition may terminate, I think the country is under lasting obligation to the Senator from Mississippi for his efforts to terminate the existing difficulties. While he has proved himself true to his own section of the country, he has proved himself true to the whole country. He has stood up manfully for the rights of the South, but he has stood up, also, for the obligations of the constitution. And I must say, too, that I have seldom seen an instance of greater moral courage than has been displayed by him. The distinguished Senator from South Carolina occupies, we all know, a high position in the country; and from the zeal, and energy, and ability, with which he has long advocated the cause of the South, he has almost rendered himself the representative of southern opinions. When, in the name of that section of country, he advanced claims which, if persisted in, would have presented insurmountable obstacles to the amicable adjustment of these difficulties, the Senator from Mississippi came forward to disavow the sentiments thus advanced. He came as a messenger of peace, to pour oil upon the troubled waters. He deserves the gratitude of the country for this noble effort. I must confess, my own impressions agreed with the impressions of the honorable Senator from Mississippi. I thought the speech of the Senator from South Carolina was calculated to produce most unfavorable results.

I listened, Mr. President, with great regret, to the speech of the distinguished Senator from South Carolina, (Mr. Calhoun.) I am not going to criticize it—my great respect for that gentleman will prevent me from doing so. I will merely say, that there was a strange collection of facts, as well as a strange collocation of them, and that these were followed by strange conclusions. I think, Mr. President, I may say, and I imagine this feeling is general in the Senate, that a sombre hue pervaded his whole speech, in consequence of its being prepared in the recesses of a sick chamber. Had he been able to walk abroad in the light of heaven, and felt the breezes blowing upon him, I am sure his remarks would not have been as gloomy, nor the results as desponding. We have all felt this, sir, and know how to sympathize with him.

I repeat, that I am not going to criticize the speech of the honorable Senator; but there was one expression, I remember, which grated harshly upon my ear. He denominated Washington the *illustrious southerner!* Not the renowned warrior—not the eminent statesman—not the distinguished citizen—not the great American—not the beloved Virginian—but the illustrious southerner! Our Washington—the Washington of our whole country—receives in this Senate the epithet of "southerner," as if the glory of his name and fame could be divided or assigned to a single section of his beloved country—as if that great man, whose distinguished characteristic was his attachment to his country, and his whole country, who was so well known, and who, more than any one, deprecated all sectional feeling and all sectional action—loved Georgia better than he loved New Hampshire, because he happened to be born on the southern bank of the Potomac. I repeat, sir, that I heard with great pain, that expression from the distinguished Senator from South Carolina.

I heard the disavowal of the honorable Senator from Mississippi (Mr. Foote) with the more gratification, because it was followed by an explanation from the distinguished Senator from South Carolina, (Mr. Calhoun,) which, though it did not remove my apprehensions, certainly diminished them. If the impression which I, as well as many others, received, respecting the nature of these propositions, was correct, the handwriting upon the wall, "God hath numbered thy kingdom and finished it," announced with no more certainty to the wondering king of Babylon the destruction of his empire, and the termination of his life, than would these propositions—if the continuance of our Union depended upon their adoption—have announced that, "God hath numbered our Republic and finished it." To what new Medes and Persians we should have been delivered, is known only to Him who holds in his hands the fate of nations.

We have been three months here, and what have we done? Nothing. We have not passed a single law of the least national importance. We have occupied the whole time by the discussion of this question, and no practical result has been attained; and present appearances do not indicate that such a result is near. But, though we have done nothing, we have ascertained that some things cannot be done. We have ascertained (I think I may say with certainty) that no Wilmot proviso can be passed through this Congress. That measure is dead. It is the latest, and I hope it is the last, attempt that will be made to interfere with the right of self-government within the limits of this Republic. I think we may also say, that no Missouri compromise line can pass, and that no one expects or desires that it should pass.

Mr. President, what was the compromise line? Allow me to read the law which established it:

"Sec. 8. *And be it further enacted*, That in all that territory ceded by France to the United States, under the name of Louisiana, which lies north of thirty-six degrees and thirty minutes north latitude, not included within the limits of the State contemplated by this act, slavery and involuntary servitude, otherwise than in the punishment of crimes, whereof the parties shall have been duly convicted, shall be, and is hereby, forever prohibited."

Now, sir, what is that provision? It is intervention north of the line of 36° 30′ and non-intervention south of that line. Why, sir, there is not one southern Senator on this floor, and not one southern member of the other house, nor indeed a southern man who understands the subject, who would accept that line as a proper settlement of this question.

Mr. Foote, (in his seat.) I would not.

Mr. Cass. Why, sir, the whole doctrine of equal rights and of non-intervention is taken away by it at once. Why, sir, putting out of view the constitutional objections to such an arrangement, it gives the South nothing, while it prohibits the people north of 36° 30′ from exercising their own will upon the subject. The true doctrine of non-intervention leaves the whole question to the people, and does not divide their right of decision by a parallel of latitude. If they choose to have slavery north of that line, they can have it.

Mr. Calhoun, (in his seat.) We are very competent to judge of that matter ourselves.

Mr. Cass. Is there a Senator on this floor who would accept of a proposition to apply the principle of non-intervention to a part of the territory, leaving to the people of the other portion to do as they please? No, sir; there is not a southern Senator here who would vote for it. I will tell you, what would be voted for, has already been announced—a law declaratory, mandatory, or permissory, for the establishment of slavery south of the line of 36°

30′. The distinguished Senator from South Carolina might be willing to accept a declaration that slavery does now exist, or that it shall exist, or may exist, south of a certain line; but I take it for granted that no Senator from the South would be willing to abandon the ground of non-intervention, without some provision like that.

Mr. FOOTE. Permit me freely to say, that I would no sooner vote for a southern Wilmot proviso than I would for a northern one. I rely, and am content to rely, upon the constitution. I was not convinced by the argument of the Senator from South Carolina, of the necessity or expediency of going further than that. I rely with entire confidence, upon our rights under the constitution, and the treaty by which the territories were acquired. I ask for no legislation upon the subject, but simply that the whole matter be let alone. I ask nothing but the doctrine of non-intervention.

Mr. CASS. Mr. President, I will not argue this point. I was about to say, that what the law is, is a question for the decision of the judiciary; but what the law shall be, belongs to the legislative department to declare. If we have the power to pass a law declaring the existence of slavery, which is to be attended with any practical result, we necessarily possess jurisdiction over the whole subject-matter. We have the same power to pass a mandatory law, commanding the existence of slavery, as a declaratory one, recognizing its existence. And I will appeal to every Senator, northern or southern, eastern or western, if there is any probability, I may say, possibility—of such a law passing this Congress? No one asks it—no one expects it. The Missouri compromise line is, therefore, as much out of the question as the Wilmot proviso. The fact is, Mr. President, it is not any way applicable to the existing state of things, though it was applicable to the country when it was established, because slavery was then an existing institution, and it was left in force south of 36° 30′. Insuperable objections, therefore, exist to such an arrangement, where the condition of the country is entirely changed.

Well, then, Mr. President, if these things are impossible—if they cannot be done—it remains to inquire what it is in our power to do.

My own opinion is, sir, that we should take up the bill for the recapture of fugitive slaves, reported by the Judiciary Committee. I am disposed to suspend all our discussions, and to lay aside all other business, with a view to act upon that bill, without unnecessary delay, and to pass it in such form as would be acceptable to a majority of this body. That is a point upon which the South feels most acutely, and in regard to which it has the most serious cause of complaint. I have heard but one man in this body deny the existence of this evil, or the justice and necessity of providing an adequate remedy.

The act of 1793 provided that the State magistrates in the various cities and countries of the Union should carry that law into effect. This provision has been since rendered nugatory, as these officers will not now act, and consequently the judges of the United States alone have jurisdiction over the subject. They are not enough for that purpose, and the law, therefore, requires an amendment. I, for one, am willing to take up the subject, and provide the necessary means of carrying the provision of the constitution into full effect. Such a procedure would have the very best effect upon the South at this time. It would be a pledge of our sincerity, and of our desire to do justice to that great section of our common country.

If I understood the Senator from New York, (Mr. SEWARD,) he intimated his belief that it was immoral to carry into effect the provision of the constitution for the recapture of fugitive slaves. That, sir, is a very strange view of the duties of a Senator in this body. No man should come here who believes that ours is an immoral constitution; no man should come here, and, by the solemn sanction of an oath, promise to support an immoral constitution. No man is compelled to take an oath to support it. He may live in this country, and believe what he chooses with regard to the constitution; but he has no right, as an honest man, to seek office, and obtain it, and then talk about its being so immoral that he cannot fulfil its obligations. It is the duty of every man, who has sworn to support the constitution, fairly to carry its provisions into effect; and no man can stand up before his fellow-citizens and maintain any other doctrine, whatever reasons he may urge in his vindication.

In one of the most disingenuous portions of the speech of the honorable Senator from New York, (Mr. SEWARD)—which itself was one of the most disingenuous I have ever heard—he speaks of "slavery having a reliable and accommodating ally in a party of the free States," and he says he "bears witness to its fidelity to the interests of slavery."

Now, I ask the Senator from New York, if he believes there is a man in this Senate from the North, whose course is influenced by his fidelity to slavery; and if he does, what right he has to cast odium upon gentlemen who are associated with him in the high duties which belong to his position?

Mr. SEWARD. The Senator addresses a question to me, and I rise for no other purpose than to answer it. I think it was Mr. Jefferson who said that the natural ally of slavery in the South, was the Democracy of the North. I have heard it attributed to Mr. Jefferson. However this may be, I believe it. I assail the motives of no Senator. I am not to be drawn into personal altercations by any interrogatories addressed to me. I acknowledge the patriotism, the wisdom, the purity of every member of this body. I never have assailed the motives of honorable Senators in any instance, I never shall. When my own are assailed, I stand upon my own position. My life and acts must speak for me. I shall not be my own defender or advocate.

Mr. Foote. Do I understand the Senator from New York as saying Mr. Jefferson asserted that the northern Democracy was the natural ally of slavery? He never said such a word.

Mr. Cass. I will not touch upon that question; but I will ask the Senator from New York in relation to another point—and that is, if he meant it in the sense which Mr. Jefferson, or whoever may have used it, intended? The one was intended as a commendation for their attachment to constitutional principles—the other as a slur upon a great party.

Mr. Seward. I answer promptly and freely; I had no purpose of casting reproach upon, or of reflecting upon, any member of this body, or upon any person anywhere. The remark had no such connection. I ask leave now to say, that such as I described, is, in my view, the political organization of the parties of this country; that slavery has the support, the toleration (given honestly, and from patriotic motives, I admit) of the party to which I referred; and that its alliance with slavery constitutes its tower of strength. On the other hand, the party to which I belong, is a party which is more distinctly identified with the progress of the sentiment of freedom or emancipation, and therefore it is weaker in its alliances with the South. I again disavow, as I always shall, any reflections upon the conduct of Senators here. I know the motives which govern me. I have no reason to question—I never do question—the motives of others with whom I am associated.

Mr. Dawson, (interposing.) Will the Senator permit me to inquire if I understood him to say this: that these were the sentiments of the party to which he belongs? I want to know if he claims to belong to the Whig party? (Laughter.) If he does, it will be known to every true Whig that I do not belong to his party; and I hope that when he speaks for the party to which he belongs, he will not put under his banner the Whig party of the United States, the conservative party of this country, together with the Democratic party, which I admit to be conservative too.

Mr. Seward. I will not detain the honorable Senator from Michigan with categorical replies to my friend from Georgia, (Mr. Dawson.) I pretend to speak no man's sentiments, and for no man but myself. I am a citizen of the United States. My duty is to promote the welfare, interest, and happiness of the people of the United States; and I hold, that I can do so in no effectual way by going alone and independent. That is always the error of schismatics. Therefore, in the discharge of my duty, I ally myself to such a party as I find most approximate to the principles and sentiments that I entertain. I will do the Whig party the justice or the injustice to say, that I have been a member of it all my active life; and I will do it the great disservice to say, that no matter what may happen, and who may put me under the ban, I shall be the last to leave it, however individuals may disown me or the principles I maintain. I shall adhere to it, because I think, of the two great parties it is the most devoted to the cause of freedom and emancipation. I will, however, do the Whig party the justice, if it be such, to say that these sentiments of mine upon that point, are not in accordance with the sentiments of that party throughout the whole country—that I do not profess to speak for it, but for myself alone. I have, however, great hopes that the Whig party, and the party claiming to be the party of progress, to which I refer, and ultimately all parties, will come to precisely the same conclusions which are the guide and governing principles of my own conduct.

Mr. Cass, (resuming.) I was going to remark that, with respect to the creed of the Whig party, or the orthodoxy of the Senator from New York, it is a matter with which I have no concern; but with respect to progress, I have something to say. My progress is within the constitution. My age of progress is circumscribed there. If the Senator from New York is going out of it, I do not believe in his progress at all. No, sir! My object is to support the constitution which, under God, is the source of our prosperity and happiness.

Mr. Seward, (in his seat.) That is mine.

Mr. Cass. The Senator from New York says, that also is *his* object. If it is, I think he has a very strange way of showing it, by pronouncing it immoral, and denying the validity of its obligations. It would last scarcely a day, if that Senator, with this avowed principle of action, had the direction of the Government. I do not say that it would be dissolved immediately, but the seeds of dissolution would be sown, and would ripen into a harvest of misfortune as speedily as the rankest vegetation gains maturity under a tropical sun.

The honorable Senator from Illinois (Mr. Douglas) has the floor to-day, and I do not wish to interfere with that arrangement. I have not concluded my remarks, and I would move to postpone the further consideration of this subject until to-morrow, at half-past twelve o'clock.

Mr. Calhoun. I have a few words to say in reply to the observations of the Senator from Michigan, and, as it is in reference to a point of some importance, I desire that what I say shall go out with his remarks. I regret very much that the state of my health does not permit me to enter fully into the argument, and that I shall be under the necessity of economizing my words, as well as my strength.

Mr. President, the Senator could not have heard me with more regret, make the declaration to which he has alluded, than I have heard him this morning make the declaration which he has made. Sir, the Senator and myself have two distinct and different conceptions as to the mode of saving this Union. His whole course has been a course of palliatives. And, sir, of all courses, that is far the worst. Why, sir, you might as well treat a cancer, that is about striking into a vital part, with palliatives, as to treat this question with palliatives. No, sir! my idea has been from the first, that it was a disease that would be fatal if not finally arrested; and I have acted upon that impression. If I am wrong, it is because the impression is wrong; and in order to arrest it, it is necessary at every stage of it, to understand the real causes and progress of the disease, and the causes by which it endangers the Union. In my late speech, which the Senator has heard with such profound regret—and I am amazed that my meaning should be so utterly misunderstood by the honorable Senator from Michigan—I stated simply, and in as few words as I could, what would certainly, according to my judgment, save the Union, promote conciliation, and restore harmony and good feeling throughout all sections of the Union. That was the amount of what I said. Now, I ask, can the Senator believe that the South is safe, while one portion of the community hold entire possession of the power of the Government, to wield it for their own benefit, in any manner they please, and while they see fit to interfere between the two sections of the Union? Can any man believe that the South is safe while this state of things exists? No man can say that he believes it. I do not, at least; and, therefore, all the wonder of the honorable Senator upon that point may cease. But the Senator says, it is impossible to comply with the requisition of giving us a new constitutional gurantee. Well, that very declaration goes to show—

Mr. Cass. The honorable Senator entirely mistakes. I certainly did not say any thing of the kind.

Mr. Calhoun. I said, in my remarks the other day, that such amendment in the constitution must be made as would give to the South—

Mr. Cass. The Senator will pardon me, I have not alluded to the subject of an amendment to the constitution. I was coming to it, however, and should have spoken of it before concluding my remarks. I should prefer, therefore, that the distinguished Senator from South Carolina should hear me before he undertakes to reply.

Mr. Calhoun. I understood the argument of the Senator as leading to that.

Mr. Cass. I hope the honorable Senator will defer his remarks until to-morrow morning.

Mr. Calhoun. I do not know that an opportunity will then be afforded me of saying what I desire to say upon this point. The Senator says that new guarantees cannot be given by amendments to be made in the constitution. Sir, I insist that that is the legal and constitutional mode—it is the mode pointed out by the constitution itself. Why, who ever before heard of such a suggestion as, that to amend the constitution, would be treason? It shows a state of feeling existing in the mind of the Senator which, in my opinion, is inconsistent with judicious action.

I intended to branch off here, and to show, that the distinguished Senator, if this Union is ever to be dissolved, will have contributed his full share to its dissolution; that the very entanglement we are now in, originated in the last Presidential election, and, as I think I have demonstrated, originated in a violation of the constitution, and in a violation and disregard of the sovereignty of the States. Whenever the Senator chooses to go into a discussion upon this point, I am ready to meet him.

Mr. President, I must necessarily abbreviate what I have to say. The distinguished Senator heard me with painful feelings designate Washington as the illustrious Southerner. Why, the Senator ought to remember, that every effort has been made to take Washington out of our hands; but it seems that the morality of the present time is, that the assailant is perfectly innocent, and the assailed the only guilty party. Yes, sir! it was endeavored to take him out of our hands; and we are to be stigmatized as disunionists, and his message—his farewell address—to be quoted against us, while I venture to assert, that the greater part of that message bears directly upon the assailants, and not the assailed. It was to meet this, that I reminded the Senate and the world—and rightly reminded them—that Washington was an illustrious Southerner; he was not the less an illustrious American; but I must say, that the whole proceeding here, for the last fifteen years, has been such that, if carried out and consummated, as it will be, unless some definite understanding is arrived at, the end of the whole will be the holding up of Washington as a miserable slaveholder. I do not insinuate that Washington should be regarded exclusively as a Southern man; I only say, we have a right to claim him as an illustrious Southerner, for he was a Southern man—a Southern planter—and we do not intend that he shall be taken out of our hands.

Mr. President, with these remarks, I will content myself for the present, without detaining the Senate further.

Mr. Cass. One word, Mr. President, for I do not wish to be misunderstood: I have not uttered a syllable in regard to the constitution, or the constitutional amendment suggested by the distinguished Senator from South Carolina—not a word. The honorable Senator supposed that I had arraigned him for seeking a constitutional amendment. Such an idea never entered my head; and allow me to tell the Senator, that that was not the difficulty at all.

Mr. Calhoun. What was it, then?

Mr. Cass. The ground upon which it was put by the honorable Senator was, that if a guarantee were not given to the South, by an amendment to be made to the constitution, it would be fatal to the country.

Mr. Calhoun. Certainly; it would, in the end, be fatal.

Mr. Cass. But the honorable Senator said it must be done immediately, or it would be fatal to the interests of the country.

Mr. Calhoun. No, sir; that is not the language I used.

Mr. Cass. I beg the honorable Senator's pardon; it is so stated in the speech: "If the question is not now settled," says the Senator, "it is uncertain whether it can ever be settled hereafter."

Mr. Calhoun. Certainly.

Mr. Cass. And one of the processes by which it is to be done is, by amending the constitution. There were two points stated by the honorable Senator. One was, that there must be an amendment made to the constitution—and I merely mention this because it excited some surprise in my mind—and the other, that the admission of California be made a test question.

Mr. Calhoun. Certainly.

Mr. Cass. That if California were admitted, it would be followed by a dissolution of the Union.

Mr. Calhoun. No, sir. I wish the Senator would read the remarks I made in reference to that point.

Mr. Cass. I will read them, sir, with pleasure:

"If the question is not now settled, it is uncertain whether it ever can hereafter be; and we, as the representatives of the States of this Union, regarded as governments, should come to a distinct understanding as to our respective views, in order to ascertain whether the great questions at issue can be settled or not. If you who represent the stronger portion, cannot agree to settle them on the broad principles of justice and duty, say so; and let the States we both represent agree to separate and part in peace. If you are unwilling we should part in peace, tell us so, and we shall know what to do when you reduce the question to submission or resistance. If you remain silent, you will compel us to infer what you intend. In that case California will become the *test* question."

Mr. Calhoun. Read on—read the whole.

Mr. Cass. I will, sir:

"If you admit her, under all the difficulties that oppose her admission, you compel us to infer that you intend to exclude us from the whole of the acquired territories, with the intention of destroying, irretrievably, the equilibrium between the two sections. We would be blind not to perceive, in that case, that your real objects are power and aggrandizement, and infatuated not to act accordingly."

Now, is there a Senator here who does not know what that means? I do not affirm that it is objectionable to propose an amendment to the constitution. Far from it—that is one of the most harmless things in the world; but the admission of California, according to the honorable Senator, is to be made a test question; and it went to my heart's core when I heard the declaration, for I knew very well, if that were to be a test questien—if such was the sentiment of the South—the Union was gone. An immediate amendment of the constitution, I consider almost impossible. I do not say that amendments may not be made; but it should be done only under the pressure of extreme cases, and extreme difficulties; for if we commence to make changes and alterations, he who is the Ruler of nations, alone knows what changes may be made, and what sort of a Government this will become.

In commenting on the honorable Senator's remarks, I have connected these two subjects—the amendment of the constitution now or at a reasonable time, and the point that was made by him, that the admission of California was to be a test question.

Mr. Calhoun. I must say there has been a strong disposition manifested on the part of the honorable Senator, to misconstrue my expressions—and plain expressions they are. The Senator says I asserted, that a dissolution of the Union would follow the admission of California. I did not assert that. I stated that it ought to be considered a test question; but I leave it to my constitutents to determine what course they will take. Let the gentleman give the words I used, and I am willing to stand by them; but he must not expect me to be responsible for his interpretation of them. Well, in regard to the word "now," I did not intend to be understood as asserting that the amendment must be made instanter, but that an indication should be given now, that such amendment would be agreed to, and let it then be carried through the ordinary process.

Mr. Foote. I promise not to occupy the attention of the Senate long. Senators will perceive that my position is rather a peculiar one. I am certainly exposed to misapprehension, in consequence of what has fallen from the honorable Senator from South Carolina, if I do not make some explanation. He undertakes to express surprise at the course I have pursued, in protesting against certain portions of his speech the other day, when he must know, that there are but few persons, here or anywhere, who do not understand the speech of the honorable Senator precisely as I understand it—nor a member of the other House who did not understand it in the same way. In fact, I have only declared what is the plain interpretation of the speech. But the honorable Senator is surprised that I should take the liberty of guarding myself, and those associated with him in this great contest, against that misconstruction of our motives and plans, which I did believe would arise in the public mind, if no seasonable effort were made to guard against it. Why, sir, I hoped, as I said at the time, in giving the honorable Senator an opportunity to explain, that a ready explanation would be afforded, that would satisfy the country. But I must say, his explanation was not entirely satisfactory to me or to others; for what do we now hear from the honorable Senator? He frankly avows that he did not intend to raise an additional issue—a new issue—without consulting other Senators from the South, who were equally involved in this contest, with himself, and who were entitled to be conferred with, before so important a movement was hazarded. This issue has not been openly made known to any portion of the South; nor is there any one here, besides the honorable Senator himself, able at this moment to make known the precise constitutional amendment at which the honorable gentleman is aiming. I have said, and must continue to say, that the honorable gentleman, throughout this proceeding, has not acted with his accustomed discretion, and, without intending it, has done serious injustice to some of his most confiding friends, in undertaking to make an issue of this sort—of this vital character—without consulting them beforehand. To speak plainly, I almost felt that a noose was put around my neck, while asleep, and without having antecedently obtained my consent. Never did the honorable Senator, on any former occasion, announce the necessity of raising this new issue; and the whole country will be found entirely unprepared for it. Now, sir, what would be the probable effect of the honorable Senator's conduct in this affair, had I not interposed in the manner now complained of? The honorable Senator has had it in his power for several years past, to propose the amendment of the constitution, of which he seems now solicitous; but he has made no such movement, nor intimated his intention to do so at any future time. He knows well, that the meeting of the great Nashville Convention is but little more than two months distant, and that, meanwhile, this contest between the free and slave States of the Union, is waxing still warmer and more warm—that the excitement on the unadjusted questions, growing out of the subject of slavery, is becoming every day more and more intense. Yet he has deliberately undertaken to throw this new issue before the country, when he knows that it is only calculated to increase our difficulties, add to the existing irritation, and postpone, if not utterly defeat, all satisfactory settlement. Meanwhile, the honorable Senator is not only engaged in thus obstructing all compromise, but is heard to denounce the very name of compromise. He is actively opposing, at this moment, the raising of the committee of thirteen, proposed by me.

Now he must know, that if, in the next two months, something is not done, the Nashville Convention will have all the questions, which are at present the subject of discussion here, before that high tribunal for final decision—at least so far as the South is concerned. Does he not perceive, that the very delay which he is now producing, may devolve upon that body a most fearful responsibility, only to be avoided, if possible, consistently with Southern honor and Southern safety? Suppose the excitement to which I have alluded continue its progress, and that certain healing influences had not been interposed—as I rejoice that they have been—suppose no such conciliatory and patriotic speeches as have emanated from gentlemen in both Houses of Congress had been made—I appeal to the Senator, and to all men, if the Nashville Convention had been permitted to assemble, with this new issue submitted to them under such circumstances, whether it is not likely that the honorable Senator's influence would have been potential enough to induce the convention to demand that such a change in the constitution as he desires should be accorded? Had such a demand as an amendment of the constitution been made, does not the Senator well know that it would have been, in the present temper of the public mind, wholly impossible to be effected? And had the demand been formally made and refused, does he doubt—does any one doubt—that a dissolution of the Union would have occurred? I do not charge improper motives to the honorable Senator—I never have done so; yet I hold it not improper for me to express surprise, that the honorable Senator should have failed to place the only interpretation upon his own words of which they seemed susceptible. The Senator knows that no man is more devoted to the South than I am; but I admit the right of no man to make a grave issue for the people whom I represent here, or for myself, without consulting either them or me, especially if, in my judgment, that issue not only puts the Union in serious and unnecessary danger, (whether intended or not,) but subjects the cause, which I have been so long endeavoring to sustain, to certain overthrow.

The honorable Senator from Illinois will please accept my thanks for the courtesy exercised by him, in allowing me this opportunity of explanation.

Mr. DAVIS, of Mississippi. I do not intend to consume the time of the Senator from Illinois, or now to enter into any discussion or argument, but merely to say that when the Senator from South Carolina delivered his speech, I did not understand it as it has been construed in the debate of this morning. The Senator said, that to finally and forever settle this question, certain things were necessary, which the North could easily provide. This I believed. These certain things were, he said, to do justice, by conceding to the South an equal right in the acquired territory—so I think: to do her duty by causing the stipulations relative to fugitive slaves, to be faithfully fulfilled; to cease the agitation of the slave question—these I think necessary to insure tranquillity: to provide, by amendment of the constitution, for a restoration to the South of the power she possessed of protecting herself before the equilibrium between the sections was destroyed. Events, however unwillingly, have forced upon me the conviction, that such additional protection, if not now, will become necessary. What that amendment should be, I am not prepared to say; what the Senator from South Carolina desired, I did not, nor do I now, know. He says, several were thought of. When the constitution was made, each section had the power to protect itself, by its numerical strength, in the Legislature of the General Government. But if we reach a period in the progress of the country, when one section cannot protect itself against the manifested, settled hostility of another—when the rights of the minority become subject to the will of a self-sustaining, powerful majority—then it becomes requisite that the compact shall be so amended as to give that protection to the minority, which it was originally designed to afford to all. Whether that time has come now or not, I am not prepared to say. I think that the indications of this morning are such as to show that the time has arrived. I think that the votes taken this morning, in regard to the reception of the petitions presented by the Senator from New York, declare the opinion of the Senate to be, that it may take cognizance of the subjects referred through those petitions. Another indication is, that the Senator from Michigan, whose opinions and knowledge I always highly respect, has said this morning, that the Missouri compromise cannot be extended—cannot be applied—to the remaining territories. Here, then, we have the doctrine of non-intervention overthrown at one blow, by the Senate; and immediately follows the announcement, that the Missouri compromise cannot be extended—that is, the power is to be exercised, but we are to have neither joint nor separate right. When we have reached this point, it is time that there should be an amendment of a compact, the equal operation of which seems to be at end.

Mr. Foote. I know that my colleague did not intend to misrepresent the statement of the Senator from Michigan; but I think he has not understood him aright. He said that he was for non-intervention; and he thought that the Missouri compromise is not such, as it interfered with the northern part, although it did not with the southern. He did not state his opposition to the compromise, but said only that it was not non-intervention.

Mr. Davis, of Mississippi. I understood the honorable Senator from Michigan as standing upon the ground of non-intervention. If we could have that, it would give the South the most we have claimed—that is, an equal right to go into all the territories—all property being alike protected. In default of this, I have said that I would take the Missouri compromise line, and that was my ultimatum. But when we see the Senate, by a vote this morning, overturn the doctrine of non-intervention of the Senator from Michigan, and when the Senator from Michigan comes forward and declares that the Missouri compromise cannot be extended, it is quite time that the South should look to something besides Congressional action.

Mr. Butler. I shall speak more for testimony than any thing else.

Mr. Davis, of Mississippi. I certainly did not intend to say that Northern votes had decided the question of referring the petitions this morning. Here is my friend from New York, the Bayard of the North, (Mr. Dickinson,) who has stood by us on this, as on all occasions. I regret much more deeply that this vote should have succeeded, by the aid of Southern men, and this but heightens my estimate of the danger.

Mr. Butler. I will only occupy the time of the Senate with a few words. When my friend from Mississippi moved this committee, I was opposed to it, and it was without consultation with any one. I do not think I had seen my colleague upon the subject at all. If any one stands responsible for opposing it at that time, I am the man. I did not do it for the purpose of defeating the committee, or to defeat the adjustment of this question. I have spoken to my colleague upon the subject, and have understood him to vindicate the views which I have expressed to-day. While he was willing, ultimately, to consent to a committee of this kind, he thought it premature to take it out of the hands of the Senate.

The question being taken upon the motion to postpone the further consideration of the resolutions submitted by Mr. Bell, until to-morrow, it was agreed to.

Thursday, March 14.

Mr. Bell's Resolutions—Select Committee.

The Senate, on motion by Mr. Foote, resumed the consideration of the motion to refer the resolutions proposed by Mr. Bell, to a select committee of thirteen.

Mr. Cass resumed, and concluded as follows:

Mr. President: Before I resume my remarks at the point where I left off yesterday, I have a question to put to the Senator from Mississippi, who, (said Mr. Cass, looking round,) I am sorry to see, is not in his seat. I regret he is not; but I will postpone the reference I designed making to him until the close of my remarks, when perhaps he may be here. I spoke to him this morning on the subject, and therefore he is perfectly aware of the question I wish to put to him.

I was remarking yesterday, when I resigned the floor, that there were certain things we could not accomplish, and others that, with equal certainty, we might take for granted we could do. Among the latter, was the bill providing for the recapture of fugitive slaves; and another object, which I trust will be accomplished, is the providnig of a government for the new territories. I think it essential to calm this agitation, and so long as these territories are left without a government, so long will the present state of things continue, and this agitation be kept up, which is so harassing to the tranquillity, and dangerous to the peace, of the Union.

That a law may be passed authorizing the people of the territories to govern themselves, without any Wilmot proviso being attached to it, is my wish and my hope. I am not going to say much upon the propriety of the admission of California, for the remarks that have fallen from my friend from Illinois (Mr. Douglas) are so well expressed and so pertinent, that they preclude the necessity of entering anew into that topic at any length.

I understood the distinguished Senator from South Carolina to admit, yesterday, that he did make it expressly a test question. As I remarked before, it was this demand of the honorable Senator, that excited in my mind serious apprehensions as to the result; for I knew, that if this was made a test question, upon which the fate of this Republic depended, that fate was sealed. I trust I may be permitted to say, with regard to this issue, that it appears to me not only unwise but useless, for the reasons so well expressed by the Senator from Illinois, in his speech to-day.

No gentleman on this floor, from the North or the South, the East or the West, will rise in his seat, and say he believes that slavery will ever go into the Territory of California; no one can believe this for a moment. What, sir, would the southern States gain by sending California, after she has come here with a constitution in her hands, back again, to undergo the process of a territorial government, and then to return here a year hence—every year perhaps for ten years—and revive the question anew? What would be gained by it for any portion of the country? Is it a battle worth fighting? Is the object to be accomplished really worth the contest? Sir, there is no object that can be accomplished by such a course of procedure. Under existing circumstances, what kind of territorial government can be established there? Can any territorial government be established? And is this unsettled state of things to go on from year to year, perpetuating the bitter feelings that have already sprung up between one section of the Union and the other? But I have said, also, that such a course is unwise; and I trust my southern friends will pardon me for saying, that they are making a very unwise issue.

Sir, we cannot stand before the country, and before the world, and object to the admission of California on the ground that has been urged. The objection is not to her boundaries, though that topic has been much debated. The honorable Senator from Illinois, whom we have all just heard with so much pleasure, has discussed the subject so ably and clearly, that it would be a work of supererogation in me to renew it. I myself was at first startled at the boundary claimed, stretching as it does along the coast of the Pacific one thousand miles—a much greater extent than any one State in the Union ought to possess. As the Senator from Illinois, and myself, are together in the same house, we have conversed repeatedly upon this subject, and with an earnest desire to reduce these boundaries if the nature of the country would permit. With this view he examined various lines proposed—the parallel of 36° 30′, and the southern range of mountains—to ascertain what proper limitation could be imposed upon the new State. But he ultimately became satisfied that no change could be made. The country between the ocean and the sea is a narrow one, and east of the mountains is a desert; and in proportion to its extent, the quantity of arable land is small. Be the boundaries as they may, it is not probable that its population will ever be as great as that of some of the other States of this Union. And if its southern boundary were to stop at the mountains, there would be left between them and the Mexican possessions a small district of country, which would have to remain for an indefinite period, perhaps forever, in a colonial condition.

The Senator from South Carolina, (Mr. Calhoun,) who I regret to see is not in his seat to-day, does not assume this ground as an objection to the admission of California. That objection rests upon her present position and mode of application; because she has established a government of her own without passing through a territorial process, and comes here of her own accord, and asks admission into this Union. This ground of objection cannot be maintained in this age of the world, before the people of this country, and, I may add, the people of Christendom.

One hundred thousand American citizens on the shores of the Pacific are, or might be, so far as depends upon our action, in a perfect state of anarchy. Three sessions of Congress have intervened since these new territories came under the jurisdiction of the United States, and you have not legislated for them in a single instance, except to make provision for the collection of revenue at their ports. All other duties, devolving upon you as legislators for the entire Union, have been totally neglected. You have used them only for the purpose of collecting taxes from them. Are we, sir, to be told, in the middle of the nineteenth century, that these people, under such circumstances, have no right to form a government? No man can stand up here, and assert this doctrine, and expect to receive the support of the people of this country. My friend from Illinois (Mr. Douglas) correctly said, that the right of government—of some kind of government—was a right inherent in all people upon the face of the earth, and that the establishment of civil and social order was among the first necessities of men entering into civil society. Without government, they cannot exist; and you have provided no government for the people of California, and it is now contended that they have no right to provide one for themselves. You have neglected your own duty toward them for the last three sessions, and now, when they come here acknowledging your jurisdiction, and with a constitution in their hands, you are about to send them back to the shores of the Pacific, to enter into a territorial condition, and return again at some future time as supplicants for your favor. They love the Union; they have felt its blessings, and desire to secure them to themselves and posterity. They will have no other standard to wave in the breezes of the Pacific, on their coast, but the standard of their fathers —the stars and stripes of their country. Would to God that this feeling prevailed with equal intensity at the centre of the Republic, as it prevails at its distant extremity! While they wish to come in, there are those who wish to go out. It is consoling to find that the patriotic ardor of our countrymen does not diminish as they recede from the older portions of the Republic. I repeat, they come here, not as revolutionists, but as an integral part of our great community, asking admittance into the Confederacy.

Mr. King, (in his seat.) Who is it prevents them?

Mr. Cass. The Senator from Alabama inquires who is it that has prevented them from having a government, and I answer it is the Congress of the United States; and in saying this, I take the blame myself, as one of its members.

Mr. Downs. The Wilmot proviso prevents them.

Mr. Cass. I am speaking of the cause of our neglect—the Wilmot proviso is another thing. I am not examining what differences of opinion may have prevented our action. I am speaking of our neglect, and of its effect upon the people of California, and of their justification in forming a State government. What has the Wilmot proviso, or any other difference of opinion here, to do with them? They would still have remained without a government, had they not taken their own cause into their own hands, and done for themselves what we ought to have done for them. Are they to be deprived of social organization, and of all the elements of social order—I may add, of existence, and to be treated by us with contumely and mockery, under the pretence that we can do nothing for them, because some one thinks proper to introduce the Wilmot proviso into our legislative proceedings?

Mr. Butler. Will the honorable Senator allow me to ask him a question?

Mr. Cass. Certainly.

Mr. Butler. Do I understand the honorable Senator now to say, that it was the duty of Congress to have provided a competent government for these territories?

Mr. Cass. There are two positions I have always maintained with reference to this subject—first, that Congress, under the constitution, has no right to establish governments for the territories; secondly, that under no circumstances have they the right to pass any law to regulate the internal affairs of the people inhabiting them. The first may be a matter of necessity; and when the necessity exists, if a Senator votes for it, he votes upon his own responsibility to his constituents. If they believe the necessity, and support him, he is safe, but if not, he must fall. If I had voted under such circumstances, I must have looked to my constituents for my justification; but under no circumstances could I have voted for any law interfering with the internal concerns of the people of a territory. No necessity requires it; there is no necessity which would justify it.

Mr. Chase. Will the Senator allow me to ask him a question?

Mr. Cass. Certainly; I stand ready to be catechized all day on this subject, if Senators desire it.

Mr. Chase. Did I understand the Senator as saying that in voting for a bill to establish a government in the territories, he would assume the exercise of any authority not given in the constitution?

Mr. Cass. The honorable Senator will undoubtedly recollect, that in a historical document called the Nicholson letter, which subsequent circumstances have made somewhat important, I distinctly stated my views upon this subject, and those views have remained unchanged to the present hour. I maintained, that no power is given by the constitution to establish territorial governments; but that where an imperious necessity exists for such a measure, the legislator who yields to it must look to his constituents for his justification.

Mr. Chase. I understand the Senator to say, that there was no such authority given by the constitution?

Mr. Cass. I said, that if we do an act not authorized by the constitution, under a pressure of necessity, that act must be done upon our own responsibility; and I refer the gentleman to the authority of Mr. Madison, who justified the action of the Congress of the Confederation on the subject of territories upon this ground—and upon this alone. If the gentleman will take the trouble to look at my speech on the Wilmot proviso, he will find my views on this point distinctly laid down. What is the objection in principle to the admission of California? Allow me to say, that great political rights and movements, in this age of the world, are not to be determined by mere abstract or speculative opinions. There is no want of heavy books in the world, which treat of political science; but you need not go to them to ascertain the rights of men—either individuals or in communities; if you do, you will lose yourself groping in a labyrinth, and where no man can follow you. If there are rights of sovereignty, there may be wrongs of sovereignty; and this truth should be held in everlasting remembrance. And this is the case with regard to California. We have rights, and we have duties; and if the former are sacred, the latter should be sacred also. One of these duties we have neglected to perform; and we are told by gentlemen who have spoken here, that when a State wishes admission into the Union, she should come to the door of Congress and knock for admission. California has thus come, and knocked; but no door is opened to her, and she is to be told, "Go back, and wait till we are ready." There is but one door through which you can enter, and that door we keep shut. You must pass through a territorial government; but that government we have neglected to give you, and we are probably as far from establishing it as ever. And such is the paternal regard we manifest toward one hundred thousand American citizens, who are upholding the flag of our country on the distant shores of the Pacific. A good deal has been said about precedents: I am not going to examine either their application or authority, though it has been pretty clearly shown by others, that they fully justify this measure of admission.

Great political measures must be judged by themselves. When new and imposing circumstances dictate an unusual course, they furnish the justification for action, they furnish also a precedent for future proceedings; and whether such cases as this are to be found in our legislative history, our duty is still the same. That duty imperiously requires the admission of California into our Union. She comes and asks admission—not, as the honorable Senator from Illinois says, in language of equal force and beauty—not to reject your sovereignty, but because her citizens love their native country, know the value of our institutions, and desire to become bone of our bone, and flesh of our flesh. They come, I repeat, not as revolutionists, but as petitioners, asking the greatest favor we can bestow upon them. The distinguished Senator from South Carolina has objected, that we can only admit a State into our Confederacy, and that California is not a State. Well, sir, in my opinion it is a State, and as truly so as any existing under the sun. The honorable Senator from Maine asked the very emphatic question, What constitutes a State? And his answer will find a responsive cord in the heart of every American. It is said with truth that it is men who make a State. They do, sir. It is not land, nor trees, nor gold mines; but it is men, by whom and for whom States are constituted and maintained. Why, sir, any other doctrine would carry us back to the worst portion of the middle ages, when Governments were instituted for the protection of the few, and men without property were men without rights.

But, Mr. President, there are other considerations which seem to me forcibly to urge the admission of California. The Senator from Illinois truly said, that the pride of opinion is strong in the human breast, and that it belongs as well to communities as individuals. The Wilmot proviso is offensive—justly offensive—to the southern section of the Confederacy—offensive, independently of its practical consequences. It is considered an arbitrary assumption of power, and is, therefore, resisted, agreeably to the established laws of human nature. We oppose instinctively all improper assumptions of authority over us, without stopping to inquire into the pecuniary value they may affect. No man is willing to have a measure forced upon him. Now, the people of California have been driven by necessity to take this matter into their own hands. They have decided the question for themselves. There is no offence to the pride of the South or of the North. There is no invidious Wilmot proviso to be passed north or south of 36° 30′. There is no pride of opinion involved, and no overbearing act of one portion of the country against the other; and therefore the admission of California removes much of the present controversy in a manner that spares the feelings of all.

I regret, sir, that the Senator from South Carolina is not present, as I desired to extend my remarks further than I shall now do. I have already said that the speech of that honorable Senator inevitably leads us to the conclusion, that upon the admission of California depends the dissolution of the Union. He likewise contended, that an amendment to the constitution was indispensable, and his remarks on yesterday seemed to connect the fate of the country with the accomplishment of this object.

Mr. DOWNS. The Senator from Michigan states that the Senator from South Carolina remarked, in his speech, that this amendment was indispensable. Now, I may have misunderstood his words, but certainly I think he only said that it was desirable.

Mr. CASS. I do not desire to exchange words upon this point, and have not the slightest disposition to provoke debate upon it. In order to satisfy the Senator from Louisiana, I will read the Senator's own words:

"The North has only to will it, to accomplish it; to do justice by conceding to the South an equal right in the acquired territory, and to do her duty by causing her stipulations, relative to fugitive slaves, to be faithfully fulfilled; to cease the agitation of the slave question; and to provide for the insertion of a provision in the constitution, by an amendment, which will restore to the South, in substance, the power she possessed of protecting herself before the equilibrium between the sections was destroyed by the action of this Government. There will be no difficulty in devising such a provision, one that will protect the South, and which at the same time will improve and strengthen the Government, instead of impairing and weakening it. But will the North agree to do this? It is for her to answer this question. But I will say she cannot refuse, if she has half the love for the Union which she professes to have, or without justly exposing herself to the charge, that her love of power and aggrandizement is far greater than her love of the Union. At all events, the responsibility of saving the Union rests on the North, and not on the South. The South cannot save it by any act of hers, and the North may save it without any sacrifice whatever, unless to do justice, and to perform her duties under the constitution, should be regarded by her as a sacrifice. It is time, Senators, that there should be an open and manly avowal on all sides, as to what is intended to be done. If the question is not now settled, it is uncertain whether it ever can hereafter be; and we, as the representatives of the States of this Union, regarded as governments, should come to a distinct understanding as to our respective views, in order to ascertain whether the great questions at issue can be settled or not. If you, who represent the stronger portion, cannot agree to settle them on the broad principle of justice and duty, say so, and let the States we both represent, agree to separate and part in peace."

I have not another word to say, Mr. President. If these remarks do not justify the conclusion I have drawn from them, I do not know what can.

Mr. Downs. Do I understand the Senator as saying, that he understood the Senator from South Carolina as asserting that the amendment should be made now?

Mr. Cass. The Senator from South Carolina, in the explanation he gave us, said he did not require it to be done now, but that it was indispensable that it should be done. Am I not right?

Mr. Foote. The Senator from South Carolina said, I believe, that it would be indispensable ultimately. That, I think, was the word he used.

Mr. Butler. I know it may be expected that I should be able to indicate what are the precise opinions of my colleague, but I have, in reality, no more knowledge of his views, than is, or may be, in the possession of any Senator; but I did understand him distinctly to say, so far as I can infer from other sources—I believe it is his opinion—that when the Northern States shall have acquired such a predominating influence in the councils of the nation, that there shall be no security for the South against their abuse of power, then there should be inserted in the constitution some provision, by which the minority shall have it in their power to avoid becoming a despised and degraded minority. Sir, that is his idea; and I will say in this connection—and I endorse his view to this extent—that I do not see that we have any security in the forbearance of a Northern majority. I am free to say, that I do not feel security from that source, because, when I hear one gentleman say that he holds to one part of the constitution and disregards another, according to his conscience, and others come in and say that they will break it down, so far as they understand its provisions, what security have we for the preservation of our rights, unless we have something to rely upon by way of a veto?

My colleague has not intimated that the Union may not continue for many years to come; but what sort of a Union is it, by which we are bound together, when the elements of strife are introduced here every day? He has always adhered to the Union, and he wishes to restore to it the elements of its prosperity, by producing harmony and conciliation; and they are attained by the North doing justice, and conceding to the South an equal right in the acquired territory, by complying with the requisitions of the constitution in relation to the delivery of fugitive slaves, and by ceasing the agitation of the slave question, and by providing for the insertion of some provision in the constitution, which will give to the South some security that her rights will be respected.

Mr. Downs. With the permission of the honorable Senator, I will state that I believe it was not understood, without going minutely into the views expressed by the Senator from South Carolina, that I believe he was not understood by Southern members of this body generally, in the sense in which the honorable Senator from Michigan understood him. I certainly did not so understand him, and I am not aware than any Southern Senator did.

Mr. Foote. I understand now, from the explanation that has been given by the colleague of the honorable Senator from South Carolina, that it is the opinion of both these gentlemen that an amendment to the constitution is indispensable. Does the Senator from Louisiana doubt that such is their opinion?

Mr. Downs. I did not so understand the gentleman.

Mr. Cass. I am not going to dwell upon this point of construction. God knows I have not the slightest wish to misrepresent the opinions or the objects of the Senator. I have only to say, that any man who reads the speech must come to the same conclusion, that, in the opinion of the Senator, the dissolution of the Union, if not altogether, was almost inevitable. When I alluded to this subject yesterday, saying that, agreeably to the views of the Senator from South Carolina, if the amendment of the constitution did not take place *now*, "it would be fatal to the country," the honorable Senator answered "certainly it will in the end." The Senator says expressly, in his speech, the amendment must be made *now*. Yesterday he explained, and I took his explanation with the greatest pleasure—that he conceives an amendment necessary to be made, but that he does not conceive it is necessary to be done *now*. That is all I have to say in regard to this matter. What, then, is the avowed object of the Senator from South Carolina? He says he seeks to establish an equilibrium in this Government. I do not know precisely what is meant by an equilibrium in a Government. I do not know in what way legislation is to be exactly weighed or measured, with reference to the various sections or interests of the country. There has never been such a political expedient since the commencement of this Government, or indeed of any other—and there never can be. When the Government came into operation, there were six slave and seven non-slaveholding States. The majority, therefore, in this Senate was in proportion then what it is now. There was of course no sectional equality, and if a disposition had been felt to oppress the South, it could have been as easily indulged by the Northern statesmen at that day as at this; for if your equilibrium is not perfect, you have no security from this new-contrived equipoise. If the majority is disposed to disregard all constitutional checks, and to oppress the minority, that can as well be done by a small preponderance in the legislature as by a larger one. The security now is just what it was when the constitution went from the hands of its framers.

But what kind of equilibrium could be established? Is every section of this country—North, South, East, and West—is every interest, manufacturing, agricultural, commercial, and mechanical, to be weighed each against the other? Is each to hold the Government in a state of equipoise? What it would become in such a case, while in nominal operation, no man can tell. We can all tell, however, what it would not do: it would leave its great functions unperformed, and would, ere long, die in the affections of the people, as it would be already dead to their interests. Who ever heard or dreamed of such a Government? I believe the constitution was intended to provide for every interest; but each must be cultivated and protected as the circumstances of the country may require, without the vain attempt at mathematical accuracy in the progress of public affairs.

In the days of Solomon it was said that there was nothing new under the sun; but I confess, that a perfect equilibrium, for all time and for all interests, be these interests greater or smaller, would be something new. There is a difference of opinion respecting the constitutionality of the Wilmot proviso. The attempt to enforce it is not the result of an arbitrary disposition to injure the South, but rises from a belief that the measure is legal and salutary. These differences of construction are inseparable from human language; and he who expects to prepare a written constitution, carrying with it universal concurrence of opinion, in all its constructions, indulges a chimera as wild as ever presented itself to any man, sleeping or waking. I ask, sir, when did the North seek to injure the South, or when did the South seek to injure the North, in the mere wantonness of oppression? This charge of sectional rivalry, I know, has been a fruitful theme of discussion among the political parties of the day, but it has no real foundation in the progress of our history. We have gone on, sir, increasing in power, in all the elements of prosperity, with a rapidity unknown among the nations of the earth. The charge, indeed, is not new—it goes back to the days of Mr. Jefferson. When the aggressions of England required counteracting measures to be adopted by this country, non-intercourse, and the embargo, and finally war, were resorted to in defence of the rights and the independence of the country. At that time a powerful party in the Eastern States desired to secede from the Union. They said then, as is said now, There is a sectional majority against us; they disregard our rights, and destroy our interests; and we will go out from among them. There was not an argument used then which is not used now; nor a measure proposed which is not now proposed. There are some of us yet here who were living at that period, and participated in these events; and the younger generation well know that these facts stand prominently forward in the history of their country.

Sir, the objection of the Senator from South Carolina is repeated here to-day by his colleague, and it amounts to this: that if you give power to a Government, it may be abused. So it may; and I should like to see the Government where power cannot be abused. It would be another new thing under the sun. We may all suppose cases of extreme oppression, where a State should be justified before the world in resisting the acts of a majority, and in seceding from this Union, or from any other. We can all suppose such a case; but sufficient unto the day is the evil thereof; and when that evil day comes, let those who have the responsibility, act upon it, and decide for themselves and for their posterity. There has generally been a sound public opinion existing in our country. Wisdom and patriotism are found in both Houses of Congress, as well as in the State Legislatures, whose influence is everywhere felt and appreciated; and these are salutary checks against the abuse of power. And we happily possess another institution—the Supreme Court—which contributes its full share to the stability of our institutions. There are nine men, advanced in years, with neither the power of the sword nor the purse, whose decisions are received with confidence, and obeyed with alacrity, from one end of this broad Republic to the other. It is an oasis in the desert of politics—a green spot for the eye to rest upon—it is a tribunal of which we may all be proud. There is none higher upon the face of the earth. By their ability, their dignity, their impartiality, their unimpeached probity, the judges have won the respect of their countrymen; and besides the performance of their judicial functions, they everywhere exert a salutary influence upon public opinion. It is refreshing to leave these chambers of discussion and dissension, and to enter the hall below us, and mark the tranquillity and wisdom with which the high interests of the community are there considered and determined.

Sir, at the last session of that court a sublime moral spectacle was presented, of which every American may justly be proud. One of the greatest States of this Union appeared at the bar and made itself a party, asking the court to judge its cause, and to remove certain impediments to the navigation of the Ohio River, which were considered an injury by the Commonwealth of Pennsylvania. Yes, like an individual, that State asked the court to sit in judgment upon the cause, and to direct the impediments to be removed. Who would witness such a spectacle if this Union were dissolved? Differences like this would then be adjusted, not by reason, but by the strong hand. Another similar scene passed in the same place a short time since, when two States, members of this Confederacy, disputing about their boundaries, asked this court to decide between them; and the court did decide; and I understand the line they fixed, is now running by commissioners armed only with a slip of paper, and through a country heretofore highly excited by this question, but now calm and satisfied, leaving the surveyors to perform their duty with as much safety as if protected by all the force of the Republic. Such lines elsewhere are run by armies, and marked by the sword. Thus it will be seen that our Government has a mode of settling difficulties—a constitutional mode—that ought to command the assent of all.

I do not deny that there may be great political cases where this court can have no jurisdiction. When such cases arise, I trust a peaceable remedy will be found for their adjustment. I leave that to time and events. It is one of national characteristics to neglect our immediate advantages, and to look forward to some great calamity, which is to overtake us after the lapse of centuries.

The Senator from South Carolina (Mr. Calhoun) has not stated the amendment by which he proposes to secure the equilibrium of the Government. There are, however, two indications in his speech which leave but little doubt as to the nature of the remedy, though its details must of course be conjectural. He pointed out two difficulties in the operations of the Government, which it would be necessary to obviate:

First, that it claimed to use force in order to carry into effect the powers it felt authorized to exercise. Well, sir, what Government exists, or ever existed, which does not use force? Human beings are influenced by hope and fear, (I leave higher considerations out of view in this discussion,) and, as no Government is rich enough to buy obedience, it must compel it by force.

The second difficulty is, that the Government assumes to judge of the extent of its own powers. It does so, and necessarily; and so must every other Government, in a greater or less degree. I do not propose to enter into any argument upon this point, nor to investigate the course necessary to pursue in the event of collisions of opinion between the General and State Governments. That must be determined by events as they arise. I merely allude to these topics briefly, in order, by ascertaining the evils supposed to exist by the Senator from South Carolina, to ascertain the nature of the remedy he is desirous of applying to them. He is seeking a constitutional remedy, which shall produce an equilibrium, by which the rights of every section and of every interest of the country can be preserved from aggression. The South is not the only section which is liable to oppression. There are also the East, the West, and the remote West, which may have the same cause of complaint; and the various interests I have already enumerated may, in like manner, each demand peculiar protection. There is to be some controlling principle within the constitution, by which its operations may be regulated, when these several sections or interests may consider their rights assailed or endangered; for I do not suppose the honorable Senator is so local in his views as to propose a remedy which shall not be applicable, under similar circumstances, to every portion of the country. And that remedy is an equilibrium, as it is called, which, when translated into English, means a plan by which a sectional minority may, at its pleasure, control or suspend the operations of the Government. I have already said, that the general plan is more easily ascertained, than the specific details. Well, sir, such an equilibrium, instead of being a balance-wheel, would be a check-wheel—it would stop the whole operations of the Government—it would, in fact, place it under the control of a minority.

Now, sir, these minority Governments are not new in the world; they have existed since the institution of civil society, and will continue, I suppose, until it is terminated. There are many of them found in Europe, and in other parts of the world. There is one at St. Petersburg, another at Constantinople, and another at Vienna; and these Governments take very good care of the rights of the minority; but I do not see the advantage of the plan, for I believe the rights of the majority are very little regarded—at any rate, such is the opinion of the Poles and of the Hungarians, and of many an oppressed people beside. It is all idle, sir, to talk of such a plan. Provide proper checks and limitations for all sections and interests as a just foresight may require; but after this is done by the constitution, the Government must be conducted agreeably to the will of a majority, unless you choose to intrust your rights to a single man, and thus establish a despotism. That, I suppose, is the perfection of a minority Government. No intellect, however profound, can give plausibility to such a scheme, or obviate the insuperable difficulties which would present themselves in any political organization thus strangely constituted. The machine would stop by its own inherent arrangements. Such minorities would, in fact, become majorities, controlling public affairs at their pleasure.

Mr. President, I will terminate my remarks as speedily as possible, and I trust the Senate will bear with me a little longer. There are one or two circumstances, alluded to by the Senator from South Carolina, which I desire to notice, and which appear to me not a little extraordinary. I hold in one hand the speech of the Senator from South Carolina, and in the other the speech of a gentleman from Pennsylvania, (Mr. STEVENS,) delivered the other day in the House of Representatives—a gentleman who, in all his opinions upon the subject before us, so far as we know, is directly the opposite of the Senator from South Carolina—aye, as far as the antipodes—as far asunder as the poles. *The bane and antidote are both before me.* The distinguished Senator from South Carolina says in that speech, that this Government is one as absolute as that of the Autocrat of Russia. The expression is strong, and I will read it from the speech, so that I may not be accused of misrepresentation:

"What was once a constitutional Federal Republic, is now converted in reality into one as absolute as that of the Autocrat of Russia, and as despotic in its tendency as any absolute Government that ever existed."

Mr. BUTLER. Who says that?

Mr. CASS. Your colleague, the distinguished Senator from South Carolina.

Mr. BUTLER. I thought you were reading from another speech.

Mr. CASS. No, sir; from the speech of your colleague. He says, that this is the most despotic Government on the face of the earth. Well, sir, the Representative from Pennsylvania reiterates a similar sentiment, and speaks of this Government as a despotic one. All this shows how often extremes meet in this world; and it is not a little curious that both these gentlemen, in the illustration of their views, refer to the Autocrat of Russia.

We lose all our confidence in the force of language, and in the authority of years and intellect, when such extravagant assertions are presented to us. Is there a man in this broad land, who does not know, and feel instinctively, that he is free? And yet he is told seriously —not in an extemporaneous debate, such as we are now engaged in, when no man should be held to a rigid accountability for his expressions—but in a prepared speech, written and printed before its delivery, and laid upon our tables immediately after—and I believe, sent through all parts of our country contemporaneously—we are told, I say, that this is the most despotic Government on the face of the earth!

There is another subject to which I must allude. Almost at the time the Senator from South Carolina was endeavoring to show how the North had injured and oppressed the South, and how the Government, or rather the majority, had gone on to assume despotic power —almost at that very time, a distinguished member from Virginia, in the House of Representatives, (Mr. MEADE,) was placing in singular contrast, the authority which the South had gained and exercised over the Government of the country.

"Though we have been in a numerical minority in the Union for fifty years, yet, during the greater part of that period, we have managed to control the destinies of the Union. Whether on the battle-field, or in the council, the sons of the South have taken the lead; and the records of the nation afford ample testimony of their superior energy and genius."

Well, sir, put this and this together, and then we see who is right. I state the facts. I leave these gentlemen to settle their own controversy. I do not deny—no man is more ready than I am to acknowledge—the obligations we owe to the South, to Washington, to Jefferson, to Madison, to Monroe, to Jackson, and to the distinguished men the South has sent here to preside over the Executive department of the Government, or to assist in its operations. They have won imperishable fame for themselves, and imperishable honor for their country. I accord to them the full meed of praise, for I have no sectional feeling to interfere with my sense of justice, and I love the South as well as the North or West. I have been so much of a wanderer, during my life, that sectional feeling is absorbed in a general one, and I love my country, and my whole country, with equal ardor. Abroad, it is the name of American which inspires honor and confidence, and not the name of Virginia, or Pennsylvania, or any other less eminent in our country. I repeat, that Southern statesmen, when conducting our affairs, have conducted them with ability and success; and the best proof of this is the prosperity we enjoy, and the proud eminence we have attained.

I desire to refer to another fact. The distinguished Senator from South Carolina speaks of the disastrous effects of the Union upon the material interests of the South, while the Senator from Louisiana (Mr. DOWNS) endeavored to prove, the other day, that in all the elements of prosperity the South were better off than the North. Let any man who will, reconcile these differences if he can. It is an effort I shall not undertake. I think it proves to the satisfaction of every moderate man, that the whole matter is greatly exaggerated, and that expressions are used, and facts assembled together—sometimes indeed in an imposing form —which furnish no justification for the serious conclusions presented to the country. But, sir, instead of depreciating one section and exalting another, let us all join together to thank that God who enabled our fathers to assert their rights, and who, we may humbly hope, will enable their sons, if they are not struck by judicial blindness, to maintain them, and to transmit them, unimpaired, to their posterity.

Mr. DAVIS, of Mississippi. I understand that the honorable Senator from Michigan expressed a wish to ask me a question.

Mr. CASS. Yes, sir. I wished to ask the

honorable Senator from Mississippi if he would vote for the Missouri compromise?

Mr. Davis, of Mississippi. I will answer the Senator from Michigan with great pleasure. I have stated on several occasions that I would take the Missouri compromise. This I have said deliberately and decidedly, on several occasions, and explained at some length in a recent speech on the resolutions of the Senator from Kentucky. I have stated that I considered it as an ultimatum, less than I believed to be the rights of the South, but which I would accept, to stop the agitation which now disturbs and endangers the Union.

Mr. Cass. As I had a conversation with the Senator on this subject in the morning, I supposed he understood the precise object I had in view. As this, however, appears not to be the case, I will ask him if he would accept the Missouri compromise, as it was regulated by the statute providing for the admission of Missouri into the Union?

Mr. Davis, of Mississippi. I understood the Senator, in a conversation this morning, to make that inquiry. I then told him that I would not. I now answer before the Senate, No. To meet this inquiry, I waited in the Senate chamber, expecting that he would, at the expiration of the morning hour, address the Senate; but, as he did not, I left here, (when the Senator from Illinois was addressing the Senate,) to answer a summons to see a sick friend. I returned a few minutes, as I was informed, after the Senator from Michigan commenced his address, and learned that he had signified a wish to ask me a question. It seemed to me proper to remind him, at the close of his remarks, of the wish he had announced. I now answer his question in its modified form. I would not take the terms of the Missouri act, but would accept its spirit if presented in terms applicable to this case. When I spoke of the Missouri compromise, I spoke of it as an arrangement by which the territory was divided between the slaveholding and the non-slaveholding interests; I spoke in reference to the result—the intent of that compromise—which gave to each a portion. I have always been ready to rebuke that mean spirit that would evade its true meaning by a delusive adherence to its words.

I would not take the compromise in the terms by which it was applied to the remaining part of the territory acquired under the name of Louisiana. I would not take it as applied to Texas, when that State was admitted into the Union, because the circumstances of both were different from those of the Mexican territory; but I would take it, if made applicable to the existing case, and extended to the Pacific. I considered that, when the Senate had yesterday voted to receive petitions, and to refer them to committees, to consider upon the power of this Government over slavery in the territories, over slavery in the District of Columbia, and over the future admission of slave States, we had taken one great step in advance, and one which should awaken the apprehension of the South; and when, in close connection with this action of the Senate, followed the remark of the honorable Senator from Michigan, that the Missouri compromise could not be extended to the recent acquisitions from Mexico, I looked upon it as a conjunction in our political firmament, which boded evil to those likely to be destroyed by the joint attraction of these planets. It was therefore that I spoke of the declaration as a thing to be noted—marked as the foreshadow of an event. If we are not to have non-intervention, the right to go into these territories and there claim whatever may be decided to be ours by the decree of nature—if we are to be debarred from acquiring—by emigration, by enterprise, by adventure, by toil, and labor—equally with others, from the common domain of the Union—if we are to be forbidden to use the commons belonging to the common field, of which we are joint owners—if, in addition to all this, we are told that no division can be made—that all of that which we owe in common must finally become the exclusive property of the other partners—in truth, sir, we are rapidly approaching to that state of things contemplated by the Senator from South Carolina, (Mr. Calhoun,) when, without an amendment of the constitution, the rights of the minority will be held at the mercy of the majority. Give us our rights under the constitution—the constitution fairly construed—and we are content to take our chance, as our fathers did, for the maintenance of position in the Union. We are content to hold on to the old compact; and, as we believe in the merits of our own institutions, we are willing to trust to time and fair opportunity for the working out of our own salvation. If we are to be excluded, by Congressional legislation, from joint possession on the one hand, and denied every compromise which, by division, would give us a share on the other—neither permitted to an equality of possession as a right, nor a divided occupation as a settlement, between proprietors—I ask what is the hope which remains to those who are already in a minority in this Confederacy? What do we gain by having a written constitution, if sectional pride or sectional hate can bend it, as passion, or interest, or caprice may dictate? What do we gain by having a Government, based upon this written constitution, if, in truth, the rights of the minority are held in abeyance to the will of the majority? And now, I ask the Senator from Michigan a question: Will he not, under the crisis which hangs upon the fate of the country—will he not support the Missouri compromise—the spirit of the compromise—for a division of the territories between the two interests of the Confederacy?

Mr. Cass. I will answer the Senator. I spoke of the Missouri compromise, which established a line that ran through a country in which slavery existed, and which declared that slavery should be excluded north of that line, and left the country south of it as it found it, to continue slavery or to exclude it, as the people might judge best. I say that my doctrine for the whole territory is non-intervention.

Mr. DAVIS, (in his seat.) I prefer that, too.

Mr. CASS. I agree, therefore, with the Senator from Mississippi. I say that this Government has no right to interfere with the institution of slavery in the territories; and I say, if the South think they have rights there under the constitution, in God's name, let the Supreme Court determine the question. No one can object to that.

Mr. DAVIS, (in his seat.) But we cannot get there.

Mr. CASS. I do not know that. I think otherwise. I would observe, and the Senate will remember, that the point in issue was the Missouri compromise; and now I understand the Senator from Mississippi would not vote for that measure unless it was accompanied with the declaration that slavery should, or may, or does, exist south of that line. Do I understand him aright?

Mr. DAVIS, of Mississippi. I have several times had occasion to explain that point, which has been attacked by gentlemen of the North as an inadmissible claim. I will agree to the drawing of the line 36° 30′ through the territories acquired from Mexico, with this condition, that in the same degree as slavery is prohibited north of that line, it shall be permitted to enter south of the line; and that the States which may be admitted into the Union, shall come in under such constitutions as they think proper to form.

Mr. CASS. With respect to the last point, I imagine there would be no difference between us. With respect to the other, the proposition is intervention north, and non-intervention south of the line, without conferring any rights on the South. It would be of no practical utility whatever to that section of country, unless accompanied by some legislative declaration on the subject. I repeat the belief, that we have no authority to say that slavery shall or shall not exist in the territories of the United States. It is a matter to be left wholly to the people of the country to decide. That is, I think, the true doctrine. I have ever maintained it, and unless I change greatly, I shall abide by it.

Mr. DAVIS, of Mississippi. The Senator does not exactly comprehend my meaning. He and I do not differ much as to the powers of Congress over the territories. The difference between the honorable Senator and myself seems to begin just where he ceases to answer. I say that if we cannot be permitted, free from Congressional interference, to go into these territories, and test our rights, and opportunities under the constitution and by the law of nature, and before the Supreme Court of the United States, shall this agitation continue—shall this sectional strife be unassuaged? Will not the Senator, like myself, come down in this stage of the question, and take less than his own standard—take the Missouri compromise in terms adapted to these territories?

Mr. CASS. What I would do to save this Union from dissolution, if dissolution were impending over it, and to be averted only by one course of action, it is difficult to say. I would do almost any thing.

I desire to advert to another topic, and that is, one relating personally to myself. I need not remind the Senate, that within a short time I have passed through a very severe ordeal for any man. I said, and I said truly, when the Senator from Kentucky remarked, a few days since, he was the best abused man in the country, that he was so with one exception. That exception my modesty prevents me from naming. During that campaign I was silent, and left the falsehoods which in this country seem to belong to such a contest, to serve out their purpose, and then to die; but when these things are resuscitated and repeated here, or in the other branch of the National Legislature, I choose to defend myself. I am not now in a position which precludes me from the exercise of that right, and I will exercise it in my place, when the nature of the assault, or the standing of the assailant, may render this necessary. I owe this duty to my constituents, by whose favor I am here, not less than to myself. A gentleman from North Carolina (Mr. STANLY) said, in the House of Representatives a few days since, that "Taylor beat Cass, who thanked God he never owned a slave," &c. I never said this; it is one of the unfounded stories, whose functions having been fulfilled, is thus suddenly called from its resting-place, for some purpose, I know not why. It is an expression I never used—it conveys a meaning I utterly disavow. I do not arraign the motives of the gentleman who has thus arraigned me; he had heard the story, and, I presume, believed it; but he should have ascertained the facts, before he thus summoned me—not in the heat of an excited contest, but in the cool hours of legislation—to the bar of the House of Representatives, and, in effect, to the bar of the country. The charge, sir, places me in the position of a Pharisee, thanking God that I am better than the men of the South, and free from offences which they commit. All this is as contrary to my feelings as to my habits. I cast no reflections upon the South then, or at any other time.

What I said and did, I will now state, and if a single Senator on this floor will condemn my course, I will then confess that this charge is not as wholly groundless as it appears to me.

While I was in France, it is well known that Great Britain had formed a plan by which she intended to gain the command of the seas. There is no secret about this now, and it has been openly avowed. Her object was, under the pretext of putting an end to the slave-trade, to board our vessels, which would have been followed by the imprisonment of our seamen, and other acts of aggression incident to her naval superiority. My friend, Mr. Stevenson, was then our representative in London. It is the first and great duty of an American minister abroad, when the rights of his country are assailed, to assert and defend them. Mr. Stevenson did so in an able and fearless manner, in a correspondence marked with signal ability. During the progress of the controversy, the public mind in England became much excited, and there was a strong effort made to connect the continuance of the slave-trade with the condition of slavery in our country, as though the former were essential to the latter. All the tirades against slavery we sometimes hear at home, were poured out there.

Mr. Foote. I had intended to-day, had I enjoyed a favorable opportunity of doing so, to make a few remarks explanatory of my own attitude in reference to the questions under discussion; but the Senate will perceive that it is too late to do so now. I will state in general terms, what I came here prepared to show. I may be in error or not, in regard to the questions referred to; I may be in advance of the South generally, or the reverse, in regard to the measures proper to be adopted at the present crisis; but one thing is certain, that I am perfectly in unison with my own State, as I hope to be always hereafter. Sir, I hold in my hand a document, from which I intend to read an extract or two, which I am sure will be listened to with patience, and even satisfaction, by a majority of this body, and which I am certain will be found far more edifying than any thing which I could originate. It is the opening address of Chief Justice Sharkey, at the late Mississippi Convention, in the proceedings of which originated the grand scheme of the Nashville Convention; and I beg leave simply to say, that hereafter I shall rely upon this address and the resolutions adopted by our convention, to prove that I have not said a word here, during the last four days, in which I was not justified by mature public sentiment at home, and in which I am not likely to be sustained hereafter by that high-spirited and patriotic constituency whom it is my highest pride to serve and to obey. I need not add, sir, that I intend to stand by the position of Mississippi, as asserted in the proceedings of her convention, now and hereafter, firmly, faithfully, and fearlessly—neither going to the right nor to the left, to please or displease, to gratify or to affront, any man or set of men, here or elsewhere.

Before I proceed to read the extracts promised, allow me to introduce to honorable Senators, the distinguished author of the address referred to, the Hon. William L. Sharkey. It was thus that I had occasion lately to write of him, in a communication addressed to the editor of the *Union*, in October last, preliminary to this same address, the publication of which I was then soliciting:

"William L. Sharkey has been known for more than twenty years as one of the ablest jurists in the south-western section of the Republic. He is as remarkable for all the virtues which belong to social and domestic life, as he is for legal learning and elevated patriotism. He is distinguished above most men for sweetness and placidity of temper, a bland courtesy of manners, and a discreet and cautious circumspection and forbearance, under all circumstances of trial and irritation. He has, for many years past, had no particular connection with scenes of political strife, but has been recognized by all who know him as a uniform and inflexible Whig; and he voted in the late Presidential election, for the present Chief Magistrate of the United States, as did precisely one half of the members of the convention over which he was, on this occasion, called to preside. When all these facts come to be duly considered, it is to be hoped that his words of stern remonstrance and solemn warning, will not be disregarded by those who love the Union, and are desirous that our free institutions shall be perpetuated."

So much for the author of the address. Now listen, if you please, to the extracts promised:

"The subject of your contemplated deliberations is an important one—nothing less than a question involving in its consequences, the liberty of this people—perhaps directly or remotely the liberty of other nations. I trust that you will approach it dispassionately—that you will lay aside your party predilections, and meet it, not as politicians, but as patriots—as statesmen. We had flattered ourselves that the capacity of man for self-government was no longer a subject of doubt. We have boasted of ours, as an example of a free Government, based on an enduring foundation. I trust it may prove so; but events of recent occurrence seem to forebode danger. The convocation of this assembly—the intense interest manifest in every countenance here—are proofs that there is cause of alarm. For a time we have been prosperous and happy under a free Government, but that time, in the great history of man, is but a brief space—a mere point. The page of history is yet fresh which records our existence as a nation of freemen. Scarce has the stain of revolutionary blood, shed for liberty, faded from the face of the land, before it has been found necessary for the people of the South to prepare to check threatened aggression. And whence this danger? No foreign foe threatens us. Our countrymen—our brothers—are arrayed against us in civil strife. They seem to forget that they are allied to us by the most sacred ties, and to forget the value of the Union. Blinded by the poison of fanaticism, they seek to abridge our constitutional rights in the enjoyment of our property, under the mask of false humanity. If the right to do so was unquestionable, in Christian charity, it should be asserted without inflicting remorseless stings to our sensibilities. The entire independence of the States was achieved by the most memorable struggle that history records. They were separate and independent sovereignties, and first united under articles of confederation. These articles were defective, mainly in not having provided proper means for raising a revenue, and in not giving Congress sufficient power to regulate commerce. These defects gave rise to our present constitution. In the Convention which formed it, the States met as equals in political power. The small States were unwilling to relinquish their equality of power—the slaveholding States were unwilling to confederate, unless their slaves should be made a basis of representation, and the owners secured in their right. These were exciting subjects. After great difficulty, they were compromised. The second section of the first article provides, that Representatives and direct taxes should be apportioned according to numbers, to be ascertained by adding three-fifths of the slaves to the number of whites. The second section of the fourth article provides for recapturing slaves escaping into those States where slavery did not exist. In these provisions we have an acknowledgment of the existence of slavery, and a guarantee for its protection, as the basis of representation and as property. The constitution did not create property in slaves. Such right existed anterior to, and above, the constitution. As slaves were owned in many of the States, they would not, of course, have entered into the Confederacy on such terms as would weaken the right of the owner to his slave, or diminish the value. One of the great objects of the constitution was, that it should, in its consequences, protect property by giving protection and strength to the several States; but as the States were sovereign, they could not surrender to Congress the right to control, by legislation, the property of their citizens. Such a grant of power would have been a complete surrender of sovereignty. A great consolidated Government would have risen up, which was an evil, of all others, most dreaded, and most rigidly guarded against, by declaring that all power, not expressly granted to Congress, was reserved to the States or to the people. Hence no power can be exercised unless it has been granted by the constitution. The safety of the States and of the people is best preserved by holding Congress strictly within the limit of the delegated powers. No rule of construction can be safe which encroaches upon individual rights. The right to hold slaves as property became a fixed principle, inseparable from the other provisions of the constitution. Indeed, that description of property seems to have been thought worthy of specific and special protection. The constitution must exist and harmonize in all its parts. Every principle it contains is inseparably connected together. It is an entire thing—being the great frame-work of the Government—indissolubly united in all its parts. It would not have been formed without the insertion of every feature; it is an infraction to violate any of them; the symmetry is broken.

"Notwithstanding this unqualified recognition of property in slaves, and the protection provided for its enjoyment as such, it is still contended that Congress may prohibit and abolish it in the territories of the United States. The territories are common property, and cannot be appropriated by Congress to the use of one portion of the common owners, to the exclusion of another. Equality of right must, then, prevail; and any act which would destroy that equality, cannot be valid. It is a principle in the law of nations, that 'all the members of the community have an equal right to the use of their common property.' Rules may be prescribed by the sovereign power, regulating the manner of its use, provided they are not inconsistent with that entire equality which ought to be preserved. If the sovereign authority in a State or nation can do nothing which shall produce inequality in the enjoyment of the public domain or property, surely such authority is not possessed by the Federal Government, which has but a limited power. The attempt by Congress to prohibit slavery in the Territory of California, has caused this meeting. That territory is common property. There each citizen of the United States has equal rights—is entitled to equal freedom—in the enjoyment of the territories. I am proud to say, that in acquiring it, Mississippians displayed as much valor as any other portion of their brethren in arms, and shed as much blood, in proportion to their numbers, as the citizens of any of the States. They were distinguished for their prowess in many a hard-fought battle; but now they are to be told that restrictions must be imposed on their right to enjoy the conquest. Can we—should we—yield the fruits of our valor, and surrender with our constitutional right of equality? Congress cannot deprive us of it, and ought not, if it could—cannot say, that if we go, we must leave our property behind us. Property constitutes the means of enjoyment; and to exclude the property of the people of the southern States, is in effect to exclude the people, and appropriate the country to the northern States. Such a power is not possessed by a Government possessing sovereignty; it could not be rightfully exercised even by a monarchy. The property of the South consists mostly in slaves; and to interdict its use on our own soil, would not only be unjust, but an arbitrary violation of the constitution. It is vain to talk of our right to the territories, if we may be deprived of the means of enjoying those rights. The mere soil is nothing; it is the use that we may make of it, which renders it valuable. As well might Congress interdict the use of any other property there; if it can exclude a slave, it may exclude a horse or an ox. * * * * *

"But in the efforts to exclude our property from that territory, another false doctrine is promulgated, which is equally disastrous to us. We are told that, as slavery was prohibited by the laws of Mexico, we cannot take slaves there without the authority of a law permitting it. This is the doctrine of a class of politicians in our country who look no further than the surface of the law. If this error were confined to politicians, it might be passed over as harmless; but it is also the doctrine which has been unceremoniously promulgated by a member of the supreme bench. We could overlook the groundless fallacies of a few politicians; but when the sanctity of the bench is perverted, and its influence thrown as an element into the exciting cause of malcontent and strife, there is just ground of complaint. If this could be a judicial question in any shape, that was the tribunal before which it might come. With the decision, the American people would have rested satisfied—quiet would have been restored. It was a great constitutional question, and on such questions, the people of the United States have been taught to look to the decisions of the Supreme Court with veneration; but they have not been accustomed to having them promulgated in advance, and are startled at thus seeing them. The effect is almost as injurious to us as a decision regularly pronounced, because it has deterred the South from an equal participancy in the territories, while it has emboldened the North to persist in its efforts. It has caused one party to believe that it was right, and the other to fear that it was wrong. From position, it has made the 'worse appear the better cause.' It is not true, that slavery does not exist in California, although it may have been prohibited by the laws of Mexico. True, the conquering country may permit the municipal laws of the conquered country to remain in force; but this is only true of private or strictly municipal laws. It is not true as regards political laws. By elementary writers, laws are divided into public and private, or political and municipal. Political laws are such as are organic, and confer power and form on the Government. They give it vitality as an organized body. These political laws are sometimes reduced to the form of a constitution, which becomes supreme and paramount to all other laws, either public or private. Our constitution is the law of our being—it is the essence of our Government—it is the combination of certain great principles, between each one of which, there is a connection and dependency, and the aggregate constitutes a unit. To withdraw or destroy any one of them, would break the entire fabric—it would lop off an essential part of our political power. When we acquired California, it became subject to our constitution—our whole constitution—our constitution as an entire thing. The territory did not become subject to part of our Government only; but every principle of the constitution prevailed there as an active principle, and superseded, of necessity, whatever was repugnant to any one of them. No abridgment of the rights of the new-comers could be permitted. The vested rights of the citizens there, at the time we acquired it, may be protected by a principle not inconsistent with this position. The consequence is, that we have a right to take our slaves there, because they are our property, secured to us, as such, by the principles of our paramount political law. If it were true that slavery was then prohibited by the laws of Mexico, and could not be established there without positive law, then the constitution went there a mere cripple—but not so. Wherever the stars and stripes float over a territory, as an emblem of political dominion, they rest upon a perfect pedestal—formed by every principle in the constitution—indissolubly cemented together. As well may it be said, that our constitution must give place to the established religion of Mexico.

"How strange it is, that while Congress has no power over the subject of slavery, in consequence of an inhibition, it should be contended that the laws of the conquered country should secure a prohibition, and thus triumph over our constitutional rights!

"Thus, as I conceive, stands the question of right; but if it were a question of expediency merely, how ungenerous the conduct of the North! We are united as a family of nations. We may have different local interests, but our obligations to each other, require an observance of good faith, of good feeling, of mutual support, and forbearance. With them, it is a matter of feeling only—with us, it is a question of interest. Are they not prepared to yield their feelings and prejudices, for the sake of protecting our interest? If not, they have forgotten the objects of the Union: mutual safety, prosperity, and happiness, dictated it. Are they willing to risk all these for the gratification of a mere imaginary philanthropy? It would seem so. The Wilmot proviso is but the entering wedge; that accomplished, the rest will follow. Emancipation in the States is doubtless the ultimate object; and we have reason to fear that at no point short of this will the effort cease. The Union must be dissolved, and the blessings which we enjoy under our Government must become a sacrifice on the altar of fanaticism. We must become a degraded people, or abandon our country to the African race. We would say to them, Beware! you but rush on to your own destruction.

"It is a subject of deep regret, that the powerful engine of prejudice is arrayed against us. Enormities are falsely ascribed to us, with a view to excite indignation; they add insult to injury. We are held out as destitute of common mercy—degraded at home and abroad. The means employed are calculated to excite our slave population, and endanger our lives. We hope and believe that there are still a few at the North, who value the Union, and do not engage in this unnatural warfare. Our Union should be social as well as political—amity should prevail between the different divisions. But the ties that bind us are being daily weakened, and the love of the Union diminished. We have remonstrated, but in vain. We yield to none, in a deep and abiding love for the Union. We wish not to sever it, but to re-cement it. We can vindicate it only by keeping it inviolate. We would preserve it in all its purity. We want it as our fathers gave it to us, and must defend it against infraction, as a sacred duty we owe to their memory. The South has borne with these encroachments, under a hope that a sense of justice would ultimately correct the evil; but of this there seems now to be but little hope. We must take our stand. Let us survey the ground well, and occupy that position on which we can stand within the pale of the constitution; and when taken, let us maintain it, like men who know their rights and are determined to protect them. We are not the aggressors; and if the result should prove disastrous, let the blame rest on those who have provoked the quarrel."

It will readily be perceived, Mr. President, that Judge Sharkey contented himself with a bold, nervous, and irresistible vindication of the constitutional rights of the South, of the assailment of which he justly complained, and against further aggressions, upon which he most solemnly and earnestly protested. He confined himself, and wisely, too, as I conceive, to "*the pale of the Constitution.*" He did not feel authorized to recommend any amendment of the constitution, as indispensable to the safety and honor of the South. He did not suggest the adoption by Congress of any act for amplifying, adding to, or strengthening, the existing rights of the slave States of the Union in any part of our territorial domain. He regarded our rights, under the constitution, as full and complete—Mexican laws to the contrary notwithstanding. He occupied strict *non-intervention* ground throughout this address, and demanded only that Congress should refrain from all legislation hostile to southern rights. He firmly and proudly relied upon an enlightened judiciary for the decision of all questions which might arise in regard to the *legality* of slavery in the territories. This is precisely the ground which, for several sessions past, southern members in Congress have assumed, and maintained, as I think, with arguments of irresistible and conclusive force. Territorial government, without the Wilmot proviso, or any restriction on the subject of slavery, is all that we have claimed. To be sure, we have declared—and I understand every State of the South, including Mississippi, to declare—that if the course of aggression, heretofore pursued, should be obstinately persisted in —if tyranny and injustice should be practised, which might be justly regarded as amounting to *intolerable oppression*—then would the right of *secession* arise as an extra-constitutional, or, if you please, a revolutionary remedy—authority to resort to which, in such a case, no freeman, worthy of the name, will ever gainsay. Such, sir, do I understand to be the precise attitude of the State of Mississippi, upon whose suggestion the proposition to hold a Southern Convention, in Nashville, was first entertained by the southern States of the Union. This convention was recommended by the State of Mississippi, as I have several times had occasion to state here, not for *disunion purposes*—not for the purpose of adding to the unhappy excitement now existing—not for the purpose of raising up insuperable obstacles of any kind, to the ultimate adjustment of the pending questions —but for the purpose of holding calm, fraternal and patriotic counsel, and, by embodying the whole moral force of the South in favor of such fair, reasonable, and constitutional measures of redress and prevention, as the crisis might seem to demand, to rescue the Union from impending jeopardy, effectually to shield the honor of the South from menaced discredit, and secure to the slave States of the Republic that perfect domestic security to which, by the constitution itself, they are undeniably entitled. Such, according to my understanding of the matter, is the position of the State of Mississippi—such the objects of the Nashville Convention, the holding of which, I hope, may still be rendered unnecessary, by the adoption of certain healing measures here, which are beginning, as I think, to be generally regarded as more than likely to be ultimately matured and carried into effect.

And now, sir, before I conclude, I will say, that I have more confident hopes than several of my friends, who have spoken in the last day or two, of a satisfactory adjustment of all the questions growing out of slavery at the present session of Congress. My honorable colleague will allow me to suggest, that I do not concur with him in the rather despondent opinion he has just now expressed, that there is no prospect of passing a bill through both Houses of Congress for the establishment of territorial governments, without any restriction in regard to slavery. I will not positively predict future results; but I will venture to declare that, from the best information which I have been able to obtain from members of the two Houses of Congress, I have been led to the conclusion, that such a territorial bill as I have described, will unquestionably pass both the Senate and House of Representatives, if we can ever put it fairly in progress. Other questions, I doubt not, may be also satisfactorily adjusted, whenever we conclude to terminate angry and unprofitable discussion, and enter in the proper spirit upon the pathway of practical duty.

Mr. President, I had hoped that the Senate would have granted the motion, now under consideration, several days since. I entertained a very decided wish, that the special committee that I have been so long endeavoring to raise, might enter upon their important task under the auspicious influences awakened by the noble speech of the honorable Senator from Massachusetts, (Mr. WEBSTER,) whose attitude and political connections are such as to give him peculiar efficiency as a pacificator at this period. In this wish I have not been gratified. As I anticipated and apprehended, other speeches have been made less conciliatory in their character. The honorable Senator from New York (Mr. SEWARD) has been especially active since in stirring up the embers of discord, and in reawakening that fell spirit of contention which has been already productive of so much mischief. It is probable that no injury will now result from a still longer postponement of final action upon my motion for a special committee; and as several gentlemen, who profess to be willing to vote for the motion hereafter, when they shall have had an opportunity of addressing the Senate, have requested me not to urge immediate action, I acquiesce very willingly in the motion of the honorable Senator from New Jersey, (Mr. DAYTON,) and hope that the question under consideration may be made the order of the day for Wednesday next.

Mr. BUTLER. My friend from Mississippi (Mr. FOOTE) has understood me as having endorsed the course that he says has been taken by my colleague. Now, sir, as to the course which my colleague may think proper to take, it is upon his own responsibility, and his speech has been deliberately prepared, and is fairly the subject of parliamentary criticism. I do not object to the remarks made upon it by the honorable Senator from Michigan; for the speech has been given to the public, with a claim to public attention, and it cannot lose any thing by public discussion; and, of course, public men have a right to comment freely on it. I am sorry my colleague is not here, to make such a reply as the assaults upon it would have demanded. He is not quite so well to-day as he was yesterday; but, absent or present, he must share the fate of all public men who have a historical reputation. The authority of his name is derived from his services to the Union for an eventful lifetime; and that authority is not to be destroyed by the ephemeral criticism of the moment, or the evanescent censure dictated under the influence of a confident majority. The reputation of distinguished men is more like the promontory in the deep, than the fluctuating waves that beat upon its base, or the winds that assail its bosom. It preserves its identity in spite of them, and looks the prouder when it has withstood them.

I do not choose to say more now, nor do I know that I shall hereafter say any thing in the way of personal vindication. I do not understand any one to say that this Government may not last, by a faithful adherence to the provisions of its constitution, or the original and honest construction of it; and my colleague, I suppose, thinks, as long as there was self-sustaining power in what he regards the equilibrium of the different sections of the country, there was an ample guarantee of the continuance of the Union. But he has intimated his opinion, that there is no security against the abuse of an irresponsible majority; and when he speaks of this Government, as tending to an irresponsible despotism, like that of Russia, he says nothing more or less, than that if the majority assume a power not in the constitution, and use force to carry out their ends, it would be like any other irresponsible despotism, to all intents and purposes. Can any one doubt that? I do not think it can be denied, that others must respect our rights, or we must have guarantees to maintain them when they are wrongfully violated.

Mr. Dayton moved that the further consideration of this question be postponed till Wednesday next, at one o'clock.

The motion was agreed to, and,

On motion, the Senate then adjourned.

Thursday, March 21.

Mississippi—Nashville Convention.

Mr. Foote. I hold in my hand several joint resolutions, recently adopted by the Legislature of the State of Mississippi, having a vital connection with the important questions which have, for some time past, almost exclusively occupied the attention of the two Houses of Congress, and which have awakened an amount of solicitude and anxiety in the public mind of the country, that has been seldom heretofore called forth by any questions whatever. I shall ask presently that these resolutions may be read, but shall desire no action of any kind thereupon, until my honorable colleague and myself shall receive an attested copy thereof—the arrival of which is confidently to be expected a few days hence. I trust, Mr. President, that the Senate will bear with me patiently, while I offer a few remarks upon the subject embraced in these resolutions—necessary, as I conceive, to the vindication of the State of Mississippi against certain unjust and unkind allegations, and important at this time, as explanatory of the true attitude of that State, in regard to the convocation of the Nashville Convention. I should not be willing to occupy the attention of the Senate with these matters at the present moment, but for two reasons, which I will concisely state. The first is this: the National Intelligencer of this city, in several recent editorial articles, has dealt very freely in language of censure, in regard to the action of the State of Mississippi, in originating the call of a Southern Convention. The editors of this old and respectable journal have not hesitated to run a regular parallel between the action of the southern States at this time—in resolving to assemble in convention, for the vindication of their constitutional rights from assailment, and for the counteraction of certain well-known measures of threatened hostility—and the famous Hartford Convention, the very name of which has long been odious and abhorrent to all true patriots. I shall not now, sir, indulge in the language of recrimination, to which I am so strongly invited. It is not my desire at this moment to do or to say any thing which may beget feelings of sectional unkindness, and thus obstruct that speedy compromise and settlement of all existing difficulties, which all good citizens now so ardently desire. One of the points of similitude between the expected Nashville Convention and that of Hartford is, as urged by the editors of the National Intelligencer, that the Hartford Conventionists demanded an amendment of the constitution, as indispensable to the security of those whom they represented, which expedient of a constitutional amendment, is asserted to be also one of the expedients to which the southern States have avowed their determination to resort, through the medium of the Nashville Convention. On yesterday, this view of the subject was earnestly insisted upon by the honorable Senator from New Hampshire, (Mr. Hale,) who formally accused the whole South of designing to demand some constitutional amendment, impossible to be obtained, in order to pave the way to a dissolution of the Union. This assertion of the Senator from New Hampshire, constitutes my second reason for undertaking, at this time, a defence of those who have participated in getting up the Nashville Convention. I do not know how I can prove more satisfactorily the injustice of all that has been said in regard to the designs and motives of the Southern States, in agreeing to meet, in convention, at Nashville, than by reading a few extracts from a document which lies before me, which is nothing more nor less than the very "Address to the Southern States" which has been so emphatically denounced by the editors of the National Intelligencer, as one of a treasonable character. Those who will dispassionately consider what I am about to read, will not only be satisfied that there has been, as yet, no organized movement in the South for a dissolution of the Union, but that no radical change in the fundamental law of the Republic has been seriously contemplated, much less insisted upon, in any part of the South. It would be highly gratifying to me, and I have no doubt, under different circumstances, equally agreeable to the Senate, to have the whole of this able and patriotic address read on the present occasion. But as I have only a few minutes of the morning hour, during which to perform the task which I am now executing, I shall merely lay before the Senate a few of the concluding paragraphs, assuring honorable Senators that there is no part of the address which will not be found, upon examination, perfectly to harmonize with the portions now to be read in their hearing. After a clear and forcible statement of historic facts, and an able argument upon constitutional and other grounds, the address proceeds as follows:

[Here the Senator caused the concluding paragraphs to be read.]

These, sir, are the views of the people of the sovereign State of Mississippi, as declared by our convention, through a committee of seven gentlemen, who, in ability, patriotism, moral worth, and I will add, *devotion to the Union*, are not inferior to any seven individuals to be found in the whole Republic. Who doubts now the truth of what I have so often declared here, that the people of Mississippi stand alone upon their constitutional rights; that they rely exclusively upon the fundamental guarantees so wisely provided by our venerated forefathers, and that they are resolved to do all in their power to preserve this Union, by the only means capable of securing its preservation—*the maintenance of the integrity of the constitution itself?*

But the National Intelligencer, in one of its late numbers, instead of publishing the whole, or any considerable portion, of this address, has torn a single paragraph from its context, in order to prove that the South, or at least the people of Mississippi, have unconditionally resolved upon a dissolution of the Union, and the establishment of a Southern confederacy. That paragraph is as follows:

"Besides and beyond a popular Convention of the southern States, with the view and the hope of arresting the course of aggression, and if not practicable, then to concentrate the South in will, understanding, and action, the convention of Mississippi suggested, as the possible ultimate resort, the call by the legislatures of the assailed States of still more solemn conventions—such as should be regularly elected by the people of those States—to deliberate, speak, and act, with all the sovereign power of the people. Should, in the result, such conventions be called and meet, they may lead to a like regularly-constituted convention of all the assailed States, to provide, in the last resort, for their separate welfare, by the formation of a compact and a Union, that will afford protection to their liberties and rights. In such a crisis, in the language of Mr. Madison, 'one spirit will animate and conduct the whole.'"

Now, Mr. President, does not every one perceive the gross injustice done the committee who prepared this address, in deducing from the paragraph cited, the inference that the Mississippi people are so resolved upon secession that nothing else can satisfy them? Sir, the true and obvious import of the language objected to, is simply this: *the constitution is to be maintained, if possible, by all legitimate and honorable means.* The obligations of that sacred instrument are to be scrupulously observed and executed, on the part of the southern States, while its faithful observance by other members of the confederacy, is to be demanded and insisted upon. The *guarantees* in which the South is peculiarly interested, are to be respected by the free States of the Union in all their scope and amplitude. If in all these important points, the North should prove unwilling to do justice—which Heaven forbid—if the offensive enactments menaced shall be adopted, and the grievances already confessedly inflicted shall remain unredressed—then the southern States will assemble in convention, to consult for their own safety and welfare; and if justice shall still be withheld, after all pacific and constitutional expedients have been tried, and tried in vain, why then the southern States *may* feel it to be a duty, forced upon them, of seceding in the last resort from the Union.

This, I repeat, is the real and full import of that portion of the Mississippi address, to which the editors of the Intelligencer have applied language of the most unmeasured denunciation. What is this but to assert, sir, that we live under a system of Government which renders all tyranny justifiable, and oppression too sacred a thing to be complained of—under which power, however obtained or wielded, is entitled to triumph over right—under which, in fine, freedom is but a name, and the written organic law a ridiculous mockery! It was not thus that our noble forefathers thought and acted, under which non-resistance to the most hideous usurpation, is the bounden duty of all good citizens, and even of sovereign States; nor was it thus that, in a purer and more high-spirited generation, public men either wrote or spoke. It was not thus that Andrew Jackson expressed himself in that famous proclamation, in which, though rebuking nullification, he declared secession to be a just and proper remedy—to be resorted to in any case of *intolerable oppression.* It was not thus that the honorable Senator from Massachusetts (Mr. Webster) spoke the other day, in our hearing, when he emphatically declared the same doctrine. Such was not the doctrine of Philip P. Barbour, who asserted secession to be the *political arsenic* of our system, to be resorted to when all other remedies might fail. Such, finally, was not the doctrine of Mr. Jefferson, who oftentimes declared secession (or "scission," as he denominated it) to be, in certain cases of enormous and long-continued outrage, the proper and only remedy. I find the opinion of Mr. Jefferson, on this point, very precisely set forth in the eulogy delivered some years since upon the life and character of Mr. Madison, by Mr.

John Quincy Adams. Here are Mr. Adams's own words, as printed in the volume from which I now read:

"Concurring in the doctrines that the separate States have a right to *interpose*, in cases of palpable infractions of the constitution by the Government of the United States, and that the alien and sedition acts presented a case of such infraction, Mr. Jefferson considered them as absolutely null and void, and thought the State legislatures competent, not only to declare, but to *make* them so, to resist their execution within their respective borders by physical force, and to *secede from the Union* rather than to submit to them, if attempted to be carried into execution by force."

I will not enlarge upon this fruitful topic: it would be quite easy to do so, and to retaliate upon the editors of the Intelligencer, the illiberal reproaches cast upon millions of their fellow-countrymen, who have given their formal, solemn, and deliberate adhesion to those measures of resistance; but I forbear; such unkind comments would be as unprofitable to others as they would be disagreeable to myself. But I cannot conclude, Mr. President, without announcing to these venerable gentlemen, that they were never in grosser error in their lives, than when they asserted, in this morning's Intelligencer, that "there is in the State of Mississippi no general acquiescence in the propriety or expediency" of the Nashville Convention. So far as I know or believe, more than ninety-nine hundredths of all parties in Mississippi recognize the expediency of this measure, and will sustain the expected convention in every proceeding which may be deemed necessary for vindicating southern honor against menaced indignity, and southern safety against threatened assaults. The worthy editors of the Intelligencer do not err less surprisingly when, in the same number of their paper, after publishing the names of the eminent gentlemen who will have the honor of representing the State of Mississippi in the Nashville Convention, they express themselves as follows: "Very respectable gentlemen, but who, we cannot but think, should all or any of them get to Nashville at the time appointed, will, when they find themselves so ill-seconded by other States, feel very much like fish out of water." Sir, I earnestly hope that all occasion for the assembling of the Nashville Convention may be shortly removed, and that healing, temperate, and patriotic counsels may prove efficient in warding off the dangers which now environ our beloved institutions. But if the aggressions, to counteract and avert which the Nashville Convention has been called, should be persevered in, I can assure the editors of the Intelligencer—and I speak advisedly when I say so—that there will not be two southern States—I doubt if there will be a single one—that will not be represented at Nashville; and despite domestic treachery, and all other causes, obstructive of united action, ninety-nine hundredths of the whole southern population will prefer any fate whatever to an unconditional submission to tyranny.

THURSDAY, March 28.

The Compromise.

The VICE PRESIDENT announced that the hour had arrived for the consideration of the special order, namely, the series of resolutions presented by Mr. CLAY.

Mr. CHASE resumed and finished the speech which he commenced yesterday.

Mr. BALDWIN moved that the further consideration of the subject be postponed until to-morrow.

The motion was agreed to.

Mr. BALDWIN. I now move that the resolutions of the Senator from Tennessee be taken up, with a view to make them the special order of the day for to-morrow, at 1 o'clock.

Mr. FOOTE. I understood the motion of the Senator from Connecticut, in regard to the subject which has been under consideration, to be, to postpone it until to-morrow. I trust that, under the circumstances, the subject which was before the Senate this morning will be allowed to have precedence. I hope the Senate will permit my motion for referring to a committee the resolutions of the Senator from Tennessee, to be acted upon to-morrow, and afterward give an opportunity for the discussion of the general subject upon the propositions that will remain before the Senate. I trust that I may be permitted to say, that I have been forbearing and conciliatory in regard to this matter; and I hope that, at the least, the friends of the proposition will co-operate in hastening its final decision.

The question being taken on the motion to take up the resolutions of the Senator from Tennessee, it was agreed to.

Mr. MANGUM. I now move, for the benefit of the Senator from Connecticut, that these resolutions be made the special order of the day for 1 o'clock to-morrow, to take precedence over all other matters.

The motion was agreed to.

HOUSE OF REPRESENTATIVES.

MONDAY, April 1.

A Recess.

Mr. VINTON rose and said: We may expect in a little time, Mr. Speaker, to receive from the Senate a message announcing the melancholy event which is already known to us as a national calamity. Instead of proceeding to the discharge of the ordinary business of the House, I move that the rules be suspended, and that the House take a recess until we receive the message from the Senate.

The SPEAKER. If there be no objection, the motion made by the gentleman from Ohio will be considered as agreed to, and the House will take a recess until such time as the message is received from the Senate.

No objection being made,

The Speaker left the chair, and the House took a recess.

At ten minutes past 1 the Speaker resumed the chair.

The Decease of Mr. Calhoun.

A message was received from the Senate, by the hands of A. Dickins, Esq., their Secretary, who said that he was directed to communicate to the House information of the decease of the Hon. John C. Calhoun, a Senator in Congress from the State of South Carolina, and the proceedings of the Senate thereon.

The message having been read,

Mr. Holmes, of South Carolina, rose and addressed the House as follows:

It becomes, Mr. Speaker, my solemn duty to announce to this House the decease of the honorable John C. Calhoun, a Senator of the State of South Carolina. He expired at his lodgings in this city, yesterday morning, at 7 o'clock. He lives no longer among the living: he sleeps the sleep of a long night which knows no dawning. The sun which rose so brightly on this morning, brought to him no healing in its beams.

We, the Representatives of our State, come to sorrow over the dead; but the virtue, and the life, and the services of the deceased, were not confined by metes and bounds; but standing on the broad expanse of this confederacy, he gave his genius to the States, and his heart to his entire country. Carolina will not, therefore, be suffered to mourn her honored son in secret cells and solitary shades; but her sister States will gather around her in this palace of the nation, and bending over that bier, weep as she weeps, and mourn with the deep, afflictive mourning of her heart. Yes, sir; her honored son—honored in the associations of his birth, which occurred when the echoes and the shouts of freedom had not yet died along his native hills, born of parents who had partaken of the toils, been affected by the struggles, and fought in the battles for liberty —he seemed as if he were baptized in the very fount of freedom. Reared amid the hardy scenery of nature, and amid a stern, pious, and reserved population, yet unseduced by the temptations, and unnerved by the luxuries of life, he gathered from surrounding objects, and from the people of his association, that peculiar hue and coloring which so transcendently marked his life. Unfettered by the restraints of the school-house, he wandered in those regions which surrounded his dwelling, unmolested, and indulged those solitary thoughts, in rambling through her mighty forests, which gave that peculiar cast of thinking and reflection to his mighty soul. He was among a people who knew but few books, and over whose minds learning had not yet thrown its effulgence. But they had the Bible; and with his pious parents, he gathered rich lore, which surpasses that of Greek or Roman story. At an age when youths are generally prepared to scan the classics, he was yet uninitiated in their rudiments. Under the tuition of the venerable Doctor Waddle, his relative and friend, he quickly acquired what that gentleman was able to impart, and even then began to develop those mighty powers of clear perception, rapid analysis, quick comprehension, vast generalization, for which he was subsequently so eminently distinguished. He remained but a very short time at his school, and returned again to his rustic employments. But the spirit had been awakened—the inspiration had come like a spirit from on high; and he felt that within him were found treasures that learning was essential to unfold. He gathered up his patrimony, he hastened to the College of Yale, and there, under the tuition of that accomplished scholar and profound theologian, Rev. Dr. Dwight, he became, in a short period, the first among the foremost, indulging not in the enjoyments, in the luxuries, and the dissipation of a college life, but with toil severe, with energy unbending, with devotion to his studies, he became (to use the language of a contemporary) "a man among boys." In a conflict intellectual with his great master, the keen eye of Dr. Dwight discerned the great qualifications which marked the man, and prophesied the honors that have fallen in his pathway. He was solitary, and associated not much with the class. He indulged his propensity to solitude; he walked among the elms that surround that ancient college; and in the cells, in the secret shades of that institution, he felt that dawning on his mind which was to precede the brighter and the greater day; and raising himself from the materiality around him, he soared on the wings of contemplation to heights sublime, and whirling his flight along the zodiac, raised his head among the stars. The honors of the college became his meed, and departing thence with the blessings and the benedictions of his venerable instructor, he repaired for a short period to the school of Litchfield, and there imbibed those principles of the common law, based upon the rights of man, and throwing a cordon around the British and the American citizen. He left, and upon his return home, was greeted by the glowing presence of his friends, who had heard from a distance the glad tidings of his studies and his success. He took at once his position among his neighbors. He was sent by them to the counsels of the State; and there, amid a glittering array of lofty intellects and ennobled characters, he became first among the first.

But that sphere was too limited for the expansibility of a mind which seemed to know no limit but the good of all mankind. At the age of twenty-eight he was transferred to this hall. He came not, sir, to a bower of ease; he came not in the moment of a sunshine of tranquillity; he came when the country was disturbed by dissension from within, and pressed from without by the great powers of Europe, then contending for the mastery of the world, and uniting and harmonizing in this, and this alone — the destruction of American institutions, the annihilation of American trade. The whole country (boy as I then was, I well remember) seemed as if covered with a funeral gloom. The spirits of the best men seemed crushed amid that pressure, and the eye of hope scarce found consolation in any prospect of the future. But he had not been long in these halls, before he took the gauge and measurement of the depth of these calamities, and the compass of its breadth. He applied himself most vigorously to the application of the remedies for so vital a disease. He found that a mistaken policy had added to the calamities on the ocean, that still further calamity of fettering, with a restrictive system, the very motions and energies of the people. He looked down and saw that there was a mighty pressure, a great weight upon the resources of this country, which time had gradually increased, and he resolved at once, with that resolution which characterized him—with that energy which impelled him direct to his purpose—to advise what was considered a remedy too great almost for the advice of any other—"at once, weak as we were in numbers, unprepared as we were in arms, diminished as were our resources, to bid defiance to Britain, and assume the attitude of a conflicting nation for its rights."

Fortunately for the country, that advice was taken; and then the great spirit of America, released from her shackles, flamed up, and caused her to arouse from her prostrate condition, and, standing erect, shake her spear in bold defiance. In that war, his counsels contributed as much, I am informed, as those of any man, to its final success. At a period when our troops on the frontier, under the command of the Governor of New York, were about to retire from the line, and that Governor had written to Mr. Madison that he had exhausted his own credit, and the credit of all those whose resources he could command, and his means were exhausted; and unless, in a short period, money was sent on to invigorate the troops, the war must end, and our country bow down to a victorious foe,—sir, upon that occasion Mr. Madison became so disheartened, that he assembled his counsellors, and asked for advice and aid; but advice and aid they had not to give. At length Mr. Dallas, the Secretary of the Treasury, said to Mr. Madison, You are sick—retire to your chamber—leave the rest to us. I will send to the Capitol for the youthful Hercules, who hitherto has borne the war upon his shoulders, and he will counsel us a remedy. Mr. Calhoun came. He advised and appealed to the States for the loan of their credit. It seemed as if a new light had burst upon the cabinet. His advice was taken. The States generously responded to the appeal. These were times of fearful import. We were engaged in war with a nation whose resources were ample, while ours were crippled. Our ships of war, few in number, were compelled to go forth on the broad bosom of the deep to encounter those fleets which had signalized themselves at the battles of Aboukir and Trafalgar, and annihilated the combined navies of France and Spain. But there was an inward strength—there was an undying confidence—in the hearts of a free people; and they went forth to battle and to conquest.

Sir, the clang of arms and the shouts of victory had scarcely died along the dark waters of the Niagara—the war upon the plains of Orleans had just gone out with a blaze of glory—when all eyes were instinctively turned to this youthful patriot, who had rescued his country in the dark hour of her peril. Mr. Monroe transferred him to his Cabinet; and upon that occasion, so confused was the Department of War, so complicated and disordered, that Mr. William Lowndes, a friend of Mr. Calhoun, advised him against risking the high honors he had achieved upon this floor, for the uncertain victories of an Executive position. But no man had pondered more thoroughly the depths of his own mind, and the purposes of his own heart—none knew so well the undaunted resolution and energy that always characterized him, and he resolved to accept, and he did. He related to me, what was extremely characteristic—he went into the department, but became not of it for a while. He gave no directions—he let the machinery move on by its own impetus. In the mean time he gathered, with that minuteness which characterized him, all the facts connected with the working of the machinery. With that power of generalization for which he was so remarkable, he combined together in one system all the detached parts, instituted the bureaus, imparting individual responsibility to each, and requiring from them that responsibility in turn, but uniting them all in beautiful harmony, and creating in the workings a perfect unity. And so complete did that work come from his hand, that at this time there has been no change material in this department. It has passed through the ordeal of another war, and it still remains fresh, and without symptoms of decay. He knew that if we were to have wars, we should have the science to conduct them; and he therefore directed his attention to West Point, which, fostered by his care, became the great school of tactics and of military discipline, the benefits of which have so lately been experienced in the Mexican campaign.

But, sir, having finished this work, his mind instinctively looked for some other great object on which to exercise its powers. He beheld the Indian tribes, broken down by the pressure and the advances of civilization, wasting away before the vices, and acquiring none of the virtues, of the white man. His heart expanded with a philanthropy as extensive as the human race. He immediately conceived the project of collecting them into one nation, of transferring them to the other side of the great river, and freeing them at once from the temptations and the cupidity of the Christian man. Sir, he did not remain in office to accomplish this great object. But he had laid its foundation so deep, he had spread out his plans so broad, that he has reared to himself, in the establishment of that people, a more enduring monument than battles ever gave, and gathered more glorious trophies, than can be plucked upon the plains of war. The triumphs of war are marked by desolated towns and conflagrated fields; his triumphs will be seen in the collection of the Indian tribes, constituting a confederation among themselves, in the school-houses in the valleys, in the churches that rise with their spires from the hill-top, in the clear sunshine of heaven. The music of that triumph is not heard in the clangor of the trumpet and the rolling of the drum, but swells from the clang of the anvil, and the tones of the water-wheel, and the cadence of the mill-stream, that rolls down for the benefit of the poor red man.

Sir, he paused not in his career of usefulness; he was transferred, by the votes of a grateful people, to the chair of the second officer of the Government. There he presided with a firmness, an impartiality, with a gentleness, with a dignity, that all admired. And yet it is not given unto man to pass unscathed the fiery furnace of this world. While presiding over that body of ambassadors from sovereign States —while regulating their councils—the tongue of calumny assailed him, and accused him of official corruption in the Riprap contract. Indignantly he left the chair, demanded of the Senators an immediate investigation by a committee, and came out of the trial like gold refined in the furnace. From that time, to the day that terminated his life, no man dared to breathe aught against the spotless purity of his character.

But while in that chair, Mr. CALHOUN perceived that there was arising a great and mighty influence to overshadow a portion of this land. From a patriotic devotion to his country, he consented on this floor, in 1816, upon the reduction of the war duties, to a gradual diminution of the burdens, and thus saved the manufacturers from annihilation. But that interest, then a mere stripling, weak, and requiring nurture, fostered by this aliment, soon increased in strength, and became potent, growing with a giant's growth, and attained a giant's might, and was inclined tyrannously to use it as a giant. He at once resigned his seat, gave up his dignified position, mingled in the strifes of the arena, sounded the tocsin of alarm, waked up the attention of the South, himself no less active than those whom he thus aroused, and at length advised his own State, heedless of danger, to throw herself into the breach for the protection of that sacred constitution, whose every precept he had imbibed, whose every condition he had admired. Sir, although hostile fleets floated in our waters, and armies threatened our cities, he quailed not; and at length the pleasing realization came to him and to the country, like balm to the wounded feelings, and by a generous compromise on all parts, the people of the South were freed from onerous taxation, and the North yet left to enjoy the fruits of her industry, and to progress in her glorious advancement in all that is virtuous in industry and elevated in sentiment.

But he limited not his scope to our domestic horizon. He looked abroad at our relations with the nations. He saw our increase of strength. He measured our resources, and was willing at once to settle all our difficulties with foreign powers on a permanent basis. With Britain we had causes of contention, of deep and long standing. He resolved, if the powers of his intellect could avail aught before he departed hence, that these questions should be settled for a nation's honor and a nation's safety. He faltered not: I know (for I was present) that when the Ashburton treaty was about to be made—when there were apprehensions in the cabinet that it would not be sanctioned by the Senate—a member of that cabinet called to consult Mr. CALHOUN, and to ask if he would give to it his generous support. The reply at that moment of Mr. CALHOUN was eminently satisfactory, and its annunciation to the cabinet gave assurance to the distinguished Secretary of State, who so eminently had conducted this important negotiation. He at once considered the work as finished; for it is the union of action in the intellectual, as in the physical world, that moves the spheres into harmony.

When that treaty was before the Senate, it was considered in secret session; and I never shall forget, that sitting upon yonder side of the House, the colleague of Mr. CALHOUN—who at that time was not on social terms with him—my friend, the honorable Mr. Preston, whose heart throbbed with an enthusiastic love of all that is elevated, left his seat in the Senate, and came to my seat in the House, saying, I must give vent to my feelings; Mr. CALHOUN has made a speech which has settled the question of the north-eastern boundary. All his friends—nay, all the Senators—have collected around to congratulate him, and I have come out to express my emotions, and declare that he has covered himself with a mantle of glory.

Sir, after a while he retired from Congress; but the unfortunate accident on board the Princeton, which deprived Virginia of two of her most gifted sons, members of the cabinet, immediately suggested the recall of Mr. Calhoun from his retirement in private life, and the shades of his own domicil, to aid the country in a great exigency. His nomination, as Secretary of State, was sent to the Senate, and, without reference to a committee, was unanimously confirmed. Sir, when he arrived here, he perceived that the southern country was in imminent peril, and that the arts and intrigues of Great Britain were about to wrest from us that imperial territory which is now the State of Texas. By his wisdom, and the exercise of his great administrative talents, the intrigues of Great Britain were defeated, and that portion of the sunny South was soon annexed to this Republic.

With the commencement of Mr. Polk's administration, he retired once more from public life, but he retired voluntarily. Mr. Buchanan (for I might as well relate the fact) called upon me, took me to the embrasure of one of those windows, and said: "I am to be Secretary of State; the President appreciates the high talents of Mr. Calhoun, and considers the country now encircled by danger upon the Oregon question. Go to Mr. Calhoun, and tender to him the mission to the Court of St. James—special or general, as he may determine—with a transfer of the Oregon question entirely to his charge."

Never can I forget how the muscles of his face became tense, how his great eye rolled, as he received the terms of the proposal. "No, sir—no, (he replied.) If the embassies of all Europe were clustered into one, I would not take it at this time; my country is in danger; here ought to be the negotiation, and here will I stand." Sir, he retired to his farm; but the President, in his inaugural, had indicated so strongly his assertion of the entirety of the Oregon treaty—and inspirited the people of the West almost to madness, and in like manner had dispirited the merchants of the East, and of the North and South, that a presentiment of great dangers stole over the hearts of the people, and a war seemed inevitable with the greatest naval power of the earth. Impelled by their apprehensions, the merchants sent a message to Mr. Calhoun, and begged him again to return to the councils of the nation. His predecessor generously resigned. He came, and when he came, though late, he beheld dismay on the countenances of all. There was a triumphant majority, in both parts of this Capitol, of the Democratic party, who, with a few exceptions, were for carrying out the measures of Mr. Polk. The Whigs, finding that they were too few to stem the current, refused to breast themselves to the shock. But when Mr. Calhoun announced on the floor of the Senate, the day after his arrival, his firm determination to resist and save from the madness of the hour, this great country, they immediately rallied, and soon his friends in this House, and in the Senate, gathered around him, and the country was safe. Reason triumphed, and the Republic was relieved of the calamities of war. This was the last great work he ever consummated.

But he saw other evils; he beheld this Republic about to lose its poise from a derangement of its weights and levers; he was anxious to adjust the balance, and to restore the equilibrium; he exercised his mind for that purpose; he loved this Union, for I have often heard him breathe of that love; he loved the equality of the States, because he knew that upon that equality rested the stability of the Government; he admired that compact—the constitution of our fathers—and esteemed it as a great covenant between sovereign States, which, if properly observed, would make us the chosen people of the world.

At length the acting of the spirit chafed the frail tenement of mortality, and to the eye of his friends, the tide of life began to ebb; but, sir, with an undying confidence in his powers; with a consciousness of the dangers which encircled his physical nature, but without regard to his own sufferings in the solitude of disease, unable even to hold a pen, he dictated his last great speech. That speech has gone forth to the world, and the judgment of that world will now impartially be stamped upon it.

Sir, when his health began gradually to recover, his spirit impelled him, against the advice of his friends, into the Senate chamber; and there, with a manliness of purpose, with a decision of tone, with a clearness of argument, with a rapidity of thought, he met and overthrew his antagonists one by one, as they came up to the attack. But weakened by the strife, although he retired victorious, and encircled with a laurel wreath, he fell exhausted by his own efforts, and soon expired on the plains. And now where is he? Dead! dead! sir; lost to his country and his friends.

"For him no more the blazing hearth shall burn"—

nor wife nor children more shall he behold, nor sacred home. But he shall shortly rest amid his own native hills, with no dirge but the rude music of the winds, and after a while, no tears to moisten his grave but the dews of heaven.

Though dead he still liveth; he liveth in the hearts of his friends, in the memory of his services, in the respect of the States, in the affections—the devoted affections of that household he cherished. He will live in the tomes of Time, as they shall unfold their pages, rich with virtues, to the eyes of the yet unborn. He lives, and will continue to live, for countless ages, in the advance of that science to which, by his intellect, he so much contributed, in the disenthralment of man from the restrictions of Government, in the freedom of intercourse of nations, and kindreds, and tongues, which makes our common mother earth throw from her lap her bounteous plenty unto all her children. And it may be, that with the example set to other nations, there shall arise a union of thought and sentiment, and that the strong ties of interest, and the silken cords of love, may unite the hearts of all, until, from the continents and the isles of the sea, there will come up the congratulation of voices, that shall mingle with the choral song of the angelic host—"Peace on earth; good will to all mankind."

I move, sir, the adoption of the following resolutions:

Resolved, That this House has heard, with deep sensibility, the announcement of the death of the Hon. JOHN C. CALHOUN, a Senator in Congress from the State of South Carolina.

Resolved, That as a testimony of respect for the memory of the deceased, the members and officers of this House will wear the usual badge of mourning for thirty days.

Resolved, That the proceedings of this House, in relation to the death of the Hon. JOHN C. CALHOUN, be communicated to the family of the deceased by the Clerk.

Resolved, That this House will attend the funeral of the deceased in a body, and as a further mark of respect for his memory, that it do now adjourn.

Mr. WINTHROP rose to second the resolution offered by Mr. HOLMES, and proceeded as follows: I am not unaware, Mr. Speaker, that the voice of New England has already been heard, to-day, in its most authentic and most impressive tones, in the other wing of this Capitol. But it has been suggested to me, and the suggestion has met with the promptest assent from my own heart, that here, also, that voice should not be altogether mute on this occasion.

The distinguished person, whose death has been announced to us in the resolutions of the Senate, belonged not, indeed, to us. It is not ours to pronounce his eulogy. It is not ours, certainly, to appropriate his fame. But it is ours, to bear witness to his character, to do justice to his virtues, to unite in paying honor to his memory, and to offer our heartfelt sympathies—as I now do—to those who have been called to sustain so great a bereavement.

We have been told, sir, by more than one adventurous navigator, that it was worth all the privations and perils of a protracted voyage beyond the line, to obtain even a passing view of *the Southern Cross*—that great constellation of the southern hemisphere. We can imagine, then, what would be the emotions of those who have always enjoyed the light of that magnificent luminary, and who have taken their daily and their nightly direction from its refulgent rays, if it were suddenly blotted out from the sky.

Such, sir, and so deep, I can conceive to be the emotions at this hour, of not a few of the honored friends and associates whom I see around me.

Indeed, no one who has been ever so distant an observer of the course of public affairs for a quarter of a century past, can fail to realize that a star of the first magnitude has been struck from our political firmament. Let us hope, sir, that it has only been transferred to a higher and purer sphere, where it may shine on with undimmed brilliancy forever!

Mr. Speaker, it is for others to enter into the details of Mr. CALHOUN's life and services. It is for others to illustrate and to vindicate his peculiar opinions and principles. It is for me to speak of him only as he was known to the country at large, and to all, without distinction of party, who have represented the country, of late years, in either branch of the National Councils.

And speaking of him thus, sir, I cannot hesitate to say, that, among what may be called the second generation of American statesmen since the adoption of the Federal Constitution, there has been no man of a more marked character, of more pronounced qualities, or of a wider and more deserved distinction.

The mere length and variety of his public services, in almost every branch of the National Government, running through a continuous period of almost forty years—as a member of this House, as Secretary of War, as Vice President of the United States, as Secretary of State, and as Senator from his own adored and adoring South Carolina—would alone have secured him a conspicuous and permanent place upon our public records.

But he has left better titles to remembrance than any which mere office can bestow.

There was an unsullied purity in his private life; there was an inflexible integrity in his public conduct; there was an indescribable fascination in his familiar conversation; there was a condensed energy in his formal discourse; there was a quickness of perception, a vigor of deduction, a directness and a devotedness of purpose, in all that he said, or wrote, or did; there was a Roman dignity in his whole senatorial deportment; which, together, made up a character which cannot fail to be contemplated and admired to the latest posterity.

I have said, sir, that New England can appropriate no part of his fame. But we may be permitted to remember, that it was in our schools of learning and of law that he was trained up for the great contests which awaited him in the forum or the Senate chamber. Nor can we forget how long and how intimately he was associated in the Executive or deliberative branches of the Government, with more than one of our own most cherished statesmen.

The loss of such a man, sir, creates a sensible gap in the public councils. To the State which he represented, and the section of the country with which he was so peculiarly identified, no stranger tongue may venture to attempt words of adequate consolation. But let us hope that the event may not be without a wholesome and healing influence upon the troubles of the times. Let us heed the voice, which comes to us all, both as individuals and as public officers, in so solemn and signal a providence of God. Let us remember that, whatever happens to the Republic, *we* must die! Let us reflect how vain are the personal strifes and partisan contests in which we daily engage, in view of the great account which we may so soon be called on to render! As Cicero exclaimed, in considering the death of Crassus: "*O fallacem hominum spem, fragilemque fortunam, et inanes nostras contentiones!*"

Finally, sir, let us find fresh bonds of brotherhood and of union in the cherished memories of those who have gone before us; and let us resolve that, so far as in us lies, the day shall never come, when New England men may not speak of the great names of the South, whether among the dead or among the living, as of Americans and fellow-countrymen!

Mr. Venable rose and said,

Mr. Speaker: In responding to the announcement just made by the gentleman from South Carolina, (Mr. Holmes,) I perform a sad and melancholy office. Did I consult my feelings alone, I would be silent. In the other end of this building, we have just heard the touching eloquence of two venerable and distinguished Senators, his contemporaries and compatriots. Their names belong to their country as well as his; and I thought, while each was speaking, of the valiant warrior, clothed in armor, who, when passing the grave of one with whom he had broken lances and crossed weapons, dropped a tear upon his dust, and gave testimony to his skill, his valor, and his honor. He whose spirit has fled, needs no effort of mine to place his name on the bright page of history, nor would any eulogy which I might pronounce, swell the vast tide of praises which will flow perennially from a nation's gratitude. The great American statesman, who has fallen by the stroke of death, has left the impress of his mind upon the generations among whom he lived—has given to posterity the mines of his recorded thoughts, to reward their labor with intellectual wealth—has left an example of purity and patriotism on which the wearied eye may rest,

> "And gaze upon the great,
> Where neither guilty glory glows,
> Nor despicable state."

For more than forty years, his name is conspicuous in our history. Born at the close of the revolutionary war, he was in full maturity to guide the councils of his country in our second contest with England. Never unmindful of her claims upon him, he has devoted a long life to her service, and has closed it, like a gallant warrior, with his armor buckled on him. "Death made no conquest of this conqueror; for now he lives in fame, though not in life." The only fame, sir, which he ever coveted—an impulse to great and honorable deeds—a fame which none can despise, who have not renounced the virtues which deserve it. It is at least some relief to our hearts, now heaving with sighs at this dispensation of Heaven, that he now belongs to bright—to enduring history; for his was one of "the few immortal names that were not born to die." Of his early history, the gentleman who preceded me has spoken; of his illustrious life, I need not speak; it is known to millions now living, and will be familiar to the world in after times.

But, sir, I propose to say something of him in his last days. Early in the winter of 1848–9, his failing health gave uneasiness to his friends. A severe attack of bronchitis, complicated with an affection of the heart, disqualified him for the performance of his senatorial duties with the punctuality which always distinguished him. It was then that I became intimately acquainted with his mind, and above all, with his heart. Watching by his bedside, and during his recovery, I ceased to be astonished at the power which his master mind and elevated moral feelings had always exerted upon those who were included within the circle of his social intercourse. It was a tribute paid spontaneously to wisdom, genius, truth. Patriotism, honesty of purpose, and purity of motive, rendered active by the energies of such an intellect as hardly ever falls to any man, gathered around him sincere admirers and devoted friends. That many have failed to appreciate the value of the great truths which he uttered, or to listen to the warnings which he gave, is nothing new in the history of great minds. Bacon wrote for posterity, and men of profound sagacity always think in advance of their generation. His body was sinking under the invasion of disease before I formed his acquaintance, and he was passing from among us before I was honored with his friendship. I witnessed with astonishment the influence of his mighty mind over his weak physical structure. Like a powerful steam-engine on a frail bark, every revolution of the wheel tried its capacity for endurance to the utmost. But yet his mind moved on, and as if insensible of the decay of bodily strength, put forth without stint his unequalled powers of thought and analysis, until nature well-nigh sunk under the imposition. His intellect preserved its vigor, while his body was sinking to decay. The menstruum retained all its powers of solution, while the frail crucible which contained it was crumbling to atoms. During his late illness, which, with a short intermission, has continued since the commencement of this session of Congress, there was no abatement of his intellectual labors. They were directed as well to the momentous questions now agitating the public mind, as to the completion of a work which embodies his thoughts on the subject of government in general, and our own constitution in particular—thus distinguishing his last days by the greatest effort of his mind, and bequeathing it as his richest legacy to posterity.

Cheerful in a sick chamber, none of the gloom which usually attends the progress of disease annoyed him; severe in ascertaining the truth of conclusions, because unwilling to be deceived himself, he scorned to deceive others; skilful in appreciating the past, and impartial in his judgment of the present, he looked to the future as dependent on existing causes, and fearlessly gave utterance to his opinions of its nature and character; the philosopher and the statesman, he discarded expedients by which men "construe the times to their necessities." He loved the truth, for the truth's sake, and believed that to temporize, is but to increase the evil which we seek to remove. The approach of death brought no indications of impatience—no cloud upon his intellect. To a friend, who spoke of the time and manner in which it was best to meet death, he remarked, "*I have but little concern about either; I desire to die in the discharge of my duty; I have an unshaken reliance upon the providence of God.*"

I saw him for days after his last appearance in the Senate chamber, gradually sinking under the power of his malady, without one murmur at his affliction; always anxious for the interest of his country, deeply absorbed in the great question which agitates the public mind, and earnestly desiring its honorable adjustment; unchanged in the opinions, which he had held and uttered for many years, the ardent friend of the Union and the constitution, and seeking the perpetuity of our institutions, by inculcating the practice of justice, and the duties of patriotism.

Aggravated symptoms, on the day before his death, gave notice of his approaching end. I left him late at night, with but faint hopes of amendment; and on being summoned early the next morning, I found him sinking in the cold embrace of death. Calm, collected, and conscious of his situation, but without any symptom of alarm—his face beaming with intelligence, without one indication of suffering or of pain. I watched his countenance, and the lustre of that bright eye remained unchanged, until the silver cord was broken, and then it went out in instantaneous eclipse. When I removed my hand from closing his eyes, he seemed as one who had fallen into a sweet and refreshing slumber. Thus, sir, closed the days of JOHN CALDWELL CALHOUN, the illustrious American statesman. His life and services shall speak of the greatness of by-gone days with undying testimony. Another jewel has fallen from our crown; an inscrutable Providence has removed from among us one of the great lights of the age; but it is not extinguished. From a height, to which the shafts of malice or the darts of detraction never reach, to which envy cannot crawl, or jealousy approach, it will shine brighter and more gloriously, sending its rays over a more extended horizon, and blessing mankind by its illumination. The friend of constitutional liberty will go to his writings for truth, and to his life for a model. We, too, should be instructed by his experience, while his presages for the future should infuse caution into our counsels, and prudence into our actions. His voice, now no more heard in the Senate, will speak most potentially from the grave. Personal opposition has died with his death. The aspiring cannot fear him, nor the ambitious dread his elevation. His life has become history, and his thoughts the property of his countrymen.

Sir, while we weep over his grave, let us be consoled by the assurance that "honor decks the turf that wraps his clay." He was our own, and his fame is also ours. Let us imitate his great example, in preferring truth and duty to the approbation of men, or the triumphs of party. Be willing to stand alone for the right, nor surrender independence for any inducement. He was brought up in the society of the men of the Revolution, saw the work of our constitution since its formation, was profoundly skilled in construing its meaning, and sought by his wisdom and integrity to give permanency to the Government which it created. If such high purposes be ours, then our sun, like his, will go down serenely, and we shall have secured "a peace above all other dignities—a calm of quiet conscience."

The question was then taken upon the adoption of the resolutions;

Which were unanimously agreed to,

And the House adjourned.

IN SENATE.

MONDAY, April 1.

Death of Mr. Calhoun.

Mr. BUTLER rose and said:

Mr. PRESIDENT: I rise to discharge a mournful duty, and one which involves in it considerations well calculated to arrest the attention of this body. It is, to announce the death of my late colleague, the Hon. JOHN CALDWELL CALHOUN. He died at his lodgings in this city, on yesterday morning, at half-past seven o'clock. He was conscious of his approaching end, and met death with fortitude, and uncommon serenity. He had many admonitions of its approach, and without doubt he had not been indifferent to them. With his usual aversion to profession, he said little for effect on the world, and his last hours were an exemplification of his life and character, truth and simplicity.

Mr. CALHOUN, for some years past, had been suffering under a pulmonary complaint, and under its effects could not have reckoned on a long existence. Such was his own conviction. The immediate cause of his death was an affection of the heart. I few hours before he expired, he became sensible of his situation; and when he was unable to speak, his eye and look evinced recognition and intelligence of what was passing. One of the last directions he gave was to a dutiful son, who had been attending him, to put away some manuscripts which had been written a short time before, under his dictation.

Mr. CALHOUN was the least despondent man I ever knew; and he had, in an eminent degree, the self-sustaining power of intellect. His last days, and his last remarks, are exemplifications of what I have just said. Mental determination sustained him, when all others were in despair. We saw him, a few days ago, in the seat near me, which he so long occupied; we saw the struggle of a great mind exerting itself to sustain and overcome the weakness and infirmities of a sinking body. It was the exhibition of a wounded eagle, with his eyes turned to the heavens in which he had soared, but into which his wings could never carry him again.

Mr. President, Mr. Calhoun has lived in an eventful period of our Republic, and has acted a distinguished part. I surely do not venture too much when I say that his reputation forms a striking part of a glorious history. Since 1811, until this time, he has been responsibly connected with the Federal Government. As Representative, Senator, Cabinet Minister, and Vice President, he has been identified with the greatest events in the political history of our country. And I hope I may be permitted to say, that he has been equal to all the duties which were devolved upon him in the many critical junctures in which he was placed. Having to act a responsible part, he always acted a decided part. It would not become me to venture upon the judgment which awaits his memory. That will be formed by posterity before the impartial tribunal of history. It may be that he will have had the fate, and will have given to him the judgment, that have been awarded to Chatham.

I should do the memory of my friend injustice were I to speak of his life in the spirit of history. The dignity of his whole character would rebuke any tone of remark which truth and judgment would not sanction.

Mr. Calhoun was a native of South Carolina, and was born in Abbeville district, on the 18th March, 1782. He was of an Irish family. His father, Patrick Calhoun, was born in Ireland, and at an early age came to Pennsylvania, thence moved to the western part of Virginia, and after Braddock's defeat moved to South Carolina, in 1756. He and his family gave a name to what is known as the Calhoun settlement in Abbeville district. The mother of my colleague was a Miss Caldwell, born in Charlotte county, Virginia. The character of his parents had no doubt a sensible influence on the destiny of their distinguished son. His father had energy and enterprise, combined with perseverance and great mental determination. His mother belonged to a family of revolutionary heroes. Two of her brothers were distinguished in the Revolution. Their names and achievements are not left to tradition, but constitute a part of the history of the times.

Mr. Calhoun was born in the Revolution, and in his childhood felt the influence of its exciting traditions. He derived from the paternal stock, intellect and self-reliance, and from the Caldwells enthusiasm and impulse. The traditions of the Revolution had a sensible influence on his temper and character.

Mr. Calhoun in his childhood had but limited advantages of what is termed a literary tuition. His parents lived in a newly-settled country, and among a sparse population. This population had but a slight connection with the lower country of South Carolina, and were sustained by emigrants from Virginia and Pennsylvania. There was of course but limited means of instruction to children. They imbibed most of their lessons from the conversation of their parents. Mr. Calhoun has always expressed himself deeply sensible of that influence. At the age of thirteen he was put under the charge of his brother-in-law, Dr. Waddel, in Columbia county, Georgia. Scarcely had he commenced his literary course before his father and sister died. His brother-in-law, Dr. Waddel, devoted himself about this time to his clerical duties, and was a great deal absent from home.

On his second marriage he resumed the duties of his academy; and in his nineteenth year Mr. Calhoun put himself under the charge of this distinguished teacher. It must not be supposed that his mind before this had been unemployed. He had availed himself of the advantages of a small library, and had been deeply inspired by his reading of history. It was under such influences that he entered the academy of his preceptor. His progress was rapid. He looked forward to a higher arena with eagerness and purpose.

He became a student in Yale College in 1802, and graduated two years afterwards with distinction—as a young man of great ability, and with the respect and confidence of his preceptors and fellows. What they have said and thought of him would have given any man a high reputation. It is the pure fountain of a clear reputation. If the stream has met with obstructions, they were such as have only shown its beauty and majesty.

After he had graduated, Mr. Calhoun studied law, and for a few years practised in the courts of South Carolina, with a reputation that has descended to the profession. He was then remarked for some traits that have since characterized him. He was clear in his propositions, and candid in his intercourse with his brethren. The truth and justice of the law inculcated themselves on his mind, and when armed with these, he was a great advocate.

His forensic career was, however, too limited to make a prominent part in the history of his life. He served for some years in the Legislature of his native State; and his great mind made an impression on her statutes, some of which have had a great practical operation on the concerns of society. From the Legislature of his own State he was transferred to Congress; and from this time his career has been a part of the history of the Federal Government.

Mr. Calhoun came into Congress at a time of deep and exciting interest—at a crisis of great magnitude. It was a crisis of peril to those who had to act in it, but of subsequent glory to the actors and the common history of the country. The invincibility of Great Britain had become a proverbial expression, and a war with her was full of terrific issues. Mr. Cal-

HOUN found himself at once in a situation of high responsibility—one that required more than speaking qualities and eloquence to fulfil it. The spirit of the people required direction; the energy and ardor of youth were to be employed in affairs requiring the maturer qualities of a statesman. The part which Mr. CALHOUN acted at this time has been approved and applauded by contemporaries, and now forms a part of the glorious history of those times.

The names of CLAY, CALHOUN, CHEVES, and LOWNDES, GRUNDY, PORTER, and others, carried associations with them that reached the *heart of the nation.* Their clarion notes penetrated the army; they animated the people, and sustained the administration of the Government. With such actors, and in such scenes—the most eventful of our history—to say that Mr. CALHOUN did not play a second part, is no common praise. In debate he was equal with Randolph, and in council he commanded the respect and confidence of Madison. At this period of his life he had the quality of Themistocles—*to inspire confidence*—which, after all, is the highest of earthly qualities: it is a mystical something which is felt, but cannot be described. The events of the war were brilliant and honorable to both statesmen and soldiers, and their history may be read with enthusiasm and delight. The war terminated with honor; but the measures which had to be taken, in a transition to a peace establishment, were full of difficulty and embarrassment. Mr. CALHOUN, with his usual intrepidity, did not hesitate to take a responsible part. Under the influence of a broad patriotism, he acted with an uncalculating liberality to all the interests that were involved, and which were brought under review of Congress. His personal adversary at this time, in his admiration for his genius, paid Mr. CALHOUN a beautiful compliment for his noble and national sentiments.

At the termination of Mr. Madison's administration, Mr. CALHOUN had acquired a commanding reputation; he was regarded as one of the sages of the Republic. In 1817 Mr. Monroe invited him to a place in his Cabinet; Mr. CALHOUN's friends doubted the propriety of his accepting it, and some of them thought he would put a high reputation at hazard in this new sphere of action. Perhaps these suggestions fired his high and gifted intellect; he accepted the place, and went into the War Department, under circumstances that might have appalled other men. His success has been acknowledged; what was complex and confused, he reduced to simplicity and order. His organization of the War Department, and his administration of its undefined duties, have made the impression of an *author*, having the interest of originality and the sanction of trial.

To applicants for office Mr. CALHOUN made few promises, and hence he was not accused of delusion and deception. When a public trust was involved, he would not compromise with duplicity or temporary expediency.

At the expiration of Mr. Monroe's administration, Mr. CALHOUN's name became connected with the Presidency; and from that time to his death he had to share the fate of all others who occupy prominent situations.

The remarkable canvass for the President to succeed Mr. Monroe, terminated in returning three distinguished men to the House of Representatives, from whom one was to be elected. Mr. CALHOUN was elected Vice President by a large majority. He took his seat in the Senate, as Vice President, on the 4th of March, 1825, having remained in the War Department over seven years.

While he was Vice President he was placed in some of the most trying scenes of any man's life. I do not now choose to refer to any thing that can have the elements of controversy; but I hope I may be permitted to speak of my friend and colleague in a character in which all will join in paying him sincere respect. As a presiding officer of this body he had the undivided respect of its members. He was punctual, methodical, and accurate, and had a high regard for the dignity of the Senate, which, as a presiding officer, he endeavored to preserve and maintain. He looked upon debate as an honorable contest of intellect for truth. Such a strife has its incidents and its trials; but Mr. CALHOUN had, in an eminent degree, a regard for parliamentary dignity and propriety.

Upon General Hayne's leaving the Senate to become Governor of South Carolina, Mr. CALHOUN resigned the Vice Presidency, and was elected in his place. All will now agree that such a position was environed with difficulties and dangers. His own State was under the ban, and he was in the national Senate to do her justice under his constitutional obligations. That part of his life posterity will review, and will do justice to it.

After his senatorial term had expired, he went into retirement by his own consent. The death of Mr. Upsher—so full of melancholy association—made a vacancy in the State Department; and it was by the common consent of all parties that Mr. CALHOUN was called to fill it. This was a tribute of which any public man might well be proud. It was a tribute to truth, ability, and experience. Under Mr. CALHOUN's counsels, Texas was brought into the Union. His name is associated with one of the most remarkable events of history—that of one Republic being annexed to another by the voluntary consent of both. Mr. CALHOUN was but the agent to bring about this fraternal association. It is a conjunction under the sanction of his name, and by an influence exerted through his great and intrepid mind. Mr. CALHOUN's connection with the Executive department of the Government terminated with Mr. Tyler's administration. As a Secretary of State, he won the confidence and respect of foreign ambassadors, and his despatches were characterized by clearness, sagacity, and boldness.

He was not allowed to remain in retirement

long. For the last five years he has been a member of this body, and has been engaged in discussions that have deeply excited and agitated the country. He has died amidst them. I had never had any particular association with Mr. Calhoun until I became his colleague in this body. I had looked on his fame as others had done, and had admired his character. There are those here who know more of him than I do. I shall not pronounce any such judgment as may be subject to a controversial criticism. But I will say, as a matter of justice, from my own personal knowledge, that I never knew a fairer man in argument, or a juster man in purpose. His intensity allowed of little compromise. While he did not qualify his own positions to suit the temper of the times, he appreciated the unmasked propositions of others. As a Senator, he commanded the respect of the ablest men of the body of which he was a member; and I believe I may say, that where there was no political bias to influence the judgment, he had the confidence of his brethren. As a statesman, Mr. Calhoun's reputation belongs to the history of the country, and I commit it to his countrymen and posterity.

In my opinion, Mr. Calhoun deserves to occupy the first rank as a parliamentary speaker. He had always before him the dignity of purpose, and he spoke to an end. From a full mind he expressed his ideas with clearness, simplicity, and force, and in language that seemed to be the vehicle of his thoughts and emotions. His thoughts leaped from his mind, like arrows from a well-drawn bow. They had both the aim and force of a skilful archer. He seemed to have had little regard for ornament; and when he used figures of speech, they were only for illustration. His manner and countenance were his best language; and in these there was an exemplification of what is meant by action in that term of the great Athenian orator and statesman. They served to exhibit the moral elevation of the man.

In speaking of Mr. Calhoun as a man and a neighbor, I hope I may speak of him in a sphere in which all will like to contemplate him. Whilst he was a gentleman of striking deportment, he was a man of primitive tastes and simple manners. He had the hardy virtues and simple tastes of a republican citizen. No one disliked ostentation and exhibition more than he did. When I say he was a *good neighbor*, I imply more than I have expressed. It is summed up under the word *justice.* I will venture to say, that no one in his private relations could ever say that Mr. Calhoun treated him with injustice, or that he deceived him by professions. His private character was characterized by a beautiful propriety, and was the exemplification of truth, justice, temperance, and fidelity to his engagements.

I will venture another remark; Mr. Calhoun was fierce in his contests with political adversaries. He did not stop in the fight to count losses or bestow favors. But he forgot resentments, and forgave injuries inflicted by rivals with signal magnanimity. Whilst he spoke freely of their faults, he could with justice appreciate the merits of all the public men of whom I have heard him speak. He was sincerely attached to the institutions of this country, and desired to preserve them pure, and make them perpetual.

In the death of Mr. Calhoun, one of the brightest luminaries has been extinguished from the political firmament. It is an event which will produce a deep sensation throughout this broad land.

I have forborne to speak of his domestic relations. They make a sacred circle, and I will not invade it.

Mr. Butler then offered the following resolutions:

Resolved unanimously, That a committee be appointed by the Vice President, to take order for superintending the funeral of the Hon. John Caldwell Calhoun, which will take place to-morrow, at 12 o'clock meridian, and that the Senate will attend the same.

Resolved unanimously, That the members of the Senate, from a sincere desire of showing every mark of respect due to the memory of the Hon. John Caldwell Calhoun, deceased, late a member, thereof, will go into mourning for him for one month, by the usual mode of wearing crape on the left arm.

Resolved unanimously, That, as an additional mark of respect to the memory of the deceased, the Senate do now adjourn.

Mr. Clay. Mr. President, prompted by my own feelings of profound regret, and requested at the same time by some highly esteemed friends, I wish, in rising to second the resolutions which have been offered, and which have just been read, to add a few words to what has been so well and so justly said by the surviving colleague of the illustrious deceased.

My personal acquaintance with him, Mr. President, commenced upwards of thirty-eight years ago. We entered at the same time, together, the House of Representatives at the other end of this building. The Congress of which we thus became members, was that amongst whose deliberations and acts was the declaration of war against the most powerful nation, as it respects us, in the world. During the preliminary discussions which arose in the preparation for that great event, as well as during those which took place when the resolution was finally adopted, no member displayed a more lively and patriotic sensibility to the wrongs which led to that momentous event, than the deceased, whose death we all now so much deplore. Ever active, ardent, able, no one was in advance of him in advocating the cause of his country, and denouncing the foreign injustice which compelled us to appeal to arms. Of all Congresses with which I have had any acquaintance since my entry into the service of the Federal Government, in none, in my humble opinion, has been assembled such a galaxy of eminent and able men, as were in the House of Representatives of that Congress which declared the war, and in that immediately following the peace; and amongst that splendid assemblage, none shone more bright and brilliant than the star which is now set.

It was my happiness, sir, during a large part of the life of the departed, to concur with him on all great questions of national policy. And, at a later period, when it was my fortune to differ from him as to measures of domestic policy, I had the happiness to agree with him generally as to those which concerned our foreign relations, and especially as to the preservation of the peace of the country. During the long session at which the war was declared, we were messmates, as were other distinguished members of Congress from his own patriotic State. I was afforded, by the intercourse which resulted from that fact, as well as the subsequent intimacy and intercourse which arose between us, an opportunity to form an estimate, not merely of his public, but of his private life; and no man with whom I have ever been acquainted, exceeded him in habits of temperance and regularity, and in all the freedom, frankness, and affability of social intercourse, and in all the tenderness and respect and affection which he manifested towards that lady who now mourns more than any other the sad event which has just occurred. Such, Mr. President, was the high estimate I formed of his transcendent talents, that, if at the end of his service in the executive department under Mr. Monroe's administration, he had been called to the highest office in the Government, I should have felt perfectly assured that under his auspices, the honor, the prosperity, and the glory of our country would have been safely placed.

Sir, he is gone! No more shall we witness from yonder seat the flashes of that keen and penetrating eye of his, darting through this chamber. No more shall we behold that torrent of clear, concise, compact logic, poured out from his lips, which, if it did not always carry conviction to our judgment, commanded our great admiration. Those eyes and those lips are closed forever!

And when, Mr. President, will that great vacancy which has been created by the event to which we are now alluding, when will it be filled by an equal amount of ability, patriotism, and devotion, to what he conceived to be the best interests of his country?

Sir, this is not the appropriate occasion, nor would I be the appropriate person to attempt a delineation of his character, or the powers of his enlightened mind. I will only say, in a few words, that he possessed an elevated genius of the highest order; that in felicity of generalization of the subjects of which his mind treated, I have seen him surpassed by no one; and the charm and captivating influence of his colloquial powers have been felt by all who have conversed with him. I was his senior, Mr. President, in years—in nothing else. According to the course of nature, I ought to have preceded him. It has been decreed otherwise; but I know that I shall linger here only a short time, and shall soon follow him.

And how brief, how short is the period of human existence allotted even to the youngest amongst us! Sir, ought we not to profit by the contemplation of this melancholy occasion? Ought we not to draw from it the conclusion how unwise it is to indulge in the acerbity of unbridled debate? how unwise to yield ourselves to the sway of the animosities of party feeling? how wrong it is to indulge in those unhappy and hot strifes, which too often exasperate our feelings and mislead our judgments in the discharge of the high and responsible duties which we are called to perform? How unbecoming, if not presumptuous, it is in us, who are the tenants of an hour in this earthly abode, to wrestle and struggle together, with a violence which would not be justifiable if it were our perpetual home!

In conclusion, sir, while I beg leave to express my cordial sympathies and sentiments of the deepest condolence toward all who stand in near relation to him, I trust we shall all be instructed by the eminent virtues and merits of his exalted character, and be taught, by his bright example, to fulfil our great public duties by the lights of our own judgment and the dictates of our own consciences, as he did, according to his honest and best conceptions of those duties, faithfully, and to the last.

Mr. WEBSTER. I hope the Senate will indulge me in adding a very few words to what has been said. My apology for this presumption is the very long acquaintance which has subsisted between Mr. CALHOUN and myself. We are of the same age. I made my first entrance into the House of Representatives in May, 1813. I there found Mr. CALHOUN. He had already been a member of that body for two or three years. I found him then an active and efficient member of the assembly to which he belonged, taking a decided part, and exercising a decided influence, in all its deliberations.

From that day to the day of his death, amidst all the strifes of party and politics, there has subsisted between us, always, and without interruption, a great degree of personal kindness.

Differing widely on many great questions respecting our institutions and government of the country, those differences never interrupted our personal and social intercourse. I have been present at most of the distinguished instances of the exhibition of his talents in debate. I have always heard him with pleasure, often with much instruction, not unfrequently with the highest degree of admiration.

Mr. CALHOUN was calculated to be a leader in whatsoever association of political friends he was thrown. He was a man of undoubted genius and of commanding talent. All the country and all the world admit that. His mind was both perceptive and vigorous. It was clear, quick, and strong.

Sir, the eloquence of Mr. Calhoun, or the manner of his exhibition of his sentiments in public bodies, was part of this intellectual character. It grew out of the qualities of his mind. It was plain, strong, terse, condensed, concise; sometimes impassioned—still always severe. Rejecting ornament, not often seeking far for illustration, his power consisted in the plainness of his propositions, in the closeness of his logic, and in the earnestness and energy of his manner. These are the qualities, as I think, which have enabled him through such a long course of years to speak often, and yet always command attention. His demeanor as a Senator is known to us all—is appreciated, venerated by us all. No man was more respectful to others; no man carried himself with greater decorum, no man with superior dignity. I think there is not one of us but felt, when he last addressed us from his seat in the Senate—his form still erect, with a voice by no means indicating such a degree of physical weakness as did in fact possess him, with clear tones, and an impressive, and I may say, an imposing manner—who did not feel that he might imagine that we saw before us a Senator of Rome, when Rome survived.

Sir, I have not, in public nor in private life, known a more assiduous person in the discharge of his appropriate duties. I have known no man who wasted less of life in what is called recreation, nor employed less of it in any pursuits not connected with the immediate discharge of his duty. He seemed to have no recreation but the pleasure of conversation with his friends. Out of the chambers of Congress, he was either devoting himself to the acquisition of knowledge pertaining to the immediate subject of the duty before him, or else he was indulging in those social interviews in which he much delighted.

My honorable friend from Kentucky has spoken in just terms of his colloquial talents. They certainly were singular and eminent. There was a charm in his conversation not often found. He delighted, especially, in conversation and intercourse with young men. I suppose that there has been no man among us who had more winning manners, in such an intercourse and such conversation, with men comparatively young, than Mr. Calhoun. I believe one great power of his character, in general, was his conversational talent. I believe it is that, as well as a consciousness of his high integrity, and the greatest reverence for his talents and ability, that has made him so endeared an object to the people of the State to which he belonged.

Mr. President, he had the basis, the indispensable basis, of all high character; and that was unspotted integrity, unimpeachable honor and character. If he had aspirations, they were high, and honorable, and noble. There was nothing grovelling, or low, or meanly selfish, that came near the head or the heart of Mr. Calhoun. Firm in his purpose, perfectly patriotic and honest, as I am sure he was, in the principles that he espoused, and in the measures that he defended, aside from that large regard for that species of distinction that conducted him to eminent stations for the benefit of the Republic, I do not believe he had a selfish motive or selfish feeling. However, sir, he may have differed from others of us in his political opinions or his political principles, those principles and those opinions will now descend to posterity, under the sanction of a great name. He has lived long enough, he has done enough, and he has done it so well, so successfully, so honorably, as to connect himself for all time with the records of his country. He is now a historical character. Those of us who have known him here, will find that he has left upon our minds and our hearts a strong and lasting impression of his person, his character, and his public performances, which, while we live, will never be obliterated. We shall hereafter, I am sure, indulge in it as a grateful recollection that we have lived in his age, that we have been his contemporaries, that we have seen him, and heard him, and known him. We shall delight to speak of him to those who are rising up to fill our places. And, when the time shall come that we ourselves shall go, one after another, in succession, to our graves, we shall carry with us a deep sense of his genius and character, his honor and integrity, his amiable deportment in private life, and the purity of his exalted patriotism.

Mr. Rusk. Mr. President, I hope it will not be considered inappropriate for me to say a word upon this solemn occasion. Being a native of the same State, with the distinguished Senator whose death has cast such a gloom upon this Senate and the audience here assembled, I had the good fortune, at an early period of my life, to make his acquaintance. At that time, he was just entering upon that bright career which has now terminated. I was then a boy, with prospects any thing but flattering. To him, at that period, I was indebted for words of kindness and encouragement; and often since, in the most critical positions in which I have been placed, a recurrence to those words of encouragement has inspired me with resolution to meet difficulties that beset my path. Four years ago, I had the pleasure of renewing that acquaintance, after an absence of some fifteen years; and this took place after he had taken an active part in the question of annexing Texas to the United States, adding a new sense of obligation to my feeling of gratitude.

In the stirring questions that have agitated the country, it was my misfortune sometimes to differ from him; but it is a matter of heartfelt gratification for me to know, that our personal relations remained unaltered. And, sir, it will be a source of pleasant, though sad reflection, to me, throughout life, to remember, that on the last day on which he occupied his seat in this chamber, his body, worn down by disease, but his mind as vigorous as ever, we held a somewhat extended conversation on the exciting topics of the day, in which the same kind feelings which had so strongly impressed me in my youth, were still manifested toward me by the veteran statesman. But, sir, he is gone from among us; his voice will never again be heard in this chamber; his active and vigorous mind will participate no more in our councils; his spirit has left a world of trouble, care, and anxiety, to join the spirits of those patriots and statesmen who have preceded him to a brighter and better world. If, as many believe, the spirits of the departed hover around the places they have left, I earnestly pray that his may soon be permitted to look back upon our country, which he has left in excitement, confusion, and apprehension, restored to calmness, security, and fraternal feeling, as broad as the bounds of our Union, and as fixed as the eternal principles of justice, in which our Government has its foundation.

Mr. CLEMENS. I do not expect, Mr. President, to add any thing to what has already been said of the illustrious man whose death we all so deeply deplore; but silence upon an occasion like this would by no means meet the expectations of those whose representative I am. To borrow a figure from the Senator from Kentucky, the brightest star in the brilliant galaxy of the Union has gone out, and Alabama claims a place among the chief mourners over the event. Differing often from the great Southern statesman on questions of public policy, she has as yet always accorded due homage to his genius, and still more to that blameless purity of life which entitles him to the highest and noblest epitaph which can be graven upon a mortal tomb. For more than forty years an active participant in all the fierce struggles of party, surrounded by those corrupting influences to which the politician is so often subjected, his personal character remained not only untarnished, but unsuspected. He walked through the flames, and even the hem of his garment was unscorched. It is no part of my purpose to enter into a recital of the public acts of JOHN C. CALHOUN. It has already been partly done by his colleague; but even that, in my judgment, was unnecessary. Years after the celebrated battle of Thermopylæ, a traveller, on visiting the spot, found a monument with the simple inscription, "Stranger, go tell at Lacedæmon that he died in obedience to her laws." "Why is it," he asked, "that the names of those who fell here, are not inscribed on the stone?" "Because," was the proud reply, "it is impossible that any Greek should ever forget them." Even so it is with him of whom I speak. His acts are graven on the hearts of his countrymen, and time has no power to obliterate the characters. Throughout this broad land "the meanest rill, the mightiest river, rolls mingling with his fame forever." Living, sir, in an age distinguished above all others for its intelligence, surrounded throughout his whole career by men, any one of whom would have marked an era in the world's history, and stamped the time in which he lived with immortality, Mr. CALHOUN yet won an intellectual eminence, and commanded an admiration, which was not only unsurpassed, but unequalled, in all its parts, by any of his giant compeers. That great light is now extinguished; a place in the Senate is made vacant which cannot be filled. The tidings have been borne upon the lightning's wings to the remotest corners of the Republic, and millions of freemen are now mourning with us, over all that is left of one who was scarcely "lower than the angels."

I may be permitted, Mr. President, to express my gratification at what we have heard and witnessed this day. Kentucky has been heard through the mouth of one, who is not only her geatest statesman, but the world's greatest living orator. The great expounder of the constitution, whose massive intellect seems to comprehend and give clearness to all things beneath the sun, has spoken for the Commonwealth of Massachusetts. From every quarter the voice of mourning is mingled with notes of the highest admiration. These crowded galleries, the distinguished gentlemen who fill this floor, all indicate that here have

"Bards, artists, sages, reverently met,
To waive each separating plea
Of sect, clime, party, and degree,
All honoring him on whom Nature all honor shed."

The resolutions were then unanimously adopted.

The VICE PRESIDENT appointed the following as the Committee of Arrangements: Messrs. MASON, DAVIS of Mississippi, ATCHISON, DODGE of Wisconsin, DICKINSON, and GREENE.

Ordered, That the Secretary communicate these proceedings to the House of Representatives.

Whereupon the Senate adjourned.

TUESDAY, April 2.

Obsequies of the Hon. John C. Calhoun.

The Senate met at twelve o'clcok, for the purpose of attending the funeral obsequies of the Hon. JOHN C. CALHOUN, late a Senator in Congress from the State of South Carolina.

The galleries, and every avenue thereto, were crowded with spectators, and hundreds left the doors unable to obtain admittance.

At twelve o'clock, the House of Representatives, preceded by its officers, entered the chamber, and took seats assigned them.

Numerous officers of the army and navy, and many distinguished strangers, occupied the sofas in the lobbies.

The Supreme Court of the United States entered the chamber, and took seats at the left of the Vice President.

The President of the United States and the Cabinet soon followed; the President being conducted to a seat at the right of the Vice President.

The diplomatic corps, which was very fully represented, occupied seats near the centre of the chamber.

At twenty minutes past twelve, the corpse was brought into the chamber, in charge of the Committee of Arrangements, and placed immediately in front of the Secretary's desk. Several relatives and friends of the deceased, Senator BUTLER, and the South Carolina delegation of the House of Representatives, accompanied the corpse as mourners.

The Rev. C. M. Butler, Chaplain to the Senate, read the passage of Scripture, found in the 1st Epistle of Paul to the Corinthians, 15th chapter, beginning at the 20th verse, to the end of the chapter.

Mr. B. then delivered a brief discourse from the words, in the 82d Psalm, 6th and 7th verses:

"*I have said, Ye are gods; and all of you are children of the Most High. But ye shall die like men, and fall like one of the princes.*"

The address being ended, the Senate and audience left the chamber, and formed in procession in the following order:

The Chaplains of both Houses of Congress
Physicians who attended the deceased.
Committee of Arrangements:

Mr. Mason,	Mr. Dodge, of Wis.,
Mr. Davis, of Miss.,	Mr. Dickinson,
Mr. Atchison,	Mr. Greene.

Pall-bearers:

Mr. Mangum,	Mr. Cass,
Mr. Clay,	Mr. King,
Mr. Webster,	Mr. Berrien.

The family and friends of the deceased.
The Senator and Representatives from the State of South Carolina, as mourners.
The Sergeant-at-Arms of the Senate of the United States.
The Senate of the United States, preceded by the Vice President of the United States and their Secretary.
The Sergeant-at-Arms of the House of Representatives.
The House of Representatives, preceded by their Speaker and Clerk.
The President of the United States.
The Heads of Departments.
The Chief-Justice and Associate Justices of the Supreme Court of the United States, and its Officers.
The Diplomatic Corps.
Judges of the United States.
Officers of the Executive Departments.
Officers of the Army and Navy.
The Mayor of Washington.
Citizens and Strangers.

The line having been formed, the procession moved to the Congressional Burying Ground, where the remains of the deceased were deposited, with the usual solemnities, in the receiving vault.

The Senate then returned to their chamber, and adjourned.

HOUSE OF REPRESENTATIVES.

TUESDAY, April 2.

The House was called to order by the Speaker at 12 o'clock, M.

After prayer by the Chaplain of the House,

The Journal was read and approved.

The Speaker stated that, in accordance with the orders taken yesterday, the House would proceed in a body to the Senate, to unite with them in attending the funeral of the Hon. JOHN C. CALHOUN, deceased.

The Speaker accordingly left the chair,

And the House, preceded by its Speaker and other officers, proceeded to the Senate.

The funeral services having been performed,

The House returned to its chamber,

And on motion, adjourned.

IN SENATE.

THURSDAY, April 4.

Mr. Bell's Resolutions.

The Senate proceeded to the consideration of the series of resolutions submitted some time since by Mr. BELL, which Mr. FOOTE had moved to refer to a select committee of thirteen.

Mr. BORLAND. As my colleague desires to address the Senate on this subject, I hope the question will not now be taken, that he may have an opportunity to do so.

Mr. FOOTE. I have conversed with the Senator's colleague, and I understand that he is willing to be heard on some other measure. However, if he desires to be heard before this question is taken, I am willing to give way to him. I therefore move, sir, that the further consideration of this subject be postponed until to-morrow at one o'clock, and that it be made the special order for that hour.

Mr. WEBSTER. Mr. President, I am far from entertaining any wish to prevent the honorable member from Arkansas addressing the Senate on this topic, but I think it my duty to remind the Senate that we have now gone through the first four months of the session, and although I am willing to admit that the circumstances were such as to excuse or even justify a great deal of delay in the despatch of the public business, yet, after all, the time seems now to have come at which, with all convenient despatch, and without encroaching in any degree upon the freedom of debate, we should proceed to some action. Sir, I may be permitted to say that it will require weeks, and perhaps months, and our most deliberate attention and active co-operation in legislation, to do the things and pass the laws which will be necessary when the question of the admission of California shall be decided one way or the other. I wish therefore to say, that so far as my opinion and conduct in the Senate go, I shall endeavor to take such a course of voting and acting as may bring this question of the admission of California *per se* to a decision by the Senate. I am then willing to go on and take up the territorial question—the question of a government for the territories; and I may say upon the whole, that I am inclined to think it will be the best way to proceed, to take up the territorial bills and act upon them.

Sir, the honorable member from Kentucky, (Mr. CLAY,) who moved a series of resolutions on these subjects, whom I have now the honor of addressing as the occupant of the chair, will, as a matter of right, if he choose to exercise it, at a convenient hour, be entitled to reply to the remarks which have been made upon his propositions. That is a matter of courtesy due to every member of the Senate, and it is especially due to him. There is also an honorable member from Tennessee (Mr. BELL) who has brought forward a series of resolutions. He too, is entitled to be heard in reply to objections which have been suggested to his propositions. I do not mean to say that the debate should extend no further, but it is my judgment that it becomes us to consider whether we will discuss one question to-day, and another to-morrow, without coming to any result upon the great question before us.

Sir, as far as depends upon me, as I have said, there will be by no vote of mine any restraint upon debate at all—none at all. But I think we ought to bring the subjects so as to have a tendency to some point—that, instead of postponing these resolutions, one or the other series, from day to day, and keeping them all open to debate, we ought pretty soon to come to a resolution to take up some measure of a practical character, and debate it till we are ready to act upon it. That is my view. The two precise questions, or the two forms in which the questions are presented, most fit I think for practical action, are the amendments moved by an honorable member from Missouri (Mr. BENTON) to the resolution of an honorable member from Illinois, (Mr. DOUGLAS,) by way of amendment to that resolution, instructing the Committee on the Territories to bring in a bill for the admission of California, unconnected with any other subject; and the bill which, before we had time to come to any resolution upon that point, or to any vote upon that question, has been reported.

Now, it appears to me, sir, with great deference to the judgment of others, that our true course now is to take up the bill reported from the Committee on Territories, for the admission of California, and debate it. I mean to say that it is our true course, in my opinion, to adopt that procedure, after the honorable member from Kentucky (Mr. CLAY) and the honorable member from Tennessee (Mr. BELL) have had a proper opportunity to reply to the objections which have been urged against their respective propositions. At the same time, I wish to say to the honorable member from Mississippi, (Mr. FOOTE,) that, though I have no objection to come to a vote upon his proposition, yet I cannot conceal from him—and I do not wish to conceal from the country—that my opinion is, that we have now come to a point upon this general subject, which every one is as well informed of as he can possibly be after any report of the committee. My opinion is, that we had better proceed to take up these subjects, beginning at the beginning. I am unwilling, I will take occasion to say—if the Senate will not consider me as too much trespassing on its attention—I am unwilling to leave any of these questions open, to be the cause of heart-burnings, and dissension, and dissatisfaction through the recess, (if we are to have any recess—which may be much doubted.) I am for acting on California, and then on the territorial bills reported to us from the Committee on Territories. I am for taking them up and voting upon them; and if any amendments are made, such as have been suggested, I am ready to vote upon any such amendments. And my opinion is, sir, that we can do nothing so important to the satisfaction of the country—nothing that will relieve men's minds from apprehension—nothing that will give such general quietude, as to act as soon as is convenient and proper upon the bill for the admission of California, and then upon the bill or bills for the creation of the territorial governments in New Mexico and the rest of the territories, and pass a bill such as the majority of the Senate shall approve. That is my judgment, and in pursuance of these opinions, and according to these opinions, will be my conduct here.

I wish this body to come to a conclusion upon California; my opinion is made up. I wish this body then to come to a conclusion upon the character of the territorial bills. I am willing to act upon them on the principles and opinions which I have already avowed; and I do apprehend, sir, an entire concurrence in these opinions by a majority of this body; and my conviction is, that when these bills shall come up, and this body shall come to a decision upon them—upon what may be called the contested part of them—the majority of this body will come to a conclusion exceedingly useful to the country, in extending to it more harmony, quiet, and satisfaction.

Sir, I desire—if I may say so—to preserve the credit of this great republican Government in the estimation of men all over the world. I do not wish to hear it said on the other side of the Atlantic, that this great, constitutional, free, representative Government cannot go on with certainty and despatch, and without impediment; that it is liable to a great *hiatus* every now and then; that the great principle of free government is likely, after all, not to be so satisfactorily exemplified in this great Republic as its friends at home and abroad have fondly hoped and predicted. I am desirous that we should take such a course in regard to these exciting questions, as will enable us to dispose of them, and to resume and go through with our ordinary duties of legislation. And I will take occasion to say, sir, that I do not expect to see harmonious legislation upon any of the subjects which touch the great interests of the country until this question shall be settled. There are great questions—highly-important questions—for the decision of which the country, North and South, and in the centre, have looked with great interest to the action of Congress at this session. For one, I despair of any wise, and temperate, and just legislation, until these disturbing questions be removed; and therefore I wish, that the questions that have been brought upon us by the events of the last two or three years, somewhat unexpectedly, shall be settled. I wish them to be settled upon the true principles of the Constitution of the United States. I want no new platform. I ask no new concessions on the one side or on the other—no new compromises; the constitution is enough; it is broad enough, full enough, efficient enough; and if we can bring ourselves to act with moderation, and temperance, and candor, and magnanimity, and I will add, with, what is equally important, a fraternal regard and sympathy upon the questions before us, in the spirit of the constitution, we shall be able to rescue the country from its present perils. We who sit here, clothed with this high authority for the moment, are, I firmly believe, able to rescue the country from its present embarrassing condition, and to satisfy the public judgment and the public feeling of the extreme North, and the extreme South, and from one ocean to the other.

Sir, I beg the indulgence of the Senate for wandering into these general remarks. I had no intention so to do when I rose; but I must now express my sincere, deliberate conviction, that our true course is to proceed onward, step by step, with the great subjects that have been devolved on us by recent events, by the acquisitions that have been made by this Government of these great territories, and to take them up, and act upon one and all in the spirit which the Constitution of the United States prescribes to us all, enjoins upon us all, as it is our duty to conform to that spirit in all our legislation.

Well, when gentlemen shall have satisfied themselves on these propositions, and when, as I have said, the movers of the propositions shall have had all the opportunity they desire for replying to the remarks that have been made, I shall feel it my duty to bring to the attention of the Senate practical measures, with the view to their being decided upon, one after the other, in the order in which they may have been presented.

Friday, April 5.

Mr. Bell's Resolutions.

The Senate proceeded to the consideration of the special order, being Mr. Foote's motion to refer Mr. Bell's resolutions to a committee of thirteen members—the pending question being upon an amendment proposed by Mr. Baldwin, to except from the reference so much as relates to the admission of California into the Union as a State.

The Vice President stated, that the pending question, at the adjournment yesterday, was the motion of the Senator from Mississippi, (Mr. Foote,) to postpone the further consideration of the subject until to-morrow at 1 o'clock, and that at that time it be made the special order of the day; and on this motion the Senator from Illinois (Mr. Shields) was entitled to the floor.

Mr. Clay. That motion has exhausted itself, and is now dead.

The Vice President. Unless it is to operate from the day on which it may be adopted.

Mr. Foote. Mr. President, I withdraw that motion.

The Vice President. The motion is withdrawn; and, in that case, the Senator from Mississippi is entitled to the floor.

Mr. Foote. Then I yield, with great pleasure, to the Senator from Illinois.

Mr. Shields. Mr. President, it was not my intention, when this debate commenced, to take any part in it. I had not the vanity to suppose that any thing I could say, would contribute in the slightest degree to the work of conciliation; and I felt extremely anxious, if I could do no good, to abstain, at all events, from doing any injury. But sir, the discussion has become so general, and so many have participated in it, that I fear, if I remain any longer silent, my silence may be misconstrued, and my course misunderstood; and that it is due to myself, and my constituents, to make a few explanatory observations; and I promise that these observations will be the honest convictions of my mind.

The Senate, sir, has hardly yet recovered from the effects of its recent great loss. Death has bereaved this body of one of its most illustrious members. This bereavement will be long felt in this Senate, and in every city, town, and hamlet, throughout this broad land, from the Atlantic to the Pacific ocean. Sir, one of the great lights of this continent has just been extinguished; one of the most brilliant stars of our political galaxy has disappeared forever. A star that shed its lustre, not only on the proud and noble State of South Carolina, but on this whole country, has been removed from our sight—translated, I trust, to a higher and purer region, to shine in a brighter firmament. Sir, it is with feelings subdued and deepened by this sad event, that I enter this morning upon the simple and humble duty of defining my position, and explaining the motives that will govern my future action in this body, upon the delicate questions now under consideration.

The State of Illinois, which I have the honor in part to represent, has thought proper to give me instructions for my guidance and government on the subject of slavery in the territories. I recognize the full right of my State to give me such instructions, and I consider it to be my duty, as one of the Senators from that State, to obey them. I regard the will of my State, when fairly expressed, as a political trust, which it is my duty to discharge in good faith, if I can do so without any violation of the constitution of my country. The resolutions of the Legislature of Illinois instruct me to vote for the application of the Wilmot proviso, to all the territories acquired by the late war with Mexico. These resolutions I consider constitutional, and, as such, it is my duty to obey them. In my humble opinion the Congress of the United States has full power and authority to govern all the territories, including the District of Columbia, in all respects whatsoever, including the introduction and the exclusion of slavery, subject to no limitation or restriction, except that contained in the Constitution of the United States. In other words, I believe that Congress can exercise all governmental control over the territories, which is not in conflict with the provisions of the constitution. I cannot understand the argument I have heard urged in this chamber, that Congress can declare war, conquer a country, subjugate a people, and annex both country and people to the United States, and yet that it has no power to govern them after they have been annexed. Upon this principle Congress can destroy a government, but cannot replace it; can annex a people, but cannot govern them; can regulate a territory, but cannot regulate the people; can govern the land and the habitations, but cannot govern the inhabitants of the territories. Sir, there is something so incomprehensible in this argument, something so unreasonable in this proposition, that I cannot believe it, or accept it, on the authority of any man, however distinguished as a statesman. But I do not wish to pursue this argument any further. I have merely alluded to it for the purpose of declaring that I regard the instructions as constitutional, and that it is my duty, as well as my determination, to obey them.

Sir, in saying this, I do not wish to be understood as laying down any rule for the government of others in similar cases. I merely wish to prescribe a rule in this particular case for my own government—and that is, to obey *constitutional instructions*, or *resign*. This, I take it, is a good, honest, old-fashioned, democratic rule, upon which I can stand, and act with honor and safety.

It will be readily perceived that this restriction upon my action, will prevent me from giving my support to the proposition now under consideration, or to any compromise on the question of slavery in the territories. I am a little afraid of this committee of thirteen, any how. I hardly think it can do any good, and I am afraid it may do much injury. In my opinion, the mind of every member of this Senate has been long made up on all these questions. A great senatorial committee like this will excite great public expectation, and if this expectation be disappointed, the effect may be extremely prejudicial.

Mr. Foote, (interposing.) I wish to make one single suggestion to my honorable friend, that he has misunderstood the motion which I have had the honor to present. A "compromise" is not mentioned; "adjustment" is the word. And, if he is in favor of adjusting the questions, he must go for the motion.

Mr. Shields. Well, sir, I am not so critical perhaps in my knowledge of words, as my honorable friend from Mississippi, and I will change the word *compromise* for the word *adjustment.* However, in acting under the instructions of my State, I am determined to act in good faith; and, therefore, I cannot support the proposition of my honorable friend from Mississippi for what he calls the "*adjustment*" of these questions, or any of the propositions of compromise on this subject. But, sir, while this is the case, I am far from thinking that it is my duty, as a Senator from Illinois, knowing as I do the spirit and patriotism of the people of that State, to stand here in my place, and wage a war of fierce denunciation against this and every other proposition, which may have been matured and brought forward by the highest minds of this body, for the settlement and adjustment of our unfortunate difficulties. It would be especially unworthy of me, who have been the recipient of the generous, though perhaps unmerited sympathy of this whole country, to contribute my puny efforts in this body to widen the breach between the North and the South, and to excite the passions and prejudices of one section of this great country against another. I think I ought to be one of the last of living men to be guilty of such conduct.

Sir, I have seen northern men and southern men stand together shoulder to shoulder in many a struggle. I have seen northern and southern blood mingle on many a field. I have seen northern and southern men follow the glorious standard of a common country to common victory, and to many a victory. And, with all these recollections still around me, I would consider myself criminal to take advantage of my present position, to excite hate and animosity between brethren of the same country, having the same glorious history and the same common destiny, the same pride in the past and the same hope for the future; especially as I sincerely believe that the very men now engaged in this unfortunate controversy, would to-morrow, if necessary, unite in a common struggle, for their common country, against a hostile world. Sir, I have no sympathy—no communion of feeling—with those men who employ their energies, in exciting and maddening one portion of their countrymen against another. I have seen and felt the ruin and wretchedness, that have followed the success of such unhallowed efforts in other lands, and

I am persuaded that a similar result would attend the success of such efforts here. Yes, sir, the full and complete success of these unholy efforts here would be the ruin of this republican Government, the destruction of this great temple of American liberty.

Mr. President, I regret to say that the proceedings of Congress, during the present session, have been characterized by extraordinary passion and excitement. Criminations, invectives, and personalities have too often disfigured our debates, and have even threatened, on some occasions, to bring us into angry personal collision. These were ominous indications in an American Congress, and particularly in an American Senate, which has been uniformly distinguished heretofore for the dignity, propriety, and decorum of its proceedings. But, sir, not only here, but throughout the whole country, the indications seemed ominous of some impending evil. The North was in a state of perfect apathy, while the South was in a state of furious excitement; the North was glorifying the virtues of the Wilmot proviso, while the South was organizing the Southern States, and preparing to assemble a great Southern Convention at Nashville, that could have no purpose—I mean to say no practical purpose—but the dissolution of this Union. I say practical purpose, because I hold that, unless the South is prepared to urge matters to the last extremity, that Convention ought never to be held. In my opinion, it would prove deeply injurious to the character of the South. Mr. President, I looked upon this unnatural state of things—this singular national discordance—one portion of the same country in apathy, and another palpitating with excitement; one portion unmoved and indifferent, and the other preparing for revolution, as the presage of some great national evil. I know, sir, there may be others less timid than I am, who may have looked upon all this with something like indifference; but I am not one of these indifferent men; I can be indifferent in nothing, and least of all upon questions that involve, not only the existence of this Government, but the existence of liberal government throughout the world. To me this is not merely an American question; it is a mundane question. I look upon it in connection with the question of civil liberty and human progress in other countries, because I am convinced, that if the great experiment of republican government fails on this continent, it need never be attempted again in this world.

And, sir, I began to fear that the experiment was about to fail; that the glorious institutions which you have received as a legacy from a wise and noble ancestry, and which you hold in trust, not for yourselves only, not for this generation alone, but for future generations, for posterity, and humanity, were, by some fatality, by some judgment perhaps of Divine wrath, or by some of those terrible conjunctures, which destroy the best of human institutions, approaching a dark, premature, and inglorious end. And was there not cause, sir, for serious alarm? Was it not felt by every member of this body? The South complains of grievances and aggressions, and complains vehemently. I think the South exaggerates these grievances; but doubtless it has some grounds of just complaint. But let me say, the North complains of grievances also, and it has some just grounds of complaint also. Individual, sectional, and national grievances exist under every Government on the face of the earth; and grievances, I fear, will continue to exist forever, under every form of human government. But suppose, sir, all the grievances of which the South complains to be wholly imaginary, (and some of our northern friends think so,) does this lessen the imminence of the danger? No, sir; by no means. On the contrary, imaginary grievances are often more dangerous than real ones. Real grievances can be redressed; for imaginary grievances there is no remedy. Sir, more than half the great convulsions that have shaken this world have sprung from imaginary grievances.

It is not real dangers that are present to us; it is prospective dangers—dangers that loom and lower in the distant future—that frighten and alarm us most. These are the dangers that excite men to acts of folly, and urge them on to the most fearful extremities. And, sir, there are times and seasons when it is impossible to account for the folly of human conduct any how. There are periods when men and nations rush blindly, or, rather, with their eyes open, on certain and inevitable destruction. This is the history of the world. The annals of nations are filled with instances of this kind—with periodical instances of folly and frenzy. One generation builds up, and another pulls down—one generation founds empires, and another destroys them. This has been the history of the world for six thousand years, and will continue, I fear, to be its history forever. And without meaning to cast any reflection upon the generation to which I belong, I must say that when I saw the total failure of the people of Europe, in their recent struggles, their unsuccessful efforts, to ameliorate their condition and reform their institutions, I began to fear that there was something wrong in the character of the present age, and that the responsibilities of this great Government had fallen, perhaps, on a generation unequal to the present crisis, and incapable of wielding, at this critical juncture, the destinies of this great Republic. But, sir, when we see assembled in this chamber, as if by the special ordination of Providence, the highest intellects of this nation—minds matured and moderated by experience, and exalted and ennobled by patriotism—men capable of comprehending the dangers and difficulties of the crisis, and having the courage and capacity—and I may add, the national reputation, to grapple with these dangers, and triumph over them—I think we may conclude, and conclude joyfully, that Heaven still smiles on this favored land; that the glorious stars, the appropriate emblem of this great Republic, are not yet destined to set in darkness and blood, but to illumine for ages—I hope forever—the broadest and brightest political firmament that ever sheltered liberty, civilization, and humanity. My admiration and enthusiasm have been often excited this session, at the extraordinary efforts of the great statesmen of this body, to work out some just and equitable plan for the settlement of our unfortunate difficulties. When I saw the distinguished Senator from Kentucky, now in the chair, present his great plan of national compromise, and when I listened to his thrilling eloquence and fearless enunciation of great moral truths, in favor of liberty and humanity—truths as old as the laws that govern the moral world, and which will live and kindle the hearts of millions, when the present generation is mouldering in the dust—I felt that there is a heroism higher and holier than any that ever inspired a conqueror to tread his way through blood and battle to victory and immortality. I forgot, on that occasion, that I was a Democrat, and that he was the great leader of the Whig party. I remembered nothing but the great cause and the great advocate. I saw nothing but the great Republican, and the great American. I do not allude to the distinguished Senator from Kentucky for the purpose of invidious distinction; on the contrary, I refer to him as the type, or rather as the central figure of a host of intellectual giants, who have employed their time, and talents, and energies, this session, in the great Republican and American work of compromise. I call the work of compromise emphatically American. A fearful controversy has raged here, and throughout the country, this whole session. A controversy that excites the strongest and deepest feelings of our nature—a controversy, as it were, between sentiment and interest, liberty and slavery. And yet, no man now, either in this body or the other Hall, seriously contemplates any other result than its amicable adjustment, by an honorable and a national compromise. Well, sir, my notion is, that this controversy could not have raged one month, in any other country on earth, without a national convulsion. Why is this, sir? Because the people of this country are trained and educated to settle all their difficulties, public and private, by just and honorable compromise, while the people of other countries, in great national difficulties, are accustomed to have immediate recourse to force. Sir, there are only two principles employed in the government of the political world—*force* and *compromise*. Some nations are governed by both principles, others by *force alone;* but this is the only nation that has always been governed by compromise since the foundation of the Government, and it must continue to be so governed as long as it continues to be a Republic. Sir, where *compromise ends force begins*, and when *force* begins *war* begins; and the tocsin of civil war is the death-knell of Republicanism.

Mr. President, I am in favor of the admission of California into the Union as a State. Here there is no room for compromise. I am also in favor of keeping the question of admission unconnected with any of the other exciting questions now before the Senate. A great measure, like the admission of an independent State, should, in my opinion, be determined on its own intrinsic merits, and not in connection with any other question, however important. If California is entitled to admission, it is unjust to the people of that territory, and unwise as a principle of legislation, to make that admission depend upon the doubtful issue of any other question. You have done injustice enough to the territories already; you have refused to give them governments of any kind; and when they come here with governments formed by themselves, you refuse to sanction them. Sir, upon the annexation of New Mexico and California, it was the imperative duty of Congress to extend the blessings of government to the people of those territories within a reasonable time. No considerations of policy could exonerate Congress from this obligation. The highest trust that God commits to man is that of government; and when he disregards this trust, he sins against God's appointment, and does grievous wrong, to those whom fortune has made dependent upon him for government and protection. Sir, you have done wrong, and grievous wrong to the people of the territories: you tore them from their own government; you severed them from their own people; you annexed them to your country; you made them a part of your people—and all by force; and you refused to give them government of any kind, and left them in a state of anarchy. You poured out blood and treasure to win these territories, and when you acquired them you abandoned them. Sir, Congress has consumed more time in talking, quarrelling, and wrangling over these territorial acquisitions, without doing any thing for them, than your army took to conquer Mexico, dismember that country, and annex the territories to the United States. So far as my experience goes, I can vouch for it, that your soldiers perform their duty much more promptly and efficiently than your statesmen.

The people of the territories, it is true, have formed governments for themselves, and governments perhaps better adapted to their anomalous condition than any that could be fashioned for them by the wisdom of Washington. And this only proves, that, when their Government fails to provide for any portion of the American people, they are competent to provide for themselves. In my opinion, California has worked out the most hope-giving problem of this age. It has demonstrated the capacity of man for self-government. The mind of man can scarcely conceive of any condition in which human beings could be placed, more unfavorable to the establishment of order and government than that of California. The people were an assemblage of every kindred, tongue, and nation—thrown together promiscuously in a wild, distant, desert region of the world—away from all the restraints of civilization, and engaged, not in the peaceful pursuits of agriculture, but in wild adventure, and a reckless grapple for gold, "the root of all evil," and certainly the cause of more than half the evils of civilized society. Now, sir, I should like to know how the experiment of leaving such a people, under such circumstances, without any government, would have worked in any other country in the world. The rulers of Europe think it necessary to employ armies of soldiers, and armies of policemen, and dungeons, racks, and scaffolds, to keep their loyal people in order and subjection. What would such rulers have predicted of California? Why, that it would prove to be an earthly *tophet*, a sort of *terrestrial pandemonium*. But no such thing, sir. To the honor of human nature, and to the eternal honor of American character, that imbued that society with American loyalty to law and order, the people of California established a government, and that government, from the hour of its establishment till this hour, has given more effectual protection to life and property and the pursuits of industry, than any Government of Europe during the same period.

Sir, California furnishes the strongest demonstration of this age in favor of the inherent capacity of man for self-government, when left to the free exercise of his native faculties. And it is the loudest condemnation of those systems of government which first debase and brutalize man, and then punish and oppress him because he is debased. Without the aid of law, or rather, by virtue of a better law than ever was enacted by Congress—the law of truth and justice in their own hearts—the people of California organized their society, framed a constitution, and established a government, and they now present that constitution for our acceptance; and, sir, if we have the law of truth and justice in our hearts, we will receive this constitution at once, and welcome California into the Union.

But, sir, it is said by some that California must be remanded back to a territorial condition; that it must remain quietly in that condition, until Congress finds it convenient to give it a government. Others say that California can have no government until Congress agrees upon some general plan for the settlement of all our difficulties: first, our territorial difficulties—a government for Utah, and another for New Mexico; secondly, the settlement of the boundary between New Mexico and Texas, and whether we are to have a slave State or a free State carved out of Texas; and finally, the settlement of the question of slavery and the slave-trade in the District of Columbia. Now, sir, my opinion is, that if you keep California out of the Union until you settle all these questions by satisfactory adjustment, it needs a vast amount of Christian patience; because, at the rate you despatch business here, California may stand some chance of admission at some indefinite time between now and the millennium. Sir, this is perfect mockery. It is to say substantially to the people of California: "You must break up your government, resolve yourselves again into a state of anarchy, go back and live quietly and peaceably, and behave yourselves well, and neither rob nor kill one another, if you can avoid it, until we can settle all our difficulties, all questions connected with slavery, to the satisfaction of the North and the South, and then we will extend the blessing of government to you—we will give you a government exactly suited to your condition." This, sir, I suppose, is Congressional justice to California. I wish to say, most respectfully to my southern friends, that I cannot conceive what advantage they expect to derive from the rejection of California. It puzzles me to divine the secret of southern policy on this point. Whether California is a State or a Territory, whether it has any government or no government, no southern slave-owner will ever venture to carry his slaves to that country. Slavery can never be established there. With law or without law, southern men will never dare to carry their slaves there. The people of California are working out a great social problem—a problem that has never yet been worked out successfully anywhere else: and that is to make *labor—hard labor*, dignified and respectable. I trust in God they may succeed. But do you think the people engaged in this work will suffer themselves to be jostled by slaves? No, sir, never. The sons of southern planters, the high-spirited sons of southern gentlemen, would be the first to resist and resent such an experiment. Sir, the whole united South dare not venture to carry slaves to California for the purpose of establishing slavery there. In California, at this moment, there are one hundred and fifty thousand men; not old men, women and children, but young, active, daring, adventurous men—the flower of the youth of our country—men such as never settled a new country before. Before a year rolls round, California will number half a million of the same sort. If I searched this world for an army, I would take the men collected in California. I tell you, sir, the South, and the North, and the whole country united, can never force slavery on them. Napoleon trampled down Europe with fewer men and worse material. Sir, they are laying the foundation of a great empire on the shores of the Pacific—a mighty empire—an empire that at some future day will carry your flag, your commerce, your arts, and your arms into Asia, and through China, Hindostan, and Persia, into Western Europe. Talk about carrying slavery there—of imposing such a blight upon that people—of withering their strength and paralyzing their energies by such an institution! No, sir; such a thing was never intended by God, and will never be permitted by men.

I am one of those who believe that the laws of Mexico abolishing slavery, are still in force and operation in California and New Mexico. I understand the great principle of law to be this: When one country conquers another, the political laws, that is, the laws prescribing the duty of the subject or citizen to the Government, are abrogated. And why? Because the conquered Government goes out of existence, and the conquering Government takes its place; but municipal laws—laws between man and man, made for the protection of life and property—remain in force, and must of necessity remain in force, for the preservation of society, until modified or repealed by positive enactment on the part of the conquering Government. Now, this is an old principle of law, a little older than modern civilization, yet it has been as seriously questioned and denied on this floor, as if it had arisen for the first time on the conquest of Mexico. It is sometimes urged here, that our constitution carries slavery with it wherever it goes, unless positively excluded by law; in other words, that slavery is the *normal law* of this Republic. I think the principle is just the reverse. Slavery, being in violation of natural right, can only exist by positive enactment; and the constitution of this country only tolerates slavery where it exists, but neither extends nor establishes it anywhere. But, sir, I have heard it seriously argued in the Senate, that the laws and edicts abolishing slavery in Mexico were all irregular, and therefore void; and that slavery was in full force in that country at the time of the annexation of these territories. It is extremely hard to answer such an argument as this. This is emphatically a chivalrous argument, which, though it may not convince a man, is well calculated to astound him. I will merely say that the poor Mexicans made a great many honest and earnest attempts to abolish slavery, and if they have failed to accomplish that object, they have been very unfortunate in all their efforts. I have no doubt that the people of Mexico will be highly edified when they learn that their old acquaintances, the "*Norte Americanos*," about the time they discovered the "El Dorado," in California, made another discovery, and that is, that their laws, edicts, and constitution, to the contrary notwithstanding, slavery was in full force and operation in that country, without the people themselves being aware of the fact. I think when they hear this, they will come to the conclusion that we are as invincible in logic as we are in battle.

But, sir, I will drop this subject. I care not whether there is any Mexican law or American law there, or whether the Wilmot proviso or the Jefferson proviso ever be extended over those territories, slavery can never be established in California or New Mexico. The climate, the soil, the productions forbid it. In a word, the principle of the Wilmot proviso is extended over the country by the law of nature—by the law of God—as the distinguished Senator from Massachusetts (Mr. WEBSTER) emphatically expressed it. And were I permitted to act upon my own judgment, I would leave it under the operation of that law. Sir, you might as well undertake to plant orange groves in Siberia, as establish slavery in California or New Mexico.

I will now notice the question of boundary between New Mexico and Texas. I admire Texas as highly as any man living; I like the State and the people; they fought gallantly and successfully, and achieved their independence by a struggle as glorious and extraordinary as any of the present age. I will say, also, that we ought not to criticize the claim of Texas too closely; that we ought to be liberal to that young and gallant State. If there be a doubt, it ought to be resolved in her favor. But, to my mind, there is no doubt in the case. Texas has no right, claim, or title, to any portion of New Mexico, either on this side or on the other side of the Rio Grande. She never conquered it, never occupied it, never reduced it to possession, and never exercised any authority over it. She has no more title to Santa Fe than she has to San Francisco—not a particle. That country, and the whole of that country, was under the law, jurisdiction, and authority of Mexico, when it was wrested from that country by the arms of the United States. I care nothing about maps; I take facts, and these are the facts. I venture to say, further, that in my opinion Texas never conquered all the country to the lower Rio Grande. There is a portion of Coahuila, south of New Mexico, on the Texas side of the Rio Grande, which I scarcely think she ever conquered. At all events I can say, that when at one time during the Mexican war, I was wandering along the Rio Grande, I found Mexican towns in the State of Coahuila, on the Texan side of the river, living quietly under Mexican law and Mexican authority; and if they had ever been conquered by Texas, it was wholly without their knowledge, for they were living in the most happy ignorance of such conquest. But while this is my opinion, I am ready and willing to pay to Texas, for such claim as she has, enough to wipe out her whole State debt. That debt was contracted in a noble cause—the struggle for liberty—the war of her independence. The United States have got the benefit of that struggle, by the annexation of the country, and I hold that it is only a generous duty, which the Government ought to fulfil, to pay Texas a sufficient sum to wipe out the whole of her State debt.

On the question of making a new State in Texas, I am prepared to say that I feel myself bound to comply with every stipulation, condition, and obligation of the resolutions of annexation. Whatever the stipulations are, we are bound by them. This nation is bound, by every principle of honor and good faith, to fulfil its obligations with Texas. No man can give any reason for the violation of these stipulations that he cannot give for the violation of every human obligation. I do not know, sir, the opinion of my State on this subject, but I take it for granted, that the State of Illinois will never so far forget her duty to this nation, and her own character, as to violate the plighted faith of this Government. I do not think there is a man in my State who will not consider himself bound by the engagements of his Government. The Mormons, while they lived in that State, were accused of assuming that they had authority from God to violate their engagements with men. But they have left the State, and I do not think we have any political Mormons in Illinois now. But I must be permitted to say, that I think Congress has no right to take the initiative in this matter. I think there is a wrong here; the initiative ought to be taken by Texas. It is for her to take the preliminary steps, designate the territory, and organize a new State, and when that State asks for admission into the Union, if it comes within the conditions of the resolutions of annexation, it is the duty of Congress to admit it. But I suppose the reason our southern friends are so anxious to squeeze a State out of Texas at this time, is to bring a slave State into the Union in conjunction with California, to preserve the balance of power, to maintain the equilibrium in the Senate. Now, sir, I think there is one thing to which southern gentlemen must make up their minds, and that is, to submit to what is inevitable. The whole world must submit to what is inevitable, and the South must submit to it, like the rest of mankind. I tell you, sir, what I think is inevitable—that the free States will outnumber the slave States, and that the power of the free States will preponderate over the power of the slave States. The South will lose its relative power in this nation. It is doing so every day; not by the action of Government, but by the action of irresistible laws—laws that control the moral, social, and political condition of man. You may as well talk of equalizing the population as of equalizing the States. There is another thing the South may as well understand, (I mention this as a prediction,) and that is, that the people of the North will never consent to see one foot of free soil converted into slave soil, if they can prevent it by constitutional resistance. I believe the North does not contemplate any other mode of resistance. If free territory be annexed, it must remain free, until as a State it may choose to change its condition. If slave territory be annexed, (Cuba for instance,) let it remain slave territory until as a State it chooses to change its condition. Sir, it seems to me there is nothing unfair in all this; on the contrary, that it is just and equitable. No one, I think, in this advanced age of the world should attempt to convert a free man into a slave, or free territory into slave territory.

Mr. President, I sincerely believe that if the South had not assumed the extraordinary position, that slavery is the normal law of this country; that, like the electric fluid, it pervades all space; that it exists throughout this whole land, where not expressly excluded by law; that slaveholders can carry their slaves like their horses, to California and New Mexico, by force and virtue of the Constitution of the United States, and contrary to the municipal laws of Mexico still in force there, the terrible feeling awakened in the North on the subject of the Wilmot proviso, would never have found such general expression in that portion of the country. When southern men declare that slaves are like horses, mere chattels; that they can carry them with them into California and New Mexico by virtue of the constitution; that the constitution protects the right of property in chattels, and consequently in slaves, the northern feeling revolts against such claim. And even the very best friends of the South are compelled to reject such untenable pretensions. Sir, I cannot believe that you southern men (Mr. Clay in the chair) have absolute property in your slaves. You have property in their service, and that service is perpetual. Slavery is a state of perpetual servitude, and you have a right to employ all necessary power over the man to enforce such service. But you have no absolute property in the *man*, in that mysterious being composed of *body* and *soul;* you do not own him as you own your horse, because no human law can give you such property in him. Sir, slavery never was understood in this sense in any country, neither amongst the Romans, the Greeks, or even the Mohammedans, and it is to be deeply regretted that such a claim should be urged by Christians.

I have already said that the South may give up all idea of an equilibrium. Here it never existed, and never can exist. It is a most fanciful notion at best—the mere dream of a political visionary. You cannot balance political power; you cannot weigh it in scales; you cannot regulate it by any system of equipoises. The thing is simply impossible. Why, sir, South Carolina—a proud little State, spirited and intelligent—has wielded more political power in this Confederacy for several years past, than some of the larger States of the Union. The equilibrium has been often tried, but has always failed. The French tried it, as they have tried every kind of experiment. After their first revolution they established a Government, most fancifully constructed, upon an equilibrium compounded of territory and population. It was the delight of the enthusiasts of that age. No liberal politician of that day seemed fully to appreciate the absurdity of the experiment but Edmund Burke; and that great English statesman, I should say Irish statesman—but England appropriated him to herself, as she does all renowned Irishmen—that great statesman, I mean to say, ridiculed the whole scheme, pointed out its absurdity and impracticability, and predicted its speedy destruction. And, sir, the prediction was soon verified. The very first heave of the great political mass, shattered the Government into a thousand fragments, and buried its projectors under its ruins. The experiment, therefore, wholly failed in France. After the fall of Napoleon, the Holy Alliance tried a similar experiment, and if any body of men possessed the power to carry out such an experiment, the members of the Holy Alliance did at that time. They settled the relative power and condition of the several States, and established a free continental system, upon what they called the equilibrium of Europe. Sir, I should like to know what has become of that system? I should like to find out the state of the equilibrium of Europe now? Sir, in my opinion, the Czar of Russia could throw the whole of Europe at this moment, with the exception perhaps of France and England, into one scale; and he would only have to throw his sword into the same scale, and in twelve months Europe would be Cossack, from the Bosphorus to the British Channel. So the experiment of an equilibrium has utterly failed in Europe. Sir, it never has succeeded, and never can succeed. The thing is impossible and impracticable. You never can maintain a permanent equilibrium between States, or nations, or parts of nations. But I am wasting time unnecessarily upon such a subject.

Now, sir, if all the dangers which the South sees in the far distant future, were, at this moment, present and pressing upon us, I would most respectfully ask southern gentlemen to tell me what remedy they would propose in such a case? Say, a dissolution of this Confederacy—the peaceable separation of the States—an amicable destruction of this Government? I would just as soon expect to see a high-spirited southern gentleman stand up quietly to have the whip applied to his back, as to see the people of this country sit down quietly, and look tamely and unmoved on the destruction of their Government. No, sir; the very attempt would be war; the beginning of a war of which none but God could foresee the end; a war of extermination and desolation; a continuous, ceaseless, perpetual war; a war to be transmitted from father to son, from generation to generation, until your great Anglo-American race, now the pride, and boast, and glory of this continent, would become a by-word, a scorn, and a warning to the world. The very energy of your race, that terrible energy which is making you masters of this continent, would be the motive power to accelerate its own destruction—you would devour yourselves. But does any sane man suppose that the great Northwest, with all its millions—that world that is growing up between the headwaters of the Ohio and the headwaters of the Missouri, between the Alleghany and the Rocky Mountains—will ever peaceably submit to see the mouth of the Mississippi River in the possession of a foreign Government? Never, sir, never. With that people it would not be a question of reason; it would be above all reason; it would be a question of necessity and of existence; a thing which they never would quietly submit to. But there is no danger of any thing of the kind. The people of the valley of the Mississippi can never separate. They may talk about it, and threaten it, but they never will attempt any thing so disastrous. They are one people, tied together by the indissoluble bonds of physical nature. For weal or woe, for good or evil, the whole people of the Mississippi valley must share the same fate and the same destiny. And does any man suppose that this people, occupying about one-eighteenth of the habitable globe, will ever submit quietly and peaceably to see the southeastern States establish a separate confederacy? The idea is preposterous—very little short of insanity.

But suppose the Southern Confederacy was now established—that it was quietly and peaceably established this moment, what would be the actual condition of that Confederacy? It could not exist a single day without a close and intimate connection with some great nation, having all the elements of industrial, financial, and commercial power. The South possesses none of these elements. It has plenty of cotton, and it has brave men, and lovely women, but it is wholly destitute of all the other material elements of national power. Every man that knows any thing knows this. The Southern Confederacy, therefore, would be compelled by necessity to enter into a strict alliance with some great nation—that nation would doubtless be England. Now, Old England is not a whit more partial to slavery than New England; and Englishmen have a peculiar fondness for enforcing their own views upon their loving allies. But, sir, what would be the character of an alliance between such a nation and such a Confederacy? It would be supremacy on the one hand, and dependence on the other: it would be the worst kind of dependence, having all the disadvantages, and none of the advantages, of colonial dependence.

In fact, the Southern Confederacy would be a mere colony of masters and slaves, to raise cotton for the factories of England. Besides, sir, it is my firm conviction that the institution of slavery, as it now exists in the South, would not last, in its present shape, for the space of twenty years in that Southern Confederacy. The South might as well attempt to shut out the pressure of the atmosphere, as to shut out the whole pressure of the civilized world on its cherished institutions. Another Chinese wall would not be sufficient to protect the Confederacy from the influences of Abolitionism flowing in upon it, and invading it from every quarter of the civilized world. Sir, in saying this, I may be permitted to add, that the effect of abolition at this time in the South would prove most disadvantageous to the slaves. I think the negroes would be the principal sufferers by the change.

I listened the other day to the eloquent remarks of the gentleman from Virginia, (Mr. Hunter,) and I heartily concur with him in nearly all his opinions and statements on this subject. All I have seen, and heard, and read, convince me that where there are two distinct races in the same community, one inferior and the other superior, like the negro and the white race; a state of mild and gentle slavery is the safest and happiest condition for the inferior race. Equality of rights, and equality in the hard struggle of life, result in the insensible but certain extermination of the inferior race. You may give the slave liberty if you please, but that very liberty is his destruction. If you emancipate the slaves, and wish to save the negro, you must separate the races. God only knows how this is to be done; but it is my solemn conviction that the universal emancipation of the African race of this country, would lead to the gradual and insensible, but certain extinction of that race.

Sir, the history of this very country proves the truth of this assertion. Where now are the Indian tribes that once roamed in wild freedom over this continent? The history of Mexico proves it. Where now are the Tlascalans, the Tolucans, the Aztecs, and the other numerous Indian nations of that country? The history of the French and British West Indies proves it. It is a melancholy fact, but it is a fact, that the negroes in these islands are rapidly becoming extinct. But, sir, let the consequence be what it may to the negro, or the white, my opinion is, that if a Southern Confederacy ever be constituted, (which God in his mercy avert!) the institution of slavery, as it now exists, will not continue in existence, in its present shape, for a quarter of a century.

Mr. President, I firmly believe that the rights of the South, notwithstanding all the annoyances to which they are subjected, are better protected under our present constitution and Government, than they could possibly be by any other scheme or plan which the ingenuity of man could devise. They are protected against the foreign world, the world abroad—by the character, and power, and majesty of this great nation. They are protected from the North by the obligation and guarantees of the constitution. You will say no; you will say the North does not respect these guarantees. But I say the constitution is a restraint upon the North, a powerful restraint; it imposes some restraint on all, even on the rankest abolitionists; and it imposes a binding restraint upon all those, whatever may be their abstract opinions, who love their constitution, and their Government, and their country—their whole country—and who prefer the safety and perpetuity of this great Republic to the abolition of slavery or the emancipation of the negro; and I need scarcely say that these constitute a vast majority of the northern people.

It is my opinion, then, that the true policy as well as the duty of the South, is loyalty to the constitution and fealty to the Government. This is the policy and the duty of the North also—the policy and duty of the whole American people. Let us preserve our constitution, and fulfil all its obligations with true American honor and honesty, if we wish to preserve this great American republican Government. I will no longer detain the Senate.

Several Senators. Go on as long as you wish.

Mr. Shields. I thank the members of the Senate for their kindness and patience, but I do not wish to trespass any further. However, there is one matter I forgot to allude to. I have said that it is the duty and policy of the North as well as the South to stand honestly and faithfully by the constitution—that every patriot and honest man is bound by its guarantees. In this spirit I am prepared to vote for any reasonable bill for the restoration of fugitive slaves. The clause of the constitution which provides for this subject is as binding on me as any other provision of that instrument; and I am ready and willing to perform my obligation in this matter. I have done.

Mr. Mason. I do not mean now to go at large into a consideration of the questions that are pending before this Senate and before the country. I am restrained, sir, because I feel that both the State and the section of country which I represent, are standing in a decided and ascertained minority. I have been made to feel, that what is, or what is not to be done in reference to this question, has not yet been disclosed by the majority. I do not know what their purpose is, but I feel that I might do a wrong to those whom I represent, and possibly to the Southern States, were I at present to take any position that might interfere with the future settlement of these questions. Sir, the point of division between the States where slavery exists, and the States where slavery does not exist, is this: We claim, under the constitution, a right in law, for all or any of our citizens to go into any territory belonging to the United States, with all or any of their property, and to reside there, and to enjoy it as their property, without molestation or hindrance, under the protection of the constitution, as long as it remains a territory. We hold that a territory is, in the terms of the constitution, "the property of all the United States;" and so long as the Southern States where slavery exists, are constituents of these United States, they have the right to go into that territory, to reside there with their property, and to enjoy it under the protection of the constitution. That is the right, clearly, and I hope distinctly, defined upon the part of the South, so far as I understand it. What is said upon the other side? It is said, that the majority of those who represent the people of the United States in Congress, have a right by law, to prohibit the people of the Southern States from taking one species of property into their territory; and that there is nothing in the constitution to prevent it. What is the position on the other side? Now, sir, notwithstanding what we just now heard from the Senator over the way, (Mr. Shields,) as to the consequence of the assertion of this right on the part of the Southern States—notwithstanding what may be his opinions of the impolicy of maintaining such a right on their part, they are prepared to assert it, and to make it good, cost what it may. Sir, the State of Virginia has asserted it; Mississippi has asserted it; Carolina has asserted it; Georgia has asserted it; Alabama has asserted it; and what they shall do in such event, is no longer a matter to be controverted. Their position is taken.

Now, sir, I have said, and I repeat it, that I do not mean now to go into the discussion of the questions involved in this sectional division. I must wait until they are presented in a more practical point of view. I have arisen principally to present, not so much to this Senate as to those I represent at a distance, what is the present posture of these questions. It is the motion of the honorable Senator from Mississippi (Mr. Foote) to refer all these controverted questions to a select committee, in the hope and the belief, expressed by that Senator, that it will be in the power of a committee so raised to adjust them. What are the questions? The organization of governments for the territories —the expediency of creating one or more new States in Texas—the proposition for the purchase of her public lands—a proposition to define her boundaries, and a proposition to admit the territory of California under the State Government which she has recently assumed. These are the questions. We are met at the threshold by a motion, coming from the State of Connecticut, by the honorable Senator over the way, (Mr. Baldwin,) modified and adopted, I believe, by a Senator from Missouri, (Mr. Benton,) to except from that reference the question of the admission of California; and the reason avowed is, that the admission of California, as she is now presented under the constitution which the inhabitants of California have adopted, and with the boundaries which that constitution has prescribed, must be taken up and entertained in this Senate as a separate question, to be decided upon its own merits, separate from, and unconnected with what we consider as kindred questions, and necessarily to be considered and adjusted at the same time.

Now, sir, we were told yesterday, by the Senator from Mississippi, (Mr. Foote,) who moved this committee, that, in his judgment, the act admitting California into this Union, before the other questions were settled, would be taken by the Southern States as offensive—as indicating the purpose of the majority of Congress to exclude their people from all the territories; and further, as he believed, the admission of California as a separate and independent question, would involve a dissolution of this Union. Sir, upon this floor, under the grave and heavy responsibilities belonging to all of us, we are bound to form the best judgment of which we are capable, in the difficulties that surround us, and to express it. Sir, what the consequences may be of the admission of California as she stands now, by a separate and independent vote, I am not prepared to say. It rests with others, not with me. But I am prepared to say this: that if it be done as the act of a majority, and against the united dissenting vote of all the slaveholding States, it will require no prophet to foretell what the consequences will be upon the minds of the Southern people. Sir, I am not one of those, if there be any, who are opposed to the admission of California. Far from it. There is no man who sympathizes more deeply than I do with the people now in that territory. There is no man who would go further, consistently with safety to others, to provide a government for them, or to ratify that which they have provided for themselves. And it is that I may be saved from the necessity of voting against their admission into the Union, that I depreciate the action thus proposed by a separate vote upon the admission of California. Sir, the point, at which the action of the States of the South has been levelled, in the settlement of this question, is the interdiction of slavery in the territories, passing under the modern historical name of the Wilmot proviso—the interdiction of slavery in the territories.

Now, sir, what is California at this day, at the moment that I speak? What are the federal relations of that people to the United States? California is a territory, nothing but a territory —and I say it without the least disparagement to the action of her people in convention—California is at this day, and this moment, a territory, and known only as a territory to the constitution and the laws. She cannot become a State, either in the acceptation of national law, or within the interpretation of our constitution, until she becomes so by the assent of the Government of the United States, the owner of the territory, or unless she should place herself in opposition to the Government, and make good her claim, vindicating it by force of arms. She now remains a territory; and with every disposition which I cordially entertain to throw no obstacle in the way of the people there in the formation of a State government, or of a recognition of a State government already formed, I am not prepared to do it, and I cannot do it, while it is in derogation of the rights of others —the rights of citizens of the Southern States.

The Senator from New Jersey, (Mr. Dayton,) who addressed the Senate some time ago, took the ground distinctly, and avowed it in his place upon this floor, that the question of the admission or non-admission of California, was the weakest form for the South in which the question of slavery or no slavery could be presented. Why did he say so? He said so because it might be considered as complicated with the right of a people to govern themselves, and it might be ascribed to the South that their true objection to the admission of California, should such objection be made, was, that in deciding for themselves, the people had excluded slavery. Now, sir, circumstances and events over which none have control, have placed it in the power of those representing the free States here to change the issue in form, although not in fact. The attraction of the gold mines has hurried an immense population into that territory, and they have felt themselves strong enough to assume an independent government. In doing this, they have assumed a boundary embracing the entire Pacific front, and they have, by their fundamental law, excluded the people of all the Southern States from removing there with their slave property. Now, sir, I have no desire, for all this, to remand them to a territorial state, and, under proper conditions, to refuse them admission into the Union, with such institutions as they deem best for themselves; but, before this is done, I am bound to insist on such a division of the common property that the rights of all shall be regarded.

I understood the honorable Senator from Massachusetts, (Mr. Webster,) in speaking of the admission of this State of California, to say that his opinions upon that question were reserved; that he could see no reason at a future day to refuse admission to California with suitable boundaries. Since then, he has announced his purpose to be to admit her with her present boundaries. Now, Mr. President, what I wish to say to honorable Senators who are prepared to vote for the admission of California with her limits as now prescribed—if their true purpose be, as I doubt not it is, to do no act gratuitously, which may prevent the adjustment of our differences—is this: Forbear that vote until some disposition is made of the remaining territories. Why should it be done? California has assumed the form of a State government, and is now, as we are informed, regularly organized—two houses of legislation, a judiciary, and an executive, all appointed, all in operation. I am perfectly aware that their authority must be, to a certain extent, weakened, and their resources not fully under the control of their people, that new vigor and new life will be infused into them as soon as their existence is acknowledged upon the part of the United States, and they are admitted into the Union. But I cannot see so great a necessity for it as to have it done now, in a hurried manner, and prematurely, and before other kindred questions are considered, the adjustment of which is to be vitally affected by such preference to California. After the State is carved out, there remains a territory in California two or three times as large in extent, and with some forty or fifty thousand people, to be provided with a government. Again, there is the territory of New Mexico, pressing, by a petition on our tables, for a government to protect them. I do not see why one is more pressing upon us than the other; but I do see, although I cannot express it more forcibly than it was yesterday expressed by the Senator from Mississippi, (Mr. Foote,) why a proper regard to a large portion of the States should require us to act upon the territories before we act upon the State of California.

Sir, if there be a man upon this floor who has a more sacred regard—a more superstitious attachment, if I may so express it—to the constitution which now binds these States together than he who now addresses you, I do not know who he is. If there be a State in this Union which has given more undoubted proofs of loyalty to the constitution than the State which I represent in part, I know not what State it is. But, sir, knowing that people as I know them, they would not regard the constitution as worth the parchment on which it is impressed, if it is to be maintained at the expense of rights which they intended it should secure. No, sir, just as cordially as they came into this Union, so will they go out of it, when they are satisfied that the bonds of union are regarded by the majority only for the purpose of oppression.

Now, Mr. President, I submit it to honorable Senators who have at heart, as I know they have, the preservation of the Union, and the design to save any or all from the consequences of disunion, which have been so strikingly depicted here—I call upon them to pause before they bring into it the State of California, under the constitution adopted by her people, before some final disposition has been made of the great questions yet undecided in reference to the government of the remaining territories.

Sir, I hope I am no alarmist; I feel no alarm myself; but I know the people of the country from which I come, well. I believe I know the people of the southern States, through their reputation and by their acts. I know their deeply excited feeling; and I know that nothing can bring home to them a keener sense of their condition as a hopeless minority, nothing will more fill them with alarm, than the admission of another free State carved out of the territory in dispute, before the question of prohibiting slavery in the territories that remain, is finally disposed of.

Mr. President, I repeat again, and I believe, in so doing, I express the sentiment of the people of those States, that there are none who are against the admission of California as a State, or who desire to have her delayed longer than is necessary to the protection of their rights and their safety: I mean California with suitable boundaries—a question which I may discuss when the proposition to admit California comes directly before us—boundaries which will leave to the people of those States the liberty of enjoying a portion of that territory, should they think proper to do so, or it be found adapted to their condition.

We have heard here from various quarters, and from high quarters, and repeated on all hands—repeated here again to-day by the honorable Senator from Illinois, (Mr. Shields,) that there is a law of nature which excludes the southern people from every portion of the State of California. I know of no such law of nature—none whatever; but I do know the contrary, that if California had been organized with a territorial form of government only, and for which, at the last two sessions of Congress, she has obtained the entire southern vote, the people of the southern States would have gone there freely, and have taken their slaves there in great numbers. They would have done so, because the value of the labor of that class would have been augmented to them many hundred fold. Why, in the debates which took place in the convention in California which formed the constitution, and which any Senator can now read for himself, after the provision excluding slavery was agreed upon, it was proposed to prohibit the African race altogether, free as well as bond. A debate arose upon it; and the ground was distinctly taken, as shown in those debates, that if the entire African race was not excluded, their labor would be found so valuable, that the owners of slaves would bring them there, even though slavery were prohibited, under a contract to manumit them in two or three years. And it required very little reasoning on the part of those opposed to this class of population, to show that the productiveness of their labor would be such as to cause that result. An estimate was gone into with reference to the value of the labor of this class of people, showing that it would be increased to such an extent in the mines of California that they could not be kept out. It was agreed that the labor of a slave in any one of the States from which they would be taken, was not worth more than one hundred, or one hundred and fifty dollars a year, and that in California it would be worth from four to six thousand dollars. They would work themselves free in one or two years, and thus the country would be filled by a class of free blacks, and their former owners have an excellent bargain in taking them there.

I do not mean to go now into what may be suitable boundaries. I may do so when the question is properly before us, and shall be disposed to deal as liberally as a proper regard to the rights of others will admit. The people now in California have gone from every quarter of this country. There are among them my neighbors and friends, and in large numbers, in whose success and welfare I feel a deep interest. Those with whom I act, can have no interest or object in defeating or in delaying their elevation to the platform of the States—no purpose to interfere with any policy they may deem most conducive to their welfare. But, on their part, they can have no just ground of complaint if, while portioning them off in independence, we retain for others, who may come after them, a reasonable share of the common property.

The question of boundary, sir, is one not proper to be left altogether to the interested party. Congress should determine it with due regard certainly to the interests of those in possession, but with an eye always to the rights and interests of all the people of all the States.

But, sir, to come back to the matter in reference to which principally I have risen. The Senator from Mississippi, (Mr. FOOTE,) who has taken this subject in charge, informs us that the territorial bills are in posture of legislative precedence, and that to act first on the California bill, will be to put them back in order to give precedence to California.

The same effect will be produced if we detach the California bill from the proposed reference. I suggest, therefore, that we take up these territorial bills, and pass them in the order in which they stand, and as they have been reported. And, that, being done, the way is open for the admission of California as one of the States of the Union, subject only to such modifications of boundary as may be found right, or such conditions, if any be suggested, as the terms of the constitution may require.

Mr. UNDERWOOD. I will venture to submit a few remarks upon the proper course of proceeding in relation to this subject. When the Senator from Mississippi first submitted his resolution, I was against raising this committee, and making the reference at that time, because I thought there were other members who might be desirous of submitting their views, and that they ought to have the whole subject before them to debate upon, as broad as it had been presented by my colleague's resolutions. If there be any member on this floor who wishes that broad latitude to speak upon, I would still be disposed to continue the whole subject before the Senate, so as to give them opportunity; but if there be no such, I am willing to adopt the resolution offered by the gentleman from Mississippi, in the hope of avoiding the disagreeable predicament in which some Senators will consider themselves to be placed, as is indicated by the Senator from Virginia. I think that in matters of great moment, such as those we now have to act upon, we ought to consult, as far as we can, the feelings of every one, and try, as far as we can, not to create any just foundation for complaint on the part of any one. With these views, I shall vote against the amendment proposed by the Senator from Connecticut, hoping that if the committee be raised at all—and I believe, sir, I shall vote for raising it—that not only the bill for the admission of California, but the territorial bills, shall also go to that committee; and trusting also that the committee will first act upon the bill providing for the reclamation of fugitive slaves, and then make a recommendation to the Senate and the country in relation to all the other bills; and that when they come back again, we shall take them up in the order the committee present them, and act upon them in that order. There will then be a pledge, sir, as far as the recommendation of the committee can operate, that a compromise in relation to these bills shall be carried out.

In that order I would advise the committee to proceed. In the first place, proceed with the bill for the reclamation of fugitive slaves. That is the first step towards settling the agitations of the country. In the next place, take up either the territorial bills, or the bill admitting California as a State, and admit California, regulating the boundaries, either changing them or letting them remain as they are; and then pass the territorial bills without any proviso, thus leaving the question of slavery, its existence or non-existence, its introduction or non-introduction, to depend entirely upon the legislation of the people of the territories, or upon the judicial interpretation of the constitution as contended for by some gentlemen of the South. It then becomes a judicial question; for, if a slave be introduced into New Mexico or Utah, the question arises for the judges to decide under the constitution, as it now exists, unless the legislature of the territory acts upon it, whether the slave can be held in bondage in a land made free by Mexican law? If that course would be adopted by the committee, and they should give to it the weight of their high recommendation, it would relieve, to some extent, the embarrassment which some gentlemen seem to labor under in regard to the admission of California under present circumstances.

I do not think that, if even the California bill was taken up first, and she was admitted, the consequences are to result which my friend from Virginia has pointed out, and which were somewhat more plainly indicated by the Senator from Mississippi on yesterday. I do not think, sir, that any such consequences ought to result, or will result; but I have so much respect for the opinions and feelings of those gentlemen, and for others with whom they are associated, and for whom they no doubt feel themselves authorized to speak, that I will not force upon them the adoption or rejection of measures, or a vote upon these highly important subjects, of such vital interest, as they conceive, to their constituents—I say I will not force it upon them, when they protest against it, and thus bring them to do an act which they think will lead to such injurious consequences. Therefore, for one, I am willing to adopt the resolution which was originally proposed to raise this committee, and refer all the subjects to their consideration; and I trust that the committee will be able to make their report in a week or two at the furthest.

Mr. Foote, (in his seat.) By Monday.

Mr. Underwood. The sooner the better, in my opinion. Meantime, I think the remarks of the Senator from Virginia are entitled to some weight. The government of California is organized; the State government is going on; and she can suffer no inconvenience or injury from a slight procrastination of her admission. To be sure, it may be a matter of some little personal convenience to herself that her respected delegation should be admitted on this floor as soon as possible; but it will be but a temporary delay; at all events, one which will be remedied in a few weeks, if the course pursued here is one tending to harmony.

The Vice President. The question now before the Senate is, the motion of the Senator from Connecticut, to amend the resolution offered by the Senator from Missouri.

Upon this motion Mr. Benton asked the yeas and nays; and they were ordered.

Mr. Butler. I have no idea of detaining the Senate long, and I have arisen only to state, that I concur entirely with what has been said by my friend from Virginia, and to offer a suggestion or two before the vote is taken on this question. It is now in the power of a majority to rescue the Union, and to save one portion of this country from mortification and insult, by making such issues as at least will be consistent with their rights. Suppose that, under the existing state of things, California is admitted with her present boundaries—as some of us propose—by a disregard of a practical and fundamental principle in the Constitution of the United States. There are those who can reconcile it to their consciences to waive all objection, and organize California into a State. I do not say that I am one of them; but I do say, that if you admit California, with her present boundaries, separately, you do an act of usurpation. And what comes next? Why, the territorial bills will be brought forward, the Wilmot proviso incorporated into them, or you refuse to give any government at all, on the ground that by waiting, they can gradually be brought in, as California seeks now to be brought in, by assuming a position which the constitution itself would not have authorized, under the original practice of this Government. The Wilmot proviso, then, is put into these territorial governments, or else no government is given to them at all—leaving them to come in, in the course of time, as California seeks to come in. And the result of this action will be nothing more nor less than the exclusion of slavery. I do not undertake to say whether slavery will go there or not. If it may not go there because of the laws of nature, it is an insult to the South to have it prohibited by special enactment. But if the Wilmot proviso is put upon these territorial bills—I shall utter no threat—I shall not say what influence it will have upon the temper of the southern people—I never have stated it—but I think I understand our people very well, and I think they fully understand their rights, and will maintain them. Sir, to make experiments of this kind upon the feelings of the South, I consider an act—if I may be allowed so to speak—of almost criminal temerity. You would force California upon us, and then put into the territorial bills the Wilmot proviso, or what is equivalent to it. If California is associated with those measures which are intended to be presented in one general compromise, I will not say there will not be acquiescence in the course; for I am not prepared to state how far an adjustment of that character will satisfy every section of this Union; but if you take these issues one by one, and leave the majority at liberty to use its power on the other questions which have been raised, you are presenting a most terrific and disagreeable issue to the American people.

Mr. Clay. I believe that the immediate question before the Senate is a proposition for amendment, made either from this or the other side of the House, to the motion of the honorable Senator from Mississippi, to refer this subject to a committee of thirteen; a proposition, the object of which is to except from the general reference the particular subject of California.

Mr. President, no one more than I do, can deplore what is the manifest state of feeling and relation of parties at this time, in both Houses of Congress. It is in a great measure the result of those most unhappy agitations which prevail in Congress, and throughout the country. These agitations have engendered feelings of distrust of the honor and fidelity with which one portion of the common subject being disposed of, the other portions of the same subject may be finally disposed of. Sir, I do not partake of these feelings to the extent which, I apprehend, some others may. From the first moment of my entry into this House until this, my anxious desire has been to see these great questions settled and adjusted amicably, and to see harmony and concord, and fraternal affection, once more restored to this divided, and, for the moment, unhappy, country; and, sir, acting upon this feeling, I have favored every proposition which has been offered, which looked to such a termination of the subject as I have described. Less confident, perhaps, than others may be, in regard to particular modes of adjusting the question, I have been for embracing them all, no matter from what quarter they might come—every one which looked toward restoring union and harmony among this people. When, therefore, the Senator from Mississippi presented the proposition that is now under consideration, I was ready to vote for it; if no good could be accomplished by it, I believed at least that it would do no harm. And it is a great recommendation to any project that it has the object in view to which I have referred.

Sir, I am ready, for one, to vote for the admission of California separately, or in conjunction with the other territories, for which governments are proposed, of the recently acquired or conquered provinces. I am ready to vote for them, either separately or conjointly, with or without the boundaries which she has prescribed for herself, but rather acquiescing, under all the circumstances of the case, in the boundary which she has herself prescribed. I repeat, I am ready to vote for her admission, at any time, and under any circumstances, separately or conjointly. I confess to you, sir, that when the message of the President, communicating the constitution of California, was first received in the Senate chamber, I was inclined to immediate and prompt action upon the message, so as to admit at once the delegation from California, who had come so far, and travelled at such an inclement season of the year, under such unfavorable circumstances, and thus constituting this infant and inchoate State one of the States of this Union. I think it ought to have been done instantly, promptly; but it has not been done.

Causes which I did not anticipate have brought into existence excited feelings, and a degree of opposition, and have produced procrastination in reference to the subject, of which we were totally unaware. And now, sir, I say to those who are friendly to the admission of California, and who constitute, I believe, a large majority of this body, and who are friendly to a prompt and immediate admission of California, that I have been forced by circumstances to come to the conclusion and belief, that the most rapid mode in which you can get California admitted as a member of the Union, is by combining in the same bill provisions for her admission and provisions for the government of the new territories; that if you propose—though I will not go into minute circumstances—if you propose the admission of California separately, there will be danger of opposition to the passage of the measure, which will delay, if it do not ultimately defeat, its passage, a much longer time than would be consumed by taking the course of uniting the admission of California with measures for establishing governments for the other territories. I have heard it said that it was disrespectful to California. How, I would ask, is it disrespectful to California to combine her in a bill which shall not only provide for her speedy admission, but shall also provide governments for the territories? I can conceive of no disrespect being offered to her by pursuing such a course. There is no more disrespect in putting her in a bill with other kindred measures, than there would be in placing a bill for her admission exclusively, on the statute books, which shall contain other bills and laws in relation to the government of the territories. There is no disrespect in this; it is imaginary—in my humble conception it is idle to affirm it. If you want her speedily admitted, give her admission, and provide at the same time for the government of the territories. And, sir, is there not something exceedingly suitable in a combination of these measures? By doing so, you at once make an arrangement for the government of all the territories acquired from Mexico; giving a government, to be sure, of one description to one and another to another, but still giving them all governments suited to their respective conditions. Is there any thing injurious, any thing improper in it? Then, sir, there is another great recommendation in favor of this course, which is, that we are aiming at a compromise, a specific settlement—a compromise that shall lead to the restoration of peace and harmony among this disturbed and distracted people. As a compromise, you may put into the bill as many kindred subjects as it is practicable to insert. I do not wholly concur with my colleague—though I am happy to say we generally agree—in regard to his suggestion of adding to this bill a provision for the restoration of fugitive slaves; but I insist upon it, that all that relates to California, and all that relates to governments for the territories, and, if you please, the adjustment of the boundary of Texas—although, perhaps, it would be better to leave that out—are kindred subjects, and are all proper to be inserted in the same common bill.

Mr. Underwood. My colleague is mistaken in supposing that I want the bill for the reclamation of fugitive slaves to be made a part of the same bill which provides for the admission of California. I only suggested that it should go to the same committee.

Mr. Clay. I was not present during the whole time my colleague was addressing the Senate; but I understood him to signify that the subjects should all be embraced in the same bill. The condition of my health scarcely justifies my being here at all; but such is the deep, inextinguishable anxiety I feel on this subject, that, even at the risk of injury to my personal health, I feel an irrepressible inclination always to be at my post.

Sir, I have explained what I am inclined to think is the best course to be pursued in relation to this subject. I think that the whole subject, and all parts of the subject, in reference to propriety and concurrence, and common character and sympathy between them, should be treated in combination, as I have suggested. That combination can be disrespectful to no one and to no portion of the country; and it is a combination that is most likely to terminate the unhappy difficulties in which we find ourselves placed at the earliest day, and in the most satisfactory manner.

Entertaining these views, I had risen for the purpose of stating that I cannot vote for the amendment which has been proposed by the Senator from Connecticut; I had hoped indeed that, on reflection, that amendment would have been withdrawn. Sir, it seems to me wholly incompatible with the purposes and the circumstances under which the committee is to be formed. Why, sir, when you constitute a committee of thirteen, for the purpose of endeavoring to arrange all these subjects, will you manacle them, will you tie their hands in regard to one of the most important branches of the subject? No, sir; if the amendment prevail, there will be no advantage in raising a committee of thirteen, and, for one, I would as soon vote against it as for it.

Mr. Benton. On the reception of the President's message transmitting the constitution of California, a proposition was made to refer this subject to the Committee on the Territories, and I believe I was the first to propose that the question of the admission of California as a State should be excepted from the general subjects which went to that committee. And when that proposition got overslaughed—I do not know how, for things get overlooked and run over here, and I cannot pretend to follow them up—when it was afterward proposed by my friend from Connecticut, (Mr. Baldwin,) to except the question of the admission of the State of California from the particular motion to refer all these subjects to a committee of thirteen, having been thinking somewhat on the subject, I suggested to him a modification of his motion, which he accepted. It is to be supposed, then, that I have been thinking on this subject, and that I have some reasons for my opinion that California ought to be considered separately. I had reasons then, and they have become stronger, much stronger to-day than they were then. And I had intended, after hearing every thing gentlemen had to say on this subject, if no one proclaimed the sentiments which I myself entertained, to take an occasion, before the question was disposed of, to give the reasons to the Senate which induced me to believe that the admission of California should be considered as a separate question. It has been my intention to do so; and, sir, I will say that, at the head of the considerations which appeal for the admission of California, stands the course of honorable action. And I, for one, will never consent to make the admission of that State weigh in the balance against the catching of runaway negroes; I never will consent to the bringing of a State into the Union in that way. No one State has ever yet been subjected to such a condition. Nor will I go through the forms of adopting a system of measures which is to have the obligatory form of a compromise, and that upon California, while she herself stands as an outcast repulsed from our doors—to our binding her to a system of measures, and she not here to say aye or no to it. Sir, I entertain this feeling, and I have some reasons for it, more than I can give to-night.

Mr. Cass. If the Senator will permit, I will move an adjournment.

Mr. Benton. Very well, sir; I can hardly expect to go on with a subject of this kind to-night.

And then, on motion, the Senate adjourned until Monday next.

Monday, April 8.

Mr. Bell's Resolutions.

The Senate proceeded to the consideration of the special order, being Mr. Foote's motion to refer Mr. Bell's resolutions to a committee of thirteen, the pending question being upon an amendment proposed by Mr. Baldwin, to except from the reference so much as relates to the admission of California as a State.

Mr. Benton. It is proposed to make the admission of California a part of a system of measures for the settlement of the whole slavery question in the United States. I am opposed to this mixing of subjects which have no affinities, and am in favor of giving to the application of California for admission into this Union a separate consideration, and an independent decision, upon its own merits. She is a State, and should not be mixed up with any thing below the dignity of a State. She has washed her hands of slavery at home, and should not be mixed up with it abroad. She presents a single application, and should not be coupled with other subjects. Yet it is proposed to mix up the question of admitting California with all the questions which slavery agitation has produced in the United States, and to make one general settlement of the whole, somewhat in the nature of a compact or compromise. Now, I am opposed to all this. I ask for California a separate consideration, and object to mixing her up with any, much more with the whole, of the angry and distracting subjects of difference which have grown up out of slavery in the United States.

What are these subjects? They are:

1. The creation of Territorial Governments in New Mexico, and in the remaining part of California.

2. The creation of a new State in Texas, reduction of her boundaries, settlement of her dispute with New Mexico, and cession of her surplus territory to the United States.

3. Recapture of fugitive slaves.

4. Suppression of the slave trade in the District of Columbia.

5. Abolition of slavery in the District of Columbia.

6. Abolition of slavery in the forts, arsenals, navy-yards, and dock yards of the United States.

7. Abolition of the slave trade between the States.

8. Abolition of slavery within the States.

And a non-enumerated catalogue of oppressions, aggressions, and encroachments upon the South. This is the list of the subjects to be mixed up with the question of admitting the State of California into the Union; and I am against the mixture, and that for reasons which apply to the whole in the lump, and to each separate ingredient in the detail.

I am against it in the lump.

California is a State, and has a right to be treated as other States have been, when asking admission into the Union, and none of which have been subjected to the indignity of having their application coupled with the decision of other, inferior, and to them, foreign questions.

I object to the process. I object to mixing California with any thing else. I have objected in the lump; I will now take the ingredients in detail.

1. The government for the two territories. This brings up the Wilmot proviso, which is unconstitutional in the opinion of some members—inexpedient in the opinion of others—and both constitutional and expedient in the opinion of some others. It is an angry, distracting, and sectional question, with which California, for herself, has determined to have nothing to do. She has put it into her constitution, that slavery and involuntary servitude shall not exist in her borders. This settles the question of the Wilmot proviso for her, and was intended to settle it, and intended to free the question of her admission from the impediment of that question. And now, how wrong to her,—how unjust,—how mortifying—how unexpected and incomprehensive to her, to have the question of her admission connected with this proviso in two neighboring territories, and her admission made actually dependent upon its settlement—precedent settlement—in New Mexico and the Great Basin. She had as well have remained a territory herself, subject to the question upon her own soil, as thus to be subjected to it abroad. And better, too. There is more dignity in being tried at home than abroad—more consonance to our notions of fair trial, to be tried in her own person than by proxy. After all, there is a positive incongruity and incompatibility in mixing these two questions. One is clearly constitutional. The power for it is written down in the constitution. Congress may admit new States; and this is an appplication for the admission of a new State out of territory belonging to the United States; and there is no question of constitutionality in it. Not so the Wilmot proviso. Power for it is not written down in the constitution. Its constitutionality is denied, and that by many members on this floor. Here, then, is a coupling of an undisputedly constitutional with a strenuously disputed constitutional measure; and in voting upon them as a whole, or as mutual and dependent measures, as a system of measures, as a compromise, members may find themselves in a state of impossibility. Oaths to the constitution cannot be compromised; and, therefore, questions of disputed should never be mixed with questions of undisputed constitutionality.

I am ready to vote for governments to the territories; and, believing in what I have alleged from the beginning, that slavery is extinct in New Mexico, and in all California, and cannot be revived in either, or in any part of either, without positive enactment, I am ready to vote them governments without any provisions on the subject of slavery.

2. Texas, with her large and various questions, is the second subject proposed to be coupled with the admission of California. It is a large and complex subject, presenting in itself many and distinct points. A new State, to be carved out of her side—reduction of boundaries—settlement of the dispute with New Mexico—cession of her surplus territory to the United States: such are the large and various points which the Texan question presents. They deserve a separate consideration. Texas herself

should object to this conjunction with California, as much as California should object to it with Texas. They present incompatible subjects—incongruous—and large enough each to demand a separate consideration. They are subjects of equal dignity. Each concerns a State, and States should be considered alone. But there is another objection to this conjunction, of higher order, still, and which concerns this Congress, and the exercise of its powers. By the constitution, Congress is to admit new States: by this coupling of Texas and California, it would be Texas which would admit the new State of California. Thus: Texas has four questions to be settled, not one of which can be settled without her consent. A new State cannot be carved out of her—her boundaries cannot be reduced—her dispute with New Mexico cannot be settled—her surplus territory cannot be had, without her consent! This gives her a vote upon the admission of California, if coupled as proposed—gives her four vetoes! for there are four points at which her consent would be necessary, and the withholding of which upon any one point would be a veto upon the admission of California. In fact it would give her still more vetoes. For the subjects coupled together, and acted upon as a whole, must all stand or fall together; so that the veto of Texas upon any part of her own subject, would be the veto of the whole with which they were coupled.

The Texas questions ought to be settled—ought to have been before she was admitted into the Union, and I proposed it then, five years ago, and have proposed it again at the present cession. My proposition, heretofore printed by order of the Senate, contains my sentiments. I am ready to vote for them; or for better, if offered; but always as a separate and substantive measure.

3. Fugitive slave bill. This is a case of runaway negroes, and in which California has no concern. She will have no slaves to run away, and none can run to her. She is too far off for that. She has no interest on the subject, and it is a degradation to her to have the question of her admission mixed up with it. In her name I protest against this dishonor, against this disgrace of having the high question of her admission thrown into *hotch-potch* with a fugacious bill for the capture of runaway negroes.

We have a bill now—an independent one—for the recovery of these slaves. It is one of the oldest on the calendar, and warmly pressed at the commencement of the session. It must be about ripe for decision by this time. I am ready to vote upon it, and to vote any thing, under the constitution, which will be efficient and satisfactory. It is the only point, in my opinion, at which any of the non-slaveholding States, as States, has given just cause of complaint to the slaveholding States. I leave out individuals and societies, and speak of States, in their corporate capacity; and say, this affair of the runaway slaves is the only case in which any of the non-slaveholding States, in my opinion, have given just cause of .complaint to slaveholding sisters. But how is it here, in this body, the appropriate one to apply the legal remedy? Any refusal on the part of northern members to legislate the remedy? We have heard many of them declare their opinions; and I see no line of East and West, dividing North from South, in these opinions. I see no geographical boundary dividing northern and southern opinions. I see no diversity of opinion but such as occurs in ordinary measures before Congress. For one, I am ready to vote at once for the passage of a fugitive slave recovery bill; but it must be as a separate and independent measure.

4. Suppression of the slave trade in the District of Columbia. This again is a subject in which California has no concern, and with which she should not be mixed. It is a subject of low degree, and not fit to be put into the balance against the admission of a State. It is a thing right in itself, and to be done by itself; and I see no reason why it is not done. The opinion of this chamber seems to be unanimous; then why not act? I have been here thirty years, and have seen no state of parties in which this revolting traffic might not have been suppressed.

5. Abolition of slavery in the District of Columbia. I object to mixing this question with California, or with any thing else, or taking it singly. I will send it to no committee. I will not even consider it. I will do as I have done for thirty years—let it alone. I will do as Congress has done for sixty years—let it alone. I will do, as I believe this Congress will do—let it alone. I will give no committee power to act upon it, either by special authorization, or by general words large enough to cover it.

6. Abolition of slavery in the ports and arsenals, navy-yards, and dock-yards of the United States. I make the same objection to mixing this subject with California, or with any thing else. I eschew it in *toto*, and will vote to give no committee any sort of jurisdiction over it.

7. Abolition of the slave trade between the States. Still the same answer. I will mix it with nothing, nor take it by itself. Congress has shown no disposition to meddle with it, and has no power to do so. The clause quoted by some—no one in Congress that I ever heard of—the clause to regulate commerce between the States, gives no such power; and if it did, would be precisely the contrary of what has been claimed. To "regulate" is not to destroy, but to guide and direct—to conduct with order and method, for the better success of the thing regulated. It is to protect and to promote commerce among the States that Congress is authorized to regulate it between them; and, in that sense, it is probable that Congress will have no applications to regulate the sale of slaves between the States, nor have any disposition to do it of its own accord.

8. Abolition of slavery in the States. This

again is a subject which I would not touch. The slave States are much agitated about it; but without reason and against reason. Congress has done nothing to alarm them, and much to quiet them. Disclaimer of power—disclaimer of desire; sixty years' refusal to touch it is the highest evidence which Congress can give of its determination to abide the constitution and its duty. This ought to be satisfactory to all slaveholders. If any one is not satisfied with this test, let him try another; let him go to the market—that quick and truthful reporter of all danger to property; and he will quickly find, from the price that is offered him, that nobody is afraid of abolition but himself.

No, sir! These four last-named subjects—abolition of slavery in the District—its abolition in the forts and arsenals, dock-yards and navy-yards—its abolition in the States—and the suppression of the slave trade between the States—all belong to a class of subjects not to be touched—which Congress never has touched, and has no disposition now to touch. They are subjects which require no additional guarantees from congressional compromises. The constitution is the compromise. It is the binding compromise, and has been faithfully kept by every Congress from 1789 to 1850; and there is no reason to suppose it will not continue to be kept. If it shall not be kept, it will be time enough after the breach is committed, to think of the remedy—the remedy of disunion. We should no more look ahead for causes of disunion, than we should look ahead for causes of separation from our wives or for the murder of our mothers.

These are all the specified causes of alarm to the slave States from any conduct or apprehended conduct on the part of Congress, of which I have heard complaint. I do not trouble myself with those who have no power to act—with individuals or societies. Congress is the effective power—the representation of all the States—and of that I speak, and say that I know of nothing in its conduct which can give the slave States any cause for complaint or alarm.

Undefined complaints of aggressions, encroachments, and oppressions are made from some parts of the South. So far as these undefined complaints apply to Congress, and the northern States, I know of no foundation for them. Some legislative resolutions are offensive, but they do not amount to aggression, encroachment, oppression. But I do know of forbearance in Congress to exercise an undisputed power which might be exercised to the annoyance and oppression of the South. I allude to the power of direct taxation. The slave property of the slaveholding States is estimated at more than a thousand millions of dollars. It would be a rich subject of taxation. No Government in the world leaves such a mass of wealth untaxed. We have taxed it, and when it was worth much less than now—taxed it in 1798 and in 1813. No one dreams of it now! Yet it would be a mode of taxation to oppress the slaveholding States, because the burden of it would fall exclusively upon them. It would be a mode of annoying the slave States from the right it would involve to count and value the slaves, and verify returns by actual inspection. It might be a mode of abolishing slavery, upon the principle of suppressing, by fining, under the name of taxing; which was a mode of suppressing, or banishing, branches of the Bank of the United States, once resorted to, in order to get rid of that institution, in some of our western States. The abstinence in Congress to exercise this undisputed power—the fact that no northern member has ever proposed or hinted it—this great fact of not using this undisputed power, when it might, should be received by all candid minds as the highest earthly evidence that Congress has no disposition to usurp disputed powers, much less to commit flagrant violations of the constitution, to harass or destroy slave property in the slaveholding States of this Union.

But we do not stop at forbearance—at abstinence from using undisputed power to annoy the slave States. We do not stop at negative proof to show the just and kind disposition of Congress towards these States. We proceed to positive acts, and by them prove the same thing. And here let us be precise. The year 1835 is named as the year of the commencement of the slavery agitation, and the aggressions upon the South. Granted, as to the time. Granted, also, as to individuals and societies. But how was it as to States and Congress? That is the point. And the answer is, that so little was Congress affected by the abolition societies—so little inclined to abolish slavery, or to restrict its area—that it actually increased it; and that repeatedly and largely, and within the obnoxious time. It was in the year 1836—the very year after this slavery agitation is dated, and the very year after the leading papers in the South had made it a question of *time* only for a convention of the slaveholding States to assemble and provide for a southern confederacy, that Congress actually increased the area of slavery in one of the largest of the slave states; and that at a sacrifice of a part of the Missouri compromise line, and by the actual conversion of a large extent of free soil into slave soil. I speak of the annexation of the Platte country to the State of Missouri. By that act of annexation, a part of the Missouri compromise line—one hundred miles of it on a straight line—was abolished; and a new line substituted, near three hundred miles long on its two sides, cutting deep into free soil, and converting it into slave soil. The six beautiful counties of the Platte country were gained to Missouri by this operation—gained to a slave State, and carved out of free territory, made free by the compromise of 1820—and all by the help of northern votes. I say by the help of northern votes, and without referring to the journal; for the fact proves tself. The northern members were the majority; and without help from their votes, the law could not have passed to alter the compromise line. Their Senators were equal on this floor; and without help from them, the two-thirds of the Senate could not have been obtained to ratify the treaty which removed the Indians from the ground promised to them for a permanent home, and which removal was indispensable to the annexation of the country to the State of Missouri. All this done, and by the help of northern votes, and in the very time laid as the period of northern designs for the abolition of slavery in the States! It was done without even an array of North and South. And so powerless were the abolitionists at home, so unable to make an agitation at home, that, so far as I am informed, they were not able to turn a single member out of Congress for the vote he gave in favor of the extension of slavery under such extraordinary circumstances. This is a fact which stands for an answer; and as such I produce it and leave it.

This is a great fact, but small in comparison to another. Behold that Texas ceded to the king of Spain by a southern administration in 1819, recovered by the help of northern votes in 1844! the greater part of it slave territory. This recovery carries slavery from the Sabine to the Rio Grande—from the Red River to the Bay of Matagorda—from the frontiers of Louisiana to the frontiers of New Mexico—ten degrees of longitude—above five hundred miles on a straight line! All this was done for the extension of slavery, and by the help of northern votes, and within five years past, and during the very time that the southern convention was under advisement on account of the designs of the northern people to abolish slavery in the States. This was done, and in that time. And now, away with idle fears and groundless accusations! They sink into nothing in the presence of such facts as these.

But this is not all—hardly the beginning of Congress legislation for the actual extension of slavery. Look at all the south-western and some of the western and southern States. Look at them as they were some thirty years ago. Look at Kentucky, Tennessee, Alabama, Mississippi, Georgia, North Carolina, Arkansas, and Missouri; all of them more or less encumbered with an Indian population, keeping out the white man and his slave. Now, all redeemed from the Indian, and actual slavery extended where it could not go before! And all this again by the help of northern votes; for without that help the laws could not have been passed, nor the treaties have been ratified by which this great extension of actual slavery in so many great States has been accomplished.

I say, then, that these fears are idle—this agitation groundless—that Congress has no design to disturb slave property—and that there is no necessity for any settlement or adjustment about it—no necessity for compromising California into the Union by a grand scheme of settling the whole slavery agitation, at the expense of her honor, dignity, and rights.

Having shown that the admission of California ought not to be mixed up with any other subject, I now come to the question of admission itself, and say that all the objections which have been made to her admission are groundless in fact, or insignificant in their nature. What are they?

1. That no act of Congress has been passed to authorize the people of California to form a State constitution. The fact is admitted, but its consequence is denied. Congress has full power over the admission of new States, and may dispense with all preliminary forms, when it pleases, and come direct to the question of admission. This is what it may do, and what it has done. It has admitted more new States without than with the previous authorization of an act of Congress to form a constitution. Eight have been so admitted—Vermont in 1791; Kentucky, 1792; Tennessee, 1796; Maine, 1820; Arkansas, 1836; Michigan, 1837; Florida, 1845; and Iowa, 1846. Eight in all—a majority of the whole number ever admitted—and stretching over a period of sixty years, and reaching back to the venerable times of our early history, when Washington was President, and the fathers of our political church were still at the altar. Eight! and there would have been another if Congress had not passed the act in March, 1820, to authorize the people of Missouri to assemble their convention to form a constitution. They would have assembled the convention themselves, as other territories had done before them, if Congress had not passed the act at the session it did. I was contemporary with that event, and know something about it. Certainly the authorization by Congress is a convenience—it regulates the process and pays the expense; but it is not a necessity, and may be dispensed with in all, and has been in a majority of the cases of admission, and ought to be in every case in which Congress does not do its duty by the territory. This was the case with California. She had been scandalously neglected—left without any legal government, or any American law, but a tax law; and she had no alternative but to make some sort of a government for herself. The choices lay between a provisional government—such as Oregon had established under similar circumstances—and a State government. Her population and wealth, and the rapidity of her march to the rank of a great State, decided her in favor of the latter; and she decided well; I rejoiced when I heard it. It was the course which I deemed she ought to take from the moment Congress adjourned, 3d of March, 1849, without giving her a legal government, and which I then expressed to several persons, and among the rest to the present Secretary of State, Mr. Clayton. Sir, this is a subject which I have studied—twice studied; once in 1820, when the law for the Missouri Convention was so long delayed—and again in 1837,

when Michigan was admitted; and when, as the chairman of the Senate's committee which reported the bill for her admission, it became my duty to study her case, and to hold myself ready to answer all objections; I did so study and answer; and the answers were satisfactory to the Senate, for the State was admitted. There is nothing in this objection, and I dismiss it.

2. Aliens voting at the election of members of the convention. The fact may be so—probably was so, in some degree—and might have been so to a large degree, and still no insuperable objection. The framers of the Texan constitution were all aliens; and yet that did not prevent her admission into this Union with the identical constitution which these aliens had formed. No, sir! the question is not so much who made it, as what is it? Its character is what concerns us, and the only point at which we have power over it and on which we can reject it. What is it? And that is a question that every Senator can answer for himself; for it has been printed by our order for our use, and laid upon our tables. Any thing in it contrary to the paramount constitution of the Union? any thing contrary to our republican institutions? any thing smelling of alienism? Nothing! nothing at all! A fair American republican constitution! and one of the best, if not the very best, that has been made in any one of the thirty States which now compose this Union; and being thus good in itself, it is not to be met by the question, who made you? It is well made; and that is all the business that anybody has with it. It is a *republican* constitution; and that is the only test to which *we* can subject it. Finally, this very objection of alien voters was made in the case of Michigan, and truly, and stood for nothing; and for nothing, I trust, it will stand here.

3. Insufficient numbers—not people enough—is another of the objections. And how many are enough? I speak of men who exercise political rights and constitute the State. How many are enough according to the practice of Congress in admitting new States? About ten or twelve thousand; for that is the number of men which the usually required population of a new State would give. One man to six souls is the usual proportion in civilized communities; and sixty thousand souls would give ten thousand men; and upon that number or thereabouts, have most of our new States been admitted. Now apply that rule to California, and see what would be the result. Her *man* population was computed at about one hundred thousand when her constitution was formed; that would imply a population, women and children included, of six hundred thousand souls. True, all these women and children are not there yet; but that is their own business, and not ours. We look to the population which sustains a State—which constitutes political power—which pays taxes, gives votes, and fights battles. That is all we want. The rest is their want; and they will supply it, even if they have to repeat the drama of the Sabine women; for there is no law of gravitation and attraction—none ever discovered by Sir Isaac Newton—more universal in its application, or invincible in its force, than the law that brings the sexes together. Where the men are, the women will be, and that by strong arm, if gentle arm will not do; and the children also. They will all be there in due time. Six hundred thousand would be the census population now. No, not now—last fall. It is double now, for it rains men upon California, and all the year round; no dry season in that; and the census of 1860 will probably place her at the head of the populous States. She has population enough now for two members at least; and I will vote her the two that she has asked. The rule is to admit a State when she has population to give one representative. California has enough for several at this day.

4. Boundaries, that is to say, extent, is another objection. The State is said to be too large—that she cut and carved too largely for herself. That objection comes with an ill grace from us, who took in Texas, five years ago, three times as large as California, refusing my proposition to provide for her reduction, and refusing to propose reduction to her now. California is only the third part of Texas, and her extent is more apparent than real. Mountains and desert spots abstract greatly from her arable acres, and reduce them to the area of some of our large States—to a less magnitude than Missouri or Illinois. But California, as now made into a State, is conformable to natural boundaries, and could not, without violence to the features of nature, undergo division. She is a slip—a long and narrow one—between the sea and the mountains—between the Pacific Ocean and the Sierra Nevada: and that strip bound together in its centre by the union of its waters, and the concentration of its wealth and power on the Bay of San Francisco. That bay is the heart of California, and it cannot be split by a line through it. The Sacramento and San Joaquin Rivers, and their affluents, are the arteries and viens of that heart, and cannot be cut off from it. The slip is long, but it is narrow—only an average of one hundred and fifty miles, and the one-third of that consisting of the slope—the western slope—of the Great Sierra Nevada. What is east of the summit of that mountain, and out to the lower Colorado, as the line actually runs, is no addition to the strength or power of the State, and can only sustain some scattered and discontented people—to be discontented because they can have no political weight—and had better have been left out. All the real elements of her wealth and power are in the slip along the coast; and that is not divisible, either length-

wise or crosswise. It is too narrow for one of these operations; and could not suffer the other without being cut through the heart.

5. Interference of the President. It is objected that President Taylor interfered to induce the people of California to make this State government. Even if he had so interfered, it would not vitiate the constitution which they have formed, and which is the only thing that we have to judge. Even if true in fact, the objection would be of no application to her constitution. It would be, as Judge Chase said of the young lawyer's argument at Richmond, a *non sequitur*. But it is not founded in fact. President Taylor did not interfere. He was not in California to interfere personally; he could only have done it vicariously; and accordingly he was so charged. But the imputed agents deny the agency. And if they did not, his character ought to stand for an answer to a vague accusation. He has the character of an honest and a fair man; and that character should shield him from charges which have nothing but suspicion (and that of adversaries, intent upon defeating a measure which he has responsibly recommended) to rest upon. This objection, of Presidential interference, receives, then, the twofold answer, of being unfounded in fact, and a *non sequitur*, if it was not.

These are the named objections, strenuously urged at first, but more faintly now. In fact they seem to be abandoned, and a bargain offered for the admission of the State, with a threat of total defeat if the offer is not accepted. I allude to what was said by the Senator from Kentucky, who sits farthest over the way, (Mr. Clay,) on Friday last, and which then had the effect of starting me from my tranquil seat. He said, as I find it reported, and I think correctly, in the morning papers:

"He would say now to those who desired the speedy admission of California, the shortest and most expeditious way of attaining the desired object, was to include her admission in a bill giving governments to the territories."

"He made this statement, because he was impelled to do so from what had come to his knowledge. If her admission as a separate measure be urged, an opposition is created which may result in the defeat of any bill for her admission."

"Another reason for such a course was that we are all aiming at a compromise, and whatever would be productive of harmony and peace to the distracted country, should be done."

These are the points of that Senator's remarks which struck me so forcibly as to spring me from my seat at the time they were delivered, and upon which, after full time for deliberation, I feel bound to comment now. I had heard such things before, but did not attach any very great practical consequence to them; but when I see them reproduced by that Senator—a man of head and nerve—a head to measure, and a nerve to master any danger; and see the consequence which he attaches to them, I can no longer consider them as words without intents. Words are sometimes deeds, and these now become so; and as such they deserve grave consideration.

The Senator from Kentucky is in favor of the proposition to couple the admission of California with some other subject. I think he limited himself to the territorial governments, and recommends that conjunction as the most speedy way of accomplishing the admission of the young State. Sir, I say, honor first,—speed afterwards. I say, an honorable admission, no matter upon what time, in preference to a dishonorable one, no matter how speedy. The subjects proposed to be coupled with California under the motion from which we move to except her, are all the subjects impending in the Senate, and which grow out of the institution of slavery in the United States. If she goes to the intended grand committee of thirteen under this proposition, she goes there to be coupled in the consideration, and weighed in the balance, and mixed up in the concoction, and brought out in the product, of all these subjects moulded and amalgamated into one measure, or into a system of measures of mutual dependence, and called a compromise. I qualify this as dishonorable to California; and say that the latest admission, without it, is preferable to the speediest with it.

Speedy admission is doubtless desirable to California. Her position is anomalous, and disadvantageous. A young government without the means of living—without character to borrow—soliciting loans, and that in vain, at three per cent. a month. If she was a State of the Union, Wall street would relieve her of her bonds; but being as she is, without acknowledged legal existence, the capitalist eschews her; and this young State, rich in inherent resources, and sitting upon gold, is driven to the resource of State bonds, and a paper medium, which nobody will touch. All her operations are carried on at a disadvantage, for want of a fixed legal character. The sum of six hundred thousand dollars has been taken from the people, without law, and when they were without government, and ought to be paid back to the State—but being no State, *in the law*, her name cannot be put into a bill to pay it back. This six hundred thousand dollars refunded, would relieve the young State, and allow time for the development of her own resources. It is justly due, being illegally collected for duties when there was no law to warrant it, no correlative protection to justify taxation, and when the necessaries and comforts of life, were dear enough without being subjected to a military tariff. That money should be refunded, not to the merchant who paid it to the military chest, but to the people who restored it, with his *per centum* upon it, to the merchant; and who are the rightful party to have it back, and their State government their rightful agent to receive it.

Want of a branch mint; and before that could be got ready, an assayer to fix the value of gold in the lump, is another want of California, neglected because she is not a State. The laborer loses largely on all his diggings for want of this test of value. All the gold that is used in the country is used at a great loss—two dollars in the ounce, as I have been informed, equal to twelve per cent. on the amount dug. That is an enormous tax upon labor—such as no country ever beheld; yet it has to be endured until the State is admitted; and even after that, until Congress can legislate for her.

These are some of the reasons for the speedy admission of California; they are great, and many remain untold; but, great as they all are, dishonorable admission is worse than their still longer endurance.

The Senator from Kentucky made this statement because he was impelled to it by what had come to his knowledge, namely, that if her admission was urged as a separate measure, an opposition is created which may result in the defeat of the admission; and, thereupon, he declares his own determination not to urge the separate measure. Now, this strikes me exactly in the contrary sense. Threats are not good arguments with me, even when I may be going a little wrong, much less when I am going precisely right. It is right to consider the admission of California as a separate measure. It is right to do so upon parliamentary principles. It is right to do so upon the principle of fair legslation. It is right to do so upon uniform practice. All other new States have been so admitted; and it is an indignity to California to make her an exception. We have a right under the constitution, upon parliamentary law, and upon sixty years' practice, to give her case a separate consideration: and are we to be deterred from it by a threat? By a threat of creating an opposition which may keep the State out of the Union, if we persist in doing what we have a clear right to do? Are we to capitulate to that threat? Sir, let Washington answer that question. This is what he says of it:

"All obstructions to the execution of the laws, all combinations and associations, under whatever plausible character, with the real design to control, counteract, or awe the regular deliberation and action of the constituted authorities, are destructive of this fundamental principle (obedience to the established Government) and of fatal tendency. They serve to organize faction, to give it an artificial and extraordinary force, to put in the place of the delegated will of the nation, the will of a party, often a small, but artful and enterprising minority of the community: and, according to the alternate triumphs of different parties, to make the public administration the mirror of the ill-concerted and incongruous projects of faction, rather than the organ of consistent and wholesome plans, digested by common counsels, and modified by mutual interests."

After an impressive pause, Mr. B. continued: Sir, this threat comes under the ban of the Farewell Address of the Father of his Country. I have often read that address, and pondered every part of it, but never expected to have occasion to produce any part of it in the American Senate. That time has now come, and I produce this clause against combinations to defeat public measures, or to overawe the constituted authorities, as the part which the statements of the Senator from Kentucky extorts from me. He yields to that threat: I do not. On the contrary, I see additional reason in it for adhering to what I deem a right course in legislation. The threat is, indeed, a serious one; otherwise the Senator from Kentucky would not have felt himself impelled to communicate it to the Senate, and to present it as an argument to influence our deliberations. The nature of the opposition is not explained; but it is obliged to be a combination in some minority in Congress to control or awe the majority; and it may connect itself with that approaching convention at Nashville, of which the want of a clearly-defined object, and many deplorable indications, permit and justify the most unhappy suspicions. Connected or not, each in itself, and much more both together, fall under the ban of Washington's Farewell Address; and the spirit of the address, and the character of the man, forbid a surrender on the part of the constituted authorities to such combinations to control or overawe them. I cannot surrender. I cannot capitulate. No garrison, not even the weakest, will surrender until it sees the force of the enemy, and learns the terms of the capitulation. Some will not surrender at all—will resist at all hazards, and to the last extremity: and that I hold to be the duty of the Senate in the present crisis. Sir, it may be temperament, or it may be reason, that governs my resolve; but, be it which it may, I adhere to it with the tenacity of religious conviction, that it is our duty to resist this attempt to overawe us. It is among the first of such attempts, and we should resist at the beginning. All history tells us that confederacies are ruined by anarchy among the members, rather than by tyranny in the head; and if this threat connects itself with the Nashville Convention, we have the case of anarchy among the members, against which ten impressive numbers of The Federalist so prophetically warned us.

The Senator from Kentucky says, another reason for joining all these subjects together is, that we are all aiming at a compromise, and at the restoration of peace and harmony to a distracted country. Certainly these are desirable objects, and already near about accomplished. The Senator's own speech—his own frank, manly, noble speech delivered on this floor—and for which I thank him from the bottom of my heart—has done much to quiet the public mind—far more than any hugger-mugger work that he could do in a committee room, could ever accomplish. His own great speech, and the speeches of others—I name him because I am addressing myself to him—has already done the good work of quieting the country. The public press, also, has done its part; many papers have done nobly—too many to be enumerated; but there is one which, from its position, its presence here among us, its long standing and wide circulation, and its risk of losing friends in the very quarter of its greatest support, and the firm stand which it has taken in favor of the Union, single it out from all the rest, and entitle it to be named: *It is the National Intelligencer.*

The Senator from Kentucky speaks of compromise. He says we are all aiming at compromise, and seems to look to the committee of thirteen for the desirable work. Certainly the spirit of compromise is good; and where there is room for it, the thing itself is good. The compromises of the constitution are good; they are fundamental, permanent, and obligatory upon us all. But the little patch-work of statutory legislation, though dignified with the name of compromise, and celebrated when they are brought forth for all the virtues of the real genuine Brandreth pills, yet in the end, they turn out to be quack medicines, and often produce worse diseases then they are intended to cure. I have no faith in such patch-work. I can have none in any thing that the committee of thirteen shall produce, if it is raised. But I have faith in open, manly, responsible declarations and votes, in which every Senator speaks for himself and stands for a Senator, baring his heart, and letting the people see what is in it. There is hugger-mugger in that—no leading or being led. A Senator stands for a Senator. He counts one. He speaks for himself. He shows what is in him. And I fully believe that if this Senate, at this moment, was permitted to vote man by man, on each and every of the slavery questions which now disturb the country, it would kill agitation so dead, by showing there is foundation for it, that human power could not resuscitate it during this generation.

I am for open and independent voting upon every point, and against any concoction of a committee. I am against letting it be supposed, either at home or in Europe, that the preservation of this Union depends upon the consultation of political doctors over the sick body of the Republic. Its preservation is not there—nor here—in a committee room, nor in this chamber, nor in the hands of politicians; but in the hearts of the people, who are at home attending to their own affairs, and who will attend to the public affairs also when necessary; and who know that they themselves have enjoyed, and are enjoying, more blessings under THIS UNION than ever fell to the lot of man upon earth; and who are determined that their children shall have the same right to the blessings of civil and religious liberty, and the same equal chance for the wealth and honors of the country which they themselves have had. There is where the salvation of the Union lies, and not in the contrivances of politicians, or the incubations of committees.

Let us vote upon the measures before us, beginning with the admission of California. Let us vote her in. Let us vote, after four months' talk. The people who have gone there have done honor to the American name. Starting from a thousand points, and meeting as strangers far removed from law or government, they have conducted themselves with the order, decorum, and justice, which would have done honor to the oldest established and best regulated community. They have carried our institutions to the farthest verge of the land—to the coast of the Pacific, and lit it up with the lights of religion, liberty, and science—lights which will shine across the broad ocean, and illuminate the dark recesses of benighted Asia. They have completed the work of the Pilgrim Fathers. Would to God that those who landed on the Rock, and on the banks of the James River, more than two hundred years ago, and who crossed the stormy Atlantic in search of civil and religious liberty, and who did so much for both in their day and generation, could now see what has been done in our day! could look down from their celestial abodes, and see the spark which they struck from the flint, now blazing with a light which fixes the gaze of the world—see the mustard seed which they planted, now towering to the skies, and spreading its branches from the Atlantic to the Pacific. With what rapture would they welcome the Pilgrims of California into the family circle, while we, their descendants, sit here in angry debate, repulsing our brethren, calculating the value of the Union, and threatening to rend it asunder if California is admitted!

Mr. Clay. Mr. President, I will thank the Secretary to read the motion and the proposed amendment to the motion.

The resolutions, together with the amendment proposed to them, were then read.

Mr. Clay. Mr. President, although far from being well, suffering still under the common malady of the times—the influenza I suppose—I feel myself called upon to make some reply to a portion of the arguments which we have just heard from the Senator from Missouri. Sir, I have to express an unfeigned regret that it is not my fortune to concur in opinion with that Senator, in reference to the mode of accomplishing a common object which we both have very much at heart. My respect for the ability, and my deference to the long service and great experience of that Senator, and my knowledge of the deep interest which he takes, and in which I most heartily share, in the admission of this new State as soon as practicable, render it extremely unpleasant, and as I think unfortunate, that we should differ as to the means of accomplishing a common object.

Mr. President, I stated on Friday last, and I have on various occasions stated, that, for one, I was ready to vote for the admission of California separately, by itself, and unconnected with any other measures, or in conjunction with other measures. And I stated on that occasion to the Senate, and to the Senator from Missouri, that I believed, as I yet believe, that the most speedy mode of accomplishing the object which both he and I have in view, is by combining some of these measures in connection with California, and by this combined bill presenting subjects, which I shall presently show are fairly connected in their nature, to the consideration of Congress at one and the same time. The whole question between the Senator from Missouri and myself, is which is the best mode of accomplishing the object. I say, connect the several measures together: he says no; take California separately and alone. Sir, I should be glad if the experiment could be made without injury to the public, that the two modes should be tested by experience, and it would then be ascertained whether the Senator from Missouri or myself was correct. He has made an allusion to a remark of mine on Friday last, with reference to the difficulties that may arise on the passage of a bill alone for the admission of California, and he has inquired what I had in contemplation at the time I made that remark. Mr. President, I had various matters in contemplation at that time, and one was this. About California we all know there is no difficulty as to her admission, either separately or conjointly with other measures: We all know perfectly well that there are large majorities in both Houses in favor of the admission of California. We know at the same time, that there are great difficulties with reference to the passage of territorial governments unconnected with the Wilmot proviso. We know that one portion of Congress desire very much the admission of California, when many members comprising that portion are opposed—some to the establishment of any governments at all for the territories, and many of them to the establishment of such governments without the introduction of the proviso. Thus, whilst that party, anxious for the accomplishment of its own views, and the satisfaction of its own wants, are pressing on for the passage of a bill for the separate admission of California, they are holding back in reference to other subjects equally important in the great object which I trust animates the breasts of all—the great object of quiet and pacific action to the country. And, besides, there are those who desire the establishment of governments for the territories without the proviso, but who are willing to take the admission of California in combination with governments for the territories without the proviso. I did allude to other considerations, not likely to happen in this House, but which have happened, and may again happen, in the other house of Congress; I did allude to what we heard said, not in approbation—far from it—but with most decided disapprobation of it on my part. I did hear—as we know has occurred once at least on one day during this session—that if it was attempted to force on the minority of that House, a measure which is unacceptable to it, and abhorrent to its feelings, without its association with other objects in view, that minority would resort, in resistance of it, not, I trust, to acts of violence, but to those parliamentary rules and modes of proceeding of which we have had before instances in this country, and which I myself witnessed forty years ago, in a most remarkable degree, in the House of Representatives, and which we know some consider lawful at any time to be employed. For myself, I differ perhaps from most members of this body, or of any deliberative body, on this subject. I am for the trial of mind against mind, of argument against argument, of reason against reason, and when, after such employment of our intellectual faculties, I find myself in the minority, I am for submitting to the act of the majority. I am not for resorting to adjournments, calls for the yeas and nays, and other dilatory proceedings, in order to delay that which, if the constitution has full and fair operation, must inevitably take place. There is great loss of sleep, with great physical discomfort, in the one mode of proceeding, without any in the other. But whilst this is my judgment of what is proper, in deliberative bodies, other gentlemen entertain different opinions. They think it fair to employ all the parliamentary means that are vested in them by the constitution, or by the rules which regulate the body to which they belong, to defeat, impede, or delay to any extent, the passage of the measure which they consider odious. I repeat, sir, I do not justify such a course; but we must take man as he is, with all his weaknesses and infirmities, and we can never expect to make him as we could wish him to be.

Now, the Senator from Missouri has chosen to characterize this measure with unfairness of proceeding. Sir, if I were disposed to retort, which I am far from doing, I could say that there had been some unfairness in the argument of the Senator from Missouri, when he endeavored to show that the pending proposition was to combine California, the territorial governments for the two proposed territories, the fixation of the line of Texas, the fugitive slave bill, the bill for abolishing the slave-trade in this District, abolition, and God Almighty knows how many other subjects, which his imagination depicted as contemplated to be introduced into our omnibus bill, and to be considered in that way. The Senator from Missouri knows perfectly well that no such purpose existed, and he has no right to infer any purpose of the kind. No longer ago than Friday last, when I misunderstood my colleague, and supposed that his object was to combine this fugitive slave bill with these measures, he rose at once and disclaimed any such intention. Sir, nobody has gone further in this proposed combination of subjects, than the admission of California, the establishment of territorial governments, and —doubting its propriety, as I did on Friday, not being absolutely determined in my own mind—adding to these two measures the establishment of a suitable boundary for Texas, with the offer of an equivalent for the surrender of any title which she might be supposed to have in the territory so surrendered. Let us look, whilst on this subject of Texas, to another part of the Senator's argument, and I put it to the candor of the Senator to admit how unfair, how improper, at least, it is to suppose that, by such a combination as I have indicated, the result would be to give Texas a veto on California? Who imagines that? You pass a bill with the separate section for the admission of California, other sections in the same bill establishing governments in the two Territories, and other sections in relation to the proposition to Texas for the settlement of her boundary, making her certain offers, and this latter proposition dependent on the consent which Texas might, or might not give. But suppose Texas does not give her consent, does anybody say that the other parts of the bill would become dead, or nugatory? Each portion of the bill is of force and effect according to the object in view, and each might stand, although the other portion of the bill might be rendered null, in consequence of the non-concurrence of Texas in any other power.

It has been said that it is wrong to make those who might be in favor of the admission of California, and against the establishment of territorial governments, or *vice versa*, vote on such a combination—that it would be wrong to combine them in one bill, because they would have to vote against both, not liking a portion of the bill, or for both, still disliking a portion of the bill. And we are told that what the wisdom of California suggested in her constitution—that is to say, the keeping of subjects separate and distinct—is thereby to be disregarded. Now there is very little of practicability in this idea of a total separation of subjects. Suppose you have the California bill alone before you; is that a single idea? There is first the admission of the State, and secondly the proper boundaries of the State. Now there may be Senators, if you had this single bill before you, who would say, we are willing to admit a State, to be carved out of this territory, but we are against the boundaries proposed; and why not separate it into two bills, one for the admission of the State, and the other for the fixation of its limits. Why, thus you might go on, cutting subjects up into as many parts as they are capable of being divided into, and say that each one of them shall contain a single, and only a single, idea. Take the tariff bill. It contains five hundred items usually, and we have never passed a tariff bill, or given a vote upon it, without some parts of it being objectionable to some, or that did not contain items for which some man voted against his judgment, but which he did vote for, because of other items in the same bill. And so with the course we propose. If we combine together a bill for the admission of California, and for governments for the territories, in the first place those who opposed the combination may oppose it. If it is introduced already in the bill, it may be proposed to strike out what relates to the territories; or if it is proposed that they shall be added to the bill for the admission of California, they can move amendments, call for the yeas and nays, and thus show their opposition to the association of the measures together. But suppose the majority overrules them. Suppose there is a majority in favor of the association of the measures, and then the final question is put: Will you vote for, or against the bill? And what are you to do in a case of that kind? Exactly what we would do in all human concerns. There is bad and good mixed together. You may vote against it if you please in toto, because of the bad there is in it, or you may vote for it, because you approve of the greater amount of good there is in it. The question for the time is, whether there is more of the good than of the bad in the bill; and if the good outweighs the bad, that will be a further consideration for voting for the whole measure.

But, sir, my object now is to show that there is a perfect connection between the subjects proposed to be united, and I refer not to what the Senator from Missouri has charged, but to the State of California, territorial governments for the territories, and at most the fixation of the boundary of Texas. Sir, are these subjects connected together, or are they not? Let us look at facts and at history. Let us appeal to the very facts which the Senator from Missouri himself insists ought to be so influential on our judgment. Well, sir, California, New Mexico, and Utah, all were component parts of the Mexican Republic, and they were ceded together, in association, to the Republic of the United States. They were of a like grade of government in Mexico. All of them were provinces; none of them were States under the Mexican Republic. They came here together, in association, under the treaty by which we acquired them. They came here at the last session together, all imploring the establishment of territorial governments within their respective limits. It was not done. Why was it not done? The South reproaches the North for not doing it by saying, you insisted upon the introduction of the Wilmot proviso. The North reproaches the South by saying, you are responsible for it by opposing the Wilmot proviso.

Mr. President, both parties were wrong, and neither was wrong. They were wrong in the aggregate, but not wrong separately. They were wrong in the aggregate, because Congress failed to devise and establish governments, which it was called upon to do by all the solemn obligations of treaty stipulations, and all the solemn duties whch resulted from the fact of the acquisition of those territories by this country. They were not wrong separately, because, you who contended for the proviso, did so, I have no doubt, honestly; and you who opposed the proviso, did so, I have no doubt, honestly. It was a case, therefore, of irreconcilable difference of opinion between two large parties in Congress; and their convictions, their consciences, respectively restrained them from yielding the one to the views of the other. No reproaches, therefore, I think, can justly be made by one party upon the other. It was a subject of deep and profound regret that proper governments were not then devised, but it was attributable solely to those unhappy divisions which sometimes exist in deliberative bodies, and prevent legislation. But, sir, these territories were all together—Utah, California, and New Mexico. One short year ago they were all territories; and allow me to say, however much it may be emphasized, that California is no State yet, and she can be no State until she has the seal and sanction of the paramount authority which pervades all this country. It is in the power of Congress, if it chooses to exercise the right, to put down the present State government which has been established there, and establish a territorial government there. I am not disposed to charge on a community the misconduct or peculiar opinions of any individual of that community, but I must say what I have been constrained to feel, that I am pained to see with what contumacy, with what disregard of the allegiance due from the States, old and new, they sometimes treat the parental and paramount authority. And I was lately—I will not say provoked, for the annoyance was too slight—somewhat grieved at seeing some letter-writers from California talking already of breaking off from this Union, and setting up for themselves. They will venture on no such hazardous experiment as that. If they do, I venture to say the common authority of the Union will recall them to obedience and a sense of their duty very quickly. But, sir, these three territories, one of which is now called a State, were component parts of Mexico, and they are now component parts of the United States; and allow me to say, in reference to that part of the argument of the Senator from Missouri which speaks of the wretched condition of California at this moment, with her mines of boundless extent of gold—that desperate condition, that anarchy with which she is threatened, that want of law which exists, that danger of breaking into pieces (for such I believe was the remark of the honorable Senator) if there is not some legislation here—do not all these considerations, every one of them, apply with equal force, and ought they not to receive equal application, to the territories of Utah and New Mexico? Why, in regard to New Mexico especially, she is not only at present without any government, except some patched-up military form of government, but she is at this moment threatened with civil war with her neighbor Texas, and if I were to single out of these three Territories, that in regard to which it was the most imperative duty of Congress at once to legislate, I would say it was New Mexico, and the adjustment of the boundary between her and Texas. Every consideration derived from anarchy, confusion, the want of government, the want of law, the danger from disorder which the Senator has arrayed in reference to California, applies with full force and vigor to New Mexico. Well, how does this matter stand? The three sisters came here at the last session of Congress; New Mexico the eldest, California next, and Utah the youngest. They came here all soliciting territorial governments. Attempts were made to give them all territorial governments, but they failed. In the mean time, Miss California has made a runaway match of it—and she has not only done that, but she has taken as large a portion of the common patrimony of the whole as she pleases. She comes here now with her two sisters—the one older and the other younger—and cocks up her nose, and asks if you will associate her with those two girls, [laughter.] Mr. President, I might laugh, if I did not feel the profoundest respect toward California; but, as was asked, on another memorable occasion, "Ye gods, on what meat has our Cæsar fed, that he has grown so great?" I believe the meat of California would seem to be gold; for although it appears to abound in all parts of the country, yet it is said that they cannot carry on the government without some loan. I have seen some documents of late from the legislature of California, and I find in one of them a very sensible report to one branch of the legislature, in which it is proposed to levy a poll tax of five dollars, which it is said will collect an ample revenue by July next for all the purposes of the government. But is there not, in the nature of the subject—which is the establishment of governments for our recent acquisitions—is there not in the fact of their community of existence heretofore, and in the community of their present existence—is there not in the fact that we propose government for the one, matured, it is true, in the form of a State government, and for the others, governments also adapted to their peculiar condition, ample reason why they should be combined? And what is there, I ask, in the nature of the case, that offends the dignity of California, or renders it less to her honor to be associated hereafter, where she has always been associated heretofore, with Utah and New Mexico?

But, sir, the honorable Senator from Missouri has endeavored to place himself behind precedent, and he asserted, that in every instance of the admission of a new State, the question of admission has stood by itself, unconnected with any measure whatever. Now, it is very remarkable that that honorable Senator did not recollect the case of the admission of the very State of which he is such an able and efficient Senator. Why, sir, that State was not admitted alone. Other subjects were connected with the act by which she was admitted. Here it is:

"An act to authorize the people of the Missouri Territory to form a constitutional and State government, and for the admission of such State into the Union, upon an equal footing with the original

States, and to prohibit slavery in certain territories."

And the eighth section of the bill provides expressly, not merely for the establishment of a temporary territorial government, but a permanent, perpetual, fundamental law in reference to those other territories:

"That in all the territory ceded by France to the United States, under the name of Louisiana, lying north of 36° 30′ north latitude, not included within the State contemplated by this act, slavery and involuntary servitude, otherwise than as a punishment for crime, whereof the parties shall be duly convicted, shall be, and is hereby, forever prohibited."

What did we do in the case of Louisiana? In 1805 two territorial governments were established—one for the territory of Orleans, and the other for the territory of Louisiana; the latter one embracing the very State to which this provision in reference to slavery was applied. But if I were to open the records of this body, what would they disclose? Not a territory and a State combined, but two States, as far separated from each other as possible, were combined by the Senate of the United States in the same bill, and by a perseverance almost unexampled in the history of legislation, each House, having disagreed with the other—vote after vote was taken without any practical result. But they finally saw land, and the question was settled by the Senate yielding to the separation of the two States, Maine and Missouri, in consideration of the introduction of the free clause to which I have referred. But, if there were no precedent in the case, I might very properly say that the peculiar situation of affairs would supply a precedent. There is, I admit, no case exactly in all points like that of California, and the two territories adjacent to it, which are seeking the establishment of territorial governments.

In most of the cases to which the honorable Senator has referred, Vermont, Kentucky, Tennessee, and others, there was but one single Territory to be admitted, and that was clearly defined; and its muniments ascertained by the parent States. But here we have the subject before us, and I put it to you, sir, and to every member of this body, if there is not a connection, and fitness, and propriety, and sympathy, in the subjects themselves, that not only warrant, but demand that you should connect them together.

But, sir, see the enormity of this proposition. I hope it will be distinctly understood that I am equally anxious with the honorable Senator from Missouri for the admission of California. I think her admission has been improperly delayed; it has been unavoidably delayed, by causes which we all know and understand. But not only does the honorable Senator require that this elder sister, who treats with so much contempt the other poor members of her family—not only does he require that her superior honor and dignity shall be recognized, but he exacts from us that she shall be kept separate and alone; that she shall not be contaminated by any sort of connection with her sisters, lest she might contract some contagious and fatal disease. The honorable Senator is not satisfied that she should stand alone, but she must lead off in the dance; she must precede all the others. He insists that it will be treating her with indignity, with contempt, if you take up the territorial bills in the first instance, and act upon them before you act upon the question of the admission of California.

Mr. President, I hope I am doing a less imprudent thing in the attempt I am making to keep these subjects together, than I am doing in regard to my personal condition in occupying so much of your time. If I had supposed otherwise, I should not have said a word. But, sir, I hope I have said enough to show, first, that California would be more speedily admitted by being connected with the territories in a common bill than if it should stand separated from them: secondly, that there is no incongruity in the association of the subject; and, thirdly, that according to precedents and all the analogies to be drawn from precedents, not exactly like, but somewhat similar to, the present case, there is no impediment in the way of the course which I have proposed. And if am right in this view, I am sure no difficulty need be apprehended. Every member of this body is desirous of restoring once more peace, harmony, and fraternal affection to this distracted people. Various projects have been suggested to accomplish that patriotic object. Amongst them a proposition has been made by the Senator from Mississippi, to refer all the subjects to one committee, to be appointed by the Senate, with power to report as that committee may, upon consideration, deem it best, either a separate or a conjoint measure. The purpose of the committee is to settle, if they can, the causes of difference which exist in the country by some proposition of compromise. There are, no doubt, many who are very wise in their own estimation, who will reject all propositions of compromies, but that is no reason why a compromise should not be attempted to be made. I go for honorable compromise whenever it can be made. Life itself is but a compromise between death and life, the struggle continuing throughout our whole existence, until the Great Destroyer finally triumphs. All legislation, all government, all society, is formed upon the principle of mutual concession, politeness, comity, courtesy; upon these, every thing is based. I bow to you to-day because you bow to me. You are respectful to me because I am respectful to you. Compromise is peculiarly appropriate among the members of a republic, as of one common family. Compromises have this recommendation, that if you concede any thing, you have something conceded to you in return. Treaties are compromises made with foreign powers contrary to what is done in a case like this. Here, if you concede any thing, it is to your own brethren, to your own family. Let him who elevates himself above humanity, above its weaknesses, its infirmities, its wants, its necessities, say, if he pleases, I never will compromise, but let no one who is not above the frailties of our common nature disdain compromises.

Well, what does the honorable Senator from Mississippi propose? Here is a proposition to refer all the subjects to a committee with a view to a compromise. The honorable Senator from Missouri rises up and says no; here is one subject that you must not refer to the committee; another Senator may rise up and say, here is another subject that you must not refer; and a third may rise up and say, here is a third subject that you must not refer to the committee. This proposition establishes a committee the object of which is to compromise all the differences that arise out of the subject of slavery. Constitute your committee for such a purpose, and then take from them the consideration of one branch of the subject. Would this be right, sir? Can you not trust your committee? Whatever is done by the committee has to be brought before the Senate for its consideration, for confirmation or rejection at the pleasure of the Senate. If they report an improper bill, either as a separate measure, or a connected measure, you have the controlling power. Will you not allow the subject to be considered, examined, determined upon by the committee, according to the best judgment of those to whom you confide the great and responsible duty? Sir, I am done; I ought not to have said so much, and I beg pardon of the Senate for occupying so much of their time.

Mr. BENTON. I rise to set the honorable Senator from Kentucky right in his recollection about Missouri. I remember it well, and so ought he, for he had a good deal to do with her admission, for which Missouri was very thankful to him. She was admitted by joint resolution, and the act from which the Senator has read was merely a law authorizing the holding of a convention *pro forma;* that is all.

Now, if I had been answering the speech of the honorable Senator from Kentucky, it might have been unjust to him to have treated him as proposing that all subjects connected with slavery should be placed in the hands of the committee; for, in the brief remarks that he made the other day, I believe he only maintained that the territorial governments should be connected with the question of the admission of California. But I was not answering him. I was speaking to the motion which was then depending, and which motion is broad enough to cover every thing which I enumerated; so broad that it goes far beyond what the Senator proposed on Friday last, when he addressed the Senate, and I shall therefore claim his vote against the motion upon his own speech. He is only in favor of coupling California with the territories. The motion on which we shall have to vote, and on which the Senator from Kentucky must cast his vote, includes every thing connected with the subject of slavery; and of those things connected with it which are not enumerated, there are four over which I would give no committee jurisdiction, either by express reference or by implied reference. I would give no committee jurisdiction over the subject of the abolition of slavery in the District of Columbia; I would give no committee jurisdiction over the abolition of slavery in the forts, arsenals, and dockyards of the United States; I would give no committee jurisdiction over the slave-trade between the States; and I would give no committee jurisdiction over the abolition of slavery in the States of this Union. These are four subjects which disturb the country—and which would be necessarily comprehended on the motion—over which I would give no committee jurisdiction, and, on account of which, I would vote against the whole motion, even if I were in favor of a portion; and I think now I can claim the vote of the honorable Senator from Kentucky himself against it.

Mr. FOOTE. I ask for the reading of the motion, and I have then a single remark to make in reference to it.

The Secretary read Mr. FOOTE's motion, as follows:

"*Resolved*, That the resolutions [submitted by Mr. BELL] be referred to a select committee of thirteen, with instructions to exert themselves for the purpose of maturing a scheme of compromise for the adjustment of all pending questions growing out of the institution of slavery, with power to report by bill or otherwise."

Mr. FOOTE. The motion simply proposes, as has been argued so successfully this morning by the honorable Senator from Kentucky, that this committee shall have power to examine all questions growing out of the institution of slavery, and mature, if they can, a general scheme of adjustment and compromise; with this addition, simply, that they are authorized to report by bill or otherwise—either by bill or bills, as may to them seem expedient. There is no design, then, to connect necessarily and inevitably in one bill the various subjects involved in the inquiry. That is all I have to say.

Mr. DOUGLAS. I rise for the purpose of making one remark, and then of making the motion of which I gave notice this morning, which is, to lay this resolution on the table, and proceed to the consideration of the bill for the admission of California into the Union as a State. My object in making this motion is not necessarily to make it a test question, as to whether any thing else shall be connected with the question of the admission of California or not, but to get a vote upon something practical, in order that we may see what is likely to be the result. If it be the desire of the Senate to unite the California bill with the territorial bills, it can be done by the Senate, upon a motion to that effect. Let the Senate declare, one way or the other, its determination upon that point. Any Senator who desires to have them included in the same bill, can move the territorial bills as amendments to the California bill. There is a bill now pending for the admission of California as a State, and there are bills pending for establishing territorial governments in New Mexico and Deseret. And there is a fugitive slave bill now pending. I can see no reason for appointing a committee to take these bills into their consideration, and bring them in again, and report them back to the Senate. If it be the sense of the Senate to unite them, it can be done without sending them to a committee. I move that the resolution lie upon the table, and that the Senate proceed to the consideration of the bill for the admission of California.

Mr. Cass. Will the honorable Senator withdraw his motion for a moment?

Mr. Douglas. Certainly, if the honorable Senator will renew it.

Mr. Cass. I have a very few observations to make before the vote is taken upon this question, as it may be considered a test question, in explanation of my own views in relation to it. I wish to say nothing that has been already so well said by others; but before I vote, I desire to state to the Senate how the matter strikes my mind as to the condition in which the country is at present placed. What does it grow out of? We have been here four or five months, and have done practically nothing at all. We have been going on from worse to worse, and how is this deplorable condition to be remedied? So long as every member stands upon the ground which he occupied at first, with no disposition to compromise, God alone knows where the question is to end; for I agree with every word that the honorable Senator from Kentucky has said. Here is a proposition to refer the whole matter to a committee. An extended debate has taken place upon the question, and it is not my purpose to extend that discussion. A committee is proposed to be raised to consider this matter, and why should we not accede to the proposition, and refer all the subjects to them for consideration? You will have one chance the more for arriving at a favorable termination, without any danger of injury being done. Then why not adopt the proposition? In the collision of minds among the thirteen men who are to compose the committee, some practical plan of adjustment may be struck out. Why conjure up evils that do not exist? Why talk of indignity to California by associating the question of her admission with other propositions? What is the objection? Why, it is presupposed that the committee will bring in a bill embracing all these subjects, and that we should necessarily be compelled to vote upon them all conjointly. Who knows that? That is one of the subjects for the committee to consider. It is for them to determine whether they will report one bill containing the various subjects, or whether they will report separate bills. This is one of the very subjects for their consideration, and if they do report a general bill, it will still be under our control. If the committee report a bill embracing all the topics, and a majority of the Senate think that that course is inexpedient, and that it is essential that each should be considered separately, the whole matter will be in our control just as well then as now, and it will be time enough to consider that question when the committee shall have reported. If that is the only practical objection, it amounts to nothing. As to the admission of California, it is a foregone fact. I suppose you will not be able to find in either House a member who will declare that California, in his opinion, will not be admitted. There are those who object to it, and, of those who favor it, there are some who urge that the proposition for her admission should be considered by itself, and some others who are for connecting that proposition with other topics. But I believe you will not find in either House a member who does not believe that California will be admitted, unless prevented by a state of feeling which I trust will not be exhibited. I concur in what has been so well said by the distinguished Senator from Kentucky. I have no doubt that the propositions, if considered simultaneously—I do not say necessarily in the same bill—would pass through both Houses more readily than if each were brought forward by itself. In the latter case the admission of California might encounter opposition the nature of which has been distinctly announced, and which can alone render that important measure doubtful. I am not afraid to refer any or all of the topics to the committee, for the best reason in the world, because I believe the committee can have no disposition to do wrong, and because the measure will not commit any member of this body to any step that may be taken by the committee, and it is making one experiment more to restore harmony to this distracted country. After the committee reports, we shall be just as free to act as we are now; not at all bound by any thing they may do. One would suppose, to listen to the objections we have heard, that the report of a committee would carry some binding force to which we must submit. I repeat, it is an experiment which, if successful, may produce incalculable benefits, and if unsuccessful, places us in no worse position than we are now.

Mr. Hale. I concur entirely with the honorable Senator from Massachusetts, that the people of California have an undoubted right to insert such prohibition in their constitution. This being clearly their right, then, I am opposed to any scheme of compromise that can be offered in relation to California. I am opposed to compromising a clear and undoubted right.

The question was taken on the motion to postpone, and it was agreed to.

And then, on motion, the Senate adjourned.

THURSDAY, April 11.

Mr. Bell's Resolutions.

Mr. FOOTE. I would ask if the hour has not arrived for the consideration of the special order?

The VICE PRESIDENT. The hour has arrived.

Mr. FOOTE. I suppose that the special order was my motion of the other day; if it be not, I am certainly anxious to have the motion taken up and acted upon.

The VICE PRESIDENT. The chair is informed that the first business in order will be the resolutions submitted by the Senator from Kentucky. If it be not moved, the next business in order will be the California message. If that be not moved, the next business in order will be the resolutions of the Senator from Tennessee, and the motion of the Senator from Mississippi.

Mr. DOUGLAS. In regard to the California message, unless there is some Senator who is desirous to speak upon it, it may as well be laid on the table. The same question comes up on the bill reported for the admission of the State.

Mr. UPHAM. I believe I had the floor on this subject some ten or fifteen days ago, but I have been confined to my room since then, and am not able to-day to speak on the subject. I move that it be passed over.

The VICE PRESIDENT. The other subjects will be considered as having been passed over, and the next business in order is the resolution of the Senator from Tennessee, and the motion of the Senator from Mississippi in reference thereto.

Mr. FOOTE. I move that subject be now considered.

The motion was agreed to.

Mr. BENTON. Mr. President, I gave, as one of the reasons why the Senate should mix up nothing with this bill for the admission of California, the fact, that in the sixty years of legislation on the subject, and in the admission of seventeen States, there has been no example of mixing up any other matter with the admission of a State, but that every one has been admitted by itself, or, at all events, in company with another, so that the circumstances were equal. It was supposed that there was some error in that statement of mine, and I deem it a very material thing, as it is proposed that we should now commence with doing by a new State what is without precedent in the annals of legislation, and which many feel to be a deep indignity to that State, that I shall, by reference to the cases of admission of new States, show that such a thing has never been done before.

The first of the States which was admitted was Vermont. She was admitted by the act of the 1st of February, 1791, and nothing could be more brief and simple than that act of admission. It is entitled "An act for the admission of the State of Vermont into the Union"—a title which, of itself, excludes the idea of any thing being mixed up with it. It says:

"The State of Vermont having petitioned the Congress to be admitted a member of the United States, be it enacted by the Senate and House of Representatives of the United States of America in Congress assembled, and it is hereby enacted and declared, that on the fourth day of March, one thousand seven hundred and ninety-one, the said State, by the name and style of 'the State of Vermont,' shall be received and admitted into this Union as a new and entire member of the United States of America," approved 18th February, 1791. (1 *Stat. at Large*, *p.* 191.)

That is the act, sir, for the admission of the first State, and its simplicity and unity is worthy of all praise.

The next was the act for the admission of Kentucky, of the 4th of February, 1791. It consents to the formation of the new State, and provides that, "on the 1st day of June, 1792," it "shall be received and admitted into this Union as a new and entire member of the United States of America." The act embraces no other subject. (See 1 *Stat. at Large*, page 189.)

Then comes Tennessee. She was admitted by the act of June 1, 1796. The act is in the briefest possible form, and contains no other subject whatever. (See 1 *Stat. at Large*, page 491.)

Then comes Ohio. The act was to authorize the formation of a constitution and State government, "and for the admisson of such State into the Union." In this case, the acts authorizing the people to form a constitution and providing for the admission of the State into the Union, were one and the same. The admission was to take effect upon their complying with the requirements set forth, and it was therefore a complete act, and contained nothing but what related to the admission of the State. Afterward there was an act passed for the due execution of the laws of the United States within the State of Ohio, and that act declares the State to have become one of the States of this Union. (See 2 *Statutes at Large*, page 201.) Neither of these acts embraces any subject but what relates to Ohio, and the making of the laws of the United States obligatory upon her.

Then comes Louisiana. She was admitted on the 8th of April, 1812. That act includes nothing that does not relate to that State. (See 2 *Stat. at Large*, page 701.) It has been supposed that it did, but on examination of it, it will be found that it contains nothing but what relates to the admission of the State, and to perfect that admission by giving force to the laws of the United States within the State. The first section is, that Louisiana be admitted into the Union as an independent State, and provides for her admission. The next section is to give effect to it, by allowing her one Representative in the House of Representatives.

The next is, that the laws of the United States shall be enforced there, and then judicial circuits and some officers are provided for. There is nothing in it but what provides for perfecting the admission, and what would have been contained in an act by itself, if it had not been joined to the act of admission. In this particular there is a little diversity of action. On some occasions, the act which admits a State provides for the extension of the laws of the United States to the State, but in a majority of cases it is all reserved, and put in an act by itself, and the admission stands alone.

Indiana was admitted by joint resolution of the 11th December, 1816. (See *Stat. at Large*, p. 399.) The resolution is entirely clear of any other matter than the mere admission.

Mississippi was admitted by joint resolution of 10th December, 1817, and it contains nothing besides the simple admission. (3 *Stat. at Large*, p. 472.)

Illinois was admitted by the joint resolution of 3d December, 1818. It contains nothing but the simple admission. (3 *Stat. at Large*, p. 436.)

Alabama was admitted by joint resolution of 14th December, 1819. It contains nothing but the admission. (3 *Stat. at Large*.)

Maine was admitted by the act of 3d March, 1820. It is a naked admission—nothing more. (3 *Stat. at Large*, p. 544.)

Missouri was admitted by joint resolution of March 2, 1821. It contains nothing but admission, and a condition for the State to perform. (3 *Stat. at Large*, p. 645.)

This is the case in which the Senator from Kentucky (Mr. Clay) had supposed something else was mixed up with the act of admission; but it is clear he confounded the act which authorized the meeting of the convention to form a State constitution, with the joint resolution for the admission of the State itself. The joint resolution was posterior to that time; it was passed the year after; and for that joint resolution the State of Missouri, and the whole Union, were indebted to the Senator from Kentucky himself. It is, that the State should comply with certain conditions, and upon a certified copy of the constitution being filed in the Department of State, the President should by proclamation declare the admisson complete, and the State to be in the Union; all of which was done, and in fact occasioned very little delay, for the General Assembly of Missouri met very soon after the adjournment of Congress, and passed an act of compliance, which was sent to the President, and he, by proclamation, declared the State in the Union.

Michigan was admitted by the act of the 22d January, 1837, and it is a naked admission.

Iowa and Florida were admitted by the same act on the 3d March, 1845. The act contains nothing that does not relate to those States. I have the acts here, and have looked over them, and that is the only instance in which two States were coupled together in the same bill at the time of their admission. They were put together, it is true, but they were subjects of equal dignity, and there was nothing in the act which related to any thing upon earth but themselves and the extension of the laws of the United States. Here is the only exception up to that time, and that exception has been overruled before, as I will show. Before that time, I say, it was overruled, since it was before that Arkansas and Michigan were admitted. They were before this body at the same time. Their constitutions were referred to the several committees at the same time, and they were reported upon in separate bills. They were conducted through this chamber, *pari passu*, but they were not put in the same bill. It was held to be the right of each State to have a separate consideration, and, that being pressed, there was no junction at all—they passed separately.

Arkansas was admitted by the act of the 26th of January, 1837. It was a naked admission. (See *Stat. at Large*, p. 144.)

Texas was admitted by joint resolution on the 1st of March, 1845, and Wisconsin was admitted by the act of 3d March, 1847. The act for the admission of Texas relates only to what concerns the State, as does the act admitting Wisconsin.

Now, the admission of a new State into the Union is a mere question of constitutional authority. Congress has written authority for the admission of States, and in some cases the duty becomes obligatory upon Congress to admit a new State. That is the case in every instance in which the Government of the United States is under obligation or compact to admit a new State when it shall fulfil certain conditions. That is the case with respect to California. By our treaty with Mexico, new States are to be admitted from the acquired territory as soon as it can be done consistent with the principles of the constitution. That is the treaty, sir.

So we have our constitutional authority and a treaty obligation upon us for acting on the subject. California has fulfilled every requirement which is necessary to entitle her to the rank of a State, and has a population far beyond what has been required from any other new State; for while it is certain that there was from one hundred to one hundred and fifty thousand men there at the time her constitution was formed, which would imply what we call a census population of six or seven hundred thousand souls, yet in all cases of admission heretofore, ten or twelve thousand men, resulting in a population of sixty or seventy thousand souls, according to the census account, was deemed sufficient.

California then has the constitution in her hands, which gives the Senate of the United States undisputed constitutional authority to admit her. She has the treaty with Mexico in her hands, which makes it obligatory on the Congress of the United States to admit her when she presents herself under the circumstances of that treaty. She has done so. Here, then, is the case of a State—the constitution in one hand, and the treaty with Mexico in the other, and sixty years of the uniform practice of the Government in such cases in her favor. Constitution, treaty, and sixty years' practice, with one single deviation, all in her favor. And now, sir, it is proposed that she shall be made an exception, and subjected to the indignity of being mixed up with a subject of which she has washed her hands—and washed them too, sir, for the precise, deliberate purpose of preventing her admission from being made dependent upon or mixed up with any such subjects. Sir, this is what she has done, and now to undertake to mix her up with all these subjects—the subjects connected with slavery in the United States—is, in my opinion, wrong to her, and an indignity. Sir, it is an indignity to her, and such an indignity as goes to rebuke her, and to tell her that she has done what she ought not to do, in undertaking to clear herself of a subject which she knew was an annoying and distracting one in the United States, and with which she therefore wanted nothing to do. Now, to mix her up with these subjects, after she has, in the most solemn manner in her constitution, cleared herself from them, and for the express purpose of having free admission here, is a great indignity to her.

Mr. Dickinson. If this debate is to proceed further now, I shall move to lay the subject on the table, for the purpose of taking up the appropriation bill. If the vote is to be taken, however, I will make no such motion.

Mr. Clay. I trust the Senator will permit me to say a word or two. I pledge myself not to occupy more than five minutes of time.

Mr. Dickinson. Certainly.

Mr. Clay. Mr. President, in reference to the cases referred to by the Senator from Missouri, of the admission of States heretofore, I can only remark, that each of those cases depended upon a particular state of circumstances existing at the time of its admission. With regard to Missouri, it was the only State in which there was that species of agitation and division prevailing in this country which unfortunately exists now; and in that case only, of the States admitted into the Union, was a course somewhat similar to that now proposed adopted. And what was that course? In the act which was passed by Congress for the admission of Missouri into the Union—that is to say, authorizing her to form a State constitution and government for herself, and to come here for admission—in that very act was inserted a clause on the subject of slavery north and south of the line of 36° 30′. What was done on her final admission? Upon her final admission, it was made to depend on a condition relating to the African population of the United States. Missouri had inserted in her constitution a provision against the admission within her limits of free negroes; and that occasioned division and agitation in Congress. Well, she was admitted, upon the condition that she should, by a solemn and effective act of her Legislature, declare that no portion of her constitution should be so interpreted as to violate the Constitution of the United States—in other words, that if free negroes had the right by the constitution of going to Missouri, that she should not exclude them under the provisions of her constitution. Well, in order to exclude any legislation or action by Congress on the subject afterward, the President was authorized by proclamation to declare the compliance of Missouri to the requirement made in the resolution of admission; and upon her complying with that requirement, and the President's proclaiming that fact, then, and only then, was she admitted into the Union.

Now, sir, the Senator places himself behind precedents. I say, sir, that each case of the admission of a State was under peculiar circumstances, and I shall not take up the time of the Senate to go over the whole of them. But here is a great subject agitating and distracting the country, and it is proposed, in the spirit of compromise and concession, to connect together two or three analogous subjects—perfectly analogous; and the Senator gets up, and intrenching himself behind various precedents, talks about the indignity to be inflicted upon California. Will the Senator tell me how she is threatened with indignity? Suppose she is admitted, and a territorial government established, and all in one bill, California comes forward through her representatives and is admitted. And where is the indignity? We have heard it again and again announced, in the most emphatic terms, that indignity was to be rendered to her, without any definition, without any explanation, and without any showing how this indignity is to arise.

Sir, I said I would not take up more than five minutes of the time of the Senate, and I will redeem my pledge. The simple question is, whether it is an indignity or not on California to connect her in a great scheme of national compromise, the object of which is the restoration of harmony, peace, and concord to this people? If there is any indignity inflicted on her in that, it is an indignity in which the whole country shares with her, but which I am utterly unable to comprehend, from any thing said, or which has taken place.

Mr. Benton. What, sir! California concur in some scheme of pacification! California, standing outside of the Union, a stranger, to be associated as regards the question of admission, with other topics, in a scheme of pacification in which she is to concur! The Senator from Kentucky puts it on the ground that she is not to be allowed to come in here without having the question of her admission associated with other questions, with a view to pacification, and talks about California concurring in such a proposition! Compromise! Talk of

California concurring in such a proposition! Sir, she is concurring in the sense in which a slave bound to a stake concurs in relation to what is done to him. That is the sense in which she concurs. Sir, she has no voice in the matter. She is not consulted—not allowed to come in. And is she to be bound by a general scheme of which she is to be a party, and yet to have no voice in it? I have always understood, sir, that it takes two to make a bargain, but it would seem that in this case it takes thirty—thirty States—to make a bargain; and one of the parties to be bound by that bargain—the party to be the most bound by it, to be the subject of the binding—is to have no voice in the matter. That party is only to receive the bonds, to acquiesce—to concur in them, without the power of a negative. That is the proposition. Sir, it is an indication of what is intended. But it is to me an incomprehensible thing, that such a proposition should be made. It will be inflicting a serious injury upon California, as I have heretofore urged, if you swell the bill up with doubtful questions, some of which are denied in point of constitutionality—some of which are disputed on the ground of expediency—all of which are brimful of points of difficulty. It is an injury to California, first to be delayed, and next to be subjected to the contingencies of agreement on all these points. That is the injury.

Sir, it is an indignity to California to be mixed up with things that do not belong to her admission as a State. If there was another State at this moment ready to come into the Union, it would not be an indignity to put such State into the same bill. Still I say it would be wrong. The bill should rest upon its own foundation. It should have a separate consideration. Each State has a right, under the constitution, to be admitted upon her own merits, and each should have a separate consideration. I will not again go over the subjects with which it is proposed that California shall be mixed up. God Almighty only knows how many they will be, under the latitudinous, boundless order given to this committee. I know not, sir, how many subjects there are to take cognizance of, but I intend to endeavor to ascertain before they go to the committee. I, sir, according to my reading of the constitution, am of opinion that there are very few points on which Congress has jurisdiction in connection with the subject of slavery—very few points; and those few arise out of the construction of the constitution. And of those few, Mr. President, in which there is a clear constitutional authority in Congress to interfere with the subject of slavery, there are several which this Congress and all former Congresses have refused to touch—which I would myself refuse to touch; and therefore I will not delegate to any committee the power to touch them. I care not what gentlemen may compose the committee. There are subjects, it is true, which may be taken up by the committee—ordinary subjects—in regard to which it will be perfectly immaterial as to how the committee is constituted—whether they are taken from either side of the great dividing line, or whether taken from either of the two great political parties. I believe that the result will be the same in either case, and that there is no necessity for drawing geographical lines, or party lines, in any thing that the committee has to do upon the subject here. That is a point that I will not go into now, but I shall have occasion to do so hereafter. I come back to the main point; and I say that there are but few points upon which Congress has the right to touch slavery at all, and of these few there are several—there are four at least, and I have heretofore referred to them—which I would not grant any committee the power to touch.

For the present, sir, the question is to exempt California from the consideration of this committee. Now, sir, we have debated, thoroughly debated, the subject, but it is very questionable in my mind whether it is not a mere question of order, which refers itself to the chair—whether, under an attempt of the committee to take cognizance of the subject of California, a question of order may not be made to ascertain whether or not, under the words of this resolution, California is referred, and that without any debate on the subject. Sir, it would have to be shown that the State government of California, her constitution, is something that has grown out of the institution of slavery in the United States, in order to give the committee jurisdiction. I deny that it has grown out of the institution of slavery in the United States, or anywhere else. It has no connection with it at all; and to be forced into violent conjunction with it, or to be treated as having been born of slavery, is a thing which I undertake to say will be resisted to the last.

I wish, sir, to say to the honorable Senator from Kentucky, to whom we are all so much indebted for the admission of Missouri, that the act which he quotes is a bill, not for her admission as a State, but a territorial bill. Missouri was a territory at the time when the compromise act of 1820 was passed. It was as a territory that that act was made applicable to it. And what has since taken place, has illustrated the truth and correctness of the decision made by President Monroe's cabinet at the time, when one of these questions was submitted to their decision, whether Congress had jurisdiction over slavery within the territories outside of the limits of the States, and to what the word "forever" applied—whether it applied to the territory while it continued a territory, or whether it applied to the State after a State was formed. Their opinion, as we are informed, was, that the word "forever" applied only to the territory, and had no application to a State at all; and that, sir, has been the decision on the part of this identical territory, as I remarked to the Senate some days ago, thus left outside by the compromise act of 1820, when annexed to the State of Missouri. From territorial soil, from which slavery was forever excluded, it became State soil, and subject to State authority, and slavery went into it *instanter*, and has been there ever since. This full and practical illustration of the principle I have affirmed, is the decision of Mr. Monroe's cabinet. Yes, sir; it was the Territory of Louisiana to which the act applied which the Senator from Kentucky has quoted, and which is called the compromise act.

But now comes the act of admission itself, and for which, I again repeat, we were so much indebted to the Senator from Kentucky—that is, that Missouri should be admitted into the Union upon an equal footing with the original States in all respects; and with respect to the fundamental condition, it is contained in the fourth clause of the twenty-sixth section of the third article of the constitution, submitted on the part of said State to Congress, to the following effect: It shall not be construed to authorize the passing of any law, and that no law shall be passed in conformity thereto, by which any of the citizens of the other States shall be excluded from the enjoyment of any of the privileges and immunities to which such citizens are entitled under the Constitution of the United States; provided that the Legislature of said State, by a solemn public act, shall declare the assent of said State, and shall transmit to the President of the United States, on or before the fourth Monday of November next, an authenticated copy of said act; whereupon, and without further proceeding on the part of Congress, the admission of said State into the Union shall be considered as complete. That is the substance of the provision of the act, sir. I was here at the time—I was contemporary with these proceedings, and had occasion to admire the manner in which superior minds could remove apparent obstacles. It was, to be sure, like the case of Columbus making the egg stand on its end. The admission of the State of Missouri was resisted—great resistance was made to her admission, which seemed to divide the whole Union, and from which fearful consequences were apprehended. At that time the point of admission hung upon this, that by the clause in the Missouri constitution, which is here particularized, free negroes were prohibited from coming into the State. That was the clause. The objection was, that it would interfere with the Constitution of the United States, and be the cause of difficulty between the States; because in many of the States now, and perhaps in all of them once, free negroes had the privileges of citizens. That was the objection. The answer to that was, that if there was a provision in the constitution of Missouri that would come into opposition to the Constitution of the United States upon that point, it would be null and void; and every authority in the State—every judge in the State, every executive officer—was under oath to disregard whatever might be repugnant to the Constitution of the United States. It was a clear case, sir, and so represented and argued at the time; but it was not satisfactory.

On motion of the Senator from Kentucky, the case was referred to a committee, which committee brought in a declaration—it was nothing in the world but a declaration—that gave to the General Assembly of Missouri, and to all the authorities of Missouri who have the execution of the laws in their hands, that they should not permit any constitutional provision of Missouri to interfere with the Constitution of the United States, or, in other words, that they would perform their duty under the oath which they had taken to support the Constitution of the United States; and if they found any thing in the State constitution repugnant to the Constitution of the United States, they would hold it to be imperative upon them to maintain the latter, or, in other words, that they would not violate the Constitution of the United States—that is all. Now, this case of Missouri is affirmed by the practice of sixty years' legislation in regard to the same subject. But I do not rest upon precedent alone—that is a lawyer business. It belongs to form. It belongs to a case-hunting lawyer to search the files for precedents. I do not go by precedent, except as it illustrates the case in hand. I go by reason rather than precedent. I require these things to have a separate consideration; and I refer to over sixty years of legislation, not as a precedent to govern this body, but as an example to show what has been deemed proper by every Congress that has preceded us. That is what I want.

Mr. Dayton. I am opposed, Mr. President, to the proposition, and though not intending to discuss it at all, yet as this proposition has had very little discussion, as compared with the general questions which have been discussed by the Senate and the country, I feel constrained to say a few words. The distinct question now is, to refer California, in connection with other matters, to this committee, in the hope that they may unite in some satisfactory adjustment for the compromise of all the pending questions in regard to slavery. Now, Mr. President, I beg leave to ask the Senate, and to submit it to the country, whether, in this matter of referring California, it is not an act of indignity to her—whether you are not doing an act of injustice to her? I submit to the members of this body now, whether there is the slightest doubt that California will come into the Union as a State, standing alone? Has it not been said again and again on all sides of this chamber, and by the representatives of all shades of political opinion, that California will come into this Union; that she has a right to come here; and that she will be admitted by a large majority? Why then is it, I ask again, that she is to be sent back to this committee of conference, except for the purpose of using her with a view to making more palatable some more objectionable proposition? You take the hazard, by referring California, of defeating her admission, in the hope that you may bring something in along with her—she serving as a sugar-plum to sweeten the dose, that you may swallow them all together. I ask now, with very great respect to gentlemen of all opinions in this chamber, whether it is just to California to place her in this peculiar position? She has a certain class of rights—not legal perhaps—which we are bound to recognize; and when we use her, not in matters connected with her own advantage, but simply for the purpose of subserving the interests of party, I submit, with great respect, that we commit an injustice upon her. Can any man doubt that this reference of California to this committee, and bringing her back here connected with bills for territorial governments and the settlement of the Texan boundary, will tend to hazard to some extent her admission, or if not to hazard her admission, at least to decrease the amount of votes which would be given for that admission? Is she not now, I submit, kept back simply for the purpose of sweetening the dose, and making it more palatable to a majority of this body? This, I submit very respectfully, is what strikes me as obvious on the face of this matter. If it is unjust to California, is it not equally unjust to us, who desire to vote for the admission of California, that you send her to your committee of conference? They will take the question of her admission into consideration, and connect it with other matters, making the whole bill obnoxious to us, as would be any bill of such a character, whereby we are compelled to vote against California. It is not only unjust to California, but unjust to the members of this body who are disposed to vote for her admission standing alone. It is, I think, a false principle of legislation. It is wrong in itself. Here is one matter conceded to be a clear question of right. The parties are here making claim at our hands for admission, which we refuse; and here are other matters more doubtful in their character. Hence it is proposed to go to log-rolling a little, and see if they may not all be brought in together. I have no wish to occupy the time of the Senate on this matter, but it seems to me, with great respect to the opinions of others, that the question of the admission of California should be considered by itself. She has rights of her own. If she is entitled to admission, let us admit her; if she is not, let us keep her out; but do not let us trammel California, by connecting her with other subjects, so that we cannot vote for her admission without doing her injustice. I am opposed to such a course of proceeding.

Mr. King. I do not intend, sir, to detain the Senate with any protracted remarks, but merely to appeal to gentlemen to let the vote be taken. Sir, I suspect that the Senator from New Jersey would not be so exceedingly desirous of admitting California instantly, promptly, and without a moment's delay, had there not been a clause in her constitution prohibiting slavery. I know very well, sir, that when we tried here, time and again, to give this very California a government that would protect the rights of her citizens—that would afford the means of punishing crime and preserving order—that honorable Senator, with others, resisted every effort that was made for that purpose. Why, sir? Because there was not a clause introduced prohibiting slavery. Those gentlemen, then, had no such great desire to protect that people, or to put them in a situation in which they would be under the protection of the law, unless they could get a provision which they knew involved what is calculated to distract and divide the country, to the extent almost of the destruction of the Government itself. And the consequence was, that California, New Mexico, and all the territories acquired from Mexico, had no government and no laws, except such as were found existing there at the time of the acquisition. In that state of things, California set about forming a constitution for herself—whether stimulated to it or not, is not for me to say—she set about establishing a State government for herself, from the necessity of the case, with the view of securing the public peace and tranquillity. In her anxiety to do something to protect herself, and to preserve peace in that country, to which emigration is so rapidly flowing, she thought proper to form a constitution. Well, sir, the constitution formed in that way—in that irregular way, as even the Senator from Missouri is bound to admit—is presented to the Congress of the United States, in order that California may be received into the Union. And we are told, that in making an effort to protect ourselves and our property, to protect the rights of the citizens of the United States, we are doing a great injustice to California. Now, sir, I was here when Missouri was admitted. I know very well that it was considered not a party measure, but as a very favorable indication that Congress gave of a willingness to bring her in without delay, by requiring her assent to a particular provision that was introduced by the Senator from Kentucky; but her Senators did not take their seats until after this assent was given.

But we are told that California is a State. Well, if she is a State, what are we debating about? If she comes here with all the rights of a State, there is no further question about the matter. No, sir; she is but a territory; and a territory she must remain until we, by our action, bring her into the confederacy of States. California, in forming her constitution, has done—what? Has she complied with the requisitions of the Constitution of the United States, which have always heretofore been considered necessary to entitle a new State to come into the Union? Will gentlemen tell me that they are prepared to relinquish all the territory of California? Will they tell me that they are prepared to give up the whole of the public domain? And where is the guarantee that it is not surrendered the moment you admit California into the Union? Heretofore such guarantees have always been introduced into the compact that we have formed with a new State when seeking for admission. Instructions have been always given to the territory, that when she held a convention for the purpose of forming a constitution, these stipulations should be introduced: that all navigable streams should be open forever to the citizens of the United States, and that the State should not impose tolls. Another was, that the territory of the State should be given up—that the public domain should be secured to the Government of the United States, and not to the State herself. New States relinquished all claim to the territory. Where is there any such relinquishment in the constitution of California? Do you find it anywhere? No, sir; there is no such relinquishment on its part. And will any Senator, who is a lawyer, and who understands the force of terms, tell me that unless there is some such relinquishment, the Government of the United States does not lose the domain the moment the territory becomes a State, if such new State should think proper to claim all the territory within her limits? Are not these considerations sufficient to induce the Senate to pause before they act upon the subject, and ascertain whether it is not proper to send the subject to a committee, whose duty it shall be to investigate, and see if some mode of proceeding cannot be adopted by which this omission may be remedied—by which the evil that will be inflicted upon us, if California be admitted without some such provision, may be averted? And I tell the Senator from New Jersey, that he is entirely mistaken, if he supposes that every Senator on this floor is ready and willing to permit the State of California to come in instantly—if he supposes that every Senator on this floor is willing to acknowledge that California must and will come in by an overwhelming majority. Sir, the honorable Senator, if he supposes this, will find himself mistaken; he will find that unless some mode be devised, that will render it agreeable to gentlemen to admit California, as a separate question, as a matter disconnected with all others, to induce them to waive their objections to these unexampled irregularities, which there is an almost absolute obligation on the part of the Government to discountenance — unless some such thing is done, California cannot come in; for let the intelligence be spread before the country—not before one section only, but before the whole country—let it be understood in New England, that we are to lose our domain there; that we have ascertained that California, if she chooses to grasp it, has it in her power to do so; that it is to go out of our hands; and that we shall have no means of getting it back, unless she voluntarily surrenders it—let this be understood, and rest assured, that even that section of the country will not justify or approve the admission of California under such circumstances.

Well, where is the great evil, if it should become necessary to send California back, as Missouri was sent back? We are told, and no doubt it is the truth, that the people in California are almost in a state of anarchy; that they cannot move along; that they cannot get funds to support their government; that one portion of the territory is arrayed against the other; that San Diego is arrayed against San Francisco. And, by the by, all that portion of the territory lying south of San Francisco was opposed to the formation of a State government. They were anxious for a territorial government; and in that they showed their good sense; for I have no doubt a territorial government, properly organized, would have been much better for them, for some years to come, than any State government they could possibly establish. I have no question of that.

My object in rising, sir, was to say, that while I am most anxious to see this distracting question settled on some reasonable basis, one that can be acquiesced in in every quarter of the Union; while I am anxious to see fraternal relations and harmony restored; and while, for the purpose of securing these objects, I would be disposed to yield every thing that I could yield consistently with my duty to my constituents and to the country; while I would be disposed, I say, to yield every thing that I could yield under the oath that I have taken to sustain the constitution, and consistently with the duty that I owe to the people whom I represent, and the country generally, I shall not be driven by any kind of proceedings to adopt a course which I believe, if persevered in, will neither be beneficial to the country nor put an end to these agitations, but which would undoubtedly augment them; in consequence of which they would go on from day to day increasing, and continually becoming worse and worse.

When you come upon the question, you will probably get a majority to act upon this question alone, and determine to do nothing in reference to the other questions, but leave them open to be acted upon for political or other purposes. But, sir, I tell you that if gentlemen attempt to interfere with our rights, there will be no division among us in the controversy. When every one feels, as he should feel, that his rights have been set at naught—that insult and injustice have been heaped upon him—they will stand together, shoulder to shoulder, in defiance of what they honestly believe to be oppression. Are gentlemen prepared to bring about this state of things? Are they prepared to goad the southern people almost to desperation? We are willing to bear with oppressions as long as possible; we are prepared to sacrifice every thing that can reasonably be demanded or expected of us, and even more, in order to preserve the Union; but they must not drive us to extremities, or they will find themselves at that point when they will be compelled to calculate the value of the Union.

Mr. President, few men perhaps have been more attached to the Union than myself; few men have manifested, on every occasion where the opportunity was presented to show it, a stronger desire to maintain every principle that binds the States of this Confederacy together. I never lent myself to any of the wild schemes that were got up some years ago; I considered them visionary and unnecessary, and in some degree dangerous; and therefore I made all the opposition to them I could, notwithstanding the action that was attempted by gentlemen, whose motives I respected, but whose course I deprecated, and would not sustain.

I had no design, Mr. President, of detaining the Senate when I rose to speak; but I must add, that I trust in God that there will be patriotism, good sense, and fraternal feeling enough in this body, to enable it to act upon these great and distracting questions in such a way as will restore harmony and peace to the country. We have been told at times, by various gentlemen, of the glory, the power, the magnificence of this country; and I feel the truth of all these glowing descriptions as an American; and I feel also that we are destined, if we can avoid internal dissensions, to become the greatest among the nations of the earth; but in order to this, we must preserve peace at home—peace at home. We have nothing at all to fear from abroad. It is our internal dissensions, our internal bickerings and strife, got up in some instances by unprincipled politicians, to advance their own selfish purposes, and carried forward through the medium of miserable fanatics, that are becoming stronger and stronger every day, that is leading to results of which God only knows the end. I hope that the good sense of the Senate of the United States will avert the evils resulting from the efforts to which I have alluded, and that we will be enabled to save this glorious Union from sectional division, and fulfil the destiny which I have no doubt awaits us.

Mr. Douglas. The remarks of the Senator from Alabama are of such a character, that I feel compelled to say a few words in reply. Upon the discussion of a proposition to create a committee to consider the questions at issue, he goes into a discussion of the bill for the admission of the State of California. And, sir, I cannot but think that it would be much better to defer that discussion until we get the bill up, or rather to proceed at once to the consideration of the bill providing for the admission of California. I feel bound, sir, to say, that I think the Senator is entirely mistaken in the fact which he asserts, that if the present bill for the admission be adopted, the public domain of that country will not belong to this Government. But, sir, he is mistaken entirely, for my bill for the admission of California is in the usual form. It is framed on the same principle that bills for the admission of States heretofore have been framed, and the Senator will find, upon examination, that it is an exact transcript of two or three of the bills that have been presented for the admission of new States into this Union. I am well aware of the compacts of which he speaks. Those compacts are not generally parts of bills admitting new States into the Union. They have been generally separate bills, passed at different times. They were matters of compact, not generally embraced in the same bill; and the one referring to my own State was not a part of the bill admitting my own State. Hence my attention has been drawn to this subject, and I am prepared, when the bill for the admission of California comes up for consideration, to vindicate it against any charges which may be made. I think that the turn this discussion has taken ought to admonish us at once to proceed to the consideration of the bill for the admission of California, which is a practical question.

Mr. Downs. I would inquire of the Senator from Illinois, if he is aware that any new State having public lands within her limits, has been admitted into the Union until the government, or the constitutional authority of the State, had entered into a formal compact to cede the public domain to the General Government?

Mr. Douglas. The question of the Senator from Louisiana fully proves the propriety of the motion which I am about to make. If the Senate will proceed to the consideration of the bill for the admission of California, I am prepared then to vindicate it from all the charges that may be brought against it. I desire to have a discussion upon the merits of the question, and upon the bill itself. And, sir, if I cannot show that the bill is precisely as it ought to be, and that not one of the objections really exists which Senators advance, I will offer amendments myself that will obviate those objections, so that they shall not be able to make even criticisms on the subject.

Mr. Foote. Will the Senator from Illinois allow me to say one word?

Mr. Douglas. Certainly, if it is by way of suggestion.

Mr. Foote. I would state that, in my opinion, immediate action upon the resolution I had the honor to offer is in perfect harmony with the objection raised by the Senator from Illinois. It is certainly true that this committee will be raised, probably, in a few moments, and the Senator can then move to proceed to the consideration of his bill—a motion which I shall always be happy to sustain. I know that gentlemen here are desirous of voting upon the question, and having the proposition immediately before us. Let us raise this committee without any further discussion.

Mr. Douglas. As I have said, the whole merits of the bill for the admission of California can be discussed on this resolution, and the consequence is, that discussion is to go on indefinitely. My object in rising was simply to state that when the California bill came up, I would be prepared to show that it was framed in the manner in which it should be. If I do not show this, I will offer an amendment, as I before said, to obviate any objections that may be made. In the progress of the bill Senators will be at liberty to offer any amendments they may deem proper. The bill must go through the ordinary stages before it is passed, and there may be some alterations to be made in it; for I do not undertake to say that it is perfect; I do not pretend that it contains no errors; every bill is liable to them. And now, for the purpose of making a test vote on this question of raising a committee at this time, I move that the question of raising this committee lie upon the table.

Mr. WEBSTER. Will the Senator withdraw his motion for a moment?

Mr. DOUGLAS. Certainly.

Mr. WEBSTER. I have a very few words to say, sir. When the question of raising this committee was before the Senate a month or six weeks ago, I said to the Senate, that, although I did not perceive that any considerable good was likely to result from this proposed measure, yet if it was desired by any considerable portion of the Senate, and especially those who have taken a lead on the subject, (the honorable member from Kentucky, and the honorable member from Tennessee, and others,) that such a committee should be raised, I should not oppose the motion. I suppose that it would hardly have had much opposition in the Senate, if it had not happened that the honorable Senator from Mississippi has used a phrase, or prescribed a mode of proceeding in his resolution, calculated to alarm in a measure some Senators. The instruction, according to his resolution, is, that the committee shall mature some scheme of compromise. Well, probably this word scheme created some little apprehension.

Mr. FOOTE. That is not the phraseology of the resolution.

Mr. WEBSTER. I am quite certain it is, sir; let the resolution be read.

The Secretary read the resolution as follows:

"That the resolutions be referred to a select committee of thirteen, with instructions to exert themselves for the purpose of maturing a scheme of compromise for the adjustment of all pending questions growing out of the institution of slavery, with the right to report by bill or otherwise."

Mr. WEBSTER. Not that I suppose a meaning was intended to be attached correspondent to the phrase, or that it was to be taken in a strict sense; but as I have said, taken in this sense, the resolution has given rise to alarm in the minds of Senators; and I am free to say, if it is to be taken in that sense, I shall not agree to it in any way whatever; because it seems to imply, or might imply—I do not suppose that such is its purpose—that something is to be compromised away—something that is of importance to the country; and as we are dealing with the rights of the country, this should not occur. Sir, I am inclined to unite with those Senators who have taken the lead in this discussion, and also a very large portion of the Senate, and allow the committee to be appointed, so far as by my vote it can be appointed; but to avoid all possible misapprehension hereafter, I beg to say that I shall not commit myself, and do not now commit myself, to support any measure which shall make the admission of California dependent upon the success of any other proposition whatever. I wish to say one other thing, sir. The honorable member from Kentucky yesterday observed, that the subjects which he regarded or supposed proper for the committee to consider, were the admission of California, provision for the government of the territories, and the question of the boundary of Texas. Now, I am afraid, sir, that the question of the boundary of Texas is a question which will necessarily call for much examination, and probably bring on much discussion; both in the committee and in the Senate.

One word further, sir. It does seem to me that the importance of the measure now before us, take it either one way or the other, is greatly overrated—very much overrated. Mr. President, the honorable gentlemen before me, from the State of Illinois, (Mr. DOUGLAS,) desires to bring up his bill—his clean bill—for the admission of California, and I am ready to vote for it. But, then, if this bill were now before us, the member himself must see, and all the Senate must see, that it would be quite competent for any gentleman, wishing to unite the question of California, and the question of the territories, to move to insert territorial governments on the bill, and you would thus raise the same question. Well, if this committee bring in a combined bill, any member of the Senate may move to strike out the territorial portions of the bill, and take a vote for the admission of California alone—so that, after all, we arrive at the opinion of the majority of the Senate in one way just as well as in the other. We cannot avoid the question of its separation and of the combination any way. It must come up, and must come up in any way that we proceed. Therefore, I do not think it of much importance, nor indeed of any considerable importance, because it stands upon the ground of appointing a general committee to consider what is best to be done to allay the existing agitation and to satisfy all parties, according to the usual proceeding in ordinary cases. I have no objection; something good may come out of it. They may express the opinion that it will not much, if it should in any degree, facilitate the settlement of these questions. We have got a question now upon which to take the votes of the Senate, and see what is the opinion of the majority of the Senate as to the separate or combined consideration of these questions. I make these remarks merely to prevent any unjust inference that may be drawn from my vote, for I shall feel bound to support any measure, as I have said, which shall make the admission of California independent of any other measure.

One word more, and I take my seat. We are acting under discretionary power, devolved on us by the constitution, and for the exercise of which we have entered into stipulations with Mexico by the treaty of 1848.

I do not think it will advance us toward a conclusion, to set up at present any rights of California. Nor do I think, on the other hand, that it advances us toward that just conclusion at all, by indulging in criminatory remarks upon the proceedings which have taken place in California, without any previous authority derived from this Government.

The facts are before us. The case is before us. The constitution of California is before us. We are by the treaty to exercise our own discretion as to the time of admitting her. When she comes with her constitution in conformity with the requsitions of our constitution, and as she has undoubtedly the requisite number of inhabitants that will constitute her a State, according to the usage of the Government in cases of a similar character heretofore arising, I am prepared, in the exercise of the discretion which devolves upon me as a member of this body, to admit her as a State; and in voting for this committee, I repeat here, that I do it out of deference to the leading gentlemen who have taken part in this discussion, and who have brought forward these resolutions—particularly the resolutions of the Senator from Tennessee—rather than from being sanguine of any benefit to arise from it.

Mr. Foote. I rise simply to make a remark with reference to the phraseology of my motion. It will be recollected, sir, that I submitted a new motion in a different form upon this subject; therefore it has happened that, with reference to this motion, I forgot its particular terms. But I would say, that if any one has felt alarm concerning it—if the Senator from Massachusetts has experienced any alarm—I think that that alarm would be relieved by a proper consideration of the words used in the resolution. If the word compromise had been the only word used, there might have been some cause for entertaining fears that the motion was destined to sacrifice the rights of either one or the other section of the confederacy; but, as I was desirous of avoiding that, the motion was prepared with reference to that particular object; and it purports, according as it has been read in our hearing, to authorize this committee to assemble for the purpose of making every effort to mature some scheme of compromise for the adjustment of all pending questions. All must be desirous of having the questions at issue adjusted, and to unite upon some scheme of adjustment that will not involve a sacrifice of our rights. Still, as my honorable friend from Massachusetts suggests, there may be some occasion for alarm in the particular terms of the resolution. After the pending amendment of the Senator from Connecticut is rejected, as I doubt not it will be, we can modify the original resolution where it speaks of a scheme of compromise. I am perfectly willing to strike out the word "scheme," and insert the word "plan," although I cannot understand how the phrase "scheme of adjustment" can imply the sacrifice of the rights of any portion of the Union. I will move, however, that the word "scheme" be stricken out, and the word "plan" substituted.

The modification was made accordingly.

Mr. Douglas. I now renew my motion to lay the subject on the table.

Mr. Turney. On that I call for the yeas and nays.

Mr. Foote. It will be recollected that this is intended as a test question.

The yeas and nays were ordered; and being taken, were as follows:

Yeas. — Messrs. Baldwin, Benton, Bradbury, Chase, Clarke, Corwin, Davis of Massachusetts, Dayton, Dodge of Iowa, Dodge of Wisconsin, Douglas, Felch, Greene, Hale, Hamlin, Jones, Miller, Norris, Phelps, Seward, Shields, Smith, Spruance, Upham, Wales, and Walker—26.

Nays.—Messrs. Atchison, Badger, Bell, Borland, Bright, Butler, Cass, Clay, Clemens, Davis of Mississippi, Dickinson, Downs, Foote, Hunter, King, Mangum, Mason, Morton, Pearee, Pratt, Rusk, Sebastian, Soulé, Turney, Underwood, Webster, Whitcomb, and Yulee—28.

So the motion was not agreed to.

The question then recurred on the amendment.

Mr. Baldwin called for the yeas and nays.

Mr. Benton. I have several times stated to the Senate that there are two or three points on which the Congress of the United States has no right to touch slavery at all. These points have been too often mentioned to need repetition, but I have embodied them in the shape of amendments which I shall offer, and I shall call for the yeas and nays upon each amendment, in order that my vote may stand recorded against giving to any committee of this body the right to take into consideration these questions.

The Vice President. The question is now upon the amendment of the Senator from Connecticut. Does the Senator from Missouri offer his amendment to that amendment.

Mr. Benton. No, sir; I do not intend to interfere with that amendment.

Mr. Bradbury. Mr. President, I do not rise to enter into a general consideration of the questions involved in the resolutions before the Senate. Time enough has already been consumed in such discussions, and I desire action. But before I vote upon the amendment now pending, I feel bound to state the reasons for the vote I shall give. The Legislature of the State I have the honor in part to represent, have instructed me to vote for no bill for the organization of governments for the territories, unless such bill shall contain an express inhibition of slavery therein. I recognize the right to give such instructions, and I have no constitutional difficulty in the way of implicit obedience to them. I think it competent for Congress to give a government to our territories, and to prohibit slavery therein. It is a power that has been exercised from the foundation of this Government to the present day, a power that results from the right to acquire; for if our Government can acquire, it must have the power to take care of its acquisitions, to govern them, to make all necessary laws for them; and under the constitution, Congress must judge what laws are necessary.

While instructed to vote, and feeling bound to vote for no bill which does not contain a prohibition of slavery, I am impressed with the conviction that the feeling of my constituents is universal in favor of the immediate admission of California into the Union as a State. In this opinion I heartily concur, and I think she should be admitted without delay. It is understood that one great object of the resolution of the Senator from Mississippi is, to have incorporated into one bill the admission of California and territorial governments for New Mexico and Utah. If that is done, the Senate will perceive that I shall be placed in the position, by voting against the bill, to vote against California, which I am unwilling to do, or by voting for the bill, to vote against the explicit instructions of the Legislature of my State. Now, sir, I cannot voluntarily place myself in this dilemma.

One word more upon this subject. I think it due to truth to say, that while I recognize the right of Congress to prohibit slavery in the territories, for which we are attempting to prepare governments, I am not so fully impressed with the *necessity* of such prohibition under existing circumstances as some gentlemen appear to be. I concur, mainly, with the honorable Senator from Missouri, (Mr. BENTON,) who expressed the conviction that the "proviso," as applicable to these territories, was a cloud without rain—an unnecessary enactment of a law that is already there.

As practical men, we must take cognizance of known facts. It is now perfectly understood that there is a decided and fixed majority in this body against the "proviso." This fact was declared the other day by the honorable Senator from Connecticut, (Mr. SMITH.) He reiterated it as well known and beyond all doubt. The admission of California, as is well understood, will add two more votes to that majority. We must then regard it as settled, that neither at this nor any future session can that measure pass this body.

What, then, are the alternatives? Either non-action and no bill, or a bill giving a government, but without Congressional prohibition of slavery in either case. Which course, then, is the best and safest to be pursued, and which ought to be adopted? The Senator from Missouri (Mr. BENTON) demonstrated a few days ago that slavery was prohibited in these territories at the time of our acquisition of them, by the laws and constitution of Mexico. These laws remain in force; and the proviso is now there, prohibiting slavery throughout their entire extent. It is a well-settled principle of law, repeatedly recognized by the most eminent jurists, and by the Supreme Court, that upon the acquisition of territory by one government from another, the *political* laws of that territory are changed, but the *municipal* laws remain in force. Political laws are those which regulate the relations between the people and their government. Municipal laws are those which regulate the relations of the inhabitants with each other, and nothing is more obvious than that the laws respecting slavery are embraced in the latter class. Nor is slavery carried into these territories by the Constitution of the United States; for if carried there by the force of that instrument, it is also extended into every territory and State of the Union, notwithstanding any law to the contrary, by the same authority, which is the paramount law of the land. It would therefore seem, that slavery is as fully inhibited by the Mexican laws as it could be by any act of Congress.

Again: we have seen the action of the people of California upon this subject, and it gives assurance that these questions are safe in the hands of the people themselves.

Again: the geographical character and insulated position of New Mexico and Utah forbid the establishment of slavery there. They are so many hundreds of miles from a market, that the cost of transportation of agricultural products would in many cases exceed their value at the place of sale; and slavery can only be profitable where the productions of its labor can find a market.

I wish to add, that I desire to see the questions that are disturbing the harmony of the country and delaying the business of Congress, settled. It is due to the country, that questions which cause irritation and create sectional prejudice should be put to rest; it is due to a just regard for the public business. If not disposed of now, the future sessions of Congress will be occupied precisely as the present has been, and the general business of the country entirely neglected. So long as these questions remain open, no other subjects can command the calm and dispassionate consideration of Congress. Non-action, then, is the worst possible policy that can be pursued. It settles nothing, gives no proviso, and leaves every thing open for future agitation, without the possibility of any other practical result than that which would now be attained. It will tend, moreover, to the premature introduction of these territories into the Union as States.

I oppose the reference of this subject to a committee for another reason. We have a bill before us for the admission of California, and a bill for the government of the territories, both matured with great care, and reported by the appropriate committee; and if a majority of the Senate should determine to unite the two measures in one bill, it would be infinitely better to do so, by uniting these bills, than to send the subject to a new committee to report another bill, which will require to be again examined, and open new discussions. I think it better, therefore, to have action upon practical measures already before the Senate. I beg Senators, favorable to the success of these measures, and who wish them all to pass, to consider whether, by their union in one bill, they increase the probability of their success? The test vote which any bill will have to encounter, is the proviso, and that can as well be put upon the double bill as the single one for the territories. Can any good result, therefore, from this combination of two subjects, so distinct in their character, and which may compel Senators to vote against their convictions or their instructions? Certainly not. California, moreover, presents stronger claims for immediate action than other territories, however urgent their case may be. We should consider the situation of a population of one hundred thousand inhabitants, coming from different quarters of the world, thrown together in large masses, under circumstances of extreme exposure of life and property, without government having legal sanction, and therefore without credit or authority to procure the means to sustain those laws which they have provided for their protection. The exigency of their case demands immediate action at our hands, and they ought not to be subject to that delay which would arise from a connection with other questions. What are the objections to the admission of this State? It is said that Congress did not authorize the formation of a constituton. True; but it is in our power to ratify the act of the people. It is said the South has been excluded from the country, and has a right to complain. In the convention which formed their constitution, the South was fully represented, and both of the Senators elect, as well as the Governor, were from that section of the Union, and cannot be presumed to feel any other than the most friendly sentiments in regard to every just measure for the promotion of its interests.

It is alleged that there has been an improper interference on the part of the Executive in forming the State government. If this be so, the result shows a singular degree of magnanimity; for this interference has resulted in sending to each House of Congress two gentlemen opposed to every political principle of the Administration, and distinguished for their adherence to the policy of the Democratic party.

One other remark before I conclude. The proposition before the Senate is, to refer the resolutions of the Senator from Tennessee, (Mr. Bell,) which contemplate the erection of a new State from Texas; and this reference might, by implication, be regarded as giving the sanction of the Senate to the policy of admitting such State at this time. While I concur in the remarks of the honorable Senator from Massachusetts, (Mr. Webster,) that at the proper time, when there shall be the requisite population, and Texas shall apply, we shall carry out in good faith all the stipulations upon this subject in the resolutions of annexation, it is not for Congress to take the initiative, and carve out States, without the request or assent of the State from which they are taken, and without the requisite population to authorize it.

I have refrained, Mr. President, from engaging in the discussions which have occupied the Senate almost exclusively since its commencement; and I now omit many remarks which under other circumstances I would like to make, confining myself to the reasons of my vote, that we may have an immediate vote upon the question. I desire action. I desire the time to come when we can hear something else than the never-ending discussion upon the subject of slavery.

The yeas and nays on the amendment were then ordered.

Mr. Webster. I did not hear the amendments, presented by the honorable member from Missouri, which he intends to offer. I will thank the Chair to allow the Clerk to read them, if there is no objection.

The Secretary read the amendments, as follows:

Provided, That nothing in this instruction shall be construed to authorize the said committee to take into consideration any thing that relates to either of the four following subjects:

1. The abolition of slavery within the States.
2. The suppression of the slave trade between the States.
3. The abolition of slavery within the forts, arsenals, dock-yards, and navy-yards of the United States.
4. Abolition of slavery within the District of Columbia.

And provided further, That said committee shall not take into consideration any question in relation to the subject of domestic slavery in the United States, which shall not be specially referred to it by order of the Senate.

Mr. Webster. It is quite obvious that we are making no progress at all. The original motion was for a reference. Now, the Senator proposes to instruct that committee, and there is work enough cut out to last that committee a fortnight. I really wish some gentleman, who has an interest in this subject, and has matured some plan, would make some motion, so that we can vote upon the reference of the resolutions of the honorable member from Tennessee, or that in some way we may dispose of them, and bring ourselves to the consideration of what is pertinent and german to our duties. This amendment of the honorable member from Missouri opens a great field for discussion, and we shall make no progress.

The VICE PRESIDENT. That amendment is not pending.

Mr. WEBSTER. I understand the Chair very well, that that amendment is not now pending; but when the pending amendment is disposed of, the one way or the other, it will become pending; and I say, therefore, that there is a disposition to raise all possible questions upon this general question of reference; and if that be so, I do not know but that it would be better to proceed at once upon the bill for the admission of California; for really, if we go on in this way, and are to discuss all sorts of questions under these instructions to the committee, we shall be here a fortnight before we take the question on this reference. If there can be any way suggested to refer generally the resolutions of the member from Tennessee, I shall continue to vote as I have voted. I wish these resolutions to go to a committee for consideration.

Mr. FOOTE. I do not wish to take any leading part in this matter. So far as I and a few other Senators are concerned, there will be no difficulty at all. As it regards the form of proceeding, I certainly am not very anxious that the instructions which I drew up should go to the committee. Such a committee as will be selected, will doubtless be as fully able to act without instructions as with them. It has been supposed by some Senators, who have looked into the matter, that the resolutions of the honorable Senator from Tennessee are not quite so comprehensive as they should be, to give this committee a sufficiently wide scope for action. I would suggest, what I think will readily be agreed to on all sides, that I am perfectly willing, instead of instructing the committee, the motion should be so modified as to submit the resolutions of the honorable Senator from Tennessee, in conjunction with those of the honorable Senator from Kentucky, to this committee of thirteen; leaving them, in the exercise of their discretion, to make such a report as they may deem best. I am willing to accept the modification; it appears to be approved on all sides; and if so, I will move that the resolutions of the Senator from Tennessee, and those of the Senator from Kentucky, should be referred to a committee of thirteen.

The VICE PRESIDENT. It can only be done by unanimous consent of the Senate.

Mr. MANGUM. I will move, with the permission of the honorable Senator from Mississippi, an amendment to his motion, that the resolutions offered by the honorable Senator from Kentucky (Mr. CLAY) likewise go to the committee.

Mr. FOOTE. I beg leave now to state, that I accept the amendment of the honorable Senator from North Carolina, and move that the resolutions of the Senator from Tennessee, and those of the Senator from Kentucky, be referred to a committee of thirteen.

Mr. KING. I think the Senator from Missouri will see that his amendment now proposed is not applicable to the subject. There are no instructions to the committee—none whatever. The proposition is, to refer the resolutions of the Senator from Tennessee, and those offered by the Senator from Kentucky, to a select committee of thirteen, to take into consideration the subjects of which these resolutions treat. Now, there are no instructions that they should take into consideration any thing else, and although I entirely concur in the view of the Senator from Missouri, that Congress has no power whatever to legislate on the subject of which these amendments treat, yet I suppose there are those who have entertained, and yet entertain the opinion that they have power over one of the subjects, and perhaps over two. I could not myself vote against them, were they relevant to the subject; but I do not consider them as relevant to the subject. No beneficial object can be accomplished by pressing these amendments; for though I think there is a decided majority in regard to the two subjects, the others would lead to a division, and probably much debate. If the Senator perseveres in his amendments, I shall certainly call for the vote on each subject, and give my vote in favor of the whole of them. At the same time, I know that there will be division in relation to the other two points. But why send to a committee to determine what we all believe and know is literally in violation of the Constitution of the United States, if they should attempt to take jurisdiction of it? The prohibiting of the slave-trade between the States is a question over which it has been decided by the highest tribunal in the land, that Congress has no power. As regards the abolition of slavery within the forts, dock-yards, and arsenals, that also comes under the same rule; and I think, therefore, that under all the circumstances, it is scarcely german to the subject, and perhaps, strictly speaking, is not in order.

Mr. BENTON. I ask the Clerk to strike out the word "instructions," and insert the word "reference."

The amendment, as thus modified by Mr. BENTON, was then read.

Mr. BENTON. I wish to say to the honorable Senator from Alabama, that it was with no view of embarrassing the Senate, or any member, that I introduced this proposition. It was with precisely the opposite view, and in accordance with what I said the other day, in the poor remarks in which I gave my opinion that the speeches of individual Senators will go further to quiet the country, than any thing in the world which a committee can do; and it was with a view of having the question presented, so that the vote might be taken on each of these points, and for the express purpose of letting the people of the United States see that they have been alarmed without reason and against reason; that there is not the least foundation in the world for supposing that the Senate is going to interfere with the subject about which they are so alarmed, and that there is no necessity for any scheme or contrivance to be hatched up to settle these questions. It is in the bosom of every Senator to speak out at once in a way to silence the agitation that exists in the country. Sir, what is that agitation caused by? It is about the abolition of slavery in the States, and in the forts, and arsenals, and dock-yards in the bosom of the States, so situated as to make asylums for runaway negroes; the abolition of the slave-trade between the States and in this District, which is said to be an entering wedge for the accomplishment of the others. Now, sir, I know the country is alarmed about these things. We see it manifested in the resolves of public bodies. I have seen as good and candid people as there are on God's earth laboring under the most serious alarm, and in the greatest nervous excitement, when they talked on the subject of slavery, supposing that Congress was going to abolish slavery in the States. I endeavored to convince them that, whereas for sixty years Congress had done nothing on this subject, they should be satisfied that Congress would not touch it, and especially when there is abundant proof that they will not exercise their undisputed powers over it.

It has, therefore, been my determination from the beginning, and is still, to obtain a vote in this body upon each of these four points, so as to remove the alarm which now exists in the country, and I have endeavored to frame them in such a way as to embarrass no one. If you give reason for embarrassment, you must expect it; and as the Senator from Alabama thinks there may be embarrassment in voting on the question of the power of Congress to touch the subject of slavery, I think that embarrassment will be removed by showing the fact that Congress does not authorize the committee even to think upon the subject.

Mr. President, I rejoiced yesterday when I saw the honorable Senator from Kentucky add to the long list of benefits he has conferred upon his country, another benefit, by making that extraordinary motion. I think he was fully justified under the circumstances in making that motion, because when that motion was made, it implied not merely that the measure ought not to pass—it implied not merely that we could give no parliamentary sanction to such a measure—but it rebukes it as an improper thing. The motion to reject them is a strong one, and I think it was strongly made yesterday; and I do hope that the same motion will be made upon each class of petitions which come here to annoy us on the subject—one motion of the same kind upon each class. And it is my opinion that the motion made yesterday in the Senate, in which the Senator spoke for himself and upon the spot, will have more influence upon the public mind than all the arrangements that can be made by committees, and that will be precisely the effect if this amendment is adopted. Sir, when the thing is carried into a committee, and considered there, especially when the word "compromise" is used in connection with it, there is a belief among the people that there was a giving and taking—that the people are to be brought together by mutual concessions, by giving an inch here, and taking an inch there, and that at last a compromise is made up. But the idea is, that it is a result made up by some sort of patch-work, each yielding something to the other. How, different, then, when every Senator stands in his place, and speaks at once when his name is called, and speaks from his heart, and bares his heart to the view of the country, and lets the country see what he feels—that he is leading nobody and is led by nobody—that he is speaking the sentiments of a man alike unawed by the frowns and uninfluenced by the smiles of any.

Now, it is my design to have a vote of the Senate upon each of the four great subjects which agitate the country. I have paid some attention to them all; and it seems the total abolition of slavery is to be got at the end of a series of measures leading to it, especially the slave trade between the States, and the abolition of slavery in the forts, the arsenals, and the dock-yards. Sir, upon this latter subject, as well as upon the other, no thought has ever been entertained by any human being that I know of, that Congress designs to legislate. So, far from abolishing slavery within the grounds occupied by the United States for erections for military and naval purposes, so far as I know, Congress has never legislated upon these subjects at all. They are all in the same category with the abolition of slavery in the District of Columbia. Exclusive jurisdiction is given to Congress over such ground as is given for the seat of government, and for other specified purposes; but, sir, I do not recollect that Congress has ever exercised jurisdiction in a single case.

And does not that stand as an argument that Congress has no desire to meddle with the States at all? There are perhaps two or three hundred concessions by the States; there is an immense number of them; and I do not recollect that Congress has ever interfered with them in the slightest degree.

Then, Mr. President, with respect to the abolition of slavery in this District, I am one of those that believe it is covered by the constitutional power of Congress. I am one of those who believe, from the foundation of the government to the present day, that it ought not to be touched while slavery exists in the States from which the District was ceded. And surely Congress has shown no disposition to touch it.

I declare to the Senator from Alabama, that I have no desire to embarrass, and I see no earthly objection that can be made to this amendment. My object is, that we shall all vote together, and I believe we shall vote unanimously on this question, because it leaves every gentleman free to vote as he pleases. I believe the vote of the Senate will be unanimous upon the great points as to the abolition of slavery in the States, the ports, dock-yards, and arsenals, and nearly unanimous with regard to the power to abolish it in the District of Columbia. I believe that; and I believe, as I must repeat again and again, that it will have a better effect to quiet the country and restore harmony, than all the compacts prepared by any committee. Let us all vote together, and we shall silence agitation. I believe that is the way to quiet agitation in the country.

Now, Mr. President, the Senator from Kentucky thinks it is nothing to send these questions to a committee, because the committee will report against them. I do not agree to that. Is it nothing to give jurisdiction? Is it nothing to set the example of giving the right to think upon the subject, when I myself will not think upon it, and when this body will not think upon it? It will be creating real cause for alarm among the people in the States when they find any committee vested with jurisdiction on the subject of slavery. No committee, I care not on what side of the line, should have jurisdiction of it. I have no idea of setting an example which can be followed hereafter. I have no desire to depart from what has been the practice of the Government from its foundation to the present time.

Now, if we vote to lay this on the table, I shall ask the yeas and nays upon each of these points. It is with that view that I have offered this amendment. I have offered this as my compromise; I have offered it as my peacemaker, my healer, my restorer—as my balm of Gilead; it is to leave the hearts of the Senators open, and let the people look inside and see what is in them, and they will see there is no cause for agitation, and that is what I want to show.

Mr. WEBSTER. I regret that the Senator from Missouri should think it expedient or useful to attach these propositions of amendment to the general question of reference. It is quite evident, as I have once or twice before said today, that if we make all these questions upon a mere matter of the reference of these resolutions, these questions may be the subjects of debate for many days, keeping the main question of the admission of California in the mean time in abeyance. I acknowledge that I consider the reference of the resolutions to a committee rather a collateral proceeding. It is but yielding to a suggestion, that some good may come from it with a view of quieting the agitation which exists. And the honorable member will allow me to suggest, that it has already been intimated by the chairman of the Committee on Territories, that to-morrow morning he will call up the bill for the admission of California.

Mr. BENTON, (in his seat.) I will vote for it.

Mr. WEBSTER. I shall vote with the Senator for taking up the subject, and the Senator from Mississippi has promised to do the same. Then why does the Senator wish to use more time, and pursue a course likely to throw embarrassment upon this collateral measure, this trial for peace and harmony, by bringing up these most difficult and embarrassing questions, the whole of which we have got to meet? I was sorry that my friend from Connecticut attempted to refer the matter with instructions, and what I have seen to-day, but confirms me in the opinion that California makes no advance toward admission, while we are discussing these questions which run over the whole subject of constitutional law. Every thing contained in the constitution in any way relating to slavery comes up under a subject of that kind. I appeal to the judgment of the Senator whether there is any utility in this? I have not the power to stop it, of course; but if these propositions of the Senators from Kentucky and Tennessee may not be considered in a spirit of some kindness, and with some disposition to settle the agitation of the country, why, then, we make more excitement than we allay, and more difficulties than we compromise. I wish those resolutions to be disposed of. I think it better that they should be, and that leaves nothing on our hands; and unless to-morrow we begin with the deficiency bill, which my friend from New York has in charge, I am ready at once to take up the bill admitting California. Then we shall have something before us, to which all sorts of amendments cannot be presented, because none can be considered that are not in some way or other connected with the subject. I only wish therefore to get rid, if we can, of these series of propositions to amend, and then let the resolutions be referred or not, and proceed to take up the California bill immediately.

Mr. FOOTE. I only rise to explain what might otherwise be misapprehended, in the remarks just made by the Senator from Massachusetts. It is perfectly true, as the Senator states, and I authorized him in conversation, this morning, to say what I have before said in debate, that I would vote for the motion to take up the California bill whenever it was made. At the same time, the Senator will do me the justice to say, that I declared to him and to others, that in doing so, it was not my intention, nor could I consent, to do any thing that would in the least degree interfere with the action of the select committee raised.

Mr. WEBSTER, (in his seat.) Certainly.

Mr. FOOTE. If it be a practical thing, in the course of parliamentary proceeding, to take up the California bill as a separate measure for consideration and amendment, while that very subject is before the committee of thirteen, I have no objection, though it certainly seems to me to be inconsistent with parliamentary law, and a very inexpedient and improper course. All this was in connection with an understanding that has existed for some days past to this effect. The Senator from Illinois (Mr. Douglas) was to call up the California bill, when the Senator from Kentucky was to present as an amendment to that bill the territorial bill, and some other Senator was to present, as another amendment, the bill settling the Texas boundary question; so that we should have all the measures likely to be considered by the committee properly before us. I saw no objection to that plan of operations, if the committee was not raised. I did myself the justice, in the exercise of courtesy and liberality toward the Senator from Illinois, on yesterday morning to say to him, that so far as I was concerned, he could introduce the California bill first, with the understanding that no opposition was to be presented to the amendment expected to be proposed by the Senator from Kentucky, by the introduction of the territorial bill, and that I, for one, was not willing to give up the scheme of raising the select committee, but to postpone action upon it, so far as I was concerned, for a day or two, in deference to the Senator from Illinois, who seems perhaps not justly treated by us, in referring to the select committee of thirteen a matter which he himself, as chairman of the Committee on Territories, had reported upon. These are the facts of the case. I have no hesitation in saying that, so far as I am concerned, I am willing to take up the California bill, with a view to bringing in as an amendment the territorial bill, and otherwise amending it. To this end my vote shall be given, provided always that this can be effected without in the least degree interfering with the action of the committee of thirteen.

Mr. Butler. If this matter is to take the course indicated, I am satisfied that the result will be that the committee will gravely deliberate on all the subjects spoken of, and that, while the committee is out, the California bill will be taken up and disposed of by the Senate.

Mr. Foote. It cannot be reached before Monday.

Mr. Butler. I do not know how long the committee may be out.

Mr. Foote. We can propose the amendments to the bill, then.

Mr. Butler. I have understood from the beginning, that the great object to be attained was this, to use an illustration: there were three vessels at sea—one of them (California) was strong enough to carry the other and weaker vessels into port, if connected with her. California was a large and safe ship, and the other smaller boats in danger were to be attached to her, and she would carry them all safely into port. This I have all along understood to be the object. California was to be used for a beneficial, a generous purpose, and I had resolved to throw no obstacle in the way—without, however, giving up any objection I might have entertained. But now, according to the course indicated, I find that the committee is to be deliberating in the committee room while the Senate is to take from them the most important matter—the consideration of the California bill. That would indeed be taking the oyster and leaving the shell. I do not certainly understand what is to be referred to them, if the Senate is still to go on and consider the California bill; and if such is likely to be the result, I am ready at once to move to lay this whole subject on the table.

Mr. Benton. The Senator from Massachusetts has made an appeal to me in the spirit of candor, and I desire to reply to him in the same spirit, and to give him a reason for what I do. Now, it is certain that the agitation which has existed in one part of the country during the past summer—I do not wish to allude to any thing which will have the slightest effect on the feelings of any gentleman, and I allude to it for no such purpose—but it is incontestable that this agitation was produced by a certain address from members of Congress here. Now, what produced that address, and the meeting of members of Congress by whom it was reported? It was a motion to abolish slavery in this District. Sir, that is the root of all the trouble which the country has felt, and it is for that purpose I want that vote of the Senate which I know will quiet the agitation. It is for that purpose, and for no other. But the Senator from Massachusetts asked me a question. He comes from a quarter of the Union in which, according to the wisdom of Dr. Franklin, they are good at putting questions. I do not come from that part of the Union, but I am not absolutely a slouch at putting a question myself. The Senator from Massachusetts wishes to know why I will persist in these amendments when no practical consequence, as he thinks, is to result from it? I ask him why, on the other side, they will persist in sending these matters to a committee, when no practical consequence is to result from it? I put the question to him, and his action is precedent for it, why persist in sending these questions to a committee, when the adoption of the amendments I propose, which find a response in the heart of every Senator, will quiet this agitation beyond the possibility of any human being to re-establish it?

Mr. Foote. I have a suggestion to make, which, perhaps, is unnecessary, as the matter must be obvious to the whole Senate. The great object of the committee of thirteen was to embody a moral influence in favor of some plan of settlement which it is hoped may have a good effect here and elsewhere, and that is not to be attained by referring this matter to the Territorial Committee. It was supposed that a report from a committee of thirteen of the most distinguished men of this body—I speak without indelicacy, for I have expressly declined being on the committee myself—would have the most beneficial moral influence. It would not only be a combination of moral influence, so far as those thirteen gentlemen were concerned, but also of the whole moral influence of the committee.

The motion to refer the whole subject to the Committee on the Territories was rejected, as follows:

Yeas.—Messrs. Baldwin, Benton, Bradbury, Chase, Clarke, Corwin, Davis of Massachusetts, Dayton, Dodge of Iowa, Dodge of Wisconsin, Felch, Greene, Hale, Hamlin, Jones, Miller, Phelps, Seward, Shields, Smith, Upham, and Walker—23.

Nays.—Messrs. Atchison, Badger, Bell, Borland, Bright, Butler, Cass, Clay, Clemens, Davis of Mississippi, Dickinson, Douglas, Downs, Foote, Hunter, King, Mangum, Mason, Morton, Pearce, Pratt, Rusk, Sebastian, Soulé, Spruance, Turney, Underwood, Wales, Webster, Whitcomb, and Yulee—31.

The question then recurred on the amendment of the Senator from Missouri.

Mr. Benton. The extreme disposition I have to get on harmoniously, disposes me to adopt the amendment of the Senator from Kentucky. It is not, however, as strong as the amendment I offer. My object is to prevent the committee taking any jurisdiction of those subjects; the amendment of the Senator from Kentucky permits the committee to take jurisdiction, and at the same time denies them the power to do any thing. And while I certainly prefer my own, I can see no objection to a reference which tells the committee to do nothing in the world on the subject.

The Vice President. Is the Senator from Missouri understood to accept the amendment of the Senator from Kentucky?

Mr. Benton. Why, all this comes suddenly upon me. It is not so strong as my own.

Mr. Davis, of Massachusetts. I should like, for one, to have as a matter of information these propositions printed and laid on our tables.

Mr. Benton. This debate to-day has been conducted in a way pleasant to my feelings, and I doubt not to the feelings of the Senate. Agitating, exciting, and distracting as is the subject, yet we are acting upon it like a calm and deliberate Senate, and I am willing to go home and sleep upon it, and come back to-morrow, and finish it up harmoniously and understandingly to all. Intelligibility and harmony, that is all I wish.

Mr. Foote. There are, no doubt, several Senators who are desirous of postponing and avoiding action.

The Vice President. The question is on the amendment of the Senator from Kentucky; or is the Senator from Missouri understood to accept of that amendment?

Mr. Benton. Yes, sir; it is not so strong as my own, yet I will accept of it. I am for harmony and compromise.

Mr. Clay. Ah! very well.

Mr. Foote moved that the Senate do now adjourn.

And the Senate adjourned accordingly.

Tuesday, April 16.

The Compromise Committee.

Mr. Foote. I rise for the purpose of asking the consent of the Senate to renew a certain motion, which I had the honor of introducing the other day, for raising a committee of thirteen.

Mr. Dayton. It appears to me that, as the hour is far advanced, it is hardly worth while to go into a discussion of the questions involved in that motion; and, as there is much business pressing upon us of an Executive character, with the consent of the Senator from Mississippi, I will move now that the Senate go into an Executive session.

Mr. Foote. I cannot consent to withdraw my motion, sir.

Mr. Downs. I am as anxious as the Senator from Mississippi, or the Senator from Kentucky, or any other Senator can possibly be, that this question should be disposed of, and disposed of speedily. I have not delayed the disposition of it by saying a single word upon it. But it is very evident to me, and I think must be evident to every Senator present, that it cannot be disposed of now. However a majority of the Senate may be disposed to despatch this resolution forthwith, it cannot be done without the unanimous action of the Senate. Where, then, is the use of attempting to do a thing that cannot be done? What is the state of things? Here is a long string of amendments to this resolution, each of which, in all probability, will elicit debate, and there may be twenty others before the final question is taken.

Mr. Foote. If the honorable Senator from Louisiana will allow me to interrupt him for a moment, I think I can save him the necessity of proceeding further with his remarks at present. Some of us have thought it better to take up the resolution to-morrow, at half-past twelve o'clock, than to press it at this time. I therefore now only desire that it may be taken up for the purpose of making it the special order to-morrow.

Mr. Downs. That is just what I was going to do.

Mr. Foote. I now move, Mr. President, that this resolution be taken up for the purpose of making it the special order of the day for to-morrow, at half-past twelve o'clock.

The question was then taken on the motion to take up the resolution, and it was agreed to.

Mr. Foote. I now move, Mr. President, that the further consideration of this subject be postponed until to-morrow, and that it be made the special order of the day for half-past twelve o'clock.

The question was taken on the motion to postpone, and it was agreed to.

On motion by Mr. Butler, the Senate then proceeded to the consideration of Executive business, and, after some time spent therein, the doors were reopened, and

The Senate adjourned.

HOUSE OF REPRESENTATIVES.

Wednesday, April 17.

Election of Clerk of the House—Ninth Vote—Richard M. Young Elected.

The roll was called the ninth time; and the tellers reported that the whole number of votes given in was 188; necessary to a choice 95; of which

Mr. Young received	96
Mr. Walker	82
Mr. Prindle	5
Mr. Stansbury	4
Mr. Clarke	1
	188

[Mr. Stanly did not vote, having paired off with Mr. Cleveland.]

So there was an election.

The Speaker declared that Richard M. Young, of the State of Illinois, was duly elected Clerk of the House of Representatives.

On motion, the House then adjourned.

IN SENATE.

Wednesday, April 17.

The Select Committee of Thirteen.

The Senate proceeded to the consideration of the special order, being the motion of the Senator from Mississippi, (Mr. Foote,) to refer the resolutions of the Senator from Tennessee (Mr. Bell) and of the Senator from Kentucky (Mr. Clay) to a committee of thirteen.

The Vice President announced the first question to be on the amendment of the Senator from Missouri, a modification of which by Mr. Clay he had accepted.

The amendment, as originally proposed by the Senator from Missouri, was in these words:

Provided, That nothing in the motion shall be construed so as to affirm the existence of any power in Congress over the four following points:

1. The abolition of slavery within the States.
2. The suppression of the slave trade between the States.
3. The abolition of slavery within the forts, arsenals, dock-yards, and navy-yards of the United States.
4. The abolition of slavery in the District of Columbia.

The Senator from Kentucky proposed to amend so that it should read—

Provided, That nothing in the reference shall be so construed as to assert or imply the existence of any power whatever in Congress for the abolition by Congress of slavery within the States; nor to authorize the suppression by Congress of the slave trade between the States; nor that Congress ought to abolish slavery in the forts, arsenals, dock-yards, and navy-yards of the United States; nor that Congress ought to abolish slavery in the District of Columbia.

Mr. Clay. Mr. President, I desire to offer an amendment to the amendment proposed by the Senator from Missouri. It will be recollected by the Senate that the Senator from Missouri proposed an amendment, when this subject was last before the Senate, to restrict the committee in its consideration of these resolutions to thirteen topics, which are enumerated in his motion; and that I afterwards moved an amendment to that amendment, which the Senator from Missouri accepted. Therefore, the amendment as it now stands is the one which I proposed to modify, and which the Senator from Missouri has accepted. I now wish to propose an amendment to the proposition as modified by the Senator from Missouri.

The amendment which I now propose is to strike out all the propositions of the Senator from Missouri, after the word "provided," and insert the following:

"That the Senate does not deem it necessary to express or advance any opinion, or to give any instructions, either general or specific, for the guidance of the said committee."

Mr. President, I will make a single remark. The amendment of the Senator from Missouri, as it now stands, proposes to declare that Congress possesses no power upon certain subjects therein mentioned. Such a declaration on the part of the Senate, it seems to me, is wholly unnecessary, as the Senate would, by a unanimous voice, declare the belief that Congress has no power to abolish slavery in the several States, and so forth. I think it, therefore, useless as it at present stands; and I propose this amendment, declaring that the Senate does not deem it necessary, in advance, to express any opinion, or give any instructions whatever to the committee. I hope the amendment may be adopted.

Mr. Benton. Mr. President, the amendment which is called that of the Senator from Missouri, is the amendment of the Senator from Kentucky himself, which was accepted by the Senator from Missouri on Thursday last in a spirit of compromise. The Senator from Kentucky now proposes to amend his own amendment by rubbing it all out. Why, sir, I will withdraw it, and fall back upon my own original amendment, which I will undertake to get through, if I can, and I will call for the vote upon each point. I withdraw that amendment.

The Vice President. The amendment of the Senator from Missouri having been withdrawn, the amendments to that amendment fall with it.

Mr. Benton. Mr. President, I now offer my own amendment—

"*Provided*, That nothing in this reference shall be construed to authorize the said committee to take into consideration any thing that relates to either of the four following subjects:

"1. The abolition of slavery within the States.

"2. The suppression of the slave trade between the States.

"3. The abolition of slavery within the forts, arsenals, dock-yards, and navy-yards of the United States.

"4. The abolition of slavery in the District of Columbia.

"*And provided further*, That said committee shall not take into consideration any questions relating to the subject of domestic slavery in the United States, which shall not be specially referred to them by order of the Senate."

Mr. CLAY. Mr. President, I now move my amendment, as just now proposed, to the amendment of the Senator from Missouri. Strike out all after the word "provided," and insert the following:

"That the Senate does not deem it necessary to express in advance any opinion, or to give any instructions, either general or specific, for the guidance of the said committee."

Mr. CASS. It seems to me that the two amendments are in conflict. Do I understand that the amendment of the Senator from Kentucky is to be a substitute for the amendment of the Senator from Missouri?

Mr. CLAY. Certainly.

Mr. BENTON. I rise with great reluctance and deference to the honorable Senator from Kentucky, who is confessedly one of the best skilled parliamentarians, and perhaps is equal in that respect to any in America or Europe—I say, it is with great deference that I would suggest that he is not proceeding parliamentarily, when he offers such a resolve as that is, and calls it an amendment. I do not think it can come under the name, style, or description of an amendment at all. The object of it can be attained in a parliamentary way by voting down the proposition I have submitted. An amendment is to improve a thing, to make it better; but here is a design to obtain a resolution from the Senate declaring that they will not act upon the subject at all. Now, Mr. President, it is my intention, before we go into the question of amendments, in consequence of what was communicated yesterday as to the absence of a portion of the Senate on Monday next, to bring a motion before the Senate, which I communicated yesterday. Half a dozen Senators are to be absent by order of the Senate, and it follows, of course, that no question in which the States they represent are interested will be taken up during that time. If half a dozen members of the Senate go away on Monday on a mission that must keep them away one or two weeks, it will be one week or two weeks—no one can tell how long—before any thing that concerns California can again be taken up in the Senate. Now, we have three days and a half of this week to work in, and, during these three days and a half, it seems to me that what concerns California can be disposed of one way or the other; and before these gentlemen go away, that State will have a decision upon her application for admission. If any thing is done which prevents a decision upon her application, it stands over for one or two weeks more, in addition to the eight weeks which have already elapsed since the President communicated his message with the constitution of California. It is my desire, Mr. President, after having lost eight weeks, to avoid the loss of two more, which will be a dead loss, because we cannot touch the subject during that time, and all of us are sufficiently acquainted with what happens in parliamentary bodies, when any thing is laid down for two weeks and gets cold. When you take it up again, you take it up *de novo*, and give us a rehash of every thing that has been said before, with the addition of as much more as has been thought of in the mean time. To proceed in a way which will not bring the Senate to a decision upon the admission of California this week, is to make a dead loss of two more weeks, to be followed by as many more weeks as the discussion may last. I feel it to be my duty, in consequence of what was communicated to the Senate yesterday, and have made up my mind accordingly, to move, before we enter into the question of the committee, to take up the bill No. 169, reported by the Committee on Territories, for the admission of the State of California. I deem it my duty to make that motion, upon the belief that, having had this subject upon our hands, in some shape or other, since the meeting of the Senate in December—after having had the question of the admission of California, in some shape, upon our minds the whole of that time, we shall be able, in the three or four remaining days of this week, to act upon it in one way or another, if our action is confined to that bill, and nothing else.

Now, sir, I will read that bill, and let the Senate see how brief and to the point it is, and how comprehensive are the points which the bill contains. They are these, sir: That the State of California shall be and she is hereby declared to be one of the United States of America, on an equal footing with the original States in all respects whatever. That is the whole bill, as far as it respects the admission of California, and it is drawn in plain terms, according to the early precedents of our Government. The number of words is about the same as those used in the time of Washington, in the cases of Vermont, Kentucky, and Tennessee. Then just about the same number of terms were employed, and the same identical questions were presented. That is all that relates to the admission of the State. Then the second section of the bill, which might be here or anywhere else, provides that, until the representation in Congress shall be apportioned according to the enumeration of the inhabitants of the United States, the State of California shall be entitled to two representatives in Congress.

Sir, from there to there is the whole bill—not half a span by my hand, which is not a large span either. Now, sir, it is my opinion—and I shall make a motion to that effect, and ask the yeas and nays upon it—that if the Senate will lay down the motion which is now before them, and postpone other subjects, and proceed to the consideration of this bill for the admission of California, we can finish it this week, while we have the benefit of the presence of those gentlemen who will be absent next week, under the order of the Senate. We shall save a great deal of time, besides doing what is proper in itself with regard to this subject; that is, to admit California as a separate measure. If, on the contrary, Mr. President, this motion shall not prevail, and we go on with the motion for raising a committee, there will be some time inevitably taken up by the consideration of that motion, and after that is decided, the committee of thirteen will necessarily be required by the imposing gravity of their mission, to consider it some length of time before they report. Dr. Franklin, sir, in his wisdom—and his wisdom was such that it picked out whatever was wise or even decorous in the conduct of nations or individuals—relates an anecdote of an Indian chief, who, when called upon to sign a treaty of peace, considered it disrespectful to answer any propositions which were made to him till the next day, in order that he might seem, at least, to have considered the question. On the principle of the action of this Indian chief, who took one night to seem to consider a question which he was to decide upon, this committee of thirteen, acting under such impressive circumstances, with nothing less than the salvation of the Union in its hands, will have to consider many nights, before they can come back and tell us they have performed the duty which the Senate gave them. If they return incontinently, the Senate may suppose they had not considered it at all; or, what might be supposed much more material, that they had considered it beforehand, and that it therefore was a solemn farce to go out and come back with what, in the vernacular, had been "cut and dried" beforehand. They must consider; they are obliged to consider a week, perhaps two or three weeks, under such grave circumstances as they will be placed in. Here, then, is to be a great deal of lost time, if the proposed committee is raised. This week is gone beyond all question; and the committee will need that, and perhaps all the time while others be absent, to consider. Any attempt, then, Mr. President, to go on and raise a committee, I consider as a postponement of the question for weeks, and then to stand the chance of being brought forward incumbered with questions which do not belong to it, and which must necessarily give rise to debate here, and possibly a disagreement between the two Houses; and this long delay may result in the loss of the California bill by the disagreement between the two Houses. I see nothing, sir, but long delay and imminent danger to the California bill, by proceeding any further with this motion to refer to a committee. We have no need of it; we have the bill here, brief, pointed, exactly in the words in which the bills in all such cases were introduced in the early part of our history. I shall, therefore, make the motion which I intended to make yesterday, that when the question shall be taken up this day, before the pending amendment is gone into, to lay the subject of raising a committee on the table, for the purpose of taking up the bill No. 169, for the admission of the State of California, and upon that motion I ask the yeas and nays.

Mr. Clay. I hope the honorable Senator from Missouri will withdraw his motion for a moment.

Mr. Benton. Oh, certainly, certainly; any thing in a spirit of compromise, except the compromising of California away.

Mr. Clay. With respect to the parliamentary objection made by the Senator from Missouri to my amendment, if he chooses to present that objection in form, I am ready to meet it. The amendment was drawn after the fullest consideration that I could give to any possible question of form that might arise.

I pass that by, sir. It is a most unhappy non-concurrence for poor California between the honorable Senator from Missouri and myself. He wants California to be admitted. So do I. He regrets the lapse of time before her admission can take place. So do I. But it is a little singular that the honorable Senator himself—I must say it, in all respect and deference—is one of the causes which prolong the admission of California into the Union. Sir, I made a proposition to that Senator on Friday last, I think, which I will renew to-day. Let this committee be appointed without further opposition; which opposition, I think, will be found to be wholly unavailing, and to be productive of no consequence but that of an additional consumption of time. Let opposition to the appointment of the committee be withdrawn; let the committee be raised; let the bill for the admission of California be reported and acted upon in the Senate. Sir, when taken up, I have already intimated the purpose, which I shall not abandon, to propose as an amendment to that bill provisions to give territorial governments to the two new territories, without the Wilmot proviso. But, sir, short as that bill is, not occupying more space than the honorable Senator's hand, does he suppose that bill is going to pass in the shape in which it is, even supposing the rejection of my proposition? He talks about early precedents. If he means to refer to early precedents for the admission of new States, we shall violate all of them if California be admitted. For how were they admitted, from Ohio upward, but by the passage of a previous law proposing certain articles of compact to the new States, which were to be assented to by a convention of the people of the new States, and brought here in the shape of a compact, binding and obligatory forever upon both parties? How is it with California? Why, upon the subject of the public domain and the rights of the United States in California, if the bill were to pass in that little, brief space, which the honorable Senator has read and exhibited to the Senate, the consequence will be the loss of the public domain in California. I know my honorable friend from Illinois, who has seen this objection to the bill, has turned his attention to it, and I hope he will add to the valuable labors he has rendered the country and the Senate, by proposing a suitable provision to protect the rights and interests of the United States in California. But if California be admitted at all, she can only be admitted by annexing the condition to the act for her admission, that nothing in that act shall contravene or impair the rights of the United States in the public domain. I confess that, although I have rather brought my mind to her admission, upon the condition of the reservation of the rights of the United States in California, I do not think it quite equal to what it would be if it were a solemn compact between the people of California and the United States before it was admitted.

Now, sir, the honorable Senator talks of the delay which will ensue if the California bill be not now taken up and acted upon, as a committee will in a few days depart upon a melancholy occasion, and probably be absent about two weeks. He thinks we may get through with this in two or three days. Let all opposition to the appointment of the committee be withdrawn; let it be appointed; then we can take up the California bill and act upon it. So that, really, I say, without any intentional disrespect towards the Senator from Missouri, he is prolonging the admission of California in thus continuing to oppose the appointment of this committee.

Sir, let us look at all the facts connected with this matter. Suppose it were practicable to pass a bill for the admission of California, with suitable guards and protection to the public property; suppose it were practicable to pass it this week; why, then, we must turn our attention to the condition of things in the other House. The passage of a bill through the Senate, for the admission of California, does not admit California. It must first have the concurrence of the co-ordinate branch of the Nationl Legislature, and another co-ordinate department of the Government. If we are to judge of the future by the past, I should be very happy to be perfectly assured that the other branch of the Lgislature will be in a condition to transact the public business two weeks hence. If they consume any thing like the amount of time in electing an officer to supply the place of the lamented individual who has died, as they did in organizing at first, it may be weeks before that body will be even prepared to act upon any bill. I am willing to give California a chance, without our consuming time. It is so much waste of time, sir, to object to the committee. Let opposition to the committee cease. Let its fate be decided. If the Senate decide against it, there will be an end to it. But if there be a majority in favor of it, no dilatory proceedings, no parliamentary proceedings, no attempt to thwart the will of a majority of this Senate, (and I hope no such attempt will be made, and I charge no one with making it,) will, I trust, finally prevail. Let us then go to work and act like men, talk less and act more, and decide upon the question, and after that, take up the bill for the admission of California. That is my view of what we should do.

Mr. Benton. I propose the point of my objection, if there be any point in it, to his specious amendment. My objection to it is, that it is a resolve to govern the conduct of the Senate; that it is an independent resolve to govern the conduct of the Senate. It has nothing to do with the business which is included in the motion. It is simply a resolve, which can be introduced and considered by itself—a resolve, I repeat, to govern the conduct of the Senate in their action upon a certain case. In that point of view, it seems to me that what is called an amendment is not an amendment, but an independent resolve.

But the Senator from Kentucky makes a proposition, or renews one made yesterday, and, in his extreme good nature, supposes that all parts of the Senate are in the most amicable temper possible. It is nothing more nor less than that a jury should go out with the case, and after the jury has gone out with it, the counsel and advocates may proceed to argue it. That is his proposition, and whether the case is sent to a jury of twelve or thirteen, makes no difference. The jury of thirteen is to go out in this case. Sir, it is nothing more nor less than a proposition to send a jury out with the case, and we have been sufficiently advertised of the fact that that jury is to consist of the distinguished and leading members of the Senate. These distinguished and leading gentlemen will go out, and will deliberate upon the case, and while they are deliberating, why, the remainder—those perhaps who would necessarily fall into the category of led members—may be amusing themselves—with discussing the subject and presenting their views; and, whenever the jury of thirteen shall have made up their verdict, they will come in, and whoever may happen to be upon his feet at the moment, will have to take his seat, and will be cut off exactly where he stood; the delivery of the verdict putting an end to the whole case he is arguing. This is rather a new proceeding in the Senate of the United States, and I object to the idea of sending out a jury with a case, and leaving other Senators here to argue it.

The Senator from Kentucky, sir, charges me with occasioning all the delay in the admission of California. And how do I occasion it? By resisting a motion to send this question to a committee. Have I not a right to do that?

If I have no right to do it, it is a question of order, which the Chair may decide; and if it is decided that I have no right, I will sit down at once. But while I have a parliamentary right to proceed in a certain way, all efforts to deter me from proceeding, by throwing on me the blame of obstructing business, will be of no avail. But this is no novelty. We have great examples for throwing the blame of being promoters of disturbances upon those who are innocent. I believe, Mr. President, there were never more professions made in favor of peace, there were never more encomiums delivered upon peace, nor ever greater sentiments of devotion to peace uttered or professed by any being upon the face of the earth, than were uttered by him who was the greatest of warriors—the great emperor. He was always for peace; how, then, came he to be always in war? Because, when his armies entered a country, the people would resist, and that made war, and made him a disturber of the peace which he was so anxious to preserve. That is exactly the way the great emperor got the name of being a disturber of the peace—the people would resist when his armies entered their country. All that he asked of them was to submit; all that he asked was, that they should be quiet, and let his armies move over their country. They had come for their good, and perhaps for something else. Yes, sir, when one of the ladies that George I. brought from Hanover, and afterwards made a duchess, was once passing through the streets of London, she was hooted at, if not pelted; and when for the purpose of pacifying the mob, she declared she had come for their "*goots*," meaning their good, one of the populace replied readily, supposing that goods were meant, "and for our chattels, too." And so of the great emperor; he entered all those countries for the good of the people, and for their chattels also; and, as they did not choose to have good performed for them in that way, war was the result. They resisted, and thereby made war, and made the emperor a disturber of the peace, lover of peace as he was.

In the same identical manner, Mr. President, with a parallelism which has been drawn here somewhat too close for a parody, the Senator from Kentucky charges me with delaying the admission of California, because I resist where I have a right to resist; and more than that, where I hold it to be my duty to resist, and where I am sustained by sixty years of uninterrupted legislation of the two Houses of Congress. Sir, three times Washington, the Father of his Country, sent in Messages for the admission of new States, precisely under the same circumstances as those under which President Taylor sent in a Message in this case. Tennessee, Kentucky, and Vermont, were all admitted precisely under these circumstances, and upon the presentation of Messages precisely like this. Five other States were admitted afterwards, under the same circumstances, and by Messages of the Presidents of the time in which those States were admitted, making eight in the whole, being as near half as eight can be of seventeen. I am doing what has been done for sixty years. Every State that has been admitted for sixty years has been admitted in a bill by itself, except in one single case, and then two were put together in the same bill. Two States applied for admission at the same time, and had no more right than California now has, for they made their constitutions for themselves, without the previous authority of Congress. I am doing what I have a right to do, what I feel it to be my duty to do, what sixty years of legislation justifies me in doing; and while this is the case, it will be lost labor to undertake to scare me off the track, by saying that I am obstructing legislation on the subject.

The honorable Senator from Kentucky has said on several occasions, and repeated it again here to-day, that California will come in sooner if all these subjects be taken together, exciting as they appear. Come in sooner! Now, it is hard for me to conceive that the Senator has an insight into this matter which I have not. Though I profess to be able, when I have a view of things, to see as far into a millstone as he that picks it, yet I cannot see the pickers here. The Senator from Kentucky undertakes to say that these things will go on, and California will come in sooner, if she is mixed up with all these foreign questions—foreign to her certainly. Now, he certainly understands what he says. I do not. I do not understand why one subject, complicated with an immense number of others, is to go faster than it could go by itself. There may be a question in this, as to the public lands. I here repeat what I said the other day, that when the question of the admission of the State is up before the Senate, it will be proper to discuss the question of admission, and then I shall expect the Senator from Illinois, who has reported this bill, to satisfy me and the Senate upon this point. It will be sufficient time to discuss that, when we come to discuss the bill. The supposition is, that the bill is to go faster when complicated and loaded with all these subjects than it can go alone. There is something in that which is inexplicable to me. I know there is an idea, which may be called vernacular, prevalent in some parts of the country, that a horse can pull stronger if he has a weight upon his back, and I have often seen large packs with two or three bushels of grain upon a horse's back, while he was straining every nerve in pulling a load up hill. The argument was, that it kept the backbone straight, and enabled him to draw directly against the centre of every joint. [Laughter.] That was done in the case of drawing; but this is a case of running. California has to run, and as it seems to me, she has to run the gauntlet and a long line. I never heard it supposed that a horse ran faster for having a load upon his back; but when we come to look at what is proposed to California, we shall find she has not only three hundred pounds upon her back, but we shall have a hundred pounds to tie to each leg, and still a pretty considerable weight to tie to the tail. I should like to see how Californa would run with three hundred pounds upon her back, and a hundred to each leg, and fifty pounds to the tail. It will be a strange thing for the people of California to learn that, in the opinion of the American Senate, their State is to run faster precisely in proportion as she is loaded down.

I have been occupied, Mr. President, wholly with the preliminary question of laying this resolution upon the table, and postponing its consideration for the purpose of taking up the California bill. I am not arguing the admission of California; I have not got to that. I am not arguing the motions which will be made to amend the motion to send out this committee; much less, sir, am I arguing the question of such a committee at all. All these things are in advance of what I want. All that I want, as I have made known, is to put this in a shape which will admit of no dispute. The question is now as to the delay, the almost indefinite delay, with the chance of eventually losing the admission between the two Houses. We have now three full days remaining of this week, and I think, if we proceed, we can in these three days come to a decisive vote on the California bill, and in doing that, we shall have washed our hands and done our duty; and it will then be for the House of Representatives to do their duty, a thing with which we have nothing to do.

Mr. DOUGLAS. Mr. President, when the objection was raised the other day, by the Senator from Alabama, that if the bill reported by the Committee on Territories was passed, all the public lands within the limits of that State would be lost to the Government, would belong to the State of California, I promised the Senate that when that bill should be taken up, I would vindicate the bill entirely from all apprehensions on that score; and that, if I could not do it by argument, I would certainly do it by amendment. I had hoped, therefore, that criticisms upon that part of the bill would have been deferred, and that the public mind would not have been prejudiced by allusions to that supposed defect, until the California bill came up for consideration. It has, however, been alluded to, and the high authority of the Senator from Kentucky has been given to sanction the correctness of the opinion expressed by the Senator from Alabama.

Sir, I hold myself entirely capable of removing all apprehensions upon that point, on reference to well-established authority—a large number of cases—forming such a current of authority, as, I apprehend, that no one, after investigating the facts, can question the correctness of the opinion which I expressed. Sir, as a Senator from the State of Illinois, I may rejoice if the Senator from Kentucky, or the Senator from Alabama, would succeed in maintaining the position that they have here assumed in regard to California. If that position be correct, I am prepared to show that this Government owes the State of Illinois nineteen millions of dollars, for lands sold within that State, and that fifteen millions of acres of unsold lands, held by the Government of the United States within the limits of that State, now belong to the State of Illinois. Yes, sir, and also that this Government owes Ohio twenty millions, and owes Indiana twenty-one millions; and other States large sums, to the amount of ninety odd millions of dollars, for lands sold within those States, the money for which has been received by this Government, when the proceeds belonged to those States, if the position assumed by the honorable Senators from Alabama and Kentucky be correct.

Mr. FOOTE. I rise to a question of order. But if my friend from Illinois desires to make only a few remarks in vindication of his bill, I will certainly withdraw it. If, however, he designs extending his remarks, I feel bound, as the proposer of this resolution, to insist upon the point of order.

Mr. DOUGLAS. I will state the limit of my remarks, and the Chair can then decide. I propose to extend my remarks just so far, and not one iota farther, than is necessary to reply to the charge made by the Senator from Kentucky.

Mr. FOOTE. I understood the honorable Senator from Kentucky to throw out a single suggestion, which may or may not have been in order, accompanied by the additional suggestion to the Senator from Illinois, which I thought in order. Now, sir, my point of order is, that it is not in order, on the question now before the Senate, to go into the discussion of the general question.

The VICE PRESIDENT. It is the opinion of the Chair that the remarks made by the Senator from Illinois (Mr. DOUGLAS) were foreign to the question under consideration, and consequently out of order.

Mr. DOUGLAS. I will refrain, then, from any expression of opinion on the point on which I was proceeding to address the Senate.

Mr. HALE. I move that the Senator from Illinois have liberty to proceed.

Mr. FOOTE. If he desires it, I will not interpose any objection.

Mr. DOUGLAS. I do not desire the Senate to depart from its usage on my account. The Senator from Kentucky was simply arguing a position, with the best of motives, which I thought would throw an imputation upon me as the chairman of a committee. Hence I thought it my duty to myself and to my committee, to vindicate the California bill from that imputation. And if the motion of the Senator from Missouri prevails, I shall take the floor and make that vindication. If not, I shall feel bound to do it on this resolution, when the subject comes up in the course of debate.

Mr. Foote. I rise to make a personal explanation. I trust my friend from Illinois will understand, that if I had not considered that he had already combated with considerable effect the suggestion thrown out by the honorable Senator from Kentucky, and other Senators—if I had not considered the war about even—I would not have raised the point of order.

Mr. Clay. Mr. President, I wish to make a single remark. I certainly expressed no deliberately formed opinion whether the admission of California, without any provision as to the disposition of the public lands of the United States in that State, would prevent the United States from holding the public domain there located. But, sir, notwithstanding all that has been said, I shall insist, as a precautionary measure, that some clause be inserted declaring the retention by the Government of the United States of the public lands in California. It is not necessary, however, to go into the discussion of the subject now. I trust the honorable Senator from Illinois, at the proper time, will enlighten us on the point. For myself, I should be glad that the enactment of such a law would not be necessary.

Mr. Douglas. I would state to the honorable Senator from Kentucky, that although I am prepared to show that it is unnecessary, yet, by way of precaution, I am prepared to offer an amendment, which I hold in my hand, to remove every doubt on the subject. But I can show that such an amendment will not be necessary.

Mr. Butler. Mr. President, what is the question before the Senate?

The Vice President. The question is on the motion to amend submitted by the Senator from Kentucky, (Mr. Clay.)

Mr. Benton. I withdrew my motion to lay the subject on the table, in order to give the Senator from Kentucky an opportunity to say a few words. Other Senators also embraced the opportunity.

Mr. Butler. I do not rise to make any remarks. I merely wish to know whether the motion of the honorable Senator from Missouri, to take up the California bill alone, or the amendment offered by the Senator from Kentucky, be pending?

The Vice President. There can be no motion to take up the California bill until the question now before the Senate be disposed of.

Mr. Benton. I move to lay this subject on the table, for the purpose of taking up the California bill, and on that motion I ask the yeas and nays.

The question was then taken on the motion to lay the subject on the table, and it was rejected, as follows:

Yeas.—Messrs. Baldwin, Benton, Bradbury, Chase, Clarke, Corwin, Davis of Massachusetts, Dayton, Dodge of Iowa, Dodge of Wisconsin, Douglas, Felch, Greene, Hale, Hamlin, Jones, Miller, Norris, Phelps, Seward, Shields, Smith, Walker, and Webster—24.

Nays.—Messrs. Atchison, Badger, Bell, Borland, Bright, Butler, Cass, Clay, Clemens, Davis of Mississippi, Dickinson, Downs, Foote, Hunter, King, Mangum, Mason, Morton, Pearce, Rusk, Sebastian, Soulé, Spruance, Sturgeon, Turney, Underwood, Whitcomb, and Yulee—28.

Mr. Mangum. I understand the question now to be on the motion of the Senator from Kentucky.

The Vice President. That is the only question before the Senate now.

Mr. Miller. I wish to make a suggestion in regard to the amendment of the Senator from Kentucky. It appears to me to be out of order, and not coming within the rules of the Senate. The Senator from Missouri proposes to amend the original resolution by the adoption of certain instructions to the committee proposed to be raised. The Senator from Kentucky moves to amend that amendment by striking it out, and to declare in substance that no instructions shall be given to the committee. So that the amendment not only strikes out the amendment proposed by the Senator from Missouri, but if adopted, it declares that no further instructions on any other point shall be given to the committee. Now, can that be done? If it can, I mistake the rule in regard to a bill. Suppose this amendment is offered to a bill, and a Senator moves to strike out all of the amendment, and to substitute in lieu thereof a declaration that no further amendment shall be made to the bill: can that be done? The amendment goes further than the amendment offered by the Senator from Missouri, for it not only strikes out his amendment, but declares that no further instructions shall be given on any other point. Now, by the rules of the Senate, when a resolution or bill is under consideration, it may be amended at any time, and we cannot declare by an amendment that no further amendment shall be made to the bill. Neither can we declare that no other or further instruction shall be made to a committee. We can strike out these instructions, but we cannot by an amendment declare that there shall be no other amendment.

Mr. Clay. Of all unprofitable subjects, these questions of parliamentary law and usage are the most so. I have had, sir, in another branch of the Legislature, some little experience on this subject. But, sir, what is the objection which the Senator from New Jersey makes upon the ground of order to my proposition? The Senator from Missouri proposes to affirm certain instructions which I propose to negative. Now, are we not at liberty to vote in the negative upon those instructions? Well, if we have a right to vote against them, have we not a right to put that negative in the form of an amendment, and vote for it? But I will state a case which every man of three days' service in a deliberative body understands perfectly well. A report is made by a Special Committee —for example, on a claim. It concludes, "resolved, therefore, that the claim ought not to be allowed." Now, is any thing more common in a legislative body, than to strike out the words "ought not to" and to insert the words "should be"? Every man at all acquainted with parliamentary law knows that if a new subject is proposed—one which has no connection with the one under consideration—it is not in order. But whether they are substitutes for the amendment, or propositions to amend it, they are precisely the same. They relate to instructions to the committee. The amendment of the Senator from Missouri proposes to give such and such instruction to the committee. My amendment says that the Senate will give none, and it is perfectly german to the subject, and perfectly consistent with all parliamentary law that I have ever heard of in any deliberative body.

Mr. MILLER. I do not make this point of order in any captious spirit, and the Senator from Kentucky has not understood the point I make. I do not object to this motion that it is a negative of the proposition made by the Senator from Missouri. The Senator is perfectly correct there, but his amendment goes further, and cuts off all further instructions that the Senate may think proper to give to the committee. That is the point, sir.

Mr. CLAY. That is the design of the amendment, and I ask of the Senator from New Jersey, who I am glad has given up half of his objection—

Mr. MILLER. I have not given it up, for I never made that to which the Senator refers.

Mr. CLAY. I understood the Senator from New Jersey to object, first, that my proposition was a negative to affirmative instructions. Now I understand him to say, his objection is not that it comprehends all that was offered by the Senator from Missouri, but that it laps a little over; that, in other words, it declares we will give no instructions to the committee. And has not the Senate the right to do that—to say that it will give no such instructions? And has it not a right, either through the medium of an amendment, or in any other form? There cannot be a doubt on the subject.

Mr. MILLER. That is the very point I wish to raise before the Senate—whether the Senate, by an amendment to a bill or resolution, can declare that it will not give any instructions to a committee?

Mr. BENTON, (in his seat.) That's it, sir.

Mr. MILLER. That is the question. Can a Senator, when an amendment is offered to a bill, move to strike out the amendment, and declare subsequently that no amendment shall be offered to the bill? Can you, in a resolution where an amendment is offered to instruct, strike out these instructions, and declare that no other shall be given? Why, we have on the table several other instructions offered by the Senator from Missouri, and are they to be cut off?

Mr. FOOTE, (in his seat.) They have not yet been offered, but merely suggested.

Mr. MILLER. I may think proper to offer instructions, or other Senators may so intend, and it cannot be done if this amendment is adopted.

The VICE PRESIDENT. The Chair will consider the point of order as raised.

Mr. KING. I hope the Chair will decide it.

The VICE PRESIDENT. The Chair is of opinion that the objection is not well taken. The amendment, which proposes to restrict the action of the committee, is moved to be stricken out by another amendment. That is clearly in order. It is then proposed to substitute, in lieu thereof, the declaration that the Senate do not deem it necessary to express in advance any opinion, or give any instruction, either general or specific, for the guidance of said committee. The utmost that can be said of the amendment is, that it decides nothing. And, if it expressed nothing but the mere motion, it would leave the matter just where it was left before the amendment was proposed. Therefore, though it may be a consideration to induce a Senator to vote against it, it is not a question upon which to raise a point of order as to its reception.

Mr. BENTON. This, which is called an amendment, and which strikes me as being nothing but a rule of action, which the Senate is called upon to adopt for itself, was objected to by me as being unparliamentary, at the time it was offered, but I was so unfortunate as not to make the point of my objection intelligible. I will endeavor to do so now, and let it be seen that here is—

Mr. KING. If the Senator intends to discuss the question of order, he must appeal from the decision of the Chair. In the absence of any such appeal, the decision is binding upon the Senate, and every Senator is bound to acquiesce in it. The Senator from Missouri, therefore, if he is dissatisfied with the decision, must take an appeal before he can discuss the point of order.

Mr. BENTON. What I say is for the Senate, and not by way of appeal.

The VICE PRESIDENT. Does the Senator appeal?

Mr. BENTON. I am speaking merely to the Senate, and not by way of appeal. I am speaking on the proposition submitted by the Senator from Kentucky, and I mean to give my reasons—very poor ones to be sure—why it should not be adopted. I take that to be in order.

The VICE PRESIDENT. Yes, sir.

Mr. BENTON. Well, I have learned something. If I cannot teach, I can be taught. Yes, sir, here is a proposition, which is called an amendment, that the Senate does not deem it necessary to express in advance any opinion, or give any instructions, either general or specific, for the guidance of said committee. Now, here is a declaration, very proper perhaps to be adopted in a caucus, but not belonging to the Senate at all, by which the Senator asks that the Senate shall cut itself off from its parliamentary rights, of offering amendments to bills and resolutions while going through the body. All this might do in caucus, but it will not do in the Senate. The Senate does not deem it necessary (why not deem it necessary?) to give any instructions at all on any subject to the committee. It is a committee, as is frequently proclaimed—though its appointment is not yet entered on the Journal—composed of distinguished and leading men, and it may be that they have all the wisdom of the Senate in their hands, and that when they go out, nothing will be left behind, and all the rest of the Senate, put together, can give them no information. All this may be so, but it is the first time that the American Senate was ever called upon to make such a declaration. It is not to do it in advance. Why not do it in advance? Has not the Senate been in the practice of giving instructions to committees, from the foundation of the Government to the present day? Is it not done in regard to all committees, whenever Senators choose? And was it ever proposed before to tie up the hands of the Senate by a previous declaration, that they will not give opinions in advance? They may give them afterwards, and may agree to what may be done, but beforehand the body of the Senate is to do nothing. It is not to give any instructions, either general or specific, for the guidance of the said committee! Sir, the objection is well taken by the Senator from New Jersey, that this goes beyond the amendment which I have offered, and which is before the Senate. It goes beyond what is before the Senate, and declares at once that, no matter what amendments any Senator may have in his bosom, no matter what may be offered, the Senate will not consider them. This, sir, is a new declaration to be made in the American Senate, and one of those which, if it pass, will pass after going through such parliamentary forms as will mark it as an epoch in our parliamentary history. Sir, it is a new method of applying the previous question—a question never applied in this body. It is a new method of applying the gag—a thing never done in this body. It is a new way of stultifying the whole body of Senators, except those who go out of the committee. Sir, all this is new; and is it not as impotent as it is new? Suppose the Senate resolve itself into what seems to me to be nothing more than a caucus, and adopt this resolution. What next? The moment they have adopted it, has not every member here a parliamentary right to offer amendments on the spot, regardless of what the Senate has decided upon? The attempt is impotent. We have a right to offer instructions after instructions, and when offered, the only way for the Senate to do, if it will not adopt them, is to refuse them; that is, to vote them down when presented. That is the only way—the only sensible method. If the Senate adopts this resolution, that it will not give any instructions, they cannot get rid of the question. We have the right, every one of us, while we remain Senators, to offer our propositions for instruction. And I presume there will be enough to offer those instructions, and test their parliamentary right to do so; and Senators will be brought to the point on each instruction for itself, while there is enough to call the yeas and nays to vote on each for itself. All this must be apparent. And now, sir, why persevere in endeavoring to get a declaration from the Senate which is to cut off a parliamentary proceeding, when you cannot do it? It will end in impotency; of that, gentlemen may rest assured. It is the first time that ever such a thing was attempted in the American Senate. It is cutting us off from deliberation. It is cutting us off from our right of instruction, and it is forestalling debate. It is an assumption, the like of which never before was known in this body.

Now, sir, this great committee—we have had their names in the newspapers, though they have not yet been elected by the Senate. Grant that they have all the wisdom of the Senate, and will carry it out with them; yet the Senate is not to declare upon this proceeding that it could give them no instruction. They are not to adopt a resolution which admits that the Senate cannot enlighten them at all. It is not for the Senate to say that they would sit here in Egyptian darkness, until the committee comes in and illuminates the Chamber. And now, if it should be the fact that every thing is ready, that the report is ready, and that the committee have nothing to do in the world after it goes out, but to come back again—like the French king who marched up the hill and down again—if such should be the case, would it not better become the American Senate that it should be produced, and let us have the illumination from it at once? Would it not be better to produce the report at once, and act on this bill for the admission of California as it came along?

I have taken up more time than I intended on this preliminary point. I consider it wholly nugatory, that, after what is called an amendment, but is nothing but a resolve to govern the action of the Senate, shall be voted upon and adopted—as it may be, though I think, if the thirteen gentlemen who are to compose the committee will abstain from voting, it will not be adopted; and really, delicacy, I think, should forbid them to vote—after all that is done, I say it is nugatory; for we shall undertake to exercise our parliamentary right of offering instructions; and we think that some of us have been here just about long enough to know how to do it, and to get a vote upon every instruction, in some form or other, that lies upon the table, and upon every instruction that may hereafter be offered.

Mr. Clay. I am very sorry, Mr. President, for this unnecessary consumption of the time of the Senate; but there are two or three remarks which the honorable Senator from Missouri has made, which seem to me to require some notice. The honorable Senator has spoken of a caucus, and intimated that there has been one. On what authority does the Senator make such an assertion? I now pronounce it a mistake—an absolute and entire mistake. There has been no caucus, that I know of; although, God knows, I would attend a caucus of any and everybody, to settle this most unhappy question, which is now distracting the country; and I would attend it without any feeling of reproach, from whatever quarter it might be ventured to be hurled. The honorable Senator speaks of his rights. Yes, sir; and other Senators have their rights also; and other Senators are just as well prepared as the Senator from Missouri is, to assert their rights. And the Senate has its rights. Now, sir, I put it to the Senate and the country, what has been the progress of this matter? The Senator from Missouri proposes an amendment embracing four propositions, and, as a sort of menace, I suppose, he shells out eight or ten others, and speaks of his having others yet in reserve. Well, my dear sir—Mr. President, I mean—has not this body a right to protect itself? Has not the majority of this Senate a right to say whether they will or will not create a committee without any instructions? The resolution will be adopted. The Senator offers his set of amendments—for the purpose I will not say, because I have no right to go into the intention of the Senator—but the effect of them would be delay, procrastination, embarrassment; and that effect is attempted, or will be attempted to be produced against these distinct and emphatic expressions of the opinion of the majority of this body. The question, then, comes to this—whether the Senate shall or shall not have the power—I speak always of the majority of the Senate—to act? I say, sir, it ought to have it; and I care not by what name you call it. The previous question!—ah, sir, not many years will elapse before you will find the indispensable necessity of this valuable mode of terminating a useless and unnecessary debate in this House. In my reflections upon the past, in respect to my parliamentary career —my Congressional career—I look back to none with more satisfaction than the introduction of that previous question in the other wing of this building. But, sir, it seems that all at once there has been some extraordinary violation of the rights of the Senator; and what is it? That we create a committee without giving that committee any instructions—a thing which happens every day, and sometimes two or three times a day, either to a special or standing committee—every day of the session, either in this House or in the other.

Now, sir, is it not known that if you refer a subject to a committee, you must, to some extent, confide in that committee; leave it untrammelled, unshackled, to the exercise of its best judgment? for, at last, when it does any thing, it is reported back to you, subject to your decision, to your power, to your control. Sir, what was done with the committee proposed in the case of the very State which the Senator represents, appointed in the other House in the year 1822? Were any instructions given to that committee? Not one. Was any embarrassing mode of procrastination attempted on that occasion? And afterwards, in relation to the constitution of the committee, that happened which had never happened before, and which, perhaps, will not happen again for many years. When I proposed in the House of Representatives the constitution of a joint committee, to consist of twenty-three on the part of the House, and a suitable number on the part of the Senate, to consider the question of California—of Missouri, I mean. Why, sir, it is not at all extraordinary that I speak of California; for if we listen to the honorable Senator on the other side of the House, there are no United States—California has absorbed every thing. [Laughter.] When I proposed a joint committee of twenty-three on the part of the House, and a suitable number on the part of the Senate, was there any motion in the other body to instruct, to manacle, to chain down that committee? No, sir; they were left free as air, to explore through the whole region of patriotic intellect, for the purpose of devising a mode by which that unhappy question should be settled. Sir, what is proposed? The honorable Senator has several times talked and presented, in his witty and humorous manner, the figure of a horse borne down by a grievous weight cast upon its back. Why, sir, the Senator knows perfectly well, that the whole amount of what was intended by anybody, is to connect and combine together the government of territories acquired in common, and to establish for these territories a suitable form of government adapted to their respective situations.

And, sir, what is the condition of the case? Let us look at the facts. There is a certain portion of this body that is for California. Give us California, California, and nothing but California. There is another portion of this body and of Congress that says, we are willing to give you California, but we want something more than California; we want to establish governments for a people thrown by the vicissitudes of war and of political events under our care. And, to my utter surprise, I have heard Senators upon this floor express the opinion that we should leave all New Mexico and all Utah—New Mexico with a population of one hundred thousand, and a military—yes, I have heard Whigs, Whigs express the opinion that we should leave the military government which is in operation in New Mexico to continue; Whigs who denounced the existence of the military government established under the authority of the late Administration during a season of war; and yet now, in a state of profound peace, it is proposed to pass California, pass California, pass California, and leave New Mexico and Utah to take care of themselves. Sir, it is contrary to every obligation of duty resulting from the treaty, resulting from the constitution, resulting from the position and character which we hold as American statesmen and legislators; and as soon as leave New Mexico and Utah without government—of all others the portions of that country the most in want of governments—I would, as a father, as lief turn out my son at the age of fifteen into the streets of a corrupt city, and say to him, "Go, my boy, take care of yourself until you are twenty-one, and then come back to me, and I will tell you what honorable vocation in life to select." Sir, it is our duty, our bounden, our solemn duty, to make at least an attempt to establish governments for Utah and New Mexico; and if we cannot do it after making the effort, we shall stand reproachless for not having done it. If we cannot do it, it will be the result of differences of opinion unfortunately existing amongst us, which will prevent its being done. The error of those Senators who talk of leaving Utah and New Mexico to their fate, is exactly this: they begin where they ought to end. Begin to discharge your duty; try to make governments for these territories, and if you fail to do it, you will stand unreproached in the eyes of God and man in having made the effort to discharge your duty.

I have said that one portion of Congress wants California, and nothing but California; another portion, whilst for bringing in California, says, Let us settle this distracting question; let us establish territorial governments without the proviso, and connect them with California. And why should not we do it? I have heard the "dignity of California" alluded to, as if all the gold and dignity of the nation had sought refuge and found an asylum on the shores of the Pacific. I have been utterly unable to comprehend this derogation from the dignity of California. Sir, I go for both measures; both ought to be carried; both, in my opinion, ought to be associated together; and I do not see the slightest evidence of disrespect to California, or to anybody else, in doing it.

Sir, I framed this resolution deliberately, and I framed it for the purpose of getting rid of the unnecessary instructions, which the Senator from Missouri has proposed, and to dispose of any other instructions which his ingenuity—and no man possesses a greater amount of it than he does—might suggest to be brought before this body. Let my amendment be adopted, and let the Senator offer his other instructions, from one to ninety-nine, if he pleases, and we will see whether the question of order will not silence them all.

Mr. Benton. Mr. President, the State of California is not here, and unless somebody stands up for her, it seems likely that she will go to the wall; for she not only gets hard knocks, but she gets also what is called trumps. She is spoken of to-day as absorbing the whole United States. So far as I can see, she only wants to get in among the United States—to be one of thirty-one, and to be the last of the thirty-one. That is all I can see in her wants. But the Senator from Kentucky not only presents California in this aspect, but he presented her some days ago in an attitude which I did not then remark upon, and which I should not do now, but for the manner in which he has brought her up to-day. It was said by the Senator from Kentucky the other day, that California had made a runaway match, and now turned up her nose at her unmarried sisters. Well, sir, if she did make a runaway match, she did not marry a runaway negro: and if her unmarried sisters should marry into that family, it may be that, when they come about her and into her company, she may not only turn up her nose, but snub their noses. California has made a constitution for herself, and in that constitution she has left out slavery in every form, and the proposition now to unite her with the fugitive slave bill—

Mr. Clay. Will the Senator allow me to say that there is no such proposition?

Mr. Benton. The Senator from Kentucky, it is due to him to say, has in his speeches disclaimed it; but the Senator from Kentucky, eminent as he is, and leading as he is, is not the record. The motion is to refer two sets of resolutions. One is the honorable Senator's own set of resolutions, and the other that of the Senator from Tennessee, (Mr. Bell,) and those two sets of resolutions do include the subject of runaway negroes, and the original motion now pending will carry with it all these subjects. Here is a proposition, then, to unite California with a subject of which she has washed her hands, and which has already delayed her, is now delaying, must continue to delay her, and may in the end lead to her rejection. She will have nothing to do with the slavery question. There is nothing in her constitution about slavery, because she did not wish to have it impede her admission into the Union; but if the territorial measures are to be added, and those measures are to have the question of slavery mixed up with them, then we shall have a question brought up by which the whole admission of California, after being delayed for such a length of time, may be lost in disagreement between the two Houses. Sir, I cannot be driven off the track by hearing it urged that there is nothing in this proceeding injurious or derogatory to California. In my opinion it is both injurious and derogatory; injurious already in the delay it has created, dangerous in the conjunction which it may make of questions which may result in a disagreement between the two Houses, and by which she may be lost. We all remember the Oregon bill, and the contest between the two Houses on that bill.

The honorable Senator from Kentucky says that it may become necessary to introduce the previous question here. Whenever the Senate by resolve shall introduce the previous question here, though I shall struggle against the adoption of it, as I have done heretofore, to the utmost—for I go for full debate in this Chamber—yet whenever the Senate adopts the previous question, I shall submit to it; but until the Senate adopts it, I will resist its unauthorized and disguised execution upon this body. Sir, we now have it admitted that here is the previous question, in a different form from that which is known to the parliamentary law; that here is the previous question, intended to cut off all amendments; every thing in the world which the previous question contains, except the form and except the rule which leads to it. It is now a bastard rule, surreptitiously introduced and attempted to be forced upon us by a declaration that the Senate will not pass upon any amendment. It is the previous question, sir, and it is most revolting, and if it were anybody else than the eminent Senator from Kentucky who had proposed it, I should say that it was a most unparliamentary motion.

But, Mr. President, this committee is to go out for compromise. Now, what is a compromise, and how long are such things kept? What was the validity of the compromise made between the Senator from Kentucky and myself—how long was it inviolable? I offered a set of resolutions which I deemed good ones; the Senator from Kentucky got up and moved to have them amended, by substituting another set. I did not think his equal to my own at all, but in a spirit of compromise, and as a compromise, I accepted them, and did what a compromiser ought to do, immediately give up his own. And yet, what is the state of the case to-day? I thought then that the Senator from Kentucky was going to vote for his own amendment; I thought he was going to accept the compromise which he had made; and yet to-day, sir, he flies from that amendment, he does not stand to it; he objects to the whole of his own amendment, which I accepted the other evening in a spirit so conciliatory that it ought to have brought us all to harmonious conciliation. Now, sir, we are going to have another compromise, a plan of compromise with this experience of compromising before our eyes. I have no great faith in compromises at any time. There are compromises in the constitution; they are fundamental, they are permanent, they are obligatory; we are sworn to observe them, and these compromises I wish religiously to keep. But as for these, which seem to me like the compromises of lovers, made one evening to be broken the next morning—as for these compromises which I have referred to, really after this experience—this, I would say, flagrant experience, in the face of the Senate, between myself and the Senator from Kentucky—I do think that the idea of bringing a compromise into this body ought to be abandoned altogether.

Mr. President, we ask the yeas and nays upon this motion; and if the Senator's resolution—for I can call it nothing but a resolution—for the guidance and conduct of the Senate shall be adopted, we shall immediately undertake to test it, and to see whether the rules in your book are not in force which allow Senators to offer instructions; and we are entitled to a vote upon this resolution, and which cannot be laid on the table without carrying the whole subject with it.

The yeas and nays having been ordered on the amendment of the Senator from Kentucky—

Mr. DOUGLAS said: I feel inclined to vote for the amendment of the Senator from Kentucky, and I will very briefly give my reasons for that vote. My object in resisting the appointment of the select committee, was to get at the practical question of the admission of California into the Union. A majority of the Senate has on three different occasions, by the yeas and nays, declared that the Senate is in favor of the appointment of a committee. We are authorized to infer from these three test votes, that that majority is determined to appoint this committee. Sir, if they are determined upon it, they have a right to the appointment of a committee. I hold that, if I occupy the position of making factious opposition to the majority of this body, I give a license to a factious opposition from the other side, in the manner that has been threatened, in order to keep California out of the Union. I will do no act, here or elsewhere, that shall be a precedent, that shall be a license to an opposition under the rules of the body, but which can only have the effect to occasion delay by thwarting the majority. I will sanction no course of proceedings which may give that license when California shall be put upon her passage. For this reason, I feel disposed to vote for the amendment offered by the Senator from Kentucky, and on the ground avowed by him; that is, to cut off all amendments, and let this matter go to a committee, if there is a majority to send it there, for them to act according to their discretion. When they come to report, there will be a vote taken on the proposition as a whole, if it shall be one, or upon their several propositions, if there shall be more than one. Those who think it wise to separate the measures will have an opportuuity then of testing that course, by the yeas and nays, in this body, and they will then have an opportunity of recording their own opinions upon the record. I deprecate this course. I would prefer the consideration of the California State bill at once, and let the motion to unite be made here in the Senate; but if I cannot have my own way, I will not delay the Senate by preventing the majority from having theirs. I shall vote to cut off all these amendments, in order that the committee may be appointed at once, if it is to be appointed at all. And, sir, the remarks of the Senator from Missouri have relieved my doubt upon this point, when he informed us that there was reason to suppose that this matter was all cut and dried, and arranged; that the committee had been formed, that the measures had been agreed upon, that the whole matter had been arranged, and that it is but a farce to go out, and bring in the verdict. If that be true, it will take but a very short time to get through with the farce, and I would rather laugh at the farce than wrangle and quarrel, and make it a tragedy instead of a farce. The objection urged by the Senator from Missouri has convinced me upon this point—that we had better submit to the farce, allow them to go out, and to come in. This is not my opinion, but I have come to this conclusion simply in order to save time, and to get at the practical question. I see no use in prolonging this controversy, against the express will of the majority of the Senate. I speak for myself, and for no one else. I felt it due to myself to express my own opinion, in order to put myself before the country in the light in which I wish to stand before my own constituents.

Mr. Webster. I merely wish to suggest, sir, what I conceive to be an irregularity in the motion of the honorable Senator from Kentucky, (though he is as competent to judge of the order or irregularity of a proceeding as any gentleman in the country.) I care not, sir, how this motion to raise a committee be decided. I have no interest in it, because I am inclined to think that no great benefit can now be derived from it; but I must say that I do not think that the motion of the honorable member from Kentucky is in order. I do not think that it is a motion that can be received and entertained by the Chair; because I think it is the direct reversal of one of the standing rules of the Senate. Any proposition may be made——

Mr. Foote. The honorable Senator from Massachusetts, I know, is not aware that this is *res judicata.*

The Vice President. Does the Senator from Mississippi rise to a point of order?

Mr. Foote. I do, sir. I know that the Senator from Massachusetts was not in the house at the time, and I am sure he would not pursue the present course of discussion if he knew that this point had been decided by the Chair already.

Mr. Webster. I did not so understand it.

Mr. Foote. The point of order was raised, and the Chair decided that the motion was in order.

Mr. Webster. I suppose, if the amendment is in order, I may give my reasons for voting for it or against it; if it is not in order, I shall not say any thing about it. The rule of the Senate is, that the proposition under consideration may be amended. Now, suppose that this were a bill, could it contain a proposition that it should not be subject to amendment? Or could any gentleman move as an amendment to it, that this bill should be carried through the Senate without any proposition to amend? I apprehend that he could not; and I submit to the honorable member from Kentucky whether his motion is strictly in order? If I understand his resolution, it expresses the opinion that we ought to go clear of all propositions to amend. Is that the sentiment that will be expressed in the amendment if we adopt it?

Mr. Clay. I do not wish to interrupt the Senator, but here is a proposition to raise a committee of thirteen, and to refer to that committee of thirteen certain subjects. Very well. The Senator from Missouri proposes to do what? To impose certain restrictions upon that committee. Well, what is my proposition? The negative of his, accompanied by a declaration that we do not wish to give any instructions to the committee, and especially not those proposed by the Senator from Missouri. We have the right to vote these amendments down one by one: my proposition amounts to the same thing. The original motion is to raise a committee and refer certain subjects to it. The amendment is, to restrict that committee. My proposition is, that we will not adopt the restrictions proposed, or any other, but leave the committee free and untrammelled.

Mr. Webster called for the reading of Mr. Clay's amendment; which was read accordingly.

Mr. Webster. The Senator from Kentucky will excuse me if I doubt the propriety of his motion. I suppose it will not be in order, if this resolution is passed, to have any further amendments. I very much doubt whether such a motion should be received by the Chair. I doubt whether it is not a question for the Senate to decide, whether any amendments that may be proposed shall be adopted. It is my opinion that it is.

Mr. Mangum. Some question has been raised by the Senator from New Hampshire, or rather some objection made in regard to the phraseology of the amendment proposed by the Senator from Kentucky, to wit: "That the Senate does not deem it necessary to instruct the committee." They may not deem it necessary at this instant, and an hour hence there may be a change of opinion. The modification that I propose, and which I trust the Senator will accept—for I cannot offer it in the shape of an amendment, there being an amendment to an amendment, already pending—is, that it shall read thus: "The Senate does not deem it necessary, and therefore declines to instruct the committee."

Mr. Clay. I accept the modification, sir.

The question being put upon the amendment as modified, the yeas and nays were taken and resulted as follows:

Yeas.—Messrs. Atchison, Badger, Bell, Borland, Butler, Clay, Cass, Clemens, Davis of Mississippi, Dickinson, Dodge of Iowa, Douglas, Downs, Foote, Hunter, Jones, King, Mangum, Mason, Morton, Pearce, Rusk, Sebastian, Soulé, Spruance, Sturgeon, Turney, Underwood, and Yulee—29.

Nays.—Messrs. Baldwin, Benton, Bradbury Bright, Chase, Clarke, Corwin, Davis of Massachusetts, Dayton, Dodge of Wisconsin, Felch, Greene,

Hale, Hamlin, Miller, Norris, Phelps, Seward, Shields, Smith, Walker, and Whitcomb—22.

So the amendment to the amendment was adopted.

Mr. Hamlin. I desire to have the original motion read by the Secretary; I mean the motion made by the Senator from Mississippi.

The Vice President. That motion was to refer the resolutions of the Senator from Tennessee and those of the Senator from Kentucky to a select committee.

Mr. Hamlin. Yes, sir, I am aware of the purport, but I want the precise words, because I desire to amend the motion. I propose to amend by inserting these words: "Except so much of the same as relates to the admission of California as a State." I take it, sir——

Mr. Turney. I rise to a question of order. I understand there is a question before the Senate. The question now is upon the amendment of the Senator from Missouri as amended.

Mr. Foote. In addition to that I would suggest——

The Vice President. The Senator from Tennessee is correct; the question will be on the amendment as amended.

The amendment as amended was then adopted.

Mr. Hamlin. I suppose it will now be in order to move to amend the original motion?

The Vice President. It is in order.

The proposed amendment was again read.

Mr. Clay. I believe, sir, that is the precise proposition that was made the other day by the Senator from Missouri, and which was voted down.

Mr. Hamlin. If the gentleman had waited for a moment, I would have explained the reason why I offer this amendment. It is true that another proposition, similar to this, but embracing a larger number and greater variety of questions, was submitted a few days since, and it was voted down. The motion of the Senator from Mississippi now is less extensive than it was then, consequently the vote of the Senate to connect or dissever the questions then, cannot be considered tantamount to a vote to exclude a portion of them now; although I have myself no doubt that the action of the Senate will be the same now as it was then. It is my intention, and it is also, I believe, the intention of my colleague, to vote for no territorial bill that does not contain an express prohibition of slavery. We have been instructed by the Legislature of our State to that effect, and those instructions accord fully with our own views. Well, sir, being so instructed, and cordially approving of those instructions, I desire to present this proposition to the Senate, so that I may exhibit the evidence of my willingness to carry out that doctrine in good faith, and to vote for no measure by indirection which shall cover up a subsequent vote, and thus relieve me from those instructions. Therefore, I ask that I may have the privilege now of voting to dissever them, so that if they should be connected by the committee, as I suppose we all understand they are to be, that then, when I am compelled to vote against the admission of California, on account of its being connected with other questions, if that contingency should arise, this amendment will show my desire to disconnect them.

Mr. Clay. The motion made the other day is precisely that which is now offered. It is in these words:

"But nothing in the resolution shall be construed to authorize the said committee to take into consideration any thing that relates to the admission of California into the Union."

That is the resolution that was voted down.

Mr. Hamlin. I do not desire to offer any other reason than I have already offered, except to say that, upon the proposition then pending, no committee was then raised, and nothing grew out of it. There was an expression of the opinion of the Senate, it is true; but under that motion no committee was raised, and the motion was subsequently withdrawn. If, under the present motion, a committee is to be raised, as I doubt not there will be, I desire to record my vote in favor of the separation of the subjects.

Mr. Cass. Mr. President, I would suggest to the honorable Senator from Maine, whether he would not attain his object in a better manner by awaiting the report of the committee, and then by moving to separate California from the other subjects, should it be associated in the same bill with any other? The Senator desires that his position should not be misunderstood, and therefore wishes to have a vote now upon this question. As to the appointment of a committee, there is no danger of misunderstanding, because he has announced his objection to the measure, and will record his vote against it. He is presupposing that the committee will unite various subjects in the same bill, and wishes in advance in effect to pronounce upon it. This interpretation may not be correct. There may be no such reason, and in that event this measure would be wholly unnecessary. It would be a mere work of supererogation. If, on the contrary, the union should take place, it will then be as competent for the Senator to move a separation, as it is now to move a prohibition against it. The subject will be just as much in our power then as now, and it will be much more proper to act in that case, for we shall then be dealing with existing facts, and not with imaginary ones.

And this same error, as to the course of the committee, seems to pervade all our discussions upon this subject. It is assumed that, because different subjects are to be referred to this committee, they must therefore be included in the same bills, and the one, therefore, made dependent upon the other; and this assumption, made, it appears to me, without the least authority, is then urged as a decisive argument against this proposition of reference.

In the first place, sir, no one has a right to assume that such will be the case, and to make this bare assumption a ground of opposition to the proceeding. I agree with the distinguished Senator from Kentucky, that no committee would thus unite all the questions referred to it. I consider such a course out of the question; so much so as not to furnish, even to the most cautious, a reason for voting against this measure. I go further, sir: I do not believe that there will be any further union of subjects in the same bill than the junction of the admission of California with the governments of the territories; and I see a great fitness in that. But, sir, should the committee go further, and include more topics, what effect will that have? Just none at all, in opposition to the will of the majority.

Gentlemen seem to suppose that the report of the committee is to be like the laws of the Medes and Persians, not subject to any alteration or amendment whatever. And the Senator from Maine evidently acts upon the same supposition, when he makes his motion beforehand, to guard against a particular course of action on the part of the committee which he happens to disapprove. And permit me here to remark, that a great deal has been said about an understanding among Senators—a caucus of the leading members of this body, and much more of the same sort. This is certainly making a great matter out of a very small one. It is of little consequence whether there has been any caucus or not, or whether there be in reality such an understanding or not. I will say, however, that I have heard of no caucus, and know of no understanding upon the subject. If there be any such, I am utterly ignorant of it. And I repeat, it is a small matter to be placed so prominently before the Senate and the country—to talk so earnestly about caucuses and about leaders. I know nothing of either. I, for myself, am as little disposed to lead as I trust I am to be led.

Now, here is a proposition to refer to a committee a grand subject, affecting the very existence of the Confederation. It is said to be unusual; but it must be remembered that the present condition of the country is unusual also. There is a proposition to refer all the questions connected with this grave subject to a committee. Well, what is the objection that is urged against this reference? A good deal has been said about instructions to the committee, and about an effort to check debate. Now, it seems to me that no reasonable man, who has listened to the debate that has taken place to-day, can suppose that there is any disposition to check debate. If this debate has been checked, it would require a wiser man than I am to tell what would be a free debate, or to what length of time or topics its course would lead us. Senators have pursued their own course in their own way, and a more discursive debate I have never listened to. I have little apprehension that, here or elsewhere, any martyrs can be made to the great cause of free discussion by the proceedings of to-day. All such allusions are, to say the least of them, in very bad taste. And what is to be the practical disposition of the labors of the committee? The subjects will come back to us reported upon by the committee; the whole matter will be within the jurisdiction of the Senate, and any proposition to amend can then be made as well as now. Let the subject go to the committee, and let them make the best report they can; no man will be committed by the report whatever it may be; we shall be pledged to nothing the committee may do. All that is proposed is that, in the difficulties in which we find ourselves involved, a committee shall deliberate, and ascertain if some practicable plan cannot be devised for the settlement of the agitating subjects which now distract the country. Can any reasonable man object to this course? I freely confess I cannot see how he can. I have listened to every word that has been said in the course of the debate, and my surprise has increased rather than diminished at the opposition which is exhibited. The proposition affords one hope the more for an accommodation of the differences that divide us. I said when this measure was first introduced, that my hopes of the advantages to be derived from it were by no means sanguine; and the course of proceeding in the Senate since that time has by no means increased my confidence in the result. I followed the honorable Senator from Kentucky in his declaration of similar views, as I am happy to follow him in his noble effort to preserve this Union, equally dear, I have no doubt, to him and me. But, whether my hopes or my appprehensions preponderate, as to the effect of this measure my course will be still the same. It may do good, and can do no harm. As I have said, it affords one chance the more of a happy termination of our troubles. If the committee make a report that will be satisfactory, we can adopt it and rejoice heartily at the happy result. If they do not, we shall then be no worse off than we are now, and must proceed to look our difficulties in the face, and to apply the best remedy which may then be left to us; and in any event it will be a grateful reflection that we have taken this step, deemed so important by many members of this body, and so urgently demanded by a large portion of the Union. And this consideration, were there no other, is decisive with me for supporting the proposition. It is indeed a small, a very small matter to yield in a spirit of conciliation; but it seems to be opposed with as much sternness of purpose, as if a sacrifice of the dearest interests of the country were demanded. I sympathize, sir, with no such feeling, nor indeed do I understand it. North or South, East or West, when great sectional questions are involved, if I could not yield the principle at issue, certainly I would yield much as to the mode of its consideration, and as to the process of adjustment. In no country under heaven is such a spirit more required than this; and if it prevailed more extensively, I should anticipate with more confidence than I now do, not merely the speedy settlement of the questions in dispute, but the restoration of those fraternal feelings without which, though there may be a political union, there can be no union of affection. It seems to be distinctly understood that the discussion of the subject of the admission of California is to go on, notwithstanding the reference to this committee; and before the discussion can be terminated under any circumstances, to judge by the progress made, the report will be received, and we shall then have made some progress towards a solution of our difficulties; we shall have done something, much indeed, I trust, towards the admission of California, and the establishment of the necessary territorial governments.

I repeat what I have before said, that I consider the admission of California as certain as any event which has not yet happened, unless prevented by some process or machinery of legislation in the other House, such as has been alluded to here and elsewhere. I trust, however, that no such measures will be resorted to. I should consider it a course of action greatly to be deprecated. All we have to do is, to permit the committee to consult and bring back a report. A good deal has been said about compromises, as though, by the appointment of this committee, we were proposing to surrender some great principle lying at the foundation of our Government. Indeed, one might suppose, from the temper and earnestness displayed, that our whole social and political system was to be put to hazard by this very harmless attempt to adjust our troubles by a compromise committee. And such are our fears of this terrible word, that we have actually struck it out of the resolutions, where it had been very properly introduced, and made ourselves safe behind the shelter of its substitute, *adjustment*. Why, sir, neither the word nor the thing is so very terrible. This world is a world of compromise. From the cradle to the grave, human life is full of compromises. A man gives up some portion of his natural rights to secure the remainder; and from the beginning to the end of his years, the same principle marks his progress. He who stands upon his position with rigid inflexibility, and expects the world to bow before him, will soon find by experience, how much he has deceived himself. In the operations of all Governments there must be compromises. I suppose there never was a law passed which precisely met the views, in all particulars, of every one taking part in legislation. Each can see something which, in his opinion, might be improved; but each has to surrender something TO COMPROMISE, in order to attain the object in view. What mutual concessions are to be made to lead to a compromise in any given case, is always ready to be determined by the circumstances. I suppose no one dreams of the cession of any of the questions connected with the application of California. With the views I entertain, and have expressed upon that subject, I never can consent to *compromise* away her rights. Such a measure is disavowed in all parts of this chamber. But measures far short of that, from the indications we have received, would afford satisfactory grounds for adjustment. Many who object to the admission of California as an insulated proposition, have avowed their willingness to abandon their opposition, if that measure is connected to a bill for the government of the territories. Is that a compromise which involves any surrender of principle, or, indeed, of expediency? Is it not a small peace-offering upon the altar of our country, if it is followed by the restoration of peace and harmony? As has been well remarked by the distinguished Senator from Kentucky, it will be fulfilling an obligation we have solemnly taken; it will give equally to the people acquired by the same treaty, the governments suited to their condition.

It is, in fact, no compromise, but the performance of a duty. It is doing precisely what we ought to do, and what we have engaged to do. If the opposition to California can be removed by such an act—compromise, if you please to call it—and that State brought into the Union more easily and more speedily, as I believe it can, I am in favor of it; as I should be opposed to it, were that great measure put to hazard. And I hold myself as free to act after the report of the committee as I am now—under no obligation, however slight, to accept it, unless I think it just and reasonable. And I am well satisfied that we shall secure the admission of California much sooner by this process than by any other, especially by endless opposition and endless discussion, of which this day has had its full share, as has many a day before, and as will many a day hereafter, if the same spirit prevails; and while we are thus talking about delay in the admission of California, that very delay is produced more by this cause than by all other causes put together.

I am opposed to any instructions, for a most obvious reason. Would you make a farce of what should be a solemn measure? If you select thirteen members of this body as a committee of reference, have you not confidence enough in them to trust something to their discretion? If you have not, you had better abandon the project. Cannot you trust them to talk over this whole matter, and to tell you what they think of it, without fettering their thoughts and their tongues, and saying omit this and that subject, for we cannot trust you even to offer us an opinion upon it? Why, sir, no honorable man would serve upon such a committee, purporting to be organized for a great national purpose, and responsible in the eyes of the country for its proceedings and its recommendations, but divested of all means of effecting any valuable object, and rendered impotent by the very act of its creation. I am willing to have the opinion of any thirteen members of this Senate upon this whole subject, and then I shall be as free as I am willing to consider their report in a spirit of respect, and to adopt just as much of it as I think the public interest requires. In the mean time, and while the committee is deliberating, I shall vote with the distinguished Senator from Kentucky for proceeding with the discussion respecting the admission of California, and making all the progress we can.

Mr. Benton. The amendment proposed by the Senator from Maine is now pending.

The Vice President. The Chair has been making inquiries, and now learns that this amendment was submitted to the original motion first, and that it was withdrawn, and was appended by the Senator to the motion now pending. The Chair, in comparing the amendments, finds a verbal difference.

Mr. Benton. Then the Chair decides that the amendment of the Senator from Maine is not now pending before the Senate?

The Vice President. That is the impression of the Chair. The Chair is of opinion that it is out of order.

Mr. Hamlin. Will the Chair allow me to make an inquiry? Was there any amendment to the motion now pending?

Mr. Foote. If the Senator from Maine will allow me, I think I can explain this. The other day, pending the amendment of the honorable Senator from Missouri, I submitted an amendment which gave the motion its present shape, so far as I recollect. I have a tolerably distinct memory of the fact, and I think the record will also show it.

The Vice President. The Chair understands, that after the present motion to refer the resolutions of the Senator from Tennessee and those of the Senator from Kentucky to a select committee, that then the Senator from Missouri submitted to that motion the following amendment:

"But nothing in these resolutions shall be construed to authorize the said committee to take into consideration any thing which relates to the admission of California into the Union."

And the vote was taken on it, and it was rejected; and now the Senator submits the following:

"Except so much as relates to the admission of California as a State."

Mr. Hamlin. There are certain resolutions to accompany this resolution of the Senator from Mississippi to the Select Committee. My amendment is simply to prevent a part of these resolutions from going to that committee, leaving the rest of the resolutions to go to it. The other amendment was that the whole of the resolutions should go, but that they should not act upon them. I think there is a difference in the two propositions. I proposed to keep from that committee a certain portion of the resolutions proposed to be submitted by the Senator from Mississippi. The amendment offered by the Senator from Missouri did not propose to withhold any of the resolutions, but to instruct the committee how to act after they had got there.

The Vice President. The Chair reads the first amendment, in the following words:

"But nothing in this resolution shall be construed to authorize the said committee to take into consideration any thing which relates to the admission of California as a State into the Union."

The present amendment is to except from the reference so much of the same as relates to the admission of California as a State. The only difference is, that in the one case they are proposed to be referred to the committee with instructions, and in the other without.

Mr. Foote. Certainly; the action of the committee must be the same in both cases. I now understand the question to be decided by the Chair.

The Vice President. The Chair thinks it is a proper question for the Senate to decide.

Mr. Benton. Then I understand that the amendment is pending, and I offer as an amendment to the amendment the fourteen points of instruction; and I shall ask the vote of the Senate and the yeas and nays up n each of these fourteen points; and I will see whether or not the previous question is in force here yet.

The Vice President. The Senator from Missouri moves to amend the amendment by adding thereto the following:

1. With instructions that, in any bill, scheme, or other measure or measures they may report, they shall not connect the admission of the State of California with any other proposed legislation which shall require the assent of any other State to its completion.

2. That they shall not connect the admission of the State of California with any measure which is connected with a question of boundary or other controversy with any other State.

3. That they shall not connect the admission of the State of California with any other measure of less dignity than the reception and admission of a sovereign State to be a new and entire member of this Union.

4. That they shall not make California a party to, or in any way include or connect her with, any provision in the nature or intent of a compact relating to slavery, or to any slave State or slave territory, other than the compacts of the constitution.

5. That they shall not make California a party to, or in any way include or connect her with, any provisions in the nature or intent of a compact of any description, other than the compacts of the constitution, and those compacts relating to the domain which have been heretofore required of new States formed out of the territory of the United States.

6. That they shall not report any measure proposing any alteration in the boundaries of the State of California.

7. That they shall not make the State of California a party to, or in any way connected with, or the question of her admission in any way connected with or dependent on, any provision in the nature of a compact which has not been required of either of the following named States: Ohio, Indiana, Illinois, Michigan, Louisiana, Mississippi, Alabama, Arkansas, Missouri, Iowa, Wisconsin, and Florida.

8. That they shall not make a party to, or in any manner bind to, include in, or connect with, any provision having the character or intent of a compact, any State, or people having the political organization of a State, not represented in this body.

9. That they shall not connect the admission of the State of California with any matter foreign to the admission of that State in a direct manner, on a precisely equal footing with the original States, and unincumbered with any other conditions, responsibilities, or considerations.

Mr. BENTON. There were five others offered before these, which I wish would take precedence of them:

They were read as follows:

Provided, That nothing in this instruction shall be construed to authorize the said committee to take into consideration any thing that relates to either of the four following subjects:

1. The abolition of slavery within the States.

2. The suppression of the slave trade between the States.

3. The abolition of slavery within the forts, arsenals, dock-yards, and navy-yards of the United States.

4. Abolition of slavery within the District of Columbia.

And provided further, That said committee shall not take into consideration any question in relation to the subject of domestic slavery in the United States, which shall not be specially referred to it by order of the Senate.

Mr. DICKINSON. I understood the Chair to decide that it is a question for the Senate to determine, whether the amendment now proposed by the Senator from Maine is not the same in substance as that offered by the Senator from Missouri.

The VICE PRESIDENT. The Chair decided that it was not so identical as to make it the same.

Mr. DICKINSON. I understood that the Chair was going to submit the question to the Senate?

Mr. UNDERWOOD. This, if I understand it, is a proposition by the Senator from Missouri to amend a proposition submitted by the Senator from Maine. The Chair doubts as to the point of order in reference to the proposition submitted by the Senator from Maine, but I wish the decision of the Chair upon the point of order embraced in the proposition offered by the gentleman from Missouri. Now, we have just adopted a resolution that we will not instruct the committee. The resolution, or rather amendment, proposed by the Senator from Maine, does not propose to send any instructions to the committee, but is an exception of a portion of the subject to be committed. It seems to me, however, that the amendment of the Senator from Missouri contemplates an instruction as to what the committee shall, and what it shall not do; and it therefore presents itself to my mind that, so far as they propose to direct the committee, that it shall, or shall not, do such and such a thing, it is in violation of the amendment of my colleague, which has already been decided, and therefore not in order, although the proposition of the gentleman from Maine may be in order.

While I am up, permit me to make one or two other remarks. I must say that I concur entirely with the remarks which have been made by the honorable Senator from Michigan on this subject. I think they were very seasonable, and hope they may have their due weight. I regret exceedingly that we should be here hour after hour, and day after day, discussing things of no importance; and I would submit to the honorable Senator from Missouri whether there can be any utility in proposing such instructions, or in taking the course he is now pursuing. Sir, would it do any good, if I were to take up the Constitution of the United States, and propose that the committee should not interfere with the establishment of religion in the country; that it should not interfere with liberty of speech; that it should not grant titles of nobility, or do any other of the hundreds of things which may be prohibited by the constitution, or by the whole tenor of our institutions? Certainly, sir, if a young member like myself, a gentleman unknown to fame, as humble and unpretending as I am, should do a thing of that sort, what little reputation I do possess would very soon be lost.

Now, sir, it seems to me that these general abstract propositions, although perfectly true, and although no one would gainsay one of them, we should not be alarmed at rejecting in this way. It does seem to me that if we ever intend to come to any practical result, we will allow the committee to go out, as proposed by the Senator from Michigan, to give us the benefit of their consultations; and when they present the result of their labors before us, we can consult them, and we will get rid of all these abstract propositions, which the gentleman from Missouri must see are only calculated to embarrass the question it is so desirable should be settled.

Mr. President, I present the point of order. I think it is out of order to propose these points of instruction, when the Senate have already decided that they will not instruct the committee.

The VICE PRESIDENT. The amendment of the Senator from Missouri is objected to on the ground that it is an instruction to the committee, and therefore inconsistent with the resolution in relation to the instruction of the committee, which the Senate has adopted. The

Chair is of opinion that the proposition presented by the honorable Senator from Missouri is in the nature of instructions to the committee, to except from their deliberations a certain subject. But the question that presents itself is, whether inconsistencies are questions of order. On the 169th page of the Manual I find that

"If an amendment be proposed inconsistent with one already agreed to, it is a fit ground for its rejection by the House, but not within the competence of the Speaker to suppress, as if it were against order. For, were he permitted to draw questions of consistence within the vortex of order, he might usurp a negative on important modifications, and suppress, instead of subserving, the legislative will."

The Chair is of opinion that the amendment is in order, but it is for the Senate to decide.

Mr. Clay. I rise to perform the painful duty of appealing from the decision of the Chair, and I ask the yeas and nays on the question. I do not mean to take up time. My opinion is, that when the Senate has decided that it will not do a given thing, it is out of order for that thing to be proposed to be done, and it is within the province of the Chair to decide it to be out of order. The question is, whether the Senate will maintain its power, whether it will maintain its dignity, whether it will maintain its consistency; and upon that ground I must take an appeal from the decision of the Chair.

Mr. Benton. I believe that the amendment, as it is called, though it is nothing but a rule for the government of the conduct of the Senate, has not been adopted by the Senate.

The Vice President. The question is on the appeal.

Mr. Benton. And now, Mr. President, I must recur to the main point, that here is an open attempt to enforce the previous question without any rule of the Senate, and to press the previous question against the rule. It is admitted that it is to cut off all amendments; it is admitted to be the previous question in a different form, and it is even treated as a factious attempt to arrest the enforcement of the previous question here; to cut off all amendments where there is no rule to authorize them. I am opposed to this course, and determined to resist it as long as the parliamentary law permits me. I understand that the Senate declines to give instructions to this committee; but I have a parliamentary right to offer them; and, when they are offered, there is no way to get rid of them but by a vote upon them. That is all. I have a right to offer them. The rules are not altered. The Senator from Kentucky has got a resolve adopted, but that cannot alter the rules of the Senate. They cannot be altered by a side move; they cannot be altered, pending a question, for the purpose of cutting off debate. Rules must be known, and they must be adopted beforehand; and if they are to be altered, there must be notice given that they are to be altered; and the process must be gone through in a regular manner. The rules of the Senate cannot be overturned; they cannot be obliterated; they cannot be expunged by a vote adopted in the progress of a case that the Senate will do a thing contrary to the existing rule. Sir, the motion of the honorable Senator from Kentucky, and which has been adopted, is a motion to overrule the rules of the Senate; to trample the rules of the Senate under foot, for the purpose of stifling debate; for the purpose of cutting off amendments; and when we come to these amendments, we will see whether or not they are abstractions, which have been made the root of all the agitation that has taken place in the United States. Sir, I intend by these amendments to cut at the root of all that agitation, and to cut up the whole address of the Southern members, by which the country was thrown into a flame. I mean to show that there was no foundation for any such thing; that is, I mean to offer a proposition upon which the votes will show that there has been a cry of "wolf," when there was no wolf; that the country has been alarmed without reason, and against reason; that there is no design in the Congress of the United States to encroach upon the rights of the South, nor to aggress upon the South, nor to oppress them upon the subject of their institutions. I propose, sir, to give the Senate an opportunity of showing that all this alarm has been without foundation; and I further propose to give to the people of the United States the highest declaration that can be given upon earth, that they have been disturbed about nothing; and when we come to that part of the question, we will see whether they are abstractions or not; and if these are abstractions, then the country has been alarmed about abstractions. In the mean time, Mr. President, I propose my amendments, and I ask that a separate vote may be taken upon each of the fourteen.

Mr. Foote. Mr. President, I think——

Mr. Butler. Will the Senator from Mississippi allow me to say one word?

Mr. Foote. Certainly; I yield with great pleasure to the honorable Senator from South Carolina.

Mr. Butler. I wish to say to the Senator from Missouri, that if he supposes that the Southern people are to be satisfied with votes upon truisms, or which all the country should regard as such, he is mistaken. He is equally mistaken, if he supposes votes of that kind are to be safely-valves for the dangerous and aggressive agitations of the North. Sir, the Senator must see as plainly as I do, that there is danger—that this thing has progressed to such lengths, that it will be but a feeble palliative to quiet it, to offer a resolution which merely declares that Congress has no right to interfere with slavery in the States; that the South and the whole country is in no danger, and that all the agitation is caused by the Southern Address. He is mistaken if he supposes that this thing, which may reach further than he supposes, is to be cut up by the roots by votes of this kind. We may differ as to the extent of the danger, but this is not to be the safety-valve by which it is to be avoided. Gentlemen will not satisfy the South, I can assure them, by any such declarations.

Mr. Clay withdrew his appeal from the Chair.

On motion of Mr. Butler, the Senate adjourned.

Thursday, April 18.

The Select Committee of Thirteen.

The Senate then proceeded to the consideration of the unfinished business of yesterday, being the resolutions submitted by the honorable Senator from Tennessee, (Mr. Bell,) and by the honorable Senator from Kentucky, (Mr. Clay,) and the motion to refer them to a select committee.

Mr. Mangum. I will inquire whether the appeal from the decision of the Chair yesterday had been withdrawn? If it has not, I hope it will be.

Mr. Clay. It has.

Mr. Mangum. I am gratified that the Senator has withdrawn the appeal from the decision of the Chair. It is always unpleasant to come in collision with any decision which has been made by the Chair.

While I am up, sir, I will remark that I hope we shall vote upon all these propositions. I hope the fullest latitude will be given by our friends to discussion, and, when that discussion is ended, that they will take the vote. I further hope that those who have voted with the majority upon these questions hitherto, will give an answer only by yea or nay; and if any matter should be adverted to that may hereafter require notice, I hope that that notice will be bestowed upon it at a period which shall not tend to retard the action of the Senate upon these vastly important questions. I think, sir, there is a disposition universal amongst this body to bring to a close the whole of this matter at the earliest day——

The Presiding Officer, (Mr. Atchison.) The Senator from Mississippi is entitled to the floor. The gentleman from North Carolina is therefore out of order.

Mr. Foote. I have yielded the floor.

Mr. Mangum. The Senator from Mississippi has declined to occupy it, with a view of bringing this matter to the earliest possible termination. I do hope that no person who votes with the majority upon this question, will be either provoked, entrapped, or induced, by any mode or by any course of observations, to speak, except to say yea or nay.

Mr. Clay. I rise to express my hearty concurrence in the sentiments expressed by the Senator from North Carolina. The Senate, sir, has decided, by a solemn vote, that it will give no instructions whatever to the committee. The propositions now before the Senate are to reverse this decision of the Senate—to detach California, and to give instructions which the Senate has declared it will not do. But if the gentlemen choose to persevere in this course, I concur heartily in the object of the Senator from North Carolina, which is to exempt ourselves (I mean those who co-operate together on this subject) from any portion of the responsibility which may arise out of the further protraction and delay of this subject.

Mr. Benton. The present occupant of the chair, not having been in the chair yesterday evening at the time the motions were made, may not perhaps have got the pending motion precisely correct. The Senator from Maine (Mr. Hamlin) offered an amendment; a question of order arose; it was finally withdrawn; the question, therefore, is on the amendment of the Senator from Maine.

The Presiding Officer. The Chair so understands it.

Mr. King. I wish to say one word. The amendment that was offered by the Senator from Maine, was received by the Chair. I thought then, and stated so at the time, that it was not in order; that that proposition, made by the Senator from Maine, had been disposed of by a solemn vote of the Senate on a former occasion; and that, although the phraseology in some degree differed, yet that it was as much out of order as if it was a literal copy of the original proposition; but feeling, as I did, unwilling to protract the discussion on that point, I was, as the Senator from Kentucky well knows, disposed to withdraw opposition on the question of order. Well, sir, the amendment was received, and a string of amendments have been offered by the Senator from Missouri. How many more he has given notice that he intends to present, I know not. So far as I am concerned, I concur entirely in the view taken by the Senators from North Carolina and Kentucky. I think that we owe it to ourselves, we owe it to the country, we owe it to this body, not to be consuming, upon questions of no importance in themselves, the time of the Senate, when a question of the first magnitude—of the greatest importance—is under consideration, and ought to be brought to as speedy a conclusion as is consistent with the proper action of this body. For myself, therefore, (and I hope I may speak for my friends around me,) I am not disposed to consume any time; and I would suggest, with all proper respect, to those gentlemen who are opposed to us, and who have no disposition to consume the time of the Senate upon this question, to let it go to the committee, as there is a decided majority in favor of that course, and try to arrange this matter so as to produce quiet everywhere—as well in this Chamber as out of it.

Mr. Benton. Mr. President, we seem to have made some progress, and the way seems to have been entirely cleared for me to make the motion which was suggested to me by the gentlemen on the other side. I asked to take up the California bill; it was objected to, because there was unfinished business. It was objected to because the business of yesterday ought to take precedence. Good; I have nothing to say against that now. That business has been taken up; now the objection of "unfinished business" is removed. And now I act upon the suggestion of the gentleman upon the other side of the Chamber, and move, though it involves a double motion, to lay this question upon the table for the purpose of taking up the California bill; and, as the gentlemen have given you a programme of the manner in which they will act, I will give you mine. My programme is this: That, if this bill be taken up, as I suppose it may be now, in conformity to the suggestion of the gentleman opposite, and after the reasons given for not taking it up have passed away, my course will be, if gentlemen on the other side offer amendments which may be in the nature of adding further measures to that bill—of attaching other bills to that bill. Why, sir, I have said enough already to let the Senate know that I am what is called uncompromisingly opposed to it; and as I have given as many reasons for my opposition as can be necessary, now, therefore, I am willing to content myself with the vote of "nay" on the different propositions to add other measures to the California bill when it comes up. Now, sir, my opinion is, that in this way we can finish the California bill in this sitting to-day, while the six gentlemen are here who will be absent next week by order of the Senate. We are now all for action; we are now all for speedy action, and here is the way to get action, and I apprehend that there is not a single amendment intended to be made or thought of to the California bill, that is not in the minds of members at this time, and which cannot be offered here at once in the progress of the bill through this body. I think, then, sir, that we can finish the whole throughout this afternoon's sitting, in the way in which I propose, and either admit or reject California. I therefore make the motion, which I think will accomplish that object, and I ask for the yeas and nays.

The Vice President. It is moved that the question now under consideration be laid on the table, and on that motion the yeas and nays are demanded.

The yeas and nays were then ordered by the Senate, and being taken, resulted as follows:—Yeas 24; nays 28.

So the motion to lay on the table was lost.

The question then recurred upon the amendment proposed by the Senator from Missouri, (Mr. Benton,) to the amendment offered by the Senator from Maine, (Mr. Hamlin.)

Mr. Benton asked for a vote upon every point in his amendment by the yeas and nays.

The yeas and nays were ordered to be taken.

Mr. Butler. I will make a single remark, and that is, that I shall vote nay upon every one of the points in this amendment, on the ground that it would be a palpable inconsistency with what was done by the Senate yesterday.

Mr. Yulee. Allow me to inquire whether the division of the question results necessarily from the request of a single member of the body, or whether it would require a vote of the body? If it requires a vote of the body, I should be disposed to vote against the division, for the reason that the Senate having already decided, by what appears to me to be a conclusive vote, that they would not give instructions to this committee, it will be unnecessary for this body (unless, indeed, it should have changed its opinion) to go through the labor of a divided vote upon the motion now made. If it be competent to the Senate to refuse the division of the amendment, I hope the question will be put to the Senate.

The Vice President. The Chair will read the rule for the information of the Senator:

"If the question in debate contains several points, any member may have the same divided."

The first proposition before the Senate will now be read; it is as follows:

"With instructions that in any bill, scheme, or other measure or measures they may report, they shall not connect the admission of the State of California with any other proposed legislation which shall require the assent of any other State to its completion."

Mr. Benton. I will state that this is an amendment which is offered to the amendment of the Senator from Maine, and is the same in substance as it.

Mr. Borland. I will very briefly state the reason of the vote I shall give upon the propositions now before the Senate. These propositions are in direct opposition to the deliberate and emphatic decision of the Senate yesterday; and if they have any purpose, it seems to me to be in contempt of that deliberate and emphatic decision. That decision was, that the Senate would give no instructions to the committee, and I concurred in that decision. For that reason, as stated by the Senator from South Carolina, (Mr. Butler,) I shall vote against the first proposition. For the same and for other reasons, I shall vote against each and every one of the long list of amendments offered by the Senator from Missouri, (Mr. Benton.) What are those amendments? Every Senator must admit that they are unnecessary, as all must also agree that the most of them are merely declaratory of truisms which need no enactment here at this time. I feel no necessity, and feel under no obligation to adopt, by formal vote, any abstract truisms upon any subject. It would be just as well, and just as becoming in the Senate to occupy itself with declaring, by formal legislative action, that the constitution is in force in the United States, or that the Senate itself is now in session. It is a sort of expedient for consuming the time of the Senate, and delaying its legitimate business—a sort of legislative trifling, which I can neither approve nor hesitate to condemn. I shall vote against each and every one of the propositions already submitted by the Senator from Missouri, (Mr. Benton,) and against all others of the same sort which may hereafter be brought forward by him, or any one else. I have no fear that my votes will be misunderstood, either by the Senate or my constituents.

Mr. Turney. I wish to say one word. I shall not vote except on the final amendment, respecting the union of California with other measures; and my reason will be that we were told yesterday that the object of these propositions was not for the purpose of legislation, but for the purpose of giving quiet to the country and of calming excitement. Now, sir, I am not for adopting a string of propositions for no practical purpose, but I am in favor of leaving the committee free and unrestricted, and I shall vote against all the amendments.

Mr. Dickinson. I beg our friends to proceed at once to the vote on the amendments that have already been offered, as the honorable member from Missouri has signified that there may be more of the same sort. I think that we can best dispose of the matter by voting.

Mr. Cass. Mr. President, I beg the Senate not to be alarmed; I am not going to discuss this matter at all. I rise merely to state the reason which will govern my vote.

The Senator from Missouri (Mr. Benton) has displayed great powers of analysis in the preparation of his propositions. There are fourteen of them, nine of which relate to California, and the other five to other topics. Those respecting California, each and all, merely amount to the exception of that subject from the powers of the committee. As I have already explained my views upon that question, and have voted for the appointment of a committee, I shall vote against all measures such as these, which are merely calculated to defeat the expressed will of the Senate, and which must operate only to delay the very admission which so many of us are desirous of insuring in the shortest possible time.

As to the five last propositions, some of them at least are still more exceptionable. They undertake to affirm the principles of the constitution, and to protect the rights of the States. Now, sir, as to the rights of the States, I believe they are fully competent to protect themselves, and, I am sure, if they are not, they can derive no protection from any act of mine.

As to the reaffirmance of the provisions of the constitution, should that measure ever become necessary, it belongs to the people of the United States, of whom I am but an infinitesimal fraction. I did not come here to declare what the constitution is, but to legislate in conformity with its provisions. If, indeed, a law is proposed, and there are constitutional doubts about our power to pass it, I am prepared to discuss it, and to vote according to the dictates of my judgment. But, if we once begin to reaffirm the provisions of the constitution, where are we to stop? We may begin at the beginning, and go on to the end, affirming that the constitution makes provision for the election of a President, for the establishment of a Legislature, and so on to the end of the chapter. And what then, after such a vote? We are just where we were before. The vote has not the slightest effect, except to expose us to public reprobation. Even if we had the necessary power, it would be a mere abstract declaration destitute of the least practical effect. Our time may be much more properly and profitably employed. I am opposed to the whole matter, being as anxious as any member of the Senate for the admission of California, and satisfied that these proceedings will merely tend to delay that measure.

The several amendments were then rejected by vote.

The question then recurred on the adoption of the original resolution of Mr. Foote, as amended, so as to embrace the resolutions of Mr. Bell and Mr. Clay, together with the amendment of Mr. Clay refusing to give instructions.

The question being taken, it resulted as follows:

Yeas.—Messrs. Atchison, Badger, Bell, Borland, Bright, Butler, Cass, Clay, Clemens, Davis of Mississippi, Dickinson, Dodge of Iowa, Downs, Foote, Hunter, Jones, King, Mangum, Mason, Morton, Pearce, Rusk, Sebastian, Soulé, Spruance, Sturgeon, Turney, Underwood, Whitcomb, and Yulee—30.

Nays.—Messrs. Baldwin, Benton, Bradbury, Chase, Clark, Corwin, Davis of Massachusetts, Dayton, Dodge of Wisconsin, Douglas, Felch, Greene, Hale, Hamlin, Miller, Norris, Phelps, Seward, Shields, Smith, Walker, and Webster—22.

So the motion to refer was agreed to.

Mr. Foote. I move that the balloting now take place.

The motion was agreed to.

The Vice President. Senators will please to prepare their votes for the committee of thirteen.

Mr. Mangum. Will not the chairman of the committee be first elected?

The Vice President. There is no order of the Senate to that effect.

Mr. Mangum. I move that the chairman be first elected by separate ballot.

The question being put, the motion was agreed to.

Mr. Davis, of Mississippi. I am not at all prepared for the balloting for this committee. I think it requires some reflection at least before the Senate takes any further action on the subject. I will move, therefore, that the balloting be postponed until to-morrow at one o'clock, and that the Senate adjourn.

The question being put on the motion to postpone balloting for the committee until one o'clock to-morrow, it was, upon a division, agreed to: Ayes 30, noes not counted.

FRIDAY, April 19.

Election of the Select Committee.

Mr. MANGUM. It will be remembered, that by the decision of the Senate yesterday, the chairman of the Select Committee is first to be elected.

The VICE PRESIDENT. The Senate has fixed this time for the election of the Select Committee of thirteen. The chairman will be elected first, and Senators will please prepare their ballots accordingly.

The ballots were then collected and reported.

The VICE PRESIDENT. The question presents itself whether blanks can be counted? There are thirty-four votes cast; of which Mr. CLAY received 27, Mr. BELL 1, Mr. MANGUM 1, Mr. BENTON 1, and blank 4. It will be perceived that, unless the four blanks can be counted, a quorum of the Senate has not voted. The Chair is informed that the usage has been not to count the blanks. If so, there has been no election for the want of a quorum.

Mr. BENTON. Mr. President—

Mr. WEBSTER. Mr. President, I was not in early enough to vote. If it is in order, I should be glad do so, in order to make a quorum.

Mr. MANGUM. I move that the Senator have permission to vote.

The VICE PRESIDENT. If there be no objection, the vote will be received. The Chair hears none.

Mr. BENTON. I owe it to the Senate to say that, contrary to my usual custom, I did not vote at all, because I am wholly opposed to the raising of such a committee. But I would not see the Senate in trouble for want of a quorum, and I would be willing to throw in a vote that would count, if it be the sense of the Senate, in order to save going through with the whole ballot again.

The VICE PRESIDENT. Does the Senator desire to vote?

Mr. BENTON. Yes, sir.

Mr. MANGUM. I move the Senator have permission to vote.

The VICE PRESIDENT. There is an additional vote for Mr. CLAY, on receiving Mr. WEBSTER'S ballot.

Mr. BENTON. Very well; that makes a quorum.

The VICE PRESIDENT. The vote now stands: For Mr. CLAY 28, Mr. BELL 1, Mr. BENTON 1, Mr. MANGUM 1, and blank 4. Mr. CLAY having received a majority of the votes, is of course elected chairman of the committee.

Senators will prepare to vote for the remaining twelve members of the committee on one ballot.

The VICE PRESIDENT announced that the votes cast were as follows:

Mr. Cass	30	Mr. Cooper	29
Mr. Dickinson	31	Mr. King	29
Mr. Bright	28	Mr. Mason	29
Mr. Webster	30	Mr. Downs	29
Mr. Phelps	31	Mr. Mangum	29
Mr. Bell	30	Mr. Smith	1
Mr. Berrien	29	Mr. Underwood	1
Mr. Badger	2	Mr. Corwin	1
Mr. Rusk	2	Mr. Davis, Miss	1
Mr. Dodge, W	2	Mr. Clarke	1
Mr. Dayton	2	Mr. Sturgeon	1
Mr. Atchison	1	Mr. Benton	1

The result is, that the remaining twelve members of the committee will consist of Messrs. CASS, DICKINSON, BRIGHT, WEBSTER, PHELPS, COOPER, KING, MASON, DOWNS, MANGUM, BELL, and BERRIEN, those gentlemen having received a majority of all the votes cast.

Mr. PHELPS. I regret, sir, that I must beg to be excused from acting on this committee. The state of my health forbids that I should devote that attention to its duties which the importance of the subjects referred to it demands. There are other reasons, which will naturally suggest themselves to gentlemen of the Senate, why I should be excused from any participation in this proceeding; but the reason that I decline on account of the state of my health will, I trust, be a sufficient reason why I should not be on the committee.

The VICE PRESIDENT. The question is on excusing the Senator from Vermont from serving on the committee.

Mr. MANGUM. I very much hope that my friend will withdraw that motion. The committee will accommodate their action so as to afford every convenience to the gentleman. I hope, therefore, he will withdraw his request.

Mr. PHELPS. I think there can be no difficulty about this matter. I have considered from the outset, that the appointment of this committee would result in nothing more nor less than the expression of opinion on the one side and the other, and probably we shall get nothing new upon the subject—nothing except what Senators have already expressed in their places on this floor. But, sir, this question has assumed an importance in the country, which will render it necessary for every man on this committee to be prepared to vindicate his course. And I may be permitted to say that I think, in all human probability, to say nothing more, that the result of the whole proceeding will be unsatisfactory to my constituents and to myself. Under these circumstances, I should feel myself compelled, if assigned to the committee, to prepare my own opinions for my own vindication, to be spread before the country, which is more than my feeble health would possibly allow. I hope, therefore, that I shall be excused.

Mr. WEBSTER. I hope the honorable member from Vermont will withdraw his application, and the committee will doubtless act in view of the state of his health. If the mere fact of having been opposed to the raising of the committee, and having expressed great doubts whether good results would come from it, be allowed as a reason for being excused—if that example should be set, I should be obliged perhaps to follow it. I hope, sir, the honorable member will be kind enough to withdraw his application. If not regularly, the state of his health may at least allow him to meet occasionally with the committee, who, I doubt not, will make their sessions convenient for him. He will, therefore, be conferring a favor on the Senate by withdrawing his application.

Mr. PHELPS. A word more. I cannot, in justice to myself, withdraw this application. The subject is with the Senate, and if they do not see fit to gratify me in this particular, why, of course, I must make the best of my position.

Mr. MANGUM. I hope for the present the Senate will not accord the request. If my friend is put to any inconvenience, on the score of health, in this matter in the future, I will yield to any request for his personal convenience and comfort.

The question was then taken, and the Senate refused to excuse the Senator from Vermont from serving on the Select Committee.

HOUSE OF REPRESENTATIVES.

THURSDAY, April 25.

The Franklin Expedition.

Mr. STANTON, of Tennessee, from the Committee on Naval Affairs, reported a joint resolution to authorize the President of the United States to accept and attach to the navy the two vessels offered by Mr. Henry Grinnell, of New York, to be sent to the Arctic seas in search of Sir John Franklin and his companions.

The joint resolution was read a first time by its title.

Mr. JOHNSON, of Arkansas, rose and objected.

Mr. BAYLY. I move that the resolution be referred to the Committee of the Whole on the state of the Union.

The SPEAKER. The resolution has not yet been read a second time. The gentleman from Tennessee (Mr. STANTON) proposes that this joint resolution be now put upon its engrossment. The resolution will therefore be read through.

And the joint resolution having been read—

Mr. STANTON said he desired to say one word in relation to it. It was this: If these vessels were to be placed under the control of the rules and regulations of the naval service of the United States, (which was the principal object of the resolution,) it was important that the resolution should be passed immediately, because the vessels were to put to sea in a few days.

The question, "Shall this resolution be laid upon the table?" was then taken, and decided in the negative, as follows:

YEAS.—Messrs. Albertson, Ashe, Averett, Bay, Bayly, Bingham, Bissell, Bowlin, Boyd, Breck, Albert G. Brown, William J. Brown, Joseph Cable, W. R. W. Cobb, Colcock, Disney, Dunham, Ewing, Featherston, Fuller, Gerry, Gorman, Hall, Hamilton, Hammond, Haralson, Isham G. Harris, Sampson W. Harris, Thomas L. Harris, Hibbard, Holliday, Howard, Hubbard, Joseph W. Jackson, Andrew Johnson, Robert W. Johnson, Jones, Preston King, Leffler, Littlefield, Mason, McClernand, McDonald, McDowell, Miller, Millson, Olds, Peaslee, Peck, Phelps, Potter, Powell, Richardson, Ross, Savage, Sawtelle, Alexander H. Stephens, Stetson, Sweetser, Thomas, Jacob Thompson, J. B. Thompson, William Thompson, Toombs, Wallace, Watkins, Willborn, Wildrick, and Wood—70.

NAYS.—Messrs. Allen, Alston, Baker, Bennett, Bocock, Booth, Bowden, Briggs, Brooks, Buel, Burrows, Chester Butler, T. B. Butler, J. P. Caldwell, Calvin, Campbell, Casey, Chandler, Clarke, Cleveland, Clingman, Conger, Conrad, Corwin, Crowell, Deberry, Dickey, Dimmick, Dixon, Doty, Duer, Duncan, Durkee, Fitch, Fowler, Freedly, Giddings, Goodenow, Gould, Halloway, Harlan, Haymond, Hebard, Henry, Hoagland, Howe, Inge, Julian, Kerr, Daniel P. King, George G. King, John A. King, La Sère, Job Mann, Matteson, McGaughey, McKissock, McLanahan, Robert M. McLane, McQueen, McWillie, Moore, Morehead, Morse, Morton, Nelson, Orr, Otis, Outlaw, Pitman, Putnam, Reed, Risley, Robbins, Rockwell, Root, Rumsey, Sackett, Schermerhorn, Shepperd, Sylvester, Spaulding, Sprague, Stanly, Frederick P. Stanton, Richard H. Stanton, Strong, Taylor, Thurman, Tuck, Underhill, Van Dyke, Vinton, Walden, White, Williams, Wilson, and Winthrop—99.

So the House decided that the resolution should not be laid upon the table.

Mr. BROOKS then obtained the floor. He said he desired to say a very few words in explanation of these resolutions, and he would be very brief. The object of this expedition was not to obtain money from the Government, as had been insinuated—

Several MEMBERS. Not *now!* not *now!*

Mr. BROOKS. No, not now, nor hereafter. The projector of the expedition, (Mr. Henry Grinnell,) impelled by the highest impulses that could move a man, proposed to fit out two vessels, costing, as he understood, some $30,000 and over, and to fit them out at his own expense, asking of the Government nothing, save that it extend over them the protection of its flag, and give them the discipline of its navy. No money was asked for now, and Mr. Grinnell was not the man who, while contributing thus liberally for a philanthropic and national object, would ask any thing of Congress hereafter. What was wanted of Congress now, with the protection and sanction of its flag, was the discipline of its navy. It was felt and known, that a private vessel, with sailors enlisted only under our mercantile laws, as for the mercantile marine, could not have that discipline on board —that salutary and efficient government, which might be necessary in high northern latitudes, under the most trying circumstances in which human beings might be placed. To prevent mutiny—to enforce law—to compel, if necessary, self-sacrifice—the discipline and government of the navy were wanted; and it was unwise, if not unsafe, to send two vessels to the Arctic seas for the purposes contemplated, with only the discipline of the mercantile marine to govern them. The distinguished merchant, the starter of this expedition, who so generously —nay, so gloriously—opened his own purse-strings, and who was doing for his country what his country ought to do for itself, had no dishonorable nor selfish purposes to gratify, "now nor hereafter." He comes to you, and offers to share with you all the glory and honor of this expedition; and all he asks in return, is the discipline, the aid of your navy. The princely merchants of New York, whose hearts are as liberal as his, and whose conceptions of national duty are as exalted as his, stand ready, I doubt not, to contribute more money, more means, if desired; but there is asked of you only what no money can give—no liberality, ever so princely, can contribute—and that is, the protection of your flag—the discipline of your navy. While other nations are sending out their expeditions to this continent, to rescue a gallant British sailor and his crew from the horrors of Arctic starvation, their feelings are warmed up, their ideas of American honor are aroused, and they stand ready, I doubt not, to open their purses as freely as water runs, if necessary; but they can do nothing well—they can do nothing satisfactorily and surely—without your co-operation; and for that co-operation, Mr. Grinnell offers to share with you all the honor and glory. Will you refuse it? Can you look other nations in the face if you do, and let them have all the honor of exploring even your own North American continent?

But, says the gentleman from Virginia, (Mr. Bayly,) "it's all, or only, a wild-goose chase!" Well, it may be. It may be, and perhaps is; but I do not know by what wonderful foreknowledge, by what amazing second sight, or by what astonishing power of divination, the gentleman from Virginia has come to this sudden conclusion. To ascertain and settle whether there is, or is not, a south-west passage, has been a problem all mankind has been trying to solve for a century; but if the gentleman from Virginia is all right, and it is "a wild-goose chase," why, the problem is solved, and there is no use to talk and write any more about it, unless it is worth the while, for the sake of humanity, to rescue Sir John Franklin and his sailors from starvation. I am afraid, however, that all mankind, and especially that portion whom I represent, will not acquiesce in the judgment of the gentleman from Virginia, and will be as earnest as ever to solve the problem, and to rescue the officers and sailors in the Arctic Sea. But if this is "a wild-goose chase," what was the Dead Sea expedition?—which was far from our own continent; and which had no useful, no humane, no charitable purpose; but which, nevertheless, gratified and satisfied every reader of the Bible, every student of Christian topography, and which highly honored the country; or what was the exploring expedition? But this is an expedition which humanity invokes, which science calls for, which continental pride demands from you, and you alone of all other nations, and an expedition that costs you nothing, save the honor of your flag, and the aid of the discipline of your navy. I should blush, if I did not see by the vote just given, that your aid would not be refused.

IN SENATE.

Wednesday, May 1.

Credentials of Hon. Jefferson Davis.

Mr. Foote, in consequence of an error being discovered in the credentials of the Hon. Jefferson Davis, of Mississippi, elected a Senator from that State for the constitutional term of six years, from the 4th of March, 1851, which were presented yesterday, asked leave to withdraw them from the files of the Senate, and that the Journal be so amended as not to state the fact that they had been presented. The error consisted in the use of a wrong figure, 1852 instead of 1851, as the period when the honorable Senator's next term will commence, the correction of which renders it necessary to return the credentials to Mississippi. The motion was agreed to.

Wednesday, May 8.

Compromise Report from the Committee of Thirteen.

Mr. Clay. Mr. President, I have risen to present to the Senate a report from the Committee of Thirteen, which was appointed some weeks ago.

The report is of some length, sir, and there have been some erasures and alterations in it; and therefore, if the Senate will allow me, there may be some expediency in reading it myself. If there is no objection, I will do so.

"The Senate's Committee of Thirteen, to whom were referred various resolutions relating to California, to other portions of the territory recently acquired by the United States from the Republic of Mexico, and to other subjects connected with the institution of slavery, have, according to order, had these resolutions and subjects under consideration, and beg leave to submit the following report:

"The committee entered on the discharge of their duties with a deep sense of their great importance, and with earnest and anxious solicitude to arrive at such conclusions as might be satisfactory to the Senate and to the country. Most of the matters referred have been not only subjected to extensive and serious public discussion throughout the country, but to a debate in the Senate itself, singular for its elaborateness and its duration; so that a full exposition of all those motives and views which, on the several subjects confided to the committee, have determined the conclusions at which they have arrived, seems quite unnecessary. They will, therefore, restrict themselves to a few general observations, and to some reflections which grow out of those subjects.

"Out of our recent territorial acquisitions, and in connection with the institution of slavery, questions most grave have sprung, which, greatly dividing and agitating the people of the United States, have threatened to disturb the harmony, if not to endanger the safety, of the Union. The committee believe it to be highly desirable and necessary speedily to adjust all those questions, in a spirit of concord, and in a manner to produce, if practicable, general satisfaction. They think it would be unwise to leave any of them open and unsettled to fester in the public mind, and to prolong, if not aggravate, the existing agitation. It has been their object, therefore, in this report, to make such proposals and recommendations as would accomplish a general adjustment of all those questions.

"Among the subjects referred to the committee which command their first attention, are the resolutions offered to the Senate by the Senator from Tennessee, Mr. BELL. By a provision in the resolution of Congress annexing Texas to the United States, it is declared that 'new States of convenient size, not exceeding four in number, in addition to said State of Texas, and having sufficient population, may hereafter, by the consent of said State, be formed out of the territory thereof, which shall be *entitled to admission* under the provisions of the Federal Constitution; and such States as may be formed out of that portion of said territory lying south of 36° 30′ north latitude, commonly known as the Missouri compromise line, *shall be* admitted into the Union with or without slavery, as the people of each State asking admission may desire.'

"The committee are unanimously of opinion, that whenever one or more States, formed out of the territory of Texas, not exceeding four, having sufficient population, with the consent of Texas, may apply to be admitted into the Union, they are entitled to such admission beyond all doubt, upon the clear, unambiguous and absolute terms of the solemn compact contained in the resolution of annexation adopted by Congress, and assented to by Texas. But whilst the committee conceive that the right of admission into the Union of any new States carved out of the territory of Texas, not exceeding the number specified, and under the conditions stated, cannot be justly controverted, the committee do not think that the formation of any such new States should now originate with Congress. The initiative, in conformity with the usage which has heretofore prevailed, should be taken by a portion of the people of Texas themselves, desirous of constituting a new State with the consent of Texas. And in the formation of such new State, it will be for the people composing it to decide for themselves, whether they will admit or will exclude slavery. And however they may decide that purely municipal question, Congress is bound to acquiesce, and to fulfil in good faith the stipulations of the compact with Texas. The committee are aware that it has been contended that the resolution of Congress annexing Texas was unconstitutional. At a former epoch of our country's history, there were those (and Mr. Jefferson, under whose auspices the treaty of Louisiana was concluded, was among them) who believed that the States formed out of Louisiana could not be received into the Union without an amendment of the constitution. But the States of Louisiana, Missouri, Arkansas, and Iowa have been all, nevertheless, admitted. And who would now think of opposing the admission of Minnesota, Oregon, or other new States formed out of the ancient province of Louisiana, upon the ground of an alleged original defect of constitutional power? In grave national transactions, while yet in their earlier or incipient stages, differences may well exist; but when once they have been decided by a constitutional majority, and are consummated, or are in a process of consummation, there can be no other safe and prudent alternative than to respect the decision already rendered, and to acquiesce in it. Entertaining these views, a majority of the committee do not think it necessary or proper to recommend at this time, or prospectively, any new State or States to be formed out of the territory of Texas. Should any such State be hereafter formed, and present itself for admission into the Union, whether with or without the establishment of slavery, it cannot be doubted that Congress will, under a full sense of honor, of good faith, and of all the high obligations arising out of the compact with Texas, decide, just as it will decide under the influence of similar considerations in regard to new States formed of or out of New Mexico and Utah, with or without the institution of slavery, according to the constitutions and judgment of the people who compose them, as to what may be best to promote their happiness.

"In considering the question of the admission of California as a State into the Union, a majority of the committee conceive that any irregularity by which that State was organized without the previous authority of an act of Congress ought to be overlooked, in consideration of the omission by Congress to establish any territorial government for the people of California, and the consequent necessity which they were under to create a government for themselves best adapted to their own wants. There are various instances, prior to the case of California, of the admission of new States into the Union without any previous authorization by Congress. The sole condition required by the Constitution of the United States in respect to the admission of a new State is, that its constitution shall be republican in form. California presents such a constitution; and there is no doubt of her having a greater population than that which, according to the practice of the Government, has been heretofore deemed sufficient to receive a new State into the Union.

"In regard to the proposed boundaries of California, the committee would have been glad if there existed more full and accurate geographical knowledge of the territory which those boundaries include. There is reason to believe that, large as they are, they embrace no very disproportionate quantity of land adapted to cultivation. And it is known that they contain extensive ranges of mountains, deserts of sand, and much unproductive soil. It might have been, perhaps, better to have assigned to California a more limited front on the Pacific; but even if there had been reserved on the shore of that ocean a portion of the boundary which it presents for any other State or States, it is not very certain that an accessible interior of sufficient extent could have been given to them to render an approach to the ocean through their own limits of any very great importance.

"A majority of the committee think that there are many and urgent concurring considerations in favor of admitting California with the proposed boundaries, and of securing to her at this time the benefits of a State government. If, hereafter, upon an increase of her population, a more thorough exploration of her territory, and an ascertainment of the relations which may arise between the people occupying its various parts, it should be found conducive to their convenience and happiness to form a new State out of California, we have every reason to believe, from past experience, that the question of its admission will be fairly considered and justly decided.

"A majority of the committee, therefore, recommend to the Senate the passage of the bill reported by the Committee on Territories for the admission of California as a State into the Union. To prevent misconception, the committee also recommend that the amendment reported by the same committee to the bill be adopted, so as to leave incontestable the right of the United States to the public domain and other public property in California.

"Whilst a majority of the committee believe it to be necessary and proper, under actual circumstances, to admit California, they think it quite as necessary and proper to establish governments for the residue of the territory derived from Mexico, and to bring it within the pale of the Federal authority. The remoteness of that territory from the seat of the General Government; the dispersed state of its population, the variety of races—pure and mixed—of which it consists; the ignorance of some of the races of our laws, language, and habits; their exposure to inroads and wars of savage tribes; and the solemn stipulations of the treaty by which we acquired dominion over them—imposes upon the United States the imperative obligation of extending to them protection, and of providing for them government and laws suited to their condition. Congress will fail in the performance of a high duty if it does not give, or attempt to give, to them the benefit of such protection, government, and laws. They are not now, and for a long time to come may not be, prepared for State government. The territorial form, for the present, is best suited for their condition. A bill has been reported by the Committee on Territories dividing all the territory acquired from Mexico, not comprehended within the limits of California, into two Territories, under the names of New Mexico and Utah, and proposing for each a territorial government.

"The committee recommend to the Senate the establishment of those territorial governments; and, in order more certainly to secure that desirable object, they also recommend that the bill for their establishment be incorporated in the bill for the admission of California, and that, united together, they both be passed.

"The combination of the two measures in the same bill is objected to on various grounds. It is said that they are incongruous, and have no necessary connection with each other. A majority of the committee think otherwise. The object of both measures is the establishment of government suited to the conditions, respectively, of the proposed new State and of the new territories. Prior to their transfer to the United States, they both formed a part of Mexico, where they stood in equal relations to the Government of that Republic. They were both ceded to the United States by the same treaty. And in the same article of that treaty the United States solemnly engaged to protect and govern both. Common in their origin, common in their alienation from one foreign Government to another, common in their wants of good government, and conterminous in some of their boundaries, and alike in many particulars of physical condition, they have nearly every thing in common in the relations in which they stand to the rest of this Union. There is, then, a general fitness and propriety in extending the parental care of Government to both in common. If California, by a sudden and extraordinary augmentation of population, has advanced so rapidly as to mature her for State government, that furnishes no reason why the less fortunate Territories of New Mexico and Utah should be abandoned and left ungoverned by the United States, or should be disconnected with California, which, although she has organized for herself a State government, must be legally and constitutionally regarded as a territory until she is actually admitted as a State in the Union.

"It is further objected, that, by combining the two measures in the same bill, members who may be willing to vote for one and unwilling to vote for the other, would be placed in an embarrassing condition. They would be constrained, it is urged, to take or to reject both. On the other hand, there are other members who would be willing to vote for both united, but would feel themselves constrained to vote against the California bill if it stood alone. Each party finds in the bill which it favors something which commends it to acceptance, and in the other something which it disapproves. The true ground, therefore, of the objection to the union of the measures, is not any want of affinity between them, but because of the favor or disfavor with which they are respectively regarded. In this conflict of opinion, it seems to a majority of the committee that a spirit of mutual concession enjoins that the two measures should be connected together; the effect of which will be, that neither opinion will exclusively triumph, and that both may find in such an amicable arrangement enough of good to reconcile them to the acceptance of the combined measure. And such a course of legislation is not at all unusual. Few laws have ever passed in which there were no parts to which exception was taken. It is inexpedient, if not impracticable, to separate these parts, and embody them in distinct bills, so as to accommodate the diversity of opinion which may exist. The Constitution of the United States contained in it a great variety of provisions, to some of which serious objection was made in the Convention which formed it by different members of that body; and when it was submitted to the ratification of the States, some of them objected to some parts, and others to other parts of the same instrument. Had these various parts and provisions been separately acted on in the Convention, or separately submitted to the people of the United States, it is by no means certain that the constitution itself would ever have been adopted or ratified. Those who did not like particular provisions found compensation in other parts of it. And in all cases of constitutions and laws, when either is presented as a whole, the question to be decided is, whether the good it contains is not of greater amount, and does not neutralize any thing exceptionable in it. And, as nothing human is perfect, for the sake of that harmony so desirable in such a Confederacy as this, we must be reconciled to secure as much as we can of what we wish, and be consoled by the reflection that what we do not exactly like is a friendly concession, and agreeable to those who, being united with us in a common destiny, it is desirable should always live with us in peace and concord.

"A majority of the committee have, therefore, been led to the recommendation to the Senate that the two measures be united. The bill for establishing the two territories, it will be observed, omits the Wilmot proviso, on the one hand, and on the other, makes no provision for the introduction of slavery into any part of the new territories. That proviso has been the fruitful source of distraction and agitation. If it were adopted and applied to any territory, it would cease to have any obligatory force as soon as such territory were admitted as a State into the Union. There was never any occasion for it, to accomplish the professed object with which it was originally offered. This has been clearly demonstrated by the current of events. California, of all the recent territorial acquisitions from Mexico, was that in which, if anywhere within them, the introduction of slavery was most likely to take place; and the constitution of California, by the unanimous vote of her convention, has expressly interdicted it. There is the highest degree of probability that Utah and New Mexico will, when they come to be admitted as States, follow the example. The proviso is, as to all these regions in common, a mere abstraction. Why should it be any longer insisted on? Totally destitute, as it is, of any practical import, it has, nevertheless, had the pernicious effect to excite serious, if not alarming consequences. It is high time that the wounds which it has inflicted should be healed up, and closed; and that, to avoid, in all future time, the agitations which must be produced by the conflict of opinion on the slavery question—existing, as this institution does, in some of the States, and prohibited, as it is, in others—the true principle which ought to regulate the action of Congress, in forming territorial governments for each newly-acquired domain, is to refrain from all legislation on the subject in the territory acquired, so long as it retains the territorial form of government—leaving it to the people of such territory, when they have attained to a condition which entitles them to admission as a State, to decide for themselves the question of the allowance or prohibition of domestic slavery. The committee believe that they express the anxious desire of an immense majority of the people of the United States, when they declare that it is high time that good feelings, harmony, and fraternal sentiments should be again revived; and that the Government should be able once more to proceed in its great operations to promote the happiness and prosperity of the country, undisturbed by this distracting cause.

"As for California—far from feeling her sensibility affected by her being associated with other kindred measures—she ought to rejoice and be highly gratified that, in entering into the Union, she may have contributed to the tranquillity and happiness of the great family of States, of which, it is to be hoped, she may one day be a distinguished member.

"The committee beg leave next to report on the subject of the northern and western boundary of Texas. On that question a great diversity of opinion has prevailed. According to one view of it, the western limit of Texas was the Nueces; according to another, it extended to the Rio Grande, and stretched from its mouth to its source. A majority of the committee, having come to the conclusion of recommending an amicable adjustment of the boundary with Texas, abstain from expressing any opinion as to the true and legitimate western and northern boundary of that State. The terms proposed for such an adjustment are contained in the bill herewith reported, and they are, with inconsiderable variation, the same as that reported by the Committee on Territories.

"According to these terms, it is proposed to Texas that her boundary be recognized to the Rio Grande, and up that river to the point commonly called El Paso, and running thence up that river twenty miles, measured thereon by a straight line, and thence eastwardly to a point where the hundredth degree of west longitude crosses Red River; being the south-west angle in the line designated between the United States and Mexico, and the same angle in the line of the territory set apart for the Indians by the United States.

"If this boundary be assented to by Texas, she will be quieted to that extent in her title. And some may suppose that, in consideration of this concession by the United States, she might, without any other equivalent, relinquish any claim she has beyond the proposed boundary: that is, any claim to any part of New Mexico. But, under the influence of a sentiment of justice and great liberality, the bill proposes to Texas, for her relinquishment of any such claim, a large pecuniary equivalent. As a consideration for it, and considering that a portion of the debt of Texas was created on a pledge to her creditors of the duties on foreign imports, transferred by the resolution of annexation to the United States, and now received and receivable in their treasury, a majority of the committee recommend the payment of the sum of —— millions of dollars to Texas, to be applied in the first instance to the extinction of that portion of her debt for the reimbursement of which the duties on foreign imports were pledged as aforesaid; and the residue in such manner as she may direct. The said sum is to be paid by the United States in a stock, to be created, bearing five per cent. interest annually, payable half-yearly at the Treasury of the United States, and the principal reimbursable at the end of fourteen years.

"According to an estimate which has been made, there are included in the territory to which it is proposed that Texas shall relinquish her claim, embracing that part of New Mexico lying east of the Rio Grande, a little less than 124,933 square miles, and about 79,957,120 acres of land. From the proceeds of the sale of this land, the United States may ultimately be reimbursed a portion, if not the whole of the amount of what is thus proposed to be advanced to Texas.

"It cannot be anticipated that Texas will decline to accede to these liberal propositions; but if she should, it is to be distinctly understood that the title of the United States to any territory acquired from Mexico east of the Rio Grande, will remain unimpaired and in the same condition as if the proposals of adjustment now offered had never been made.

"A majority of the committee recommend to the Senate that the section containing these proposals to Texas shall be incorporated into the bill embracing the admission of California as a State, and the establishment of territorial governments for Utah and New Mexico. The definition and establishment of the boundary between New Mexico and Texas has an intimate and necessary connection with the establishment of a territorial government for New Mexico. To form a territorial government for New Mexico, without prescribing the limits of the territory, would leave the work imperfect and incomplete, and might expose New Mexico to serious controversy, if not dangerous collisions, with the State of Texas. And most, if not all, the considerations which unite in favor of combining the bill for the admission of California as a State and the territorial bills, apply to the boundary question of Texas. By the union of the three measures, every question of difficulty and division which has arisen out of the territorial acquisitions from Mexico will, it is hoped, be adjusted, or placed in a train of satisfactory adjustment. The committee, availing themselves of the arduous and valuable labors of the Committee on Territories, report a bill, herewith annexed, (marked A,) embracing those three measures, the passage of which, uniting them together, they recommend to the Senate.

"The committee will now proceed to the consideration of, and to report upon, the subject of persons owing service or labor in one State escaping into another. The text of the constitution is quite clear: 'No person held to labor or service in one State, *under the laws thereof*, escaping into another, shall, in consequence of any law or regulation therein, be discharged from such service or labor, but *shall be delivered up* on the claim of the party to whom such service or labor may be due.' Nothing can be more explicit than this language—nothing more manifest than the right to demand, and the obligation to deliver up to the claimant, any such fugitive. And the constitution addresses itself alike to the States composing the Union and to the General Government. If, indeed, there were any difference in the duty to enforce this portion of the constitution between the States and the Federal Government, it is more clear that it is that of the former than of the latter. But it is the duty of both. It is now well known and incontestable that citizens in slaveholding States encounter the greatest difficulty in obtaining the benefit of this provision of the constitution. The attempt to recapture a fugitive is almost always a subject of great irritation and excitement, and often leads to most unpleasant, if not perilous, collisions. An owner of a slave, it is quite notorious, cannot pursue his property, for the purpose of its recovery, in some of the States, without imminent personal hazard. This is a deplorable state of things, which ought to be remedied. The law of 1793 has been found wholly ineffectual, and requires more stringent enactments. There is, especially, a deficiency in the number of public functionaries authorized to afford aid in the seizure and arrest of fugitives. Various States have declined to afford aid and co-operation in the surrender of fugitives from labor, as the committee believe, from a misconception of their duty arising under the Constitution of the United States. It is true that a decision of the Supreme Court of the United States has given countenance to them in withholding their assistance. But the committee cannot but believe that the intention of the Supreme Court has been misunderstood. They cannot but think that that court merely meant that laws of the several States which created obstacles in the way of the recovery of fugitives were not authorized by the constitution, and not that State laws affording facilities in the recovery of fugitives were forbidden by that instrument.

"The non-slaveholding States, whatever sympathies any of their citizens may feel for persons who escape from other States, cannot discharge themselves from an obligation to enforce the Constitution of the United States. All parts of the instrument being dependent upon, and connected with each other, ought to be fairly and justly enforced. If some States may seek to exonerate themselves from one portion of the constitution, other States may endeavor to evade the performance of other portions of it; and thus the instrument, in some of its most important provisions, might become inoperative and invalid.

"But, whatever may be the conduct of individual States, the duty of the General Government is perfectly clear. That duty is, to amend the existing law, and to provide an effectual remedy for the recovery of fugitives from service or labor. In devising such a remedy, Congress ought, while on the one hand securing to the owner the fair restoration of his property, effectually to guard on the other against any abuses in the application of that remedy.

"In all cases of the arrest, within a State, of persons charged with offences; in all cases of the pursuit of fugitives from justice from one State to another State; in all cases of extradition provided for by treaties between foreign powers—the proceeding uniformly is summary. It has never been thought necessary to apply, in cases of that kind, the forms and ceremonies of a final trial. And when that trial does take place, it is in the State or country from which the party has fled, and not in that in which he has found refuge. By the express language of the constitution, whether the fugitive is held to service or labor or not, is to be determined *by the laws of the State from which he fled*; and, consequently, it is most proper that the tribunals of that State should expound and administer its own laws. If there have been any instances of abuse in the erroneous arrest of fugitives from service or labor, the committee have not obtained knowledge of them. They believe that none such have occurred, and that such are not likely to occur. But, in order to guard against the possibility of their occurrence, the committee have prepared, and herewith report, (marked B,) a section to be offered to the fugitive bill now pending before the Senate. According to this section, the owner of a fugitive from service or labor is, when practicable, to carry with him to the State in which the person is found, a record, from a competent tribunal, adjudicating the facts of elopement and slavery, with a general description of the fugitive. This record, properly attested and certified under the official seal of the court, being taken to the State where the person owing service or labor is found, is to be held competent and sufficient evidence of the facts which had been adjudicated, and will leave nothing more to be done than to identify the fugitive.

"Numerous petitions have been presented, praying for a trial by jury, in the case of arrest of fugitives from service or labor, in the non-slaveholding States. It has been already shown that this would be entirely contrary to practice and uniform usage in all similar cases. Under the name of a popular and cherished institution—an institution, however, never applied in cases of preliminary proceeding, and only in cases of final trial—there would be a complete mockery of justice, so far as the owner of the fugitive is concerned. If the trial by jury be admitted, it would draw after it its usual consequences, of continuance from time to time, to bring evidence from distant places; of second or new trials, in cases where the jury is hung, or the verdict is set aside; and of revisals of the verdict and conduct of the jurors by competent tribunals. During the progress of all these dilatory and expensive proceedings, what security is there as to the custody and forthcoming of the fugitive upon their determination? And if, finally, the claimant should be successful, contrary to what happens in ordinary litigation between free persons, he would have to bear all the burdens and expense of the litigation, without indemnity, and would learn, by sad experience, that he had by far better have abandoned his right in the first instance, than to establish it at such unremunerated cost and heavy sacrifice.

"But, whilst the committee conceive that a trial by jury in a State where a fugitive from service or labor is recaptured, would be a virtual denial of justice to the claimant of such fugitive, and would be tantamount to a positive refusal to execute the provision of the constitution, the same objections do not apply to such a trial in the State from which he fled. In the slaveholding States full justice is administered, with entire fairness and impartiality, in cases of all actions for freedom. The person claiming his freedom is allowed to sue in *forma pauperis;* counsel is assigned him; time is allowed him to collect his witnesses and to attend the sessions of the court; and his claimant is placed under bond and security, or is divested of the possession during the progress of the trial, to insure the enjoyment of these privileges; and if there be any leaning on the part of courts and juries, it is always on the side of the claimant for freedom.

"In deference to the feelings and prejudices which prevail in the non-slaveholding States, the committee propose such a trial in the State from which the fugitive fled, in all cases where he declares to the officer giving the certificate for his return that he has a right to his freedom. Accordingly the committee have prepared, and report herewith, (marked C,) two sections, which they recommend should be incorporated in the fugitive bill pending in the Senate. According to these sections, the claimant is placed under bond, and required to return the fugitive to that county in the State from which he fled, and there to take him before a competent tribunal, and allow him to assert and establish his freedom, if he can, affording to him for that purpose all needful facilities.

"The committee indulge the hope that if the fugitive bill with the proposed amendments shall be passed by Congress, it will be effectual to secure the recovery of all fugitives from service or labor, and that it will remove all causes of complaint which have hitherto been experienced on that irritating subject. But if in its practical operation it shall be found insufficient, and if no adequate remedy can be devised for the restoration to their owners of fugitive slaves, those owners will have a just title to indemnity out of the Treasury of the United States.

"It remains to report upon the resolutions in relation to slavery and the slave trade in the District of Columbia. Without discussing the power of Congress to abolish slavery within the District, in regard to which a diversity of opinion exists, the committee are of opinion that it ought not to be abolished. It could not be done without indispensable conditions, which are not likely to be agreed to. It could not be done without exciting great apprehension and alarm in the slave States. If the power were exercised within this District, they would apprehend that, under some pretext or another, it might be hereafter attempted to be exercised within the slaveholding States. It is true, that at present all such power is almost unanimously disavowed and disclaimed in the free States. But experience in public affairs has too often shown that where there is a desire to do a particular thing, the power to accomplish it, sooner or later, will be found or assumed.

"Nor does the number of slaves within the District make the abolition of slavery an object of any such consequence as appears to be attached to it in some parts of the Union. Since the retrocession of Alexandria county to Virginia, on the south side of the Potomac, the District now consists only of Washington county, on the north side of this river; and the returns of the decennary enumeration of the people of the United States show a rapidly progressive decrease in the number of slaves in Washington county. According to the census of 1830, the number was 4,505; and in 1840 it was reduced to 3,320: showing a reduction in ten years of nearly one-third. If it should continue in the same ratio, the number, according to the census now about to be taken, will be only a little upwards of two thousand.

"But a majority of the committee think differently in regard to the slave trade within the District. By that trade is meant the introduction of slaves from adjacent States into the District, for sale, or to be placed in depôt for the purpose of subsequent sale or transportation to other and distant markets. That trade, a majority of the committee are of opinion, ought to be abolished. Complaints have always existed against it, no less on the part of members of Congress from the South, than on the part of members from the North. It is a trade sometimes exhibiting revolting spectacles, and one in which the people of the District have no interest, but, on the contrary, are believed to be desirous that it should be discontinued. Most, if not all, of the slaveholding States have, either in their constitutions or by penal enactments, prohibited a trade in slaves as merchandise within their respective jurisdictions. Congress, standing in regard to the people of this District on this subject, in a relation similar to that of the State Legislatures to the people of the States, may safely follow the examples of the States. The committee have prepared, and herewith report, a bill for the abolition of that trade, (marked D,) the passage of which they recommend to the Senate. This bill has been framed after the model of what the law of Maryland was when the General Government was removed to Washington.

"The views and recommendations contained in this report may be recapitulated in a few words:

"1. The admission of any new State or States formed out of Texas, to be postponed until they shall hereafter present themselves to be received into the Union, when it will be the duty of Congress fairly and faithfully to execute the compact with Texas by admitting such new State or States.

"2. The admission forthwith of California into the Union, with the boundaries which she has proposed.

"3. The establishment of territorial governments without the Wilmot proviso for New Mexico and Utah, embracing all the territory recently acquired by the United States from Mexico not contained in the boundaries of California.

"4. The combination of these two last-mentioned measures in the same bill.

"5. The establishment of the western and northern boundary of Texas, and the exclusion from her jurisdiction of all New Mexico, with the grant to Texas of a pecuniary equivalent; and the section for that purpose to be incorporated in the bill admitting California and establishing territorial governments for Utah and New Mexico.

"6. More effectual enactments of law to secure the prompt delivery of persons bound to service or labor in one State, under the laws thereof, who escape into another State.

"And, 7. Abstaining from abolishing slavery; but, under a heavy penalty, prohibiting the slave trade in the District of Columbia.

"If such of these several measures as require legislation should be carried out by suitable acts of Congress, all controversies to which our late territorial acquisitions have given rise, and all existing questions connected with the institution of slavery, whether resulting from those acquisitions or from its existence in the States and the District of Columbia, will be amicably settled and adjusted, in a manner, it is confidently believed, to give general satisfaction to an overwhelming majority of the people of the United States. Congress will have fulfilled its whole duty in regard to the vast country which, having been ceded by Mexico to the United States, has fallen under their dominion. It will have extended to it protection, provided for its several parts the inestimable blessing of free and regular government adapted to their various wants, and placed the whole under the banner and flag of the United States. Meeting courageously its clear and entire duty, Congress will escape the unmerited reproach of having, from considerations of doubtful policy, abandoned to an undeserved fate territories of boundless extent, with a sparse, incongruous, and alien, if not unfriendly, population, speaking different languages, and accustomed to different laws, whilst that population is making irresistible appeals to the new sovereignty to which they have been transferred for protection, for government, for law, and for order.

"The committee have endeavored to present to the Senate a comprehensive plan of adjustment, which, removing all causes of existing excitement and agitation, leaves none open to divide the country and disturb the general harmony. The nation has been greatly convulsed, not by measures of general policy, but by questions of a sectional character, and, therefore, more dangerous and more to be deprecated. It wants repose. It loves and cherishes the Union. And it is most cheering and gratifying to witness the outbursts of deep and abiding attachment to it which have been exhibited in all parts of it, amidst all the trials through which we have passed and are passing. A people so patriotic as those of the United States, will rejoice in an accommodation of all troubles and difficulties by which the safety of that Union might have been brought into the least danger. And, under the blessings of that Providence who, amidst all vicissitudes, has never ceased to extend to them His protecting care, His smiles, and His blessings, they will continue to advance in population, power, and prosperity, and work out triumphantly the glorious problem of man's capacity for self-government."

I do not know (said Mr. Clay) whether it will be the pleasure of the Senate that the bills should be read otherwise than by their titles, or that the several amendments proposed to the fugitive bill should be read. I hardly think it can be required. They are stated and referred to in the report in such a clear manner, that they can be printed without being read. I think it would be trespassing too much upon the time of the Senate to read them; unless the reading is called for, I do not think it desirable. I therefore send to the Clerk's table the bills which have been prepared.

[The bills were laid on the table.]

The Secretary having read the first bill by its title, as follows:

"A bill to admit California as a State into the Union; to establish territorial Governments for Utah and New Mexico; and making proposals to Texas for the establishment of her western and northern boundaries"—

The Vice President. This bill has had its first reading. Shall it be read a second time?

Mr. Clay. Mr. President, still cherishing the desire which has always actuated me, and which is, I am sure, shared by the committee in common with me, I am anxious that the Senate should get on with as much promptness as possible. I think that by to-morrow the bills may be printed. Although there are slight amendments to the Utah and New Mexico bills, they are very slight—some accidental clerical omissions. It is hardly necessary that they should be printed again. But the order to print them need not interrupt action on the bill to-morrow, if it be desired. I move, then, that the report, with the bills accompanying it, be printed, and that they be made the order of the day for to-morrow.

[On this motion to print, a general discussion of the whole subject broke out, which was checked by the presiding officer, as a question of order; and the printing was ordered as moved.]

Wednesday, May 15.

The Compromise Bill.

The hour of one o'clock having arrived,

The Vice President announced the special order of the day, being the bill reported from the Select Committee of thirteen to admit California as a State into the Union, to establish territorial governments for Utah and New Mexico, and making proposals to Texas for the establishment of her western and northern boundaries. This bill was announced to be under consideration as in Committee of the Whole, and open to amendment.

Mr. DAVIS, of Mississippi. I offer the following amendment. To strike out in the sixth line of the tenth section the words "In respect to African slavery," and insert the words "with those rights of property growing out of the institution of African slavery as it exists in any of the States of the Union." The object of the amendment is to prevent the territorial legislature from legislating against the rights of property growing out of the institution of slavery.

Mr. CLAY. Mr. President, I am not perfectly sure that I comprehend the full meaning of the amendment offered by the Senator from Mississippi. If I do, I think he accomplishes nothing by striking out the clause now in the bill, and inserting that which he proposes to insert. The clause now in the bill is, that the territorial legislation shall not extend to any thing respecting African slavery within the territory. The effect of retaining the clause as reported by the committee will be this: that if in any of the territories slavery now exists, it cannot be abolished by the territorial legislature; and if in any of the territories slavery does not now exist, it cannot be introduced by the territorial legislature. The clause itself was introduced into the bill by the committee, for the purpose of tying up the hands of the territorial legislature in respect to legislating at all, one way or the other, upon the subject of African slavery. It was intended to leave the legislation and the law of the respective territories in the condition in which the act will find them. I stated on a former occasion that I did not, in committee, vote for the amendment to insert the clause, though it was proposed to be introduced by a majority of the committee. I attached very little consequence to it at that time, and I attach very little to it at the present. It is, perhaps, of no practical importance whatever.

Now, sir, if I understand the measure proposed by the Senator from Mississippi, it aims at the same thing. I do not understand him as proposing that if any one shall carry slaves into the territory—although by the law of the territory he cannot take them there—the legislative hands of the territorial government should be so tied as to prevent its saying he shall not enjoy the fruits of their labor. If the Senator from Mississippi means to say that—

Mr. DAVIS, of Mississippi. I do mean to say it.

Mr. CLAY. If the object of the Senator is to provide that slaves may be introduced into the territory contrary to the *lex loci*, and, being introduced, nothing shall be done by the legislature to impair the rights of owners to hold the slaves thus brought contrary to the local laws, I certainly cannot vote for it. In doing so, I shall repeat again the expression of opinion which I announced at an early period of the session. I think that the language of the amendment which the Senator from Mississippi has offered, is just as much restricted as is the language of the bill which he proposes to strike out. His amendment does not provide in express terms for the privilege of introducing slaves, but merely declares that the territorial legislature shall not interfere with the rights of property in slaves, as that property exists in a certain class of States. Very well. The legislature is already restrained from so interfering, unless slaves are brought in contrary to the *lex loci*. If they be so brought in, then the amendment of the gentleman—although its language does not comprehend it—might secure to the introducer of slaves the protection of his property.

If the object of the Senator, however, is as he states, the language of it, I think, does not necessarily imply it. I repeat what I have before said, that I cannot vote to convert a territory already free into a slave territory. I am satisfied, for one, to let the *lex loci*, as it exists, remain. Now, let us see what will be the effect of this in that portion of New Mexico east of the Rio Grande. Three opinions prevail upon that subject in the Senate. According to my opinion, the laws of Mexico still prevail in that country, because Texas never had possession of that country, never legislated for that country, and her laws never stretched over that country; but, on the contrary, the country remained in the possession of Mexico until, by the treaty of Guadalupe Hidalgo, it was ceded to the United States. In my opinion, therefore, the local law which prevails in New Mexico—as well in New Mexico east of the Rio Grande as west of it—is the law of Mexico, as pronounced by the Dictator of Mexico, by the constitutional authority of Mexico, and by the legislative power of Mexico. That is my own opinion.

FRIDAY, May 24.

The Compromise Bill.

The Senate proceeded to the consideration of the special order, being the bill to admit California as a State into the Union, to establish territorial governments for Utah and New Mexico, and making proposals to Texas for the establishment of her western and northern boundaries.

Mr. SOULE replied to the speech of Mr. DOWNS, which was delivered on Wednesday. His speech occupied upwards of an hour in the delivery.

Explanations were afterwards made by Messrs. FOOTE, DOWNS, DAVIS of Mississippi, CLAY, and others, and then the further consideration of the subject was postponed to Monday next.

HOUSE OF REPRESENTATIVES.

Friday, May 31.

Death of Mr. Elmore.

A message was received from the Senate by the hands of Asbury Dickins, Esq., their Secretary, informing the House of the decease of Hon. F. H. Elmore, a Senator from the State of South Carolina, and communicating the proceedings of the Senate with respect thereto.

The message having been read—

Mr. Woodward rose and addressed the House as follows:

Mr. Speaker: It is not only expected but desired by every one present that we should spend a few moments in enlivening our remembrance of the distinguished person whose much lamented and untimely death is the subject of the resolutions just received from the Senate. Not that the solemnities about to be entered upon can add any thing to the reputation of the deceased, or increase the estimation in which he was and is to be held by the country. No eulogy of mine could add to a fame from which aspersion could never be able to detract. I have not risen, therefore, to do justice to the dead. The dead has done full justice to the dead. The death of Franklin H. Elmore holds no claim upon his life uncancelled. I rise to discharge a debt due to you, to ourselves, and the country—due to the proprieties growing out of the relations under which we stood to the deceased when living and the relations under which we stand to those who in his death have suffered bereavement. It is not necessary that any one should here, on this occasion, bear testimony to his uncommon intellectual endowments or his pure and elevated character. The knowledge of these and the deep impression they have made on the public mind, will impart much greater interest to an unadorned narrative of his life than any elaborate eulogium could possess.

Franklin Harper Elmore was born in the year 1799, in the District of Laurens, State of South Carolina. He was the second son of Gen. John Elmore, who served in the war of the Revolution, under Gen. Greene. He received his education in his native State, and was graduated at the South Carolina College, in the year 1819. In 1821 he was admitted to the bar, and the year after was elected by the Legislature Solicitor, or State's Attorney, for the judicial circuit which included Columbia, the seat of Government. The duties of this office he continued to discharge with ability and distinction for fourteen years, having been successively re-elected, at periods of four years. From this office he was, in December, 1836, transferred to the House of Representatives of the United States, to fill the vacancy occasioned by the resignation of the Hon. James H. Hammond, subsequently a distinguished Governor of South Carolina. He was again chosen Representative at the next regular election. The whole period of his service in this body was three years. He was here known and marked as the man of thought, and counsel, and action. He but seldom mingled in debate, though he was gifted with parliamentary powers. He was, however, destined to pass to a different sphere.

In 1839 the Presidency of the Bank of the State of South Carolina became vacant. This bank, owning a large capital, and being the fiscal agent of the State, holds a responsible position relative to neighboring monetary institutions. The weight of this responsibility had been increased by the general crash and derangement of 1837–'8. Circumstances made it peculiarly necessary to place at its head a man of deep and comprehensive mind, capable of discipline and system—of complex combinations, and full of circumspection and forecast. Colonel Elmore was the individual fixed upon. For upwards of ten years he continued at the head of the institution, unceasing in assiduity, and indefatigable in labor. It was mainly during this period that he achieved his reputation as a financier and commercialist. And if results were not altogether as favorable as could have been desired, the explanation, doubtless, will be found in the reflection that there are conditions which impose a limit upon possible success in all affairs, and no degree of human talent or effort is capable of transcending this limit. It is confidently believed that the laborious career just referred to undermined his constitution, disabling it to withstand the assaults of an accidental malady. He is believed to have died of erysipelas.

It would hardly seem appropriate to detail the circumstances, so recently commemorated, under which he appeared amongst us as a Senator from his native State. I cannot, however, refrain from remarking, how striking and impressive is the thought, that, having been called so unexpectedly to take the post of his great predecessor, he should also have been called so speedily to follow his footsteps to the grave; as if drawn by some strong affinity for the one who had gone before him; as though he had been beckoned still onward to a happier state by the friendly spirit of a just man made perfect. I believe that Mr. Elmore's voice was heard but once in the Senate, and that was in answering to his name when called by the Secretary.

The intellectual endowments of Col. Elmore, his mental culture and acquirements, his elevated character, the purity of his morals, his unexceptionable good breeding, and the perfection of his social qualities, all conspired to bind his fellow-men to him; some by one law of human sympathy, some by another.

Not unfrequently engaged in the honorable competitions of life, he was, of course, sometimes the object of those irritations of feeling which rivalries are apt to engender. These heartburnings, however, could scarcely ever survive a social interchange of ten minutes, or even a transitory greeting upon the street. And, strange as the verbal contradiction may seem, I speak with perfect sincerity when I say, that his enemies, if he had an enemy, were also his friends. And yet his popularity was not of an intense character: it was too universal to be intense. It did not meet with sufficient resistance to give it the highest degree of compactness. It seemed to exist, or rather live by a general law of nervous connection with the community; and there is no portion of the community whose sensibilities will not be touched by his death.

Upon the nearer social ties that have been broken, I choose not to make any remarks. The disconsolate heart shrinks from the gaze of the world, and what our eyes may not look at, let our lips forbear to mention.

Mr. W., at the close of his remarks, submitted the following resolutions:

Resolved, That this House has heard with deep sensibility the announcement of the death of the Hon. Franklin H. Elmore, a Senator in Congress from the State of South Carolina.

Resolved, That, as a testimony of respect for the memory of the deceased, the members and officers of this House will wear the usual badge of mourning for thirty days.

Resolved, That the proceedings of this House in relation to the death of the Hon. Franklin H. Elmore, be communicated to the family of the deceased by the Clerk.

Resolved, That this House will, as a body, forthwith repair to the Senate Chamber, to attend the funeral of the deceased.

The resolutions were unanimously adopted.

After a pause—

The Speaker stated, that in compliance with the resolutions just adopted, the House would now proceed to the Senate Chamber.

And thereupon, the members of the House, preceded by their Speaker and Clerk, repaired to the Senate Chamber, to attend the funeral proceedings.

After having deposited the corpse in the Congressional burying-ground, the officers and members returned to the House.

And then the House adjourned to Monday.

IN SENATE.

Friday, May 31.

Obsequies of the Hon. Franklin H. Elmore.

The funeral services over the remains of the Hon. F. H. Elmore, Senator from the State of South Carolina were performed this morning in the Senate Chamber, in the presence of the President of the United States, and the Heads of Departments, Senators, Members of the House of Representatives, members of the Diplomatic Corps, (among whom the young Sandwich Island Princes, in their court dresses, were conspicuous,) United States Judges, and others.

Monday, June 17.

The Compromise—Admission of California.

Mr. Webster. On the 7th of March, sir, I declared my opinion to be, that there is not a square rod of territory belonging to the United States, the character of which, for slavery or no slavery, is not already fixed by some irrepealable law. I remain of that opinion. The opinion, sir, has been a good deal canvassed in the country, and there have been complaints—sometimes respectful and decorous, and sometimes so loud and so empty as to become mere clamor. But I have seen no argument upon any question of law embraced in that opinion, which shakes the firmness with which I hold it, nor have I heard any discussion upon any matter of fact, as to that part of the opinion which rests on facts, which leads me to doubt the accuracy of my conclusions as to that part of the opinion which regarded the true construction, or I might with more propriety say, almost the literal meaning, of the resolutions by which Texas was admitted into the Union. I have heard no argument calculated, in the slightest degree, to alter that opinion. The committee, I believe, with one accord, concurred in it. A great deal of surprise, real or affected, has been expressed in the country at the announcement by me of that opinion, as if there were something new in it. Yet there need have been no surprise for there was nothing new in it. Other gentlemen have expressed the same opinion more than once; and I myself, in a speech made here on the 23d day of March, 1848, expressed the same opinion, almost in the same words; with which nobody here found any fault—at which nobody here cavilled or made question, and nobody in the country.

With respect to the other ground on which my opinion is founded, that is, the high improbability, in point of fact, that African slavery could be introduced and established in any of the territories acquired by us in pursuance of the late treaty with Mexico, I have learned nothing, heard nothing, from that day to this, that has not entirely confirmed that opinion. That being my judgment on this matter, I voted very readily and cheerfully to exclude what is called the Wilmot proviso from these territorial bills, or to keep it out, rather, when a motion was made to introduce it. I did so, upon a very full and deep conviction that no act of Congress, no provision of law, was necessary in any degree for that purpose; that there were natural and sufficient reasons and causes excluding forever African slavery from those regions. That was my judgment, and I acted on it; and it is my judgment still. Those who think differently, will, of course, pursue a different line of conduct, in accordance with their own judgments. That was my opinion then, and it has been strengthened by every thing that I have learned since, and I have no more apprehension to-day of the introduction or establishment of African slavery in these territories, than I have of its introduction into, and establishment in, Massachusetts.

Well, sir, I have voted not to place in these territorial bills what is called the Wilmot proviso, and by that vote have signified a disposition to exclude the prohibition, as a thing unnecessary; I am now called upon to vote upon this amendment, moved by the honorable member from Louisiana, (Mr. Soule,) which provides that the States formed out of New Mexico and Utah shall have the right and privilege of making their own constitutions, and of presenting those constitutions to Congress conformably to the Constitution of the United States, with or without a prohibition against slavery, as the people of those Territories, about to become States, may see fit to declare, I have not seen much practical utility in this amendment, I agree. Nevertheless, if I should vote, now that it is presented to me, against it, it might leave me open to suspicion of intending or wishing to see that accomplished in another way hereafter which I did not choose to see accomplished by the introduction of the Wilmot proviso. That is to say, it might seem as if, voting against that form of exclusion or prohibition, I might be willing still that there should be a chance hereafter to enforce it some other way. Now, I think that ingenuousness and steadiness of purpose, under these circumstances, compel me to vote for the amendment, and I shall vote for it. I do it exactly on the same grounds that I voted against the introduction of the proviso. And let it be remembered that I am now speaking of New Mexico and Utah, and other territories acquired from Mexico, and of nothing else. I confine myself to these; and, as to them, I say that I see no occasion to make a provision against slavery now, or to reserve to ourselves the right of making such provision hereafter. All this rests on the most thorough conviction, that, under the law of nature, there never can be slavery in these Territories. This is the foundation of all. And I voted against the proviso, and I vote now in favor of this amendment, for the reason that all restrictions are unnecessary, absolutely unnecessary; and as such restrictions give offence, and create a kind of resentment, as they create a degree of dissatisfaction, and as I desire to avoid all dissatisfaction as far as I can, by avoiding all measures that cause it, and which are in my judgment wholly unnecessary, I shall vote now as I voted on a former occasion, and shall support the amendment offered by the honorable member from Louisiana. I repeat again, I do it upon the exact grounds upon which I declared upon the 7th day of March that I should resist the Wilmot proviso—the precise grounds.

Sir, it does not seem to strike other Senators as it strikes me, but if there be any qualification to that general remark which I made, or the opinion which I expressed on the 7th of March, that every foot of territory of the United States has a fixed character for slavery or no slavery; if there be any qualification to that remark, it has arisen here, from what seems to be an indisposition to define the boundaries of New Mexico; that is all the danger there is. All that is part of Texas was by the resolutions of 1845 thrown under the general character of the Texan territory; and if, for want of defining the boundaries of New Mexico, by any proceeding or process hereafter, or by any event hereafter, let me say to gentlemen, that if any portion which they or I do not believe to be Texas should be considered to become Texas, then, so far, that qualification of my remark is applicable. And therefore, I do feel, as I had occasion to say two or three days ago, that it is of the utmost importance to pass this bill, to the end that there may be a definite boundary fixed now, and fixed forever, between the territory of New Mexico and Texas, or the limits of New Mexico and the limits of Texas. Here the question lies. If gentlemen wish to act efficiently for their own purposes, here it is, in my poor judgment, that they are called upon to act. And the thing to be done, and done at once, is to fix the boundaries of New Mexico.

Mr. President, when I see gentlemen from my own part of the country, no doubt from motives of the highest character, and for most conscientious purposes, not concurring in any of these great questions with myself, I am aware that I am taking on myself an uncommon degree of responsibility. The fact that gentlemen with whom I have been accustomed to act in the Senate took a different view of their own duties in the same case, naturally led me to reconsider my own course, to re-examine my own opinions, to rejudge my own judgment. And now, sir, that I have gone through this process, without prejudice, as I hope—and certainly I have done so under the greatest feeling of regret at being called upon by a sense of duty to take a course which may dissatisfy some to whom I should always be desirous of rendering my public course and every event and action of my public life acceptable—yet I cannot part from my own settled opinions. I leave consequences to themselves. It is a great emergency, a great exigency, that this country is placed in. I shall endeavor to preserve a proper regard to my own consistency. And here let me say, that neither here nor elsewhere has any thing been advanced to show that on this subject I have said or done any thing inconsistent, in the slightest degree, with any speech, or sentiment, or letter, or declaration that I ever delivered in my life; and all would be convinced of this, if men would stop to consider, and look at real differences and distinctions. But where all is general denunciation, where all is clamor, where all is idle and empty declamation, where there is no search after truth, no honest disposition to inquire whether one opinion is different from the other, why, everybody, in that way of proceeding, may be proclaimed to be inconsistent.

Now, sir, I do not take the trouble to answer

things of this sort that appear in the public press. I know it would be useless. Those who are of an unfriendly disposition would not publish my explanations or distinctions, if I were to make them. But, sir, if any gentleman here has any thing to say on this subject—though I throw out no challenge—yet, if any gentleman here chooses to undertake the task—and many there possibly are, who think it an easy task—to show in what respect any thing that I said in the debate here on the 7th of March, or any thing contained in my letter to the gentlemen of Newburyport, or anywhere else, is inconsistent with any recorded opinion of mine, since the subject of the annexation of Texas began in 1837, I will certainly answer him with great respect and courtesy, and shall be content to stand or fall by the judgment of the country.

Sir, my object is peace. My object is reconciliation. My purpose is, not to make up a case for the North, or to make up a case for the South. My object is not to continue useless and irritating controversies. I am against agitations, North and South. I am against local ideas, North and South, and against all narrow and local contests. I am an American, and I know no locality in America: that is my country. My heart, my sentiment, my judgment, demand of me that I shall pursue such a course as shall promote the good, and the harmony, and the Union of the whole country. This I shall do, God willing, to the end of the chapter.*

The honorable Senator resumed his seat amidst general applause from the gallery.

The debate was continued by Messrs. NORRIS, SEWARD, FOOTE, and BALDWIN, who moved to amend the amendment of Mr. SOULE, viz:

"And when the said Territory, or any portion of the same, shall be admitted as a State, it shall be received into the Union with or without slavery, as their constitution may prescribe at the time of their admission;"

By striking out all after the word "State" and inserting the following:

"At the proper time, to be judged of by Congress, the people of said Territory shall be admitted to the enjoyment of all the rights of citizens of the United States, according to the principles of the constitution."

After debate by Messrs. CASS, KING, HALE, SEWARD, BALDWIN, and SOULE, the question was taken on the amendment to the amendment, and resulted as follows:

* It is impossible to read the speeches of this session, and hear, as it were, the last words of the last great men of that wonderful time, without having the feelings profoundly moved by the deep dangers to the Union which stood before them, and the patriotic attempts they made to avert that danger. This brief speech of Mr. Webster is a noble illustration of the feelings of the patriotic sages of that portentous day. They labored to save their country, and believed that they had done it.

YEAS.—Messrs. Baldwin, Chase, Clark, Davis of Massachusetts, Dayton, Dodge of Wisconsin, Greene, Pale, Miller, Smith, Upham, and Walker—12.

NAYS.—Messrs. Atchison, Badger, Bell, Benton, Berrien, Bright, Butler, Cass, Clay, Clemens, Cooper, Davis of Mississippi, Dawson, Dodge of Iowa, Douglas, Downs, Foote, Houston, Hunter, Jones, King, Mason, Morton, Norris, Pearce, Pratt, Rusk, Sebastian, Shields, Soulé, Spruance, Sturgeon, Turney, Underwood, Wales, Webster, Whitcomb, and Yulee—38.

So the amendment was rejected.

The question then recurred on the amendment offered by Mr. SOULE, and a debate ensued, in which Messrs. MILLER, DODGE of Iowa, BUTLER, DAYTON, SEWARD, and DOUGLAS participated.

The yeas and nays having been demanded and ordered on the amendment, resulted as follows:

YEAS.—Messrs. Atchison, Badger, Bell, Benton, Berrien, Bright, Butler, Cass, Clay, Clemens, Cooper, Davis of Mississippi, Dawson, Dodge of Iowa, Douglas, Downs, Foote Houston, Hunter, Jones, King, Mason, Morton, Norris, Pearce, Pratt, Rusk, Sebastian, Shields, Soulé, Spruance, Sturgeon, Turney, Underwood, Wales, Webster, Whitcomb, and Yulee—38.

NAYS.—Messrs. Baldwin, Chase, Clark, Davis of Massachusetts, Dayton, Dodge of Wisconsin, Greene, Hale, Miller, Smith, Upham, and Walker—12.

So the amendment was agreed to.

Mr. HALE offered the following amendment to be added to the first section of the bill:

"New States, not exceeding two in number, of convenient size, and having sufficient population, may hereafter, by the consent of the said State of California, be formed out of the territory thereof, which shall be entitled to admission under the provisions of the Federal Constitution."

The further consideration of the bill was then postponed until twelve o'clock to-mor row.

MONDAY, June 24.

Mr. HUNTER presented the credentials of the honorable R. W. BARNWELL, appointed by the Governor of South Carolina to fill the vacancy occasioned by the death of the honorable FRANKLIN H. ELMORE, which were read.

Mr. BARNWELL was then duly qualified and took his seat.

TUESDAY, July 9.

The Compromise Bill—Admission of California—Impressive Interruption.

The Senate resumed the consideration of the bill for the admission of California as a State into the Union, to establish territorial governments for Utah and New Mexico, and making proposals to Texas for the establishment of her western and northern boundaries.

Mr. Butler, who obtained the floor yesterday, proceeded to address the Senate; and, having spoken an hour, on a private communication from Mr. Webster, he suspended his remarks.

Illness of the President.

Mr. Webster. Mr. President, I have permission from the honorable member from South Carolina to interrupt the progress of his speech, and to make a solemn and mournful suggestion to the Senate. The intelligence which, within the last few moments, has been received, indicates that a very great misfortune is now immediately impending over the country. It is supposed by medical advisers and others that the President of the United States cannot live many hours. This intimation comes in a shape so authentic, and through so many varieties of communication, and all tending to the same result, that I have thought it my duty to move the Senate to follow the example which has already been set in the other branch of the National Legislature.

At half-past eleven o'clock to-day, I called at the President's mansion to inquire after his health. I was informed that he had had a very bad night; that he was exceedingly ill this morning, but that at that moment he was more easy and more composed. I had hardly reached my seat in the Senate when it was announced to me that the fever had suddenly returned upon him with very alarming symptoms ; that appearances of congestion were obvious; and that it was hardly possible his life would be prolonged through the day.

With the permission, therefore, of my honorable friend from South Carolina, who, I am sure, like the rest of us, has those feelings on this occasion which quite disqualify us for the performance of our duties, even in this very important crisis of public affairs, I venture to move the Senate that it do now adjourn.

The Senate accordingly adjourned.

Wednesday, July 10.

Death of the President of the United States.

A few minutes past 11 o'clock the Senate was called to order by Asbury Dickins, Esq., its Secretary, and an impressive prayer was delivered by the Rev. C. B. Butler, its Chaplain.

The Secretary then said: With the permission of the Senate, I will read a communication from the late President of the Senate:

Washington, *July* 10, 1850.

To the Senate of the United States:

In consequence of the lamented death of Zachary Taylor, late President of the United States, I shall no longer occupy the chair of the Senate; and I have thought that a formal communication to that effect, through your Secretary, might enable you the more promptly to proceed to the choice of a presiding officer.

MILLARD FILLMORE.

The following message was then received by the hands of George P. Fisher, Esq., from the late Vice President of the United States:

Washington, *July* 10, 1850.

Fellow-citizens of the Senate and of the House of Representatives:

I have to perform the melancholy duty of announcing to you that it has pleased Almighty God to remove from this life Zachary Taylor, late President of the United States. He deceased last evening, at the hour of half-past ten o'clock, in the midst of his family, and surrounded by affectionate friends, calmly, and in the full possession of all his faculties. Among his last words were these, which he uttered with emphatic distinctness: "I have always done my duty;* I am ready to die; my only regret is for the friends I leave behind me."

Having announced to you, fellow-citizens, this most afflicting bereavement, and assuring you that it has penetrated no heart with deeper grief than mine, it remains for me to say that I propose, this day at twelve o'clock, in the Hall of the House of Representatives, in the presence of both Houses of Congress, to take the oath prescribed by the constitution, to enable me to enter on the execution of the office which this event has devolved on me.

MILLARD FILLMORE.

Mr. Webster then submitted the following resolutions:

Resolved, That the two Houses will assemble this day in the Hall of the House of Representatives, at twelve o'clock, to be present at the administration of the oath prescribed by the constitution to the late Vice President of the United States, to enable him to discharge the powers and duties of the office of President of the United States, devolved on him by the death of Zachary Taylor, late President of the United States.

Resolved, That the Secretary of the Senate present the above resolution to the House of Representatives, and ask its concurrence therein.

The resolutions were unanimously agreed to.

A message was received from the House of Representatives by Richard M. Young, Esq., their Clerk:

"Mr. President, the House of Representatives have passed the following resolution, in which they request the concurrence of the Senate:

"*Resolved*, That the Hon. Messrs. Winthrop, Morse, and Morehead, be appointed a committee on the part of this House, to join such committee as may be appointed by the Senate, to wait on the President of the United States, and inform him that the Senate and House of Representatives will be in readiness to receive him in the Hall of the House of Representatives this day, at twelve o'clock, for the purpose of witnessing the administration of the oath prescribed by the constitution, to enable him to enter upon the execution of the office."

The Senate then proceeded to consider the resolution, and, having concurred therein, it was ordered that Mr. Soule, Mr. Davis of

---

* Happy the public man who in the moment of death can say, "*I have always done my duty.*"

Massachusetts, and Mr. UNDERWOOD, be the committee on their part.

Ordered, That the Secretary notify the House of Representatives accordingly.

After a short absence the committee returned, and

Mr. SOULE, on behalf of the committee, reported that they had discharged the duty confided to them, and that the President would be in attendance in the House of Representatives at twelve o'clock.

The Senate then proceeded to the House of Representatives, preceded by their Sergeant-at-arms and Secretary.

The Senate having returned from the House of Representatives, a Message was received from the President of the United States.

[This Message will be found in the House proceedings of this day.]

The Message having been read—

Mr. DOWNS said:

Mr. President: I rise, as a member of the delegation of the State whose citizen the late President of the United States was, to offer resolutions suitable to the occasion. The announcement of his death has been already made officially here and elsewhere; and on the wings of lightning, and almost as swift as thought, the sad intelligence has been conveyed to remote portions of this great Republic. How sublime, as well as melancholy, is the scene in which we are now engaged! But a few days since—less than a week—many of us sat near the then President of the United States, and saluted him in health, at the base of that monument which the hands of a grateful posterity are now raising to the memory of the first and the greatest of his predecessors—hero, statesman, like himself—and where we had assembled to pay devotion to the memory of the man "first in war, first in peace, and first in the hearts of his countrymen," and to rekindle anew, in the breasts of all, that spirit of union, fraternity, and liberty, without which we shall prove ourselves unworthy of our revolutionary ancestors, and a reproach to their memory. Yes, there sat, quiet and placid as the gentle breeze from the Potomac that cooled his heated brow, the man, whose very pathway to his log-cabin schoolhouse in Kentucky, the "Bloody Ground," was beset by the tomahawk of the savage, and who had passed through four wars and many of the bloodiest and most glorious battle-fields of his country unscathed—at the head of the greatest Republic of this or any other country, protected, not by bayonets, but by the affections of his countrymen: yet, in a few short days, in the midst of this quiet, peace, prosperity, and fame, he was to approach that doom which awaits us all.

ZACHARY TAYLOR was born in 1784, in Orange County, Virginia. In early life he gave evidence of extraordinary energy and force of character. In 1808 he was appointed, during the Presidency of Mr. Jefferson, lieutenant in the army of the United States; rose, in 1812, to the rank of captain; and, after the declaration of war with Great Britain in that year, he was breveted major by President Madison for his memorable and gallant defence of Fort Harrison, with a handful of men, against a large body of savages. In 1832, then advanced to the rank of colonel, he distinguished himself in the Black Hawk war; was ordered into Florida in 1836, and for his signal services against the savage Seminoles was created a brevet brigadier general and commander-in-chief in Florida. Subsequently, he was transferred to the command of the division of the army in the south-western portion of the Union; was ordered into Texas in 1845; advanced to the banks of the Rio Grande; and afterwards, beginning with the battles of the 8th and 9th of May, 1846, at Palo Alto and Resaca de la Palma, and ending with Buena Vista, he overthrew, with fearful odds against him, and signally defeated the most skilful of the Mexican generals, Ampudia, Arista, Paredes, and even the President of Mexico himself, and, by a series of brilliant victories, gained for himself and the brave armies under his command, a world-wide renown, commanding the verdict and admiration of Europe and America, and securing an enviable and proud place in the brightest chapters of the history of American arms.

But why attempt to portray his life or describe his actions? This is not the time nor place for such a purpose, if I had the ability to do it justice. His history is part of the history of his country, and therefore needs no aid of friends to preserve it. The battle-fields of Fort Harrison, of Okeechobee, Palo Alto, Resaca de la Palma, Monterey, and, the most glorious of them all, Buena Vista, are at once his monuments and his eulogiums. He needs no others. Of his political history this is not the place nor I the person to speak. Yet I may, I hope, be pardoned a single remark. The wisest and best counsels of public men in a free country—free in speech, in the press, and in the ballot—cannot be expected to go unquestioned. It would not be a free country, if they were. But it is consolatory to know that, whatever differences of opinion may have existed as to the policy of him whose untimely death we all so much lament, they are already, before the tomb has been closed over him, buried in oblivion forever. He is hereafter to belong to no party, to no section, but to the whole American family, and his memory will be revered and cherished by them all alike.

But let not the tears we are shedding over our departed President blind us to the grandeur of the scene in which we stand. Did the world ever witness such a one before? How soon, if ever, can it be witnessed in other countries? The Chief of a nation, of more than twenty millions of freemen, is suddenly withdrawn from the world by an act of God, followed by no disturbance of the perfect equipoise of our institutions. The gentlemen composing the Cabinet of the late President, after his decease, and at the approach of midnight, without ostentation, quietly repair to the residence of the Vice President, and there announce the national bereavement. Within twenty-four hours thereafter he will have taken the oath of office, without any military parade, and been installed in command of the ship of State, which moves on over the billows of time, more bright and buoyant than ever, bearing at her masthead the proud emblems of national glory and greatness, and presenting to the world a sublime spectacle of the beauty and perfection of self-government.

Such a scene as this ought to make us a happier and a better people. It should make us sensible of the great and manifold advantages we enjoy as a free and united people. Let us, then, bury in the tomb of our departed President all sectional feelings and divisions, and unite, once more, in that spirit of cordial good-will and brotherly love which united our forefathers in the earlier days of the Republic. Let us renew before we leave his grave our vows to support the Union, and our determination to perpetuate our constitution in all its primeval simplicity and purity. There is room enough, glory enough, and honors for us all, while we preserve the Union, and know how wisely and prudently to enjoy it.

Whereas it has pleased Divine Providence to remove from this life Zachary Taylor, late President of the United States, the Senate, sharing in the general sorrow which this melancholy event must produce, is desirous of manifesting its sensibility on this occasion: Therefore,

Resolved, That a committee, consisting of Messrs. Webster, Cass, and King, be appointed on the part of the Senate, to meet such committee as may be appointed on the part of the House of Representatives, to consider and report what measures it may be deemed proper to adopt to show the respect and affection of Congress for the memory of the illustrious deceased, and to make the necessary arrangements for his funeral.

Ordered, That the Secretary of the Senate communicate the foregoing resolution to the House of Representatives.

Mr. Webster. Mr. Secretary, at a time when the great mass of our fellow-citizens enjoy remarkable health and happiness throughout the whole country, it has pleased Divine Providence to visit the two Houses of Congress, and especially this House, with repeated occasions for mourning and lamentation. Since the commencement of the session, we have followed two of our own members to their last home; and we are now called upon, in conjunction with the other branch of the Legislature, and in full sympathy with that deep tone of affliction which I am sure is felt throughout all the country, to take part in the last and due solemnities of the funeral of the late President of the United States.

Truly, sir, was it said in the communication read to us, that a "great man has fallen among us." The late President of the United States, originally a soldier by profession, having gone through a long and splendid career of military service, had, at the close of the late war with Mexico, become so much endeared to the people of the United States, and had inspired them with so high a degree of regard and confidence, that without solicitation or application, without pursuing any devious paths of policy, or turning a hair's breadth to the right or the left from the path of duty, a great, and powerful, and generous people saw fit, by popular vote and voice, to confer upon him the highest civil authority in the nation. We cannot forget that as in other instances so in this, the public feeling was won and carried away, in some degree, by the eclat of military renown. So it has been always, and so it always will be, because high respect for noble feats in arms has been, and always will be, outpoured from the hearts of the members of a popular government. But it will be a great mistake to suppose that the late President of the United States owed his advancement to high civil trust, or his great acceptability with the people to military talent or ability alone. I believe, sir, that associated with the highest admiration for those qualities possessed by him, there was spread throughout the community a high degree of confidence and faith in his integrity, and honor, and uprightness, as a man. I believe he was especially regarded as both a firm and a mild man in the exercise of authority; and I have observed more than once, in this and in other popular Governments, that the prevalent motive with the masses of mankind for conferring high power on individuals, is a confidence in their mildness, their paternal, protecting, secure, and safe character. The people naturally feel safe where they feel themselves to be under the control and protection of sober counsel, of impartial minds, and a general paternal superintendence.

I suppose, sir, that no case ever happened in the very best days of the Roman republic, when every man found himself clothed with the highest authority in the State, under circumstances more repelling all suspicion of personal application, all suspicion of pursuing any crooked path in politics, or all suspicion of having been actuated by sinister views and purposes, than in the case of the worthy, and eminent, and distinguished, and good man, whose death we now deplore.

He has left to the people of his country a legacy in this: He has left them a bright example, which addresses itself with peculiar force to the young and rising generation; for it tells them that there is a path to the highest degree of renown, straight, onward, steady, without change or deviation.

Mr. Secretary, my friend from Louisiana (Mr. Downs) has detailed shortly the events in the military career of General Taylor. His service through his life was mostly on the frontier, and always a hard service—often in combat with the tribes of Indians all along the frontier for so many thousands of miles. It has been justly remarked by one of the most eloquent men whose voice was ever heard in these Houses, that it is not in Indian wars that heroes are celebrated, but that it is there that they are framed. The hard service, the stern discipline, devolving upon all those who have a great extent of frontier to defend, and often with irregular troops of their own, being called on suddenly to enter into contests with savages, to study the habits of savage life and savage war, in order to foresee and overcome their stratagems—all these things tend to make hardy military character.

For a very short time, sir, I had a connection with the executive government of this country; and at that time very perilous, embarrassing circumstances existed between the United States and the Indians on the borders, and war was actually raging between the United States and the Florida tribes; and I very well remember that those who took counsel together on that occasion officially, and who were desirous of placing the military command in the safest hands, came to the conclusion that there was no man in the service more fully uniting the qualities of military ability and great personal prudence than ZACHARY TAYLOR; and he was, of course, appointed to the command.

Unfortunately his career at the head of this Government was short. For my part, in all that I have seen of him, I have found much to respect and nothing to condemn. The circumstances under which he conducted the Government for the few months he was at the head of it, have been such as perhaps not to give to him a very favorable, certainly not a long, opportunity of developing his principles and his policy, and to carry them out; but I believe he has left on the minds of the country a strong impression, first, of his absolute honesty and integrity of character; next, of his sound, practical good sense; and, lastly, of the mildness, kindness, and friendliness of his temper towards all his countrymen.

But he is gone. He is ours no more, except in the force of his example. Sir, I heard with infinite delight the sentiments expressed by my honorable friend from Louisiana, (Mr. DOWNS,) who has just resumed his seat, when he earnestly prayed that this event might be used to soften the animosities, to allay party criminations and recriminations, and to restore fellowship and good feeling among the various sections of the Union. Mr. Secretary, great as is our loss to-day, if these inestimable and inappreciable blessings shall have been secured to us, even by the death of ZACHARY TAYLOR, they have not been purchased at too high a price; and if his spirit from the regions to which he has ascended could see these results flowing from his unexpected and untimely end—if he could see that he had entwined a soldier's laurel around a martyr's crown, he would say, exultingly, "Happy am I, that by my death I have done more for that country which I loved and served than I did or could do by all the devotion and all the efforts that I could make in her behalf during the short span of my earthly existence."

Mr. Secretary, great as this calamity is, we mourn, but not as those without hope. We have seen one eminent man, and another eminent man, and at last a man in the most eminent station, fall away from the midst of us. But I doubt not there is a Power above us exercising over us that parental care that has marked our progress for so many years. I have confidence still that the place of the departed will be supplied; that the kind, beneficent favor of Almighty God will still be with us, and that we shall be borne along, and borne upward and upward on the wings of his sustaining Providence. May God grant that in the time that is before us, there may not be wanting to us as wise men, as good men for our counsellors, as he was whose funeral obsequies we now propose to celebrate!

Mr. CASS. Again and again, during the present session, has a warning voice come from the tomb, saying to all of us, "Be ye also ready." Two of our colleagues have fallen in the midst of their labors, and we have followed them to the narrow house where all must lie. In life we are in death; and this lesson, which accompanies us from the cradle to the grave, is among those merciful dispensations of Providence which teach us how transitory are the things around us, and how soon they must be abandoned for an existence with no hope but that which is held out by the Gospel of our Saviour. And now another solemn warning is heard; and this time it will carry mourning to the hearts of twenty millions of people. Impressively has it been said and repeated, "A great man has fallen in Israel." In the providence of God the Chief Magistrate of the Republic, to whom his fellow-citizens had confided the high executive duties of the country, has been suddenly taken from us—ripe, indeed, in years and honors, and but the other day in the full possession of his health, and with the promise of years of faithful and patriotic services before him. The statesman, occupying as proud a position as this world offers to human hopes, has been struck down in a crisis which demanded all his firmness and wisdom. The conqueror upon many a battle-field has fought his last fight and been vanquished. The soldier who had passed unharmed through many a bloody fray has fallen before the shaft of the great destroyer. How truly are we told, that *there is one event unto all!* The mighty and the lowly descend to the tomb together, and together are covered with the cold clod of the valley; and thus pass away the honors and the cares of life!

The moment is too solemn and impressive for labored addresses. Thoughts, not words, are the tribute which it demands. History will do justice to the deceased patriot. He will live in the memory of his countrymen, as he lived in their hearts and affections. His active life was spent in their service, and in those scenes of peril, of exertion, and of exposure, which it is the lot of the American soldier to encounter, and which he meets without a murmur, faithful to his duty, lead him where it may, in life or in death. His splendid military exploits have placed him among the great captains of the age, and will be an imperishable monument of his own fame and of the glory of his country. In the disparity of force, they carry us back for similar examples to the early ages of the world—to the combats which history has recorded, and where inequality yielded to the exertion of skill and valor. But I need not recur to them: are they not written in burning characters upon the heart of every American?

Strong in the confidence of his countrymen, he was called to the Chief Magistracy at a period of great difficulty—more portentous, indeed, than any we have ever experienced. And now he has been called by Providence from his high functions, with his mission unfulfilled, leaving us to mourn his loss and to honor his memory. His own last words, spoken with equal truth and sincerity, constitute his highest eulogy: "I am not afraid to die," said the dying patriot. "I have done my duty." The integrity of his motives was never assailed or assailable. He had passed through life, and a long and active one, neither meriting nor meeting reproach; and in his last hour the conviction of the honest discharge of his duty was present to console, even when the things of this life were fast fading away.

Let us humbly hope that this afflicting dispensation of Providence may not be without its salutary influence upon the American people and upon their representatives. It comes in the midst of a strong agitation, threatening the most disastrous consequences to our country, and to the great cause of self-government through the world. It is a solemn appeal, and should be solemnly heard and heeded. His death—whose loss we mourn—will not be in vain, if it tends to subdue the feelings that have been excited, and to prepare the various sections of our country for a mutual spirit of forbearance, which shall insure the safety of all by the zealous co-operation of all. We could offer no more appropriate nor durable tribute to departed worth than such a sacrifice of conflicting views upon the altar of our common country. In life and in death he will have equally devoted himself to her service and her safety.

Mr. Pearce. Mr. Secretary, I must ask the Senate to pardon me for venturing to add to what has been said, the expression of the profound regret with which, in common with the Senate and the country, I have learned the sad event which has been announced to-day.

A life of public service, hardship, danger, and glory has been suddenly closed. That Providence which protected the late President amidst the perils of his long, faithful, and splendid military career, and which permitted him to reap the harvest of admiration and affection which had grown up for him in the hearts of his countrymen, has removed him from us before the measure of his usefulness was full. That life which was ever devoted to the service of his country, was yielded up while he was in the discharge of the highest civil trusts—trusts not sought by him, but imposed upon him by the people. To the perfomance of those trusts he had brought the pledges of an unstained life, of a pure and fervent patriotism, of stern integrity, of a kind and benignant temper, of unyielding firmness, and of unmixed devotion to the welfare of that country which he has served so well, and which so freely and worthily bestowed its confidence on him.

Few men have had better fortune than he—none better deserved it. The virtues of his simple and modest, but heroic character, had so endeared him to his fellow-citizens, that I am sure I may venture to say, that, even in the midst of the political strife which he ever sought to moderate and soften, there is not one whose heart will not throb with emotion when he learns the death of Zachary Taylor.

Mr. King. Mr. Secretary, it is not my design, after the eloquent tribute that has been paid to the memory of the deceased President of the United States, to add many words to what has already fallen from the honorable gentlemen. It was my fortune to have been personally and intimately acquainted with the distinguished individual, who has been called away from among us, for more than five-and-twenty years past. My relations with him, at that period, were of such a character as enabled me to form, I think, a correct estimate of the man, and to appreciate, as I did most highly, his many estimable qualities; and I can say that, in all the relations of life, he so bore himself as to command the respect of his acquaintances, the ardent regard of his friends, and the devoted attachment of his countrymen. As a man he was surpassed by none in honesty of purpose. He was without guile. As a soldier, all know, and none more than those I address, that he had won laurels that would have graced the brow of the first soldier of Europe or America. It was my fortune, Senators, to be in Europe at the time when the news reached there that the gallant General of our forces on the Rio Grande, the late President of the United States, was surrounded, or supposed to be surrounded, by an overwhelming force, he commanding a small but gallant band. Every American heart beat with anxiety and fear. We felt, as Americans should feel, that a reverse then would cast in some degree a cloud over the country of our birth. When the news reached us that the gallant General of that little band had marched from his position, regardless of the danger, had retraced his footsteps and conquered the foe at Resaca de la Palma, no man but he who was away from his country in a foreign land could have felt what we, as

American citizens, felt at those tidings. Senators, the gallantry of that man was appreciated not only by his countrymen, but it was felt and appreciated by the first military men of Europe. The living hero of the age, the great Duke of Wellington, declared, as Napoleon had declared of him on a certain occasion, "General Taylor is a General indeed." I, therefore, Senators, am not surprised that the enthusiastic spirit of the American people led them to support a man whose patriotism, whose devotion to his country, whose gallantry, and whose successful services on the field, must have endeared him to the hearts of all. As a man, I have said, he was honest of purpose. His patriotism, his devotion to the constitution of his country, under which he cherished these free institutions, I have never questioned. I think I knew him well, and I believe there was no man more patriotic. If errors were committed, I shall draw the curtain over them. No longer would I feel justified in holding them up to the public gaze, even if they had been ten times as glaring as they were. The country has reason to deplore the death of a great man, and, I must be permitted to add, a good man. He has gone from among us, and the afflictive event has been appealed to to cultivate and cherish kind relations. I trust in God that these kind relations will be cherished, and that we shall on this day vow on the altar of our country to discard all bickering and strife, all sectional dissensions, and live and die as Americans should, in support of the Union.

Mr. Berrien. Senators, I yield to a suggestion which has been made to me, since our assembling here this morning, by a highly respected associate, in making this brief trespass on your time. It is not my purpose, in these brief and unpremeditated remarks, to pronounce an eulogium on the departed Chief Magistrate. That has been amply done already, in terms at once impressive and eloquent. Nor is it my design to give expression to individual and personal feeling; such feeling may be left appropriately to repose in the bosom of him who cherishes it. Nor yet do I seek to give feeble and imperfect utterance to a nation's grief; that will be done by our countrymen in their primary assemblages, as this melancholy intelligence flies with lightning speed to the remotest borders of the Republic, and with a freshness, and vividness, and force which the feelings of a free and sensitive people will impart to the expression of emotions springing directly from their own sorrowing hearts. We should vainly attempt by anticipation to give utterance to their feelings. Still less would I venture to intrude upon the mourning inmates of that domestic circle, who are still clustering round the mortal remains of a departed husband and father; for the sorrows of widowhood and of orphanage are sacred. But concurring, as I do most cordially, in the sentiments which have been so touchingly and eloquently expressed in various portions of this chamber, if I could succeed in adding one, even the slightest motive—in furnishing one, even the feeblest incentive, to the suggestion which honorable Senators have urged of the use which we ought to make of this solemn and afflictive dispensation of Providence, my purpose will have been accomplished—my duty will have been fulfilled. In my reflections upon this subject, I have felt that this dispensation of Providence is, in its results, to be eminently productive of good or of evil to our common country; and in humble reliance on the blessing and guidance of a beneficent Providence, it depends upon us, Senators, and our associates, in the discharge of the important trusts which are committed to this highest legislative assembly of a free people—it depends essentially upon us and the coordinate department of the Government to improve this afflictive dispensation of Almighty God to purposes at once salutary and beneficial to the great interests of the country. If we can feel that in the sudden death of our patriot chieftain—in this abrupt summons of one "without fear and without reproach"—in the vigor of life, and in the full enjoyment of the highest honors—the most gratifying reward which the unbought homage of a free people could accord to him—if we can feel the solemnity of this sudden call of an individual so esteemed, so honored, so surrounded with all that could contribute to the happiness of man—if we can truly appreciate the lesson which such a dispensation is calculated to impart, then, Senators, consequences the most beneficial may result from it. If it shall teach us to realize the comparative littleness of sublunary things—if it shall enable us in sincerity to feel that this transitory life in which we are sometimes struggling, in the bitter dissensions which political parties or sectional divisions are but too apt to engender—that the brief term of our continuance here is but a single step in the series of infinite existence—a mere point at which man pauses to look around him before he launches on eternity's ocean—if we can justly estimate ourselves, and rightly appreciate the duties which devolve upon us, we shall indeed have extracted from this melancholy event that salutary and beneficent lesson which, in the goodness of Providence, it was designed to impart. If, on the altar of our common country, we can sacrifice the bitterness of party and of sectional feeling—if, at this moment, when the heart of a great nation is palpitating with anxiety, we can come to the discharge of the high and solemn duties which devolve upon us with hearts purified by affliction, in the singleness and sincerity of purpose, and in the humility of spirit which becomes us, this melancholy dispensation of Providence will indeed have been productive of results most salutary to the great interests of the American people. And believe me, Senators, if a result so propitious could have been foreshadowed to that departed patriot in the last struggling moments of his existence, it would have cheered the agonies of his dying hour.

I am permitted to say, in illustration of the strong and patriotic feeling which animated him in the latest moments of his existence, even when the light of intellect was flickering in its socket—I am permitted to repeat the expression of the departed patriot, as his recollection turned to the recent visit he had made to the monument now being erected to the memory of Washington: "Let it rise, (he said;) let it ascend without interruption; let it point to the skies; let it stand forever as a lasting monument of the gratitude and affection of a free people to the Father of his Country."

The resolutions were then unanimously adopted.

A message was received from the House of Representatives, informing the Senate that it had appointed a committee of thirteen on its part, to make the necessary arrangements for the funeral of the late President of the United States.

On the motion of Mr. Webster, the resolution of the House was unanimously concurred in, and it was ordered that Messrs. Webster, Cass, and King, be the committee on the part of the Senate.

The Senate then adjourned.

HOUSE OF REPRESENTATIVES.

Wednesday, July 10.

The Speaker called the House to order at eleven o'clock.

The Rev. Doctor Butler, Chaplain of the Senate, made the following prayer:

"Almighty God, King of kings, and Lord of lords, who only hath immortality, dwelling in the light which no man can approach unto, thou doest according to thy will in the army of Heaven and among the inhabitants of the earth. Just and true are thy ways, thou King of saints. Clouds and darkness are about thy throne; but righteousness and judgment are the habitation of thy seat!

"Thou hast seen fit, Almighty God, to take out of this world our beloved and honored Chief Magistrate, the President of these United States. Thou didst cover his head in the day of battle; and thou hast given his life to the sickness that destroyeth at the noon-day. We desire to bow in resignation to thy blessed will, and to realize that thou doest all things well. Now that thy judgments are abroad in the land, make us to learn and love and practise righteousness.

"We ask thy special blessing for thy servant upon whom thy providence hath devolved the momentous duties of the Chief Magistracy of this Republic. Thou hast seen fit to summon him to the great duties of his new position in a crisis of gloom, and storm, and danger. Let thy fatherly hand ever be over him. Let thy Holy Spirit ever be with him. Give him the spirit of wisdom and understanding; the spirit of counsel and ghostly strength; the spirit of knowledge and true godliness; and fill him with thy holy fear now and forever. Preserve him in health and prosperity; and so bless his administration, that all the States of this vast Republic, reconciled, happy, and fraternal, may be able unitedly to adore Thee for thy goodness, and to declare that The Lord of Hosts is with us—the God of Jacob is our refuge.

"Bless the deliberations of the Senate and Representatives in Congress assembled, to the advancement of thy glory, the good of thy church, the safety, honor, and welfare of thy people; that peace and happiness, truth and justice, religion and piety may be established among us for all generations.

"Look with pity upon the sorrows of thy servants, the family of the departed Chief Magistrate of this land. Remember them, O Lord, in mercy; sanctify thy fatherly correction to them; endow their souls with patience under their affliction, and with resignation to thy blessed will; comfort them with a sense of thy goodness; lift up thy countenance upon them, and give them peace.

"Grant, O Lord, that when we shall be summoned to go the way of all the earth, we may die in the communion of thy church, in the confidence of a certain faith, in the comfort of a religious and holy hope, in favor with Thee, our God, and in charity with the world.

"All which we ask and offer in the name and for the sake of Jesus Christ, our Lord and Saviour, Amen!"

The Speaker then vacated the Chair.

A pause of some minutes followed.

At eighteen minutes past eleven o'clock, the Speaker resumed the Chair.

Mr. Stanly moved that the reading of the Journal of yesterday be dispensed with.

Ordered accordingly.

George P. Fisher, Esq., appeared at the bar, and stated that he was directed by the President of the United States to deliver to the House of Representatives a Message in writing.

The Speaker. The Message will be laid before the House.

And it was read, as follows:

Washington, *July* 10, 1850.

Fellow-citizens of the Senate
and of the House of Representatives:

I have to perform the melancholy duty of announcing to you, that it has pleased Almighty God to remove from this life Zachary Taylor, late President of the United States. He deceased last evening, at the hour of half-past ten o'clock, in the midst of his family and surrounded by affectionate friends, calmly and in the full possession of all his faculties. Among his last words were these, which he uttered with emphatic distinctness: "I have always done my duty; I am ready to die. My only regret is for the friends I leave behind me."

Having announced to you, fellow-citizens, this most afflicting bereavement, and assuring you that it has penetrated no heart with deeper grief than mine, it remains for me to say, that I propose this day at twelve o'clock, in the Hall of the House of Representatives, in the presence of both Houses of Congress, to take the oath prescribed by the constitution, to enable me to enter on the execution of the office which this event has devolved on me.

MILLARD FILLMORE.

The reading of the Message having been concluded—

Mr. MORSE rose and said, that, in accordance with the suggestion contained in the melancholy announcement which had just been read from the Clerk's desk, he (Mr. M.) would move that the House now take a recess until twelve o'clock—at which time they would be in readiness to receive the Senate, and the President of the United States, who would then take the oath of office prescribed by the constitution.

Mr. WINTHROP said it seemed to him that, as the President of the United States had expressed his intention to present himself in the House of Representatives for the purpose of taking the oath of office, it would be no more than becoming that the House should appoint a committee to wait upon him and inform him that the House would be ready to receive him at twelve o'clock, for the purpose indicated.

Mr. MORSE. I accept the suggestion.

Mr. WINTHROP. I therefore move that a committee be appointed on the part of the House to join such committee as may be appointed by the Senate, to wait upon the honorable MILLARD FILMORE, and inform him that the House will be in readiness to receive him this day at twelve o'clock, in order that the oath required by the Constitution of the United States may be administered to him.

The SPEAKER stated the question on the motion of Mr. WINTHROP, and it was unanimously agreed to.

The SPEAKER. Of what number does the gentleman from Massachusetts (Mr. WINTHROP) propose that the committee shall consist?

Mr. WINTHROP. Three on the part of the Senate and three on the part of the House—being, I believe, the usual number.

Ordered accordingly.

And the following gentlemen were appointed by the Speaker the committee on the part of the House, viz., Messrs. WINTHROP, MORSE, and MOREHEAD.

The SPEAKER then stated the question to be on the motion of the gentleman from Louisiana, (Mr. MORSE,) that the House take a recess until twelve o'clock.

Mr. MORSE suggested that the motion should be modified so as to read "five minutes before twelve."

The SPEAKER said there was no necessity for any formal change in the motion. The Speaker could, if necessary, resume the chair a few minutes before the time designated.

The House thereupon took a recess.

At thirteen minutes before twelve o'clock—

The SPEAKER resumed the Chair.

A message was received from the Senate, by L. H. MACHIN, Esq., Chief Clerk thereof, informing the House that that body had passed a resolution proposing the assembling of the two Houses in the Hall of Representatives, to witness the administration to the President of the United States of the oath to support the constitution, to enable him to enter upon the discharge of his duties; and, also, that the Senate had concurred in the resolution of the House for the appointment of a joint committee to wait upon the President of the United States, and that they had appointed Messrs. SOULE, DAVIS of Massachusetts, and UNDERWOOD, on their part.

The message having been read—

Mr. ASHMUN suggested, that as each House, acting separately, had adopted resolutions of a similar purport, which had passed each other between the two Houses, he supposed it would not be necessary to act upon the resolution just communicated from the Senate; and he moved, therefore, that it be laid upon the table.

Mr. STANTON, of Tennessee, suggested, that the more appropriate mode would be, to concur in the resolution, rather than to lay it upon the table.

The SPEAKER said that a similar resolution had already been passed by the House, and that there was no necessity for concurrence in this.

Thereupon the resolution of the Senate was laid upon the table.

The SPEAKER again vacated the chair.

At six minutes before twelve the SPEAKER resumed the Chair. A pause of several minutes followed.

At twelve o'clock—

Mr. MORSE appeared at the bar, introducing the honorable WILLIAM CRANCH, Chief Justice of the District and Circuit Court of the United States, who ascended the Clerk's platform and took a seat thereon, a little to the right of the Speaker.

At four minutes past twelve—

The Senate of the United States, preceded by their Sergeant-at-arms and Secretary, entered the Hall (the Speaker and members of the House rising to receive them) and took the places assigned to them in the area in front of the Speaker's chair.

The Speaker and the members of the House then resumed their seats.

Immediately afterwards—

His Excellency MILLARD FILLMORE, President of the United States, appeared at the bar of the House, supported by Messrs. SOULE of the Senate, and WINTHROP of the House of Representatives, and accompanied by the other members of the joint committee, and by the cabinet of the late President of the United States.

The Speaker and members of the House rose to receive them.

The President of the United States was conducted to a seat on the Clerk's platform, immediately in front of the Speaker's chair.

The Speaker and members of the House then resumed their seats.

After a pause of a few moments—

The Speaker rose and said: "The oath of office will now be administered to the President of the United States, by Chief Justice Cranch."

The President and the Chief Justice thereupon rose—

And the President read, in a firm and audible voice, the following oath of office, prescribed by the Constitution of the United States:

"I, Millard Fillmore, do solemnly swear that I will faithfully execute the office of President of the United States, and will, to the best of my ability, preserve, protect, and defend the Constitution of the United States."

The Chief Justice (Cranch) then administered the oath.

After which the President and Chief Justice resumed their seats.

A brief pause followed.

And then the President rose, and, accompanied by the committee, left the Hall, followed by the Cabinet, the Senate, &c., (the Speaker and members of the House rising as when they entered.)

A further pause followed.

A Message, in writing, was then received from the President of the United States, by the hands of George P. Fisher, Esq.

Whereupon,

The Speaker rose and addressed the House, as follows:

Gentlemen: Your session of yesterday was brought to an early close by the announcement of the dangerous illness of the President. It is my duty to-day to lay before you an official communication of his death. It is my purpose simply to make the announcement, not to dwell upon it; that duty will more properly devolve upon others. Whilst, gentlemen, our own body has been peculiarly exempt during its present sittings, from the fatality which usually attends a protracted session, we should not be regardless of the solemn warnings which Providence has extended to us in the death of those associated with us in the administration of our National Government. The victims who have been summoned to the tomb have been less remarkable for their number than their exalted character and position.

For the first time in our history has the Chief Executive of the Union been stricken down during the session of Congress. It devolves a novel and solemn duty upon the representatives of the people. As the organ of this House, delegated with the mere expression of its resolves, I feel it appropriate to indulge in no suggestions of my own, or expressions of personal emotions. I cannot, however, forbear from uttering the confident assurance that it will be your melancholy satisfaction to adopt the most appropriate manifestations of the profound sensibility which this afflicting dispensation must awaken throughout the Union, and to concur in every mark of respect to the memory of the distinguished patriot who has been so suddenly summoned from the high honors and responsibilities of the Chief Magistracy, to which he had been called by his grateful countrymen, to the repose of the grave.

The Message was then read, as follows:

Fellow-Citizens of the Senate and of the House of Representatives:

A great man has fallen among us, and a whole country is called to an occasion of unexpected, deep, and general mourning.

I recommend to the two Houses of Congress to adopt such measures as in their discretion they may deem proper, to perform with due solemnities the funeral obsequies of Zachary Taylor, late President of the United States; and thereby to signify the great and affectionate regard of the American people for the memory of one whose life has been devoted to the public service; whose career in arms has not been surpassed in usefulness or brilliancy; who has been so recently raised by the unsolicited voice of the people to the highest civil authority in the Government—which he administered with so much honor and advantage to his country; and by whose sudden death, so many hopes of future usefulness have been blighted forever.

To you, Senators and Representatives of a nation in tears, I can say nothing which can alleviate the sorrow with which you are oppressed. I appeal to you to aid me, under the trying circumstances which surround me, in the discharge of the duties, from which, however much I may be oppressed by them, I dare not shrink; and I rely upon Him, who holds in his hands the destinies of nations, to endow me with the requisite strength for the task, and to avert from our country the evils apprehended from the heavy calamity which has befallen us.

I shall most readily concur in whatever measures the wisdom of the two Houses may suggest, as befitting this deeply melancholy occasion.

MILLARD FILLMORE.

Washington, *July* 10, 1850.

The reading of the Message having been concluded—

Mr. Conrad said:

Mr. Speaker: In accordance with a wish expressed by many members, I have prepared a resolution adapted to the melancholy event which has just been announced, and which I purpose to offer to the House. Before doing so, however, I would do violence to my own feelings, as a representative of that State of which the illustrious deceased was a citizen and the brightest ornament, if I did not offer some remarks appropriate to the melancholy occasion on which we are assembled. Seldom has an event occurred which more strikingly illustrates the uncertainty of life and the instability of all earthly greatness than the one we are called upon to deplore.

A few days ago General Taylor was in his usual robust health. On the fourth of this month he attended some ceremonies which took place in commemoration of the anniversary of our national independence. As the ceremonies occurred in the open air, it is believed that the exposure to a heat of unusual intensity produced the malady which, at about half-past ten last night, terminated his earthly career. A great patriot has fallen! A great benefactor of his country has departed from among us! In a few hours a nation will be plunged in mourning, and the voice of lamentation will ascend from twenty millions of people!

It is not my purpose, Mr. Speaker, to dwell at length, on this occasion, on the public career and the military achievements of General Taylor. These belong to the history of his country, and are deeply engraven on the memories and the hearts of his countrymen. I prefer to dwell on those minor traits of his character which, as they exert a less perceptible influence on the destinies of nations, are too often overlooked by historians.

General Taylor's was not one of those characters, of which history furnishes many conspicuous examples, in which many defects are concealed amid the dazzling splendor of a single virtue. On the luminous disc of his character no dark spots are discernible. *His* biographer will have no great follies to conceal, or faults to excuse, or crimes to palliate or condemn. There is no dark passage in *his* life which justice will be called upon to condemn, or morality to reprove, or humanity to deplore. Like the finished production of an artist, the details of the picture are as correct and as beautiful as the general outline is grand and imposing.

His heroic courage and military genius are those qualities to which he is chiefly indebted for his fame, and yet those who knew him best would not consider them the prominent attributes of his character. On the contrary, this courage appeared only an adventitious quality, occasionally developed by circumstances requiring its exercise. His prominent characteristics, always manifest, were an unaffected modesty, combined with extraordinary firmness, a stern sense of duty, and of justice tempered and softened by a spirit of universal benevolence, an inflexible integrity, a truthfulness that knew no dissimulation, a sincerity and frankness which rendered concealment or disguise absolutely impossible.

These were the traits that endeared him to his friends, and inspired with confidence all who approached him. These were the qualities which in private life made him the upright man, the valuable citizen, the devoted friend, the affectionate husband, the fond father, the kind and indulgent master, and which, brought into public life, made him the disinterested patriot, and the faithful and conscientious functionary. His martial courage was set off and relieved by this group of civic virtues, as the brilliancy of the diamond is enhanced by the gems of softer ray by which it is encircled.

The mass of the people in all countries possess a wonderful sagacity in detecting the prominent traits of their distinguished men. The American people are inferior to none in this quality; and they soon discovered and appreciated the merits of General TAYLOR. It is not surprising, therefore, that they called him, almost by acclamation, to fill the first office in their gift.

It is so common for the most ambitious men to affect a reluctance in accepting those very honors which they have long and ardently sought, that we are apt to consider all such professions as indicating feelings the very reverse of those they express. Those, however, who knew General TAYLOR well, entertained no doubt of the entire sincerity of his declarations when he was called upon to be a candidate for the office of President.

The excitement of politics had no charm for one who had always been extremely averse to political controversy. The pomp and splendor of the presidential mansion had no temptations for one who was always remarkable for the simplicity of his tastes and the frugality of his habits. Add to this that his unaffected modesty and inexperience in public affairs led him sincerely to distrust his ability to discharge the duties of this high and responsible station.

At no period of our history, indeed, was the executive chair surrounded by more difficulties than those which encompassed it when he was called on to occupy it. Party spirit was still raging with unabated fury; a dark cloud was visible on the horizon, which portended that a storm of unusual violence was approaching, and would shortly burst forth. Under such circumstances, a man even of stouter heart than his might well hesitate before he consented to embark on this "sea of troubles." Yielding, however, to the public voice, and to the arguments and persuasion of his friends, he did embark. The tempest arose; and in the midst of its fury, while the vessel of State was tossed to and fro, and all eyes were turned with a confidence not unmingled with anxiety on the pilot who, calm and collected, guided her course, that pilot was suddenly swept from the helm!

Here let us pause! Let us avail ourselves of the momentary calm which this sad event has produced, and calmly survey the perils that surround us—the lowering heavens above, the raging billows below, the breakers on our right, the shoals on our left. Let us prepare to meet these dangers like men, and like patriots, to overcome them. Let us not despair of the Republic. On the contrary, let us determine that she *must* be saved, and she will be saved. The clouds that overhang us will be dispersed, and the glorious stars of our Union will again shine forth with their wonted splendor.

I beg leave to submit the following resolutions:

Whereas it has pleased Divine Providence to remove from this life ZACHARY TAYLOR, late President of the United States, the House of Representatives, sharing in the general sorrow which this melancholy event must produce, is desirous of manifesting its sensibility on the occasion; Therefore,

Resolved, That a committee, consisting of —— members, be appointed on the part of this House, to meet such committee as may be appointed on the part of the Senate, to consider and report what measures it may be deemed proper to adopt in order to show the respect and affection of Congress for the memory of the illustrious deceased, and to make the necessary arrangements for his funeral.

Resolved, That this resolution be communicated to the Senate.

Mr. Winthrop rose to second the resolutions, and proceeded as follows:

It would not be easily excused, Mr. Speaker, by those whom I represent in this Hall, if there were no Massachusetts voice to respond to the eulogy which has been pronounced by Louisiana upon her illustrious and lamented son. Indeed, neither my personal feelings nor my political relations to the living or to the dead, would permit me to remain altogether silent on this occasion. And yet, sir, I confess, I know not how to say any thing satisfactory to myself, or suitable to the circumstances of the hour.

The event which has just been officially announced, has come upon us so suddenly—has so overwhelmed us with mingled emotions of surprise and sadness—that all ordinary forms of expression seem to lose their significance, and one would fain bow his head to the blow in silence, until its first shock has in some degree passed away.

Certainly, sir, no one can fail to realize that a most momentous and mysterious Providence has been manifested in our midst. At a moment when, more than almost ever before in our history, the destinies of our country seemed, to all human sight, to be inseparably associated with the character and conduct of its Chief Executive Magistrate, that Magistrate has been summoned from his post, by the only messenger whose mandates he might not have defied, and has been withdrawn forever from the sphere of human existence!

There are those of us, I need not say, sir, who had looked to him with affection and reverence as our chosen leader and guide in the difficulties and perplexities by which we are surrounded. There are those of us, who had relied confidently on him, as upon no other man, to uphold the constitution and maintain the Union of the country in that future, upon which "clouds and darkness" may well be said to rest. And, as we now behold him, borne away by the hand of God from our sight, in the very hour of peril, we can hardly repress the exclamation, which was applied to the departing prophet of old: "My father, my father! the chariot of Israel, and the horsemen thereof."

Let me not even seem to imply, however, that the death of General Taylor is any thing less than a national loss. There may be, and we know there is, in this event, a privileged and preëminent grief for his immediate family and relatives, to which we can only offer the assurance of our heartfelt sympathy. There is, too, a peculiar sorrow for his political friends and supporters, which we would not affect to conceal. But the whole people of the United States will feel and will bear witness when they receive these melancholy tidings, that they have all been called to sustain a most afflicting national bereavement.

I hazard, nothing, sir, in saying, that the roll of our Chief Magistrates, since 1789, illustrious as it is, presents the name of no man, who has enjoyed a higher reputation with his contemporaries, or who will enjoy a higher reputation with posterity than Zachary Taylor, for some of the best and noblest qualities which adorn our nature.

His indomitable courage, his unimpeachable honesty, his Spartan simplicity and sagacity, his frankness, kindness, moderation, and magnanimity, his fidelity to his friends, his generosity and humanity to his enemies, the purity of his private life, the patriotism of his public principles, will never cease to be cherished in the grateful remembrance of all just men and all true-hearted Americans.

As a soldier and a general, his fame is associated with some of the proudest and most thrilling scenes of our military history. He may be literally said to have conquered every enemy he has met, save only that *last enemy*, to which we must all, in turn, surrender.

As a civilian and statesman, during the brief period in which he has been permitted to enjoy the transcendent honors which a grateful country had awarded him, he has given proof of a devotion to duty, of an attachment to the constitution and the Union, of a patriotic determination to maintain the peace of our country, which no trials or temptations could shake. He has borne his faculties meekly, but firmly. He has been "clear in his great office." He has known no local partialities or prejudices, but has proved himself capable of embracing his whole country in the comprehensive affections and regards of a large and generous heart.

But he has fallen almost at the threshold of his civil career, and at a moment when some of us were looking to him to render services to the country, which we had thought no other man could perform. Certainly, sir, he has died too soon for everybody but himself. We can hardly find it in our hearts to repine, that the good old man has gone to his rest. We would not disturb the repose in which the brave old soldier sleeps. His part in life had been long and faithfully performed. In his own last words, "he had always done his duty, and he was not afraid to die." But our regrets for ourselves and for our country are deep, strong, and unfeigned.

Sir, it was a fit and beautiful circumstance in the close of such a career, that his last official appearance was at the celebration of the

Birthday of our National Independence, and, more especially, that his last public act was an act of homage to the memory of *him* whose example he had ever revered and followed, and who, as he himself so well said, "was, by so many titles, the Father of his Country."

And, now, Mr. Speaker, let us hope that this event may teach us all how vain is our reliance upon any arm of flesh. Let us hope that it may impress us with a solemn sense of our national as well as individual dependence on a higher than human power. Let us remember, sir, that "the Lord is king, be the people never so impatient; that he sitteth between the cherubim, be the earth never so unquiet." Let us—in language which is now hallowed to us, as having been the closing and crowning sentiment of the brief but admirable Inaugural Address with which this illustrious patriot opened his presidential term, and which it is my privilege to read at this moment from the very copy from which it was originally read by himself to the American people, on the 4th day of March, 1849—let us, in language in which "he, being dead, yet speaketh"—"*Let us invoke a continuance of the same Protecting Care which has led us from small beginnings to the eminence we this day occupy; and let us seek to deserve that continuance by prudence and moderation in our councils; by well-directed attempts to assuage the bitterness which too often marks unavoidable differences of opinion; by the promulgation and practice of just and liberal principles; and by an enlarged patriotism, which shall acknowledge no limits but those of our own wide-spread Republic.*"

Mr. BAKER said: Mr. Speaker, it is often said of sorrow, that, like death, it levels all distinctions. The humblest heart can heave a sigh as deep as the proudest; and I avail myself of this mournful privilege to swell the accents of grief which have been poured forth to-day with a larger though not more sincere utterance. A second time since the formation of this Government a President of the United States has been stricken by death in the performance of his great duties. The blow which strikes the man falls upon a nation's heart, and the words of saddened praise which fall upon our ears to-day, and here, are but echoes of the thoughts that throng in the hearts of the millions that mourn him *everywhere.* You have no doubt observed, sir, that in the first moments of a great loss the instincts of affection prompt us to summon up the good and great qualities of those for whom we weep. It is a wise ordination of Divine Providence; a generous pride tempers and restrains the *bitterness* of grief, and noble deeds and heroic virtues shed a consoling light upon the tomb. It is in this spirit that I recur for an instant, and for an instant *only*, to the events of a history fresh in the remembrance of the nation and the world. The late President of the United States has devoted his whole life to the service of his country. Of a nature singularly unambitious, he seems to have combined the utmost gentleness of manner with the greatest firmness of purpose. For more than thirty years the duties of his station confined him to a sphere where only those who knew him most intimately could perceive the qualities which danger quickened and brightened into sublimity and grandeur. In the late war with Great Britain he was but a captain; yet the little band who defended Fort Harrison saw amid the smoke of battle that they were commanded by a man fit for his station. In the Florida campaign he commanded but a brigade; yet his leadership not only evinced courage and conduct, but inspired these qualities in the meanest soldier in his ranks. He began the Mexican campaign at the head only of a division; yet as the events of the war swelled that division into an army, so the crisis kindled him into higher resolves and nobler actions, till the successive steps of advance became the assured march of victory.

Mr. Speaker, as we review the brilliant and stirring passages of the events to which I refer, it is not in the power even of sudden grief to suppress the admiration which thrills our hearts. When, sir, has there been such a campaign—when such soldiers to be led—and when such qualities of leadership so variously combined? How simple, but yet how grand, was the announcement, "In whatever force the enemy may be, I shall fight him." It gave Palo Alto and Resaca to our banner. How steadfast the resolution that impelled the advance to Monterey! How stirring the courage which beleaguered the frowning city—which stormed the barricaded street—which carried the embattled heights, and won and kept the whole! Nor, sir, can we forget that in the flush of victory, the gentle heart stayed the bold hand, while the conquering soldier offered sacrifices on the altar of *pity*, amid all the exultation of triumph.

Sir, I may not stop to speak of the achievements of Buena Vista: they are deeds that will never die—it was the great event of the age, a contest of races and institutions. An army of volunteers, engaged not in an impetuous advance, but in a stern defence of chosen ground against superior force, and in a last extremity—men who had never seen fire faced the foe with the steadiness of veterans. Sir, as long as those frowning heights and bloody ravines shall remain, these recollections will endure, and with them, the name of the man who steadied every rank, and kindled every eye, by the indomitable resolution which would not yield, and the exalted spirit which rose highest amid the greatest perils. It was from scenes like these he was called to the Chief Magistracy. It was a summons unexpected and unsought—the spontaneous expression of a noble confidence, the just reward of great actions. It may not be proper to speak here and now of the manner in which these new duties were executed; but I may say, that here, as everywhere else, he exhibited the same firmness and decision which had marked his life. He was honest and unostentatious; he obeyed the law and loved the constitution; he dealt with difficult questions with a singleness of purpose which is the truest pilot amid storms. Nor can it be doubted that when impartial history shall record the events of his administration, they will be found worthy of his past life, and a firm foundation for his future renown.

You remember, Mr. Speaker, that when the great Athenian philosopher was inquired of by the Lydian king as to who was the happiest among men, he declared that no man should be pronounced happy till his death. The President of the United States has so finished a noble life, as to justify the pride and admiration of his countrymen—he has faced the last enemy with a manly firmness and a becoming resolution. He died where an American citizen would most desire to die—not amid embattled hosts and charging squadrons, but amid weeping friends and an anxious nation—in the house provided by its gratitude, only to be taken thence, to a "house not made with hands, eternal in the Heavens."

Sir, in the death which has caused so much dismay, there is a becoming resemblance to the life which has created so much confidence. His closing hours were marked with a beautiful calmness; his last expressions indicated a manly sense of his own worth, and a consciousness that he had done his duty. Nor can I omit to remark, that it is this sense of the obligation of duty which appears to have been the true basis of his character. In boyhood and in age—as Captain and as General—whether defending a fort against savages, or exercising the functions of the Chief Magistracy, duty, rather than glory—self-approval, rather than renown, have prompted the deeds which have made him immortal.

Mr. Speaker, the character upon which death has just set his seal is filled with beautiful and impressive contrasts;—a warrior, he loved peace; a man of action, he sighed for retirement. Amid the events which crowned him with fame, he counselled a withdrawal of our troops. And, whether at the head of armies, or in the Chair of State, he appeared as utterly unconscious of his great renown as if no banners had drooped at his word, or as if no gleam of glory shone through his whitened hair. It is related of Epaminondas, that when fatally wounded at the battle of Mantinea, they bore him to a height from whence, with fading glance, he surveyed the fortunes of the fight, and when the field was won, laid himself down to die; the friends who gathered around him wept his early fall, and passionately expressed their sorrow that he died childless. "Not so," said the hero, with his last breath, "for do I not leave two fair daughters, Leuctra and Mantinea?" General Taylor is more fortunate, since he leaves an excellent and most worthy family to deplore his loss and inherit his glory. Nor is he fortunate in this only, since, like Epaminondas, he leaves not only two battles, but four—Palo Alto, Resaca, Monterey, Buena Vista—the grand creations of his genius and valor, to be remembered as long as truth and courage appeal to the human heart.

Mr. Speaker, the occasion and the scene impress upon us a deep sense of the instability of all human concerns, so beautifully alluded to by my friend from Massachusetts, (Mr. Winthrop.) The great southern Senator is no longer among us. The President during whose administration the war commenced, sleeps in "the house appointed for all the living;" and the great soldier who led the advance and assured the triumph, "lies like a warrior taking his rest." Ah! sir, if in this assemblage there is a man whose heart beats with a tumultuous and unrestrained ambition, let him to-day stand by the bier upon which that lifeless body is laid, and learn how much of human greatness fades in an hour; but if there be another man here whose fainting heart shrinks from a noble purpose, let him, too, visit those sacred remains, to be reminded how much there is in true glory that can never die.

Mr. Bayly said: Mr. Speaker, representing in part the native State of the illustrious dead, it may not be improper for me, in behalf of her delegation, to add a word to what has already been said. However much she may have differed with him while living, there is not one that mourns more deeply his sudden death. No State felt a loftier pride in his military achievements, or admired more his private virtues. None will drop a tear of more heartfelt sorrow upon his bier.

I hope it will not be deemed inappropriate for me to indulge in some reflections suggested by the occasion. For the second time, Mr. Speaker, in our political history, our National Government is to be subjected to the trial of being administered by a President not elected by the people to that office. The first was severe enough; but this must be still more so. How different is our situation now from what it was then! Then, it is true, we were in a condition of high political excitement. But it was the elevation or downfall of parties which depended upon the result. Now we are in the midst of an angry sectional strife, threatening the very existence of the Government itself. If that crisis required prudence, moderation, and wisdom to insure success to the experiment, how much more will the one in which we now find ourselves demand the exercise of those high qualities! Sir, in the very midst of the tempest, when the storm is howling about us, and when all is uncertainty and alarm, the Captain has been unexpectedly swept from the deck, and the second in command has just taken charge of the helm. If this loss has added to their anxiety, it but increases the obligation of fidelity on the part of the crew, upon whose fidelity at last the safety of the ship depends.

Sir, we, that crew, owe it to ourselves, to those who have trusted us where we are—we owe it to mankind to save her from her perils.

Heretofore, when deluges have swept over the eastern continent, heaving off before them the vestiges of liberty, our country has been looked to as the Mount Ararat, upon which the Ark, laden with all that was dear to liberty, might rest in safety. Shall we now fan the internal fires which are kindling in its bosom, and convert it into a terrible volcano, eructating its dreadful lava, and spreading ruin and devastation around—an object to be avoided rather than sought? My ardent prayer is, that there is still enough of the spirit of our fathers among us to save mankind from this awful catastrophe.

Sir, as much as I have always admired our institutions, I am free to admit that I have never seen their beauties in bolder relief than to-day. The scene which has just been enacted before us, has converted my admiration, as I doubt not it has that of all of us, almost into idolatry itself. In the midst of such a crisis as the Union of these States never found itself in before—one threatening its downfall—in the very focus of the excitement which has produced it, we have seen the executive branch of the Government, with all of its enormous power, pass, without the conflict of dynasties, without the presence of a soldier, or even a police officer, so quietly from one set of hands to another, that but for the sadness which rests upon the brows of those around me, no one would conjecture that any thing unusual had occurred! Where else could such a scene be witnessed? In the history of what other Government is its parallel to be found? Is there not enough—I appeal to my countrymen—in the reflections suggested by what is passing around us to awaken the nation to a sense of that justice and patriotism by which alone can the blessings we enjoy be preserved to ourselves and mankind?

Mr. HILLIARD rose and said: Mr. Speaker, at the suggestion of those in whose judgment I have confidence, I rise to offer an humble tribute to the memory of the great man who has just fallen in our midst. If he were living I should leave others to eulogize him—as he is dead, I choose to speak of him. And yet I am so overwhelmed by the event which has just occurred, that I can scarcely find language to express what I feel. Some events are so impressive that they leave little occasion for words—they are too great to be enlarged on. I am almost ready to follow the example of a great French orator, who, when called on to pronounce a funeral oration upon a deceased monarch, laid his hand upon the head of the dead king, and exclaimed: "There is nothing great but God." Sir, there *is* nothing great but God.

General TAYLOR's whole career illustrated the high qualities which so eminently distinguished him. I do not dwell upon his battle-fields—they belong to history, and they will find a place upon the brightest pages which record such exploits. Nor shall I speak of his courage—it is unnecessary; that is attested by hard-fought fields, and brilliant victories won under his eye against overwhelming numbers. But I wish to speak of that high sense of duty which characterized his whole life—that steady purpose to do what he believed to be right, at all times and in all places. In the performance of duty, nothing could move him—he marched directly upon the road where that called him. The reference to this trait in his character has been appropriately made by the gentleman from Illinois, (Mr. BAKER,) and it deserves to be observed and dwelt upon. To him, as fully as to any one I have ever known, may be applied the high eulogium of "*incorrupta fides*"—he kept his faith with all men. You might dissent from his opinions—you might find fault with his judgment, but when he took his position, he kept it—his sense of duty sustained him, and opposition only served to make him the more steadfast in holding it.

It is said of Napoleon, that the great quality which distinguished him, next to his genius, was his love of glory; so that when he marched his army into Egypt, the appeal which he made to them on the eve of battle was, "Soldiers, forty centuries look down upon you from these pyramids."

General TAYLOR rather resembled Lord Nelson, who, when about to engage the enemy's fleet, sent to his several officers in command of his ships the words, "England expects every man to do his *duty*."

This was the constant aim of the illustrious man who has just been called away from us. This great quality which sheds such lustre upon his name, gave him that success which so uniformly attended him. When about to engage in battle at Buena Vesta with the overwhelming army opposed to him, he comprehended the danger which invested him, but he had made up his mind that it was his duty to stand there, and in his own beautiful language, written before the engagement, he "looked to Providence for a good result."

General TAYLOR's character was American—distinctly and decidedly American. He was invited to quit the army and take the Chief Magistracy of the Government. He did so with unaffected reluctance, from a sincere distrust of his fitness for such a station. But as in the army he had obeyed every order of his Government, he now obeyed the call of his countrymen, and laying aside his plumed hat, his epaulets, and his sword, he entered upon the functions of his new and great position with an honest purpose to do his duty.

Unlike Cæsar, who repelled the proffered crown while he coveted it, he came with diffidence to the high position to which he had been called, and unostentatiously employed himself with its appropriate duties; his whole course evincing his profound sense of the value of constitutional liberty, and his manners illustrating the beautiful simplicity of his character.

Sir, this illustrious man is called away from us at a moment most critical. Never have I known the Republic in such peril as now surrounds it. My friend from Massachusetts (Mr. Winthrop) has well said that it is so clearly an interposition of Providence, that he is ready to exclaim, "The chariots of Israel and the horsemen thereof."

Sir, I agree to this. It is an interposition of Providence; and it comes to us in a trying hour. But I am not dismayed. My trust in Providence is unshaken. Our country has been delivered, guided, made glorious, by a good Providence. It will be so still. I remember, when the prophet referred to by the gentleman from Massachusetts, (Mr. Winthrop,) was surrounded by a hostile force, and all hope of escape seemed cut off, that a young man who was with him cried out in great fear; and the reply of the prophet was, a prayer that the young man's eyes might be opened. He then saw that all within the hostile lines were "chariots and horsemen of fire" ready to succor and to deliver the beleaguered city. So will it be with us. The dangers which threaten us will be averted, and, I trust, forever disposed of. The solemn event which has just occurred, will arrest the angry current which has swept us on so fiercely. It imposes a truce, at least for a season, upon contending parties. In the meanwhile, a better feeling may spring up; and we may ask, "Why do we struggle with each other? Are we not brethren?" The nation will be impressed with the bereavement which it has suffered, and the tide of sorrow which sweeps throughout the country, will admonish us to agree in wise, patriotic, and fraternal counsels. The very event which we deplore, and which we regard as a calamity, will be overruled for good; and He that sitteth on high, mightier than the water-floods, will put forth his power and cause a great calm.

Sir, death is at all times a solemn event; it touches both time and eternity; it terminates an earthly existence; it opens an immortal one. But this death will strike the world as an event marked by more than common solemnity. We mingle our tears over the bier of the Chief Magistrate of a great nation. We will honor his memory, and we will claim his fame for his whole country. Henceforth he belongs to his country, and his name is a part of our common inheritance. His last public act was in honor of the memory of Washington: he fixed his eyes upon that noble monument which is rising to the skies, built up by the present generation for one whom all called blessed. By this time he has, it may be hoped, met the revered Father of his Country in a world where their companionship will be eternal. His memory is safe—no human events can now affect it; the great qualities, the private virtues, the public services—all that is precious in his memory, has received the seal of death.

> "The love where death hath set his seal,
> Nor age can chill, nor rival steal,
> Nor falsehood disavow."

A message was received from the Senate, by L. H. Machin, Esq., informing the House that that body had passed a resolution for the appointment of a committee, to join such committee as might be appointed on the part of the House, to consider and report measures proper to be adopted, to show the respect and affection of Congress for the memory of the illustrious deceased, and to make the necessary arrangements for his funeral; and that they had appointed Messrs. Webster, Cass, and King, the committee on the part of the Senate.

The reading of the message having been concluded—

Mr. J. A. King said: Mr. Speaker, I desire to say a few words on the sad and overwhelming event which has caused us to assemble here this day. In grief and in sorrow, in honor and respect, we are called upon to bow with submission to the inevitable will of Him, in whose hands are the issues of life and death—to mourn the loss of one, who, during a long career of distinguished and patriotic services, had endeared himself to the hearts of the American people—to look firmly, but without despair, at the sudden death of the Chief Magistrate of the millions of freemen over whose destinies he but yesterday presided in health and in honor—to acknowledge and confess the eminent services which in war he rendered to his country—to bear our testimony to the moderation, the wisdom, and the firmness of his conduct, as the chosen head of the nation—to declare the hope which sprang in every bosom, while the short struggle for life endured, that that life, if not for his, for their sakes, might be spared—to manifest, so far as words can express them, the feelings of desolation which reign unchecked in every bosom on account of the sad bereavement. The character of him whom we mourn, was made up of elements which never fail to win the attachment and confidence of the American people. Frank, direct, humane, yet firm of purpose, he brought to the consideration of questions of difficulty a clear and unbiassed judgment—a decision which, once fairly made, never swerved. The consequences were, success and honor for himself and his country. Few ever could boast a greater or a better influence over the hearts of the people; and that generous attachment which cheered him while living, will mourn him—dead. We lament him as our glory and defence—as the head and hope of this great Confederacy.

But yet we are not left without hope, without alleviation. One yet remains to us, who is to fill the honored chair of State—one whose public and private character needs no eulogy—one in whom the mild and best qualities of a statesman are fairly mingled. Let us give him our confidence; let us cheer him in the performance of this, his unexpected and most undesired duties. Let us cast upon him the mantle of our hopes and our confidence, for he deserved and will honorably wear it.

Mr. Speaker, there are those of the household of the distinguished and lamented dead, whose bereavement is deepest, and whose broken hearts no human consolation can reach. Let our anxious thoughts be directed, and our warmest sympathies be poured out in their behalf; for they have borne themselves gently, in the position they have been called upon to fill. I cannot close, sir, these brief remarks, without expressing my abiding trust that the dispensations of an overruling Providence, whose will we may not question, may still be ordered for the honor, the safety, and the glory of the Republic.

Mr. McLANE, of Maryland. Mr. Speaker, I hope, sir, late as the hour is in this day's proceedings, I may be indulged in responding to an invitation of some friends around me, by giving public expression to those sentiments of personal friendship and respect which I entertain for the illustrious deceased; and when I say, sir, that my acquaintance with General TAYLOR had its origin long before either he or I had engaged in the heated strifes of political life—when we both served under the same flag, as brethren in arms—I shall not be deemed obtrusive. He was then, sir, in command of the army in Florida, and I was an humble officer of one of the corps of that army. At this period of his life, he was already distinguished by those high qualities of courage, fortitude, and virtue, in the discharge of his public duties, as he was for that extraordinary benevolence and kindness which so endeared him to his family and friends. Sir, I formed for him then a respect and friendship which I retained undiminished to the hour of his death, and which shall be cherished for his memory, now that the hand of God has translated him from the scene of his early life and trial.

Subsequently, sir, I again met General TAYLOR at the head of his army in the valley of the Rio Grande. I delivered to him in his camp at Monterey, the orders of his Government, which announced to him, that the military plans and policy of the country were to be materially modified and changed. The northern States of Mexico, then about to be invaded, were to be left unmolested, and the entire military power of our people was to be directed upon the city of Mexico, by a new line of operations. Those operations, sir, left him to the comparatively humble task of a defensive campaign in the valley of the Rio Grande, while the more glorious and decisive movement upon the city of Mexico, seemed likely to fall to the lot of some more fortunate commander. On this occasion, sir, it was my privilege and my duty to confer with him fully and confidentially on the part of his Government, and it afforded me, sir, the opportunity to witness once more a rare display of those qualities to which I have already referred, of fortitude, and courage, and patience, and I must add fidelity to the Government which he served. It is not for me, at this moment, when I have so unexpectedly, but I hope not intrusively, touched this topic, to refer to those extraordinary events, which soon followed, and which invested his defensive position with singular and startling importance, and which finally led him to the field of *Buena Vista*, where he accomplished a victory so brilliant and wonderful, that it must rest, sir, as the crown of glory to that war, while it will through all time adorn his fame as an illustrious soldier. My reference to these events, sir, is that I may mark my association with General TAYLOR, to events near to his own personal fame and honor, and apart from those passages in life, when he was necessarily associated with the political and partisan excitements of the country; this course enables me, sir, not only to forego, but to be together insensible to any influences they might excite, and to render his memory, on this occasion, my most profound homage and respect. As a statesman, sir, he was necessarily exposed to encounter the strife of contending sentiment and opinion, and I feel happy, sir, at this instant, that I knew him in a life of high and noble action, in which he developed the highest attributes of American character—patriotism. And whatever might be the relation we would respectively hold to his political opinions or policy, it is cheering to feel that his life has left us all an example, displaying qualities of the head and heart, which to cultivate and cherish, should be our first and chief duty. This humble tribute, plainly and I fear imperfectly expressed, I beg to submit on my own part, and for the people I represent, with a further expression of condolence for those who remain to mourn the loss of a husband, father, brother and friend.

Mr. MARSHALL said: Mr. Speaker, silence is the eloquence of woe, and most appropriate sign of submission to Him whose inscrutable decree afflicts the people.

Were the emotions of my own bosom at this moment the accepted counsellors of my action, content to mingle mine with the nation's tears, I should permit this solemn occasion to pass without the obtrusion of a single remark. But custom, and the known relations I held to the late President of the United States, induce me to express here the profound sensibility with which intelligence of his lamented death will be received by the Commonwealth of Kentucky. In no quarter of our country will this blow fall with more crushing force than upon the district I represent. *There* are the graves of his parents—the habitations of his kindred—the surviving associates of his youth—the especial friends of his matured manhood—the companions of his military adventures—and the most numerous branches of his family connection. There his name was a tower of strength, as his fame was the pride of the people.

I have not risen to dwell upon his exploits, or to recount his many virtues. These can derive no additional lustre from the voice of exaggerated eulogy. Comparison between Zachary Taylor and celebrated ancients, illustrious in life or death, will neither diminish nor increase his claim to the admiration of mankind. His character was formed on no pre-existing model. Reared amidst the solitudes of a western wilderness, his principles were fashioned by the precepts of the pioneer, and his career has vindicated their christianity, their wisdom, and their patriotism. The column is complete. Omniscience has withdrawn the workman. Time and earth have but "the sign and token" of the great original. The pencil of history must fill the bold outline for the contemplation of posterity. Great, without pride; cautious, without fear; brave, without rashness; stern, without harshness; modest, without bashfulness; sagacious, without cunning; apt, without flippancy; intelligent, without the pedantry of learning; benevolent, without ostentation; sincere, and honest as the sun, the "noble old Roman" has lain down his harness—his task is done. He has fallen, as falls the summer tree in the bloom of his honors, before the blight of autumn has seared a leaf that adorns it. The image of his great character is indelibly impressed upon the hearts of his countrymen, and the lines thereof,

> "By just degrees will every moment rise,
> Fill the wide earth, and gain upon the skies."

At the honored urn which holds the remains of our beloved and departed chief, Kentucky asks a place among her sisters, to baptize it with the tears of sincere sorrow, and to attest her sense of the common loss. Participating entirely in the feeling which follows into retirement the bereaved family of the illustrious deceased, I desire to offer to them, in behalf of the representatives and people of the Commonwealth of Kentucky, (and I am sure I may well add, of all the States of the Union,) the expression of our sincerest sympathy under their deep affliction. May the Hand which "tempers the wind to the shorn lamb," bring to their relief the consolation imparted by the assurance, that of General Taylor, as a friend, citizen, soldier, patriot,

> "None knew him but to love him,
> None named him but to praise."

To them the beauties of his domestic life remain, and I shall not presume to intrude upon their sacred recollections, or the satisfaction they must inspire. To us, as public men, may the bright example of the departed be ever present through all the watches of the night; may *we*, too, be able to repeat, as the last of earth is present to each of us, before a grateful country, the simple and touching declaration of his death scene, "I am not afraid to die—I have done my duty."

Mr. White moved that the blank in the resolution of the Senate (for the appointment of a committee) be filled with the number 13.

Ordered accordingly, and the following gentlemen were appointed by the Chair to constitute said committee, viz.: Messrs. Conrad, McDowell, Winthrop, Bissell, Duer, Orr, Breck, Strong, Vinton, Cabell, of Florida, Kerr, Stanly, and Littlefield.

The resolution was then unanimously concurred in.

And, on motion of Mr. Thompson, of Mississippi, the House adjourned until to-morrow at 11 o'clock.

IN SENATE.

Thursday, July 11.

Election of President pro tem.

The Secretary called the Senate to order at 11 o'clock.

Mr. Dickinson. Mr. Secretary, I am aware that, in the course I am about to pursue, I differ from that which is prescribed by our rules. I trust, however, for the sake of despatch, and in view of the good feeling which prevails in this body, that unanimous consent will be given to it. I, therefore, move that the Senior Senator from Alabama, the honorable William R. King, be appointed President *pro tem.* of this body.

Mr. Berrien. Mr. Secretary, I desire to express for myself my entire assent to the resolution which has been offered by the Senator from New York, and I trust that it will meet with unanimous acceptance on the part of the Senate.

The motion was unanimously agreed to.

Mr. King, having been conducted to the chair by Messrs. Dickinson and Berrien, rose and said:

Senators: Words could but feebly express the warm and gratified feelings which have penetrated my heart by this manifestation of kindness and confidence, so unanimously displayed by the representatives of the sovereign States of this Union. Had it been the pleasure of my political friends to have placed me in this distinguished position, it would have been to me a source of gratification and pride. I should have felt, as I trust I shall always feel in every situation in which I may be placed, that there was imposed upon me a solemn obligation to discharge the duties of the position with faithfulness and impartiality. How much higher, then, Senators, is the obligation imposed upon me to discharge these duties with the utmost faithfulness and impartiality, when I am called to this place by no political party, by no sectional feeling, but by the unanimous expression of the wishes of the Senators in Congress assembled.

While I preside here I shall endeavor to enforce mildly, but firmly, and I trust impartially, all the rules for the government of this body. I shall endeavor to apply the parliamentary law as it is laid down in the books, upon every occasion, believing, as I honestly do, from long experience and observation, that it is promotive of the harmony of the body and of sound legislation. Should I err, I look to my brother Senators, in a spirit of kindness, to correct my errors. To such corrections I shall always submit with the greatest pleasure.

Committee of Arrangements.

Mr. WEBSTER. Mr. President, the joint committee of the two Houses, appointed yesterday to make arrangements for the funeral of the late President of the United States, have assembled this morning, and, as far as practicable, have agreed upon a report, which I am directed to present to the Senate. I hope the Senate will adopt that report in part; for there are still remaining some subordinate arrangements to be attended to by the committee.

Mr. UNDERWOOD. Mr. President, the report just made having brought up again to the attention of the Senate the death of the late President of the United States, and being absent yesterday when the gentleman from Louisiana (Mr. DOWNS) made his eloquent and appropriate address, and offered his resolutions upon that subject—that absence having been occasioned by the fact that I was appointed as one of the committee on the part of the Senate to wait upon Mr. FILLMORE, to make arrangements preparatory to his taking the oath of office—I throw myself upon the indulgence of the Senate, and beg permission to make a few remarks.

I was among the earliest to advocate the election of General Taylor, and, in common with a very large majority of the people of my State, gave him a most cordial support. He had been raised among us. His character was formed and developed by associations with the pioneers of the western wilderness; with those who encountered the difficulties and privations of settling and improving the most fertile region of the globe; and who, almost unaided by Government, relying exclusively upon their own individual resources and energies, successfully resisted the persevering efforts of numerous hordes of warlike savages to expel them from the country. His father, Richard Taylor, a soldier of the Revolution, was eminently qualified to infuse into the mind of his son those sentiments of ardent patriotism and lofty heroism which pervaded all classes with whom Zachary Taylor associated when a boy. Well do I remember that father; for I was associated with him in the Legislature of Kentucky, at a time when questions of constitutional law deeply agitated the entire State, and when rancorous and bitter politicians threatened the public peace, and dared to talk of bloodshed. I remember how conciliatingly, how calmly, and yet how firmly, that father demeaned himself amidst the storms of debate and the fierce collisions of conflicting opinions. In these respects he was the admirable prototype of the hero of Buena Vista.

With such a father, and under the influences of the society and circumstances by which General Taylor was surrounded in his boyhood, it would have been indeed strange had he grown up without a strong predilection for military life. Fortunately for his own fame, fortunately for the glory of his country, in youth he put on the armor of a soldier. What followed is well-known history, and needs no repetition here.

A grateful country, penetrated by a deep conviction of the intuitive sagacity and elevated patriotism of General Taylor, united with military achievements of unsurpassed splendor, and a personal character for truth and honesty without a superior, made him Chief Magistrate. The providence of God has terminated his earthly career, during this the first session of Congress since his inauguration. His father was permitted to live and take an efficient part in accomplishing those measures which relieved Kentucky from the threatened horrors of civil war. The son has been taken hence to the world of spirits, before those agitating questions which now excite Congress and the people, and threaten the destruction of the Government, have been settled. Mysterious Providence! There were thousands and hundreds of thousands of our countrymen, who looked for help in this time of need to the unbending integrity and firmness of purpose which ever characterized our late President. God has taken from them this staff of their reliance. It will be manifested in time whether, the measure of General Taylor's honors and usefulness being full and overflowing, he was removed by the Ruler of the Universe to give place to those equally or better able to calm political dissensions, and to extricate the country from impending dangers, or whether the awful judgments of God are to rest upon us for national sins, and for the want of that wisdom and spirit of conciliation which have heretofore enabled such men as Zachary Taylor to secure national prosperity and happiness. Whatever purposes of the Deity the future may unfold, the present is a day of mourning; and certain I am that no portion of our extensive country will feel more sensibly the general bereavement than the State in which our dead and yet unburied Chief Magistrate spent the morning of his life. Kentucky will long remember and mourn for him as one of her own sons, and as the commander who led her McKee, her Clay, her Hardin, her Barbour, her Willis, and a host of her less distinguished children, to the glorious sacrifice of life, to secure the triumph of their country.

And while we sympathize and condole with the family of the great and good man gone from earth forever, let us indulge the hope that his bright example will be of immense value to succeeding generations, and that his spirit with kindred spirits now constitute a blessed society in Heaven.

On motion of Mr. Webster, the report of the committee was concurred in.

On motion of Mr. Atchison, it was ordered that when the Senate adjourns, it adjourn to meet on Saturday at 11 o'clock.

On motion of Mr. Dickinson, the Secretary of the Senate was directed to inform the President of the United States and the House of Representatives that the Senate have appointed a President *pro tem.*

On motion of Mr. Webster, the Senate adjourned.

Saturday, July 13.

The Senate met, in pursuance of resolutions previously adopted, for the purpose of attending, in a body, the funeral services of the late President of the United States; and having performed that duty, and returned to their chamber,*

On motion, the Senate adjourned.

---

* The following order was observed in the burial of the late President of the United States:

The Military portion of the Funeral Procession of Saturday is worthy of a special notice. It was anticipated that many volunteer companies, and indeed military men generally, would be anxious to attend the obsequies of the illustrious Chieftain and President of the Republic; and this anticipation was fully realized. Baltimore contributed largely and patriotically to the military display, than which we never witnessed a more imposing one in this city. The whole was under the command of the distinguished General-in-Chief of the United States Army, whose manly form and martial bearing, mounted as he was on a noble charger, and surrounded by a numerous staff, attracted all eyes, as the funeral cortege moved solemnly from the Presidential Mansion to Congress Burying Ground. From a favorable and commanding position that we occupied, at the corner of one of the cross streets, we noticed the troops marching in slow time, in the following order:

Patapsco Riflemen, of Baltimore, Captain Swain, preceded by their Band.

Independent Greys' Band, of Baltimore.

Light Infantry, from Wilmington, Delaware.

German Yeagers, of Baltimore, Captain Pracht.

Maryland Cadets, of Baltimore, Captain Poor.

National Blues, of Baltimore, Captain Chesnut.

Taylor Light Infantry, from Catonsville, Maryland, under the command of Lieutenant Brown, of the Independent Greys, Baltimore. This interesting corps consisted of two companies of youths, who are being educated at St. Timothy Hall. Their uniform was handsome and they were well drilled.

German Washington Guards, of Baltimore, Captain Hoffman.

National Greys, of Washington, Captain Bacon.

Independent Greys, of Baltimore, Captain Hall.

A platoon of commissioned officers representing volunteer companies of the fifty-third regiment of Baltimore.

A portion of the patriotic volunteer Defenders of Baltimore in the year 1814, with their banner. Amongst them we recognized General Anthony Miltenberger, Joseph K. Stapleton, and Wm. P. Mills, Esqs.

First Baltimore Sharp Shooters, of Baltimore, Captain Lilly.

Jackson Guards, of Baltimore.

Independent Blues, of Baltimore, Captain Shutt.

Independent Greys, of Georgetown, Captain Goddard.

National Guards, of Philadelphia, Captain Lyle.

Mount Vernon Guards, of Alexandria, Captain Fields.

Richmond (Va.) Blues, Lieutenant Regnault, accompanied by their Band.

Worth Infantry, of York, Pennsylvania.

Eagle Artilery, of Baltimore, Captain Phillips.

A platoon of officers representing volunteer companies of the fifth regiment of Baltimore.

Mounted Carbineers, of Baltimore, Captain S. C. Owings.

The Marine Band attached to the Washington Navy Yard.

Two companies of United States Marines, Captain Tansill.

Walker Sharp Shooters, of Washington, Lieutenant Birkhead.

Washington Light Infantry, of Washington, Captain Tate.

Four companies (C, E, F, G) U. S. Artillery, acting as infantry, under the command, respectively, of Capt Bowen, Lieutenant Doubleday, Captain Williams, Captain Brannan, and Lieutenant Nichols.

1st Artillery Band, from Fort Columbus, New York.

One company of U. S. Flying Artillery, mounted and fully equipped, under the command of Major Sedgwick, from Fort McHenry, Baltimore.

Officers of the United States Navy, in uniform, on foot.

Maj. Gen. Jones, commanding the Militia of the District of Columbia, and Staff.

Maj. Gen. Scott, General-in-Chief of the United States Army, and Staff.

Marshal of the District of Columbia, and his Aids.

Mayors of Washington and Baltimore.

Joint Committee of Arrangements on the part of the two Houses of Congress, as follows:

Committee of the Senate.

Mr. Webster of Massachusetts, Mr. Cass of Michigan, and Mr. King of Alabama.

Committee of the House.

Mr. Conrad of Louisiana,	Mr. Strong of Pennsylvania,
Mr. McDowell of Virginia,	Mr. Vinton of Ohio,
Mr. Winthrop of Mass.,	Mr. Cabell of Florida,
Mr. Bissell of Illinois,	Mr. Kerr of Maryland,
Mr. Duer of New York,	Mr. Stanly of North Carolina,
Mr. Orr of South Carolina,	Mr. Littlefield of Maine.
Mr. Breck of Kentucky,	

Chaplains to Congress and Officiating Clergymen.

The Pall Bearers, as follows:

Hon. Henry Clay,	Hon. T. H. Benton,
Hon. Lewis Cass,	Hon. Daniel Webster,
Hon. J. M. Berrien,	Hon. Truman Smith,
Hon. R. C. Winthrop,	Hon. Lynn Boyd,
Hon. Jas. McDowell,	Hon. S. F. Vinton,
Hon. Hugh White,	Hon. Isaac E. Holmes,
G. W. P. Custis, Esq.,	Hon. R. J. Walker,
Chief Justice Cranch,	Joseph Gales, Esq.,
Major General Jesup,	Major General Gibson,
Commodore Ballard,	Brig. Gen. Henderson.

Funeral Car, drawn by eight white horses, each horse attended by a groom.

General Taylor's horse, "Old Whitey," fully caparisoned, attended by a groom.

The Family of the late President in three carriages.

The President of the United States.

The Cabinet.

The Senate of the United States, preceded by its Officers.

The House of Representatives, preceded by its Officers.

The City Councils of Washington.

A representation of the Firemen and of the Temperance Societies of Washington.

The Band of the Independent Blues, of Baltimore.

Clerks of the Executive Departments of the Government.

The Mayor and City Councils of Baltimore, in mourning.

Judges of Courts, Citizens, Strangers, &c., &c.

It is not extravagant to state that the Procession was from one mile and a half to two miles in length. The line occupied three-quarters of an hour in passing before us.

Of the good conduct of the soldiery who formed the military escort at the funeral, it is unnecessary to speak. The United States troops, under Captain Brannan, (a native of this city,) Major Sedgwick, Captain Bowen, and Lieutenant Nichols, deported themselves in a soldier-like and becoming manner. The same may be said of the volunteer companies and the young Cadets. The Taylor Infantry, from Catonsville, Maryland, for the most part juvenile, behaved admirably.

The arrangements made by the Marshal of the District and the Mayor of the city were admirably carried out by the Aids of the former, and the police officers appointed by the latter. The line of the Funeral Procession was kept clear of carriages and vehicles of every description, as the cortege passed along. No accident occurred, that we have heard of, during the whole day.

The Boards of Aldermen and Common Council of the City of Baltimore, at the head of whom was Mayor Stansbury, of that city, attended the Funeral, and did themselves much honor by their full attendance and dignified deportment. They unfortunately did not arrive until past one o'clock, owing to the breaking of the locomotive, which caused a delay of two hours. They were met by a committee of our City Councils, consisting of Messrs. French, Maury, Brent

MONDAY, July 15.

The Compromise Bill.

The Senate, as in Committee of the Whole, resumed the consideration of the bill for the admission of California as a State into the Union, to establish Territorial Governments for Utah and New Mexico, and making proposals to Texas for the settlement of her western and northern boundaries.

Mr. BUTLER, having the floor, resumed and concluded his remarks commenced on Tuesday last.

Mr. CLAY rose, after a brief pause, and said: Mr. President if there is no other gentleman disposed to speak, I hope we shall take up the amendments and act upon them.

The PRESIDING OFFICER. There is no amendment before the Senate. Several amendments have been laid upon the table, but there have been none offered.

Mr. CLAY. Then the question will be on reporting the bill to the Senate.

MONDAY, July 22.

The PRESIDENT *pro tem.* laid before the Senate the following communication from the Hon. DANIEL WEBSTER, which was read:

WASHINGTON, *July* 22, 1850.

To the Hon. WM. R. KING,
President pro tem. of the Senate of the United States:

SIR: I have to request that you will lay before the Senate the accompanying copy of a communication addressed by me to the Governor of Massachusetts.

With the highest regard, I have the honor to be your obedient servant,

DANIEL WEBSTER.

WASHINGTON, *July* 22, 1850.

To his Excellency GEO. N. BRIGGS,
Governor of Massachusetts:

SIR: I have to inform you that I have been appointed Secretary of State for the United States, and that my seat in the Senate will be vacant from this day.

I have the honor to be, with regard, your Excellency's obedient servant,

DANIEL WEBSTER.

The Compromise Bill—Mr. Clay's Great Speech—Danger to the Union—His Noble Devotion to the Union—His Paternal Vindication of the Truth of History in Relation to the Missouri Compromise.

The Senate resumed the consideration of the bill; and the pending question being on the amendment of Mr. FOOTE, proposing to reduce the boundaries of California—

The PRESIDENT. It has been printed.

Mr. CLAY. Mr. President, it is known to the Senate that it has been my hope and expectation that we should dispose of all the amendments either proposed or to be proposed to the bill, and that upon the question of its engrossment I intended, with the permission of the Senate, to occupy some portion of its time in taking a rapid review of some of the objections that have been made to the adoption of the measure under consideration, and then to submit it into those hands in which, by the constitution of the country, the responsibility is placed. The events of Saturday, of which we possess information, deprived us of the opportunity of employing that day in the consideration of those amendments which were intended to be submitted, or were yet before the Senate. But as some rather impatient anxiety has been manifested to arrive at the conclusion of this important subject—an anxiety in which, to some extent, I share with others—I have risen this morning to perform a duty toward the committee and to the subject which my position prompts me to endeavor to execute.

Mr. President, in the progress of this debate it has been again and again argued that perfect tranquillity reigns throughout the country, and that there is no disturbance threatening its peace, endangering its safety, but that which was produced by busy, restless politicians. It has been maintained that the surface of the public mind is perfectly smooth and undisturbed by a single billow. I most heartily wish I could concur in this picture of general tranquillity that has been drawn upon both sides of the Senate. I am no alarmist; nor, I thank God, at the advanced age at which His providence has been pleased to allow me to reach, am I very easily alarmed by any human event; but I totally misread the signs of the times, if there be that state of profound peace and quiet, that absence of all just cause of apprehension of future danger to this confederacy, which appears to be entertained by some other Senators. Mr. President, all the tendencies of the times, I lament to say, are towards disquietude, if not more fatal consequences. When before, in the midst of profound peace with all the nations of the earth, have we seen a convention, representing a considerable portion of one great part of the Republic, meet to deliberate about measures of future safety in connection with great interests of that quarter of the country? When before have we seen, not one, but more—some half a dozen—legis-

---

and WHEELER, who immediately conducted the Baltimore authorities to the City Hall, and thence to the Funeral Procession. The Mayor of Washington and the Mayor of Baltimore rode to the burying ground in the same carriage. After the Funeral Ceremonies, the Baltimore authorities dined with the Mayor and Corporate authorities of this city, at Brown's Hotel, where a handsome entertainment was provided. Although the occasion of the visit forbade any social festivity, the exchange of mutual civilities and courtesies was characterized by the kindest feelings. The Baltimore guests of the Washington Corporation, amongst whom was the President of the Baltimore and Washington Railroad Company, the President of the Baltimore Board of Health, and the President of the Baltimore Board of Aldermen, returned to their homes in the extra train that started at half-past seven o'clock.

lative bodies solemnly resolving that if any one of these measures—the admission of California, the adoption of the Wilmot proviso, of the abolition of slavery in the District of Columbia, —should be adopted by Congress, measures of an extreme character, for the safety of the great interests to which I refer, in a particular section of the country, would be resorted to? For years, this subject of the abolition of slavery, even within this District of Columbia, small as is the number of slaves here, has been a source of constant irritation and disquiet. So of the subject of the recovery of fugitive slaves who have escaped from their lawful owners; not a mere border contest, as has been supposed—although there, undoubtedly, it has given rise to more irritation than in other portions of the Union—but everywhere through the slaveholding country it has been felt as a great evil, a great wrong which required the intervention of Congressional power. But these two subjects, unpleasant as has been the agitation to which they have given rise, are nothing in comparison to those which have sprung out of the acquisitions recently made from the Republic of Mexico. These are not only great and leading causes of just apprehension as respects the future, but all the minor circumstances of the day intimate danger ahead, whatever may be its final issue and consequence.

Mr. President, I will not dwell upon other concomitant causes, all having the same tendency, and all well calculated to awaken, to arouse us—if, as I hope the fact is, we are all of us sincerely desirous of preserving this Union —to rouse us to dangers which really exist, without underrating them upon the one hand, or magnifying them upon the other.

It was in this stage, or state, rather, of the Republic, that my friend from Mississippi, (Mr. Foote,) something more than four months ago, made a motion for the appointment of a committee of thirteen. Unlike what occurred at an analogous period of the Republic, when it was my duty to make a similar motion in the other end of the Capitol, and when, on account of the benefits which might result from the reconciliation of a distracted country, the proposition was immediately adopted—on the present occasion, unlike what occurred at that historical period, the proposition of the honorable Senator from Mississippi was resisted from day to day, from week to week, for four or five weeks. An experiment to restore the harmony of the country met with the most determined and settled resistance, as if the measures which the committee might report, whatever might be its character, would not still be under the power and control of the Senate, to be disposed of by it according to its own best judgment. Finally, however, the motion prevailed.

Well, the committee was finally raised and went out. Of its composition it does not become me to speak, nor is it necessary to say any thing. The country, the Senate will judge of that. Without, however, saying a word in respect to the humble person who now addresses you, I may be permitted to say that a large portion of that committee consisted of gentlemen who had honorably served their country in the highest stations at home and abroad—men of ripe experience, and whose large acquaintance with public affairs entitled them at least to respectful consideration when they were engaged in the holy office—if I may use the expression—of trying to reconcile the discordant parts of this distracted country.

It has been objected against this measure that it is a compromise. It has been said that it is a compromise of principle, or of a principle. Mr. President, what is a compromise? It is a work of mutual concession—an agreement in which there are reciprocal stipulations —a work in which, for the sake of peace and concord, one party abates his extreme demands in consideration of an abatement of extreme demands by the other party; it is a measure of mutual concession—a measure of mutual sacrifice. Undoubtedly, Mr. President, in all such measures of compromise, one party would be very glad to get what he wants, and reject what he does not desire, but which the other party wants. But when he comes to reflect that, from the nature of the Government and its operations, and from those with whom he is dealing, it is necessary upon his part, in order to secure what he wants, to grant something to the other side, he should be reconciled to the concession which he has made, in consequence of the concession which he is to receive, if there is no great principle involved, such as a violation of the Constitution of the United States. I admit that such a compromise as that ought never to be sanctioned or adopted. But I now call upon any Senator in his place to point out from the beginning to the end, from California to New Mexico, a solitary provision in this bill which is violative of the Constitution of the United States.

Sir, adjustment in the shape of compromise may be made without producing any such consequences as have been apprehended. There may be a mutual forbearance. You forbear upon your side to insist upon the application of the restriction denominated the Wilmot proviso. Is there any violation of principle there? The most that can be said, even assuming the power to pass the Wilmot proviso, which is denied, is that there is a forbearance to exercise, not a violation of, the power to pass the proviso. So, upon the other hand, if there was a power in the Constitution of the United States authorizing the establishment of slavery in any of the Territories—a power, however, which is controverted by a large portion of this Senate—if there was a power under the constitution to establish slavery, the forbearance to exercise that power is no violation of the constitution, any more than the constitution is violated by a forbearance to exercise numerous powers that might be specified that are granted in the constitution, and that remain dormant until they come to be exercised by the proper legislative authorities. It is said that the bill presents the state of coercion—that members are coerced in order to get what they want, to vote for that which they disapprove. Why, sir, what coercion is there? Is there any coercion in the numerous treaties made by the United States—the treaty in settling the Maine boundary; the treaty coming down from 54° 40′ to 49° in Oregon; all treaties which have been made upon commerce, upon boundaries, and other questions from time to time by the United States upon the principles of mutual and reciprocal concession on the part of those who made them? Is there any more coercion in this case than in the passage of a bill containing a variety of provisions, some of which you approve and others of which you disapprove? Can it be said upon the part of our northern friends, because they have not got the Wilmot proviso incorporated in the territorial part of the bill, that they are coerced—wanting California, as they do, so much—to vote for the bill, if they do vote for it? Sir, they might have imitated the noble example of my friend (Mr. COOPER) from that State upon whose devotion to this Union I place one of my greatest reliances for its preservation. What was the course of my friend upon this subject of the Wilmot proviso? He voted for it; and he could go back to his constituents and say, as all of you could go back and say to your constituents, if you chose to do so, "We wanted the Wilmot proviso in the bill; we tried to get it in, but the majority of the Senate was against it." The question then came up whether we should lose California, which has got an interdiction in her constitution, which, in point of value and duration, is worth a thousand Wilmot provisoes; we were induced, as my honorable friend would say, to take the bill and the whole of it together, although we were disappointed in our votes with respect to the Wilmot proviso—to take it, whatever omissions may have been made, on account of the superior amount of good it contains.

Why, Mr. President, incongruous as it may be supposed, this measure has not half the incongruity of the elements of opposition to the bill. While upon this part of my subject, allow me to answer an argument delivered with all possible self-complacency by the honorable Senator near me (Mr. HALE) the other day. He said he had gone into a certain apartment of this Capitol, and there he had found my friend from Michigan (Mr. CASS) and myself in close conversation; and the Senator from Mississippi (Mr. FOOTE) with a Senator now no longer in his place, but a Senator called by a grateful country to a more responsible station, and who has left us only this morning, (Mr. WEBSTER.) I might have inquired how the Senator came there. May I ask to what keyhole he applied his ear or his eye—in what curtain he was ensconced—to hear and perceive these astonishing circumstances, which he narrated with so much apparent self-satisfaction? (Laughter.) Sir, I have been in repeated consultation with my friend (Mr. CASS)—for so I will call him, and he has shown himself to be the friend of the peace of his country—during the progress of this measure, and also with other Democratic friends upon this measure. Repeatedly have I been in consultation with them upon the subject of this bill and the amendments which have been proposed. I regret only that our consultations have not been more numerous and of longer duration. But how stands the matter with us, with the friends of this bill? On the subject of slavery, the treatment of California, the Territories, the adjustment of the boundary of Texas, the fugitive slave bill, and the bill for abolishing the slave-trade, there is no difference of opinion between my Democratic friends whom I have consulted and myself; but there has been perfect union during all our consultations. Allow me to say that there is not a solitary instance in which a subject connected with party politics, upon which we might have heretofore differed in the progress of the administration of our Government, has been adverted to. We spoke of that measure which absorbed all our thoughts, which engrossed all our hopes, which animated all our anxieties—the subject of pacifying, if possible, the distracted parts of this country—a subject upon which, between us, there was a perfect coincidence of opinion.

But how does the matter stand with the extremes who are united against this measure? Why, they are extremes upon this very measure, and upon this very subject of slavery! Upon the very subject under consideration there is among them no union of sentiment, no coincidence of opinion, and yet a most cordial and confidential co-operation. In our meetings upon this subject, in our consultations, Democrats and Whigs convened and consulted together. They threw aside, as not germane, and as unworthy of their consideration, all the agitating party politics of the day, and I venture to say that, in those meetings between my Democratic friends and myself, there was no diversity or contrariety of opinion upon the only subject that brought us together. If I am not utterly mistaken, there are no such union and coincidence of opinion between the opponents of this bill, who, upon the very subject of slavery to which it relates, are as wide apart as the north and south poles.

But, Mr. President, I am not only fortified in my convictions that this will be the salutary and healing effect of this great plan of compromise and settlement of our difficulties, but I am supported by the nature of man and the truth of history. What is that nature? Why, sir, after perturbing storms a calm is sure to follow. The nation wants repose. It pants for repose, and entreats you to give it peace and tranquillity. Do you believe, when the nation's Senators and the nation's Representatives, after such a continued struggle as we have had, shall settle these questions, it is possible for the most malignant of all men longer to disturb the peace, and quiet, and harmony of this otherwise most prosperous country? But I said, not only according to the nature of man, but according to the universal desire which prevails throughout the wide-spread land, would the acceptance of this measure, in my opinion, lead to a joy and exultation almost unexampled in our history. I refer to historical instances occurring in our Government, to verify me in the conviction I entertain of the healing and tranquillizing consequences which would result from the adoption of this measure. What was said when the compromise was passed? Then, as now, it was denounced. Then, as now, when it was approaching its passage, when being perfected, it was said, "It will not quell the storm, nor give peace to the country." How was it received when it passed? The bells rang, the cannons were fired, and every demonstration of joy throughout the whole land was made upon the settlement by the Missouri compromise. Nor is it true, as has been unkindly suggested, I think by the Senator who sits at my left, (Mr. Hale,) that northern men were obliged to remain at home and incur the displeasure of their constituents. There was Henry Baldwin, of Pittsburg, Henry Storrs, of New York, and others, if I had time to enumerate them, who voted for a settlement of the Missouri question, and who retained the confidence and affection of their respective constituents. I suppose the Senator was understood, as I understood him, to throw out something by way of menace to northern Senators, to make them swerve from the patriotic duty which lies before them of healing the agitation of the country. They did not lose the confidence of their country. They may have in particular instances, but I speak of those of which I had a distinct recollection. Yes, sir, the Missouri compromise was received with exultation and joy. Not the reception of the treaty of peace negotiated at Ghent, nor any other event which has occurred during my progress in public life, ever gave such unbounded and universal satisfaction as the settlement of the Missouri compromise. We may argue from like causes like effects. Then, indeed, there was great excitement. Then, indeed, all the Legislatures of the North called out for the exclusion of Missouri, and all the Legislatures of the South called out for her admission as a State. Then, as now, the country was agitated like the ocean in the midst of a turbulent storm. But now, more than then, has this agitation been increased. Now, more than then, are the dangers which exist, if the controversy remains unsettled, more aggravated and more to be dreaded. The idea of disunion then was scarcely a low whisper. Now, it has become a familiar language in certain portions of the country. The public mind and the public heart are becoming familiarized with that most dangerous and fatal of all events, the disunion of the States. People begin to contend that this is not so bad a thing as they supposed. Like the progress in all human affairs, as we approach danger it disappears, it diminishes in our conception, and we no longer regard it with that awful apprehension of consequences that we did before we came into contact with it. Everywhere now there is a state of things, a degree of alarm and apprehension, and determination to fight, as they regard it, against the aggressions of the North. That did not so demonstrate itself at the period of the Missouri compromise. It was followed, in consequence of the adoption of the measure which settled the difficulty of Missouri, by peace, harmony, and tranquillity. So now, I infer, from the greater amount of agitation, from the greater amount of danger, that, if you adopt the measures under consideration, they, too, will be followed by the same amount of contentment, satisfaction, peace, and tranquillity which ensued after the Missouri compromise.

Mr. President, I wish I had the physical power to give utterance to the many, many ideas which I still have; but I have it not. I must hasten towards a conclusion.

The responsibility of this great measure passes from the hands of the committee, and from my hands. They know, and I know, that it is an awful and tremendous responsibility. I hope that you will meet it with a just conception and a true appreciation of its magnitude, and the magnitude of the consequences that may ensue from your decision one way or the other. The alternatives I fear, which the measure presents, are concord and increased discord; a servile civil war, originating in its causes, on the lower Rio Grande, and terminating, possibly, in its consequences, on the upper Rio Grande in the Santa Fé country—or the restoration of harmony and fraternal kindness.

I believe, from the bottom of my soul, that the measure is the reunion of this Union. I believe it is the dove of peace, which, taking its aërial flight from the dome of the Capitol, carries the glad tidings of assured peace and restored harmony to all the remotest extremities of this distracted land. I believe that it will be attended with all these beneficent effects. And now let us discard all resentment, all passions, all petty jealousies, all personal desires, all love of place, all hankering after the gilded crumbs which fall from the table of power. Let us forget popular fears, from whatever quarter they may spring. Let us go to the limpid fountain of unadulterated patriotism, and, performing a solemn lustration, return divested of all selfish, sinister, and sordid impurities, and think alone of our God, our country, our consciences, and our glorious Union; that Union without which we shall be torn into hostile fragments and sooner or later become the victims of military despotism, or foreign domination.

Mr. President, what is an individual man? An atom, almost invisible without a magnifying glass—a mere speck upon the surface of the immense universe—not a second in time, compared to immeasurable, never-beginning, and never-ending eternity; a drop of water in the great deep, which evaporates and is borne off by the winds; a grain of sand, which is soon gathered to the dust from which it sprung. Shall a being so small, so petty, so fleeting, so evanescent, oppose itself to the onward march of a great nation, to subsist for ages and ages to come—oppose itself to that long line of posterity which, issuing from our loins, will endure during the existence of the world? Forbid it God! Let us look at our country and our cause; elevate ourselves to the dignity of pure and disinterested patriots, wise and enlightened statesmen, and save our country from all impending dangers. What if, in the march of this nation to greatness and power, we should be buried beneath the wheels that propel it onward. What are we—what is any man worth who is not ready and willing to sacrifice himself for the benefit of his country when it is necessary?

Now, Mr. President, allow me to make a short appeal to some Senators—to the whole of the Senate. Here is my friend from Virginia, (Mr. MASON,) of whom I have never been without hopes. I have thought of the revolutionary blood of George Mason which flows in his veins—of the blood of his own father—of his own accomplished father—my cherished friend for many years. Can he, knowing, as I think he must know, the wishes of the people of his own State; can he, with the knowledge he possesses of the public sentiment there, and of the high obligation cast upon him by his noble ancestry, can he hazard Virginia's greatest and most glorious work—that work, at least, which she, perhaps more than any other State, contributed her moral and political power to erect? Can he put at hazard this noble Union, with all its beneficial effects and consequences, in the pursuit of abstractions and metaphysical theories—objects unattainable, or worthless, if attained—while that honor of our own common native State, which I reverence and respect with as much devotion as he does, while the honor of that State, and the honor of the South are preserved unimpaired by this measure?

I appeal, sir, to the Senators from Rhode Island and from Delaware; my little friends, which have stood by me, and by which I have stood, in all the vicissitudes of my political life; two glorious patriotic little States, which, if there is to be a breaking up of the waters of this Union, will be swallowed up in the common deluge, and left without support. Will they hazard that Union, which is their strength, their power, and their greatness!

Let such an event as I have alluded to occur, and where will be the sovereign power of Delaware and Rhode Island? If this Union shall become separated, new unions, new confederacies will arise. And with respect to this—if there be any—I hope there is no one in the Senate—before whose imagination is flitting the idea of a great Southern Confederacy to take possession of the Balize and the mouth of the Mississippi, I say in my place never! *never!* NEVER will we who occupy the broad waters of the Mississippi and its upper tributaries consent that any foreign flag shall float at the Balize or upon the turrets of the Crescent city—never—never! I call upon all the South. Sir, we have had hard words—bitter words, bitter thoughts, unpleasant feelings towards each other in the progress of this great measure. Let us forget them. Let us sacrifice these feelings. Let us go to the altar of our country and swear, as the oath was taken of old, that we will stand by her; we will support her; that we will uphold her constitution; that we will preserve her Union, and that we will pass this great, comprehensive, and healing system of measures, which will hush all the jarring elements, and bring peace and tranquillity to our homes.

Let me, Mr. President, in conclusion, say that the most disastrous consequences would occur, in my opinion, were we to go home, doing nothing to satisfy and tranquillize the country upon these great questions. What will be the judgment of mankind, what the judgment of that portion of mankind who are looking upon the progress of this scheme of self-government as being that which holds the highest hopes and expectations of ameliorating the condition of mankind—what will their judgment be? Will not all the monarchs of the Old World pronounce our glorious Republic a disgraceful failure? What will be the judgment of our constituents, when we return to them and they ask us, How have you left your country? Is all quiet—all happy—are all the seeds of distraction or division crushed and dissipated? And, sir, when you come into the bosom of your family, when you come to converse with the partner of your fortunes, of your happiness and of your sorrows, and when in the midst of the common offspring of both of you, she asks you, "Is there any danger of civil war? Is there any danger of the torch being applied to any portion of the country? Have you settled the questions which you have been so long discussing and deliberating upon at Washington? Is all peace and all quiet?" What response, Mr. President, can you make to that wife of your choice and those children with whom you have been blessed by God? Will you go home and leave all in disorder and confusion, all unsettled, all open? The contentions and agitations of the past will be increased and augmented by the agitations resulting from our neglect to decide them. Sir, we shall stand condemned by all human judgment below, and of that above it is not for me to speak. We shall stand condemned in our own consciences, by our own constituents, and by our own country. The measure may be defeated. I have been aware that its passage for many days was not absolutely certain. From the first to the last I hoped and believed it would pass, because from the first to the last I believed it was founded on the principles of just and righteous concession—of mutual conciliation. I believe that it deals unjustly by no part of the Republic; that it saves their honor, and, as far as it is dependent upon Congress, saves the interests of all quarters of the country. But, sir, I have known that the decision of its fate depended upon four or five votes in the Senate of the United States, and upon whose ultimate judgment we could not count upon the one side or the other with absolute certainty. Its fate is now committed to the hands of the Senate, and to those five or six votes to which I have referred. It may be defeated. It is possible that, for the chastisement of our sins or transgressions, the rod of Providence may be still applied to us, may be still suspended over us. But, if defeated, it will be a triumph of ultraism and impracticability—a triumph of a most extraordinary conjunction of extremes; a victory won by abolitionism; a victory achieved by free-soilism; the victory of discord and agitation over peace and tranquillity; and I pray to Almighty God that it may not, in consequence of the inauspicious result, lead to the most unhappy and disastrous consequences to our beloved country. [Applause.]

Mr. Barnwell. It is not my intention to reply to the argument of the Senator from Kentucky, but there were expressions used by him not a little disrespectful to a friend whom I hold very dear, and to the State which I in part represent, which seem to me to require some notice. I believe, sir, that character does not depend upon words; it does not live in eulogy; it is not to be destroyed by obloquy. It rests upon a higher and more stable foundation—upon intelligence, honesty, disinterestedness, accompanied with the manifested determination to exercise these high qualities in the best mode, for the best ends. To this test I am willing to bring the character of my friend; one with whom my friendship, commencing almost with the cradle, and strengthening through life, will, I doubt not, terminate only with the grave. I do not intend to pronounce his eulogy. It is well for us both that he is no unknown man; nor is he, in this assembly or in the other House, without many who know him and appreciate him. I am very willing to intrust the defence of his character to the judgment of all who know him. It is true that his political opinions differ very widely from those of the Senator from Kentucky. It may be true that he, with many great statesmen, may believe that the Wilmot proviso is a grievance to be resisted "to the utmost extremity" by those whose rights it destroys, and whose honor it degrades. It is true that he may believe—and he will not be very singular in the opinion, especially among those who have heard and may read the able and triumphant argument of the distinguished Senator from Georgia—that the admission of California will be the passing of the Wilmot proviso, when we here in Congress give vitality to an act otherwise totally dead, and by our legislation exclude slaveholders from that whole broad territory on the Pacific; and, entertaining this opinion, he may have declared that the contingency will then have occurred which will, in the judgment of most of the slaveholding States, as expressed by their resolutions, justify resistance as to an intolerable aggression. If he does entertain and has expressed such sentiments, he is not to be held up as peculiarly a disunionist. Allow me to say, in reference to this matter, I regret that you have brought it about; but it is true that this epithet "disunionist" is likely soon to have very little terror in it in the South. Words do not make things. Rebel was designed as a very odious term when applied by those who would have trampled upon the rights of our ancestors, but I believe that the expression became not an ungrateful one to the ears of those who resisted them. It was not the lowest term of abuse to call those who were conscious that they were struggling against oppression; and let me assure gentlemen that the disunionist is rapidly assuming at the South the meaning which rebel took when it was baptized in the blood of Warren at Bunker's Hill, and illustrated by the gallantry of Jaspar at Fort Moultrie.

As to the State of South Carolina, I do not, as I need not, defend her by words. I have said that the character of an individual does not live in words or die from obloquy. Much more strongly may this be said of a State. South Carolina has a history for the past and a character for the present. To that history and that character I am perfectly willing to leave her, to repel any reproach which may be attempted to be cast upon her. Allow me to say, in this connection, that whilst I listened, a few days since, with a high admiration to the eloquent eulogium which the Senator from Massachusetts (now no longer in his place) pronounced upon his own State; whilst I freely accorded to her the honor which he attributed, it did not seem to me, sir, that he had selected the highest attribute of her character as the subject of his eulogium. He spoke of her attachment to this Union as the highest subject of his commendation, but he had previously and very pointedly alluded to motives, not addressed to the most honorable sentiments of mankind, which might justly render this Union very dear to her. Sir, I prefer to honor Massachusetts for the devotion which, in times past, she has exhibited for freedom, and which I doubt not still animates her, because I believe that, as in former days, she justified the proud motto with which she emblazoned her escutcheon. So should any, in future time, invade her rights, or disturb her peaceful liberty, she would again with the sword maintain the heritage sought and gained by it. To this criterion I willingly commit my native State; by this standard do I desire that she may be ever judged. Small she may be, and weak in numbers, but it is not by the extent of territory, or in the number of inhabitants, that a State is to be measured. Rather by the spirit of its people—a spirit which prepares them in the maintenance of their liberty to live with her or die for her. I will not speak of my devotion to South Carolina:

> "I would rather be beloved on trust for what I feel
> Than prove it in her griefs, which might not yield to any cares of mine."

But this I may claim, in common with all her sons, in the hour of her peril, to be found at her side, to sustain or perish with her.

Mr. CLAY. Mr. President, I said nothing with respect to the character of Mr. RHETT, for I might as well name him. I know him personally, and have some respect for him. But, if he pronounced the sentiment attributed to him of raising the standard of disunion and of resistance to the common Government, whatever he has been, if he follows up that declaration by corresponding overt acts, he will be a traitor, and I hope he will meet the fate of a traitor. [Great applause in the galleries, with difficulty suppressed by the Chair.]

The PRESIDENT. The Chair will be under the necessity of ordering the gallery to be cleared if there is again the slightest interruption. He has once already given warning that he is under the necessity of keeping order. The Senate Chamber is not a theatre.

Mr. CLAY resumed. Mr. President, I have heard with pain and regret a confirmation of the remark I made, that the sentiment of disunion is becoming familiar. I hope it is confined to South Carolina. I do not regard as my duty what the honorable Senator seems to regard as his. If Kentucky to-morrow unfurls the banner of resistance unjustly, I never will fight under that banner. I owe a paramount allegiance to the whole Union—a subordinate one to my own State. When my State is right—when it has a cause for resistance—when tyranny, and wrong, and oppression insufferable arise—I will then share her fortunes; but if she summons me to the battle-field, or to support her in any cause which is unjust against the Union, never, *never* will I engage with her in such a cause.

Mr. HALE. I do not intend to occupy the attention of the Senate but a moment. As the Senator from Kentucky has taken issue with me on a point of history, I want to give what I understand to be the truth of the case. He says the Missouri compromise was a very beneficial measure. I do not undertake to say whether it was or not; but if there is any truth in history, though I was a boy at the time, when the New England States were of considerably more relative and numerical importance than they are now, the history of those men who went for the Missouri compromise has been a warning from that day to this to northern men who come here on the floor of congress to surrender northern right to propitiate power. I think the Senator from Massachusetts in my eye, (Mr. DAVIS,) will tell you that some of the most promising and talented of the public men in the State, who went for that measure, have never recovered from the odium with which they were overwhelmed from that day. I think the Senator from Rhode Island could stand up and show that they have living monuments of public odium in the persons of northern representatives who went for that measure in that State. I know it was so in New Hampshire; and I believe in that part of the country there was but one solitary instance of a northern statesman that had vitality and elasticity enough to rejuvenize himself from the obloquy with which that measure overwhelmed him, and he was an individual well known to the honorable Senator.

Mr. CLAY. One or two words in reply to the honorable Senator. He has confounded two very different epochs in the history of the country. I spoke first of the Missouri compromise; and I think I know the names much better than the Senator does, though there were not a great many—not above ten or twelve from the free States—who voted with us for that compromise. I knew at that time every one of them, and I preserve the most friendly recollection of them at this moment. If the Senator says they were all sacrificed, I am sure he is mistaken. I remember the names of Henry Baldwin, of Pittsburg; Henry Storrs, of Whitestown, near Utica, New York; Judge Ford; Henry Shaw, formerly of Lanesboro', who, although he did not return to Congress, went to the Legislature of his own State whenever he chose, and was one of its honored influential members long after the passage of the compromise. I cannot recollect them all at this time. But as to New Hampshire, and some of the other States, we got very few supporters from them. I believe Governor Tomlinson was one who favored it at heart; and Mr. Foot voted for it, and was here long after that. I am sure, if you were to look over the list of northern members who voted for the Missouri compromise, you would find that a majority of them were sustained.

Sir, Mr. Monroe was in office at the time of the passage of the Missouri compromise, and I do not believe one word of any man getting into office in consequence of, or as a price for, his vote upon that occasion—I care not whence the charge may come. I know most of the men; and if I had been aware of the Senator's intention to go over again the list of northern men who voted for that compromise, I would have fortified my own recollection by a resort to the Journals of the House. Henry Baldwin got no office; Henry Storrs got none; Henry Shaw got none; Judge Ford got none; and I suppose they constitute about half the northern vote for that measure. Mr. Foot got no office. Mr. Holmes got none from the General Government until long after, when he was appointed district attorney. Some ten or twelve years after, when Mr. Adams was in power, he may have got an office. Here, then, we have six or eight out of the number who got no office; and when Mr. Livermore, or anybody else, ventures to make a charge against the memory of that virtuous patriot, Monroe, and hold out the idea that offices were distributed as a reward for the votes given, let him specify the men and the offices. I do not believe one word of it. It is a mistake. I dare say the Senator believes what he has stated; but his informer is mistaken.

Sir, really these little posthumous debates, after one has become exhausted by the main battle of the day, are very unpleasant. But I stand up here for this measure, and I do not want the Senator to deal in declamation. I ask him *what* right is sacrificed by the North in this measure? Let him tell me if the North does not get almost every thing, and the South nothing but her honor—her exemption from usurped authority to the Texas land which I have mentioned, together with the fugitive slave proposition, and an exemption from agitation on the subject of slavery in the District of Columbia. I do not want general broadcast declamation, but specifications. Let us meet them like men, point upon point, argument upon argument. Show us the power here to which northern sacrifice is made. Show what sacrifices, *what* is sacrificed by the North in this bill. That is what I want.*

HOUSE OF REPRESENTATIVES.

Saturday, July 27.

Death of Hon. Daniel Putnam King.

Mr. Rockwell rose and said: Mr. Speaker, at the suggestion of the members of the delegation from Massachusetts, I rise to announce the death of our colleague, the Hon. Daniel Putnam King, who represented in this House the second congressional district of that State. He died at his residence in Danvers, in the county of Essex, on the evening of Thursday last. He left this city on the 10th instant, for the purpose of visiting his family, and attending some indispensable business arrangements. His visit to his home was, perhaps, somewhat hastened by a slight temporary indisposition, of which he had several times spoken, which however occasioned no alarm. It seems that soon after his arrival at home, he was attacked with the acute and distressing disease which so speedily terminated his life. He met his death as he wished to meet it, when his time had come, in the bosom of his affectionate family, with the wife of his youth, and the children of his love, to solace his dying hour, and hear his last earthly words.

Mr. King was graduated at Harvard University, in the year 1823. His classical and scientific studies, however, were not discontinued at the termination of his collegiate course. Without pursuing any particular profession, he became a ripe and sound general scholar. Devoted principally to Agricultural pursuits, for which he cherished an enthusiastic regard, his easy fortune gave him leisure for varied and rich intellectual acquirements. Such a man, in so intelligent a community as that in which he lived could hardly avoid public employments and distinction. He first entered the House of Representatives of his native State in 1836, where he served with reputation during that and the succeeding year. In 1838, he first took his seat in the Senate of that State. In 1840 he was elected President of the Senate, and discharged the duties of that station to the general satisfaction, in a time of high party excitement. In 1843 he was again a member of the popular branch of that Legislature, and was chosen the Speaker, under circumstances highly honorable to his character. He discharged the duties of that office in a House almost equally divided in political sentiment, with the general favor. In June, 1843, while holding the office of Speaker of the House of Representatives of Massachusetts, he was elected to the twenty-eighth Congress, in which he took his seat in December of that year. He has been, by the unsolicited suffrages of the same constituency, three times re-elected. This is the fourth Congress to which he has been elected, and the seventh year of his service upon this floor. In each of these situations, his course has been marked by an unassuming, industrious, conscientious discharge of every duty.

Upon that portion of the legislation of his State, which has been manifested in behalf of the suffering and the unfortunate, his influence has been repeatedly and effectually exerted. He was for five years an active and diligent member of the Board of Trustees of the State Lunatic Hospital; and contributed while in the Legislature to the enlargement and extended usefulness of that institution. Highly distinguished as he had been in Massachusetts, other paths of usefulness would there have been opened before him, had his life been spared, and other honorable distinctions awaited him.

Of his character and conduct in this House, it is scarcely necessary for me to speak. In

---

* This reference to the truth of history in relation to the Missouri Compromise comes here with a fulness and particularity which are not seen elsewhere, and under circumstances to claim for it the most absolute verity. The person who speaks is Mr. Clay, the great champion of the measure; and he speaks under circumstances to take on himself the full responsibility of what he says. It was thirty years after the event, and after it had given peace and quiet to a distracted country. Now he saw the country going into the same distraction; disunion threatened; and a seeming breaking up of the Government in the death of great men. One who had been Vice President of the United States had just died, and died at his post. Another who had just been elected President had also died, and died at his post. Those who were still acting their parts were verging toward the termination of their public and natural lives. Every thing combined to give solemnity, and the seal of truth, to all they said. In these awful and impressive circumstances, Clay renews his testimony to the Missouri Compromise as a Southern Measure, of thirty years' duration, and he adheres to it as the crowning principle in the measures of 1850.

your hearing, Mr. Speaker, who knew him well, and in the hearing of the older members of this House, I hesitate not to say, that no member has more constantly and faithfully devoted his time and talents to the public service than my deceased colleague. He was daily, hourly, almost continually in his seat, with a clear and constant understanding of the business under consideration. In the discharge of his duties upon the various committees upon which he has been placed, he has been alike industrious and exemplary. In attending to the interests of his constituents, which were manifold, as his district was a highly commercial one, his diligence could not be exceeded. He acted and voted always; he spoke seldom.

In all the relations of private life, he was without reproach; nay, more, his life was an active blessing to all around him. It was made such by the religious principle which was the living spring of all his conduct. He was an humble, active, devoted Christian. No pressure of public duty, no desire for ease or relaxation, induced him to neglect the religious duties which he deemed as essential and proper here as at home; or the ordinances of the church to which he belonged. If to a stranger ear this seems the language of eulogy, I can only say, I cannot change it, for it is the simple truth.

Mr. Speaker, the power of death, which has been repeatedly during the present session exhibited in the other Chamber of Congress, and in the Executive Mansion, has now for the first time manifested itself here. Although our departed friend had not an iron constitution, he had never before, I believe, suffered any severe sickness. He was perhaps as little likely as any man among us to become the victim of disease. The plain language of so sudden an end, of such a life, is, "Be ye *also* ready."

Sir, when the resolutions which I am about to propose shall have been adopted, the great tide of public events will obliterate here the memory of my friend. His name will be stricken from the roll, and will pass from recollection here. But in the circle of his particular acquaintances, by those of us who have shared his domestic and social relations, his memory will be borne with us to the gates through which his gentle and noble spirit has just passed. And, in that district which he so faithfully represented, and of which he always spoke with such tender and proud regard, there will be a future of sincer emourning, for the loss of a private friend and a public benefactor.

I move, sir, the following resolutions:

Resolved, That this House has received with deep sensibility, the intelligence of the death of the Hon. DANIEL P. KING, a member of this House, from the State of Massachusetts, which took place at his residence in that State on Thursday last.

Resolved, That, as a testimony of respect for the memory of the deceased, the members and officers of this House will wear the usual badges of mourning for thirty days.

Resolved, That the Clerk of the House be directed to communicate a copy of these proceedings to the family of the deceased.

Resolved, That the Clerk be also directed to communicate a copy of these resolutions to the Senate; and that, as a further testimony of respect to the memory of the Hon. DANIEL P. KING, this House do now adjourn.

Mr. WINTHROP. If mere custom had prevailed on this occasion, Mr. Speaker, it would have fallen to me, as the senior member of the Massachusetts Delegation in this Hall, to perform the sad duty, which has been so faithfully and feelingly discharged by my friend and colleague who has just taken his seat. I trust, therefore, that I may be allowed to say that, in yielding as I readily have done, to the claims of a more intimate association and immediate companionship with the excellent person whose death has been announced to us, I have not been wanting in the deepest regret for his loss, or in the most sincere respect for his memory.

It has been my good fortune to be connected with Mr. KING for many years in the Legislature of our own Commonwealth, as well as to be with him here, during the whole period of his seven years' service as a member of this House; and I can truly say, that I have rarely met with a juster or worthier man, or with one more scrupulously faithful to every obligation to his neighbor, his country, and his God.

His devotion as a public servant, his integrity as a private citizen, and the high moral and religious character which he sustained in all the relations of life, had endeared him not merely to his immediate constituents, but to the whole people of Massachusetts; and there is no one who was more likely to have received at their hands, at no distant day, the reward of his honorable ambition, in the highest honors of his native State.

Though he had enjoyed the advantage of an education, which would have fitted him for entering upon either of what are commonly called *the learned professions*, his tastes had led him to Agricultural pursuits. He prided himself, as any one may well pride himself, on being a good Farmer; and the farmers of his neighborhood were justly proud of him as one of the most intelligent, observing, and scientific of their number.

We may well count it, sir, among the consolations of this hour, that he was permitted by a kind Providence, after so long a detention amid these scenes of strife, to revisit his native fields, to die beneath his own roof, surrounded by his family and friends, and to lie down at last beneath the soil which he had adorned with his hand, and which was so dear to his heart.

In the beautiful village in which he lived, and which is now the scene of so much unaffected sorrow for his loss, I venture to say that no sod will be kept greener than that which covers his ashes, and that his name will long be sadly but fondly associated with "the Flower of Essex."

Mr. Chandler. I have waited till the members of the Massachusetts delegation should have given expression to the feeling which the death of their colleague (and such a colleague) must naturally inspire. It seemed to me to be a sort of sacrilege to anticipate their lamentation, or to break the chain of communication by which from mouth to mouth the voice of sorrow and of eulogy had utterance. It must be that these home-companions of the deceased have deeper griefs than the comparative stranger, and I am not one who would invade the holy rights of sorrow. But, Mr. Speaker, it would, I think, be injustice to our late fellow-member--to the claim which his abundant virtues had upon the respect of all with whom he was in any way associated—to imagine that the afflictive rod of Providence had not reached beyond the State of which the deceased was one of the Representatives in this House.

Wherever the Hon. Daniel P. King cultivated an acquaintance he made a friend; and though he was not ambitious of enlarged social intercourse yet the public positions to which he was called, and the fidelity with which he discharged all the duties connected with these trusts, extended his connections and multiplied the number of those who admired his character and rejoiced in his distinction. And that circumstance, sir, has bowed a thousand hearts to the blow which Providence has inflicted in the death of our lamented friend. On that ground, sir, I speak, not for myself alone, nor to occupy the attention of this House with any expression of my proper sorrows; but in this solemn moment, when the eyes of the House are turned towards the seat now left vacant, to say that the associates—the household companions —the members of the mess of which Mr. King formed a part—have a peculiar grief in the deprivation which his death has brought. We had found him, sir, accomplished in all the riches of classic study, and able to command, for the delight of social intercourse, the treasures of science and the arts, while his attainments, and the profitable use to which he could apply them, were exhibited with a modesty that seemed to be alarmed at the admiration which such attainments and such a use of them naturally excited.

The honorable gentleman who announced to this House the fearful intelligence upon which we are now acting, and the honorable gentleman who followed him, took occasion to say, that Mr. King, though enjoying the advantages of high collegiate education, declined professional pursuits that he might indulge in his taste for Agriculture; and it was with his landed estate as with his mental gifts, it was not the bare possession that he prized, but the improvement; nothing with him remained unproductive—the wide-spread farm, the well-stored intellect, and the treasures of domestic affection, year by year augmented in beauty and usefulness, by well-directed skill and careful cultivation.

Mr. King, sir, was a gentleman—a gentleman of that school which teaches self-abnegation when the feelings and views of others are concerned. The apparent diffidence of his manners for a moment concealed the merit which lay beneath, but the solid, substantial qualities of his heart, and the full cultivation of his intellect, combined, with the gentleness of his manners and the purity of his morals, to insure in a little time the respect and the affection of his associates.

Mr. King, sir, was a christian. The virtues to which I have already alluded, owed their greatest attraction to the christian spirit in which they originated, and in which they were exhibited. He was kind and forbearing; watchful over his own words and manners; and ever prompt to aid, by all appropriate means, those whose condition appealed to his superior attainments or larger possessions. And the bland courtesy of the gentleman blended in perfect harmony with the meekness and purity of the christian. And if I were called on to present, from public life, the true exemplification of the christian gentleman, I know of no character that would more beautifully illustrate the idea and supply the model than that of Daniel P. King.

The loss which the Commonwealth of Massachusetts sustains in the death of such a son and such a Representative, has been eloquently set forth by some of those who shared with him the honor of that representation, and who shared among themselves the delight of his association.

The terrible affliction that has made desolate the home of those that gathered into the domestic circle of the deceased, is not to be described. The arm upon which filial reverence leaned with much confidence is palsied by death—the heart, which the purest affections shared, has ceased to beat; and sorrow that springs from such a visitation, is too sanctified for us to disturb—the expression of sympathy itself might be an intrusion.

We have lost from our midst, Mr. Speaker, one who did honor to his association—he is the first indeed that has fallen among us, but we cannot conceal the monitory fact, that he has been swept away by a disease that is prevalent around us, and among us, and yesterday, when the news of the death of our late colaborer reached this House, some of us who speak, and many who listen, were startled, not only with the painful intelligence, but with the consciousness of bending beneath the very disease which has deprived our House of so useful a member, and the nation of so faithful a servant. May we not hope, Mr. Speaker, that the hand of afflictive Providence thus visible among us, will direct us to a more faithful discharge of the high duties imposed upon us; and that while we pause to do honor to the memory of so good a man, we shall resolve to dedicate our services more effectually to the nation, and in our grief to bury our passions, our pride, and our selfishness.

One word more, Mr. Speaker, and I will cease to trespass on the patience, or to tax the courtesy of this House. One word more, and I will unite with you and my brother members, in the adoption of those resolutions which give expression to our feelings on this painful bereavement, and then we will separate, that we may, in silence and solitude, extract from this Providence, the benefits which it is capable of conferring by a right use.

There are few in this Hall, I imagine, Mr. Speaker, who had not some knowledge of the character of the deceased; and none, I venture to say, who had not a respect for him just in proportion to that knowledge. I confess that, though older than he, I had learned to love the man for the beautiful simplicity of his character, to admire him for his social virtues, and to respect him for his enviable attainments. The friendship which was consequent upon intercourse, was a prize which made life delightful, and the pain consequent upon his unexpected death deprives the grief of utterance. I was proud of his friendship as I was covetous of his intercouse. He was kind in granting both to me;

> "But greater gifts were his—a happier doom,
> A brighter genius, and a purer heart;
> A fate more envied, and an earlier tomb."

The question was then taken on the resolutions, and they were unanimously agreed to.

And the House accordingly adjourned.

IN SENATE.

SATURDAY, July 27.

Mr. DAVIS, of Massachusetts, presented the credentials of the Hon. THOMAS EWING, appointed by the Governor of Ohio to fill the vacancy occasioned by the resignation of the Hon. THOMAS CORWIN. Mr. EWING, having been duly qualified, took his seat.

Death of Hon. Daniel P. King.

A message was received from the House of Representatives by the Clerk, announcing the death of the Hon. DANIEL P. KING, a member of the House from the State of Massachusetts, and the proceedings had thereon.

Mr. DAVIS, of Massachusetts. Mr. President, in listening to the painful intelligence which has been announced to us by the message from the House, I may be pardoned if I give utterance to feelings in which I am sure many will sympathize. The grave should not close over the remains of a co-laborer so pure in heart, and so upright in purpose, without some expression of our sense of his merit —of our regret at his decease—of our sympathy with his surviving friends.

I have known Mr. KING for many years; and, without entering into the details of a life usefully and honorably spent, I may observe that he was a graduate of Harvard University, in his native State; but, unlike most persons who go through that course of education, instead of engaging in professional pursuits, he devoted himself to Agriculture. In this employment upon his own estate in Danvers, he will be long remembered for the zeal with which he prosecuted his business, and the influence which he exercised in promoting and encouraging useful improvements in the arts of husbandry.

His character and intelligence in the profession which he had chosen to be the business of his life, combined to recommend him for places of public trust and confidence. His townsmen frequently solicited him to represent them in the Legislature of the Commonwealth, and he was once chosen to preside over the House as its Speaker. He was also elected by the county of Essex one of her Senators, and was, during his service in the Senate, made its presiding officer. In these stations he acquitted himself in a manner so creditable, that in a district distinguished for gentlemen of learning and other intellectual accomplishments, he was selected as a candidate for Congress, and had, when brought to his untimely end, entered upon a fourth period of service. Honored as he had been with many and repeated marks of confidence by those who knew best his worth, still his rural pursuits had stronger charms than public life, and it was his purpose to leave these chambers at the end of this Congress, to enjoy the pleasures of his farm and his home.

Mr. President, death has disappointed these anticipations. He who was with us, uniting in our counsels only a few days ago, has left a seat vacant and gone to his account.

While we were gathering round the bier of that great and good man of whose counsels we have been recently bereaved, he embraced the opportunity afforded by a suspension of business to visit his family. While at his home, and in the midst of those most dear to him, he was seized with the disease which terminated his life.

Many greater men have died, but few better —few whose virtues shine more conspicuously —whose patriotism was warmer, or whose pure, unblemished character entitled them more emphatically to be called good men.

Mr. D. concluded by offering the following:

Resolved, That the Senate has received with deep sensibility the message from the House of Representatives, announcing the death of the Hon. DANIEL P. KING, a Representative from Massachusetts.

Resolved, That, in token of respect for the memory of the deceased, the Senate will wear the usual badge of mourning thirty days.

Resolved, That the Secretary of the Senate be directed to communicate a copy of these proceedings to the family of the deceased.

Resolved, That, as a further token of respect for the memory of the deceased, the Senate do now adjourn.

And the Senate adjourned.

TUESDAY, July 30.

Mr. DAVIS, of Massachusetts, presented the credentials of the Hon. ROBERT C. WINTHROP, appointed a Senator by the Governor of the Commonwealth of Massachusetts, to fill the vacancy occasioned by the resignation of the honorable DANIEL WEBSTER, which were read, and the oath prescribed by law having been administered to Mr. WINTHROP, he took his seat.

WEDNESDAY, July 31.

Admission of California—The Compromise Bill.

The Senate resumed the consideration of the bill for the admission of California as a State into the Union, to establish Territorial Governments for Utah and New Mexico, and making proposals to Texas for the establishment of her western and northern boundaries.

The pending question was the amendment of the Senator from New Hampshire, (Mr. NORRIS,) to strike out of the tenth section the words "nor establishing nor prohibiting African slavery."

A debate ensued, in which Messrs. DAVIS, of Mississippi, BALDWIN, EWING, and MASON took part.

The question was then taken, and the result was:

YEAS.—Messrs. Badger, Baldwin, Bell, Bradbury, Bright, Cass, Chase, Clarke, Clay, Cooper, Dayton, Dickinson, Dodge of Iowa, Douglas, Felch, Greene, Hamlin, Jones, Mangum, Miller, Norris, Phelps, Pratt, Seward, Shields, Smith, Spruance, Sturgeon, Underwood, Upham, Wales, and Winthrop—32.

NAYS.—Messrs. Atchison, Barnwell, Benton, Berrien, Butler, Davis of Mississippi, Dawson, Downs, Ewing, Hunter, King, Mason, Morton, Pearce, Rusk, Soulé, Turney, Whitcomb, and Yulee—19.

So the amendment was agreed to.

The bill was then ordered to be engrossed for a third reading; yeas 32, nays 18.

And the Senate then adjourned.

FRIDAY, August 2.

The Compromise Bill.

The Senate resumed the consideration of the bill for the admission of California as a State into the Union, to establish Territorial Governments for Utah and New Mexico, and making proposals to Texas for the establishment of her western and northern boundaries.

The bill as amended came up on its third reading, and it was read a third time and passed.

On motion by Mr. DOUGLAS, the title of the bill was changed to, "A bill to establish a Territorial Government for the Territory of Utah."

The Senate then adjourned.

MONDAY, August 5.

New Mexico and Texas.

Mr. PEARCE, pursuant to notice, asked and obtained leave to introduce the following bill:

A BILL proposing to the State of Texas the establishment of her northern and western boundaries, the relinquishment by said State of all territory claimed by her exterior to said boundaries, and of all her claims upon the United States.

The bill having been read a first time—

Mr. PEARCE asked for its second reading, and he addressed the Senate for more than half an hour in explanation of his plan.

The bill was then read a second time, ordered to be printed, and was made the order of the day for to-morrow.

WEDNESDAY, August 7.

Final Vote on the Boundary of Texas.

Mr. PEARCE. I ask that the bill may now have its third reading.

Mr. YULEE. Do I understand the Chair that it is in order for the bill to have more than one reading the same day?

The PRESIDENT. It is not in order to read it more than once on the same day if objected to. This bill was read two separate times a week ago, on the day on which it was introduced.

Mr. YULEE. But has it been engrossed since it was amended?

Mr. BADGER. The bill is engrossed.

Mr. YULEE. The question on engrossment is one question, and I supposed that the bill would come up the next day for its third reading.

Mr. BERRIEN. I understand the rule to be, that the bill must be read three times on two separate days. This bill has been read twice before, and if it is engrossed it can certainly be put upon its passage now.

The PRESIDENT. There can be no question about the propriety of the order of proceeding. The bill has been read twice on a previous day, has been ordered to be engrossed, and, being engrossed, it is now presented to the Senate for its third reading. The Senate can postpone it until to-morrow if it chooses to do so.

Mr. YULEE. I merely desire to call the attention of the Senate to the fact that we are very far from having a full Senate. The last vote was but 27 to 24.

Mr. BADGER. The absentees have paired off.

Mr. YULEE. How do you know?

The bill was then read a third time, and the question was stated, "Shall the bill pass?"

Mr. BRADBURY called the yeas and nays, and they were ordered, and were as follows:

YEAS.—Messrs. Badger, Bell, Berrien, Bradbury, Bright, Cass, Clarke, Clemens, Cooper, Davis of Massachusetts, Dawson, Dickinson, Dodge of Iowa, Douglas, Felch, Foote, Greene, Houston, King, Norris, Pearce, Phelps, Rusk, Shields, Smith, Spruance, Sturgeon, Wales, Whitcomb, and Winthrop.—30.

NAYS.—Messrs. Atchison, Baldwin, Barnwell, Benton, Butler, Chase, Davis of Mississippi, Dodge of Wisconsin, Ewing, Hale, Hunter, Mason, Morton, Seward, Soulé, Turney, Underwood, Upham, Walker, and Yulee—20.

So the bill was passed, and is as follows:

A Bill proposing to the State of Texas the establishment of her northern and western boundaries, the relinquishment by said State of all territory claimed by her exterior to said boundaries, and of all her claims upon the United States.

Be it enacted, &c., That the following propositions shall be and the same hereby are offered to the State of Texas, which, when agreed to by the said State, in an act passed by the General Assembly, shall be binding and obligatory upon the United States and upon the said State of Texas. *Provided*, That the said agreement by the said General Assembly shall be given on or before the 1st day of December, 1850.

First. The State of Texas will agree that her boundary on the north shall commence at the point at which the meridian of one hundred degrees west from Greenwich is intersected by the parallel of thirty-six degrees and thirty minutes north latitude, and shall run from said point due west to the meridian of one hundred and three degrees west from Greenwich; thence her boundary shall run due south to the thirty-second degree of north latitude; thence on the said parallel of thirty-two degrees of north latitude to Rio Bravo del Norte; and thence with the channel of said river to the Gulf of Mexico.

Second. The State of Texas cedes to the United States all her claim to territory exterior to the limits and boundaries which she agrees to establish by the first article of this agreement.

Third. The State of Texas relinquishes all claim upon the United States for liability for the debts of Texas, and for compensation or indemnity for the surrender to the United States of her ships, forts, arsenals, custom-houses, custom-house revenue, arms and munitions of war, and public buildings, with their sites, which became the property of the United States at the time of annexation.

Fourth. The United States, in consideration of said establishment of boundaries, cession of claim to territory, and relinquishment of claims, will pay to the State of Texas the sum of ten millions of dollars, in a stock bearing five per cent. interest, and redeemable at the end of fourteen years, the interest payable half-yearly at the Treasury of the United States.

Fifth. Immediately after the President of the United States shall have been furnished with an authentic copy of the act of the General Assembly of Texas accepting these propositions, he shall cause the stock to be issued in favor of the State of Texas, as provided for in the fourth article of agreement. *Provided*, That not more than five millions of said stock shall be issued until the creditors of the State holding bonds and other certificates of stock of Texas for which duties on imports were specially pledged, shall first file at the Treasury of the United States releases of all claim against the United States for or on account of said bonds or certificates, in such form as shall be prescribed by the Secretary of the Treasury, and approved by the President of the United States: *Provided, also*, That nothing herein contained shall be construed to impair or qualify any thing contained in the third article of the second section of the joint resolution for annexing Texas to the United States, approved March 1, 1845, either as regards the number of States that may hereafter be formed out the State of Texas, or otherwise.

The Senate then adjourned.

MONDAY, August 12.

Admission of California.

The Senate resumed the consideration of the bill for the admission of California as a State into the Union.

The pending question was stated to be on the passage of the bill.

A long debate ensued, in which Messrs. DAVIS, of Mississippi, CLEMENS, HOUSTON, BARNWELL, EWING, BERRIEN, CASS, ATCHISON, FOOTE, and others, took part.

The PRESIDENT. The question is on the passage of the bill.

Mr. EWING called for the yeas and nays, and they were ordered; and being taken, were as follows:

YEAS. — Messrs. Baldwin, Bell, Benton, Bradbury, Bright, Cass, Chase, Cooper, Davis of Massachusetts, Dickinson, Dodge of Wisconsin, Dodge of Iowa, Douglas, Ewing, Felch, Greene, Hale, Hamlin, Houston, Jones, Miller, Norris, Phelps, Seward, Shields, Smith, Spruance, Sturgeon, Underwood, Upham, Wales, Walker, Whitcomb, and Winthrop —34.

NAYS.—Messrs. Atchison, Barnwell, Berrien, Butler, Clemens, Davis of Mississippi, Dawson, Foote, Hunter, King, Mason, Morton, Pratt, Rusk, Sebastian, Soulé, Turney, and Yulee—18.

So the bill was passed.

New Mexico.

Mr. DOUGLAS. I now move that the Senate take up Senate bill No. 170, to establish a Territorial Government for the Territory of New Mexico.

Mr. BUTLER. Mr. President, I rise with the permission of the Chair, to say that a portion of the minority on the bill which has just passed will, to-morrow, ask leave to place upon the Journal a protest.

WEDNESDAY, August 14.

Protest against Admitting California.

Mr. HUNTER. I rise, not to present a petition, but to address a motion to the courtesy of the Senate—a motion which I am aware I cannot make as a matter of right and parliamentary privilege. It is to ask that a protest, which has been prepared and signed by ten members of this body, against the passage of the bill admitting California into the Union as a State, which passed yesterday, may be received and spread upon the Journals of the Senate. We ask it, because we deem it one of the most, if not perhaps the most important measure that has passed during our experience here, and we wish to give whatever emphasis we legitimately can to our opposition to it. We wish, so far as we can, to break the force of a precedent, which we regard as mischievous and dangerous, for the admission of States into this Union. I ask that it may be read, and spread upon the Journals of the Senate.

Mr. Hale. Do I understand the Senator to ask that it may be read? It ought to be read, that the Senate may understand what it is.

Mr. Hunter. Yes, sir.

The Secretary read the Protest, as follows:

"We, the undersigned Senators, deeply impressed with the importance of the occasion, and with a solemn sense of the responsibility under which we are acting, respectfully submit the following protest against the bill admitting California as a State into this Union, and request that it may be entered upon the Journal of the Senate. We feel that it is not enough to have resisted in debate alone a bill so fraught with mischief to the Union and the States which we represent, with all the resources of argument which we possessed; but that it is also due to ourselves, the people whose interest have been intrusted to our care, and to posterity, which even in its most distant generations may feel its consequences, to leave in whatever form may be most solemn and enduring, a memorial of the opposition which we have made to this measure, and of the reasons by which we have been governed, upon the pages of a journal which the constitution requires to be kept so long as the Senate may have an existence. We desire to place the reasons upon which we are willing to be judged by generations living, and yet to come, for our opposition to a bill whose consequences may be so durable and portentous as to make it an object of deep interest to all who may come after us.

"We have dissented from this bill because it gives the sanction of law, and thus imparts validity to the unauthorized action of a portion of the inhabitants of California, by which an odious discrimination is made against the property of the fifteen slaveholding States of the Union, who are thus deprived of that position of equality which the constitution so manifestly designs, and which constitutes the only sure and stable foundation on which this Union can repose.

"Because the right of the slaveholding States to a common and equal enjoyment of the territory of the Union has been defeated by a system of measures which, without the authority of precedent, of law, or of the constitution, are manifestly contrived for that purpose, and which Congress must sanction and adopt, should this bill become a law.

"Because, to vote for a bill passed under such circumstances, would be to agree to a principle, which may exclude forever hereafter, as it does now, the States which we represent from all enjoyment of the common territory of the Union; a principle which destroys the equal rights of their constituents, the equality of their States in the Confederacy, the equal dignity of those whom they represent as men and as citizens in the eye of the law, and their equal title to the protection of the Government and the constitution.

"Because all the propositions have been rejected which have been made to obtain either a recognition of the rights of the slaveholding States to a common enjoyment of all the territory of the United States, or to a fair division of that territory between the slaveholding and non-slaveholding States of the Union—every effort having failed which has been made to obtain a fair division of the territory proposed to be brought in as the State of California.

"But, lastly, we dissent from this bill, and solemnly protest against its passage, because, in sanctioning measures so contrary to former precedent, to obvious policy, to the spirit and intent of the Constitution of the United States, for the purpose of excluding the slaveholding States from the territory thus to be erected into a State, this Government in effect declares, that the exclusion of slavery from the territory of the United States is an object so high and important, as to justify a disregard not only of all the principles of sound policy, but also of the constitution itself. Against this conclusion we must now and forever, protest, as it is destructive of the safety and liberties of those whose rights have been committed to our care, fatal to the peace and *equality* of the States which we represent, and must lead, if persisted in, to the *dissolution* of that confederacy, in which the slaveholding States have never sought more than *equality*, and in which they will not be content to *remain* with less."

J. M. MASON, } Virginia.
R. M. T. HUNTER, }
A. P. BUTLER, } South Carolina.
R. B. BARNWELL, }
H. L. TURNEY, Tennessee.
PIERRE SOULE, Louisiana.
JEFFERSON DAVIS, Mississippi.
DAVID R. ATCHISON, Missouri.
JACKSON MORTON, } Florida.
D. L. YULEE, }

Senate Chamber, *August* 13, 1850.

Mr. Davis, of Massachusetts. What is the question before the Senate?

The President. The proposition to receive the protest, and have it entered upon the Journals of the Senate.

On this proposition a lengthy debate ensued in which Messrs. Davis, of Massachusetts, Hunter, Foote, Baldwin, Hale, Winthrop, Hamlin, and others took part.

Mr. Pratt. I would, if in order, move that the pending question to receive and enter on the Journal lie over until to-morrow, in order that we may all vote understandingly.

The motion was agreed to, and the further consideration of the subject was postponed until to-morrow.

Thursday, August 15.

Protest against Admitting California.

The Senate resumed the consideration of the motion of the Senator from Virginia, (Mr. Hunter,) to receive the Protest presented yesterday, and to spread it upon the Journal of the Senate.

Mr. Hunter. I would state, that by the

unanimous consent of the protestants, another paragraph has been added, which I desire may be read by the Secretary.

Mr. PRESIDENT. The protest had been modified, which the protestants had a right to do, the document not having yet been received.

The additional paragraph was then read as follows:

"Because the admission of California as a State into the Union, without any previous reservation assented to by her of the public domain, might involve an actual surrender of that domain to, or, at all events, places its future disposal at the mercy of that State; and, as no reservation in the bill can be binding upon her until she assents to it, her dissent 'hereafter' would in no manner affect or impair the act of her admission."

The debate was then continued by Messrs. BADGER, WALKER, HUNTER, BENTON, BUTLE, HOUSTON, CASS, PRATT, DAVIS of Mississippi, DOWNS, WHITCOMB, and TURNEY.

Mr. NORRIS moved to lay upon the table the question of reception and the motion to spread the protest upon the Journal.

Mr. BADGER called for the yeas and nays, and they were ordered, and were as follows:

YEAS.—Messrs. Badger, Benton, Bradbury, Bright, Chase, Cooper, Davis of Massachusetts, Dodge of Wisconsin, Downs, Greene, Hamlin, Houston, Miller, Norris, Phelps, Pratt, Smith, Underwood, Upham, Wales, Walker, Winthrop—22.

NAYS.—Messrs. Atchison, Barnwell, Berrien, Butler, Cass, Davis of Mississippi, Dawson, Dickinson, Dodge of Iowa, Hunter, Mason, Morton, Rusk, Sebastian, Shields, Soulé, Sturgeon, Turney, and Yulee—19.

So the whole subject was laid upon the table.

New Mexico.

On motion of Mr. DOUGLAS, the Senate took up the bill to establish a territorial government in the Territory of New Mexico, and it was read a third time.

Mr. WINTHROP called for the yeas and nays upon the question "Shall the bill pass?" and they were ordered.

Mr. DICKINSON. The final passage of this bill was one of those questions upon which I have paired off with my colleague. If I were to vote I should vote for the passage of the bill, but under the circumstances, I am not at liberty to vote upon this question.

Mr. SMITH. Upon this particular bill I too have paired off with the honorable Senator from Mississippi, (Mr. FOOTE,) and therefore I shall not record my name upon its passage.

The vote was then taken, and resulted as follows:

YEAS.—Messrs. Atchison, Badger, Benton, Berrien, Bradbury, Bright, Cass, Cooper, Dawson, Dodge of Iowa, Douglas, Downs, Felch, Houston, Hunter, King, Mangum, Mason, Norris, Pratt, Rusk, Sebastian, Shields, Sturgeon, Underwood, Wales, and Whitcomb—27.

NAYS.—Messrs. Chase, Davis of Massachusetts, Dodge of Wisconsin, Greene, Hamlin, Miller, Phelps, Upham, Walker, and Winthrop—10.

So the bill was passed.

On motion of Mr. DOUGLAS, the title was made to conform to the body of the bill, omitting "Utah;" and as agreed to, it is "A bill to establish a Territorial Government for New Mexico.

The Senate then proceeded to the consideration of Executive business, and after some time the doors were reopened, and the Senate adjourned.

WEDNESDAY, August 21.

The Fugitive Slave Bill.

The Senate resumed the consideration of the bill to provide for the more effectual execution for the third clause of the second section of the fourth article of the Constitution of the United States.

Mr. MASON. I move to amend the amendment of the Senator from Maryland, in such way as to provide that the jury who are to try these issues, shall try the issue whether or not there has been any collusion on the part of the claimant. I have submitted the amendment to the Senator from Maryland, and he is willing to accept it as a modification.

The PRESIDENT. It is proposed to amend the amendment of the Senator from Maryland, by inserting after the word "issues," in the fifth line of the fourth section, the following words:

"And whether or not there has been collusion on the part of the claimant, either in the escape of said fugitive or in the proceedings for his recovery."

Mr. PRATT. I accept the modification.

The PRESIDENT. It is further proposed to amend the amendment, by inserting after the word "court," where it first occurs in the tenth line of the same section, "that in the opinion of the jury there was no such collusion."

Mr. PRATT. I accept that modification also.

The PRESIDENT. The question is on the amendment of the Senator from Maryland, as modified.

Mr. DAYTON. I ask for the yeas and nays.

The yeas and nays were ordered.

Mr. DICKINSON. My colleague is not here. On this question and all those involved in it, I agreed to pair off with him until his return. I am anxious to vote on this bill, and I hope he will return this evening, so as to enable me to do so.

A long debate ensued, in which Messrs. DAYTON, ATCHISON, FOOTE, PRATT, MASON, and BERRIEN participated, and for which, see Appendix.

The Senate then adjourned

SATURDAY, August 24.

The Fugitive Slave Bill.

The Senate resumed the consideration of the bill to provide for the more effectual execution of the third clause of the second section of the fourth article of the Constitution of the United States.

Several amendments were offered to the bill, which were debated at length and disposed of, and the bill was finally ordered to be engrossed for a third reading by yeas and nays, as follows:

YEAS.—Messrs. Atchison, Badger, Barnwell, Bell, Berrien, Butler, Davis of Mississippi, Dawson, Dodge of Iowa, Downs, Foote, Houston, Hunter, Jones, King, Mangum, Mason, Pearce, Rusk, Sebastian, Soulé, Spruance, Sturgeon, Turney, Underwood, Wales, and Yulee—27.

NAYS.—Messrs. Baldwin, Bradbury, Chase, Cooper, Davis of Massachusetts, Dayton, Dodge of Wisconsin, Greene, Smith, Upham, Walker, and Winthrop—12.

MONDAY, August 26.

The Fugitive Slave Bill.

The bill to provide for the more effectual execution of the third clause of the second section of the fourth article of the Constitution of the United States came up on its third reading, and having been read a third time, the question was upon its passage.

Mr. DICKINSON. Mr. President, having consented not to vote on this bill, to enable my colleague, who is opposed to it, to be absent a few days to recover his health, I deem it proper to state my opinions concerning it.

The act of 1793, providing for the restoration of fugitive slaves under the constitution, would, in my judgment, have answered the purposes for which it was designed, if it had been fairly construed and faithfully executed. And, although we may obviate some defects which experience has detected, and add to its force by prescribing penalties for resisting its mandates, yet, as the whole difficulty has rested in a neglect to comply with a plain provision of the constitution, the remedy will be sooner found, if sought, in cultivating a sound state of public feeling and constitutional obligation, among the people of the free States, by Executive recommendations and State legislation, than in multiplying penal enactments by Congress. The passage of a bill with suitable provisions will do much good, but its discussion here, going out as it will to the people of the States, will do much more; for it will turn public attention back from the contemplation of a spurious philanthropy, and more spurious morality, to the allegiance which all owe and all good citizens acknowledge to the constitution and laws of their country.

In entering into a common compact, the several States of the Union solemnly covenanted with each other to restore fugitives from justice and from service, and these provisions are too plainly written in the constitution to be mistaken or disregarded with impunity.

The constitution, article fourth, second subdivision of the second section, relating to fugitives from justice, is as follows:

"A person charged in any State with treason, felony, or other crime, who shall flee from justice and be found in another State, shall, on demand of the Executive authority of the State from which he fled, be *delivered up*, to be removed to the State having jurisdiction of the *crime*."

The third subdivision of the same section, relating to fugitives from service, is as follows:

"No person held to service or labor in one State, under the laws thereof, escaping into another, shall, in consequence of any law or regulation therein, be discharged from such service or labor, but *shall be delivered up* on claim of the party to whom such service or labor may be due."

In both cases the fugitive is to be "delivered up," summarily, upon proper evidence; and in neither case, nor in one more than the other, is he to be put upon trial in the State to which he has fled, nor can Congress do more than to provide that he shall be "delivered up." The theory of the compact is, that the fugitive will be justly dealt with in the jurisdiction to which he is returned. It was assented to in this confiding spirit, and I have yet to learn that the practice is otherwise. And if we may distrust their sense of justice on the one hand, and therefore violate the constitution, they may with far greater propriety distrust ours on the other; and thus, having the sanction of that instrument, for a just and necessary provision of the fundamental law a system of conflict and violence will be substituted.

The grievance upon the subject of fugitive slaves will be redressed, whenever the masses of the people in the free States are aroused to the abuses which have been practised in their name, under the garb of benevolence and superior sanctity; and, to the end that it may be seen how the question has been viewed by courts and judges of the highest character in the free States, and what are our constitutional obligations, I shall append to these remarks brief extracts from the opinions of Chancellor Walworth, and Justices Nelson, McLean, and Story, upon the subject.

In the supreme court of New York, in the matter of Jack, a colored man, charged as a fugitive, Mr. Justice Nelson, then a justice of that court, in speaking of the clause of the constitution requiring the restoration of fugitives, said:

"It is peremptory and unqualified that he 'shall be delivered up upon the claim of the party to whom such service or labor may be due.'

"The right of the owner to reclaim the fugitive in the State to which he has fled has been yielded to him by the States. Without this provision, it would have been competent for them to have wholly denied such claim, or to have qualified it at discretion.

"All this power they have parted with, and the owner now has not only an unqualified right to the possession, but he has the guarantee of the constitution in respect to it."

In the same matter, in the court for the correction of errors, Chancellor Walworth says:

"Independent, however, of any legislation on the subject, either by the individual States or by Congress, if the person whose services are claimed is in fact a fugitive from servitude under the laws of another State, the constitutional provision is imperative that *he shall be delivered up to his master upon claim made;* and any State officer or private citizen, who owes allegiance to the United States, and has taken the usual oath to support the constitution thereof, cannot, without incurring the moral guilt of perjury, do any act to deprive the master of his right to recapture, when there is no real doubt that the person whose services are claimed is in fact the slave of the claimant."

In the Supreme Court of the United States, in the case of Prigg *vs.* Commonwealth of Pennsylvania, Mr. Justice Story says:

"The clause was of the last importance to the safety and security of the Southern States; and could not have been surrendered by them without endangering their whole property in slaves. The clause was accordingly adopted into the constitution by the unanimous consent of the framers of it—a proof at once of its intrinsic and practical necessity.

"How, then, are we to interpret the language of the clause? The true answer is, in *such a manner as consistently with the words shall fully and completely effectuate the whole objects of it.* If, by one mode of interpretation, the right must become shadowy and unsubstantial, and without any remedial power adequate to the end, and by another mode it will attain its just end and secure its manifest purpose, it would seem, upon the principles of reasoning, absolutely irresistible that the latter ought to prevail. No court of justice can be authorized so to construe any clause of the constitution as to defeat its obvious ends, when another construction, equally accordant with the words and sense thereof, will enforce and protect them.

"The clause manifestly contemplates the existence of a positive, unqualified right on the part of the owner of the slave, which *no State law can in any way qualify, regulate, control, or restrain.* The slave is not to be discharged from service or labor *in consequence of any State or law regulation.* Now, certainly, without indulging in any nicety of criticism upon words, it may fairly and reasonably be said that any State law or State regulation which interrupts, limits, delays, or postpones the right of the owner to the immediate possession of the slave, and the immediate command of his service and labor, operates, *pro tanto*, a discharge of the slave therefrom.

In the same case Mr. Justice McLean says:

Without adverting to other conflicting views and interests of the States represented in the General Convention, the subject of slavery was then, as it is now, a most delicate and absorbing consideration. In some of the States it was considered an evil, and a strong opposition to it, in all its forms, was felt and expressed. In others it was viewed as a cherished right, incorporated into the social compact, and sacredly guarded by law.

"Opinions so conflicting, and which so deeply pervaded the elements of society, could be brought to a reconciled action only by an exercise of exalted patriotism.

"Fortunately for the country, this patriotism was not wanting in the Convention and in the States. The danger of discord and ruin was seen, and felt, and acknowledged; and this led to the formation of the Confederacy. The constitution, as it is, cannot be said to have embodied in all its parts the peculiar views of any great section of the Union; but was adopted by a wise and far-reaching conviction that it was the best which, under the circumstances, could be devised; and that its imperfections would be lost sight of, if not forgotten, in the national prosperity and glory which it would secure.

* * * * * * *

"The language of the provision is general. It covers the whole ground, not in detail, but in principle. The States are inhibited from passing 'any law or regulation which shall discharge a fugitive slave from the service of his master;' and a positive duty is enjoined on them to deliver him up, 'on claim of the party to whom his service may be due.'"

The bill was then passed, and its title was amended on the motion of Mr. MASON, so that it now stands as follows:

"An act to amend, and supplementary to the act, entitled 'An act respecting fugitives from justice, and persons escaping from the service of their masters,' approved February 12, 1793."

FRIDAY, September 6.

Line of the Treaty of Utrecht.

Mr. BENTON. I ask leave to communicate to the Senate, and to move for the printing of a letter from the Department of State, received by me a few days ago, in relation to the line of the treaty of Utrecht. It had been made known to me that in a letter from the then Minister of the United States to Great Britain, (Mr. Everett,) in the year 1843, to the then Secretary of State, (Mr. Webster,) it is stated that he had seen that line upon a map shown to him since the settlement of our boundary question by Sir Robert Peel and Lord Aberdeen. I applied for it at the time I made the little speech about printing books, but it could not be found. I now ask leave to communicate it to the Senate and have it read, and I hope it will be ordered to be printed. It relates both to the line of the treaty of Utrecht and to our north-eastern boundary, both of which Mr. Everett saw after the controversy on the subject was over.

The letter was then read by the Secretary, as follows:

"DEPARTMENT OF STATE,
WASHINGTON, *August* 18, 1850.

"The Secretary of State presents his compliments to Mr. Benton, and has the honor to transmit herewith a copy of the paragraph from one of Mr. Everett's letters, requested by Mr. Benton. The paragraph has just been discovered.

"*Extract from a letter from Mr. Everett to Mr. Webster, dated London,* 31*st March*, 1843.

"The above was chiefly written before I had seen Mr. Oswald's map, which I have since, by the kindness of Sir Robert Peel and Lord Aberdeen, been permitted to do. It is a copy of Mitchell's, in fine preservation. The boundaries between the British and French possessions in America, '*as fixed by the treaty of Utrecht*,' are marked upon it in a very distinct line, at least a tenth of an inch broad, and these words written in several places.

"In like manner, the line giving our boundary, as we have always claimed it—that is, carrying the north-east angle of Nova Scotia far to the north of St. John's, is drawn very carefully in a bold red line, full a tenth of an inch broad, and in four different places along the line distinctly written, '*the boundary described by Mr. Oswald*.' What is very noticeable is, that a line narrower, but drawn with care with an instrument, runs from the lower end of Lake Nipissing to the source of the Mississippi, as far as the map permits, and has since been partially erased, though distinctly visible."

The motion to print was referred to the Committee on Printing.

Monday, September 9.

California, Texas, New Mexico, Utah.

The Clerk of the House of Representatives, R. M. Young, Esq, appeared below the bar, and announced that the House of Representatives had passed Senate bills entitled:

An act for the admission of the State of California into the Union.

An act to establish a territorial government for Utah.

He also said the House of Representatives has passed Senate bill entited "An act proposing to the State of Texas the establishment of her northern and western boundaries, the relinquishment by the said State of all the territory claimed by her exterior to said boundaries, and of all her claims upon the United States," with an amendment, in which I am directed to ask the concurrence of the Senate.

The President *pro tem.*, at a later period of the day, laid before the Senate the bill "proposing to the State of Texas the establishment of her northern and western boundaries," which had been agreed to by the House, with an amendment, establishing a territorial government for New Mexico.

Mr. Douglas. I would suggest to the Senate the propriety of dispensing with the reading of the amendment of the House of Representatives. Their amendment is, word for word, the New Mexican territorial bill which passed the Senate some days since, which they have added to the Texan boundary bill, without altering either. I therefore move that the Senate concur in the amendment of the House.

Mr. Chase. Mr. President, if I am not laboring under a misapprehension, there is an amendment of the House to that bill other than that of which the Senator from Illinois speaks. I would ask for the reading of that amendment of the House.

The President. There is an amendment other than that mentioned by the Senator from Illinois.

Mr. Douglas. I beg pardon; I recollect the other amendment.

The Secretary read the following amendment of the House:

"Sec. 19. *And be it further enacted*, That no citizen of the United States shall be deprived of his life, liberty, or property in said Territory, except by judgment of his peers or the laws of the land."

Mr. Chase. I move to amend that amendment of the House by striking out the word "citizen," and inserting the word "person;" and by striking out the words, "except by judgment of his peers and the laws of the land," and insert "without due process of law." This will conform it precisely to the language of the constitution.

Mr. Foote. I hope there will be no debate on this question. We will vote down the amendment.

Mr. Chase. Nor do I wish to debate this motion. It is nothing more than a proposition to substitute the language of the constitution for the language of the House. If we are wiser than our fathers, let it be voted down.

Mr. Foote. The amendment is wholly unnecessary, any way. We all know that; and I do not want any delay in this matter.

The President. The question will first be taken on the first amendment of the Senator from Ohio, to strike out "citizen," and insert "person."

The amendment was rejected.

The question was next taken on the second amendment of Mr. Chase, to strike out "without judgment of his peers or the laws of the land," and insert "without due process of law," and it was rejected.

The question then recurred on concurring with the amendment of the House.

Mr. Seward and Mr. Chase asked for the yeas and nays on the question of concurrence.

The yeas and nays were ordered; and, being taken, were as follows:

Yeas.—Messrs. Atchison, Badger, Bell, Berrien, Bright, Cass, Clay, Dawson, Dickinson, Dodge of Iowa, Douglas, Downs, Felch, Foote, Houston, Jones, King, Mangum, Morton, Norris, Pearce, Pratt, Rusk, Sebastian, Shields, Smith, Spruance, Sturgeon, Underwood, Wales, and Whitcomb—31.

Nays.—Messrs. Baldwin, Benton, Chase, Davis of Massachusetts, Dodge of Wisconsin, Ewing, Hamlin, Seward, Upham, and Winthrop—10.

So the amendment was concurred in.

The House had also amended the title of the

bill by adding to it, "and to establish a territorial government for New Mexico."

On motion by Mr. BADGER, the Senate concurred in this amendment of the House.

At a still later period of the day, the three enrolled bills, embracing four important measures, were received from the House, with the signature of the Speaker, and were signed by the President of the Senate.

TUESDAY, September 10.

Senators Elect from California.

Mr. DOUGLAS. Mr. President, I have been requested to present the credentials of WILLIAM M. GWIN, as a member of the Senate elect from the State of California. I move that they be read, and that the oath of office be administered to Mr. GWIN.

The Secretary read the credentials accordingly.

Mr. BARNWELL. Mr. President, I have been requested to present the credentials of JOHN C. FREMONT as a Senator from California. It is well known, sir, that I entertained the strongest constitutional objections to the admission of California into the Union. But Congress having passed an act for her admission, Mr. FREMONT'S admission could not be otherwise than very acceptable.

The credentials were read by the Secretary.

Mr. DAVIS, of Mississippi. Mr. President, if I were governed by either personal or party considerations, I certainly should make no objection to the ordinary course which is pursued when the credentials of Senators are received here. But believing, as I do, that the constitutional provisions for the election of Senators could not have been complied with in this case, it is with me a sacred matter of duty to interpose such objection as requires me to move the reference of these credentials to the Committee on the Judiciary, with instructions to report on the law and the facts. I make that motion.

The Secretary read the motion, when it was reduced to writing, as follows:

Resolved, That the credentials of the Senators elect from the State of California be referred to the Committee on the Judiciary, with instructions to report on the law and the facts.

Mr. DOUGLAS. Mr. President, I see no necessity for taking up time by this reference. If this were the forepart of the session I would interpose no objection to the reference. But now less than three weeks of the session remain, and much legislation must take place for California. Hence it is important that these Senators should take their seats. In order that they may do so, there being many precedents for this case, certainly one or two precisely in point, as no one can doubt, I hope the motion will not prevail.

Mr. DAVIS called for the yeas and nays on his motion, and they were ordered.

Mr. DAVIS. If it be in order, and if the chairman of the Judiciary Committee thinks he will then be ready to report, I would move, as additional instructions, that the committee report to-morrow morning.

The PRESIDENT. Such instructions are not in order.

Mr. FOOTE. As the yeas and nays have been ordered, I wish to make a single remark. I shall not vote for the reference of these credentials, because this matter has been thoroughly investigated heretofore. And I am very well satisfied that if the Judiciary Committee, for every member of whom I entertain the highest respect, were to take the matter into consideration for twenty centuries, and were fifty times as well qualified to discharge the duties connected with this matter as they are, they could not, in my opinion, throw one single particle of new light on the question. Under such circumstances, I shall oppose the reference.

Mr. BUTLER. Mr. President, if this matter should be referred to the Committee on the Judiciary, I certainly will, in good faith, report on it as speedily as possible. That is, I would not postpone the consideration of what rights these gentlemen may have. But what course will be taken in the committee I cannot tell. It may be discussed, and a long report written upon it. I can make no other than this general statement.

Mr. TURNEY. Mr. President, I shall vote for the reference, upon the principle that no other case of the kind has ever occurred since the formation of the Government. I believe there is no instance where a State has been admitted without there first being some organization on the part of the community to be admitted. No community has been admitted as a State unless there was some vestige of legal existence to such community. In the present instance there was none. There have been States admitted where there was no law of Congress authorizing the formation of a constitution and State government. But in all such cases there was previously a territorial government, and jurisdiction on the part of Congress conferred upon such communities as a territorial government. And in every such case, the territorial legislative authorities enacted laws for the calling of a convention for the purpose of forming a State constitution; which, in my judgment, gave it something of a legal existence as a State, although the election of Senators by a Legislature, under a constitution formed in that way, without the sanction of Congress, would not to a certain extent be in compliance with the constitution, which requires the Legislature of a "State" to elect Senators. But, sir, California was no State, in any sense of the word, in my judgment; consequently I must vote for the reference, and against the admission of her Senators.

Mr. MASON. Mr. President, I had occasion to look into this question when the bill for the admission of California was before the Senate, as one properly involved in the considerations relating to that subject. I did not then find any precedent directly in point, but in the case of the admission of the State of Michigan. I considered that a precedent directly in point. I did not consider that the fact that Michigan had previously been organized into a territorial government, could make any discrimination whatever. But I entertained very serious doubts whether the Senators whom we then admitted, were Senators within the meaning of the constitution. I have the same doubts in the case of California. As far as my personal feelings are concerned, I should certainly welcome the Senators from California as peers upon this floor. But I have a constitutional doubt; and I should be glad to have that doubt solved, if it can be solved by this reference.

Mr. Foote. I wish to make one other observation in addition to what I have already said. Although all those Senators who opposed our plan of adjustment did not take the ground which I am about to state, yet some of them, and among them some very influential and leading gentlemen, did take the ground, that if we would reduce the territorial boundaries of California, all constitutional difficulty in regard to the admission of California as a State would be thereby removed. I suppose those gentlemen, at least, can have had no difficulty in allowing the gentlemen whose credentials have been presented, to be qualified and take their seats, as I suppose a mere alteration of territorial boundaries cannot alter the constitutional aspect of this particular question.

One other observation, and I have done. I am very happy that the credentials of these gentlemen have been in part presented from the State of South Carolina, whose attitude is perfectly well known to the whole country. This movement, originating in part from the State, seems to me to lend a gracious sanction to what we have done heretofore on the subject, upon which I congratulate the country.

Mr. Berrien. I do not mean to enter upon this discussion, but I do mean to protect myself from the remark made, that there would have been no objection to the admission of California——

Mr. Foote. I said in certain quarters, and I certainly did not intend to allude to the Senator from Georgia, because he and I discussed the precise point, and I understood him to take the opposite ground.

Mr. Berrien. I wish merely to say, for self-protection, that when I urged restrictions upon the limits of California, it was with the entire conviction, in my own mind, that if the limits were restricted, the constitution presented here would not be the constitution of the people of California, as then constituted, and we should certainly be obliged to refer the instrument back to the people for their action upon it.

Mr. Mason. I do not know to what opinion, or to what Senator, the Senator from Mississippi alluded, but I was one of those who felt an earnest desire, and frequently expressed it in debate, to limit the boundaries of California to the parallel of 36° 30′; and I never went further, after having done that, than to declare my willingness to allow California to be admitted, after its boundaries had been restricted, upon the proclamation of the President, in order to avoid unnecessary delay.

Mr. Foote. I did not intend to refer to the Senator from Virginia; for I have understood that he was utterly opposed to the admission of California under any circumstances whatsoever. [Mr. Mason shook his head in dissent.] Certainly, however, his mistake was natural enough, inasmuch as I alluded to the leading and influential gentlemen who opposed the admission. It is natural, therefore, that in himself he should recognize one of those persons to whom I alluded.

Mr. Mason. I can assure the Senator from Mississippi, that so far from looking upon myself as an individual of any great influence, it has been a matter of deep regret to me, since I have had a seat here, that I was not entitled to more influence than I have been able to exercise. I have never obtruded myself upon the Senate except when I thought the occasion imperatively required it, in the solemn discharge of my duty. The Senator is also mistaken in ascribing to me an opinion adverse to the admission of California on any grounds; and if he had listened, as I doubt not he did as a matter of courtesy, to my remarks when I addressed the Senate on the admission of California, he would have known that I expressed myself ready, so far as I could, to harmonize the difficulties which had arisen on the acquisition of this territory, in any way I could, with a proper regard to my constitutional obligations; and that I was willing, from devotion to the Union, to agree, in order to avoid delay, to admit California on the proclamation of the President, if her constitution should be returned to her for the proper action upon it.

Mr. Clay. Prior to yesterday, California was a State *de facto*, out of the Union. Upon the approbation of the President of the United States of the bill for her admission into the Union, she became, and now is, one of the States of the Union, having equal and all the privileges which belong to any State in the Union. Among those privileges is that of being represented on this floor by two Senators. She has presented through her Senators the regular credentials of their election; and as she has the same privileges as Kentucky, New York, or any other State, I do not see upon what ground we can treat her differently, or make any reference of those credentials not made in the case of any other State. If we do, then she does not in all respects whatsoever stand on that equal footing which the constitution has prescribed.

Mr. Davis, of Mississippi. I do not consider that California was a State out of the Union, but that it was a Territory of the United States—territory obtained by conquest and purchase—over which the United States had full authority, and over which Congress failed to exercise that authority, from considerations, as I believe, discreditable to the Government itself. It was this failure of the Government to take charge of this Territory which constituted the best argument for the action of the people of California themselves. California became a State by the action of Congress, and the action of the President approving the bill which Congress passed; and she was not a State before that action was had. The constitution provides that Senators shall be elected by the Legislature of a State, and, if there was no State, there should be no Legislature of a State. I do not propose to go into an argument upon this subject, and I only moved the reference to a committee which I thought might best judge of a constitutional question, and I do not believe now that the committee would have detained us more than one or two days. I seek for no delay—I wish the question fairly presented, and I took this mode of reaching it. I am one of those who opposed the admission of California—who sought to restrict its boundaries; and I am not one of those who at any time was prepared to enter into a compact to admit her with reduced boundaries. I considered the defect in the whole proceeding to be inherent and radical, and beyond any reduction of the boundaries. I am one of those who stand here instructed by my State Legislature to resist the admission of California by all honorable and constitutional means. This is taken as an incident to State existence prior to the admission of California, and this is the ground taken by the Senator from Kentucky. If, then, I am under instructions to use all honorable and constitutional means to resist the admission of California as a State, I am also necessarily instructed to oppose every thing which is an incident to the assertion of State existence prior to our action for admission.

I did not wish to be drawn into any remarks on this subject, and personal considerations rendered me very reluctant to do so; nor did I wish to consume the time of the Senate by debate. Whatever views I have entertained on this subject have been heretofore expressed, and I have merely sought now to refer the question to that committee to whom we have supposed we might intrust the examination of questions of constitutional law.

Mr. DOUGLAS. I desire to state only one of the grounds upon which I base this proceeding. California has been admitted into the Union as a State, and, by the act of admission, she becomes a State from the day of the date of her constitution. The principle of relation, known to the law applying to it, is, when the act is consummated it becomes a valid act from the beginning. It was upon that principle, and that only, that the Michigan Senators were enabled to take their seats here. It was upon that principle, and that only, that the Senators from Indiana first elected were enabled to take their seats here. And it is upon that principle, and that only, that the two gentlemen now representing Texas on this floor are now eligible, they not having been for nine years citizens of the United States at the time of their election. But when we annexed Texas to the Union, by the principle of relation, they having been nine years citizens of Texas, they thereby became for nine years citizens of the United States. It is upon this principle of relating back that the defects in the case of Texas, of Indiana, and of Michigan were remedied; and so in this case; California being a State now, she was a State from the time she adopted her constitution. She has had a Legislature from that time, and all the acts of that Legislature from that day relate back and become valid from the time of their adoption. These are the grounds upon which I place my vote, and upon which I suppose these gentlemen will be sworn in.

Mr. FOOTE. I was instructed also to vote against the admission of California, and I have done so, and complied with my instructions, and obeyed them to the letter. I was not instructed, after the admission had taken place, to oppose the admission of the Senators elect upon the floor of the Senate, and therefore I present no such opposition. And I am free to say, that it would have been exceedingly disagreeable to me, if not a duty impossible for me conscientiously to perform, to obey such instructions if I had received them; for, according to my judgment, it would be an act improper in itself, extremely improper with my views of constitutional duty, to oppose the admission on this floor of Senators from a sovereign State of the Union, so recognized, and already admitted into the confederacy. Such being my view, it was not a matter upon which I conceived we could hesitate or delay, and hence I rose and first objected to the proposed reference.

Mr. BUTLER. Perhaps it is proper, as I am on the committee to which it is proposed to refer this matter, that I should make a single remark. My opinion, so far as regards the faculty or the power of the people of California to erect themselves into a State, is well known, and in regard to the body of men said to be a Legislature, I do not believe that they have the faculty of being a Legislature. They have not had the previous assent of Congress, or passed through a territorial condition, and they cannot, in my opinion, have the faculty in legal phrase, without that consent of Congress being given, without a violation of the constitution.

Mr. DAVIS, of Mississippi, again modified his motion, so that it stood as follows:

Resolved, That the credentials of William M. Gwin and John C. Frémont, presenting themselves as Senators elect from the State of California, be referred to the Committee on the Judiciary, with instructions to report on the law and the facts.

The question was then taken by yeas and nays, and they were:

YEAS.—Messrs. Atchison, Barnwell, Berrien, Butler, Davis of Mississippi, Hunter, Mason, Morton, Pratt, Sebastian, Soulé, and Turney—12.

Nays.—Messrs. Badger, Baldwin, Bell, Benton, Bright, Cass, Chase, Clay, Davis of Massachusetts, Dawson, Dayton, Dickinson, Dodge of Wisconsin, Dodge of Iowa, Douglas, Downs, Ewing, Felch, Foote, Greene, Hamlin, Jones, King, Mangum, Norris, Phelps, Seward, Shields, Smith, Spruance, Sturgeon, Underwood, Wales, Walker, Whitcomb, and Winthrop—36.

So the motion to refer was not agreed to.

Slave Trade in the District of Columbia.

The Senate resumed the consideration of the bill to suppress the slave trade in the District of Columbia.

Mr. Mason moved to strike out the first two sections which were a part of the bill as it was reported from the Committee of Thirteen. The first of these sections prohibits the introduction of any slave into the District of Columbia for the purpose of being sold, or placed in depot to be subsequently transported to another market. The second section provides for the abolition of the depots themselves in which the slaves are confined in the District of Columbia. If, therefore, the motion to strike out should prevail, all that portion of the bill relating to the abolition of the slave trade in the District of Columbia will be stricken out, and its character changed, as it will only provide for the punishment of persons enticing slaves from the District, and invest a power in the corporation to prohibit free persons of color from coming into the District.

Mr. M. advocated his amendment, and the debate was continued by Messrs. Clay and Pearce.

Before the vote was taken on that motion—

Mr. Pearce moved to amend the first section by striking out from the end the words, "Such slave shall thereupon become liberated and free," and inserting the words:

"Such owner, or the agent of such owner, shall be subject to a penalty of five hundred dollars, to be recovered by action of *qui tam*, one-half to the informer, and the other half to the corporation within whose limits the offence may be committed; and in every such case bail shall be required, any law to the contrary notwithstanding."

The penalties thus proposed to be inflicted are for bringing slaves into the District of Columbia.

After debate, in which Messrs. Clay, Foote, Pearce, Ewing, and Underwood, took part—

Mr. Pearce modified his amendment by omitting the closing words: "and in every such case bail shall be required, any law to the contrary notwithstanding."

The debate was continued by Messrs. Berrien, Badger, Baldwin, Davis of Mississippi, Pratt, and Turney.

Mr. Seward called for the yeas and nays, and being ordered, were as follows:

Yeas.—Messrs. Atchison, Bell, Berrien, Dawson, Downs, Foote, Houston, King, Mason, Morton, Pearce, Pratt, Rusk, Sebastian, Underwood, and Yulee—16.

Nays.—Messrs. Badger, Baldwin, Benton, Chase, Clay, Davis of Massachusetts, Dayton, Dickinson, Dodge of Wisconsin, Dodge of Iowa, Ewing, Felch, Greene, Hamlin, Jones, Mangum, Norris, Seward, Shields, Smith, Spruance, Sturgeon, Wales, Walker, Whitcomb, and Winthrop—26.

So the amendment was rejected.

The question recurred on the motion to strike out the first two sections of the bill.

Mr. Underwood asked for a division of the question, and the vote was taken on striking out the first section, and resulted thus:

Yeas.—Messrs. Atchison, Berrien, Butler, Davis of Mississippi, Dawson, Downs, Houston, Hunter, King, Mason, Morton, Pratt, Rusk, Sebastian, Soulé, Turney, Underwood, and Yulee—18.

Nays.—Messrs. Badger, Baldwin, Bell, Benton, Bright, Chase, Clay, Davis of Massachusetts, Dayton, Dickinson, Dodge of Wisconsin, Dodge of Iowa, Ewing, Felch, Foote, Greene, Hamlin, Jones, Mangum, Norris, Phelps, Seward, Shields, Smith, Spruance, Sturgeon, Wales, Walker, Whitcomb, and Winthrop—30.

So the motion to strike out was not agreed to.

The Senate also refused to strike out the second section, by yeas and nays as follow:

Yeas.—Messrs. Atchison, Barnwell, Berrien, Butler, Davis of Mississippi, Dawson, Downs, Houston, Hunter, Mason, Morton, Pratt, Rusk, Sebastian, Soulé, Turney, and Yulee—17.

Nays.—Messrs. Badger, Baldwin, Bell, Benton, Bright, Chase, Clay, Davis of Massachusetts, Dayton, Dickinson, Dodge of Wisconsin, Dodge of Iowa, Douglas, Ewing, Felch, Greene, Hamlin, Jones, Mangum, Norris, Phelps, Seward, Shields, Smith, Spruance, Sturgeon, Underwood, Wales, Walker, Whitcomb, and Winthrop—31.

Mr. Dayton submitted the following amendment:

In the third line of the fifth section strike out all after the word "power," and insert the following:

"To pass all necessary ordinances or police laws not inconsistent with the constitution, touching the residence and conduct of free negroes residing and coming to reside within their respective jurisdictional limits, and to enforce such ordinances or laws, upon the breach thereof, by fine and imprisonment, or either, at their discretion."

After a few words of conversation he withdrew the amendment for the present.

Mr. Seward submitted the following as a substitute for the whole bill after the enacting clause:

Sec. 1. Slavery shall forever cease within the District of Columbia, and all persons held in bondage therein shall be free. The Secretary of the Interior shall audit and pay to all persons holding slaves within the District at the time that this act takes effect, such damages as they shall suffer by the passage thereof, and the sum of two hundred thousand dollars is hereby appropriated to carry this act into execution, out of any money in the Treasury not otherwise appropriated.

SEC. 2. An election shall be held in the District of Columbia, to ascertain whether this bill is approved by the people thereof. Those who approve the act shall express their approbation by a ballot containing the words, "For emancipation in the District." Those who are opposed shall vote by ballot, containing the words, "Against emancipation in the District." All persons entitled to vote for any municipal officer in the District, and all citizens of the United States residing within the District permanently, shall be deemed qualified to vote at such election. Such election shall be held within six months from the passage of this act, and on public notice of not less than three months, to be given by the marshal of the District. If a majority of the votes given at such election shall be in favor of this act, it shall go into effect immediately. If a majority of votes shall be against the same, this act shall be void and of none effect.

Debate ensued, in which Messrs. BALDWIN, MANGUM, DAWSON, DAYTON, PRATT, ATCHISON, MASON, CHASE, FOOTE, WINTHROP, BADGER, and others took part.

Pending the question, the Senate adjourned.

FRIDAY, September 13.

Death of Hon. Henry Nes.

A message was received from the House of Representatives by Mr. YOUNG, their Clerk:

Mr. PRESIDENT: I am directed to inform the Senate of the decease of the Hon. HENRY NES, a Representative from the State of Pennsylvania, and to communicate the proceedings of the House thereupon:

The SECRETARY read the resolutions of the House.

Mr. STURGEON. Mr. President, the painful intelligence that has just been announced to the Senate by a message from the House of Representatives, has warned us that death has again been in our midst. These frequent calls of the invisible upon the visible world, speak to us in language that cannot be misunderstood. We are admonished that all must die, and that we must set our "house in order," that we may be prepared to undertake the inevitable journey to that bourn from which no traveller returns.

In the absence of my colleague occasioned by sickness, the duty devolves upon me to say a few words on the life and character of the deceased.

Doctor HENRY NES was born in the town of York, York county, in Pennsylvania. There he spent his early childhood. There he spent his manhood. There, amidst his friends, he descended to his grave. Mr. NES qualified himself for the medical profession, which he commenced to practise at an early day. His urbanity of manners, his kind disposition and his disinterested benevolence, soon introduced him to a large and lucrative practice. That practice was continued for years, occasionally and partially interrupted by the calls that were made upon him to fill places of trust and responsibility in his native town.

It was not until the year 1843 that Mr. NES was elected a Representative in the Congress of the United States. This was his first appearance on the theatre of public life. Mr. NES did not represent his district in the next Congress. He was, however, elected in 1846, and again re-elected in 1848. And as an evidence of his popularity, I may mention the fact that he was elected, although his district usually gave six or seven hundred Democratic majority. This speaks highly for his character and standing among the people of Pennsylvania. The voice of Mr. NES was seldom heard in the Hall of the House, but he was assiduous in his application to the duties that were devolved upon him by the several committees of which he was a member. Owing to his retiring character his acquaintances were perhaps not many. But he had warm and ardent friends among those who were more immediately around him.

Mr. NES died in the 52d year of his age. He will be missed much by his friends. To his children, whom he has left without the care of a mother or the protection of a father, the loss will be irreparable. But they have the consolation to know that he died leaving them the inheritance of an irreproachable character.

Without saying any thing more, Mr. President, I offer the following resolutions:

Resolved, That the Senate has received with deep sensibility the message from the House of Representatives announcing the death of the Hon HENRY NES, a Representative from the State of Pennsylvania.

Resolved, That, in token of respect for the memory of the deceased, the Senate will wear the usual badge of mourning for thirty days.

Resolved, That as a further mark of respect to the memory of the deceased, the Senate do now adjourn.

The resolutions were unanimously adopted, and

The Senate adjourned.

WEDNESDAY, September 18.

Enticing Slaves from the District.

Mr. PRATT. I ask the Senate now to take up a bill introduced a day or two since, to prevent the enticing or assisting of slaves to escape from their owners in the District of Columbia, and for other purposes, that it may have a second reading.

Mr. CLAY. One word only, sir. I consider the passage of this bill as part of that great system of policy which has for its object peace and quiet. I agree entirely with the Senator that we ought to put an end to all these "aggressions." This bill proposes to put an end to an aggression. If the Senator will only agree that this aggression shall terminate—if he will enter into bond and security that no more slaves shall be stolen from the District of Columbia—I presume gentlemen will not ask for the passage of this bill.

Mr. Cass. Mr. President, I desire to say one word. I am not at all afraid of discussion on this matter. It is the last expiring effort to raise a party in this country. I do not believe any party could now be built up in relation to this question of slavery. I think the question is settled in the public mind. I do not think it worth while to make speeches upon it.

Mr. Gwin. Will the Senator from Maryland withdraw his motion, in order to allow me to introduce a bill of which I have given notice?

Mr. Pratt. I cannot withdraw my motion, lest I should not have a chance to renew it. If there is to be a contest on this subject, I shall call for the yeas and nays on my motion.

Mr. Walker. If Senators cannot have the privilege of using the morning hour for the ordinary morning business, I should like to know it. I shall concur in taking the yeas and nays.

Mr. Chase. Mr. President, what is the question before the Senate? Is the question upon taking up the bill of the Senator from Maryland? (Mr. Pratt.)

The President. That is the question. But the merits of that bill are not open for discussion.

Mr. Chase. I withdrew a moment since, in deference to what seemed to be the general desire of the Senate, that no further discussion should take place upon questions of this character, a bill which I regard as infinitely more important than that of the Senator from Maryland. If it be the pleasure of the Senate now, to be indicated by the vote to take up this bill, and protract discussion upon these questions to the hindrance of other business, I shall feel it my duty again to ask leave to introduce that bill. I know no reason why the security of slavery in the District of Columbia should be preferred to the security of freedom in the Territories.

The honorable Senator from Kentucky tells us that this is a part of the scheme of adjustment, and that, therefore, it ought to be taken up for consideration. If it be a part of that scheme, it has recently been adopted as such. It received no consideration, so far as I am aware, from the Committee of Thirteen. It was brought in by the Senator from Maryland, and affects this District only. It is a measure which has never been called for by the people of this District, during the fifty years that slavery has existed here by act of Congress.

Mr. Pratt. I call the Senator to order.

The President. The Senator must confine himself to the subject under consideration, which is, Shall the bill of the Senator from Maryland be taken up for consideration?

Mr. Chase. I am urging reasons why it should not be taken up, and I have only followed the course of the Senator from Kentucky.

I deny, sir, that this bill is a part of the scheme of compromise and adjustment, because it has never received the consideration of the committee which was appointed to consider the questions relating to slavery. The honorable Senator from Kentucky has said that all these questions are settled. Some of them are, indeed, settled. The question of the Texan boundary is settled, contingent only upon the acceptance of Texas, which I apprehend will be given very promptly. The question of the admission of California is settled. The question of the admission of slavery in the Territories has been avoided. It has not been settled.

The President. The Chair must interfere. The Senator is not speaking to any question before the Senate.

Mr. Chase. I am pursuing the line of remark which the Senator from Kentucky adopted. If that be out of order, I shall submit.

Mr. Clay. The Senator should recollect that the question is on the second reading of the bill—a mere matter of form.

The motion of the honorable Senator from Ohio (Mr. Chase) was to introduce a bill, and therefore the whole subject was fully open for discussion. The motion now is simply to take up a bill as a matter of form, to give it its second reading, and it ought to be recollected by the Senator from Ohio, that when it was proposed the other day, according to almost invariable custom, to give this bill its second reading, it was objected to by the Senator who now sits before me, (Mr. Hale.) This is merely a question of form. It comes up regularly for its second reading, and when it is taken up it will be in order to make objections to and discuss it.

Mr. Hale. I wish to say a single word in answer to the honorable Senator from Kentucky, (Mr. Clay.) The Senator suggests that the other day I objected to the second reading of the bill, which is merely a matter of form. It is true that I did object, and now I want to mention another fact. When a motion was made fifteen minutes ago to introduce a bill—a thing which I have never heard objected to during all the time that I have been in Congress, in either House—the Senator from Kentucky objected, and called for the yeas and nays upon it. So that, if mine was an offence, I should think his must be *magnum scandalatum*, or something worse, because it is an every-day thing to object to a second reading, but to object to the introduction of a bill is certainly a very extraordinary one.

The motion to take up the bill was carried on division—ayes 26, noes not counted.

The bill was then read a second time, and considered as in Committee of the Whole.

Mr. Clay. I do not wish to take up the time of the Senate at all upon the subject of this bill; but I propose to strike out the third section, which excludes free persons of color from this District. I have no doubt that they have been increasing a great deal, and that something ought to be done. But before we drive them away we should ascertain where they are to go, and where they can go. The subject ought to be taken up and most deliberately examined, and some provisions made, in the spirit of the age and of humanity, in reference to persons of color. The other provisions of the bill, if that is stricken out——

Mr. Pratt. If the Senator will permit me to interrupt him, I will say that I think he misapprehends the section of the bill to which he refers. The retrospective action of this section has been altered.

Mr. Clay. Ah! indeed.

Mr. Pratt. It is only to prevent free negroes coming into the District hereafter.

Mr. Clay. Very well. Then I agree to it, and will withdraw my motion to strike out.

The motion was accordingly withdrawn.

Mr. Hale. I rise now to make a motion for the special benefit of those of my friends that are in favor of abolishing slavery in the District of Columbia, but who have been waiting for a good time and an appropriate measure by which it may be done. I do not propose to trust myself with the details of such a measure, but I propose to give those gentlemen a fair chance of expressing upon the record what their sentiments are, untrammelled by any "inexpedient" and "indiscreet" details; and in order to give the largest scope for discretion, I move that the bill be committed to the Committee on the District of Columbia, with instructions so to amend it as to abolish slavery in the District of Columbia. On that motion I ask for the yeas and nays.

Mr. Clay. Then I hope we shall have them without discussion.

Mr. Hale. I hope so too.

The yeas and nays were ordered, and being taken, resulted as follows:

Yeas.—Messrs. Baldwin, Chase, Davis of Massachusetts, Dodge of Wisconsin, Ewing, Hale, Hamlin, Seward, and Winthrop—9.

Nays.—Messrs. Atchison, Badger, Barnwell, Bell, Benton, Bright, Butler, Cass, Clay, Cooper, Davis of Mississippi, Dawson, Dayton, Dickinson, Dodge of Iowa, Douglas, Downs, Felch, Foote, Frémont, Gwin, Houston, Hunter, Jones, King, Mason, Morton, Norris, Pratt, Rusk, Sebastian, Shields, Smith, Soulé, Spruance, Sturgeon, Turney, Underwood, Wales, Whitcomb, and Yulee—41.

So the proposition to commit the bill was rejected.

Mr. Baldwin. I move to amend the bill by adding the following:

Be it further enacted, That the seventh section of the act entitled "An act additional to and amendatory of an act entitled an act concerning the District of Columbia," approved May 3, 1802, be, and the same is hereby, repealed.

The section proposed to be repealed is section seven, of chapter LII., of the United States Statutes at Large, volume 2, in the following words:

Sec. 7. *Be it further enacted*, That no part of the laws of Virginia or Maryland, declared by an act of Congress passed the 27th day of February, 1850, "concerning the District of Columbia," to be in force within the said District, shall ever be so construed as to prohibit the owners of slaves to hire them within or remove them to the said District, in the same way as was practised prior to the above recited act.

This clause in the act of 1802 has reference now only to the State of Maryland, and if it continues to be a part of the code of the District, it gives to the people of Maryland a right to introduce their slaves into the District of Columbia, which is denied to the people of Virginia and to every other slaveholding State. While the county of Alexandria continued a part of the District of Columbia, this provision of the act of 1802 had relation as well to the State of Virginia as to the State of Maryland. Slaves might be introduced from the State of Virginia into that part of the District which was ceded by Virginia, and slaves might be introduced from the State of Maryland into that part which was ceded by Maryland. But as the law then stood, although they might thus be introduced by Maryland and Virginia into the parts of the District respectively ceded by those States, they could not, when thus introduced, be passed from one of those counties to the other.

In 1812, an act of Congress was passed authorizing slaves who had thus been introduced lawfully from Virginia into the county of Alexandria, and from Maryland into the county of Washington, to be transferred from one county to the other in the District, and there held in slavery in the same manner as they might have been in the county into which they were originally introduced. But since the retrocession of Alexandria to Virginia, no slave can be introduced into the District from the State of Virginia, or from any slave State except Maryland, (unless when accompanying their owners on their removal to the District.) We were assured a few days since by the Senator from Maryland, that probably five-sixths of the slaves now in the District of Columbia had been introduced in consequence of this clause in the act of 1802. Now, why, I ask, if it be the policy of this District and of Congress to refuse to permit the introduction of slaves into this District from the State of Virginia, or any other slave State, should it be permitted to Maryland to have the exclusive privilege of peopling the District with their slaves, by bringing them here to hire them out to service, and thus adding to the slave population, to the manifest injury of the free laborers of the District? I see no reason why this monopoly should be allowed to Maryland, and I think therefore the provision of the act of 1802, under which so many slaves have been introduced into the District, should be now repealed.

Mr. Pratt. I wish merely to offer a word of explanation, and certainly I shall not enter upon a debate on this question, which I know will be fatal to the bill. The Senator from Connecticut has stated, with a considerable degree of correctness, the law as it stands, and as I had the honor to explain it a week or two ago to the Senate. The Senator complains that the citizens of Maryland are enjoying, under the act of Congress of 1802, a privilege which the people of no other State may enjoy. I say to him if he is sincere in that objection, that we are perfectly willing to authorize Virginia, Kentucky, and every other slave State in the Union, which may choose to do so, to bring their slaves into the District. It is an exclusive privilege to Maryland, under the laws as they exist, because this territory belonged to Maryland, and the people who originally inhabited it were citizens of Maryland, the people when the territory was ceded going with it. It was, therefore, thought right and proper that the people of Maryland, who were inhabitants of the territory when it was ceded, should enjoy the laws of their native State. Now, I ask the attention of the Senate and the Senator himself to the only effect of the proposition which he has made to repeal the act of 1802. The Senator has not adverted at all to the action of both Houses during the present session, in passing the bill introduced by the Senator from Kentucky. Under that bill, no one either from Maryland or anywhere else, can bring his servants here for sale. They cannot be brought here for sale under the Maryland law if left in force, and the act of Congress be repealed to which the Senator has referred. Maryland does not desire or propose to interfere with any person coming to Washington or to the District to reside. He may bring with him his servants, but he is not privileged to sell his servants so brought here, under the Maryland law, until he has resided in the District for a period of three continuous years. That is the old law of Maryland; that is the present law of the District; and the law introduced by the Senator from Kentucky, and which has already passed both Houses of Congress, prohibits any citizen of Maryland, or of any other State, from bringing his servants here for the purpose of sale. I think that under the law of Maryland, which the Senator does not propose to interfere with, the citizen of Virginia, or of any other part of the United States, who may come to the District to reside, is now privileged to bring his servants with him. The repeal of the act of 1802, as proposed by the Senator from Connecticut, would have a most limited operation, indeed, in view of the law which has already passed, as introduced by the Senator from Kentucky. I am not prepared to say whether it would have any operation. I am certain that the Senator will find this to be the effect of his amendment upon examination. I do not propose to discuss the question at all, and will not detain the Senate further.

I am reminded that, under the law of Maryland, in order to produce a reciprocity between the people of the District and the people of the State of Maryland, the former have the privilege of taking their servants into Maryland for the purpose of working them, many of the residents of the District having farms in the State of Maryland; or that they may have the privilege of hiring out their servants into the State of Maryland, and of bringing them back again to this District. Now, the only effect of this amendment is to do away with this reciprocity, so far as Maryland is concerned, and to prevent the citizens of Maryland from bringing their servants here for the purpose of hiring them: or a citizen of Maryland, living here a part of the year, from bringing his servants with him. That is the only effect of the amendment.

The motion to postpone was agreed to.

Monday, September 23.

Hickey's Edition of the Constitution.

The following resolution came up in its order, and was read a third time:

"*Resolved*, That the Secretary be directed to procure from the proprietor for the use of the Senate, ten thousand copies of Hickey's edition of the constitution, with an alphabetical analysis, Washington's Inaugural and Farewell Addresses, and other important statistical matter illustrative of the genius of the American Government, and the development of its principles: *Provided*, That they be furnished at the same price as those last procured for the use of the Senate."

The question was then stated to be upon its passage.

Mr. Atchison. This resolution is for the purchase of ten thousand copies of the constitution. My recollection is, that we have ordered twenty or thirty thousand copies of this work before, at different sessions. I do not know the exact number; but I know that I have got tired of franking and distributing these books. If this resolution has any other object than merely to purchase the book for the benefit of the vender, I cannot perceive it. For any such purpose, I am unwilling to vote.

Mr. Badger. The object of purchasing these books is very obvious. It is to circulate them among our constituents; and I know of no book which either House of Congress has at any time circulated which is so valuable, and so general acceptable, and so much desired by our constituents as this very book. I hope, therefore, the resolution will be adopted.

Mr. Atchison. I fully admit the value of this work. I think I have given evidence of it by voting for the purchase of some twenty or thirty thousand copies of it before.

Mr. Badger. Oh, no; we have never purchased but fourteen thousand copies of it.

Mr. Atchison. Very well; fourteen thousand copies will answer for my purpose. I acknowledge the value of the book. I have voted for it heretofore, for the benefit of the gentleman who compiled the book. But it strikes me that the Constitution of the United States is now more generally diffused, and more easily obtained, than any other book whatsoever. It prefaces the constitution of every State in the Union; it is a part of the digest of the laws of every State in this Union; and it is to be had, I presume, at every bookstore in the Union.

Who will get these books, if we purchase these ten thousand copies? They must be distributed among twenty millions of people. Only a favored few will receive them. Like all other documents printed for distribution, they will fall into the hands of the favored few. Perhaps not one man in five hundred will receive a copy of this book. The distribution of all these books is very partial. I think it is time now to stop this book business. I thought we had done with it. I thought this business had been stopped by a large, a very large vote given at this session. I thought that our refusal to purchase the work of Aaron H. Palmer would put an end to this system of purchasing books for distribution. I ask the yeas and nays on the passage of this resolution, that I may record my vote against it.

The yeas and nays were ordered.

Mr. RUSK. As the yeas and nays have been called, I desire to record my vote in favor of this resolution. We pay ten times what this work will cost in printing and distributing much inferior documents. If Congress never goes into extravagance till it does it in circulating the Constitution of the United States among the people, we shall be a very economical Government, indeed.

Mr. GWIN. As the Senator from Missouri (Mr. ATCHISON) is tired of franking these books, I will relieve him of that trouble, if he will only furnish me with the books. My country has not had these books, and we want our share.

Mr. WALKER. I believe this book has done more good than all the other books that Congress has ever printed. I have received letters even from persons in favor of the abolition of the franking privilege—and I have received a great many letters on that subject—that have seen this work, who say that if the Government would put that book in the hands of every citizen of the United States, it would be a benefit; and the post office might well be made to bear the burden of transporting it. It has been made an exception, I believe, in every letter I have received on the subject of the franking privilege, and I have received some violent ones on that subject. It seems to be a favorite work. I believe I can say that in Wisconsin it has had a good effect on the sentiments and political opinions of the people, and has introduced a high feeling of patriotism wherever it has been read.

Mr. SEWARD, (jocularly.) I suppose this is one of the great measures of "pacification."

Mr. ATCHISON. I do not wish to be understood as depreciating the value of this book. Not by any means. But it is now said, that of all the documents Congress has ever printed for distribution, this is the most valuable. I admit it. But this purchasing of books is an abuse. The argument is that this is not a great abuse; but I contend the whole system is an abuse. I admit that this is, perhaps, the least abuse that attaches to the system of buying and distributing books, for I believe it is the most valuable work we have ever distributed. But I am unwilling even to distribute the Constitution of the United States among the people, because I consider this book business an abuse. As I before observed, the distribution is partial. It will fall into the hands of very few, and into the hands of those few who, perhaps, have already the constitution. I know that I have received letters in regard to this work. So has every Senator. Every book that is printed at the public expense is gratefully received by those to whom it is sent, whether it be valuable or not.

Mr. BADGER. I desire to add but one remark. I am surprised at the zealous opposition made by the Senator from Missouri to the purchase of a book which he thinks the best which Congress has ever circulated. I will merely mention one fact. I received a letter from a very intelligent man in North Carolina, to whom I had sent a copy of this book, in which he expressed the opinion that it was not only the most valuable book Congress had ever circulated, but that if a sufficient number of copies were circulated to put it into the hands of every reading man in the country, it would be money well laid out. It contains not only the Constitution of the United States, which my friend says is printed at the head of the digest of the laws of every State, but also a compilation of information which I venture to say no man can find in any one private library in the United States. If he were to sit down and look through all the books, a compilation could not be found so carefully made as that put in conjunction with the Constitution of the United States in this book.

Mr. DICKINSON. This is the only book worth one cent ever published by Congress, according to my view. It is an exceedingly valuable book, and one of the very best compilations for public use I ever saw. I cannot vote for this motion, because I am determined to vote against all Congress books; but I deemed it due to say this much, though I have made up my mind to vote against the motion.

The yeas and nays were then taken, and resulted:

YEAS.—Messrs. Badger, Baldwin, Bell, Berrien, Cass, Clarke, Downs, Ewing Frémont, Greene, Gwin, Hale, Jones, Morton, Rusk, Seward, Shields, Smith, Soulé, Walker, Winthrop, and Yulee—22.

NAYS.—Messrs. Atchison, Barnwell, Benton, Chase, Dawson, Dickinson, Dodge of Wisconsin, Dodge of Iowa, Felch, Hamlin, Hunter, King, Mason, Sebastian, Spruance, Sturgeon, Turney, Underwood, and Whitcomb—19.

Wednesday, September 25.

The Galphin Claim.

The joint resolution from the House of Representatives to authorize the President of the United States to cause suit to be brought against George W. Crawford, late Secretary of War, was read a first time by its title.

The joint resolution was read a second time with a view to reference.

Mr. Badger. I can see no reason why that resolution should not be passed without reference to a committee. It is a measure which was introduced into the House at the request of Mr. Crawford. I suppose there can be no objection to gratify his wish on the subject, and I hope the resolution will be put upon its passage.

Mr. Butler. I hope the resolution will be acted on at once, with a decided opinion on my part that it ought not to pass.

Mr. Dawson moved to refer the resolution to the Judiciary Committee, which motion did not prevail, and the resolution was considered by the Senate as in Committee of the Whole.

Mr. Turney. I have but a single remark to make. I think the resolution itself will not raise the question which it is proposed to raise and to investigate before the courts: that is, to test the correctness of the decision of the departments here in paying the interest upon this claim. It cannot do it, in the first instance, because Mr. Crawford only acted as agent or attorney for the Galphins, and if he received the money in the character of agent or attorney, the presumption is that he has paid it over to the owners, retaining, no doubt, the fee which was to be paid him by the contract with them. If this question is to be tested, you must sue the parties who received the money, and not the attorney who prosecuted the claim. It is mere humbug to say that Mr. Crawford was justified, or that the departments were justified in paying it, on account of any decision which the courts might make under this resolution. The suit must be brought, not against the agent or attorney who prosecuted the claim, but against the man who recovered the money. And besides, from the provisions of this resolution, I take it, that even if Mr. Crawford was the proper party to be sued, you could not get behind the decisions of the auditors and comptrollers, and of the treasurer who paid the money. Their decisions would be final and conclusive before the courts. Thus it would be a mere matter of mockery to authorize the President to bring a suit in order to whitewash the character of some man. I am opposed to passing this resolution to authorize a judicial investigation for the purpose of whitewashing the character of Mr. Crawford in this transaction. You cannot reach the question of the correctness of the decision of the department in paying this money by any suit that can be instituted under this resolution, because you cannot sue Mr. Crawford, the attorney, and, secondly, because in any such suit the decision of the auditor and treasurer would be conclusive upon the court. The court would have no right to reverse it. Their decision would be the law of the case. An act of Congress confers the duty of making such decisions upon these accounting officers, and there is no law authorizing the courts to correct or reverse them. No appeal can be taken, nor is there any mode of revising the decisions of the accounting officers; and hence I say this is a mere mode of whitewashing the character of Mr. Crawford, without any possible hope even of submitting to the court the correctness of those decisions. The court would have no power to reverse or revise them and render judgment against Mr. Crawford, even if he was the proper man to be sued to recover this money back. I hold that it is utterly unnecessary, therefore, to pass any such resolution. In fact, I think it is "throwing good money after bad" to incur the expense of a lawsuit merely for the purpose of whitewashing the character of these parties.

Mr. Ewing. I think the Senator from Tennessee is entirely mistaken in all the positions he has taken in this matter. In the first place, he says that the proposed suit is not against the proper individual, and that the suit cannot be sustained against him, because he is only the attorney, and not the party. Now, sir, this attorney received the money, or a portion of the money, no matter how much; but whatever portion of that money he received, if he be sued for it, and if in his pleadings he do not set up the defence that he was attorney, the suit can be sustained. The case has to be decided upon the declaration and the plea, and you can sustain the action against him if he admits that he received the money, and does not plead that he received it as attorney. Now, he says in his communication to the House, that he will not put in that plea. If he does, he is a dishonored man, as a matter of course, and there is no "whitewashing" of character at all. But I undertake to say that he will not plead nor set up as a defence that he received this money as attorney. So that, as to that particular point, it settles it without any difficulty at all, just as if you sued the individual party instead of suing the attorney.

As to the next position, that the settlement of this account by the accounting officer is conclusive, Mr. Crawford says in his letter that he will not set up that as a defence, nor will he set up any thing as a defence except the legal right, conferred by law, to pay this money, and every part of it, over to the parties. He will not set up as a defence the fact that the accounting officers have acted upon it at all. In his pleadings, he will present the single and sole question, that the law of 1848 and the previous obligations of the Government gave him the right to receive this money. Well, if he does not—if the pleadings are presented in that form, I need not say to every lawyer that the question will be settled by our courts upon the pleadings, and settled, therefore, upon the law of the original case. It is no matter of whitewashing at all. If the pleadings be made fairly —if the pleadings be set forth *bona fide*, as he says he will cause them to be set forth, the actual law of the case will be presented; and if there has been blackballing by the decision of the committee, there will be nothing more than the wiping off of that blackballing by the decision of the court, entitled to decide upon the question of law, and having the direct question before them, and nothing but the question.

Mr. BUTLER. I was one of those who thought that this resolution ought not to go to the committee. I think it unnecessary, because the subject is well understood. I object to the bill upon this obvious ground, that we have no right to make use of the courts of the United States to perform the office of arbitrator. We have no right to devolve upon them the office of arbitrator between gentlemen who may conceive their honor involved in any matter in the administration of the Federal Government. To say the least, this mode of proceeding is unusual. Candor requires me to say that I believe that Mr. Crawford, as a man of honor, would be guided by what he has said, because I know the man: I believe he is willing to have the matter fully investigated before a court. But the court derives its jurisdiction from the Constitution and laws of the United States, and ought not to be made a reviewing power of the executive decisions; and no matter what he may say with regard to what he will do or will not do, it will, to all intents and purposes, be making use of that court as arbitrator to decide between him and the Government. Now, how would the matter stand? Mr. Crawford, in good faith—and his *parole* would go very far with me, and I would regard his word as his bond—says that he will not plead any thing in bar, but will go into a full and fair investigation, and let the judgment of the court turn entirely on the validity of that judgment made under an authoritative decision of the Treasury Department. Well, it may be so, or it may not be so; but suppose the judgment of the court below is against Mr. Crawford, in honor he would be bound by the state of the pleading on which the judgment was rendered. His sense of honor, and not legal obligation, would lead him. In the event of his death—the suit abating—it could not be revived; or if revived, his executors might be under a high duty to file a plea in bar to defeat the action.

Mr. EWING. No, sir. I need not say to my learned friend that they would have to abide by the pleadings below.

Mr. BUTLER. There are a great many ways of amending the pleadings below.

Mr. EWING. No, they cannot do it.

Mr. BUTLER. I do not undertake to say that it would be so in this case. I know very well that the pleadings and judgment in appellate tribunals must rest entirely on the pleadings and the judgment upon them in the court below. But I say that this mode of entertaining a matter of this kind, is making use of the courts for purposes not contemplated by the Constitution of the United States. It never has been done. Now with regard to the present state of the law: This money was paid over under the adjudication of the auditor, and approved by the Secretary of the Treasury. That judgment or proceeding is final. It was paid, therefore, on a judgment, or that which has the operation of a judgment, and that judgment secures Mr. Crawford against any right, *per lege*, of the Government to recover it back, and I have no idea of interposing. Mr. Crawford has given his word, and as I have said, I believe he will abide by it, but there is no security that Milledge Galphin or others may not be sued by the Federal courts, and brought within the scope of the judgment. I conclude as I began, by saying that it is making the court an arbiter, which is not a part of its office, nor within its usual and proper jurisdiction. It will, in effect, give it the office of review over a distinct department of this Government.

Mr. DAWSON. I regret very much the tone and manner of the Senator from Tennessee (Mr. TURNEY) on this subject. Mr. Crawford has had a great deal said in relation to him in connection with his particular claim; and when gentlemen use the term "whitewashing" in relation to this character, they ought first to understand the nature of the imputation that they are making, and whether they can sustain the accusation against Mr. Crawford in relation to this matter. I demand, as the friend of Mr. Crawford, to know what part of his conduct in relation to this matter needs "whitewashing?" What infamy or impropriety has been attached to him in relation to this matter? Where are the occasions upon which he has not acted openly, fairly, and boldly, in relation to this matter? When was it that he ever forfeited his honor or his character either as an individual or as a politician? What part of his conduct during his administration of the War Department needs "whitewashing," even by a decision of the Supreme Court of the United States? I know the Senator from Tennessee did not, in using the word "whitewashed," intend to convey a charge inconsistent with honor; at least, I think not.

Mr. TURNEY. If the Senator will allow me, I will say that I made no charge—I intended to make none when I spoke of whitewashing. Mr. Crawford himself feels that there is something hanging suspended over him, otherwise he would have never made the application to Congress. He felt it when he first asked an investigation in the House. That investigation resulted unfavorably to him, and now to get rid of that—for it only plunged him lower in the public estimation—he sends here a proposition for a judicial investigation, in order to whitewash those reflections which have been cast upon him by the proceedings of the House and by what has transpired.

Mr. Dawson. What part of the proceedings of the House casts any imputation upon Mr. Crawford?

Mr. Turney. They speak for themselves.

Mr. Dawson. And they cast no imputation. Sir, it is ungenerous and unkind, in the absence of this gentleman, where he has not the opportunity of vindicating his own honor by taking part in the debate, to insinuate any thing against him, calculated to do him injury before the country that he has served. Mr. Crawford, in this transaction, has acted with a marked honor and propriety. His hand, his finger has not been laid upon this claim improperly. The claim was passed by the proper departments of the Government, and its payment was sustained by the late Attorney-General of the United States, who, with an honor and magnanimity which I trust will always accompany him, said that if there was any blame in relation to this matter, it was upon him, and he published it to the world. The late Attorney-General (Mr. Johnson) has published his opinion and evidence, and assumed the whole responsibility like a man. Then how can it be brought up here, before the American people, and charged that this is a measure to "whitewash" George W. Crawford? But, Mr. President, what is he to do? When the bitterness of party, and the unkindness of personal relations will circulate reports throughout the country injurious to his reputation, how is he to meet it? He can only to do it by the mode he has adopted. What is it? He comes before the country, and notwithstanding that he is shielded by the constitution and laws in the possession of the money, yet as doubts have been expressed whether that money went honestly and justly to the representatives of Galphin, he says, so far as he is concerned, here is every dollar of that money. Now, adjudicate it before any tribunal you may select. Congress proposes to select the Supreme Court of the United States, commencing in the district court and carrying it up to the Supreme Court. What for? To "whitewash" the character of George W. Crawford by a decision of the Supreme Court? And will the Supreme Court make a decision to whitewash his character, against their oaths and the high obligations of their dignified position? Why, it is a charge against them. And, when Mr. Crawford has pursued only the course which justice, honor, and propriety demanded of him, he is charged here as coming with a view to "whitewash" his reputation, stained of course by some previous conduct? But, as the Senator from South Carolina said, Mr. Crawford's honor is known, and his *parole* would carry weight wherever honor and honesty are to be found. Gentlemen say they will not grant this investigation. And why? Because the Supreme Court may support the construction of that law given to it by the departments of this Government, and their sanction would be a prôtection to the past Administration from this slander, and that is the thing to be feared. It is not a "whitewashing," but it is subjecting the vindication of Mr. Crawford and the last Administration to the decision of the Supreme Court as the final arbiter; and their decision, when pronounced, will give satisfaction to the entire country, where party motives and personal feelings do not interfere to prevent.

I did not expect, at any time, to be called up in relation to this claim. I was not in Congress when it passed. Other gentlemen passed the law, and they passed the law subject to that construction which had been made by the proper departments of the Government, and we are willing to abide by it. But others are not, and the only way to give the whole matter a proper bearing, is before the Supreme Court of the United States. Mr. Crawford abandons his legal right to defend himself against any suit whatsoever. He abandons all that, and comes here and says, I will abide by the decision of the Supreme Court, and not put in any plea——

Mr. Gwin. Will the gentleman give way for a motion to postpone the bill till to-morrow?

Mr. Dawson. No, sir; I have but a few more remarks to make. I did not know before of the existence of the report of this committee, nor did I know what its contents were until I heard it read by the Secretary. I wished to have the resolution referred to the Judiciary Committee, for the purpose of placing before that intelligent committee, having a full knowledge of the laws of the country and of the constitution, the question whether, by an agreement between the parties, this suit could be ordered. As it has been declared by the immediate representatives of the people that a suit shall be instituted against Mr. Crawford, I go for the institution of it, and if Mr. Crawford is not sustained by the decision of the Supreme Court, then let him pay back every dollar, as he will do without a moment's hesitation.

Mr. Cooper. I have but a word to say. I desired to obtain the floor after the Senator from Tennessee, to say that I did not concur with him in the views which he has expressed. And I desired to suggest, what was very properly suggested by the Senator from South Carolina, that in the event of Mr. Crawford's decease, there are pleas that may be taken advantage of that would preclude recovery on the part of the United States, notwithstanding originally there was no right on the part of the Government to pay the money to Mr. Crawford. There is a distinction, well known to every lawyer, between the recovery of money paid through a mistake of law, and that paid through a mistake of fact. Here, if there is any mistake at all, it was a mistake of law, and according to the decisions of the courts, both of this country and of England, money paid through a mistake of law cannot be recovered back, and if advantage of this be taken by the executors of Mr. Crawford, of course the merits of this question could not be inquired into. On that point, the case would turn, and it would turn in favor of the defendant in the suit. If Mr. Crawford lives, under his letter he would not take advantage of that plea, or any other of that nature. And no doubt, as the gentleman before me (Mr. EWING) stated, the money was received by him, he would not set up that it was received by him as attorney, or plead any plea that would prevent the merits of the case from being investigated. But, as life is uncertain, he may die, and as his administrators and executors would feel bound themselves to take every legal advantage, the bill before us therefore is imperfect. It does not present, under all the circumstances which may occur, an issue to decide what was intended by Mr. Crawford to be decided when he addressed his letter to the House. I believe him to be a man of high honor, and have no doubt whatever that he would be governed by the propositions in that letter; but if he should die, the case would be different.

Mr. GWIN. I move to lay the resolution on the table, so that we may proceed with other business.

The motion was not agreed to.

Mr. BADGER. I desire to engage for a moment or two the attention of the Senate on the question presented in this joint resolution. In the first place, I desire to say that I do not agree with my friend from South Carolina, that there is any objection in the form proposed by the House of Representatives to be given to this investigation. I do not understand how it is, in any sense, making a court of the United States an arbitrator to decide this question. There is a very clear general principle, that if a man is in possession of money which belongs to the Government of the United States, that Government has a right to institute a suit, and by that suit in the proper tribunals to compel the payment of the money which this individual holds, and which belongs to them.

Mr. BUTLER. I will, with the Senator's permission, ask him a question, which perhaps may shorten this argument. It is, whether the Government could at this time sue Mr. Crawford?

Mr. BADGER. My friend generally anticipates. An argument consists of steps, and I was going on step by step to present my views on this question, when my friend asks me a question which I must inevitably answer before I get through, and while I am stating premises which lead to that conclusion. The general principle is, as I stated, that if A is in the possession of money belonging to B, B has a right to sue and recover it; and I suppose there is nothing clearer than that the United States have the same right to recover the money which A is in possession of, belonging to them. I believe there is nothing to prevent it.

It would be very strange, indeed, if, when there is in the possession of an individual money belonging to the United States, the Government would not have the faculty which every individual or corporation has, to institute a suit for its recovery. Then, that being clear, the only difficulty that could arise with regard to the institution of a suit against Mr. Crawford, would arise from the proceedings in the executive department. That is all. The nature of the claim is properly a judicial one, the right is properly assertable in a court of law. The United States is a proper and competent party to assert such a claim, and the only reason why there is any embarrassment on the subject, arises from the proceedings which have taken place in the executive department. Now, they have nothing more to do with the subject than they would have in an ordinary case of a claim by a party, or a release which might be pleaded in law against him. The fact of the existence of the release would not change the nature of the claim. Quite the contrary. It is still a legal claim, and the release is a legal impediment to its recovery. If the release be moved out of the way, the legal claim, in its own character, still subsists; the legal right is retained, and the action can be supported.

Now, Mr. Crawford comes here and proposes that he will withdraw, and not insist upon any bar which technically he might have a right to plead against the claim of the United States to recover this money, supposing that the facts that constitute that legal bar did not exist. It seems to me, then, clear that the commencement of this action is perfectly analogous to the case I have supposed, of one man having a claim against another, and his supposed debtor having in his possession a release. If he surrenders that release, if he does not plead it, there is no more difficulty in testing the merits of the original claim than if the release had never been executed. This is, then, a proper investigation for this claim, in a proper court. In its nature judicial, the functions to be exercised by the judges are functions which are exercised by them in the regular discharge of their ordinary official duties. So, in no aspect and shape in which I can see it, is it the establishment of an arbitration. The action is to be brought in the circuit court of the United States, and if that was constituted an arbitrator, all know that its decision would be final; but the same writs of appeal and error are to be allowed as in every other cause of action brought in that court.

I am not going to enter into any of those investigations brought here in regard to whitewashing and other matters, but I desire, however, to say this: In the first place I have no personal acquaintance with Mr. Crawford. It so happens that I have not had even an introduction to that gentleman; and I know nothing of him, except as I know from his general reputation in the country. One thing is certain, however; he has been most cruelly assailed in regard to the particular transaction to which this resolution relates. When I say that, I do not refer to any thing which has taken place in the Senate; I mean abroad throughout the country. Mr. Crawford thinks he has a right to this money, but he is not willing to retain it unless he has that right; and he comes to the House and asks that an action shall be brought to ascertain whether he is entitled to the money or not.

My own opinion, from the examination I have given to the case, is, that all that was done in the executive department of the Government was rightly done, and that under the act of Congress, this claim was adopted and made one against this Government, in the same condition and in every respect as it formerly stood against the Government of Georgia. Against the State of Georgia it was a claim valid for principal and interest both, and therefore when adopted by the United States, it became a just claim for principal and interest against the United States. When this gentleman comes and asks that this question may be investigated, and proposes to put every obstacle out of the way, and submit this legal question to a legal court, it would be cruel and harsh treatment to him for the Congress of the United States to refuse what he thus asks, and what I think a fair and just respect for his character and standing requires.

Mr. Foote. Mr. President——

Mr. Butler. I understand your object is to move to lay this motion on the table.

Mr. Foote. I understand that my friend desires to close his remarks with a motion to lay this subject on the table; and so understanding, I give way to him with pleasure.

Mr. Butler. I have but two propositions to state, and those very briefly. I did not understand that under any law we may propose, Mr. Crawford may not release the judgment, so far as he is concerned, under which this money was paid. If it was paid, it was to all intents and purposes a proceeding having all the validity of a judgment, and so far as he is concerned, he may undoubtedly release the judgment, but he has not a right to release it so far as the other party is concerned. But that was not the gravamen of the remarks I made. I say that Mr. Crawford has no right to bring the Supreme Court of the United States into collision with the executive departments of the Government. It is not in accordance with the genius of our Government, and I believe it to be inconsistent with the independence of those two departments of the Government. I believe they ought to be kept separate, and that neither should have any supervisory power over the other. I move to lay the resolution on the table.

Mr. Ewing demanded the yeas and nays, and they were ordered.

The question was then taken on the motion to lay the resolution on the table, and resulted as follows:

Yeas.—Messrs. Atchison, Benton, Bright, Butler, Cass, Chase, Clay, Davis of Mississippi, Dickinson, Dodge of Wisconsin, Dodge of Iowa, Felch, Foote, Frémont, Gwin, Hale, Hamlin, Houston, Jones, Norris, Pearce, Rusk, Sebastian, Soulé, Sturgeon, Turney, and Whitcomb—27.

Nays.—Messrs. Badger, Baldwin, Barnwell, Bell, Berrien, Clarke, Cooper, Davis of Massachusetts, Dawson, Dayton, Ewing, Greene, Hunter, King, Mason, Morton, Pratt, Seward, Smith, Spruance, Underwood, Wales, Walker, Winthrop, and Yulee—25.

So the resolution was laid on the table.

Monday, September 30.

Bounty Land Bill.

Mr. Walker. In consequence of an unfortunate error in engrossing and enrolling what is called the bounty land bill, it becomes necessary this morning to pass an explanatory act. I therefore ask unanimous consent to introduce an act supplementary to an act entitled "An act granting bounty lands to certain officers and soldiers who have been engaged in the military service of the United States."

Unanimous consent to introduce the bill was granted, and it was read a first and second time, and considered as in Committee of the Whole.

Mr. Walker. The bill, as it finally passed, was intended to provide that no warrant should be assignable prior to the issue of the patent. In engrossing and enrolling the bill, the words "of the patent" were left out; so that these warrants will be assignable. This supplementary bill is only to correct that error. It provides that the act shall be construed as if the words "of the patent" were inserted after the word "issue." That is all. There will be no sense in the section if this amendment is not made.

Mr. Hale. If I understand it, this amendment of the Senator from Wisconsin is to prevent the assignability of the warrant.

Mr. Walker. It was an error in the engrossment, which cannot now be remedied. The only way to correct that error is to pass this bill. The departments, the President, and everybody else connected with the matter would be in an embarrassed situation if the bill should be left as it now is.

After an objection made by Mr. Dawson was withdrawn, the bill was read a third time and passed.

Adjournment.

The Senate appointed a committee to wait upon the President of the United States, in conjunction with a committee of the House of Representatives, to notify him that the two Houses, having finished the legislative business before them, were ready to adjourn if he had no further communication to make to them.

Mr. EWING, from that committee, reported that they had performed the duty assigned them, and that the President replied that he had no further communication to make.

On motion, it was ordered that a message be sent to the House of Representatives, to inform the House that the Senate, having finished the business before them, are about to adjourn.

On motion, it was

"*Resolved, unanimously,* That the thanks of the Senate are due, and are hereby tendered, to the Hon. WILLIAM R. KING, for the ability, dignity, and impartiality with which he has performed the duties of President of the Senate *pro tem.*"

Mr. KING, President *pro tem.*, then rose, and addressed the Senate as follows:

SENATORS: Our protracted session is about to close. The causes which have led to its unusual extension were of a character well calculated to produce an excited state of feeling, and occasionally to lead to altercations of a very unpleasant character. Whether the action of Congress will allay the excitement, restore harmony, and bring about a better state of feeling in the country, remains to be seen. As an American citizen, devotedly attached to the institutions of my country, I sincerely hope it may; and I trust that the dangers with which we have been threatened will serve as a warning to all future Congresses to deal justly by every section, and to respect the constitutional rights of all, if they would insure the permanency of our Union. In discharging the duties imposed upon me as your presiding officer, I may, in the opinion of some, have been too strict in the enforcement of the rules adopted for the government of this body. Should this be the case, I can only say that it gives me no pleasure to exercise authority, and I have only been led to do so when the occasion called for it by an imperious sense of duty to the Senate, over which your kindness has called me to preside. In taking leave of you, Senators, I can but express my grateful sense of the kindness and courtesy with which I have uniformly been treated. I wish you all a safe return to your respective homes.

He then proclaimed that the Senate was adjourned *sine die.*

INDEX TO VOL. XVI.

A

B

C

D

E

F

I

J

K

M

Y

www.ingramcontent.com/pod-product-compliance
Lightning Source LLC
LaVergne TN
LVHW021100110826
845150LV00001B/130

* 9 7 8 1 4 2 5 5 6 6 1 9 7 *